STUDY GUIDE

STUDY GUIDE

to accompany

Microeconomics

in Modules Third Edition

Krugman | Wells

Elizabeth Sawyer Kelly
University of Wisconsin-Madison

WORTH PUBLISHERS
A Macmillan Higher Education Company

Study Guide
by Elizabeth Sawyer Kelly
to accompany
Krugman/Wells: Microeconomics in Modules, Third Edition

ISBN 10: 1-4641-4347-1
ISBN 13: 978-1-4641-4347-2

First Printing

Printed in the United States of America

Worth Publishers
41 Madison Avenue
New York, NY 10010
www.wortheconomics.com

Contents

Key to Corresponding Modules Numbers

Module Title	Microeconomics in Modules	Economics in Modules
The Study of Economics	1	1
Models and the Circular Flow	2	2
The Production Possibilities Frontier Model	3	3
Comparative Advantage and Trade	4	4
Demand	5	5
Supply and Equilibrium	6	6
Changes in Equilibrium	7	7
Income Effects, Substitution Effects, and Elasticity	8	8
Interpreting Price Elasticity of Demand	9	9
Other Elasticities	10	10
Consumer and Producer Surplus	11	11
Efficiency and Markets	12	12
Price Controls	13	13
Quantity Controls	14	14
Taxes	15	15
Gains from Trade	16	16
Supply, Demand, and Trade	17	17
Making Decisions	18	18
Behavioral Economics	19	19
Maximizing Utility	20	20
The Production Function	21	21
Firm Costs	22	22
Long-Run Costs and Economies of Scale	23	23
Introduction to Market Structure	24	24
Perfect Competition	25	25
Graphing Perfect Competition	26	26
Long-Run Outcomes in Perfect Competition	27	27
Monopoly in Practice	28	28

Module Title	Microeconomics in Modules	Economics in Modules
Monopoly and Public Policy	29	29
Price Discrimination	30	30
Oligopoly	31	31
Game Theory	32	32
Oligopoly in Practice	33	33
Monopolistic Competition	34	34
Product Differentiation and Advertising	35	35
Externalities	36	36
Externalities and Public Policy	37	37
Public Goods and Common Resources	38	38
The Economics of the Welfare State	39	39
Factor Markets	40	40
Marginal Productivity Theory	41	41
The Market for Labor	42	42
The Cost-Minimizing Input Combination	43	43
The Time Value of Money	44	
The Economics of Information	45	44

Preface

This Study Guide is designed for use with ***Microeconomics in Modules, Third Edition*** by Paul Krugman and Robin Wells. It is intended to help you evaluate your understanding of the material covered in the textbook and thereby reinforce the key concepts you need to learn.

For each module, the Study Guide is organized as follows:

Before You Read the Module

- Summary: an opening paragraph that provides a brief overview of the module.
- Objectives: a numbered list outlining and describing the material that you should have learned in the module. These objectives can be easily used as a study tool.
- Key Terms: a list of bold key terms with their definitions. This section includes room for note-taking.

After You Read the Module

- Tips: a numbered list of learning tips with graphical analysis.
- Worked Problems: a set of worked-out problems that take the student step-by-step through a particular problem/exercise.
- Problems and Exercises: a set of comprehensive problems.

Before You Take the Test

- Module Review Questions: a set of multiple-choice questions that focus on the key concepts from the text that you should grasp after reading the module. These questions are designed for quick exam preparation.

Answer Key

- Answers to Problems and Exercises: detailed solutions to the Problems and Exercises in the Study Guide.
- Answers to Module Review Questions: solutions to the multiple-choice questions in the Study Guide—along with thorough explanations.

Answers as well as explanatory solutions can be found at the end of each module. Students often use an answer section to simply check if they have gotten the "right" answer. I caution you to use the answer section accompanying each module with an eye to getting the highest possible value from the exercises provided. In economics, the reasoning used in coming to conclusions and correctly modeling the problems are as important as coming to an accurate answer. Explanations for each problem have been provided in order for you to check that your understanding of the concepts has been appropriately applied.

The study of economics has the potential of altering the way you evaluate and understand the world. I hope that your use of this guide will help you in your study of basic microeconomics principles and will provide a jumping-off point for further study in the economics field.

Elizabeth Sawyer Kelly

STUDY GUIDE

module 1

The Study of Economics

BEFORE YOU READ THE MODULE

Summary

This module introduces and discusses the concepts of scarcity, choice, opportunity cost, positive and normative economics, and the distinction between microeconomics and macroeconomics. The module also discusses agreement as well as disagreement among economists.

Module Objectives

This module introduces a set of principles that will guide your study of economics.

Objective #1. Resources—land, labor, physical capital, and human capital—are scarce, so individuals as well as societies must make choices about how to use these resources.

Objective #2. A market economy determines both production and consumption decisions for an economy through the decentralized decisions that are made by individual producers and consumers.

Objective #3. Societies must make decisions about how to allocate their scarce resources. These resource allocation decisions are sometimes the result of many individual choices but sometimes they are the result of decisions made at a higher, community-wide level.

Objective #4. The opportunity cost, or the real cost of something, is what you must give up to get it.

Objective #5. Microeconomics studies the choices that are made by individuals, households, or firms while macroeconomics studies the overall performance of the economy.

Objective #6. Macroeconomics focuses on the aggregate economy, or the economy as a whole. Macroeconomics considers how individual and firm behavior in the aggregate interact to produce a particular level of economic performance in the economy. Central topics in macroeconomics include the determination of the overall level of output, the overall level of prices, and the overall level of employment in the economy.

Objective #7. Positive economics is factual and descriptive, whereas normative economics is about what ought to be or what should be. Positive economics is objective and can be tested for accuracy, and often involves forecasting. Normative economics is subjective and prescriptive, and it is value based. However, it is possible to rank normative policies designed to achieve a certain prescription on the basis of the efficiency of each policy.

Objective #8. Economists may come to different conclusions because they have different values or because they use different economic models.

Key Terms

economics the study of scarcity and choice.

individual choice the decision by an individual of what to do, which necessarily involves a decision of what not to do.

economy a system for coordinating a society's productive and consumptive activities.

market economy an *economy* in which decisions of individual producers and consumers largely determine what, how, and for whom to produce, with little government involvement in the decisions.

resource anything, such as land, labor, and capital, that can be used to produce something else; includes natural resources (from the physical environment) and human resources (labor, skill, intelligence).

land all resources that come from nature, such as minerals, timber, and petroleum.

labor the effort of workers.

physical capital manufactured goods used to make other goods and services.

human capital the educational achievements and skills of the labor force, which enhance its productivity.

scarce in short supply; a *resource* is scarce when there is not enough of the resources available to satisfy all the various ways a society wants to use them.

opportunity cost the real cost of an item: what you must give up in order to get it.

microeconomics the branch of *economics* that studies how people make decisions and how those decisions interact.

macroeconomics the branch of *economics* that is concerned with the overall ups and downs in the *economy*.

Notes

Key Terms *(continued)*

Notes

economic aggregates economic measures that summarize data across different markets for goods, services, workers, and assets.

positive economics the branch of economic analysis that describes the way the *economy* actually works.

normative economics the branch of economic analysis that makes prescriptions about the way the *economy* should work.

AFTER YOU READ THE MODULE

Tips

Tip #1. The study of economics is cumulative. You should master each topic as it is presented since later topics build on earlier topics.

Tip #2. Pay attention to new vocabulary and make sure you know, understand, and can apply these terms. Your instructor will expect you to do more than just define the terms: you must also be able to indicate through your work an ability to apply these terms in a meaningful manner.

Tip #3. Plan to spend time every day studying economics. Review your lecture notes, review the vocabulary, work on the practice questions, and identify what questions you have about the material. Once you formulate your questions, seek out answers by returning to your text, your lecture notes, your classmates, or your professor.

Tip #4. Think about the topics that might be on an exam and the kinds of questions that might be asked about these topics—questions that are strictly definitional, questions that apply the definitions in a problem-solving setting, and questions that force you to really think about the material and apply your knowledge. Most college-level exams include questions designed to make you think about the material.

Tip #5. Studying economics requires learning both new vocabulary and a new way of thinking. You will need to familiarize yourself with this information and vocabulary. You may find it helpful to make a set of flash cards for all the vocabulary you learn while studying economics. For each flash card you will find it helpful to write the term on one side of the card and its definition on the other side of the card. You might also find it helpful to identify on the first side of the card the module number where the term is first introduced. After you make a set of flash cards for the module, review these flash cards until you are thoroughly familiar and comfortable with each term.

Tip #6. Macroeconomics focuses on the economic behavior of the overall economy, while microeconomics focuses on the economic behavior of individuals, firms, and specific markets. Macroeconomics studies topics like the determination of the aggregate level of output, the aggregate price level, the level of employment, short-run economic fluctuations, and long-run economic growth. Microeconomics considers topics like supply and demand in particular markets, profit maximization by firms, and utility maximization by individuals.

WORKED PROBLEMS

1. This module defines and describes four types of resources: land, labor, physical capital, and human capital. For each of the following items identify the type of resource and explain why you chose this answer.
   a. Frank is an experienced heart surgeon.
   b. Mary works at an assembly line job that does not require any particular training or educational background.
   c. A large moving truck is used to haul people's furniture across country.
   d. A machine molds plastic into car doors.
   e. A coal seam is still in the ground.
   f. Water flows in a river.

STEP 1: Start by reviewing the four types of resources and their definitions.

There are four types of resources: land, labor, physical capital, and human capital. Land includes all resources that come from nature, such as minerals, timber, and petroleum. Labor is the effort of workers. Physical capital is manufactured goods used to make other goods and services. Human capital is the educational achievements and skills of the labor force, which enhance its productivity.

STEP 2: Classify each of the examples as one of the four types of resources, and explain why you chose this classification.

a. Frank is a worker, but he also possesses a high degree of training and education that is required for this work. This is an example of human capital.

b. Mary is a worker, but the work she does on the assembly line does not require any special training or education: this is labor.

c. A moving truck is physical capital, since it is a manufactured good that is used to provide moving services.

d. The machine that molds plastic into car doors is physical capital, since it is used to provide another good: car doors.

e. The coal seam in the ground is a land resource, since coal comes from nature.

f. Water in a river is a land resource.

2. For each of the following scenarios identify the opportunity costs of the decision.
   a. Mary needs to study for her economics exam tonight, but she is also considering going to the band concert this evening. The band concert will last for two hours and requires her to purchase a ticket for $10. What is Mary's opportunity cost of going to the band concert?
   b. Joe is considering studying in Mexico next semester rather than attending the university where he is enrolled. The cost of studying abroad is equal to his current tuition payment plus $1,000. His room and board would cost the same with either choice. What is Joe's opportunity cost of studying abroad?
   c. Chen is debating going to the hockey game Friday night or joining a group of friends to see a movie. The hockey game will last three hours and cost $15, while the movie will last three hours and cost $5. What is Chen's opportunity cost of going to the hockey game?

STEP 1: **Review the concept of opportunity cost.**

The opportunity cost of an item is what you must give up to get that item. So for each of the scenarios it will be important to figure out what the individual must give up when choosing a particular activity.

STEP 2: **For each scenario, identify the opportunity costs of the choices that are being considered.**

a. The opportunity cost to Mary of attending the band concert includes the two hours of studying for economics that she must give up as well as the $10 she must pay for the ticket to attend the concert. If she did not attend the concert, she would be able to spend this $10 on some other item or activity.

b. The opportunity cost to Joe of studying abroad includes the extra $1,000 he must pay for this experience. The opportunity cost of studying abroad would not include his regular tuition or his fees for room and board, since no matter where he chooses to study (at home or abroad) he would have these costs. However, if the question had included the possibility that Joe might choose to work (or travel, for example) rather than attend college, then his opportunity costs of studying abroad would have included the $1,000 plus his tuition, since he is choosing between studying and doing something else that does not include enrollment at an institution. No matter what Joe's choices are, the room and board are not a part of his opportunity costs, since he will have living costs no matter what he chooses to do.

c. The opportunity cost to Chen of attending the hockey game includes the $10 difference between the price of the ticket to the hockey game and the cost of the movie. The opportunity cost also includes the movie that she will not be able to see because of this choice.

Problems and Exercises

1. For each of the following situations describe the opportunity costs of each decision.

a. Sarah considers two options for Saturday night: she can attend a concert that costs $10 per ticket or she can go to the free movie offered at the student union. She decides to attend the concert.

b. A new business in town debates paying $20,000 for a prime location versus $10,000 for a less perfect location. The business estimates that it will eventually serve the same number of customers in either location, but that it will take 6 months before the sub-optimal location provides the same outcome as the prime location. The business decides to purchase the $10,000 property.

c. Jamie is given a choice for his next holiday from school: he can be an unpaid intern at a company or he can earn $2,000 working as a camp counselor. He decides to take the internship.

d. Roberto is studying for two midterms this week. He figures he has 20 available hours to study for both midterms. If he studies all 20 hours for the economics exam he will undoubtedly get an A on the exam, but he will at best earn a C on his organic chemistry test. If he studies all 20 hours for the organic chemistry test he will get an A on the organic chemistry exam, but he will likely earn a D on his economics test. Roberto decides to devote all of his available time to economics since he has determined that he does not wish to pursue a premed major.

2. The following table presents the possible combinations of study time available to Roberto this week as he prepares for his two midterms (one in economics and the other in organic chemistry). Assume Roberto has 20 hours available to study and that he will use all 20 hours studying economics and chemistry.

Hours of study time spent on economics	Hours of study time spent on organic chemistry	Grade in economics	Grade in organic chemistry
0	20	60	90
5	15	70	85
10	10	80	75
15	5	86	73
20	0	90	70

Roberto currently plans to study 10 hours for economics and 10 hours for organic chemistry.

a. If he alters his plan and studies 15 hours for economics, what is the opportunity cost of that decision?

b. If he alters his plan and studies 15 hours for organic chemistry, what is the opportunity cost of that decision?

c. If he alters his plan and studies 20 hours for economics, what is the opportunity cost of that decision?

d. If he alters his plan and studies 20 hours for organic chemistry, what is the opportunity cost of that decision?

3. Decide whether each of the following statements is a normative statement or a positive statement, then explain your answer.

a. The gasoline tax is projected to yield $10 million in tax revenue next year.

b. If the gasoline tax was raised by 10 cents per gallon, the tax revenue from this tax would increase by 4%.

c. The state should raise the gasoline tax for the coming year. An increase in the tax will reduce congestion and smog, which is more important than the cost to commuters if they shift from private car transportation to public transportation.

d. Mandatory school enhances the work skills of students.

e. The age of mandatory school attendance should be extended, since this will provide greater benefits to our economy.

f. An extension of mandatory school attendance will increase government education costs by $2 million for the state.

4. Economists sometimes disagree about positive economics, but more often they disagree about normative economics. Briefly define both of these terms and then explain why economists do not always agree.

5. For each of the following questions identify whether the question is more appropriate for the study of microeconomics or macroeconomics, and why.
   a. What will happen to the wages in our community if corporation X, an employer of 1,000 people (that's 40% of our workforce), decides to relocate its plant to a different state?
   b. What will happen to the level of overall economic production in our economy if the federal government continues to run record levels of government deficit?
   c. If the government engages in monetary policy and increases the money supply, what will happen to the interest rate in our economy?
   d. How has the recent increase in the price of a barrel of oil affected the prices of bicycles, cars, and airplane fares?
   e. What will the effect of recent tropical storms be on the price of bananas?

BEFORE YOU TAKE THE TEST

Module Review Questions

1. Camillo is offered two jobs: one pays a salary of $30,000 per year and offers four weeks of vacation, and the other job pays a salary of $32,000 per year and offers two weeks of vacation. What is the opportunity cost for Camillo of taking the job offering $32,000 per year?
   a. $2,000 plus two weeks of vacation per year
   b. $2,000 per year
   c. two weeks of vacation per year
   d. $30,000 plus two weeks of vacation per year

2. Ning decides to attend a special speaker presentation tonight at her college instead of staying in her dorm and listening to her music collection. Which of the following statements is true?
   a. Ning faces no opportunity cost with regard to her decision since listening to music or attending the speaker are both free events.
   b. The opportunity cost of Ning's decision is so small that it is not worth calculating.
   c. The opportunity cost of Ning's decision is the loss of her evening of music listening.
   d. The opportunity cost of Ning's decision includes the cost associated with hearing the speaker.

3. Scarcity of resources implies that
   a. people can do whatever they want and do not need to worry about making choices.
   b. life involves making choices about how to best use these scarce resources.
   c. societies need to invest time and money to discover more resources.
   d. only very wealthy individuals are not constrained by their resources.

4. Each day people make decisions about what to wear, what to eat, or where to work,
   a. since they all face constraints that mean they cannot do everything they would like to do.
   b. without regard to the level of resources that are available to them.

5. The university in Smart, USA, has a parking problem and is looking into programs to alleviate the parking shortage. Which of the following ideas is likely to decrease the number of cars parking on campus each day by the greatest amount?
   a. Faculty and staff at the university all receive free parking permits.
   b. Faculty and staff at the university all pay a set fee per year for parking permits.
   c. Faculty and staff at the university must pay an hourly fee for each hour that they park on campus.
   d. Faculty and staff are exempt from any parking policies at the university since they need to be able to come to campus to do their jobs.

6. Salespeople working at Department Store of Suburbia are offered two compensation plans. Plan A pays the worker $4 per hour plus a 5% sales commission on the total dollar value of sales that this worker makes. Plan B pays the worker $6 per hour and does not include a sales commission. Total sales per hour per salesperson averages $100. Which of the following statements is true?
   a. Plan A will result in the salespeople being less helpful to customers than does plan B.
   b. Plan A will result in the salespeople being more helpful to customers than does plan B.

7. Which of the following statements is true about positive economics?
   I. Positive economics is about how the world should work.
   II. Positive economics is about how the world works.
   III. Positive economics is descriptive.
   a. Statements I, II, and III are all true.
   b. Statements I and III are true.
   c. Statements II and III are true.
   d. Statement II is true.

8. Which of the following statements is an example of normative economics?

I. The United States should pass a value-added tax, since this is a tax that will work best for the country.

II. A value-added tax will add $10 billion to the administrative costs of the U.S. tax system.

III. A value-added tax will increase the economic burden of taxes on poor people by 15%.

a. Statements I, II, and III are all examples of normative economics.
b. Statements I and III are examples of normative economics.
c. Statements I and II are examples of normative economics.
d. Statement I is an example of normative economics.

9. Macroeconomics, unlike microeconomics,

a. considers the behavior of individual firms and markets.
b. focuses on the production and consumption of particular goods.
c. tries to explain increases in living standards over time.
d. finds that the behavior of individuals is more important in determining economic activity than is the aggregate summation of this behavior.

10. Macroeconomics

a. focuses on how the behavior of individuals and firms in the aggregate economy interact to produce a market price for each good and service offered in the economy.
b. focuses on how the actions of individuals and firms in the economy interact to produce a particular economy-wide level of economic performance.
c. considers how specific markets for goods and services determine their equilibrium prices and quantities.
d. Answers (a), (b), and (c) are all correct.

ANSWER KEY

Answers to Problems and Exercises

1. a. Sarah's decision to attend the concert has two opportunity costs: attending the concert means that she will be unable to attend the movie, and in addition, to attend the concert she must pay $10 for a ticket. Her decision to attend the concert means that she is giving up whatever she could have purchased with the $10.

   b. The business gives up $10,000 to get the property, but this is not an opportunity cost since the business must have a business location to exist. However, there is an opportunity cost to this decision: the business gives up the additional business it would have gotten at the prime location during the first six months.

   c. When he decides to take the internship, Jamie incurs an opportunity cost of $2,000, since he is giving up this income to work in the intern position.

   d. Roberto's opportunity cost with regard to his studying is his diminished grade in organic chemistry. (Obviously Roberto might want to consider some combination of studying that allows him to prepare for both exams, but this question did not offer that possibility.)

2. Remember that opportunity cost measures what is given up, so when Roberto studies more for his economics exam, he is giving up time he could devote to his organic chemistry exam. This decision will therefore affect his organic chemistry grade. Similarly, if Roberto devotes more time to studying for his organic chemistry exam, then he will be giving up points on his economics exam.

   a. The opportunity cost of studying 15 hours for the economics exam instead of 10 hours is two points on the organic chemistry exam.

   b. The opportunity cost of studying 15 hours for the organic chemistry exam instead of 10 hours is ten points on the economics exam.

   c. The opportunity cost of studying 20 hours for the economics exam instead of 10 hours is five points on the organic chemistry exam.

   d. The opportunity cost of studying 20 hours for the organic chemistry exam instead of 10 hours is twenty points on the economics exam.

3. a. Positive: this statement is a forecast of the tax revenue from the gasoline tax. It is verifiable and hence positive.

   b. Positive: this is also a forecast, and although it may be wrong, it can be verified through the data once the data are available.

   c. Normative: this is a value statement that reflects one person's viewpoint of the way the world should work. It is not refutable since it reflects a person's opinion and not a set of facts.

   d. Positive: this statement can be tested for its accuracy.

   e. Normative: this statement reflects the opinions of the speaker.

   f. Positive: this is a forecast.

4. Positive economics is descriptive, whereas normative economics is prescriptive—that is, positive economics is objective and expresses how the world works, while normative economics is subjective and expresses how the world should work. Economists may differ because of positive economics: they may use different models with different assumptions

that lead to different conclusions. Economists may also disagree over normative economics: economists may not share the same values and will therefore reach different conclusions about how the world should work. Economists can evaluate alternative policies in terms of their efficiency at reaching stated goals.

5. **a.** Microeconomics: this question is directed at understanding the local effect of this corporation's move instead of its total effect across the aggregate economy.

   b. Macroeconomics: this question focuses on the aggregate performance of the economy.

   c. Macroeconomics: this question considers the impact of monetary policy on the aggregate economy.

   d. Microeconomics: this question addresses the effect of a change in the price of a barrel of oil on specific markets like the market for bicycles or cars.

   e. Microeconomics: this question considers the price of a specific good rather than the overall price level in the economy.

Answers to Module Review Questions

1. **Answer c.** The opportunity cost of taking the job includes what must be given up. In this case, Camillo is giving up two weeks of vacation since the other job offers four weeks of vacation instead of two weeks. He is not giving up any salary when he selects the job paying $32,000.

2. **Answer c.** Ning's opportunity cost is measured by what she must give up when she chooses to do something else. In this case, when Ning decides to attend the lecture she is giving up a night of listening to music in her dorm room.

3. **Answer b.** When resources are scarce, this implies that people and societies must make decisions about how to use those scarce resources since the scarcity of resources is a constraint on production and consumption.

4. **Answer a.** People must make decisions every day because they do not have an infinite amount of time, income, or resources that would allow them to do everything they might want to do.

5. **Answer c.** To get the university community to curtail their parking on campus by the greatest amount, the university should adopt a program that makes drivers aware of the cost of bringing a car on campus every time they drive on campus. Thus, charging an hourly parking fee is the best choice offered, since this fee will serve to remind drivers that it will cost them something each time they drive on campus and park. In contrast, a single annual fee does not reward the purchaser for reducing the number of times they park on campus during the year; free parking indicates that parking on campus does not cost anything and will result in people parking on campus more often; and exempting the staff from parking fees eliminates incentives to get staff to think about alternatives to driving on campus and parking.

6. **Answer b.** When salespeople are awarded the base salary plus a commission, they are encouraged to be helpful to shoppers in the hope of boosting their sales figures. When offered a flat hourly rate, they have no incentive to provide helpful service beyond the minimum required by the store, since their compensation will not be impacted by their extra effort.

7. **Answer c.** Positive economics is objective, factual, and can be subject to proof. In contrast, normative economics is subjective and expresses what ought to happen or what should happen. Statements II and III are both statements that describe positive economics, since positive economics describes and analyzes how the world works.

8. **Answer d.** Normative economics is subjective and value oriented. Both statements II and III are positive statements that can be evaluated as to their factual accuracy. Statement I is a normative statement since it expresses someone's subjective opinion and therefore cannot be proven true or false.

9. **Answer c.** Macroeconomics studies the aggregate economy, not individual action; in studying the aggregate economy, macroeconomics seeks to explain the factors that determine a country's standard of living. In macroeconomics we are reminded that the aggregation of individual behavior often has a larger impact than just the sum of these individual behaviors.

10. **Answer b.** Macroeconomics is focused on the aggregate economy and its overall performance. Microeconomics focuses on specific markets and how the behavior of firms and individuals interact to determine the prices in those markets as well as the quantities in those markets.

module 2

Models and the Circular Flow

BEFORE YOU READ THE MODULE

Summary

This module introduces the concept of model building and then presents a simple model of the circular flow diagram of the economy. Models are a simplified representation of reality, and the study of economic models will be a crucial aspect of your study of economics. The module also discusses how individual decisions affect the larger economy.

Module Objectives

Objective #1. A model is a simplified representation of reality that is used to better understand real-life situations. Underlying every model is a set of assumptions.

Objective #2. The other-things-equal assumption allows economists to focus on the effects of only one change at a time on an economic outcome. This is a simplifying assumption. This assumption is often used in thought experiments that allow economists to examine the economic impact of a change.

Objective #3. The circular-flow diagram is a simple model of the aggregate economy. This model illustrates the relationship between firms and households. In this simple model:

- Households receive income from selling factors of production to firms. Households gain the income they earn from selling factors of production and then use this income to purchase goods and services.
- Firms hire factors of production to produce goods and services.

Objective #4. In the simple circular-flow diagram presented in this module many real world complications are left out. For example, the simple model does not include the rest of the world that imports goods and services as well as exports goods and services;

the simple model does not include the sale of goods by firms to other firms; the simple model does not include the government; and the simple model does not include the financial markets.

Objective #5. The simple circular-flow diagram in this module is a reminder that one person's spending is another person's income. That is, many people make a living selling things to other people. Since one person's spending is another person's income, this implies that a decrease in spending will lead to reduced family incomes, which in turn will lead to more decreases in spending.

Key Terms

model a simplified representation of a real situation that is used to better understand real-life situations.

other-things-equal assumption in the development of a model, the assumption that all relevant factors except the one under study remain unchanged.

circular-flow diagram represents the transactions in an *economy* by two kinds of flows around a circle: flows of physical things such as goods or labor in one direction and flows of money to pay for these physical things in the opposite direction.

household a person or a group of people that share their income.

firm an organization that produces goods and services for sale.

product markets where goods and services are bought and sold.

factor markets markets in which *firms* buy the *resources* they need to produce goods and services.

Notes

AFTER YOU READ THE MODULE

Tips

Tip #1. This module introduces the concept of models. This is a crucial concept that forms the basis of the majority of material you will study in the rest of the course. In working with models it is important to understand the simplifying assumptions underlying whatever model you are using.

Tip #2. Many of the models you will encounter in this course make the other-things-equal assumption, which means that the model considers only one change at a time while holding everything else constant. Make sure you understand this basic assumption before working with the models introduced in the module.

WORKED PROBLEMS

1. Mario and Julio live in the same town, and initially only Julio has a job. If Mario gets a job, how will this alter the flow of income going to households and the flow of expenditures on goods and services in this community? In your answer use the circular-flow model of the economy.

STEP 1: Review the circular-flow model of an economy.

The circular-flow diagram of the economy illustrates the flows of goods and services from businesses to households and the flow of resources from households to businesses. With the addition of money, this diagram allows us to see a flow of goods, services, and resources to households and a flow of expenditures on goods and services from households to businesses. It also reveals a flow of income from businesses to households.

STEP 2: Relate this scenario to the circular-flow model of the economy.

Before Mario gets a job, Julio is earning income by selling his labor resources. Julio uses this income to purchase goods and services. There is an income–expenditure stream due to Julio's activities that can be illustrated with a circular-flow diagram: income flows from Julio's place of employment (a business) to Julio's household, and then Julio's household uses this income to purchase (make expenditures on) goods and services. When Mario gets a job, the flow of income from businesses to households increases, since the number of workers has increased. In addition, Mario now has income that he will spend in the market for goods and services: thus, the level of expenditures in this economy increases when Mario procures a job.

Problems and Exercises

1. Suppose that you wish to travel from your college campus to a nearby community. You go online to download a map to guide you on your trip. How is this map an example of a model? How does it simplify reality? How do you evaluate whether or not your map helps you better understand the world?

2. An economy experiences a recession in which the level of production of goods and services is lower than the level the economy is capable of producing. As the level of production falls, people decrease their level of spending. What can you conclude in general about the level of people's income in this economy?

3. An economy has a fixed amount of resources available to it during any given period. If there is too much spending in the economy during this time, how will the economy respond?

BEFORE YOU TAKE THE TEST

Module Review Questions

1. Models
a. are an exact replica of reality.
b. bear no resemblance to real life.
c. are a simplification of the real world.
d. are made more complicated by the assumptions that underlie the model.

2. There are a limited number of possible economic models.
a. True b. False

3. The other-things-equal assumption means that
a. all economic models hold the same variables constant.
b. all economic models vary only one variable at a time, and that variable is always the same for all economic models.
c. only one variable is allowed to change in a model at a time so that the analyst using the model can focus on the effect of that change on the model.
d. lots of variables are allowed to change in a model at one time so that the analyst using the model can focus on the effect of all these changes on a single variable of interest.

4. When one group of people in an economy decreases their spending, this will
a. have no effect on the level of income of other people in the economy.
b. increase the level of income of other people in the economy.
c. decrease the level of income of other people in the economy.
d. lead to inflationary pressures in this economy.

5. When one group of people in an economy increases their spending, this will
a. have no effect on the level of income of other people in the economy.
b. increase the level of income of other people in the economy.
c. decrease the level of income of other people in the economy.
d. lead to inflationary pressures in this economy.

ANSWER KEY

Answers to Problems and Exercises

1. The map is an example of a model because it simplifies the real world while trying to enable the user to better understand that world. It simplifies the real world by leaving out many things—for example, your map may only show the main roads in your community, or it might leave out major landmarks that you might find helpful, such as park and school names. The map is helpful to you provided it enables you to get from your starting point to your destination. Although it simplifies the real world, it should still provide key insights into that world.

2. When people reduce their spending and purchase fewer goods and services, the level of income that other people in the economy earn is reduced since the purchases by one group of people represent income for another group of people. In a recession, the level of spending and the level of income fall in an economy.

3. With a fixed amount of resources in an economy during a given period, there is a limit to the amount of goods and services the economy can produce. If spending is greater than this economic capacity, then this puts pressure on the prices of goods and services to rise, leading to inflationary pressures. Too much spending in an economy results in inflation.

Answers to Module Review Questions

1. **Answer c.** This is a simple definition of "model."

2. **Answer b.** This is not a true statement since there are an infinite number of possible models. Models can vary, for example, due to their focus of attention, their underlying assumptions, and their degree of complexity.

3. **Answer c.** The assumption "other things equal" implies that everything else is being held equal or constant while considering the effect of changing one variable. Answer (a) is incorrect since different economic models have different economic variables. Answer (b) is incorrect since different variables may be varied in different models or even within a particular model. Answer (d) is incorrect with regard to the other-things-equal assumption, which is used to isolate the effect of a single change on the rest of the model.

4. **Answer c.** This is true by definition. If spending is reduced by one group in an economy, then some other individuals in the economy will not receive as much income as they initially did due to this reduction in spending.

5. **Answer b.** This is true by definition. An increase in spending in an economy indicates that some people in that economy will receive that additional spending and, hence, their incomes will rise.

module 3

The Production Possibility Frontier Model

BEFORE YOU READ THE MODULE

Summary

This module develops a simple model of the production possibility frontier in order to more fully examine the idea of trade-offs. The module uses this model to explore the concepts of efficiency, opportunity cost, and economic growth. The module discusses two sources of economic growth: increases in the amount of resources available and improvements in technology.

Module Objectives

Objective #1. The production possibility frontier is a model that represents the production possibilities available to an individual or to an economy. The production possibility frontier model assumes that the individual (or country) has a set amount of resources, a set level of technology, and a set amount of time. Then the production possibility frontier delineates a set of points that indicates the maximum amount of two goods that can be produced by this individual (or country) given their resources, technology, and available time. For simplicity, this Study Guide refers to production possibility frontiers in terms of production by countries rather than individuals, but the arguments made from the perspective of countries also hold for individuals. Figure 3.1 illustrates a linear production possibility frontier for a country, where the frontier indicates the maximum amount of goods X and Y that can be produced from the available resources and technology. Points *A* and *B* are points that lie on the production possibility frontier and are feasible production points for this country. Points *C* and *D* are points that lie inside the production possibility frontier: this country can produce these points—they are feasible—but the country is not using its available resources fully. Points *C* and *D* are therefore feasible points, but not efficient points. Points *E* and *F* lie outside the production possibility frontier and are therefore not feasible points of production for this country.

Figure 3.1

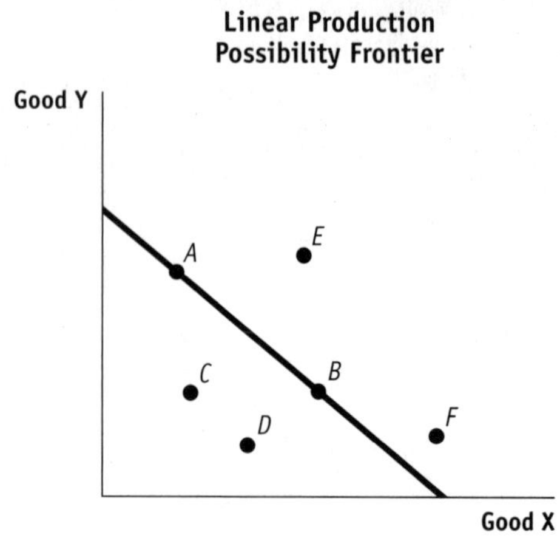

Objective #2. The simplest version of this production possibility frontier model assumes that the frontier is linear and thus has a constant slope. This implies that the opportunity cost of producing another unit of the good measured on the *x*-axis stays the same as you move along the production possibility frontier. In Figure 3.2 the opportunity cost of moving from point *A* to point *B* and the opportunity cost of moving from point *C* to point *D* are illustrated. Remember that opportunity cost measures what you give up to get something: thus, when moving from point *A* to point *B*, opportunity cost is measured in terms of good Y, the good you give up to get more of good X; whereas, when moving from point *C* to point *D*, opportunity cost is measured in terms of good X, the good you give up to get more of good Y. The lines that are bold in Figure 3.2 indicate the opportunity cost of moving from point *A* to point *B* or from point *C* to point *D*.

Figure 3.2

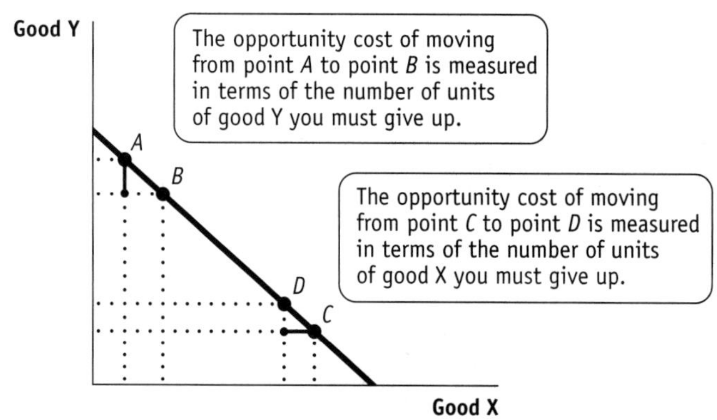

Objective #3. A more realistic production possibility frontier is one that is bowed out from the origin: this implies that as the country produces more and more of one of the goods, the opportunity cost of producing this good increases. The production possibility frontier has this shape due to specialization of resources: some of the resources available to the country are more suited to produce good X than they are good Y. When the country decides to increase the production of one type of good, the first few units can be produced at relatively low opportunity cost since resources can be shifted from the production of one good to the production of the other good that are not particularly well suited to the production of the first good. However, the opportunity cost eventually will rise since the increased production of this good eventually will require the use of resources that are ill-suited to produce this good. Figure 3.3 illustrates a bowed-out production possibility frontier and the opportunity cost of getting one more unit of the good measured on the *x*-axis. Notice that as we get more and more units of good X, the opportunity cost of each additional unit of X is larger than the opportunity cost of the preceding unit.

Figure 3.3

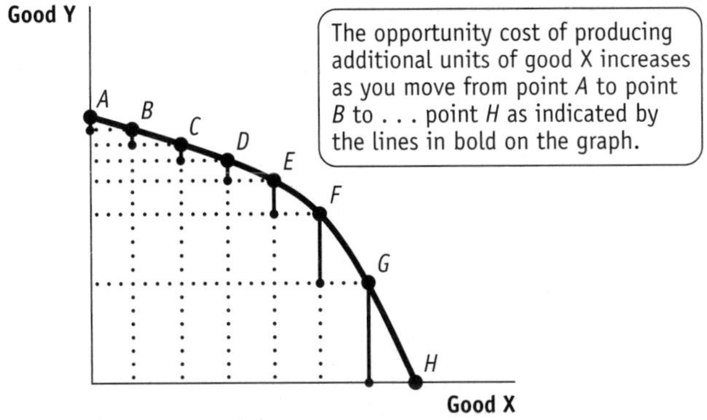

Objective #4. There are two types of efficiency to discuss with respect to production possibility frontiers: productive efficiency and allocative efficiency. Productive efficiency refers to producing at a point that lies on the production possibility frontier. Points that lie inside the frontier are inefficient, since it is possible to increase the level of production from the given set of resources. Allocative efficiency refers to producing the right mix of goods from the available resources. For an economy to be allocatively efficient it must allocate its resources in such a way as to make consumers as well off as possible. Another way of saying this is that an allocatively efficient economy produces the mix of goods that people want.

Objective #5. For an economy to be efficient it must achieve productive and allocative efficiency: it must not waste resources and it must produce the right mix of goods.

Objective #6. The production possibility frontier illustrates scarcity in that there are points of production that cannot be produced because the level of resources and/or technology constrain production. The production possibility frontier illustrates trade-offs: getting more of good X requires giving up some of good Y.

Objective #7. Economic growth can be illustrated with the production possibility frontier model. When the frontier shifts away from the origin, this means that the represented economy can now produce more of good X and good Y. The production possibility frontier shifts out when there are increases in resources or increases in the available level of technology.

Key Terms

trade-off when you give up something in order to have something else.

production possibility frontier illustrates the trade-offs facing an economy that produces only two goods. It shows the maximum quantity of one good that can be produced for any given quantity produced of the other.

efficient describes a market or economy that takes all opportunities to make some people better off without making other people worse off.

factors of production resources used to produce goods and services.

technology the technical means for producing goods and services.

Notes

AFTER YOU READ THE MODULE

Tips

Tip #1. Economic models can be described verbally, but they can also be represented by graphs or equations. You will want to be comfortable working with all three types of representations.

Tip #2. Throughout the course you will find it helpful to be able to sketch graphs to illustrate the ideas you are analyzing. You should practice making precise, numerically significant graphs, but you also should practice less formal graphs that sketch the nature of the relationship rather than the precise mathematical relationship.

Tip #3. Opportunity cost can be measured using the production possibility frontier model. To do this calculation pick a point on the production possibility frontier and identify how much of each good is being produced. Then pick a second point on the production possibility frontier and identify the new levels of production. The opportunity cost is measured as the number of units of the good you must give up to get more of the other good. Note that both points must be on the production possibility frontier. Figure 3.4 illustrates the measurement of opportunity cost when moving from point *A* to point *B*. In this example, the opportunity cost is measured as the amount of good Y, $Y_1 - Y_2$, that must be given up to increase the production of good X from its initial value of X_1 to the new level X_2. The bold line indicates the amount of good Y that is given up to increase the production of good X from X_1 to X_2.

Figure 3.4

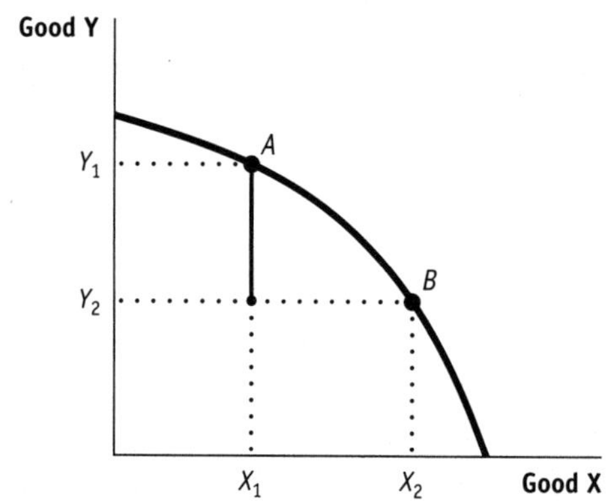

Tip #4. If you are using flash cards, make sure you include the following cards: (a) a linear production possibility frontier indicating feasible and infeasible points as well as efficient and inefficient points, and (b) a production possibility frontier bowed out from the origin showing these same concepts. Also, don't forget to include a card for each new vocabulary word as well as the module heading on each card.

Tip #5. Calculating opportunity cost in a problem is often challenging for students initially. Let's explore a fail-safe method for this calculation based on a linear production possibility frontier (this is the type of production possibility frontier that we will use in the comparative advantage model). First, construct the production possibility frontier and, since it is linear, calculate the slope of the frontier. Then use this slope measure to generate the opportunity costs you want: the opportunity cost of producing one more unit of the good measured on the *x*-axis is given by the slope, since the slope tells us the change in the *y*-variable divided by the change in the *x*-variable. Thus, if the slope of the production possibility frontier is −2, then the opportunity cost of producing an additional unit of good X is 2 units of good Y. To find the opportunity cost of the good produced on the *y*-axis, we simply need to use the reciprocal of the slope. Thus, if the slope of the linear production possibility frontier is −2, then the opportunity cost of producing one more unit of good Y is ½ unit of good X, since this is the amount of good X we must give up to get one more unit of good Y. The problems in this module will give you a chance to practice this reasoning and this technique.

WORKED PROBLEMS

1. People often face trade-offs about the use of their resources. In this problem, Joe can produce either bicycles or sweaters. The following points lie on Joe's production possibility frontier and represent points where Joe is maximizing his production of the two goods given his available resources, technology, and time. Assume that Joe's production possibility frontier for these two goods is linear.

Production point	Bicycles per year	Sweaters per year
A	160	20
B	120	40
C	60	70
D	40	80

a. Draw a graph of Joe's production possibility frontier. In your graph measure bicycles on the *y*-axis and sweaters on the *x*-axis.

STEP 1: Draw a graph of Joe's production possibility frontier using the given points in the table. The following figure provides a graph of the Joe's production possibility frontier based upon the points given in the provided table.

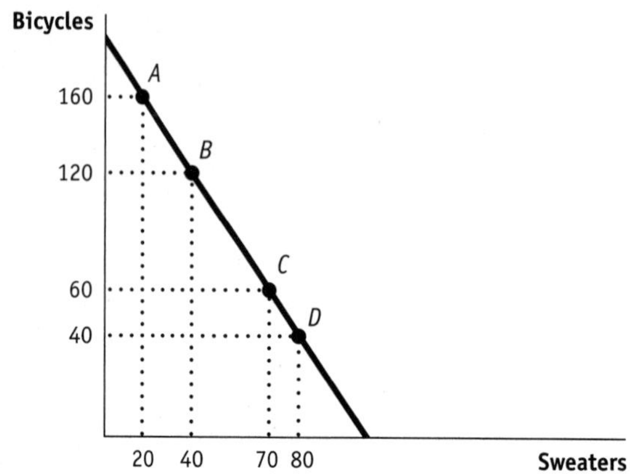

b. Write an equation for Joe's production possibility frontier.

STEP 2: Use the slope-intercept form to write an equation for Joe's production possibility frontier. The slope-intercept form is given as $y = mx + b$, where y is the variable measured on the vertical axis (in this case bicycles, B), x is the variable measured on the horizontal axis (in this case sweaters, S), m is the slope of the equation, and b is the y-intercept.

To write the equation for Joe's production possibility frontier, you will need to know the slope of the frontier as well as the y-intercept for the frontier. Since the frontier is linear, the slope will be constant and equal to the change in the bicycles divided by the change in sweaters. Thus, moving from point A to point B, the slope is equal to $(160 - 120)/(20 - 40) = -2$. To find the y-intercept, you can use the general formula for a linear equation, $y = mx + b$, and substitute in the slope measure you just computed for m, and replace the y and x with B and S (where B is the number of bicycles and S is the number of sweaters). Thus, $y = mx + b$ is now $B = -2S + b$. To find the y-intercept, b, you need to replace (S,B) with values that you know are on the line. For example, you know that point A is on the line and that point A consists of 20 sweaters and 160 bicycles. Thus, $B = -2S + b$ can be written as $160 = -2(20) + b$. Solving for b, you will find that $b = 200$. You can use any of the points you are given in the table to find this y-intercept: the only requirement is that the point must lie on the production possibility frontier. The following figure illustrates Joe's production possibility frontier while identifying both the y-intercept and the x-intercept (to find the x-intercept, use the basic formula $B = -2S + 200$ and substitute $B = 0$ into this equation: thus, $S = 100$).

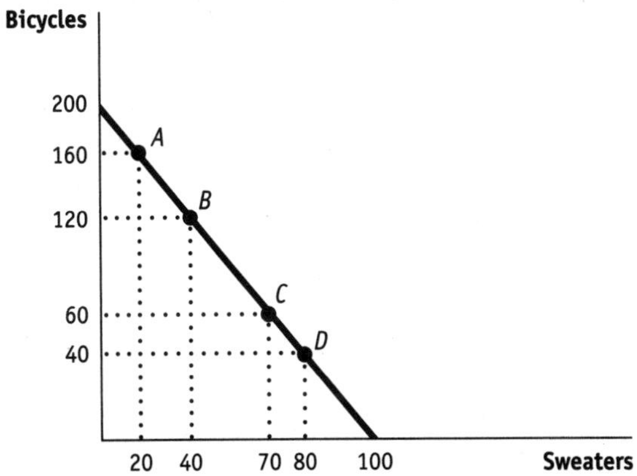

c. Consider each of the following production points and determine whether the production point is (1) feasible and efficient; (2) feasible and inefficient; or (3) infeasible (that is, the point lies beyond the production possibility frontier). Hint: you may find the equation you wrote in part (b) helpful in determining the attributes of these production points.

i. 30 sweaters and 150 bicycles
ii. 15 sweaters and 170 bicycles
iii. 90 sweaters and 15 bicycles
iv. 75 sweaters and 55 bicycles

STEP 3: Using the equation for Joe's production possibility frontier you found in part (b), check each of the previously mentioned points to see if they lie on his production possibility frontier, lie beyond his production possibility frontier, or lie inside his production possibility frontier.

i. This point is infeasible. To see this, use the equation you found in part (b) and plug in the value for *S*. Thus, $B = -2S + 200$ and you are told that sweater production is 30. So, $B = -2(30) + 200 = 140$. The maximum number of bicycles that can be produced when 30 sweaters are produced is 140 and not 150. The point (30, 150) lies beyond Joe's production possibility frontier and therefore is not feasible.

ii. This point is feasible and efficient. To see this, use the equation from part (b) and this point. Thus, $B = -2(15) + 200 = 170$. The point (15, 170) lies on Joe's production possibility frontier: it is both feasible and efficient.

iii. This point is feasible but inefficient. To see this, use the equation from part (b) and this point. Thus, $B = -2(90) + 200 = 20$. The point (90, 15) lies inside Joe's production possibility frontier since the point (90, 20) lies on his frontier. This point is therefore feasible but inefficient.

iv. This point is infeasible. To see this, use the equation from part (b) and this point. Thus, $B = -2(75) + 200 = 50$. The point (75, 55) lies outside Joe's production possibility frontier since the point (75, 50) lies on his frontier. This point is therefore not feasible.

d. Suppose that Joe experiences an improvement in his sweater-making technology so that he can now produce twice as many sweaters as he could initially. Assume that his ability to produce bicycles has not changed. Draw this new production possibility frontier for Joe and then write an equation for this new production possibility frontier.

STEP 4: **Draw Joe's new production possibility frontier and compare it with his original production possibility frontier.**

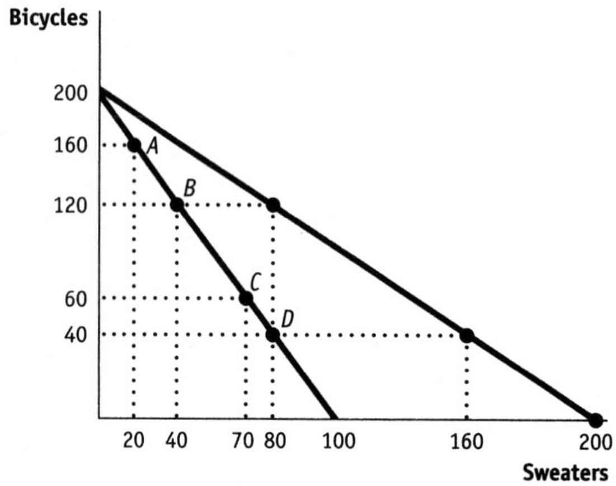

The equation for this new production possibility frontier is $B = -S + 200$.

2. The following graph depicts Susie's production possibility frontier for producing widgets and gadgets. In this problem assume that Susie is initially producing only widgets and no gadgets.

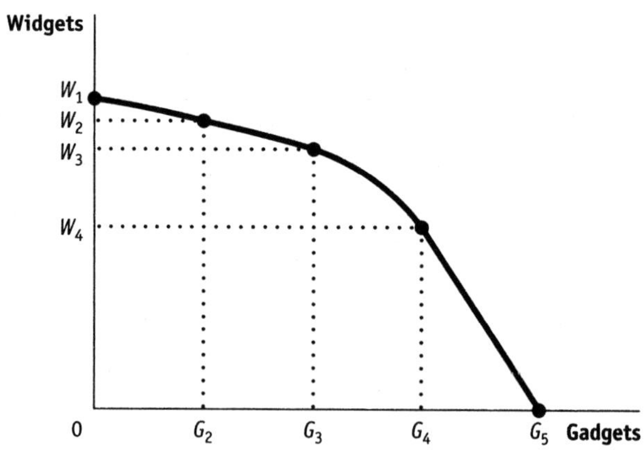

Use this graph to evaluate Susie's opportunity cost of moving from one point of her production possibility frontier to another point on her production possibility frontier.

a. What is Susie's opportunity cost of producing G_2 units of gadgets if she is currently producing zero gadgets?

STEP 1: **For questions (a), (b), and (c), refer to the previous graph and measure Susie's opportunity cost by what she must give up when moving from one point on her production possibility frontier to another point on her production possibility frontier.**

The opportunity cost of producing G_2 units of gadgets is the number of widgets that must be given up. Initially Susie is producing W_1 widgets and 0 gadgets. When Susie moves along her production possibility frontier to produce G_2 units of gadgets, she finds that she must decrease her widget production to W_2. The opportunity cost of this gadget production is therefore equal to $(W_1 - W_2)$ units of widgets.

b. Suppose that Susie is now producing G_2 units of gadgets and that she is producing at a point on her production possibility frontier. What is the opportunity cost of producing G_3 units of gadgets?

The opportunity cost of producing G_3 units of gadgets is the number of widgets that must be given up. Using the same logic as in the answer to part (a), this opportunity cost can be calculated as the distance $(W_2 - W_3)$ since this distance measures the number of widgets that Susie must give up in order to increase her gadget production from G_2 units to G_3 units.

c. Suppose that Susie is now producing G_3 units of gadgets and that she is producing at a point on her production possibility frontier. What is the opportunity cost of producing G_4 units of gadgets?

The opportunity cost of producing G_4 units of gadgets is the number of widgets that must be given up. Using the same logic as in the answer to part (a), this opportunity cost can be calculated as the distance $(W_3 - W_4)$ since this distance measures the number of widgets that Susie must give up in order to increase her gadget production from G_3 to G_4 units.

d. What happens to Susie's opportunity cost of producing gadgets as she decides to produce increasing amounts of gadgets? Provide a verbal explanation and then use the preceding graph to illustrate what happens to Susie's opportunity cost as she produces more and more gadgets.

STEP 2: Refer to the graph and use it to see what happens to Susie's opportunity cost as she increases her production of gadgets by one unit at a time starting with zero units of gadgets. Remember that her opportunity cost of producing a gadget is measured by the number of widgets she must give up.

As Susie produces more and more gadgets, her opportunity cost increases. Since her production possibility frontier is bowed outward from the origin, this indicates that Susie's available resources are specialized, with some of those resources being more suited to widget production while others are more suited to gadget production. This idea of increasing opportunity cost is illustrated on the following graph.

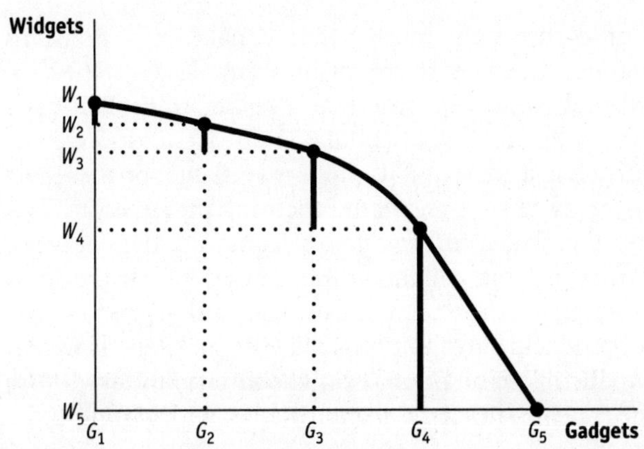

Notice that the bold vertical lines get longer and longer as we move from 0 units of gadgets to a larger level of gadget production (e.g., G_4). The length of the bold vertical lines measures the opportunity cost of that level of gadget production: for example, the opportunity cost of moving from 0 units of gadgets to G_2 units of gadgets is given by the vertical distance ($W_1 - W_2$).

e. Suppose that Susie had initially produced only gadgets and no widgets. Does the opportunity cost of producing widgets increase as Susie increases her widget production by one unit at a time from 0 units of widgets to W_1 units of widgets? Use a graph to illustrate your answer.

STEP 3: Now, you want to use the graph to think about moving from the point that corresponds to G_5 units of gadgets and 0 units of widgets to the point that corresponds to 0 units of gadgets and W_1 units of widgets. As you move upward along the curve increasing widget production by one unit at a time, remember that the opportunity cost of this increased widget production will be measured by the number of gadgets that must be given up.

The law of increasing opportunity cost holds if Susie moves from producing only gadgets to producing a mix of gadgets and widgets. The following graph illustrates this idea by considering changing the production of widgets by one unit at a time. Notice that in this case the opportunity cost is measured as a horizontal distance since increasing widget production implies giving up gadget production: thus, the opportunity cost of producing widgets is measured by the number of gadgets that must be given up.

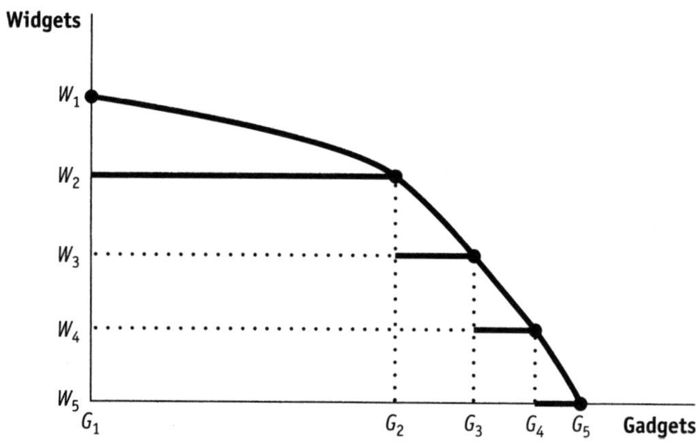

3. All countries face scarcity of resources and must therefore make tough decisions about what they should produce. Consider the following example about the allocation of resources toward health care. Suppose that a kidney transplant costs \$50,000, while immunizations against major childhood diseases cost \$500 per child. Assume that a country has a total of \$10 million available for these two programs and that there is no issue with regard to procuring the necessary kidneys for transplants. Use the provided information to construct the country's production possibility frontier, placing childhood immunizations on the horizontal axis and kidney transplants on the vertical axis. Use your graph to measure the opportunity cost of producing an additional kidney transplant as well as the opportunity cost of producing an additional childhood immunization. Use this example to discuss the trade-offs that an economy faces with regard to the production of these two goods.

STEP 1: Use the given information to construct a production possibility frontier for these two goods. Then use this figure to measure the opportunity cost of producing an additional unit of either good.

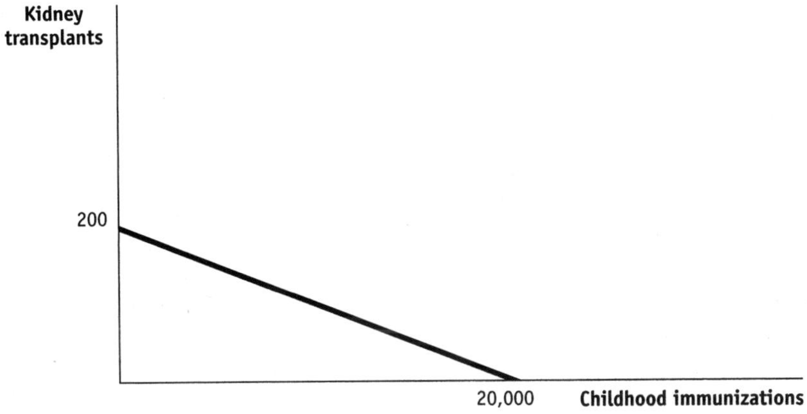

The opportunity cost of a kidney transplant is 100 immunizations. The opportunity cost of an immunization is (1/100) of a kidney transplant.

STEP 2: Use this example to discuss the trade-offs an economy faces with regard to the production of these two goods.

If a country is faced with a limited amount of resources, it cannot produce an unlimited amount of goods and services. In this example, the country has only so many financial resources available for the production of kidney transplants and immunizations: the country will have to decide how to allocate these scarce resources, and in allocating these scarce resources it will face a trade-off where the decision to produce more kidney transplants implies a decision to provide fewer immunizations and vice versa.

Problems and Exercises

1. The production possibilities frontier model holds resources, technology, and the time period constant in order to construct a path of points that represents the maximum amount of two goods an economy can produce given the constraints of their resources and technology during the given time period. This model allows us to consider the effect of an increase in resources while holding everything else constant. In this example, what is it that we are holding constant? Describe the effect of this change in resources on this economy's production possibility frontier.

2. Suppose you are stranded on an island by yourself and must therefore produce all the goods you consume. You consume clams and mangos exclusively. If you devote all your available time to harvesting clams, you can harvest 100 clams in a week. If you devote all your available time to collecting mangos, you can find 200 mangos in a week.

   a. Imagine it is possible for you to divide your time between harvesting clams and collecting mangos and that you can even find fractional amounts of both goods. Draw a sketch of your production possibility frontier for a week, placing mangos on the *x*-axis and clams on the *y*-axis.

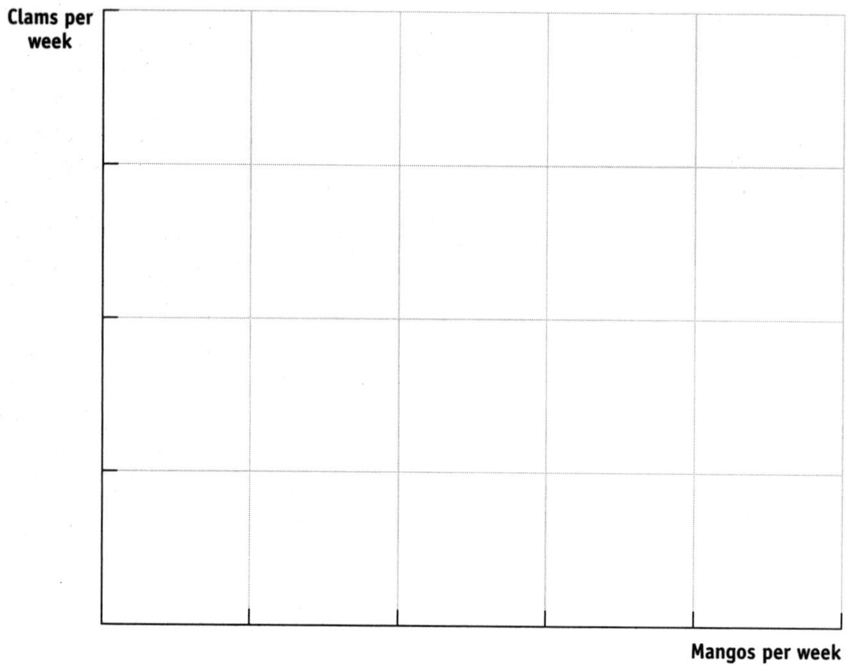

   b. Now, sketch your production possibility frontier for a two-week period. Describe what happens to your production possibility frontier when you increase the amount of time available for production.

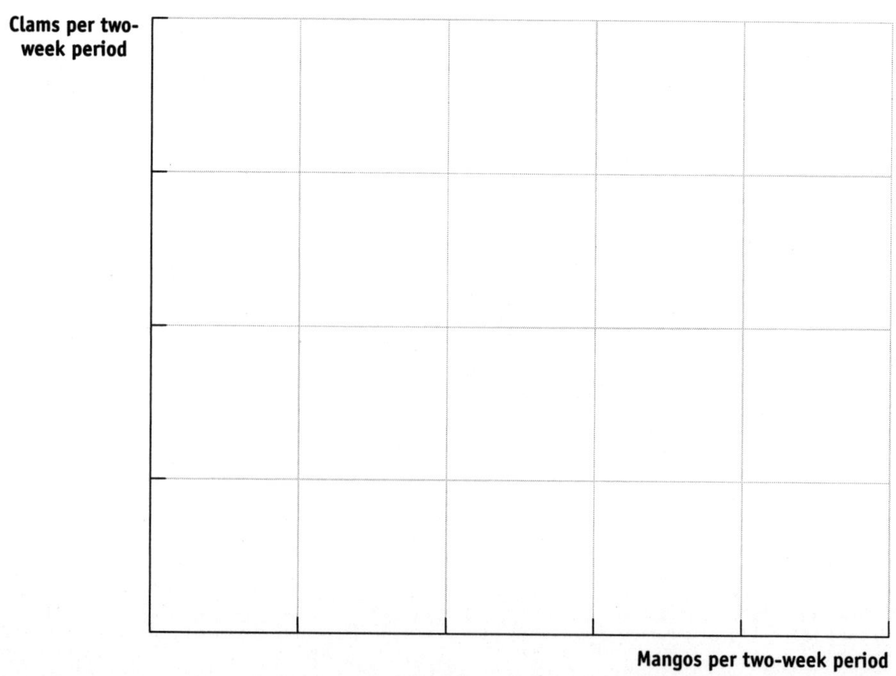

c. Now, imagine you invent a clam rake that enhances your ability to harvest clams. With this invention you are able to increase your clam harvest to a maximum of 200 clams per week if you spend all your time on clams. Your invention has no effect on your ability to collect mangos. Sketch your new production possibility frontier. Describe in words the effect of a change in technology that affects the ability to produce one of the goods, but not both of the goods.

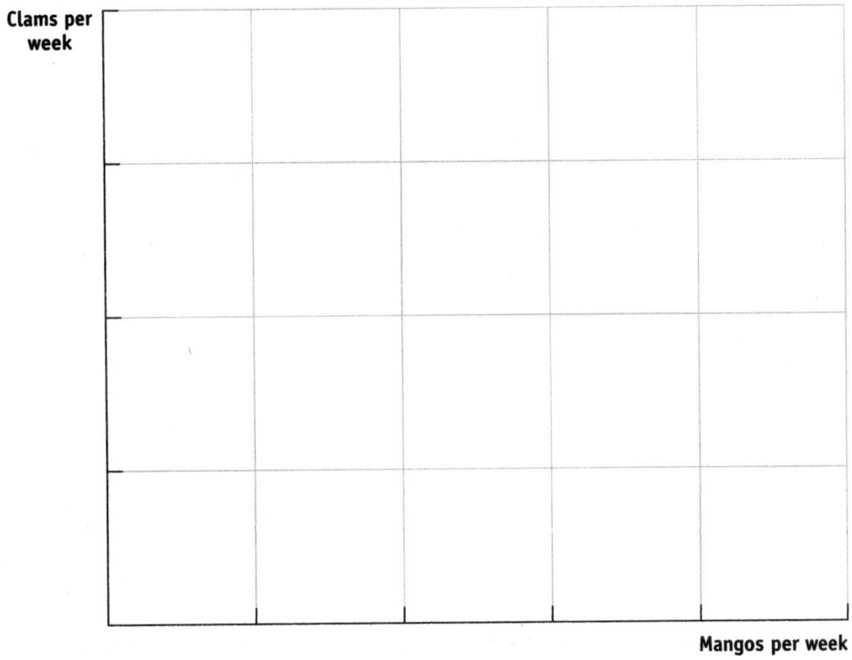

d. Suppose you have your clam rake and, in addition, you procure knowledge over time that enhances your ability to collect mangos. Your ability to gather mangos increases to 300 mangos per week because of this knowledge. Sketch your new production possibility frontier based on this knowledge and your use of the clam rake. In effect you have experienced a change in technology that has a positive effect on the production of both goods. Describe in words the effect of this change on the production possibility frontier.

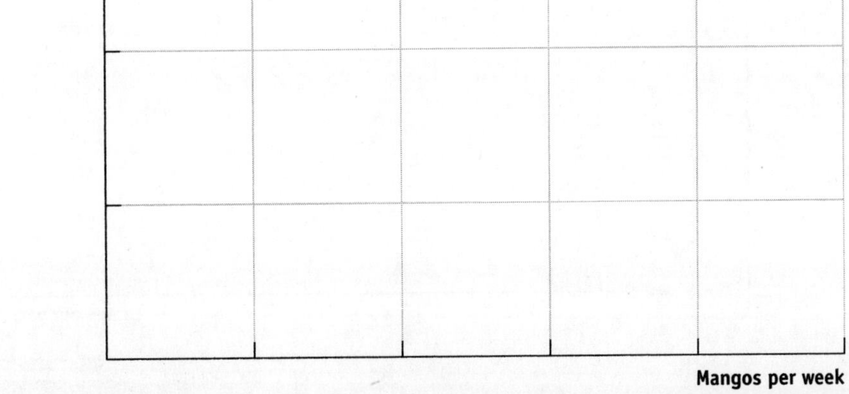

3. Let's return to the example given in problem 2.

   a. What is the opportunity cost of harvesting a clam given the original information in problem 2?

   b. What is the opportunity cost of collecting a mango given the original information in problem 2?

   c. What is the slope of the production possibility frontier that you sketched in your answer to problem 2a? How does this slope measure relate to the answers you provide in parts (a) and (b) of this question?

   d. What happened to the slope of the production possibility frontier once you invent the clam rake (problem 2c)? What happens to the opportunity cost of harvesting clams once you invent the clam rake? What happens to the opportunity cost of collecting mangos once you invent the clam rake?

4. The country of Orange manufactures sofas and lamps. With its available resources and technology, Orange can manufacture in a year 1,000 sofas and 0 lamps or 0 sofas and 250 lamps. It can also manufacture any combination of sofas and lamps that lie on the straight line connecting these two points.

   a. Sketch Orange's production possibility frontier, placing sofas on the *y*-axis and lamps on the *x*-axis.

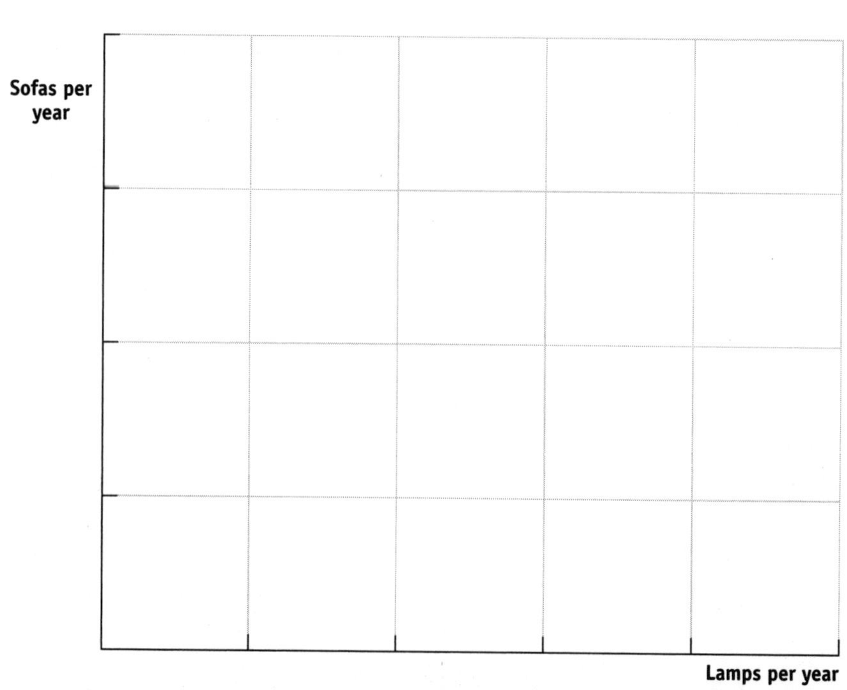

b. Fill in the following table by listing some of the feasible and efficient combinations of production available to Orange each year given its resources and technology.

Combination	Number of lamps possible	Number of sofas possible
A	0	
B	50	
C		500
D		200
E	225	
F	250	

c. What is the slope of the production possibility frontier for Orange?

d. What is the opportunity cost of producing one additional sofa for Orange?

e. What is the opportunity cost of producing one additional lamp for Orange?

f. What is the value of the y-intercept for Orange? (Hint: In this example, the y-intercept is the number of sofas Orange can produce if it does not produce anything else.)

g. Write an equation for the production possibility frontier for Orange using S to stand for sofas and L to stand for lamps. Write this equation in y-intercept form. (Hint: This means that the equation will be written with S on the left-hand side of the equation, where the S stands for the value of the variable measured on the vertical axis of your sketch.) Verify that each of the combinations you found in part (b) of this problem are true in the equation you wrote.

5. The country of Utopia produces two goods from its available resources and technology. The only resource that Utopia has is labor. It takes 3 hours of labor to produce 2 widgets and 4 hours of labor to produce 1 gadget. For this question assume that the production possibility frontier for Utopia is a straight line.

   a. Sketch the production possibility frontier for the country of Utopia. (Hint: To do this, you must first decide on a relevant period. You might pick 120 hours, or 1,200 hours, or 1.2 million hours as your labor constraint, for example, and then you would sketch your production possibility frontier based on this amount of available time and labor.) Draw your production possibility frontier with widgets on the *y*-axis and gadgets on the *x*-axis.

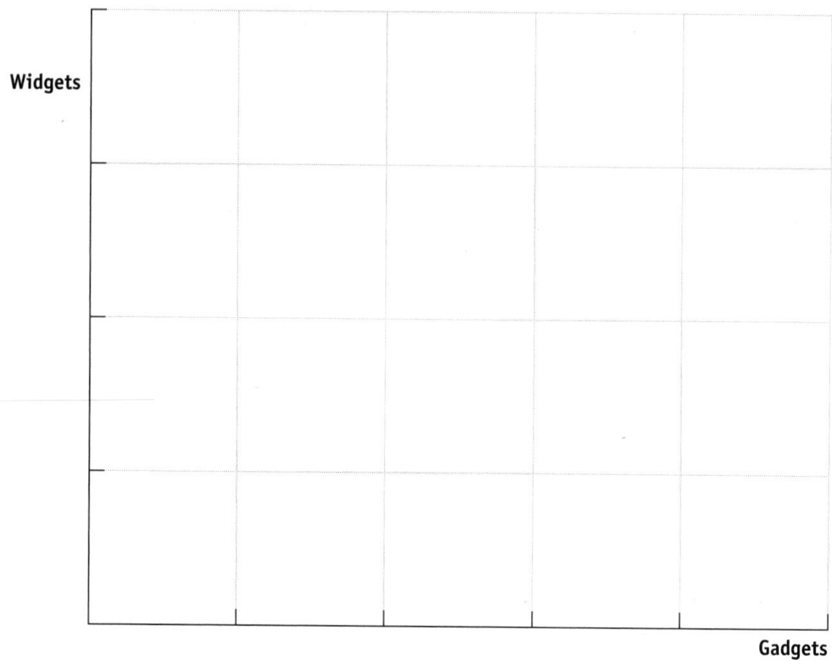

   b. What is the slope of your production possibility frontier?

   c. What is the opportunity cost of producing an additional widget in Utopia?

   d. What is the opportunity cost of producing an additional gadget in Utopia?

6. The country of Jonesville produces two goods from its available resources and technology. The only resource that Jonesville has is labor. The following table gives the amount of labor necessary to produce a widget or a gadget. For this question assume that the production possibility frontier for Jonesville is a straight line.

	Number of hours of labor needed to produce a gadget	Number of hours of labor needed to produce a widget
Jonesville	2	5

a. Suppose that you want to draw a production possibility frontier for Jonesville. What must you do first to draw your sketch?

b. Sketch the production possibility frontier for Jonesville assuming that Jonesville has 120 hours of labor available. Place gadgets on the *x*-axis and widgets on the *y*-axis.

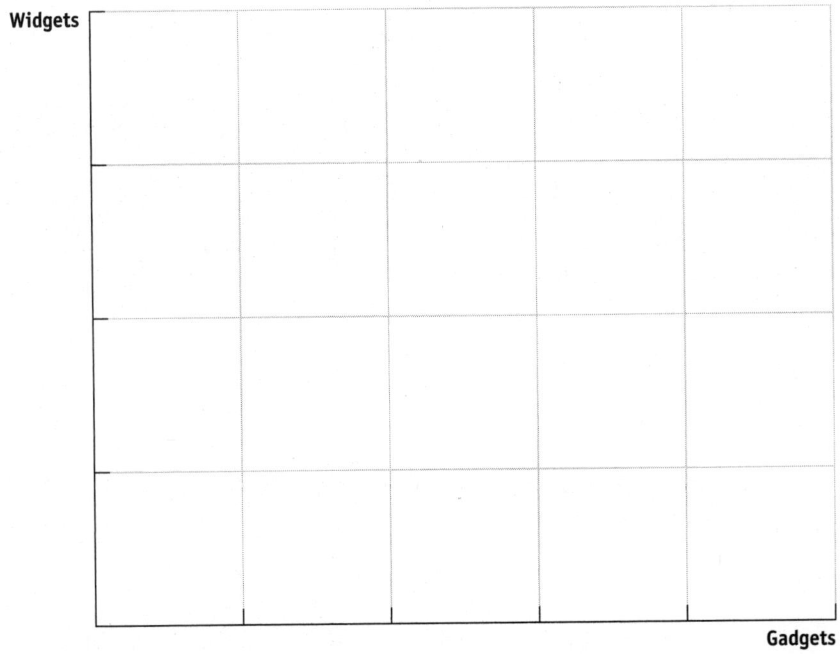

c. What is the slope of the production possibility frontier?

d. What is the opportunity cost of producing an additional gadget?

e. What is the opportunity cost of producing an additional widget?

f. Suppose that Jonesville has 240 hours of labor instead of 120 hours of labor. Does this affect the opportunity cost of producing widgets or gadgets? Explain your answer.

7. The following table provides six possible production combinations that Smithtown can produce from their available resources and technology during this year. Assume that Smithtown only produces bicycles and tents from their available resources.

Combination	Bicycles	Tents
A	100	0
B	90	10
C	70	25
D	40	36
E	10	42
F	0	44

a. Sketch Smithtown's production possibility frontier. Measure bicycles along the *x*-axis and tents along the *y*-axis.

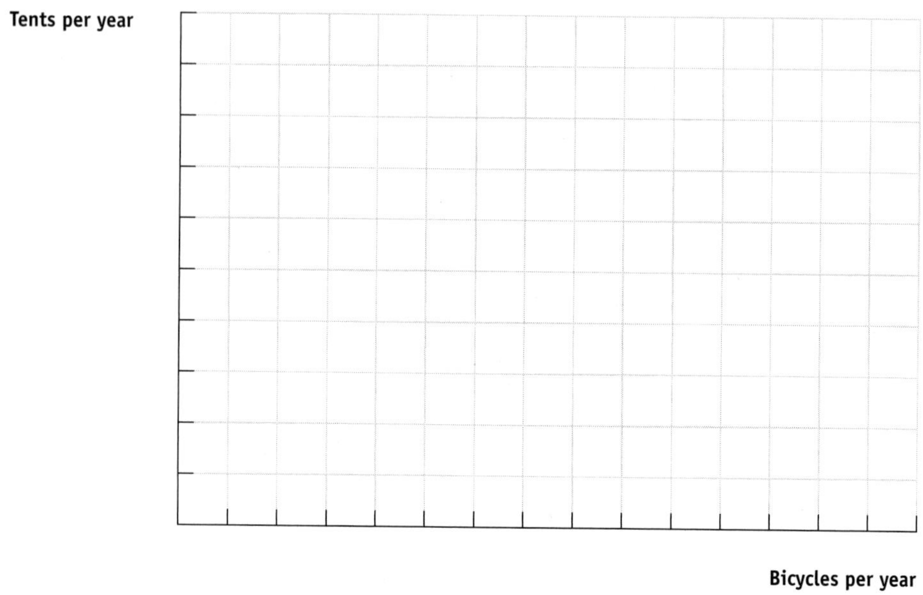

b. Suppose Smithtown is currently producing at combination *C*. If Smithtown chooses to produce at combination *B*, what is the opportunity cost of moving from combination *C* to combination *B*?

c. Suppose Smithtown is currently producing at combination *C*. If Smithtown chooses to produce at combination *D*, what is the opportunity cost of moving from combination *C* to combination *D*?

d. Smithtown's production possibility frontier is not linear. Provide an explanation for why the production possibility frontier is not linear.

8. Suppose an economy produces two goods in a year using its available resources and technology. This economy's resources are specialized.

a. Describe the general shape of this economy's production possibility frontier.

b. If this economy currently produces only one of these two goods, what do you know must be true about the opportunity cost of producing more and more units of the good that is not being currently produced?

c. If this economy is to be productively efficient, what must be true about its production of these two goods?

d. If this economy is to be allocatively efficient, what must be true about its production of these two goods?

e. Suppose this economy is deemed to be efficient. What must occur for this statement to be true?

BEFORE YOU TAKE THE TEST

Module Review Questions

1. Suppose Mike has a linear production possibility frontier in the production of potatoes and tomatoes. If Mike devotes all his time to the production of potatoes, he can produce 1,000 pounds of potatoes a year; if he devotes all his time to the production of tomatoes, he can produce 2,000 pounds of tomatoes a year. Which of the following combinations of potatoes and tomatoes are not feasible for Mike?

a. 1,000 pounds of potatoes and 2,000 pounds of tomatoes per year
b. 1,000 pounds of potatoes and 0 pounds of tomatoes per year
c. 0 pounds of potatoes and 2,000 pounds of tomatoes per year
d. 500 pounds of potatoes and 1,000 pounds of tomatoes per year

2. Suppose Mike has a linear production possibility frontier in the production of potatoes and tomatoes. If Mike devotes all his time to the production of potatoes, he can produce 1,000 pounds of potatoes a year; if he devotes all his time to the production of tomatoes, he can produce 2,000 pounds of tomatoes a year. Which of the following combinations of potatoes and tomatoes are not efficient for Mike?

a. 500 pounds of potatoes and 500 pounds of tomatoes per year
b. 500 pounds of potatoes and 1,000 pounds of tomatoes per year
c. 750 pounds of potatoes and 500 pounds of tomatoes per year
d. 250 pounds of potatoes and 1,500 pounds of tomatoes per year

3. Utopia has a linear production possibility frontier in the production of widgets and gadgets. It can produce three gadgets per hour of labor time or four widgets per hour of labor time. What is the opportunity cost of producing one widget in Utopia?

a. 3 gadgets
b. 4 widgets
c. 0.75 gadget
d. 1.33 gadgets

4. Jonesville produces widgets and gadgets and its production possibility frontier is linear. The following table provides the number of units of labor necessary to produce 1 gadget or 1 widget in Jonesville.

	Number of hours of labor needed to produce a gadget	Number of hours of labor needed to produce a widget
Jonesville	5	10

Suppose that Jonesville has 100 hours of labor. What is the maximum number of widgets it can produce?

a. 10 widgets
b. 20 widgets
c. 1 widget
d. 100 widgets

5. Jonesville produces widgets and gadgets and its production possibility frontier is linear. The following table provides the number of units of labor necessary to produce 1 gadget or 1 widget in Jonesville.

	Number of hours of labor needed to produce a gadget	Number of hours of labor needed to produce a widget
Jonesville	5	10

Suppose that Jonesville has 100 hours of labor. What is the maximum number of widgets and gadgets it can produce if it devotes half of its labor time to the production of gadgets and half of its labor time to the production of widgets?

a. 20 gadgets and 5 widgets
b. 10 gadgets and 5 widgets
c. 5 gadgets and 20 widgets
d. 5 gadgets and 10 widgets

6. Jonesville produces widgets and gadgets and its production possibility frontier is linear. The following table provides the number of units of labor necessary to produce 1 gadget or 1 widget in Jonesville.

	Number of hours of labor needed to produce a gadget	Number of hours of labor needed to produce a widget
Jonesville	5	10

Suppose that Jonesville initially has 100 hours of labor. What happens to the opportunity cost of producing a widget if Jonesville's labor resource increases to 200 hours of labor?

a. The opportunity cost of producing a widget decreases.
b. The opportunity cost of producing a widget increases.
c. The opportunity cost of producing a widget does not change.
d. The opportunity cost of producing a widget may increase, decrease, or remain unchanged depending on the number of gadgets that are produced in Jonesville.

7. Jonesville produces widgets and gadgets and its production possibility frontier is linear. The following table provides the number of units of labor necessary to produce 1 gadget or 1 widget in Jonesville.

	Number of hours of labor needed to produce a gadget	Number of hours of labor needed to produce a widget
Jonesville	5	10

Suppose that Jonesville has 100 hours of labor. Which of the following combinations of gadgets and widgets is not feasible for Jonesville to produce?

a. 4 gadgets and 8 widgets
b. 7 gadgets and 7 widgets
c. 8 gadgets and 6 widgets
d. 0 gadgets and 10 widgets

8. Utopia has a linear production possibility frontier in the production of widgets and gadgets. It can produce 3 gadgets per hour of labor time or 4 widgets per hour of labor time. Suppose that Utopia has 120 hours of labor time and that it chooses to divide its labor time equally between the production of widgets and gadgets. What is the maximum number of widgets Utopia can produce given this decision?

a. 480 widgets
b. 240 widgets
c. 60 widgets
d. 15 widgets

9. Suburbia has a production possibility frontier bowed out from the origin for the two goods, guns and butter, that Suburbia produces from its available resources and technology. The following table describes six points that lie on Suburbia's production possibility frontier.

Combination	Number of guns	Pounds of butter
A	0	80
B	10	75
C	20	65
D	30	50
E	40	30
F	50	0

Suppose Suburbia is initially producing at point *D*. What is the opportunity cost of moving to point *E*?

a. 10 guns
b. 40 guns
c. 20 pounds of butter
d. 30 pounds of butter

10. Suburbia has a production possibility frontier bowed out from the origin for the two goods, guns and butter, that Suburbia produces from its available resources and technology. The following table describes six points that lie on Suburbia's production possibility frontier.

Combination	Number of guns	Pounds of butter
A	0	80
B	10	75
C	20	65
D	30	50
E	40	30
F	50	0

Suppose Suburbia is initially producing at point *D*. What is the opportunity cost of moving to point *B*?

a. 25 pounds of butter
b. 20 guns
c. 10 guns
d. 75 pounds of butter

11. Suburbia has a production possibility frontier bowed out from the origin for the two goods, guns and butter, that Suburbia produces from its available resources and technology. The following table describes six points that lie on Suburbia's production possibility frontier.

Combination	Number of guns	Pounds of butter
A	0	80
B	10	75
C	20	65
D	30	50
E	40	30
F	50	0

Suburbia is currently producing 50 pounds of butter and 20 guns. This combination is

a. allocatively efficient, since butter is tastier than guns.

b. productively efficient, since it is a feasible point for Suburbia to produce.

c. infeasible, because Suburbia cannot produce this combination given its resources and technology.

d. feasible but inefficient, since it is a combination that lies inside the production possibility frontier.

12. Which of the following statements is true?

I. Points that lie on the production possibility frontier are allocatively efficient.

II. Points that lie on the production possibility frontier are productively efficient.

a. Statement I is true.

b. Statement II is true.

c. Statements I and II are true.

d. Statements I and II are false.

13. An economy is allocatively efficient provided that

a. it produces at any point along its production possibility frontier.

b. it produces the right mix of goods from its available resources.

c. no resources are wasted.

d. All of the statements are true about allocative efficiency.

ANSWER KEY

Answers to Problems and Exercises

1. Technology and the time period are being held constant so that we can focus on the effect of a change in the level of resources on this economy's production possibility frontier. If resources increase, we would expect the production possibility frontier to shift out because the economy should be able to produce more of both goods now that there are more resources to work with.

2. a.

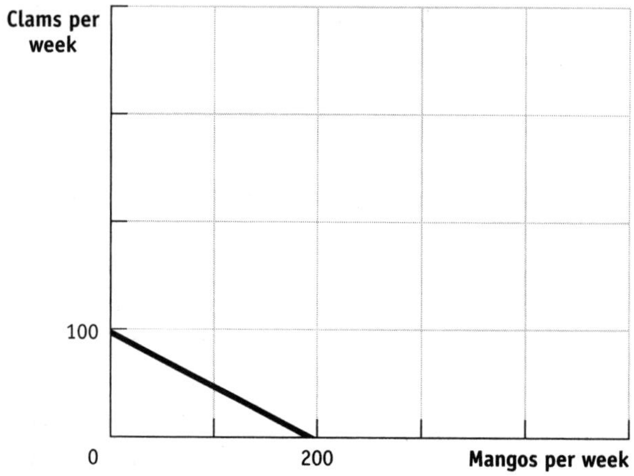

b. An increase in the time period, holding everything else constant, increases the level of production.

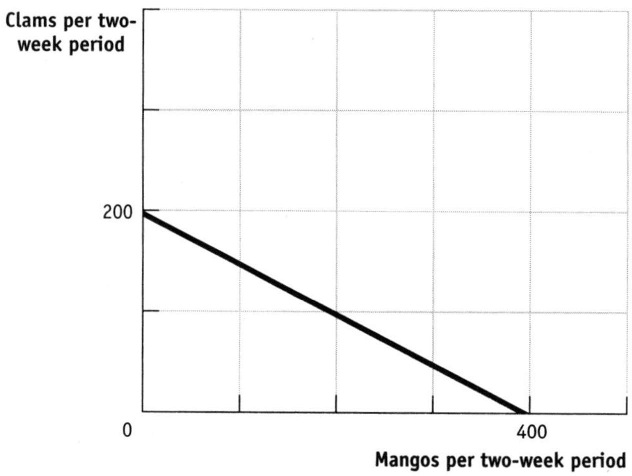

c. The invention of the clam rake shifts the production possibilities frontier out along the clam axis since it is now possible to produce more clams in the same time period.

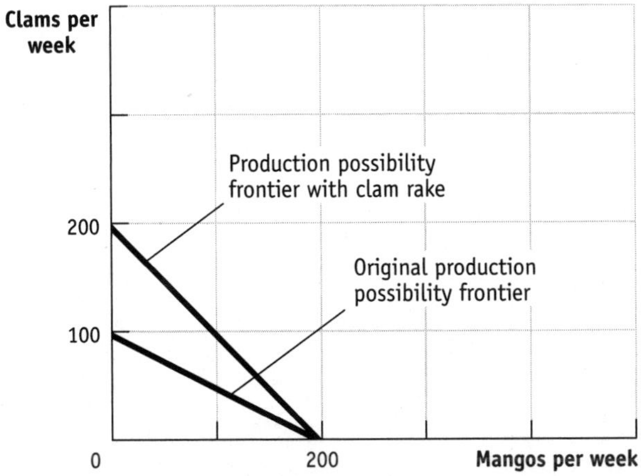

d. Technological change shifts the production possibility frontier away from the origin and therefore results in the possibility of greater production of both goods.

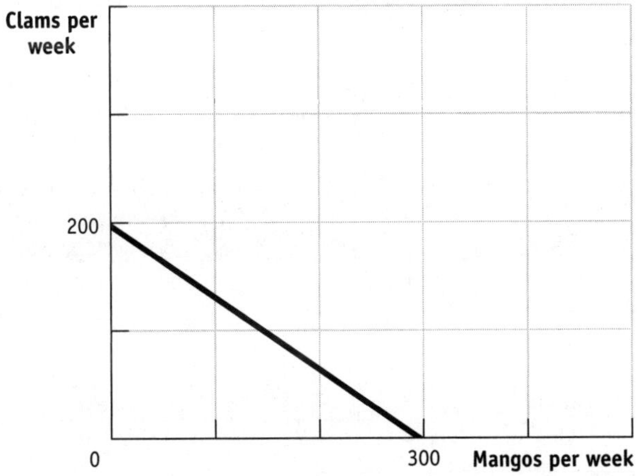

3. a. The opportunity cost of harvesting a clam is measured in terms of the number of mangos you must give up when you harvest a clam. In the original example, you must give up 2 mangos for every clam you harvest.

b. The opportunity cost of collecting a mango is measured in terms of the number of clams you must give up when you collect a mango. In the original example, you must give up ½ of a clam for every mango you collect.

c. The slope of the production possibility frontier is –½ (remember, you calculate this as the rise/run, or the change in the *y*-variable divided by the change in the *x*-variable). The slope tells us what the change in the *y*-variable is for a 1-unit change in the *x*-variable. In this case, the slope tells us what the change in the number of clams is for a 1-unit change in mangos: when mango collection increases by 1 unit, then clam harvesting decreases by ½ unit; when mango collection decreases by 1 unit, then clam harvesting increases by ½ unit. The negative sign of the slope tells us that these two variables move in opposite directions: an increase in mangos requires a decrease in clams, or a decrease in mangos requires an increase in clams. The slope measure tells us what the opportunity cost of one more mango is, since mangos are measured on the horizontal axis in this example. If we take the reciprocal of the slope (in this case, –2), it would give us the opportunity cost of producing one more unit of the good on the *y*-axis. In this case, harvesting one more clam has an opportunity cost of 2 mangos since that is the number of mangos we must give up to get one more clam.

d. The invention of the clam rake changed the slope of the production possibility frontier from –½ to –1 and therefore changed the opportunity cost of producing both goods. The opportunity cost of collecting a mango is now 1 clam and the opportunity cost of harvesting one clam is 1 mango.

4. a.

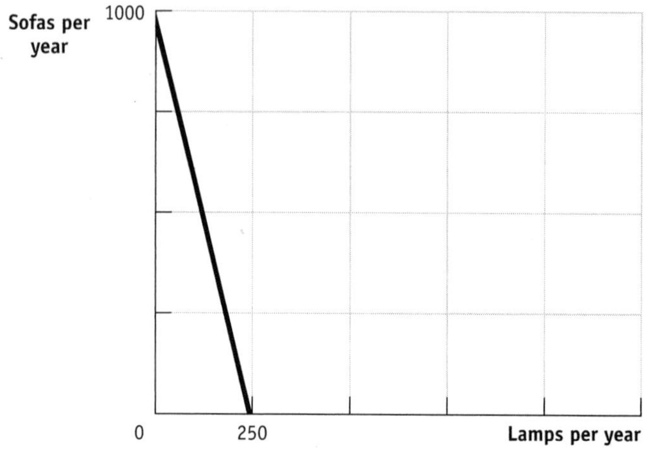

b.

Combination	Number of lamps possible	Number of sofas possible
A	0	1,000
B	50	800
C	125	500
D	200	200
E	225	100
F	250	0

c. The slope of the production possibility frontier is –4 (you can find this by looking at the rise/run, or in this case, –1,000/250).

d. The opportunity cost of producing one more sofa is ¼ lamp. (Hint: Remember that because sofas are measured on the *y*-axis, you can find the opportunity cost by taking the reciprocal of the slope measure.)

e. The opportunity cost of producing one more lamp is 4 sofas. (Hint: Remember that because lamps are measured on the *x*-axis, you can find the opportunity cost by using the slope measure.)

f. The *y*-intercept is 1,000, since if Orange uses all of its resources and technology to produce sofas, this is the maximum number of sofas it can produce in a year.

g. The equation for Orange's production possibility frontier is $S = 1{,}000 - 4L$. You can verify that all the combinations work in this equation by substituting the value of the number of lamps in one of the combinations and verifying that the equation generates the number of sofas you found in the table. For example, if L equals 225, then $S = 1{,}000 - 4(225)$ or $S = 100$ (the value you found in the table).

5. **a.** To draw the production possibility frontier, you first need to identify the number of hours of labor that Utopia has available. Since it takes 3 hours of labor to produce 2 widgets (or 1.5 hours of labor to produce 1 widget) and 4 hours of labor to produce 1 gadget, you will find it helpful to select an amount of time that is divisible by both three and four. So, for instance, 12 hours would work, as would 120 hours, or 240 hours, or an infinite number of other numbers that are divisible by both three and four. For our sketch let's suppose that there are 120 hours of labor available to Utopia and that its citizens can produce either widgets or gadgets or some combination of the two goods. If they devote all of their labor time to widget production, they can produce 80 widgets since (120 hours of labor/3 hours of labor) × (2 widgets) = 80 widgets. If they devote all of their labor time to gadget production, they can produce 30 gadgets since (120 hours of labor/4 hours of labor) × (1 gadget) = 30 gadgets. The graph below illustrates Utopia's production possibility frontier.

Utopia's Production Possibility Frontier Based on 120 Hours of Labor

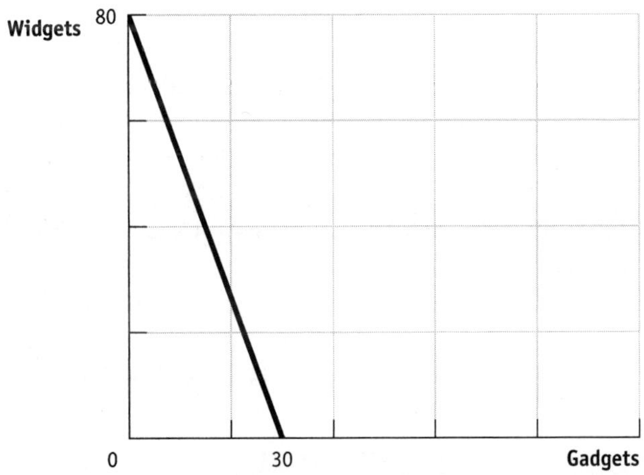

The values of your intercepts will be different depending on the number of hours of labor you assume Utopia has, but the slope of the production possibility frontier should be the same as the one drawn above.

b. The slope of the production possibility frontier is –8/3.

c. The opportunity cost of producing an additional widget in Utopia is 3/8 gadget.

d. The opportunity cost of producing an additional gadget in Utopia is 8/3 widget.

6. **a.** You must first decide how much labor Jonesville has so that you can calculate the maximum amount of widgets and gadgets Jonesville can produce. Since you know gadgets take 2 hours of labor and widgets take 5 hours of labor, you will want to pick a number of hours that is divisible by both two and five. For example, 10 hours would work, or 100 hours, or 20 hours, or 2,000 hours—there is an infinite number of labor quantities that would work in constructing this production possibility frontier.

b.

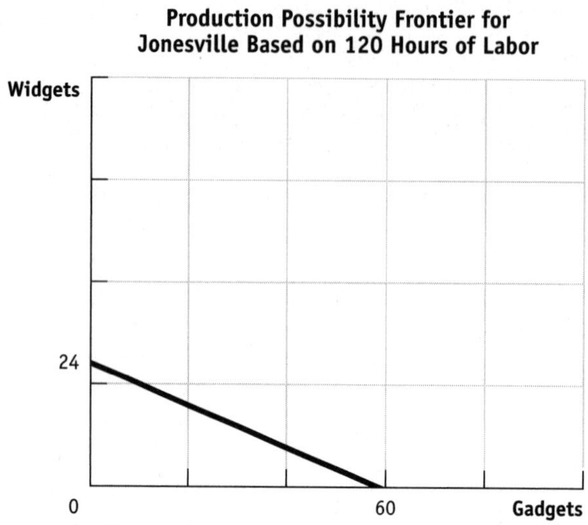

c. The slope of the production possibility frontier is –24/60, or –4/10, or –0.4.

d. Recall that you can use the slope measure to quickly find the opportunity cost of producing one more unit of the good measured on the *x*-axis. To produce one more gadget, you must give up 0.4 widget, therefore the opportunity cost of an additional gadget is 0.4 widget.

e. Recall that you can use the reciprocal of the slope measure to quickly find the opportunity cost of producing one more unit of the good measured on the *y*-axis. To produce one more widget, you must give up 1/0.4 gadgets, therefore the opportunity cost of an additional widget is 2.5 gadgets.

f. If Jonesville has an increase in the amount of labor available to use in producing gadgets and widgets, it can produce more gadgets and more widgets. That is, Jonesville's production possibility frontier will shift out from the origin. But the slope of the new production possibility frontier will be the same as the one drawn based upon 120 hours of labor, thus the opportunity cost of producing widgets or gadgets will not change for Jonesville.

7. a.

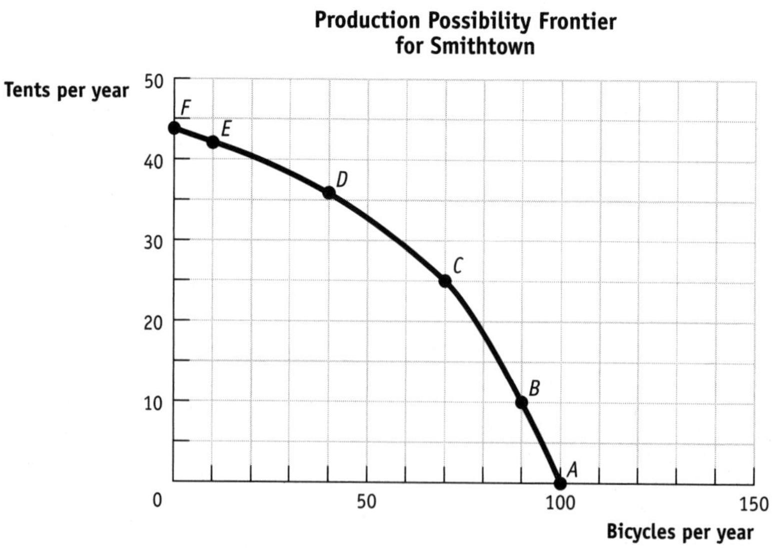

b. The opportunity cost of moving from point *C* to point *B* is measured in terms of the number of units of production you give up. In this case you give up 15 tents, so this is the opportunity cost.

c. The opportunity cost of moving from point *C* to point *D* is 30 bicycles.

d. Smithtown's resources are not equally well suited to produce bicycles and tents. If Smithtown initially devotes all of its resources to producing bicycles, then some of its resources that are currently going into the production of bicycles are not particularly productive at producing bicycles. Smithtown can move some of these resources away from bicycle production and into tent production without decreasing its bicycle production significantly. However, as Smithtown decides to produce more and more tents, this will eventually require moving resources that are well suited to bicycle production into tent production where they are less productive. This specialization of resources results in a production possibility frontier that is bowed out from the origin.

8. a. This economy's production possibility frontier must be bowed out from the origin if the economy's resources are specialized: this implies that the opportunity cost of producing more and more units of one of the goods increases because increased production of this good requires the economy to use resources that would be more productive producing the other good.

b. The opportunity cost of producing more and more units of the good will increase due to the shape of the production possibility frontier, which is bowed out from the origin.

c. To be productively efficient, this economy must be producing at a point that is located on the production possibility frontier.

d. To be allocatively efficient, this economy must be producing at a point that represents the optimal mix of these two goods for the economy.

e. To be efficient, the economy must be both productively and allocatively efficient—that is, it must produce not only on the production possibility frontier, but it must also produce the right mix of goods.

Answers to Module Review Questions

1. Answer a. Mike can produce 1,000 pounds of potatoes and 0 pounds of tomatoes a year or he can produce 2,000 pounds of tomatoes and 0 pounds of potatoes a year. His resources do not allow him to produce a combination of 1,000 pounds of potatoes and 2,000 pounds of tomatoes in a year. Thus, answer (a) is not feasible, while answers (b) and (c) are feasible. Answer (d) is also feasible since if Mike devotes half of his resources this year to producing potatoes and half of his resources this year to producing tomatoes, he will be able to produce 500 pounds of potatoes and 1,000 pounds of tomatoes this year.

2. Answer a. Any combination of production of potatoes and tomatoes that lies on Mike's linear production possibility frontier is an efficient combination. An inefficient combination must lie inside his production possibility frontier. His linear production possibility frontier includes the two points (1,000 pounds of potatoes, 0 pounds of tomatoes) and (0 pounds of potatoes, 2,000 pounds of tomatoes), and we can use these two points to write an equation for his production possibility frontier. If potatoes are measured on the *y*-axis and are denoted by *P*, and tomatoes are measured on the *x*-axis and denoted by *T*, then Mike's production possibility frontier is $P = 1{,}000 - \frac{1}{2}T$. Substitute the number of tomatoes provided in each answer into this equation to calculate the number of potatoes Mike can produce when he produces that level of tomatoes. Thus, for answer (b), when Mike produces 1,000 pounds of tomatoes, the equation states that he will be able to produce 500 pounds of potatoes, which is the number of potatoes given in answer (b). Answers (c) and (d) also fit the equation. Thus, answers (b), (c), and (d) all identify production combinations that are on the production possibility frontier. But answer (a) does not fit the equation: when Mike produces 500 pounds of tomatoes, the equation says that he will be able to produce 750 pounds of potatoes, while answer (a) says that he will produce 500 pounds of potatoes. The combination in answer (a) is a combination that lies inside Mike's production possibility frontier.

3. **Answer c.** Since 4 widgets can be produced in the same amount of labor time as 3 gadgets in Utopia, then 1 widget can be produced in the same amount of labor time as ¾ gadget. Thus, the opportunity cost of producing 1 widget is measured by the number of gadgets that must be given up. In this case, ¾ of a gadget.

4. **Answer a.** Jonesville uses all of its labor to produce widgets. With 100 hours of labor, it can produce 10 widgets since the production of each widget takes 10 hours of labor.

5. **Answer b.** When Jonesville devotes 50 hours of labor to widget production, it can produce 5 widgets. When Jonesville devotes 50 hours of labor to gadget production, it can produce 10 gadgets. Thus, when Jonesville divides its labor equally between widget and gadget production, the maximum number of gadgets it can produce is 10 while the maximum number of widgets it can produce is 5.

6. **Answer c.** Since the number of hours needed to produce each widget and each gadget has not changed in Jonesville, the opportunity cost of producing these goods does not change. Jonesville does see its linear production possibility frontier shift out due to the increase in the amount of available labor, but the new production possibility frontier has the same slope as the original production possibility frontier.

7. **Answer b.** A combination of gadgets and widgets is not feasible for Jonesville if that combination lies outside of its production possibility frontier. If gadgets are measured on the vertical axis and widgets are measured on the horizontal axis, then the production possibility frontier can be written as $G = 20 - 2W$, where G is the symbol for gadgets and W is the symbol for widgets. Answer (a) lies on the production possibility frontier since $G = 20 - 2(8) = 4$. Answer (c) lies on the production possibility frontier since $G = 20 - 2(6) = 8$. Answer (d) lies on the production possibility frontier since $G = 20 - 2(10) = 0$. Answer (b) does not lie on the production possibility frontier nor does it lie inside the production possibility frontier: $G = 20 - 2(7) = 6$, but the answer in (b) has gadgets equal to 7 and not 6. The combination of 7 widgets and 7 gadgets lies beyond the production possibility frontier for Jonestown.

8. **Answer b.** Utopia plans to devote 60 hours of labor to the production of widgets. If the production of 4 widgets takes 1 hour of labor time, then 60 hours of labor is enough labor to produce 240 widgets.

9. **Answer c.** The opportunity cost of moving from point *D* to point *E* is measured by what Suburbia must give up when it makes this move. At point *D*, Suburbia has 50 pounds of butter, while at point *E* Suburbia has only 30 pounds of butter; thus, when moving from point *D* to point *E*, Suburbia must give up 20 pounds of butter. Notice that when measuring the opportunity cost of moving from one point of a production possibility frontier to another point on the production possibility frontier, it is important to provide the unit of measurement as well as the numerical value.

10. **Answer b.** The opportunity cost of moving from point *D* to point *B* is measured by what Suburbia must give up when it makes this move. In this case, Suburbia is giving up guns to get more butter. Moving from point *D* to point *B*, Suburbia gives up 20 guns.

11. **Answer d.** From the table, we know that Suburbia can produce 50 pounds of butter and 30 guns (point *D* on the production possibility frontier). When Suburbia produces 50 pounds of butter and 20 guns, it is producing at a point that is inside its production possibility frontier and hence it is producing at a feasible but inefficient point, since the point does not lie on the production possibility frontier. Alternatively,

Suburbia could produce 20 guns and 65 pounds of butter (point C) according to the table. Its choice of 20 guns and 50 pounds of butter is also not efficient from this perspective.

12. **Answer b.** Allocative efficiency focuses on producing the right mix of goods and services. Without additional information, we cannot identify which point is the allocatively efficient point on the production possibility frontier. Productively efficient refers to the maximum production feasible from the available resources. All points on the production possibility frontier are productively efficient.

13. **Answer b.** This is true by definition.

module 4

Comparative Advantage and Trade

BEFORE YOU READ THE MODULE

Summary

This module explores trade and how trade between individuals or between economies can lead to gains. The module also discusses the distinction between absolute and comparative advantage and then uses the production possibility frontier model to illustrate how comparative advantage leads to gains from trade in the global marketplace.

Module Objectives

Objective #1. Specialization and trade is beneficial for individuals as well as societies since it allows a higher standard of living than is possible without specialization and trade.

Objective #2. An individual has a comparative advantage in the production of a good or service if they can produce that good or service at a lower opportunity cost than can another individual. A society has a comparative advantage in the production of a good or service if they can produce that good or service at a lower opportunity cost than can another society.

Objective #3. Absolute advantage refers to the ability to produce more of a good or service from a given amount of resources than anyone else can produce. Absolute advantage is not the same as comparative advantage.

Objective #4. Trade among individuals or among economies is beneficial when it is based upon comparative advantage since it allows the individuals or the economies to consume a greater amount of goods and services than would be possible if there was not trade.

Objective #5. The model of production possibility frontiers can also be used to illustrate the gains from trade, which is referred to as the model of comparative advantage. This model assumes that there are two countries, that there are two goods that the countries produce, and that each country has a set amount of resources, technology, and time available to them. Furthermore, this model assumes that the two countries have different opportunity costs of production. In this model, countries benefit from specializing in the production of that good for which they have the comparative advantage, or lower opportunity cost of production, and then trade with each other. Countries do not have to have absolute advantage in production to benefit from trade: the benefits from trade only require that countries have different opportunity costs of production for the two goods and that each country specialize in producing the good that it can produce at a lower opportunity cost relative to the other country.

Key Terms

Notes

trade when individuals provide goods and services to others and receive goods and services in return.

gains from trade an economic principle that states that by dividing tasks and trading, people can get more of what they want through *trade* than they could if they tried to be self sufficient.

specialization a situation in which different people each engage in the different task that he or she is good at performing.

comparative advantage the advantage conferred on an individual or nation in producing a good or service if the *opportunity cost* of producing the good or service is lower for that individual or nation than for other producers.

absolute advantage the advantage conferred by the ability to produce more of a good or service with a given amount of time and resources; not the same thing as comparative advantage.

AFTER YOU READ THE MODULE

Tips

Tip #1. In the previous module you practiced finding the opportunity cost of producing a good or service using the production possibility frontier. In this module you continue with that concept but now you compare the opportunity cost of producing the good for one country or individual to the opportunity cost of producing the good by another country or individual.

Tip #2. The comparative advantage in the production of the good or service belongs to that individual or country that can produce the good or service at lowest opportunity cost. Specialization based upon comparative advantage leads to a higher standard of living than would otherwise be possible.

Tip #3. Once you can calculate the opportunity cost of producing good X or good Y, then you can compare the opportunity costs faced by two countries. The model of comparative advantage illustrates that countries will benefit from trade when they specialize and produce the good that has the lowest opportunity cost of production relative to the other country.

WORKED PROBLEM

1. The following provides a numerical example of how trade is advantageous to two countries that decide to trade with each other. Suppose there are two countries, Arcadia and Supreme, that produce bricks and windows. Arcadia and Supreme use only labor to produce these two goods, and each country has 200 units of available labor. The following table provides information about the number of hours of labor needed in each country to produce one unit of bricks or one unit of windows.

	Hours of labor to produce one brick	Hours of labor to produce one window
Arcadia	2 hours of labor	4 hours of labor
Supreme	5 hours of labor	2 hours of labor

Use the table's information to draw production possibility frontiers for Arcadia and for Supreme. In your graph, measure bricks on the *x*-axis and windows on the *y*-axis. Then use your graph to find each country's opportunity cost of producing one brick. Identify each country's comparative advantage. Finally, calculate a range of prices for one brick in terms of windows.

STEP 1: Draw and label the production possibility frontiers for Arcadia and Supreme.

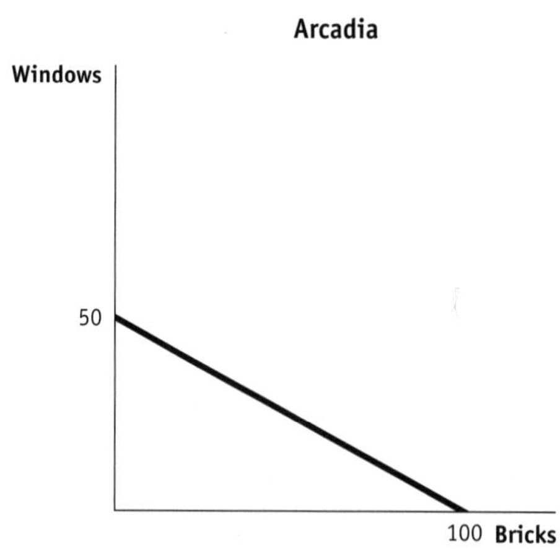

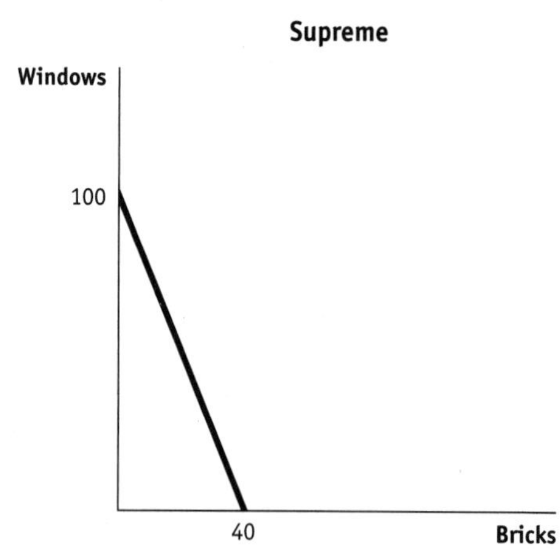

STEP 2: Find each country's opportunity cost of producing one brick, as measured by the number of windows that must be given up when the country produces one additional brick.

The opportunity cost of producing one brick for Arcadia is ½ of a window. To see this, remember that the slope of the production possibility frontier tells you how many units of the good on the *y*-axis must be given up in order to get one more unit of the good on the *x*-axis. Since the slope of Arcadia's production possibility frontier is equal to −1/2, we know that the opportunity cost of one more brick is equal to ½ of a window. The opportunity cost of producing one brick for Supreme is 2.5 windows.

STEP 3: Identify each country's comparative advantage by comparing their opportunity cost of production for each good: a country has the comparative advantage in producing the good when its opportunity cost of producing the good is lower than the other country's opportunity cost of producing the good.

Arcadia has the comparative advantage in producing bricks since Arcadia can produce an additional brick at lower opportunity cost than can Supreme. One additional brick costs Arcadia ½ of a window, while it costs Supreme 2.5 windows: Arcadia can produce bricks at lower opportunity cost and therefore has a comparative advantage in brick production.

STEP 4: Find the range of prices for one brick in terms of windows.

Arcadia is willing to produce bricks for any price equal to or greater than ½ of a window. Supreme is willing to purchase one brick for any price equal to or less than 2.5 windows. The range of prices for one brick will therefore fall between ½ window and 2.5 windows.

Problems and Exercises

1. Economists believe that specialization and trade are beneficial when they are based on comparative advantage. Briefly explain why economists believe this to be true.

2. There are two islands in the middle of the ocean and these two islands produce fish and baskets. Big Island can produce either 100 fish per day and 0 baskets per day or 0 fish per day and 200 baskets per day. Big Island can also produce any combination of fish and baskets that lies on their linear production possibility frontier. Small Island can produce either 80 fish per day and 0 baskets per day or 0 fish per day and 80 baskets per day. Like Big Island, Small Island has a linear production possibility frontier.

a. Sketch two graphs. Sketch Big Island's production possibility frontier on the first graph and sketch Small Island's production possibility frontier on the second graph. Place fish/day on the *y*-axis and baskets/day on the *x*-axis.

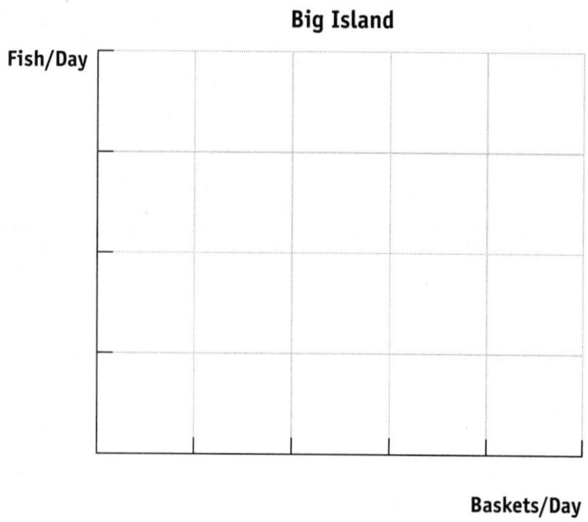

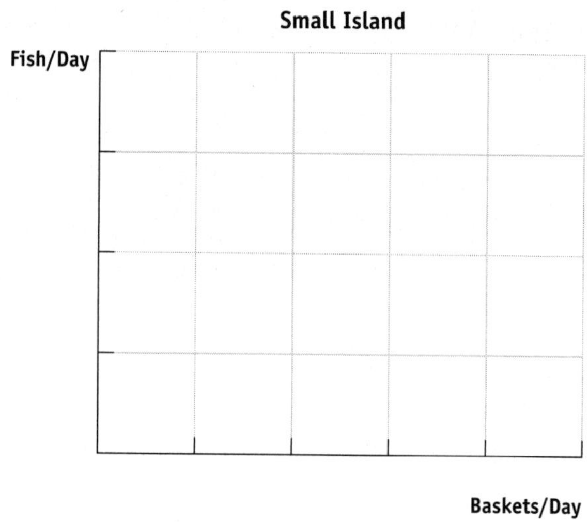

b. What is the slope of Big Island's production possibility frontier?

c. What is the slope of Small Island's production possibility frontier?

d. What is the opportunity cost of producing an additional basket on Big Island? What is the opportunity cost of producing an additional basket on Small Island? Which island can produce baskets at a lower opportunity cost?

e. What is the opportunity cost of producing an additional fish on Big Island? What is the opportunity cost of producing an additional fish on Small Island? Which island can produce fish at a lower opportunity cost?

f. What good should Big Island specialize in producing?

g. What good should Small Island specialize in producing?

3. There are two islands in the middle of the ocean, and these two islands produce fish and baskets. Big Island can produce either 100 fish per day and 0 baskets per day or 0 fish per day and 200 baskets per day. Big Island can also produce any combination of fish and baskets that includes these two combinations and lies on their linear production possibility frontier. Small Island can produce either 80 fish per day and 0 baskets per day or 0 fish per day and 80 baskets per day. Like Big Island, Small Island has a linear production possibility frontier. Currently there is no trade between the two islands. The current production for both islands is given in the table below.

Initial production	Fish	Baskets
Big Island	80	40
Small Island	30	50
Total production	110	90

a. Is Big Island producing at a productively efficient point? Explain your answer.

b. Is Small Island producing at a productively efficient point? Explain your answer.

Referring back to problem 2, let's analyze what happens to total production if these countries decide to specialize and trade according to their comparative advantage.

c. Suppose that Big Island decides to produce 50 baskets instead of 40 baskets. How many fish will Big Island be able to produce if its basket production is increased to 50 baskets?

d. Suppose that Small Island decides to produce 40 fish instead of 30 fish. How many baskets will Small Island be able to produce if its fish production is increased to 40 fish?

e. Fill in the table below showing the new levels of production given the information in parts (c) and (d).

New production	Fish	Baskets
Big Island		50
Small Island	40	
Total production		

f. Do specialization and trade benefit both islands in this example? Explain your answer.

Referring back to problem 2, let's analyze what happens to total production if these countries decide to specialize and trade without regard to their comparative advantage.

g. Suppose that Big Island decides to produce 30 baskets instead of 40 baskets. How many fish will Big Island be able to produce if its basket production is increased to 30 baskets?

h. Suppose that Small Island decides to produce 20 fish instead of 30 fish. How many baskets will Small Island be able to produce if its fish production is increased to 20 fish?

i. Fill in the table below showing the new levels of production given the information in parts (g) and (h).

New production	Fish	Baskets
Big Island		30
Small Island	20	
Total production		

j. Do specialization and trade benefit both islands in this example? Explain your answer.

k. What must be true for specialization and trade to be beneficial? (Hint: Think about the two examples in this problem and how they differ before you write your answer.)

4. Suppose that Jane and Bob live on an island far away from any other countries. Jane and Bob both produce widgets and gadgets from their available resources, but they do not currently trade with one another. The table below gives the number of hours of labor needed to produce one widget or one gadget for Bob and Jane. For this example let's assume that Jane and Bob each have 120 hours of labor time.

	Hours of labor needed to produce a widget	Hours of labor needed to produce a gadget
Bob	2	4
Jane	3	1.5

a. Sketch two graphs: on the first graph draw Bob's production possibility frontier and on the second graph draw Jane's production possibility frontier. Place widgets on the *y*-axis and gadgets on the *x*-axis. Label both graphs carefully.

Bob's Production Possibility Frontier

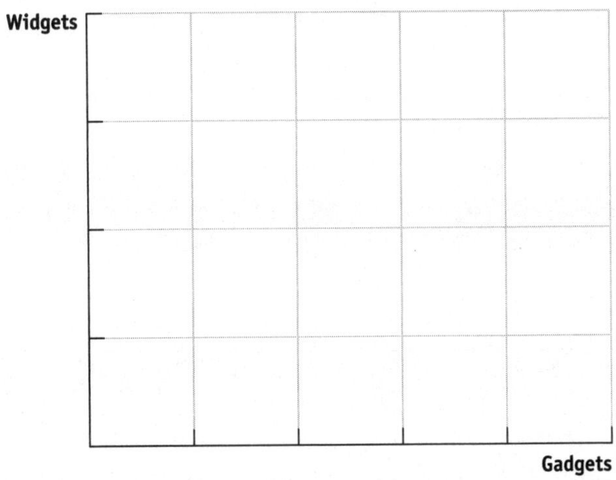

Jane's Production Possibility Frontier

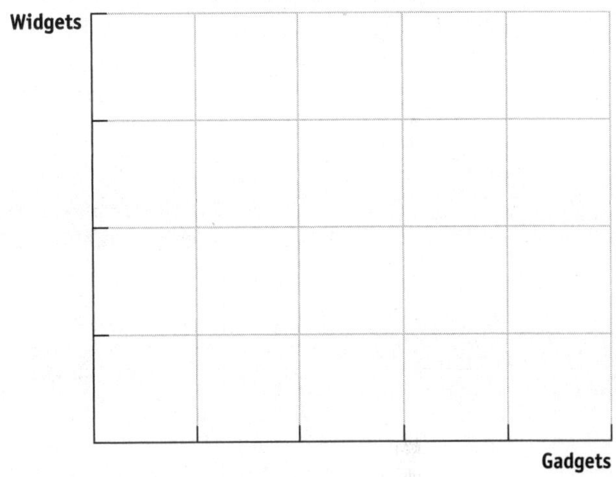

b. Suppose that Bob and Jane devote half of their labor time to producing gadgets and half to producing widgets. Fill in the following table based on this allocation of labor.

Initial production	Widgets	Gadgets
Bob		
Jane		
Total production		

c. What is Bob's opportunity cost of producing an additional gadget? What is Jane's opportunity cost of producing an additional gadget? Who can produce gadgets at a lower opportunity cost?

d. What is Bob's opportunity cost of producing an additional widget? What is Jane's opportunity cost of producing an additional widget? Who can produce widgets at a lower opportunity cost?

e. Bob and Jane decide to specialize and trade. What good should Bob specialize in producing?

f. Bob and Jane decide to specialize and trade. What good should Jane specialize in producing?

g. Bob and Jane specialize according to their comparative advantage and give us this partially filled-in table that provides some information about their production. Fill in the missing information on the table assuming that Bob and Jane are both productively efficient.

New production	Widgets	Gadgets
Bob	46	
Jane		60
Total production		

BEFORE YOU TAKE THE TEST

Module Review Questions

1. Suppose there are two countries, Texia and Urbania, that produce food and clothing and currently do not trade. Both countries have linear production possibility frontiers. Texia, if it devotes all of its resources to food production, can produce 1,000 units of food this year and 0 units of clothing. If Texia devotes all of its resources to clothing production this year, it can produce 500 units of clothing and 0 units of food. Urbania can either produce 500 units of food this year and 0 units of clothing, or it can produce 200 units of clothing this year and 0 units of food. _________ has the absolute advantage in the production of clothing and _________ has the absolute advantage in the production of food.

   a. Texia; Texia
   b. Texia; Urbania
   c. Urbania; Texia
   d. Urbania; Urbania

2. Suppose there are two countries, Texia and Urbania, that produce food and clothing and currently do not trade. Both countries have linear production possibility frontiers. Texia, if it devotes all of its resources to food production, can produce 1,000 units of food this year and 0 units of clothing. If Texia devotes all of its resources to clothing production this year, it can produce 500 units of clothing and 0 units of food. Urbania can either produce 500 units of food this year and 0 units of clothing, or it can produce 200 units of clothing this year and 0 units of food. _________ has the comparative advantage in the production of clothing and _________ has the comparative advantage in the production of food.

   a. Texia; Texia
   b. Texia; Urbania
   c. Urbania; Texia
   d. Urbania; Urbania

3. Suppose there are two countries, Texia and Urbania, that produce food and clothing and currently do not trade. Both countries have linear production possibility frontiers. Texia, if it devotes all of its resources to food production, can produce 1,000 units of food this year and 0 units of clothing. If Texia devotes all of its resources to clothing production this year, it can produce 500 units of clothing and 0 units of food. Urbania can either produce 500 units of food this year and 0 units of clothing, or it can produce 200 units of clothing this year and 0 units of food. Each country devotes half of its resources to the production of food and half of its resources to the production of clothing. Total clothing production is equal to _________ and total food production is equal to _________.

   a. 600; 500
   b. 250; 500
   c. 100; 250
   d. 350; 750

4. Suppose there are two countries, Texia and Urbania, that produce food and clothing and initially do not trade. Both countries have linear production possibility frontiers. Texia, if it devotes all of its resources to food production, can produce 1,000 units of food this year, and 0 units of clothing. If Texia devotes all of its resources to clothing production this year, it can produce 500 units of clothing and 0 units of food. Urbania can either produce 500 units of food this year and 0 units of clothing, or it can produce 200 units of clothing this year and 0 units of food. Suppose that Texia and Urbania decide to specialize and trade. If Texia increases its clothing production to a total of 400 units, how many units of food will Texia be able to produce if it is productively efficient?

   a. 100 units
   b. 200 units
   c. 300 units
   d. 400 units

5. Specialization and trade benefit
   a. usually only one of the trading partners.
   b. the wealthier country more than the poorer country.
   c. the poorer country more than the wealthier country.
   d. both countries if they specialize according to their comparative advantage.

6. True or False: "Provided that their opportunity costs of production are not equal, two countries will find that specialization of production and trade according to their comparative advantage with one another increases the overall level of production."
   a. True   b. False

Use the following information to answer the next two questions.

Each time country A decides to produce 1 bicycle it must give up 2 radios. Each time country B decides to produce 1 radio if must give up 3 bicycles.

7. If the two countries specialize according to their comparative advantage, then country B should produce
   a. radios.   b. bicycles.

8. If the two countries specialize according to their comparative advantage, then country A should produce
   a. radios.   b. bicycles.

9. Suppose that both Tom and Sue each have 100 hours of labor available to them. Tom needs 10 hours of labor to produce a table and 4 hours of labor to produce a chair. Sue needs 5 hours of labor to produce a table and 2 hours of labor to produce a chair. Assuming that labor is the only resource that constrains Tom or Sue, what is the maximum amount of tables that the two of them can produce?
   a. 30 tables
   b. 20 tables
   c. 10 tables
   d. 15 tables

10. Suppose that both Tom and Sue each have 100 hours of labor available to them. Tom needs 10 hours of labor to produce a table and 4 hours of labor to produce a chair. Sue needs 5 hours of labor to produce a table and 2 hours of labor to produce a chair. Assuming that labor is the only resource that constrains Tom or Sue, who has the comparative advantage in the production of chairs?
   a. Tom
   b. Sue
   c. Tom and Sue have the same opportunity cost of producing a chair: thus, neither Tom nor Sue has the comparative advantage in the production of chairs.
   d. Tom and Sue both have the comparative advantage in the production of chairs.

11. Suppose that both Tom and Sue each have 100 hours of labor available to them. Tom needs 10 hours of labor to produce a table and 4 hours of labor to produce a chair. Sue needs 5 hours of labor to produce a table and 2 hours of labor to produce a chair. Assuming that labor is the only resource that constrains Tom or Sue, who has the absolute advantage in the production of chairs?

a. Sue b. Tom

12. Suppose that both Tom and Sue each have 100 hours of labor available to them. Tom needs 10 hours of labor to produce a table and 4 hours of labor to produce a chair. Sue needs 5 hours of labor to produce a table and 2 hours of labor to produce a chair. Assuming that labor is the only resource that constrains Tom or Sue, who has the absolute advantage in the production of tables?

a. Sue b. Tom

ANSWER KEY

Answers to Problems and Exercises

1. Economists believe that specialization and trade based on comparative advantage result in a greater level of production than is possible without specialization and trade. Economists argue that, so long as opportunity costs differ, specialization in the production of the good that has a lower opportunity cost will enhance the overall level of production available and will therefore be beneficial.

2. a.

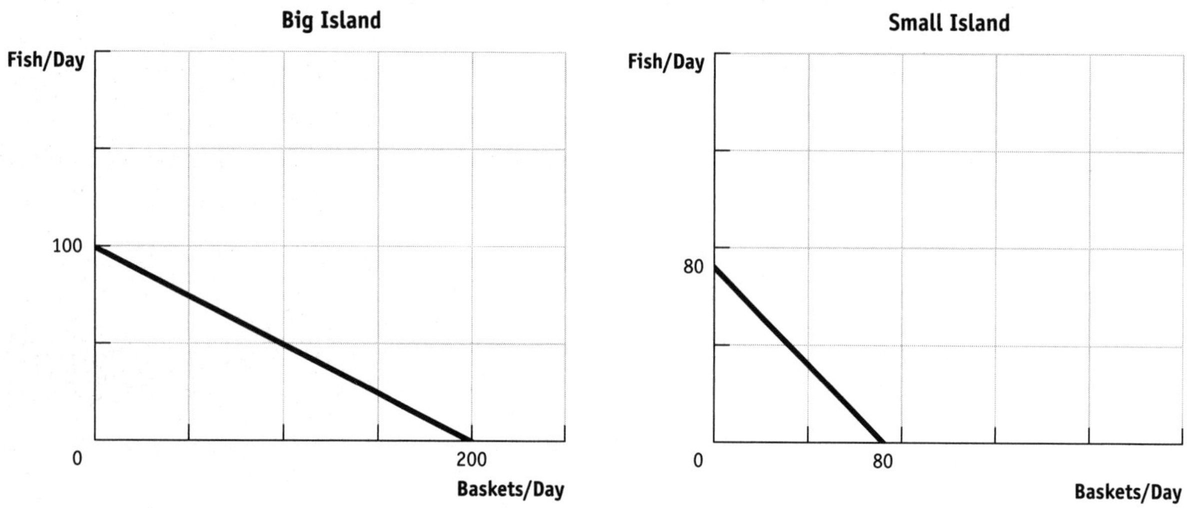

   b. The slope of Big Island's production possibility frontier is –½.

   c. The slope of Small Island's production possibility frontier is –1.

   d. The opportunity cost of producing an additional basket for Big Island is ½ of a fish. The opportunity cost of producing an additional basket for Small Island is 1 fish. Big Island can produce an additional basket at a lower opportunity cost than can Small Island.

   e. The opportunity cost of producing an additional fish for Big Island is 2 baskets. The opportunity cost of producing an additional fish for Small Island is 1 basket. Small Island can produce an additional fish at a lower opportunity cost than can Big Island.

   f. Big Island should specialize in producing baskets, since it can produce baskets at a lower opportunity cost than can Small Island.

   g. Small Island should specialize in producing fish, since it can produce fish at a lower opportunity cost than can Big Island.

3. a. Big Island is producing at a productively efficient point because 80 fish and 40 baskets lies on its linear production possibility frontier.

   b. Small Island is producing at a productively efficient point because 30 fish and 50 baskets lies on its linear production possibility frontier.

   c. Big Island will be able to produce 75 fish. The easiest way to calculate this answer is to write an equation for Big Island's production possibility frontier: $F = (-½)B + 100$, where F is the symbol for fish and B is the symbol for baskets. Thus, if $B = 50$ then F must equal 75 according to this equation.

   d. Small Island will be able to produce 40 baskets. The easiest way to calculate this answer is to write an equation for Small Island's production possibility frontier: $F = (-1)B + 80$, where F stands for fish and B stands for baskets. Thus, if $F = 40$ then B must equal 40.

e.

New production	Fish	Baskets
Big Island	75	50
Small Island	40	40
Total production	115	90

f. Specialization and trade are beneficial to both islands since the total production of fish is increased to 115 fish instead of the original 110. This change in fish production does not change the level of basket production. Thus, the two islands can increase the amount of goods available to them if they specialize according to their comparative advantage and then trade with one another.

g. Big Island will be able to produce 85 fish. One way to calculate this answer is to write an equation for Big Island's production possibility frontier: $F = (-\frac{1}{2})B + 100$, where F is the symbol for fish and B is the symbol for baskets. Thus, if $B = 30$ then F must equal 85 according to this equation.

h. Small Island will be able to produce 60 baskets. One way to calculate this answer is to write an equation for Small Island's production possibility frontier: $F = (-1)B + 80$, where F stands for fish and B stands for baskets. Thus, if $F = 20$ then B must equal 60.

i.

New production	Fish	Baskets
Big Island	85	30
Small Island	20	60
Total production	105	90

j. Specialization and trade are not beneficial to both islands in this example since the total production of fish decreased to 105 fish instead of the original 110. This change in fish production does not change the level of basket production. Thus, the two islands decrease the amount of goods available to them when they specialize and trade with one another without paying attention to their comparative advantage.

k. For specialization and trade to be beneficial for two countries, they must have different opportunity costs of production, and they must also specialize according to their comparative advantage.

4. a.

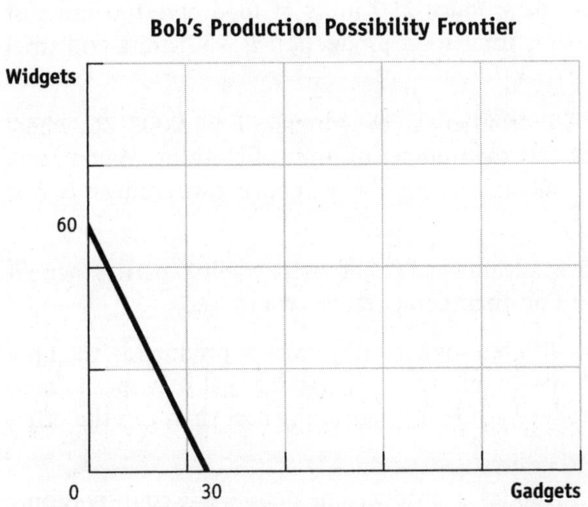

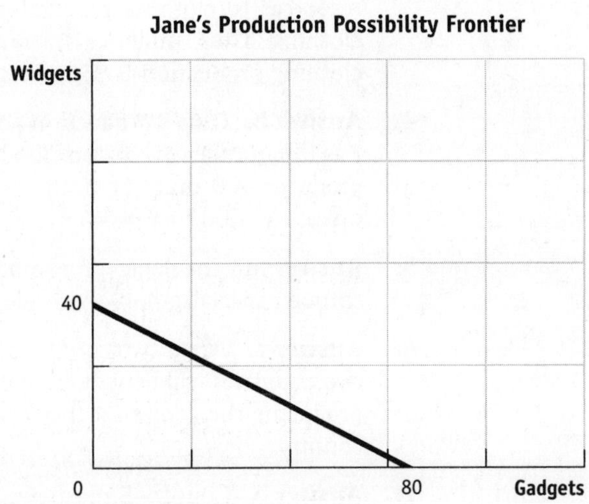

b.

Initial production	Widgets	Gadgets
Bob	30	15
Jane	20	40
Total production	50	55

c. Bob's opportunity cost of producing an additional gadget is 2 widgets, whereas Jane's opportunity cost of producing an additional gadget is ½ of a widget. Jane can produce gadgets at a lower opportunity cost than can Bob.

d. Bob's opportunity cost of producing an additional widget is ½ of a gadget, whereas Jane's opportunity cost of producing an additional widget is 2 gadgets. Bob can produce widgets at a lower opportunity cost than can Jane.

e. Bob should specialize in producing widgets.

f. Jane should specialize in producing gadgets.

g.

Initial production	Widgets	Gadgets
Bob	46	7
Jane	10	60
Total production	56	67

Answers to Module Review Questions

1. **Answer a.** Given the resources that Texia and Urbania have this year, Texia is able to produce more food and more clothing than Urbania this year.

2. **Answer b.** For every unit of clothing that Texia produces it must give up 2 units of food, while for Urbania the opportunity cost of producing 1 unit of clothing is 2.5 units of food. Thus, the opportunity cost of producing clothing is lower for Texia than it is for Urbania. Texia therefore has the comparative advantage in producing clothing while Urbania has the comparative advantage in producing food.

3. **Answer d.** When Texia devotes half of its resources to food production and half of its resources to clothing production, it can produce 500 units of food and 250 units of clothing. When Urbania devotes half of its resources to food production and half of its resources to clothing production, it can produce 250 units of food and 100 units of clothing. Thus, under this arrangement, total food production is 750 units and total clothing production is 350 units.

4. **Answer b.** Texia's production possibility frontier can be written as $F = 1{,}000 - 2C$, where F is the number of units of food and C is the number of units of clothing. When Texia produces 400 units of clothing, the maximum amount of food it can produce is 200 units: $F = 1{,}000 - 2(400) = 200$.

5. **Answer d.** The logic of comparative advantage is that both trading parties benefit through specialization and trade based on their comparative advantage.

6. **Answer a.** When two countries have different opportunity costs of production then the two countries will benefit from trading with one another provided that they specialize in producing the good that they can produce at lower opportunity cost than can the other country.

7. **Answer b.** Country B must give up 3 bicycles to produce one radio while country A only gives up ½ of a bicycle to produce one radio. country B's opportunity cost of producing one radio is greater than country A's opportunity cost of producing one radio. Country B should produce bicycles while country A produces radios.

8. **Answer a.** See answer to previous question.

9. **Answer a.** If both Tom and Sue devote all of their labor to the production of tables, Tom will be able to produce 10 tables while Sue will be able to produce 20 tables. Together they will be able to produce 30 tables.

10. **Answer c.** If you draw Tom's production possibility frontier you will see that he can produce a maximum of 10 tables and 0 chairs or 25 chairs and 0 tables. From this information you can construct Tom's linear production possibility frontier and see that the slope of this production possibility frontier is equal to $-2/5$ if chairs are measured on the horizontal axis. If you draw Sue's production possibility frontier you will see that she can produce a maximum of 20 tables and 0 chairs or 50 chairs and 0 tables. From this information you can construct Sue's linear production possibility frontier and see that the slope of this production possibility frontier is equal to $-2/5$ if chairs are measured on the horizontal axis. Thus, the opportunity cost of producing one chair is equal to $2/5$ of a table for both Tom and Sue. There is no comparative advantage in this example.

11. **Answer a.** With 100 hours of labor Sue can produce a maximum of 50 chairs while Tom can only produce a maximum of 25 chairs. Sue can absolutely produce more chairs than can Tom from the same amount of resources (in this case, 100 hours of labor).

12. **Answer a.** With 100 hours of labor Sue can produce a maximum of 20 tables while Tom can only produce a maximum of 10 tables. Sue can absolutely produce more tables than can Tom from the same amount of resources (in this case, 100 hours of labor).

module 5

Demand

BEFORE YOU READ THE MODULE

Summary

This module introduces the model of supply and demand in the context of a competitive market and discusses the demand for a good or service. It develops the concept of the demand curve and then discusses what causes a movement along the demand curve and what factors cause a shift in the demand curve.

Module Objectives

Objective #1. A competitive market is a market that has many buyers and many sellers of the same good or service. No buyer or seller can affect the price of the good or service in a competitive market.

Objective #2. A demand schedule shows the relationship between possible prices of the good or service and the quantity of that good or service demanded at those different prices. As the price increases, the quantity demanded decreases: price and quantity demanded are inversely related to one another. A demand curve is the graphical representation of the demand schedule. The demand curve is drawn with the price of the good on the vertical axis and the quantity demanded on the horizontal axis. Demand curves usually slope downward: this is referred to as the "law of demand." Demand refers to the entire demand curve, while quantity demanded refers to a specific quantity demanded at a specific price.

Objective #3. The quantity demanded depends on many factors, but the primary determinants of the quantity demanded are the price of the good, the changes in the price of related goods, and changes in income, tastes, expectations, and the number of consumers. A change in the price of the good, all other things being equal, will cause a movement along the curve and a change in the quantity demanded. A change in any other determinant of demand, all other things being equal, will cause a shift in the demand curve. At any given price, the quantity demanded will increase when demand shifts to the right and decrease when demand shifts to the left.

Objective #4. The module discusses several kinds of specific types of goods.

- Two goods are substitutes if a decrease in the price of one of the goods causes a decrease in the demand for the other good. As the price of the first good decreases, people increase the quantity of this good they demand, which results in a reduction in the overall demand for the other, substitute good. Two goods are complements if a decrease in the price of one of the goods causes an increase in the demand for the other good. As the price of the first good decreases, people increase the quantity of this good they demand, which results in an increase in the overall demand for the other, complementary, good.
- A good is a normal good if a decrease in income causes a decrease in the demand for the good. A good is an inferior good if a decrease in income causes an increase in the demand for the good.

Objective #5. A market demand curve illustrates the combined quantity demanded by all consumers in the market. The market demand curve is found by horizontally adding the individual demand curves. At each price the quantity demanded by each individual is added to give the total quantity demanded at that price.

Key Terms

competitive market a market in which there are many buyers and sellers of the same good or service, none of whom can influence the price at which the good or service is sold.

supply and demand model a model of how a *competitive market* works.

demand schedule a list or table showing how much of a good or service consumers will want to buy at different prices.

quantity demanded the actual amount of a good or service consumers are willing to buy at some specific price.

demand curve a graphical representation of the *demand schedule,* showing the relationship between quantity demanded and price.

law of demand a higher price for a good or service, other things equal, leads people to demand a smaller quantity of that good or service.

change in demand a shift of the demand curve, which changes the quantity demanded at any given price.

movement along the demand curve a change in the quantity demanded of a good that is the result of a change in that good's price.

substitutes pairs of goods for which a rise in the price of one of the goods leads to an increase in the demand for the other good.

complements pairs of goods for which a rise in the price of one good leads to a decrease in the demand for the other good.

normal good a good for which a rise in income increases the demand for that good—the "normal" case.

inferior good a good for which a rise in income decreases the demand for the good.

individual demand curve a graphical representation of the relationship between *quantity demanded* and price for an individual consumer.

Notes

AFTER YOU READ THE MODULE

Tips

Tip #1. A full understanding of this module is critical for your study of economics. The model of supply and demand is used repeatedly in a variety of settings throughout the remainder of this course. You should work with the material in this module until you are confident that you know it well and that you understand the techniques, vocabulary, and information in the module. Pay particular attention to the distinction between demand and the quantity demanded, and shifts of a demand curve versus movements along a demand curve. You also should know the determinants of demand.

Tip #2. A demand curve is usually downward sloping. The negative slope of a demand curve implies that the quantity demanded of a good or service is inversely related to its price. Another way to express this idea is that as the price of the good decreases, holding everything else constant, consumers will want to buy more units of the good. Figure 5.1 illustrates this law of demand: at P_1, Q_1 units of the good are demanded; as the price of the good falls from P_1 to P_2, the quantity demanded of the good increases from Q_1 to Q_2.

Figure 5.1

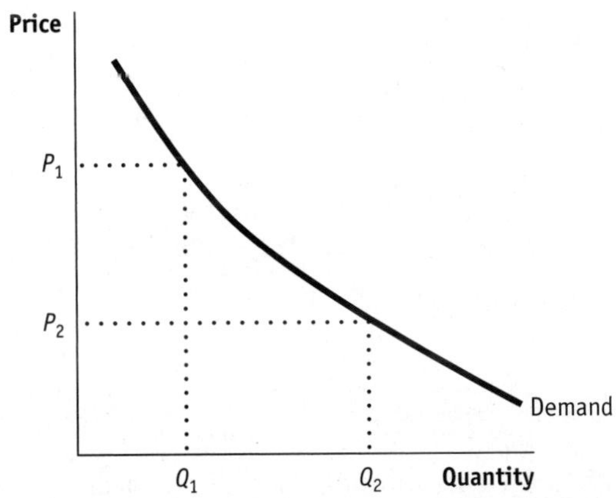

Tip #3. A demand curve illustrates the relationship between the price of the good and the quantity demanded at each specific price. In drawing the demand curve, the other determinants of demand are held constant; this constancy is referred to as the other-things-equal assumption. This assumption allows economists to consider a change in a single variable while holding all other potentially important variables constant. In the examples throughout the remainder of the course, we typically consider a single change in a situation while holding the other variables constant. Students often struggle with this concept and have trouble working with the model of supply and demand because they do not limit themselves to considering a single change at a time.

Tip #4. Besides the price of the good, the quantity demanded of a good is affected by the following variables: changes in the price of related goods, changes in income, changes in tastes and preferences, changes in expectations, and changes in the number of consumers. You will need to know this list of variables as well as how each of these variables affects the demand curve.

Tip #5. Economists make a distinction between demand and the quantity demanded. The quantity demanded refers to a specific quantity associated with a specific price (as in Figure

5.1, where Q_1 is associated with P_1 and Q_2 is associated with P_2). Demand refers to the entire demand curve. Although this may sound like a matter of semantics, economists view this distinction as highly important.

Tip #6. Economists also make a distinction between a movement along a demand curve and a shift of the demand curve. A movement along a demand curve is caused by a change in the good's price, while a shift in a curve is caused by a change in some demand determinant other than the price of the good.

- Figure 5.2 illustrates this distinction for a demand curve. There is a movement from point *A* to point *B* when the price decreases from P_1 to P_2, and there is a shift in the demand curve from D_1 to D_2 due to a change in some other determinant of demand. A shift causes the quantity demanded of the good to change at every price—for example, at P_1 in Figure 5.2, the shift causes the quantity demanded to increase from Q_1 to Q_3 (compare point *A* to point C). Figure 5.2 illustrates an increase in demand when the demand curve shifts to the right from D_1 to D_2. A decrease in demand would be illustrated by the demand curve shifting to the left (in Figure 5.2 this would be a shift from D_2 to D_1).

Figure 5.2

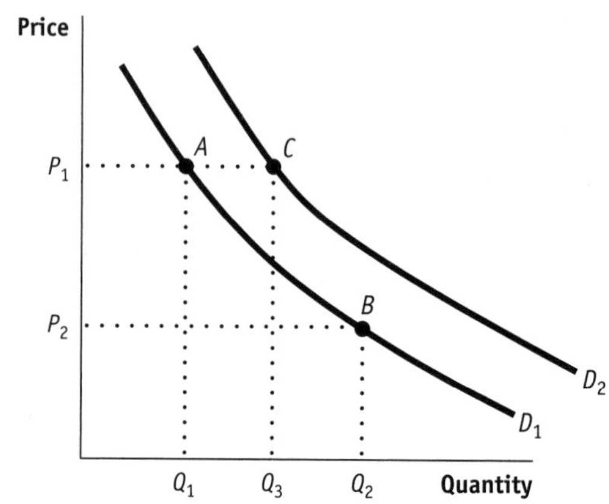

Tip #7. Students initially find it easier to understand the concepts of substitutes and complements if they think about concrete examples. For example, consider soft drinks and popcorn. Two different brands of soft drinks are substitutes: holding all other demand determinants constant, if the price of one brand increases, then the demand for the other soft drink will increase since it is now relatively cheaper and the two goods can easily serve as substitutes for one another. In contrast, if the price of soft drinks increases, holding everything else constant, then the demand for popcorn will decrease. Popcorn and soft drinks are consumed together: they are complements to one another, which implies that if one of these goods gets more expensive (and therefore, you move upward along that good's demand curve), the quantity demanded of that good decreases. This in turn leads to a decrease in the demand for the complementary good. Questions about substitutes and complements are far easier to interpret if you take the time to think of two specific goods.

Tip #8. You will find it easier to understand questions about normal and inferior goods if you think of specific examples. A normal good is a good that you will choose to increase the quantity demanded at every price as your income increases (demand shifts to the right as income increases). For example, as your income increases you will increase the quantity demanded of vacations, car travel, and recreation. An inferior good is a good that you will choose to decrease the quantity demanded at every price as your income increases (demand shifts to the left as income increases). For example, as your income increases you will likely consume fewer fast-food restaurant meals or generic pasta dinners.

WORKED PROBLEMS

1. The supply and demand model is often used to analyze the effect of a change in the market on the equilibrium price and quantity of a good. Consider each of the following markets and the given situation to determine whether the demand curve shifts or there is a movement along the demand curve. For any shift in the demand curve, indicate whether the curve shifts to the left or to the right. The examples are given in a table to help you consolidate your answers.

Market under consideration	Situation	Shift of or movement along the demand curve
Automobile market	The price of gas, a complement to cars, increases.	
Pizza market	The Surgeon General announces that pizza consumption is detrimental to one's health.	
Soap market	Health officials release a study showing the advantages of frequent hand washing.	
Automobile market	The price of cars increases.	
Insulation market	Homeowners are granted a tax credit for installing home insulation.	

STEP 1: Review the determinants of demand that result in the demand curve shifting.

The demand curve will shift when there is a change in the price of a related good, either a substitute or a complement. It will also shift because of a change in the level of income; the good under consideration may be either a normal good or an inferior good. The demand curve will also shift because of a change in tastes and preferences, in expectations about future prices, or in the number of consumers in the market.

STEP 2: For each of the markets determine whether the change in the price of the good will cause a movement along the demand curve or a change in some other demand determinant that will shift the demand curve.

For each of the given situations except the increase in the price of automobiles, the change described in the table will cause a shift in the demand curve. A change in the price of gas is a change in the price of a complementary good to automobiles. The Surgeon General's announcement about pizza and the health officials' report on soap will change people's tastes and preferences for eating pizza or washing their hands, respectively. A government program to reduce homeowners' taxes when they install insulation will change homeowners' tastes and preferences for home insulation.

STEP 3: For each demand curve that shifts, determine the direction of the shift and record your responses in the provided table.

Market under consideration	Situation	Shift of or movement along the demand curve
Automobile market	The price of gas, a complement to cars, increases.	The increase in the price of gas will cause the demand curve for cars to shift to the left: at every price fewer cars will be demanded.
Pizza market	The Surgeon General announces that pizza consumption is detrimental to one's health.	The Surgeon General's announcement will cause the demand curve for pizza to shift to the left: at every price fewer units of pizza will be demanded.
Soap market	Health officials release a study showing the advantages of frequent hand washing.	The release of this study will cause the demand curve for soap to shift to the right: at every price more units of soap will be demanded.
Automobile market	The price of cars increases.	An increase in the price of cars will cause a movement along the demand curve: the quantity of cars demanded will fall.
Insulation market	Homeowners are granted a tax credit for installing home insulation.	The tax credit for home insulation will shift the demand curve for home insulation to the right: at every price more home insulation will be demanded.

2. Suppose you are told that the initial demand curve for good X is $P = 100 - Q$. You are then told that incomes increase in this economy and that good X is a normal good. If you know that the quantity demanded of good X changes by 5 units at every price, what is the equation for the new demand curve?

STEP 1: **Start by drawing a graph of the initial demand curve. The figure that follows illustrates this demand curve.**

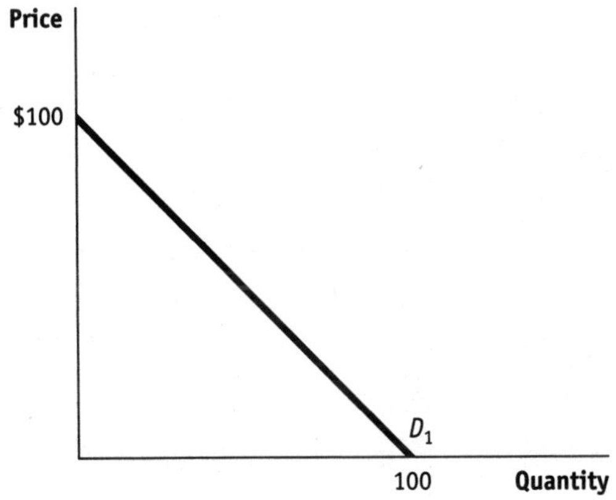

STEP 2: **You are told that incomes increase in this economy and that this is a normal good. A change in income will cause the demand curve to shift: since incomes increase and the good is a normal good, the demand curve will shift to the right.**

STEP 3: **Calculate the exact location of the new demand curve. You know that, at every price, 5 more units are being demanded than were demanded initially. Thus, if the price was initially \$0, the quantity demanded was initially 100 units (use the demand equation to get the quantity demanded when the price is \$0). Now, at a price of \$0, the original 100 units plus an additional 5 units will be demanded. Thus, you know that the point $(Q,P) = (105,\$0)$ sits on the new demand curve. The new demand curve has the same slope as the original demand curve, so all you need to find is the new *y*-intercept: use the point you know that is on the new demand curve to find this *y*-intercept. Thus, $P = b - Q$, and when $Q = 105$ and $P = \$0$, then $b = 105$. Thus, the new demand equation is $P = 105 - Q$. The figure**

that follows illustrates the new demand curve, D_2, along with the initial demand curve. Alternatively, the initial demand curve can be written as $Q = 100 - P$. The new demand curve has the same slope as the initial demand curve and an *x*-intercept of 105: thus, the new demand curve can be written as $Q = 105 - P$.

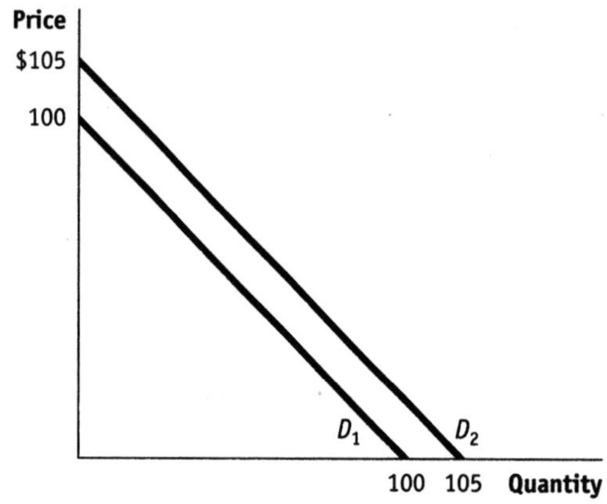

Problems and Exercises

1. Why is the assumption that there are many buyers and many sellers in a competitive market important?

2. You are given the following information about demand in the competitive market for bicycles.

Price per bicycle	Quantity of bicycles demanded per week
$100	0
80	100
60	200
40	500
20	800
0	1,000

a. Graph this demand schedule placing price on the vertical axis and quantity on the horizontal axis.

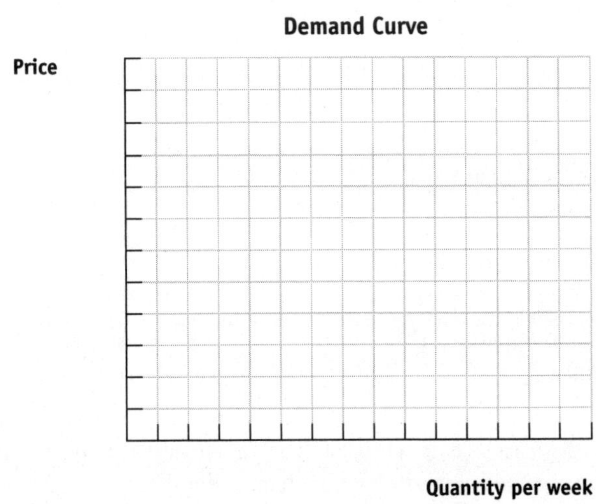

b. Suppose the price is initially $40. If the price rises by $20, what happens to the quantity demanded?

c. Suppose the price is initially $40. If the price falls by $40, what happens to the quantity demanded?

3. For each of the following situations in the table below, fill in the missing information. First, determine whether the situation causes a shift or a movement along the demand curve; then, if it causes a shift, determine whether the demand curve shifts to the right or to the left.

Situation	Specified market	Movement or shift	Rightward or leftward shift in demand
People's income increases	Market for exotic vacations		
People's income decreases	Market for goods sold in secondhand shops		
Price of bicycles increases	Market for bicycles		
Price of tennis balls increases	Market for tennis racquets		
Price of movie tickets decreases	Popcorn at movie theaters		
Popularity of music-playing device increases	Market for music-playing device		
Popularity of branded clothing items decreases	Market for brand-name designer clothing		
Winter clothing to go on sale next month	Market for winter clothing		
Increase in urban residents	Market for apartments in urban areas		

4. Suppose a market has three consumers (this will simplify the work you need to do!): Joe, Maria, and Chao. Their demand schedules are given in the table below.

Price	Quantity demanded by Joe	Quantity demanded by Maria	Quantity demanded by Chao
$0	10	20	5
1	8	16	4
2	6	12	3
3	4	8	2
4	2	4	1

a. On the following graphs, sketch a graph of Joe's demand curve, Maria's demand curve, and Chao's demand curve. Then sketch the market demand curve based on the demand of these three individuals.

Joe's Demand

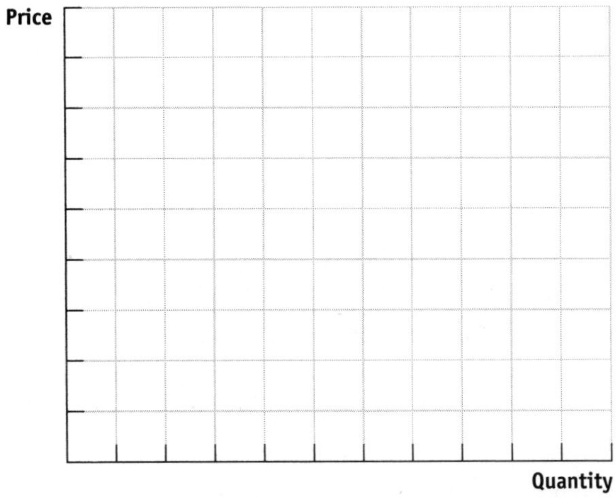

Maria's Demand

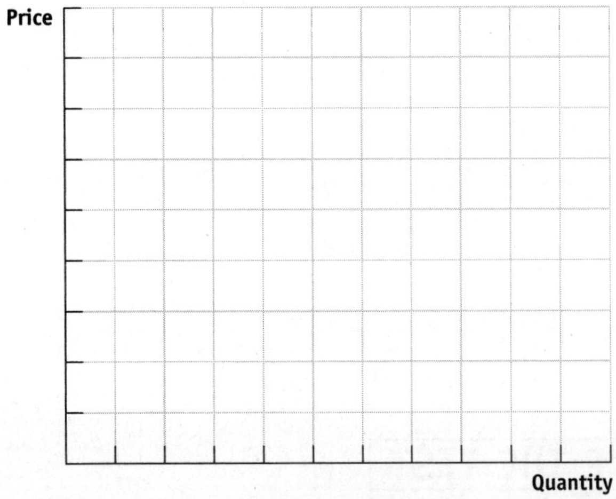

Chao's Demand

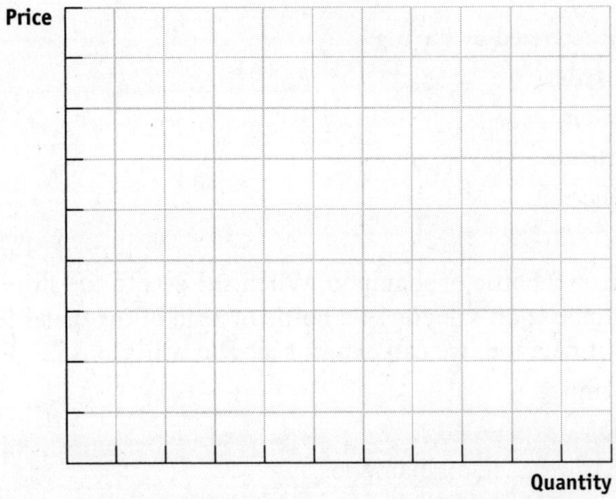

Market Demand

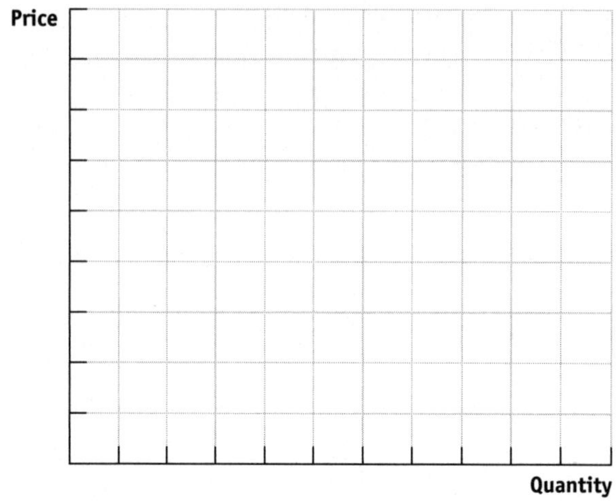

b. Summarize the market demand curve you found by filling in the following table.

Price	Quantity demanded in market
$0	
1	
2	
3	
4	

BEFORE YOU TAKE THE TEST

Module Review Questions

1. Competitive markets are characterized as having
a. many buyers and a single seller.
b. many buyers and a few sellers.
c. many buyers and many sellers.
d. a few buyers and many sellers.

2. Sue goes to the store to purchase a bottle of shampoo. When she gets to the store she discovers that her brand of shampoo is on sale for $4 a bottle instead of the usual $5.99 per bottle. According to the law of demand, we can expect that Sue will
a. purchase one bottle of shampoo.
b. not purchase the shampoo.
c. likely purchase more than one bottle of shampoo.
d. substitute away from her usual brand of shampoo and instead purchase an alternative brand.

3. The law of demand states that the quantity demanded is an inverse function of its price. This means that
   a. as price increases, the quantity demanded decreases.
   b. as price increases, the quantity demanded increases.
   c. the demand curve shifts to the left with increases in price.
   d. the demand curve shifts to the right with increases in price.

4. Consider the market for mangos. Suppose researchers discover that eating mangos generates large health benefits. Which of the following statements is true?
   a. This discovery will not affect the market for mangos.
   b. This discovery will cause the demand for mangos to shift to the right.
   c. This discovery will cause the price of mangos to decrease due to a movement along the demand curve for mangos.
   d. This discovery will cause a movement along the demand curve for mangos.

5. Consider the demand curve for automobiles. An increase in the price of automobiles due to a leftward shift in the supply curve will
   a. cause a movement along the demand curve for automobiles.
   b. result in an increase in the quantity of automobiles demanded.
   c. have no effect on the quantity of automobiles demanded since the change occurred on the supply side of the model.
   d. Answers (a) and (b) are both true statements.

6. The prices of flat-screen TVs are expected to fall next year. Which of the following statements about the market for flat-screen TVs this year are true?
   I. Consumers will decrease their demand for flat-screen TVs at all prices this year in anticipation of the decrease in flat-screen TV prices next year.
   II. Prices today for a given quantity of flat-screen TVs are likely to decrease due to these expectations.
   III. Prices today for a given quantity of flat-screen TVs are likely to increase due to these expectations.
   a. Statement I is true.
   b. Statement II is true.
   c. Statement III is true.
   d. Statements I and II are true.
   e. Statements I and III are true.

7. Peanut butter and jelly are considered to be complements in the diet of many people. Holding everything else constant, if the price of peanut butter increases, then the demand for
   a. peanut butter will shift to the left.
   b. peanut butter will shift to the right.
   c. jelly will shift to the left.
   d. jelly will shift to the right.

8. Ham and turkey are considered to be substitutes in the diet of many people. Holding everything else constant, if the price of ham decreases, then the demand for
   a. turkey will shift to the left.
   b. turkey will shift to the right.
   c. ham will shift to the left.
   d. ham will shift to the right.

9. Consider two goods: good X and good Y. Holding everything else constant, the price of good Y increases and the demand for good X decreases. Good X and good Y are
   a. complements.
   b. substitutes.
   c. not related to each other.

10. Consider two goods: good X and good Y. Holding everything else constant, the price of good Y decreases and the demand for good X decreases. Good X and good Y are
   a. complements.
   b. substitutes.
   c. not related to each other.

11. Holding everything else constant, Jon's income increases. If Jon's demand for good X decreases, then it must be the case that good X is a(n)
   a. inferior good.
   b. normal good.
   c. complement.
   d. substitute.

12. Jon's income increases by 10% this year while his purchases of steak increase by 4% this year over last year's purchases of steak. Holding everything else constant, Jon considers steak to be a(n)
   a. inferior good.
   b. normal good.
   c. complement.
   d. substitute.

13. Smalltown experiences an increase in its population due to the economic opportunities available in Smalltown. This event is likely to
   a. cause the demand curve for many products in Smalltown to shift to the right.
   b. cause the demand curve for many products in Smalltown to shift to the left.
   c. have little effect on the demand for products in Smalltown.
   d. cause the supply curve for many products in Smalltown to shift to the left.

14. A market is initially composed of 100 buyers. Holding everything else constant, if an additional 100 buyers join this market, then this will
   a. have no effect on the market demand curve since there is a limit to how many units of the good can be demanded at any price.
   b. cause the market demand curve to shift to the left since the good's price will necessarily increase when there are more buyers.
   c. cause the market demand curve to shift to the right as the additional demand of these new consumers is added to the initial demand curve.
   d. cause a movement along the demand curve as the price of the good rises due to the increase in the number of buyers.

15. Consider a market composed of three consumers: Peter, Anya, and Pablo. The market demand schedule is given in the table below. Which of the possible individual demand schedules provided in the answer selection is most likely to correspond to this market demand schedule?

Price	Market quantity demanded
$10	100
20	75
30	50
40	25

a.

Price	Quantity demanded by Peter	Quantity demanded by Anya	Quantity demanded by Pablo
$10	25	25	40
20	20	20	35
30	15	14	16
40	10	10	5

b.

Price	Quantity demanded by Peter	Quantity demanded by Anya	Quantity demanded by Pablo
$10	25	25	50
20	20	15	35
30	15	10	25
40	10	10	5

c.

Price	Quantity demanded by Peter	Quantity demanded by Anya	Quantity demanded by Pablo
$10	25	25	55
20	15	20	35
30	10	15	20
40	5	10	5

d.

Price	Quantity demanded by Peter	Quantity demanded by Anya	Quantity demanded by Pablo
$10	25	25	50
20	20	20	35
30	15	15	20
40	10	10	5

16. The market demand curve for a product is the horizontal summation of the individual demand curves for the product, holding the

a. quantity demanded constant.

b. price constant.

ANSWER KEY

Answers to Problems and Exercises

1. This assumption results in a market situation in which no buyer (or group of buyers) and no seller (or group of sellers) can affect the market price. In a competitive market the interaction of demand and supply determines the equilibrium price and the equilibrium quantity rather than the behavior of a particular buyer and/or seller.

2. a.

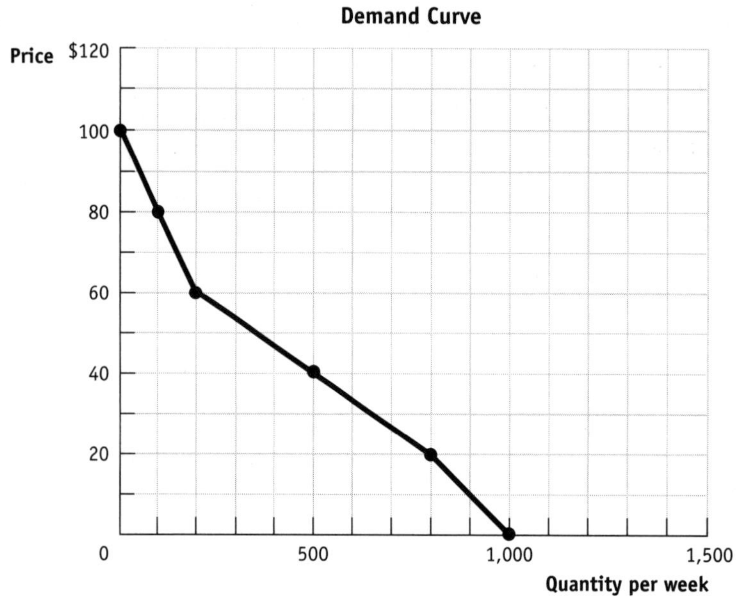

b. If the price rises to $60, the quantity demanded will fall by 300 units, from 500 bicycles to 200 bicycles.

c. If the price falls to $0, the quantity demanded will increase by 500 units, from 500 bicycles to 1,000 bicycles.

3.

Situation	Specified market	Movement or shift	Rightward or leftward shift in demand
People's income increases	Market for exotic vacations	Shift	Rightward
People's income decreases	Market for goods sold in secondhand shops	Shift	Rightward
Price of bicycles increases	Market for bicycles	Movement	
Price of tennis balls increases	Market for tennis racquets	Shift	Leftward
Price of movie tickets decreases	Popcorn at movie theaters	Shift	Rightward
Popularity of music-playing device increases	Market for music-playing device	Shift	Rightward
Popularity of branded clothing items decreases	Market for brand-name designer clothing	Shift	Leftward
Winter clothing to go on sale next month	Market for winter clothing	Shift	Leftward
Increase in urban residents	Market for apartments in urban areas	Shift	Rightward

4. **a.** Note: these sketches are not drawn to scale since they are meant to be a guide rather than a perfect mathematical rendering of the data in the table. To find the market demand curve, hold price constant and ask how many units are demanded by all the consumers at this price. For example, at a price of $3, Joe demands 4 units, Maria demands 8 units, and Chao demands 2 units for a total market demand of 14 units at a price of $3. Repeat this for another price (e.g., for a price of $4, Joe demands 2 units, Maria demands 4 units, and Chao demands 1 unit for a total market demand of 7 units).

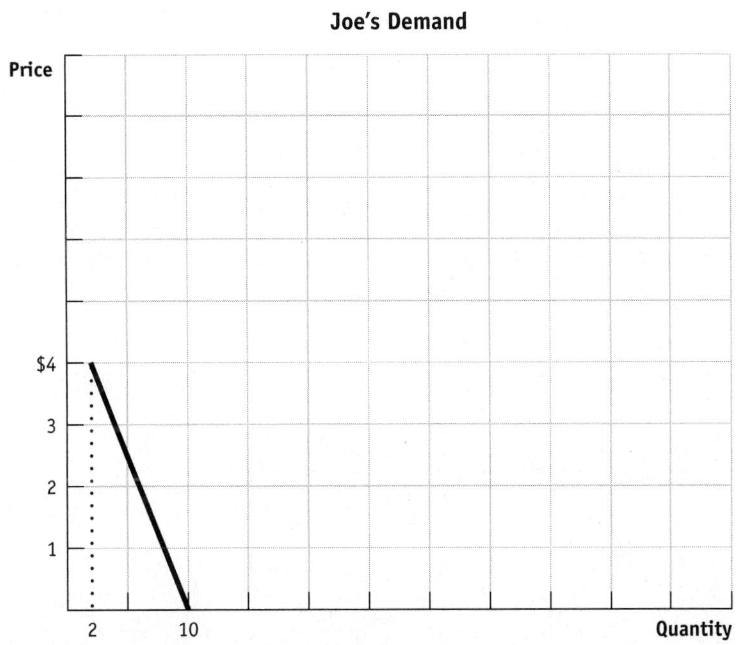

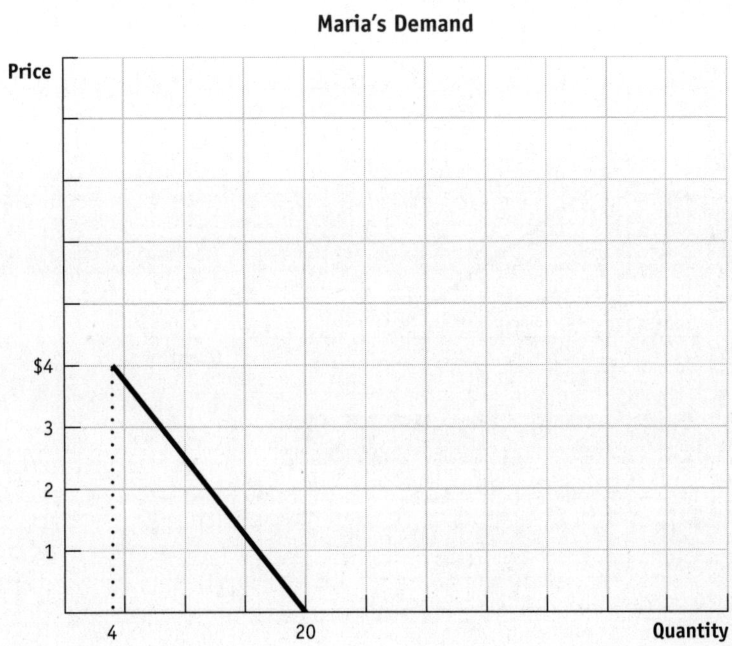

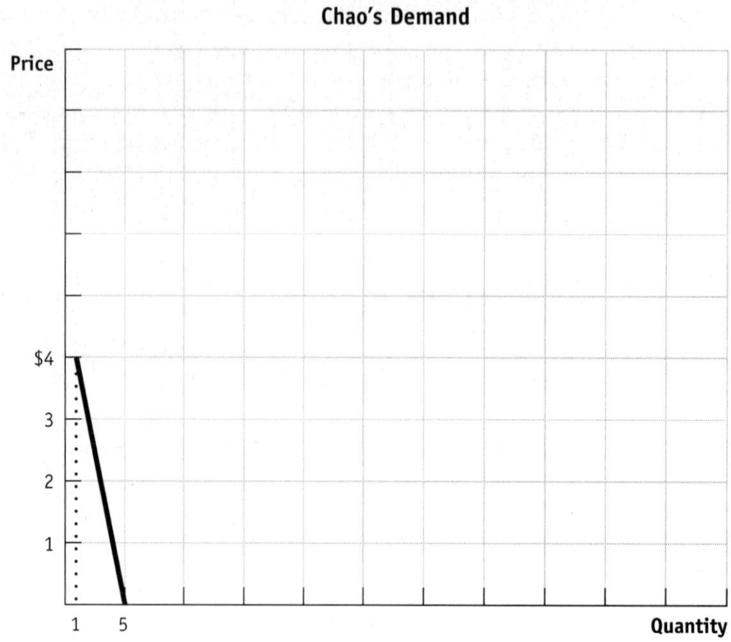

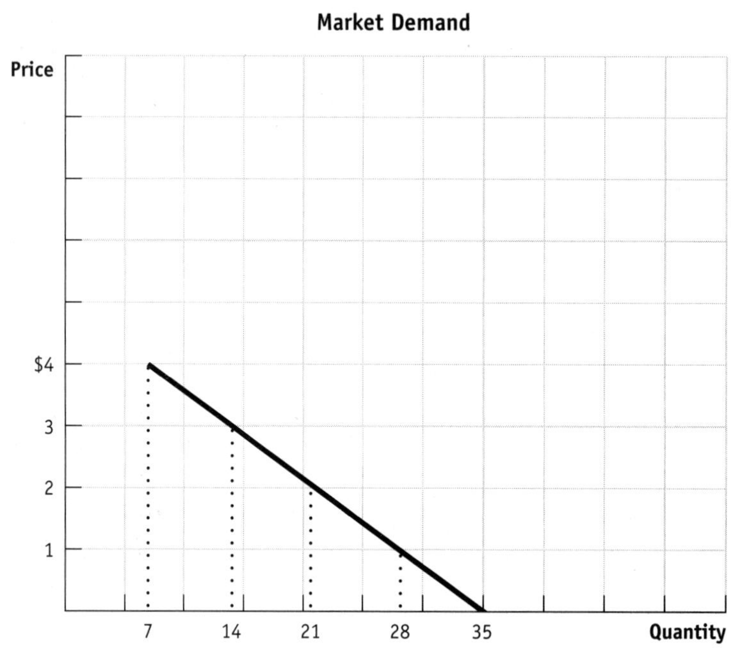

b.

Price	Quantity demanded in market
$0	35
1	28
2	21
3	14
4	7

Answers to Module Review Questions

1. **Answer c.** This is a definitional statement.
2. **Answer c.** The law of demand states that as the price of the good decreases, the quantity demanded of the good increases. Since the shampoo is on sale, its price has fallen and the law of demand suggests that the quantity demanded should therefore increase.
3. **Answer a.** This is a definitional statement. An inverse function of two variables means that an increase in one of the variables will result in a decrease in the other variable, or a decrease in one of the variables will result in an increase in the other variable. The law of demand states that as the price of the good increases, the quantity demanded of the good decreases; thus, price and quantity are inversely related.
4. **Answer b.** This research finding is likely to result in an increase in tastes and preferences for mangos, which will cause the demand curve for mangos to shift to the right.
5. **Answer a.** A leftward shift in the supply curve holding everything else constant will cause the price of the good to increase. An increase in price will result in a movement along the demand curve, since as the price increases, the quantity demanded of the good decreases.
6. **Answer d.** The expected fall in flat-screen TV prices next year will cause the demand curve for flat-screen TVs this year to shift to the left as consumers decrease the quantity of flat-screen TVs they demand at every price. At any given quantity of flat-screen TVs the price demanders are willing to pay will be lower because of the change in expectations.
7. **Answer c.** Since peanut butter and jelly are considered complements in this example, an increase in the price of peanut butter will cause the demand curve for jelly to shift to the left, since as fewer units of peanut butter are demanded due to the higher price of peanut butter, fewer units of jelly will also be demanded at any given price for jelly.
8. **Answer a.** Since ham and turkey are substitutes, when the price of ham decreases, this causes the quantity of ham demanded to increase. As more units of ham are demanded, fewer units of turkey are demanded at every price. The demand for turkey therefore shifts to the left.
9. **Answer a.** As the price of good Y increases, this results in a decrease in the quantity demanded of good Y. Since the demand for good X decreases, this implies that good Y and good X are consumed together; thus good X and good Y are complements.
10. **Answer b.** As the price of good Y decreases, this results in an increase in the quantity demanded of good Y. Since the demand for good X decreases when the quantity demanded of good Y increases, this implies that good X is a substitute for good Y.
11. **Answer a.** When Jon's income increases, the quantity of good X he demands at any given price falls, which implies that good X is an inferior good.
12. **Answer b.** Both Jon's income and the quantity of steak he demands increases; therefore steak is a normal good.
13. **Answer a.** An increase in population shifts the demand curve to the right, as the increase in population implies a larger number of consumers of the product.
14. **Answer c.** An increase in the number of buyers causes the quantity demanded of the good to increase at every price, and the demand curve shifts to the right.
15. **Answer d.** To find the market demand curve, hold price constant and then add the quantity of the good demanded by each of the consumers. Thus, if the price of the good is \$10, then the total of Peter's, Anya's, and Pablo's demand must add up to 100 units according to the table provided in the question.
16. **Answer b.** This is a definitional statement. The market demand curve is found by holding price constant and then adding together the quantities demanded by each consumer in the market. This process is repeated for other prices.

module 6

Supply and Equilibrium

BEFORE YOU READ THE MODULE

Summary

This module describes the supply curve, explains the distinction between movements along a supply curve versus a shift of the supply curve, and also discusses the primary determinants of supply. The module defines the meaning of equilibrium in the model of demand and supply. The module examines how demand and supply interact to determine a market's equilibrium price and equilibrium quantity. The module also discusses how a market eliminates shortages and surpluses through changes in price and quantity so that the market returns to its equilibrium.

Module Objectives

Objective #1. The quantity of a good or service supplied by a producer depends on the price producers are offered for their product. The supply schedule illustrates the relationship between various prices and the quantity of the good supplied at each of these prices. Generally speaking, the quantity supplied increases as the price increases, holding everything else constant. A supply curve is the graphical representation of a supply schedule. Usually a supply curve is upward sloping: the quantity supplied increases as the price increases.

Objective #2. The quantity supplied depends on many factors, but the primary determinants of the quantity supplied are the price of the good, the price of its inputs, the price of related goods, and changes in technology, expectations, and the number of producers. A change in the price of the good causes a movement along the supply curve; a change in one of the other supply determinants, other than price, causes a shift in the supply curve. A rightward shift in the supply curve is an increase in supply; a leftward shift in the supply curve is a decrease in supply. An increase in the price of inputs, holding everything else constant, will cause a decrease in supply. This means that the supply curve shifts to the left, and at every price the quantity supplied is now less than it was initially.

Objective #3. Two goods are substitutes in production when an increase in the price of one of these goods results in greater production of this good and reduced production of the other good. Two goods are complements in production when an increase in the price of one of these goods results in greater production of both goods.

Objective #4. The market supply curve is found by horizontally adding together the individual supply curves. At each price, the quantity supplied by each firm is added together to create the market supply curve. As the number of individual producers increases there is an increase in supply.

Objective #5. A competitive market is in equilibrium at the price at which the quantity demanded equals the quantity supplied. This price is called the equilibrium price. The quantity associated with this equilibrium price is called the equilibrium quantity. The equilibrium price is the market-clearing price, since at this price the quantity demanded equals the quantity supplied. The equilibrium in a market occurs at the point of intersection between the demand and supply curves.

Objective #6. At a given price, if the quantity supplied of the good is greater than the quantity demanded of the good, there is a surplus, or excess supply, in the market. If there is excess supply, prices will fall until the quantity supplied equals the quantity demanded. At a given price, if the quantity supplied of the good is less than the quantity demanded of the good, there is a shortage, or excess demand, in the market. If there is excess demand, prices will rise until the quantity supplied equals the quantity demanded.

Key Terms

quantity supplied the actual amount of a good or service producers are willing to sell at some specific price.

supply schedule a list or table showing how much of a good or service producers will supply at different prices.

supply curve a graphical representation of the *supply schedule,* showing the relationship between *quantity supplied* and price.

law of supply the general proposition that, all else constant, a higher price leads to higher quantity supplied and a lower price leads to lower quantity supplied.

change in supply a shift of the supply curve, which changes the quantity supplied at any given price.

movement along the supply curve a change in the *quantity supplied* of a good that results from a change in the price of that good.

input a good or service used to produce another good or service.

individual supply curve a graphical representation of the relationship between *quantity supplied* and price for an individual producer.

equilibrium the state in which no individual would be better off doing something different.

equilibrium price the price at which the market is in *equilibrium,* that is, the quantity of a good or service demanded equals the quantity of that good or service supplied; also referred to as the *market-clearing price.*

equilibrium quantity the quantity of a good or service bought and sold at the *equilibrium* (or *market-clearing*) *price.*

Notes

market-clearing price the price at which the market is in *equilibrium*, that is, the quantity of a good or service demanded equals the quantity of that good or service supplied; also referred to as the *equilibrium price.*

surplus the excess of a good or service that occurs when the quantity supplied exceeds the quantity demanded; surpluses occur when the price is above the *equilibrium price.*

shortage the insufficiency of a good or service that occurs when the quantity demanded exceeds the quantity supplied; shortages occur when the price is below the *equilibrium price.*

Notes

AFTER YOU READ THE MODULE

Tips

Tip #1. A supply curve is usually upward sloping. The positive slope of a supply curve implies that the quantity supplied of a good or service is directly related to its price. Another way to express this idea is that as the price of the good decreases, holding everything else constant, producers will want to supply fewer units of the good. Figure 6.1 illustrates this idea: at P_1, Q_1 units of the good are supplied; as the price of the good falls from P_1 to P_2, the quantity supplied of the good decreases from Q_1 to Q_2.

Figure 6.1

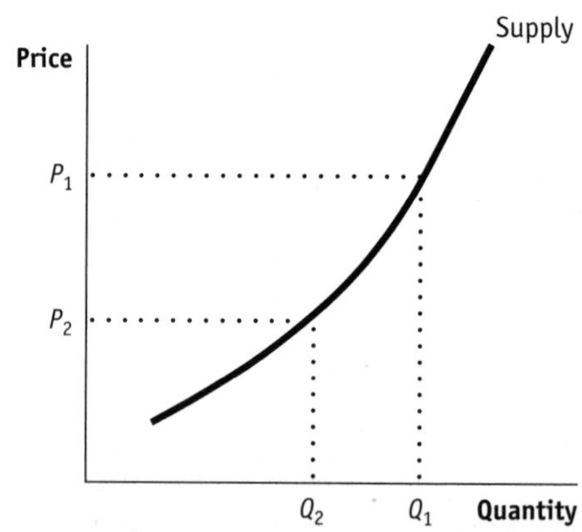

Tip #2. A supply curve illustrates the relationship between the price of the good and the quantity supplied at each specific price. In drawing the supply curve, the other determinants of supply are held constant; this constancy is another example of the other-things-equal assumption.

Tip #3. Besides the price of the good, the quantity supplied of a good is affected by the following variables: changes in input prices, changes in the price of related goods, and changes in technology, expectations, and the number of producers. You need to know this list of variables as well as how each of these variables affects the supply curve.

Tip #4. Economists make a distinction between supply and the quantity supplied. The quantity supplied refers to a specific quantity associated with a specific price (as in Figure 6.1 where Q_1 is associated with P_1 and Q_2 is associated with P_2). Supply refers to the entire supply curve.

Tip #5. Economists also make a distinction between a movement along a supply curve and a shift of the supply curve. A movement is caused by a change in the good's price, while a shift in a supply curve is caused by a change in some supply determinant other than the price of the good.

- Figure 6.2 illustrates this distinction for a supply curve. There is a movement from point *A* to point *B* when the price decreases from P_1 to P_2, and there is a shift in the supply curve from S_1 to S_2 due to a change in some other determinant of supply. A shift causes the quantity supplied of the good to change at every price—for example, at P_1 in Figure 6.2, the shift causes the quantity supplied to increase from Q_1 to Q_3 (compare point *A* to point C). Figure 6.2 illustrates an increase in supply when the supply curve shifts to the right from S_1 to S_2. A decrease in supply would be illustrated by the supply curve shifting to the left (in Figure 6.2 this would be a shift from S_2 to S_1).

Figure 6.2

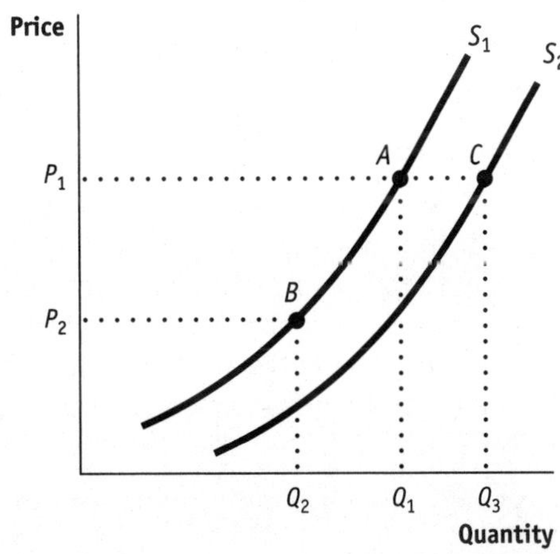

Tip #6. The market equilibrium occurs at the point of intersection of the demand and supply curves. Figure 6.3 indicates that equilibrium at point E, where the equilibrium price is P_1 and the equilibrium quantity is Q_1. If the price is greater than the equilibrium price, there is excess supply, or a surplus, in the market. Figure 6.3 illustrates a situation of excess supply at the price P_2. Note that at price P_2 the quantity supplied is Q_3, while the quantity demanded is Q_2. If the price is less than the equilibrium price, there is excess demand, or a shortage, in the market. Figure 6.3 illustrates a situation of excess demand at the price P_3. Note that at price P_3 the quantity demanded is Q_5, while the quantity supplied is Q_4.

Figure 6.3

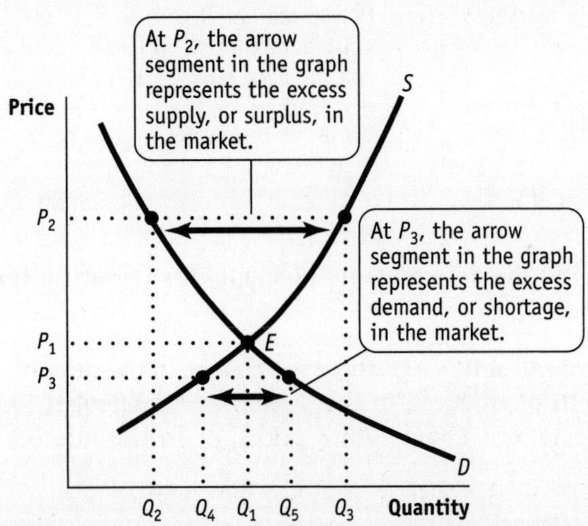

Tip #7. If you are given an equation for the demand curve and an equation for the supply curve, you can solve these two equations for the equilibrium price and equilibrium quantity. For example, suppose demand is given by the equation $P = 10 - Q$ and supply is given by the equation $P = Q$. To find the equilibrium, recall that in equilibrium the quantity demanded equals the quantity supplied; thus, $10 - Q = Q$, or the equilibrium quantity equals 5. Replace Q in either equation with 5 and you will find that the equilibrium price is 5.

Tip #8. Often a quick sketch of a demand and supply curve is all that you need to answer questions about the effect of a change in the market on the equilibrium price or equilibrium quantity. Practice drawing a quick representation of the demand and supply curves as you do this module's problems, recognizing that you do not always need a precisely plotted graph to find a solution or to guide your solution of a problem.

Tip #9. As always, if you are making a set of flash cards, make one for each new definition or concept and then review these cards (as well as the cards from the earlier modules).

WORKED PROBLEMS

1. The supply and demand model is often used to analyze the effect of a change in the market on the equilibrium price and quantity of a good. Consider each of the following markets and the given situation to determine whether the supply curve shifts or there is a movement along the supply curve. For any shift in the supply curve, indicate whether the curve shifts to the left or to the right. The examples are given in a table to help you consolidate your answers.

Market under consideration	Situation	Shift of or movement along the demand curve
Automobile market	The price of steel, a key input in the production of cars, increases.	
Pizza market	The number of pizza shops in town doubles.	
Shampoo market	The price of plastic used in shampoo bottles decreases.	
Automobile market	Manufacturers of cars anticipate that car prices will increase next year.	
Leather belt market	The price of leather wallets increases.	

STEP 1: Review the determinants of supply that result in the supply curve shifting.

The supply curve will shift when there is a change in the price of an input, in the price of a substitute in production, in the price of a complement in production, in technology, in expectations about future prices, or in the number of producers in the market.

STEP 2: For each of the markets determine whether there is a change in the price of the good, which will cause a movement along the supply curve, or a change in some other supply determinant, which will shift the supply curve.

For each of the given situations the change described in the table will cause a shift in the supply curve. The table in Step 3 summarizes these shifts and their causes.

STEP 3: For each supply curve that shifts, determine the direction of the shift and record your responses in the provided table.

Market under consideration	Situation	Shift of or movement along the demand curve
Automobile market	The price of steel, a key input in the production of cars, increases.	The supply curve will shift to the left: at every price, the quantity of cars supplied will decrease because of an increase in the price of an input.
Pizza market	The number of pizza shops in town doubles.	The supply curve will shift to the right: at every price, the quantity of pizzas supplied will increase because of an increase in the number of producers.
Shampoo market	The price of plastic used in shampoo bottles decreases.	The supply curve will shift to the right: at every price, the quantity of shampoo supplied will increase because of a decrease in the price of an input.
Automobile market	Manufacturers of cars anticipate that car prices will increase next year.	The supply curve will shift to the left: at every price, the quantity of cars supplied will decrease because of expectations that prices will increase in the future.
Leather belt market	The price of leather wallets increases.	The supply curve will shift to the left: at every price, the quantity of leather belts supplied will decrease because of an increase in the price of a substitute in production.

2. Suppose you are told that each firm in an industry is identical and that there are two firms in the industry. Furthermore, you are told that one firm's supply curve is given by the equation $P = 10 + 2Q$. Find the market supply curve in this industry.

STEP 1: To find the market supply curve, you will want to horizontally add all the individual supply curves of the firms in the industry. This will be relatively easy if you draw three horizontally aligned graphs where the first graph illustrates firm 1's

supply curve, the second graph illustrates firm 2's supply curve, and the third graph illustrates the market supply curve. The following figure represents this concept.

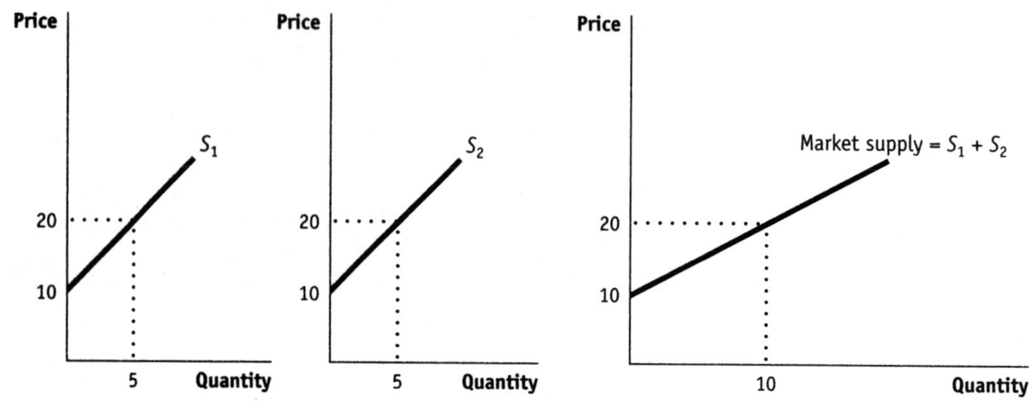

STEP 2: To find the market supply curve, you will want to horizontally add all the individual supply curves of the firms in the industry. Use your sketch to help you write this equation.

From the third graph you can see that the y-intercept is 10. You can also calculate the slope of the market supply curve as the change in price divided by the change in quantity. Using the points (0,10) and (10,20), the slope is equal to 1. The market supply curve can thus be written as $P = Q + 10$.

Problems and Exercises

1. The following graph represents the supply curve for the production of widgets in Town Center.

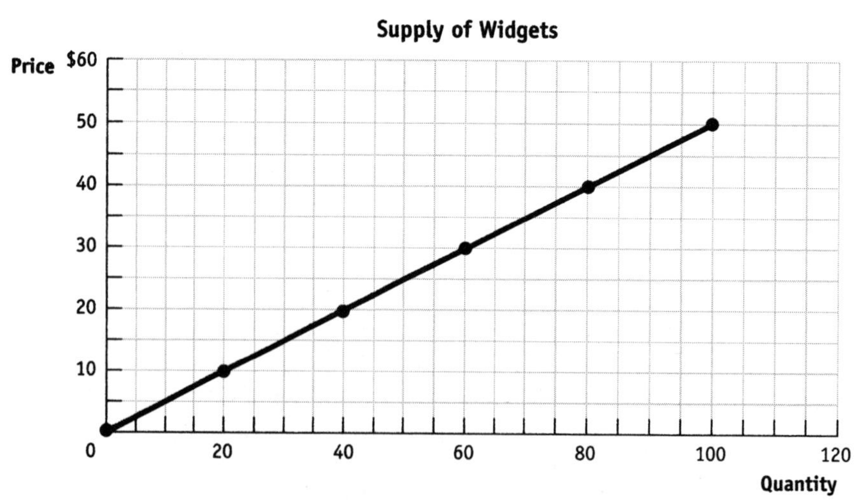

a. At a price of $20, how many widgets are producers willing to supply?

b. At a price of $40, how many widgets are producers willing to supply?

c. Suppose there are ten widget producers in Town Center and that the price of widgets is $50. If each widget producer produces exactly the same number of widgets as every other widget producer, how many widgets will each producer produce at this price?

d. Suppose the price is initially $30 but then falls to $20. What is the change in the quantity supplied?

e. Suppose the price is initially $30 but then increases to $50. What is the change in the quantity supplied?

f. What price must suppliers receive in order to be willing to supply 80 widgets?

g. What price must suppliers receive in order to be willing to supply 40 widgets?

h. What does the slope of a typical supply curve imply about the relationship between price and the quantity supplied?

2. For each of the following situations in the table below, fill in the missing information: first, determine whether the situation causes a shift or a movement along the supply curve; then, if it causes a shift, determine whether the supply curve shifts to the right or to the left.

Situation	Specified market	Movement or shift	Rightward or leftward shift in supply
Labor costs for air travel and cruise ships increase	Market for exotic vacations		
Prices of office equipment and phone service rise by 40%	Market for call center services		
Price of bicycles increases	Market for bicycles		
Price of leather boots increases	Market for beef products		
Price of leather boots increases	Market for leather belts		
New technology for music-playing device revealed	Market for music-playing devices		
Price of brand-name designer clothing increases	Market for brand-name designer clothing		
Stock market prices expected to fall next quarter	Stock market today		
Increase in number of coffee shop owners in the metro area	Market for coffee shops in the metro area		

3. The demand and supply schedules for Healthy Snacks, Inc., is provided in the table below.

Price	Quantity demanded	Quantity supplied
$ 0	1,000	0
10	800	125
20	600	275
30	400	400
40	200	550
50	0	675

a. Draw a sketch of the demand and supply curves for Healthy Snacks, Inc. Don't worry about drawing a precise graph but instead focus on drawing a simple rendering of the underlying relationships captured in the above table. This drawing should be accurate with regard to x-intercepts and y-intercepts and it should also indicate the point of equilibrium.

Demand and Supply Curves for Healthy Snacks, Inc.

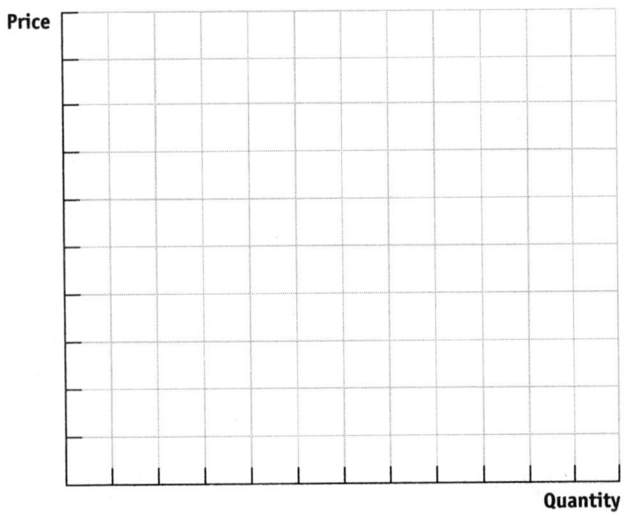

b. From the table, what are the equilibrium price and the equilibrium quantity in this market? Indicate these on your graph.

c. Fill in the following table based on the data given to you. Assume that for each row in the table, the price is as given and that you are calculating the number of units of excess demand or excess supply. (Hint: Some of the cells in your table will be left empty—for example, if there is excess supply, then there isn't excess demand.)

Price	Excess demand	Excess supply
$ 0		
10		
20		
30		
40		
50		

d. Why is a situation of excess demand referred to as a shortage? Explain using a simple graph to illustrate your answer.

e. Why is a situation of excess supply referred to as a surplus? Explain using a simple graph to illustrate your answer.

4. Use the following graph to answer this next set of questions. The graph illustrates the competitive market for garbage cans in Cleantopia.

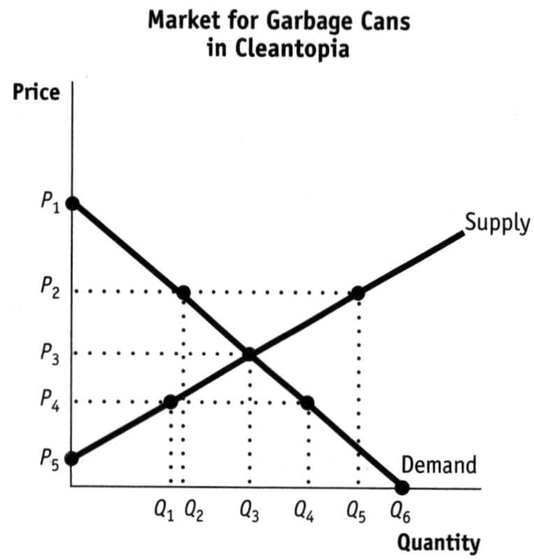

a. What is the equilibrium price in this market?

b. What is the equilibrium quantity in this market?

c. Suppose the current price of garbage cans in Cleantopia is P_2. Describe this market in detail and explain what you think will happen in this market.

d. Suppose the current price of garbage cans in Cleantopia is P_4. Describe this market in detail and explain what you think will happen in this market.

e. Suppose at the current market price the quantity demanded equals Q_4. Describe this market and identify the quantity supplied given this information. What do you expect will happen in this market?

f. Suppose at the current market price the quantity supplied equals Q_5. Describe this market and identify the quantity demanded given this information. What do you expect will happen in this market?

g. At what price is the quantity demanded equal to zero? What does it mean to have the quantity demanded equal to zero?

h. At what price is the quantity supplied equal to zero? What does it mean to have the quantity supplied equal to zero?

5. The competitive market for bicycles in Pedal City is described by the demand curve $P = 2{,}000 - 2Q$ and the supply curve $P = 6Q$. There are twenty bicycle manufacturers in Pedal City and each of these manufacturers produces the same number of bicycles as every other manufacturer.

a. Using the two equations for the demand and supply curves, fill in the following table describing the demand and supply schedules for bicycles in Pedal City.

Price	Quantity demanded	Quantity supplied
$ 0		
240		
480		
720		
960		
1,200		
1,440		
1,680		
1,920		

b. Examine the table you created in (a) and provide a range of prices that you expect the equilibrium price to fall between. Why do you expect the equilibrium price to fall within this range?

c. Sketch a graph of the demand and supply curves for bicycles in Pedal City.

Market for Bicycles in Pedal City

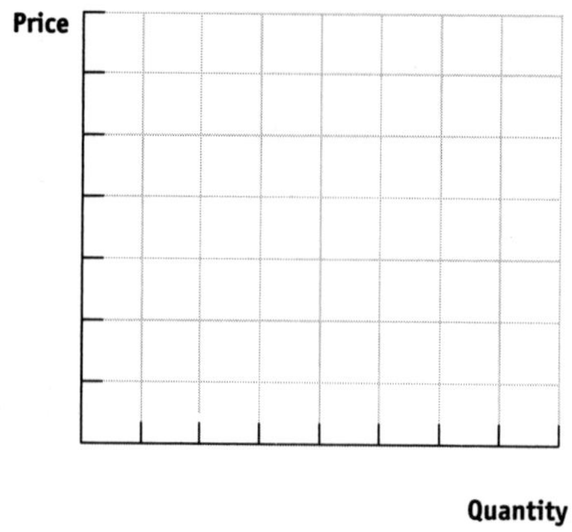

d. If the current price for bicycles is $240, how many bicycles will be supplied in Pedal City and how many bicycles will a single manufacturer produce? At a price of $240, how many bicycles will be demanded? At a price of $240, is the market in equilibrium? Explain your answer.

e. If the current price for bicycles is $480, how many bicycles will be supplied in Pedal City and how many bicycles will a single manufacturer produce? At a price of $480, how many bicycles will be demanded? At a price of $480, is the market in equilibrium? Explain your answer.

f. If the current price for bicycles is $1,680, how many bicycles will be supplied in Pedal City and how many bicycles will a single manufacturer produce? At a price of $1,680, how many bicycles will be demanded? At a price of $1,680, is the market in equilibrium? Explain your answer.

g. Calculate the equilibrium price and the equilibrium quantity in the market for bicycles in Pedal City.

BEFORE YOU TAKE THE TEST

Module Review Questions

1. Consider a supply curve. When the price of the good increases, then this results in a movement along the supply curve resulting in a greater
   a. supply of the good.
   b. quantity supplied.

2. The cost of ground beef used to produce Fast Wally's hamburgers increases. Holding everything else constant, this will result in
   a. the supply curve shifting to the left.
   b. the supply curve shifting to the right.
   c. a movement along the supply curve to a smaller quantity supplied.
   d. a movement along the supply curve to a greater quantity supplied.

3. The cost of raw materials used to produce Ever Strong Batteries decreases. Holding everything else constant, this will result in
   a. the supply curve shifting to the left.
   b. the supply curve shifting to the right.
   c. a movement along the supply curve to a smaller quantity supplied.
   d. a movement along the supply curve to a greater quantity supplied.

4. Input prices decrease for a manufacturer. Holding everything else constant, this implies that at any given price the manufacturer will supply
   a. more of the good.
   b. less of the good.

5. A manufacturer produces two different products from its fixed set of resources. When the manufacturer increases the production of the first good, it must necessarily reduce the level of production of the second good due to these fixed resources. These two goods are
   a. complements in production.
   b. substitutes in production.

6. A sawmill operator produces lumber used in the construction industry as well as sawdust used for pet bedding. An increase in the supply of lumber is likely to
   a. increase the supply of sawdust, since lumber and sawdust are complements in production.
   b. decrease the supply of sawdust, since lumber and sawdust are complements in production.
   c. increase the supply of sawdust, since lumber and sawdust are substitutes in production.
   d. decrease the supply of sawdust, since lumber and sawdust are substitutes in production.

7. Research and development result in the discovery of a new technology for electricity generation. Holding everything else constant, this discovery will
   a. increase the supply of electricity.
   b. increase the quantity supplied of electricity.
   c. decrease the supply of electricity.
   d. decrease the quantity supplied of electricity.

8. The sawmill industry expects lumber prices to rise next year due to growing demand for the construction of new homes. Holding everything else constant, this expectation will shift

a. the supply curve for lumber this year to the left.
b. the supply curve for lumber this year to the right.

9. The graph below illustrates the supply curve for the competitive market for widgets. Currently there are sixteen producers in this market and each producer produces exactly the same number of widgets as every other producer. Suppose the price of widgets is $40. If all the producers continue to produce the same number as every other producer, what will be the level of production for each producer?

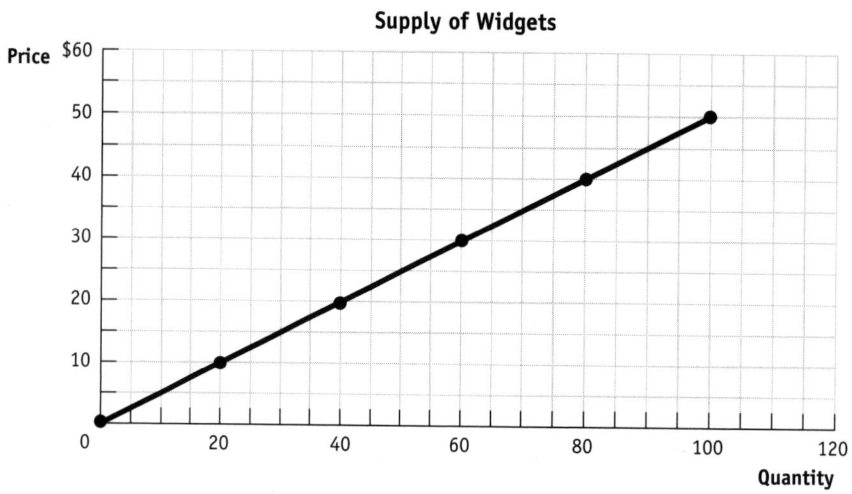

a. 8 widgets
b. 10 widgets
c. 5 widgets
d. 20 widgets

10. Which of the following statements is true about equilibrium in a competitive market for a good?

I. In equilibrium, the quantity demanded equals the quantity supplied.
II. The equilibrium price and the equilibrium quantity correspond to the price and quantity at which the demand curve intersects the supply curve.
III. In equilibrium, every consumer who wishes to consume the product is satisfied.

a. Statement I is true.
b. Statement II is true.
c. Statement III is true.
d. Statements I and II are true.
e. Statements I, II, and III are true.

11. The competitive market for widgets is described by the following table.

Price	Quantity demanded	Quantity supplied
$ 0	400	0
20	300	100
40	200	200
60	100	300
80	0	400

If the current price is $20, then there is a(n)

a. excess supply of 200 widgets.
b. shortage of 200 widgets.
c. excess demand of 100 widgets.
d. surplus of 100 widgets.

12. The competitive market for widgets is described by the following table.

Price	Quantity demanded	Quantity supplied
$ 0	400	0
20	300	100
40	200	200
60	100	300
80	0	400

If the current price is $60, then there is a(n)

a. excess supply of 200 widgets.
b. excess demand of 200 widgets.
c. shortage of 100 widgets.
d. surplus of 100 widgets.

13. The competitive market for widgets is described by the following table.

Price	Quantity demanded	Quantity supplied
$ 0	400	0
20	300	100
40	200	200
60	100	300
80	0	400

The equilibrium quantity in this market is _________ widgets and the equilibrium price is _________.

a. 300; $20
b. 200; $20
c. 200; $40
d. 200; $60

14. The competitive market for widgets is described by the following table. Furthermore, you are told that both the demand curve and the supply curve are linear.

Price	Quantity demanded	Quantity supplied
$ 0	400	0
20	300	100
40	200	200
60	100	300
80	0	400

Which of the following equations is the demand equation for widgets?

a. $Q = 80 - 5P$
b. $P = 80 - 5Q$
c. $Q = 400 - 5P$
d. $Q = 1/5P$

15. The competitive market for widgets is described by the following table. Furthermore, you are told that both the demand curve and the supply curve are linear.

Price	Quantity demanded	Quantity supplied
$ 0	400	0
20	300	100
40	200	200
60	100	300
80	0	400

Which of the following equations is the supply equation for widgets?

a. $P = 5Q$

b. $P = 1/5Q$

c. $Q = 1/5P$

d. $Q = 100 + 1/5Q$

16. Use the following graph of a competitive market for candles to answer this question.

Market for Candles

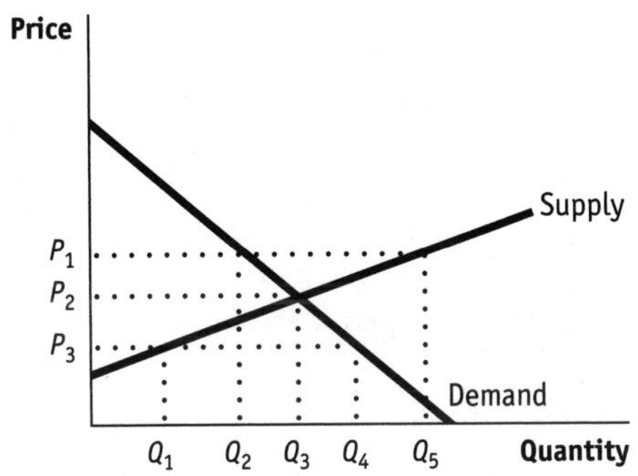

At a price of P_1, there is an excess

a. supply of the good equal to $Q_2 - Q_5$.

b. supply of the good equal to $Q_5 - Q_2$.

c. supply of the good equal to $Q_3 - Q_2$.

d. demand for the good equal to $Q_3 - Q_2$.

17. Use the following graph of a competitive market for candles to answer this question.

Market for Candles

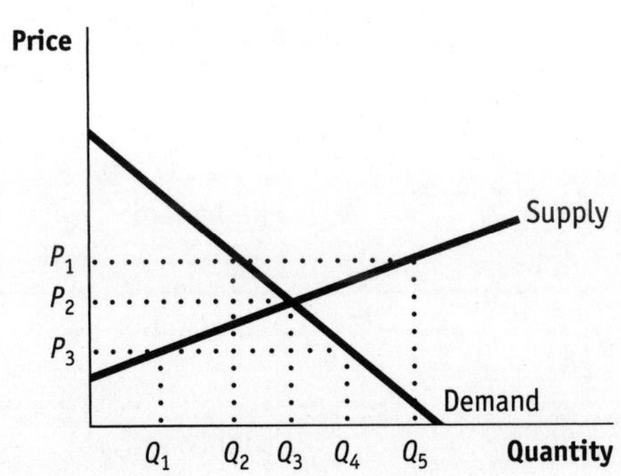

At a price of P_3, there is an excess

a. demand for the good of $Q_4 - Q_1$.

b. demand for the good of $Q_1 - Q_4$.

c. demand for the good of $Q_3 - Q_2$.

d. supply of the good of $Q_3 - Q_2$.

ANSWER KEY

Answers to Problems and Exercises

1. **a.** At a price of \$20, producers are willing to supply 40 units.

   b. At a price of \$40, producers are willing to supply 80 units.

   c. At a price of \$50, 100 widgets are supplied. Thus, if there are ten producers producing exactly the same number of widgets, then each producer must produce 10 widgets.

   d. When price falls from \$30 to \$20, the number of widgets supplied decreases by 20 widgets (from 60 widgets to 40 widgets).

   e. When price rises from \$30 to \$50, the number of widgets supplied increases by 40 widgets (from 60 widgets to 100 widgets).

   f. Suppliers are willing to supply 80 widgets if the price is \$40.

   g. Suppliers are willing to supply 40 widgets if the price is \$20.

   h. The typical supply curve is upward sloping: its slope is positive. This implies that the quantity supplied increases when price increases and that the quantity supplied decreases when price decreases.

2.

Situation	Specified market	Movement or shift	Rightward or leftward shift in supply
Labor costs for air travel and cruise ships increase	Market for exotic vacations	Shift	Leftward
Prices of office equipment and phone service rise by 40%	Market for call center services	Shift	Leftward
Price of bicycles increases	Market for bicycles	Movement	
Price of leather boots increases	Market for beef products	Shift	Rightward
Price of leather boots increases	Market for leather belts	Shift	Leftward
New technology for music-playing device revealed	Market for music-playing devices	Shift	Rightward
Price of brand-name designer clothing increases	Market for brand-name designer clothing	Movement	
Stock market prices expected to fall next quarter	Stock market today	Shift	Rightward
Increase in number of coffee shop owners in the metro area	Market for coffee shops in the metro area	Shift	Rightward

3. a.,b. Equilibrium occurs at the price at which the quantity demanded equals the quantity supplied. From the table we can see that the quantity demanded equals the quantity supplied at a price of $30. The equilibrium price is thus $30 and the equilibrium quantity is 400 units. This point is illustrated in the graph in part (d).

c.

Price	Excess demand	Excess supply
$ 0	1,000 units	
10	675 units	
20	325 units	
30	Equilibrium	Equilibrium
40		350 units
50		675 units

d. When there is excess demand this means that the quantity demanded by consumers is greater than the quantity supplied by producers. The market for some reason does not provide an adequate amount of the good, and thus there is a shortage of the good. The figure below illustrates a shortage at a price of P_1. Note that at P_1, the quantity demanded is Q_1, the quantity supplied is Q_2, and the excess demand is equal to $Q_1 - Q_2$. When a market has excess demand, this implies that the current price of the good is less than the market-clearing price.

Illustration of a Situation of Excess Demand, or a Shortage

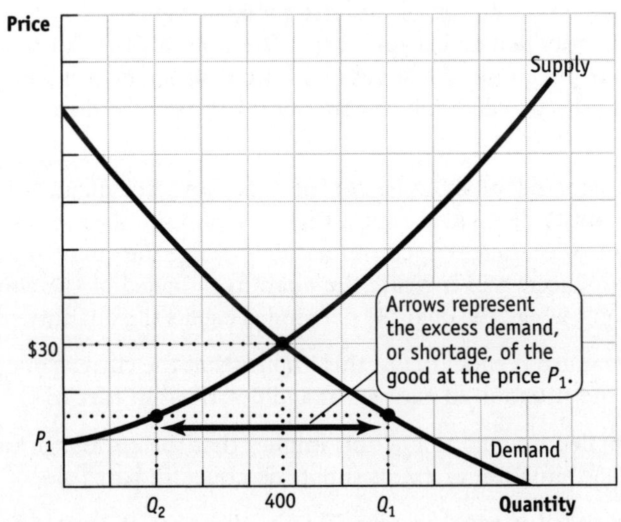

e. When there is excess supply this means that the quantity demanded by consumers is less than the quantity supplied by producers. The market for some reason provides too much of the good, and thus there is a surplus of the good. The figure below illustrates a surplus at a price of P_1. Note that at P_1, the quantity demanded is Q_1, the quantity supplied is Q_2, and the excess supply is equal to $Q_2 - Q_1$. When a market has excess supply of a good, this implies that the current price in the market is greater than the market-clearing price.

Illustration of a Situation of Excess Supply, or a Surplus

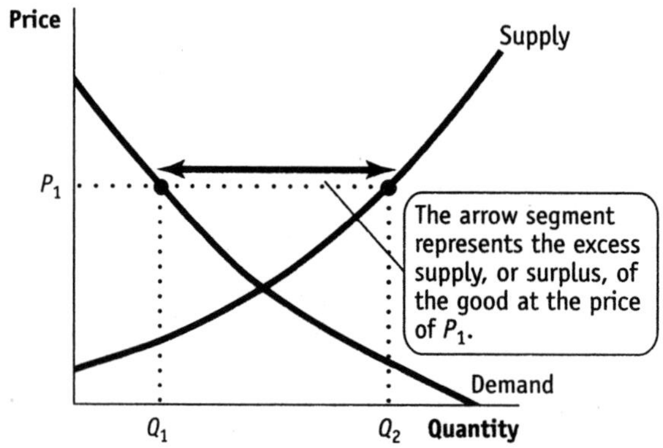

4. **a.** The equilibrium price in this market is P_3 since the quantity demanded (Q_3) equals the quantity supplied (Q_3) at this price.

b. Q_3.

c. At P_2 there is an excess supply, or surplus, of the good, since the quantity supplied equals Q_5 while the quantity demanded equals Q_2. The price should fall toward the equilibrium price. As the price falls, consumers will increase the quantity demanded of the good while producers will decrease the quantity supplied of the good until the price reaches the point where the quantity demanded equals the quantity supplied.

d. At P_4 there is an excess demand, or shortage, for the good, since the quantity supplied equals Q_1 while the quantity demanded equals Q_4. The price should rise toward the equilibrium price. As the price increases, consumers will reduce the quantity demanded of the good while producers will increase the quantity supplied of the good until the price reaches the point where the quantity demanded equals the quantity supplied.

e. When the quantity demanded is equal to Q_4, this implies that the current price in the market is P_4, which is the situation of excess demand described in part (d).

f. When the quantity supplied is equal to Q_5, this implies that the current price in the market is P_2, which is the situation of excess supply described in part (c).

g. At P_1 the quantity demanded is equal to zero. This implies that at a price of P_1 the price is too high for consumers to be willing to demand the product.

h. At P_5 the quantity supplied is equal to zero. This implies that at a price of P_5 the price is too low for producers to be willing to supply the good.

5. a.

Price	Quantity demanded	Quantity supplied
$ 0	1,000	0
240	880	40
480	760	80
720	640	120
960	520	160
1,200	400	200
1,440	280	240
1,680	160	280
1,920	40	320

b. Examination of the table reveals that prices less than or equal to $1,440 result in a situation of excess demand, while prices greater than or equal to $1,680 result in a situation of excess supply. Thus, the equilibrium price will fall somewhere in the range of $1,440 to $1,680 in this market.

c. **Market for Bicycles in Pedal City**

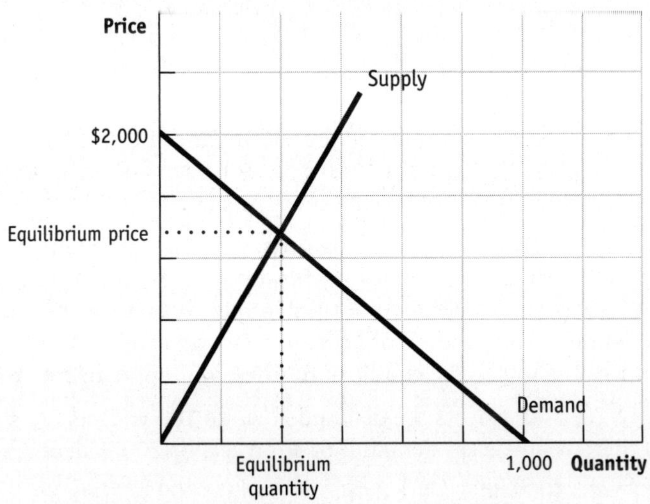

d. At a price of $240, 40 bicycles will be supplied and each manufacturer will produce 2 bicycles. At a price of $240, 880 bicycles will be demanded. The market is not in equilibrium since there is an excess demand for bicycles.

e. At a price of $480, 80 bicycles will be supplied and each manufacturer will produce 4 bicycles. At a price of $480, 760 bicycles will be demanded. The market is not in equilibrium since there is an excess demand for bicycles.

f. At a price of $1,680, 280 bicycles will be supplied and each manufacturer will produce 14 bicycles. At a price of $1,680, 160 bicycles will be demanded. The market is not in equilibrium since there is an excess supply of bicycles.

g. Since $P = 2{,}000 - 2Q$ and $P = 6Q$, we can use this information to write $2{,}000 - 2Q = 6Q$. Solving this equation gives us the equilibrium quantity of 250 bicycles. Substituting this quantity into either the demand equation or the supply equation yields the equilibrium price: $P = 2{,}000 - 2(250) = \$1{,}500$, or $P = 6(250) = \$1{,}500$.

Answers to Module Review Questions

1. **Answer b.** This question is asking you to recall that a change in the price of the good, holding everything else constant, results in a movement along the curve. This movement along the curve causes a change in the quantity supplied and not a change in the supply curve.

2. **Answer a.** Ground beef is an input in the production of Fast Wally's hamburgers. When ground beef gets more expensive, this increases the cost of producing hamburgers, which causes the supply curve to shift to the left.

3. **Answer b.** When the cost of raw materials decreases, more batteries can be produced at any given price. This decrease in the cost of raw materials causes the supply curve for batteries to shift to the right.

4. **Answer a.** When input prices decrease, producers are willing to supply more units of the good at every price.

5. **Answer b.** Since an increase in the production of one of the goods results in a decrease in the production of the other good, these two goods must be substitutes in production.

6. **Answer a.** Sawdust and lumber are complements in production. As the producer increases its production of lumber, the production of sawdust is also increased since sawdust is a by-product of lumber production.

7. **Answer a.** New technology causes the supply curve to shift to the right, resulting in an increase in the quantity supplied of the good at every price.

8. **Answer a.** The sawmill industry will want to decrease the supply of lumber it provides to the market this year due to the expectation that next year's lumber prices will be higher. At every price the quantity of lumber supplied this year will be decreased, and the supply curve for lumber this year shifts to the left.

9. **Answer c.** When the price is \$40, 80 widgets are produced. Since there are sixteen producers in this market and each of these producers produce the same number of widgets, this implies that each producer must be producing 5 widgets.

10. **Answer d.** The first two statements are fairly straightforward, but statement III may be somewhat appealing at first glance. At equilibrium, however, even though the quantity demanded equals the quantity supplied, this does not imply that every potential consumer of the good is consuming the good. Those consumers who would like to consume the good, but who are unwilling to pay the equilibrium price, will not consume the good.

11. **Answer b.** At a price of \$20, 300 widgets are demanded while 100 widgets are supplied. Thus, at a price of \$20 there is an excess demand, or shortage, of 200 widgets.

12. **Answer a.** At a price of \$60, 100 widgets are demanded while 300 widgets are supplied. Thus, at a price of \$60 there is an excess supply, or surplus, of 200 widgets.

13. **Answer c.** The equilibrium quantity is the quantity at which demand equals the quantity supplied. The equilibrium quantity is 200 widgets, and the equilibrium price is \$40.

14. **Answer c.** To find the demand curve, you can either plot the demand curve (although this is time consuming) or you can calculate the slope (rise/run = –20/100 = –1/5) and then use the slope-intercept form, $y = mx + b$, to write the equation. Thus, $P = (-1/5)Q + 80$, or solving for Q, $Q = 400 - 5P$.

15. **Answer b.** To find the supply curve, you can either plot the supply curve (although this is time consuming) or you can calculate the slope (rise/run = 20/100 = 1/5) and then use the slope-intercept form, $y = mx + b$, to write the equation. Thus, $P = (1/5)Q + 0$.

16. **Answer b.** At P_1 the quantity demanded is Q_2 units while the quantity supplied is Q_5 units. The quantity supplied is greater than the quantity demanded at P_1: this excess supply is equal to $Q_5 - Q_2$.

17. **Answer a.** At P_3 the quantity demanded is Q_4 units while the quantity supplied is Q_1 units. The quantity demanded is greater than the quantity supplied at P_3: this excess demand is equal to $Q_4 - Q_1$.

module 7

Changes in Equilibrium

BEFORE YOU READ THE MODULE

Summary

This module describes how the equilibrium price and equilibrium quantity are affected when there is a change in either the supply or demand curves. The module also describes the effect of a simultaneous shift in the demand and supply curves on the equilibrium price and equilibrium quantity.

Module Objectives

Objective #1. A shift in the demand curve, holding everything else constant, causes a change in the equilibrium price and quantity. The shift in the demand curve causes a movement along the supply curve. An increase in demand leads to a rise in both the equilibrium price and equilibrium quantity. A decrease in demand leads to a fall in both the equilibrium price and equilibrium quantity. A shift in the supply curve, holding everything else constant, causes a change in the equilibrium price and quantity. The shift in the supply curve causes a movement along the demand curve. An increase in supply leads to a fall in the equilibrium price and a rise in the equilibrium quantity. A decrease in supply leads to a rise in the equilibrium price and a fall in the equilibrium quantity.

Objective #2. If demand and supply both change simultaneously but without specific information about the relative magnitude of these changes, there will be ambiguity about the value of either the new equilibrium price or the new equilibrium quantity. The four possible outcomes of these changes are summarized in Table 7.1.

Table 7.1

Shift in demand	Shift in supply	Effect on equilibrium price	Effect on equilibrium quantity
Right	Left	Increase	Ambiguous
Right	Right	Ambiguous	Increase
Left	Left	Ambiguous	Decrease
Left	Right	Decrease	Ambiguous

AFTER YOU READ THE MODULE

Tips

Tip #1. A shift in the demand or supply curve causes a movement along the supply or demand curve. Figure 7.1 illustrates this idea for a demand curve shift. Notice that when demand shifts to the left (a decrease in demand) this causes a movement along the supply curve: the equilibrium price falls from P_1 to P_2 and the equilibrium quantity falls from Q_1 to Q_2.

Figure 7.1

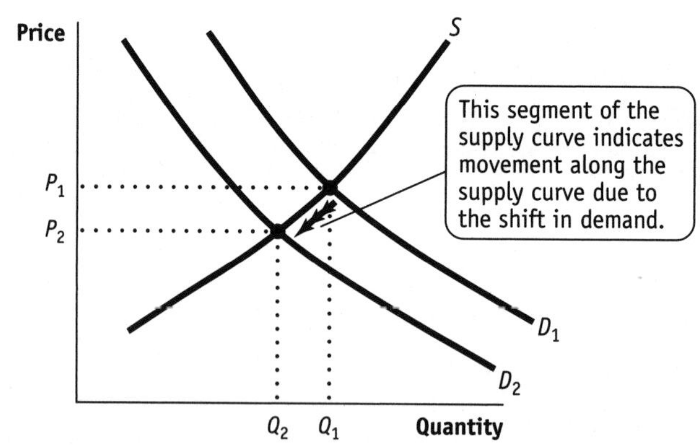

Figure 7.2 illustrates this idea for a supply curve shift. Notice that when supply shifts to the right (an increase in supply) this causes a movement along the demand curve: the equilibrium price falls from P_1 to P_2 and the equilibrium quantity increases from Q_1 to Q_2.

Figure 7.2

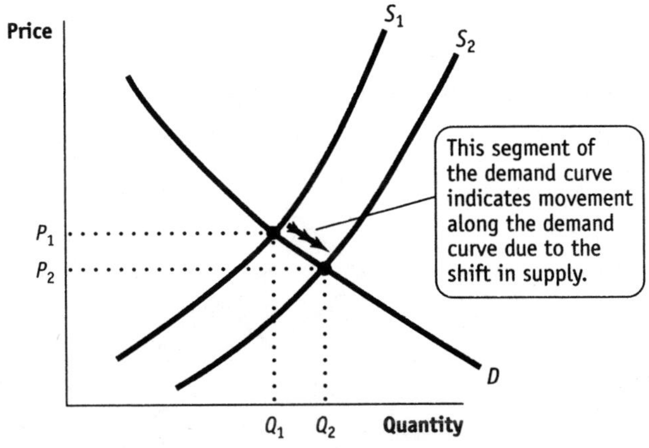

Tip #2. When both supply and demand shift simultaneously it may be impossible to determine what happens to the equilibrium price or the equilibrium quantity unless you are given specific numeric information about the demand curve, the supply curve, and the size of the shifts.

- For example if demand and supply both shift to the right simultaneously the equilibrium quantity will increase but the equilibrium price will be ambiguous. Figure 7.3 illustrates two possible outcomes for this type of situation.

Figure 7.3

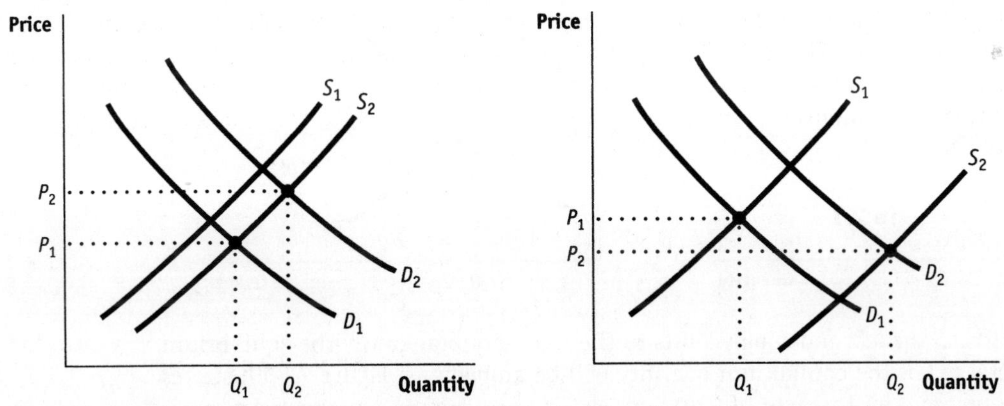

- If demand and supply both shift to the left simultaneously the equilibrium quantity will decrease but the equilibrium price will be ambiguous. Figure 7.4 illustrates two possible outcomes for this type of situation.

Figure 7.4

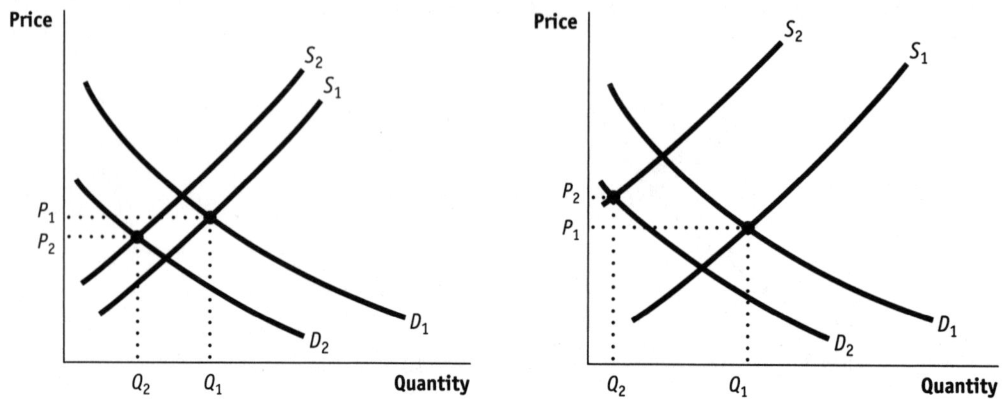

- If demand shifts to the right and supply shifts to the left simultaneously the equilibrium price will increase but the equilibrium quantity will be ambiguous. Figure 7.5 illustrates two possible outcomes for this type of situation.

Figure 7.5

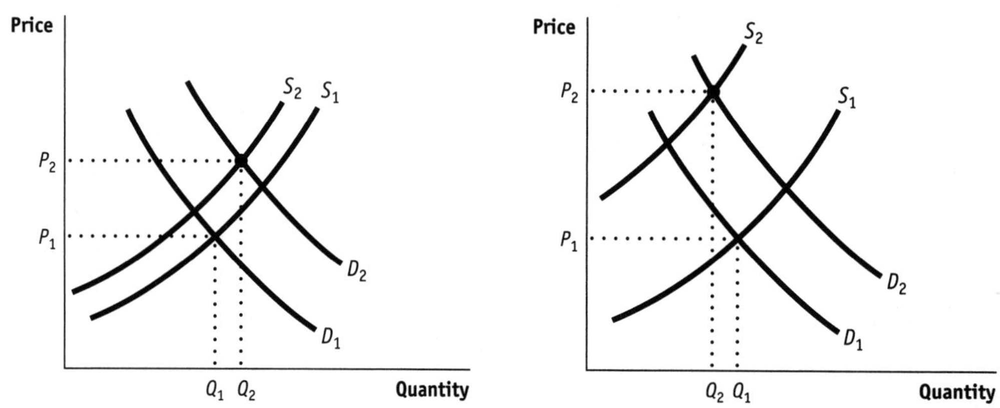

- If demand shifts to the left and supply shifts to the right simultaneously the equilibrium price will decrease but the equilibrium quantity will be ambiguous. Figure 7.6 illustrates two possible outcomes for this type of situation.

Figure 7.6

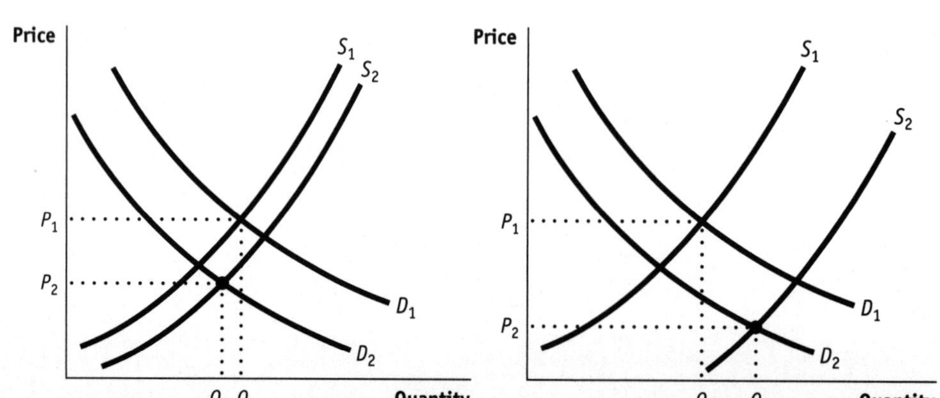

WORKED PROBLEMS

1. The supply and demand model is often used to analyze the effect of a change in the market on the equilibrium price and quantity of a good. Consider each of the following markets and the given situation to determine whether the demand and/or supply curve shift(s), and what the impact on the equilibrium price and equilibrium quantity will be relative to the initial equilibrium price and equilibrium quantity. For any shift in the demand or supply curve, indicate whether the curve shifts to the left or to the right. The examples are given in a table to help you consolidate your answers.

Market under consideration	Situation	Shift or movement along the demand curve	Shift or movement along the supply curve	Effect on equilibrium price	Effect on equilibrium quantity
Automobile market	War in the Middle East disrupts petroleum exports substantially				
Pizza market	Price of cheese increases				
Shampoo market	Health advisors release study showing danger of frequent hair washing				
Oil market	Oil-producing countries form cartel and agree to restrict output				
Insulation market	Homeowners granted tax credit for installing home insulation				

STEP 1: For each of the situations, draw the initial market situation and then label the initial equilibrium price and equilibrium quantity.

STEP 2: **Next look at the situation and decide whether the situation will cause a movement or a shift of the demand curve, or a movement or a shift of the supply curve. Draw the appropriate shift on your base graph.**

STEP 3: **Mark the new equilibrium price and equilibrium quantity and then compare the new equilibrium to the initial equilibrium. For example, when war in the Middle East disrupts petroleum exports substantially, this will cause the price of gas to rise, and since cars and gas are complements, the demand for cars will shift to the left due to the increase in the price of gas. As demand shifts left, there is a movement along the supply curve resulting in a reduction in the equilibrium quantity and the equilibrium price of cars.**

STEP 4: **Record your answers on the given table.**

Market under consideration	Situation	Shift or movement along the demand curve	Shift or movement along the supply Curve	Effect on equilibrium price	Effect on equilibrium quantity
Automobile market	War in the Middle East disrupts petroleum exports substantially	Demand shifts left as the price of gas rises: cars and gas are complements	Movement along the supply curve as price falls	Decrease in the price of cars	Decrease in the quantity of cars
Pizza market	Price of cheese increases	Movement along the demand curve as price increases	Supply shifts left since cheese is an input in making pizza	Increase in the price of pizza	Decrease in the quantity of pizza
Shampoo market	Health advisors release study showing danger of frequent hair washing	Demand shifts left due to change in tastes and preferences for washing hair: people wish to wash their hair less often at any price of shampoo after the study	Movement along the supply curve as the price of shampoo falls	Decrease in the price of shampoo	Decrease in the quantity of shampoo

Market under consideration	Situation	Shift or movement along the demand curve	Shift or movement along the supply curve	Effect on equilibrium price	Effect on equilibrium quantity
Oil market	Oil-producing countries form cartel and agree to restrict output	Movement along the demand curve due to the shift in the supply curve	Supply shifts left due to the cartel restricting output at every price	Increase in the price of oil	Decrease in the quantity of oil
Insulation market	Homeowners granted tax credit for installing home insulation	Demand shifts right due to the government subsidizing consumption of home insulation: at every price, the quantity of insulation demanded increases	Movement along the supply curve due to the shift in the demand curve	Increase in the price of home insulation	Increase in the quantity of home insulation

2. In the market for corn flakes, the price of cardboard used in packing the cereal has risen at the same time that the Surgeon General releases a report detailing the dangers of a diet high in corn products. What happens to the equilibrium price and equilibrium quantity relative to the equilibrium before these two changes?

STEP 1: First identify that there are two different changes occurring in the market for corn flakes: the price of cardboard used in packing the cereal is increasing and the Surgeon General has released a report that reveals the danger of eating corn products. In this question you will want to model each of these changes to see what the overall effect is in the market for corn flakes.

STEP 2: Draw the initial market situation and label the initial equilibrium price and equilibrium quantity. The figure that follows illustrates the initial situation.

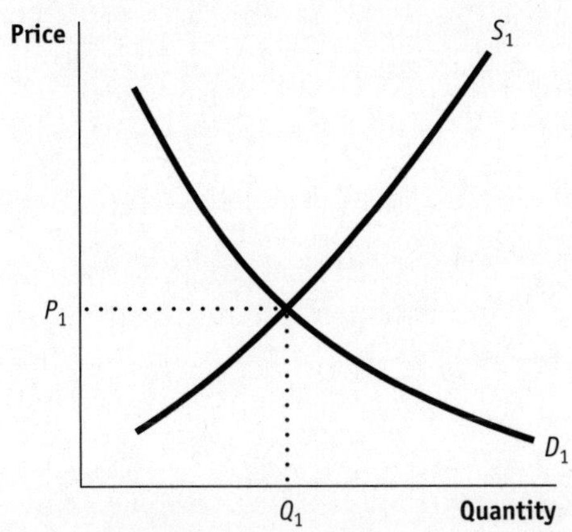

STEP 3: Consider the change in the price of cardboard: this is an input used to produce a box of corn flakes, and thus an increase in the price of cardboard will cause the supply curve for corn flakes to shift to the left. Draw the appropriate shift on your base graph and label it clearly. The figure that follows illustrates this shift.

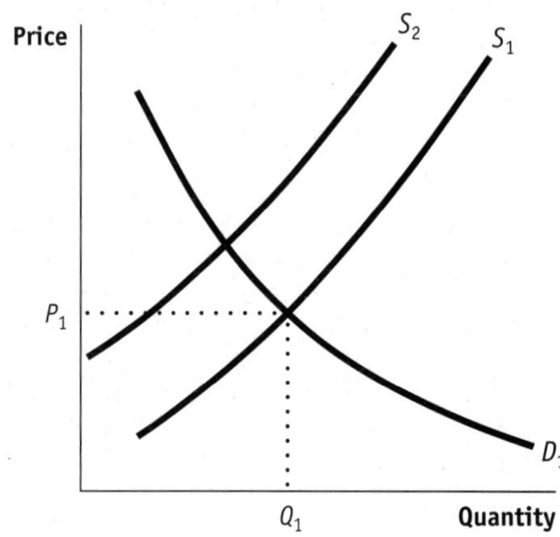

STEP 4: Next, consider the Surgeon General's report: people will decrease the quantity of corn flakes they demand at every price once this report is released. This will cause the demand curve to shift to the left. But we are not told the magnitude of the shift: a small shift will cause the equilibrium price to rise while the equilibrium quantity will fall (the intersection of D_2 and S_2, with the equilibrium occurring at Q_2 and P_2); a moderate shift might cause the equilibrium price to remain at its initial level, while the equilibrium quantity falls (the intersection of D_2' and S_2, with the equilibrium occurring at Q_2' and $P_2' = P_1$); and a large shift would cause the equilibrium price to fall, while the equilibrium quantity also falls (the intersection of D_2'' and S_2, with the equilibrium occurring at Q_2'' and P_2''). Price is therefore indeterminate, while quantity will definitely decrease with these two changes in the market for corn flakes. Study the following figure carefully to see this concept.

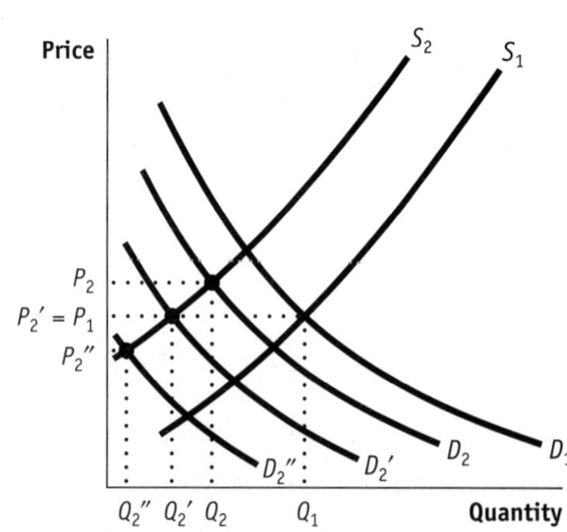

3. In the market for chocolate, people read that the consumption of chocolate has major health benefits. At the same time, the cost of growing and harvesting cocoa beans increases. What happens to the equilibrium price and equilibrium quantity relative to the equilibrium before these two changes?

STEP 1: First, identify that there are two different changes occurring in the market for chocolate: eating chocolate provides health benefits and the cost of growing and harvesting cocoa beans increases. In this question, you will want to model each of these changes to see what the overall effect is in the market for chocolate.

STEP 2: Draw the initial market situation and label the initial equilibrium price and equilibrium quantity. The following figure illustrates the initial situation.

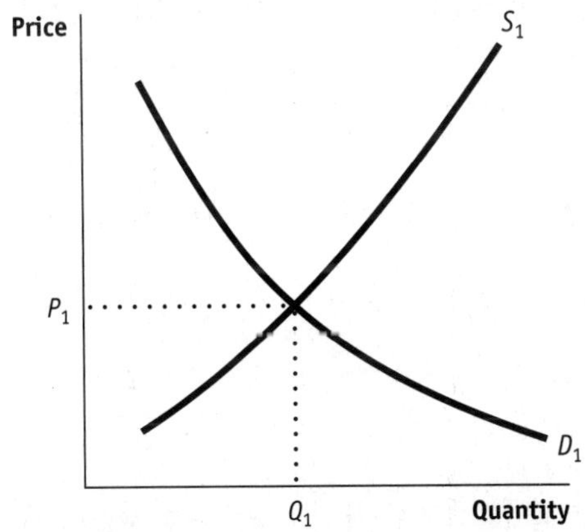

STEP 3: Consider the change in the cost of growing and harvesting cocoa beans: cocoa beans are an input used to produce chocolate, and thus an increase in the price of cocoa beans will cause the supply curve for chocolate to shift to the left. Draw the appropriate shift on your base graph and label it clearly. The figure that follows illustrates this shift.

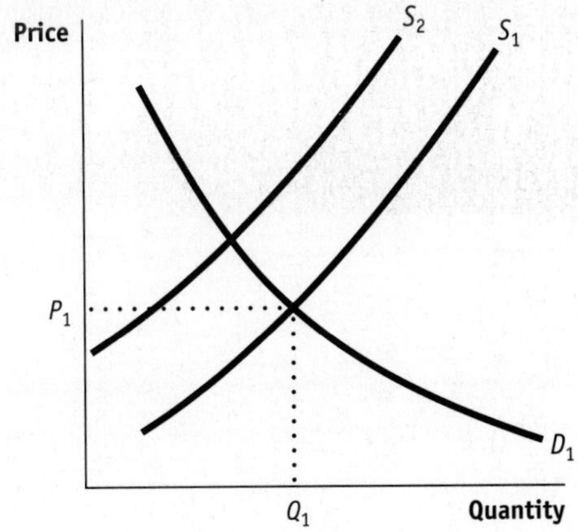

STEP 4: **Next, consider the health benefits from consuming chocolate: this will cause the quantity demanded of chocolate to increase at every price. Thus, the demand curve for chocolate will shift to the right. But we are not told the magnitude of the shift:**

- **A small shift will cause the equilibrium price to rise while the equilibrium quantity will fall (the intersection of D_2 and S_2, with the equilibrium occurring at Q_2 and P_2)**
- **A moderate shift might cause the equilibrium price to rise while the equilibrium quantity remains at its initial level (the intersection of D_2' and S_2, with the equilibrium occurring at P_2' and $Q_2' = Q_1$)**
- **A large shift would cause the equilibrium price to rise while the equilibrium quantity also rises (the intersection of D_2'' and S_2, with the equilibrium occurring at Q_2'' and P_2'').**

Price will definitely increase while quantity is indeterminate with these two changes in the market for chocolate.

Study the following figure carefully to see this concept.

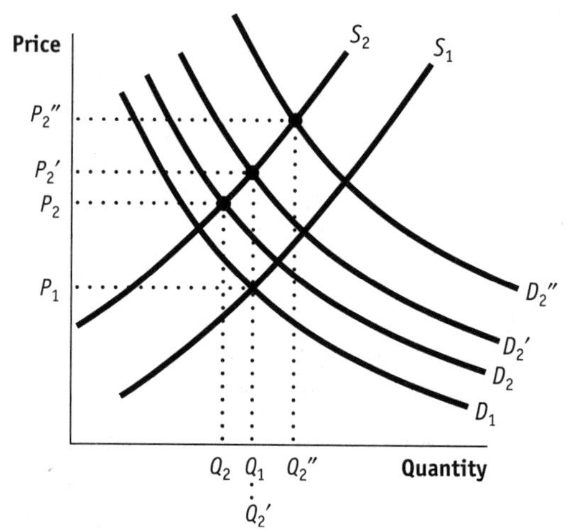

Problems and Exercises

1. For each of the following situations, sketch a graph of the initial market demand (D_1) and supply (S_1) curves and indicate the initial equilibrium price (P_1) and equilibrium quantity (Q_1). Then sketch any changes in the market demand (D_2) and supply (S_2) curves and indicate the new equilibrium price (P_2) and equilibrium quantity (Q_2). For each situation, identify which curve(s) shift and whether there is a movement along the demand or supply curves.

a. The price of gasoline increases by 40%. What happens in the market for bicycles?

Market for Bicycles

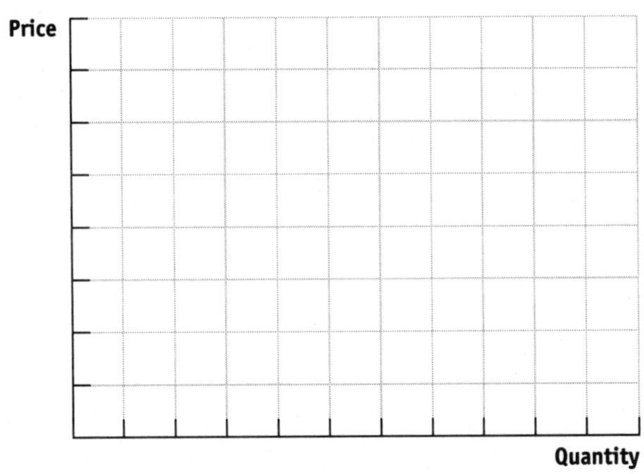

b. The price of gasoline increases by 40%. What happens in the market for fuel-inefficient SUVs?

Market for SUVs

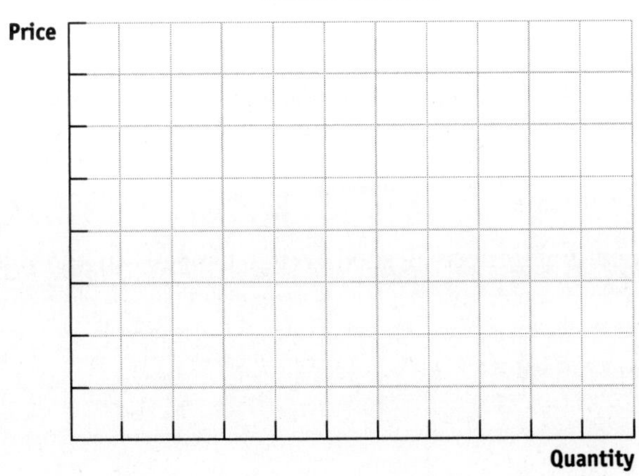

c. New technology for music-playing devices is developed. What happens in the market for music-playing devices?

Market for Music-Playing Devices

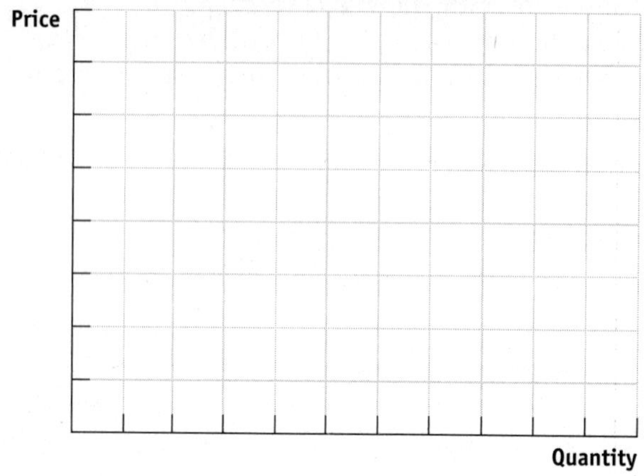

d. The price of labor decreases. What happens in the market for fast-food restaurants?

Market for Fast-Food Restaurants

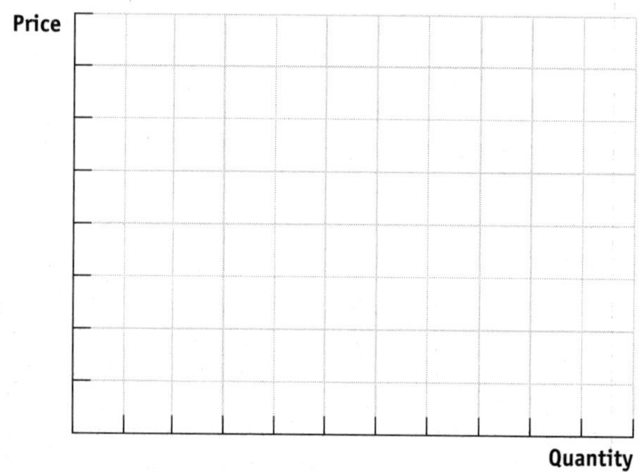

e. Income increases and good X is a normal good. What happens in the market for good X?

Market for Good X

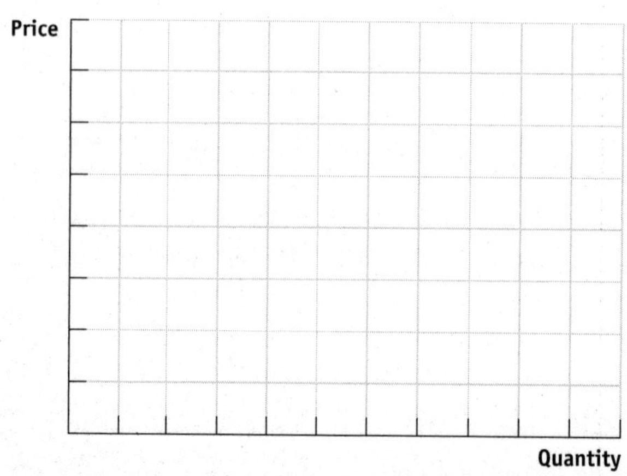

f. Income increases and good X is an inferior good. What happens in the market for good X?

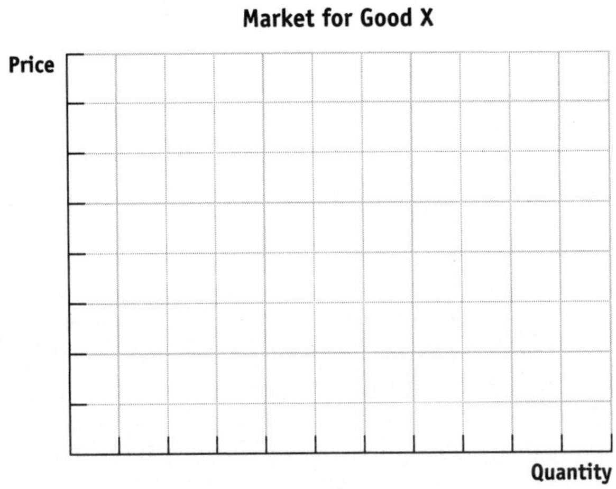

2. You are given the following information about the demand and supply schedules for gadgets in Micro Town. Assume that gadgets in Micro Town are produced in a competitive market.

Price	Quantity demanded	Quantity supplied
$ 0	100	0
2	80	20
4	60	40
6	40	60
8	20	80
10	0	100

a. From the above data, write an equation expressing the demand schedule and an equation expressing the supply schedule.

b. Using the equations you wrote in part (a), find the equilibrium price and the equilibrium quantity in this market.

c. Now suppose that the quantity demanded increases by 20 units at every price and that the quantity supplied increases by 40 units at every price. What happens to the equilibrium price and equilibrium quantity in this market relative to the initial levels of the equilibrium price and equilibrium quantity? (Hint: you might find it helpful to draw a sketch of the original demand curve and then the new demand curve to help guide you in your work. Then, once you have the new demand curve equation, you could draw a sketch of the original supply curve and the new supply curve to help you calculate the new supply curve equation.)

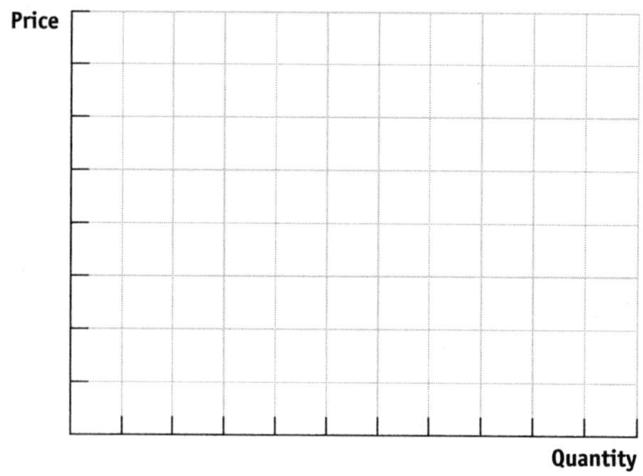

d. Now suppose that the quantity demanded increases by the same amount as in part (c), but that the quantity supplied increases by only 10 units at every price. What happens to the equilibrium price and the equilibrium quantity in this market relative to the initial levels of the equilibrium price and equilibrium quantity?

e. In parts (c) and (d), the demand and supply curves shifted to the right. If you knew the direction of these shifts, but did not know the size or magnitude of the shift, what would you know about the new equilibrium price and quantity?

3. Let's generalize the findings of question 2 for four different situations in which both the demand and supply curves shift at the same time. In each of these situations we assume that we know the direction of the shift but not the size of the shift. Fill in the table below for each of the possible situations. The first situation (the one in question 2) has already been done for you.

Situation	Effect on equilibrium price	Effect on equilibrium quantity
Demand shifts to the right and supply shifts to the right	May increase, decrease, or remain the same	Increases
Demand shifts to the left and supply shifts to the left		
Demand shifts to the right and supply shifts to the left		
Demand shifts to the left and supply shifts to the right		

BEFORE YOU TAKE THE TEST

Module Review Questions

1. In the competitive market for candles, there is an increase in the number of people purchasing candles and a decrease in the cost of beeswax, a major ingredient in the production of candles. Which of the following statements is true?
   a. The equilibrium price and the equilibrium quantity of candles will increase.
   b. The equilibrium price and the equilibrium quantity of candles will decrease.
   c. The equilibrium price may increase, decrease, or remain the same, but the equilibrium quantity will increase.
   d. The equilibrium quantity may increase, decrease, or remain the same, but the equilibrium price will increase.

2. Consumers in Mayville consider houses and apartments to be substitutes. There is an increase in the price of houses in Mayville at the same time three new apartment buildings are opened in Mayville. In the market for apartments in Mayville
   a. the equilibrium price will rise relative to its level before these two events.
   b. the equilibrium price will fall relative to its level before these two events.
   c. the equilibrium quantity will rise relative to its level before these two events.
   d. the equilibrium quantity will fall relative to its level before these two events.

3. The production of good X requires labor inputs and therefore the price of good X is directly affected by labor costs. Suppose that the price of labor increases while simultaneously people's income rises. If good X is a normal good, then we know in the market for good X
   a. the equilibrium price will increase and the equilibrium quantity may increase, decrease, or remain the same relative to their initial levels.
   b. the equilibrium price will decrease and the equilibrium quantity may increase, decrease, or remain the same relative to their initial levels.
   c. the equilibrium quantity will increase and the equilibrium price may increase, decrease, or remain the same relative to their initial levels.
   d. the equilibrium quantity will decrease and the equilibrium price may increase, decrease, or remain the same relative to their initial levels.

4. People's income rises, while simultaneously there is a technological advance in the production of good X. Good X is an inferior good. Given this information we know in the market for good X
   a. the equilibrium price will increase and the equilibrium quantity may increase, decrease, or remain the same relative to their initial levels.
   b. the equilibrium price will decrease and the equilibrium quantity may increase, decrease, or remain the same relative to their initial levels.
   c. the equilibrium quantity will increase and the equilibrium price may increase, decrease, or remain the same relative to their initial levels.
   d. the equilibrium quantity will decrease and the equilibrium price may increase, decrease, or remain the same relative to their initial levels.

5. The price of bubble gum increases at the same time that sugar, a major ingredient in candy, gets more expensive. If candy and bubble gum are substitutes, what happens to the equilibrium price and the equilibrium quantity in the market for candy?

a. The equilibrium price will increase and the equilibrium quantity may increase, decrease, or remain the same relative to their initial levels.

b. The equilibrium price will decrease and the equilibrium quantity may increase, decrease, or remain the same relative to their initial levels.

c. The equilibrium quantity will increase and the equilibrium price may increase, decrease, or remain the same relative to their initial levels.

d. The equilibrium quantity will decrease and the equilibrium price may increase, decrease, or remain the same relative to their initial levels.

ANSWER KEY

Answers to Problems and Exercises

1. a. Gasoline and bicycles are substitutes for one another. When the price of gasoline rises, people substitute away from gasoline toward bicycle transportation. This is illustrated in the graph below with the demand curve for bicycles shifting to the right, resulting in a higher equilibrium price (P_2) and a higher equilibrium quantity (Q_2). Note that there is a shift in the demand curve and a movement along the supply curve.

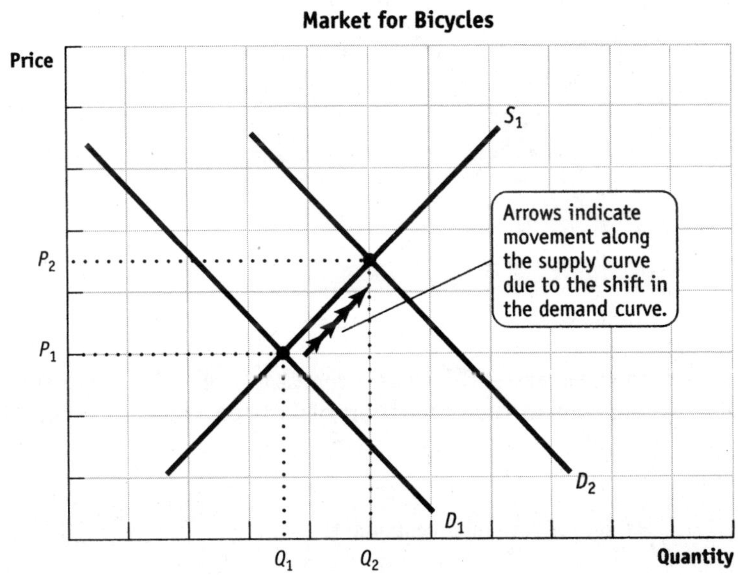

b. Gasoline and SUVs are complements for one another. When the price of gasoline rises, people find that driving SUVs is relatively more expensive and therefore decrease their demand for SUVs at every price. This is illustrated in the graph below with the demand curve for SUVs shifting to the left, resulting in a lower equilibrium price (P_2) and a lower equilibrium quantity (Q_2). Note that there is a shift in the demand curve and a movement along the supply curve.

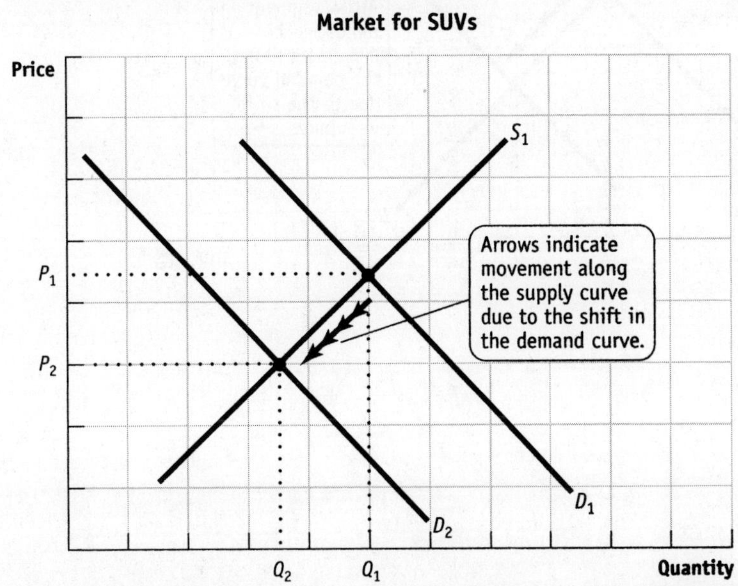

c. New technology shifts the supply curve to the right from S_1 to S_2. This causes a movement along the demand curve and results in a decrease in the equilibrium price and an increase in the equilibrium quantity. This is illustrated in the figure below.

Market for Music-Playing Devices

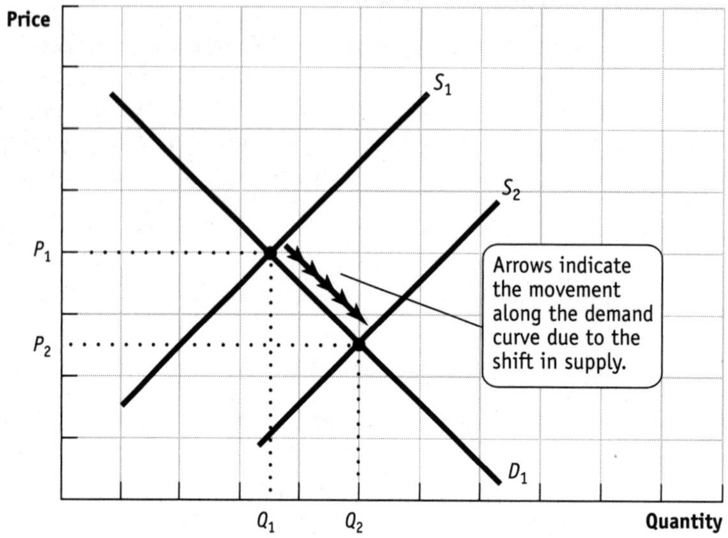

d. When the price of labor decreases, this causes the supply of fast food to shift to the right since labor is an input in the production of fast-food meals. This results in a movement along the demand curve and a decrease in the equilibrium price and an increase in the equilibrium quantity.

Market for Fast-Food Restaurants

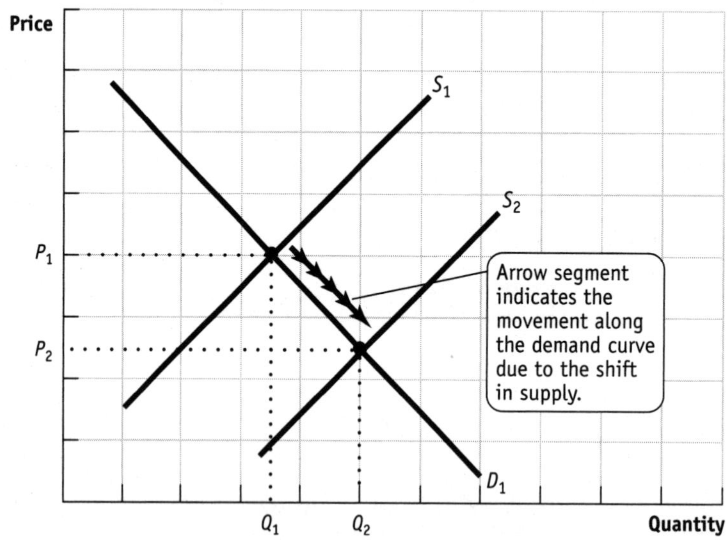

e. An increase in income shifts the demand curve to the right if the good is a normal good. This shift in demand causes a movement along the supply curve and an increase in both the equilibrium price and the equilibrium quantity.

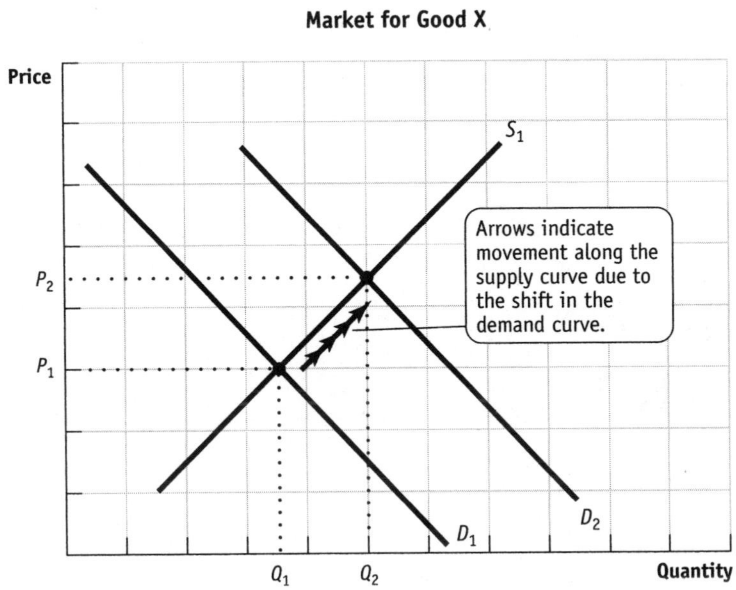

f. An increase in income shifts the demand curve to the left if the good is an inferior good. This shift in demand causes a movement along the supply curve and a decrease in both the equilibrium price and the equilibrium quantity. The graph below illustrates this situation.

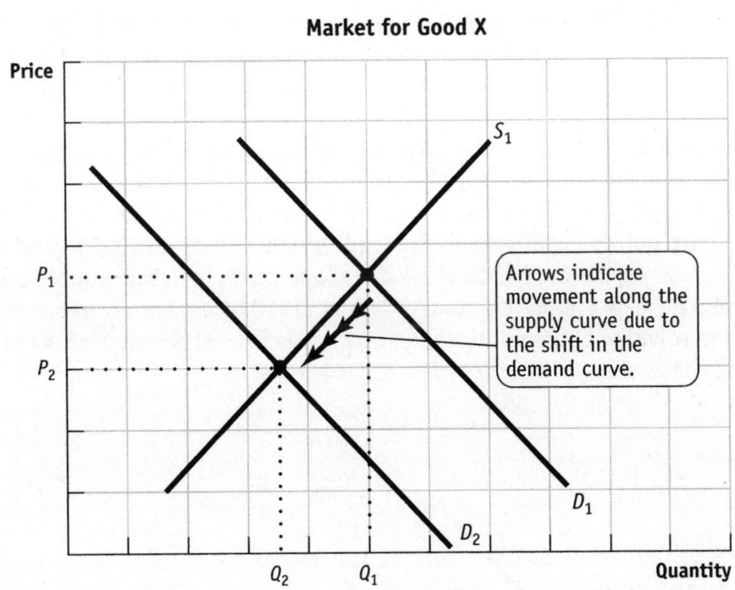

2. **a.** The demand equation is $P = 10 - (1/10)Q$ and the supply equation is $P = (1/10)Q$.

b. Solving the two equations from part (a), we find that the equilibrium price equals \$5 and the equilibrium quantity equals 50.

c. To find the new equilibrium price and quantity, we need to know the new demand and supply curves. Draw a sketch of the original demand curve and the new demand curve (shifted to the right at every price by 20 units) to guide you in your calculations. The figure below illustrates this sketch.

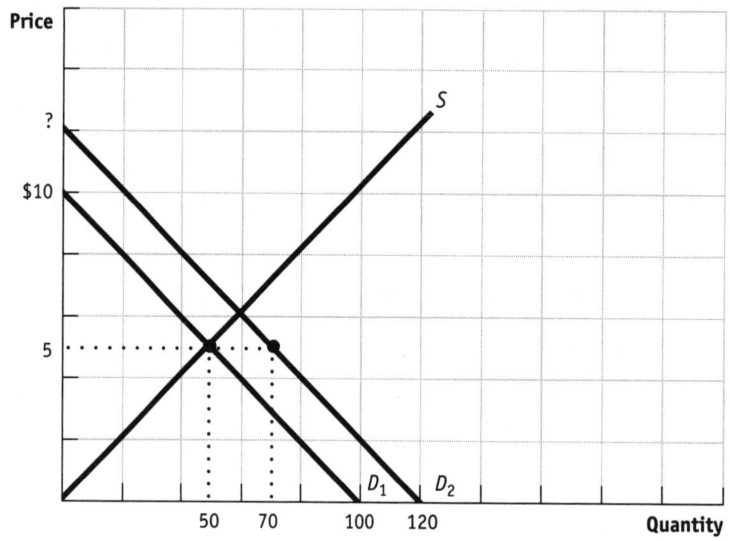

We know from part (b) that the initial equilibrium is at price \$5 and the equilibrium quantity is 50, which gives us two points on the new demand curve: (70, 5) and (120, 0). We also know that the new demand curve is parallel to the original demand curve and thus has the same slope as the original demand curve. But we do not know the *y*-intercept for the new demand curve. To find the equation, let's write the new equation as $P = b - (1/10)Q$. This equation has the same slope as the original demand curve, but has not yet identified the *y*-intercept. To find the value of *b*, let's substitute the coordinates of one of the points we know is on D_2: thus, using (70, 5) yields $5 = b - (1/10)70$, or $b = 12$. So our new demand curve equation is $P = 12 - (1/10)Q$. Use the same technique to find the new supply curve equation. The graph below sketches the original demand and supply curve and also the new supply curve, which illustrates an increase of 40 units in the quantity supplied at every price. We know the coordinates of two points on this new supply curve—(40, 0) and (90, 5)—and we also know that the new supply curve has the same slope as the original supply curve. So we can rewrite the new supply curve as $P = b + (1/10)Q$ and then use one of our known points to solve for *b*, the *y*-intercept. Thus, using (90, 5) we get $5 = b + (1/10)90$, or $b = -4$, and the new supply curve is $P = (1/10)Q - 4$.

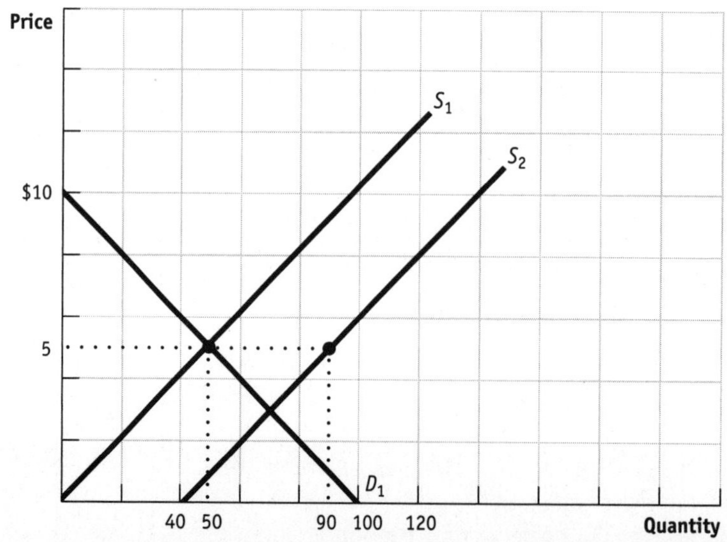

Using the new demand curve and new supply curve, we can easily solve for the equilibrium price and the equilibrium quantity in this market. Since $P = 12 - (1/10)Q$ and $P = (1/10)Q - 4$, we have $12 - (1/10)Q = (1/10)Q - 4$, or the equilibrium quantity (Q) equals 80. Then replacing Q with 80 in either the demand or supply equation, we find that the equilibrium price (*P*) equals 4. In this case, the equilibrium price decreases relative to its initial level, while the equilibrium quantity increases relative to its initial level.

d. Since the change in the quantity demanded at each price is the same as in part (c), we know that the new demand curve can be written as $P = 12 - (1/10)Q$. But we need to use the same technique as we employed in part (c) to find the new supply curve. When you do this, you will find that the new supply curve equation is $P = (1/10)Q - 1$. Solving these two equations for the equilibrium price and the equilibrium quantity, we find that the new equilibrium price is 5.5 while the new equilibrium quantity is 65 units. In this case, the equilibrium price and the equilibrium quantity increase relative to their initial quantities.

e. You would know with certainty that the equilibrium quantity increased, but you would not know if the equilibrium price increased, decreased, or remained the same, since you do not know the magnitude of the shifts in the demand and supply curves.

3.

Situation	Effect on equilibrium price	Effect on equilibrium quantity
Demand shifts to the right and supply shifts to the right	May increase, decrease, or remain the same	Increases
Demand shifts to the left and supply shifts to the left	May increase, decrease, or remain the same	Decreases
Demand shifts to the right and supply shifts to the left	Increases	May increase, decrease, or remain the same
Demand shifts to the left and supply shifts to the right	Decreases	May increase, decrease, or remain the same

Answers to Module Review Questions

1. **Answer c.** Since we do not know the relative magnitude of the shifts in the demand and supply curves, we cannot know for certain what happens to both the equilibrium price and the equilibrium quantity. The demand curve shifts to the right with the increase in the number of people purchasing candles, while the supply curve shifts to the right with the decrease in the price of beeswax. The equilibrium quantity will increase, but the equilibrium price may increase, decrease, or remain the same depending on the relative magnitude of the shifts in the two curves.

2. **Answer c.** The demand curve for apartments shifts to the right with the increase in the price of houses (houses and apartments are substitute goods for consumers in Mayville), while the supply curve for apartments also shifts to the right with the opening of the new apartment buildings. Since we do not know the magnitude of the shifts in the demand and supply curves, we know that the equilibrium quantity is now larger, but the equilibrium price may increase, decrease, or remain the same with these shifts in the demand and supply curves.

3. **Answer a.** The demand curve for good X shifts to the right since good X is a normal good and income has increased. At the same time, the supply curve for good X shifts to the left since the price of labor has increased. These two shifts result in the equilibrium price increasing while the equilibrium quantity may have increased, decreased, or remained the same depending on the magnitude of the shifts in the demand and supply curves.

4. **Answer b.** Since good X is an inferior good, the increase in income results in the demand curve for good X shifting to the left. At the same time, the technological advance causes the supply curve for good X to shift to the right. The equilibrium price will decrease, but the equilibrium quantity may increase, decrease, or remain the same depending on the magnitude of the shifts in the demand and supply curves.

5. **Answer a.** The supply curve for candy shifts to the left with the increase in the price of sugar, while the demand curve for candy shifts to the right with the increase in the price of bubble gum. The equilibrium price will increase, but the equilibrium quantity may increase, decrease, or remain the same depending on the magnitude of the shifts in the demand and supply curves.

module 8

Income Effects, Substitution Effects, and Elasticity

BEFORE YOU READ THE MODULE

Summary

This module develops the concepts of the substitution and income effects and then uses these two effects to explain why demand curves are downward sloping. The module develops the concept of elasticity, which provides a numerical measure of the responsiveness of quantity to changes in prices or income. The price elasticity of demand measures the responsiveness of the quantity demanded to changes in the price of the good. The module discusses how to measure price elasticity of demand.

Module Objectives

Objective #1. From our earlier discussion of demand curves we know that when the price of the good changes, the quantity demanded of that good changes. If the price of the good increases, then consumers will decrease the quantity demanded of that good; and if the price of the good decreases, then consumers will increase the quantity demanded of that good. This inverse relationship between the price of the good and the quantity demanded of the good is driven by two different effects: the substitution effect and the income effect. For example, when the price of the good increases:

- The substitution effect measures the change in the quantity consumed as the consumer substitutes away from the relatively more expensive good towards other relatively cheaper goods.
- The income effect measures the change in the quantity consumed that results from the change in the overall purchasing power of the consumer due to the change in the price of the good. The income effect is significant for those goods whose price represents a large share of total income, because when the price of one of these goods increases, this price increase results in a substantial reduction in the purchasing power of the individual. The individual must reduce their purchases of this good since they can no longer afford as many units of the good.

Objective #2. The price elasticity of demand measures the responsiveness of the percentage change in the quantity demanded to the percentage change in the price of the good. Thus, the price elasticity of demand can be written as

$$\text{Price elasticity of demand} = \frac{\text{\% change in the quantity demanded of good X}}{\text{\% change in the price of good X}}$$

Since demand curves typically slope downward, a positive change in price (i.e., a price increase) results in a negative change in the quantity demanded (i.e., a decrease in quantity demanded). Thus, the price elasticity of demand is usually a negative number. By convention, economists measure the price elasticity of demand in absolute value terms so that the negative sign is eliminated.

$$\text{Price elasticity of demand} = \left|\frac{\text{\% change in the quantity demanded of the good}}{\text{\% change in the price of the good}}\right|$$

a. The calculation of the percentage change in the quantity demanded of good X can be found using the formula

$$\text{\% change in quantity demanded} = \frac{\text{change in quantity demanded}}{\text{initial quantity demanded}} \times 100$$

b. The calculation of the percentage change in the price of good X can be found by using the formula

$$\text{\% change in the price of good X} = \frac{\text{change in price of good X}}{\text{initial price of good X}} \times 100$$

c. To generate consistent measures for price elasticities, regardless of an increase or decrease in price, economists calculate the percentage changes using the midpoint method. For example, consider two points on a demand curve: (Q_1, P_1) and (Q_2, P_2). The percentage change in quantity demanded using the midpoint method can be expressed as

$$\text{\% change in quantity demanded} = (Q_2 - Q_1)/[(Q_2 + Q_1)/2]$$

while the percentage change in price is expressed as

$$\text{\% change in price} = [(P_2 - P_1)/(P_2 + P_1)/2]$$

Using these two formulas, the price elasticity of demand formula using the midpoint method can be written as

$$\text{Price elasticity of demand} = \left|\frac{\dfrac{Q_2 - Q_1}{\dfrac{Q_2 + Q_1}{2}}}{\dfrac{P_2 - P_1}{\dfrac{P_2 + P_1}{2}}}\right| = \left|\frac{\dfrac{Q_2 - Q_1}{Q_2 + Q_1}}{\dfrac{P_2 - P_1}{P_2 + P_1}}\right|$$

Objective #3. Consider a numerical example illustrating the mathematical relationships described in Objective 2. Suppose the demand curve for good X is given by the equation $P = 100 - Q$ and you are asked to compute the price elasticity of demand when quantity increases from 80 units to 90 units on this demand curve. First you need to calculate the price demanders are willing to pay when the quantity demanded is equal to 90 units: this price is \$10. Then, you need to calculate the price demanders are willing to pay when the quantity demanded is equal to 80 units: this price is \$20. Figure 8.1 below provides a graph of this demand curve with point *A* on the demand curve corresponding to a price of \$10 and a quantity demanded of 90 units and point *B* on the demand curve corresponding to a price of \$20 and a quantity demanded of 80 units.

Figure 8.1

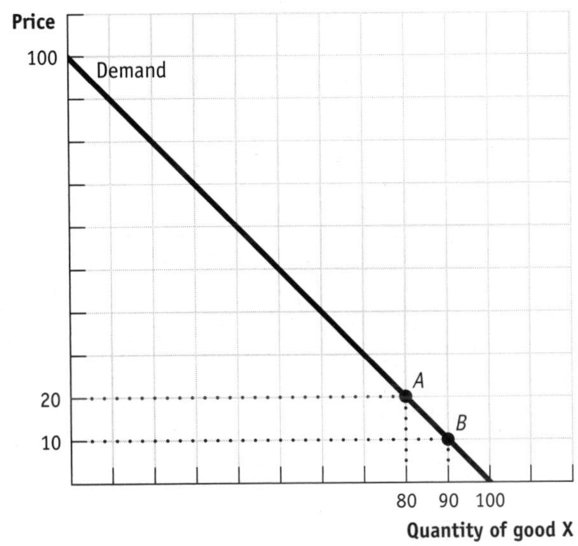

Using this information, you can then calculate the percentage change in the quantity demanded of good X and the percentage change in the price of good X using the midpoint method. Thus,

The percentage change in the quantity demanded of good X =
[(80 – 90)/2]/[(80 + 90)/2] × 100 = –5.9

The percentage change in the price of good X =
[(20 – 10)/2]/[(20 + 10)/2] × 100 = 33.3

To find the price elasticity of demand, take the absolute value of the percentage change in the quantity demanded of good X divided by the percentage change in the price of good X. Thus,

The price elasticity of demand = 5.9/33.3 = 0.18

Suppose that the price had originally been \$10 and that the price had increased to \$20. Does the price elasticity of demand change if you move from along the demand curve from the point (90, 10) to the point (80, 20)? The midpoint method of calculating the price elasticity of demand insures that the calculation of elasticity does not depend upon the direction of movement along the demand curve from one point to another. To see this recalculate the price elasticity of demand moving from point *B* to point *A*.

The percentage change in the quantity demanded of good X =
[(90 – 80)/2]/[(90 + 80)/2] × 100 = 5.9

The percentage change in the price of good X =
[(10 – 20)/2]/[(10 + 20)/2] × 100 = –33.3

To find the price elasticity of demand, take the absolute value of the percentage change in the quantity demanded of good X divided by the percentage change in the price of good X. Thus,

The price elasticity of demand = 5.9/33.3 = 0.18

The midpoint method of calculating the price elasticity of demand results in the price elasticity of demand being the same whether we move from point *A* to point *B* or from point *B* to point *A*.

Key Terms

substitution effect the change in the quantity of a good demanded as the consumer substitutes the good that has become relatively cheaper for the good that has become relatively more expensive.

income effect the change in the quantity of a good consumed that results from the change in a consumer's purchasing power due to the change in the price of the good.

price elasticity of demand the ratio of the percent change in the *quantity demanded* to the percent change in the price as we move along the *demand curve* (dropping the minus sign).

midpoint method a technique for calculating the percent change in which changes in a variable are compared with the average, or midpoint, of the starting and final values.

Notes

AFTER YOU READ THE MODULE

Tips

Tip #1. Economists calculate a variety of elasticities because these measures provide important insights into the relationship between two different variables. All elasticities are calculated as the ratio between the percentage changes in quantity (either the quantity demanded or the quantity supplied) to the percentage change in some other related variable. Elasticities are unit-free, making them an ideal measure of sensitivity of one variable to changes in another variable. In general, we can think of elasticity as being defined as

$$\text{Elasticity} = \frac{\text{\% change in quantity (either quantity demanded or quantity supplied)}}{\text{\% change in a related variable}}$$

For example, the price elasticity of demand is thus

$$\text{Price elasticity of demand} = \left| \frac{\text{\% change in the quantity demanded of good A}}{\text{\% change in the price of good A}} \right|$$

Tip #2. In general, to find the percentage change in a variable requires dividing the change in the variable by its initial value and then multiplying this value by 100. That is,

$$\text{\% change in a variable} = \frac{\text{the change in the variable}}{\text{the initial value of the variable}} \times 100$$

Tip #3. The midpoint method is used in calculating the price elasticity of demand and the price elasticity of supply. This method modifies the formula given in Tip 2 so that the results of the elasticity calculation provide a measure that is not dependent on which point on the demand or supply curve is designated the initial point.

Tip #4. The substitution and income effects are challenging concepts for students. Most students have to work hard to achieve an understanding of these concepts.

WORKED PROBLEM

1. Suppose Gretchen's demand curve for doughnuts per month is given by the equation $Q = 20 - 20P$, where Q is the quantity of doughnuts and P is the price per doughnut. You are asked to calculate Gretchen's price elasticity of demand for doughnuts when the price of doughnuts increases from \$0.10 to \$0.20. You are also asked to calculate Gretchen's price elasticity of demand for doughnuts when the price of doughnuts increases from \$0.70 to \$0.80. In calculating the price elasticities of demand, you should use the midpoint method.

STEP 1: Review the midpoint method and make sure you know the elasticity formula you will need to make this calculation.

The midpoint method for finding the price elasticity of demand uses the formula:

$$\text{Price elasticity of demand} = |\{(Q_2 - Q_1)/[(Q_1 + Q_2)]\}/\{(P_2 - P_1)/[(P_1 + P_2)]\}|$$

This formula alters the general percentage formula so that you get the same percentage change going from point *A* to point *B* as you do going from point *B* to point *A*. If this idea is still unclear to you, please review Objective 3 on page 132 of this Study Guide.

STEP 2: Find the quantities of doughnuts Gretchen will demand when the price of a doughnut is \$0.10, \$0.20, \$0.70, and \$0.80.

This is a simple matter of substituting each of these prices into Gretchen's demand curve and then calculating the quantity demanded at that particular price. For example, when the price of a doughnut is \$0.10, the quantity demanded by Gretchen is 18 doughnuts.

The table below summarizes Gretchen's demand schedule for doughnuts for the different prices of interest.

Price per doughnut	Quantity of doughnuts demanded by Gretchen
\$0.10	18
0.20	16
0.70	6
0.80	4

STEP 3: Use the elasticity formula and the prices and quantities you found in Step 2 to calculate the two measures of price elasticity of demand.

Going from (18, \$0.10) to (16, \$0.20), the price elasticity of demand can be calculated using the midpoint method as

$$\text{Price elasticity of demand} = |\{[(16 - 18)/(18 + 16)]/[(0.20 - 0.10)/(0.10 + 0.20)]\}| = 3/17 = 0.18$$

Going from (6, \$0.70) to (4, \$0.80), the price elasticity of demand can be calculated using the midpoint method as

$$\text{Price elasticity of demand} = |\{[(4 - 6)/(6 + 4)]/[(0.80 - 0.70)/(0.70 + 0.80)]\}| = 15/5 = 3$$

Problems and Exercises

1. This problem explores the midpoint method of calculating percentages and why this method is the preferred method when calculating price elasticity of demand or price elasticity of supply. Consider the demand curve in the figure below to answer this question.

a. Suppose the initial price and quantity on the above demand curve is represented by point *A* and then the price and quantity change to point *B*. Calculate the percentage change in price and the percentage change in quantity using the following formula:

$$\text{Percentage change} = \frac{\text{new value} - \text{old value}}{\text{old value}} \times 100$$

Note: we are purposefully *not* using the midpoint method for parts (a) through (e) of this problem so that we can compare these results to the results we would get if using the midpoint method.

b. Using the percentage changes you calculated in part (a), calculate the price elasticity of demand from point *A* to point *B*, using the following formula:

$$\text{Price elasticity of demand} = \left| \frac{\%\text{ change in quantity demanded}}{\%\text{ change in price}} \right|$$

c. Redo part (a) starting at point *B* and moving to point *A*. Use the same formula as that given in part (a).

d. Calculate the price elasticity of demand from point *B* to point *A* using the formula given in part (b).

e. Are your values for the price elasticity of demand the same in parts (a) and (d)?

Now, let's recalculate the price elasticity of demand using the midpoint method.

f. Suppose you are initially at point *A* and that you move to point *B*. Calculate the percentage change in price and the percentage change in quantity using the following (midpoint method) formula:

$$\%\text{ change} = \frac{\text{new value} - \text{old value}}{\dfrac{\text{old value} + \text{new value}}{2}} \times 100$$

g. Using the percentage changes you calculated in part (f), calculate the elasticity of demand from point *A* to point *B* using the following formula:

$$\text{Price elasticity of demand} = \left| \frac{\%\text{ change in quantity demanded}}{\%\text{ change in price}} \right|$$

where both percentage changes have been calculated using the midpoint method.

h. Suppose you now start at point *B* and move to point *A*. Calculate the percentage change in price and the percentage change in quantity using the formula given in part (f).

i. Calculate the price elasticity of demand from point *B* to point *A* using the formula given in part (g).

j. Are the values you calculated for the price elasticity of demand using the midpoint method the same in parts (g) and (i)? Summarize the significance of the midpoint method when calculating the price elasticity of demand or the price elasticity of supply.

2. Suppose the price of utilities (electricity, gas, water and sewer services) rose this year in Bigtown. Residents of Bigtown routinely spend 15% of their overall budget on utilities. These residents report that this price increase resulted in both an income and a substitution effect.

a. Describe the substitution effect of this price increase and how residents act to alter their consumption of utilities.

b. Describe the income effect of this price increase.

c. In this example, do the income and substitution effects reinforce each other? Explain your answer.

BEFORE YOU TAKE THE TEST

Module Review Questions

1. If the price is initially $10 and then increases to $15, the absolute value of the percentage change in price using the midpoint method is

a. 50%.

b. 40%.

c. 5%.

d. 4%.

2. The midpoint method for calculating price elasticities provides a means of

a. ensuring that all price elasticities have positive values.

b. ensuring that all price elasticities have negative values.

c. generating consistent measures of price elasticities between two points on a demand or supply curve without regard to which point is the initial point.

d. simplifying the calculation of price elasticities so that all elasticity values are whole numbers.

3. The substitution effect measures

a. the effect of a price change on the quantity of the good demanded.

b. the change in the consumer's purchasing power when the price of the good changes.

c. the degree to which good Y can be replaced by good X.

d. the total utility an individual gets from consuming a particular consumption bundle.

4. When the price of a good increases and expenditures on that good represent a substantial amount of the individual's income, then the income effect makes that individual poorer since the price increase effectively

a. reduces that individual's purchasing power.

b. increases that individual's purchasing power.

5. Consider a normal good whose consumption comprises a substantial share of the individual's income. A decrease in the price of this good will result in

a. both the income and substitution effects increasing the quantity demanded of this good.

b. the income effect increasing the quantity demanded of this good while the substitution effect decreases the quantity demanded.

c. the substitution effect increasing the quantity demanded of this good while the income effect decreases the quantity demanded.

d. both the income and substitution effects decreasing the quantity demanded of this good.

6. Suppose good Z is an inferior good. If the price of good Z changes, the income and substitution effects will

a. reinforce each other.

b. work in opposite directions.

7. Demand curves slope downwards because as the price of the good decreases

a. the opportunity cost of consuming more of the good increases.

b. the opportunity cost of consuming more of the good decreases.

8. Which of the following statements is true?

I. A Giffen good has an upward-sloping demand curve where the quantity demanded of the good increases as the price of the good increases.

II. For goods which account for a small share of consumers' incomes, the substitution effect is essentially the sole explanation for why market demand curves slope downward.

III. For goods which account for a large share of consumers' incomes, the income effect becomes important since an increase in the price of this kind of good reduces the purchasing power of households' income.

a. Statement I is true.

b. Statement II is true.

c. Statement III is true.

d. Statements I and II are true.

e. Statements I and III are true.

f. Statements II and III are true.

g. Statements I, II, and III are true.

9. The text provides a table where estimated price elasticity of demand for different goods is provided. In the table the price elasticity of demand for eggs is given as 0.1 while the price elasticity of restaurant meals is given as 2.3. Given this information which of the following statements is true?

a. The absolute value of the percentage change in the quantity of eggs demanded is greater than the absolute value of the percentage change in the price of eggs.

b. The absolute value of the percentage change in the quantity of restaurant meals demanded is greater than the absolute value of the percentage change in the quantity of eggs demanded.

c. The absolute value of the percentage change in the quantity of restaurant meals demanded is greater than the absolute value of the percentage change in the price of restaurant meals.

d. The absolute value of the percentage change in the quantity of eggs demanded is less than the absolute value of the percentage change in the quantity of restaurant meals demanded.

ANSWER KEY

Answers to Problems and Exercises

1. **a.** % change in price = [(9 – 10)/10] × 100 = – 10%
% change in quantity = [(2 – 1)/1] × 100 = 100%

b. Price elasticity of demand = $|100\%/-10\%| = 10$

c. % change in price = [(10 – 9)/9] × 100 = 11%
% change in quantity = [(1 – 2)/2] × 100 = –50%

d. Price elasticity of demand = $|-50\%/11\%| = 4.5$

e. No, the measures calculated for the price elasticity of demand using the simple percentage formula yield different price elasticities of demand measures when moving from point *A* to point *B* or from point *B* to point *A*.

f. % change in price = $\dfrac{(9-10)}{\dfrac{(10+9)}{2}} = -10.5\%$

% change in quantity = $\dfrac{(2-1)}{\dfrac{(1+2)}{2}} = 66.7\%$

g. Price elasticity of demand = $|66.7\%/-10.6\%| = 6.3$

h. % change in price = $\dfrac{(10-9)}{\dfrac{(9+10)}{2}} = 10.5\%$

% change in quantity = $\dfrac{(1-2)}{\dfrac{(2+1)}{2}} = -66.7\%$

i. Price elasticity of demand = $|-66.7\%/10.6\%| = 6.3$

j. Yes, the midpoint method yields the same measure for price elasticity of demand whether you start at point *A* and move to point *B*, or move from point *B* to point *A*. This consistent measure of price elasticity, whether for the price elasticity of demand or the price elasticity of supply, simplifies the use of elasticity by providing a value that is not dependent on the initial starting point.

2. **a.** When the price of one good rises relative to the prices of other goods, consumers will substitute away from the relatively more expensive good: in this case consumers will consume fewer utility services. They can do this by replacing appliances with more efficient models, by using fewer lights, by taking shorter showers, and by making other energy-saving choices.

b. When the price of a good increases and that good makes up a substantial part of the consumer's budget, then this price increase results in a reduction in the consumer's purchasing power. As the consumer's ability to command goods and services decreases due to their loss of purchasing power, the consumer will choose to consume less of the good, assuming it is a normal good.

c. In this case, the substitution effect that results in a change in the relative price of utilities leads consumers to decrease the quantity of utilities they demand, as does the income effect. The two effects reinforce each other, since both effects cause consumers to reduce the quantity they demand.

Answers to Module Review Questions

1. **Answer b.** To find this value, you take the absolute value of the following:

$$\left| \frac{15 - 10}{\frac{10 + 15}{2}} \right| \times 100$$

This gives you the absolute value of the percentage change in price, which is equal to 40%.

2. **Answer c.** Price elasticities may have negative values or positive values. The midpoint method for calculating price elasticities provides a method for getting identical values no matter which point is your initial point when making the calculation. Price elasticities are not always whole numbers.

3. **Answer a.** Answer (b) refers to the income effect. Answer (c) is a reference to the substitutability of one good for another good, but it does not explicitly mention a price change, which is the event that drives the substitution effect. Answer (d) has no direct relationship to the substitution effect. Answer (a) is the definition of the substitution effect.

4. **Answer a.** When the price of a good increases and the good makes up a substantial portion of the individual's budget, then the individual finds that they have less purchasing power. Answer (b) is a nonsense answer: an increase in the price of a good cannot raise the individual's purchasing power; it must reduce the individual's purchasing power.

5. **Answer a.** When the price of the good decreases, the individual purchases more of this now relatively cheaper good and fewer units of the other relatively more expensive good: this substitution effect leads the individual to purchase more units of this good. In addition, if the expenditure on the good is a substantial portion of the individual's budget, then the individual's purchasing power increases when the price of this good falls: this income effect leads the individual to purchase more units of the good.

6. **Answer b.** If the price of good Z increases, the consumer will substitute away from the relatively more expensive good Z toward some other relatively less expensive good: the substitution effect will be negative. But if the price of good Z increases, this reduces the individual's purchasing power, and the individual will also see a change in their consumption of good Z due to this change in purchasing power. When the individual's purchasing power falls, the individual will consume more units of good Z since good Z is an inferior good: the income effect is positive. Thus, the income and substitution effects for an inferior good work in opposite directions.

7. **Answer b.** Since the good is now relatively cheaper a consumer gives up less to consume the good. This implies that the opportunity cost of consuming the good has decreased.

8. **Answer g.** These are all factual statements and the text discusses each of these statements thoroughly.

9. **Answer c.** The definition of price elasticity of demand is the absolute value of the percentage change in the quantity demanded of the good divided by the percentage change in the price of the good. If the price elasticity of demand value is greater than 1, then it must be the case that the numerator (that is, the percentage change in the quantity demanded of the good) must be greater than the denominator (that is, the percentage change in the price of the good) in absolute value terms. This is true for answer c. If the price elasticity of demand value is less 1, then it must be the case that the numerator must be less than the denominator: there are no answers that provide this result.

module 9

Interpreting Price Elasticity of Demand

BEFORE YOU READ THE MODULE

Summary

This module discusses the difference between elastic and inelastic demand and then discusses the factors that determine how elastic or inelastic demand is for a good or service. The module also analyzes the relationship between elasticity and total revenue. The module discusses how price elasticity of demand changes as you move along a demand curve.

Module Objectives

Objective #1. A vertical demand curve indicates that the quantity demanded is completely unresponsive to price changes. A vertical demand curve is perfectly inelastic and its measure of price elasticity of demand equals zero.

Objective #2. A horizontal demand curve indicates that the quantity demanded is extremely responsive to price changes: even a small increase in price results in demand dropping to zero units, while a small decrease in price results in an extremely large increase in the quantity demanded. A horizontal demand curve is perfectly elastic and its measure of price elasticity of demand equals infinity.

Objective #3. A large value for the price elasticity of demand indicates that consumers are highly responsive to changes in the price of the good. A price elasticity of demand value that is greater than 1 implies that the percentage change in the quantity demanded in absolute value terms is greater than the percentage change in the price of the good in absolute value terms. When the price elasticity of demand is greater than 1, demand is elastic.

Objective #4. A small value for the price elasticity of demand indicates that consumers are less responsive to changes in the price of the good. A price elasticity of demand value that is less than 1 implies that the percentage change in the quantity demanded in absolute value terms is less than the percentage change in the price of the good in absolute value terms. Thus, when price changes, consumers respond with a relatively small change in the quantity of the good they demand. When the price elasticity of demand is less than 1, demand is inelastic.

Objective #5. When the price elasticity of demand equals 1, the demand is unit-elastic. A price elasticity of demand value of 1 implies that the percentage change in the quantity demanded of good X is exactly equal to the percentage change in the price of good X in absolute value terms.

Objective #6. For a straight line demand curve that intersects both the vertical and horizontal axes, the midpoint of that demand curve is the unit-elastic point. Above the midpoint, demand is elastic, while below the midpoint, demand is inelastic. Figure 9.1 illustrates this idea.

Figure 9.1

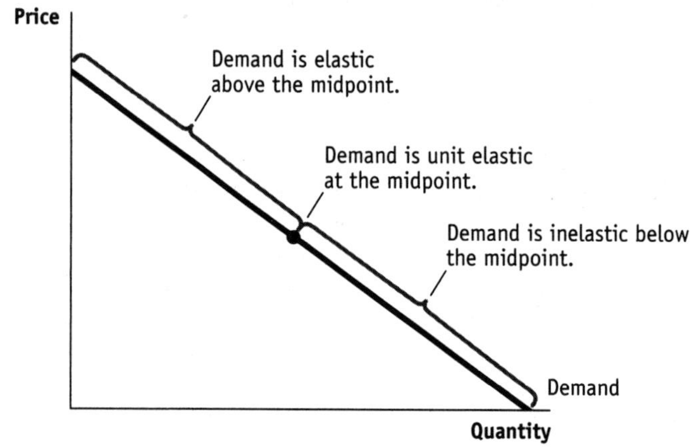

Objective #7. Total revenue is affected by the price elasticity of demand. If demand is inelastic, then an increase in price causes total revenue to increase. If demand is elastic, then an increase in price causes total revenue to decrease. An increase in price that moves symmetrically around the unit-elastic point has no effect on total revenue.

Objective #8. A change in price affects total revenue in two ways: first, the price effect is the change in total revenue due to the change in the price of the good, and second, the quantity effect is the change in total revenue due to the change in the number of units of the good sold. The price effect is stronger than the quantity effect when demand is inelastic; the quantity effect is stronger than the price effect when demand is elastic; and the price effect and the quantity effect exactly offset each other when demand is unit-elastic.

a. Figure 9.2 illustrates the effect on total revenue of an increase in price when demand is relatively inelastic. Starting at point *E*, total revenue is initially P_1Q_1, or the sum of areas *B* and *A*. When price increases to P_2 (point *F*), total revenue changes to P_2Q_2, or the sum of areas C and B. In this example, area *A* represents the quantity effect, while area C represents the price effect. When price increases, the quantity effect on total revenue is negative while the price effect on total revenue is positive, with the price effect dominating the quantity effect and leading to an increase in total revenue.

Figure 9.2

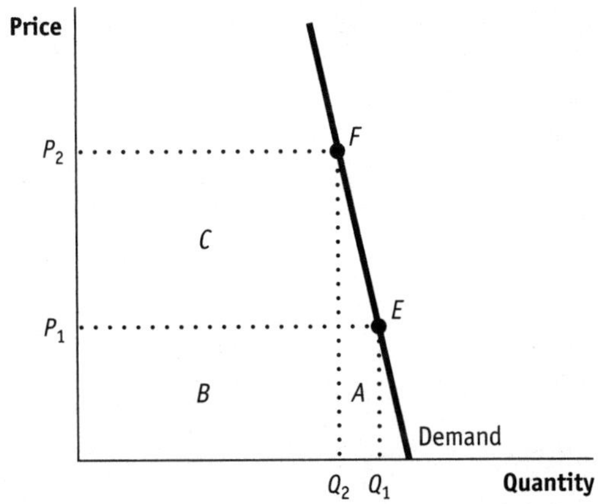

b. Figure 9.3 illustrates the effect on total revenue of an increase in price when demand is relatively elastic. When demand is elastic, the effect on total revenue of the quantity effect (area *A*) is larger than the price effect (area *C*).

Figure 9.3

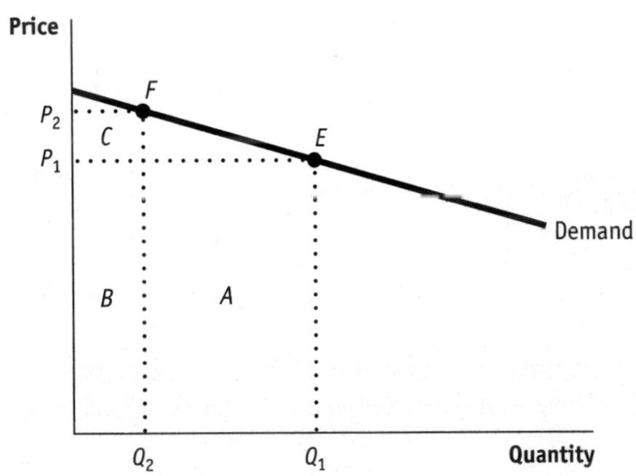

c. The table below summarizes the relationship between the price elasticity of demand and the effect of changes in price on total revenue, the price effect, and the quantity effect.

Demand	Price	Total revenue	Price effect	Quantity effect
Elastic	Increases	Decreases		Dominates
Elastic	Decreases	Increases		Dominates
Inelastic	Increases	Increases	Dominates	
Inelastic	Decreases	Decreases	Dominates	
Unit elastic	Increases	No effect	Exactly offsets quantity effect	Exactly offsets price effect
Unit elastic	Decreases	No effect	Exactly offsets quantity effect	Exactly offsets price effect

Objective #9. Price elasticity of demand is affected by the number of available substitutes, whether the good is a necessity or a luxury, and the time period for adjustment to the price change. Demand is more elastic when there are close substitutes, when the good is a luxury, and/or when there is more time to adjust to the price change. Demand is less elastic when there are no close substitutes, when the good is a necessity, and/or when there is little time to adjust to the price changes.

Key Terms

Notes

perfectly inelastic the case in which the *quantity demanded* does not respond at all to changes in the price; the *demand curve* is a vertical line.

perfectly elastic the case in which any price increase will cause the *quantity demanded* to drop to zero; the *demand curve* is a horizontal line.

elastic when the *price elasticity of demand* is greater than 1.

inelastic when the *price elasticity of demand* is less than 1.

unit-elastic the case in which the *price elasticity of demand* is exactly 1.

total revenue the total value of sales of a good or service (the price of the good or service multiplied by the quantity sold).

AFTER YOU READ THE MODULE

Tips

Tip #1. Total revenue is equal to the price per unit times the quantity. Total revenue at any given price is equal to the area of a rectangle whose height is the price and whose width is the quantity demanded at this price. Figure 9.4 illustrates this concept of total revenue for the given demand curve.

Figure 9.4

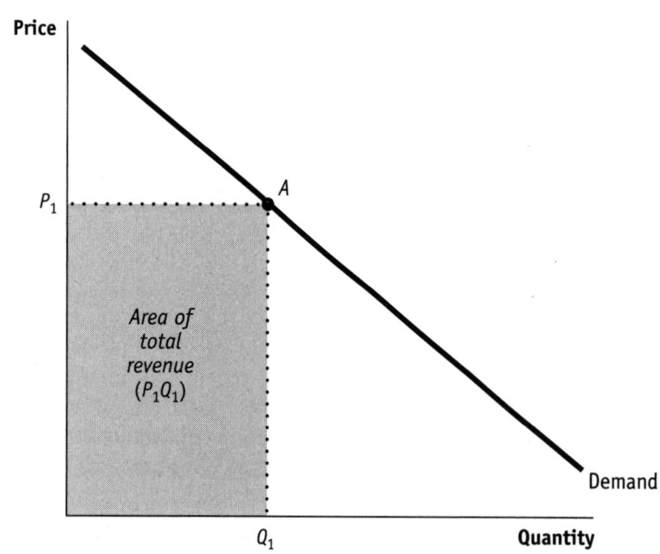

At point *A*, the price is P_1 and the quantity demanded is Q_1. The total revenue for the firm when the price equals P_1 is $P_1 \times Q_1$ (the shaded area in the graph).

Tip #2. For a given demand curve, a change in price causes total revenue to change because of two effects—the price effect and the quantity effect. Figure 9.5 illustrates these effects.

Figure 9.5

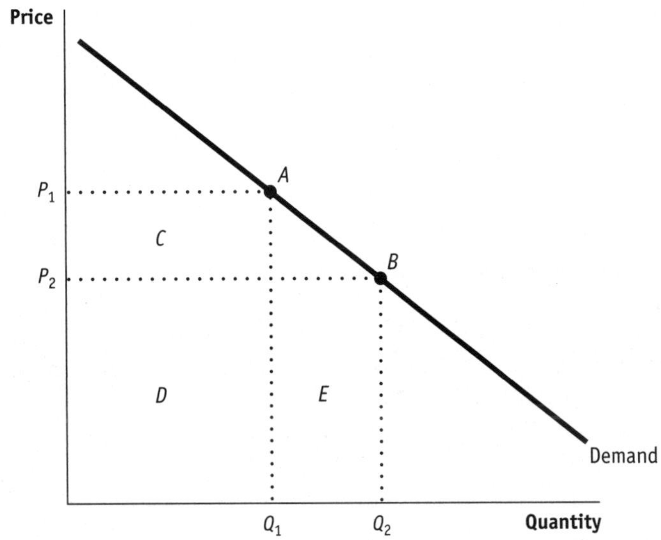

Suppose we are initially at point *A* with price P_1 and quantity Q_1. Then total revenue equals P_1Q_1, or the sum of areas *C* and *D*. If price decreases to P_2, then this causes a movement along the demand curve to point *B* with price P_2 and quantity Q_2. Total revenue is now equal to P_2Q_2, or the sum of the areas *D* and *E*. The price effect on total revenue is measured by area *C*: it reflects the change in revenue (in this case a loss in revenue) that arises from selling the original quantity Q_1 for the new price of P_2 instead of the initial price of P_1. The quantity effect on total revenue is measured by area *E*: it reflects the change in total revenue (in this case a gain in revenue) that arises from selling an additional $Q_2 - Q_1$ units of the good at the new price P_2. A similar argument holds for increases in price: you will find it helpful to redo this example starting at point *B* and moving to point *A* and thinking about the price and quantity effects.

WORKED PROBLEMS

1. George delivers lunchtime sandwiches to a variety of office buildings in his city. Over the 10 years he has been in business, he knows that he can sell 2,000 sandwiches a week if he prices each sandwich at \$2.00. He is trying to decide whether he should raise prices for his sandwiches. In two of his office buildings, he has raised the price of sandwiches to \$2.50 and found that this resulted in a 10% decline in the number of sandwiches that he sold in each of the buildings. He is not sure how to make his decision and has sought your advice about how he should price his sandwiches. George's prime concern is maximizing his revenue from his sales of sandwiches.

STEP 1: Think about how you can use George's available data to estimate the price elasticity of demand for his luncheon sandwiches.

George has some information about how price and quantity relate to each other with regard to his sandwich sales. You will need to put this information together in a way that will help you guide George toward maximizing his revenue from selling sandwiches. First, start by estimating his price elasticity of demand. Price elasticity of demand is equal to the percentage change in the quantity demanded divided by the percentage change in the price. From George's price experiment, you know that the price increase has resulted in a 10% decrease in his sales in the two office buildings. Next, calculate the percentage change in price. A simple percentage calculation (we just want to estimate price elasticity of demand) of the percentage change in price can be calculated as [(\$2.50 – \$2.00)/\$2.00] × 100, or 25%. The price elasticity of demand is approximated as 10%/25%: since this ratio is less than 1, we know that the price elasticity of demand for George's lunchtime sandwiches is inelastic.

STEP 2: Use your price elasticity of demand calculation to advise George as to his best pricing strategy.

From George's price experimentation, we can determine that George is selling sandwiches in the inelastic portion of the demand curve. Thus, George can raise his revenue by increasing the price of his sandwiches. You advise him to raise the price to \$2.50 at all of his office buildings. George may be able to raise his prices even higher and get even more revenue, but you need more information to fully determine at what price the demand for his product becomes elastic.

2. Hermione is interested in understanding the relationship between the price she receives when she sells one of her artistic creations and the revenue she earns. She estimates that she can sell 50 creations a year at a price of \$100 and that her sales decrease by 10 units for every \$20 increase in price and that her sales increase by 10 units for every \$20 decrease in price. Can you provide her guidance as to what price and quantity will result in maximum revenue per year?

STEP 1: First, you will need to construct the demand schedule for Hermione's product using the information that you have been given.

From the given information, you know that when price is \$100, the quantity demanded is 50 units. You also know that when price increases to \$120, the quantity demanded decreases by 10 units to 40 units. You also know that when price decreases to \$80, the quantity demanded increases by 10 units to 60 units. Use this constant relationship to create Hermione's demand schedule. The following table provides this demand schedule for a range of prices.

Price	Quantity demanded
\$ 20	90
40	80
60	70
80	60
100	50
120	40
140	30
160	20
180	10

STEP 2: From the demand schedule, you can calculate Hermione's revenue at each price.

Recall that total revenue is equal to price times quantity. Using the demand schedule you constructed in Step 1, now calculate the total revenue for each pair of price and quantity demanded. The following table provides this information for the demand schedule presented in step 1.

Price	Quantity demanded	Total revenue
$ 20	90	$1,800
40	80	3,200
60	70	4,200
80	60	4,800
100	50	5,000
120	40	4,800
140	30	4,200
160	20	3,200
180	10	1,800

STEP 3: Now, you can select that price and quantity that maximizes Hermione's maximum revenue for the year.

From the table, you can see that total revenue is maximized when price is equal to $100 and quantity demanded is equal to 50 units. Hermione is pricing her artistic creations optimally if she wishes to maximize her total revenue.

Problems and Exercises

1. Use the figure below to answer this set of questions.

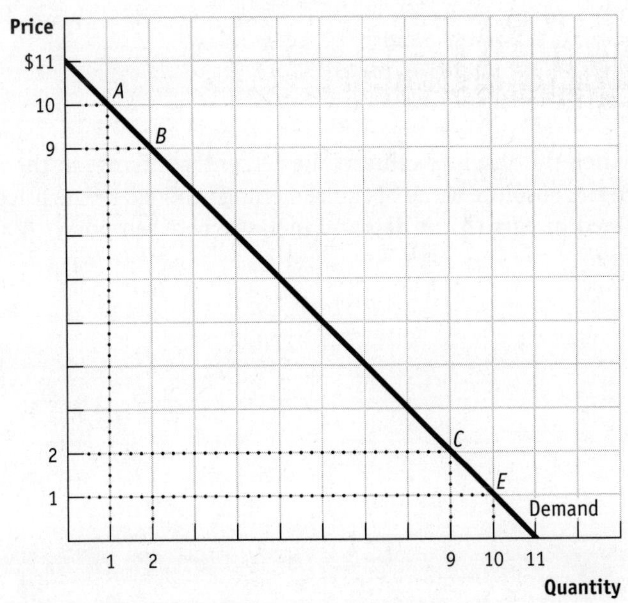

a. Calculate a value for the price elasticity of demand between points *C* and *E* using the midpoint method. Does it matter which point you select as your initial point?

b. Compare the value you calculated in part (a) of this problem with the price elasticity of demand value between points *A* and *B* calculated using the midpoint method. Are these two price elasticities of demand the same?

c. Demand is elastic when the absolute value of the percentage change in the quantity demanded exceeds the absolute value of the percentage change in the price. Given the values you compared in part (b), is demand elastic between points *A* and *B* or between points *C* and *E*?

d. Demand is inelastic when the absolute value of the percentage change in the quantity demanded is less than the absolute value of the percentage change in the price. Given the values you compared in part (b), is demand inelastic between points *A* and *B* or between points *C* and *E*?

2. Use the figure below of a linear demand curve to answer this set of questions.

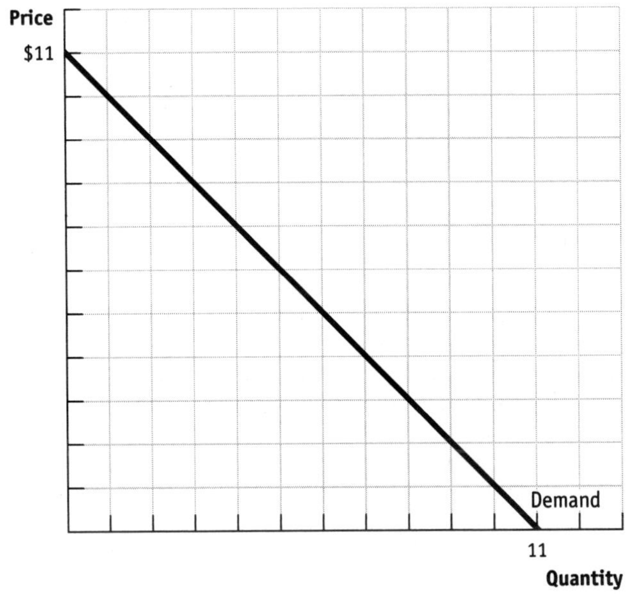

a. Based on the above figure, fill in the following table:

Price	Quantity demanded	Total revenue
$ 0		
1		
2		
3		
4		
5		
6		
7		
8		
9		
10		
11		

b. At what price is total revenue maximized? (Hint: This may be a price that is *not* included in your table.)

c. Suppose the price is initially $6, but it then decreases to $5. Calculate the elasticity of demand between these two points on the demand curve using the midpoint method.

d. Based on your calculations in part (c), describe the relationship between the absolute value of the percentage change in the quantity demanded and the absolute value of the percentage change in price when moving from a price of $6 to a price of $5.

3. For each of the following pairs of goods, identify which good is likely to have the more elastic price elasticity of demand, and then provide an explanation for your choice.

a. Golden delicious apples and all fruit

b. Gasoline and ice cream

c. Leisure travel and business travel

4. Summer Ice, a company that specializes in ice cream treats, wishes to raise its total revenue. It can identify two different groups of buyers: children and adults. Currently its ice cream treats are uniformly priced at $2.00 per serving. Summer Ice is considering reducing the price of its treats to $1 (a 67% decrease in price using the midpoint method). From its market research, it knows that the two groups of buyers are likely to respond according to the data in the table below:

Price	Quantity demanded by children	Quantity demanded by adults
$2	100	100
1	300	120

a. What is the price elasticity of demand for each of these groups? Use the midpoint method to calculate these price elasticities.

b. What is Summer Ice's current total revenue if they sell their ice cream treats at a price of $2?

c. What is Summer Ice's total revenue if they sell their ice cream treats at a price of $1?

d. What is Summer Ice's total revenue if they price their treats differently to the two groups and charge the higher price ($2) to adults and the lower price ($1) to children?

e. What is Summer Ice's total revenue if they price their treats differently to the two groups and charge the lower price ($1) to adults and the higher price ($2) to children?

f. What pricing scheme in parts (b) through (e) results in the greatest total revenue for Summer Ice? Using your knowledge of price elasticity of demand, explain why this is the best pricing scheme with regard to maximizing Summer Ice's total revenue in this market.

5. Briefly describe the factors that influence price elasticity of demand.

BEFORE YOU TAKE THE TEST

Module Review Questions

1. When the absolute value of the percentage change in quantity demanded is greater than the absolute value of the percentage change in price, demand is

a. inelastic.

b. elastic.

2. A horizontal demand curve is perfectly

a. elastic.

b. inelastic.

3. If the price elasticity of demand between two points on a demand curve is equal to 1.5, then demand between those two points is price

a. elastic.

b. inelastic.

4. If the price elasticity of demand equals infinity, then the demand curve is

a. horizontal.

b. vertical.

5. A small value (less than 1) for the price elasticity of demand indicates that consumers are very price
   a. sensitive and that a small percentage change in price will lead to a large percentage change in the quantity demanded when both changes are measured in absolute value terms.
   b. insensitive and that a small percentage change in price will lead to an even smaller percentage change in the quantity demanded when both changes are measured in absolute value terms.

Use the diagram below of a linear demand curve to answer the next three questions.

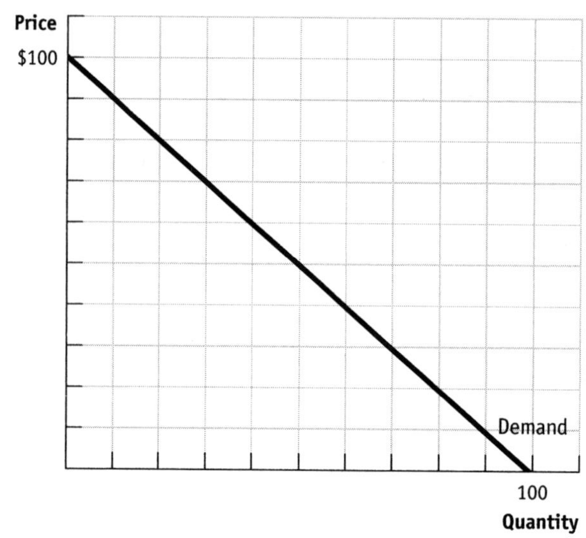

6. Suppose price is initially $60. If price increases to $70, this will cause the quantity demanded to decrease while
   a. total revenue increases.
   b. total revenue decreases.
   c. total revenue does not change.
   d. the effect on total revenue depends on consumers' reactions to the price increase.

7. Suppose you are a producer and the demand curve in the graph represents the demand for your product. Furthermore, suppose you are currently selling this product at a price of $30. If you raise the price to $40 and demand remains unchanged, total revenue will __________ because the price effect is __________ than the quantity effect.
   a. increase; larger
   b. increase; smaller
   c. decrease; larger
   d. decrease; smaller

8. Suppose you are a producer and the demand curve in the graph represents the demand for your product. To maximize total revenue you should sell the good for __________, resulting in total revenue of __________.
   a. $100; $100,000
   b. $60; $2,400
   c. $40; $2,400
   d. $50; $2,500

Use the figure below to answer the next two questions, where point *A* is the midpoint of the depicted linear demand curve.

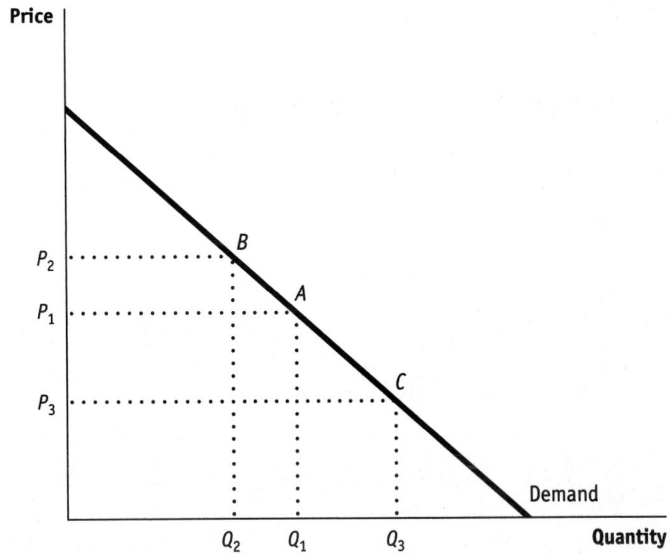

9. At prices greater than P_1 demand is __________, while at prices less than P_1 demand is __________, and at price P_1 demand is __________.

a. elastic; elastic; unit-elastic
b. inelastic; inelastic; unit-elastic
c. elastic; inelastic; unit-elastic
d. inelastic; elastic; unit-elastic

10. Suppose price is initially at P_1. Which of the following statements is true?

a. If price rises to P_2, then the quantity effect will dominate over the price effect and total revenue will increase.
b. If price falls to P_3, then the quantity effect will dominate over the price effect and total revenue will increase.
c. If price rises to P_2, then the price effect will dominate over the quantity effect and total revenue will increase.
d. If price falls to P_3, then the price effect will dominate over the quantity effect and total revenue will decrease.

11. Which of the following statements is true?

a. The longer the time period of adjustment to a change in the price of the good, the more elastic the demand for that good.
b. Goods that have many close substitutes typically have price elastic demand.
c. The demand for nonessential goods is more elastic than the demand for goods that are necessities.
d. All of the statements are true.

ANSWER KEY

Answers to Problems and Exercises

1. **a.** Price elasticity of demand = $\left|\dfrac{\text{\% change in quantity demanded}}{\text{\% change in price}}\right|$

$$\text{Price elasticity of demand} = \left|\frac{\dfrac{(10-9)}{\frac{(9+10)}{2}}}{\dfrac{(1-2)}{\frac{(2+1)}{2}}}\right| = \left|\frac{10.5\%}{-66.7\%}\right| = 0.16$$

With the midpoint method for calculating price elasticities, it does not matter which point is the initial point.

b. No, the price elasticity of demand between points *A* and *B* equals 6.3, while the price elasticity of demand between points *C* and *E* equals 0.16.

c. Demand is elastic between points *A* and *B:* we know the absolute value of the percentage change in the quantity demanded exceeds the absolute value of the percentage change in price since the ratio has a value greater than 1.

d. Demand is inelastic between points *C* and *E:* we know the absolute value of the percentage change in the quantity demanded is less than the absolute value of the percentage change in price since the ratio has a value less than 1.

2. **a.**

Price	Quantity demanded	Total revenue
$ 0	11	$ 0
1	10	10
2	9	18
3	8	24
4	7	28
5	6	30
6	5	30
7	4	28
8	3	24
9	2	18
10	1	10
11	0	0

b. From the table, we can see that total revenue equals $30 when the price is $5 or when the price is $6. At a price of $5.50—the midpoint of the demand curve—we find that total revenue equals $30.25. For a linear demand curve, total revenue is maximized at the midpoint of the demand curve.

c. Price elasticity of demand $= \left| \dfrac{\dfrac{(5-6)}{\frac{(6+5)}{2}}}{\dfrac{(5-6)}{\frac{(6+5)}{2}}} \right| = 1$

d. When the price elasticity of demand equals 1, the absolute value of the percentage change in the quantity demanded equals the absolute value of the percentage change in the price.

3. **a.** The price elasticity of demand for golden delicious apples should be far more elastic than the price elasticity of demand for all fruit since there are many possible substitutions for golden delicious apples and far fewer substitute goods for all fruit. Hence, a price increase is likely to result in a significant change in the percentage change in the quantity demanded of golden delicious apples and a far smaller percentage change in the quantity demanded of all fruit.

b. The price elasticity of demand for ice cream should be greater than the price elasticity of demand for gasoline since there are far more available substitutes for ice cream than there are for gasoline.

c. The price elasticity of demand for leisure travel should be greater than the price elasticity of demand for business travel since business travelers must get to their destination within a relatively small window of time, and hence are less sensitive to price than are leisure travelers.

4. **a.** The price elasticity of demand for children is equal to 1.5 and the price elasticity of demand for adults is equal to 0.27. Therefore, for the quantities and prices given in this example, the demand for Summer Ice is elastic for children and inelastic for adults.

b. Total revenue = ($2/treat)(200) = $400

c. Total revenue = ($1/treat)(420) = $420

d. Total revenue = ($2/treat)(100) + ($1/treat)(300) = $500

e. Total revenue = ($1/treat)(120) + ($2/treat)(100) = $320

f. Summer Ice will earn the greatest total revenue by charging children $1 per treat and adults $2 per treat: charging a higher price to the group of consumers with inelastic demand and a lower price to those consumers with elastic demand. In effect, this pricing scheme recognizes that the absolute value of the percentage change in the quantity demanded by adults is less than the absolute value of the percentage change in the price of the good, while the absolute value of the percentage change in the quantity demanded by children is greater than the absolute value of the percentage change in the price of the good. Thus, decreasing price to the adult group of buyers reduces total revenue, while reducing price to the child group of buyers increases total revenue.

5. The price elasticity of demand depends on the availability of close substitutes, whether the good is a necessity or a luxury, and how much time consumers have to adjust to the price change.

Answers to Module Review Questions

1. **Answer b.** Demand is price-elastic when the absolute value of the percentage change in the quantity demanded is greater than the absolute value of the percentage change in price. This is definitional.

2. **Answer a.** This is definitional: it is an extreme case of elasticity in which demanders are extremely price sensitive.

3. **Answer a.** Since the value of price elasticity of demand is greater than 1, this implies that the absolute value of the percentage change in the quantity demanded is greater than the absolute value of the percentage change in price, which means that demand is elastic between these two points.

4. **Answer a.** This is definitional: when the demand curve is horizontal, it tells us that consumers are very price sensitive, and at the current price there is infinite demand for the good. When the demand curve is perfectly vertical, it tells us that consumers are not price sensitive, since no matter what the price they will continue to demand the same amount of the good.

5. **Answer b.** When the price elasticity of demand has a value less than 1, this implies that the absolute value of the percentage change in the quantity demanded is less than the absolute value of the percentage change in the price of the good. Consumers are not price sensitive: they will continue to demand a similar amount of the good even though the price has increased.

6. **Answer b.** When price rises from \$60 to \$70, total revenue changes from \$2,400 to \$2,100. The price of \$60 is above the midpoint on the given demand curve, so an increase in price above \$60 implies that price is increasing in the elastic region of the demand curve. As price rises in the elastic portion of the demand curve, this results in a decrease in total revenue.

7. **Answer a.** When price rises from \$30 to \$40, you are moving along the demand curve in the inelastic region. An increase in price in the inelastic region of the demand curve results in an increase in total revenue. In this case, total revenue was initially \$2,100, and with the price increase total revenue is now equal to \$2,400.

8. **Answer d.** Total revenue is maximized at the unit-elastic point on the demand curve. For a linear demand curve, this occurs at the midpoint. In this example, the midpoint is at a price of \$50 and a quantity of 50 units.

9. **Answer c.** This is definitional: above the midpoint on a linear demand curve, demand is elastic; below the midpoint on a linear demand curve, demand is inelastic; and at the midpoint on a linear demand curve, demand is unit-elastic.

10. **Answer d.** When price rises above P_1, the quantity effect is dominant over the price effect and this dominance results in total revenue decreasing. When price falls below P_1, the price effect is dominant over the quantity effect and this dominance results in total revenue decreasing.

11. **Answer d.** All of these statements are true. When there are many substitutes available for a good, demand is more elastic. Demand is also more elastic the longer the time period for adjustment. Goods that are not necessities and therefore do not have to be consumed have more elastic demand than do goods that are necessities.

module 10

Other Elasticities

BEFORE YOU READ THE MODULE

Summary

The module discusses the price elasticity of supply which measures the responsiveness of the quantity supplied to changes in the price of the good. The module also explores the income elasticity of demand which measures the responsiveness of the quantity demanded to changes in income and the cross-price elasticity of demand which measures the responsiveness of the quantity demanded to changes in the price of another good. The module also discusses the factors that influence these elasticities.

Module Objectives

Objective #1. The cross-price elasticity of demand between goods A and B is equal to the percentage change in the quantity demanded of good A divided by the percentage change in the price of good B. That is,

$$\text{Cross-price elasticity of demand} = \frac{\text{\% change in the quantity demanded of good A}}{\text{\% change in the price of good B}}$$

Cross-price elasticity of demand may be a positive or negative number, and the sign of the cross-price elasticity of demand is critical to the interpretation of the meaning of a particular cross-price elasticity value. A positive cross-price elasticity of demand indicates that good A and good B are substitutes: if the price of good B increases, this leads to an increase in the quantity of good A demanded. A negative cross-price elasticity of demand indicates that good A and good B are complements: if the price of good B increases, this leads to a decrease in the quantity of good A demanded.

Objective #2. The income elasticity of demand is equal to the percentage change in the quantity demanded of the good divided by the percentage change in income. That is,

$$\text{Income elasticity of demand} = \frac{\text{\% change in the quantity demanded of the good}}{\text{\% change in income}}$$

Income elasticity of demand may have either a positive or negative value. A positive income elasticity of income value indicates that income and the quantity demanded move in the same direction: an increase in income leads to an increase in the quantity demanded, and thus the good is a normal good. A negative income elasticity of demand value indicates an inferior good: as income increases, the quantity of the good demanded decreases.

a. A good that is income-elastic has an income elasticity of demand that is greater than 1. When income increases, demand for income-elastic goods rises faster than income. Luxury goods tend to be income elastic.
b. Income-inelastic goods have income elasticities of demand that are positive but less than 1. When income increases, demand for income-inelastic goods rises slower than income. Necessities tend to be income inelastic.

Objective #3. The price elasticity of supply is defined as the percentage change in the quantity supplied of good A divided by the percentage change in the price of good A. To get consistent measures of the price elasticity of supply, the percentage changes in quantity supplied and price are both calculated using the midpoint method. Thus, the price elasticity of supply can be expressed as

$$\text{Price elasticity of supply} = \frac{\%\text{ change in the quantity supplied of good A}}{\%\text{ change in the price of good A}}$$

or, for two points (Q_1, P_1) and (Q_2, P_2) on a supply curve

$$\text{Price elasticity of supply} = \left| \frac{\dfrac{Q_2 - Q_1}{\dfrac{Q_2 + Q_1}{2}}}{\dfrac{P_2 - P_1}{\dfrac{P_2 + P_1}{2}}} \right| = \left| \frac{\dfrac{Q_2 - Q_1}{Q_2 + Q_1}}{\dfrac{P_2 - P_1}{P_2 + P_1}} \right|$$

a. A vertical supply curve has a price elasticity of supply equal to zero and is an example of a perfectly inelastic supply curve.
b. A horizontal supply curve has a price elasticity of supply equal to infinity and is an example of a perfectly elastic supply curve.

Objective #4. The price elasticity of supply is affected by the availability of inputs and the time period for adjustment. Supply is more price-elastic the greater the availability of inputs and/or in the long run when full adjustment to price changes has occurred.

Key Terms

Notes

cross-price elasticity of demand a measure of the effect of the change in the price of one good on the *quantity demanded* of the other; it is equal to the percent change in the quantity demanded of one good divided by the percent change in the price of another good.

income elasticity of demand the percent change in the quantity of a good demanded when a consumer's income changes divided by the percent change in the consumer's income.

income-elastic when the *income elasticity of demand* for a good is greater than 1.

income-inelastic when the *income elasticity of demand* for a good is positive but less than 1.

price elasticity of supply a measure of the responsiveness of the quantity of a good supplied to the price of that good; the ratio of the percent change in the *quantity supplied* to the percent change in the price as we move along the *supply curve.*

perfectly inelastic supply the case in which the *price elasticity of supply* is zero, so that changes in the price of the good have no effect on the *quantity supplied;* the perfectly inelastic *supply curve* is a vertical line.

perfectly elastic supply the case in which even a tiny increase or reduction in the price will lead to very large changes in the *quantity supplied,* so that the *price elasticity of supply* is infinite; the perfectly elastic *supply curve* is a horizontal line.

Notes

AFTER YOU READ THE MODULE

Tips

Tip #1. Economists calculate a variety of elasticities because these measures provide important insights into the relationship between two different variables. All elasticities are calculated as the ratio between the percentage changes in quantity (either the quantity demanded or the quantity supplied) to the percentage change in some other related variable. Elasticities are unit-free, making them an ideal measure of sensitivity of one variable to changes in another variable. In general, we can think of elasticity as being defined as

$$\text{Elasticity} = \frac{\text{\% change in quantity (either quantity demanded or quantity supplied)}}{\text{\% change in a related variable}}$$

a. The price elasticity of demand is thus

$$\text{Price elasticity of demand} = \frac{\text{\% change in the quantity demanded of good A}}{\text{\% change in the price of good A}}$$

b. The price elasticity of supply is thus

$$\text{Price elasticity of supply} = \frac{\text{\% change in the quantity supplied of good A}}{\text{\% change in the price of good A}}$$

c. The cross-price elasticity of demand is thus

$$\text{Cross-price elasticity of demand} = \frac{\text{\% change in the quantity demanded of good A}}{\text{\% change in the price of good B}}$$

d. The income elasticity of demand is thus

$$\text{Income elasticity of demand} = \frac{\text{\% change in the quantity demanded of good A}}{\text{\% change in income}}$$

Tip #2. The sign of the measure you calculate for either the income elasticity of demand or the cross-price elasticity of demand is significant. Whereas with the price elasticity of demand the measure was reported as an absolute value and thus a positive number, with the income and cross-price elasticity measures, the sign of the elasticity value carries meaning.

When the income elasticity of demand is a positive number, the good is a normal good; when it is a negative number, the good is an inferior good. When the cross-price elasticity of demand is a positive number, the two goods are substitutes; when it is a negative number, the two goods are complements.

WORKED PROBLEMS

1. Oscar's annual income increases from $40,000 to $48,000. He changes his purchases of generic cereal from 120 boxes per year to 90 boxes per year. He changes his purchases of movie theater tickets from 4 tickets per year to 12 tickets per year. He changes his purchases of fast-food dinners from 20 meals a year to 32 meals a year. For each of these goods calculate Oscar's income elasticity of demand and then determine whether the good is an inferior good or a normal good. In addition determine whether any of the goods are income-elastic.

STEP 1: Review the definition of income elasticity of demand and the formula used to calculate the income elasticity of demand.

Income elasticity of demand is the ratio of the percentage change in the quantity demanded of the good divided by the percentage change in income. The value of the income elasticity of demand may be positive or negative: a positive value indicates a normal good and a negative value indicates an inferior good. The formula to use in calculating this value is:

Income elasticity of demand = (percentage change in the quantity demanded)/(percentage change in income)

STEP 2: Calculate the percentage change in income.

To find the percentage change in income, use the following formula:

Percentage change in income = [(new value of income-initial value of income)/(initial value of income)] × 100%

The percentage change in Oscar's income is therefore equal to [(48,000 – 40,000)/(40,000)] × 100% = 20%.

STEP 3: Calculate the percentage change in the quantity demanded of each of the goods.

To find the percentage change in the quantity demanded of one of the goods, use the following formula:

Percentage change in the quantity demanded of good X =
[(new quantity of good X demanded – initial quantity of good X demanded)/(initial quantity of good X demanded)] × 100%

The percentage change in Oscar's quantity demanded of generic cereal is –25%. The percentage change in Oscar's quantity demanded of movie theater tickets is 200%. The percentage change in Oscar's quantity demanded of fast-food dinners is 60%.

STEP 4: Calculate Oscar's income elasticity of demand for each of the goods in the problem. Determine whether each good is a normal or an inferior good.

Use the formula in Step 1 to calculate the income elasticity of demand for each of the three goods.

Income elasticity of demand for generic cereal = (−25%)/(20%) = −1.25
Income elasticity of demand for movie theater tickets = (200%)/(20%) = 10
Income elasticity of demand for fast-food dinners = (60%)/(20%) = 3

If the income elasticity of demand is a negative number, the good is an inferior good: as income increases, the quantity demanded decreases. Generic cereal is therefore an inferior good for Oscar.

If the income elasticity of demand is a positive number, the good is a normal good: as income increases, the quantity demanded increases. Movie theater tickets and fast-food dinners are both normal goods for Oscar.

STEP 5: Determine whether any of the goods are income-elastic.

A good is income-elastic if the income elasticity of demand for the good has a value that is greater than 1. This indicates that the percentage change in the quantity demanded of the good increases by a greater percentage than the percentage change in income. For Oscar both movie theater tickets and fast-food dinners are income-elastic goods, since the income elasticity of demand value for both goods is greater than 1.

2. Suppose that the supply curve for a market is given by the equation $Q = P - 5$, where Q is the quantity of the good supplied in the market and P is the price per unit of the good. You are asked to calculate the price elasticity of supply using the midpoint method for this good when price increases from \$10 to \$11 and for when price increases from \$20 to \$21.

STEP 1: Review the definition of the price elasticity of supply and the forula you will need to calculate the price elasticity of supply.

The price elasticity of supply measures the ratio of the percentage change in the quantity supplied to the percentage change in the price of the good. To calculate the price elasticity of supply using the midpoint method, use the following formula:

$$\text{Price elasticity of supply} = \{[(Q_2 - Q_1)/(Q_1 + Q_2)]/[(P_2 - P_1)/(P_1 + P_2)]\}$$

STEP 2: Using the given supply equation, find the quantities that will be supplied at each of the given prices.

To find the quantity supplied at any given price, substitute that price into the supply equation and then solve for the corresponding quantity. Thus, when the price is equal to \$10, the equation is $Q = 10 - 5$, or $Q = 5$ units. This table summarizes the supply schedule for the given prices:

Price of the good	Quantity supplied
\$10	5
11	6
20	15
21	16

STEP 3: Calculate the values of the price elasticity of supply as the price changes from $10 to $11 and as the price changes from $20 to $21.

The price elasticity of supply as the price changes from $10 to $11 is {[(6 – 5)/(5 + 6)]/[(11 – 10)/(10 + 11)]} = 21/11 = 19.18.

The price elasticity of supply as the price changes from $20 to $21 is {[(16 – 15)/(15 + 16)]/[(21 – 20)/(20 + 21)]} = 41/31 = 1.32.

3. Josie has been provided the following cross-price elasticities of demand.

Goods	Cross-price elasticity of demand
Good A and good B	–0.3
Good C and good D	0.5
Good E and good F	0.2
Good G and good H	–0.15

Josie has been asked to identify whether each pair are substitutes or complements. She is unsure how to interpret the cross-price elasticity of demand and has sought your help in the matter.

STEP 1: Review the definition of cross-price elasticity of demand and how its value can determine whether two goods are substitutes or complements.

The cross-price elasticity of demand is defined as the percentage change in the quantity demanded of one good divided by the percentage change in the price of the other good.

If two goods are substitutes, this implies that when the price of one of the goods increases, consumers will substitute away from this good and toward the now relatively cheaper good. Thus, if the two goods are substitutes, then an increase in the price of one good will cause an increase in the quantity demanded of the other good. Both the percentage change in the quantity demanded of one good and the percentage change in the price of the other good will therefore move in the same direction: the cross-price elasticity of demand for substitutes is therefore a positive number.

If two goods are complements, this implies that when the price of one of the goods increases, consumers will decrease their consumption of the other, complementary good. Thus, if the two goods are complements, then an increase in the price of one good will cause a decrease in the quantity demanded of the other good. The percentage change in the quantity demanded of one good and the percentage change in the price of the other good will therefore move in the opposite direction: the cross-price elasticity of demand for complements is therefore a negative number.

STEP 2: **For each pair of goods apply the information from Step 1 to identify whether the pairs are substitutes or complements.**

Apply the information you reviewed in Step 1 to the table. The following table identifies the relationship between each pair of goods.

Goods	Cross-price elasticity of demand	Relationship between the two goods
Good A and good B	−0.3	Complements
Good C and good D	0.5	Substitutes
Good E and good F	0.2	Substitutes
Good G and good H	−0.15	Complements

Problems and Exercises

1. Suppose there are two goods, good A and good B. When the price of good A increases from \$10 to \$12, the quantity of good B demanded changes from 4 units to 6 units.

a. Calculate the cross-price elasticity of demand (use the simple formula for percentage changes rather than the midpoint method).

b. What is the relationship between good A and good B? Explain your answer and provide an example of two goods that have this relationship.

2. Suppose there are two goods, good C and good D. The cross-price elasticity of demand for these two goods is equal to −0.2.

a. What is the relationship between good C and good D? Explain your answer.

b. Suppose the price of good C increases from \$1 to \$2. What do you estimate will be the percentage change in the quantity demanded of good D? (Use the simple formula for percentage changes rather than the midpoint method.)

c. Suppose when the price of good C is \$1 that 10 units of good D are demanded. What will be the quantity demanded of good D when the price of good C increases to \$2?

d. Suppose the cross-price elasticity of demand between two goods is negative and you would like to sell more units of one of these goods. What do you hope will happen to the price of the other good? Explain your answer.

3. When Mario's income increases by 10%, his consumption of noodles decreases from 100 units a year to 70 units a year, while his consumption of salmon increases from 20 units a year to 60 units a year.

a. What is Mario's income elasticity of demand for noodles?

b. What is Mario's income elasticity of demand for salmon?

c. Is either of these goods income elastic for Mario?

d. Is either of these goods income-inelastic for Mario?

e. From Mario's perspective, is either of these goods a luxury good? Explain your answer.

f. From Mario's perspective, is either of these goods an inferior good? Explain your answer.

4. Government officials in Wonderland are concerned that the economy is entering a recession. They anticipate that this recession will lead to lower levels of production and higher levels of unemployment, thus resulting in many people experiencing a decrease in their income. Suppose there are two producers in Wonderland: producer A knows that the income elasticity of demand for his product equals –0.6 while producer B knows that the income elasticity of demand for his product equals 0.5. Which producer is likely to view this recession as a more significant problem for his company? Explain your answer.

5. The following table describes a linear supply curve for bicycles in Microland.

Price	Quantity supplied of bicycles
$ 0	0
100	200
200	400
300	600
400	800
500	1,000

a. Graph this supply curve and then write an equation for this supply curve in slope-intercept form.

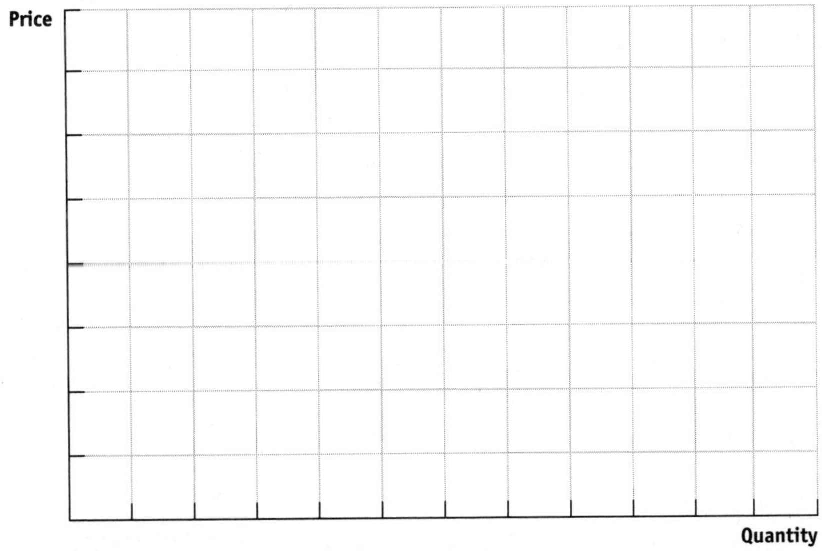

b. Suppose suppliers initially sell bicycles for $200 but then decrease their price to $100. Using the midpoint method, what is the value of the price elasticity of supply between these two points on the supply curve?

c. Suppose suppliers initially sell bicycles for $400 and then the price increases to $500. Using the midpoint method, what is the value of the price elasticity of supply between these two points on the supply curve?

d. Did your values in part (b) and part (c) of this question differ or were they the same? You might redo this problem with another set of values for a different linear demand curve that goes through the origin. Do you get the same result? Generalize your findings in a simple statement.

6. Let's redo the last example, but for a linear supply curve that does not pass through the origin. The table below describes a supply curve that has these characteristics.

Price	Quantity supplied of bicycles
$100	0
200	200
300	400
400	600
500	800

a. Graph this supply curve and then write an equation for this supply curve in slope-intercept form.

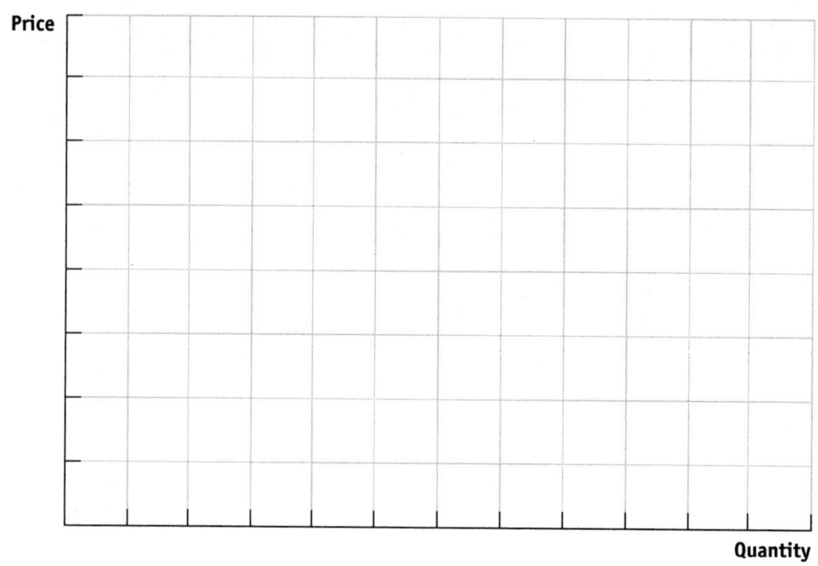

b. Suppose suppliers initially sell bicycles for $200 but then decrease their price to $100. Using the midpoint method, what is the value of the price elasticity of supply between these two points on the supply curve?

c. Suppose suppliers initially sell bicycles for $400 and then the price increases to $500. Using the midpoint method, what is the value of the price elasticity of supply between these two points on the supply curve?

d. Did your values in parts (b) and (c) of this question differ?

BEFORE YOU TAKE THE TEST

Module Review Questions

1. Tea and coffee are often viewed as substitutes for each other. Which of the following cross-price elasticity values is more likely for tea and coffee?
   a. −0.5
   b. 1.5

2. The price of movie tickets increased 10% this year. Which of the following statements is most likely to be true?
   a. The quantity of popcorn sold at movie theaters decreased this year.
   b. Video movie rentals increased this year.
   c. If the price elasticity of demand for movie tickets is greater than 1, total revenue at the movie theaters decreased.
   d. All of the statements are true.

3. The cross-price elasticity of demand between movie tickets and movie theater popcorn is estimated to equal −0.6. Suppose movie ticket prices increased by 20% this year. The percentage change in the quantity demanded of movie theater popcorn will be a(n)
   a. increase of 1.2%
   b. increase of 12%.
   c. decrease of 1.2%.
   d. decrease of 12%.

4. This year Joe's income increased by 15% while the quantity of bananas he demanded increased by 8% and the quantity of orange juice he demanded increased by 6%. Which of the following statements is true for Joe?
   a. Bananas are a normal good and orange juice is an inferior good.
   b. Bananas are an inferior good and orange juice is a normal good.
   c. Bananas and orange juice are both normal goods.
   d. Bananas and orange juice are both inferior goods.

5. Use the data in the table below to answer this question. The table provides information about prices, quantity demanded, and income for Sue for two different years.

Year	Good	Price	Quantity demanded	Income
2004	Pizza	$ 6	10	
2004	Books	9	4	
2004				$200
2005	Pizza	6	7.5	
2005	Books	9	5	
2005				250

Calculate Sue's income elasticity of demand for pizza for this time period. Sue's income elasticity of demand for pizza equals ________ and pizza is a(n) ________ good.

a. 1; normal
b. −1; inferior
c. −1.65; inferior
d. 1.65; normal

6. Use the information in the table below to answer this question.

Good	Quantity demanded initially	Price initially	Quantity demanded after price change	New price
Pizza	10	$ 6	8	$6
Books	4	12	5	9

Calculate the cross-price elasticity of demand between the quantity demanded of pizza and the price of books. What is the relationship between pizza and books given this cross-price elasticity of demand value?

a. Pizza and books are complements.
b. Pizza and books are substitutes.
c. Pizza is an inferior good and books are a normal good.
d. Pizza is a normal good and books are an inferior good.

7. Suppose the income elasticity of demand for a good is greater than 1. Which of the following statements is true?

a. The percentage change in the quantity demanded of this good is larger than the percentage change in income.
b. This good is a necessity, since as income increases the quantity demanded of the good increases.
c. This good is an inferior good, since as income increases the quantity demanded of the good increases at a much greater rate than the rate of increase in income.
d. This good could not be a luxury good, since income and the quantity demanded have a positive relationship.

8. Suppose there is an influx of new workers in a community. This will likely result in

a. an increase in the price elasticity of demand for all normal goods.

b. an increase in the price elasticity of supply for goods produced in this community.

c. a decrease in the price elasticity of demand for most goods.

d. little change in any elasticity measure for this community.

9. Acme Manufacturing produces 1,000 widgets when the price of widgets is $20 per widget, and 1,200 widgets when the price of widgets is $22 per widget. Using the midpoint method, what is the value of the price elasticity of supply?

a. 1.9

b. 0.6

c. 0.5

d. 2

10. Acme Manufacturing originally was able to produce 1,000 widgets at a price of $20 per widget, and 1,200 widgets at a price of $22 per widget. Suppose that there is an influx of new workers into the community and Acme now finds it can produce 1,200 widgets at a price of $20 per widget, and 1,600 widgets at a price of $22 per widget. Which statement best describes Acme's situation?

a. Acme's supply curve is now more price-inelastic which implies that as the price increases Acme can now supply a greater quantity of the good than it could initially.

b. Acme's supply curve is unaffected by this change in labor: a price increase for widgets simply causes a movement along the supply curve for widgets.

c. Acme's supply curve is now more price-elastic which implies that as the price increases Acme can now supply a greater quantity of the good than it could initially.

d. The availability of labor has an unpredictable effect on Acme Manufacturing.

ANSWER KEY

Answers to Problems and Exercises

1. **a.** $\text{Cross-price elasticity of demand} = \dfrac{\text{\% change in the quantity demanded of good B}}{\text{\% change in the price of good A}}$

% change in the quantity demanded of good B = (6 – 4)/4 = 50%

% change in the price of good A = (12 – 10)/10 = 20%

Cross-price elasticity of demand = 50%/20% = 2.5

b. Good A and good B are substitutes because as the price of good A increases the quantity demanded of good B increases. There are many examples of two goods that are substitutes: coffee and tea, butter and margarine, olive oil and safflower oil, taxi rides and bus rides, tennis and golf.

2. **a.** A negative cross-price elasticity of demand implies that the percentage change in the quantity demanded of one good moves in the opposite direction to the percentage change in the price of a related good. Thus, if the price of good Y increases, then the quantity demanded of good X decreases. We know that two related goods are either substitutes or complements. In this case, a negative cross-price elasticity of demand indicates that the two goods are complements. (In contrast, a positive cross-price elasticity of demand tells us the two goods are substitutes.)

b. Cross-price elasticity of demand = –0.2

$$-0.2 = \frac{\text{\% change in the quantity demanded of good D}}{\text{\% change in the price of good C}}$$

$$-0.2 = \frac{\text{\% change in the quantity demanded of good D}}{100\%}$$

% change in the quantity demanded of good D = –20%

c. With a cross-price elasticity of –0.2, a 100% increase in the price of good C will cause the quantity demanded of good D to fall by 20% (using the simple formula for percentage changes rather than the midpoint method). Thus, if the quantity demanded of good D was initially 10 units, then the quantity demanded of good D will be 8 units after the increase in the price of good C.

d. When the cross-price elasticity of demand is negative, a decrease in the price of one good will lead to an increase in the quantity demanded of the other good.

3. **a.** $\text{Income elasticity of demand for noodles} = \dfrac{-30\%}{10\%} = -3$

b. $\text{Income elasticity of demand for salmon} = \dfrac{200\%}{10\%} = 20$

c. Salmon

d. Neither good is income-inelastic since neither good has an income elasticity of demand value that is positive but is less than 1.

e. Salmon is a luxury good since the value of the income elasticity of demand for salmon is greater than 1. As Mario's income increases, his demand for salmon increases at an even faster rate.

f. Noodles are an inferior good, since as Mario's income increases his demand for noodles decreases. A negative value for the income elasticity of demand indicates that the good is an inferior good.

4. Producer B will feel the impact more than producer A since producer's B product is a normal good, so the demand for producer B's product will fall as income falls. In contrast, the negative income elasticity of demand value for producer A indicates that producer A's product is an inferior good, and as income falls, the quantity demanded of producer A's product will increase.

5. **a.** $P = (1/2)Q$

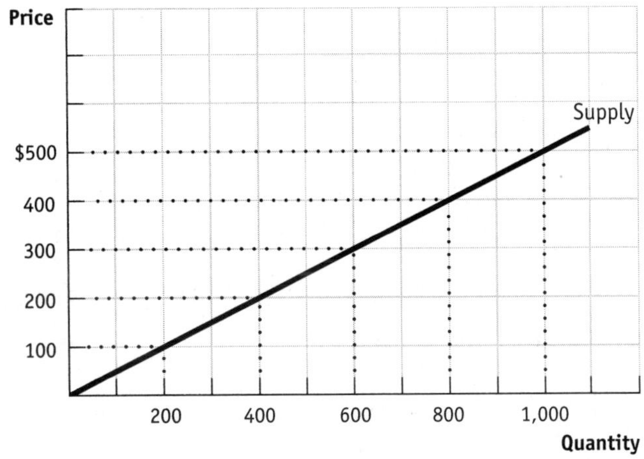

b. Price elasticity of supply $= \left| \dfrac{\dfrac{200 - 400}{\dfrac{400 + 200}{2}}}{\dfrac{100 - 200}{\dfrac{200 + 100}{2}}} \right| = 1$

c. Price elasticity of supply $= \left| \dfrac{\dfrac{1{,}000 - 800}{\dfrac{800 + 1{,}000}{2}}}{\dfrac{500 - 400}{\dfrac{400 + 500}{2}}} \right| = 1$

d. The values are the same in parts (b) and (c). Redoing the exercise for a different linear demand curve that passes through the origin yields the same value. Thus, as long as the supply curve is linear and passes through the origin, the price elasticity of supply equals 1 for all points on the supply curve.

6. **a.** $P = (1/2)Q + 100$

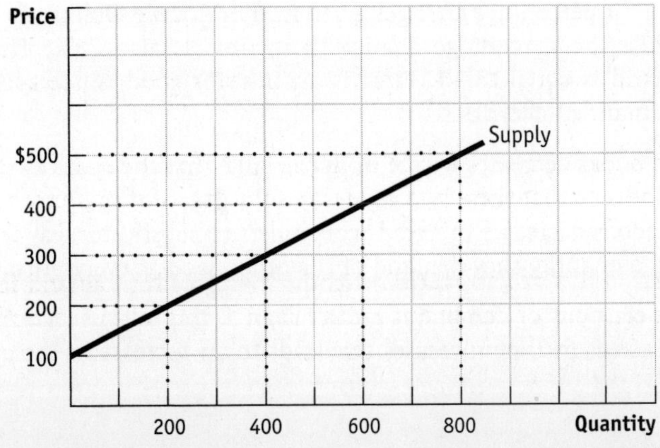

b. Price elasticity of supply = $\left| \dfrac{\dfrac{0 - 200}{\dfrac{200 + 0}{2}}}{\dfrac{100 - 200}{\dfrac{200 + 100}{2}}} \right| = 3$

c. Price elasticity of supply = $\left| \dfrac{\dfrac{800 - 600}{\dfrac{600 + 800}{2}}}{\dfrac{500 - 400}{\dfrac{400 + 500}{2}}} \right| = 1.28$

d. The values in parts (b) and (c) differ.

Answers to Module Review Questions

1. **Answer b.** Two goods are substitutes for each other when the cross-price elasticity of demand between the two goods is positive. This elasticity is positive, since as the price of one of the goods increases this leads to an increase in the quantity demanded of the other good.

2. **Answer d.** Each of these statements is likely to be true. Popcorn sold at movie theaters is likely to be a complementary good with respect to movie tickets. When movie tickets increase in price, fewer movie tickets are demanded, and this decrease in the quantity demanded results in fewer units of popcorn being sold. Similarly, movie tickets and video rentals are likely to be substitutes with respect to each other: an increase in the price of movie tickets will likely result in increased demand for video rentals. If the price elasticity of demand for movie tickets is greater than 1, this implies that demand is elastic, and an increase in price in the elastic segment of the demand curve causes total revenue to decrease.

3. **Answer d.** To compute this answer, first recall that the cross-price elasticity is the ratio of the percentage change in the quantity demanded of good A divided by the percentage change in the price of good B. The question provides the value for the cross-price elasticity of demand as well as the percentage change in the price of movie tickets. Plugging these values into our equation for cross-price elasticity of demand, we have $-0.6 = x/20\%$ where x is the percentage change in the quantity demanded of movie theater popcorn. Solving this equation, the percentage change in the quantity demanded of movie theater popcorn is a decrease of 12%.

4. **Answer c.** Joe's income increased and so did his consumption of both bananas and orange juice. Therefore they both must be normal goods.

5. **Answer b.** To find the income elasticity of demand, recall that this is the ratio of the percentage change in the quantity demanded of the good divided by the percentage change in income. The percentage change in the quantity demanded of pizza is –25% (using the simple formula for percentage changes given in the Module Objectives section of the Study Guide), while the percentage change in income is also 25%. Thus, the income elasticity of demand is equal to –1. Pizza is an inferior good, since as income increases, the quantity demanded decreases.

6. **Answer b.** As the price of books decreases we see from the table that the quantity of pizzas demanded decreases. This tells us that these two goods are substitutes for one another since as the price of one of the goods decreases this leads consumers to substitute away from the other good and decrease the quantity they demand of the other good at every price.

7. **Answer a.** When income elasticity of demand is greater than 1, this tells us that the good is not an inferior good, since as income increases this leads to an increase in the quantity

demanded of the good. From the definition of income elasticity of demand, a value greater than 1 implies that the percentage change in the quantity demanded of the good is greater than the percentage change in income. When the income elasticity of demand is greater than 1, this implies that the good is a luxury, since the percentage increase in the quantity demanded is increasing at a faster rate than the percentage increase in income.

8. **Answer b.** When there is an influx of new workers into a community, labor becomes more plentiful. Since labor is an input in the production of goods, this likely makes the supply of goods more elastic.

9. **Answer a.** To find the price elasticity of supply, use the midpoint method and calculate the percentage change in the quantity supplied divided by the percentage change in the price of the good. Thus, the price elasticity of supply equals

$$\frac{\dfrac{1{,}200 - 1{,}000}{\dfrac{1{,}000 + 1{,}200}{2}}}{\dfrac{22 - 20}{\dfrac{20 + 22}{2}}} = 1.9$$

10. **Answer c.** If you sketch out the relationships between price and the quantity supplied, you will notice that the influx of workers results in Acme Manufacturing supply's curve shifting out to the right. This causes the price elasticity of supply to increase, resulting in more price-elastic supply. Calculation of the new value of the price elasticity of supply would be equal to

$$\frac{\dfrac{1{,}600 - 1{,}200}{\dfrac{1{,}200 + 1{,}600}{2}}}{\dfrac{22 - 20}{\dfrac{20 + 22}{2}}} = 3$$

Supply is now more price-elastic.

module 11

Consumer and Producer Surplus

BEFORE YOU READ THE MODULE

Summary

This module develops the concepts of producer surplus and consumer surplus and then illustrates the connection between these two concepts and the demand and supply model.

Module Objectives

Objective #1. The demand and supply model illustrates how much consumers and producers gain from participating in a market. A consumer's willingness to pay refers to the maximum price the consumer would pay to purchase an item. The demand curve is defined by the willingness of consumers to pay.

Objective #2. An individual's consumer surplus is the difference between the individual's willingness to pay and the price he/she pays for the good: consumer surplus measures the net gain the consumer receives when he/she purchases the good. Total consumer surplus is the sum of the individual consumer surpluses achieved by all the buyers of the good. Total consumer surplus is equal to the area under the demand curve but above the price.

- The area of consumer surplus is a triangle for a smooth demand curve or a series of rectangles for a step-shaped demand curve.
- Holding everything else constant, a decrease in price increases consumer surplus while an increase in price decreases consumer surplus.

Objective #3. The seller's price is the lowest price the seller is willing to sell the good for. Individual producer surplus is the difference between the price the good sells for and the lowest price the seller is willing to accept for the good: individual producer surplus measures the net gain the seller receives from selling the good. Total producer surplus is the sum of the individual producer surplus achieved by all the sellers of the good. Total producer surplus is equal to the area above the supply curve but beneath the price.

- The area of producer surplus is a triangle for a smooth supply curve or a series of rectangles for a step-shaped supply curve.
- Holding everything else constant, a decrease in price decreases producer surplus and an increase in price increases producer surplus.

Key Terms

willingness to pay the maximum price a consumer is prepared to pay for a good.

individual consumer surplus the net gain to an individual buyer from the purchase of a good; equal to the difference between the buyer's *willingness to pay* and the price paid.

total consumer surplus the sum of the *individual consumer surpluses* of all the buyers of a good in a market.

consumer surplus a term often used to refer both to *individual consumer surplus* and to *total consumer surplus.*

cost (of seller) the lowest price at which a seller is willing to sell a good.

individual producer surplus the net gain to an individual seller from selling a good; equal to the difference between the price received and the seller's *cost.*

total producer surplus the sum of the *individual producer surpluses* of all the sellers of a good in a market.

producer surplus a term often used to refer both to *individual producer surplus* and to *total producer surplus.*

Notes

AFTER YOU READ THE MODULE

Tips

Tip #1. To master the key concept in this module, you must be able to locate the areas of surplus in the graphs of the supply and demand model. You will want to work with the concepts of consumer surplus, and producer surplus, until you feel confident that you can find these areas in your graphs.

Tip #2. Figure 11.1 illustrates the concept of consumer surplus for a step-shaped demand curve. The area of consumer surplus consists of a series of rectangles that lie under the demand curve but above the market price. Each of these rectangles has been shaded separately in Figure 11.1, but the area of consumer surplus is the entire shaded area. Those consumers whose willingness to pay is equal to or greater than the market price will purchase the good for the market price, and their consumer surplus represents the net gain they receive from purchasing the good.

Figure 11.1

Consumer Surplus for a Step-Shaped Demand Curve

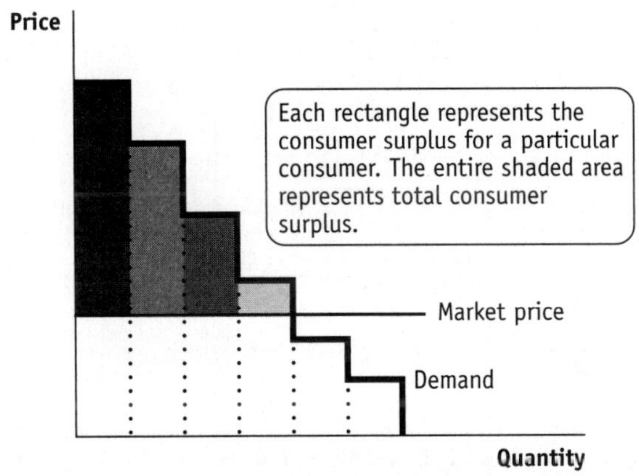

Tip #3. Figure 11.2 illustrates the concept of consumer surplus for a smooth demand curve. The area of consumer surplus consists of the area under the demand curve but above the market price. In Figure 11.2, the area of consumer surplus is shaded. The value of consumer surplus can be found by calculating the area of this shaded triangle. The consumer surplus represents the net gain consumers receive from purchasing the good.

Figure 11.2

Consumer Surplus for a Smooth Demand Curve

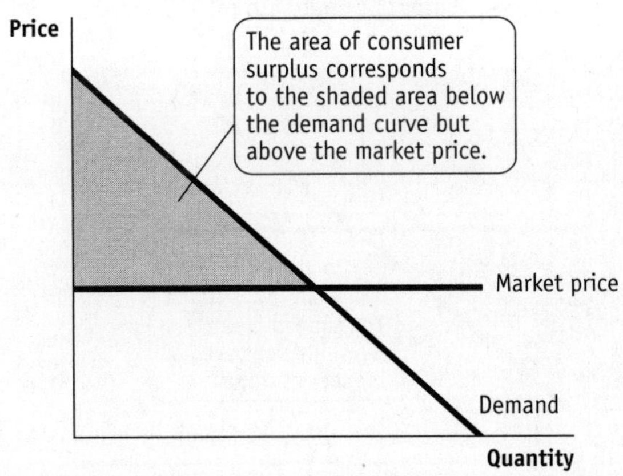

Tip #4. Figure 11.3 illustrates the concept of producer surplus for a step-shaped supply curve. The area of producer surplus consists of a series of rectangles that lie above the supply curve but below the market price. Each of these rectangles has been shaded as separate rectangles in Figure 11.3, but the area of producer surplus is the entire shaded area. Those producers whose willingness to sell is equal to or less than the market price, will sell the good for the market price, and their producer surplus represents the net gain they receive from selling the good.

Figure 11.3

Producer Surplus for a Step-Shaped Supply Curve

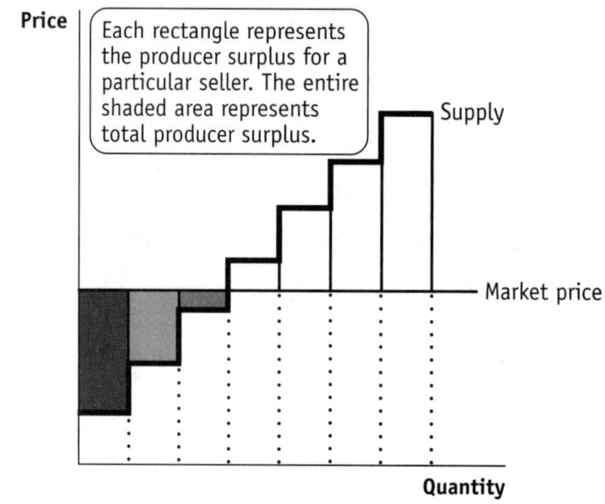

Tip #5. Figure 11.4 illustrates the concept of producer surplus for a smooth supply curve. The area of producer surplus is the shaded region above the supply curve but beneath the market price. The value of producer surplus can be found by calculating the area of this shaded triangle. The producer surplus represents the net gain producers receive from selling the good.

Figure 11.4

Producer Surplus for a Smooth Supply Curve

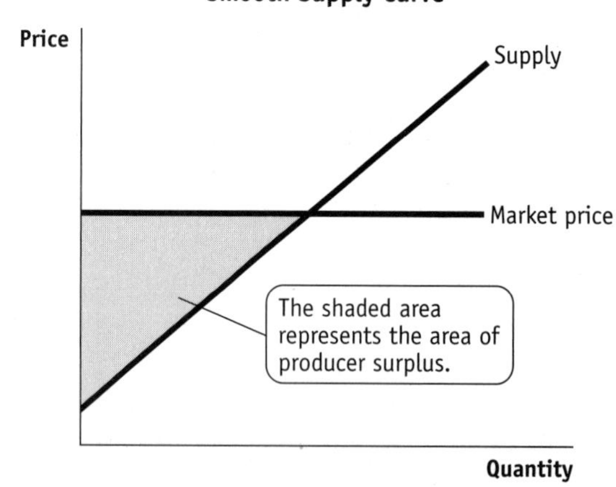

WORKED PROBLEMS

1. Mary is considering opening up a coffee shop and she has contacted three people who live and work near where she would like to open her shop. For each of these three people, she has gotten information about their willingness to buy coffee at her shop. Paul reports that he is willing to pay $4 for a daily cup of coffee. Justina reports that she is willing to pay $3 for a daily cup of coffee. Lee reports that he is willing to pay $5 for a daily cup of coffee. Given the data, determine who values coffee the least. In addition, if Mary decides to price her coffee at $3.50 a cup, how many cups will she sell on a daily basis if her market consists only of Paul, Justina, and Lee? In addition, what will be the value of consumer surplus in this market per day? Finally, construct a step-shaped demand curve illustrating the daily demand for coffee at Mary's coffee shop.

STEP 1: Determine who values coffee the least and provide an explanation for your answer.

The price people are willing to pay for the good tells you the value they place on the good: when individuals willing to pay a high price for the good, then they value the good more than when they are only willing to pay a low price. Given the data, we see that Justina places a lower value on the good than do Lee and Paul.

STEP 2: Draw the step-shaped daily demand curve for coffee at Mary's shop.

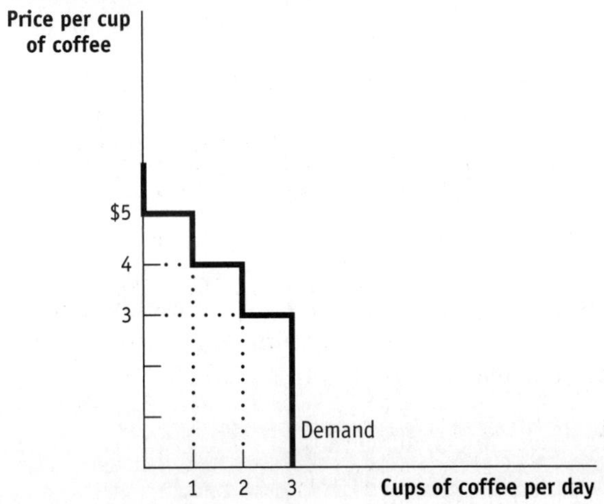

STEP 3: Determine how many cups of coffee Mary will sell daily at her coffee shop if the price of coffee is $3.50 a cup.

To determine how many cups of coffee Mary will sell daily at her coffee shop if the price of a cup of coffee is $3.50, see who is willing to pay at least that amount for a cup of coffee. Clearly Lee is willing to pay $3.50 per cup as is Paul. But Justina is unwilling to pay more than $3 per cup. Mary will be able to sell 2 cups of coffee per day.

STEP 4: Calculate the value of consumer surplus in this market per day if the price of coffee is $3.50 per cup.

First look at the step-shaped demand curve and determine where the area of consumer surplus is on the graph. Once you have found the area of consumer surplus, you can calculate its value. Alternatively, you can find consumer surplus for Lee as the difference between the price he is willing to pay and the price he does pay: in this case, Lee is willing to pay $5 per cup of coffee but he only pays $3.50 per cup, implying that his consumer surplus is equal to $1.50 per cup of coffee. Paul's consumer surplus per cup of coffee is the difference between the $4 per cup he is willing to pay and the $3.50 per cup that he pays: Paul's consumer surplus is equal to $0.50 per cup of coffee. On a daily basis then, the consumer surplus when the price of a cup of coffee is $3.50 is equal to $2.

The shaded area in the following graph depicts the area of consumer surplus.

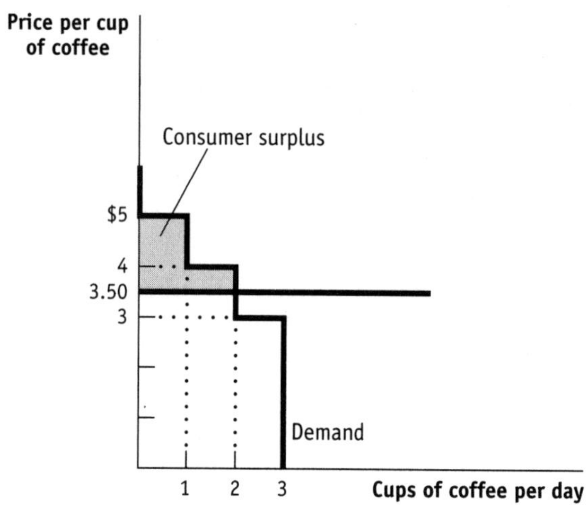

2. Quench City has five beverage companies that provide a similar range of drink options to their customers. Suppose that you are given the following information about the five companies and the lowest prices they are each willing to accept for a case of their beverages in Quench City. Assume that each company has only one case of beverages available to be sold in this market.

Beverage Company	Lowest price the company is willing to accept for a case of beverages
The Sunny Cola	$6
Bubbling Bubbles	4
Cola Cola	7
Peppy Soda	5
Afternoon Delight	4

Create a step-shaped supply curve for this market and then evaluate how many cases of beverages will be sold if the price of a case of beverages is $5.50. In addition, provide a measure of producer surplus when the price of a case of beverages is $5.50. Finally, determine which companies will not sell a case of beverages if the price per case is set at $5.50.

STEP 1: Draw the step-shaped supply curve for the beverage market in Quench City.

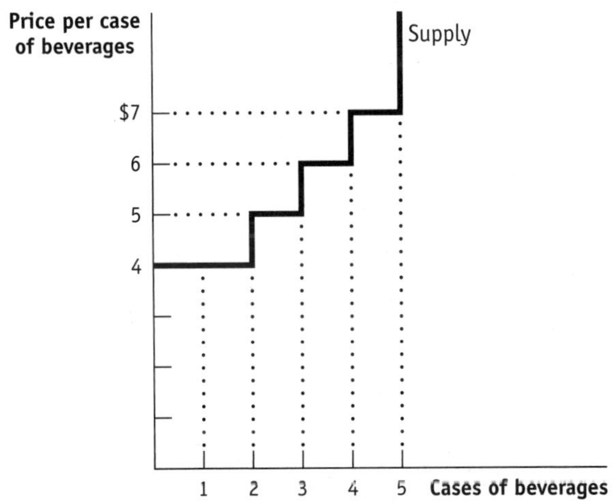

To draw the step-shaped supply curve, start with the lowest price that a company is willing to accept. In this example, both Bubbling Bubbles and Afternoon Delight are willing to sell a case of beverages for $4; the next step is occupied by Peppy Soda, which is willing to sell a case of beverages for $5; the next step is occupied by Sunny Cola, which is willing to sell a case of soda at $6; and the final step is occupied by Cola Cola, which is willing to sell a case of soda at $7.

STEP 2: Calculate the value of producer surplus when the price of a case of beverages is $5.50 in Quench City.

If the price of a case of beverages is $5.50, Sunny Cola and Cola Cola will be unwilling to sell at this price. Thus, we can calculate producer surplus as the difference between the price of $5.50 and the lowest price that the sellers are willing to accept for a case of beverages. Thus, for Afternoon Delight and Bubbling Bubbles, the producer surplus is equal to the difference between $5.50 and the $4 they are willing to accept. Since there are two producers with the same price they are willing to accept, the producer surplus for each of them is $1.50, or a total of $3. The producer surplus for Peppy Soda is the difference between the price of $5 it is willing to accept and the $5.50 it receives when it sells the case of beverages: Peppy Soda has producer surplus of $0.50. Total producer surplus is therefore equal to $3.50 when the price of a case of beverages is $5.50. The shaded area in the following graph depicts the area of producer surplus.

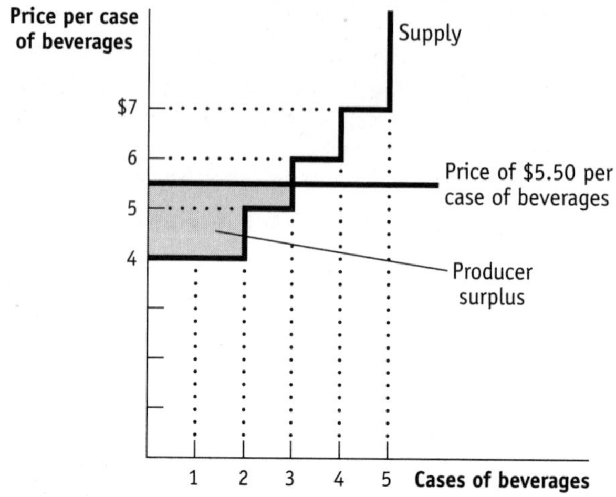

STEP 3: Determine who is willing to sell a case of beverages at $5.50 and who is not willing to sell a case of beverages at $5.50.

When the price of a case of beverages is set at $5.50 per case, Sunny Cola and Cola Cola are unwilling to sell a case since both of these companies are only willing to accept a price that is greater than this. Sunny Cola must get a price of at least $6 per case to sell a case, and Cola Cola must get a price of $7 per case to sell a case.

Problems and Exercises

1. The following table expresses the amount people are willing to pay to buy a new music-playing device. Use this information to answer this series of questions.

Name of person	Price willing to pay
Joe	$100
Mary	200
Lucinda	150
Pete	50
Mario	300

a. Who places the highest value on this good? Explain your answer.

b. Who places the lowest value on this good? Explain your answer.

c. If the good is offered at a price of $100, who would buy it?

d. If the good is offered at a price of $50, who would buy it?

e. Construct a step-shaped demand curve illustrating the demand for a music-playing device for these five consumers.

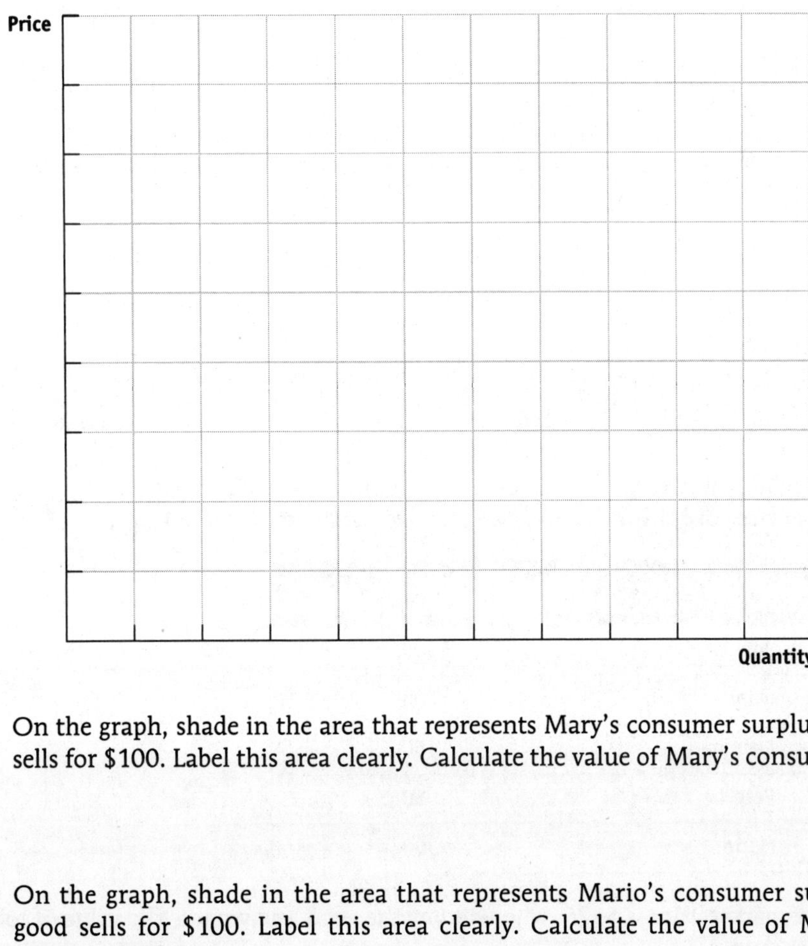

f. On the graph, shade in the area that represents Mary's consumer surplus if the good sells for $100. Label this area clearly. Calculate the value of Mary's consumer surplus.

g. On the graph, shade in the area that represents Mario's consumer surplus if the good sells for $100. Label this area clearly. Calculate the value of Mario's consumer surplus.

h. Create a new graph that is a duplicate of the one you drew for part (e) and shade in the entire area of consumer surplus if the good sells for a price of $100. Calculate the value of consumer surplus at this price.

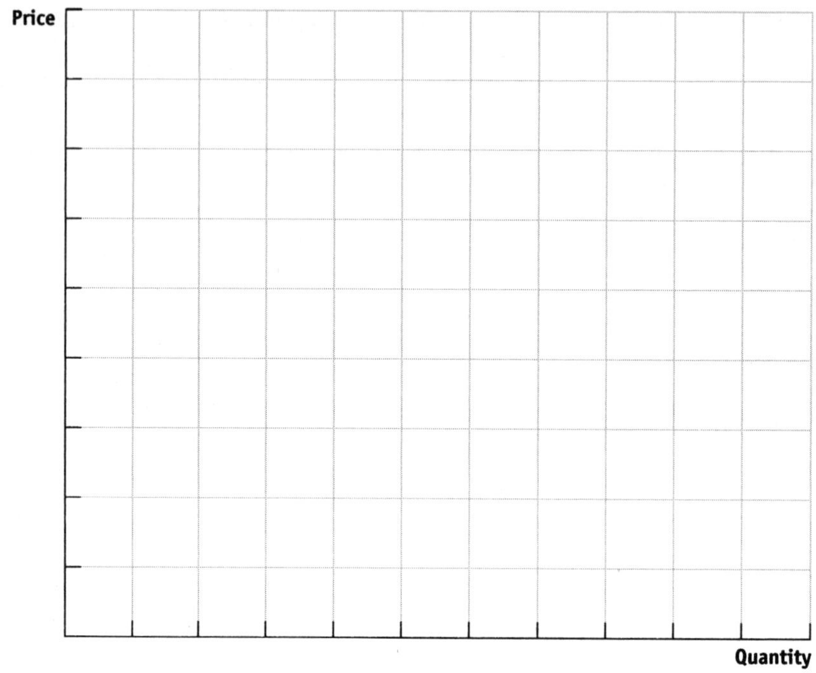

2. The following table expresses the amount people are willing to pay to buy a new music-playing device. Use this information to answer this series of questions.

Name of person	Price willing to pay
Joe	$100
Mary	200
Lucinda	150
Pete	50
Mario	300

a. If the market price is $175, who will buy the good and what is the value of total consumer surplus?

b. Suppose the market price is $175, but a decision is made to allocate the two units of the good that are demanded at that price to Mario and Lucinda. What is the value of total consumer surplus in this case?

c. Why does the reallocation of the good in part (b) reduce the value of consumer surplus? What are the implications of the reduction in consumer surplus that occurs when the good is not allocated to those buyers who place the highest value on the good?

3. Demand for widgets in Marksville is given by the equation $P = 100 - Q$.

a. If the market price of widgets in Marksville is $50, what is the value of consumer surplus in this market?

b. If the market price of widgets in Marksville is $40, what is the value of consumer surplus in this market?

c. For a linear downward-sloping demand curve, what happens to consumer surplus when the market price rises?

d. Suppose the market price of widgets is $30 in Marksville. Will at least 80 widgets be demanded at this price? Explain your answer.

e. Suppose the market price of widgets is $30 in Marksville. Will at least 60 widgets be demanded at this price? Explain your answer.

4. The following table provides a list of sellers of organic apples and the lowest price each seller is willing to accept for a bushel of apples. Assume that each seller will only offer a single bushel of apples for sale. Use this information to answer this series of questions.

Seller	Lowest price seller is willing to accept for a bushel of apples
Ski Top Orchards	$6.00
J. Appleseed's Finest	7.25
Red's Organic	5.80
Pure Apples	8.25
Nature's Medicine	8.00

a. Draw a diagram of this step-shaped supply curve.

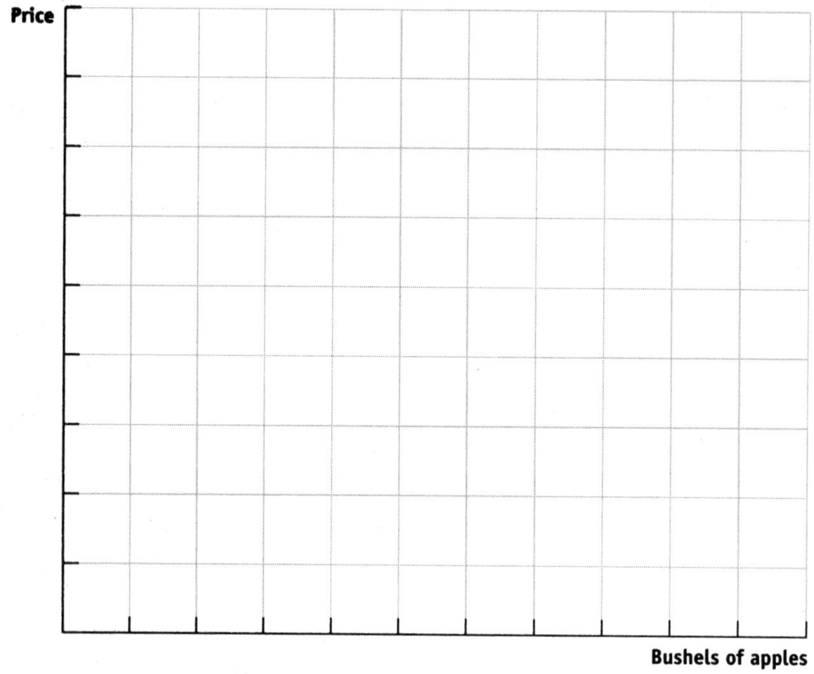

b. If only one bushel of apples is sold, which seller is most likely to make this sale? Explain your answer.

c. If the market price is \$7.50, what is the value of the producer surplus received by J. Appleseed's Finest?

d. If the market price is \$7.50, what is the value of the producer surplus received by Ski Top Orchards?

e. Redraw your sketch from part (a) and indicate the area of total producer surplus in this market if the market price is $7.50. What is the value of this producer surplus?

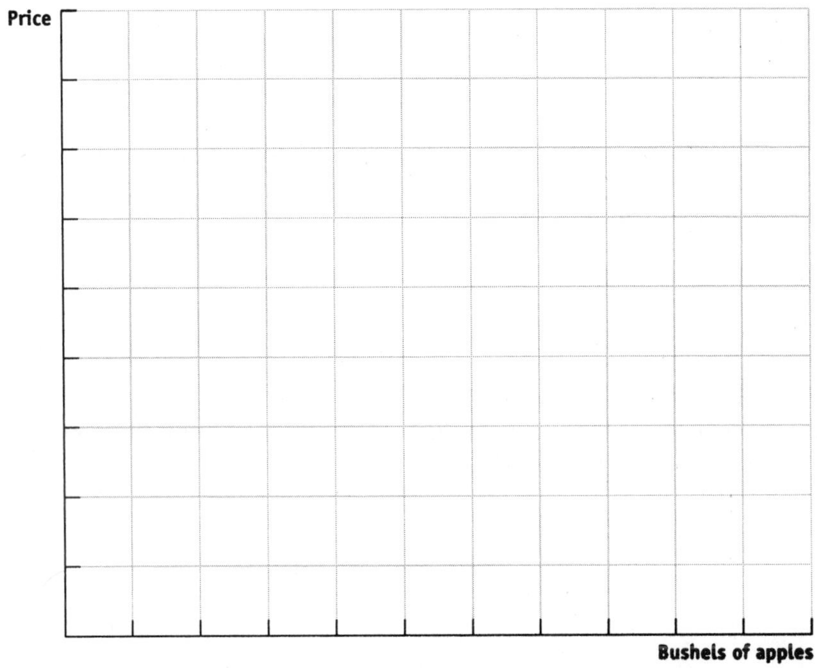

f. Which sellers will sell a bushel of apples in this market if the market price is $7.50?

5. The following table provides a list of sellers of organic apples and the lowest price each seller is willing to accept for a bushel of apples. Assume that each seller will only offer a single bushel of apples for sale. Use this information to answer this series of questions.

Seller	Lowest price seller is willing to accept for a bushel of apples
Ski Top Orchards	$6.00
J. Appleseed's Finest	7.25
Red's Organic	5.80
Pure Apples	8.25
Nature's Medicine	8.00

a. Suppose the market price of apples is $7 a bushel. At this price, which of the above potential sellers will agree to sell a bushel of apples? What is the value of producer surplus when the market price of apples is $7 a bushel?

b. Suppose the market price of apples is \$7 a bushel and that J. Appleseed's Finest is forced to sell a bushel of apples while Ski Top Orchards is forced to not sell a bushel of apples. When we reallocate sales according to this plan, what happens to the value of producer surplus in this market?

c. How does reallocation of sales away from the market-provided allocation alter the value of producer surplus? What implications does this result have if your goal is to maximize producer surplus?

6. Supply of widgets in Marksville is given by the equation $P = 1/3(Q)$.

a. Draw a sketch of this supply curve and then shade in the area of producer surplus if the market price is \$10 per widget.

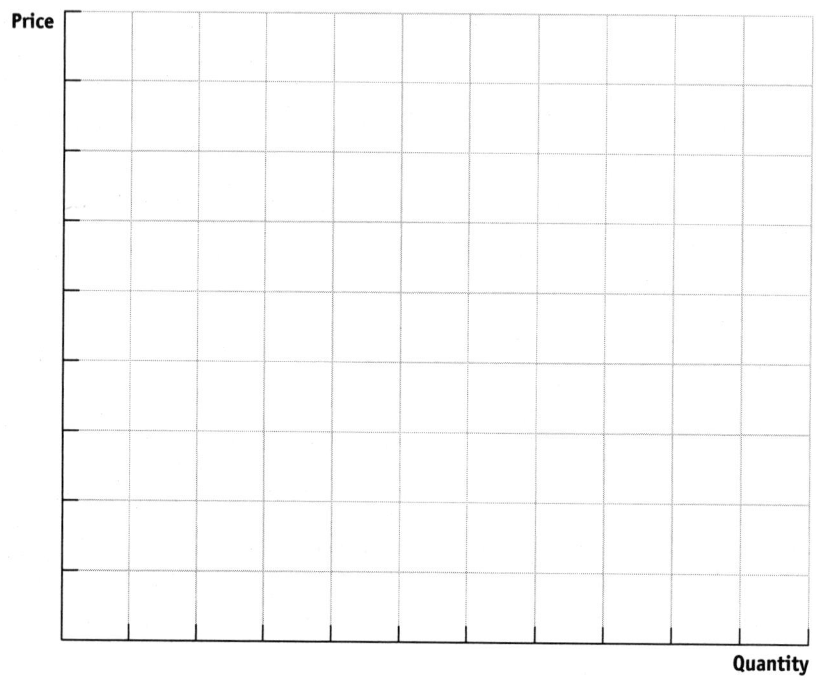

b. If the market price of widgets is \$10, what is the value of producer surplus in this market?

c. If the market price of widgets is \$20, what is the value of producer surplus in this market?

d. For a linear upward-sloping supply curve, what happens to producer surplus when the market price rises because of an increase in demand?

e. Suppose the market price is $30 per widget in Marksville. Will at least 80 widgets be supplied at this price? Explain your answer.

f. Suppose the market price is $30 per widget in Marksville. Will at least 60 widgets be supplied at this price? Explain your answer.

BEFORE YOU TAKE THE TEST

Module Review Questions

1. To answer this question, use the following table that expresses the amount people are willing to pay for a dinner tonight at Fast Eddy's Grill.

Name of consumer	Price willing to pay
Matt	$20
Donovan	15
Savannah	8
Gertrude	12
Anna	7

If a dinner at Fast Eddy's tonight sells for $10, what is the value of Donovan's consumer surplus?

a. $20
b. $15
c. $10
d. $5

2. To answer this question, use the following table that expresses the amount people are willing to pay for a dinner tonight at Fast Eddy's Grill.

Name of consumer	Price willing to pay
Matt	$20
Donovan	15
Savannah	8
Gertrude	12
Anna	7

If a dinner at Fast Eddy's tonight sells for $9, what is the value of the total consumer surplus?

a. $20
b. $15
c. $10
d. $5

3. To answer this question, use the following table that expresses the amount people are willing to pay for a dinner tonight at Fast Eddy's Grill.

Name of consumer	Price willing to pay
Matt	$20
Donovan	15
Savannah	8
Gertrude	12
Anna	7

If a dinner at Fast Eddy's tonight sells for $11, who will not purchase a dinner at this restaurant?

a. Matt
b. Donovan
c. Savannah
d. Gertrude

4. To answer this question, use the following table that expresses the amount people are willing to pay for a dinner tonight at Fast Eddy's Grill.

Name of consumer	Price willing to pay
Matt	$20
Donovan	15
Savannah	8
Gertrude	12
Anna	7

If a dinner at Fast Eddy's tonight costs $4, what is the value of the consumer surplus tonight?

a. $80
b. $42
c. $32
d. $12

5. To answer this question, use the following table that expresses the amount people are willing to pay for a dinner tonight at Fast Eddy's Grill.

Name of consumer	Price willing to pay
Matt	$20
Donovan	15
Savannah	8
Gertrude	12
Anna	7

All five of these consumers want to go out to dinner together at Fast Eddy's tonight. Assuming each consumer pays for his or her own dinner and all dinners cost the same price, what is the maximum price that Fast Eddy can charge for each dinner if they all go out?

a. $5
b. $6
c. $7
d. $8

6. The market demand curve for peanuts in Carterville is given by the equation $P = 1 - 0.001Q$, where price is measured in dollars and peanuts are sold by the bag. If the market price is $0.50 per bag, the quantity demanded will equal _________ bags and the value of consumer surplus will be _________.

a. 5; $125
b. 50; $125
c. 500; $125
d. 5,000; $125

7. The market demand curve for peanuts in Carterville is given by the equation $P = 1 - 0.001Q$, where price is measured in dollars and peanuts are sold by the bag. If the market price is $0.20 per bag, the quantity demanded will equal _________ bags and the value of consumer surplus will be _________.

a. 80; $640
b. 80; $320
c. 800; $640
d. 800; $320

8. For a given linear demand curve, the value of consumer surplus

a. decreases as the market price decreases.
b. decreases as the market price increases.
c. increases as the market price increases.
d. Answers (a) and (c) are possible.

9. For a given linear demand curve, an increase in consumer surplus must be due to a(n)

a. decrease in the market price.
b. increase in the market price.

10. To answer this question, use the following table that expresses the number of dinners Fast Eddy's Grill is willing to prepare tonight at different prices.

Total number of dinners prepared	Price per dinner
1	$ 3
2	6
3	10
4	12
5	15

If a dinner at Fast Eddy's tonight sells for $10, what is the value of Fast Eddy's producer surplus?

a. $11
b. $9
c. $16
d. $19

11. To answer this question, use the following table that expresses the relationship between each dinner and the lowest price Fast Eddy's Grill is willing to accept to prepare that dinner.

	Lowest price Fast Eddy is willing to accept
First dinner	$ 3
Second dinner	6
Third dinner	10
Fourth dinner	12
Fifth dinner	15

If a dinner at Fast Eddy's tonight sells for $13, what is the value of Fast Eddy's producer surplus?

a. $10
b. $17
c. $20
d. $21

12. To answer this question, use the following table that expresses the relationship between each dinner and the lowest price Fast Eddy's Grill is willing to accept to prepare that dinner.

	Lowest price Fast Eddy is willing to accept
First dinner	$ 3
Second dinner	6
Third dinner	10
Fourth dinner	12
Fifth dinner	15

If the price of a dinner at Fast Eddy's tonight is $9, how many dinners will Fast Eddy sell?

a. 1 dinner
b. 2 dinners
c. 3 dinners
d. 4 dinners

13. To answer this question, use the following table that expresses the relationship between each dinner and the lowest price Fast Eddy's Grill is willing to accept to prepare that dinner.

	Lowest price Fast Eddy is willing to accept
First dinner	$ 3
Second dinner	6
Third dinner	10
Fourth dinner	12
Fifth dinner	15

If the price of a dinner at Fast Eddy's tonight is $13, how many dinners will Fast Eddy sell?

a. 1 dinner
b. 2 dinners
c. 3 dinners
d. 4 dinners

14. To answer this question, use the following table that expresses the relationship between each dinner and the lowest price Fast Eddy's Grill is willing to accept to prepare that dinner.

	Lowest price Fast Eddy is willing to accept
First dinner	$ 3
Second dinner	6
Third dinner	10
Fourth dinner	12
Fifth dinner	15

Which of the following dinner prices will lead to Fast Eddy's highest value of producer surplus?

a. $9
b. $10
c. $11
d. $12

ANSWER KEY

Answers to Problems and Exercises

1. **a.** Mario places the highest value on this good, since the $300 he is willing to pay is higher than the price any other consumer in this market is willing to pay.

   b. Pete places the lowest value on this good, since the $50 he is willing to pay is lower than the price any other consumer in this market is willing to pay.

   c. If the good sells for $100, it will be purchased only by those consumers willing to pay $100 or more for the good. At this price Joe, Mary, Lucinda, and Mario will buy the good.

   d. All five consumers would buy the good at this price since their willingness to buy is equal to or greater than $50.

   e.

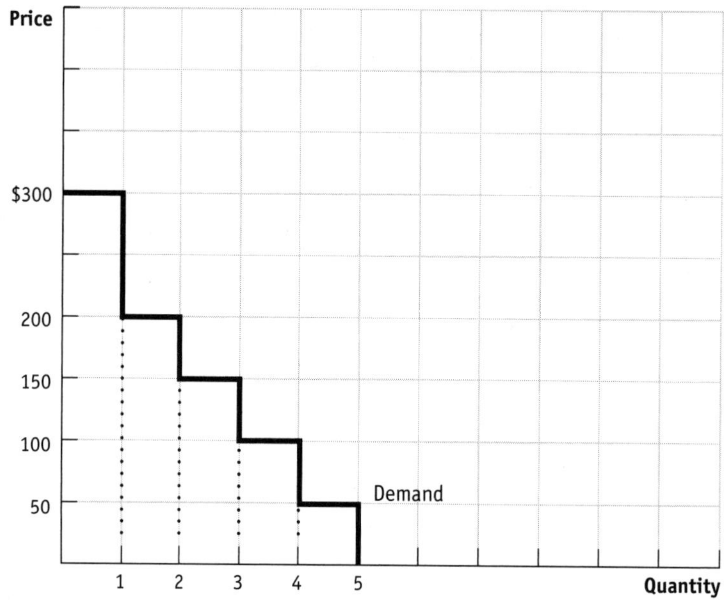

   f. Mary's consumer surplus equals $200 – $100 = $100.

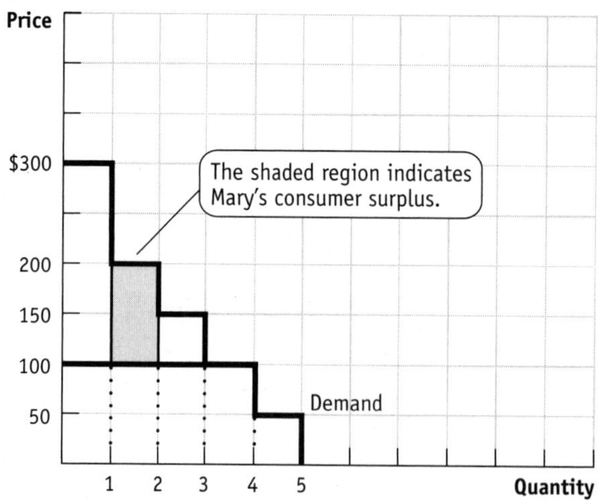

g. Mario's consumer surplus equals \$300 – \$100 = \$200.

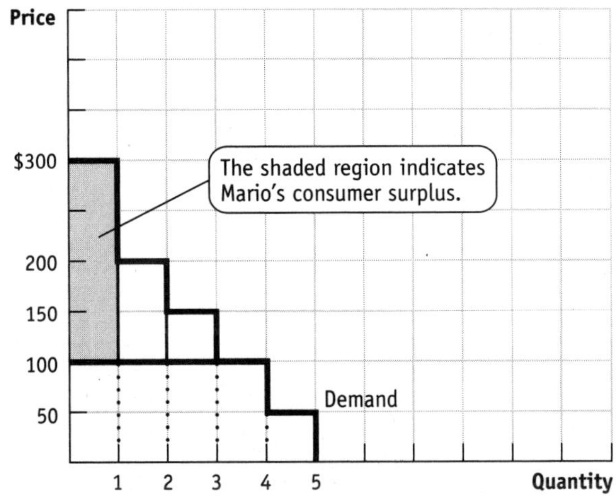

h. Total consumer surplus equals \$350.

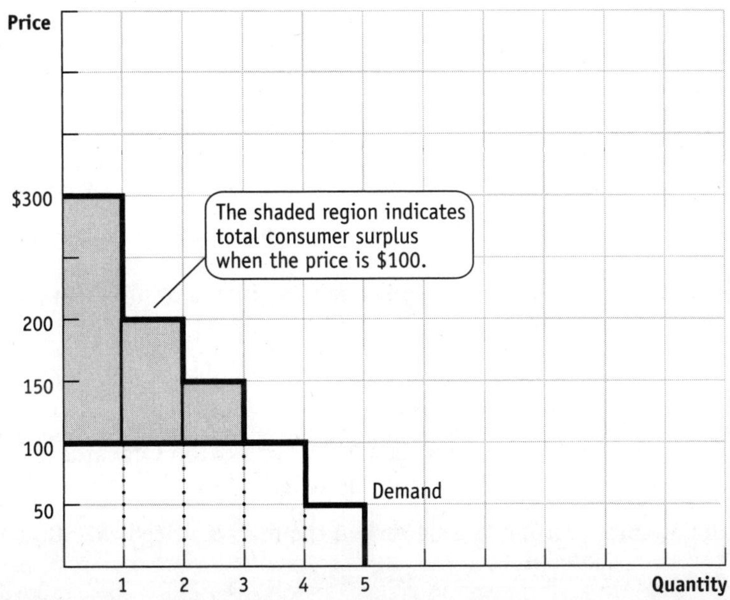

2. a. At a market price of \$175, Mario and Mary will buy the good since they are the only potential consumers who are willing to pay a price that is equal to or greater than the market price. The value of consumer surplus is \$150 (Mario receives consumer surplus of \$125 while Mary receives consumer surplus of \$25).

b. Mario has a consumer surplus of \$300 – \$175, or \$125, while Lucinda's consumer surplus is equal to \$150 – \$175, or –\$25. The total consumer surplus is therefore equal to \$100 when the two units are allocated to Mario and Lucinda.

c. Consumer surplus is reduced when the good is reallocated, because the good goes to consumers who place a lower value on the good. This type of reallocation, away from the market's allocation, results in a failure to maximize consumer surplus.

3. a. When the price of widgets is \$50, the value of consumer surplus is \$1,250. To calculate the value of consumer surplus, you need to find the *y*-intercept of the demand curve (\$100) and the quantity demanded (50 units) when the price is \$50. Since the demand curve is smooth and linear, the value of consumer surplus is equal to the area under the demand curve and above the price: CS = (1/2)(\$100/widget – \$50/widget)(50 widgets) = \$1,250.

b. Use the process outlined in part (a) but with a price of \$40 per widget instead of \$50 per widget: CS = (1/2)(\$100/widget – \$40/widget)(60 widgets) = \$1,800.

c. When the market price rises, the consumer surplus decreases.

d. When the market price of widgets is \$30, only 70 widgets will be demanded. At this price 80 widgets will not be sold.

e. Yes, when the market price is \$30, the demand curve tells us 70 widgets will be demanded.

4. **a.**

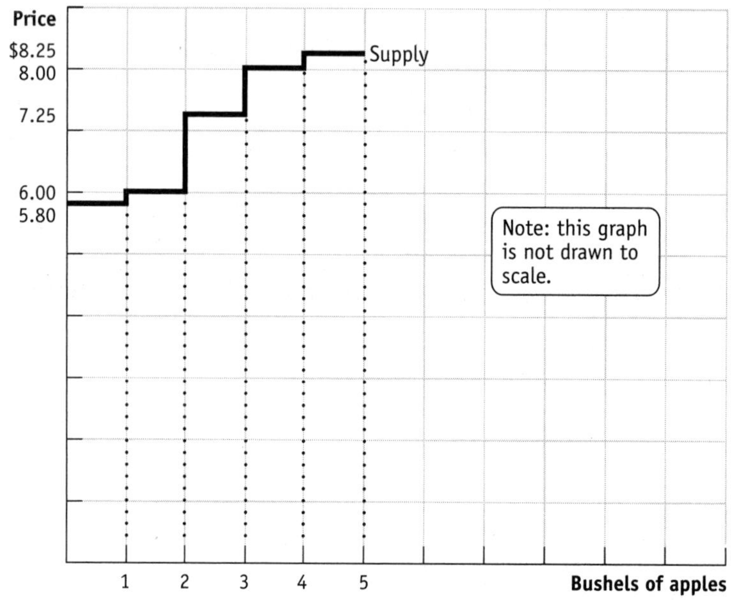

b. Red's Organic is the most likely seller at this quantity since they are willing to accept the lowest price for a bushel of apples.

c. At a price of \$7.50 per bushel, the producer surplus for J. Appleseed's Finest is \$0.25, or the difference between the market price and the seller's cost.

d. At a price of \$7.50 per bushel, the producer surplus for Ski Top Orchards is \$1.50, or the difference between the market price and the seller's cost.

e. The value of the producer surplus is \$3.45 when the market price is \$7.50.

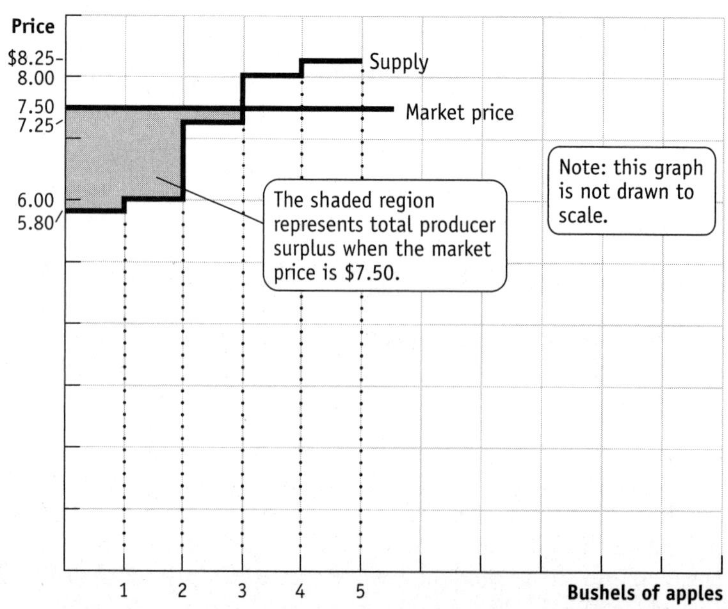

f. Ski Top Orchards, J. Appleseed's Finest, and Red's Organic will each sell a bushel of apples when the market price is $7.50.

5. a. At a price of $7.00 a bushel, Ski Top Orchards and Red's Organic will be willing to sell apples. The value of producer surplus is equal to $1.00 for Ski Top Orchards and $1.20 for Red's Organic, for a total producer surplus of $2.20.

b. When the sales in this market are reallocated away from the market-determined allocation, this reduces total producer surplus. Red's Organic's producer surplus is still equal to $1.20, while J. Appleseed's Finest's producer surplus is equal to $7.00 – $7.25, or –$0.25. Thus, total producer surplus under this reallocation plan equals $0.95.

c. Reallocation of sales away from the market-provided allocation reduces total producer surplus. Producer surplus is maximized when the market allocates sales of the good.

6. a.

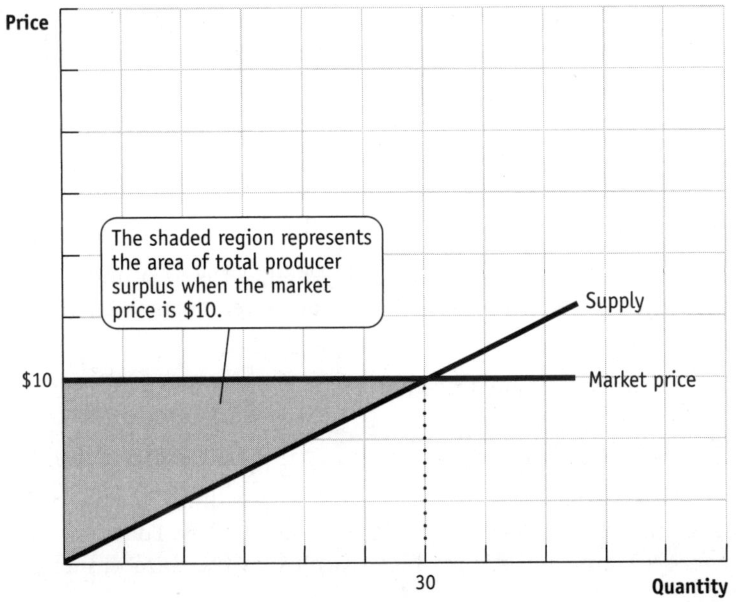

b. The value of producer surplus is equal to the area under the market price and above the supply curve. When the market price is $10, this area of producer surplus equals (1/2)($10/widget)(30 widgets) = $150.

c. When the market price is $20, the value of producer surplus equals (1/2)($20/widget)(60 widgets) = $600.

d. Holding everything else constant, for a linear upward-sloping supply curve, the value of producer surplus increases when the market price increases due to an increase in demand.

e. Yes, at a market price of $30 per widget, 90 widgets will be supplied.

f. Yes, at a market price of $30 per widget, 90 widgets will be supplied.

Answers to Module Review Questions

1. **Answer d.** The value of Donovan's consumer surplus is the difference between the price Donovan is willing to pay ($15) and the market price ($10) of the good.

2. **Answer a.** When the price of a dinner is $9, Matt, Donovan, and Gertrude are willing to purchase a dinner, since the price they are willing to pay is greater than the $9 price. Matt's consumer surplus is equal to $20 – $9, or $11; Donovan's consumer surplus is

equal to \$15 – \$9, or \$6; and Gertrude's consumer surplus is equal to \$12 – \$9, or \$3. Adding these three numbers together gives a total consumer surplus of \$20.

3. **Answer c.** At a price of \$11 per dinner, we know that Savannah and Anna are both unwilling to purchase a dinner since the prices they are willing to pay are less than the \$11 price.

4. **Answer b.** The value of consumer surplus is the difference between the price each consumer is willing to pay and the market price for all those consumers who are willing to purchase a dinner at the current dinner price. Thus, the total value of consumer surplus is equal to \$42.

5. **Answer c.** The maximum price Fast Eddy can charge per dinner is \$7, since this is the highest price that Anna is willing to pay for a dinner. Any price greater than \$7 would eliminate Anna from purchasing a dinner.

6. **Answer c.** To find the quantity demanded at a price of \$0.50 a bag, simply plug \$0.50 into the given demand equation for the price and then solve for the quantity. To find the consumer surplus, you need to calculate the area under the demand curve and above the price of \$0.50. This area is equal to (1/2)(\$1 – \$0.50)(500 – 0), or \$125.

7. **Answer d.** To find the quantity demanded at a price of \$0.20 a bag, simply plug \$0.20 into the given demand equation for the price and then solve for the quantity. To find the consumer surplus, you need to calculate the area under the demand curve and above the price of \$0.20. This area is equal to (1/2)(\$1 – \$0.20)(800 – 0), or \$320.

8. **Answer b.** Since the value of consumer surplus is equal to the area under the demand curve and above the given price, this implies that for any given demand curve an increase in the price will decrease the value of consumer surplus.

9. **Answer a.** This follows from the same reasoning as that given in the answer to question 8.

10. **Answer a.** When a dinner sells for \$10, Fast Eddy will provide 3 dinners. Eddy would have been willing to sell the first dinner for \$3, and thus his producer surplus is equal to \$10 – \$3, or \$7. Fast Eddy would be willing to sell the second dinner for \$6, and thus his producer surplus for this dinner is equal to \$10 – \$6, or \$4. Fast Eddy is willing to sell the third dinner for \$10, and thus his producer surplus on the third dinner is equal to \$0. His total producer surplus is equal to \$11.

11. **Answer d.** To answer this question, use the same reasoning as in question 10. The total producer surplus is equal to \$21.

12. **Answer b.** Fast Eddy is only willing to sell 2 dinners at a price of \$9 per dinner since the third, fourth, and fifth dinners must sell for more than this \$9 price.

13. **Answer d.** Fast Eddy is willing to sell 4 dinners at a price of \$13. He is unwilling to sell the fifth dinner since he must receive at least \$15 to be willing to provide this dinner.

14. **Answer d.** Fast Eddy will have the greatest producer surplus at a dinner price of \$12. When the price is \$11, his producer surplus is equal to \$14, and when the price is \$12, his producer surplus is equal to \$17.

module 12

Efficiency and Markets

BEFORE YOU READ THE MODULE

Summary

This module develops the concept of total surplus and its relationship to the demand and supply model. It then uses this concept to show how efficiency in markets can be illustrated. The module also discusses why markets typically work so well and why markets sometimes fail to work well.

Module Objectives

Objective #1. Total surplus is the sum of consumer and producer surplus. At the market equilibrium, total surplus is maximized: the market equilibrium allocates the consumption of the good among potential consumers and the sales of the good among potential sellers in order to achieve the maximum possible gains to society. In a well-functioning market, total surplus cannot be increased by reallocating consumption among consumers, reallocating sales among sellers, or by changing the quantity traded. In fact, each of these actions diminishes the level of total surplus in the market.

- Preventing a sale in a market that would have taken place in equilibrium reduces both consumer and producer surplus, resulting in a loss of total surplus. Increasing sales beyond the equilibrium quantity similarly reduces consumer surplus, producer surplus, and total surplus, since such a sale would represent a situation where the buyer's willingness to buy must be less than the seller's cost.

Objective #2. Total surplus is maximized at the market equilibrium: (a) the market allocates consumption of the good to those potential consumers who place the highest value on the good; (b) the market allocates sales of the good to those sellers who have the lowest cost of producing the good; (c) the market ensures that any purchase represents a situation where the buyer values the good more than the seller values the good; and (d) the market ensures that no sales are made in which the seller values the good more than the purchaser does. Markets are efficient when total surplus is maximized.

- Even though the market equilibrium maximizes total surplus, this does not imply that it maximizes the outcome for any individual buyer or seller. Subsequent modules consider situations of market intervention where individual buyers or sellers are made better off than they would be at the market equilibrium.

Objective #3. Markets can fail to achieve efficient outcomes under certain circumstances. If the market is served by a single seller of the good, the market will not produce the efficient level of output. If the market fails to take into account the side effects of a transaction on the welfare of others, the market will fail to produce the efficient level of output. Finally, some goods are unsuited for efficient management by markets. The text introduces these ideas but will develop them more fully in subsequent modules.

Key Terms

Notes

total surplus the total net gain to consumers and producers from trading in a market; the sum of the *producer surplus* and the *consumer surplus.*

property rights the rights of owners of valuable items, whether resources or goods, to dispose of those items as they choose.

economic signal any piece of information that helps people make better economic decisions.

inefficient characterized by missed opportunities: some people could be made better off without making other people worse off.

market failure lack of efficiency in a market.

AFTER YOU READ THE MODULE

Tips

Tip #1. Figures 12.1 and 12.2 illustrate total surplus, which is the sum of consumer surplus and producer surplus. Figure 12.1 illustrates this concept for step-shaped demand and supply curves, and Figure 12.2 illustrates this concept for smooth demand and supply curves.

Figure 12.1 Total Surplus for Step-Shaped Demand and Supply Curves

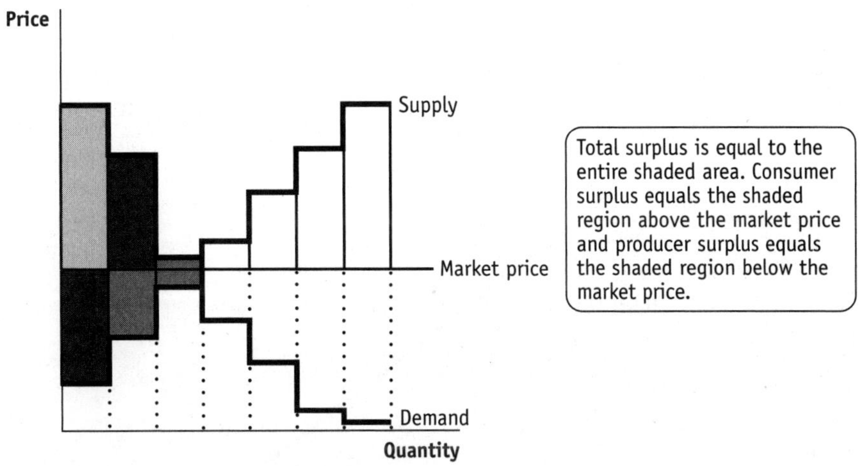

Figure 12.2 Total Surplus for Smooth Demand and Supply Curves

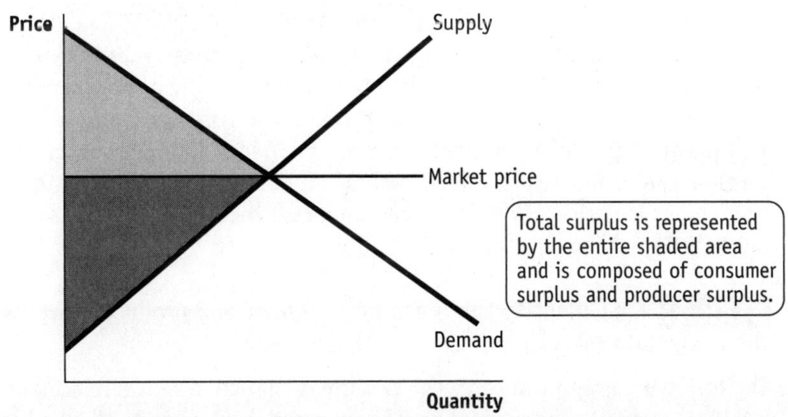

Tip #2. If you are using flash cards, make sure you make up a set with this module's new vocabulary and concepts. Review all of your flash cards on a regular basis to make sure you are not forgetting any terms or concepts.

WORKED PROBLEMS

1. Metrocity employed a consulting firm to determine what the demand for and supply of mass transit were for their community. The consultants came back and provided Metrocity with the following graph of the monthly mass transit market in their community.

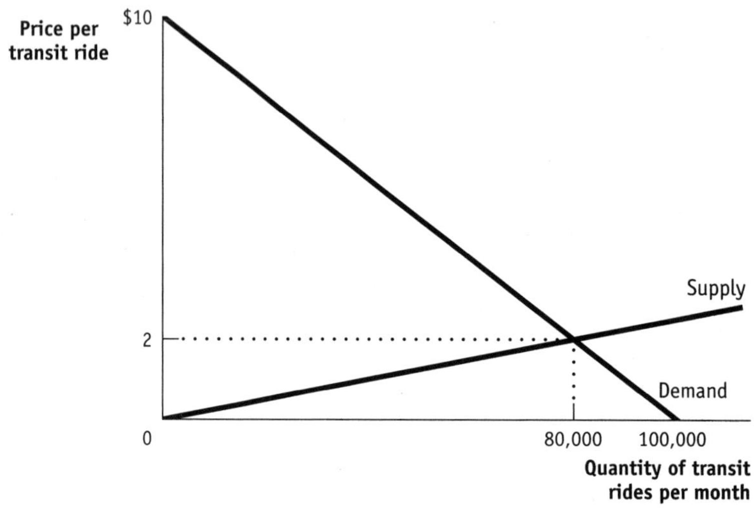

In the preceding graph, indicate the areas that correspond to consumer surplus and producer surplus and then calculate the numeric value of consumer surplus, producer surplus, and total surplus in this market. Metrocity is contemplating raising transit fares to $5. How would this policy change affect consumer surplus, producer surplus, and total surplus? Provide both a verbal explanation of the effect as well as numeric calculations. Would a fare increase increase or decrease efficiency in this market? Explain your answer. Does anyone benefit from a fare increase?

STEP 1: First identify the areas of consumer and producer surplus on the graph. Then calculate the value of each of these areas.

The following graph indicates the two areas that correspond to consumer surplus and producer surplus. The sum of these two areas is equal to total surplus.

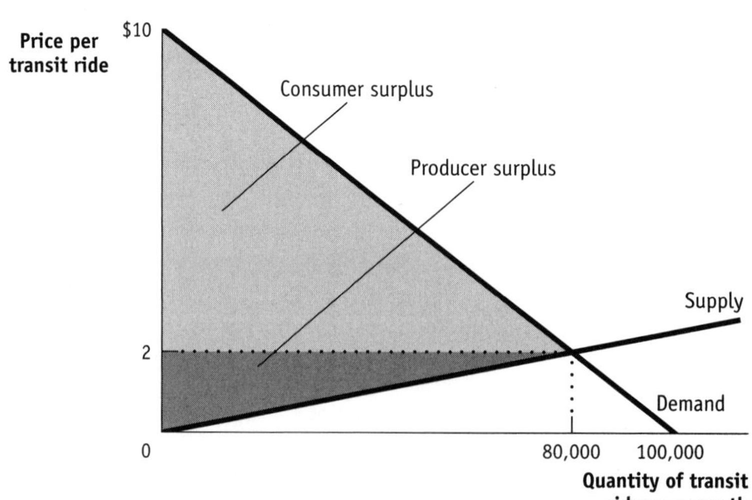

The area of consumer surplus corresponds to that area that is beneath the demand curve but above the price consumers pay for the good. In this case, consumers pay \$2 per transit ride and they demand 80,000 transit rides per month. Consumer surplus is equal to (1/2)(\$10 per ride – \$2 per ride)(80,000 rides per month) = \$320,000 per month. The area of producer surplus corresponds to that area that is above the supply curve but beneath the price producers receive when they sell the good. In this case, producers sell each transit ride for \$2 and they supply 80,000 transit rides per month. Producer surplus is equal to (1/2)(\$2 per ride – \$0 per ride)(80,000 rides per month) = \$80,000 per month. Total surplus is equal to the sum of consumer surplus and producer surplus in this example: total surplus = \$320,000 + \$80,000 = \$400,000.

STEP 2: Consider how a price increase will affect consumers and suppliers in this market. Provide a non-numerical analysis of the effect of this price increase.

In general, a price increase will decrease the area of consumer surplus and increase the area of producer surplus for a given demand curve and supply curve. To see this, let's consider what happens to these areas if the price was to change. In the following figure, we replicate the figure from Step 1 but raise the price.

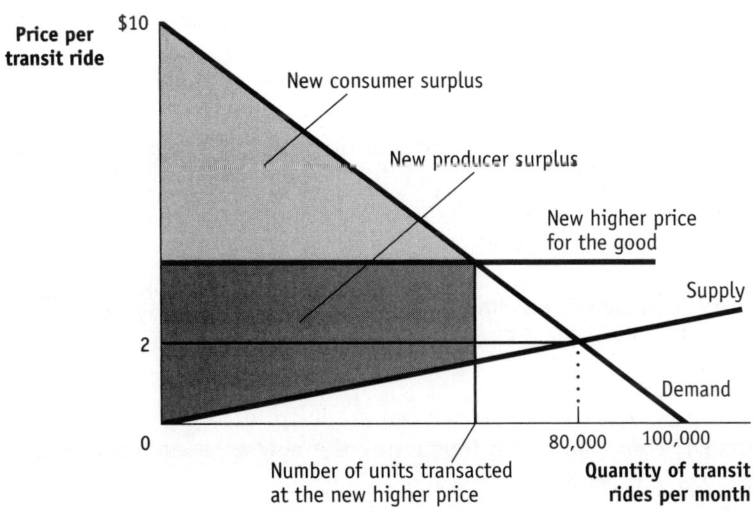

If we compare the figure from Step 1 with the preceding figure, what we see is the area of consumer surplus shrinks when the price in the market is increased: this is due to fewer transactions being made and each transaction occurring at a higher price. Consumers receive less consumer surplus. Comparing the two figures also reveals that producer surplus increases when the price is raised: producers capture some of the consumers' initial surplus. If you compare the two figures—you will note that there is an area that is shaded in the first figure but not shaded in the second figure: this area is composed of two parts—the loss in consumer surplus that occurs because consumers purchase fewer units and the loss in producer surplus that occurs because producers sell fewer units.

STEP 3: Calculate how many transit rides demanders will demand if the price of transit rides increases to \$5 per transit ride. Calculate how many transit rides suppliers will supply if the price of transit rides increases to \$5 per transit ride.

This step requires that you find the equations for the demand and supply curves and then use these equations to find the quantity demanded and supplied at a price of $5 per transit tickets.

Let's start with the demand equation. From the provided graph, we know that the y-intercept is $10 and that the point (100,000) sits on the line. Using this information and the slope intercept form, we can write the equation for the demand curve. The general slope intercept form is $Y = mX + b$. We know that b, the y-intercept, is equal to $10. Thus, $Y = mX + 10$. We also know that price (P) is the variable measured on the y-axis and quantity demanded (Q_d) is the variable measured on the x-axis. Thus, $P = mQ_d + 10$. Now, all we need is the slope, m. From the graph, we can measure the rise as 10 and the run as −100,000: thus, slope = rise/run = 10/(−100,000) = −1/10,000. The equation for the demand curve is $P = (-1/10{,}000)Q_d + 10$. When price is $5 per transit ticket that implies that $Q_d = 50{,}000$ transit tickets.

To find the supply equation, note that on the provided graph the supply curve is linear and goes through two points: $(Q_s, P) = (0, 0)$ and (80,000, 2). Use this information and the general equation in slope intercept form to find the equation for the supply curve. Thus, $Y = mX + b$ can be rewritten as $P = mQ_s + 0$ since the y-intercept is 0 and the x-axis and y-axis are Q_s and P, respectively. Since we have two points on the linear supply curve, we can write the slope as the (change in y)/(change in x) or (0 − 2)/(0 − 80,000) = 1/40,000. Thus, the supply equation is $P = (1/40{,}000)Q_s$. When price is $5 per transit ticket that implies that $Q_s = 200{,}000$ transit tickets.

Since the quantity demanded is less than the quantity supplied, at a price of $5 per transit ticket the market is not at its equilibrium. If the price is raised to $5 per transit ticket, 50,000 transit tickets will be sold and the remaining 150,000 transit tickets producers are willing to supply at that price will not be purchased.

STEP 4: Calculate the value of consumer surplus and producer surplus with the increase in the price of transit rides. Sum these two values to get the new total surplus value.

From our work in Step 3, we are ready to edit our graph from Step 2 by adding the numbers we calculated. Thus, our graph illustrating the new areas of producer and consumer surplus looks like the following graph.

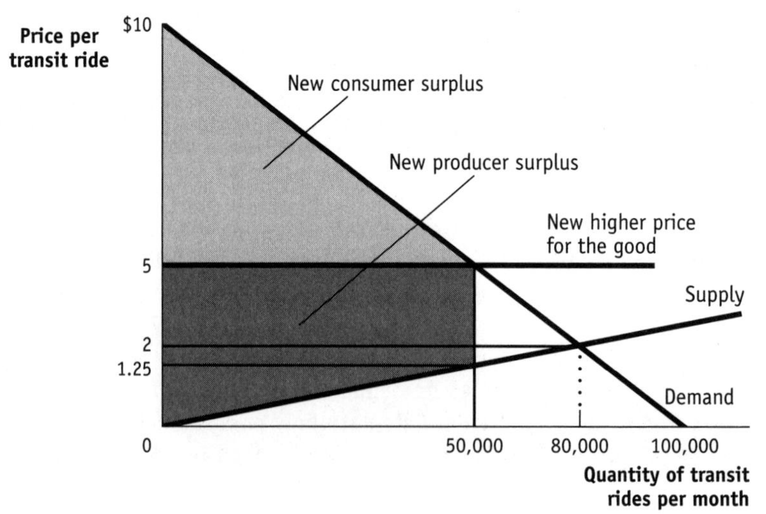

If you closely examine the preceding graph, you will realize that we need one more number: the price that corresponds to a quantity of 50,000 tickets on the supply curve. That is, we need to know the price that suppliers must receive to be willing to supply 50,000 tickets. Since we have the supply equation, it is a relatively simple matter to substitute 50,000 for Q_S and then solve for *P*. Thus, $P = (1/40{,}000)(50{,}000) =$ \$1.25 per ticket.

Now that we have all the numbers we need, it is a relatively easy proposition to calculate the areas of the new consumer surplus and new producer surplus. The area of consumer surplus is equal to (1/2)(\$10 per ticket – \$5 per ticket)(50,000 tickets) = \$125,000. The area of producer surplus is more difficult to calculate: it is the sum of the area of a rectangle and the area of a triangle. Thus, producer surplus is equal to (\$5 per ticket – \$1.25 per ticket)(50,000 tickets) + (1/2)(\$1.25 per ticket)(50,000) or (\$3.75 per ticket)(50,000 tickets) + (\$1.25 per ticket)(25,000 tickets), which is equal to \$187,500 (the part of consumer surplus captured by producers) + \$31,250 for a total of \$218,750.

STEP 5: Compare the initial total surplus when transit rides were \$2 per ride to the value of total surplus when transit rides are \$5 per ride. Relate this comparison to market efficiency.

Total surplus when the price of transit tickets is equal to \$2 per ticket is \$400,000 (review Step 1 to see where we got this amount). Total surplus when the price of transit tickets is equal to \$5 per ticket is equal to the sum of producer surplus and consumer surplus at that price; total surplus when the price of transit tickets is equal to \$5 is equal to \$343,750. Total surplus is smaller when the price is raised above the market-clearing price. This indicates a loss of efficiency: the loss of efficiency reflects how the increase in price prevents mutually beneficial trades from occurring. Rather than selling 80,000 tickets at a price of \$2 per ticket, the increase in the price of tickets to \$5 eliminates the purchase of 30,000 tickets.

Study the diagrams that have been provided in this discussion to see if you can see where the loss in consumer and producer surplus of \$56,250 (the difference between the original total surplus of \$400,000 and the new total surplus of \$343,750) is in the graph.

STEP 6: Compare the initial level of consumer surplus and producer surplus to the new levels of consumer surplus and producer surplus to determine if consumers or producers benefit from an increase in mass transit fares.

The initial level of consumer surplus is equal to \$320,000, while the level of consumer surplus after the increase in the price of transit tickets is equal to \$125,000. Consumer surplus decreases when Metrocity raises the price of transit tickets, holding everything else constant.

The initial level of producer surplus is equal to \$80,000, while the level of producer surplus after the increase in the price of transit tickets is equal to \$218,750. Producer surplus increases when Metrocity raises the price of transit tickets, holding everything else constant.

Transit producers will be in favor of a fare increase, while transit consumers will be against a fare increase. Total surplus from the consumption of transit services is maximized at the market-clearing price of \$2 per transit ticket.

Problems and Exercises

1. Demand for widgets in Marksville is given by the equation $P = 100 - Q$, while the supply of widgets is given by the equation $P = 1/3(Q)$.

a. Draw a sketch of the demand and supply curves and mark the equilibrium price and the equilibrium quantity. Solve the two equations for the specific equilibrium price and equilibrium quantity.

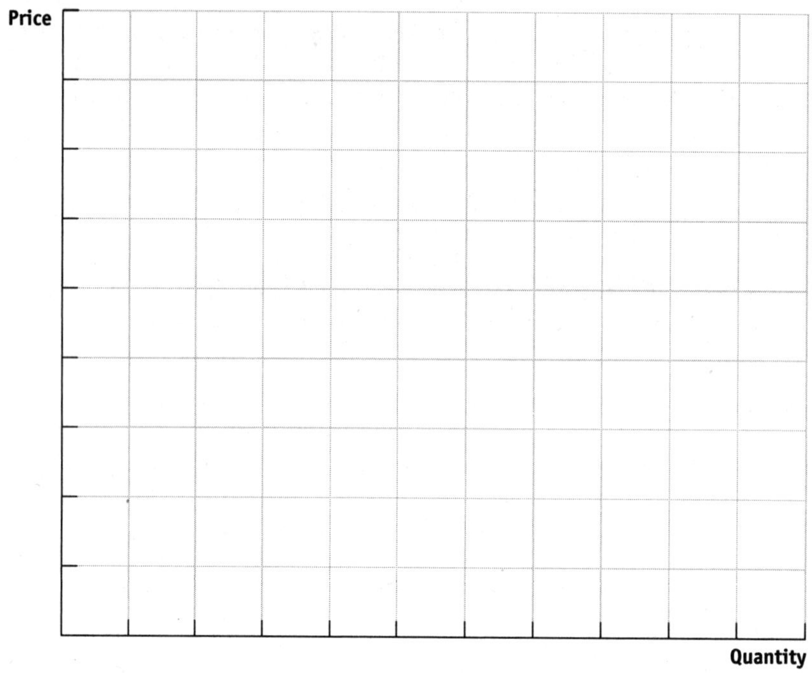

b. On the graph identify the areas of producer surplus and consumer surplus. Calculate a numeric value for each of these areas.

c. What is the value of total surplus in the market for widgets?

d. Suppose that the price of an input in the production of widgets increases so that supply is affected and changes by 60 units. Draw a new graph indicating the changes in the market for widgets due to this input price change. Label the new equilibrium price and equilibrium quantity as well as the initial equilibrium price and quantity.

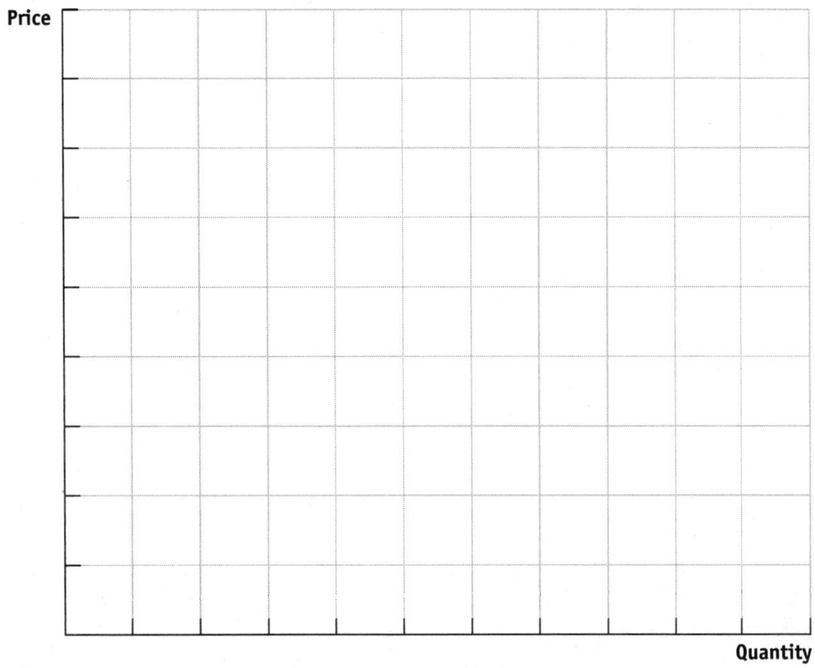

e. On the graph you drew for part (d), label the areas that correspond to producer and consumer surplus. Calculate a numeric value for consumer surplus and producer surplus. (Hint: When you calculate these values, use the graph you have drawn to guide the math steps you need to take to compute these areas.) Compare your answers in part (e) to your answers in part (b).

f. What happened to total surplus in the market for widgets when input prices increased?

2. George is considering the purchase of some new shirts for work. He is willing to pay $35 for the first shirt, $25 for the second shirt, and $15 for the third. Oxford Clothiers, his favorite shirt manufacturer, currently is selling shirts for $28 a shirt. What is the efficient number of shirts for George to buy? What is George's consumer surplus in this situation? Explain your answers.

BEFORE YOU TAKE THE TEST

Module Review Questions

1. Use the following graph to answer this question.

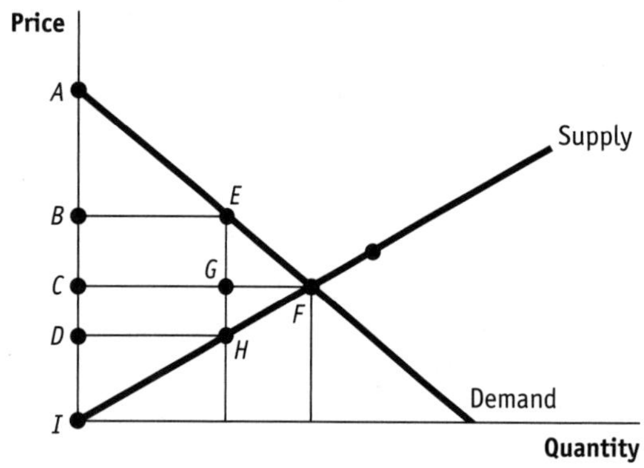

When this market is in equilibrium, consumer surplus is equal to area

a. *AEB.*
b. *EFG.*
c. *ACF.*
d. *CFI.*

2. Use the graph in question 1 to answer this question. When this market is in equilibrium, producer surplus is equal to area

a. *BEGC.*
b. *GFH.*
c. *DHI.*
d. *CFI.*

3. Use the graph in question 1 to answer this question. When this market is in equilibrium, total surplus is equal to area

a. *AFI.*
b. *BEFHD.*
c. *BEHD.*
d. *EFH.*

4. Which of the following statements is true?

I. In a well-functioning market, each transaction that occurs represents a situation in which the value the buyer places on the good is greater than or equal to the value that the seller of the good places on the good.
II. In a well-functioning market, all trades are mutually beneficial.
III. In any well-functioning market situation, it is possible to reallocate sales so as to increase total surplus.

a. Statement I is true.
b. Statement II is true.
c. Statements I and II are true.
d. Statements I, II, and III are true.

5. In a well-functioning market

a. any reallocation of the good or service away from the market equilibrium necessarily increases total surplus.

b. any purchase that does not occur must be because the value the potential consumer places on the good exceeds the value the potential seller places on the good.

c. any purchase that does not occur must be because the value the potential seller places on the good exceeds the value the potential consumer places on the good.

d. consumers who place the lowest value on the good are the first ones able to consume the good.

6. The concept of producer surplus illustrates the idea that the market works to allocate sales to

a. potential sellers who most value the right to sell the good, as indicated by their ability to produce the good at lowest cost.

b. potential consumers who most value the right to consume the good, as indicated by their willingness to purchase the good at the highest price.

ANSWER KEY

Answers to Problems and Exercises

1. a.

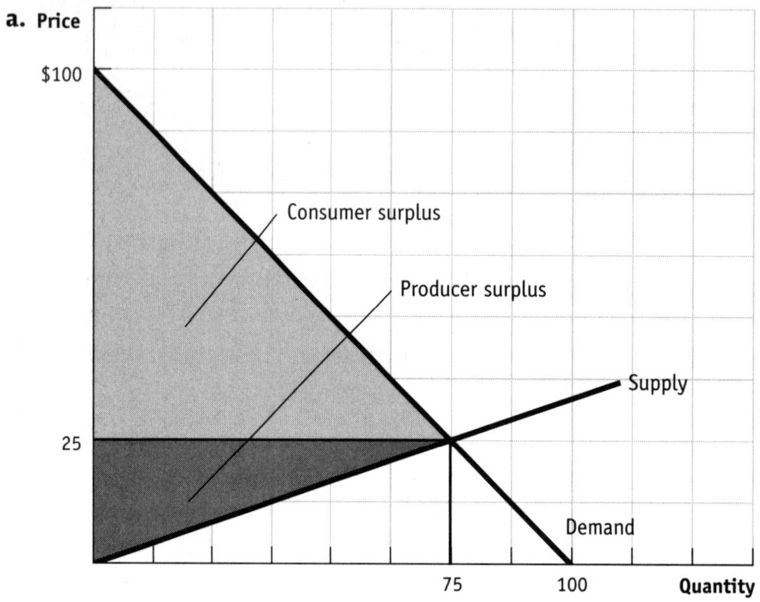

Since demand equals supply in equilibrium, we know 100 – Q = (1/3)Q. Solving for Q, we find that the equilibrium quantity equals 75 widgets and the equilibrium price is $25.

b. Consumer surplus equals (1/2)($100/widget – $25/widget)(75 widgets) = $2,812.50. Producer surplus equals (1/2)($25/widget – $0/widget)(75 widgets) = $937.50.

c. The value of total surplus in this market equals the sum of producer and consumer surplus, or $3,750.00. Alternatively, you can calculate this area as follows: TS = (1/2)($100/widget – $0/widget)(75 widgets) = $3,750.00.

d.

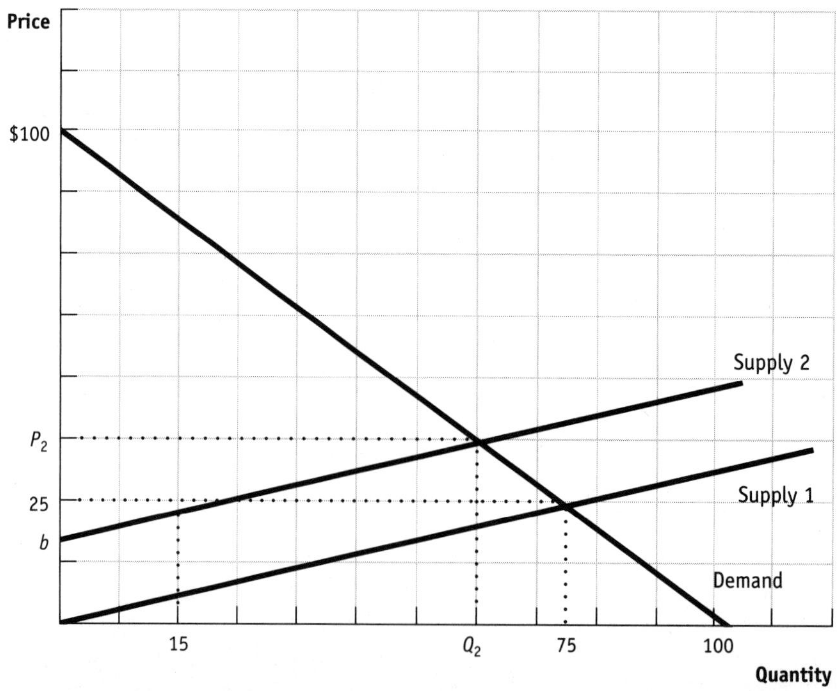

An increase in the price of an input causes the supply curve to shift to the left. In this example, the supply curve shifts to the left by a horizontal distance of 60 units. This tells us that if suppliers initially offered 75 units at a price of $25 per widget, they will now offer 15 widgets at a price of $25 per widget. This leftward shift in the supply curve causes the equilibrium price to rise from $25 to P_2 and the equilibrium quantity to decrease from 75 widgets to Q_2.

e.

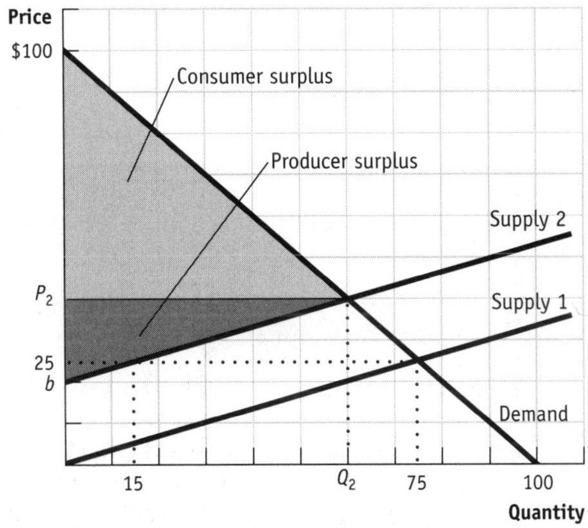

The calculation of consumer surplus and producer surplus is challenging in this problem. You need to write an equation for the new supply curve and then use this new equation with the original demand curve to calculate the numeric values of Q_2 and P_2. The new supply curve has the same slope as the original supply curve, but it has a different y-intercept. We can rewrite the new supply curve as $P = (1/3)Q + b$ and then substitute the coordinates (15, 25) into this equation to find the value of b. When you do this, you find that b, the y-intercept, has a value of 20. Thus, the new supply curve is $P = (1/3)Q + 20$. Using the new supply curve and the original demand curve, we can find Q_2 and P_2: $100 - Q = (1/3)Q + 20$, or $Q_2 = 60$ widgets and $P_2 = \$40$. To find consumer surplus, we calculate the area of the shaded region marked "consumer surplus" in the above figure: CS = (1/2)($100/widget – $40/widget)(60 widgets) = $1,800. To find producer surplus, we calculate the area of the shaded region marked "producer surplus" in the above figure: $PS = (1/2)(P_2 - b)(Q_2$ widgets$)$ = (1/2)($40/widget – $20/widget)(60 widgets) = $600. Both consumer and producer surplus are decreased when the price of an input increases.

f. Total surplus in the market initially was equal to $3,750. When input prices increased, total surplus decreased to $2,400.

2. George will purchase one shirt since the price he is willing to pay for that shirt ($35) is greater than or equal to the price Oxford Clothiers must receive ($28) to be willing to sell the shirt. George will receive a consumer surplus of $7 when he purchases this shirt. George will not purchase two shirts since the value of the second shirt from George's perspective ($25) is less than the seller's price ($28).

Answers to Module Review Questions

1. Answer c. Consumer surplus is equal to the area under the demand curve and above the equilibrium price. Since the equilibrium price is equal to C in the graph, this implies that the area of consumer surplus is equal to area *ACF*.

2. Answer d. Producer surplus is equal to the area above the supply curve and below the equilibrium price, which is area *CFI* in the graph.

3. **Answer a.** Total surplus is the sum of consumer and producer surplus, which is equal to area *AFI*.

4. **Answer c.** In a well-functioning market the equilibrium provides the maximum total surplus, and it is impossible in a well-functioning market to reallocate sales so as to increase total surplus. Statements I and II are fairly transparent, straightforward, and true while statement III is false.

5. **Answer c.** In a well-functioning market, the equilibrium provides the maximum total surplus. Hence, answer (a) is not true. Purchases of a good in a well-functioning market imply that the value the consumer places on the good is greater than or equal to the value that the producer places on the good; hence, answer (b) is not true. Answer (d) is untrue: consumers who place the lowest value on the good are not the first consumers to get the good, and the consumers willing to pay the highest price for the good are the first consumers of the good. Answer (c) is true: producers will not sell the good if the value they place on the good is greater than the value consumers have for the good.

6. **Answer a.** Producer surplus measures the difference between the price producers are willing to accept for the good and the market price. Answer (b) is not true because it is focused on consumers.

module 13

Price Controls (Ceilings and Floors)

BEFORE YOU READ THE MODULE

Summary

This module develops the ideas of price controls in competitive markets and then illustrates how the implementation of these controls reduces the efficiency of a market. In particular, the module discusses effective price ceilings, whereby the government sets the price of the good below the equilibrium price; and effective price floors, whereby the government sets the price of the good above the equilibrium price. The module also discusses the distributional impact of price controls.

Module Objectives

Objective #1. Price controls refer to the government's intervention in a market to set the price of the good or service at some level other than the equilibrium price. A price ceiling is the maximum price allowed by the government for a good or service, and a price floor is the minimum price allowed by the government for a good or service.

Objective #2. An effective price ceiling in a competitive market creates a situation of excess quantity demanded. If the price ceiling is set above the equilibrium price in the market, the price ceiling will not be effective and therefore will have no effect on the equilibrium price and the equilibrium quantity in the market.

Objective #3. An effective price ceiling prevents a market from being efficient because the price ceiling prevents transactions from occurring that would make some people better off without making other people worse off. In particular, an effective price ceiling prevents demanders who are willing to pay more for the good from consuming the good since the good's supply is artificially limited by the imposed price ceiling. Inefficiency arises because the price ceiling:

- reduces the quantity of the good available;
- reduces the value of total surplus;
- misallocates the good or service among consumers;
- wastes resources, as consumers spend resources searching for the good that is artificially scarce due to the price ceiling; and
- reduces the quality of the available units that would have been supplied in the absence of the price ceiling.

Objective #4. Price ceilings provide incentives for illegal activities. Price ceilings are primarily instituted because they benefit some particular group of demanders.

Objective #5. An effective price floor in a competitive market creates a situation of excess quantity supplied. If the price floor is set below the equilibrium price in the market, the price floor will have no effect on the equilibrium price and the equilibrium quantity in the market.

Objective #6. An effective price floor results in market inefficiency because it prevents transactions from occurring that would make some people better off without making other people worse off. In particular, an effective price floor prevents suppliers who are willing to supply the good from selling the good since the good's demand is artificially limited by the imposed price floor. Inefficiency arises because the price floor:

- reduces the quantity of the good demanded;
- reduces the value of total surplus;
- misallocates the provision of the good or service by sellers;
- wastes resources, as suppliers search the market for a potential demander of the good; and
- increases the quality of the available units above the level that would have been demanded in the absence of the price floor.

Objective #7. Price floors provide an incentive for illegal or black market activities, including the bribery and corruption of government officials. Price floors are primarily instituted because they benefit a particular group of sellers.

Key Terms

price controls legal restrictions on how high or low a market price may go.

price ceiling a maximum price sellers are allowed to charge for a good or service; a form of *price control.*

price floor a minimum price buyers are required to pay for a good or service; a form of *price control.*

inefficient allocation to consumers a form of inefficiency in which people who want the good and are willing to pay a high price don't get it, and those who care relatively little about the good and are only willing to pay a low price do get it; often a result of a *price ceiling.*

wasted resources a form of inefficiency in which people expend money, effort, and time to cope with the shortages caused by a *price ceiling.*

Notes

Key Terms *(continued)*

inefficiently low quality a form of inefficiency in which sellers offer low-quality goods at a low price even though buyers would prefer a higher quality at a higher price; often a result of a *price ceiling.*

black market a market in which goods or services are bought and sold illegally, either because it is illegal to sell them at all or because the prices charged are legally prohibited by a *price ceiling.*

minimum wage a legal floor on the wage rate. The wage rate is the market price of labor.

inefficient allocation of sales among sellers a form of inefficiency in which sellers who would be willing to sell a good at the lowest price are not always those who actually manage to sell it; often the result of a *price floor.*

inefficiently high quality a form of inefficiency in which sellers offer high-quality goods at a high price even though buyers would prefer a lower quality at a lower price; often the result of a *price floor.*

Notes

AFTER YOU READ THE MODULE

Tips

Tip #1. Students often find it confusing to remember the difference between a price floor and a price ceiling.

- A floor is a surface that you stand on and that is solid. A price floor is the *lowest* price that can be charged for a good. Figure 13.1 illustrates a price floor. To be effective, a price floor must be set at a price that is greater than the equilibrium price. At P_F, Q_1 units will be supplied and Q_2 units will be demanded. An effective price floor always results in a surplus of the good.

Figure 13.1

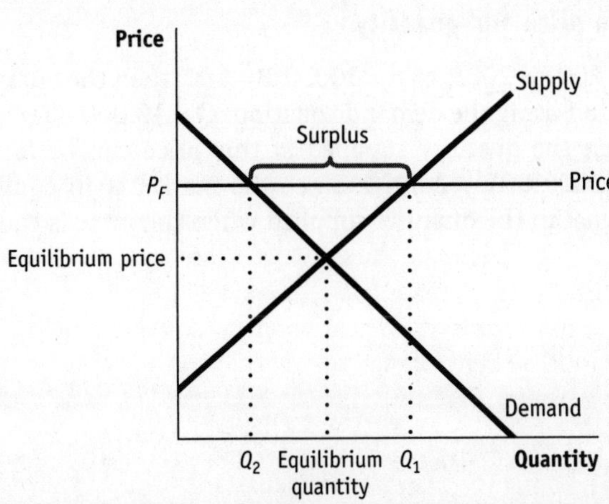

- A ceiling is a surface that you hope is solid and stays above your head. A price ceiling is the *highest* price that can be charged for a good. Figure 13.2 illustrates a price ceiling. To be effective, a price ceiling must be set at a price that is less than the equilibrium price. At P_C, Q_1 units will be supplied and Q_2 units will be demanded. An effective price ceiling always results in a shortage of the good.

Figure 13.2

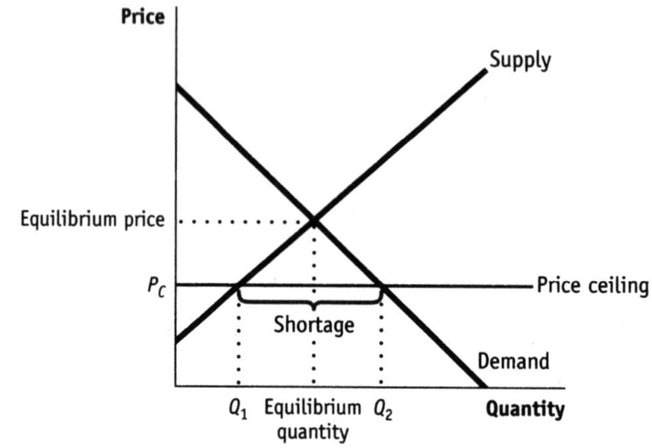

WORKED PROBLEMS

1. Consider a market for cotton in which the market demand curve is given by the equation Q = 40,000 – 200*P* and the market supply curve is given by the equation Q = 200*P*, where Q is bales of cotton and *P* is the price per bale of cotton. Suppose this market is initially in equilibrium and then cotton farmers successfully lobby the legislature to impose a price floor of $150 per bale of cotton. After imposition of this price floor, what will be the price of cotton in this market, and how does this price compare with the initial equilibrium price? Identify the number of bales of cotton consumers will purchase once the price floor is implemented. How does this quantity compare with the initial equilibrium quantity in this market? What will the surplus or shortage of cotton equal with the imposition of this price floor? If the government purchases the surplus cotton, what will be the cost of this purchase to the government?

STEP 1: First draw a graph of the market for cotton and find the initial equilibrium price and quantity in this market. Use the two equations to solve for the equilibrium price and quantity.

Thus, 40,000 – 200*P* = 200*P*, or *P* = 100. If *P* = 100, then the quantity demanded at this price can be found using the demand equation: Q = 40,000 – 200(100), or Q = 20,000. If *P* = 100, then the quantity supplied at this price can be found using the supply equation: Q = 200(100) = 20,000. Since the market is in equilibrium, the quantity demanded is equal to the quantity supplied when the price is equal to 100.

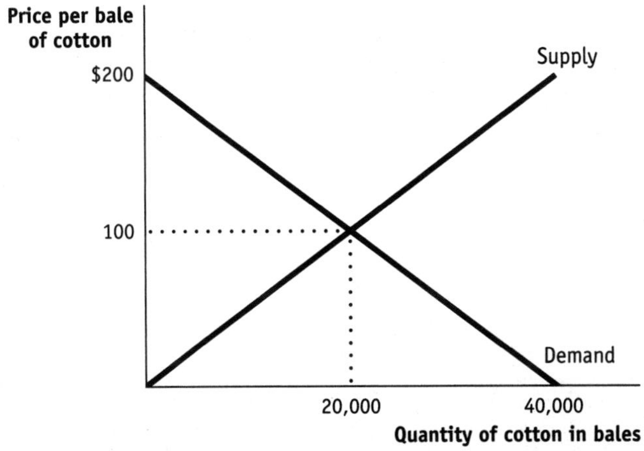

STEP 2: Draw the price floor on your graph and determine if the price floor is an effective price floor. Once you have determined if the price floor is effective, you will know whether the price in this market is the price floor price of $150 per bale or the equilibrium price of $100 per bale. Identify the number of bales of cotton that consumers demand by using the demand equation to see how many bales of cotton they are willing to demand at the new price for cotton. The effective price floor raises the price of cotton and this causes consumers to purchase fewer units of cotton.

Since the price floor is greater than the equilibrium price, the price floor is effective in this market. The price of cotton in this market will now be the price floor price of $150 per bale: the price of cotton is now higher than it was before the implementation of the price floor. When the price of cotton is $150 per bale, consumers are willing to purchase 10,000 bales of cotton.

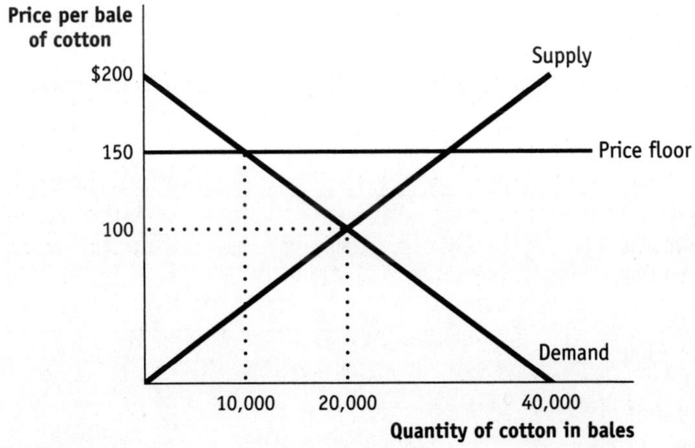

STEP 3: Identify the surplus of cotton that will be produced in this market when there is a price floor and then determine what the cost of purchasing this surplus will be for the government.

To find the surplus with the price floor requires identifying how many units of cotton suppliers are willing to supply at a price of $150, then subtracting out the number of units of cotton demanders are willing to demand at a price of $150. At a price of $150, suppliers are willing to supply 30,000 bales of cotton, but consumers are willing to purchase only 10,000 bales. Thus, the surplus of cotton is equal to 20,000 bales. If the government purchases this amount of cotton at $150 per bale, it will cost the government $4,500,000. The shaded area in the following graph identifies this cost to the government.

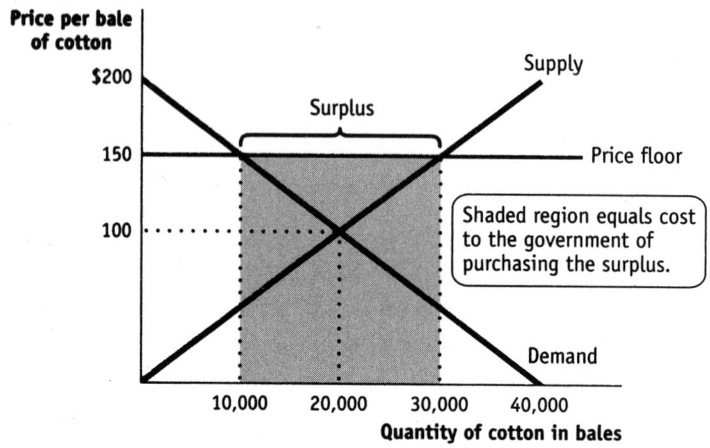

2. The following table describes several interventions in a market. Complete the table.

Situation	This is an example of a 1) Price floor, 2) Price ceiling, or 3) Quantity control or quota	What must be true for this intervention in the market to be effective?
The government decides to limit the number of taxicab licenses in Chicago		
The minimum price that can be charged for a sports car is set at $75,000 by the government		
The minimum wage that can be paid to a worker is set at $10 an hour by the government		
The maximum tuition that can be charged by a public university is set at $5,000 a year by the government		

STEP 1: To answer this question, you must first have a firm grasp of the differences among a price floor, a price ceiling, and a quantity control or quota. You need to understand what makes each of these interventions effective in the market: this will require that you understand and are comfortable with each type of market intervention.

A price ceiling is a maximum price that can be charged for a good. A price floor is a minimum price that can be charged for a good. A quantity control or quota is a maximum amount of the good that can be provided in the market. This maximum amount is set by the government. To fill in the second column of the table, you will want to consider each situation and determine whether the situation is one in which the government is setting a maximum price, a minimum price, or a maximum quantity.

STEP 2: For each type of market intervention by the government, you will want to think about what must be true in order for the intervention to have any impact on the market.

For a price ceiling to be effective, the price ceiling must be set at a price that is less than the market equilibrium amount. For a price floor to be effective, the price floor must be set at a price that is greater than the market equilibrium amount. For a quantity control or quota to have any effect on the market, the quantity control must be set at a quantity that is less than the market equilibrium quantity. The completed table follows.

Situation	This is an example of a 1) Price floor, 2) Price ceiling, or 3) quantity control or quota	What must be true for this intervention in the market to be effective?
The government decides to limit the number of taxicab licenses in Chicago	Quantity control or quota	Quota amount must be less than the market equilibrium quantity
The minimum price that can be charged for a sports car is set at $75,000 by the government	Price floor	Price floor must be set at a price that is greater than the market equilibrium price
The minimum wage that can be paid to a worker is set at $10 an hour by the government	Price floor	Price floor must be set at a price that is greater than the market equilibrium price
The maximum tuition that can be charged by a public university is set at $5,000 a year by the government	Price ceiling	Price ceiling must be set at a price that is less than the market equilibrium price

Problems and Exercises

1. Use the graph below to answer the following questions.

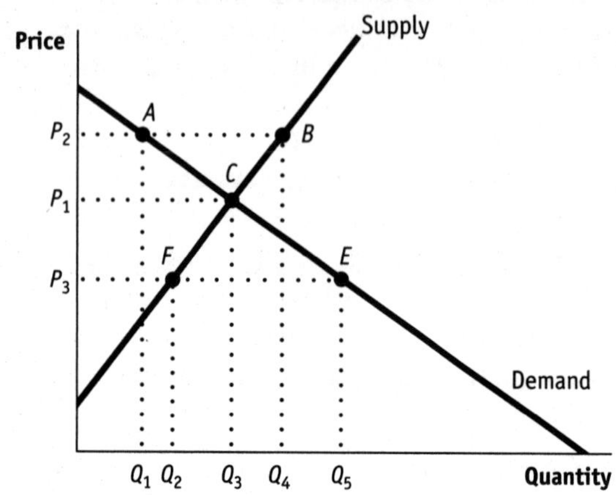

a. Identify the equilibrium price and the equilibrium quantity.

b. Suppose a price floor of P_3 is implemented by the government in this market. Describe what will happen to the price and quantity once this price floor is implemented.

c. Suppose a price floor of P_2 is implemented by the government in this market. Describe what will happen to the price and quantity once this price floor is implemented.

d. What must be true about a price floor in a market for a good or service in order for that price floor to be effective?

e. You are told that an effective price floor has been implemented in this market and that the resultant surplus is greater than $Q_4 - Q_1$. What do you know about the level of this price floor?

2. Use the graph below to answer the following questions.

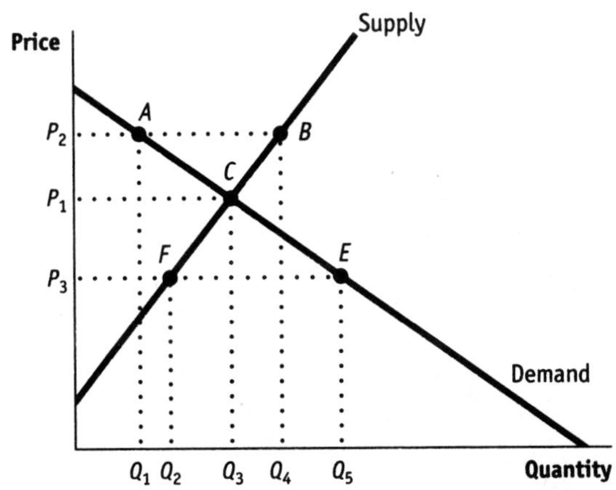

a. Identify the equilibrium price and the equilibrium quantity.

b. Suppose a price ceiling of P_2 is implemented by the government in this market. Describe what will happen to the price and quantity once this price ceiling is implemented.

c. Suppose a price ceiling of P_3 is implemented by the government in this market. Describe what will happen to the price and quantity once this price ceiling is implemented.

d. What must be true about a price ceiling in a market for a good or service in order for that price ceiling to be effective?

e. You are told that an effective price ceiling has been implemented in this market and that the resultant shortage is smaller than $Q_5 - Q_2$. What do you know about the level of this price ceiling?

3. Consider the market for housing in Metropolitan City, where all housing units are exactly the same. Currently the equilibrium price of housing is $2,000 a month and local residents consume 1,500 units of housing. The local residents argue that housing is too expensive and that an effective price ceiling should be implemented. Once the price ceiling is implemented by the local government council, only 1,200 units of housing are supplied in this market. Is this an efficient level of housing for Metropolitan City? Explain your answer. To support your answer, provide two sketches: in the first sketch indicate the equilibrium quantity, the equilibrium price, and the area of total surplus; in the second sketch indicate the price ceiling, the area of total surplus, and the area that represents the efficiency loss due to the reduction in the quantity of housing units.

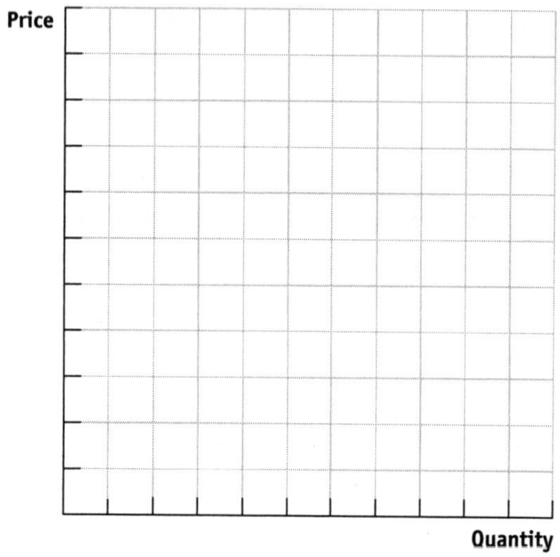

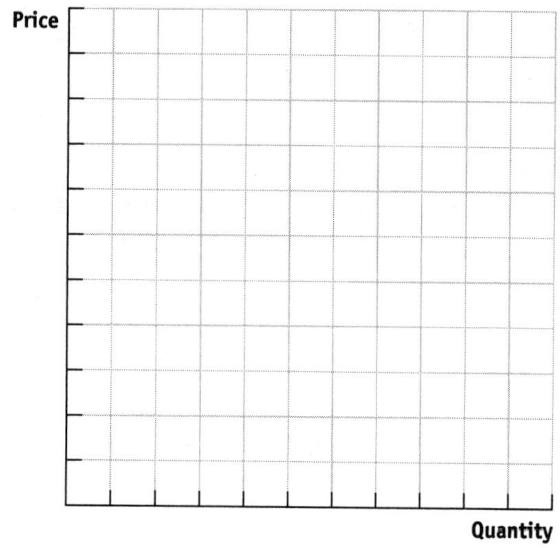

4. A price ceiling is implemented in the market for housing in Metropolitan City, where all housing units are identical. You know that before the price ceiling is implemented, the demand for housing in Metropolitan City is given by the equation $P = 1{,}000 - 0.1Q_D$ and the supply of housing is given by the equation $P = 200 + 0.3Q_S$.

a. Prior to the implementation of the price ceiling, what is the equilibrium price for housing in Metropolitan City and what is the equilibrium quantity of housing?

b. Fill in the following demand and supply schedules for this market given the above equations.

Price	Quantity demanded	Quantity supplied
$ 200		
400		
600		
800		
1,000		

c. When the price ceiling is implemented, a housing shortage develops. This shortage is equal to 4,000 housing units. Calculate the price ceiling in this market for housing. (Hint: You may find the table from part [b] helpful in thinking about this problem.)

d. Who benefits from the imposition of the price ceiling in the market for housing in Metropolitan City?

e. Who is hurt by the imposition of a price ceiling in the market for housing in Metropolitan City?

f. Why is this price ceiling apt to result in black market activities in the market for housing? Provide at least two examples of potential black market activities.

g. Does an effective price ceiling in this market result in too many or too few resources being allocated to the market for housing in Metropolitan City? Explain your answer.

5. Farmers in Corntopia successfully lobby their government to enact a price floor for their agricultural commodity. The price floor is set at $10 above the equilibrium price. The initial demand and supply curves for agricultural production in Corntopia are as follows: $P = 100 - Q$ and $P = Q$, where price is per bushel and quantity is measured in bushels.

a. What is the level of the price floor in this market?

b. How many units of the agricultural product will be demanded and supplied at this price floor level?

c. Suppose the government purchases the surplus in this market once the price floor is implemented. What will be the cost to the government of buying this surplus?

d. Given the price floor, what is the expenditure consumers make when purchasing this commodity? Do not include in your calculation the cost to the government of buying the surplus.

e. What is total farm revenue equal to in this market once the price floor is implemented? What is the relationship between total farm revenue, consumer expenditure, and government expenditure on the good, given the price floor? Does total farm revenue increase when the government enacts a price floor? Explain your answer.

f. Who benefits from the enactment of a price floor in this market?

6. a. Draw a graph of the demand and supply curves given to you in problem 5. Label the equilibrium price and the equilibrium quantity on this graph. Shade in the area that corresponds to total farm revenue in this market and label this area clearly.

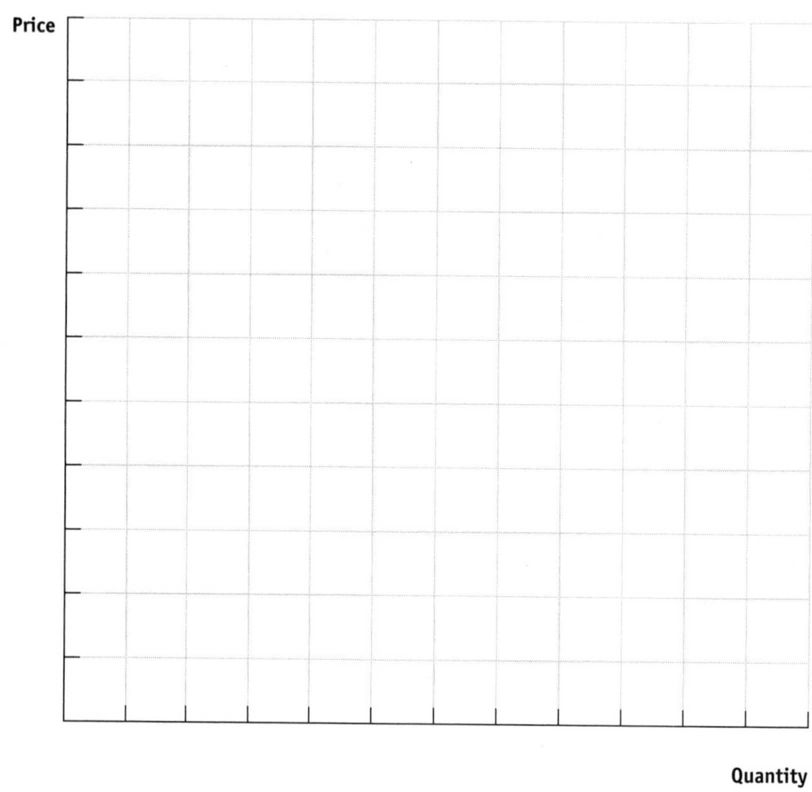

b. Redraw the graph of the demand and supply curves given to you in problem 5, and draw in a line indicating the price floor. On the graph, indicate the quantity demanded and the quantity supplied using the values you found in problem 5. Shade in and clearly label the areas that correspond to consumer expenditure on the good and government expenditure on the good, given the price floor.

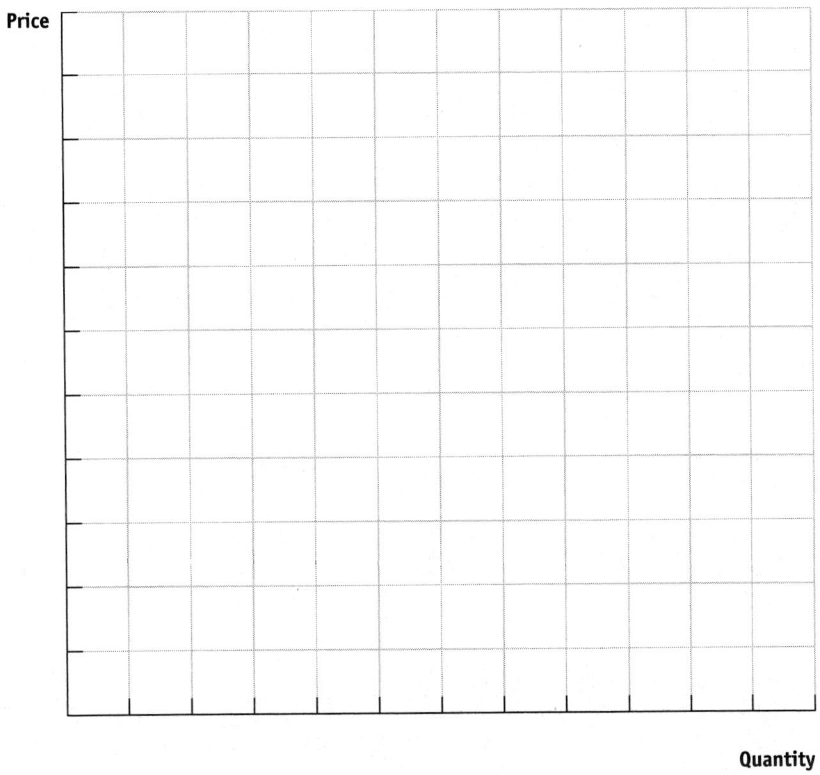

7. Consider the labor market in Utopia. You are told that the equilibrium wage in this market is \$10 per hour and that the equilibrium amount of labor in this market is 1,000 hours of labor. Furthermore, you know that at a wage of \$14 per hour, 600 hours of labor are demanded and 1,400 hours of labor are supplied. The workers in Utopia successfully lobby Utopia's government for the implementation of a price floor. This price floor results in 1,200 hours of labor being supplied and 800 hours of labor being demanded.

   a. Use the above information to derive the labor demand curve for Utopia. Assume this labor demand curve is linear. In your equation, abbreviate the price of labor, or its hourly wage rate, as *W*, and the quantity of labor demanded, measured as hours of labor, as *L*. (Hint: You may find sketching a graph of the above information helpful.)

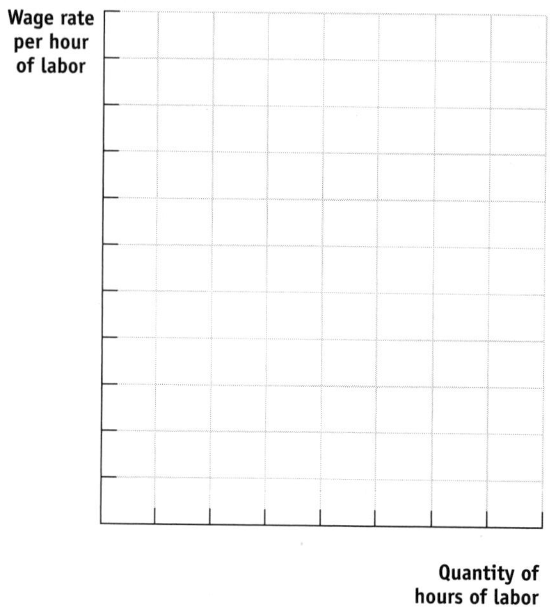

   b. Use the above information to derive the labor supply curve for Utopia. Assume this labor supply curve is linear. In your equation, abbreviate the hourly wage rate as *W* and the hours of labor supplied as *L*.

   c. What wage rate did the government set when it implemented the price floor?

   d. Describe the effects of this price floor on the labor market in Utopia. Who benefits from the price floor? Who is hurt by the price floor?

BEFORE YOU TAKE THE TEST

Module Review Questions

1. The implementation of an effective price ceiling

a. decreases the area of producer surplus.

b. increases the area of producer surplus.

2. The implementation of an effective price floor

a. decreases the area of consumer surplus.

b. increases the area of consumer surplus.

3. When demanders can make a strong moral or political case for lower prices in a market, the government may decide to enact an effective

a. price floor. b. price ceiling.

4. When suppliers can make a strong moral or political case for higher prices in a market, the government may decide to enact an effective

a. price floor. b. price ceiling.

5. Consider minimum-wage legislation requiring that all workers receive a wage payment greater than the equilibrium market wage. Which of the following two groups is more likely to have advocated for this legislation?

a. demanders of labor b. suppliers of labor

6. Use the information in the table below to answer the following question.

Price	Quantity demanded	Quantity supplied
$ 20	200	0
40	150	50
60	100	100
80	50	150
100	0	200

If the government mandates that prices in this market can fall no lower than $50, this results in

a. a situation of excess quantity demanded.

b. a situation of excess quantity supplied.

c. fewer than 100 units being supplied in this market.

d. no effect in this market, since the equilibrium price is greater than $50.

7. Use the information in the table below to answer the following question.

Price	Quantity demanded	Quantity supplied
$ 20	200	0
40	150	50
60	100	100
80	50	150
100	0	200

Suppose a price floor of $40 is implemented in this market. This results in
a. an excess demand of 100 units.
b. an excess supply of 100 units.
c. no effect in this market, since the price floor is set below the equilibrium price.
d. no effect in this market, since the price floor is set above the equilibrium price.

8. Use the information in the table below to answer the following question.

Price	Quantity demanded	Quantity supplied
$ 20	200	0
40	150	50
60	100	100
80	50	150
100	0	200

Suppose a price ceiling of $40 is implemented in this market. This results in
a. an excess demand of 100 units.
b. an excess supply of 100 units.
c. no effect in this market, since the price ceiling is set below the equilibrium price.
d. a temporary shortage of the good while prices rise, and the quantity demanded and the quantity supplied adjust until they are equal.

9. Use the information in the table below to answer the following question.

Price	Quantity demanded	Quantity supplied
$ 20	200	0
40	150	50
60	100	100
80	50	150
100	0	200

If the price ceiling is set at $40 in this market, then
a. too few resources are being allocated to the production of this good.
b. too many resources are being allocated to the production of this good.

10. Which of the following statements are true?

I. Price ceilings are inefficient because they result in too much of the good being produced in the market.

II. Price ceilings are inefficient because they result in the production of goods with too low a level of quality.

III. Price ceilings are inefficient because they lead to wasted resources since they increase the amount of time consumers must search for the price-controlled good.

a. Statement I is true.

b. Statement II is true.

c. Statements I and II are true.

d. Statements II and III are true.

11. Use the information in the table below to answer the following question.

Price	Quantity demanded	Quantity supplied
$ 20	200	0
40	150	50
60	100	100
80	50	150
100	0	200

If the price ceiling is set at $40 in this market, the loss in total surplus in this market equals

a. $2,000.

b. $1,000.

c. $500.

d. $200.

12. An effective price ceiling typically causes an inefficient allocation of the good to

a. consumers of the good.

b. producers of the good.

13. Black market or illegal activities increase with the imposition of price controls in markets. Black markets result in

a. improving the situation of all participants in the price-controlled market.

b. worsening the situation for those people who attempt to obey the rules and restrictions imposed by the government in a price-controlled market.

c. have little or no real impact in price-controlled markets.

d. the creation of greater respect in society for the need to obey all laws.

14. Use the following graph to answer this question.

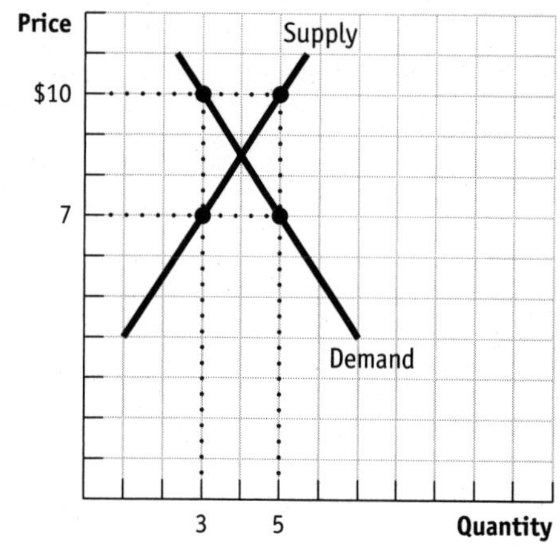

An effective price floor is implemented in the market depicted in the graph. This price floor generates an excess quantity supplied of 2 units in this market. This price floor must be equal to

a. $10.

b. $7.

15. Use the following graph to answer this question.

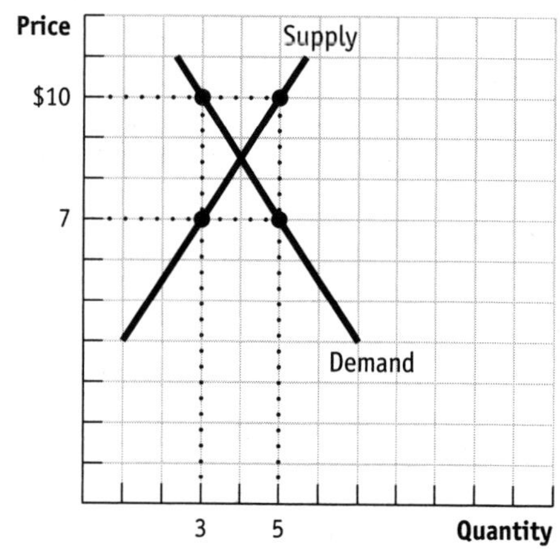

An effective price floor is enacted in this market, and with this price floor the government promises to purchase any unwanted units produced. If the price floor is set at $10, then the government will spend ________ purchasing the unwanted units of the good.

a. $50

b. $30

c. $21

d. $20

16. Use the following graph to answer this question.

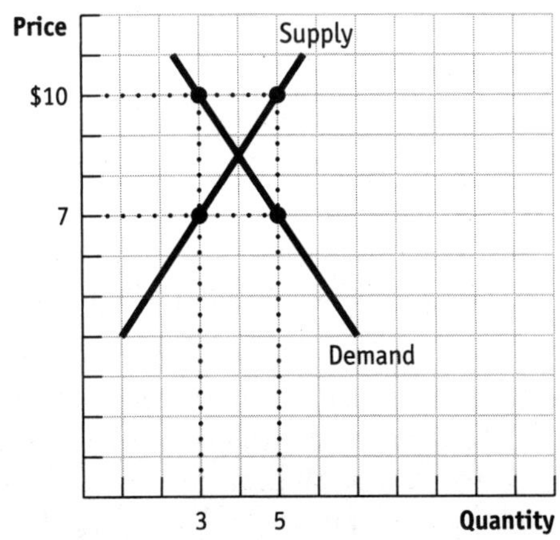

An effective price floor is enacted in this market at a price of $10. With this price floor, consumers' expenditure on this good will equal

a. $50.
b. $30.
c. $21.
d. $20.

17. Which of the following statements is true?

a. An effective price ceiling reduces the quantity of the good available to consumers, while an effective price floor increases the quantity of the good available to consumers.
b. An effective price floor reduces the quantity of the good available to consumers, while an effective price ceiling increases the quantity of the good available to consumers.
c. Government intervention in markets in the form of effective price ceilings or price floors increases the quantity of the good available to consumers.
d. Government intervention in markets in the form of effective price ceilings or price floors decreases the quantity of the good available to consumers.

18. When a price is artificially set above the equilibrium price in a market, who determines the quantity of the good bought and sold in the market?

a. demanders
b. suppliers

19. When suppliers determine the quantity of the good bought and sold in a market, this must be due to the imposition of an effective

a. price floor.
b. price ceiling.

20. An effective price floor prevents suppliers from competing for customers through lower prices, so suppliers compete for customers by offering goods with

a. greater quality than consumers desire.
b. lower quality than consumers desire.

21. Which of the following statements are true?

I. An effective price floor benefits some suppliers.
II. An effective price floor benefits all demanders.
III. An effective price floor results in a persistent surplus.
IV. An effective price floor results in an inefficiently high level of quality in the good offered by suppliers.

a. Statements I and III are true.
b. Statements I, III, and IV are true.
c. Statements III and IV are true.
d. Statements II, III, and IV are true.

ANSWER KEY

Answers to Problems and Exercises

1. a. The equilibrium price is P_1 and the equilibrium quantity is Q_3.

   b. This is not an effective price floor since the price floor of P_3 is less than the equilibrium price P_1. Since it is a nonbinding/ineffective price floor, the equilibrium price and quantity will not change.

   c. This is an effective price floor since the price floor of P_2 is greater than the equilibrium price P_1. At P_2, Q_1 units of the good will be demanded and Q_4 units of the good will be supplied. This excess supply of $Q_4 - Q_1$ will not be eliminated by price decreases since the price is artificially set at P_2 by the government and is not allowed to decrease. An effective price floor creates a situation of excess supply, or a surplus, that is not eliminated by changes in the price of the good because the price has been set at a level that is greater than the market-clearing price.

   d. For a price floor to have an effect in a market, the price floor must be set at a price that is greater than the equilibrium price.

   e. The price floor must be set at a price that is greater than P_2 since we know from part (c) that the surplus in the market at P_2 equals $Q_4 - Q_1$.

2. a. The equilibrium price is P_1 and the equilibrium quantity is Q_3.

   b. This is not an effective price ceiling since the price ceiling of P_2 is greater than the equilibrium price P_1. Since it is a nonbinding/ineffective price ceiling, the equilibrium price and quantity will not change.

   c. This is an effective price ceiling since the price ceiling of P_3 is less than the equilibrium price P_1. At P_3, Q_5 units of the good will be demanded and Q_2 units of the good will be supplied. This excess demand of $Q_5 - Q_2$ will not be eliminated by price increases since the price is artificially set at P_3 by the government and is not allowed to increase. An effective price ceiling creates a situation of excess demand, or a shortage, that is not eliminated by changes in the price of the good because the price has been set at a level that is less than the market-clearing price.

   d. For a price ceiling to have an effect in a market, the price ceiling must be set at a price that is less than the equilibrium price.

   e. The price ceiling must be set at a price that is greater than P_3 but still less than the equilibrium price of P_1. We know this because when the price ceiling is set at P_3, the shortage is equal to $Q_5 - Q_2$, and the new price ceiling results in a smaller shortage than the shortage at price P_3.

3. The market is in equilibrium when there are 1,500 units of housing offered at the price of $2,000 per month, so 1,200 is not an efficient level of housing. The price ceiling forces consumers to reduce their consumption of the good from the efficient level. In the sketch below, the shaded area represents the total surplus received when 1,500 units of housing are supplied at a price of $2,000 per unit.

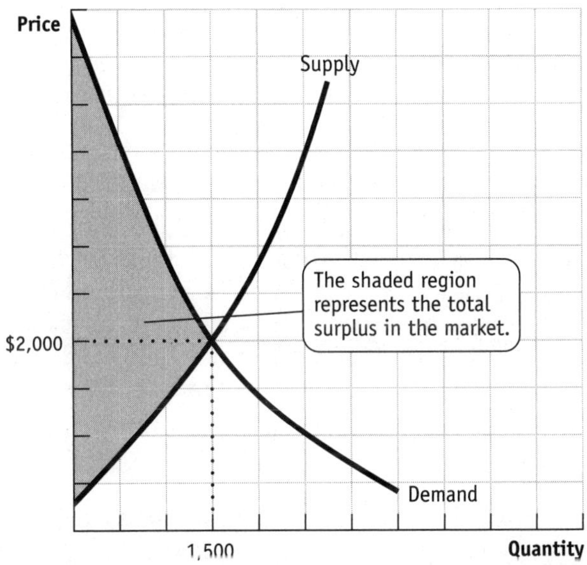

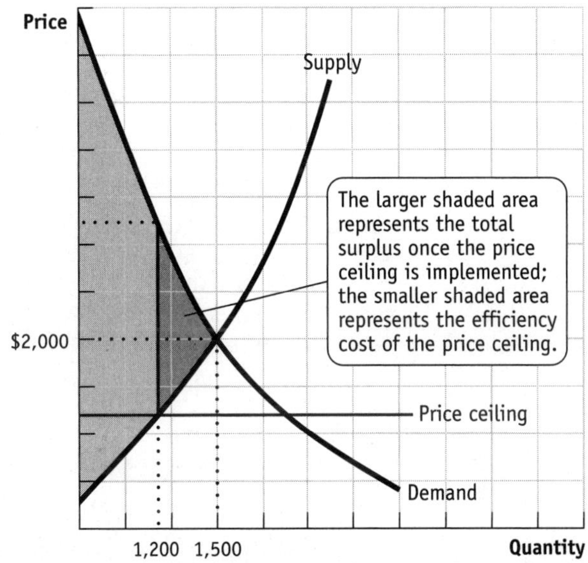

The second sketch illustrates the area of total surplus once the effective price ceiling is implemented. Notice that the area of total surplus is reduced relative to its initial level. The amount of this loss in total surplus is the measure of the efficiency cost of the reduction in quantity provided in the market due to the imposition of the price ceiling.

4. **a.** The equilibrium price is $800 per unit of housing and the equilibrium quantity of housing is 2,000 units.

b.

Price	Quantity demanded	Quantity supplied
$ 200	8,000	0
400	6,000	666.67
600	4,000	1,333.33
800	2,000	2,000
1,000	0	2,666.67

c. From the table in part (b), you know that a price ceiling of $400 is too low (the shortage is greater than 4,000 units of housing at this price) while a price ceiling of $600 is too high (the shortage at this price is less than 4,000 units of housing). You could try some prices between $400 and $600 or you could solve this problem algebraically. The shortage of 4,000 units is the difference between the quantity demanded and the quantity supplied at the price ceiling, or in other words, $Q_S + 4{,}000 = Q_D$. Thus, the demand equation can be rewritten as $P_C = 1{,}000 - 0.1(Q_S + 4{,}000)$ and the supply equation is equal to $P_C = 200 + 0.3Q_S$, where P_C is the price ceiling level. Solving this set of equations, we find that the quantity supplied is equal to 1,000 units. Thus, the quantity demanded is equal to 5,000 units while the price ceiling level is $500.

d. The people lucky enough to get one of the housing units supplied at the price ceiling price benefit from this government intervention. These individuals pay less than the market-clearing price for their housing unit.

e. Consumers who want housing but who cannot find housing due to the price ceiling are hurt by the decision to implement the price ceiling. Additionally, as landlords fail to maintain the housing units in Metropolitan City, the whole community is affected as the general condition of the housing stock deteriorates. And if a black market develops in the housing market, this will erode the general level of lawful behavior in the community.

f. Since the quantity demanded of housing exceeds the quantity supplied of housing at the price ceiling, persistent shortages will exist in this market. Consumers eager to find housing will resort to activities that are illegal—for example, subletting housing units at rates higher than the price ceiling rate or making illegal payments to landlords.

g. Too few resources are devoted to the housing market. We know this because the effective price ceiling creates a persistent shortage in the market for housing.

5. **a.** The level of the price floor in this market is \$60 per bushel. To find the price floor level, first solve for the equilibrium price in the market: set demand equal to supply. Thus, $100 - Q = Q$, and thus the equilibrium quantity is 50 bushels of the agricultural commodity. We can then substitute this quantity into either the demand or supply equation to find the equilibrium price. The equilibrium price is \$50 per bushel. If the price floor is set \$10 above the equilibrium price, we know the price floor must be at \$60 per bushel.

b. At \$60 per bushel, demanders demand 40 bushels and suppliers supply 60 bushels. There is an excess supply of 20 bushels.

c. If the government buys the surplus 20 bushels at the price floor level of \$60 per bushel, it will spend \$1,200.

d. Consumers demand 40 bushels at the price of \$60 per bushel. The expenditure by consumers on the product will equal \$2,400.

e. Total farm revenue equals the total number of bushels supplied times the price floor, or (60 bushels)(\$60 per bushel), or \$3,600. Total farm revenue equals the sum of consumer expenditure on the good plus government expenditure on the good. Total farm revenue without the price floor is equal to the equilibrium price times the equilibrium quantity, or (50 bushels) (\$50 per bushel), or \$2,500. Total farm revenue increases with the imposition of an effective price floor.

f. The farmers benefit from the imposition of the price floor since it increases total farm revenue.

6. **a.**

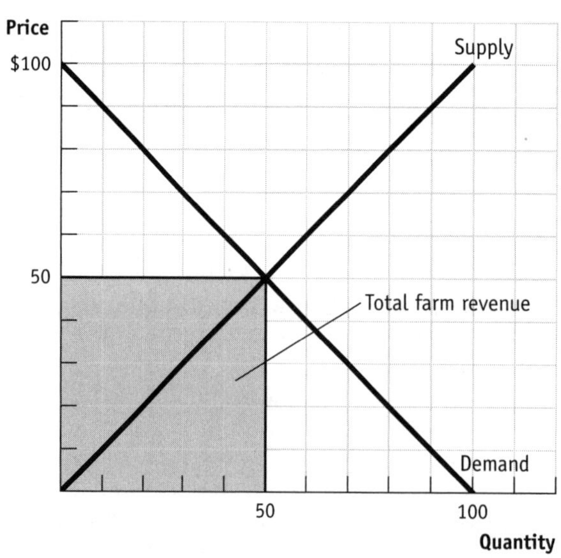

b.

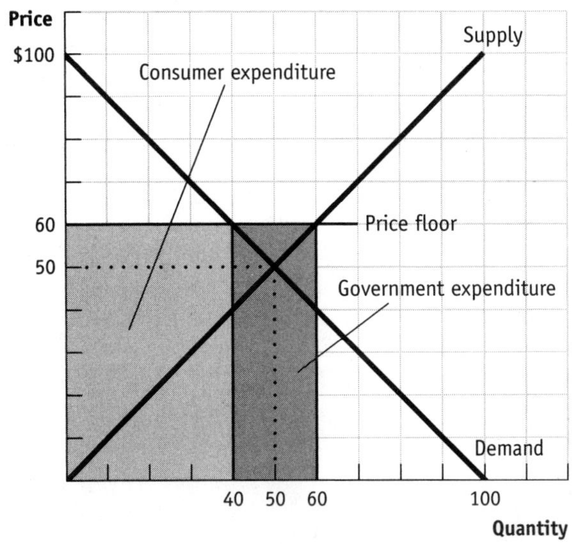

7. a. The information you are given in this problem can be represented as follows:

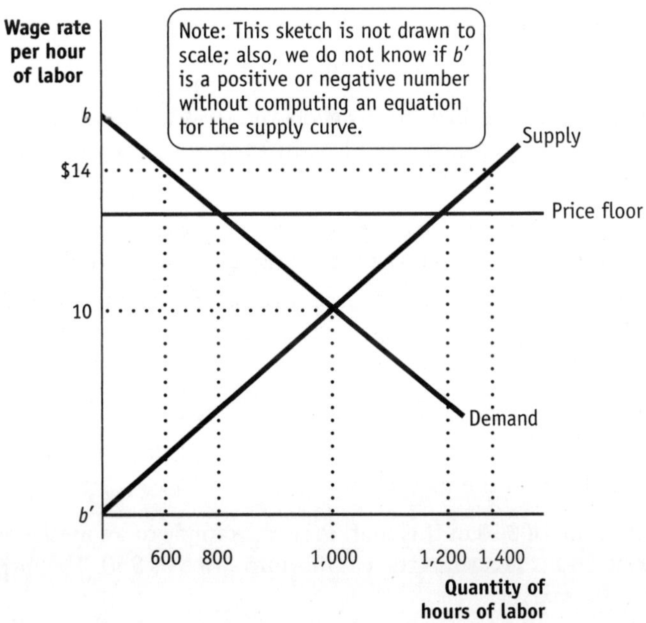

Thus, we know two points of the labor demand curve: (1,000, \$10) and (600, \$14). Use these two points to compute the slope of the demand curve: slope = rise/run = $(y_1 - y_2)/(x_1 - x_2) = (10 - 14)/(1{,}000 - 600) = -0.01$. The demand equation can be written as $W = b - 0.01L$. Then, use one of the points that you know is on the demand curve—either (1,000, \$10) or (600, \$14)—with this equation to solve for b. Thus, $W = b - 0.01L$ can be written as $10 = b - 0.01(1{,}000)$, or $b = 20$. The labor demand curve is therefore $W = 20 - 0.01L$.

b. Use a similar procedure to write the supply equation: $W = 0.01L + b'$, where b' is the y-intercept of the labor supply curve. Then use one of the points that you know is on the supply curve—either (1,000, \$10) or (1,400, \$14)—with this equation to identify the value of b'. Thus, $W = 0.01L + b'$ can be rewritten as $10 = 0.01(1{,}000) + b'$ and b' therefore equals 0. The labor supply equation is thus $W = 0.01L$.

c. At the price floor, we know that the quantity of labor demanded is 800 units. Substitute this number for L in the labor demand equation: $W = 20 - 0.01(800)$, or $W = \$12$ per hour of labor. To verify that the price floor has been set at a wage of \$12 per hour of labor, check your answer with the labor supply equation. At the price floor, we know the quantity of labor supplied is equal to 1,200 units. Using this number for L in the labor supply equation, we find $W = 0.01(1{,}200)$, or $W = \$12$ per hour of labor.

d. This price floor creates a surplus of labor when the price floor is set at a wage rate of \$12 per hour of labor. In a labor market, a surplus of labor implies that there is unemployment: workers who want to work (i.e., they are willing to supply their labor at the prevailing wage rate) cannot find work (i.e., there is insufficient demand for their services at the prevailing wage rate). Workers lucky enough to get a job paying \$12 per hour benefit from the price floor while workers who are unable to find work at that wage rate are harmed by the price floor.

Answers to Module Review Questions

1. **Answer a.** Since an effective price ceiling reduces the price that producers receive and consumers pay, this results in a decrease in producer surplus.

2. **Answer a.** Since an effective price floor increases the price that producers receive and consumers pay, this results in a decrease in consumer surplus.

3. **Answer b.** Demanders desire lower prices for the good and this can be achieved through the enactment of an effective price ceiling, since it reduces the price below the equilibrium price.

4. **Answer a.** Producers desire higher prices for the good and this can be achieved through the enactment of an effective price floor, since it raises the price above the equilibrium price.

5. **Answer b.** Suppliers of labor will receive this higher wage and therefore benefit from it. Demanders of labor will find that this higher wage increases the cost of hiring labor, and they will not benefit from it.

6. **Answer d.** Setting a lower limit on prices of \$50 in this market is an example of an ineffective price floor since a price floor of \$50 is less than the equilibrium price of \$60. This price floor would have no effect on the market.

7. **Answer c.** Setting a price floor of \$40 in this market is an example of an ineffective price floor since a price floor of \$40 is less than the equilibrium price of \$60. This price floor would have no effect on the market.

8. **Answer a.** A price ceiling of \$40 results in 150 units being demanded and 50 units being supplied. This is therefore a situation of excess demand of 100 units.

9. **Answer a.** At a price ceiling of \$40, consumers wish to consume 150 units of the good while suppliers are only willing to supply 50 units of the good. This indicates that too few resources are being allocated to this market.

10. **Answer d.** Statement I is incorrect because price ceilings result in too little of the good being produced in the market. Statement II is correct because when price is limited to a level below the equilibrium price, producers have an incentive to reduce the quality of the product they provide to the market. Statement III is correct because an effective price ceiling results in greater costs as demanders seek out the artificially scarce good.

11. **Answer b.** The total surplus in the market when there is no price ceiling is equal to \$4,000. With the imposition of the effective price ceiling the total surplus equals \$3,000. To find these areas of total surplus, sketch a graph and then calculate the relevant areas. The initial total surplus is equal to (1/2)(\$100/unit – \$20/unit)(100 units) or \$4,000. The total surplus with the effective price ceiling is equal to (1/2)(\$100/unit –\$80/unit)(50 units) +

(1/2)($40/unit – $20/unit)(50 units) + ($80/unit – $40/unit)(50 units), or $3,000. The graph below illustrates this.

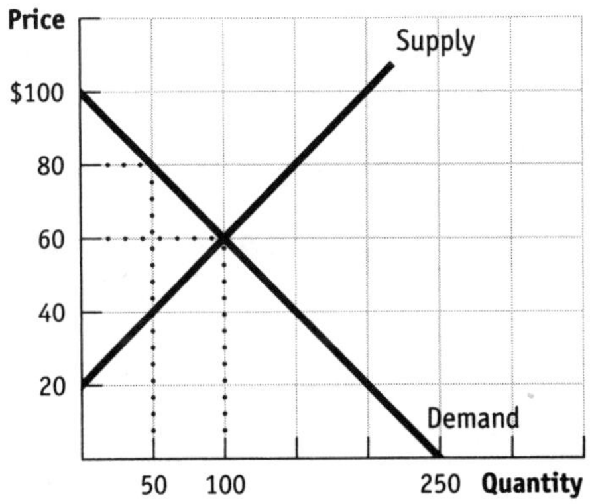

The change in total surplus is $4,000 – $3,000, or $1,000.

12. **Answer a.** An effective price ceiling limits the amount of the good available to consumers in the market by limiting the price to a level that is less than the equilibrium price. Producers produce the amount they are willing to produce at that price, and they do not expand production even though consumers are willing to consume more units of the good.

13. **Answer b.** Answers (a) and (b) are mutually exclusive: if one of these answers is correct, then the other must by necessity be incorrect. Reading answer (b) helps to identify a group that is hurt by black market activities: those individuals who decide not to engage in black market activities are left worse off because of their obedience to the rules imposed by the price-controlled market. Answer (c) is incorrect since price controls do affect markets and do have impacts when they are effective. Answer (d) is also incorrect since price-controlled markets generate black market activities, which are against the law.

14. **Answer a.** An effective price floor is the minimum price that can be charged for a good, and this price must be set above the equilibrium price. At a price of $10, the quantity demanded is 3 units while the quantity supplied is 5 units. At a price floor of $10, there will be excess supply of 2 units. The price floor must equal $10.

15. **Answer d.** At a price floor of $10, the excess supply is 2 units. If the government purchases these 2 units at $10 each, the cost to the government of this purchase is $20.

16. **Answer b.** With a $10 price floor, consumers in this market will demand 3 units of the good. Their expenditure on the good will equal ($10/unit)(3 units), or $30.

17. **Answer d.** Effective price ceilings and price floors both reduce the quantity of the good available to consumers, so answers (a), (b), and (c) are not true.

18. **Answer a.** When the price is artificially set above the equilibrium price, demanders determine the quantity demanded in the market since they select the quantity they are willing to demand based on the price of the good.

19. **Answer b.** A price ceiling is set below the equilibrium price. This limits the price that can be charged for a good in the market. Producers take this price and then determine the number of units of the good they are willing to provide in the market at this price.

20. **Answer a.** When producers cannot compete for customers through prices, they must look for other ways to compete. One way is to offer goods of higher quality, and with an effective price floor producers will compete by offering higher-quality goods.

21. **Answer b.** Statement I is correct because those suppliers who are lucky enough to sell their good at the higher price are benefited. Statement III is also correct since an effective price floor results in excess supply of the good. Statement IV is correct as well because suppliers will compete for customers by offering higher-quality goods since they cannot compete for customers by offering lower prices. Statement II is incorrect: demanders of this good now have to pay a higher price than they would have in a freely functioning market.

module 14

Quantity Controls

BEFORE YOU READ THE MODULE

Summary

This module develops the idea of quantity controls where the government limits the amount of the good available to a level lower than the equilibrium level of output. The module discusses how quantity controls reduce the efficiency of a market and includes a discussion of the distributional impact of quantity controls. The module also introduces and develops the concept of deadweight loss.

Module Objectives

Objective #1. The government may implement quantity controls or a quota in a market. In this case the government sets a limit on the total quantity of the good that can be bought and sold in the market. This quantity is usually limited through the selling of licenses that legally grant the holder of the license the right to supply the good. Quantity controls always set a maximum amount allowed. To be binding in the market, the quota must be set below the equilibrium quantity.

Objective #2. A quota or quantity control creates a wedge between the price consumers are willing to pay for the good and the price at which producers are willing to supply the good. The difference between these two prices is the quota rent, or the income that the license holder receives from their ownership of a valuable commodity (the license).

Objective #3. Quantity controls are inefficient because they prevent some mutually beneficial transactions from occurring, since the demand price for a given quantity (the quota amount) is greater than the supply price for that quantity. These missed transactions create an incentive to evade the quota limit, often through illegal activity.

Objective #4. Quantity controls are inefficient because they prevent some mutually beneficial transactions from occurring: this inefficiency implies that the quantity control, when effective, creates a deadweight loss.

Key Terms

Notes

quantity control an upper limit, set by the government, on the quantity of some good that can be bought or sold; also referred to as a *quota.*

quota an upper limit, set by the government, on the quantity of some good that can be bought or sold; also referred to as a *quantity control.*

license the right, conferred by the government, to supply a good.

demand price the price of a given quantity at which consumers will demand that quantity.

supply price the price of a given quantity at which producers will supply that quantity.

wedge the difference between the *demand price* of the quantity transacted and the *supply price* of the quantity transacted for a good when the supply of the good is legally restricted. Often created by a *quantity control,* or *quota.*

quota rent the difference between the *demand price* and the *supply price* at the *quota limit;* this difference, the earnings that accrue to the license-holder, is equal to the market price of the *license* when the license is traded.

deadweight loss the loss in total surplus that occurs whenever an action or a policy reduces the quantity transacted below the efficient market *equilibrium quantity.*

AFTER YOU READ THE MODULE

Tips

Tip #1. A quota, or quantity control, is a policy implemented by the government to set a maximum amount of the good or service that can be sold in a market. A quota has no effect if it is set at a level greater than the equilibrium quantity; to be effective a quota must be set at a level smaller than the equilibrium quantity. Figure 14.1 illustrates an effective quantity control, or quota, where the maximum allowed quantity is set by the government at Q_1. At Q_1 demanders are willing to pay P_1 for each unit of the good they consume, while suppliers are willing to supply the good at price P_2. This difference, $P_1 - P_2$, is referred to as a wedge. This wedge corresponds to the quota rent the license holder of the good receives when the quantity control is imposed in a market. This quota rent represents the additional compensation the license holder receives from selling the good in a market where the quantity of the good has been artificially restricted.

Figure 14.1

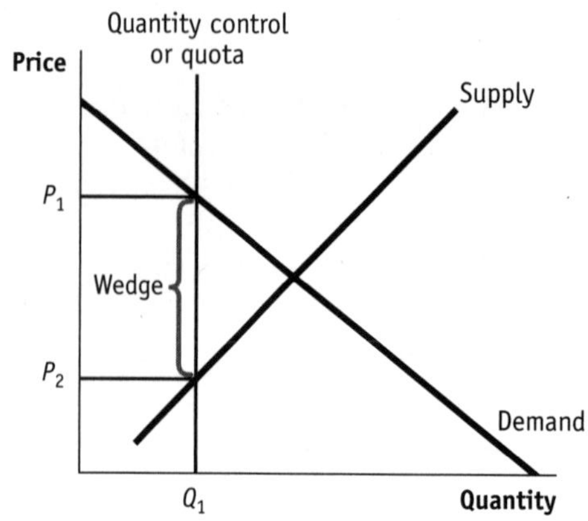

Tip #2. Notice that in Figure 14.1 consumers end up consuming less than the equilibrium quantity because of the government's imposition of a quantity control. This results in a loss in total surplus in the market. This loss in total surplus is deadweight loss. Figure 14.2 illustrates the area of deadweight loss due to a quantity control.

Figure 14.2

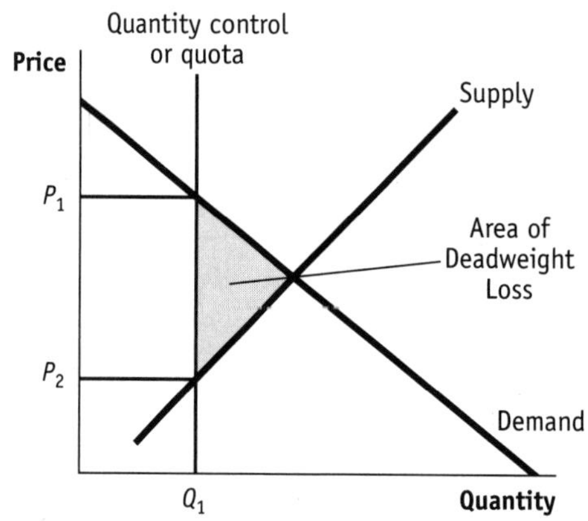

Tip #3. Thinking about the concept of deadweight loss and how the government's intervention in the market created the deadweight loss should lead you to think about other types of market intervention and the possibility that these interventions also create deadweight loss. For example, a price floor will create a deadweight loss. Figure 14.3 illustrates this idea. This idea can be generalized: when the government implements a policy that prevents the market from going to its equilibrium, one can anticipate a deadweight loss. This generalization assumes that there is no market failure. Subsequent modules will consider the issues presented by market failure.

Figure 14.3

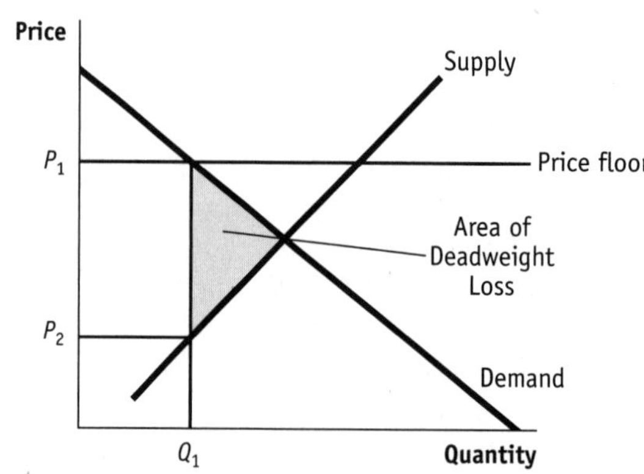

WORKED PROBLEMS

1. Consider a market for cotton in which the market demand curve is given by the equation Q = 40,000 – 200*P* and the market supply curve is given by the equation Q = 200*P*, where Q is bales of cotton and *P* is the price per bale of cotton. Suppose this market is initially in equilibrium and then cotton farmers successfully lobby the legislature to impose a quantity control, or quota, in this market of 10,000 bales of cotton. What will the "wedge" or quota rent be equal to in this market? Calculate the deadweight loss that will occur in this market if this quota is implemented.

STEP 1: Start by drawing a graph of the market for cotton, identifying the initial equilibrium price and quantity. Using the demand and supply equations, you can identify the equilibrium price as $100 per bale of cotton and the equilibrium quantity as 20,000 bales of cotton. After labeling these points on your graph, draw the quantity control or quota on your graph. The quantity control will be a vertical line where the quantity of bales of cotton is 10,000.

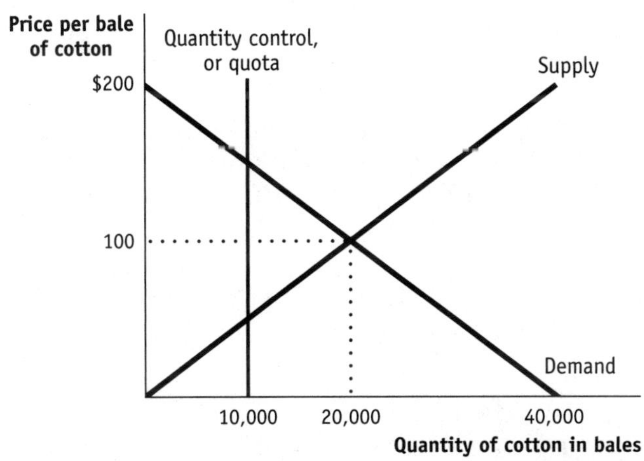

STEP 2: To find the "wedge" or quota rent, you will need to see what price consumers are willing to pay for the quota amount and what price producers must receive in order to provide the quota amount. The difference between the price consumers are willing to pay and the price producers must receive is the "wedge."

Consumers are willing to pay $150 per bale of cotton when 10,000 bales of cotton are offered in the market. Producers must receive $50 per bale of cotton if they supply 10,000 bales of cotton. The "wedge" is therefore $100, or the difference between these two prices. The following figure illustrates this wedge.

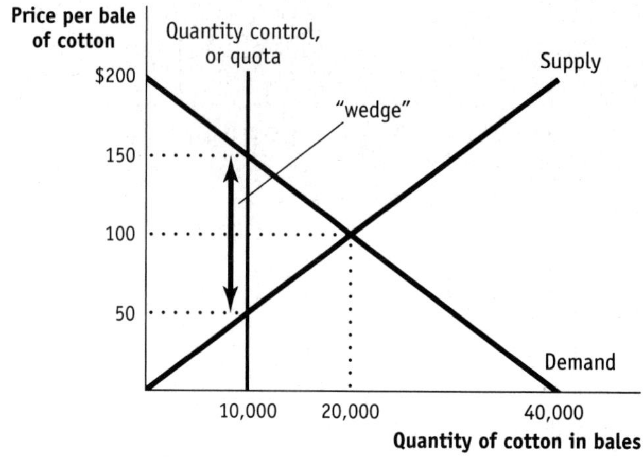

STEP 3: **Determine the area of deadweight loss.**

Deadweight loss refers to the loss of consumer and producer surplus that occurs when mutually beneficial transactions are prevented from occurring. The quota rent raises the price of cotton above its equilibrium price, and both consumers and producers find that this quota rent reduces the number of transactions that would have occurred if there had been no intervention in the market. The following diagram indicates the area of deadweight loss: we can calculate the value of the deadweight loss as the area of the shaded triangle, or (1/2)($150 per bale of cotton – $50 per bale of cotton)(20,000 bales of cotton – 10,000 bales of cotton). The deadweight loss is equal to $500,000.

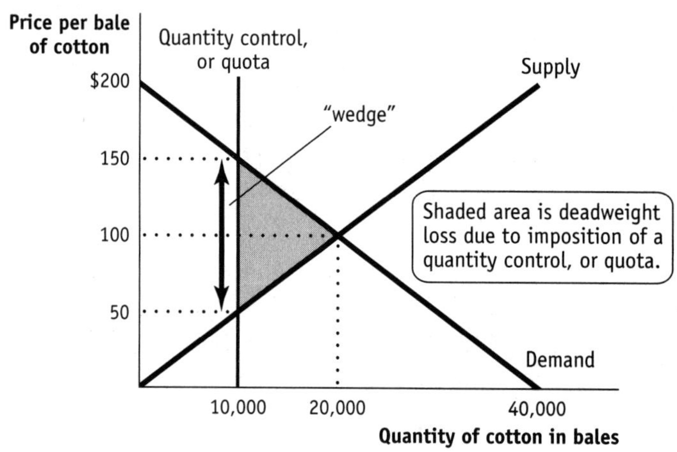

2. Consider the market for bananas in Paradise, a small country that grows all the bananas that are eaten in Paradise. Suppose that the market for bananas in Paradise is described by the demand and supply curves that are given in the following graph. You are asked to identify the equilibrium price and quantity in this market as well as the value of consumer surplus, producer surplus, and total surplus. Paradise is considering implementing a price floor of $20 per box of bananas. How will this price floor affect consumer surplus, producer surplus, and total surplus? Will the price floor create a deadweight loss, and if so, what is the value of this deadweight loss?

STEP 1: To find the equilibrium price and quantity in this market, you will need both the equation for the demand curve and the equation for the supply curve.

The demand curve has a *y*-intercept of 50 and a slope equal to –1/10. The demand curve can be written as $P = 50 - (1/10)Q$, or $Q = 500 - 10P$. The supply curve has a *y*-intercept of 0 and a slope equal to 1/40. The supply curve can be written as $P = (1/40)Q$, or $Q = 40P$. Use these two equations to find the equilibrium price and quantity: the equilibrium price is $10 per box of bananas and the equilibrium quantity is 400 boxes of bananas.

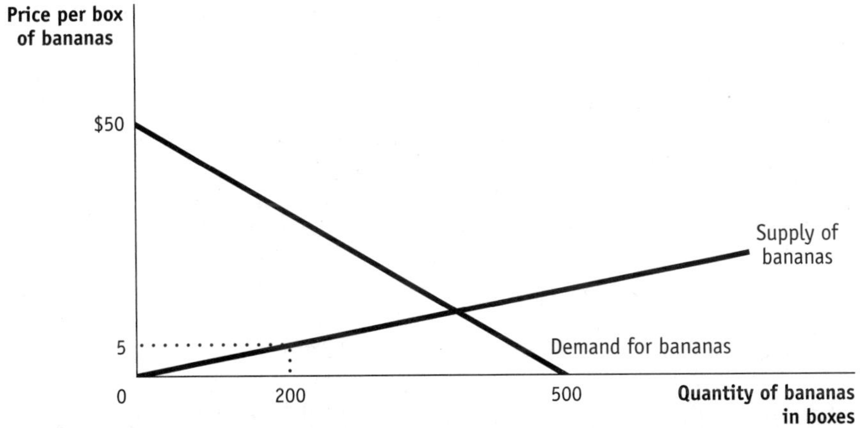

STEP 2: Identify the area of consumer surplus and the area of producer surplus, and then calculate the value of these two areas. Sum these two values to find total surplus.

First, identify on the graph the areas that correspond to consumer surplus and producer surplus. Then, use the formula for the area of a triangle to calculate the value of these areas. Remember that the area of a triangle is equal to (1/2) (the base of the triangle)(the height of the triangle). The following graph identifies the areas of consumer surplus and producer surplus. Recall that total surplus is just the sum of consumer and producer surplus.

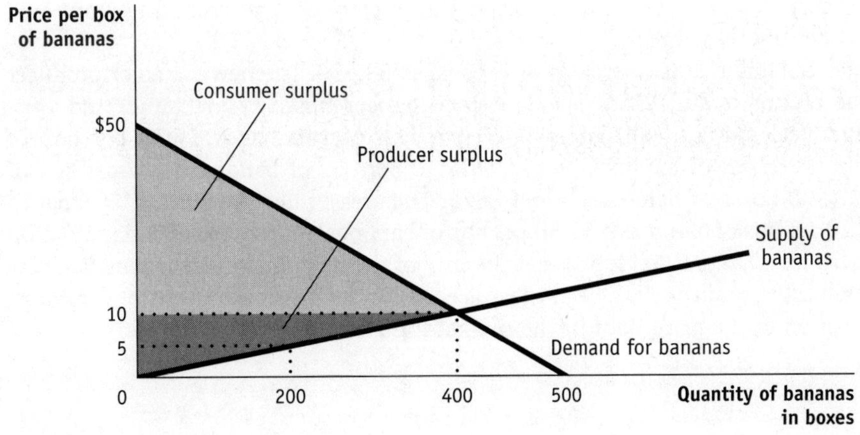

The value of consumer surplus is equal to (1/2)($50 per box of bananas – $10 per box of bananas)(400 boxes of bananas) = $8,000. The value of producer surplus is equal to (1/2)($10 per box of bananas – $0 per box of bananas)(400 boxes of bananas) = $2,000. The value of total surplus is equal to the sum of consumer plus producer surplus, or $10,000.

STEP 3: Analyze the effect of a price floor equal to $20 per box of bananas in Paradise. Determine if the price floor creates a deadweight loss.

First, check to see if the price floor is effective: recall that a price floor must be set above the equilibrium price in order for it to impact the market. In this example, the equilibrium price in the market is $10 per box of bananas, so the price floor of $20 per box of bananas will be effective. Then, determine how many bananas will be demanded at the price floor price of $20 per box of bananas. To find the number of bananas demanded when the price is $20 per box, use the demand equation. When the price is $20 per box, demanders will demand 300 boxes of bananas. Notice that suppliers need to receive a price of only $7.50 in order to be willing to supply 300 boxes of bananas.

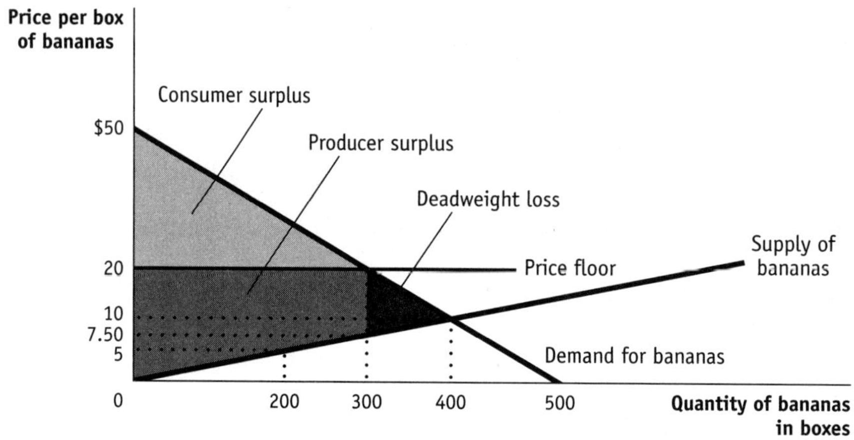

Then, determine the new areas that correspond to consumer and producer surplus. The deadweight loss will be the area that corresponds to the loss in consumer and producer surplus due to the imposition of the price floor. The preceding graph will help you identify these areas.

The new value for consumer surplus is equal to $4,500. The new value for producer surplus is a bit more difficult to calculate since it is composed of a rectangle and a triangle. Producer surplus will equal [($20 per box of bananas – $7.50 per box of bananas)(300 boxes of bananas) + (1/2)($7.50 per box of bananas – $0 per box of bananas)(300 boxes of bananas)], or $4,875. The area of deadweight loss is equal to (1/2)($20 per box of bananas – $7.50 per box of bananas)(400 boxes of bananas – 300 boxes of bananas), or $625. Notice that the sum of the new consumer surplus, the new producer surplus, and the deadweight loss is equal to the original total surplus prior to the imposition of the price floor in the market for bananas.

Problems and Exercises

1. The market for taxi rides in Metropolia this week is described in the following table. Assume that all taxi rides are the same in Metropolia.

Price of taxi rides	Quantity of taxi rides demanded per week	Quantity of taxi rides supplied per week
$ 1	200	40
2	180	60
3	160	80
4	140	100
5	120	120
6	100	140
7	80	160
8	60	180
9	40	200
10	20	220

a. What is the equilibrium price and the equilibrium quantity of taxi rides in Metropolia per week?

Suppose the government of Metropolia institutes a medallion system that limits the number of taxi rides available in Metropolia per week to 80 taxi rides.

b. At what price will consumers want to purchase 80 taxi rides per week?

c. At what price will suppliers be willing to supply 80 taxi rides per week?

d. What price will a taxi medallion rent for in this market? Explain your answer.

e. Draw a graph of the taxi ride market in Metropolia. On this graph, indicate the quota limit, the demand price, the supply price, and the medallion's rental price.

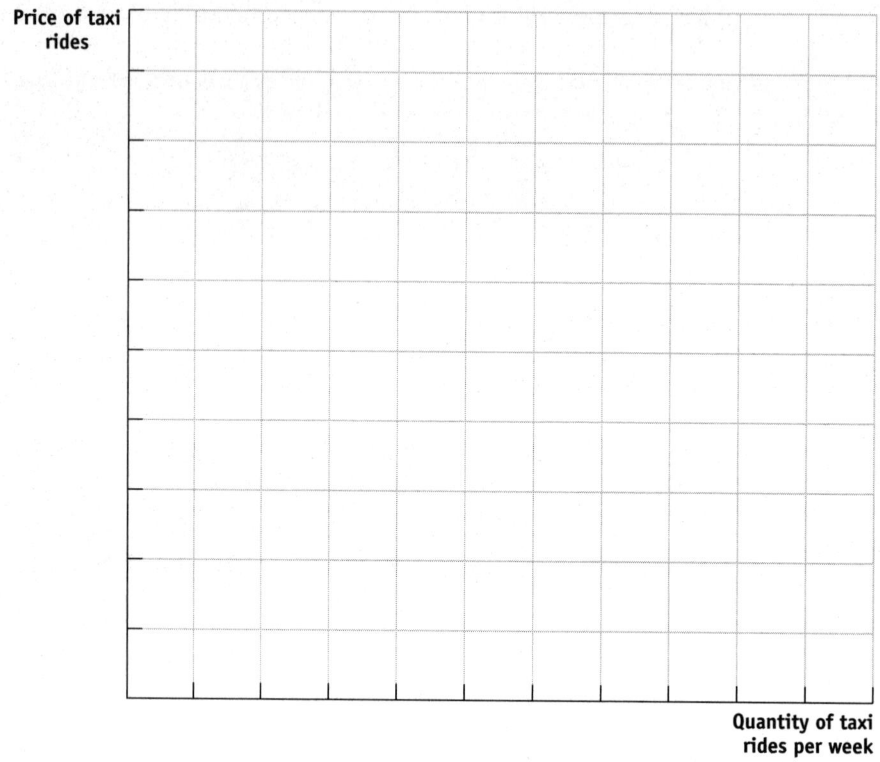

f. What is the total value of the taxi medallions per week in Metropolia?

2. Consider the following graph.

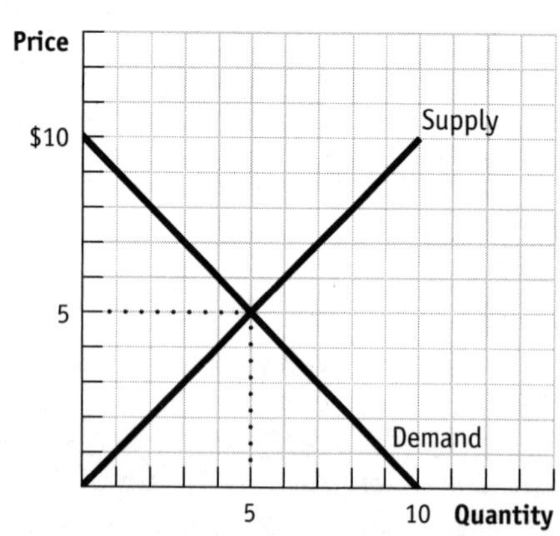

a. What price are consumers willing to pay for this good if 1 unit of the good is produced? What price must sellers receive to be willing to sell 1 unit of the good? Given that resources are scarce, should this first unit of the good be produced? Explain your answer.

b. What price are consumers willing to pay for the second unit of the good if 2 units are produced? What price must sellers receive to be willing to sell this second unit of the good? Given that resources are scarce, should the second unit of this good be produced? Explain your answer.

c. Generalize your findings from parts (a) and (b) of this question. What is the optimal amount of the good to be produced expressed in terms of the consumers' willingness to pay and the sellers' costs?

d. If this market produces a total of 4 units of this good, are resources being underallocated or overallocated to this market? Explain your answer.

e. What is the inefficiency cost or deadweight loss that occurs if this market produces and sells only 4 units of the good?

3. Consider the following graph.

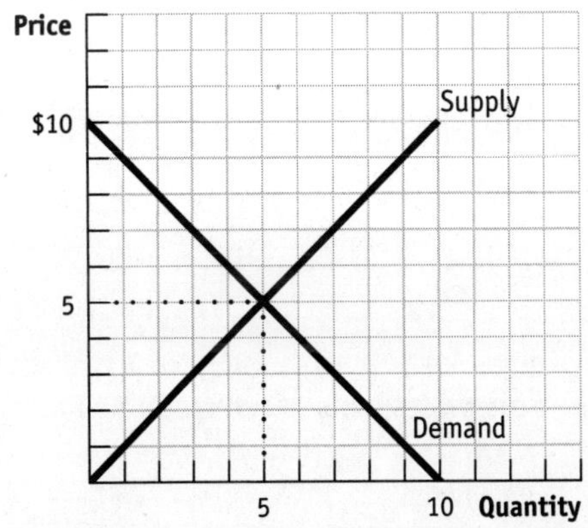

a. What price are consumers willing to pay for this good if 8 units of the good are produced? What price must sellers receive to be willing to provide 8 units of the good? Given that resources are scarce, should this market produce 8 units of the good? Explain your answer.

b. What price are consumers willing to pay if 7 units are produced? What price must sellers receive to be willing to produce 7 units of the good? Given that resources are scarce, should this market produce 7 units of the good? Explain your answer.

c. Given your findings in parts (a) and (b), make a general statement about the optimal amount of the good to produce expressed in terms of the consumers' willingness to pay and the sellers' costs.

d. If this market produces a total of 9 units of the good, are resources being underallocated or overallocated to this market? Explain your answer.

e. What is the inefficiency cost or deadweight loss that occurs if this market produces and sells 9 units of the good?

BEFORE YOU TAKE THE TEST

Module Review Questions

1. When the government intervenes in a market to regulate prices, this is an example of a
a. quantity control.
b. price floor.
c. price ceiling.
d. price control.

2. When the government institutes an upper limit on prices, this is referred to as a
a. quantity control.
b. price floor.
c. price ceiling.
d. price control.

3. When the government institutes a lower limit on prices, this is referred to as a
a. quantity control.
b. price floor.
c. price ceiling.
d. price control.

4. A quantity control or quota
a. limits the price that suppliers can charge for the good or service in the regulated market.
b. limits the price that demanders must pay for the good or service in the regulated market.
c. limits the amount of the good or service available in the regulated market.
d. increases the amount of the good or service available in the regulated market to an amount that exceeds the equilibrium quantity.

5. A quota limit imposed on a market

a. restricts the amount of the good available in that market.

b. results in a payment being made by the government to the license holder.

c. places a lower limit on the amount of the good provided in the regulated market.

d. places an upper limit on the price of the good provided in the regulated market.

6. Which of the following statements is true?

I. Quantity controls are inefficient since they prevent mutually beneficial transactions from occurring.

II. Quantity controls in a market result in too many resources being allocated to that market.

III. Quantity controls result in a wedge: the price demanders are willing to pay for the last unit is less than the price suppliers must receive to produce this last unit.

a. Statement I is true.

b. Statement II is true.

c. Statements I and III are true.

d. Statements I, II, and III are true.

7. Quantity controls

a. provide an incentive to engage in illegal activities.

b. result in underproduction of the good or service in the market where the quota limit has been imposed.

c. result in a less efficient outcome than the market outcome.

d. Answers (a), (b), and (c) are all true statements.

ANSWER KEY

Answers to Problems and Exercises

1. a. Equilibrium occurs when the quantity demanded equals the quantity supplied. From the table, we can see that the equilibrium price is \$5 and the equilibrium quantity is 120 taxi rides per week.

   b. Consumers will demand 80 taxi rides per week at a price of \$7.

   c. Suppliers are willing to supply 80 taxi rides per week for a price of \$3.

   d. The medallion will rent for \$4 per taxi ride, or the difference between the demand price and the supply price when the quantity of taxi rides is limited to 80 rides per week.

   e.

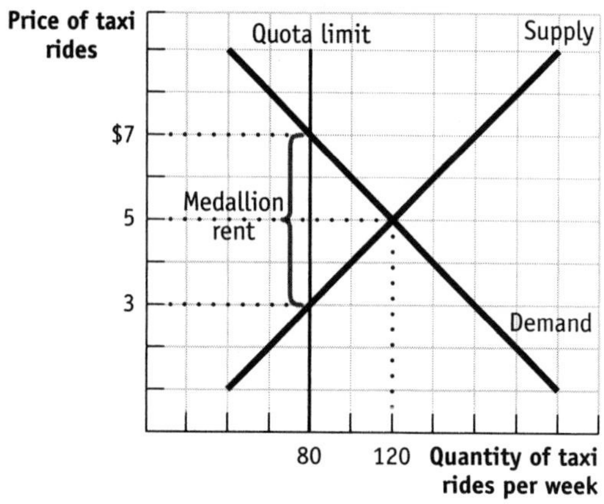

   f. The taxi medallions are worth the product of the medallion rent per ride times the number of taxi rides per week. Thus, the taxi medallions' worth per week equals (\$4 per taxi ride)(80 taxi rides), or \$320.

2. a. To answer this set of questions, you need the demand and supply equations that correspond to the graph. Using the graph as a reference, we can write the demand equation as $P = 10 - Q$ and the supply equation as $P = Q$. Plugging a quantity value of 1 into both of these equations reveals that demanders are willing to pay \$9 for the first unit and suppliers need to receive \$1 to produce this first unit. Clearly this first unit should be produced since the value to the consumer (\$9) exceeds the seller's cost of producing it (\$1).

   b. Using the equations found in part (a), we can substitute a value of 2 for the quantity in both equations to find that demanders are willing to pay \$8 for the second unit and suppliers need to receive \$2 to produce the second unit. The second unit of the good should be produced since its value to consumers (\$8) exceeds the seller's cost of producing it (\$2).

   c. The optimal amount of the good to produce is the amount at which the consumers' willingness to pay for the last unit exactly equals the producers' cost of producing the last unit. So long as the value the consumer places on the good (the price they are willing to pay) exceeds the cost the seller must receive to produce the good, not enough of the good is being produced. In this case, the optimal amount is 5 units, where the consumers' willingness to pay and the sellers' cost are equal at \$5.

d. Resources are being underallocated to this market since consumers are willing to pay \$6 for the last unit produced (the fourth unit) while suppliers are willing to sell this last unit so long as the price is at least equal to \$4. When the value the consumers place on the last unit produced is greater than the cost of producing this last unit, not enough of the good is being produced.

e. The inefficiency cost would equal \$1. The inefficiency cost is (1/2)(the price consumers are willing to pay – the price sellers must receive)(the equilibrium market quantity of the good – the actual level of production), or (1/2)(\$6/unit – \$4/unit)(5 units – 4 units), or \$1.

3. a. To answer this set of questions, you need the demand and supply equations. Using the graph as a reference, we can write the demand equation as $P = 10 - Q$ and the supply equation as $P = Q$. Plugging a quantity of 8 into both of these equations, we find that consumers are willing to pay a price of \$2 for the good and sellers need to receive a price of \$8 for the good to produce 8 units. Since the value the consumers place on the eighth unit (\$2) is less than the sellers' cost of producing the eighth unit (\$8), the eighth unit should not be produced.

b. Using the same reasoning as outlined in answer (a), we find that consumers are willing to pay \$3 per unit if 7 units are produced and sellers require a price of \$7 per unit to be willing to produce 7 units. Since the value of the seventh unit to the consumer (\$3) is less than the cost of producing the seventh unit for the producer (\$7), the seventh unit should not be produced.

c. The optimal amount of the good to produce is the amount at which the consumers' willingness to pay for the last unit exactly equals the sellers' cost of producing the last unit. So long as the value the consumers place on the good (the price they are willing to pay) is less than the cost the sellers must receive to produce the good, too much of the good is being produced. In this case, the optimal amount is 5 units, where the consumers' willingness to pay and the sellers' cost are equal at \$5.

d. Resources are being overallocated to this market: too much of this good is being produced since the value consumers place on the last unit produced is less than the cost to sellers of producing the last unit.

e. The inefficiency cost would equal \$16. The inefficiency cost is (1/2)(the price sellers must receive – the price consumers are willing to pay)(the actual level of production – the equilibrium market quantity of the good), or (1/2)(\$9/unit – \$1/unit)(9 units – 5 units), or \$16.

Answers to Module Review Questions

1. **Answer d.** The government can intervene in a market to regulate prices so that they are lower than the equilibrium level (an effective price ceiling) or higher than the equilibrium level (an effective price floor). Both are examples of price controls.

2. **Answer c.** An upper limit on prices establishes a price level for a product that is less than the equilibrium price and cannot be exceeded. This is an example of an effective price ceiling.

3. **Answer b.** A lower limit on prices establishes a minimum price level for a product that is in excess of the equilibrium price for that product. This is an example of an effective price floor.

4. **Answer c.** A quota control by definition is a limit on the number of units of the good that can be offered in the market. Answers (a) and (b) are both incorrect since they discuss price controls rather than quantity controls. Answer (d) is also incorrect since a quota limit reduces the amount of the good available rather than increasing the amount of the good available.

5. **Answer a.** Answer (a) is the basic definition of a quota limit. Answer (b) is incorrect since there is no assumption of the government making a payment to the license holder when there is a quota limit. Answer (c) is incorrect since a quota limit represents the maximum amount of the good allowed in a market rather than the minimum amount. Answer (d) is incorrect since it focuses on price controls rather than quantity controls.

6. **Answer a.** Statement I is correct because quantity controls restrict the amount of output to a level that is less than the equilibrium amount of output, and thus are inefficient since they prevent mutually beneficial trades from occurring. Because quantity controls restrict output, this implies that too few resources are devoted to the production of the good, so statement II is incorrect. Quantity controls do result in a wedge being created, but that wedge is the difference between the high price consumers are willing to pay and the low price producers must receive to provide the good, thus statement III is incorrect.

7. **Answer d.** Quantity controls restrict output, result in too few resources being devoted to the production of the good, and create an incentive for black market activities as consumers seek out alternative methods for getting the scarce good.

module 15

Taxes

BEFORE YOU READ THE MODULE

Summary

This module considers the topic of taxes and the effect of taxes on supply and demand. In addition, the module considers the issues of tax efficiency and equity; tax incidence, which analyzes who actually bears the economic burden of a particular tax; the deadweight loss associated with taxation; and the difference between progressive and regressive taxes.

Module Objectives

Objective #1. Taxes are necessary to provide governments with funds to provide services that the public wants. However, taxes usually have a cost that exceeds the money the government actually receives from the tax, because the imposition of a tax distorts the incentives to engage in mutually beneficial transactions. An efficient tax is one that distorts incentives as little as possible. An equitable tax is a tax that is considered fair. With regard to tax policy, there is a trade-off between efficiency and equity: a tax may be highly efficient, but then it is apt to be quite inequitable, and vice versa.

Objective #2. A simple tax to consider when analyzing the effects of taxes on consumers and producers is an excise tax, which is a tax that is charged on each unit of a good or service that is sold. An excise tax imposed on producers has the effect of shifting the supply curve to the left by a vertical amount equal to the excise tax. In effect, producers recognize that the excise tax effectively increases their cost of production, since now they must remit to the government an amount equal to the excise tax for every unit of the good they sell. Figure 15.1 illustrates a market in which an excise tax has been levied on producers of the good. Note that the initial supply curve and the supply curve with the excise tax are parallel to one another and that the vertical distance between these two supply curves is equal to the amount of the excise tax. Study Figure 15.1 as you read the bullet points summarizing the effects of this excise tax on this market.

Figure 15.1

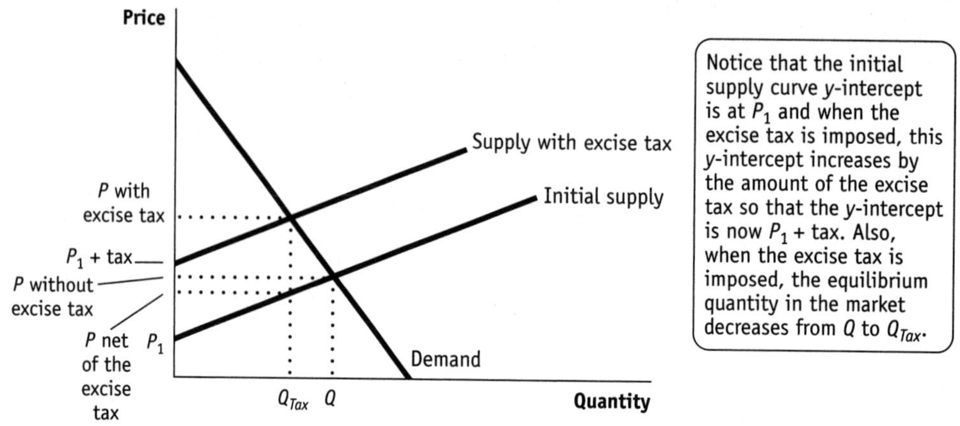

- The imposition of the tax reduces the quantity of the good sold in the market. The tax, because it effectively raises the price of the good, distorts incentives, and this distortion results in missed opportunities for mutually beneficial transactions. In the graph, the reduction in consumption from Q units to Q_{Tax} units is a measure of the missed opportunities for mutually beneficial transactions that arise with the imposition of the tax.
- When the excise tax is imposed, producers sell the good for the price marked "*P* with excise tax." But producers do not get to keep all of this money since they must pay the government the excise tax, which can be measured as the vertical distance between the two supply curves. Thus, after producers pay the tax, they get to keep the price marked "*P* net of the excise tax." From the producers' point of view the effect of the excise tax is that they are now selling fewer units of the good, Q_{Tax} instead of Q, and they are receiving the price "*P* net of the excise tax" for each unit of the good they sell rather than the original price before the imposition of the tax. The cost of the tax to producers is therefore equal to (*P* without excise tax – *P* net of the excise tax)(Q_{Tax}). Figure 15.2 illustrates the area of producer tax incidence (PTI). The area of PTI is smaller than the consumer tax incidence (CTI), but it is possible for the areas to be the same size or for PTI to be greater than the CTI, depending on the elasticities of the demand and supply curves.
- From the consumers' point of view, the excise tax raises the price of the good from "*P* without excise tax" to "*P* with excise tax" while simultaneously reducing the amount of the good transacted in the market from Q to Q_{Tax}. Thus, the cost of the excise tax to the consumer is equal to (*P* with excise tax – *P* without excise tax)(Q_{Tax}). Figure 15.2 illustrates the area of CTI. The area of PTI is smaller than the area of CTI, but it is possible for the areas to be the same size or for PTI to be greater than the CTI, depending on the elasticities of the demand and supply curves.

Figure 15.2

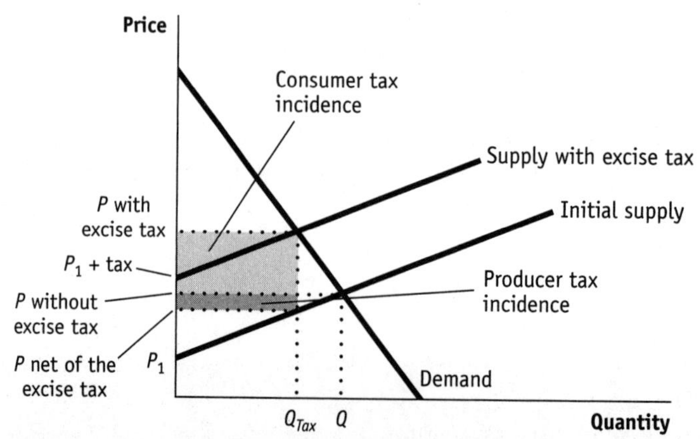

- The incidence of the tax on consumers and producers is dependent on the price elasticity of the demand and supply curves. When demand is relatively price inelastic and supply is relatively price elastic, the economic incidence of the tax falls primarily on consumers. When demand is relatively price elastic and supply is relatively price inelastic, the economic incidence of the tax falls primarily on producers. Figure 15.3 illustrates how these price elasticities can affect the CTI and PTI.

Figure 15.3

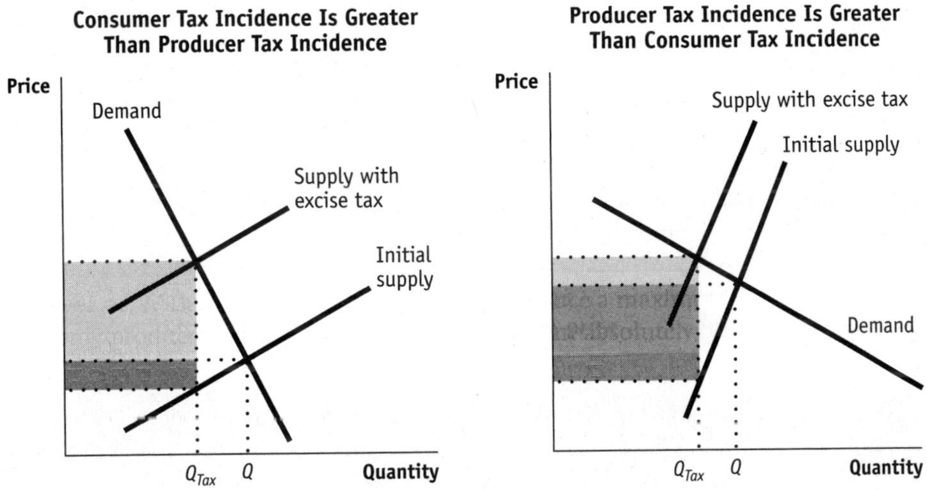

- The tax revenue from an excise tax can be calculated as the product of the tax per unit times the number of units of the good sold. The tax revenue is also equal to the sum of PTI plus CTI. In Figure 15.3, the tax revenue in each graph is equal to the sum of the two shaded rectangles. The tax revenue is equal to the area of the rectangle whose height is the tax wedge between the supply and demand curves and whose width is the quantity of the good bought and sold when the tax is imposed. The amount of tax revenue raised by an excise tax depends on the tax rate and the price elasticities of supply and demand. For a given tax rate, tax revenue is greater if the price elasticities of supply and demand are both low, since the quantity demanded of the good isn't reduced very much when the tax increases the price of the good. Theoretically it is possible to raise a tax rate to a high enough level that tax revenue falls, or to reduce the tax rate to a level at which tax revenue rises, but in practice politicians take this possibility into account when setting tax rates.
- The excise tax entails the cost that producers and consumers pay to the government, but it also imposes costs over and above the tax revenue collected in the form of inefficiency that arises when the market provides only the Q_{Tax} amount of the good instead of the original Q. This reduction in output due to the tax reflects the mutually beneficial exchanges that the tax prevents. The value to society of these lost exchanges can be measured as the deadweight loss (DWL) associated with the tax.
- All real-world taxes impose some DWL, but a badly designed tax results in a larger DWL than a well-designed tax. Figure 15.4 identifies the area of DWL and tax revenue when an excise tax is imposed. The graphs contrast two different markets and the level of DWL that occurs with the imposition of an excise tax of $*x* per unit. Taxes imposed on a good whose price elasticity of demand and/or supply is elastic results in a relatively larger DWL than the same size tax imposed on a good whose price elasticity of demand and/or supply is inelastic. This occurs because the change in the quantity demanded is greater when demand and/or supply is price elastic than when demand and/or supply is price inelastic. Thus, to minimize the inefficiency of a tax, policymakers want to tax goods whose demand and/or supply are relatively inelastic. Conversely, if policymakers wish to discourage a particular activity by taxing it, they will decrease consumption relatively more if demand and/or supply are relatively elastic.

Figure 15.4

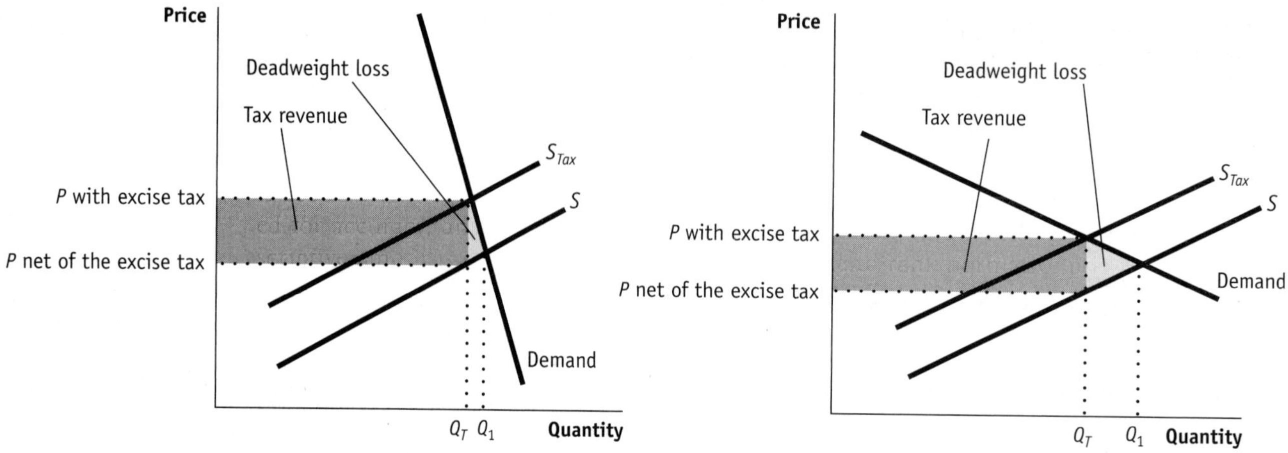

- The area of DWL is the sum of the consumer surplus and the producer surplus that is lost when the excise tax is imposed. The DWL does not include the administrative costs incurred by the government and by taxpayers to pay the tax. The total inefficiency caused by a tax is the sum of the DWL and its administrative costs.

Objective #3. A lump-sum tax is a tax that is the same for all people regardless of any actions people take. This is an efficient tax since the tax does not distort incentives. However, a lump-sum tax is perceived as a highly unfair tax since it does not distinguish among taxpayers according to their ability to pay. The example of a lump-sum tax illustrates the trade-off between efficiency and equity: taxes that are highly efficient are apt to be highly inequitable, and taxes that are equitable tend to be inefficient.

Objective #4. The simplest tax structure is a proportional tax, in which the tax is the same percentage of the base regardless of the taxpayer's income or wealth. In a regressive tax structure the tax rises less than in proportion to income. This tax structure results in high-income taxpayers paying a smaller percentage of their income than low-income taxpayers. In a progressive tax structure the tax rises more than in proportion to income: this tax structure results in high-income taxpayers paying a larger percentage of their income than low-income taxpayers.

Key Terms

progressive tax a tax that takes a larger share of the income of high-income taxpayers than of low-income taxpayers.

regressive tax a tax that takes a smaller share of the income of high-income taxpayers than of low-income taxpayers.

proportional tax a tax that is the same percentage of the *tax base* regardless of the taxpayer's income or wealth.

excise tax a tax on sales of a good or service.

tax incidence a measure of who really pays a tax.

Notes

Key Terms *(continued)*

administrative costs the *resources* used (which is a cost) by government to collect the tax, and by taxpayers to pay it, over and above the amount of the tax, as well as to evade it.

lump-sum tax a tax that is the same for everyone, regardless of any actions people take.

Notes

AFTER YOU READ THE MODULE

Tips

Tip #1. Students often struggle with finding the new supply curve once an excise tax has been imposed. This is not difficult if you start by recognizing that the new supply curve should be parallel to the old supply curve and have a *y*-intercept that is equal to the initial *y*-intercept plus the amount of the excise tax per unit. If you are working with equations, you should write the supply equation in slope-intercept form and then simply increase the constant in this term by the amount of the excise tax.

Tip #2. The imposition of an excise tax in a market in general reduces both consumer and producer surplus. Let's consider a market where there is no excise tax and then look at the same market with an excise tax. Figure 15.5 illustrates a market in which there is no excise tax: *CS* is the area of consumer surplus and *PS* is the area of producer surplus.

Figure 15.5

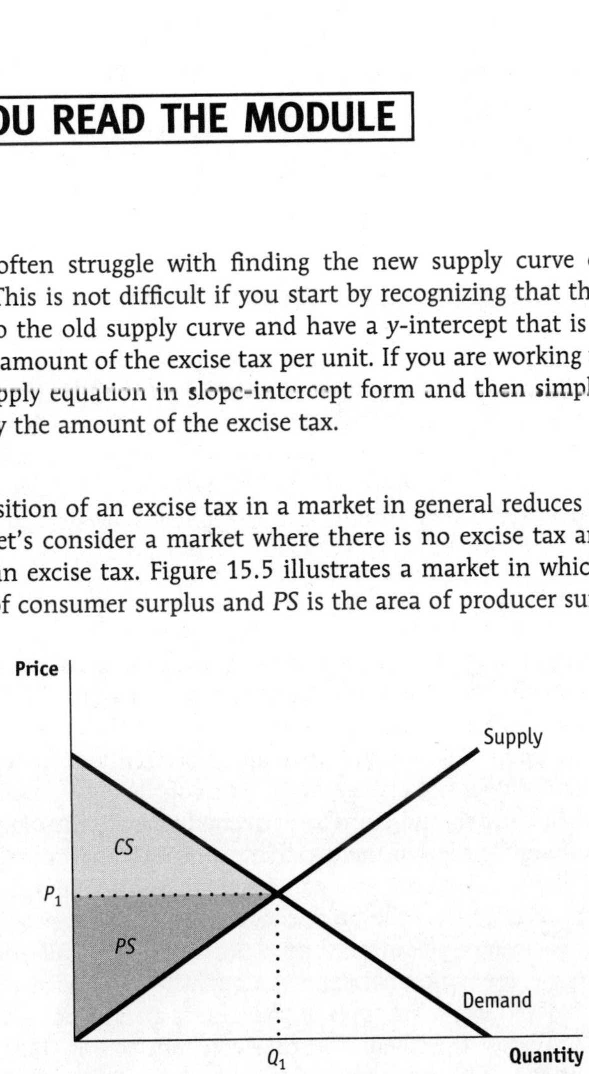

In Figure 15.6, an excise tax is imposed on this market. This excise tax shifts the supply curve to the left by a vertical distance equal to the excise tax. Once the market adjusts to this excise tax, notice that the areas of *CS* and *PS* are both decreased. Part of the original area of *CS* is now CTI and represents the economic incidence of the tax on consumers. Part of the original area of *PS* is now PTI and represents the economic incidence of the tax on producers. Part of the original area of *CS* is now DWL captured from *CS*, and part of the original area of *PS* is now DWL captured from *PS*. It is important to see that the excise tax redistributes *CS* and *PS* in two ways: some of this surplus goes to the government when it collects tax revenue from the excise tax (the tax revenue is equal to the sum of the areas of producer and consumer tax incidence), and some of this surplus is simply lost because the tax imposes an efficiency cost on this market (the area of DWL). Study this graph carefully.

Figure 15.6

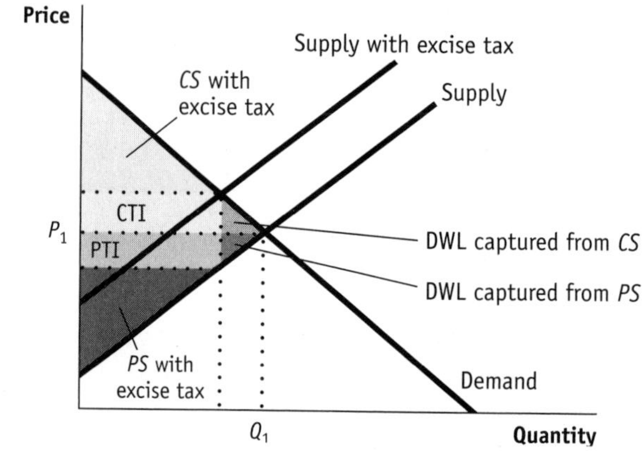

Tip #3. Students often have trouble with the analysis of the excise tax. The most common error is to think that when an excise tax is imposed on a good that this results in the price of the good increasing by the full amount of the tax. Let's go through several examples to work on this issue. Each of the examples use the following labels: P_1 is the original price of the good, Q_1 is the original equilibrium quantity of the good, Q_T is the equilibrium quantity of the good once the excise tax is imposed, P_T is the gross price of the good once the excise tax is imposed, and P_N is the net price that the producer receives after the producer pays the excise tax to the government. In addition, each example also indicates the area that corresponds to CTI, PTI, and DWL. Remember that tax revenue is always equal to the sum of the CTI and the PTI.

- In our first example, consider a market in which demand is perfectly inelastic. What happens in this market if an excise tax is imposed on producers of this good? Figure 15.7 illustrates this situation. Notice that the excise tax causes the price of the good to increase from P_1 to P_T, where the increase in the price is exactly equal to the amount of the excise tax. In this example, the excise tax does cause the price of the good to increase by the full amount of the tax: this occurs because demand is perfectly inelastic, which means that the quantity demanded does not change as the price of the good changes. Figure 15.7 also illustrates that when the demand curve is perfectly inelastic, the demanders of the good pay the entire economic burden of the tax: there is no PTI, and tax revenue in this case is exactly equal to CTI. In Figure 15.7, you can see that the original equilibrium price, P_1, is equal to the net price (P_N) that the producer receives after the producer pays the excise tax. Note that an excise tax placed on a good with perfectly inelastic demand does not create a DWL, since there is no change in the quantity demanded of the good with the increase in price due to the tax. This tells us that this is an efficient tax because it does not cause consumers to distort their behavior: they continue to buy the same amount of the good as they did prior to the imposition of the tax. Study Figure 15.7 carefully until you can easily see these points.

Figure 15.7

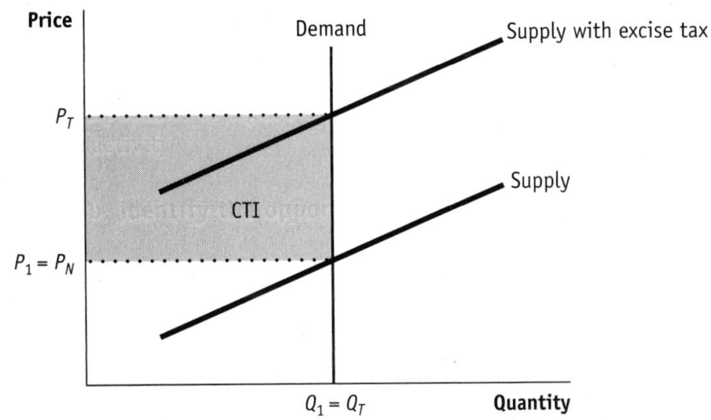

- Let's consider a second example in which the demand curve is perfectly elastic. Figure 15.8 illustrates this situation. Notice that when the demand curve is perfectly elastic, the excise tax does not cause the price of the good to increase at all. Instead, producers find that the excise tax simply results in their selling less of the good at the prevailing market price (thus, $P_1 = P_T$). In this example, there is no CTI because consumers do not end up paying more for the good with the tax. There is PTI, though, because producers find that the net price they receive when they sell the good has fallen by the full amount of the excise tax. In this example, the tax revenue is equal to PTI. The excise tax also distorts consumption decisions: notice that there is a DWL associated with the tax. The DWL can be calculated as $1/2(P_T - P_N)(Q_1 - Q_T)$. This is not an efficient tax because it results in a DWL. Again, study Figure 15.8 until these points are clear to you.

Figure 15.8

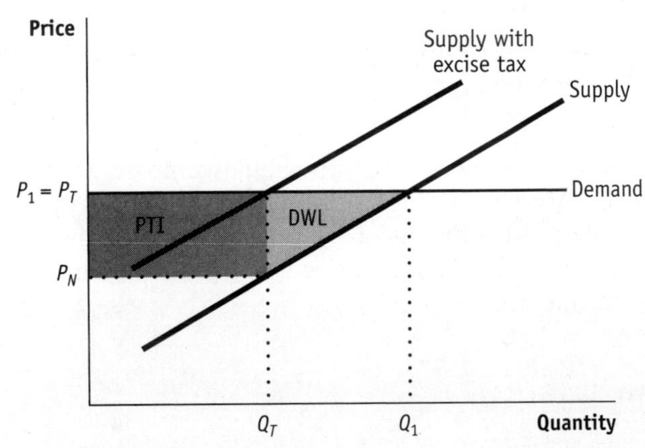

- Now for a third and more representative example, since the demand curve is neither perfectly inelastic nor perfectly elastic. Figure 15.9 illustrates this situation. Notice that when the excise tax is imposed, this causes the supply curve to shift to the left, which results in a movement along the demand curve. Because the demand curve is downward sloping, but not vertical, this movement causes the price of the good to increase relative to its initial level. But notice that P_T is not equal to P_1 plus the tax: P_T is higher than the original price before the tax, but the increase in price is not equal to the excise tax. In this example, there is both CTI and PTI. Consumers find that with the tax they purchase fewer units of the good and each unit of the good they purchase now costs P_T instead of the original P_1. From the consumer perspective, the excise tax results in the price of the good rising by $P_T - P_1$. CTI is therefore equal to $(P_T - P_1)(Q_T)$. The producer finds that the tax results in their selling fewer units of the good, and each unit of the good they sell now sells for P_N instead of the original P_1 once they pay the government the excise tax. From the producer perspective, the excise tax results in the price of the good falling by $P_1 - P_N$. PTI is therefore equal to $(P_1 - P_N)(Q_T)$. In this example, the excise tax results in fewer units of the good being sold, which indicates that the excise tax distorts choices in this market and therefore there is a DWL associated with this tax. The DWL can be calculated as the area $1/2(P_T - P_N)(Q_1 - Q_T)$. Review this graph thoroughly until you are very comfortable with it. In particular, pay close attention to the fact that the price with the excise tax does not rise by the full amount of the tax.

Figure 15.9

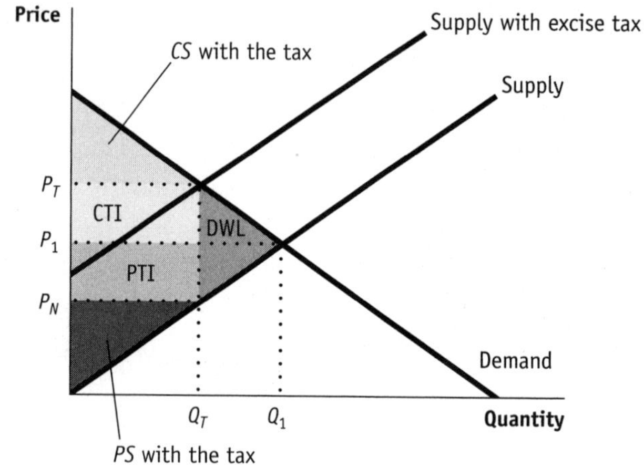

Tip #4. There is one final issue about excise taxes that requires some practice and thought: the effect of price elasticity on the effects of the excise tax on CTI, PTI, and DWL. Practice drawing some graphs with different price elasticities of demand and the same supply curve to see how the price elasticity of demand affects these three measures. Then practice drawing some graphs with different price elasticities of supply and the same demand curve to see how the price elasticity of supply affects these three measures. For each graph you draw, label the area that corresponds to CTI, PTI, and DWL.

Tip #5. When evaluating the tax structure of a tax, you should compare the tax revenue collected from a taxpayer relative to income with the tax revenue collected from another taxpayer relative to that taxpayer's income. A tax is regressive if the percentage of the tax revenue relative to income falls as income rises. A tax is progressive if the percentage of the tax revenue relative to income rises as income rises.

WORKED PROBLEMS

1. Littletown is debating implementing an excise tax on cigarettes in their community. Currently, there is agreement among city officials about the size of the excise tax that will be levied on cigarette sellers, but there is disagreement among these city officials about what the demand for cigarettes is in Littletown. One group of officials believes that demand is quite inelastic and that people who smoke will not alter their smoking behavior significantly once the excise tax is imposed. Another group of officials believes that demand is more elastic and they believe that smokers in Littletown will likely decrease their smoking of cigarettes sold in Littletown once the excise tax is implemented. This second group of officials reasons that smokers will likely drive to a nearby community to purchase their cigarettes if Littletown enacts the excise tax, and this suggests to them that even a small change in the price of cigarettes will result in a large change in the quantity demanded. Given this information, analyze the impact of this excise tax for each of the demand curves that have been described. In your description make sure you address the impact of the tax on consumer surplus,

producer surplus, and deadweight loss given the two different demand curve scenarios. Also comment on the relative amount of tax revenue to be generated by the excise tax in the two scenarios: will tax revenue be the same or will it be different depending upon the price elasticity of demand? If efficiency of the taxation is the primary goal of the city officials, which demand curve elasticity results in the greatest tax efficiency and why? Finally, comment on who bears the economic burden of the tax in the two scenarios. In your analysis assume that the supply curve is the same, the excise tax is the same per unit of cigarettes, and that the initial equilibrium price and quantity is the same.

STEP 1: Draw two diagrams depicting the same supply curve in each diagram. Label the first diagram "Inelastic Demand" and the second diagram "Elastic Demand." Draw these two diagrams next to each other so it will be easy to compare the results of your analysis. Label these supply curves S_1 on each graph.

In this step, you are trying to get a set of diagrams that allows you to easily compare how the demand elasticities affect the impact of an excise tax on consumer surplus, producer surplus, tax revenue, the economic burden of the tax, and deadweight loss. A careful rendering of this first set of graphs will make the rest of the work involved in this problem far easier.

Notice in the following graphs that the two supply curves are parallel to each other and if you extended them they would have the same y-intercept. In the diagrams, the two supply curves should be identical. Notice also that the two graphs are labeled completely and clearly so that as we continue our analysis we will not need to worry that somehow we have gotten the two scenarios mixed up.

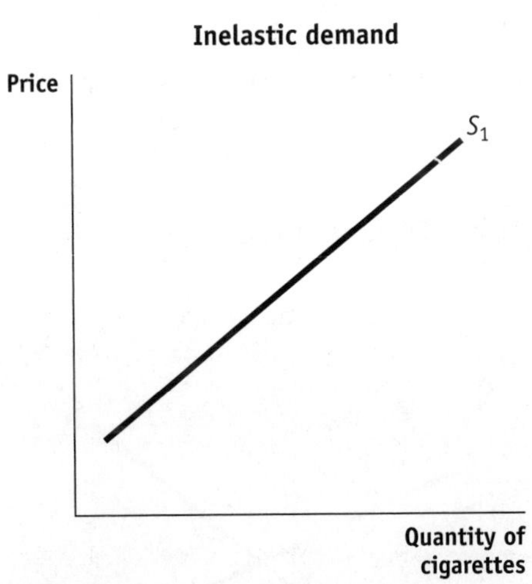

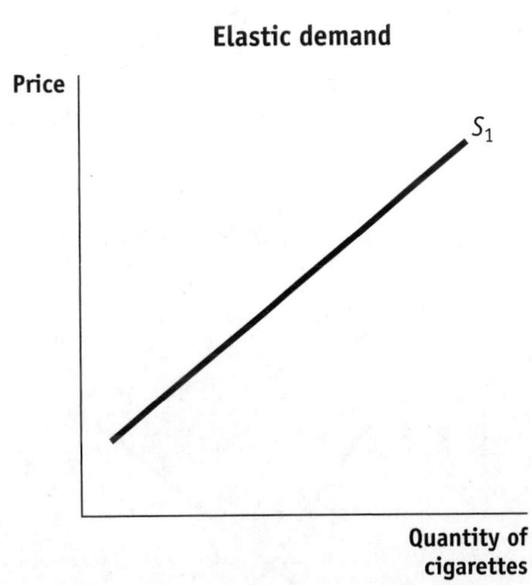

STEP 2: On the first diagram, label an initial price and quantity combination on the supply curve that will represent the initial equilibrium price and quantity. Label the same price and quantity combination of the second diagram. Label the price as P_1 and the quantity as Q_1 on both graphs.

The intent of Step 2 is to make sure that we are making a fair comparison of how demand elasticities affect the impact of an excise tax. By starting at the same initial point of equilibrium, we can focus our attention solely on how demand elasticities affect the impact of an excise tax.

To find P_1 in the two graphs, I first drew a horizontal line across both graphs so that I was effectively holding price constant. I noted on both graphs where this horizontal line crossed the supply curve and drew a vertical line down from this point of intersection. This enabled me to label Q_1 on each graph. There are an infinite number of possible Q_1 and P_1 combinations, but your work will be easier if you select a combination that is not too close to either the horizontal or the vertical axes.

Notice that I extended both the horizontal and vertical dotted lines past the point (Q_1, P_1) on the supply curve. This will be helpful particularly when we want to draw an excise tax of the same amount per unit in each graph.

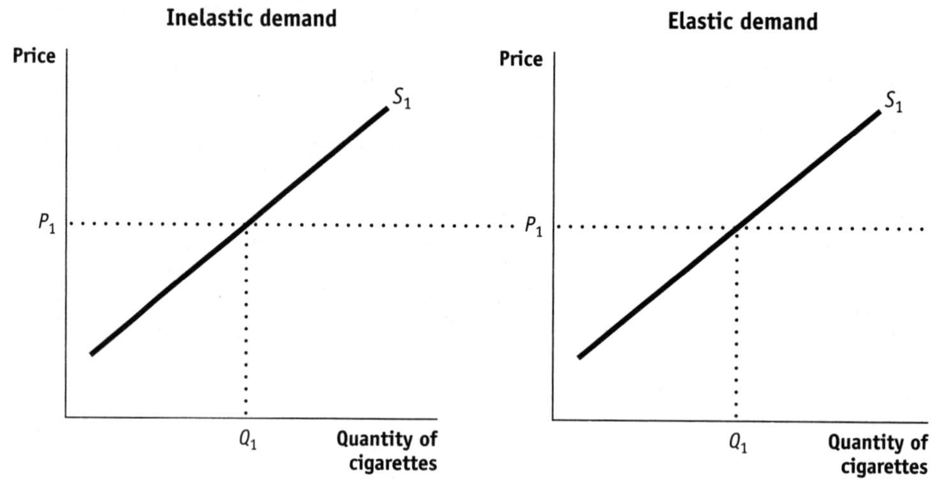

STEP 3: On the first diagram, draw an inelastic demand curve that goes through the point (Q_1, P_1) on this graph. On the second diagram, draw an elastic demand curve that goes through the point (Q_1, P_1) on this graph. Label these demand curves D_1 on each graph.

In Step 3, we are simply completing our initial diagrams so that we are ready to analyze how demand elasticities affect the impact of an excise tax. In the diagram of the inelastic demand curve, you will want to draw a relatively steeper demand curve, while in the diagram of the elastic demand curve, you will want to draw a relatively flatter demand curve. Both curves should intersect the supply curve at the point (Q_1, P_1).

STEP 4: On the first diagram and the second diagram, draw new supply curves that are parallel to the initial supply curves, to the left of the initial supply curves, and that represent the same excise tax per unit on the good. Label these new supply curves S_2 on each graph.

For our analysis to be accurate, it is vital that we have the same excise tax per unit drawn on the two diagrams. To make sure that the excise taxes are equivalent as to amount per unit, I first drew another horizontal line that was at a price greater than P_1. In a numeric example, this horizontal line would be drawn at that price that was equal to the initial equilibrium price plus the amount of the excise tax per unit. For example, if the initial price was $10 per unit of the good and the excise tax per unit was $2, then the new horizontal line would be drawn at a price of $12.

Notice on the diagrams that follow that this new horizontal line intersects the vertical line drawn from Q_1 (in the graphs there is a heavy point indicating this intersection). This heavy point on both graphs represents the same quantity and price combination: it represents how much the price would increase with the tax if the quantity was held constant at Q_1. In order for the size of the excise tax per unit to be the same in the two graphs, we will want the new supply curves to go through this point but have the same slopes as the initial supply curves in each graph. You will want to study this graph carefully to make sure you understand these ideas.

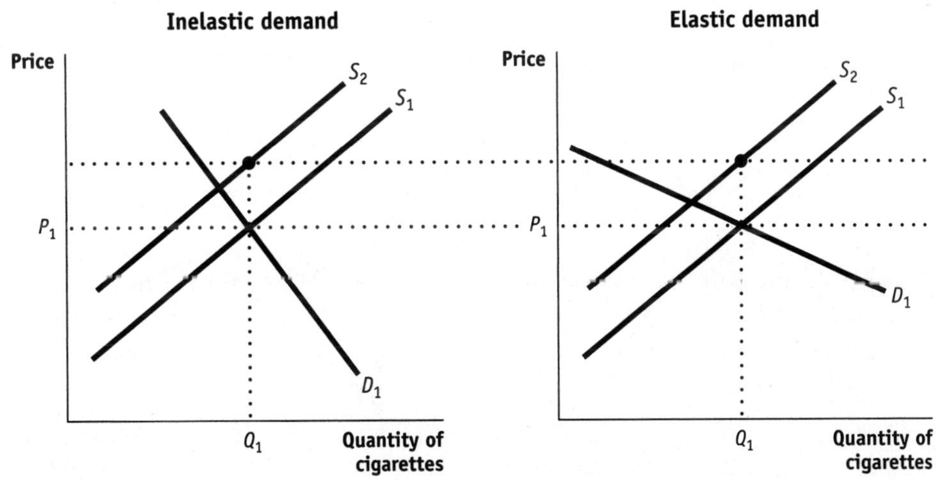

STEP 5: In your graph, label the new equilibrium price and new equilibrium quantity in each graph. Use P_2 and Q_2 in the graph labeled "Inelastic Demand" and P_3 and Q_3 in your graph labeled "Elastic Demand."

In the graphs that follow, the new equilibriums have been marked with a bold dot and labeled. Notice that in both diagrams the equilibrium price increases with the imposition of the excise tax, but the price rises by a larger amount in the diagram with inelastic demand than it does in the diagram with elastic demand. Notice also that in both diagrams the equilibrium quantity decreases with the imposition of the excise tax, but the quantity decreases by a larger amount in the diagram with elastic demand than it does in the diagram with inelastic demand.

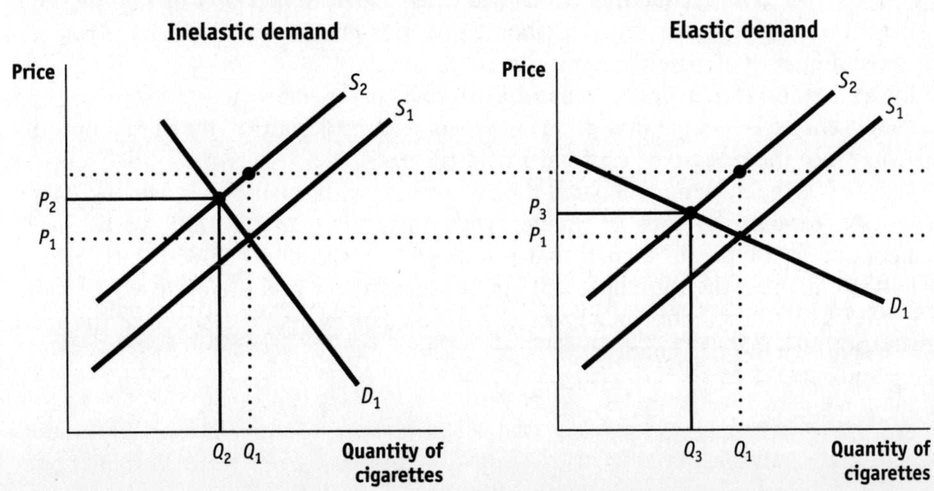

STEP 6: In each of your diagrams shade and label the areas that correspond to consumer surplus with the tax, producer surplus with the tax, tax revenue, and deadweight loss.

The diagrams that follow identify these different areas. Remember that consumer surplus is that area beneath the demand curve and above the price that consumers pay for the good; producer surplus is that area above the supply curve and beneath the price that producers receive for the good; tax revenue is equal to the tax per unit times the number of units of the good sold when the tax is implemented; and deadweight loss is equal to the sum of consumer surplus and producer surplus that is lost when the tax is imposed.

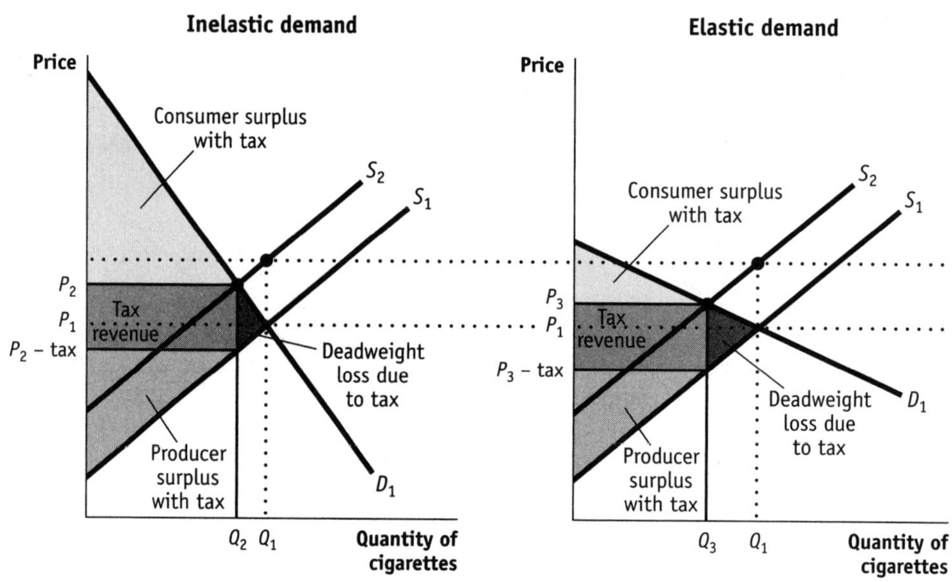

STEP 7: Analyze the two scenarios with regard to the effect of the different demand elasticities on consumer surplus, producer surplus, tax revenue, and deadweight loss.

Examination of the diagrams in Step 6 immediately makes it clear that consumer surplus is much larger when demand is inelastic than when demand is elastic, holding everything else constant. This should not be surprising since inelastic demand tells us that quantity is not very responsive to price changes: when price increases due to the imposition of the excise tax, consumers continue to purchase just about the same quantity as they did before imposition of the tax. In contrast, when demand is elastic there is a large decrease in the quantity demanded when the price increases due to the tax.

Producer surplus is also smaller when demand is elastic due to the large responsiveness of quantity to the change in price.

In the diagram with inelastic demand, the excise tax generates more tax revenue than an equivalent excise tax per unit generates when demand is elastic. This should not surprise us since in the case of elastic demand the excise tax results in a much smaller quantity of the good being purchased then is the case with the inelastic demand curve.

Finally, deadweight loss is smaller with inelastic demand than with elastic demand: an excise tax on a good that people will continue to buy with little reduction in the quantity they purchase will have less distortion, and therefore will be more efficient, than an excise tax on a good where the quantity people respond of the good is very sensitive to price changes.

STEP 8: Given your analysis in Steps 5 and 6, evaluate the relative efficiency of the tax under the two demand curve possibilities.

Referring back to the diagrams in Step 6 we can see that the area of deadweight loss is larger when the demand is elastic, holding everything else constant. This is not surprising since the quantity effect is large when price increases and the demand curve is elastic. Given the two possible scenarios, there will be less deadweight loss if the demand curve for cigarettes is inelastic.

STEP 9: Redraw the diagram you have in Step 4 and indicate on this diagram the economic burden of the tax on consumers and producers for each of the demand scenarios. Explain how demand elasticity affects the economic burden of the tax.

From the consumers' perspective, the tax they pay changes the price they pay and the quantity of the good they purchase: the price change is equal to the difference between the price with the tax and the price before the implementation of the tax, while the quantity change is equal to the reduction in purchases made by the consumers. For the diagram with the inelastic demand curve, the economic burden of the excise tax on consumers is equal to $(P_2 - P_1)(Q_2)$, and for the diagram with the elastic demand curve, the economic burden of the excise tax on consumers is equal to $P_3 - P_1)(Q_3)$. From the diagram, you can see that the economic burden of the tax is heavier for consumers when the demand is inelastic, holding everything else constant.

From the producers' perspective, the imposition of the excise tax changes the price they receive when they sell the good and the quantity of the good they sell: the price change is equal to the difference between the price they initially sold the good for and the price they receive once they collect the tax and pay that tax to the government, while the quantity change is equal to the reduction in sales of the good due to the imposition of the tax. For the diagram with the inelastic demand curve, the economic burden of the excise tax on producers is equal to $[P_1 - (P_2 - \text{tax})](Q_2)$, and for the diagram with the elastic demand curve, the economic burden of the excise tax on producers is equal to $[P_1 - (P_3 - \text{tax})](Q_3)$. From the diagram, you can see that the economic burden of the tax is heavier for producers when the demand is elastic, holding everything else constant.

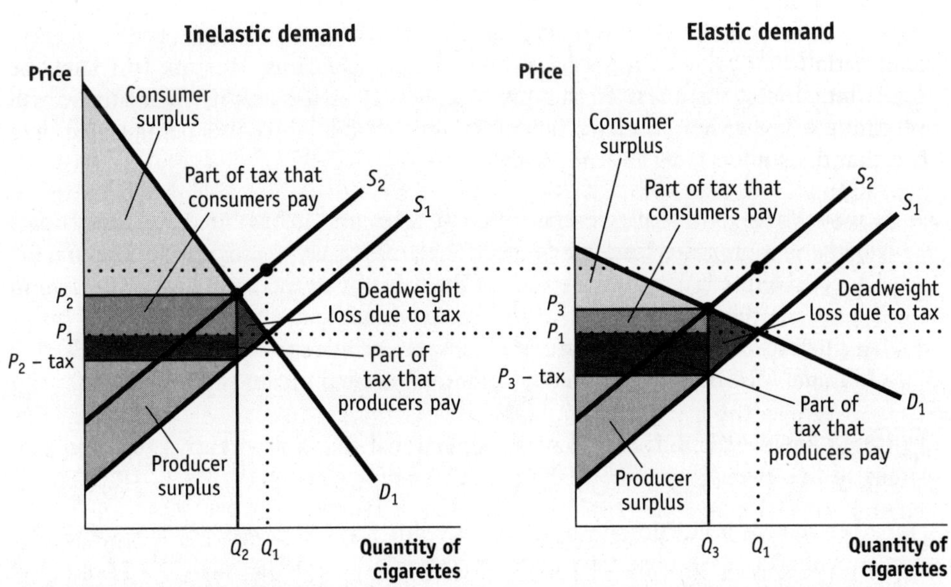

2. The mayor in your community has asked you to come up with an excise tax on a good that will be as efficient as possible. What must be true about the elasticity of demand and the elasticity of supply if the tax is to as efficient as possible? Why might this tax not be a good tax for the mayor to implement? In your answer make sure you help the mayor understand different principles of fairness that he might want to consider in designing his tax plan.

STEP 1: Focus on elasticity of demand first and how it affects the efficiency of a tax, holding everything else constant.

The more inelastic the demand for the good, holding everything else constant, the smaller will be the quantity effect of an increase in the price of the good. Since an excise tax will necessarily raise the price of the good (unless demand is perfectly elastic), there will be greater efficiency and less deadweight loss from the tax if the excise tax is imposed on a good with inelastic demand.

STEP 2: Focus on elasticity of supply and how it affects the efficiency of a tax, holding everything else constant.

The more inelastic the supply of the good, holding everything else constant, the smaller will be the quantity effect of an increase in the price of the good. As the price of the good rises with the excise tax, there will be greater efficiency and less deadweight loss from the tax if the excise tax is imposed on a good with inelastic supply.

STEP 3: Summarize your findings in Steps 1 and 2 in order to make an advisory statement to the mayor.

If the mayor's primary goal of his tax policy is efficiency, then taxing a good that has both inelastic demand and inelastic supply is superior to taxing a good that has elastic demand and/or elastic supply.

STEP 4: Advise the mayor as to why this tax might not be a good idea.

The tax, if it is highly efficient, will be levied on a good that has inelastic demand and supply. This implies that consumers of this good do not have substitutes for it readily available. It also implies that suppliers cannot alter the quantity they produce by very much even when price changes by a large percentage. Thus, this tax will likely be unpopular, since consumers of this product view it as a necessity. Consumers will find that the tax, although very efficient, is not very fair, since it is being levied on a good that consumers view as a necessity.

3. Lewistown is considering several different taxes and it has hired you to evaluate whether the proposed taxes are proportional, regressive, or progressive. The first tax it is considering is a tax equal to 5% of the value of all food purchases. The second is a tax whereby every individual in Lewistown will pay 4% of the value of his or her property each year. The third is a tax where people pay 3% on the first $30,000 of annual income, and 5% on any additional annual income above $30,000.

STEP 1: Review the definitions of a proportional tax, a progressive tax, and a regressive tax.

Remember that a proportional tax is one in which all taxpayers pay the same percentage of the tax base regardless of the taxpayer's income or wealth; a progressive tax is one in which higher-income taxpayers pay a greater percentage of their income than do lower-income taxpayers; and a regressive tax is one in which higher-income taxpayers pay a lower percentage of their income than do lower-income taxpayers.

STEP 2: Consider one tax at a time and think about how the amount of tax you pay changes as the taxpayer's income or wealth changes. Start with the first proposed tax, the tax on food purchases.

The first tax taxes all food purchases at 5%. Initially this might seem like a proportional tax, since all taxpayers are paying the same tax rate. However, the proportion of income spent on food differs between low-income individuals and high-income individuals, since there is only so much food an individual can eat in a given amount of time. So, for example, suppose a low-income individual spends 40% of her income on food and that amounts to purchases of food of $80 a month, while a high-income individual spends 5% of his income on food and that amounts to purchases of food of $200 a month. With this information, we can calculate the monthly income of each individual: the low-income individual has an income of $200 a month; the high-income individual has an income of $4,000 a month. The low-income individual will pay (.05)(80) in food taxes or $4, which is 2% of her income. The high-income individual will pay (.05)(200) in food taxes of $10 which is .25% of his income. The tax on food purchases is a regressive tax.

STEP 3: Now, consider the second tax: a tax where every individual in Lewistown will pay 4% of the value of his or her property each year.

Consider two individuals in Lewistown: one individual has property worth $400,000 and the other individual has property worth $50,000. What must they each pay under the second tax proposal? Both must pay 4% of the value of their property each year. So the first individual will pay $16,000 and the second individual will pay $2,000. The first individual will pay 4% of his property value as will the second individual. This second tax proposal is a proportional tax.

STEP 4: Now, consider the third tax: a tax whereby people pay 3% on the first $30,000 of annual income, and 5% on any additional annual income above $30,000.

Consider two individuals in Lewistown: the first individual earns $60,000 in income each year and the second individual earns $20,000 in income each year. The first individual will pay (.03)(30,000) + (.05)(60,000 – 30,000) in tax each year or $2,400 in tax each year. The second individual will pay (.03)(20,000) in tax each year or $600 in tax each year. To calculate the percentage of income this tax represents for the first individual, we would have ($2,400/$60,000) × 100, or 4%. To calculate the percentage of income this tax represents for the second individual, we would have ($600/$20,000) × 100, or 3%. Since the higher-income individual pays a greater percentage of their income in taxes than does the lower-income individual, we can conclude that this proposed tax is progressive.

4. Libertyville recently passed a law imposing a $50 per night tax on hotel rooms. During the winter, demand for hotel rooms is relatively inelastic due to the proximity of Libertyville to several excellent ski hills. During the summer, demand for hotel rooms is relatively elastic due to Libertyville's unusually hot and humid summers. Analyze the impact of this tax on hotel owners and hotel guests as well as the seasonal impact on government tax revenue from this tax. Also, discuss the deadweight loss due to the tax in each season. For simplicity assume that there are only two real seasons in Libertyville: summer and winter. Assume that the supply of hotel rooms in Libertyville is relatively inelastic, but not perfectly inelastic. Prior to the tax there was a single price charged for hotel rooms no matter what the time of year and the hotel market was in equilibrium.

STEP 1: First, it is important to recognize that this analysis actually is the analysis of two separate markets—the winter market for hotel accommodation and the summer market for hotel accommodation. You will want to model this situation with two separate graphs, with each graph depicting a different season.

Start by depicting the two seasons for hotel accommodations in Libertyville. The following graphs represent the winter season and the summer season.

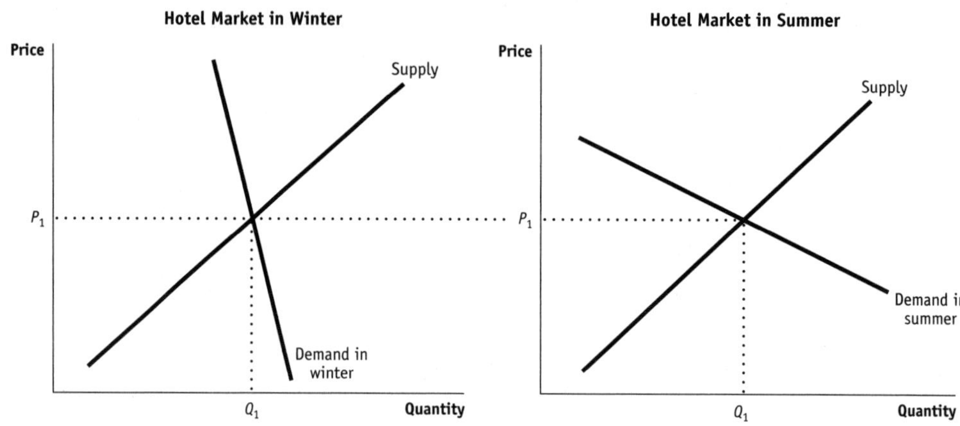

STEP 2: Depict the effect of a $50 per room tax on the market for hotel rooms in Libertyville on the two graphs you created in Step 1.

This tax will cause a $50 difference between the price that consumers pay for the room and the price that producers receive for renting the room once they have paid the room tax to the government. The following figure illustrates this room tax for both the winter and summer season in Libertyville. In your graphs, identify the loss in consumer surplus and producer surplus that is gained as tax revenue by the government.

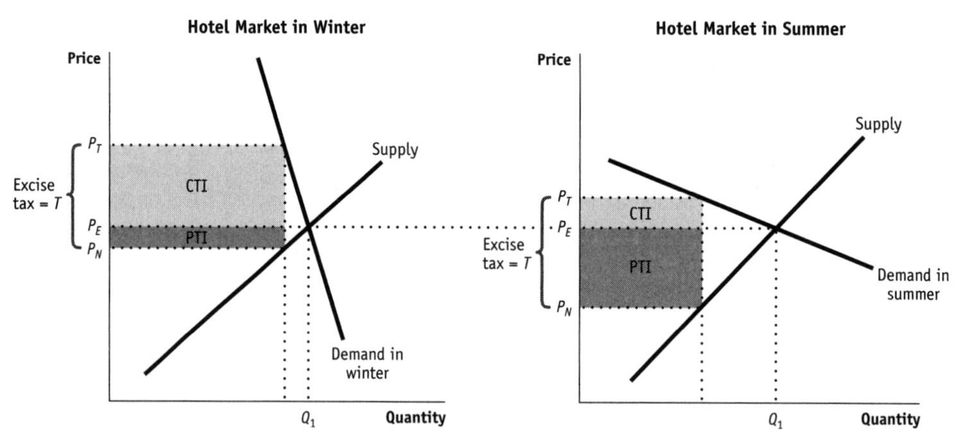

STEP 3: Analyze the effect of a $50 per room tax on hotel guests, hotel owners, and government revenue. In your analysis consider the effect of the season.

In the winter, the hotel room tax results in a relatively large increase in the price of hotel accommodations and a relatively small change in the number of hotel rooms sold. The impact of this when compared with the summer situation is that when the government collects the tax, it captures a large amount of consumer surplus and a smaller amount of producer surplus. Tax revenue from the room tax is relatively large due to the inelasticity of the demand curve: the percentage change in price far outweighs the percentage change in the quantity.

In the summer, the hotel room tax results in a relatively small increase in the price of hotel accommodations and a relatively large change in the number of hotel rooms sold. The impact of this when compared with the winter situation is that when the government collects the tax, it captures a smaller amount of consumer surplus and a larger amount of producer surplus. Tax revenue is smaller in the summer season than in the winter season due to the elasticity of the demand curve: the percentage change in price is far smaller than the percentage change in the quantity.

STEP 4: Find the deadweight loss associated with the room tax for both seasons and then compare the size of these deadweight loss areas.

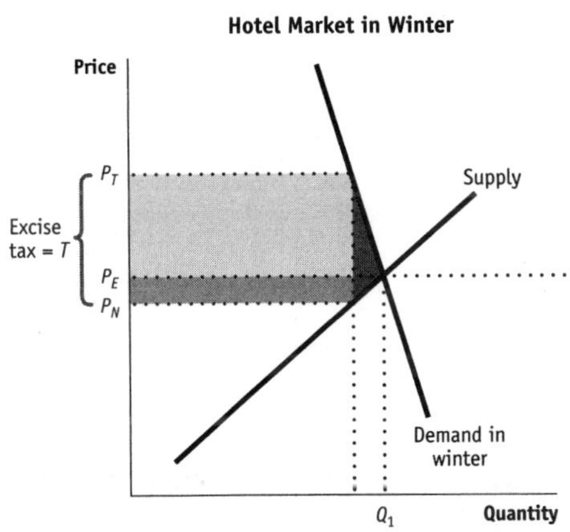

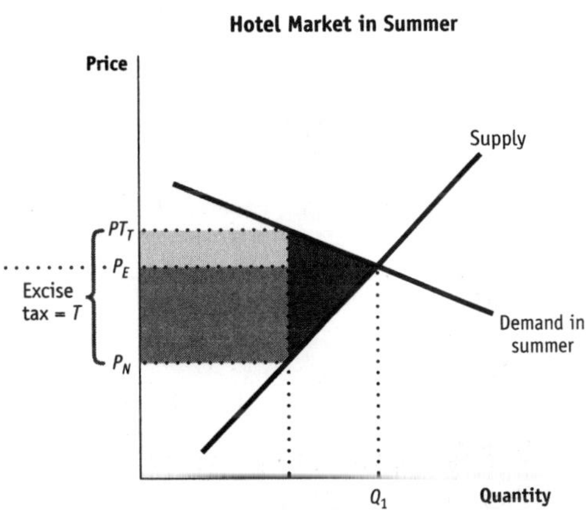

The preceding graphs depict the deadweight loss areas associated with the implementation of the room tax. During the winter season, in the hotel market the deadweight loss is smaller than it is in the summer season because of the relative inelasticity of the demand curve in winter. The room tax causes the price of a hotel room to rise, but this price increase is larger in winter than in summer: in the winter, quantity is not very price sensitive and that results in a smaller deadweight loss from the tax. In the summer, demand is elastic: quantity is very price sensitive and this results in a larger deadweight loss from the tax.

Problems and Exercises

1. The government wishes to limit the quantity of alcoholic beverages sold and therefore is considering the imposition of an excise tax on the market for alcoholic drinks. Suppose the market for alcoholic drinks can be described by the following demand and supply equations:

$$\text{Demand: } Q = 10{,}000 - 2{,}000P$$

$$\text{Supply: } Q = 2{,}000P$$

where P is the price of an alcoholic drink and Q is the quantity of alcoholic drinks sold and consumed during the time period. The proposed excise tax is \$2 per alcoholic drink.

a. Draw a graph representing the initial market for alcoholic drinks. Label the equilibrium price P_1 and the equilibrium quantity Q_1.

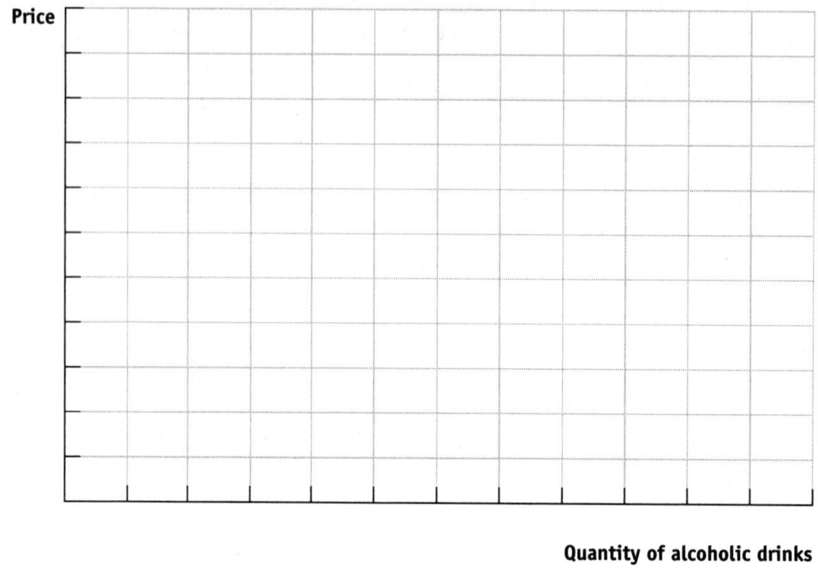

b. Compute the numeric value of P_1 and Q_1 in this market.

c. What is the value of consumer and producer surplus (*CS* and *PS*) in this market prior to the imposition of the tax? Shade in these two areas on your graph in part (a) and label these areas clearly. What is the value of total surplus before the tax?

d. Suppose the excise tax is implemented and producers are legally responsible for paying the tax. Draw a new graph representing this market now that the excise tax has been implemented. Label the new equilibrium price with the tax (P_T), the new equilibrium quantity with the tax (Q_T), and the net price received by producers after they pay the tax to the government (P_N).

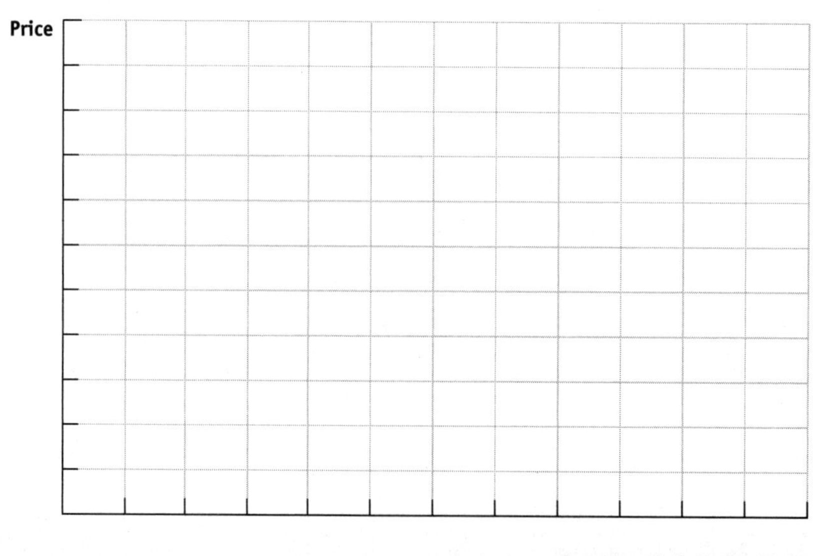

e. Calculate the numeric values of P_T, Q_T, and P_N that you marked on your graph in part (d).

f. On your graph from part (d), label the areas that correspond to consumer surplus with the tax (CS_T), producer surplus with the tax (PS_T), CTI, PTI, and DWL.

g. Calculate the value of CS_T, PS_T, CTI, PTI, tax revenue, and DWL once the tax is implemented. Is the sum of (CS_T) + (PS_T) + (tax revenue) + DWL equal to the original value of total surplus before the tax was implemented?

h. Suppose the excise tax is raised to \$3 per alcoholic drink. What is the effect of this price increase on tax revenue? Provide a qualitative answer as well as a quantitative answer.

2. The textbook emphasizes that the effect of an excise tax depends on the price elasticities of demand and supply. This problem and problem 3 explore the relationship between elasticity and the excise tax.

a. Draw two graphs side by side, and draw a demand curve that is the same in both graphs. (Hint: This means that the *y*-intercept and the *x*-intercept for these two demand curves are the same in the two graphs.) Label this curve *D* in both graphs.

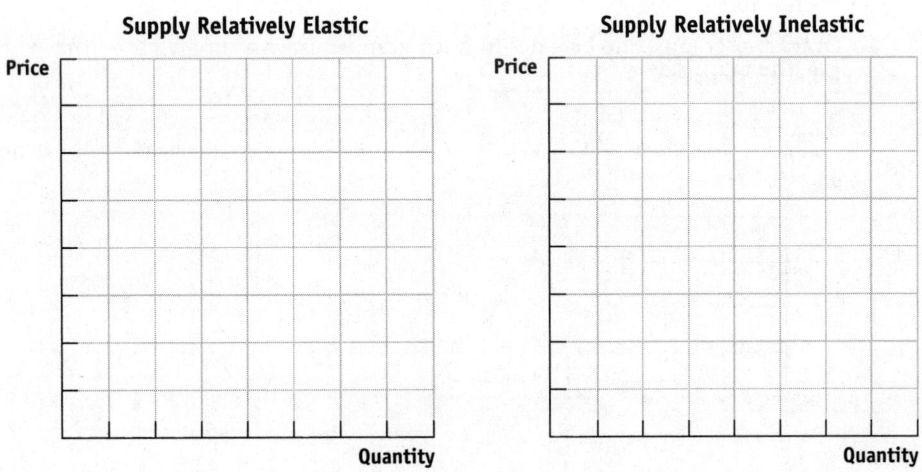

b. In the first graph, draw a relatively elastic supply curve and label the initial equilibrium price P_1 and the initial equilibrium quantity Q_1. In the second graph, mark P_1 and Q_1 (the same P_1 and Q_1 as you found in the first graph) and then draw a relatively inelastic supply curve that goes through this equilibrium point. Label the supply curve in both graphs S_1.

c. In the first graph, draw a second supply curve that shows the effect of an excise tax. This second supply curve should be drawn parallel to the first supply curve. Label the equilibrium price with the tax P_T, the equilibrium quantity with the tax Q_T, and the net price firms receive after they pay the tax P_N. In addition, on this graph, label consumer surplus with the tax (CS_T), producer surplus with the tax (PS_T), CTI, PTI, and DWL.

d. In the second graph, draw a second supply curve that shows the effect of an excise tax which is exactly the same excise tax as in the first graph. (Hint: the *y*-intercept of the new supply curve for each graph is equal to the *y*-intercept of the original supply curve plus the excise tax.) Label all the same items for this graph that you labeled in the first graph.

e. Compare the two graphs and comment on the effect of price elasticity of supply on your results.

3. **a.** Draw two graphs side by side. In both graphs, draw a supply curve that is identical. Label this curve S_1.

Demand Relatively Elastic

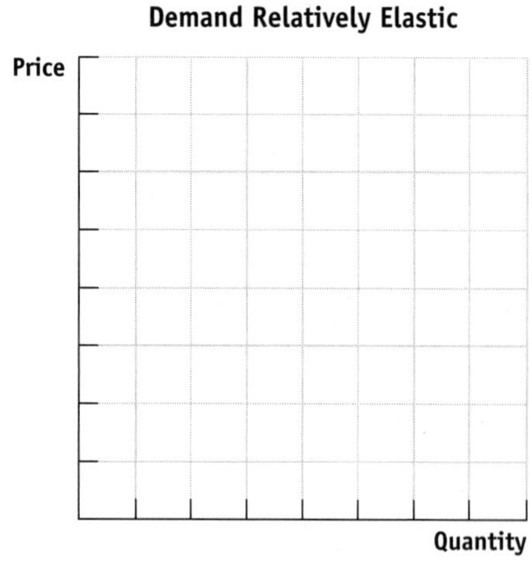

Demand Relatively Inelastic

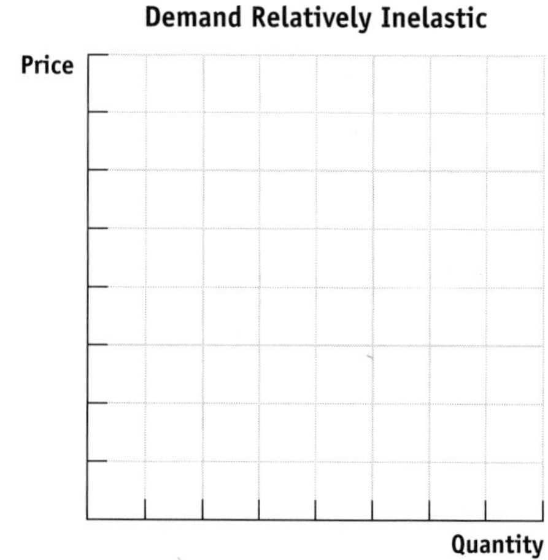

b. In the first graph, draw a demand curve (D) that is relatively elastic. Label the initial equilibrium price P_1 and the initial equilibrium quantity Q_1. In the second graph, mark P_1 and Q_1 (the same P_1 and Q_1 as in the first graph) and then draw a relatively inelastic demand curve through this equilibrium point. Label this curve D.

c. In both graphs, draw a second supply curve that illustrates an excise tax. The two supply curves should be identical and should be labeled S_T. On both graphs, label the equilibrium price with the tax P_T; the equilibrium quantity with the tax Q_T; and the net price firms receive after they pay the tax P_N. In addition, on both graphs, label consumer surplus with the tax (CS_T), producer surplus with the tax (PS_T), CTI, PTI, and DWL.

d. In which graph is the DWL greater?

e. In which graph is the CTI greater?

f. In which graph is the PTI greater?

4. For each of the following situations, identify whether the tax is proportional, regressive, or progressive. Explain your answers.

a. Inherited wealth is taxed according to the following schedule: for individuals inheriting less than $50,000 a year, there is no tax; for individuals inheriting $50,000 to $150,000 a year, the tax is 10% of the inherited amount; and for individuals inheriting more than $150,000 a year, the tax is 25% of the inherited amount.

b. A sales tax is applied to all consumer goods bought during the year.

c. A tax of $25 per individual is charged for the use of the state park system.

d. A progressive income tax is adopted that requires low-income taxpayers pay a negative tax and high-income taxpayers pay a greater proportion of their income than do middle-income taxpayers.

BEFORE YOU TAKE THE TEST

Module Review Questions

1. The cost of a tax is equal to

a. the tax revenue raised by the tax.

b. the tax revenue raised by the tax, plus the deadweight loss associated with the tax, plus whatever administrative costs that compliance with the tax incurs.

c. the tax revenue raised by the tax plus the deadweight loss associated with the tax.

d. the deadweight loss associated with the tax and the administrative costs that compliance with the tax entails.

Answer the next seven questions based on the following information. The graph that follows represents the market for cigarettes in Tinseltown. D is the demand curve, S_1 is the supply curve, and S_t is the supply curve after an excise tax has been imposed on cigarettes. Letters A through K represent areas in the graph. Prices are denoted as P_1, P_2, P_3, P_4, and P_5. Quantities are denoted as Q_1, Q_2, Q_3, and Q_4.

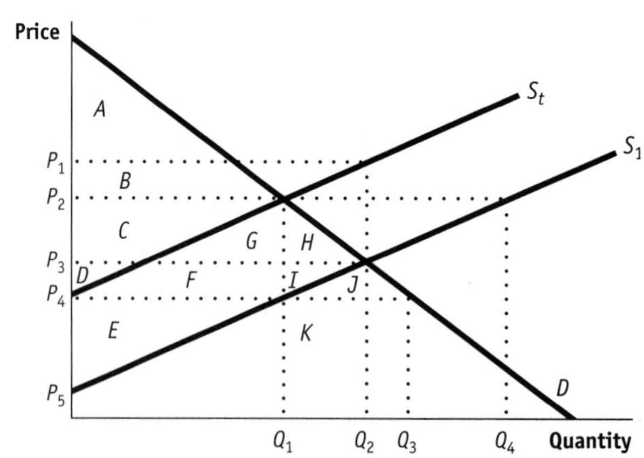

2. The excise tax in the graph is equal to

a. $P_1 - P_4$.

b. $P_2 - P_4$.

c. $P_4 - P_5$.

d. Answers (a) and (c) both measure the excise tax.

e. Answers (b) and (c) both measure the excise tax.

3. The consumer surplus before the tax is equal to the sum of areas

a. *A, B, C, G,* and *H.*

b. *A* and *B.*

c. *A, B, C, D, E, F, G, H,* and *I.*

d. *D, E, F,* and *I.*

4. The producer surplus before the tax is equal to the areas

a. *A, B, C, G,* and *H.*

b. *A* and *B.*

c. *A, B, C, D, E, F, G, H,* and *I.*

d. *D, E, F,* and *I.*

5. The tax revenue collected by the government when this excise tax is imposed is equal to

a. $(P_1 - P_3)(Q_2)$.

b. $(P_2 - P_4)(Q_1)$.

c. $(P_2 - P_4)(Q_2)$.

d. $(P_2 - P_3)(Q_1)$.

6. The deadweight loss from a consumer's perspective is equal to area(s)

a. *H.*

b. *I.*

c. *H* and *I.*

d. *C, G,* and *H.*

7. The efficiency cost of this excise tax can be measured as area(s)

a. *G* and *H.*

b. *H* and *I.*

c. *I* and *J.*

d. *H, I,* and *J.*

8. A mathematical expression for the deadweight loss caused by this excise tax is

a. $(P_2 - P_4)(Q_2)$.

b. $(P_2 - P_4)(Q_2 - Q_1)$.

c. $(1/2)(P_2 - P_4)(Q_2 - Q_1)$.

d. $(1/2)(P_2 - P_3)(Q_2 - Q_1)$.

9. The income tax in Tinseltown is a flat tax that requires everyone to pay 10% of their income to the government no matter what their level of income. This tax is

a. efficient.

b. proportional.

c. regressive.

10. In this year's presidential election in Tinseltown, one of the candidates is running on a platform that advocates a change in the income tax. This candidate proposes that individuals in the bottom half of the income distribution should pay 50% of their income to the government, while individuals in the top half of the income distribution should pay 30% of their income. This candidate reasons that the higher-income individuals will still end up paying a lot of money to the government. The tax structure advocated by this candidate is

a. regressive.

b. progressive.

c. proportional.

d. efficient.

Answer the next six questions based on the following information. The market for soft drinks in Tinseltown is given by the following demand and supply equations:

$$\text{Demand: } P = 100 - 2Q$$
$$\text{Supply: } P = 2Q$$

where P is the market price measured in cents and Q is the market quantity measured in bottles of soft drink. Tinseltown is considering imposing an excise tax on soft-drink producers of 20 cents a bottle.

11. If this excise tax is imposed, the new supply curve with the excise tax will be

a. $P = 2Q + 20$. c. $P = 2(Q + 20)$.
b. $P = 2Q - 20$. d. $P = 2(Q - 20)$.

12. If this excise tax is imposed, the price of soft drinks in Tinseltown will increase by __________ cents.

a. 20 c. 10
b. 30 d. 0

13. If this excise tax is imposed, the tax revenue collected by the government will equal

a. \$1. c. \$3.
b. \$2. d. \$4.

14. If this excise tax is imposed, the deadweight loss associated with the tax will equal

a. \$5. c. \$1.
b. \$4. d. \$0.50.

15. The loss in consumer surplus due to the imposition of this excise tax equals

a. \$6.25. c. \$2.25.
b. \$4. d. \$0.25.

16. If this excise tax is imposed, the producer tax incidence is equal to

a. \$1. c. \$2.25.
b. \$2. d. \$4.

17. An excise tax is imposed on producers of a good. For a given supply curve, the more price elastic the demand for the product, the greater the tax incidence on

a. consumers.
b. producers.

18. An excise tax is imposed on producers of a good. For a given demand curve, the more inelastic the supply of the product, the greater the tax incidence on

a. consumers.
b. producers.

19. When the price elasticity of demand is low and the price elasticity of supply is high, the burden of an excise tax falls primarily on

a. sellers of the product.
b. buyers of the product.

20. When the price elasticity of demand is high and the price elasticity of supply is low, the burden of an excise tax falls primarily on

a. sellers of the product.

b. buyers of the product.

21. You are told that the initial supply curve in a market is $P = Q$ and the initial demand curve in the market is $P = 100 - Q$. An excise tax is imposed in this market and it results in the government collecting $1,250 in tax revenue. The excise tax in this market is equal to

a. $10.

b. $20.

c. $25.

d. $50.

22. Excise taxes cause deadweight loss when the excise tax

a. raises the price of the good being taxed.

b. decreases the quantity of the good supplied and demanded in the market.

c. creates an incentive for mutually beneficial exchanges to take place.

d. Answers (a), (b), and (c) are all true.

23. The deadweight loss due to the imposition of an excise tax is lowest when demand is relatively

a. inelastic and supply is relatively elastic.

b. inelastic and supply is relatively inelastic.

c. elastic and supply is relatively elastic.

d. elastic and supply is relatively inelastic.

24. Policymakers wishing to dramatically decrease the consumption of a good by using an excise tax will find that the success of this policy depends on

a. the price elasticity of demand.

b. the price elasticity of supply.

c. the price elasticities of either demand or supply.

d. the size of the excise tax. The price elasticities of supply and demand have no impact on how successful the policy is with regard to decreasing the consumption of the good.

Use the following table to answer the next three questions. The table provides information about pre-tax income and then gives after-tax income for three different tax structure proposals.

Pre-tax income	Proposal 1: After-tax income	Proposal 2: After-tax income	Proposal 3: After-tax income
$ 20,000	$ 15,000	$ 15,000	$ 15,000
32,000	24,000	27,000	22,400
40,000	30,000	35,000	27,200
80,000	60,000	75,000	52,000
200,000	150,000	195,000	120,000

25. Policymakers wish to impose a proportional, or flat, tax based on income. Which proposed tax structure represents this choice?

a. Proposal 1

b. Proposal 2

c. Proposal 3

26. Policymakers wish to impose a regressive tax based on income. Which proposed tax structure represents this choice?

a. Proposal 1

b. Proposal 2

c. Proposal 3

27. What percentage of income does an individual pay in taxes under proposal 2 if that individual's pre-tax income is $40,000?

a. 0.125%

b. 1.25%

c. 12.5%

d. 125%

ANSWER KEY

Answers to Problems and Exercises

1. a. 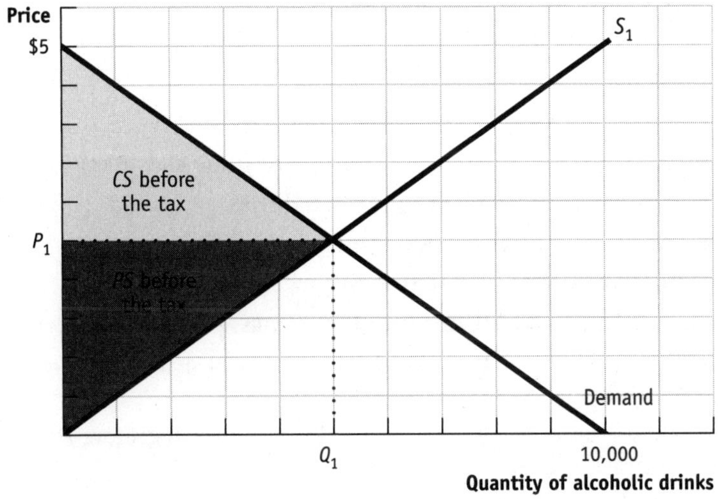

b. To find P_1 and Q_1, use the demand and supply equations: $10{,}000 - 2{,}000P = 2{,}000P$. Solving for P yields an equilibrium price of \$2.50. Plug this price into either the demand or the supply equation to find the equilibrium quantity: $Q_1 = 10{,}000 - (2{,}000)(2.50) = 5{,}000$ alcoholic drinks.

c. Consumer surplus (*CS*) before the imposition of the tax equals the area of a triangle, and can be computed as (1/2)(\$5/drink – \$2.50/drink)(5,000 drinks) = \$6,250. Producer surplus (*PS*) before the imposition of the tax equals the area of a triangle, and can be computed as (1/2)(\$2.50/drink)(5,000 drinks) = \$6,250. Total surplus is the sum of *CS* and *PS*, or \$12,500.

d. 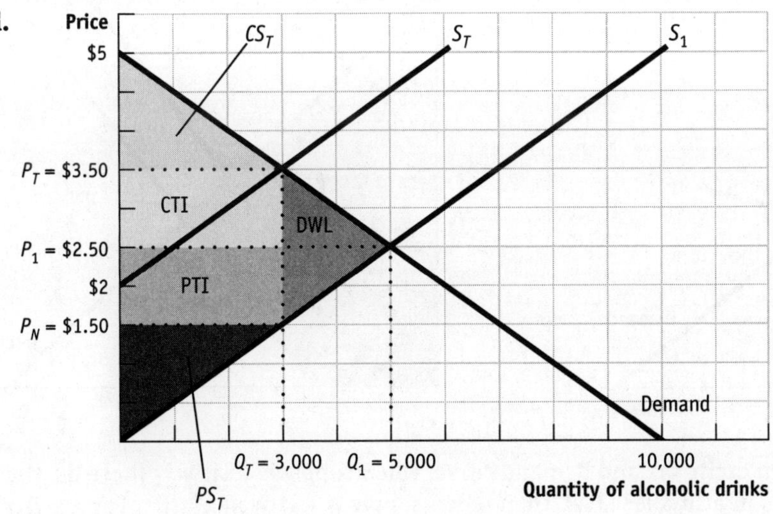

e. The new supply curve with this excise tax is $Q = 2{,}000P - 4{,}000$. To find this new supply curve, it is easiest to rewrite the initial supply curve, in slope intercept form: $P = (1/2{,}000)Q$. Then add the amount of the excise tax to the y-intercept of this equation since the excise tax shifts the supply curve vertically upward by an amount equal to the tax. Thus, $P = (1/2{,}000)Q + 2$, or $Q = 2{,}000P - 4{,}000$. Combine this new supply equation with the demand equation to find P_T and Q_T. $P_T = \$3.50$ and $Q_T = 3{,}000$ drinks. To find P_N, remember that the price producers receive after they pay the tax is equal to the price with the tax minus the excise tax, or P_T – excise tax. P_N is equal to $1.50.

f. See graph in part (d).

g. CS with the tax = CS_T = (1/2)($5/drink – $3.50/drink)(3,000 drinks) = $2,250

PS with the tax = PS_T = (1/2)($1.50/drink)(3,000 drinks) = $2,250

CTI = ($3.50/drink – $2.50/drink)(3,000 drinks) = $3,000

PTI = ($2.50/drink – $1.50/drink)(3,000 drinks) = $3,000

DWL = (1/2)($3.50/drink – $1.50/drink)(5,000 drinks – 3,000 drinks) = $2,000

Tax revenue = CTI + PTI = (excise tax per drink)(number of drinks sold) = ($2/drink)(3,000 drinks) = $6,000

The sum of $CS_T + PS_T$ + tax revenue + DWL = $12,500 and is therefore equal to the original total surplus prior to the imposition of the tax.

h. When the excise tax is raised to $3, we know this causes price to increase and quantity to decrease in this market. Quantity falls to 2,000, which would result in tax revenues of 2,000 × $3. Thus, tax revenue remains unchanged at $6,000.

2. a–d.

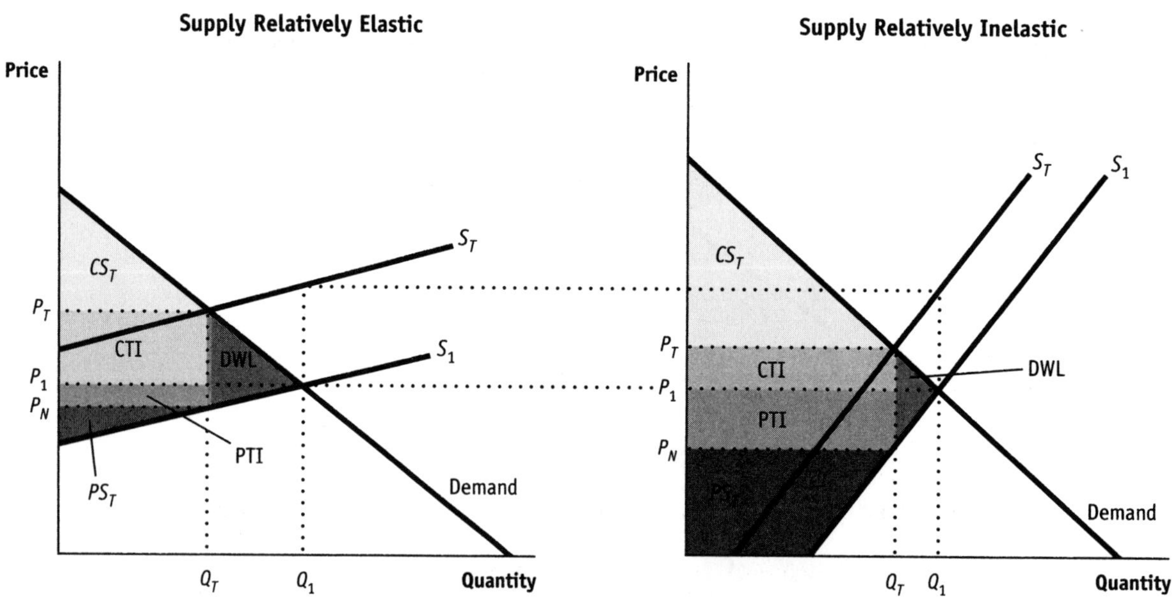

e. For a given excise tax and demand curve, when supply is relatively inelastic, the excise tax results in a smaller DWL than when supply is relatively elastic. For a given excise tax and demand curve, quantity changes by a larger amount when supply is relatively elastic. Tax revenue depends on the relative elasticities of both the demand and the supply curves.

3. a–c.

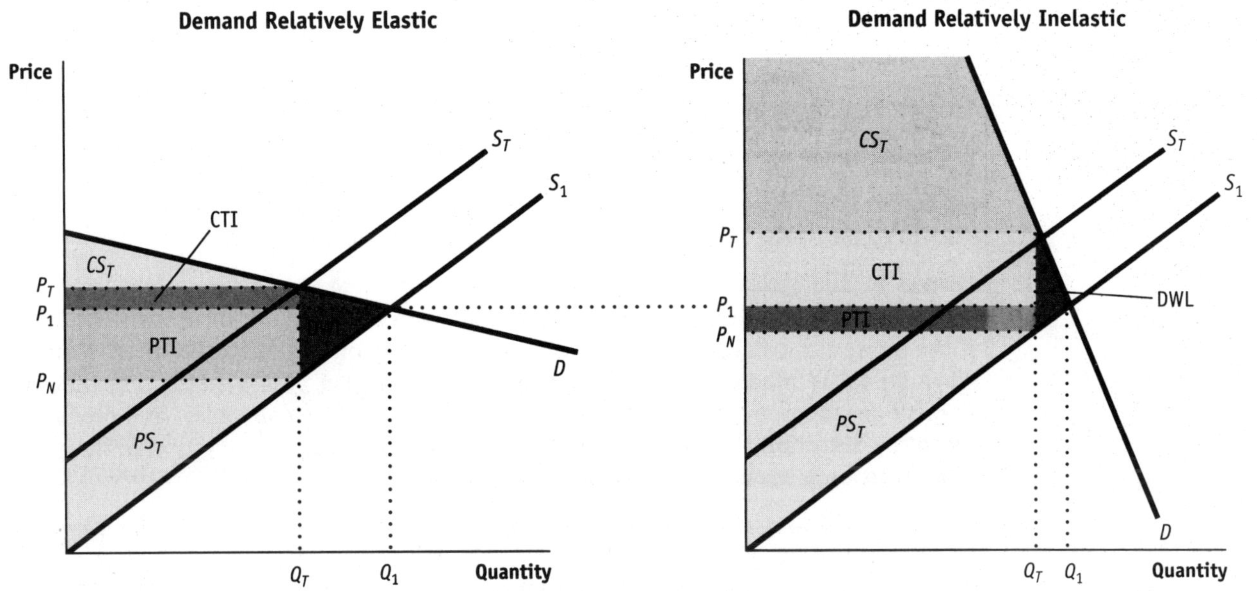

d. The DWL is greater in the graph in which demand is relatively elastic.

e. The CTI is greater in the graph in which demand is relatively inelastic.

f. The PTI is greater in the graph in which demand is relatively elastic.

4. **a.** This is a progressive tax, since as inherited wealth increases, the percentage of the tax to that wealth increases.

b. This is a regressive tax, since the tax rises less than in proportion to income: because low-income individuals spend a greater proportion of their income on consumer goods, low-income individuals pay a higher percentage of their income than high-income individuals.

c. This is a regressive tax, since it is a flat amount charged to each taxpayer without regard to income or wealth. This tax is a larger proportion of a low-income person's income and a smaller proportion of a high-income person's income.

d. This one is given to you: it's a progressive tax!

Answers to Module Review Questions

1. **Answer b.** When the government imposes a tax, this clearly results in the government receiving tax revenue which is a cost to the taxpayer, but the imposition of a tax imposes greater costs than just the tax revenue collected. The tax also imposes an efficiency cost (the DWL) as the tax causes a distortion in consumer behavior. The tax also imposes an administrative cost associated with complying with the tax.

2. **Answer e.** The excise tax is equal to the vertical distance between the original supply curve and the supply curve with the tax. At quantity Q_2, the vertical distance is equal to $P_1 - P_3$: this is the same distance as $P_2 - P_4$ or $P_4 - P_5$.

3. **Answer a.** The area of consumer surplus is the area above the equilibrium price and below the demand curve. Before the tax is implemented, the equilibrium price is P_3 and thus the area of consumer surplus is equal to the areas *A*, *B*, *C*, *G*, and *H*.

4. **Answer d.** The area of producer surplus is the area that lies beneath the equilibrium price and above the supply curve. Before the imposition of the tax, the equilibrium price is P_3 and the area of producer surplus is the sum of areas *D*, *E*, *F*, and *I*.

5. **Answer b.** The tax revenue collected by the government is equal to the product of the tax per unit and the number of units of the good sold when the tax is implemented. In this example, the tax per unit is $(P_2 - P_4)$ and the number of units sold is Q_1, so the tax revenue is equal to $(P_2 - P_4)(Q_1)$.

6. **Answer a.** When the excise tax is imposed, the consumer reduces consumption of the good. Some of the consumer's original consumer surplus is captured by the government: the consumer's tax incidence measures the economic burden of the tax borne by consumers. The consumer also loses a part of the original consumer surplus due to the efficiency cost of the tax: in this graph, this is represented as area *H*.

7. **Answer b.** The excise tax imposes an efficiency cost equal to the deadweight loss. This deadweight loss is represented by the areas *H* and *I* in the graph. Prior to the imposition of the excise tax, total surplus is equal to the sum of consumer and producer surplus. When the tax is imposed on this market, part of this total surplus is captured by the government as tax revenue, but part of the total surplus is lost to consumers and producers due to the distortion the tax causes with respect to the level of consumption of the good. This distortion is measured by areas *H* and *I*.

8. **Answer c.** The area of deadweight loss can be calculated as an area of a triangle: thus, this area is equal to one-half times the product of the excise tax per unit and the change in quantity due to the imposition of the tax. In this example, the excise tax per unit is equal to $(P_2 - P_4)$ and the change in quantity is $(Q_2 - Q_1)$.

9. **Answer b.** This is an example of a proportional tax, since the tax is the same proportion of everyone's income. High-income people pay 10% of their income as do low-income people.

10. **Answer a.** Since lower-income individuals will pay a larger percentage of their income to the government with this tax structure, this tax structure is regressive.

11. **Answer a.** The new supply curve will be parallel to the original supply curve but will have a *y*-intercept that is 20 cents greater than the original supply curve's *y*-intercept. Since the original supply curve intercepts the *y*-axis at zero, this means that the new supply curve with the excise tax will intercept the *y*-axis at 20.

12. **Answer c.** To answer this question, you must know the original price of soft drinks in Tinseltown before the excise tax and the price of soft drinks in Tinseltown after the imposition of the excise tax. The original price of soft drinks is 50 cents, and when the tax is implemented the price will rise to 60 cents. The increase in the price equals 10 cents.

13. **Answer d.** The tax revenue is equal to the tax per unit times the number of units sold. When the excise tax is implemented, 20 bottles of soft drinks will be sold at a price of 60 cents each. But 20 cents of that price represents the excise tax, so the government will collect 20 cents per bottle sold, or a total of $4.

14. **Answer d.** The deadweight loss can be calculated as the area of a triangle. The deadweight loss is equal to (1/2)(excise tax per unit)(the original equilibrium quantity – the equilibrium quantity with the excise tax), or (1/2)(20 cents per unit)(25 units – 20 units), which equals $0.50.

15. **Answer c.** The original consumer surplus is equal to $6.25 and the new consumer surplus after the imposition of the excise tax is equal to $4.00, which means the loss in consumer surplus due to the tax is equal to $2.25.

16. **Answer b.** The producer tax incidence is a measure of the economic burden of the excise tax on producers. Producers prior to the excise tax sold their good for 50 cents a bottle. With the excise tax the price of soft drinks increases to 60 cents a bottle, but the government receives 20 cents of that price. The producer therefore keeps only 40 cents for every soft drink the producer sells. From the producer's perspective, the excise tax results in a decrease in the price of soft drinks from 50 cents a bottle to 40 cents a bottle. The producer sells 20 bottles of soft drinks once the excise tax is imposed, and the producer tax incidence is therefore equal to 10 cents a bottle times the 20 bottles, or $2.

17. **Answer b.** When demand is more elastic, this implies that consumers are price sensitive and that a small change in price will result in a large change in the quantity demanded. Hence, an excise tax places a greater economic burden on suppliers in this case.

18. **Answer b.** When supply is more inelastic, this implies that a small increase in price will cause a relatively small change in the quantity demanded; when supply is more elastic, a small increase in price will cause a relatively large change in the quantity demanded. For a given demand curve, an excise tax results in greater tax incidence on producers when supply is more inelastic.

19. **Answer b.** When price elasticity of demand is low (implying a relatively steep demand curve) while price elasticity of supply is high (implying a relatively flat supply curve), the economic burden of an excise tax falls primarily on consumers since the excise tax causes a relatively large increase in price and a relatively small decrease in the quantity demanded.

20. **Answer a.** When price elasticity of demand is high (implying a relatively flat demand curve) while price elasticity of supply is low (implying a relatively steep supply curve), the economic burden of an excise tax falls primarily on producers since the excise tax causes a relatively small increase in price and a relatively large decrease in the quantity demanded.

21. **Answer d.** One way to solve this problem is to draw a graph with the initial supply and demand curves and then calculate what the tax revenue would equal for each of the excise tax rates. For each level of the excise tax, the supply curve with the tax could be written as $P_S = Q_S +$ (the amount of the excise tax), where P_S is the supply price and Q_S is the quantity supplied at that price. Then, use this equation plus the demand equation and each level of the excise tax to calculate the equilibrium quantity, the equilibrium price with the tax, and then the tax revenue generated by the tax. Thus, if the excise tax is equal to $50 per unit, then the equilibrium quantity in the market once the tax is imposed is 25 units, the equilibrium price with the tax is $75, and the tax revenue is equal to ($50/unit)(25 units) = $1,250.

22. **Answer b.** An excise tax creates a deadweight loss because it discourages mutually beneficial exchanges from taking place. The excise tax creates a deadweight loss by altering the amount of the good supplied and demanded in the market. An increase in price due to the excise tax is not sufficient to create a deadweight loss, because if the demand curve is perfectly inelastic, there is no deadweight loss due to the tax.

23. **Answer b.** The deadweight loss from an excise tax is smallest when both the demand and supply curves are relatively inelastic, since this implies that the percentage increase in the price is relatively greater than the percentage decrease in the quantity supplied and demanded in the market.

24. **Answer c.** A policy to reduce consumption of a good through the imposition of an excise tax is more successful when the activity being discouraged is elastically demanded or supplied.

25. **Answer a.** A flat tax collects the same percentage of the base regardless of the taxpayer's income or wealth. Proposal 1 represents a flat tax, since this tax is 25% of the pre-tax income regardless of the level of pre-tax income.

26. **Answer b.** A regressive tax structure is one in which the tax rises less than in proportion to income so that high-income taxpayers pay a smaller percentage of their income than do low-income taxpayers. Proposal 2 taxes individuals with income of $20,000 at a rate of 25% of their income, while individuals with income of $200,000 are taxed at a rate of 2.5% of their income.

27. **Answer c.** An individual earning a pre-tax income of $40,000 pays $5,000 in taxes under proposal 2. To convert this to a percentage, divide (5,000/40,000) and then multiply this value by 100.

module 16

Gains from Trade

BEFORE YOU READ THE MODULE

Summary

This module discusses international trade and the gains from trade that are possible through specialization according to comparative advantage. The module explores the sources of comparative advantage, and also provides a model to illustrate the distributional consequences of trade. This model provides a method for considering who benefits and who loses from international trade and why the benefits from trade outweigh the losses from trade.

Module Objectives

Objective #1. Trade is beneficial to both parties that engage in the trade, whether they are individuals or countries. Countries that specialize in producing different goods and then trade these goods with other countries benefit from this trade. Goods and services purchased from abroad are called imports, and goods and services sold abroad are called exports. Countries trade goods and services with one another, but they also invest funds: this linking of the markets for goods and services as well as financial assets between different countries is referred to as globalization.

Objective #2. A country has the comparative advantage in producing a good or service when that country can produce the good or service at a lower opportunity cost than can other countries. A simple way to model international trade is to use linear production possibility frontiers to analyze trade between two countries. The straight line production possibility frontier implies that the opportunity cost of producing the two goods does not change as the level of production of these two goods changes.

Objective #3. Autarky refers to the situation in which a country does not engage in trade with any other countries. A comparison can be made between a situation in which two countries trade with one another versus a situation in which the two countries act as autarkies and do not trade with each other. This comparison results in the following conclusions:

- When countries specialize according to comparative advantage and then trade with one another, the total amount of goods and services produced is greater than when the countries do not engage in specialization and trade.

- No country will engage in trade unless the relative price of the good traded is less than its opportunity cost of producing the good in autarky.

Objective #4. For example, consider two countries, country A and country B, that have linear production possibility frontiers for the production of two goods: good X and good Y. These two countries and their production possibility frontiers are illustrated in Figure 16.1.

Figure 16.1

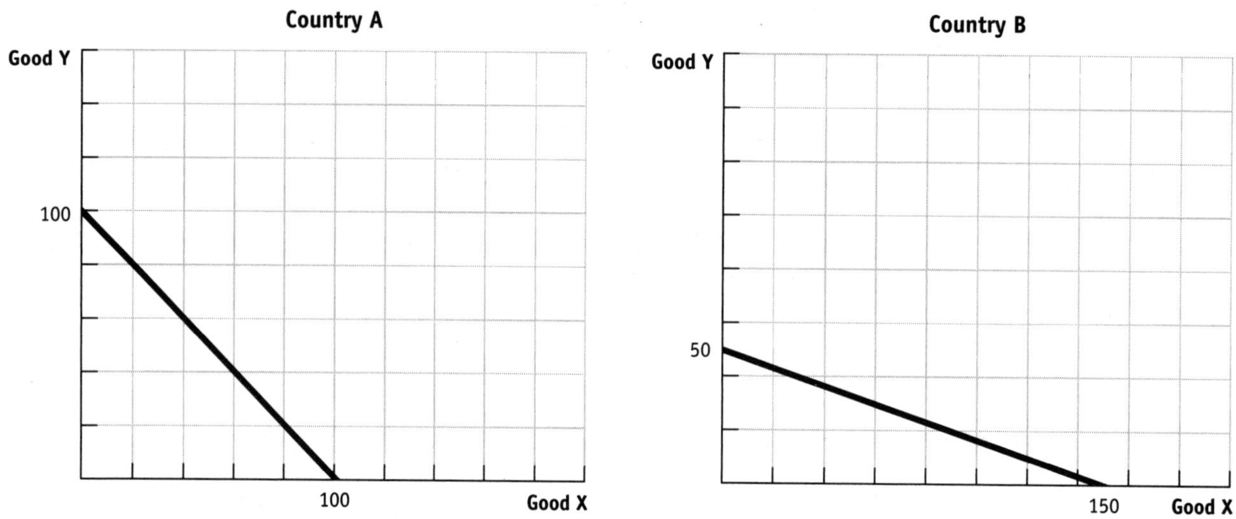

The opportunity cost of country A producing one more unit of good X is equal to 1 unit of good Y, since country A must give up 1 unit of good Y to produce an additional unit of good X according to their production possibility frontier illustrated in Figure 8.1. The opportunity cost of country B producing one more unit of good X is equal to 1/3 unit of good Y since country B must give up 1/3 unit of good Y to produce an additional unit of good X according to their production possibility frontier illustrated in Figure 8.1. Comparison of these two opportunity costs reveals that country B can produce good X at lower opportunity cost than can country A, since country B gives up fewer units of good Y to get one more unit of good X. Country B has the comparative advantage in producing good X. Country A has the comparative advantage in producing good Y, since the opportunity cost of producing 1 unit of good Y for country A is 1 unit of good X, while for country B the opportunity cost of producing 1 unit of good Y is 3 units of good X. Both countries can benefit by specializing in the production of the good they can produce at lower opportunity cost and then trading.

- As an example, suppose the two countries initially do not trade and that country A produces 50 units of good X and 50 units of good Y while country B produces 75 units of good X and 25 units of good Y. Total production without trade is summarized in the following table.

	Production of good X	Production of good Y
Country A	50	50
Country B	75	25
Total production	125	75

- Now, suppose the two countries specialize according to their comparative advantage: country A produces 0 units of good X and 100 units of good Y while country B produces 150 units of good X and 0 units of good Y. The table that follows summarizes the result of this specialization. Notice that the total production of both goods increases when the two countries specialize.

	Production of good X	Production of good Y
Country A	0	100
Country B	150	0
Total production	150	100

- Let's digress a moment and consider what would happen if the two countries specialized, but produced those goods for which they did not have the comparative advantage: this implies that country A produces good X while country B produces good Y. The table that follows summarizes what happens when countries do not specialize according to their comparative advantage: total production decreases! Specialization is beneficial only when countries produce those goods for which they have lower opportunity cost of production.

	Production of good X	Production of good Y
Country A	100	0
Country B	0	50
Total production	100	50

- Once countries decide to specialize according to comparative advantage and to trade, they then need to decide on the price of these traded goods. In our example, country A will be willing to trade good Y for any price greater than 1 unit of X (country A's opportunity cost of producing good Y). Country B, on the other hand, will be willing to trade up to 3 units of X for 1 unit of Y. Thus, country A and country B can make a mutually beneficial trade provided that the range of prices when Country A provides one unit of Y is between 1 unit of X and 3 units of X. Country A is unwilling to provide a unit of Y for less than 1 unit of X and country B is unwilling to pay more than 3 units of X for one unit of Y. Using similar reasoning, country A will be willing to trade good X for any price between 1/3 of a unit of good Y and 1 unit of good Y.

Objective #5. Gains from trade depend on comparative advantage and not absolute advantage. Comparative advantage is based on the opportunity cost of producing the good and not the absolute amount of resources used to produce the good. A country with low wage rates generally reflects low labor productivity, while a country with high wage rates reflects high labor productivity.

- One fallacy with regard to trade is the pauper labor fallacy, which is the belief that a high-wage country importing goods produced by workers in a low-wage country is an action that results in harming workers in the high-wage country.
- A second fallacy with regard to trade is the sweatshop labor fallacy, which is the belief that trade must be bad for workers in low-wage countries since the wages paid to workers in these countries is so much lower than the wages paid to workers in high-wage countries.
- Both the pauper labor fallacy and the sweatshop labor fallacy fail to recognize that trade is to the advantage of both the high-wage and the low-wage country, because both are able to achieve a higher standard of living through trade with each other.

Objective #6. Comparative advantage arises because of differences in climate, differences in factor endowments, and differences in technology.

- Climate and seasonal differences (northern hemisphere versus southern hemisphere) play a significant role in comparative advantage, since some goods can only be produced in certain climates or during certain seasons.

- The Heckscher–Ohlin model finds that a country has a comparative advantage in producing those goods whose production is intensive in the factors that are abundant in that country compared to other countries. This finding arises because the opportunity cost of a given factor is low when that factor is relatively abundant. This argument also helps to explain incomplete specialization, which is the situation when a country continues to produce a good that it also imports. A country will engage in incomplete specialization whenever that country has factor endowments that make it economically feasible for them to produce the good. A country can still gain from trade even if it does not completely specialize.
- Technological differences can also drive comparative advantage. Technological differences may arise due to accumulated experience or because of innovations that one country has made that other countries have not adopted.

Key Terms

imports goods and services purchased from other countries.

exports goods and services sold to other countries.

globalization the phenomenon of growing economic linkages among countries.

autarky a situation in which a country does not trade with other countries.

factor intensity the difference in the ratio of factors used to produce a good in various industries. For example, oil refining is capital-intensive compared with clothing manufacture because oil refiners use a higher ratio of capital to labor than do clothing producers.

Heckscher–Ohlin model a *model* of international trade in which a country has a *comparative advantage* in a good whose production is intensive in the factors that are abundantly available in that country.

Notes

AFTER YOU READ THE MODULE

Tips

Tip #1. Students often struggle with the concept of comparative advantage and how it relates to the opportunity cost of producing the good. One fail-safe method for analyzing this type of problem is to follow these steps. (1) Identify the two individuals or the two countries (for the rest of this tip we assume that we are analyzing the comparative advantage with regard to two countries) that are involved in the problem. (2) Identify the two goods that are being produced. (3) For each country, draw a graph that illustrates the production possibility frontier for that country. Make sure you label the graph with the country's name and the two axes with the goods being produced. This labeling is very important since it helps ensure that you do not confuse the two countries or the two goods. (4) Find the slope of the production possibility frontier and then use this slope to calculate the opportunity cost of producing one more unit of the good measured along the *x*-axis. You can use the slope in this manner since the slope equals the "rise/run"—that is, the slope tells you the change in the *y*-variable divided by the change in the *x*-variable. So, for example, if one more unit of the *x*-variable was produced, the slope of the production possibility frontier would tell you how many units of the *y*-variable must be given up to produce this additional unit of the *x*-variable. (5) Under each country's graph, write a statement using this slope measure that says "OC of producing 1 good X is equal to |slope value| good Y." This statement just reminds you of what the opportunity cost of producing that additional unit of good X is. Below this statement write another statement that says "OC of producing 1 good Y is equal to |1/slope| good X." (6) Compare the opportunity cost of producing good X between the two countries, and decide which country can produce good X at the lowest opportunity cost. Circle the label on the *x*-axis for this country to identify the country that has the comparative advantage in producing good X. Then, on the other country's graph, circle the label on the *y*-axis to identify the country that has the comparative advantage in producing good Y. Figure 16.2 provides an example of this method. Note the labels, the OC statements, and the circling of the relevant labels as a means of identifying the country's comparative advantage. Faithful adherence to this method will certainly assure you of getting this concept right.

Figure 16.2

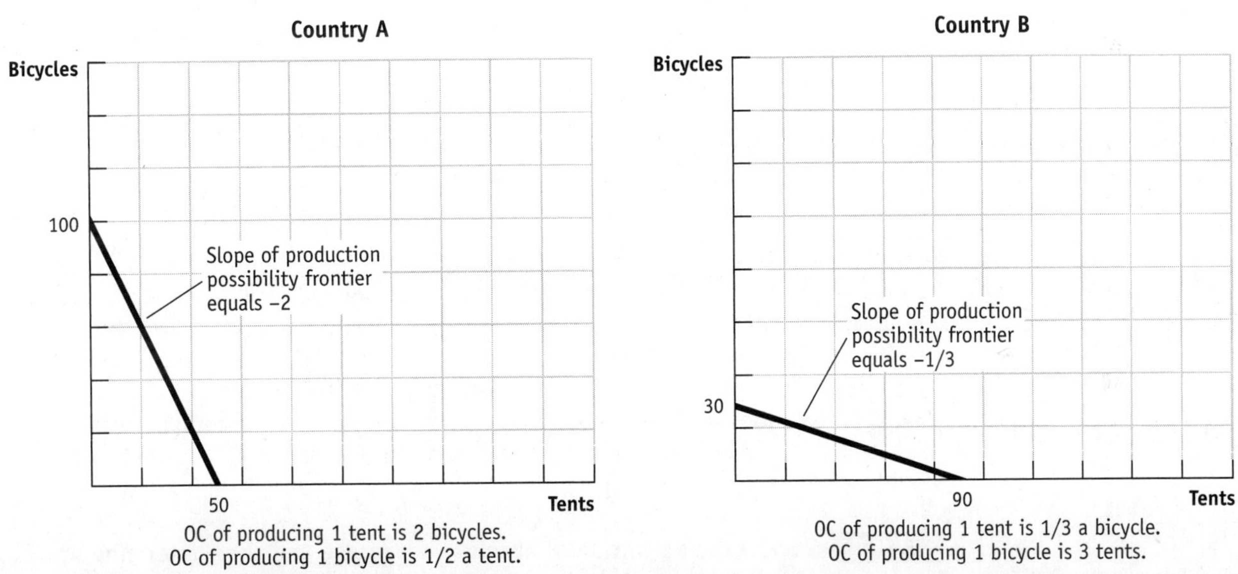

Tip #2. Students struggle with deciding what the relevant range of relative prices is for a good when countries specialize and then trade. Let's use the information in Figure 16.2 to work through a method for calculating this range of relative prices. Start with the good measured on the *x*-axis: tents. From the OC statements below the two graphs, we can see that the OC of producing 1 tent is between 1/3 a bicycle (country B's OC) and 2 bicycles (country A's OC). You can think about placing these two limits on a number line and noting that the relative price of 1 tent must fall somewhere between the lowest possible relative price of 1/3 a bicycle and the highest possible relative price of 2 bicycles. Figure 16.3 illustrates this number-line approach.

Figure 16.3

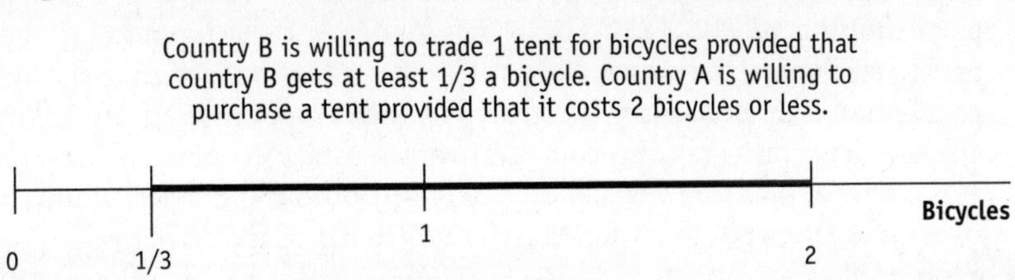

WORKED PROBLEMS

1. Bob and Mary are the only inhabitants of Littleburg. Both Bob and Mary spend their time planting vegetables and looking for berries. They currently do not trade with each other. The following graph shows their production possibilities for a day. Assume that both goods are measured in terms of some type of unit measurement (e.g., rows of vegetables or pints of berries) and that Mary and Bob have equal amounts of resources and technology available to them.

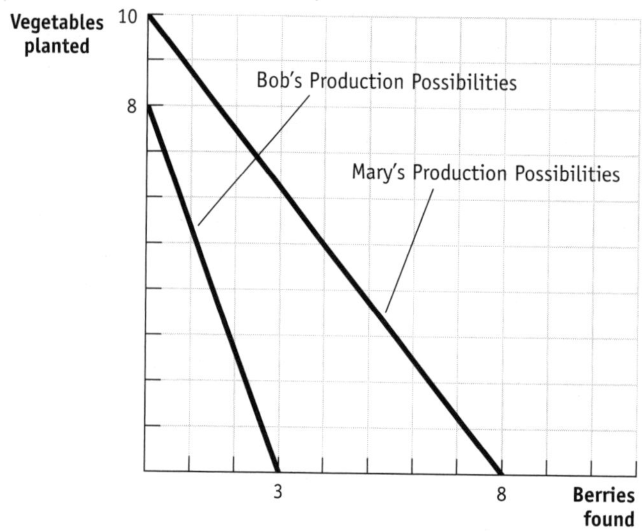

You are asked to determine who has the absolute advantage in planting vegetables and who has the absolute advantage in finding berries. You are also asked to identify who has the comparative advantage for each of these tasks. What is Mary's opportunity cost of finding berries? What is Bob's opportunity cost of finding berries? Finally, suppose that Bob and Mary decide to specialize according to their comparative advantages and then trade. What is the range of amounts of vegetables planted that both would agree to trade in exchange for one unit of berries found?

STEP 1: Review the definition of absolute advantage and then determine who has the absolute advantage in the production of each good.

From the available set of resources, Mary can produce more planted vegetables and found berries than can Bob: Mary has the absolute advantage in the production of both goods.

STEP 2: Review the definition of comparative advantage and then determine who has the comparative advantage in the production of each good.

The opportunity cost of producing a unit of berries is 8/3 units of planted vegetables for Bob and 10/8 units of berries for Mary. Mary has a lower opportunity cost of finding berries than does Bob: for each unit of berries that she finds, she gives up less than does Bob. Mary therefore has the comparative advantage in finding berries. Bob, in contrast, has the comparative advantage in planting vegetables: his opportunity cost of planting vegetables is 3/8 unit of found berries, while the opportunity cost of planting vegetables for Mary is 8/10 unit of found berries.

STEP 3: From the preceding graph determine the opportunity cost of finding berries for each of these individuals.

In Step 2, the opportunity cost of finding berries is given. Remember that you can find the opportunity cost of the good measured on the *x*-axis by using the slope measure if the production possibility frontier is linear. Thus, the slope of Mary's production possibilities curve is equal to −10/8: this indicates that for every unit of found berries she must give up 10/8 units of planted vegetables. The slope of Bob's production possibilities curve is equal to −8/3: this indicates that for every unit of found berries he must give up 8/3 units of planted vegetables. It is more costly for Bob to produce found berries than it is for Mary to produce found berries. Thus, Mary has the comparative advantage in finding berries, while Bob has the comparative advantage in planting vegetables.

STEP 4: Apply your knowledge of the opportunity cost of finding berries for each of these individuals to determine a range of amounts of vegetables planted that both would agree to trade for one unit of berries found.

Bob is willing to give up 8/3 units of planted vegetables for a unit of found berries, while Mary must receive 10/8 units of planted vegetables to be willing to give up a unit of found berries. Any time Mary can receive more than 10/8 units of planted vegetables for a unit of found berries, she is willing to trade; any time Bob pays less than 8/3 units of planted vegetables for a unit of found berries, he is willing to trade. The trading range for one unit of found berries is thus somewhere between 10/8 units of planted vegetables and 8/3 units of planted vegetables.

2. Suppose there are two individuals: Trent and Sue. Both Trent and Sue produce two different goods: clarinets and drums. Each of them has the same amount of resources, the same technology, and the same amount of time to spend producing clarinets and drums. If Trent devotes all of his time, resources, and technology to producing clarinets, he is able to produce 1,000 clarinets and 0 drums. When Trent devotes all of his time, resources, and technology to producing drums, he is able to produce 500 drums and 0 clarinets. If Sue devotes all of her time, resources, and technology to producing clarinets, she is able to produce 800 clarinets and 0 drums. When Sue devotes all of her time, resources, and technology to producing drums, she is able to produce 500 drums and 0 clarinets. Assume that the production possibility frontiers for both Trent and Sue are linear. You are asked to provide graphs of Trent's and Sue's production possibilities on which clarinets are measured on the vertical axis and drums are measured on the horizontal axis. After drawing this graph, you are asked to determine who has the absolute advantage in producing clarinets and drums. In addition, you are asked to determine who has the comparative advantage in the production of each of these goods. Suppose initially that Trent and Sue each devote half of their time and half of their resources to the production of clarinets. The rest of their time and resources goes toward producing drums. Currently Trent and Sue do not trade with each other. Fill in the following table given this information.

	Clarinets	Drums
Trent		
Sue		
Total production		

Suppose that Trent increases his production of clarinets by one unit relative to his initial production level, while Sue decreases her production of clarinets by one unit relative to her initial production level. They both adjust their production of drums so that they stay on their respective production possibility frontiers. Complete the following table, based on these assumptions.

	Clarinets	Drums
Trent		
Sue		
Total production		

Did total production increase or decrease when Trent and Sue altered their allocation of resources? Explain your answer. Suppose instead that Trent decreases his production of clarinets by one unit from the initial level, while Sue increases her production of clarinets by one unit from the initial level. They both adjust their production of drums so that they stay on their respective production possibility frontiers. Complete the following table, based on these assumptions.

	Clarinets	Drums
Trent		
Sue		
Total production		

Did total production increase or decrease when Trent and Sue altered their allocation of resources? Explain your answer. When Trent and Sue adjust their production of these two goods, total production is affected: explain how their adjustments and their impact on total production are related to specialization, comparative advantage, and trade.

STEP 1: Draw graphs of Trent's and Sue's production possibilities on which clarinets are measured on the vertical axis and drums are measured on the horizontal axis.

Trent's Production Possibility Frontier

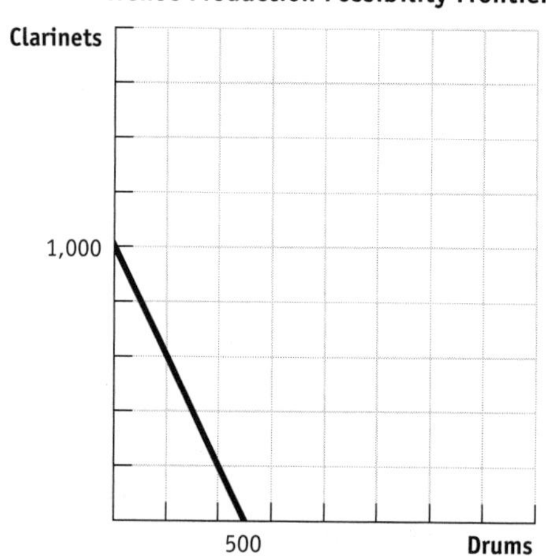

Sue's Production Possibility Frontier

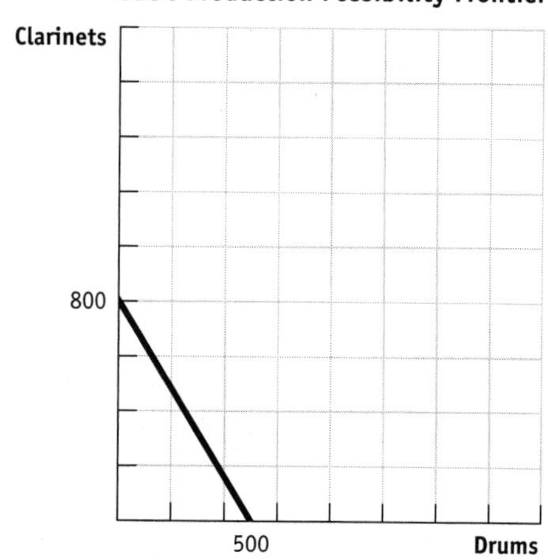

STEP 2: Determine who has the absolute advantage in the production of clarinets and who has the absolute advantage in the production of drums.

Trent can produce more clarinets than can Sue: Trent has the absolute advantage in the production of clarinets, since he is more productive than is Sue. Neither Sue nor

Trent has an absolute advantage in producing drums, since each of them can produce an equivalent amount of drums from the same amount of resources.

STEP 3: Determine who has the comparative advantage in the production of clarinets and who has the comparative advantage in the production of drums.

To determine who has the comparative advantage in producing drums, you first need to determine the opportunity cost of producing a drum for both Trent and Sue. Trent's opportunity cost of producing a drum is equal to 2 clarinets, since each time he produces a drum he must give up the production of two clarinets. Sue's opportunity cost of producing a drum is equal to 8/5 clarinets, since each time she produces a drum she must give up the production of 8/5 clarinets. Trent's opportunity cost of producing a drum is greater than Sue's opportunity cost: Sue has the comparative advantage in producing drums.

To determine who has the comparative advantage in producing clarinets, you will need to determine the opportunity cost of producing a clarinet for both Trent and Sue. Trent's opportunity cost of producing a clarinet is equal to 1/2 of a drum, since each time he produces a clarinet he must give up the production of 1/2 of a drum. Sue's opportunity cost of producing a clarinet is equal to 5/8 of a drum, since each time she produces a clarinet she must give up the production of 5/8 of a drum. Sue's opportunity cost of producing a clarinet is greater than Trent's opportunity cost: Trent has the comparative advantage in producing clarinets.

STEP 4: Fill in the following table based on the assumption that Trent and Sue each devote half of their time and half of their resources to the production of clarinets. The rest of their time and resources goes toward the production of drums.

	Clarinets	Drums
Trent		
Sue		
Total production		

To fill in the table you can consult the figures you drew in Step 1 and find the midpoints of each production possibility frontier. The results are given in the following table.

	Clarinets	Drums
Trent	500	250
Sue	400	250
Total production	900	500

STEP 5: Fill in the following table based on the assumption that Trent decides to produce one more clarinet than he did initially, while Sue decides to produce one fewer clarinet than she did initially. Make sure that the new levels of production are on Trent's and Sue's respective production possibility frontiers.

	Clarinets	Drums
Trent		
Sue		
Total production		

From the earlier discussion on comparative advantage (see Step 3), you know what the opportunity cost of an additional clarinet is for Trent: to produce one more clarinet he must give up 1/2 drum. Thus, Trent can produce 501 clarinets and 249.5 drums. A similar calculation is performed for Sue: when she produces one fewer clarinet, she is able to increase her drum production by 5/8 (this is the same as 0.625) of a drum. The following table summarizes these results.

	Clarinets	Drums
Trent	501	249.5
Sue	399	250.625
Total production	900	500.125

STEP 6: Determine the effect on total production of the change in resource allocation in Step 5. Explain your result.

When Trent moves toward more clarinet production and less drum production, while Sue moves toward more drum production and less clarinet production, we see that total production increases. Notice that in this example both Trent and Sue are moving toward specializing in the production of the good for which they have comparative advantage, and this leads to greater overall production of the goods.

STEP 7: Fill in the following table based on the assumption that Trent decides to produce one fewer clarinet than he did initially, while Sue decides to produce one more clarinet than she did initially. Make sure that the new levels of production are on Trent's and Sue's respective production possibility frontiers.

	Clarinets	Drums
Trent		
Sue		
Total production		

Do the same type of analysis that you did for Step 5, but this time have Trent produce one fewer clarinet while Sue produces one more clarinet. Use the opportunity costs that you calculated in Step 3 to help you figure out what happens to drum production for both Trent and Sue. The following table summarizes these results.

	Clarinets	Drums
Trent	499	250.5
Sue	401	249.375
Total production	900	499.875

STEP 8: Determine the effect on total production of the change in resource allocation in Step 7. Explain your result.

This time total production decreases from its initial level: Trent and Sue are specializing, but they are not specializing according to their comparative advantage, and their decisions here result in less overall production than would be possible if they specialized according to their comparative advantage. It is best for overall production if Trent produces clarinets and Sue produces drums.

STEP 9: Given your analysis in Steps 6 and 8, explain how these adjustments and their impact on total production are related to specialization, comparative advantage, and trade.

This example illustrates how specializing in the production of the good for which you have comparative advantage can result in greater overall production than is possible if there is no specialization. For specialization to be advantageous, two things must happen: you must specialize according to your comparative advantage, and you must engage in trade with others who are also specializing according to their comparative advantage.

Problems and Exercises

1. Paula and Harry both produce lawn care and window washing services, and they both have an equal number of hours available to them each week to engage in providing these services. Paula is able to clean 1/2 of a window or care for 1 yard per hour, and Harry can clean 1 window or 1/2 of a yard per hour. Currently Paula and Harry divide their work time evenly between cleaning windows and doing yard work. Both Paula and Harry work 40 hours a week.

a. Suppose that Paula and Harry initially work independently of each other. Draw two graphs, with one graph illustrating Paula's production possibility frontier and the other graph illustrating Harry's production possibility frontier. Measure windows washed on the vertical axis and yards cared for on the horizontal axis.

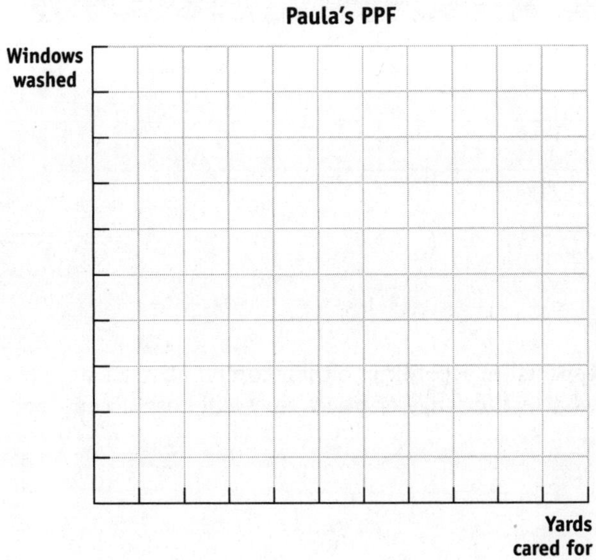

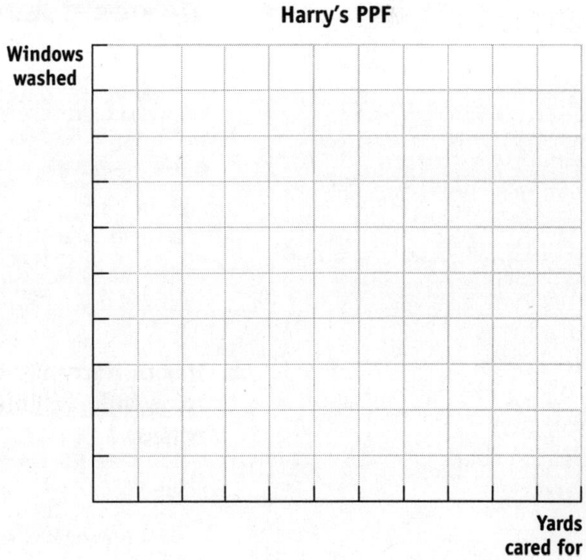

b. Who has the absolute advantage in performing yard care? Who has the absolute advantage in window washing?

c. Suppose both Paula and Harry divide their available time evenly between washing windows and doing yard care. Fill in the following table based on this assumption.

	Number of windows washed	Number of yards cared for
Paula		
Harry		
Total		

d. What is Paula's opportunity cost of washing a window? What is Paula's opportunity cost of caring for a yard?

e. What is Harry's opportunity cost of washing a window? What is Harry's opportunity cost of caring for a yard?

f. Who has the comparative advantage in washing windows? Who has the comparative advantage in caring for a yard? Explain your answers.

g. Assume that both Paula and Harry specialize according to comparative advantage and that both Paula and Harry produce only one type of good. Fill in the table that follows based on this specialization. What happens to total production of lawn care and window washing when Paula and Harry specialize according to their comparative advantage?

	Number of windows washed	Number of yards cared for
Paula		
Harry		
Total		

h. If both Harry and Paula specialize according to their comparative advantage and then trade with each other, what is the range of prices they will both accept for 1 washed window?

2. Titania and Phoenix are two countries that both produce steel and oats from their available resources. The production possibility frontiers for both countries are linear, and the following table provides information about the number of labor hours (the only resource either country uses in producing these two goods) it takes for each country to produce 1 unit of steel or 1 unit of oats. Assume that Titania and Phoenix both have 60 hours of labor available to produce either steel or oats or some combination of steel and oats.

	Number of labor hours needed to produce 1 unit of steel	Number of labor hours needed to produce 1 unit of oats
Titania	5	2
Phoenix	4	3

a. On two separate graphs, draw the production possibility frontiers for Titania and Phoenix. Place steel on the vertical axis and oats on the horizontal axis.

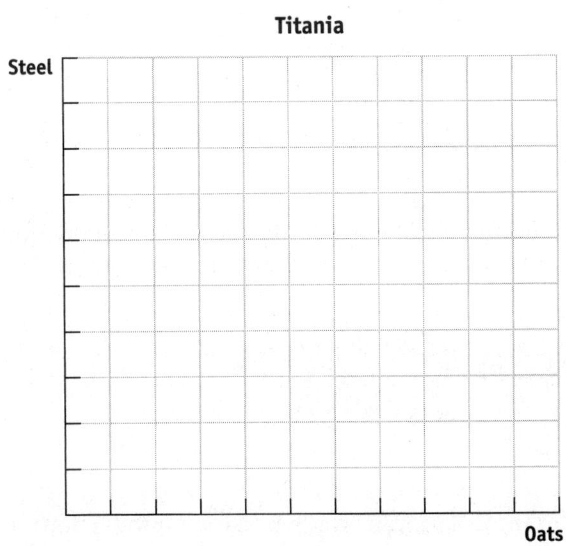

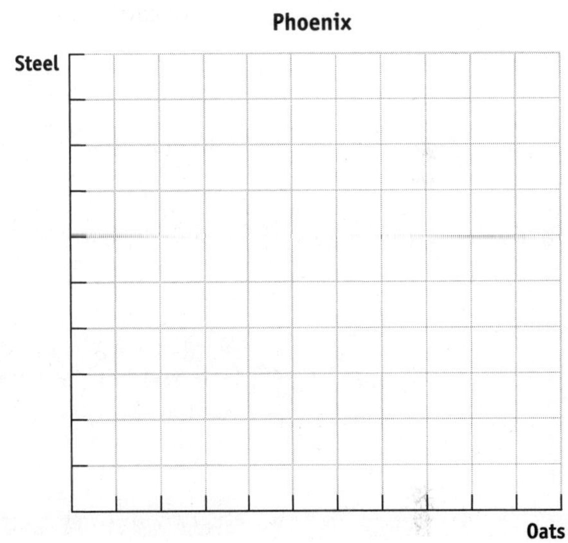

b. Which country has the absolute advantage in producing steel? Which country has the absolute advantage in producing oats?

c. What is the opportunity cost of producing 3 units of steel for Titania? What is the opportunity cost of producing 3 units of steel for Phoenix?

d. What is the opportunity cost of producing 5 units of oats for Titania? What is the opportunity cost of producing 5 units of oats for Phoenix?

e. Which country has the comparative advantage in producing steel? Which country has the comparative advantage in producing oats? Explain your answers.

f. Suppose that Titania and Phoenix both specialize according to their comparative advantage and then trade with each other. Furthermore, suppose that when they specialize these two countries only produce one type of good. What is the range of prices that steel will trade for once this specialization takes place? What is the range of prices that oats will trade for once this specialization takes place?

g. Titania proposes that Phoenix accept 1 unit of oats for 1 unit of steel. Will Phoenix agree to this trading price? Explain your answer.

3. Finlandia and Sweetland are two autarkies possessing equal resources. Both Finlandia and Sweetland produce two goods: food (*F*) and clothing (*C*). The following table provides information about the maximum amount of these two goods that these two countries can produce if they devote all of their resources to the production of just one good. Assume that the production possibility frontiers for both Finlandia and Sweetland are linear.

	Food	Clothing
Finlandia	1,000 units	2,000 units
Sweetland	600 units	1,800 units

a. On two separate graphs, draw Finlandia's and Sweetland's production possibility frontiers. Place units of food on the vertical axis and units of clothing on the horizontal axis.

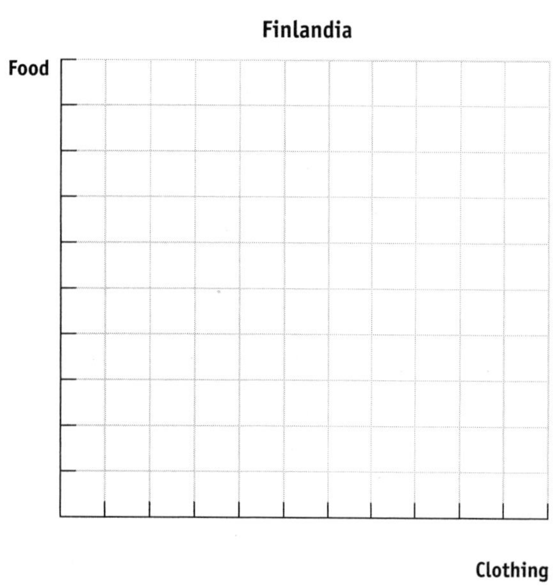

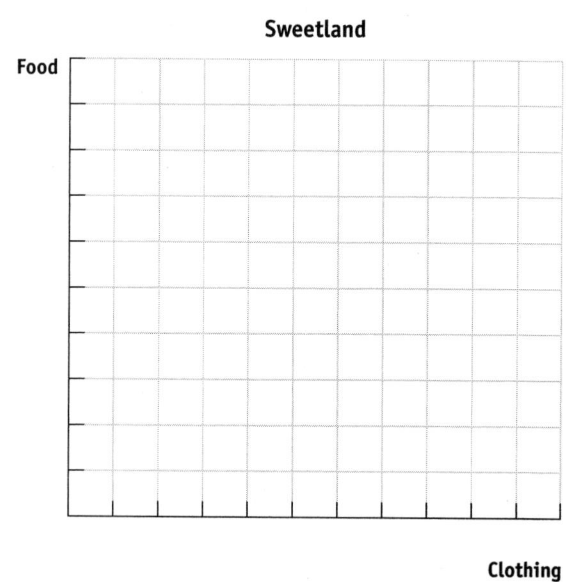

b. Both Finlandia and Sweetland currently produce at points that are located on their production possibility frontiers. Based on this information, fill in the following table. (Hint: you may find it helpful to write an equation for each country's production possibility frontier.)

	Food	Clothing
Finlandia	500 units	
Sweetland		900 units
Total production		

c. Suppose Finlandia and Sweetland open their economies to trade, but neither country fully understands the concept of comparative advantage. Suppose Finlandia and Sweetland adjust their production as given in the table that follows. Fill in the rest of the table assuming that both countries produce at points that are on their production possibility frontiers. Are Finlandia and Sweetland specializing according to their comparative advantage? Explain your answer.

	Food	Clothing
Finlandia	250 units	
Sweetland		390 units
Total production		

d. Finlandia and Sweetland alter their production once again in hopes of reaping the benefits of specialization and trade. Fill in the following table based on both countries producing on their production possibility frontiers.

	Food	Clothing
Finlandia		400 units
Sweetland		
Total production	892 units	

e. Given the production possibility choices Finlandia and Sweetland make in part (d), do these countries reap the advantages of specialization and trade?

4. Do you agree or disagree with the following statement: "Comparative advantage depends on the amount of resources used to produce a good." Explain your answer.

5. Do you agree or disagree with the following statement: "If two workers have different labor productivity, then their wage rates will usually differ from one another, with the worker with greater labor productivity earning a higher wage rate." Explain your answer.

6. What are the major sources of comparative advantage?

7. The Heckscher–Ohlin model predicts that countries have a comparative advantage in producing those goods whose production is intensive in the factors that are abundantly available in that country compared with other countries. What does the Heckscher-Ohlin model predict about factor prices for abundant resources versus less abundant resources? Explain your answer.

BEFORE YOU TAKE THE TEST

Module Review Questions

1. International trade based on comparative advantage is
   a. beneficial to some of the countries involved in the trade, but not beneficial to other countries.
   b. beneficial to all of the countries involved in the trade.
   c. rarely benefits any of the countries involved in the trade.
   d. only beneficial to relatively rich countries.

2. Sarah purchases wine from France, cheese from Italy, wheat crackers from Minnesota, potatoes from Idaho, and lamb from Australia. Sarah lives in New York.
   a. Sarah purchases imports of wine, cheese, and lamb.
   b. Sarah purchases only domestically produced goods, since she can purchase all of these goods at her local grocery store.
   c. The wine, cheese, and lamb represent exports from the perspective of the United States.
   d. Answers (a) and (c) are both true.

Use the following information to answer the next six questions. The table that follows gives information about the production possibility frontiers for two countries, Smallville and Gooseville, that each produce two types of goods, bicycles and cheese. Two possible production points on each country's production possibility frontier are given in the table. Both countries have linear production possibility frontiers.

	Bicycles	Tons of cheese
Smallville	1,000	0
Smallville	0	2,000
Gooseville	1,500	0
Gooseville	0	1,500

3. Suppose that Smallville and Gooseville have the same amount of resources and technology. Which of the following statements is true?

a. Smallville has the absolute advantage in producing bicycles and Gooseville has the absolute advantage in producing cheese.
b. Smallville has the absolute advantage in producing bicycles and cheese.
c. Gooseville has the absolute advantage in producing bicycles and cheese.
d. Smallville has the absolute advantage in producing cheese and Gooseville has the absolute advantage in producing bicycles.

4. The opportunity cost of producing one more bicycle in Smallville is

a. greater than the opportunity cost of producing one more bicycle in Gooseville.
b. less than the opportunity cost of producing one more bicycle in Gooseville.
c. equal to 2 tons of cheese.
d. Answers (a) and (c) are correct.
e. Answers (b) and (c) are correct.

5. Suppose that both countries are in autarky and do not engage in trade. In autarky, both countries choose to produce at the midpoint of their production possibility frontiers. Total cheese production is equal to ________ tons of cheese and total bicycle production is equal to ________ bicycles.

a. 1,750; 1,750
b. 1,750; 1,250
c. 1,250; 1,750
d. 1,250; 1,250

6. Suppose that both countries decide to specialize according to their comparative advantage and trade with each other. Then

a. Smallville will produce cheese and Gooseville will produce bicycles.
b. Smallville will produce bicycles and Goosevillle will produce cheese.

7. When the two countries specialize according to their comparative advantage and then trade with each other, the price of a bicycle measured in terms of cheese will be

a. less than ½ ton of cheese.
b. greater than 1 ton of cheese.
c. between 1 ton of cheese and 2 tons of cheese.
d. between ½ ton of cheese and 1 ton of cheese.

8. Suppose both countries specialize according to their comparative advantage and then trade. Which of the following represents the maximum possible amount of total production given this specialization?

a. 3,500 tons of cheese and 2,500 bicycles
b. 2,500 tons of cheese and 2,500 bicycles
c. 2,000 tons of cheese and 1,500 bicycles
d. 1,750 tons of cheese and 1,250 bicycles

9. When a production possibility frontier is linear, this implies that

a. the opportunity cost of producing either of the two goods represented is constant and does not change.
b. the country will have both a comparative and absolute advantage in producing both of the goods depicted relative to its trading partner.
c. trade of either good to other countries will always be beneficial for this country.
d. this country can not have a comparative advantage in the production of either good.

10. When a country does not engage in trade with other countries, this is referred to as

a. independence.
b. autarky.
c. home economics.
d. Heckscher–Ohlin economics.

11. Which of the following statements is true?

I. Gains from trade depend on absolute advantage.
II. Comparative advantage depends on the amount of resources used to produce a good.
III. A country's comparative advantage is translated into world markets through its wage rates: a country's wage rate typically reflects that country's labor productivity.

a. Statement I is true.
b. Statement II is true.
c. Statement III is true.
d. Statements I, II, and III are true.
e. Statements II and III are true.

12. The pauper labor fallacy refers to the idea that

a. importing goods from low-wage countries must hurt the standard of living of workers in the importing country.
b. exporting goods from low-wage countries must hurt the standard of living of those workers in the exporting country.
c. trade must be bad for workers in low-wage countries because they are paid such low wages by world standards.
d. trade must be bad for workers in high-wage countries because they are paid such high wages by world standards.

13. The sweatshop labor fallacy refers to the idea that

a. importing goods from low-wage countries must hurt the standard of living of workers in the importing country.

b. exporting goods from low-wage countries must hurt the standard of living of those workers in the importing country.

c. trade must be bad for workers in low-wage countries because they are paid such low wages by world standards.

d. trade must be bad for workers in high-wage countries because they are paid such high wages by world standards.

14. Which of the following situations illustrate one of the three sources of comparative advantage?

a. A country produces olives that can only grow in a Mediterranean climate.

b. A country specializes in producing medical equipment whose production relies on the use of highly productive labor resources.

c. A country in the southern hemisphere specializes in providing grapes to the northern hemisphere during the winter season.

d. A country uses its extensive network of fiber-optic cable to produce information technology for countries located throughout the world.

e. All of the answers illustrate at least one of the sources of comparative advantage.

15. Which of the following statements is *not* supported by the Heckscher–Öhlin model?

a. Countries specialize in producing the good whose production is intensive in the factors that are abundantly available in that country compared with other countries.

b. After they specialize, countries find that those factors that are relatively scarce in their country compared to other countries command higher factor prices than those factors that are relatively abundant in their country.

c. Countries that are labor abundant produce goods that are labor intensive relative to countries that are less labor abundant.

d. Countries that are capital abundant produce goods that are capital intensive relative to countries that are less capital abundant.

16. Which of the following statements is true?

I. Countries with highly skilled labor will tend to import goods whose production requires high levels of human capital.

II. Countries whose exporting industries focus on using a higher ratio of highly educated workers to other workers are human capital intensive.

III. Countries will find that their exporting industries utilize their relatively more abundant factors of production.

a. Statement I is true.

b. Statement II is true.

c. Statement III is true.

d. Statements I and II are true.

e. Statements II and III are true.

f. Statements I, II, and III are true.

ANSWER KEY

Answers to Problems and Exercises

1. a.

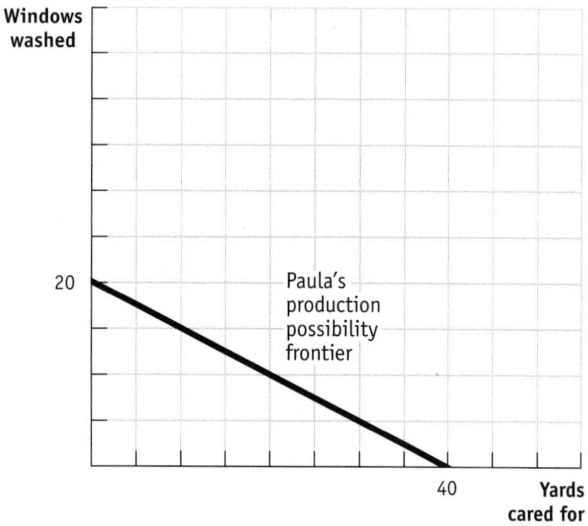

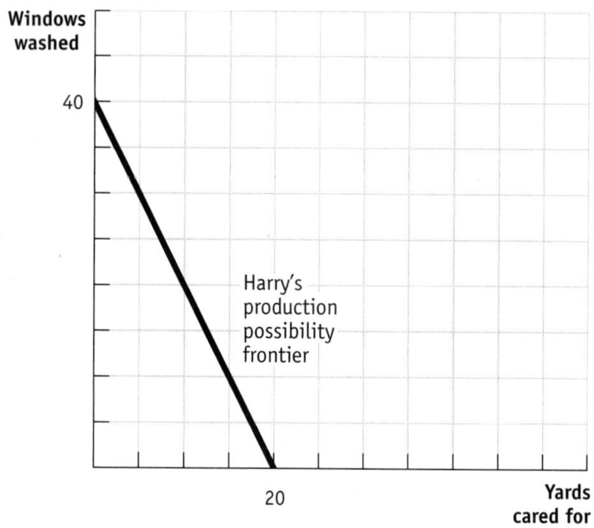

b. Paula has the absolute advantage in yard care since she can clean more yards than Harry with the same amount of resources (40 yards versus 20 yards), and Harry has the absolutc advantage in window washing since he can wash more windows than Paula with the same amount of resources (40 windows versus 20 windows).

c.

	Number of windows washed	Number of yards cared for
Paula	10	20
Harry	20	10
Total	30	30

d. Paula's opportunity cost of washing a window is 2 yards cared for, since she must give up caring for 2 yards to free up enough resources to clean 1 window. Her opportunity cost of caring for a yard is ½ of a window washed since she must give up washing ½ of a window to free up enough resources to care for a yard.

e. Harry's opportunity cost of washing a window is ½ yard cared for, since he must give up caring for ½ a yard to free up enough resources to clean 1 window. His opportunity cost of caring for a yard is 2 windows washed since he must give up washing 2 windows to free up enough resources to care for a yard.

f. Harry has the comparative advantage in washing windows, and Paula has the comparative advantage in caring for yards. Harry's opportunity cost of washing 1 window is only ½ a yard, and Paula's opportunity cost of washing 1 window is 2 yards, so Harry can produce a washed window at a lower opportunity cost than can Paula. Paula's opportunity cost of caring for 1 yard is ½ of a window washed, and Harry's opportunity cost of caring for 1 yard is 2 windows washed, so Paula can care for a yard at a lower opportunity cost than can Harry.

g.

	Number of windows washed	Number of yards cared for
Paula	0	40
Harry	40	0
Total	40	40

Through specialization according to comparative advantage, total production of both goods increases.

h. The range of prices for 1 window washed falls between ½ of a yard cared for and 2 yards cared for. Paula is willing to trade up to 2 yards cared for to get a single window washed, while Harry is willing to wash a single window provided he is compensated by ½ of a yard cared for.

2. a.

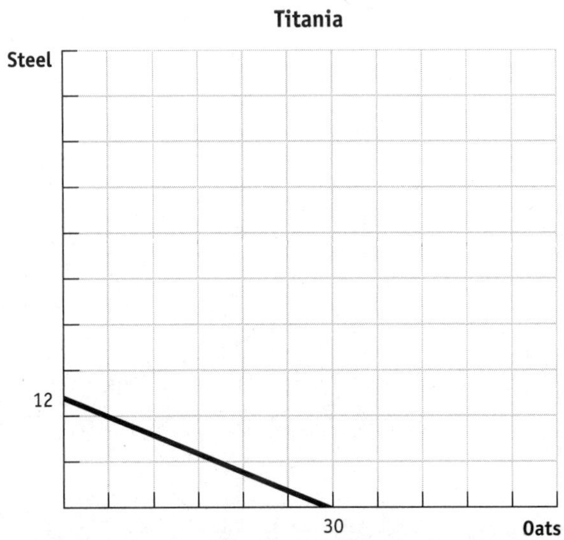

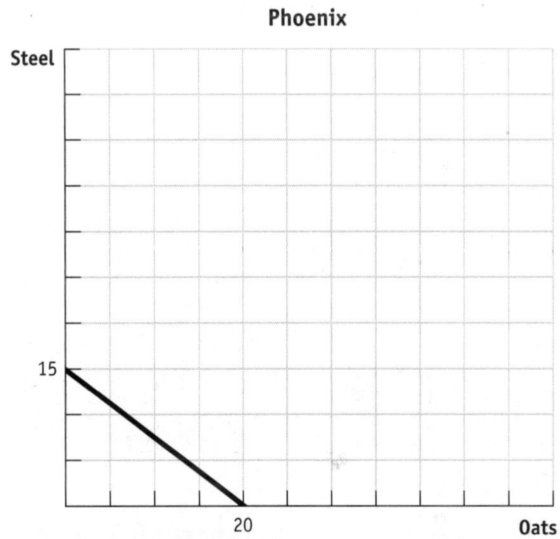

b. Phoenix has the absolute advantage in producing steel since, from the same amount of resources, Phoenix can absolutely produce more units of the good than can Titania. Titania has the absolute advantage in producing oats since, from the same amount of resources, Titania can absolutely produce more units of the good than can Phoenix.

c. The opportunity cost of producing 3 units of steel for Titania is equal to 7.5 units of oats. From the graph, the slope of the production possibility frontier for Titania is –2/5, which implies that the opportunity cost of Titania producing 1 unit of oats is 2/5 units of steel. We can take the reciprocal of this measure and get the opportunity cost of 1 unit of steel is equal to 5/2 units of oats. But since we want to know the opportunity cost of 3 units of steel, we need to multiply the 5/2 units of oats by 3 to get 15/2 units of oats, or 7.5 units of oats. The opportunity cost of producing 3 units of steel for Phoenix is equal to 4 units of oats. From the graph, the slope of the production possibility frontier for Phoenix is –3/4, which implies that the opportunity cost of Phoenix producing 1 unit of oats is 3/4 units of steel. We can take the reciprocal of this measure and get the opportunity cost of 1 unit of steel is equal to 4/3 units of oats. But since we want to know the opportunity cost of 3 units of steel, we need to multiply the 4/3 units of oats by 3 to get 12/3 units of oats, or 4 units of oats.

d. The opportunity cost of producing 5 units of oats for Titania is 2 units of steel, and the opportunity cost of producing 5 units of oats for Phoenix is 3.75 units of steel.

e. Titania has the comparative advantage in producing oats while Phoenix has the comparative advantage in producing steel. Titania's opportunity cost of producing 1 unit of oats is 2/5 units of steel, and Phoenix's opportunity cost of producing 1 unit of oats is ¾ units of steel, so Titania can produce oats at lower opportunity cost than can Phoenix. Titania's opportunity cost of producing 1 unit of steel is 5/2 units of oats, and Phoenix's opportunity cost of producing 1 unit of steel is 4/3 units of oats, so Phoenix can produce steel at lower opportunity cost than can Titania.

f. One unit of steel will trade for between 4/3 units of oats to 5/2 units of oats, and 1 unit of oats will trade for between 2/5 units of steel and 3/4 units of steel.

g. No, Phoenix is only willing to trade 1 unit of steel if the price is at least 4/3 units of oats.

3. **a.**

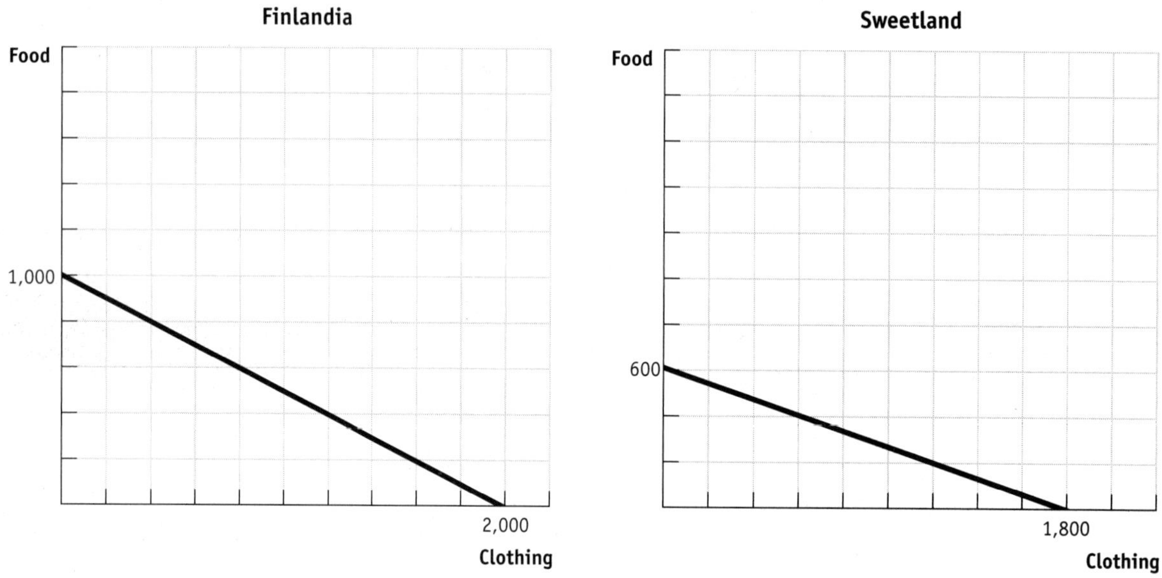

b. The equation for Finlandia's production possibility frontier is $F = 1{,}000 - (1/2)C$. When $F = 500$ units, then $C = 1{,}000$ units. The equation for Sweetland's production possibility frontier is $F = 600 - (1/3)C$. When $C = 900$ units, then $F = 300$ units.

	Food	Clothing
Finlandia	500 units	1,000 units
Sweetland	300 units	900 units
Total production	800 units	1,900 units

c. Use the equations you calculated in part (b) to fill in the table.

	Food	Clothing
Finlandia	250 units	1,500 units
Sweetland	470 units	390 units
Total production	720 units	1,890 units

Finlandia and Sweetland are not specializing according to their comparative advantage since their total production of the two goods has fallen as they altered their production.

d.

	Food	Clothing
Finlandia	800 units	400 units
Sweetland	92 units	1,524 units
Total production	892 units	1,924 units

e. Yes, by specializing according to their comparative advantage and then trading, the total level of production of the two goods increases.

4. Disagree. Comparative advantage depends on the opportunity cost of producing the good rather than the amount of resources used to produce the good.

5. Agree. Workers with lower labor productivity will earn a lower wage than workers with higher labor productivity since the competition for less-productive workers is less intense, resulting in a lower wage rate.

6. The major sources of comparative advantage are differences in climate, differences in factor endowments, and differences in technology between countries.

7. The Heckscher–Ohlin model predicts that factors of production that are abundant in a country that trades with other countries will command higher factor prices than factors of production that are less abundant. This is the result of the country's specialization in the production of the good whose production is intensive in the abundant factors of production. This specialization increases the demand for these factors and therefore increases the price of these factors.

Answers to Module Review Questions

1. **Answer b.** International trade is a source of mutual benefit to the countries involved in the trade.

2. **Answer a.** The wine, cheese, and lamb are all imported goods into the American economy since these goods are produced elsewhere in the world and then brought into the American market. Exports refers to those goods produced in the domestic economy and sold in a foreign economy.

3. **Answer d.** Since Smallville can absolutely produce more cheese than can Gooseville, Smallville has the absolute advantage in producing cheese. Gooseville, on the other hand, can absolutely produce more bicycles than Smallville from the same resources, so Gooseville has the absolute advantage in producing bicycles.

4. **Answer d.** The opportunity cost of producing one more bicycle in Smallville is equal to the number of tons of cheese that must be given up to produce one more bicycle. In this case, 2 tons of cheese must be given up to produce one more bicycle in Smallville. The opportunity cost of producing a bicycle in Smallville is 2 tons of cheese, while the opportunity cost of producing a bicycle in Gooseville is equal to 1 ton of cheese.

5. **Answer b.** If Smallville produces at the midpoint of its production possibility frontier, it will produce 1,000 tons of cheese and 500 bicycles. If Gooseville produces at the midpoint of its production possibility frontier, it will produce 750 tons of cheese and 750 bicycles. Total cheese production will equal 1,750 tons and total bicycle production will equal 1,250 bicycles.

6. **Answer a.** Smallville will produce cheese since the opportunity cost of producing cheese for Smallville is ½ a bicycle while the opportunity cost of producing cheese for Gooseville is 1 bicycle. Smallville gives up fewer bicycles to produce a ton of cheese and therefore Smallville has the comparative advantage in producing cheese.

7. **Answer c.** The opportunity cost of producing a bicycle is 2 tons of cheese for Smallville and 1 ton of cheese for Gooseville. Smallville will be willing to pay up to 2 tons of cheese for 1 bicycle, while Gooseville is willing to trade 1 bicycle for any amount of cheese greater than 1 ton. The price of a bicycle will be in the range of 1 to 2 tons of cheese.

8. **Answer c.** If both countries fully specialize, then Smallville will produce only cheese (2,000 tons of cheese) and Gooseville will produce only bicycles (1,500 bicycles).

9. **Answer a.** A linear production function is a production function with a constant slope. This constant slope tells us that for a given change in the good measured on the *x*-axis there will be a given change in the good measured on the *y*-axis. Another way to express this idea is that the opportunity cost of producing either good is constant: for the good measured on the *x*-axis, the opportunity cost of producing one more unit of that good is equal to the absolute value of the slope of the production possibility frontier; for the good measured on the *y*-axis, the opportunity cost of producing one more unit of that good is equal to the absolute value of the reciprocal of the slope of the production possibility frontier. Provided that the slopes of the two countries' production possibility frontiers are not the same, then one of these countries cannot have the comparative advantage of producing both goods: one country must have the comparative advantage in producing one of the goods, while the other country must have the comparative advantage in producing the other good. Trade is beneficial, provided countries specialize in their comparative advantage. Trade without regard to comparative advantage results in lower total production.

10. **Answer b.** This is the definition of autarky. A country may be independent of other countries when it decides not to trade, but that is not the term used to describe this trade position. Answer (d) refers to models used to analyze international trade, but they are not direct references to the term describing a closed economy.

11. **Answer c.** Gains from trade stem from a country's comparative advantage and not its absolute advantage (statement I is false). Absolute advantage focuses on the amount of resources used to produce a good (for example, the number of hours of labor it takes to produce a shirt) while comparative advantage focuses on the opportunity cost of producing the good—that is, what must be given up to produce a unit of this good (statement II is false). When a country has a comparative advantage in producing a good, this means that its opportunity cost of producing the good is lower than the opportunity cost of producing the same good in some other country: this advantage in terms of opportunity cost is translated into wage rates. When a country has less-productive labor, then the wage rate for this labor is lower than it is for a country that has more-productive labor.

12. **Answer a.** The pauper labor fallacy focuses on the erroneous idea that trade with low-wage countries must necessarily reduce the standard of living of workers in high-wage countries. This idea stems from the belief that this trade "steals" jobs from the high-wage country and does not consider the consumption benefits to the high-wage country of access to the cheaper goods that are made available to the high-wage country by the low-wage country. Trade, willingly undertaken between two parties, must be beneficial to both parties.

13. **Answer c.** This is the definition of the sweatshop labor fallacy. Here the focus is on the idea that high-wage countries are exploiting labor in low-wage countries, since the wages in the latter countries are so much less than the wages in the high-wage countries. However, this argument fails to consider the relative productivity of the labor in these two types of countries, and it does not consider the other alternatives available to labor in the low-wage countries. Sometimes a job that looks terrible from the perspective of a person in a high-wage country is highly sought after in a low-wage country.

14. Answer e. The main sources of comparative advantage are differences in climate, differences in factor endowments, and differences in technology. Answers (a) and (c) illustrate a country's specialization based on climate differences, answer (b) illustrates a country's specialization based on factor endowments, and answer (d) illustrates a country's specialization based on differences in technology.

15. Answer b. According to the Heckscher–Ohlin model, countries have a comparative advantage in producing those goods and services whose production is intensive in the factors of production that are relatively abundant in that country compared with other countries. Thus, a country that has an abundance of labor relative to other countries tends to specialize in producing labor-intensive goods and services, while a country that is capital abundant specializes in producing capital-intensive goods and services. This specialization bids up the factor price of the factors that are abundant in a country due to the increased demand for these factors, and the factor price of the factors that are scarce in a country tends to fall due to decreased demand for these factors. Answer (b) is not true because the prices of the factors are moving in the wrong direction.

16. Answer e. Countries will tend to import those goods that are produced using factors of production which are relatively scarce in the importing country (statement I is therefore false). Countries that utilize a high ratio of highly skilled workers to less skilled workers are countries that tend to produce goods that are intensive in human capital (statement II is true). Countries will export goods whose production takes advantage of the relative abundance of the factor (statement III is true).

module 17

Supply, Demand, and International Trade

BEFORE YOU READ THE MODULE

Summary

The module considers the impact of tariffs and quotas and how tariffs and quotas create market inefficiencies and reduce the area of total surplus. The module discusses why governments engage in trade protection and the effect of international trade agreements on the international flow of goods and services. The module also discusses the challenges posed by globalization.

Module Objectives

Objective #1. The model of demand and supply can be used to analyze the benefits of international trade. Figure 17.1 illustrates a market for a country that does not trade. In this figure, domestic demand represents the total demand for this good from individuals who live in this country, while domestic supply represents the total supply of this good from firms producing this good in this country. In autarky, the equilibrium in this market would be determined by the intersection of the domestic demand curve with the domestic supply curve: P_A is the equilibrium price and Q_A is the equilibrium quantity under autarky. Consumer and producer surplus are indicated in the figure, and total surplus in this market equals the sum of consumer and producer surplus.

Figure 17.1

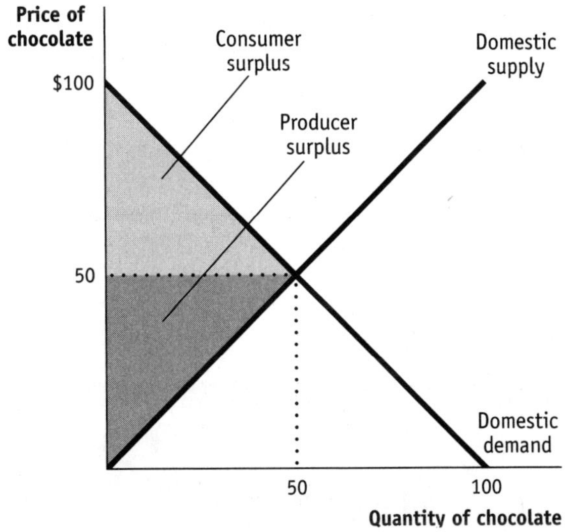

Consider what happens in this market if this country opens to trade. Suppose the world price for this good is lower than the autarky price (P_A) for this good. In Figure 17.2, this world price (P_W) is drawn on the graph. Notice that if the country opens to trade, the quantity of the good demanded domestically in this country at the world price (Q_D) will be greater than the amount of the good supplied domestically at this price (Q_S). This excess demand will be satisfied by the country importing ($Q_D - Q_S$) units of the good. Trade will also change the areas of consumer and producer surplus in this country: consumer surplus will increase as consumers get more units of the good at a lower price, while producer surplus decreases as domestic producers sell fewer units of the good at the lower price. Study Figure 17.2 carefully and recall that consumer surplus is the area that is beneath the demand curve but above the equilibrium price, while producer surplus is the area that is above the supply curve but below the equilibrium price. With trade, total surplus increases, but domestic producers of this good see a reduction in their producer surplus while domestic consumers see an increase in their consumer surplus. In the case of an imported good, domestic consumers benefit while domestic producers lose. Trade is beneficial since total surplus increases, but trade has distributional consequences as you can see from what happens to the areas of consumer and producer surplus.

Figure 17.2

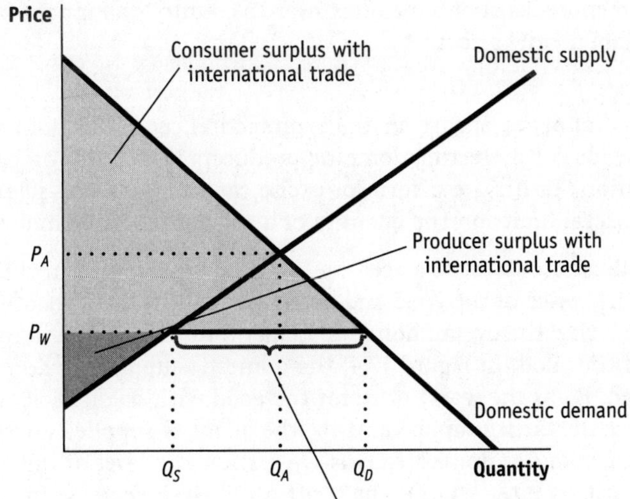

We can use the same analysis to consider the situation when the world price is greater than the autarky price. Starting from Figure 17.1, a market under autarky, let's consider a situation in which the world price exceeds the autarky price. Figure 17.3 illustrates this example: P_W is the world price and, in this case, when this country opens to trade, it finds that the quantity demanded domestically at the world price (Q_D) is less than the amount supplied domestically at this price (Q_S). This excess supply of ($Q_S - Q_D$) will be exported to other countries. Figure 17.3 also identifies the areas of consumer surplus and producer surplus once trade is allowed. As in Figure 17.2, we find that the area of total surplus is larger than in autarky. However, the distribution of the surplus has changed: in Figure 17.2, domestic consumers benefited from trade while domestic suppliers were hurt; in Figure 17.3, domestic suppliers benefit from trade while domestic consumers are hurt. In both of these examples we find that trade is beneficial since it increases total surplus, but that trade has distributional consequences.

Figure 17.3

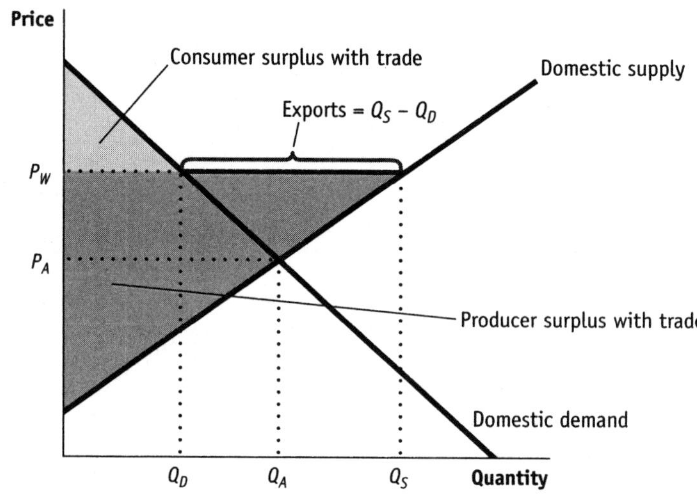

Objective #2. A country's industries can be broken down into two broad categories: exporting industries that produce goods and services to be sold abroad, and import-competing industries that produce goods and services also imported from abroad. When a country opens to trade, this leads to higher production in the exporting industries and lower production in the import-competing industries, and these changes affect the demand for factors of production in these two types of industries. The Heckscher–Ohlin model posits that international trade increases the demand for those factors of production that are relatively abundant in the country and decreases the demand for those factors of production that are relatively scarce. Thus, the price of abundant factors tends to rise while the price of scarce factors tends to fall. This price movement redistributes income toward a country's abundant factors and away from a country's less abundant factors.

Objective #3. Countries engage in trade protection, or protection, to limit the level of imports with the idea of protecting domestic producers in import-competing industries from foreign competition. Tariffs are a form of excise tax levied on the sales of imported goods, while quotas are legal limits on the quantity of a good that can be imported.

- Figure 17.4 illustrates a tariff placed on the good represented in this diagram. The tariff raises the world price of the good and therefore reduces the level of imports while simultaneously reducing the overall domestic demand for the good and increasing the domestic supply of the good. In Figure 17.4, the domestic supply and domestic demand curves are illustrated. P_W is the world price for the good with open trade, and P_T is the price of the good once the tariff is applied. At P_T, the quantity supplied domestically is Q_{ST} while the quantity demanded domestically is Q_{DT}. Thus, the level of imports with the imposition of the tariff is ($Q_{DT} - Q_{ST}$). The tariff results in a decrease in consumer surplus, an increase in producer surplus, and the capture of some of the consumer surplus as tariff revenue that the government earns. These areas are marked on the graph. In addition, the tariff results in deadweight loss: some mutually beneficial trades fail to occur and the economy wastes some resources on inefficient production since some producers produce the good even though their costs are greater than the world price of P_W. These two areas of deadweight loss are also identified on the graph. Study Figure 17.4 carefully and then compare it with Figure 17.2 to see how a tariff changes the outcome in this market. Notice that the tariff redistributes part of the consumer surplus to domestic producers and to the government as well as creates the areas of deadweight loss.

Figure 17.4

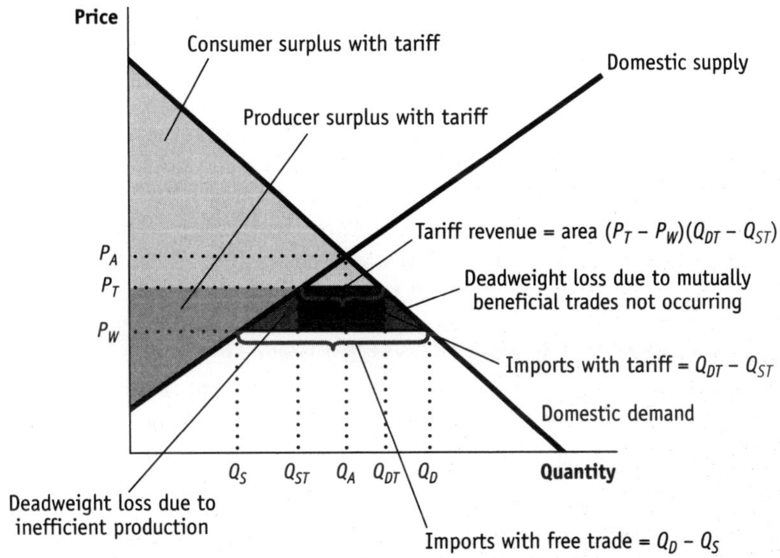

- Imposition of a quota in a market with free trade creates a limit on the number of units of the good that can be imported into the domestic market. This legal limit is typically administered through a license whereby the license holder purchases the legal right to import a certain number of units of the good into the domestic market. A quota results in a similar outcome as the tariff, but with one crucial difference. With a quota, the area labeled tariff revenue is now license-holder revenue. Instead of the government earning tax revenue from the imposition of the tariff, the quota results in the license holder earning quota rents equal to the area $(P_Q - P_W)(Q_{D\ QUOTA} - Q_{S\ QUOTA})$. The quota results in an increase in the domestic producer surplus and a decrease in the domestic consumer surplus. In addition, the quota results in the same two areas of deadweight loss that occurred with the tariff. Figure 17.5 illustrates the impact of a quota of $(Q_{D\ QUOTA} - Q_{S\ QUOTA})$ units on the market.

Figure 17.5

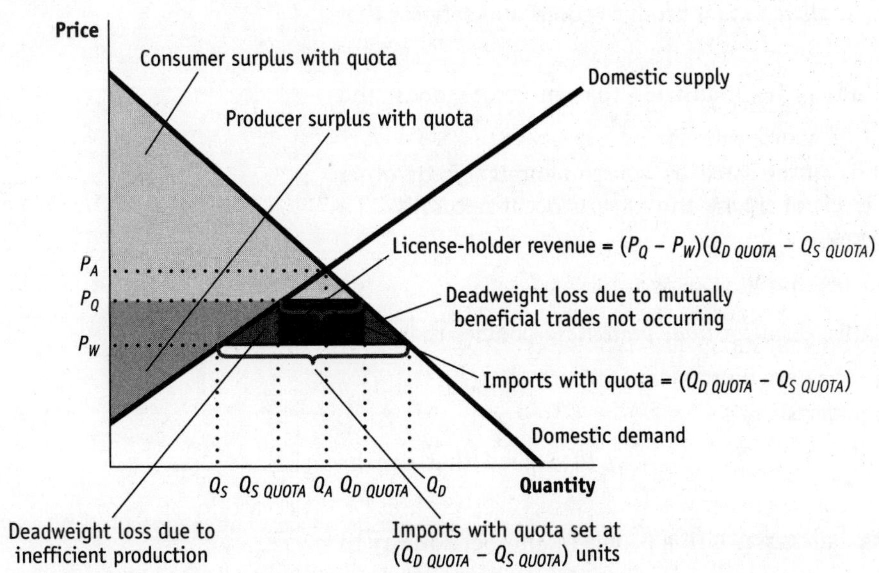

Objective #4. Advocates of tariffs and quotas offer three common arguments for trade protection: national security, job creation, and the infant industry argument. The national security argument focuses on the need to protect domestic suppliers of crucial goods from foreign competition. The job creation argument focuses on the additional jobs that are created in the import-competing industries when these industries are protected by a tariff or quota. The infant industry argument claims that newly emerging industries (those in their infancy) may need trade protection to get established. Despite these arguments, most trade protection reflects the political influence of the import-competing producers.

Objective #5. Trade protection hurts domestic consumers as well as foreign export industries. Because countries care about each other's trade policies, they engage in international trade agreements. These agreements involve treaties that pledge countries will engage in less trade protection in return for a promise from other countries that they will also engage in less trade protection. The North American Free Trade Agreement (NAFTA) and the European Union (EU) are examples of trade agreements between groups of countries. Global trade agreements that cover most of the world also are in place, and the World Trade Organization (WTO) oversees these global trade agreements. The WTO provides the framework for the extensive and complex negotiations that are involved in major international agreements; in addition, the WTO resolves disputes among its members.

Objective #6. Globalization or growing world trade has generally been seen as a positive outcome. However, concerns have arisen over the growing wage gap between more educated and less educated workers. In addition, the growth of offshore outsourcing has generated concerns about increasing economic insecurity.

Key Terms

domestic demand curve a *demand curve* that shows how the quantity of a good demanded by domestic consumers depends on the price of that good.

domestic supply curve a *supply curve* that shows how the quantity of a good supplied by domestic producers depends on the price of that good.

world price the price at which a good can be bought or sold abroad.

exporting industries industries that produce goods and services that are sold abroad.

import-competing industries industries that produce goods and services that are also imported.

free trade *trade* that is unregulated by government *tariffs* or other artificial barriers; the levels of *exports* and *imports* occur naturally, as a result of supply and demand.

trade protection policies that limit *imports.*

protection an alternative term for *trade protection;* policies that limit *imports.*

tariff a tax levied on *imports.*

import quota a legal limit on the quantity of a good that can be imported from abroad.

offshore outsourcing businesses hiring people in another country to perform various tasks.

Notes

AFTER YOU READ THE MODULE

Tips

Tip #1. Analyzing the effects of a tariff on a market for a particular good can be challenging, but it will get easier with practice. To be effective, a tariff must be set so that the domestic price of the good is above the world price and below the closed-economy price. As the good's price rises, the tariff will encourage domestic suppliers to provide more of the good and domestic consumers to demand less of the good. The results of the tariff: (1) Domestic producers can sell more of the good if the market were open to trade but had no tariff. (2) Domestic consumers purchase less of the good than they would without the tariff. (3) The price of the good rises above the world price but less than the domestic price if the economy were closed to trade. (4) The level of imports of the good is lower than if the economy were open to trade and there were no tariff. (5) The government earns tariff revenue. (6) The tariff results in deadweight loss, an efficiency cost of imposing the tariff on this market.

Tip #2. Working with quotas is often difficult for students: a quota is a legally established limit to the amount of imports a country allows during a given period. An alternative way of thinking about this legal limit is to recognize that the quota is the amount of imports that leads to the sum of the quantity supplied domestically plus the quota amount equaling the quantity demanded domestically. Thus, if you are told the quantity demanded domestically and the quantity supplied domestically at a given price, you can then calculate what the necessary quota would be in order for the total quantity supplied of the good (both the domestic production plus the world production) to equal the quantity demanded domestically. With this thought in mind, go back and revisit Figure 17.5 to see if you can apply this concept to the graph.

WORKED PROBLEMS

1. The small economy of Newville produces chocolate, and this market for chocolate is characterized by the following equations:

   Domestic Demand for Chocolate: $P = 100 - Q$
   Domestic Supply of Chocolate: $P = Q$

You are asked to determine the equilibrium price and quantity in this market if Newville continues to be a closed economy with regard to the chocolate market. You are also asked to provide a measure of the consumer and producer surplus when this market is closed to trade. Newville is considering opening this market to trade and imagines two possible scenarios: in the first scenario, the chocolate market is open to trade and the world price of chocolate is $80 per unit. Newville's government wants you to analyze the effect of opening this market to trade given this price: the government in particular wants to know the impact of opening the market on the level of imports or exports of chocolate it could anticipate as well as on the values of consumer and producer surplus when there is trade. In the second scenario, the chocolate market is open to trade, and the world price of chocolate is $20 per unit. You are also asked to provide an analysis of the impact of opening the market on the level of imports or exports of chocolate as well as on the values of consumer and producer surplus if the world price for chocolate is equal to $20 per unit. For both scenarios, you are asked to illustrate your answer with a graph to help the government officials understand the impact of opening the market to world trade. The government also wishes to understand if opening its market to trade is beneficial whether it is confronted by the first or the second scenario. Who (domestic consumers or domestic producers of chocolate) in Newville is more likely to favor opening the chocolate market to trade if the world price is anticipated to be $80 per unit?

STEP 1: **Start by drawing a graph of the market for chocolate in Newville when its economy is closed to trade. Use this graph to calculate the levels of consumer and producer surplus if there is no trade.**

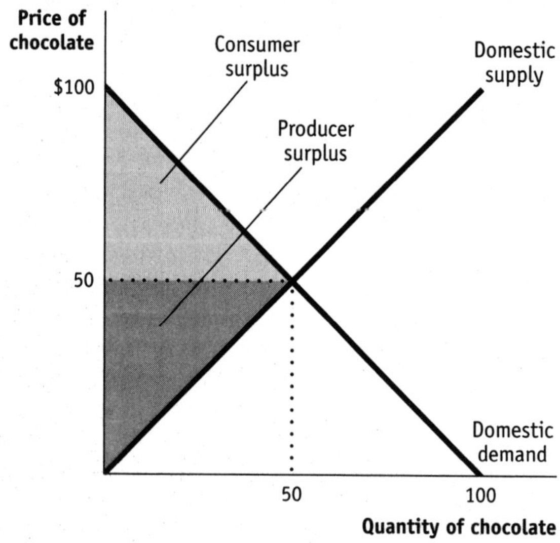

Graph the two equations and then use these two equations to find the equilibrium price and equilibrium quantity in this market when the market is closed to world competition. Using the demand and supply equations, $P = 100 - Q$ and $P = Q$ (respectively), we can solve for the equilibrium quantity and then use this quantity to find the equilibrium price. Thus, $100 - Q = Q$, or $2Q = 100$, and therefore $Q = 50$. Plugging $Q = 50$ back into either the demand or the supply equation, we can find that the equilibrium price is equal to $50.

The value of consumer surplus is equal to (1/2)($100 per unit – $50 per unit)(50 units), or $1,250. The value of producer surplus is equal to (1/2)($50 per unit – $0 per unit)(50 units), or $1,250. These areas are marked on the preceding graph. Total surplus equals $1,250 or $2,500.

STEP 2: **Modify your graph from Step 1 by adding in a line that represents a world price for chocolate of $80 per unit.**

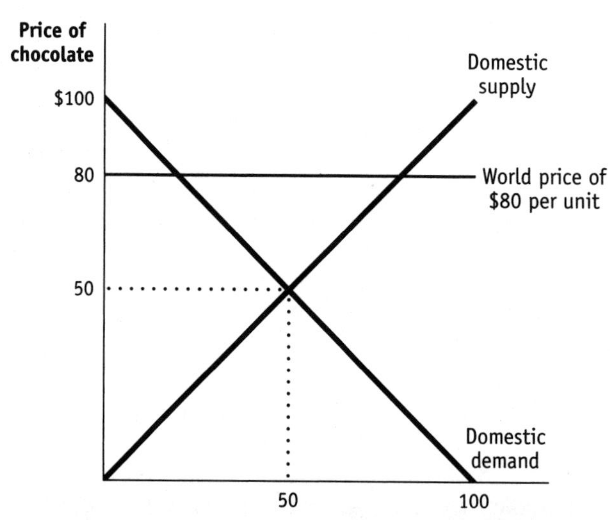

STEP 3: Analyze the impact on this market if the world price is equal to $80 and Newville opens its chocolate market. Be sure to identify whether Newville will export or import chocolate. In addition, determine the impact of this decision on consumer and producer surplus. Finally, analyze whether trade is beneficial if the world price of chocolate is equal to $80 per unit.

When Newville opens its chocolate market to international trade and the world price of chocolate is $80 per unit, domestic suppliers will be willing to supply 80 units of the good, while domestic demanders are willing to buy only 20 units of the good. This excess supply of 60 units will therefore be exported into the world market for chocolate.

To find the consumer surplus, first recognize that it is the area that is under the domestic demand curve but above the world price for chocolate. Then, calculate the value of this area: consumer surplus is equal to (1/2)($100 per unit − $80 per unit)(20 units), or $200.

To find the producer surplus, first recognize that it is the area that is under the world price for chocolate but above the domestic supply curve. Then, calculate the value of this area: producer surplus is equal to (1/2)($80 per unit − $0 per unit)(80 units), or $3,200.

The following figure illustrates the impact on consumer and producer surplus when the world price is equal to $80 per unit.

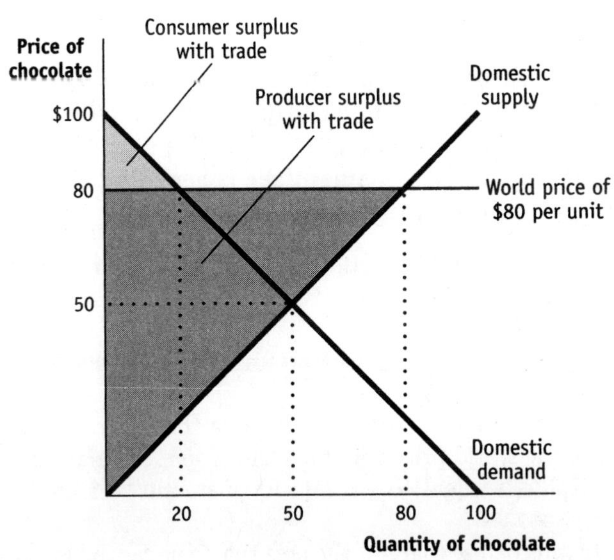

Trade is beneficial to Newville when the world price is $80 per unit since the value of total surplus, the sum of consumer and producer surplus in this case, is greater than the value of total surplus when Newville has a closed chocolate market. Total surplus is equal to $2,400 when this market is closed to trade and $3,200 + $200, or $3,400, when this market opens to trade.

STEP 4: Redraw your graph from Step 1 and revise it by adding in a line that represents a world price for chocolate of $20 per unit.

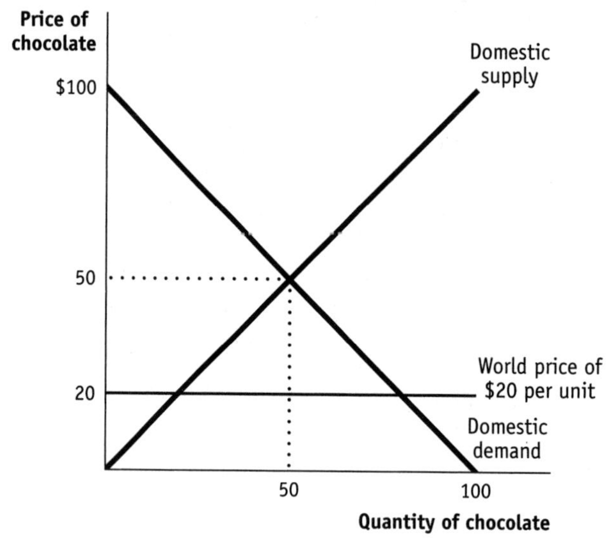

STEP 5: Analyze the impact on this market if the world price is equal to $20 and Newville opens its chocolate market. Be sure to identify whether Newville will export or import chocolate. In addition, determine the impact of this decision on consumer and producer surplus. Finally, analyze whether trade is beneficial if the world price of chocolate is equal to $20 per unit.

When Newville opens its chocolate market to international trade and the world price of chocolate is $20 per unit, domestic suppliers will only be willing to supply 20 units of the good, while domestic demanders want to buy 80 units of the good. This excess demand of 60 units will be met by Newville's importing 60 units of chocolate from the world market.

To find the consumer surplus, first recognize that it is the area that is under the domestic demand curve but above the world price for chocolate. Then, calculate the value of this area: consumer surplus is equal to (1/2)($100 per unit – $20 per unit)(80 units), or $3,200.

To find the producer surplus, first recognize that it is the area that is under the world price for chocolate but above the domestic supply curve. Then, calculate the value of this area: producer surplus is equal to (1/2)($20 per unit – $0 per unit)(20 units), or $200.

The following figure illustrates the impact on consumer and producer surplus when the world price is equal to $20 per unit.

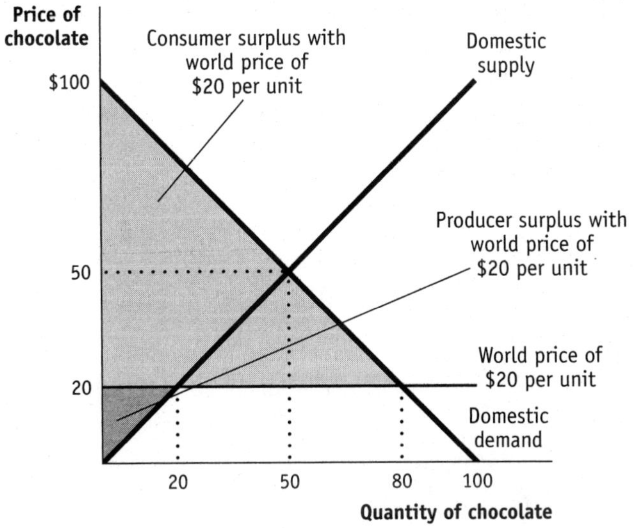

Trade is beneficial to Newville when the world price is $20 per unit since the value of total surplus, the sum of consumer and producer surplus in this case, is greater than the value of total surplus when Newville has a closed chocolate market.

STEP 6: Review your analysis in Step 3 to determine whether domestic demanders or domestic suppliers of chocolate will be more likely to favor opening the chocolate market to trade when the world price is $80 per unit.

Domestic producers will favor opening the chocolate market to trade when the world price is equal to $80 per unit, since they will be able to sell more units at a higher price. We can easily see the benefits to these producers by comparing the area of producer surplus when the economy is closed to trade (see Step 1) with the area of consumer surplus when the economy is open to trade and the world price is $80 (see Step 3). In contrast, domestic consumers of chocolate will be opposed to opening this market to trade, since their consumer surplus will shrink once the market is open to trade.

2. The small economy of Newville produces chocolate, and this market for chocolate is characterized by the following equations:

$$\text{Domestic demand for chocolate: } P = 100 - Q$$
$$\text{Domestic supply of chocolate: } P = Q$$

Furthermore, you know that the world price for chocolate is $20 per unit. Newville has decided to open its market for chocolate, and although recognizing that this will allow domestic consumers to consume more chocolate at lower prices, it has also determined that it will levy a tariff that raises the price of chocolate in Newville to $40 per unit. You are asked to compare the areas of consumer surplus with and without the tariff, the areas of producer surplus with and without the tariff, the amount of tax revenue the government of Newville will earn from this tariff, and the deadweight loss or efficiency cost of this tariff. The government of Newville has asked that you provide them with graphs that depict what happens if the market is opened to trade and what happens if this tariff is imposed.

STEP 1: Start by drawing a graph of the market for chocolate in Newville when its economy is closed to trade. Then, use the two equations to solve for the equilibrium price and quantity in this market. Once you have plotted the equilibrium price and quantity in your graph, you will then be able to use this graph to calculate the levels of consumer and producer surplus if there is no trade.

From Step 5 of problem 1, we can review the graph that represents this market if it opens to trade and the world price of chocolate is $20 per unit. In addition, we know from problem 1 that consumer surplus is equal to $3,200 and producer surplus is equal to $200.

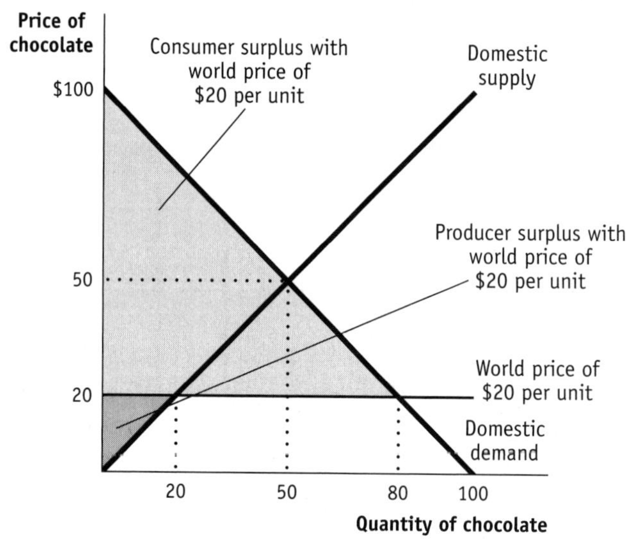

STEP 2: Draw a graph of the market for chocolate in Newville showing the effect of a tariff that raises the price of chocolate to $40 per unit. In this graph, indicate the areas that represent consumer surplus, producer surplus, tariff revenue for the government, and deadweight loss from the tariff. Calculate the values of these different areas.

The tariff raises the price of chocolate to $40 per unit. This increase in price will reduce the quantity of chocolate demanded by domestic consumers while increasing the quantity of chocolate supplied by domestic producers. When the price of chocolate is $40, domestic consumers demand 60 units while domestic producers are willing to provide 40 units. Newville will import that difference, or 20 units of chocolate. The government of Newville will collect $20 from every unit of chocolate that is imported and will therefore earn $400 in tariff revenue.

The deadweight loss for the tariff will equal $400. To find the area of deadweight loss, you first need to recognize that it is the sum of the areas of two triangles. Then, calculate the area of each triangle. From the following graph, we can see that the area of deadweight loss is equal to (1/2)($40/unit – $20/unit)(20 units) + (1/2)($40/unit – $20/unit)(20 units), or $400.

The graph that follows depicts the impact of this tariff on the market for chocolate in Newville.

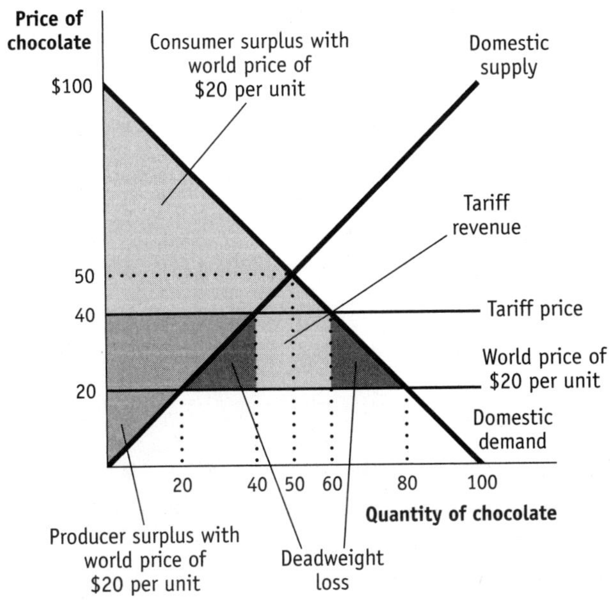

3. Suppose that Newville is still considering opening the market for chocolate that was described in problem 1, but is also now considering imposing a quota in the market once it is opened to trade. Suppose the government of Newville wishes to achieve the same outcome that it did with the tariff in problem 2, but now use a quota instead. What limit on imported chocolate would achieve the same outcome as the tariff described in problem 2, and what should the government of Newville charge the importer for the license to bring these imported chocolates into the Newville economy?

STEP 1: Review the graph in Step 2 of problem 2 to determine how many units of the chocolate are imported into Newville when there is a tariff that raises the price of chocolate to $40. This amount of imports is the amount that the quota must be set at in order to achieve the same outcome as under the proposed tariff.

From the graph we can see that Newville imports 20 units of chocolate when the price of chocolate is raised to $40 per unit. Thus, if the government of Newville limits its imports to 20 units, this will cause the price of chocolate to rise to $40 per unit, since it is only at this price that the difference between the quantity demanded domestically (60 units) and the quantity supplied domestically (40 units) is exactly equal to the amount of allowed imports (20 units).

STEP 2: Determine the price of the license for importing the chocolates by looking at the tariff revenue.

The tariff revenue represents the revenue the government receives when it places a tax on the imported good. With the quota, the government places a limit on how many units of the good can be imported, and it limits these imports by selling the right to bring the imports into the market. By selling the rights for the same price as the tariff revenue, the government imposes a quota limit that has exactly the same impact as the proposed tariff. The government of Newville should sell the rights to import chocolate for $20 per unit, or a total of $400 for all the rights.

Problems and Exercises

1. Use the following graph to answer this next set of questions. The graph depicts the domestic demand and domestic supply of bicycles in a small closed economy.

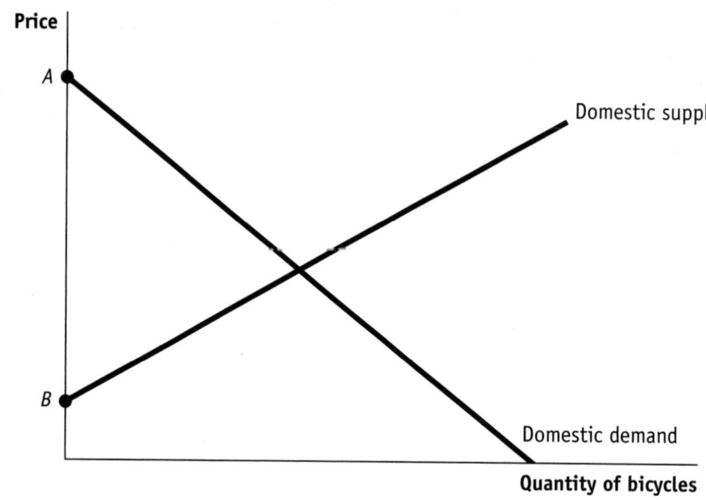

   a. In the preceding graph, label the equilibrium price (P_E) and the equilibrium quantity (Q_E) for this autarky. Label the areas that correspond to producer surplus and consumer surplus.

   b. Provide a mathematical expression for the areas of producer and consumer surplus based on the symbols and labels in the graph.

c. The same graph is replicated here, but this time the world price is also drawn on the graph. Suppose this autarky opens to trade. On the graph, indicate the quantity supplied domestically ($Q_{S_{dom}}$) and the quantity demanded domestically ($Q_{D_{dom}}$) when this country opens to trade. Identify how many bicycles this country will import or export when it opens its economy to trade.

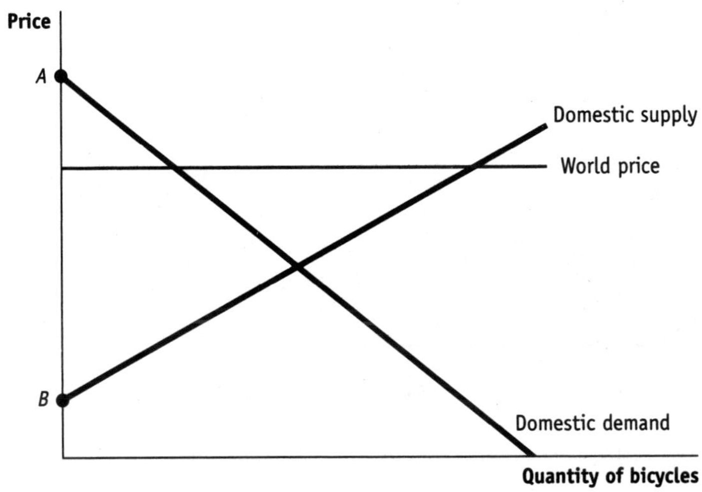

d. On the graph in part (c), label the areas that correspond to producer surplus with trade and consumer surplus with trade. Who benefits in this example from trade? Explain your answer.

e. The initial graph is replicated here, but this time the world price is also drawn on the graph. Suppose this autarky opens to trade. On the graph, indicate the quantity supplied domestically ($Q_{S_{dom}}$) and the quantity demanded domestically ($Q_{D_{dom}}$) when this country opens to trade. Identify how many bicycles this country will import or export when it opens its economy to trade.

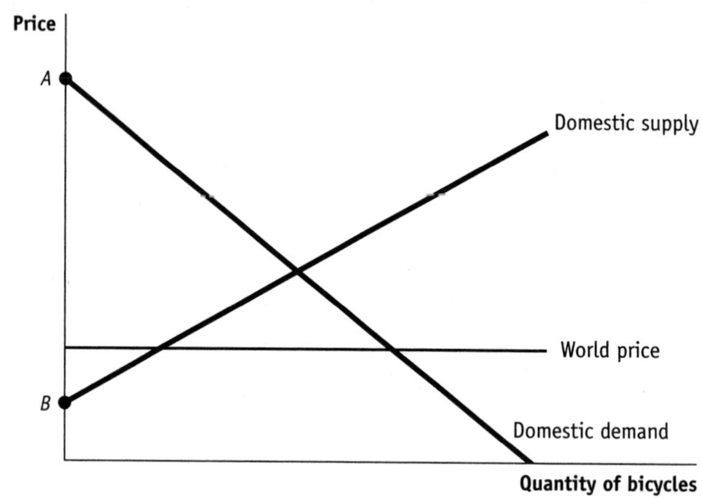

f. On the graph in part (e), label the areas that correspond to producer surplus with trade and consumer surplus with trade. Who benefits in this example from trade? Explain your answer.

2. Suppose the market for TVs in the small closed economy of Kennet can be described by the following domestic demand curve and domestic supply curve:

Domestic demand: $Q = 1{,}000 - (1/2)P$

Domestic supply: $Q = (1/2)P$

(Hint: for this question you will find it helpful to sketch graphs of the market.)

a. What is the equilibrium price and quantity in the market for TVs in Kennet? What is the value of consumer surplus, producer surplus, and total surplus?

b. Suppose Kennet opens to trade and the world price for TVs is $1,200. What is the quantity supplied domestically, the quantity demanded domestically, and the number of TVs imported into or exported out of Kennet given this world price? What happens to the value of consumer surplus, producer surplus, and total surplus when Kennet opens to trade?

c. Given the information and the analysis you did in part (b), who benefits from trade in the television market when Kennet opens its economy? Explain your answer.

d. Suppose Kennet's economy is still open to trade, but domestic demand in Kennet has significantly increased so that at every price domestic demand is now 500 units higher than it was initially. Although domestic demand in Kennet has increased, this has not impacted the world price for TVs since Kennet is a small economy. Given this change in demand, how many TVs will be domestically supplied and domestically demanded? Will Kennet import or export TVs? Calculate the numeric value of Kennet's imports or exports. What is the value of consumer surplus, producer surplus, and total surplus given this change in demand? (Hint: you will find it helpful to draw a sketch of these changes in the market for TVs and to calculate the new domestic demand equation.)

3. Pepperville is a small economy that currently operates as an autarky. In the market for green peppers, domestic demand and domestic supply can be represented as $P = 5{,}000 - 0.5Q$ and $P = 1.5Q$, respectively, where P is the price per ton of green peppers and Q is the quantity of green peppers measured in tons.

a. Identify the equilibrium price and quantity of green peppers in Pepperville. What is the value of consumer surplus and producer surplus?

b. The current world price of green peppers is \$3,000 per ton, and domestic producers of green peppers are lobbying the government of Pepperville to remain an autarky. Explain why domestic producers of green peppers are not in favor of open trade in the green pepper market.

c. Domestic consumers of green peppers in Pepperville successfully lobby the Pepperville government to open trade in the green pepper market. How many tons of green peppers will be imported into or exported out of Pepperville, given the world price of \$3,000 per ton when this market opens to trade? What is the value of consumer surplus and producer surplus with trade?

Domestic producers wage a successful campaign to enact a tariff in the market for green peppers. The tariff effectively raises the price of green peppers to \$3,450 per ton. Answer questions (d) through (g) based on this tariff. Assume the world price for green peppers is unchanged and equal to \$3,000 per ton.

d. How many tons of green peppers will be imported into Pepperville once this tariff is enacted?

e. What is the value of consumer surplus and producer surplus once this tariff is implemented?

f. What is the tariff revenue the government earns with this tariff?

g. What is the deadweight loss associated with this tariff?

h. Pepperville is considering replacing the tariff on green peppers with a quota. If consumer surplus and producer surplus are to remain the same under the quota as they are with the tariff, what must the amount of the quota equal?

i. From the domestic consumers' perspective, which trade policy—closed economy, open economy, or open economy with a tariff or quota—would they prefer? Explain your answer.

j. From the domestic producers' perspective, which trade policy—closed economy, open economy, or open economy with a tariff or quota—would they prefer? Explain your answer.

k. Given your answers in (i) and (j), why do governments frequently adopt tariffs or quotas in particular markets?

4. Evansville is a small closed economy. The domestic demand curve for shoes is given by the equation $P = 200 - Q$, where P is the price for a pair of shoes and Q is the quantity of pairs of shoes demanded. The domestic supply curve for shoes is given by the equation $P = 10 + Q$. Currently the world price of shoes is $40 a pair. Evansville is considering opening its economy to trade, and the government is debating three possible trade positions. Option I is to open the economy to trade with no trade protection intervention in the market. Option II is to open the economy to trade but limit the amount of pairs of shoes imported to a quota of 50 pairs of shoes. Option III is to open the economy to trade but impose a tariff on the shoe market that would increase the price of shoes to $80 a pair.

   a. Analyze these three policies and enter your findings in the following table.

	Option I	Option II	Option III
Pairs of shoes imported			
Consumer surplus			
Producer surplus			
Tariff revenue or quota rent			
Deadweight loss			

   b. From the perspective of domestic consumers, which is the best option?

   c. From the perspective of domestic producers, which is the best option?

   d. Which option results in the greatest efficiency cost? Explain your answer.

5. For each of the statements that follow, decide whether the statement reflects a desire for trade protection on the basis of national security, job creation, or the infant industry argument.

   a. Even though clothing can be produced more cheaply in other countries, clothing is a necessity, and if imports of clothing are disrupted by civil unrest in these foreign countries, our country will be ill prepared to provide for our citizens. The domestic clothing industry should therefore receive some form of trade protection.

   b. Since our economy is oil dependent and much of our oil comes from foreign economies, our economic well-being may be jeopardized by war or international disturbance. The domestic oil industry should therefore receive some form of trade protection from foreign oil producers.

c. As call centers are opened in foreign countries, our country is losing many entry-level positions. The industries moving these call centers overseas should be discouraged from doing this via trade measures.

d. The new product developed by corporation Z is a product that needs to be protected until corporation Z has had time to fully develop and market the idea.

e. The country of Fantasia, until recently a provider of raw materials to the rest of the world, has begun to develop a manufacturing sector in its economy. People in Fantasia argue that these industries need to have trade protection during this early period of development.

BEFORE YOU TAKE THE TEST

Module Review Questions

Use the following graph to answer the next four questions. The graph shows the market for bicycles for the country of Pedalland. The demand curve indicates the domestic demand for bicycles and the supply curve indicates the domestic supply of bicycles.

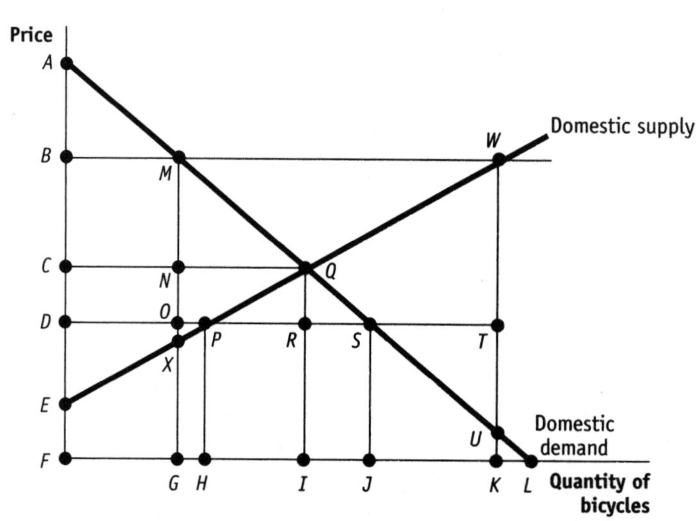

1. Suppose Pedalland is initially an autarky. In the graph, the area that corresponds to consumer surplus is equal to area __________, and the area that corresponds to producer surplus is equal to area __________.

a. *ACQ; CQIF*
b. *ADS; DPE*
c. *ACQ; CQE*
d. *BMNC; CNOD*

2. Suppose this country opens to trade and that the world price is equal to *B* in the preceding graph. Then we know that Pedalland will

a. import the number of bicycles represented by the distance between points *M* and *W*.
b. import the number of bicycles represented by the distance between points *W* and *T*.
c. export the number of bicycles represented by the distance between points *M* and *W*.
d. export the number of bicycles represented by the distance between points *W* and *T*.

3. Suppose this country opens to trade and that the world price is equal to *D* in the preceding graph. Then we know that Pedalland will import the number of bicycles represented by the distance between points

a. *R* and *S*.
b. *P* and *S*.
c. *P* and *R*.
d. *P* and *T*.

4. Suppose this country opens to trade and that the world price is equal to *B* in the preceding graph. Consumer surplus is equal to area __________, and producer surplus is equal to area __________.

a. *ABM; BWE*
b. *ABM; BMNE*
c. *ACNM; CNXE*
d. *ABM; BMQE*

Use the following graph to answer the next four questions. The graph shows the market for bicycles for the country of Pedalland. The demand curve indicates the domestic demand for bicycles and the supply curve indicates the domestic supply of bicycles.

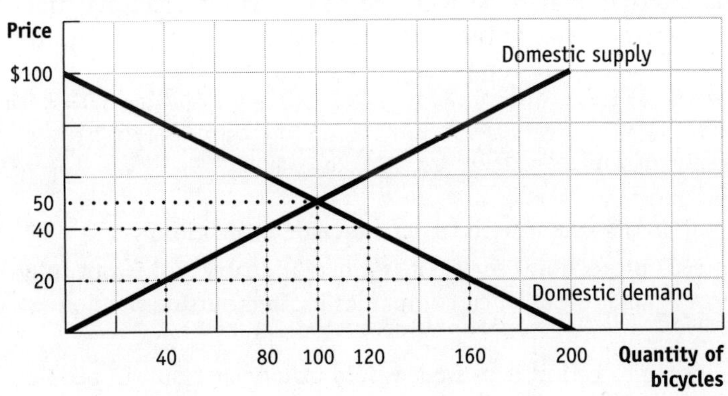

5. The world price in this market equals $20. If the market opens to trade,

a. Pedalland will import 120 bicycles, and the area of total surplus will increase by $6,800.
b. Pedalland will export 120 bicycles, and the area of total surplus will increase by $6,800.
c. Pedalland will import 120 bicycles, and the area of total surplus will increase by $1,800.
d. Pedalland will export 120 bicycles, and the area of total surplus will increase by $1,800.

6. Suppose the world price for bicycles is \$20 and Pedalland opens its bicycle market to trade. Domestic producers successfully lobby the government of Pedalland, and the government imposes a quota on the number of bicycles that can be imported into Pedalland. Suppose license-holder revenue from the quota is equal to \$800. Which of the following are possible quota limits that result in this license-holder revenue?

a. 20 bicycles
b. 40 bicycles
c. 60 bicycles
d. 80 bicycles
e. Answers (b) and (d) are both possible answers.

7. Suppose the world price of bicycles is \$20 and Pedalland opens to trade. Domestic producers of bicycles in Pedalland successfully lobby for a tariff on imported bicycles, which results in the price of bicycles being \$40. The deadweight loss associated with this tariff is equal to

a. \$400.
b. \$800.
c. \$1,600.
d. \$2,000.

8. The world price of bicycles is \$20 and Pedalland opens its economy to trade. A quota of 60 bicycles is imposed in Pedalland. This will result in consumer surplus increasing by __________ relative to the level of consumer surplus when Pedalland was an autarky.

a. \$1,725
b. \$2,500
c. \$4,225
d. \$6,725

9. A country that engages in international trade will find that this international trade increases the demand for the factors used by the exporting industries and decreases the demand for the factors used in the import-competing industries.

a. True
b. False

10. Which of the following is *not* an argument used to defend trade protection?

a. This domestic industry needs protection because it is a new industry and is not fully ready and able to compete against established companies located outside the domestic economy.
b. This domestic industry needs protection because it would otherwise result in people elsewhere in the world being paid a wage rate that is substantially lower than the wage rate in this industry in this economy.
c. This domestic industry needs protection because the good that is being produced is of vital national security for this economy.
d. This domestic industry needs protection because it provides a substantial number of jobs for people who live in this country.

11. Which of the following is *not* an example of a trade agreement?

a. NAFTA
b. EU
c. WTO

ANSWER KEY

Answers to Problems and Exercises

1. **a.**

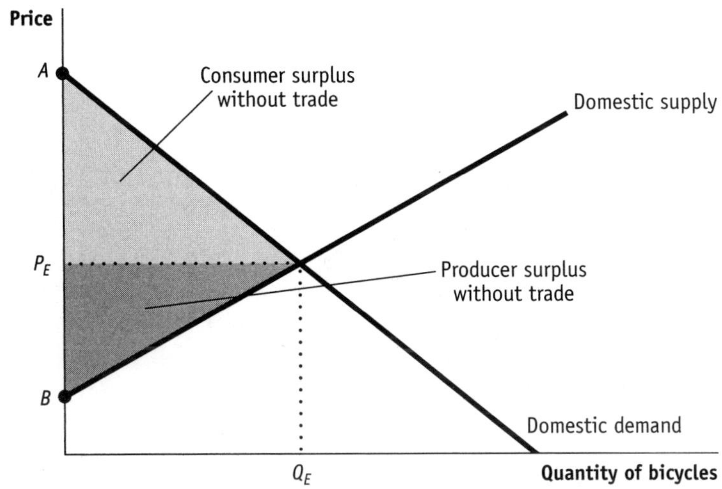

b. Consumer surplus = $(1/2)(A - P_E)(Q_E)$
Producer surplus = $(1/2)(P_E - B)(Q_E)$

c.

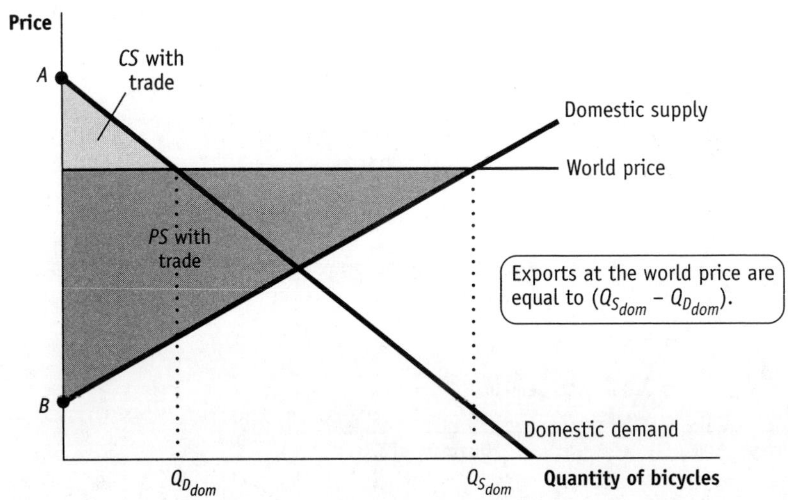

d. Domestic producers benefit from this trade because they can produce more units of the good and sell each unit at a higher price relative to the initial autarky equilibrium. Compare the graphs from part (a) and part (c) and note that the area of producer surplus is larger with trade than without trade.

e.

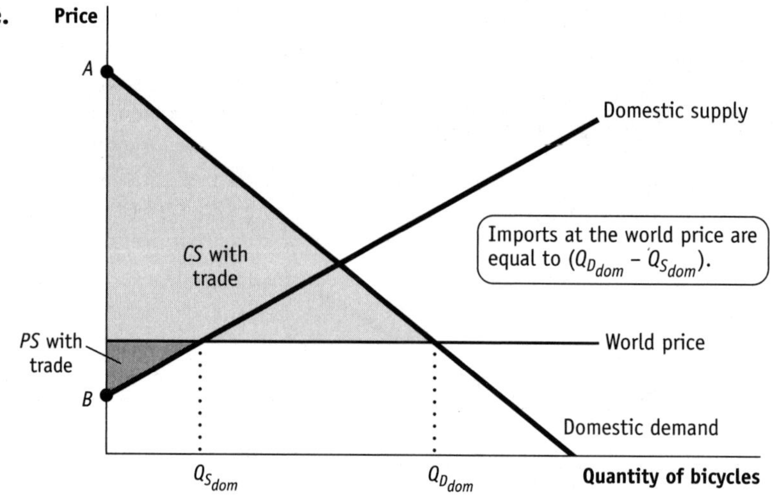

f. Domestic consumers benefit from this trade because they can consume more units of the good and purchase the good at a lower price relative to the initial autarky equilibrium. Compare the graphs from part (a) and part (e) and note that the area of consumer surplus is larger with trade than without trade.

2. **a.** Here is a sketch of Kennet's market for TVs.

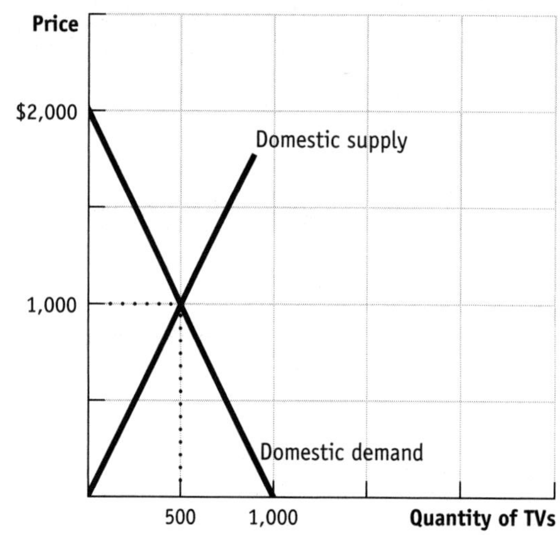

The equilibrium price is $1,000 and the equilibrium quantity is 500 TVs. Consumer surplus is equal to $250,000; producer surplus is equal to $250,000; and total surplus is equal to $500,000.

b. When Kennet opens to trade, it will buy and sell TVs at the world price since it is a small economy. Since $1,200 is greater than the domestic equilibrium price when Kennet is a closed economy, the quantity domestically demanded will fall and the quantity domestically supplied will increase. The quantity demanded domestically will equal 400 TVs, and the quantity supplied domestically will equal 600 TVs. Kennet will export the excess supply of 200 TVs. Consumer surplus with trade will decrease to $160,000 while producer surplus with trade will increase to $360,000; total surplus with trade will increase to $520,000. The following sketch illustrates this answer.

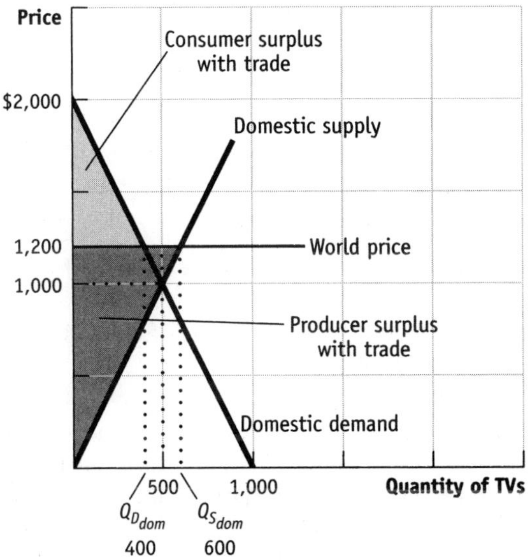

c. Domestic producers of TVs benefit from trade when Kennet opens its economy, because trade increases their producer surplus and decreases consumer surplus. The gain to producers is greater than the loss to consumers, so the net gain from trade is positive.

d. The following sketch provides a helpful guide to solving this problem.

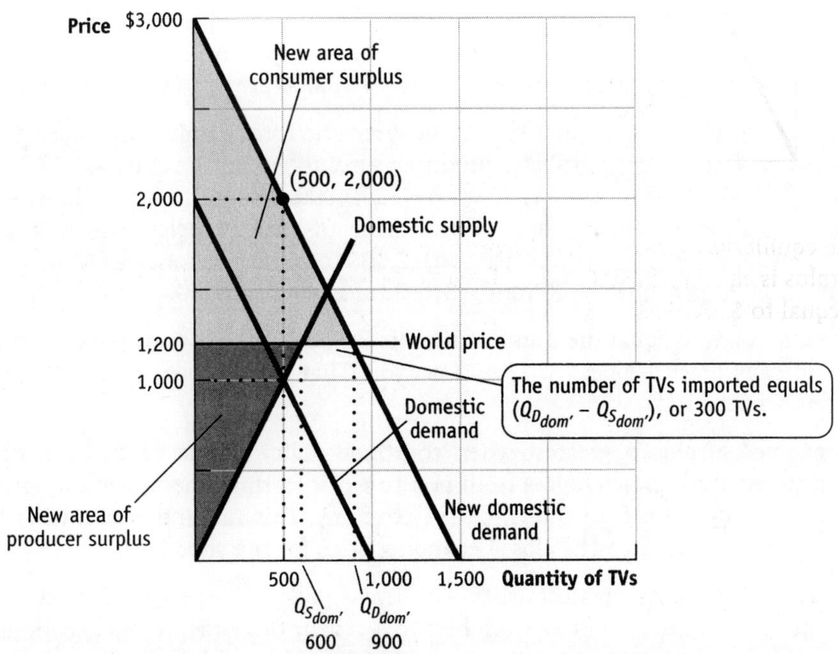

The equation for the new domestic demand curve is $Q = 1{,}500 - (1/2)P$. The domestic supply curve is still $Q = (1/2)P$. Use these two equations to analyze the effect on this market of the increase in domestic demand for TVs. At a world price of $1,200, the domestic demand for TVs is 900 while the domestic supply of TVs is 600. Kennet will import 300 TVs to meet this excess demand. Consumer surplus will now equal $810,000; producer surplus will equal $360,000; and total surplus will equal $1,170,000.

3. **a.** The equilibrium price of green peppers is $3,750 per ton, and the equilibrium quantity of green peppers in Pepperville is 2,500 tons. Consumer surplus is equal to $1,562,500 and producer surplus is equal to $4,687,500.

   b. Domestic producers are currently selling 2,500 tons of green peppers at a price of $3,750 per ton. If the market opens to trade, each ton of peppers will sell for a lower price: domestic producers will sell fewer tons of peppers as the price falls (2,000 tons instead of 2,500 tons), and they will receive a lower price per ton than they do when the green pepper market is closed ($3,000 versus $3,750).

   c. When the green pepper market is open to trade, the domestic demand for green peppers at $3,000 per ton is equal to 4,000 tons of green peppers. At a price of $3,000 per ton, the domestic quantity supplied is equal to 2,000 tons of green peppers. There is an excess demand for peppers when Pepperville opens to trade, and this excess demand will result in Pepperville importing green peppers to make up the difference between the amount domestically supplied and the amount domestically demanded. Pepperville will import 2,000 tons of green peppers. The value of consumer surplus with trade is equal to $4,000,000 and the value of producer surplus with trade is equal to $3,000,000.

   d. At a price of $3,450, the quantity of green peppers demanded domestically is equal to 3,100 tons while the quantity supplied domestically is equal to 2,300 tons. Pepperville will import 800 tons of green peppers.

   e. The value of consumer surplus is equal to (1/2)($5,000 per ton – $3,450 per ton)(3,100 tons), or $2,402,500. The value of producer surplus is equal to (1/2)($3,450 per ton)(2,300 tons), or $3,967,500.

   f. The government earns the difference between the tariff price per ton of green peppers and the world price of green peppers on every ton of green peppers imported into Pepperville. The tariff revenue is equal to ($3,450 per ton – $3,000 per ton)(800 tons), or $360,000.

   g. The deadweight loss is the difference between the total surplus with open trade and the sum of consumer surplus + producer surplus + tariff revenue, or $7,000,000 – ($2,402,500 + $3,967,500 + $360,000) = $270,000. Alternatively, the deadweight loss can be calculated as the sum of the areas of two triangles, which is equal to (1/2)($3,450 per ton – $3,000 per ton)(2,300 tons – 2,000 tons) + (1/2)($3,450 per ton – $3,000 per ton)(4,000 tons – 3,100 tons), or $270,000.

   h. The quota has to equal the number of units Pepperville imports when the tariff raises the price of green peppers to $3,450 per ton. That is, the quota must be 800 tons of green peppers.

   i. Consumer surplus is greatest when the trade policy is one of an open economy. Consumers rank these choices from best to worst in this order: open economy, open economy with a tariff or quota, closed economy. This ranking occurs whenever the world price is less than the closed economy price for the good.

   j. Producer surplus is greatest when the trade policy is one of a closed economy. Producers rank these choices from best to worst in this order: closed economy, open economy with a tariff or quota, open economy. This ranking occurs whenever the world price is less than the closed economy price for the good.

k. Governments can successfully provide a benefit to both consumers and producers by choosing this option. If you review the consumer and producer surplus under each of these options, you will see that the middle option gives consumers a greater consumer surplus than they would get with a closed economy and it provides producers with a greater producer surplus than they would get with an open economy. It is a compromise position for the government to take between these two constituencies.

4. **a.**

	Option I	Option II	Option III
Pairs of shoes imported	130 pairs	50 pairs	50 pairs
Consumer surplus	$12,800	$7,200	$7,200
Producer surplus	450	2,450	2,450
Tariff revenue or quota rent	0	2,000	2,000
Deadweight loss	0	1,600	1,600

b. From the perspective of domestic consumers, the best option is the option that results in the greatest value for consumer surplus: option I, the open economy option.

c. From the perspective of domestic producers, the best option is the option that results in the greatest value for producer surplus: option II and option III result in equivalent values for producer surplus, with the license holder earning a quota rent for option II and the government earning tariff revenue for option III. If the license holder is a domestic producer, then option II would be the best option from the perspective of domestic producers.

d. Options II and III result in the largest, and equivalent, efficiency cost as measured by the deadweight loss that occurs with the imposition of these two trade protectionist policies.

5. **a.** This argument is based on national security and the belief that, should foreign supplies of clothing be disrupted, our country's national security will be compromised.

b. This argument is based on national security and the belief that our economy will be compromised if there is a disruption in the supply of foreign-produced oil.

c. This argument is based on the job creation argument: as jobs relocate overseas, this implies a decrease in jobs in the home economy. This argument does not consider that other jobs may be created in the home economy as jobs are sent overseas.

d. This argument is based on the infant industry argument, which holds that new industries must be protected from foreign competition to give them time to get established.

e. This argument is based on the infant industry argument, which holds that new industries must be protected from foreign competition to give them time to get established.

Answers to Module Review Questions

1. **Answer c.** The area of consumer surplus is the area beneath the demand curve but above the equilibrium price, or in this example, area *ACQ*. The area of producer surplus is the area above the supply curve but below the equilibrium price, or in this example, area *CQE*.

2. **Answer c.** When the world price of the good is greater than the autarky price and the country opens to trade, Pedalland will export the good to other countries in order to sell the good at the higher world price. In this case, domestic suppliers are willing to supply the amount represented as the distance between points *B* and *W* while domestic consumers are only willing to consume the number of bicycles represented by the distance between *B* and *M*. Thus, domestic producers will export the number of bicycles represented by the distance between points *M* and *W*.

3. **Answer b.** When the world price is below the domestic equilibrium price and the country opens to trade, the country will import goods. The country will import the number of goods that represents the difference between the amount domestically supplied at the world price and the amount domestically demanded at the world price. In this case, the country will import the number of goods represented by the distance between points *P* and *S*.

4. **Answer a.** The area of consumer surplus is the area beneath the demand curve and above the equilibrium price, while the area of producer surplus is the area above the supply curve and below the equilibrium price. When this country opens to trade and the world price is equal to *B*, the country will export the good, which benefits domestic producers who are able to sell more units of the good than they could when the country was closed to trade.

5. **Answer c.** When the world price of the good is less than the autarky price, the country will import the good if it opens its economy to trade. In this case, the country will import the difference between the quantity demanded domestically at a price of \$20 and the quantity supplied domestically at a price of \$20, or 120 bicycles. The area of total surplus is initially equal to \$5,000, and when the country opens to trade, the area of total surplus has a value of \$6,800, so the increase in total surplus is \$6,800 – \$5,000 or \$1,800.

6. **Answer e.** To calculate the license-holder revenue from the quota you first need to rewrite the supply curve taking into account the quota. So, for example, if the supply equation is initially P = (1/2)(Q), then with a quota of 40 units this supply equation will be P = (1/2)q – 20. Using this new supply equation and the demand equation, P = 100 – (1/2)Q, you can find the new price with a quota of 40 units. The price with this level of quota is \$40 per bicycle. The license-holder revenue is equal to the difference between the price with the quota and the world price times the number of bicycles imported with the quota: (\$40/bicycle – \$20/bicycle), (40 bicycles) or \$800. This argument, however, also works for a quota of 80 units: when the quota is 80 bicycles the supply curve can be written as P = (1/2)Q – 30 and the new price with this quota limit is \$30 per bicycle. The license-holder revenue is equal to the difference between the price with the quota and the world price times the number of bicycles imported with the quota: (30/bicycle – \$20/bicycle)(80 bicycles), or \$800.

7. **Answer b.** The deadweight loss associated with this tariff is the result of two forces: (a) mutually beneficial trades do not take place because of the imposition of the tariff, and (b) the bicycles sold are produced at a price that exceeds the world price for bicycles. The area of deadweight loss can be calculated as the sum of the area of two triangles: (1/2)(\$40 per bicycle – \$20 per bicycle)(80 bicycles – 40 bicycles) + (1/2)(\$40 per bicycle – \$20 per bicycle)(160 bicycles – 120 bicycles) = \$800.

8. **Answer a.** This is a tough problem! You first need to figure out the price with the quota, the quantity supplied domestically with the quota, and the quantity demanded domestically with the quota. From the graph you know that if the quota price was \$40, the quota would be equal to 40 units. From the graph you also know that, at the world price, 120 bicycles are imported into Pedalland. So, logically you know that the quota price must be lower than \$40 and higher than \$20. When the quota price is \$35, the quantity demanded domestically is equal to 130 bicycles and the quantity supplied domestically is equal to 70 bicycles, for a difference of 60 bicycles. This difference is the same as the quota amount given in the question. Now you need only compute the original consumer surplus (equals \$2,500) and the consumer surplus with the quota (\$4,225) and subtract the original consumer surplus from the new consumer surplus to get the change in the value of consumer surplus that occurs with the imposition of the quota.

9. **Answer a.** When countries engage in trade, they produce those goods and services for which they have a comparative advantage. This specialization according to Heckscher–Ohlin advantage results in these countries producing those goods and services for which they have an abundant amount of resources. Thus, the exporting industries in the country will bid up the price of these resources as they increase their production of the good. The country will tend to import goods and services that are intensive in the factors that

are scarce in its economy. This effectively decreases the demand for the relatively scarce factors and increases the demand for the relatively abundant factors. Trade will cause the factor price to increase for the relatively abundant factor and to decrease for the relatively scarce factor.

10. **Answer b.** The arguments used to defend trade protection fall into three broad categories: the infant industry argument given in answer (a), the job creation argument given in answer (d), and the national security argument given in answer (c). Answer (b) is not an argument used to defend trade protection, but it is an argument that accompanies the sweatshop labor fallacy described earlier in the module.

11. **Answer c.** The World Trade Organization (WTO) is an organization composed of many member nations who meet to discuss and decide on major international trade agreements, and it works to resolve trade disputes between its members. The North American Free Trade Agreement (NAFTA) is a trade agreement between Canada, the United States, and Mexico. The European Union (EU) is a trade agreement between many countries located in Europe.

module 18

Making Decisions

BEFORE YOU READ THE MODULE

Summary

This module discusses decision making and the importance of costs and benefits for making decisions. It explores three types of economic decisions—"either-or" decisions, "how much" decisions, and decisions involving sunk costs. The module discusses the importance of implicit and explicit costs in decision making. It also compares and contrasts accounting profits and economic profits and explains why economic profit is the correct basis for making decisions. It addresses the importance of opportunity cost for making a decision about which of two possible activities to engage in (the "either-or" decision). Marginal analysis is introduced as an approach to decision making that focuses on how much of an activity is the right level (the "how much" decision). The module also explores which costs should be incorporated into decision-making analysis and which costs—the sunk costs—should be ignored.

Module Objectives

Objective #1. Due to scarcity of resources, it is not possible to do everything. This scarcity of resources implies that the true cost of anything can best be measured in terms of its opportunity cost, or the value of consumption or production that is forgone when a choice is made to consume or produce something else.

Objective #2. There are two broad categories of costs: explicit costs and implicit costs.

- Explicit costs are costs that require a direct outlay of money.
- Implicit costs do not involve an outlay of money but are instead equal to the value in dollars of all the benefits that are forgone when making a particular decision.
- Economic decision making requires consideration of both explicit and implicit costs.

Objective #3. The economic cost of any activity you do should include the cost of using any of your own resources for that activity.

Objective #4. There are two general types of profits: accounting profits and economic profits.

- The accounting profit of a business is equal to its total revenue minus its explicit cost and depreciation. Depreciation measures the dollar value of the reduction in the value of capital equipment a business owns—it is the dollar value of the capital that wears out at a business. Depreciation is measured per year.
- Economic profit for a business equals the business's total revenue minus its total costs, where those total costs include both the explicit and implicit costs of operating the business as well as depreciation costs. In particular, economic profits include the implicit cost of capital and the implicit cost of the owner's time and energy. Both capital and the owner's time and energy could be used in other ways, and the opportunity cost of these resources needs to be incorporated into the measure of total costs when measuring economic profit. The implicit cost of capital is the opportunity cost of the capital used by a business, while the implicit cost of the owner's time and energy is the opportunity cost of that time and energy.

Objective #5. Marginal analysis compares the benefit of doing a little bit more of an activity with the cost of doing a little bit more of the activity. Marginal benefit measures the benefit of doing a little bit more of the activity while marginal cost measures the cost of doing a little bit more of the activity.

- Marginal cost is measured as the change in total cost from producing one additional unit of the good. Marginal costs may be decreasing, constant, or increasing as production increases. In Figure 18.1, quantity is measured on the horizontal axis and marginal cost (*MC*) is measured on the vertical axis in dollars per unit of output. Marginal cost decreases as output increases from 0 units to Q_1 units, marginal cost is constant as output increases from Q_1 to Q_2 units, and marginal cost increases as output increases beyond Q_2 units. In other words, at outputs less than Q_1, marginal cost is greater than MC_1 but decreases as output increases; at outputs between Q_1 and Q_2, marginal cost is constant and equal to MC_1; and at outputs greater than Q_2, marginal cost is greater than MC_1 and increases as output increases.

Figure 18.1

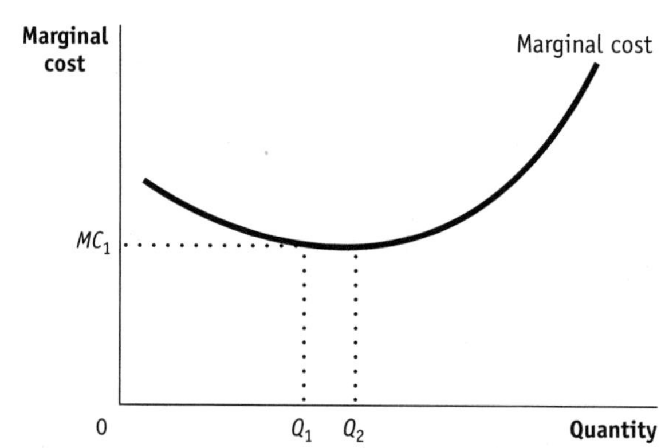

- Increasing marginal cost occurs when each additional unit costs more to produce than the previous unit.
- Decreasing marginal cost is often due to learning effects in production: for example, complicated tasks get easier to do as workers gain experience.
- Marginal benefit is the change in total benefits from consuming or producing one more unit of the good. Marginal benefit typically decreases as quantity increases: each additional unit of the good yields less benefit than the previous increase in output. Not all goods have decreasing marginal benefit: some goods exhibit constant marginal benefit, in which the benefit from producing each additional unit of the good is the same regardless of how many units have already been produced. Figure 18.2 illustrates a marginal benefit curve. Marginal benefit is measured in dollars per unit.

Figure 18.2

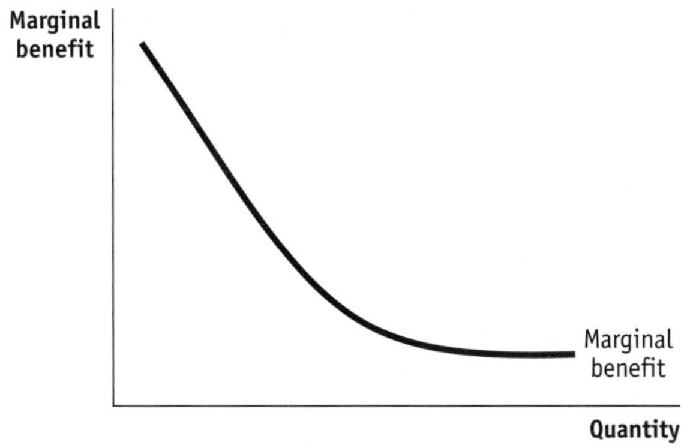

Objective #6. The principle of marginal analysis states that the optimal quantity of an activity is that quantity where the marginal benefit equals the marginal cost. When production of an activity occurs at the point where marginal benefit equals marginal cost, the total net gain from the activity is maximized. When marginal benefit is greater than marginal cost, too little of the good is being produced since the production of one more unit of the good adds more benefits than costs; when marginal benefit is less than marginal cost, too much of the good is being produced since the addition to costs from producing the last unit of the good is greater than the addition to benefits from producing the last unit. Figure 18.3 illustrates the optimal quantity of the good, Q*, where marginal costs equal marginal benefits. We can state that this general rule is known as the principle of marginal analysis: When making a decision about "how much" of a good or activity to consume, the optimal quantity is the largest quantity where marginal benefit is greater than or equal to marginal cost.

Figure 18.3

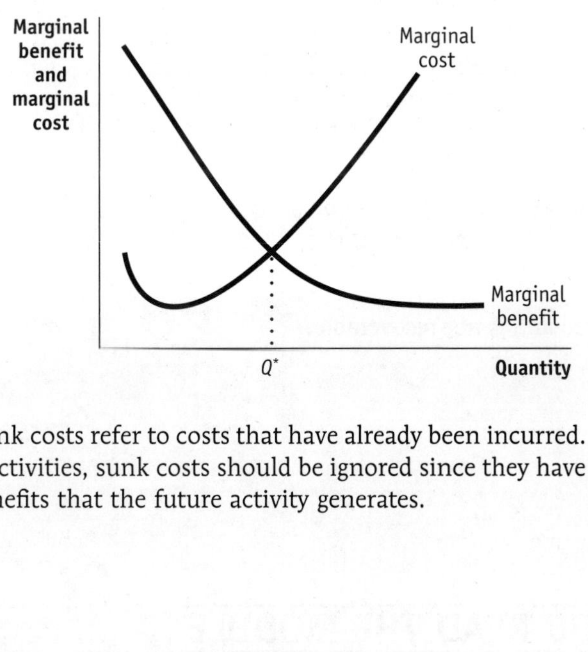

Objective #7. Sunk costs refer to costs that have already been incurred. When making decisions about future activities, sunk costs should be ignored since they have no influence on the actual costs and benefits that the future activity generates.

Key Terms

explicit cost a cost that involves actually laying out money.

implicit cost a cost that does not require the outlay of money; it is measured by the value, in dollar terms, of forgone benefits.

accounting profit a business's revenue minus the *explicit cost* and depreciation.

economic profit a business's revenue minus the *opportunity cost* of *resources;* usually less than the *accounting profit.*

Notes

Key Terms *(continued)*

principle of "either-or" decision making when faced with an "either-or" choice between two projects, choose the project with the positive economic profit.

marginal cost the additional cost incurred by producing one more unit of a good or service.

increasing marginal cost the case in which each additional unit costs more to produce than the previous one.

marginal cost curve a graphical representation showing how the cost of producing one more unit depends on the quantity that has already been produced.

constant marginal cost each additional unit costs the same to produce as the previous one.

decreasing marginal cost the condition in which each additional unit costs less to produce than the previous one.

marginal benefit the additional benefit derived from producing one more unit of a good or service.

decreasing marginal benefit the case in which each additional unit of an activity produces less benefit than the previous unit.

marginal benefit curve a graphical representation showing how the benefit from producing one more unit depends on the quantity that has already been produced.

optimal quantity the quantity that generates the maximum possible total net gain.

profit-maximizing principle of marginal analysis the proposition that the *optimal quantity* is the quantity at which *marginal benefit* is equal to *marginal cost.*

sunk cost a cost that has already been incurred and is not recoverable.

Notes

AFTER YOU READ THE MODULE

Tips

Tip #1. This module returns to the concept of opportunity cost. Economists measure costs using the concept of opportunity cost, or the value of the consumption or production forgone when a consumer or a producer chooses to consume or produce something else. You may find it helpful to review the earlier discussion of opportunity cost in this text.

Tip #2. When measuring costs, economists include both explicit and implicit costs. This means that opportunity costs are incorporated into the measures of costs that economists calculate, and it implies that decision making based on economic analysis must include implicit costs.

Tip #3. It is important that you understand the distinction between accounting and economic profits. Throughout this course, the focus will be on economic profits, since it is this measure that includes all the opportunity costs of producing a good or service. Accounting profit, although often referred to within the media and the business community, does not provide a full measure of the costs of producing a good or service. As you think about this issue, remember that the owner of the business incurs an opportunity cost associated with the use of their time and capital, and it is important to include this opportunity cost when evaluating the profitability of the enterprise.

Tip #4. The optimal level of production occurs when marginal cost equals marginal benefit. If marginal cost is greater than marginal benefit, too much of the good is being produced. If marginal cost is less than marginal benefit, too little of the good is being produced.

WORKED PROBLEMS

1. For each of the following situations determine if the decision is an "either-or" decision, a "how much" decision, or a sunk cost decision. Explain your answer for each situation.

Situation	Type of decision	Explanation
Joe can spend the next hour studying economics or chemistry		
Mary is trying to decide how often she should clean her bathroom		
Susie is trying to decide if she should expand her business		
Marcy spent $20 for theater tickets but now has a conflict on the night of the show		

STEP 1: **Review the three types of decisions.**

"Either-or" decisions are decisions about choosing between two different alternatives. "How much" decisions are decisions about how much of an activity to engage in. Both of these decisions are based on marginal analysis. Decisions involving sunk costs are decisions in which it is important *not* to consider some costs that have already been incurred and cannot be recovered.

STEP 2: In the preceding table, identify what type of decision each situation represents and provide a brief explanation for your choice.

The following table provides the answers to the missing two columns in the original table.

Situation	Type of decision	Explanation
Joe can spend the next hour studying economics or chemistry	Either-or	Joe can either spend his time on economics or on chemistry.
Mary is trying to decide how often she should clean her bathroom	How much	Mary will want to consider the marginal benefit from cleaning the bathroom and compare it with the marginal cost of cleaning the bathroom: if the marginal benefit is equal to or greater than the marginal cost, then she should clean the bath.
Susie is trying to decide if she should expand her business	How much	Susie will want to consider the marginal benefit from expanding her business and compare it with the marginal cost of expanding her business: if the marginal benefit is equal to or greater than the marginal cost, then she should expand her business.
Marcy spent $20 for theater tickets but now has a conflict on the night of the show	Sunk cost	Marcy has already spent the money on the theater tickets and she cannot recover this money. Whether she attends the theater should not depend on the money she has spent on the tickets; rather, she should compare her choices and select the one with the greater economic profit.

2. Joey owns his own business, Joe's Auto Body. He hires three people to work for him and their wages cost Joey a total of $80,000 a year. In addition, Joey owns the equipment he uses to repairs cars and he paid $100,000 for this equipment. If Joey were to close down the business, he could sell the equipment for $100,000 and invest this money in an interest-bearing account that would pay him 5% a year. Joey has revenues of $200,000 a year from his business. Joey recently was offered a job working for another shop with an annual salary of $50,000. What is the accounting profit at Joe's Auto Body and what is the economic profit? Compare your two results and explain why these two measures of profit are not equivalent. Finally, advise Joey as to whether he should continue to operate his shop or whether it would be best to close his shop and go to work for the other shop. Assume in your answer that the equipment does not depreciate.

STEP 1: Review the definition of accounting profits and economics profits.

Accounting profit is equal to the business's total revenue minus its explicit costs and its depreciation. Economic profit is equal to the business's total revenue minus its explicit costs, its depreciation, and its implicit costs. Implicit costs do not require an outlay of money but instead are measured as the value, in dollar terms, of any benefits that are foregone. For example, if the owner invests his funds in the business, he is giving up the interest return he could earn from investing his funds in some other financial instrument; or, if the owner invests his time and energy in the business, he is giving up the salary he could earn from working for someone else.

STEP 2: Calculate the value of Joey's accounting profits.

To find Joey's accounting profit requires that we identify Joey's revenue from the business ($200,000), as well as the explicit costs of the business and any depreciation. We are told that there is no depreciation. The explicit cost of the business in this example is just the cost of the labor Joey employs, or $80,000. Thus, Joey's accounting profit is equal to $200,000 – $80,000, or $120,000.

STEP 3: Calculate the value of Joey's economic profits.

To find Joey's economic profit requires that we identify Joey's revenue from the business ($200,000), as well as the explicit costs of the business ($80,000), the depreciation costs ($0), and the implicit costs of the business. In this example, the implicit costs include the interest that Joey could have earned on the $100,000 he has invested in his business, as well as the salary he could have earned by working for someone else. The interest Joey foregoes is equal to (.05)($100,000) or $5,000 per year, and the salary he could have earned is $50,000. Joey's implicit costs are therefore equal to $55,000. Joey's economic profit is $200,000 – ($80,000 + $55,000), or $65,000. Joey is making considerably less money than the accounting profits suggest when he considers his opportunity cost of running his own business.

STEP 4: Compare your two profit figures and explain why they are not equivalent.

Joey's accounting profit is $120,000 and his economic profit is $65,000. They are not equivalent because accounting profits do not include the implicit costs; accounting profits only include the explicit costs and the depreciation costs.

STEP 5: Advise Joey about which job he should take.

Joey should continue to operate his own business. Working for himself, his economic profit is $65,000 a year. If he were to work for someone else, he would earn $50,000 a year plus the $5,000 in interest on his $100,000. His total compensation therefore would be $55,000. He is better off running his own company.

3. Georgia graduates from high school in May and is debating whether to continue with her schooling. She has recognized that additional years of school will cost not only the tuition but the foregone salary she could earn if she does not attend school. But, she also recognizes that additional schooling will increase her lifetime earnings. She has provided some information to you in the table that follows and she asks that you calculate her marginal cost of each additional year of school and her marginal benefit from each additional year of school as measured by the addition to her lifetime earnings from the additional year of school. Georgia would also like you to determine the optimal number of years of schooling she should get, and, in addition, she'd like you to provide a graph of both her marginal costs and her marginal benefits from additional years of schooling.

Additional years of schooling	Total cost of schooling	Total benefit from schooling expressed as the increase in the value of lifetime earnings
0	$0	$0
1	40,000	200,000
2	100,000	280,000
3	180,000	330,000
4	300,000	360,000
5	500,000	380,000

STEP 1: Calculate the marginal cost of each additional year of schooling.

The marginal cost of each additional year of schooling is equal to the change in total cost from an additional year of schooling divided by one additional year of schooling. The following table provides the marginal cost of each additional year of schooling.

Additional years of schooling	Total cost of schooling	Marginal cost of an additional year of schooling
0	$0	
		$40,000
1	40,000	
		60,000
2	100,000	
		80,000
3	180,000	
		120,000
4	300,000	
		200,000
5	500,000	

STEP 2: Graph the marginal cost of each additional year of schooling.

The marginal cost figures from Step 1 are graphed here: note that the marginal cost amounts are graphed at the midpoint of each additional year of schooling. For example, the marginal cost of the first year of schooling is equal to $40,000, and we will graph that marginal cost at a quantity of schooling equal to half a year.

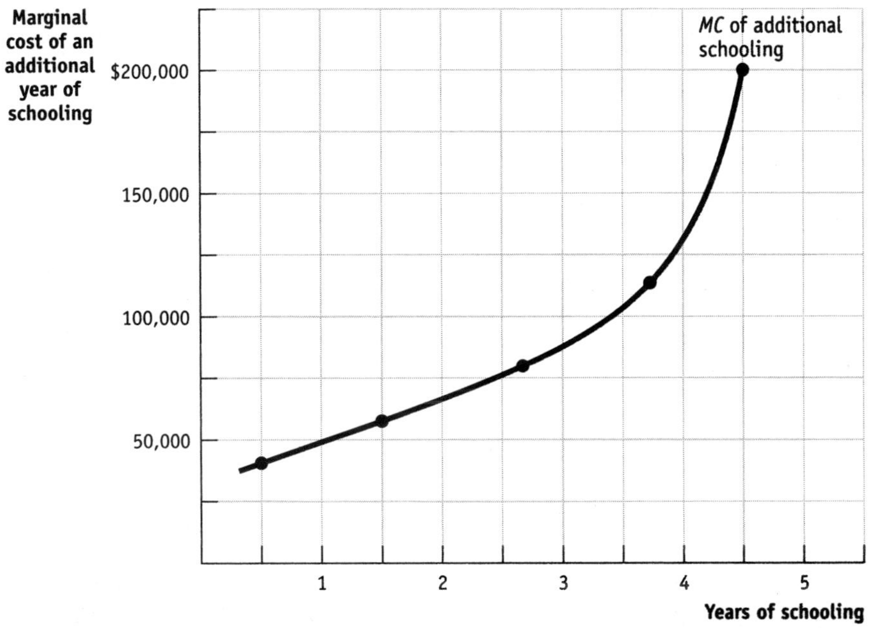

STEP 3: Calculate the marginal benefit of each additional year of schooling.

The marginal benefit of an additional year of schooling is equal to the change in total benefit from that additional year of schooling divided by the additional year of schooling. The following table provides the marginal benefit for each additional year of schooling.

Additional years of schooling	Total benefit from schooling expressed as the increase in the value of lifetime earnings	Marginal benefit of an additional year of schooling
0	$0	
		$200,000
1	200,000	
		80,000
2	280,000	
		50,000
3	330,000	
		30,000
4	360,000	
		20,000
5	380,000	

STEP 4: **Graph the marginal benefit of each additional year of schooling.**

The marginal benefit figures from Step 3 are graphed here: note that the marginal benefit amounts are graphed at the midpoint for each additional year of schooling. For example, the marginal benefit of the first year of schooling is equal to $200,000, and we will graph that marginal benefit at a quantity of schooling equal to half a year.

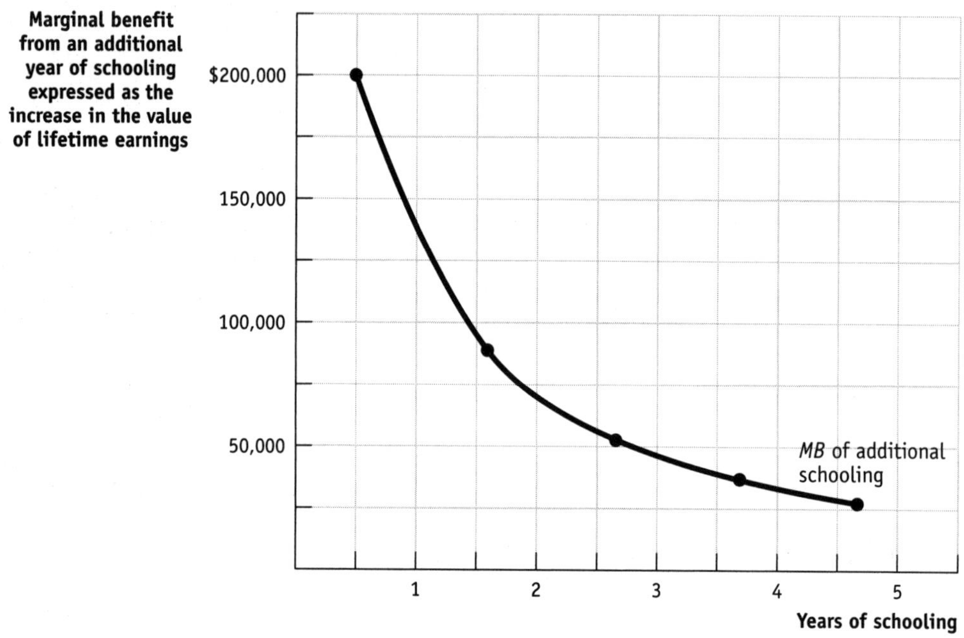

STEP 5: **Determine the optimal amount of additional schooling for Georgia.**

To determine the optimal numbers of years of additional schooling for Georgia, we should compare the marginal benefits to the additional year of schooling to the marginal cost of the additional year of schooling. The first year of additional schooling provides marginal benefits of $200,000 for Georgia while resulting in additional costs of $40,000: this additional year of schooling is definitely worth doing since the marginal benefit is greater than the marginal cost. This is also true for the second year of schooling: the marginal benefit of this year of school is $80,000, while its marginal cost is $60,000. The third year of schooling however has marginal benefits of just $50,000 and marginal costs of $80,000: Georgia will want to continue her schooling for two years and then leave school.

Problems and Exercises

1. Marty runs a bakery that employs 10 workers who each work 50 weeks a year and earn $400 a week. In addition, Marty has rent of $50,000 per year, and costs for supplies and raw materials totaling $125,000 a year. Marty occasionally is approached by another baker in town who is willing to pay Marty $75,000 a year to come work for her. Marty could sell his business for $100,000. The current interest rate on deposits at Marty's bank is 5%. Marty's revenue from the bakery is $440,000 a year. Assume that there is no depreciation of equipment at Marty's bakery.

   a. What are Marty's explicit costs?

   b. What are Marty's implicit costs?

   c. What are Marty's economic costs?

   d. What is the implicit cost of Marty's time and energy?

   e. What is the implicit cost of capital?

   f. What are Marty's accounting profits?

   g. What are Marty's economic profits?

   h. Should Marty continue to operate the bakery given the above cost and revenue figures? Explain your answer.

   i. Given the information, what is the minimum amount of revenue Marty's bakery must earn for Marty to stay in business?

2. Susie operates a business that prints designs on T-shirts. Susie's total revenue per year equals $500,000. The cost of labor per year is $125,000, the cost of raw materials and supplies is $200,000 per year, while the value of capital for the business is $200,000. Susie knows she could earn $50,000 per year working as a printer at a competitor's business. She also knows she could sell her business and the land it sits on for $600,000 and earn 10% a year on these funds. Each year her depreciation equals 5% of her capital expenditure.

a. What are Susie's explicit costs? Calculate a value for these explicit costs.

b. What are Susie's implicit costs? Calculate a value for these implicit costs.

c. What are Susie's accounting profits?

d. What are Susie's economic profits?

3. The following table provides information about Joe's Service Shop, which specializes in providing all sorts of services to customers in the metro area.

Quantity of services	Joe's total cost	Joe's marginal cost	Joe's total benefit	Joe's marginal benefit
0	$100		$ 0	
		(a)		(g)
1	110		200	
		(b)		(h)
2	118		230	
		$7		$15
3	(c)		(i)	
		10		(j)
4	(d)		255	
		(e)		8
5	150		(k)	
		20		5
6	(f)		(l)	

a. Fill in the missing cells labeled (a) through (l) in the table.

b. Define marginal cost and marginal benefit.

c. When Joe produces 2 units of services, what is the relationship between marginal cost and marginal benefit? Are 2 units of services an optimal quantity for Joe to produce? Explain your answer.

d. When Joe produces 5 units of services, what is the relationship between marginal cost and marginal benefit? Are 5 units of services an optimal quantity for Joe to produce? Explain your answer.

e. Given the preceding information, what is the optimal quantity of services for Joe to produce?

4. Use the following graph of a firm's marginal cost curve to answer this question.

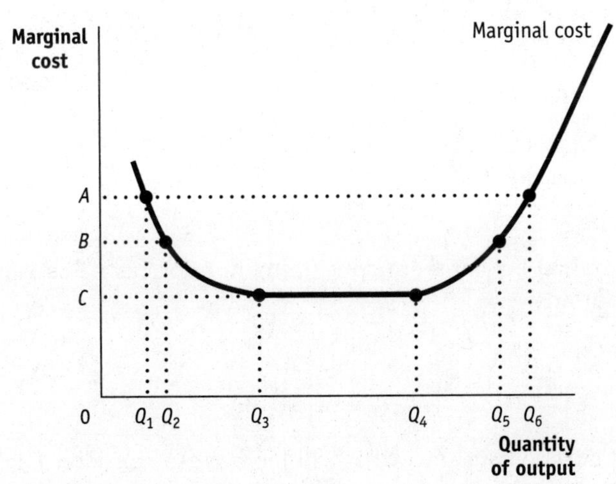

a. For what range of output is marginal cost decreasing as output increases?

b. For what range of output is marginal cost constant as output increases?

c. For what range of output is marginal cost increasing as output increases?

d. What distance measures the marginal cost of producing Q_2?

e. What distance measures the marginal cost of producing Q_6?

5. Use the following graph of the marginal benefit to Joe from consuming hot dogs to answer this question.

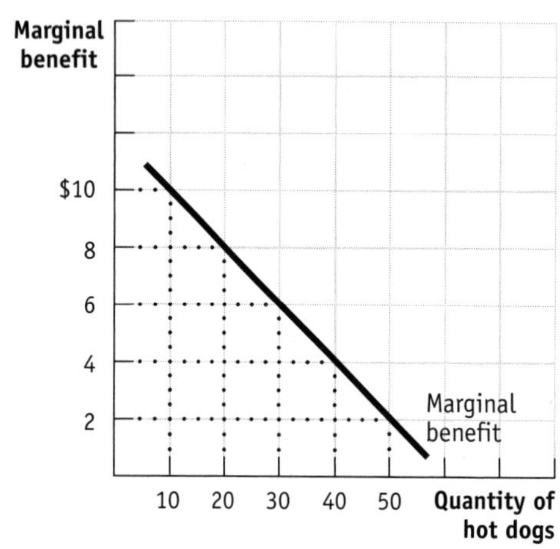

a. What happens to Joe's marginal benefit from consuming hot dogs as he consumes more hot dogs? Explain your answer.

b. In deciding how many hot dogs to consume, what will Joe want to consider? Explain your answer.

c. Suppose the marginal cost of consuming hot dogs is constant and equal to \$6. How many hot dogs will Joe want to consume given this information? Why does he choose this amount?

d. Suppose the marginal cost of consuming hot dogs is constant and equal to \$4. What will happen to Joe's consumption of hot dogs? Explain why Joe makes this choice of consumption.

6. Suppose Bob calculates that the marginal cost (MC) for his business can be expressed as $MC = Q$, where Q is the quantity of units he produces. Furthermore, suppose that the marginal benefit (MB) he gets from producing his product can be expressed as $MB = 100 - 3Q$.

a. Draw a graph illustrating Bob's marginal cost and marginal benefit. Put quantity on the horizontal axis and marginal benefit and marginal cost on the vertical axis.

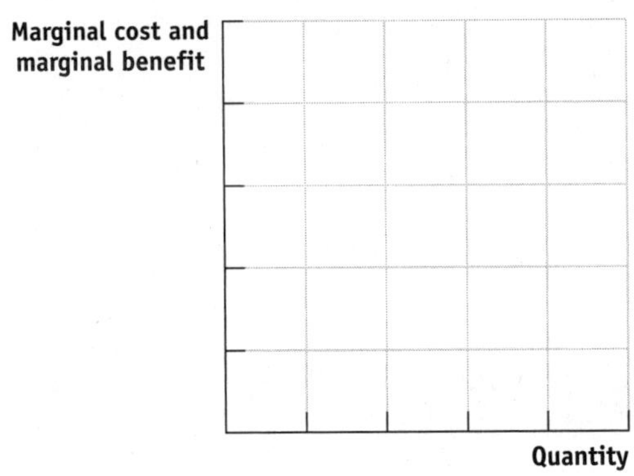

b. Calculate the optimal quantity for Bob to produce. Mark this optimal quantity on your graph.

c. If Bob produces 20 units of the good, what is the marginal cost and marginal benefit from the last unit he produces? Should Bob produce more or less of the good? Explain your answer.

7. In October, Marissa paid an annual subscription fee of \$600 to the local opera company for this season's five opera performances. This fee is nonrefundable and entitles Marissa to one ticket to each of the five performances. A friend of Marissa's invites Marissa to an all-expense paid weekend to Miami. Marissa discovers that the weekend her friend invites her to Miami is the same weekend as the first opera performance. Marissa estimates that the value of the trip to Miami is \$1,000.

a. Marissa is trying to figure out the cost of going to Miami. Since she will miss the opera, she calculates that the cost of her going to Miami is \$120 or the cost of one ticket to the opera. Do you agree with Marissa's reasoning? Explain your answer.

b. With respect to the opera, her friend says that the cost of going to Miami is $0 for Marissa, since whether she goes to the opera or not she will not get her $120 back. Do you agree with this reasoning? Explain your answer.

c. Marissa's roommate says that Marissa's cost of going to Miami is $1,120, since it should include the cost of the trip ($1,000) plus the cost of the missed opera performance ($120). Do you agree with this reasoning? Explain your answer.

BEFORE YOU TAKE THE TEST

Module Review Questions

1. Accounting profits are based on total revenue and
   a. the sum of explicit and implicit costs.
   b. the difference between explicit and implicit costs.
   c. implicit costs.
   d. explicit costs and depreciation.

Use the following information to answer the next four questions.

Jerry's Doughnut Shop employs 10 people. Each of these individuals works 1,000 hours a year, and their hourly wage is $8. In addition, Jerry's Doughnut Shop has supplies and raw materials costs of $150,000 a year and rental costs of $50,000 a year. Jerry knows that he could sell his business for $100,000, and he knows he could secure a job at Alice's Pastry Place where he would earn $60,000 a year. Currently the bank in Jerry's town is paying 5% interest per year on all funds deposited at the bank. Assume there is no depreciation of capital equipment each year.

2. Jerry's explicit costs per year include __________ and are equal to __________.
   a. Jerry's salary, the labor costs, the supplies and raw materials cost, and the rental costs; $340,000
   b. the labor costs, the supplies and raw materials cost, and the rental costs; $280,000
   c. the labor costs, the supplies and raw materials costs, the rental costs, as well as the interest Jerry forgoes; $285,000
   d. Jerry's salary he could earn at Alice's Pastry Place and the interest he forgoes when he operates his own business; $65,000

3. Jerry's explicit costs underestimate the economic costs of being in business by
   a. $0.
   b. $5,000.
   c. $60,000.
   d. $65,000.

4. Suppose Jerry sells doughnuts for $1 per doughnut. Jerry's accounting profit this year was $100,000. Jerry sold ________ doughnuts this year and his economic profit equaled ________.
   a. 380,000; $40,000
   b. 380,000; $35,000
   c. 38,000; $40,000
   d. 38,000; $35,000

5. Given the preceding information, including the $1 per doughnut price, Jerry tries to calculate the level of accounting profits where it is no longer beneficial for Jerry to operate Jerry's Doughnut Shop. You advise him to
   a. continue in the business as long as his accounting profit is positive.
   b. sell the business since he is focusing on accounting profits and not on economic profits.
   c. sell the business if his accounting profits fall below $65,000.
   d. sell the business if his accounting profits exceed $65,000.

6. Which of the following statements is true?
   a. When the marginal cost of producing one more unit of the good is greater than the marginal benefit of producing one more unit of the good, too much of the good is being produced.
   b. When the marginal benefit from producing one more unit of the good is greater than the marginal cost of producing one more unit of the good, too little of the good is being produced.
   c. Accounting profits include explicit costs, but do not include implicit costs.
   d. All of the statements are true.

7. Stella is considering producing one more unit of steel at her manufacturing plant. She calculates that her costs will increase by $5,500 if she produces this unit, while her benefits from producing this additional unit will increase by $5,600. Stella should
   a. produce the additional unit.
   b. not produce the additional unit.

8. When marginal cost is decreasing as output increases, this implies that the slope of the marginal cost curve is
   a. positive.
   b. negative.

9. Sarah's Autoshop reports that their marginal cost, no matter their level of production, is always equal to $10. This implies that the marginal cost curve for Sarah's Autoshop is

a. a vertical line.

b. a horizontal line.

c. initially downward sloping as output increases, but then eventually it is upward sloping.

d. initially upward sloping as output increases, but then eventually it is downward sloping.

10. As more and more units of a good are consumed, the marginal benefit of an additional unit typically

a. stays constant.

b. increases.

c. decreases.

d. Answers (a), (b), and (c) are all possible depending on the particular good.

Use the following table to answer the next four questions. The table provides information about Steve's Ice Cream Store's total costs and total benefits for different serving levels of ice cream.

Quantity of servings of ice cream	Total costs	Total benefits
0	$400	$0
100	450	800
200	500	900
300	550	950
400	600	975

11. The marginal cost of producing an additional serving of ice cream, if 200 servings are currently being produced, is equal to

a. $550.50.
b. $550.
c. $50.
d. $0.50.

12. Given the information in the table, as output increases from 0 units to 400 units, marginal cost

a. decreases.

b. increases.

c. stays constant.

13. What is the marginal benefit of producing one more serving of ice cream if 300 servings are currently being produced?

a. $650
b. $625
c. $25
d. $0.25

14. What is the optimal number of servings of ice cream to produce?

a. 400
b. 300
c. 200
d. 100

ANSWER KEY

Answers to Problems and Exercises

1. **a.** Marty's explicit costs include $200,000 for labor, $50,000 for rent, and $125,000 for supplies and raw materials. The sum of Marty's explicit costs equal $375,000. For this problem recall that depreciation costs equal $0.

   b. Marty's implicit costs include $5,000 for the implicit cost of capital and $75,000 for the salary Marty forgoes when he decides to work for himself. Marty could invest the value of the business ($100,000) at his bank and earn 5% interest on that deposit, yielding him $5,000 in interest income per year. In addition, Marty could close his business and earn $75,000 working for someone else. Thus, Marty's implicit costs equal $80,000.

   c. The explicit and implicit costs total $455,000.

   d. The implicit cost of Marty's time and energy is $75,000.

   e. The implicit cost of Marty's capital is $5,000.

   f. Marty's accounting profit equals his total revenue minus his explicit costs, or $440,000 – $375,000, for an accounting profit of $65,000.

   g. Marty's economic profit equals his total revenue minus his explicit costs and implicit costs, or $440,000 – $455,000, for an economic profit of –$15,000.

   h. Marty should not stay in business since he is currently earning a negative economic profit and therefore is not receiving the full value for his time and energy and the use of his capital. Since Marty's implicit costs equal $80,000, Marty must earn an accounting profit equal to $80,000 to cover his explicit costs plus his opportunity costs.

   i. The minimum amount of revenue that the bakery must earn for Marty to stay in business is $455,000: when Marty earns $455,000 in revenue, his revenue just covers his explicit and implicit costs of being in business.

2. **a.** Susie's explicit costs per year include her labor costs of $125,000 and her costs of raw materials and supplies of $200,000, for a total of $325,000.

   b. Susie's implicit costs include the value of her time as measured by the salary of $50,000 she could earn if she worked for a competitor and the earnings from her capital if it was invested at a return of 10% a year, or $60,000, for a total of $110,000.

   c. Accounting profits equal total revenue minus explicit costs and depreciation. Susie's depreciation equals $10,000, so her accounting profits equal $500,000 – $325,000 – $10,000, or $165,000.

   d. Economic profits equal total revenue minus the sum of explicit costs, implicit costs, and depreciation, or $500,000 - ($325,000 + $110,000 + $10,000), or $55,000.

3. a.

Quantity of services	Joe's total cost	Joe's marginal cost	Joe's total benefit	Joe's marginal benefit
0	$100		$ 0	
		(a) $10		(g) $200
1	110		200	
		(b) 8		(h) 30
2	118		230	
		7		15
3	(c) 125		(i) 245	
		10		(j) 10
4	(d) 135		255	
		(e) 15		8
5	150		(k) 263	
		20		5
6	(f) 170		(l) 268	

b. Marginal cost is the addition to total cost from producing one additional unit of the good, while marginal benefit is the addition to total benefit from producing or consuming one more unit of the good.

c. At 2 units of services, Joe's marginal cost of $8 is less than his marginal benefit of $30. Since the addition to benefits exceeds the addition to costs, more services should be produced.

d. At 5 units of services, Joe's marginal cost of $15 is greater than his marginal benefit of $8. Since the addition to costs exceeds the addition to benefits, fewer services should be provided.

e. When Joe provides 4 services, the marginal cost of providing the last unit of services ($10) exactly equals the marginal benefit from providing the last unit of services ($10). Thus 4 units of services is the optimal quantity to provide.

4. **a.** Marginal cost is decreasing as output increases from 0 units to Q_3 units.

b. Marginal cost is constant as output increases from Q_3 to Q_4 units.

c. Marginal cost is increasing as output increases for all output levels greater than or equal to Q_4.

d. The marginal cost of producing Q_2 is measured by the distance from the origin to *B* on the vertical axis.

e. The marginal cost of producing Q_6 is measured by the distance from the origin to *A* on the vertical axis.

5. a. Joe's marginal benefit from consuming hot dogs decreases as he consumes more hot dogs. Each additional unit of hot dog provides less benefit than the previous unit.

   b. Joe will compare his marginal cost of consuming another hot dog with his marginal benefit from consuming an additional hot dog. As long as the marginal benefit of an additional hot dog exceeds the marginal cost of an additional hot dog, Joe will consume an additional hot dog.

   c. Joe will consume 30 hot dogs since the marginal cost of the thirtieth hot dog equals the marginal benefit of the thirtieth hot dog.

   d. Joe will consume 40 hot dogs since at this quantity the marginal benefit of the last unit consumed equals the marginal cost of the last unit consumed.

6. a.

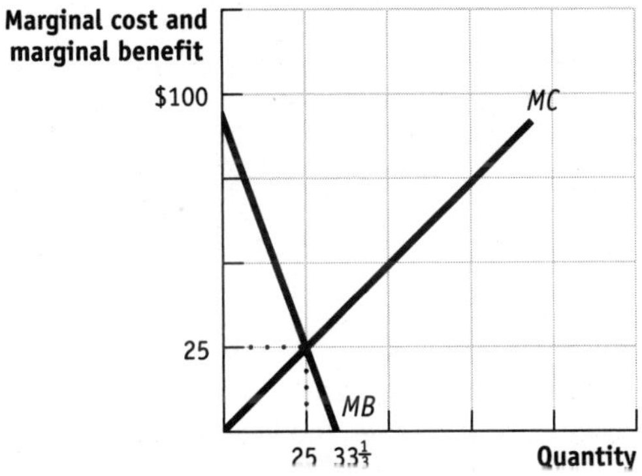

   b. The optimal quantity occurs where $MC = MB$, or where $Q = 25$. At this quantity, the marginal cost and marginal benefit are both equal to \$25 for the last unit produced.

   c. At a quantity of 20 units, the marginal cost of the last unit produced is \$20 while the marginal benefit from this last unit is \$40. Bob will add more to his benefits than his costs if he increases his production, so he should increase his production.

7. a. Since the opera tickets are nonrefundable, the expenditure on these tickets represents a sunk cost for Marissa. Marissa should ignore this cost and simply compare the costs and benefits of going to Miami. The out-of-pocket cost of going to Miami is \$0 since it is an all-expense paid trip; however, Marissa does have an opportunity cost since she will have to forgo going to the opera. Marissa should make her decision based on which choice yields the greater net benefit to her including this opportunity cost in her calculation.

   b. The opera cost is a sunk cost and the trip to Miami is all-expense paid. Marissa does have an opportunity cost in going to Miami, since she will have to forgo whatever she would have done if she had decided to not take the trip.

   c. Marissa is not paying the \$1,000 associated with the cost of the Miami trip, and the \$120 cost of the opera ticket is a sunk cost. Marissa's roommate's analysis is wrong.

Answers to Module Review Questions

1. **Answer d.** Accounting profits ignore implicit costs. Accounting profits are equal to total revenue minus the sum of explicit costs and depreciation.

2. **Answer b.** Jerry's explicit costs do not include the salary he could make if he worked for someone else, and it doesn't include the interest he could earn if he sold his business and deposited his capital in a bank deposit. His explicit costs include the labor costs, the supplies and raw materials cost, and the rental costs, for a total of \$280,000.

3. **Answer d.** Jerry's explicit costs omit the salary he could earn if he worked for someone else ($60,000) and the interest he could earn if he invested his capital ($5,000), for a total of $65,000.

4. **Answer b.** Jerry's accounting profit is equal to his total revenue minus his explicit costs (there is no depreciation in this question). His explicit costs equal $280,000 and his accounting profit equals $100,000: this implies that his total revenue must equal $380,000. If doughnuts are priced at $1 each, then this means Jerry sold 380,000 doughnuts this year. Economic profits are equal to total revenue ($380,000) minus the sum of explicit plus implicit costs ($345,000): Jerry's economic profit is equal to $35,000.

5. **Answer c.** Jerry should continue to operate his business so long as his accounting profits are equal to or greater than his implicit costs. Since his implicit costs are equal to $65,000, this means that Jerry should continue to operate provided his accounting profits are at least equal to $65,000. If his accounting profits fall below this level, then Jerry would be better off selling his business and working for someone else.

6. **Answer d.** All of these statements are true. When marginal benefit is greater than marginal cost, this means that consumers value the last unit more than the cost of producing the last unit, and more of the good should be produced. Similarly, when marginal cost is greater than marginal benefit, too much of the good is being produced. Answer (c) is a definitional statement.

7. **Answer a.** Since the marginal benefit of producing one more unit of steel is greater than the marginal cost of producing this additional unit of steel, Stella should produce this unit.

8. **Answer b.** If marginal cost is decreasing as output increases, this implies that there is an inverse relationship between quantity and marginal cost: as quantity increases, marginal cost decreases, which is represented by a downward-sloping marginal cost curve.

9. **Answer b.** Since marginal cost does not vary as output varies, this tells us that marginal cost can be represented as a horizontal line when marginal cost is measured on the vertical axis and quantity is measured on the horizontal axis.

10. **Answer c.** As people get more and more units of the good, each successive unit yields fewer additional benefits.

11. **Answer d.** Marginal cost is the change in total costs divided by the change in quantity. Total costs change from $500 to $550 when output increases from 200 units to 300 units. To get a measure of marginal cost, we can divide the change in total cost ($50) by the change in output (100 units) to get $0.50 per unit as our marginal cost.

12. **Answer c.** If you use the same technique as the one outlined in answer 12, you will find that the marginal cost is constant and equal to $0.50 per unit.

13. **Answer d.** The marginal benefit of producing one more unit of ice cream if 300 units are currently being produced is equal to ($975 – $950)/(400 units – 300 units) = $25 per 100 units, or $0.25 per unit.

14. **Answer b.** Since the marginal cost is constant and equal to $0.50, this problem is about identifying the level of output that has a marginal benefit of $0.50. This occurs when quantity is equal to 300 servings, since the marginal benefit of going from 200 to 300 servings is equal to ($950 – $900)(300 units – 200 units) = $0.50.

module 19

Behavioral Economics

BEFORE YOU READ THE MODULE

Summary

This module defines behavioral economics and discusses the origins of behavioral economics. It also discusses the difference between rational and irrational behavior before exploring why people sometimes behave irrationally in predictable ways.

Module Objectives

Objective #1. Behavioral economics studies why people make less-than-perfect decisions. This branch of economics combines economic modeling with insights drawn from human psychology. Behavioral economics is interested in studying rational decisions that individuals make that result in an outcome that they most prefer but that does not yield the greatest possible economic payoff. There are three main reasons that people might prefer a lower economic payoff: (1) concerns about fairness—people care about fairness, as well as the economic payoff to themselves; (2) bounded rationality—people make choices that are close to, but not exactly, the one that leads to the greatest possible economic payoff; and (3) risk aversion—people dislike risk, so it is rational for people to give up some potential gain to avoid risk.

Objective #2. There are six common mistakes people make when making economic decisions; these mistakes cause people to act irrationally in predictable ways. These six mistakes are (1) misperceptions of opportunity costs, (2) being overconfident, (3) having unrealistic expectations about future behavior, (4) counting dollars unequally, (5) being loss-averse, and (6) having a bias toward the status quo.

- Misperceptions of opportunity costs affect economic decision making because, when making decisions, people tend not to count nonmonetary opportunity costs while including sunk costs.
- Overconfidence refers to the human tendency to believe that we know more than we do. This can lead to poor decisions, particularly with regard to financial decisions related to investment and spending.
- Unrealistic expectations about future behavior result in people thinking that they will commit to actions and behaviors in the future, only to find that when tomorrow comes they fail to honor the commitment. People tend to push difficult actions off into the future.

- Economic decision making may be adversely affected by the human tendency to count dollars unequally. For example, people may be willing to spend more when using their credit cards than when using cash from their wallets; they may spend more at a sale because it seems like a great deal, only to regret the expenditure at a later time; or they may splurge after receiving an unexpected financial windfall. In all of these examples, the individual is not making the optimal economic decision. Effectively, the individual is placing these different dollars in different accounts so that some dollars are worth more than others.
- With loss aversion, people are reluctant to recognize a loss and to act rationally with regard to that loss. This prevents them from taking the optimal economic action.
- With status quo bias, people are reluctant to make any decision at all and find it easier to just maintain the current course, even if the current course does not result in the optimal economic outcome.

Key Terms

rational a rational decision maker chooses the available option that leads to the outcome he or she most prefers.

bounded rationality a decision maker operating with bounded rationality makes a choice that is close to, but not exactly, the one that leads to the greatest possible economic outcome.

risk aversion is the willingness to sacrifice some economic payoff in order to avoid a potential loss.

irrational an irrational decision maker chooses an option that leaves him or her worse off than he or she would choosing another available option.

mental accounting is the habit of mentally assigning dollars to different accounts so that some dollars are worth more than others.

loss aversion is an oversensitivity to loss, leading to unwillingness to recognize a loss and move on.

status quo bias is the tendency to avoid making a decision and sticking with the status quo.

Notes

AFTER YOU READ THE MODULE

Tip

Tip #1. Behavioral economics is a field of economics research that combines economic modeling with insights from psychology in order to investigate situations in which people behave irrationally but in predictable ways. These situations arise because of concerns that people have about fairness, because of bounded rationality, or because of risk aversion. Make sure you review the six common mistakes of economic decision making. Once you have reviewed these six common mistakes, take a moment to identify at least one good example of each type of mistake.

WORKED PROBLEMS

1. For each of the following situations identify the common mistake(s) being made with regard to the particular economic decision being made.
   a. Jim has recently started work for a company that offers a retirement plan for those employees interested in this benefit. Jim can join this retirement plan if he fills out the required form. Jim planned to take care of this last week, but he has yet to fill out the form and drop it off at the office.
   b. Kris has always considered herself a good judge of character. Last week she met Lelia, a woman who recently moved to her community. Lelia told Kris that she was lucky enough to be part of an investment group that for the past 10 years has earned a return of 15% on her investment. Kris, knowing the normal return on investment has been 6%, was impressed! She liked Lelia and, given her ability to judge character, she asked Lelia if she could join the investment group. Lelia took her check and Kris has not seen her since (and Lelia has not returned her calls). Lelia also cashed the check.
   c. Marcia has $5,000 in her "special fund," a savings account Marcia created with funds set aside for "fun" expenses. Marcia recently lost her job and she is not having much success finding a new job. However, her friend Mike has just invited her to go to the Super Bowl this January: Marcia's expenses will be $2,000 also. Since she has the money available in her "special fund," she told Mike she would go.

STEP 1: Review the six common mistakes people should avoid when making an economic decision.

The six common mistakes people should avoid when making an economic decision are: (1) misperceiving opportunity cost; (2) being overconfident; (3) having unrealistic expectations about future behavior; (4) counting dollars unequally; (5) being loss-averse; and (6) having a bias towards the status quo. Review the explanations and examples offered in the text for each of these common mistakes.

STEP 2: For each of the given situations, identify which of these six common mistakes are occurring.

In (a), the common mistakes being made with regard to establishing the retirement plan are having unrealistic expectations about future behavior and having a bias toward the status quo. Jim makes plans to take care of the enrollment in the future but never seems to manage to get to the future. He is unrealistic about what his future behavior is going to be: he thinks he will sign up but so far he has not. In addition, Jim's failure to sign up continues the status quo: researchers have found that humans tend to maintain the status quo, even if this is a detrimental outcome, because of the effort needed to alter the status quo.

In (b) the common mistake Kris is making is being overconfident. She prides herself on her ability to judge the character of other people, and she ends up losing money to Lelia.

In (c) the common mistake Marcia makes is counting dollars unequally. Marcia spends these dollars even though she is financially challenged with the loss of her job. This is not a rational economic decision on her part.

2. Explain three possible reasons a person might rationally choose an outcome that does not provide the best possible economic payoff to him or her.

STEP 1: Review the meaning of "rational" provided in this module.

The module discusses the concept of the rational decision maker, who chooses the available option that leads to the outcome he or she most prefers. This outcome will not necessarily provide the best possible economic payoff to this person.

STEP 2: Review the module's description of (1) concerns about fairness; (2) bounded rationality; and (3) risk aversion. Use these three concepts to explain why a rational individual might not choose the outcome with the best possible economic payoff to the individual.

"Concerns about fairness" refers to the idea that people care about fairness as well as about the economic payoff they will receive from an action. An individual who perceives that the action is unfair may choose not to pursue that action even though it might lead to the best possible economic outcome for the individual. "Bounded rationality" is the recognition that there is a cost to the individual of discerning the best payoff and that an individual may rationally decide on an action that is close to, but not exactly, the one that leads to the highest economic payoff because the effort to find the best action is too costly. Risk aversion occurs when an individual forgoes a choice that carries significant risk of a bad outcome: even though the choice might also have the potential for a good outcome, the risk of the bad outcome is so high that the individual is simply unwilling to pursue it. Each of these reasons may result in a rational individual choosing an outcome that does not provide the best possible economic payoff to the individual.

Problems and Exercises

1. Millionaire David Smith dies and his will reveals that he has left 70% of his estate to James and 30% of his estate to William. James and William are David's only children and they are twins who have always been close. James promptly decides to give William part of his inheritance so that William's share is equivalent to his share. This economic decision adversely affects James. Is this a sign of irrational behavior? Explain your answer.

2. Mike began to feel ill several months ago and after extensive medical testing has just been told by his doctor that he has cancer. The doctor provided Mike with a long document (more than 1,000 pages) detailing the likely progression of his cancer, as well as the available treatments and side effects. Mike, after thumbing through this document, sets it aside and tells the doctor to proceed with the treatment that the doctor views as optimal. Is Mike's decision not to read the entire document a sign of his irrationality? Explain your answer.

BEFORE YOU TAKE THE TEST

Module Review Questions

1. Behavioral economics is
   a. a branch of economics that considers optimal behavior.
   b. a branch of economics that combines economic modeling with insights from human psychology.
   c. a branch of economics that studies rational decision making by human beings.
   d. All of the answers are correct.
   e. Answers (b) and (c) are both correct.

2. If you are rational, you will choose the outcome you most prefer. However, this does not guarantee that this outcome is the one with the greatest economic payoff to you. You might choose an outcome that does not maximize your economic payoff because of
   a. concerns about fairness.
   b. bounded rationality.
   c. risk aversion.
   d. All of the answers are possible.

3. People can make irrational economic decisions that are systematically irrational. That is, their irrational economic decisions are based on predictable errors. Which of the following is *not* a common mistake people make when making economic decisions?
   a. miscalculating opportunity costs
   b. being overconfident
   c. having accurate predictions about future behavior
   d. being loss-averse
   e. counting dollars unequally

4. Joey knows he needs to lose a substantial amount of weight. His doctors have educated him to the health consequences of his current weight. He thinks that if he stops eating ice cream, no longer snacks between his three balanced meals a day, and foregoes seconds at mealtimes that he should be able to shed the weight. He plans to start his diet plan tomorrow. Behavioral economics suggests that Joey will have trouble losing this weight because of
   a. Joey's loss-aversion.
   b. Joey's bias towards maintaining the status quo.
   c. Joey's having unrealistic expectations about future behavior.
   d. All of the answers are correct.
   e. Answers (b) and (c) are both correct.

5. Julie has $20 in her wallet and that money must cover all of her expenses until the end of the month. But, while at the mall today, Julie sees a beautiful blouse that is on sale for $45. It is such a good deal she decides to get it. She reasons, "My credit card bill won't arrive until next month!" Julie's economic decision to buy the blouse is predictably irrational and reflects the common mistake of
   a. loss aversion.
   b. bias toward maintaining the status quo.
   c. counting dollars unequally.
   d. being overconfident.

6. Professor Smith allows his classes to select from two grading options: the first option requires students to submit three papers over the course of the semester with all papers due by the end of the semester; and the second option requires that the three papers be submitted on three specific dates within the semester that cannot be renegotiated. Each class can only select one of these options, and each member of the class must adhere to the selected option. Professor Smith finds that

a. classes selecting the second option on average earn higher grades than classes selecting the first option.
b. it makes no difference in average class grades which option is chosen.
c. classes selecting the first option on average earn higher grades than classes selecting the second option.
d. recognizing the tendency to procrastinate and then choosing a tool to address this tendency allows people to make themselves better off.
e. Answers (a) and (d) are both correct.
f. Answers (c) and (d) are both correct.

7. Jenning's Electronics, a large corporation, is in the midst of designing its retirement plans for its employees. Jenning's Electronics is debating having an opt-in plan, where employees can decide to join the retirement plan by filling out a form, or an opt-out plan, where employees are automatically enrolled in the retirement plan unless they schedule an appointment with the human resources department to fill out a form to opt-out of the plan. In terms of employee retirement plan saving, does it matter whether Jenning's Electronic institutes the opt-in or the opt-out plan?

a. Yes, because of bias toward the status quo the opt-out plan will result in more employees participating in the retirement plan and, therefore, a higher level of employee saving toward retirement.
b. No, both plans will result in those employees that wish to save for retirement saving for retirement. It does not matter which plan the company adopts if its goal is to encourage employee saving for retirement.

8. Mitchell is shopping for toothpaste, and he sees that one brand of toothpaste sells for \$2.99 a tube, while another brand sells for \$3.05. Like many shoppers, he interprets the \$2.99 price as significantly cheaper than the \$3.05 price because of:

a. risk aversion.
b. bounded rationality.
c. concerns about fairness.
d. rational decision making.

9. People's behavior is often irrational:

a. in predictable ways.
b. in unpredictable ways.
c. and research will not enable social scientists ever to understand this irrational behavior better.
d. and therefore is not worth studying.

ANSWER KEY

Answers to Problems and Exercises

1. James's decision to share the inheritance is not irrational, though it reduces his economic payoff. James is likely to share the inheritance because of his concern about fairness. He knows that William has been treated unfairly and, rather than support this treatment, James makes the decision to rectify the uneven distribution of his father's estate. People may choose to pursue a suboptimal economic payoff because of their concerns about fairness: this is not an irrational decision if the person is concerned about fairness, as well as the economic payoff.

2. Mike's decision to not read the entire document prior to making a decision reflects bounded rationality. The effort to choose an option—in this case a treatment path—requires work—identifying the options, comparing the options, considering each option's drawbacks. People often find that they make decisions that are close to, but not exactly equal to, the one with the greatest payoff because they are unwilling to expend the effort to identify the absolutely best payoff. Mike is delegating this responsibility to his doctor since his doctor likely has more expertise in the matter, as well as greater objectivity.

Answers to Module Review Questions

1. **Answer b.** This is the definition of behavioral economics. Behavioral economics explores how people act irrationally in predictable ways: thus, it is neither about how people make optimal decisions nor is it about rational decisions.

2. **Answer d.** There are three general reasons why people might rationally prefer an outcome that results in an economic payoff that is less than the maximum economic payoff that is available. Concerns about fairness may lead an individual to choose an outcome that produces a smaller economic payoff than is possible. Bounded rationality refers to making a choice that is close to, but not exactly, the one that leads to the greatest economic payoff because the effort in identifying the best payoff is too costly. Finally, risk aversion results in individuals being willing to sacrifice some potential economic payoff in order to avoid the potential of an economic loss.

3. **Answer c.** There are six common mistakes people make when making economic decisions: (1) misperceiving opportunity costs; (2) being overconfident; (3) having unrealistic expectations about future behavior; (4) counting dollars unequally; (5) being loss-averse; and (6) having a bias toward the status quo. Answer (c) is incorrect since the common mistake with regard to expectations is unrealistic expectations, rather than accurate ones.

4. **Answer e.** Diets are hard to maintain because in order to work they must successfully change our current familiar behavior to a new unfamiliar behavior. This implies that the diet is changing the status quo: we commonly find it hard to adjust to a change in the status quo because we naturally tend to prefer the familiar even if it is unhealthy for us. In addition, diets require that we project our expectations about future behavior: our expectations about future behavior are often mistaken. Although we may agree that limiting our food intake is a good idea, we typically find this difficult to actually do: we plan to start the diet tomorrow and tomorrow never comes.

5. **Answer c.** Julie purchases a blouse that costs her money she does not have. She reasons that if she pays for the blouse with her credit card the bill will come to her in the future. Her error is failing to see that she will still have to pay for the blouse and that whether she pays for the blouse now with the cash in her wallet or later when her credit card bill arrives, it still costs the same. She is counting her dollars unequally.

6. **Answer f.** People tend to procrastinate and this procrastination can result in suboptimal outcomes. Within a classroom setting flexible deadlines encourages student procrastination. Selecting the second option limits the amount of possible procrastination and provides a structure for addressing this tendency: class grades on average will be higher with this structure.

7. **Answer a.** The choice of opt-in or opt-out plan matters if the goal is to encourage employee retirement savings. The bias towards the status quo in this case means that people will be slow to do the work to change the existent situation: if the plan is opt-in, that implies that people will be slow to visit their benefits office and change to the retirement plan. The longer they wait to register for the plan, the less time they are actually saving for their retirement. The opt-out plan, however, insures that people are contributing to their retirement accounts unless they are willing to expend the energy to change the status quo: here the bias toward the status quo works in favor of creating more retirement savings rather than less retirement savings.

8. **Answer b.** Bounded rationality leads Mitchell to give more weight to the first number in the price he sees ($2 versus $3) than to the rest of the price ($0.99 versus $0.05).

9. **Answer a.** Although people often behave in irrational ways, this irrationality is often predictable; it is due to six common errors people make when they are making economic decisions. Social scientists studying decision making have been able to identify these six common mistakes. Studying this irrational behavior to learn about these errors is useful, since it lets us better understand this irrational behavior and design systems that can improve decision making.

module 20

Maximizing Utility

BEFORE YOU READ THE MODULE

Summary

This module explores how consumers pursue the general goal of utility maximization. It explains how to use marginal analysis to find the consumption bundle that maximizes the individual's utility. The module also discusses why the principle of diminishing marginal utility applies to the consumption of most goods and services.

Module Objectives

Objective #1. The model of consumer choice is based on a rational consumer who knows what he or she wants and who makes the most of his or her available opportunities.

Objective #2. Consumer utility refers to the satisfaction the consumer gets from the consumption of a bundle of goods and services. The utility function describes the relationship between an individual's consumption bundle and the total amount of utility this consumption bundle provides to the individual. Each individual evaluates the consumption bundle's utility: the level of utility depends on each person's tastes. Utility is measured in utils.

- Total utility measures the total amount of satisfaction an individual gets from consuming different amounts of a good. As the quantity consumed increases, total utility increases, but as quantity increases total utility increases at a decreasing rate. After some point of consumption, the consumer gets less satisfaction from each additional unit consumed. Figure 20.1 illustrates a total utility curve.

Figure 20.1

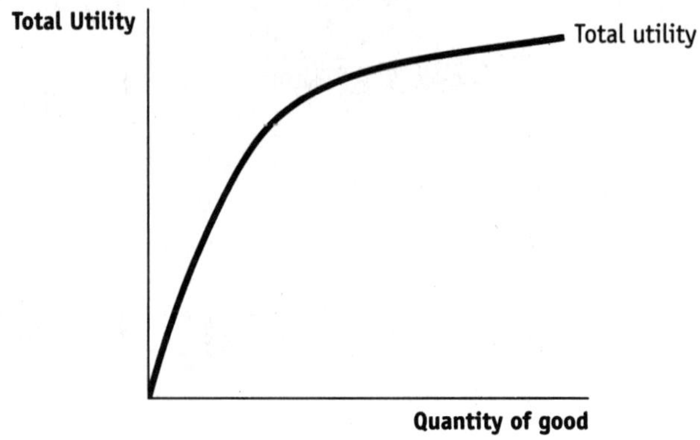

- Marginal utility measures the change in total utility from consuming an additional unit of the good. Marginal utility declines as the individual consumes more and more units of the good. The marginal utility curve illustrates the relationship between the quantity consumed and the individual's marginal utility. Figure 20.2 illustrates a marginal utility curve.

Figure 20.2

- Marginal utility curves slope downward due to the principle of diminishing marginal utility, which states that the marginal utility a consumer gets from one more unit of a good or service declines as the amount of that good or service consumed increases.

Objective #3. A consumer's budget constraint describes the consumption bundles that a consumer can afford and that exhaust the consumer's income. The budget constraint depends on the individual's income and the prices of the goods and services included in the consumption bundle. The budget constraint acts as a boundary indicating the consumer's consumption possibilities. The budget constraint for an individual with a choice of two goods can be expressed as follows:

Total income of the individual = expenditure on good 1 + expenditure on good 2

- The budget constraint when drawn on a graph is referred to as the budget line. For example, suppose an individual has income of $20,000 a year and is choosing between consuming good X, which costs $100 per unit, or consuming good Y, which costs $200 per unit. The budget line for this individual is depicted in Figure 20.3.

Figure 20.3

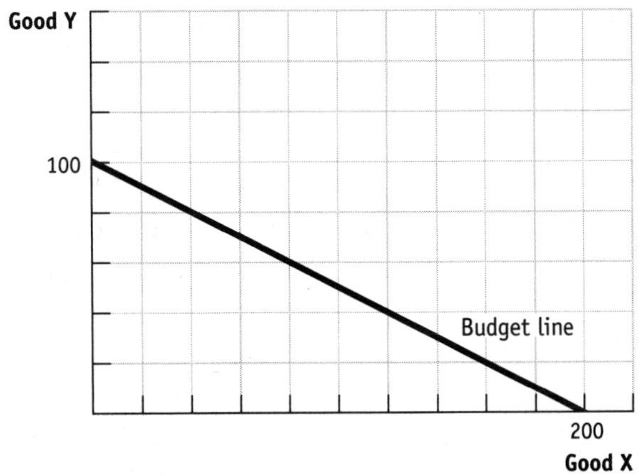

If the consumer spent all of his or her income on good X, they could consume 200 units of good X (the *x*-intercept in the graph); if the consumer spent all of their income on good Y, they could consume 100 units of good Y (the *y*-intercept in the graph). The consumer can also afford any combination of the two goods that lie on the budget line.

- The individual can afford any points that lie in the area bounded by their budget line: these affordable consumption bundles represent the individual's consumption possibilities. The individual will not choose to consume at any of these points inside the budget line provided that their utility from consuming either good is positive and the utility of saving income is zero (this amounts to the assumption that the individual spends all of their income on the two available goods).
- Budget lines are downward sloping since the individual can afford to consume more of one good only if the individual consumes less of the other good.

Objective #4. The optimal consumption bundle is the one that maximizes the individual's total utility. The top part of Figure 20.4 illustrates an individual's budget line showing all of the possible consumption bundles that the individual can afford given his income and the prices of the two goods; the lower part of Figure 20.4 is a graph of this individual's total utility function. The individual will maximize utility by selecting the consumption bundle that provides the greatest level of total utility. In Figure 20.4 this occurs at consumption bundle *D*. Study these two graphs carefully.

Figure 20.4

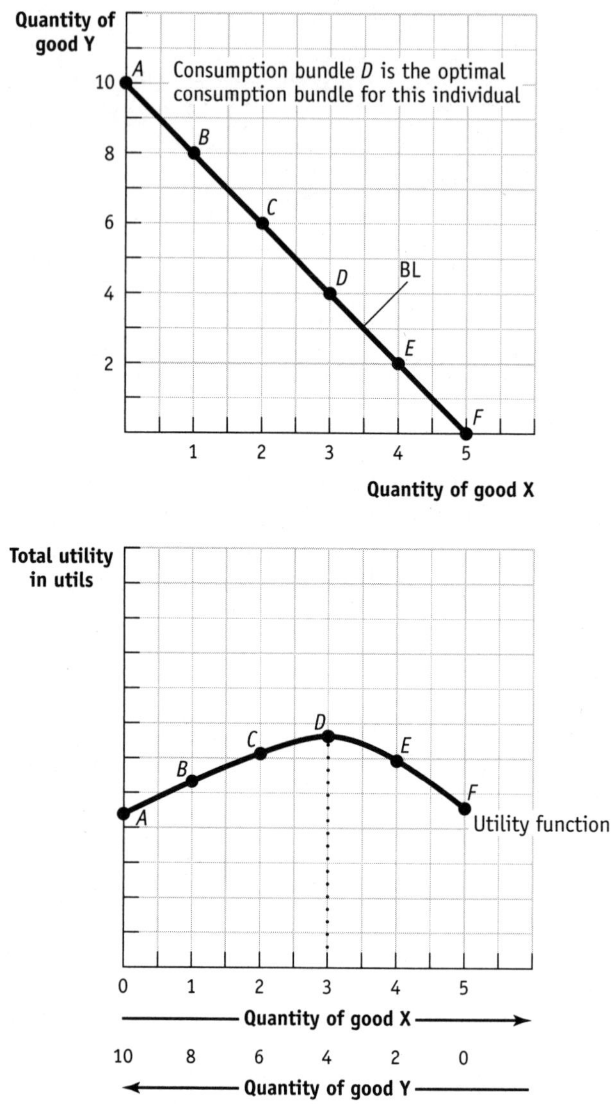

Objective #5. The marginal utility per dollar spent on a good is equal to the marginal utility of the last unit consumed divided by the price of the good. The marginal utility per dollar for good X can be written as MU_X/P_X, where MU_X is the marginal utility from consuming that unit of the good and P_X is the price of good X.

- As additional units of the good are consumed, the marginal utility per dollar spent on the good decreases, holding income and the prices of the goods constant. This is because of the principle of diminishing marginal utility: as the consumer consumes more and more units of the good, total utility increases but at a diminishing rate. When total utility increases at a diminishing rate, this implies that marginal utility is decreasing as consumption increases.
- The optimal consumption bundle for an individual is one in which the marginal utility per dollar spent on each good is equal. This idea can be expressed symbolically as

$$MU_X/P_X = MU_Y/P_Y$$

where the X and Y subscripts refer to good X and good Y, respectively.
- A graph can be constructed to depict the relationship between the marginal utility per dollar spent and the optimal consumption bundle. This graph would measure the marginal

utility per dollar spent on the vertical axis, and it would measure the consumption bundles that are affordable along the horizontal axis. Along the horizontal axis each of these consumption bundles would represent different amounts of the two goods: reading from left to right, the quantity of good X increases while the quantity of good Y decreases. (Note: because the quantity of good Y decreases as you read from left to right along the horizontal axis, this results in the marginal utility per dollar spent on good Y being drawn as an upward-sloping line.) Figure 20.5 illustrates this idea for the two goods X and Y. The consumer will maximize their utility by consuming consumption bundle C, since the marginal utility per dollar spent on good X equals the marginal utility per dollar spent on good Y with this bundle.

Figure 20.5

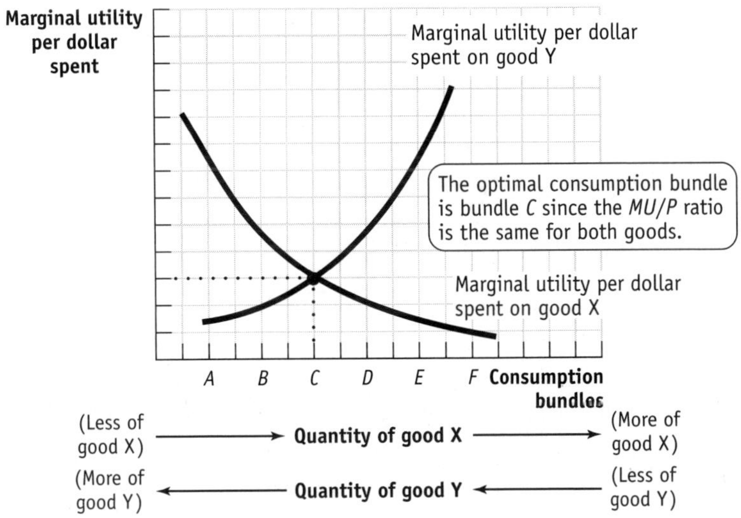

Key Terms

utility (of a consumer) a measure of the satisfaction derived from consumption of goods and services.

util a unit of *utility*.

marginal utility the change in total *utility* generated by consuming one additional unit of a good or service.

marginal utility curve a graphical representation showing how *marginal utility* depends on the quantity of the good or service consumed.

principle of diminishing marginal utility the proposition that each successive unit of a good or service consumed adds less to total *utility* than did the previous unit.

budget constraint the cost of a consumer's *consumption bundle* cannot exceed the consumer's income.

consumption possibilities the set of all *consumption bundles* that can be consumed, given a consumer's income and prevailing prices.

budget line all the *consumption bundles* available to a consumer who spends all of his or her income.

Notes

Key Terms *(continued)*

optimal consumption bundle the *consumption bundle* that maximizes a consumer's total *utility,* given that consumer's *budget constraint.*

marginal utility per dollar the additional *utility* gained from spending one more dollar on a good or service.

optimal consumption rule when a consumer maximizes *utility,* the *marginal utility per dollar* spent must be the same for all goods and services in the *consumption bundle.*

Notes

AFTER YOU READ THE MODULE

Tips

Tip #1. Construction of the individual's budget line is not difficult if you follow these steps.

- First identify the two goods the individual can choose to consume and the prices of these two goods.
- Identify the individual's income.
- In a graph, the *y*-intercept of the budget line corresponds to the individual's income divided by the price of the good measured on the *y*-axis. In other words, the total number of units of the good measured on the *y*-axis that the individual can afford if they only buy that good is found by dividing the individual's income by the price of the good. Similarly, the *x*-intercept of the budget line corresponds to the individual's income divided by the price of the good measured on the *x*-axis.
- For example, suppose an individual has a weekly income of $100 and purchases food for $5 a unit and entertainment for $20 a unit. (Although the individual obviously must buy other goods, imagine that this particular individual has $100 that they spend only on some combination of food and entertainment.) Suppose food is measured on the horizontal axis and entertainment is measured on the vertical axis. If the individual devotes all of their income to the purchase of food, they can purchase 20 units of food ($100/$5); if the individual devotes all of their income to the purchase of entertainment, they can purchase 5 units of entertainment ($100/$20); or the individual can divide their income between food and entertainment and purchase any combination of food and entertainment that lies on the line between the two endpoints of the budget line. Figure 20.6 illustrates this example.

Figure 20.6

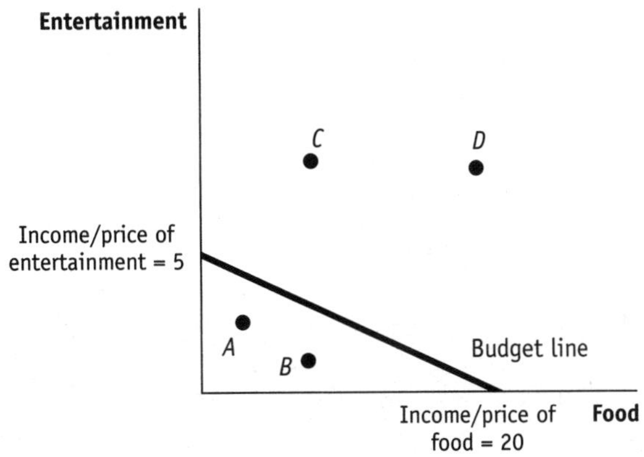

Tip #2. The individual can afford to consume any consumption bundle of food and entertainment that lies on or beneath the budget line (for example, points *A* and *B* in Figure 20.6). The individual cannot afford to consume any consumption bundle of food and entertainment that lies beyond the budget line (for example, points *C* and *D* in Figure 20.6).

Tip #3. To use marginal analysis for consumption decisions, remember that you must include the budget constraint. Thus, marginal analysis for consumption decisions involves comparing the marginal utility per dollar spent on each good and selecting that consumption bundle in which the marginal utility per dollar is the same for all goods.

WORKED PROBLEMS

1. You are given the following information about the utility that three consumers of doughnuts get from consuming various quantities of doughnuts. You have been asked to evaluate whether these individuals have diminishing marginal utility from consuming doughnuts, and you have been asked to draw diagrams depicting Anne's total utility from consuming doughnuts and her marginal utility from consuming doughnuts. When constructing her marginal utility curve, plot the marginal utility value at the midpoint of the unit intervals. For example, if the marginal utility from the second doughnut is 10 utils, then you would plot the marginal utility (10 utils) as the level that is received when the individual consumes 1.5 doughnuts (the midpoint between 1 and 2 doughnuts).

Number of doughnuts	Sam's total utility in utils	Mary's total utility in utils	Anne's total utility in utils
1	50	40	60
2	90	80	100
3	120	120	120
4	140	160	130
5	150	200	135

STEP 1: First construct a table that provides the marginal utility from consuming an additional doughnut for all of the individuals.

Marginal utility is the change in total utility from consuming one more unit of the good. Use this definition and the preceding data to construct a table that provides the marginal utility that each of the individuals gets when he or she consumes each additional doughnut.

Number of doughnuts	Sam's marginal utility in utils	Mary's marginal utility in utils	Anne's marginal utility in utils
1			
	40	40	40
2			
	30	40	20
3			
	20	40	10
4			
	10	40	5
5			

STEP 2: Evaluate the table you constructed in Step 1 to see whether any of the individuals has diminishing marginal utility from consuming doughnuts.

Sam and Anne experience diminishing marginal utility as they increase their consumption of doughnuts: from the table, we can see that their marginal utility decreases as their level of doughnut consumption increases. Mary's marginal utility from consuming doughnuts is constant: each additional doughnut she consumes provides her with the same number of utils as the last one (40 utils).

STEP 3: Draw a graph of Anne's total utility curve using the given information.

Total utility is graphed on the vertical axis, while the horizontal axis measures the units of the good. The diagram that follows illustrates Anne's total utility curve for doughnuts.

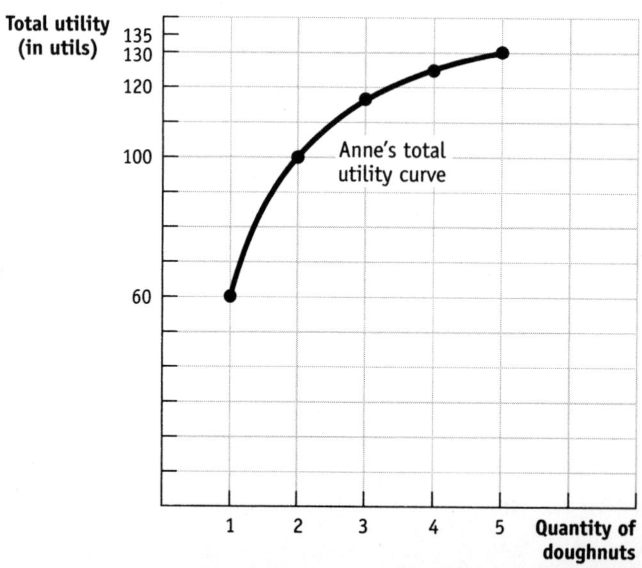

STEP 4: **Draw a graph of Anne's marginal utility curve using the information you calculated in Step 1.**

Use the data you created in Step 1 to draw a diagram of Anne's marginal utility from consuming doughnuts.

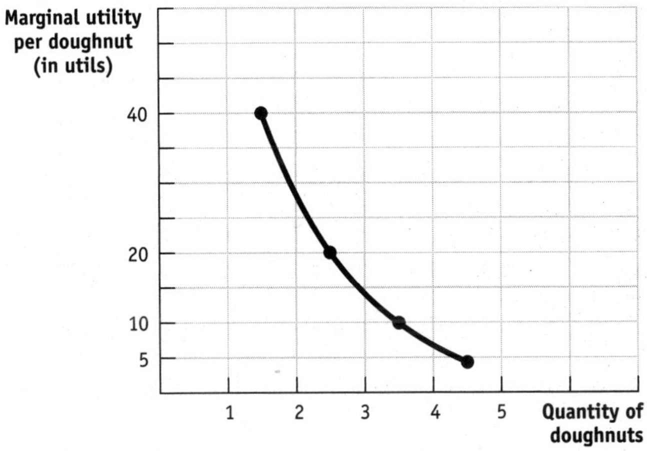

2. Brady is analyzing a budget constraint that depicts consumption bundles of apples and bananas that Leigh can afford, given her income and the prices of the two goods. The budget line is drawn in the graph, that follows. Brady has been told that the price of apples is $2 per apple but he does not know Leigh's income or the price of a banana. He has been asked to figure out Leigh's income and the price of a banana, and then to write an equation for the budget line. Finally, Brady has been asked to calculate the maximum amount of bananas Leigh can consume if she consumes 10 apples, 20 apples, or 30 apples.

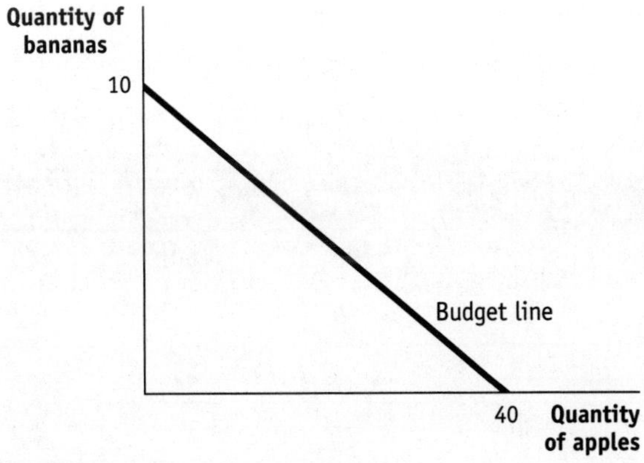

STEP 1: **Calculate Leigh's income.**

We know that Leigh can afford 40 apples if she purchases only apples and no bananas, given the graph. We also know that the price of an apple is $2. This implies that when she purchases 40 apples she must spend $80. Her income is therefore $80.

STEP 2: Calculate the price of bananas.

From the graph, we can see that if Leigh only purchases bananas she can afford to buy 10 bananas with her income. Given that her income is $80, this implies that the price of each banana must be $8.

STEP 3: Write an equation for Leigh's budget line.

From the graph, we can easily find the *y*-intercept of 10 bananas and compute the slope as −1/4. Using this information and the slope-intercept form, $y = mx + b$, we can write the equation for Leigh's budget line as $B = (-1/4)A + 10$, where *B* is bananas and *A* is apples.

STEP 4: Use the equation you wrote to figure out the maximum amount of bananas Leigh can afford when she consumes 10 apples, 20 apples, or 30 apples.

Using the equation from Step 3 it is easy to find the maximum amount of bananas Leigh can consume for any given quantity of apples consumed. For example, if she consumes 10 apples, then she can afford to consume 7.5 bananas. To see how to use the equation for this, replace *A* in the equation with 10 and then solve for the value of *B*. Thus, $B = (-1/4)(10) + 10 = 7.5$. Ten apples will cost $20 and 7.5 bananas will cost $60: when Leigh consumes 10 apples and 7.5 bananas she uses all her available income. When Leigh consumes 20 apples she can consume 5 bananas, and when Leigh consumes 30 apples she can consume 2.5 bananas.

3. Hon Ho has $200 in income available to spend on apples (*A*) and bread (*B*). The price of apples is $1 per apple and the price of bread is $2 per loaf. Hon Ho is interested in constructing a diagram that illustrates his budget constraint, given this information. He also has constructed a table in which he has analyzed five different consumption combinations that he can afford and that will exhaust his income. This information is summarized in the following table. Notice that this table is not complete and Hon Ho needs your help to complete it.

Consumption bundle	Quantity of apples	Utility from apples (utils)	Quantity of loaves of bread	Utility from bread (utils)	Total utility (utils)
A	0		100	60	60
B		15	75		67
C	100	25		45	
D	150	30			50
E			0	0	32

The table provides information about the total utility he gets from consuming various quantities of apples and bread. He has asked you to provide an illustration that will help him see the relationship between his budget constraint and his utility function from consuming apples and bread. In illustrating this relationship, measure apples on the horizontal axis for the budget constraint. Finally, Hon Ho would like your advice as to which of these bundles he should consume if his goal is to maximize his utility, and he would like you to illustrate this idea in your diagrams.

STEP 1: Complete the table by filling in the missing values.

To calculate the number of apples that Hon Ho can afford in any consumption bundle, you would first want to calculate how much of Hon Ho's income he is spending on bread in order to see how much income he has available to spend on apples. So, for example, in consumption bundle *B*, Hon Ho is purchasing 75 loaves of bread that cost him $150.That means that Hon Ho has $50 of income left to spend on apples. Since apples cost $1 per apple, this implies that Hon Ho can afford to purchase 50 apples. Use this same process to calculate the number of apples Hon Ho can afford in consumption bundle *E*.

To calculate the number of loaves of bread that Hon Ho can afford in any consumption bundle, you would first want to calculate how much of Hon Ho's income he is spending on apples in order to see how much income he has available to spend on bread. For example, in consumption bundle *C*, Hon Ho is purchasing 100 apples that cost him $100. That means that Hon Ho has $100 of income left to spend on bread. Since a loaf of bread costs $2, this implies that Hon Ho can afford to purchase 50 loaves of bread. Use this same process to calculate the number of loaves of bread Hon Ho can afford in consumption bundle *D*.

The cells with information about utility can be filled out by recognizing that the sum of the utility from apples and the utility from bread equals total utility. Thus, the utility from apples in consumption bundle *A* must equal 0 since 0 + 60 = 60. Use this same approach to fill in all the other missing values in the table. The following table provides all the missing information.

Consumption bundle	Quantity of apples	Utility from apples (utils)	Quantity of loaves of bread	Utility from bread (utils)	Total utility (utils)
A	0	0	100	60	60
B	50	15	75	52	67
C	100	25	50	45	70
D	150	30	25	20	50
E	200	32	0	0	32

STEP 2: Write an equation for Hon Ho's budget constraint and then draw a diagram of this budget constraint.

In general, Hon Ho is going to use all of his available income to purchase apples and bread. Thus, Hon Ho's income is equal to the price of bread times the quantity of bread plus the price of apples times the quantity of apples. Thus, $200 = 2B + 1A$. To graph this budget constraint, it will be easier if we write this equation in slope intercept form: since we are measuring bread on the vertical axis, we should solve this equation so that B is on the left-hand side of the equation. Thus, $B = 100 - (1/2)A$. The diagram that follows illustrates Hon Ho's budget constraint.

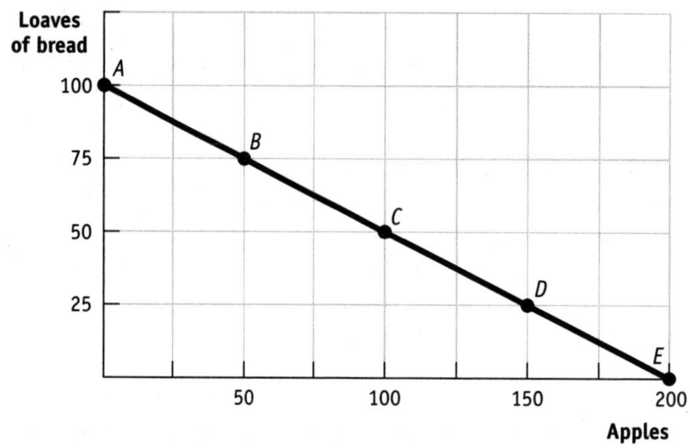

STEP 3: **Draw Hon Ho's utility function in a diagram where the quantity of apples and loaves of bread are measured on the horizontal axis, while his total utility is measured on the vertical axis.**

To draw this diagram, we must first understand how we can measure the quantity of apples and the loaves of bread on the same axis. In effect we will be measuring consumption bundles on this axis, since each consumption bundle is compose of a particular combination of apples and bread. Examine the following diagram closely to see this representation. Once the horizontal axis is constructed, it is a relatively simple matter to graph the total utility associated with each consumption bundle as a vertical distance in the graph and then to draw a line that goes through each of these points.

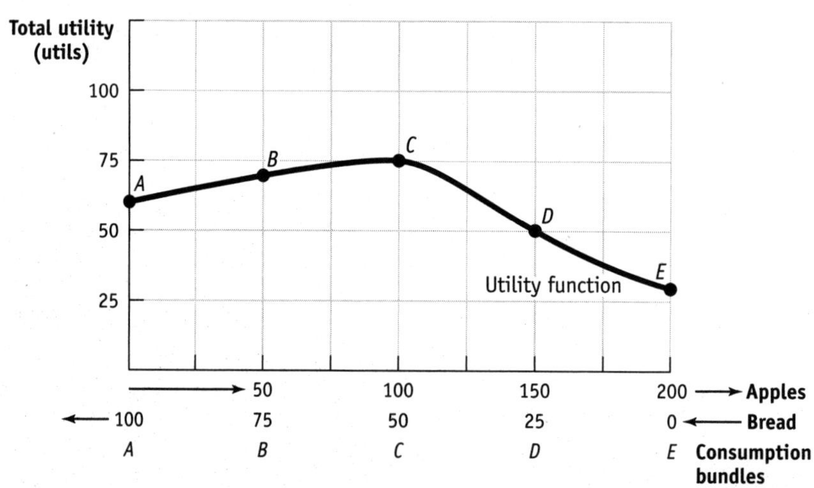

STEP 4: **Use the diagram in Step 3 to illustrate the consumption bundle that maximizes Hon Ho's utility, and then show where this bundle is on his budget constraint.**

Close inspection of the table and the diagram in Step 3 indicates that consumption bundle C provides the maximum amount of utility from the list of possible consumption bundles. Notice on the utility function bundle C is at the highest point: this is the point that maximizes Hon Ho's utility from the choices that he can afford, given his income and the prices of the two goods.

4. Suppose that Emilio's utility function can be written as $U = XY$, where U is total utility, X refers to the quantity of good X, and Y refers to the quantity of good Y. Furthermore, suppose that the price of good X is \$1, the price of good Y is \$2, and Emilio has an income of \$200. Emilio knows that his marginal utility from good X can be written as $MU_X = Y$ and his marginal utility from good Y can be written as $MU_Y = X$. He has asked you to figure out the consumption bundle of good X and good Y that will maximize his utility. He also wants to know what his total utility will equal when he maximizes his utility, and he would also like it verified that his marginal utility per dollar spent on either good X or good Y is the same when he consumes this consumption bundle. Finally, is there a simple way you might reassure Emilio that this consumption bundle maximizes his utility?

STEP 1: Construct Emilio's budget constraint from the given information. Write an equation that expresses this budget constraint.

To construct Emilio's budget constraint, we need to know his income and the prices of the two goods. Emilio has \$200 to spend on good X and good Y, and good X costs \$1 and good Y costs \$2. We can write his budget constraint as $200 = 1X + 2Y$. Rewriting this in slope intercept form, we have $Y = 100 - (1/2)X$.

STEP 2: Describe what the relationship is between the marginal utility of good X, the marginal utility of good Y, the price of good X, and the price of good Y. Explain what this relationship means.

When Emilio maximizes his utility, his marginal utility per dollar spent on each good should be equivalent, since if this was not the case it would be possible for Emilio to reallocate his budget and increase his total utility. Thus, $MU_X / P_X = MU_Y/P_Y$ or $Y/1 = X/2$. We can rearrange this as $2Y = X$. This implies that Emilio will want to consume twice as many units of good X as good Y if he is going to equate the marginal utility per dollar spent on each good.

STEP 3: Use the relationship you developed in Step 2 and the budget constraint from Step 1 to find the consumption bundle that maximizes Emilio's utility, given his income, the prices of the two goods, and his tastes and preferences described by the utility function.

We now have two equations we can use to find the consumption bundle that Emilio can afford (use the budget constraint for this) and that maximizes his utility (use the relationship we found in Step 2 for this). Thus, we have $Y = 100 - (1/2)X$ and $2Y = X$. Replacing X with $2Y$ in the first equation, we have $Y = 100 - (1/2)(2Y)$ or $2Y = 100$ or $Y = 50$. When Y is equal to 50, this implies that X is equal to 100 since $2Y = X$. Thus, Emilio will maximize his utility, given his income, the prices of the two goods, and his tastes and preferences when he consumes 100 units of good X and 50 units of good Y. Can he afford this consumption bundle? Yes, since 100 units of good X will cost \$100 and 50 units of good Y will cost \$100, for a total expenditure of \$200.

STEP 4: Calculate Emilio's total utility when he consumes this consumption bundle. Consider some other possible consumption bundles that Emilio can afford to see if these other combinations would yield him greater utility.

Emilio's total utility when he consumes the consumption bundle we found in Step 3 is equal to (100)(50) = 5,000 utils.

We could revisit problem 3 to get some combinations, since the underlying income and prices of the two goods are the same in the two problems. For instance, Emilio could afford these combinations of X and Y: (0, 100), (50, 75), (150, 25), and (200, 0). To find the total utility associated with each of these combinations, use the formula $U = XY$. Thus, when the combination is (0, 100), the total utility is zero. When the combination is (50, 75), the total utility is 3,750. When the combination is (150, 25), the total utility is 3,750. When the combination is (200, 0), the total utility is zero. This suggests that our combination of (100, 50) maximizes Emilio's total utility.

STEP 5: Confirm that the marginal utility per dollar spent is equal for good X and good Y when Emilio consumes the optimal consumption bundle.

The MU_X/P_X is equal to $Y/1$ and the MU_Y/P_Y is equal to $X/2$. Since the optimal consumption bundle is equal to (100, 50) when Emilio maximizes his utility subject to the constraint of his income, the prices of the two goods, and his tastes and preferences, this gives us 50/1 and 100/2. These two ratios are the same. When Emilio maximizes his utility subject to the previously mentioned constraints, the marginal utility per dollar spent on each good is the same.

Problems and Exercises

1. Use the information in the table below to answer this set of questions.

Servings of hot chocolate per month	Joe's total utility (utils)	Maria's total utility (utils)	Ben's total utility (utils)	Alexandra's total utility (utils)	Steve's total utility (utils)
1	100	80	100	40	20
2	180	160	150	90	40
3	240	240	200	150	60
4	280	320	250	220	80
5	300	400	300	300	100

a. Which of the individuals in the above table have constant marginal utility over the given range of hot chocolate quantities? Explain your answer.

b. Which of the individuals in the above table have decreasing marginal utility over the given range of hot chocolate quantities? Explain your answer.

2. Use the information given in problem 1 to answer this problem.

a. Complete the table below using the information from problem 1.

Servings of hot chocolate per month	Joe's marginal utility (utils)	Maria's marginal utility (utils)	Ben's marginal utility (utils)	Alexandra's marginal utility (utils)	Steve's marginal utility (utils)
1					
	80				20
2					
			50		
3					
4					
		80			
5					

b. Graph Joe's marginal utility from hot chocolate. Measure the quantity of hot chocolate on the horizontal axis and Joe's marginal utility on the vertical axis. Construct the marginal utility curve by plotting your marginal utility figures at the midpoint of the unit intervals. For example, Joe's marginal utility of the second serving of hot chocolate is 80 utils: on your graph plot this level of marginal utility (80 utils) as the level that Joe receives when he consumes 1.5 servings of hot chocolate.

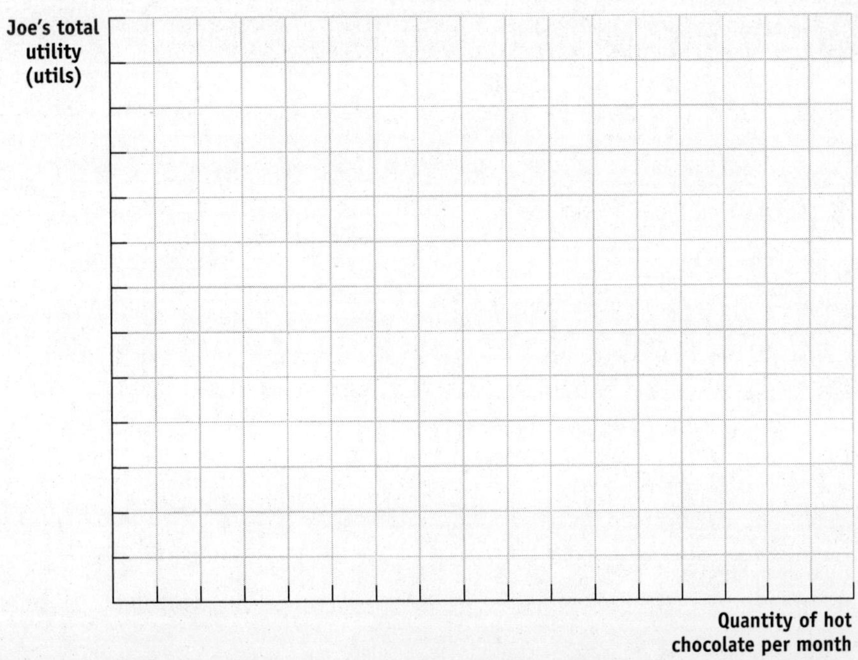

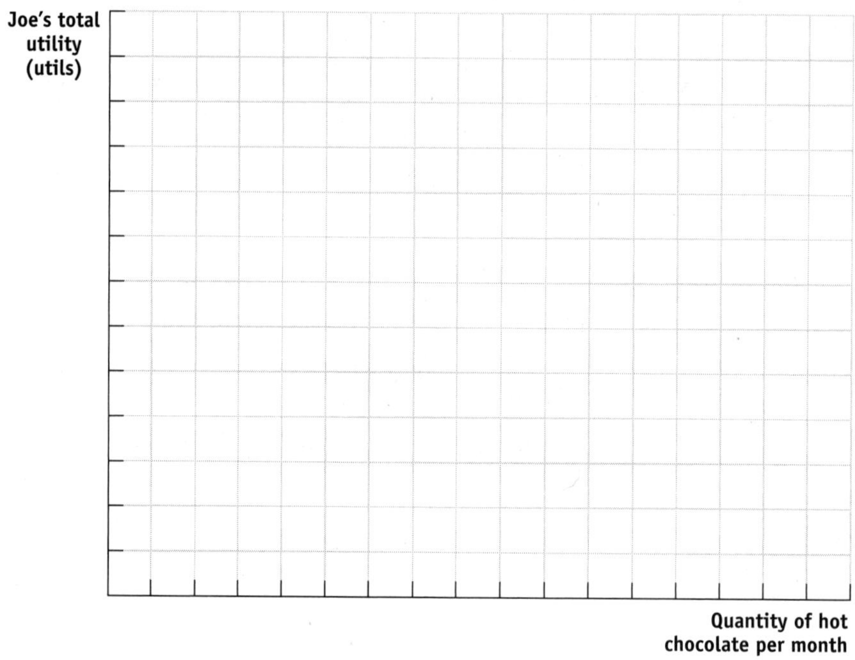

3. Sarah's total utility from consuming three slices of pizza is 120 utils while her total utility from consuming four slices of pizza is 100 utils. How is this possible and what does this mean for Sarah?

4. Why are marginal utility curves downward sloping as the level of consumption of the good increases?

5. The following table provides information about Carolyn's total utility from reading articles about current events.

Number of articles read	Total utility from reading articles (utils)
1	100
2	300
3	450
4	550
5	625
6	680
7	720
8	740

a. Using the above information, complete the following table.

Number of articles read	Marginal utility from reading articles (utils)
1	
	200
2	
	150
3	
4	
5	
6	
7	
8	

b. Does Carolyn experience diminishing marginal utility when reading articles? Explain your answer. If she experiences diminishing marginal utility, identify when this first occurs.

c. Is it possible for Carolyn to read too many articles? Explain your answer.

6. Harry's available income for spending on periodicals (P) and entertainment (E) each month equals \$40. The price of periodicals is \$2 per periodical and the price of entertainment is \$4 per unit of entertainment.

a. Fill in the following table indicating some of the consumption bundles that Harry can afford and that exhaust his income.

Consumption bundle	Number of periodicals	Units of entertainment
A	0	
B	4	
C	8	
D		2
E		0

b. Measuring periodicals on the vertical axis and entertainment on the horizontal axis, draw Harry's budget line. Assume that Harry can consume partial units of periodicals and entertainment (i.e., Harry's budget line is linear and continuous). Label each of the consumption bundles from part (a) on this graph.

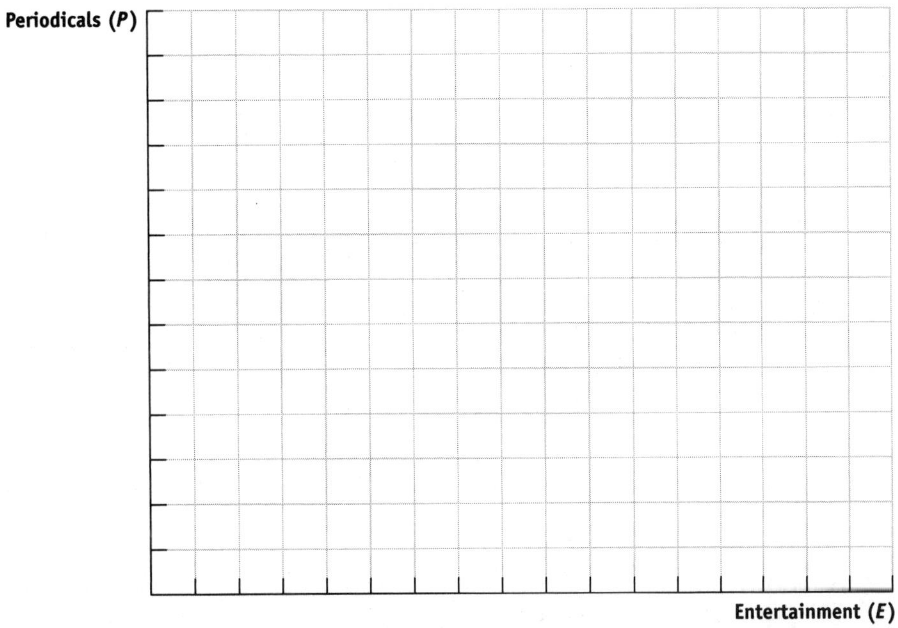

c. Suppose Harry initially consumes consumption bundle *B*. If he moves to consumption bundle *C*, what happens to his consumption of periodicals and entertainment relative to his initial situation?

d. Suppose Harry initially consumes consumption bundle *D*. If he moves to consumption bundle *C*, what happens to his consumption of periodicals and entertainment relative to his initial situation?

e. Write an equation in *y*-intercept form for Harry's budget line in which the *y*-axis variable is periodicals.

7. Katherine's available income each week for expenditures on food (F) and clothing (C) is \$40. The price of each unit of food is \$2 and the price of each unit of clothing is \$10.

   a. Draw a graph of Katherine's budget line in which food is measured on the y-axis and clothing is measured on the x-axis.

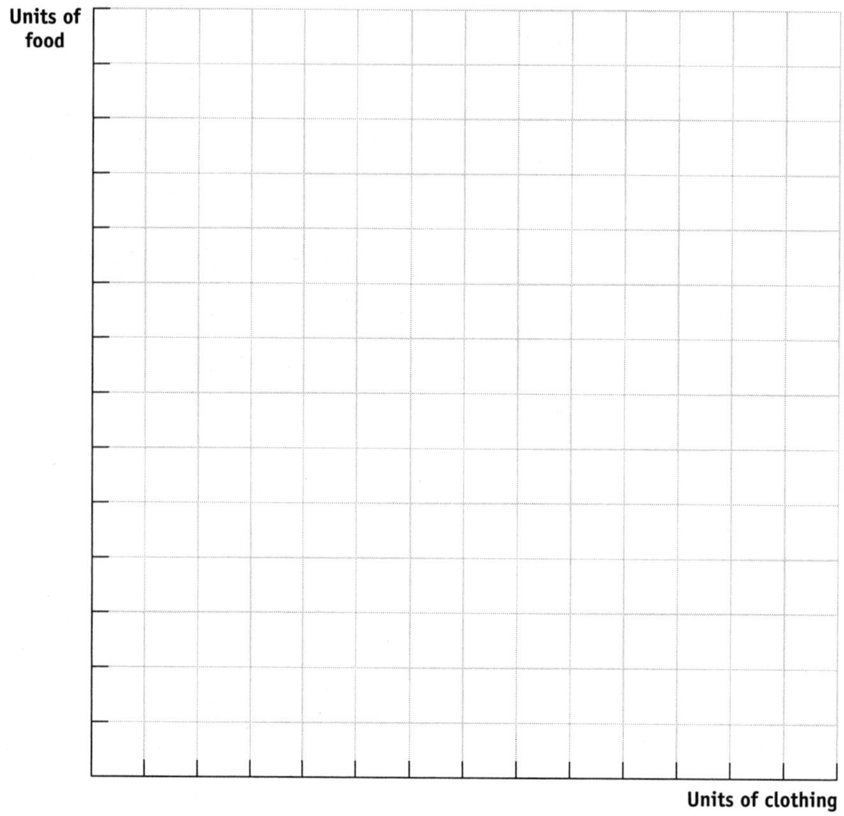

   b. For each of the consumption bundles in the table below, identify whether the bundle is on Katherine's budget line, inside Katherine's budget line, or beyond Katherine's budget line.

Consumption bundle	On, inside, or beyond the budget line
5 units of food, 3 units of clothing	
4 units of food, 4 units of clothing	
10 units of food, 1 unit of clothing	
20 units of food, 2 units of clothing	

   c. Write an equation in y-intercept form for Katherine's budget line in which food is the y-variable.

d. Suppose prices stay constant, but Katherine's available weekly income for expenditures on food and clothing doubles. Draw a graph of Katherine's initial budget line and her new budget line with food measured on the vertical axis. How does the new budget line compare to her initial budget line?

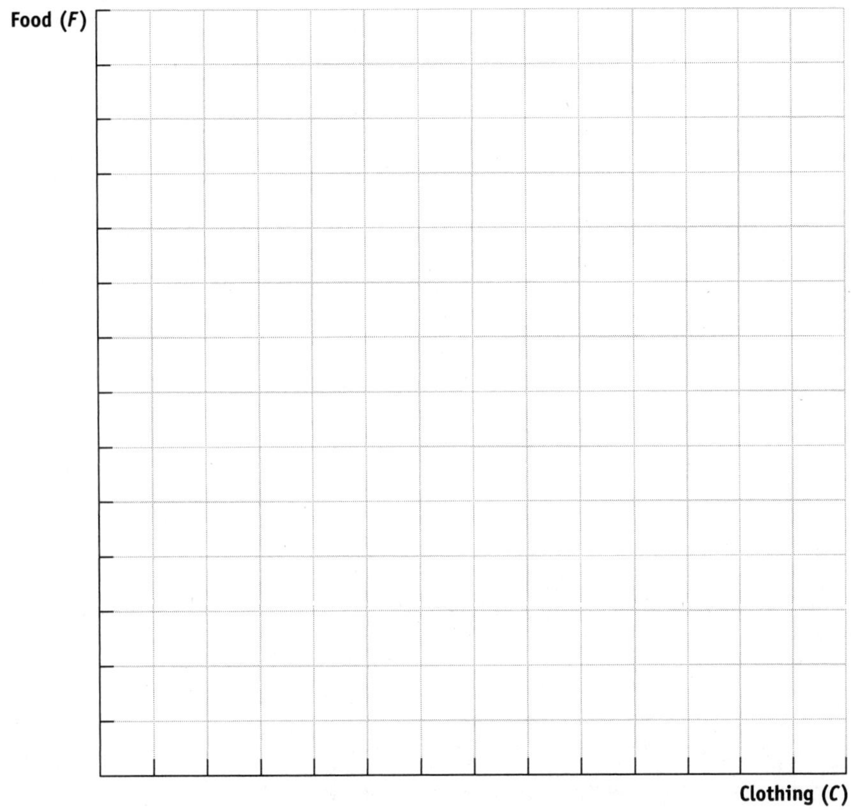

e. Suppose Katherine's weekly income is \$40 but the price of food rises to \$4 per unit while the price of clothing remains at \$10 per unit. Draw a graph of Katherine's initial budget line and her new budget line. How does this change in the price of food affect Katherine's budget line?

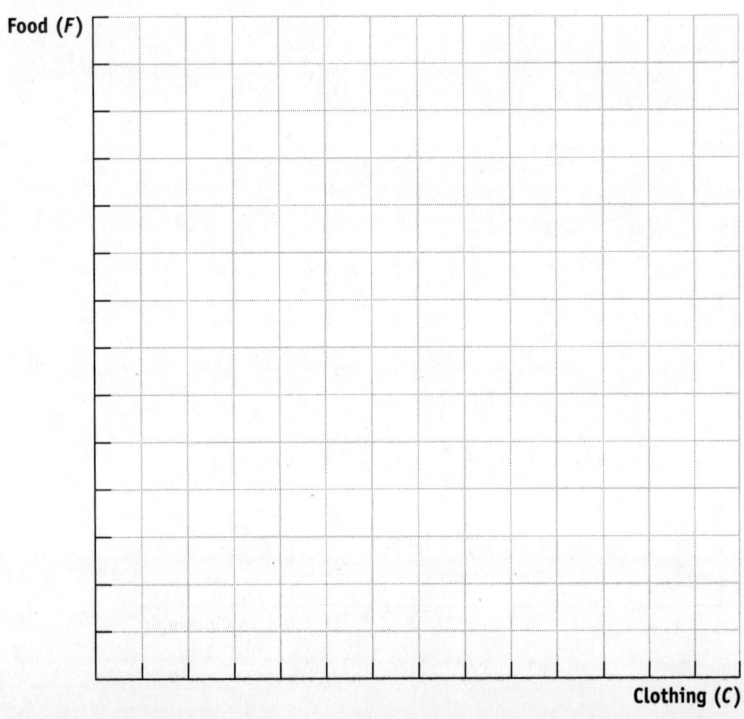

f. Suppose Katherine's weekly income is \$40 but the price of clothing falls to \$5 per unit while the price of food stays constant at \$2 per unit. Draw a graph of Katherine's initial budget line and her new budget line. How does this change in the price of clothing affect Katherine's budget line?

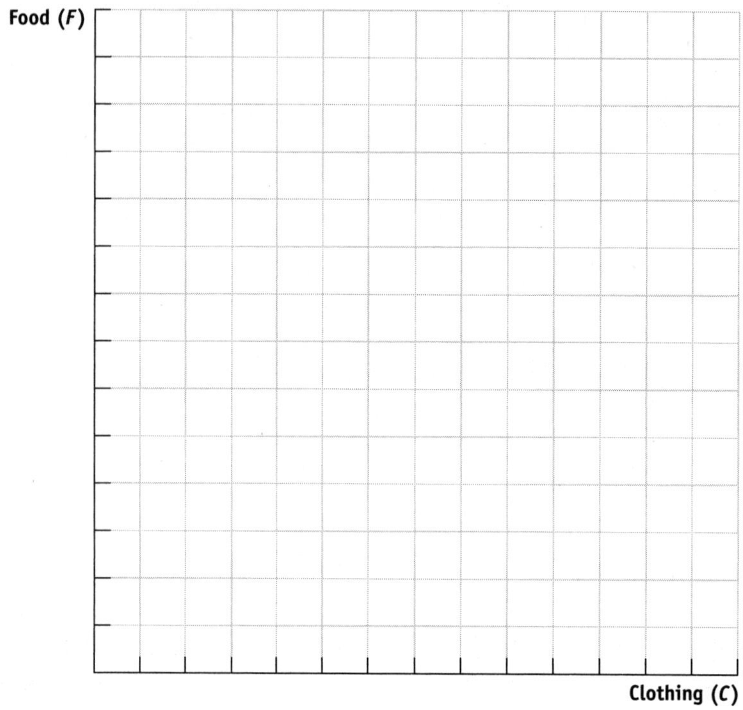

g. Suppose Katherine's weekly income increases to \$80 while the prices of food and clothing double. Draw a graph of Katherine's initial budget line and her new budget line. How does this change in income and prices affect Katherine's budget line?

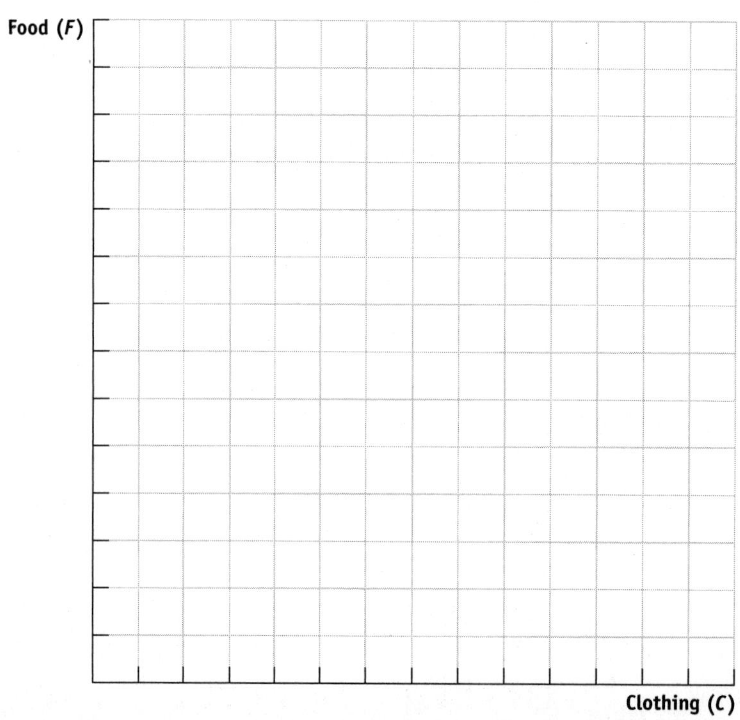

8. Use the figure below to answer this question. Bertram's marginal utility per dollar spent on good X and his marginal utility per dollar spent on good Y are illustrated in the graph. Notice that as you read from left to right along the *x*-axis, the quantity of good X increases while the quantity of good Y decreases. Each combination (*A* through *F*) of good X and good Y represented on the *x*-axis is a combination that Bertram can afford given his income and the prices of the two goods.

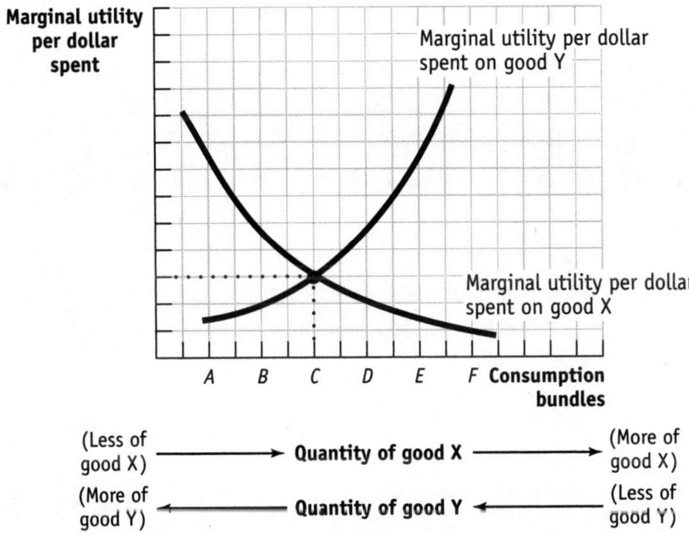

a. Suppose Bertram is currently consuming consumption bundle *B*. What is the relationship between the marginal utility per dollar spent on good X and the marginal utility per dollar spent on good Y? Is this the optimal consumption bundle for Bertram? Explain your answer.

b. Suppose Bertram is currently consuming consumption bundle *E*. If he decreases his consumption of good X and increases his consumption of good Y, what happens to his marginal utility per dollar spent on good X and his marginal utility per dollar spent on good Y? Explain your answer and make sure your answer incorporates the concept of diminishing marginal utility.

c. What is Bertram's optimal consumption bundle?

9. Mark consumes ice cream and hamburgers. The table below provides information about the relationship between the quantity of ice cream and hamburgers and the total utility Mark gets from their consumption.

Utility from Ice Cream Consumption		Utility from Hamburger Consumption	
Quantity of ice cream (cones)	Total utility from ice cream (utils)	Quantity of hamburgers	Total utility from hamburgers (utils)
0	0	0	0
1	20	1	15
2	38	2	28
3	53	3	39
4	66	4	48
5	77	5	53
6	84		
7	89		
8	92		
9	94		
10	95		

Mark's income for expenditure on ice cream and hamburgers is $50 per month, the price of ice cream is $5 per cone, and the price of hamburgers is $10 per hamburger.

a. Complete the following table based on the above information.

Consumption bundle	Quantity of ice cream (cones)	Utility from ice cream (utils)	Quantity of hamburgers	Utility from hamburgers (utils)	Total utility (utils)
A	0		5		
B				48	86
C	6		2		
D		92			107
E	10		0		

b. Draw a horizontal line and label points along this line to correspond to the different combinations of ice cream and hamburgers Mark can afford given his income and the prices of the two goods. Moving from left to right along this horizontal line, the number of ice cream cones increases while the number of hamburgers decreases.

c. Graph the results from part (a) using two different graphs. In the first graph, put the quantity of ice cream cones on the horizontal axis and the quantity of hamburgers on the vertical axis. Draw Mark's budget line and label consumption bundles *A* through *E* on this budget line. On a second graph drawn just below the first graph, draw Mark's total utility function: measure Mark's total utility on the vertical axis and the quantity of ice cream and the quantity of hamburgers on the horizontal axis—you practiced drawing this horizontal axis in part (b) of this problem. Moving from left to right along the horizontal axis, the number of ice cream cones increases while the number of hamburgers decreases. Label consumption bundles *A* through *E* on Mark's total utility curve.

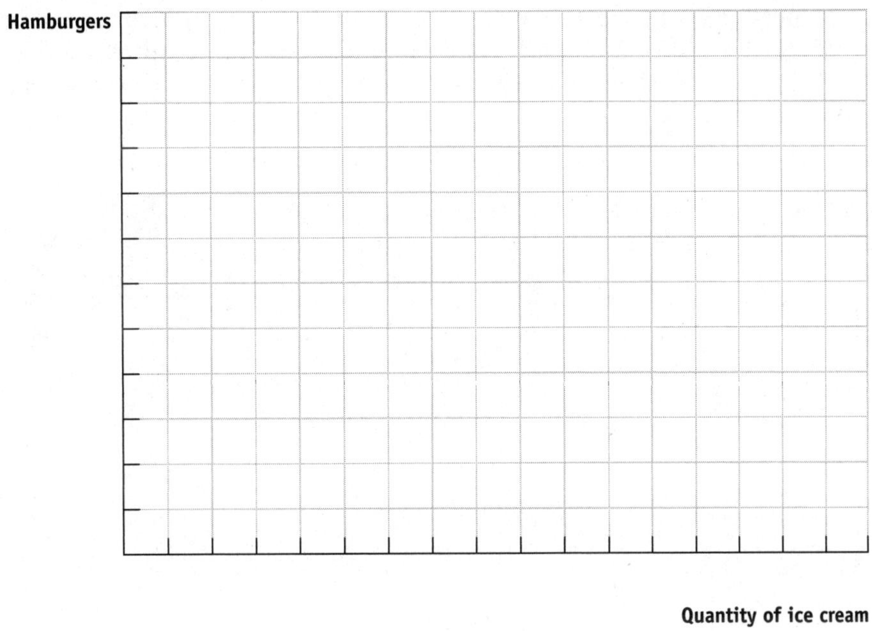

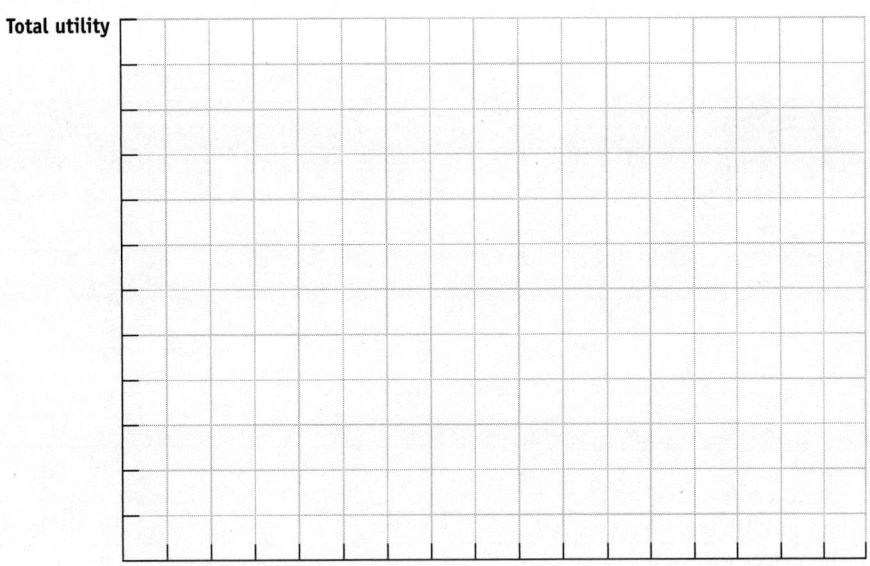

d. Given your work in part (a) and the information you graphed in part (c), which consumption bundle is the optimal consumption bundle for Mark? Why is this bundle the optimal consumption bundle?

e. In the table below, calculate Mark's marginal utility per ice cream cone (MU_{IC}), his marginal utility per dollar spent on ice cream (MU_{IC}/P_{IC}), his marginal utility per hamburger (MU_H), and his marginal utility per dollar spent on hamburgers (MU_H/P_H). Remember that the price of ice cream is $5 per cone and the price of hamburgers is $10.

Ice Cream				Hamburgers			
Quantity of ice cream (cones)	Utility from ice cream (utils)	MU_{IC} (utils)	MU_{IC}/P_{IC} (utils)	Quantity of hamburgers	Utility from hamburgers	MU_H (utils)	MU_H/P_H (utils)
0	0			0	0		
		20	4			15	1.5
1	20			1	15		
2	38			2	28		
3	53			3	39		
4	66			4	48		
5	77			5	53		
		7	1.4				
6	84						
7	89						
8	92						
9	94						
10	95						

f. Draw a graph of Mark's marginal utility per dollar spent on ice cream and marginal utility per dollar spent on hamburgers. This graph's horizontal axis should be labeled in the same manner as the one you drew in part (b) of this problem, while the vertical axis should measure Mark's marginal utility per dollar.

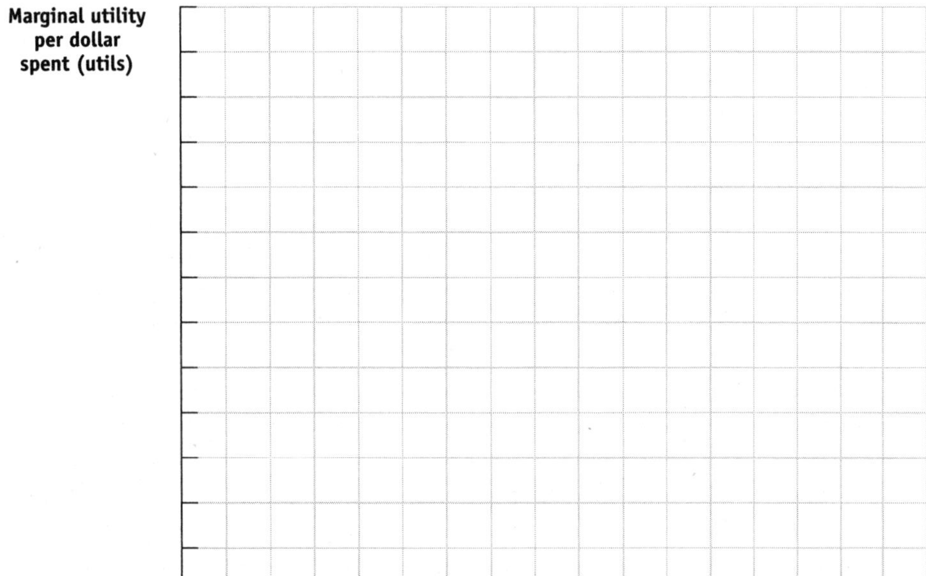

g. At the optimal consumption bundle *C*, what is the relationship between the marginal utility per dollar spent on ice cream and the marginal utility per dollar spent on hamburgers?

BEFORE YOU TAKE THE TEST

Module Review Questions

1. Rational consumers maximize

a. profits.
b. tastes.
c. utility.
d. demand.

2. An individual's utility

a. depends on everything that the individual consumes.
b. is a personal measure of the satisfaction the individual gets from their consumption of goods and services.
c. depends on the individual's tastes and preferences.
d. Answers (a), (b), and (c) are all true.

Use the following information about Joe's utility from consuming pizza to answer the next three questions.

Number of slices of pizza	Total utility
1	100 utils
2	180 utils
3	240 utils
4	280 utils
5	300 utils
6	310 utils

3. Based on the table, Joe's total utility from consuming pizza slices
a. decreases as he consumes more and more pizza slices.
b. increases at an increasing rate as he consumes more and more pizza slices.
c. increases at a decreasing rate as he consumes more and more pizza slices.
d. initially increases at an increasing rate as he consumes more pizza slices, but his total utility eventually increases at a diminishing rate.

4. Joe's marginal utility from consuming the fourth slice of pizza equals
a. 60 utils.
b. 40 utils.
c. 280 utils.
d. 20 utils.

5. Joe's utility from consuming pizza is consistent with
a. diminishing marginal utility.
b. constant marginal utility.
c. increasing marginal utility.

6. Which of the following statements is true?
I. An individual who experiences diminishing marginal utility finds that the additional satisfaction the individual gets from consuming one more unit of the good declines as the amount consumed of that good increases.
II. Marginal utility curves that exhibit diminishing marginal utility eventually become negative.
III. Marginal utility curves that exhibit diminishing marginal utility slope downward.
a. Statement I is true.
b. Statements I and II are true.
c. Statements I and III are true.
d. Statements I, II, and III are true.

7. Consider Mary whose weekly income for purchasing fruit and milk is $20. Each unit of fruit costs $1, while each unit of milk costs $2. Which of the following consumption bundles lies beyond Mary's budget line?
a. 3 units of fruit and 9 units of milk
b. 4 units of fruit and 8 units of milk
c. 6 units of fruit and 6 units of milk
d. 8 units of fruit and 6 units of milk

8. Consider Mary whose weekly income (I) for purchasing fruit (F) and milk (M) is \$20. Each unit of fruit costs \$1, while each unit of milk costs \$2. The equation expressing Mary's budget line can be written as

a. $F = 20 + 2M$

b. $F = 10 - (1/2)M$

c. $F = 20 - 2M$

d. $F = 10 - M$

9. Consider Mary whose weekly income (I) for purchasing fruit (F) and milk (M) is \$20. Each unit of fruit costs \$1, while each unit of milk costs \$2. Suppose Mary's available income for fruit and milk purchases increases to \$40 per week while the prices of fruit and milk do not change. Mary's budget line will

a. shift to the left when her income increases.

b. shift to the right when her income increases.

c. shift to the left or to the right when her income increases, depending on her tastes and preferences.

d. be unaffected by this change in income.

10. Consider Mary whose weekly income (I) for purchasing fruit (F) and milk (M) is \$20. Initially each unit of fruit costs \$1, while each unit of milk costs \$2. Suppose Mary's income for fruit and milk purchases increases to \$40 per week while at the same time the price of milk and the price of fruit double relative to their initial level. Mary's budget line will

a. shift to the left when these changes occur.

b. shift to the right when these changes occur.

c. be unaffected by these changes.

11. Sammy's budget constraint for food (F) and entertainment (E) each month is given by the equation $F = 100 - 10E$. Furthermore, you know that the price of entertainment is \$20 per unit of entertainment. The price of food per unit is __________, and the total amount of income each month that Sammy devotes to food and entertainment equals __________.

a. \$2; \$200

b. \$10; \$100

c. \$200; \$2,000

d. \$20; \$200

12. Sammy's budget constraint for food (F) and entertainment (E) each month is given by the equation $F = 100 - 10E$. Furthermore, you know that the price of entertainment is \$20 per unit of entertainment. Which of the following consumption bundles are not feasible for Sammy to consume?

a. 50 units of food and 5 units of entertainment

b. 60 units of food and 4.5 units of entertainment

c. 25 units of food and 7 units of entertainment

d. 20 units of food and 8 units of entertainment

13. Sammy's budget constraint for food (F) and entertainment (E) each month is given by the equation $F = 100 - 10E$. Furthermore, you know that the price of entertainment is \$20 per unit of entertainment. Which of the following consumption bundles lie inside Sammy's budget line?

a. 50 units of food and 5 units of entertainment

b. 60 units of food and 4.5 units of entertainment

c. 25 units of food and 7 units of entertainment

d. 20 units of food and 8 units of entertainment

14. A consumption bundle that lies beyond the individual's budget line is a consumption bundle the individual

a. does not prefer because of their particular tastes and preferences.

b. cannot afford given their income and the prices of the goods.

15. A consumption bundle that lies inside the individual's budget line is a consumption bundle that

a. does not maximize the individual's utility given their tastes, income, and the price of the goods.

b. does not exhaust the individual's income.

c. the individual can afford.

d. Answers (a), (b), and (c) are all true.

Use the following information about Maria's consumption of food and entertainment each month to answer the next four questions. Assume Maria's monthly income for spending on food and entertainment is $400 and that each of the consumption bundles in the table below are on her budget line.

Consumption bundle	Quantity of food in consumption bundle	Total utility from food consumption (utils)	Quantity of entertainment in consumption bundle	Total utility from entertainment consumption (utils)
A	200	280	0	0
B	150	240	25	80
C	100	180	50	110
D	50	100	75	130
E	0	0	100	140

16. Given the above information, the price of each unit of food is ________, and the price of each unit of entertainment is ________.

a. $2; $4

b. $4; $2

c. $2; $1

d. $4; $1

17. Maria maximizes her utility by consuming consumption bundle

a. *A*.

b. *B*.

c. *C*.

d. *D*.

18. Suppose Maria initially chooses consumption bundle *A*. She can increase her total utility by

a. consuming more units of entertainment and fewer units of food.

b. consuming more units of food and fewer units of entertainment.

19. Suppose Maria initially chooses consumption bundle *C*. She can increase her total utility by

a. consuming more units of entertainment and fewer units of food.

b. consuming more units of food and fewer units of entertainment.

20. The marginal decision for the consumer is a question of how

a. much of a good they consume relative to their neighbor's consumption of that good.

b. to allocate an additional dollar in a way to maximize utility.

c. to allocate the entirety of one's income.

21. Jamie currently consumes 4 units of tomatoes and 7 units of bread each week. The price of tomatoes is $2 per unit while the price of bread is $1 per unit. Jamie's marginal utility from the last unit of tomatoes he consumes each week is equal to 10 utils while his marginal utility from the last unit of bread he consumes each week is 6 utils. Jamie should

a. continue to consume the same level of tomatoes and bread each week.

b. consume more bread and less tomatoes, since currently his marginal utility per dollar spent on bread exceeds his marginal utility per dollar spent on tomatoes.

c. consume less bread and more tomatoes, since currently his marginal utility per dollar spent on bread exceeds his marginal utility per dollar spent on tomatoes.

d. consume more bread and less tomatoes, since currently his marginal utility per dollar spent on bread is less than his marginal utility per dollar spent on tomatoes.

22. Martin always maximizes his utility. Martin's consumption of both potatoes and steak exhibit diminishing marginal utility. Suppose the price of steak and the price of potatoes are constant and Martin's income to be spent on steak and potatoes does not change. Holding everything else constant, if Martin increases his consumption of steak

a. he must decrease his consumption of potatoes and his marginal utility per dollar spent on steak must be less than it was initially.

b. he will increase his consumption of potatoes and his marginal utility per dollar spent on steak will be less than it was initially.

23. Which of the following statements best expresses the optimal consumption rule given a consumer's budget constraint?

a. A consumer should consume the maximum amount possible of the relatively cheapest good available to them.

b. A consumer should divide their income evenly among all the possible goods they consume.

c. A consumer will maximize their utility when they specialize.

d. A consumer will maximize their utility when the marginal utilities of the last dollar spent on each and every good or service in their consumption bundle are equal.

24. An increase in the price of good X while holding income and the price of good Y constant will

a. reduce the marginal utility the individual receives from the last unit of good X they consume.

b. increase the marginal utility per dollar spent on good Y.

c. decrease the marginal utility per dollar spent on good X.

d. reduce the individual's tastes and preferences for good X.

ANSWER KEY

Answers to Problems and Exercises

1. **a.** Maria, Ben, and Steve have constant marginal utility with respect to the given levels of hot chocolate. Maria's total utility increases by 80 utils with every additional serving of hot chocolate she consumes; Ben's total utility increases by 50 utils with every additional serving of hot chocolate he consumes; and Steve's total utility increases by 20 utils with every additional serving of hot chocolate he consumes.

   b. Joe's marginal utility decreases with each additional serving of hot chocolate: each additional serving adds less to his total utility than the previous serving.

2. **a.**

Servings of hot chocolate per month	Joe's marginal utility (utils)	Maria's marginal utility (utils)	Ben's marginal utility (utils)	Alexandra's marginal utility (utils)	Steve's marginal utility (utils)
1					
	80	80	50	50	20
2					
	60	80	50	60	20
3					
	40	80	50	70	20
4					
	20	80	50	80	20
5					

   b.

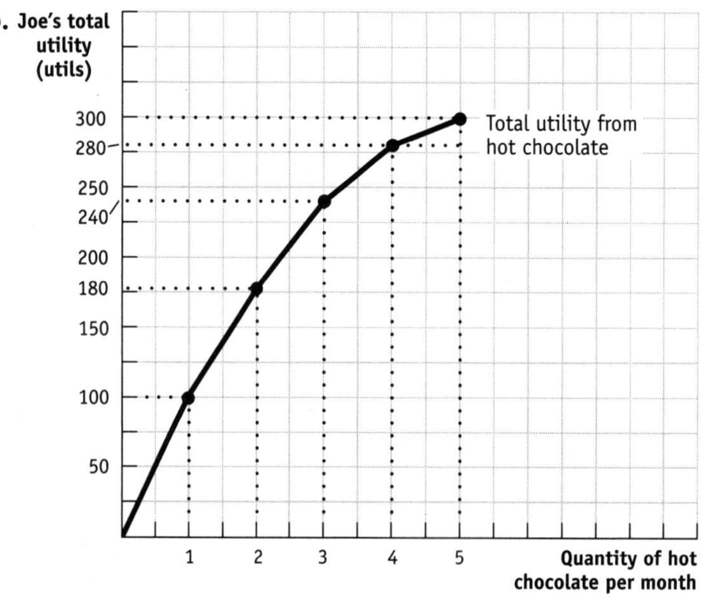

c. 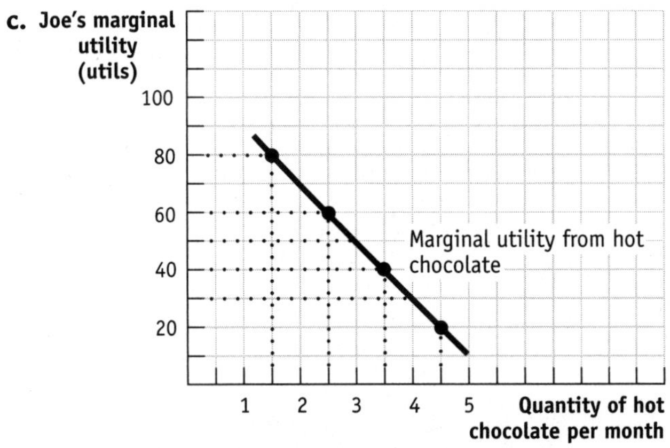

3. Sarah's total utility decreases when she increases her consumption of pizza from three slices to four slices: Sarah is worse off when she consumes four slices of pizza and she should therefore not consume the fourth slice. The marginal utility from consuming the fourth slice of pizza is equal to −20 utils.

4. The marginal utility curve is downward sloping because consumption of each additional unit of the good eventually adds less to total utility than did the consumption of the previous unit of the good. The consumption of most goods and services is subject to diminishing marginal utility.

5. a.

Number of articles read	Marginal utility from reading articles (utils)
1	
	200
2	
	150
3	
	100
4	
	75
5	
	55
6	
	40
7	
	20
8	

b. Carolyn experiences diminishing marginal utility when she reads the third article; although her total utility is increasing, it is now increasing at a diminishing rate.

c. Carolyn is reading too many articles if her reading results in less total utility than she would have if she read fewer articles. According to the data given for this question, it is not possible for Carolyn to reach this point when reading up to eight articles.

6. a.

Consumption bundle	Number of periodicals	Units of entertainment
A	0	10
B	4	8
C	8	6
D	16	2
E	20	0

b.

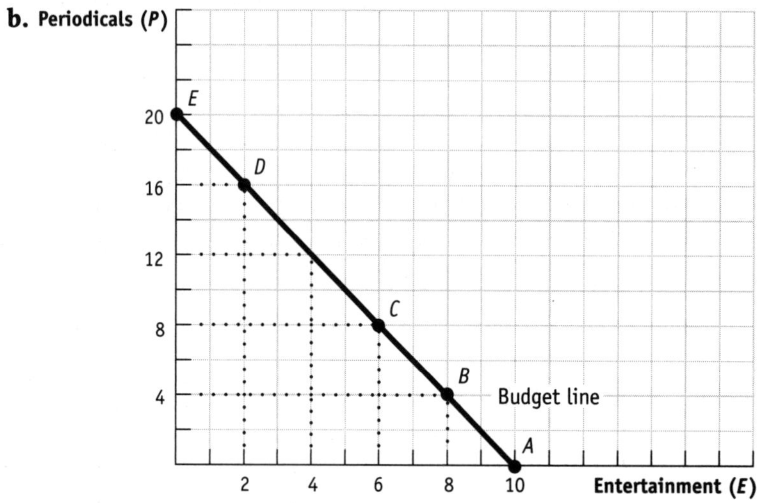

c. Harry will consume 2 fewer units of entertainment (6 units instead of 8 units) and 4 more periodicals (8 periodicals instead of 4 periodicals) when he moves from consumption bundle *B* to consumption bundle *C*. Harry cannot increase his consumption of periodicals without decreasing his consumption of entertainment.

d. Harry will consume 4 more units of entertainment (6 units instead of 2 units) and 8 fewer periodicals (8 periodicals instead of 16 periodicals) when he moves from consumption bundle *D* to consumption bundle *C*. Harry cannot increase his consumption of entertainment without decreasing his consumption of periodicals.

e. $P = 20 - 2E$

7. a.

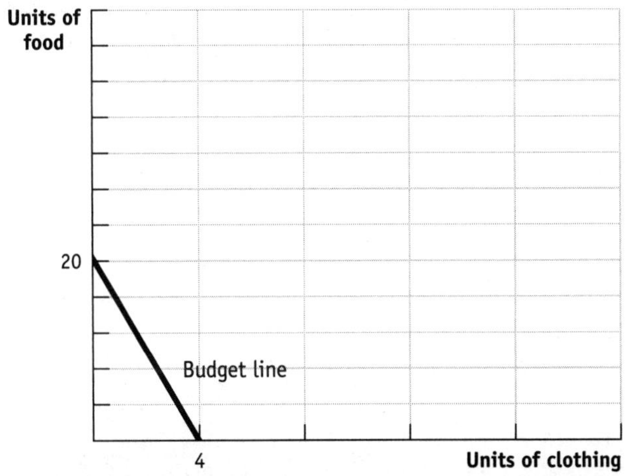

b.

Consumption bundle	On, inside, or beyond the budget line
5 units of food, 3 units of clothing	On the budget line, since 5 units of food and 3 units of clothing cost exactly $40.
4 units of food, 4 units of clothing	Beyond the budget line, since 4 units of food and 4 units of clothing cost $48, which is greater than Katherine's income.
10 units of food, 1 unit of clothing	Inside the budget line, since 10 units of food and 1 unit of clothing cost $30, which is less than Katherine's income.
20 units of food, 2 units of clothing	Beyond the budget line, since 20 units of food and 2 units of clothing cost $60, which is greater than Katherine's income.

c. $F = 20 - 5C$

d.

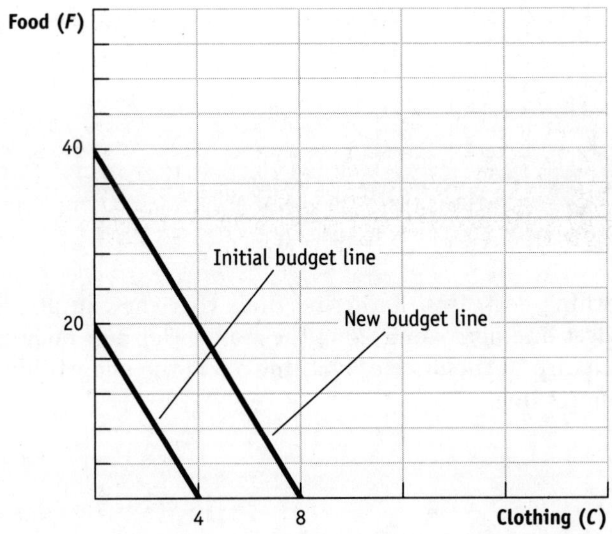

When income increases while prices stay constant, the budget line shifts out parallel to the initial budget line. The equation for the new budget line is $F = 40 - 5C$. The new budget line has a different y-intercept but the same slope as the initial budget line.

e. 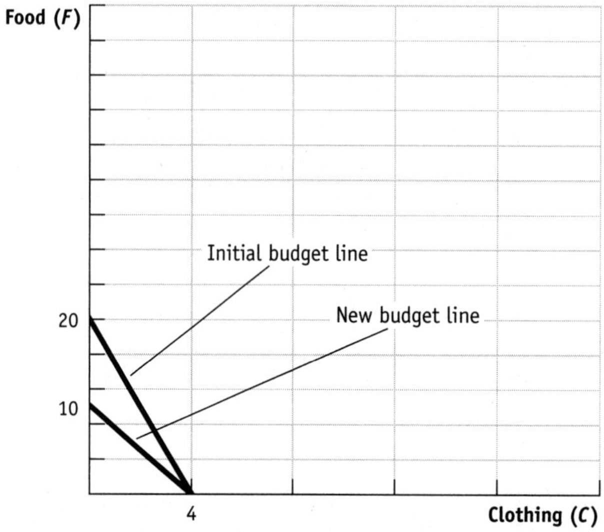

When food gets more expensive, Katherine finds that she cannot afford as much food. Her budget line pivots down along the *y*-axis, reflecting that if she devotes all of her income to food she can now afford only 10 units instead of the original 20 units. Katherine's new budget line is $F = 10 - (5/2)C$. The change in the price of food alters the *y*-intercept and the slope of the budget line relative to the initial budget line.

f. 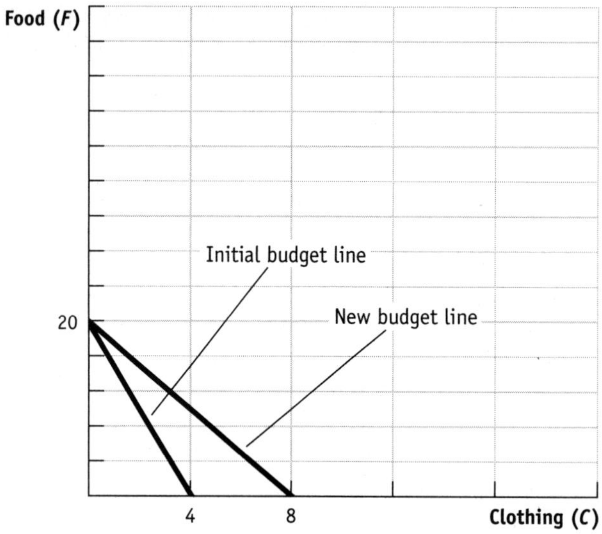

When the price of clothing decreases, Katherine finds that she can afford more of both goods. Her budget line pivots out along the *x*-axis. Her new budget line is $F = 20 - (5/2)C$. The change in the price of clothing alters the budget line's slope relative to the initial budget line.

g.

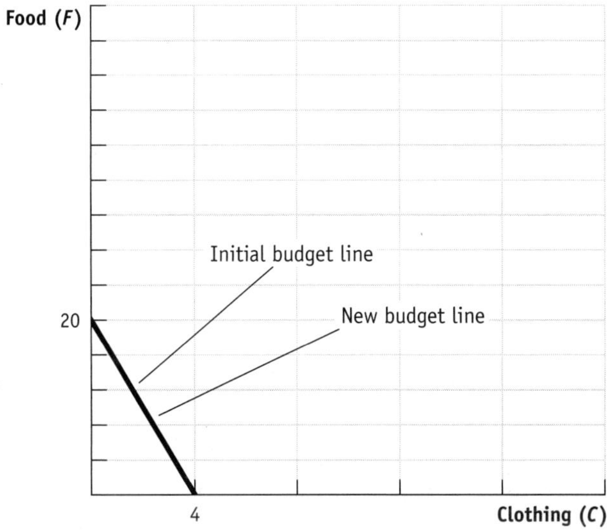

When Katherine's income and the prices of both goods double, this has no effect on her budget line. Her initial budget line can be found as $40 = 2F + 10C$, or $F = 20 - 5C$; her new budget line is equal to $80 = 4F + 20C$, or $F = 20 - 5C$.

8. **a.** With consumption bundle B, Bertram's marginal utility per dollar spent on good X is greater than his marginal utility per dollar spent on good Y ($MU_X/P_X > MU_Y/P_Y$). This cannot be Bertram's optimal consumption bundle since these ratios are not equal to one another: Bertram will want to increase his consumption of good X and decrease his consumption of good Y. This adjustment to his consumption will decrease the value of MU_X/P_X (as the marginal utility from an additional unit of good X falls) and increase the value of MU_Y/P_Y (as the marginal utility from good Y increases when fewer units of good Y are consumed).

b. A decrease in the consumption of good X increases MU_X/P_X due to diminishing marginal utility, which holds that the marginal utility from the consumption of the good decreases as consumption of the good increases; an increase in the consumption of good Y decreases MU_Y/P_Y due to diminishing marginal utility, since the marginal utility from the consumption of additional units of good Y decreases with each additional unit of good Y consumed.

c. Consumption bundle C is the optimal consumption bundle for Bertram since at that bundle the marginal utility per dollar spent on good X is equal to the marginal utility per dollar spent on good Y.

9. **a.**

Consumption bundle	Quantity of ice cream (cones)	Utility from ice cream (utils)	Quantity of hamburgers	Utility from hamburgers (utils)	Total utility (utils)
A	0	0	5	53	53
B	2	38	4	48	86
C	6	84	2	28	112
D	8	92	1	15	107
E	10	95	0	0	95

b.

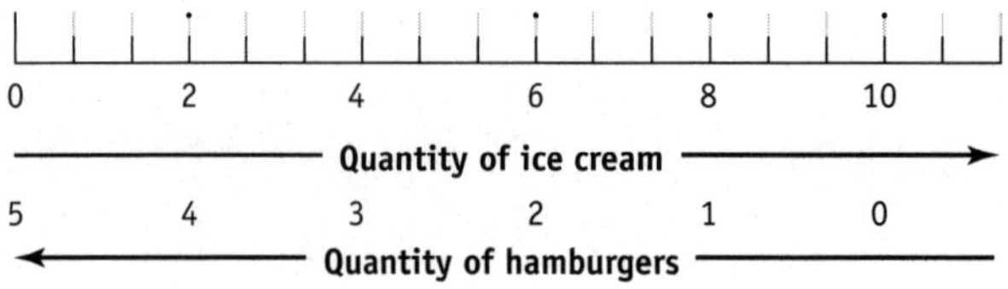

c.

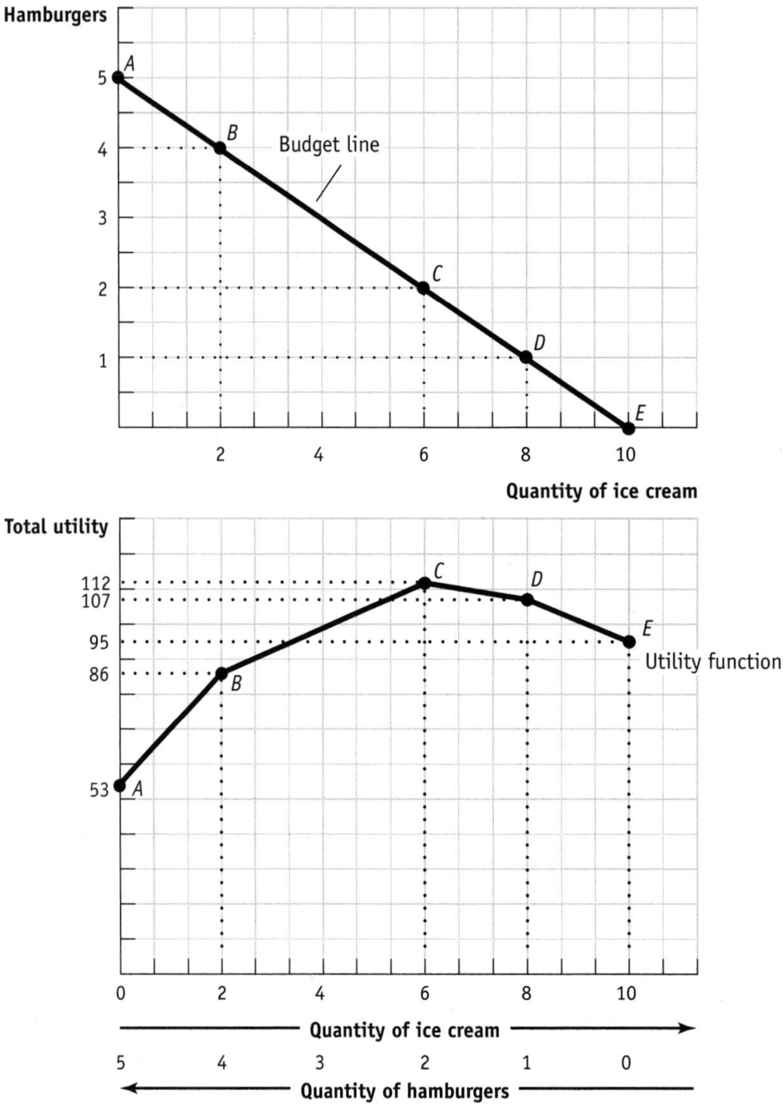

d. Consumption bundle C is the consumption bundle that maximizes Mark's utility given his tastes and preferences, his income, and the prices of the two goods.

e.

Quantity of ice cream (cones)	Utility from ice cream (utils)	MU_{IC} (utils)	MU_{IC}/P_{IC} (utils)	Quantity of hamburgers	Utility from hamburgers	MU_H (utils)	MU_H/P_H (utils)
0	0			0	0		
		20	4			15	1.5
1	20			1	15		
		18	3.6			13	1.3
2	38			2	28		
		15	3			11	1.1
3	53			3	39		
		13	2.6			9	0.9
4	66			4	48		
		11	2.2			5	0.5
5	77			5	53		
		7	1.4				
6	84						
		5	1.0				
7	89						
		3	0.6				
8	92						
		2	0.4				
9	94						
		1	0.2				
10	95						

f.

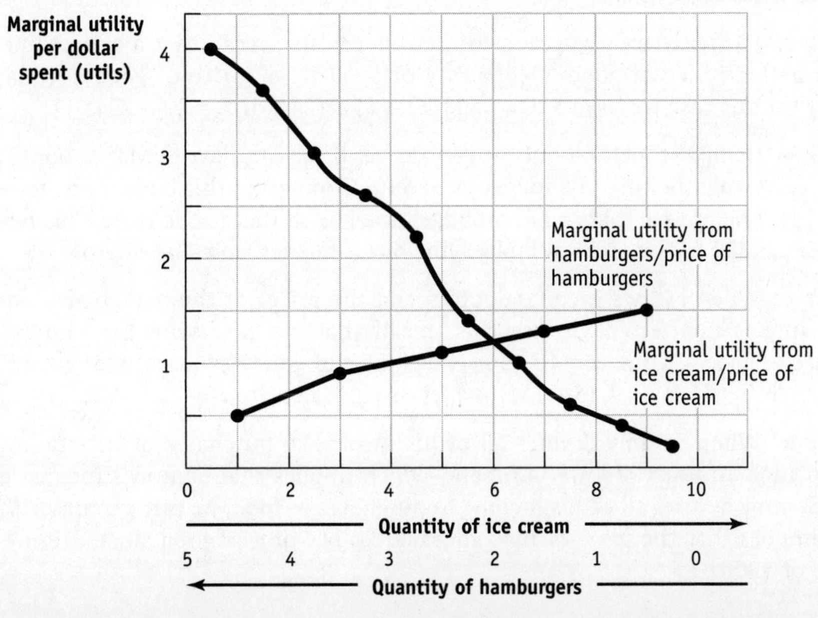

g. The optimal consumption rule states that a consumer maximizes utility in the face of a budget constraint when the marginal utility per dollar spent on each good or service in the consumption bundle is the same. Hence, the marginal utility of ice cream divided by its price (MU_{IC}/P_{IC}) equals the marginal utility of hamburgers divided by its price (MU_H/P_H) at the optimal consumption bundle (bundle C in this example).

Answers to Module Review Questions

1. **Answer c.** This is a definitional statement. Demand and tastes cannot be maximized, and profit maximization is a goal of a firm.

2. **Answer d.** A person's utility depends on the utility they get from each good that they consume. This utility is a measure of the satisfaction that the individual gets from their consumption choices. An individual's consumption choices are dependent on their tastes and preferences.

3. **Answer c.** From the table, we can see that Joe's total utility increases as he consumes more and more slices of pizza. However, Joe's total utility increases by smaller amounts with each additional slice of pizza. Joe's total utility, although increasing, increases at a decreasing rate as his level of pizza consumption increases.

4. **Answer b.** Joe's marginal utility from consuming the fourth slice of pizza is equal to his total utility from consuming four slices of pizza minus his total utility from consuming three slices of pizza. Thus, Joe's marginal utility from the fourth slice of pizza equals 280 utils minus 240 utils, or 40 utils.

5. **Answer a.** Diminishing marginal utility refers to the idea that consumption of additional units of a good increases the consumer's total utility, but at a decreasing rate. Joe's utility from pizza consumption increases with each slice he eats, but each additional slice of pizza adds less to his total utility than the previous slice.

6. **Answer c.** Statement I is a restatement of the concept of diminishing marginal utility. A marginal utility curve that exhibits diminishing marginal utility will be downward sloping over some range of consumption, but marginal utility need not be a negative value, so statement II is false and statement III is true.

7. **Answer a.** Any consumption bundle that costs more than Mary's income will lie beyond her budget line. Because 3 units of fruit and 9 units of milk cost $21, this bundle is greater than Mary's income; and she cannot afford this bundle. Mary can afford the other consumption bundles and they are therefore either on Mary's budget line or they lie inside her budget line.

8. **Answer c.** To find Mary's equation for her budget line, recall that a budget line can be written as I = (price of good X)(quantity of good X) + (price of good Y)(quantity of good Y). In this case we have $\$20 = (\$1)(F) + (\$2)(M)$, or $F = 20 - 2M$.

9. **Answer b.** Using the method outlined in answer 8, we can rewrite Mary's budget line as $F = 40 - 2M$ when her income increases to $40. Comparing this budget line to her original budget line, we see that the new budget line has shifted to the right. This new budget line is parallel to the original budget line but is farther from the origin.

10. **Answer c.** When Mary's income doubles and the prices of the two goods double, her budget line is unaffected. To see this, recall that we can write her budget line as I = (price of good X)(quantity of good X) + (price of good Y)(quantity of good Y), or in this case, $\$40 = (\$2)(F) + (\$4)(M)$, which is equivalent to $F = 20 - 2M$.

11. **Answer a.** When Sammy devotes all of his income to purchases of entertainment, he can consume 10 units of entertainment, which implies that Sammy's income is $200. When Sammy devotes all of his income to purchases of food, he can purchase 100 units, which implies that the price of food must be $2 per unit of food since Sammy has an income of $200.

12. **Answer b.** A consumption bundle for Sammy is not feasible if it costs more than his available income. From question 11 we know that Sammy's income is $200, the price of entertainment is $20, and the price of food is $2. Sixty units of food and 4.5 units of entertainment would cost Sammy $210, and he cannot afford this consumption bundle.

13. **Answer c.** A consumption bundle lies inside the budget line if the cost of the consumption bundle is less than the individual's income. From question 11 we know that Sammy's income is $200, the price of entertainment is $20, and the price of food is $2. Twenty-five units of food and 7 units of entertainment would cost Sammy $190, so he can afford this consumption bundle and still have unused income.

14. **Answer b.** A consumption bundle that lies beyond the individual's budget line may be a consumption bundle that the individual would really like to consume (such as an exotic vacation in a warm place). However, if the individual cannot consume this bundle given their income and the prices of the goods, they simply cannot afford that consumption bundle.

15. **Answer d.** A consumption bundle that lies inside the individual's budget line cannot be maximizing this individual's utility since it is possible for the individual to consume more of either good given their income and the prices they face. This interior point does not use all of the individual's income, so therefore it is affordable.

16. **Answer a.** The price of food is $2 per unit. To see this, when Maria consumes only food she can afford 200 units. Since her income is $400, this implies that the price of food must be $2 per unit. The price of entertainment is $4. To see this, when Maria consumes only entertainment she can afford 100 units. Since her income is $400, this implies that the price of entertainment must be $4 per unit.

17. **Answer b.** To answer this question, you need to calculate the total utility Maria receives from consuming each of the consumption bundles. Bundle *A* yields total utility of 280 utils; bundle *B* has total utility of 320 utils; bundle *C* has total utility of 290 utils; bundle *D* has total utility of 230 utils; and bundle *E* has total utility of 140 utils. Bundle *B* maximizes Maria's utility since it provides the highest level of total utility.

18. **Answer a.** When Maria moves to consumption bundle *B* from consumption bundle *A*, her total utility increases. At consumption bundle *B* Maria consumes more units of entertainment and fewer units of food.

19. **Answer b.** Maria can increase her utility by consuming fewer units of entertainment and more units of food. Increasing her food consumption by 50 units increases her total utility by 60 utils, while decreasing her entertainment consumption by 25 units reduces her total utility by 30 utils, leading her to a net gain in utility of 30 utils.

20. **Answer b.** Consumers decide how to best allocate their income among different goods given the prices of these goods and their individual tastes and preferences. The marginal decision for consumers is essentially a decision about how to best allocate the last dollar spent. If the marginal utility per dollar spent on one good is greater than the marginal utility per dollar spent on another good, then the consumer is best off increasing their consumption of the first good and decreasing their consumption of the second good. This analysis results in the consumer allocating their last dollar in such a way that the marginal utility per dollar spent on every good in their consumption bundle is equal.

21. **Answer b.** Jamie's marginal utility per dollar spent on bread is equal to 6 utils per dollar (6 utils/$1), and his marginal utility per dollar spent on tomatoes is equal to 5 utils per dollar (10 utils/$2). Jamie is better off consuming more bread and fewer tomatoes. As Jamie increases his bread consumption, the marginal utility from the last unit of bread consumed will fall, and as he consumes fewer tomatoes, the marginal utility from the last unit of tomatoes consumed will rise. He will adjust his consumption of these two goods until the marginal utility per dollar spent on either good is equivalent.

22. **Answer a.** Martin's consumption choices are constrained by his income and the prices of the two goods. When Martin decides to consume more steak, he must decrease his potato consumption since he will have less income available for purchasing potatoes. When Martin increases his consumption of steak, this reduces his marginal utility from steak (due to the diminishing marginal utility he gets from consuming greater amounts of steak).

23. **Answer d.** This answer is definitional. The individual does not want to consume the maximum amount of the cheapest good available for many reasons, but a primary reason is that this would not offer the individual any variety in their consumption bundle. The individual does not want to divide their income evenly among the goods available: for instance, the individual does not want to spend the same amount on table salt as they do on housing. Consumer maximization focuses on consumption decisions and not production decisions. Specialization is essentially a production decision.

24. **Answer c.** A change in the price of a good does not affect the individual's marginal utility he receives from the good, but the change in the price of the good does affect the marginal utility per dollar the individual receives. If the price of the good increases, this causes the marginal utility per dollar to decrease, since the denominator of MU/P is now bigger while the numerator is unchanged.

module 21

The Production Function

BEFORE YOU READ THE MODULE

Summary

This module develops the concept of the firm's production function and how the production function relates the level of inputs used by the firm to the level of output the firm produces. The module discusses diminishing marginal returns and the marginal product of labor.

Module Objectives

Objective #1. Firms combine inputs with technology to produce outputs. The production function for a firm describes the maximum amount of output that can be produced from a general level of inputs and technology.

- In the short run, inputs may be fixed or variable. The level of fixed input used by a firm does not change in the short run as the firm's level of output changes. In contrast, the level of variable input used by a firm does change in the short run as the firm's level of output changes.
- In the long run, all inputs are assumed to be variable since in the long run all desired adjustments to input usage are possible.

Objective #2. In the short run, a firm's ability to produce outputs from its variable inputs depends on the level of fixed input it employs. For a given level of fixed input, as the firm hires additional units of the variable input, the firm will find that its output increases. However, the firm will find that as it hires additional units of the variable input, the marginal product (*MP*) of this variable input declines. That is, as additional units of the variable input are hired, total product (*TP*) increases but it eventually increases at a diminishing rate. This principle of diminishing marginal returns is a short-run concept: in the short run, the marginal product of a variable input diminishes as the level of usage of that variable input increases, holding at least one other input fixed.

- The firm's *TP* curve graphically represents the relationship between a firm's total output and the level of variable input it is using, holding all other inputs constant. The slope of the *TP* curve at any particular level of production is equal to the marginal product of the variable input. Due to diminishing marginal returns, the slope of the *TP* curve flattens as more and more units of the variable input are hired.
- The firm's marginal product of labor is equal to the change in output divided by the change in labor. The marginal product of labor measures the addition to total output from hiring an additional unit of labor while holding all other factors of production constant. Once the firm enters the range of output for which diminishing marginal returns holds, the firm's *MP* of labor curve is downward sloping.
- The firm's *TP* and *MP* curves shift up at every level of usage of the variable input when more of the fixed input is used. For instance, suppose a firm's fixed input is capital and its variable input is labor. When the firm increases the level of its capital from its initial level to a new, higher but constant level of capital, the firm will find that every level of labor usage results in an increased level of production relative to the initial situation because the labor now has more capital resources to work with in producing the product. With more of the fixed input available, the marginal product of the variable input at every level of the variable input is now higher than it was initially.

Key Terms

production function the relationship between the quantity of *inputs* a firm uses and the quantity of output it produces.

fixed input an *input* whose quantity is fixed for a length of time and cannot be varied (for example, land).

variable input an *input* whose quantity the firm can vary at any time (for example, labor).

long run the period in which all *inputs* can be varied.

short run the period in which at least one *input* is fixed.

total product curve a graphical representation of the *production function,* showing how the quantity of output depends on the quantity of the *variable input* for a given quantity of the *fixed input.*

marginal product the additional quantity of output produced by using one more unit of a given *input.*

diminishing returns to an input the effect observed when an increase in the quantity of an *input,* while holding the levels of all other inputs fixed, leads to a decline in the *marginal product* of that input.

Notes

AFTER YOU READ THE MODULE

Tips

Tip #1. The most important tip for this module is to learn the new terminology, the abbreviations for this terminology, the graphical representations of these new terms, and how to apply these new terms. Students tend to struggle with these terms and abbreviations because there are so many of them, but understanding the material requires that you become comfortable with all the new vocabulary.

Tip #2. This module continues to develop the general concept of *marginal.* In the module, the marginal product of an input is introduced. The marginal product of an input looks at the addition to total production when an additional unit of the input is employed. The marginal concept is a critically important concept for you to understand and be able to use.

Tip #3. It is important that you understand the distinction between the short run and the long run. In the short run at least one input is fixed, while in the long run all inputs are variable. An input is fixed if its level of usage does not change even when the level of production increases. An input is variable when its level of usage varies as the level of production varies. There is no set period that determines the boundary between the short run and the long run: the short run is a period so short that full adjustment to changes cannot take place, while the long run is a period sufficiently long enough to allow full adjustment.

WORKED PROBLEMS

1. The following table gives the production function information for Rosie's Gadget Factory, where labor is the variable input and capital is the fixed input.

Quantity of labor	Quantity of output
0	0
1	20
2	38
3	53
4	65
5	70

In a graph, depict this firm's total product curve. How does this total product curve illustrate the idea of diminishing returns to an input? Calculate the marginal product of labor at Rosie's Gadget Factory. How do the numbers you calculated for the marginal product of labor illustrate diminishing returns to labor? Draw a graph of the firm's marginal product of labor curve.

STEP 1: Start by drawing a graph of the total product curve for Rosie's Gadget Factory. In this graph, measure labor along the *x*-axis and output along the *y*-axis.

STEP 2: Describe what happens to the slope of the production function as more and more units of labor are employed.

As labor increases, if output increases but at a diminishing rate, this indicates that the production function illustrates diminishing returns to labor: as more and more units of labor are employed, output increases but each successive unit of labor is less productive than the preceding unit of labor. For Rosie's Gadget Factory, we see that output is increasing, but it is increasing at a diminishing rate.

STEP 3: Calculate the firm's marginal product of labor.

The firm's marginal product of labor is equal to the (change in total product)/(the change in labor). The following table gives the firm's marginal product of labor.

Quantity of labor	Quantity of output	Marginal product of labor
0	0	
		20
1	20	
		18
2	38	
		15
3	53	
		12
4	65	
		5
5	70	

As the amount of labor increases, output increases, but the increase in output diminishes as more and more units of labor are employed: Rosie's Gadget Factory exhibits diminishing returns to labor.

STEP 4: **Draw a graph of the firm's marginal product of labor, where labor is measured on the horizontal axis and the marginal product of labor (gadgets per worker) is measured on the vertical axis.**

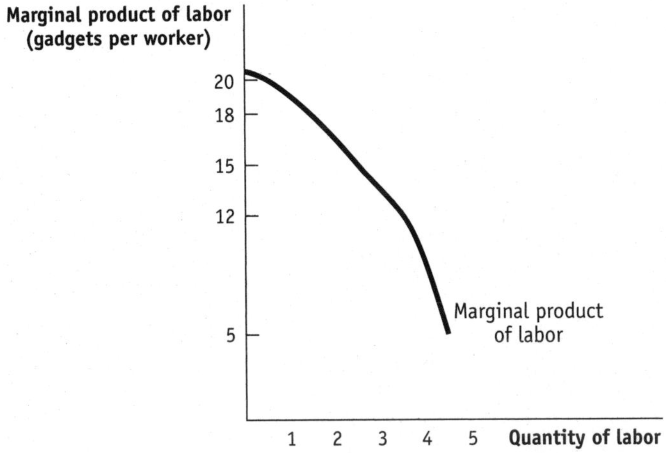

2. Otto's Computers is considering expanding its capital stock. Engineers working for the company have estimated the company's aggregate production function for two levels of capital and have provided the company management with the following table of information, where *L* is units of labor, K_1 is the first level of capital, K_2 is the second, higher level of capital, Q_1 is the quantity of output that Otto's Computers can produce using K_1, and Q_2 is the quantity of output that Otto's Computers can produce using K_2.

L	K_1	Q_1		K_2	Q_2
0	4	0		9	0
1	4	4		9	6
4	4	8		9	12
9	4	12		9	18
16	4	16		9	24
25	4	20		9	30

Provide Otto's Computers with two graphs: one depicting both its total product curve when it employs K_1 units of capital and its total product curve when it employs K_2 units of capital, and the second depicting its marginal product of labor curves for the two different levels of capital. Provide a statement about what happens to labor productivity when Otto's Computers changes its level of capital from K_1 to K_2.

STEP 1: **From the table, it is relatively easy to construct a graph representing the total product curves for the two different levels of capital that Otto's Computers is considering.**

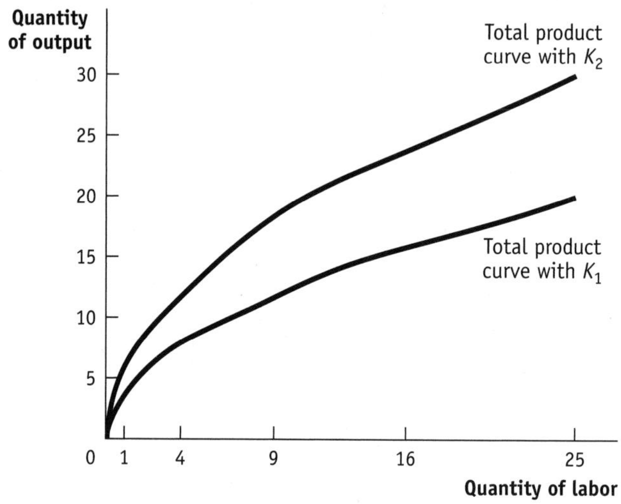

When Otto's Computers uses more capital with a given level of labor, it can produce a higher level of output. This is illustrated by the shifting up of the total product curve when capital is increased.

STEP 2: **Depicting the firm's marginal product of labor curves for the two levels of capital is a bit more work since you must first find the values of the marginal product of labor.**

It is important to realize that because labor is not increasing by one unit at a time the calculation of the firm's marginal product of labor will be more complicated. For example, when the firm uses K_1 units of capital and increases its labor usage from 1 to 4 units, the change in output is 4 units, while the change in labor is 3 units. Thus, the firm's marginal product of labor between these two levels of labor usage will be equal to 4/3, or 1.33. The following table summarizes the marginal product of labor for the two different levels of capital.

For K_1:

L	Q_1	MPL_1
0	0	
		4/1
1	4	
		4/3
4	8	
		4/5
9	12	
		4/7
16	16	
		4/9
25	20	

For K_2:

L	Q_2	MPL_2
0	0	
		6/1
1	6	
		6/3
4	12	
		6/5
9	18	
		6/7
16	24	
		6/9
25	30	

Inspection of this table of values indicates that at any given level of labor, the marginal product of labor is greater when the firm uses K_2 units of capital than when it uses K_1 units of capital. In addition, the value of the marginal product of labor gets smaller and smaller as the level of labor usage increases.

STEP 3: Graph the firm's marginal product of labor curves for each level of capital usage.

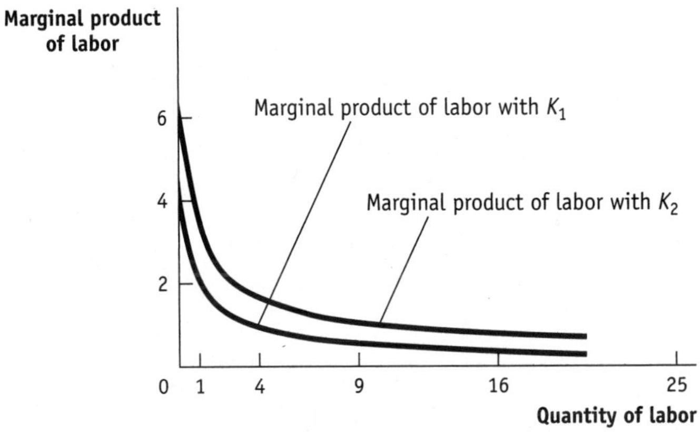

STEP 4: Assess what happens to labor productivity when Otto's Computers uses a larger amount of labor.

When Otto's Computers uses the larger amount of capital, K_2, its total product curve shifts up, as does its marginal product of labor curve. At each level of labor usage, labor is more productive.

Problems and Exercises

1. The following table describes the short-run production function for Harry's company. Harry uses labor and capital to produce can openers.

Quantity of labor (workers)	Quantity of capital (units)	Quantity of output (can openers)
0	10	0
1	10	50
2	10	80
3	10	100
4	10	115
5	10	125
6	10	133
7	10	138

a. How do you know the above table represents Harry's short-run production function? How is the short run different from the long run?

b. Economists make a distinction between variable inputs and fixed inputs. For the above short-run production function, which input is the fixed input and which one is the variable input? Explain your answer.

c. Draw Harry's total product curve for the production of can openers, holding the level of capital constant. In your graph measure the quantity of labor on the x-axis and the quantity of can openers on the y-axis.

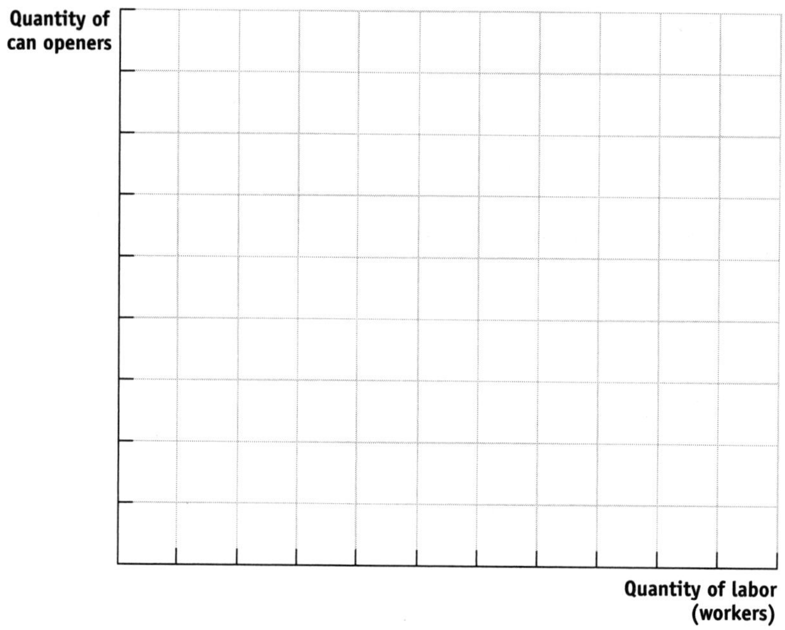

d. Complete the following table using the information given above and assuming that capital is held constant at 10 units.

Quantity of labor (workers)	Quantity of output (can openers)	Marginal product of labor $MPL = \Delta Q/\Delta L$ (can openers per worker)
0	0	
		50
1	50	
2	80	
3	100	
4	115	
5	125	
6	133	
7	138	

e. Describe the results you found in part (d). What is the relationship between the quantity of labor used and the marginal product of labor at Harry's can opener factory?

f. Graph Harry's marginal product of labor on a graph with the quantity of labor measured on the *x*-axis and the marginal product of labor measured on the *y*-axis. Plot the marginal product values you found in part (d) using the midpoint method. For example, the marginal product of labor from hiring the first unit of labor is equal to 50 can openers per worker: plot this information midway between 0 and 1 unit of labor.

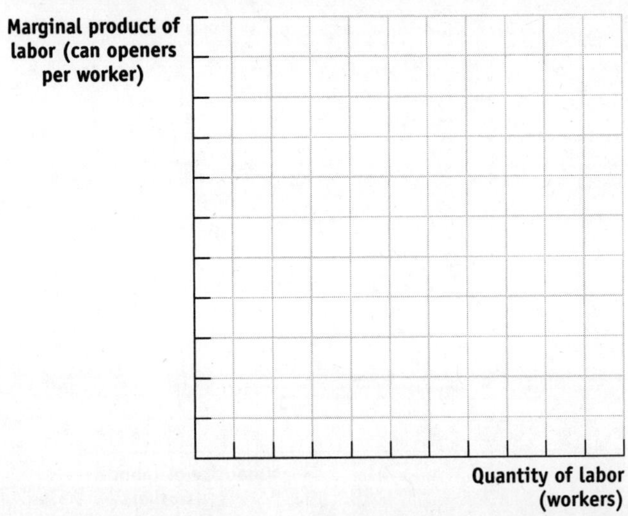

g. What does it mean if the marginal product of labor curve is downward sloping as you hire more units of the variable input?

2. Harry (from problem 1) decides to hire an additional 10 units of capital so that his capital is now fixed at 20 units. He finds that this additional capital doubles his production at every level of labor.

a. Complete the table below, which describes Harry's production function based on his using 20 units of capital.

Quantity of labor (workers)	Quantity of capital (units)	Quantity of output (can openers)
0	20	0
1	20	
2	20	
3	20	
4	20	
5	20	
6	20	
7	20	

b. Draw a graph showing Harry's original production function using 10 units of capital and his new production function using 20 units of capital. Measure total product along the *y*-axis and the quantity of labor along the *x*-axis. Describe the effect of this change in Harry's total product curve.

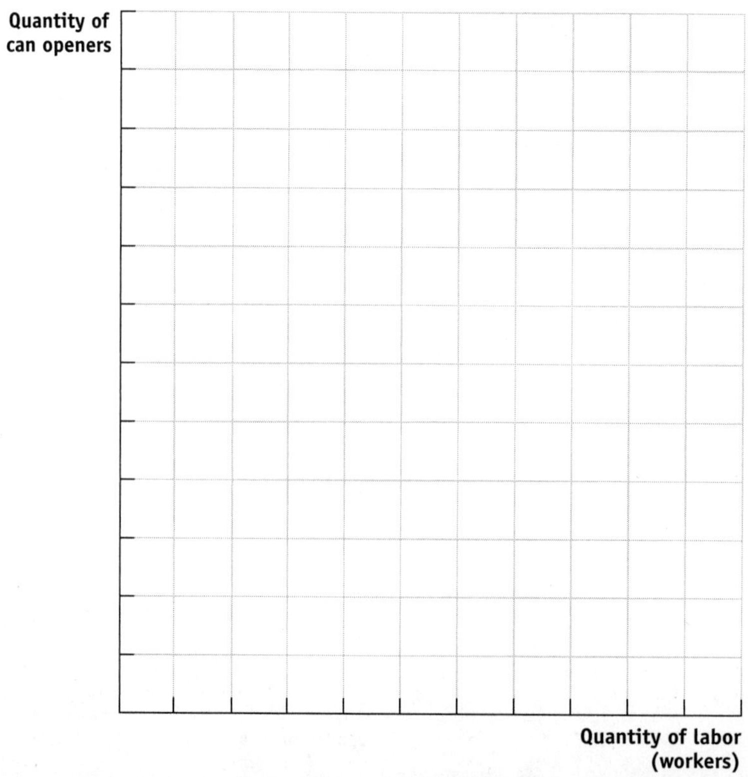

c. What happens to the marginal product of labor when Harry increases his use of capital? Provide an intuitive explanation for your answer. In your answer, sketch a graph of the original marginal product of labor curve based on 10 units of capital and the new marginal product of labor curve based on 20 units of capital.

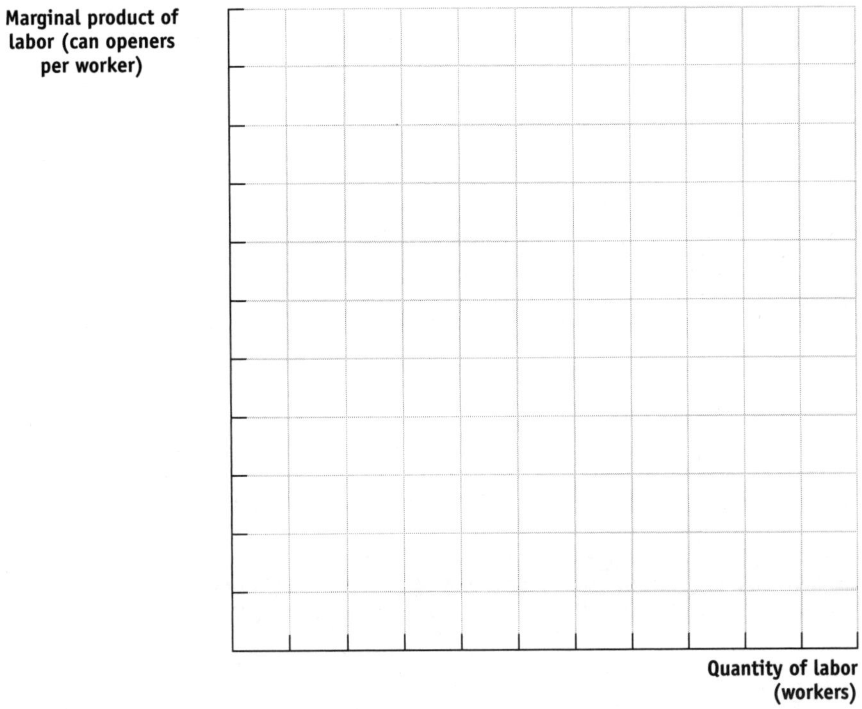

3. In the short run, it is assumed that at least one of a firm's inputs is fixed and cannot be changed. Explain why this assumption is critical for understanding diminishing marginal returns to the variable input.

4. Malthus predicted that as population grew, the economy's diminishing ability to produce food from a given set of resources would necessarily lead to insufficient food. However, population continues to grow and so does food production. What aspect of food production did Malthus fail to anticipate?

BEFORE YOU TAKE THE TEST

Module Review Questions

1. The process of transforming inputs into output is described by the firm's
a. cost function.
b. revenue function.
c. production function.
d. marginal product of labor.

2. A firm's ability to produce output depends on
a. its profitability.
b. the level of inputs it uses.
c. its stock price.
d. its location.

Use the information below about Paul's production function to answer the next five questions. Paul is a surgeon who also maintains an avid interest in economics.

Quantity of labor (hours in surgery)	Quantity of capital (operating rooms)	Total product (number of surgeries)
30	0	0
30	1	15
30	2	25
30	3	32
30	4	35

3. The information in the above table about Paul's production function depicts Paul's
a. short-run production function.
b. long-run production function.

4. The fixed input in Paul's production function for surgeries is the quantity of
a. labor. b. capital.

5. The variable input in Paul's production function for surgeries is the quantity of
a. labor. b. capital.

6. Paul's marginal product of capital from hiring a third operating room is
a. 32 surgeries.
b. 25 surgeries.
c. 7 surgeries per operating room.
d. 3 surgeries per operating room.

7. Paul's production function exhibits diminishing returns to capital because
a. output increases at a diminishing rate as additional units of capital are hired.
b. Paul cannot perform competently with more than one operating room.
c. capital, in the form of operating rooms, is highly expensive.
d. output does not increase at a constant rate as additional units of capital are hired.

Use the following table about the production function for Terry's Widget Shoppe to answer the next three questions. Assume labor is the only variable input Terry uses in the production of widgets.

Quantity of labor hired (workers)	Quantity of widgets per month
0	0
1	100
2	250
3	450
4	600
5	700

8. The marginal product of labor from hiring the third worker is
a. 450 widgets per worker.
b. 200 widgets per worker.
c. 150 widgets per worker.
d. 250 widgets per worker.

9. Diminishing returns to labor begins when Terry hires the
a. second worker.
b. third worker.
c. fourth worker.
d. fifth worker.

10. In the short run, as the level of total production for a firm increases, the firm's total product curve
a. increases but at a decreasing rate.
b. increases but at an increasing rate.
c. decreases but at a decreasing rate.
d. decreases but at an increasing rate.

Use the information below about the production function for Caroline's Ceramics to answer the following question.

Quantity of variable input (units)	Quantity of output (ceramic vases)
0	0
2	100
4	250
6	500
8	700
10	800

11. Caroline's Ceramics' production experiences diminishing returns to labor when Caroline hires

a. the second unit of labor.

b. the fourth unit of labor.

c. the sixth unit of labor.

d. the eighth unit of labor.

ANSWER KEY

Answers to Problems and Exercises

1. **a.** In the short run, at least one input is fixed and does not vary as the level of output varies. From the table, we can see that the level of capital remains constant at 10 units as output increases from 0 units to 138 units. In the long run, all inputs are variable.

b. The fixed input is the input that is held constant as output changes: in this example, it is the capital input. The variable input is labor since the level of labor used changes as the level of production changes.

c.

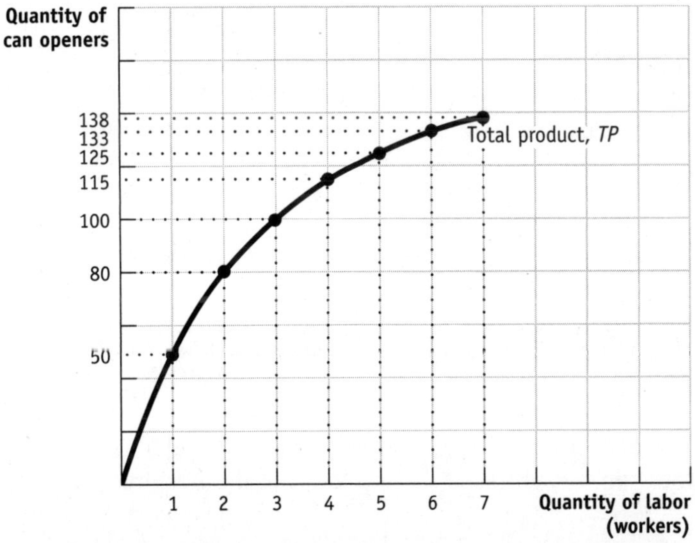

d.

Quantity of labor (workers)	Quantity of output (can openers)	Marginal product of labor $MPL = \Delta Q/\Delta L$ (can openers per worker)
0	0	
		50
1	50	
		30
2	80	
		20
3	100	
		15
4	115	
		10
5	125	
		8
6	133	
		5
7	138	

e. As Harry uses more labor, his total production of can openers increases, but it increases at a diminishing rate. The marginal product of labor describes the addition to total product from hiring an additional worker: for Harry each additional worker adds to the total production of can openers, but each additional worker adds less to total production than did the previous worker.

f.

g. When the *MP* of labor curve is downward sloping as you hire additional units of labor, this implies that the production function is subject to diminishing marginal returns to labor.

2. a.

Quantity of labor (workers)	Quantity of capital (units)	Quantity of output (can openers)
0	20	0
1	20	100
2	20	160
3	20	200
4	20	230
5	20	250
6	20	266
7	20	276

b.

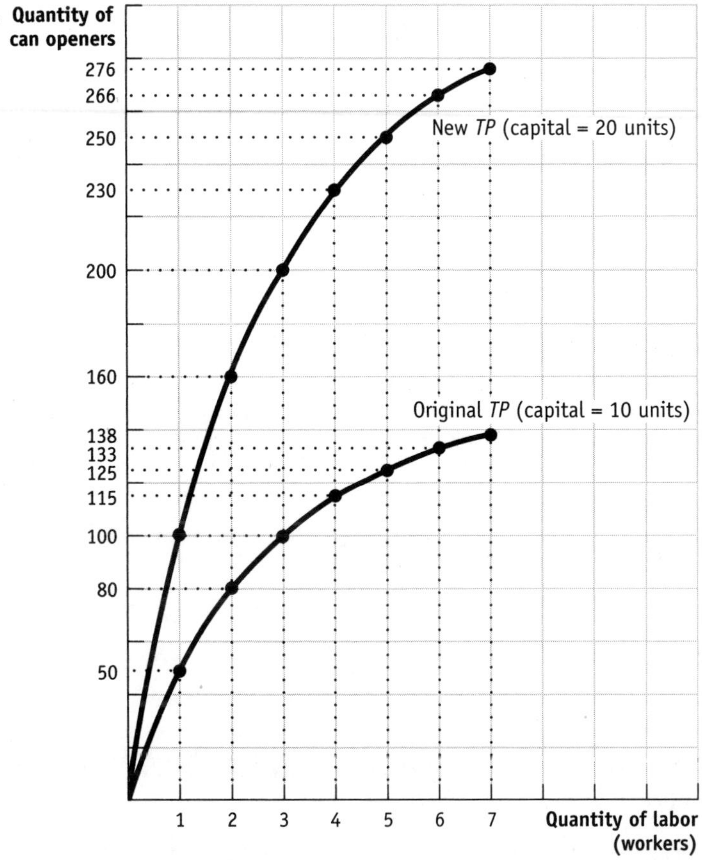

An increase in the level of capital causes Harry's total product curve to shift up; at every level of labor used, Harry can now produce a greater amount of output.

c. At every level of labor usage, Harry's marginal product of labor is higher. Each unit of labor now has more capital to work with, which enables each worker to be more productive. Each additional worker can now produce more can openers than was possible with the original level of capital. The graph below illustrates the two *MP* of labor curves based on the different levels of capital.

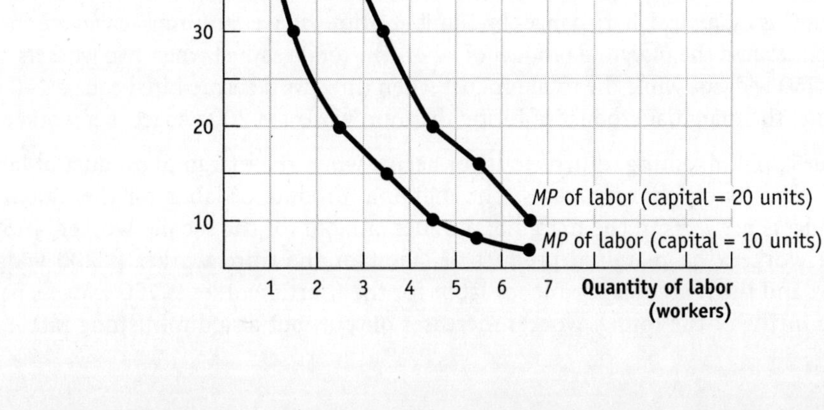

3. In the short run with at least one input fixed, a firm finds that it can expand its level of production only by hiring additional units of the variable input. But as the firm hires additional units of the variable input, each unit of the variable input has less of the fixed input to work with since the fixed input must be shared. Eventually, the addition to total product produced by the variable input increases at a decreasing rate as more units of the variable input are used. There is no reason to expect diminishing marginal returns if all the inputs can be varied: a firm that can adjust the level of all of its inputs (the long-run situation) may have increasing, decreasing, or constant returns to scale.

4. Malthus did not anticipate the scientific and technological progress in food production that occurred over the past two hundred years. The concept of diminishing marginal returns does not hold in this situation: it is possible, even if the amount of farmland cultivated is unchanged and the amount of labor involved in agricultural production is also unchanged, for production to increase when the available technology improves.

Answers to Module Review Questions

1. **Answer c.** This is a definitional statement. Inputs are combined together to produce output, and the production function describes this relationship.

2. **Answer b.** A firm's ability to produce output depends on the level of inputs it uses: this is a definitional statement.

3. **Answer a.** Since one of the inputs is fixed (the quantity of labor), a short-run production function is implied.

4. **Answer a.** The fixed input is the input that does not change in the short run as the level of output changes. Looking at the given table, the quantity of labor is fixed or constant while the quantity of capital varies.

5. **Answer b.** The variable input is the input that varies as the level of output changes. Looking at the given table, the quantity of capital varies.

6. **Answer c.** The marginal product of capital is defined as the change in total output divided by the change in capital, holding all other inputs constant. When Paul increases his number of operating rooms from two to three, his output of surgeries increases from 25 surgeries to 32 surgeries. Paul's marginal product of capital is thus 7 surgeries per operating room.

7. **Answer a.** Diminishing returns to capital occurs when total product increases at a decreasing rate as additional units of capital are hired. Diminishing marginal returns to capital implies that the marginal product of capital declines in value as additional units of capital are hired. Answer (b) is not necessarily correct: Paul finds his 30 hours of labor are more productive when spread across several operating rooms instead of a single operating room. The diminishing marginal returns to capital is due to technology and not the cost of capital—answer (c). Answer (d) is false by virtue of the definition of diminishing marginal returns.

8. **Answer b.** The marginal product of labor is the change in output divided by the change in labor. In this example, labor changes by 1 unit at a time, so we can simply calculate the change in output to find the marginal product of labor. The total product when two workers are hired equals 250 widgets, while the total product when three workers are hired equals 450 widgets; therefore, the marginal product of hiring the third worker is 200 widgets per worker.

9. **Answer c.** Diminishing returns to labor begins when the marginal product of labor falls as the quantity of labor increases. The marginal product of labor for the first worker is 100 widgets per worker; the marginal product of labor for the second worker is 150 widgets per worker; the marginal product of labor for the third worker is 200 widgets per worker; and the marginal product of labor for the fourth worker is 150 widgets per worker. The hiring of the fourth worker increases output, but at a diminishing rate.

10. **Answer a.** In the short run, the firm has at least one fixed input. To increase its production, it must hire additional units of the variable input, but the addition to total output from hiring an additional unit of the variable input eventually decreases due to the diminishing returns to the variable input. This means that output increases, but at a decreasing rate.

11. **Answer d.** To answer this question, first calculate the marginal product of labor. Recall that the marginal product of labor is the change in total product divided by the change in labor. In this example, labor increases by 2 units at a time, so the change in labor is 2 units of labor. The marginal product of labor of hiring the second unit of labor is thus (100 units of output)/(2 units of labor), or 50 units of output per unit of labor. Once you have calculated the marginal product of labor for each level of labor in the table, you can then determine at what level of labor the marginal product first declines.

module 22

Firm Costs

BEFORE YOU READ THE MODULE

Summary

This module develops different measures of a firm's costs including the firm's total cost of production, average cost of production, and marginal cost of production. The module analyzes how a firm's costs generate its marginal cost curves as well as its average cost curves.

Module Objectives

Objective #1. Producers must make a production decision about how much output they should produce. Producers are assumed to select the level of output that will result in the maximization of their economic profits.

Objective #2. A firm can construct its cost curves if it combines the information from its production function with information about the prices of inputs. The production function connects the level of input usage to the maximum level of output production possible from these inputs, while input prices allow the firm to then calculate the cost of producing that level of output.

Objective #3. The short-run costs for a firm include the following:

- Fixed cost (*FC*) is the cost of hiring the fixed input. To calculate the fixed cost, multiply the number of units of the fixed input that the firm is using by the price of a unit of the fixed input. In the short run fixed cost does not vary as the level of output varies.
- Variable cost (*VC*) is the cost of hiring the variable input. To calculate the variable cost, multiply the number of units of the variable input that the firm is using by the price of a unit of the variable input. Variable cost varies as the level of output varies: the higher the level of output, holding everything else constant, the greater the use of the variable input and, hence, the greater the variable cost.
- Total cost (*TC*) in the short run is equal to the sum of the fixed cost plus the variable cost: thus, $TC = FC + VC$.

Objective #4. A firm's total cost depends on the level of output it produces. In the short run, higher levels of output are only possible if more units of the variable input are hired. Further, as additional units of the variable input are hired, the marginal product of the variable input declines (recall the principle of diminishing marginal returns): this implies that as output increases, the variable cost of production rises, as does the total cost of production. Thus, the *TC* curve is upward sloping, and in addition, the *TC* curve gets steeper as the firm's level of output increases due to the diminishing marginal returns to the variable input.

Objective #5. Marginal cost (*MC*) is the addition to total cost from producing one more unit of output. Marginal cost is the slope of the *TC* curve. As output increases, the *MC* curve is initially downward sloping, but eventually at higher levels of output the *MC* curve becomes upward sloping due to diminishing returns. Figure 22.1 illustrates this idea: *MC* decreases as output increases from 0 units to Q_1 units, and then *MC* increases as output increases beyond level Q_1. In the downward-sloping portion of the *MC* curve, the cost of an additional unit of output is falling due to specialization. The firm, in this range of output, experiences increasing returns to scale since its cost of additional output falls.

Figure 22.1

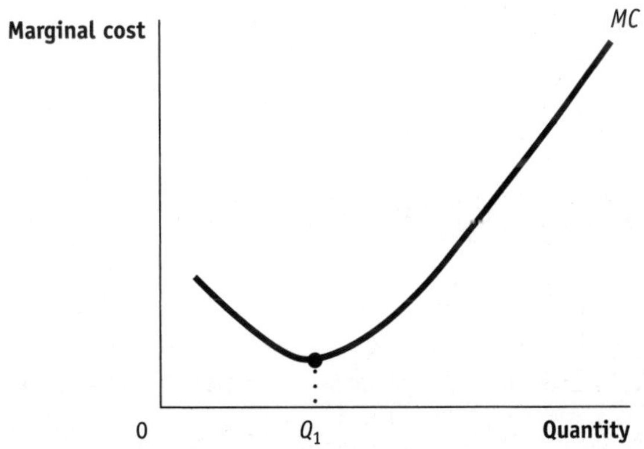

Objective #6. Average total cost (*ATC*) provides a measure of the cost per unit of output. This measure can be calculated by dividing total cost by the level of output ($ATC = TC/Q$). Average variable cost (*AVC*) is variable cost divided by output ($AVC = VC/Q$). Average fixed cost (*AFC*) is fixed cost divided by output ($AFC = FC/Q$).

- Average total cost is equal to the sum of average variable cost plus average fixed cost. To see this, recall that $TC = VC + FC$. If both sides of this equation are divided by quantity (Q), then $ATC = AVC + AFC$.
- Average total cost provides a measure of the cost per unit of production while marginal cost provides a measure of the cost of producing an additional unit of output.
- The *ATC* and *AVC* curves are U-shaped, and their minimum points intersect the firm's *MC* curve. When *ATC* is decreasing as output increases, this implies that the marginal cost is less than the average total cost: producing an additional unit of output costs less than the current cost per unit, and thus the cost per unit must decrease if that additional unit of output is produced. When *ATC* is increasing as output increases, this implies that the marginal cost is greater than the average total cost: producing an additional unit of output costs more than the current cost per unit, and thus the cost per unit must increase if that additional unit of output is produced. When *ATC* equals *MC*, this implies that the cost of producing an additional unit of output equals the current cost per unit, and thus the cost per unit will not change if that additional unit of output is produced. Figure 22.2 illustrates these relationships.
- Since fixed cost does not vary in the short run for a firm, the *AFC* must decrease as output increases. Figure 22.2 illustrates these relationships.

Figure 22.2

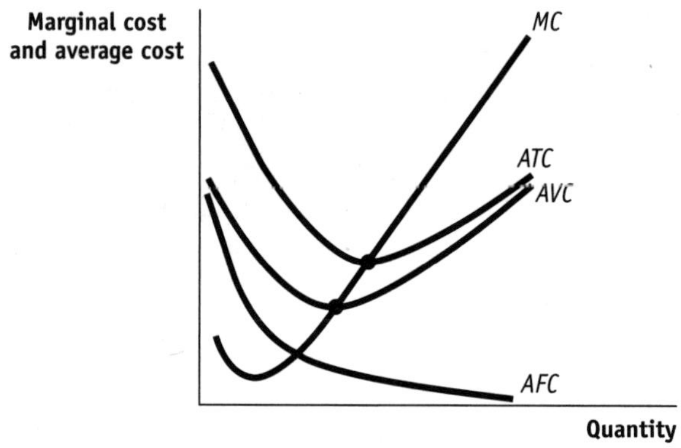

Objective #7. As the firm increases its level of production, this results in two effects on the firm's costs. The diminishing returns effect refers to the increase in the variable cost per unit (the average variable cost) of producing a higher level of output due to the diminishing returns to the variable input that the firm experiences as it increases its level of production. The spreading effect refers to the decrease in the fixed cost per unit (the average fixed cost) of producing a higher level of output due to the spreading of the fixed cost of production over more units of output. At low levels of output, the spreading effect is stronger than the diminishing returns effect, and this causes the *ATC* to decrease as the level of output increases. At higher levels of output, the diminishing returns effect is stronger than the spreading effect, and this causes the *ATC* to increase as the level of output increases. When the spreading effect exactly offsets the diminishing returns effect, the *ATC* curve is at its minimum point.

Objective #8. The minimum-cost output is the level of output at which average total cost is minimized. At this output level, the average total cost is equal to marginal cost. At output levels lower than this minimum-cost output, the marginal cost of producing an additional unit of output is less than the average total cost. At output levels greater than this minimum-cost output, the marginal cost of producing an additional unit of output is greater than the average total cost. Figure 22.3 illustrates this concept: Q_1 is the minimum-cost output; as output increases from 0 units to Q_1, *ATC* declines, and as output increases beyond Q_1 units, *ATC* increases.

Figure 22.3

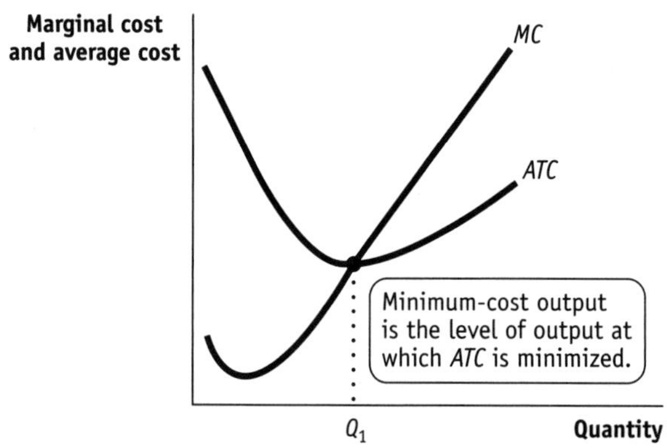

Key Terms

Notes

fixed cost a cost that does not depend on the quantity of output produced; the cost of a *fixed input*.

variable cost a cost that depends on the quantity of output produced; the cost of a *variable input*.

total cost the sum of the *fixed cost* and the *variable cost* of producing a given quantity of output.

total cost curve a graphical representation of the *total cost*, showing how total cost depends on the quantity of output.

average total cost *total cost* divided by quantity of output produced. Also referred to as *average cost*.

average cost an alternative term for *average total cost*; the *total cost* divided by the quantity of output produced.

U-shaped average total cost curve a distinctive graphical representation of the relationship between output and *average total cost*; the average total cost curve at first falls when output is low and then rises as output increases.

average fixed cost the *fixed cost* per unit of output.

average variable cost the *variable cost* per unit of output.

minimum-cost output the quantity of output at which the *average total cost* is lowest—the bottom of the *U-shaped average total cost curve*.

AFTER YOU READ THE MODULE

Tips

Tip #1. The most important tip for this module is to learn the new terminology, the abbreviations for this terminology, the graphical representations of these new terms, and how to apply these new terms. Students tend to struggle with these terms and abbreviations because there are so many of them, but understanding the material requires that you become comfortable with all the new vocabulary.

Tip #2. After you have learned the definitions of total cost, variable cost, fixed cost, average total cost, average variable cost, average fixed cost, and marginal cost, and their abbreviations, you should concentrate on learning how these terms are related to one another. Here is a summary of these relationships:

$$TC = FC + VC$$

$$ATC = TC/Q$$

$$AVC = VC/Q$$

$$AFC = FC/Q$$

$$ATC = AFC + AVC$$

$$MC = (\text{the change in } TC)/(\text{the change in } Q)$$

Think about these relationships and their implications. For example, if you know *TC* and *FC*, you can calculate *VC*; or, if you know *AVC* and *ATC*, you can calculate *AFC*.

Tip #3. Once you have learned the definitions and the abbreviations of all the new terms in the module, you should work on a thorough understanding of the graphs, particularly the graphs of *ATC*, *AVC*, *AFC*, and *MC*.

- The graph of *AFC* is a curve that decreases as output increases because the level of *FC* is constant in the short run, and as output increases, this implies that *AFC* must decline ($AFC = FC/Q$, and as Q gets larger and *FC* stays constant, this means that *AFC* must get smaller). On a graph of the *AFC* curve, the fixed cost for a particular level of production can be represented as the area under the curve. Figure 22.4 illustrates the *AFC* for Q_1 units of output as well as the fixed cost for this level of output.

Figure 22.4

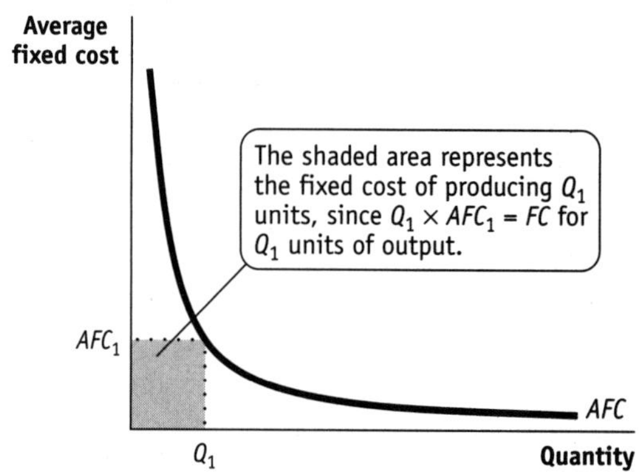

- The *AVC* curve is a U-shaped curve due to diminishing marginal returns to the variable input. Figure 22.5 represents the *AVC* curve and indicates the area that corresponds to the variable cost of producing Q_1 units of the good.

Figure 22.5

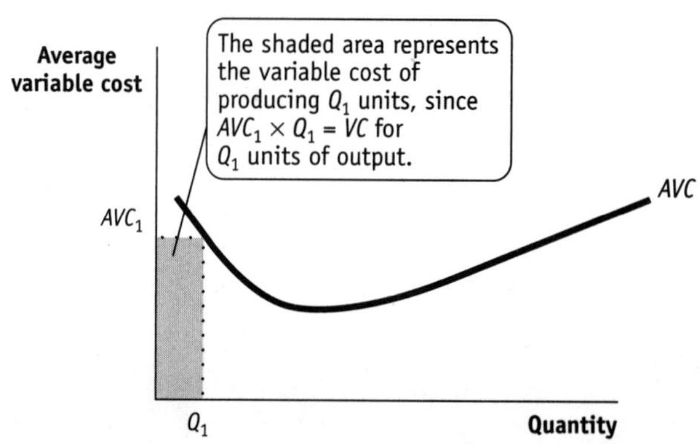

- The *ATC* curve is also U-shaped. Recall from tip 2 that $ATC = AFC + AVC$. Figure 22.6 illustrates this concept for Q_1 units of production. You should redraw this graph and see if you can locate the *AFC*, *AVC*, and *ATC* curves for a different level of output.

Figure 22.6

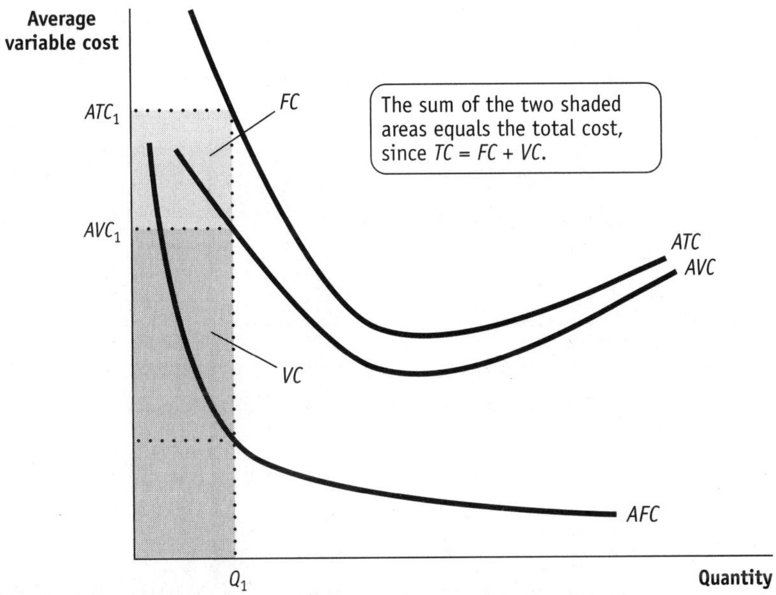

Tip #4. It is important that you understand the distinction between the marginal cost concept and the average cost concept. Marginal cost measures the cost of producing an additional unit of output, while average cost measures the cost per unit. As the firm produces an additional unit of output, it can turn to its marginal cost measure to see how this extra production affects its total cost, and it can also see that if the marginal cost of producing this last unit is less than the average total cost, then producing this additional unit will lower the unit cost of production for the firm. This relationship between marginal and average costs is difficult for many students to grasp, yet it is a relationship that almost all students know and understand in other settings. For example, suppose you form a basketball team with five players. To calculate the average height of your team you would add up the heights of the five players and then divide by 5. Then, if you added another player, this additional player would represent a marginal addition to the height of your team. If this new player were taller than the team's average height, then the team's average height would increase. But, if the player were shorter than the team's average height, then the team's average height would decrease. This basic concept can be applied to a firm's costs: when the marginal cost exceeds the average total cost, the *ATC* must rise; and when the marginal cost is less than the average total cost, the *ATC* must fall. Figure 22.7 illustrates this concept.

Figure 22.7

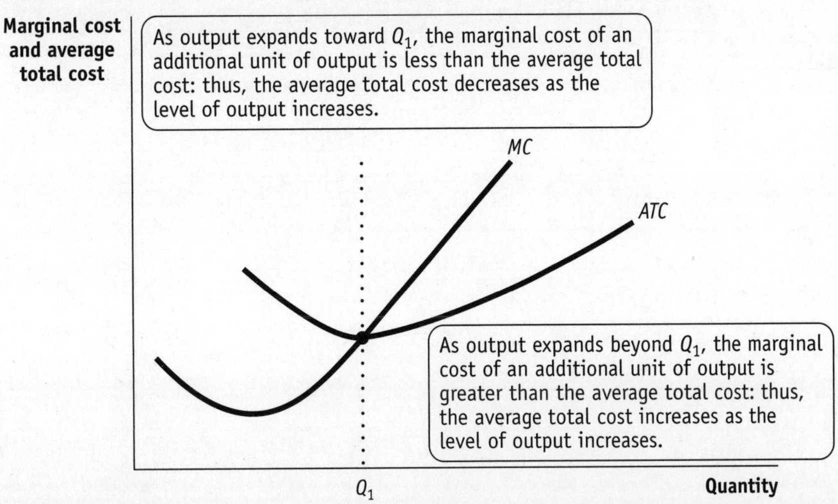

WORKED PROBLEMS

1. Otto's Computers is interested in calculating its variable costs, fixed costs, total costs, and marginal cost of production for the two possible levels of capital it is considering hiring. Otto's knows that each unit of labor employed costs $10 per unit and each unit of capital costs $5 per unit. Calculate Otto's costs and enter them in the tables that follow.

L	K_1	Q_1	Variable cost	Fixed cost	Total cost	Marginal cost ($ per unit of output)
0	4	0				—
1	4	4				
4	4	8				
9	4	12				
16	4	16				
25	4	20				

L	K_2	Q_2	Variable cost	Fixed cost	Total cost	Marginal cost ($ per unit of output)
0	9	0				—
1	9	6				
4	9	12				
9	9	18				
16	9	24				
25	9	30				

Then, calculate Otto's average variable cost, average fixed cost, and average total cost for each level of output in the table. Summarize your findings in the following tables.

Production Function and Costs when K equals 4 units:

Q_1	Variable cost	Fixed cost	Total cost	Average variable cost	Average fixed cost	Average total cost
0						
4						
8						
12						
16						
20						

Production function and costs when K equals 9 units:

Q_2	Variable cost	Fixed cost	Total cost	Average variable cost	Average fixed cost	Average total cost
0						
4						
8						
12						
16						
20						

STEP 1: Start by calculating the variable cost and the fixed cost, then sum these to find the total cost.

The variable cost of production is the cost of the variable input: in this example, labor is the variable input because it varies as the level of output varies. Since each unit of labor costs $10 per unit, it is a simple matter to calculate the variable cost by multiplying the number of units of labor times $10 per unit.

The fixed cost of production is the cost of the fixed input: in this example, capital is the fixed input. In the first table, capital is fixed at K_1 units of capital, or 4 units of capital, while in the second table capital is fixed at K_2 units of capital, or 9 units of capital. Since each unit of capital costs $5 per unit, the fixed cost can be found by multiplying this price of capital times the number of units of capital.

The total cost of production is equal to the sum of the variable cost plus the fixed cost. The tables following Step 2 summarize this work.

STEP 2: Calculate the marginal cost for each production function.

When calculating the marginal cost of production, remember that marginal cost is equal to the change in total cost divided by the change in the quantity of output. Since output is not changing by one unit at a time, you must find both the change in total cost as well as the change in output to calculate marginal cost. For example, to find the marginal cost of going from 4 units of output to 8 units of output using K_1, you must notice that the total cost of producing 4 units of output is $30 and the total cost of producing 8 units of output is $60, or a change in total cost of $30, while the change in output is 4 units since output is changing from 4 units to 8 units. Thus, the marginal cost of going from producing 4 units of output to 8 units of output is equal to $30/4 = $7.50 per unit of output.

The following tables summarize this work.

L	K_1	Q_1	Variable cost	Fixed cost	Total cost	Marginal cost ($ per unit of output)
0	4	0	$0	$20	$20	
1	4	4	10	20	30	10/4 = $2.50
4	4	8	40	20	60	30/4 = 7.50
9	4	12	90	20	110	50/4 = 12.50
16	4	16	160	20	180	70/4 = 17.50
25	4	20	250	20	270	90/4 = 22.50

L	K_2	Q_2	Variable cost	Fixed cost	Total cost	Marginal cost ($ per unit of output)
0	9	0	$0	$45	$45	—
1	9	6	10	45	55	10/6 = $1.67
4	9	12	40	45	85	30/6 = 5
9	9	18	90	45	135	50/6 = 8.33
16	9	24	160	45	205	70/6 = 11.67
25	9	30	250	45	295	90/6 = 15

STEP 3: Calculate Otto's average variable cost, average fixed cost, and average total cost and then enter your findings in the given table.

To calculate these average costs, review the formulas for average total cost, average variable cost, and average fixed cost that are given in the text.

Production function and costs when K equals 4 units:

Q_1	Variable cost	Fixed cost	Total cost	Average variable cost	Average fixed cost	Average total cost
0	$0	$20	$20	—	—	—
4	10	20	30	10/4 = $2.50	20/4 = $5	30/4 = $7.50
8	40	20	60	40/8 = 5	20/8 = 2.50	60/8 = 7.50
12	90	20	110	90/12 = 7.50	20/12 = 1.67	110/12 = 9.17
16	160	20	180	160/16 = 10	20/16 = 1.25	180/16 = 11.25
20	250	20	270	250/20 = 12.50	20/20 = 1	270/20 = 13.50

Production function and costs when K equals 9 units:

Q_2	Variable cost	Fixed cost	Total cost	Average variable cost	Average fixed cost	Average total cost
0	$0	$45	$45	—	—	—
6	10	45	55	10/6 = $1.67	45/6 = $7.50	55/6 = $9.17
12	40	45	85	40/12 = 3.33	45/12 = 3.75	85/12 = 7.08
18	90	45	135	90/18 = 5	45/18 = 2.50	135/18 = 7.50
24	160	45	205	160/24 = 6.67	45/24 = 1.88	205/24 = 8.54
30	250	45	295	250/30 = 8.33	45/30 = 1.50	295/30 = 9.83

2. Suppose that Marcy has a choice of producing her product with a set of inputs that is very capital intensive or with a set of inputs that is less capital intensive. Marcy is trying to understand how her choice of production technique will alter her firm's cost curves. She knows that this effect on her costs can be explained by both the spreading effect and the diminishing returns effect, but she is not quite sure how to apply these terms to her situation. You are asked to help out with the explanation.

STEP 1: First, you need to review what the spreading effect and the diminishing returns effect are, and then you will want to think about how to apply these terms to the decision that Marcy is contemplating.

Holding everything else constant, when Marcy uses a larger amount of capital, the greater will be her fixed cost of production. For a small level of output, this implies that Marcy's average total cost will be greater since there will be less output to spread the fixed cost over. But at higher levels of output, Marcy's average total cost will be lower since she will be able to spread her fixed cost over a larger amount of output. If Marcy anticipates producing a relatively low amount of output, she will likely want to choose the less capital-intensive production process since she will not be able to reap the full benefits of the spreading effect at low levels of production. If she anticipates producing a relatively large amount of output, she will likely want to choose the more capital-intensive production process since she will be able to take advantage of the spreading effect.

The diminishing returns effect says that as output gets larger, more of the variable input will be needed to produce that level of output, yet as more units of the variable input are employed, each successive unit is less productive and this causes average total cost to rise. Marcy will face the diminishing returns effect no matter which production process she chooses, but this effect will occur at higher levels of variable input usage if she employs the more capital-intensive production process.

STEP 2: Provide some advice or guidance for Marcy as she tries to determine the optimal production process for her business.

Marcy's optimal choice of production process ultimately rests on how much of the product she anticipates she will want to produce. If she anticipates that she will want a large quantity of output, she will find that her average costs of production will be lower with the more capital-intensive production process since the spreading effect will dominate the diminishing returns effect only at high levels of output. But if she anticipates that she will want to produce a low level of output, she will find that her average costs of production will be lower with the less capital-intensive production process since the spreading effect will dominate the diminishing returns effect at low levels of output.

Problems and Exercises

1. The following table provides the short-run production function for Sherry's Hair Salon. Sherry uses only two inputs, labor and capital, to produce her output of stylish haircuts. The price of labor is $20 an hour and the price of capital is $50 per unit.

Quantity of capital (units)	Quantity of labor (hours of work)	Quantity of haircuts
10	0	0
10	10	15
10	20	28
10	30	38
10	40	44
10	50	48

a. Complete the following table of Sherry's costs given the above information. Round your calculations to one place past the decimal point.

Quantity of capital (units)	Quantity of labor (hours of work)	Quantity of haircuts	*FC* ($)	*VC* ($)	*AFC* ($)	*AVC* ($)	*ATC* ($)	*TC* ($)	*MC* ($ per unit of output)
10	0	0			—	—	—	500	
									13.3
10	10	15							
10	20	28							
10	30	38							
10	40	44							
10	50	48							

b. Does this production function exhibit diminishing marginal returns to labor? Explain your answer.

c. Graph the total cost function for Sherry's Hair Salon. Measure total cost on the vertical axis and the quantity of haircuts on the horizontal axis. Describe how increasing the quantity of haircuts affects the slope of the total cost curve.

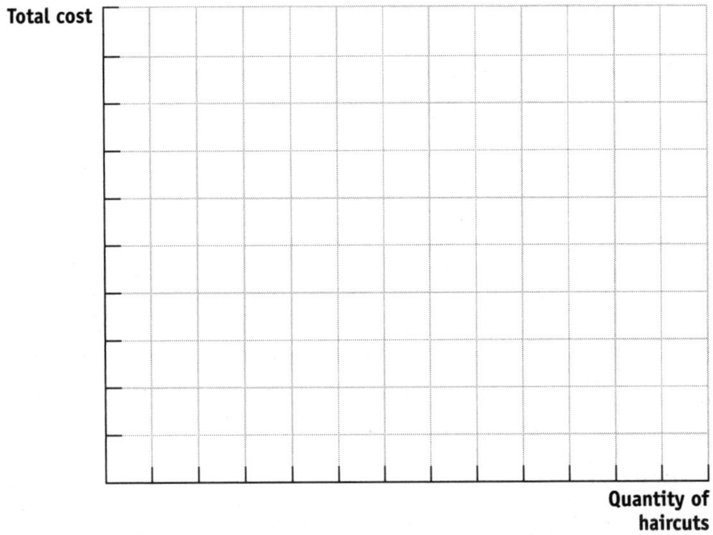

d. Graph the marginal cost function for Sherry's Hair Salon using the midpoint method. Measure marginal cost on the vertical axis and the quantity of haircuts on the horizontal axis. Describe the slope of the *MC* curve and then explain why the *MC* is sloped this way.

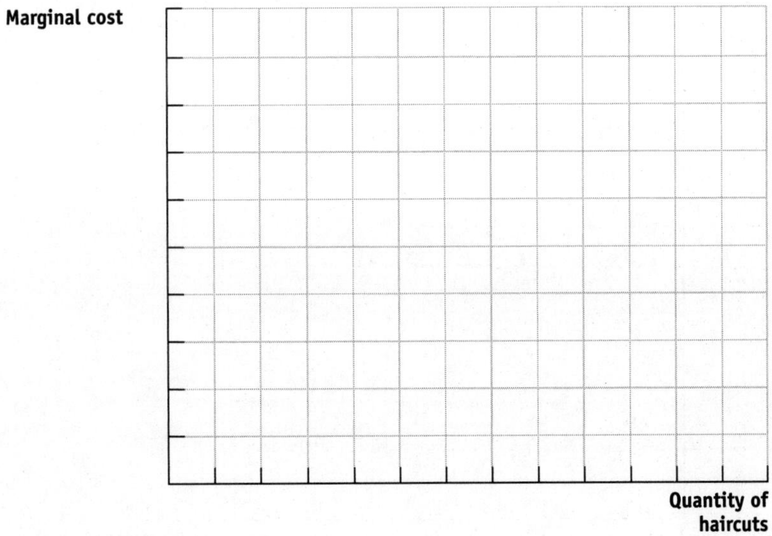

e. In a new graph, draw Sherry's Hair Salon's *AFC* curve. Measure average fixed cost on the vertical axis and the quantity of haircuts on the horizontal axis. On your graph, indicate the area that corresponds to fixed cost if 15 haircuts are currently being produced.

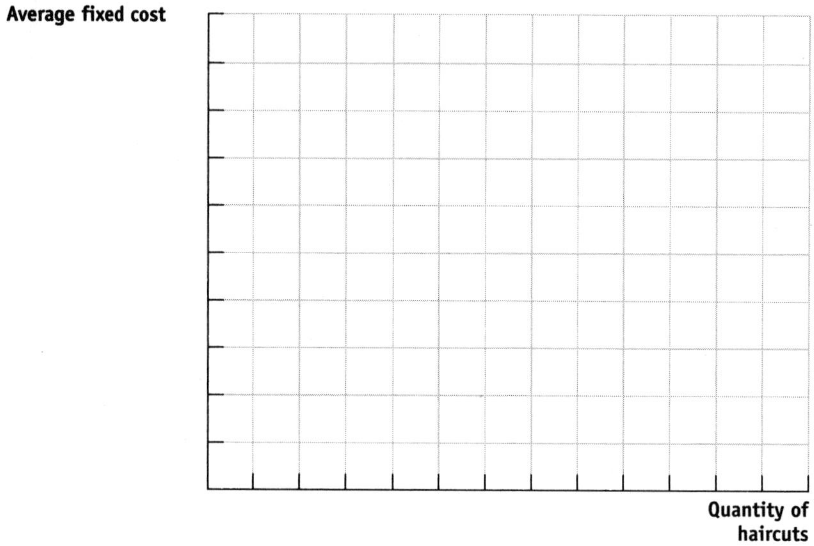

f. In a new graph, sketch Sherry's Hair Salon's *ATC*, *AVC*, *AFC*, and *MC* curves. Measure cost per unit on the vertical axis and the quantity of haircuts on the horizontal axis. What must be true about the relationship between the *ATC* and *MC* curves?

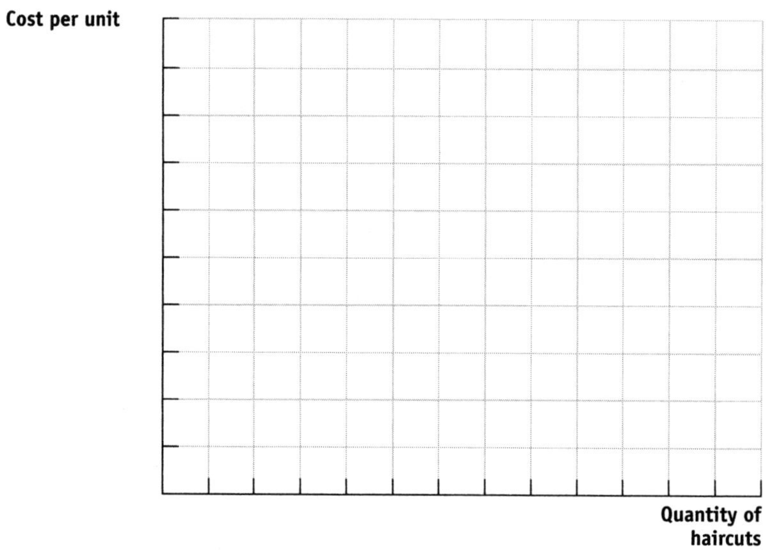

2. For each of the following costs, decide whether or not it is a fixed cost or a variable cost for the firm in the short run. Provide a brief argument for your classification of the cost.

   a. A one-year lease on the building in which the business is located.

   b. Annual property taxes that are assessed on the value of the land the business owns.

   c. The cost of a necessary metal used in the production of the firm's product.

   d. A 10-year-old metal stamping machine that has a useful life of 20 years in your business and is sufficient to produce any desired level of output for the firm.

   e. Sugar that the firm uses to make the cookies it sells.

3. Marginal cost and marginal product are both slope measures. Describe the curves that these two slope measures are derived from.

4. The following table provides some information about Stella's Delight, a business that Stella owns. Stella uses labor and capital as her only inputs in the production of her product.

a. Fill in the table below.

Quantity of labor (units)	Quantity of capital (units)	Quantity of output	*VC* ($)	*FC* ($)	*AVC* ($)	*AFC* ($)	*ATC* ($)	*TC* ($)	*MC* ($ per unit of output)
0	5	0			—	—	—		
1	5	10							
2	5	18		10					
3	5	24	15						
4	5	28							
5	5	30							
6	5	31							

b. What is the price of the variable input?

c. What is the price of the fixed input?

d. What is the marginal product of the fifth unit of labor?

e. What is the marginal cost of producing the twenty-fourth unit of output?

5. Why is the spreading effect stronger than the diminishing returns effect at low levels of output, while the diminishing returns effect is stronger than the spreading effect at high levels of output?

6. Discuss each of the following statements. Decide whether the statement is true or false and then justify your answer.
   a. As output increases, if average total cost is decreasing, then marginal cost must be less than average total cost.
   b. As output increases, if marginal cost is increasing, then marginal cost must be greater than average total cost.
   c. As output increases, if marginal cost is greater than average fixed cost, then average fixed cost must be increasing.
   d. As output increases, fixed cost decreases.
   e. As output increases, variable cost increases.

BEFORE YOU TAKE THE TEST

Module Review Questions

1. Terry spends $200 a month to rent a building for his company, $600 a month for the capital he employs to produce widgets, and $10 per hour for every worker he employs. Terry's fixed cost per month equals
   a. $200.
   b. $600.
   c. $800.
   d. $810.

2. Terry spends $200 a month to rent a building for his company, $600 a month for the capital he employs to produce widgets, and $10 per hour for every unit of labor he employs. Terry distinguishes between his fixed cost and his variable cost by

a. deciding whether he is producing in the short run or the long run.

b. whether the cost varies as his level of production changes.

c. whether the cost exceeds $500.

d. recognizing that capital is always a fixed cost while rent and labor are variable costs.

3. Larry's Auto Shop's total cost can be expressed by the equation $TC = 50 + 10Q^2$, where Q is the quantity of repairs made by Larry's Auto Shop. Which of the following statements is true for Larry's Auto Shop?

I. When Larry's Auto Shop produces 0 repairs, its fixed cost equals its total costs.

II. Larry's Auto Shop's fixed cost equals $50.

III. Larry's Auto Shop's fixed cost depends on the level of output that is produced.

a. Statement I is true.

b. Statements I and II are true.

c. Statements I and III are true.

d. Statements I, II, and III are true.

4. Larry's Auto Shop's total cost can be expressed by the equation $TC = 50 + 10Q^2$, where Q is the quantity of repairs made by Larry's Auto Shop. Larry's variable cost equals

a. $10 when 1 unit of output is produced and $40 when 2 units of output are produced.

b. $60 when 1 unit of output is produced and $90 when 2 units of output are produced.

5. As the level of output increases, the total cost curve for a firm gets

a. steeper due to diminishing returns to the variable input.

b. flatter due to diminishing returns to the variable input.

Use the following information to answer the next four questions. The table provides production function information for Jimmy's Service Shop. Assume Jimmy hires only labor and capital to produce his services. Furthermore, the price of labor is $100 per worker per week and the price of capital is $10 per unit.

Quantity of labor (workers)	Quantity of capital (units)	Quantity of output produced per week (number of services per week)
0	10	0
1	10	200
2	10	400
3	10	600
4	10	700
5	10	750

6. Jimmy's fixed cost of production equals

a. $0.

b. $100.

c. $110.

d. $500.

7. Jimmy's variable cost of production
   a. is constant and equal to $100 given the above information.
   b. varies with the level of output that is produced.
   c. is always greater than his fixed cost.
   d. decreases as the level of production increases due to diminishing marginal returns.

8. Jimmy's total cost of producing 700 units of output is
   a. equal to the sum of his fixed and variable costs of producing this level of output.
   b. $500.
   c. greater than his total cost of producing 600 units of output.
   d. Answers (a), (b), and (c) are all true.

9. Jimmy's marginal cost of producing the seven-hundredth unit of output is equal to
   a. $500 per unit of output.
   b. $400 per unit of output.
   c. $100 per unit of output.
   d. $1 per unit of output.

10. The marginal cost curve is upward sloping as output increases due to
   a. increasing returns to scale.
   b. decreasing returns to scale.
   c. diminishing marginal returns to the variable input.
   d. increasing marginal returns to the variable input.

11. In the short run, a firm's fixed cost ________ while the firm's average fixed cost ________.
   a. stays constant as output increases; increases as the firm produces higher levels of output
   b. stays constant as output increases; decreases as the firm produces higher levels of output
   c. increases as the firm produces higher levels of output; stays constant as output increases
   d. decreases as the firm produces higher levels of output; stays constant as output increases

12. The spreading effect refers to the
   a. decrease in *AVC* as the firm produces greater levels of output.
   b. decrease in *AFC* as the firm produces greater levels of output.
   c. combined effect on *AVC* and *AFC* of the firm producing higher levels of output.
   d. combined effect on *AVC*, *AFC*, and *MC* of the firm producing higher levels of output.

13. The diminishing returns effect causes the *AVC* to
   a. decline initially as output increases.
   b. decline at all levels of output.
   c. increase eventually as output increases.
   d. increase at all levels of output.

14. At high levels of output for a firm, the spreading effect is

a. stronger than the diminishing returns effect.

b. weaker than the diminishing returns effect.

15. At the minimum-cost output

a. average variable cost must equal marginal cost.

b. average fixed cost must equal marginal cost.

c. average total cost must equal marginal cost.

d. Answers (a), (b), and (c) are all true.

ANSWER KEY

Answers to Problems and Exercises

1. a.

Quantity of capital (units)	Quantity of labor (hours of work)	Quantity of haircuts	*FC* ($)	*VC* ($)	*AFC* ($)	*AVC* ($)	*ATC* ($)	*TC* ($)	*MC* ($ per unit of output)
10	0	0	500	0	—	—	—	500	
									13.3
10	10	15	500	200	33.3	13.3	46.7	700	
									15.4
10	20	28	500	400	17.9	14.3	32.1	900	
									20.0
10	30	38	500	600	13.2	15.8	28.9	1,100	
									33.3
10	40	44	500	800	11.4	18.2	29.5	1,300	
									50.0
10	50	48	500	1,000	10.4	20.8	31.3	1,500	

b. A production function exhibits diminishing marginal returns to labor if, as labor is increased while holding all other inputs constant, the level of total output increases but it increases at a decreasing rate. The marginal product of labor for this production function is summarized in the table below. As you can see from the table, the production function does exhibit diminishing marginal returns to labor.

Quantity of capital (units)	Quantity of labor (hours of work)	Quantity of haircuts	Marginal product of labor (haircuts per hour of work)
10	0	0	
			1.5
10	10	15	
			1.3
10	20	28	
			1
10	30	38	
			0.6
10	40	44	
			0.4
10	50	48	

c.

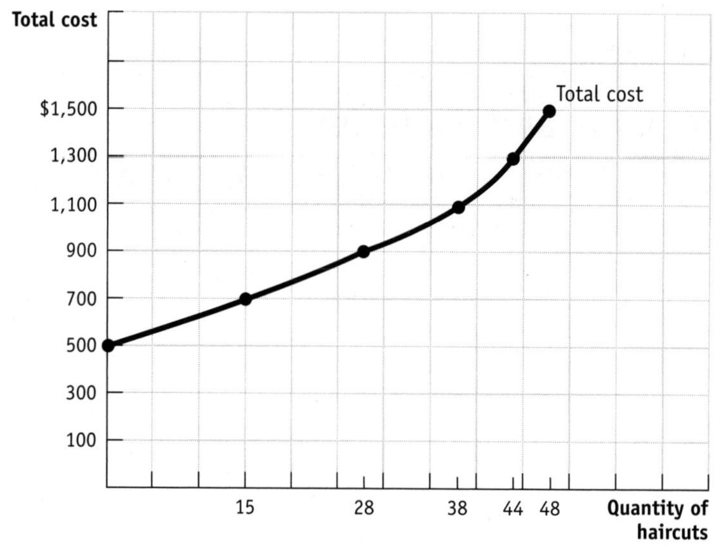

As the quantity of haircuts increases, *TC* increases at an increasing rate due to the diminishing marginal returns to labor.

d.

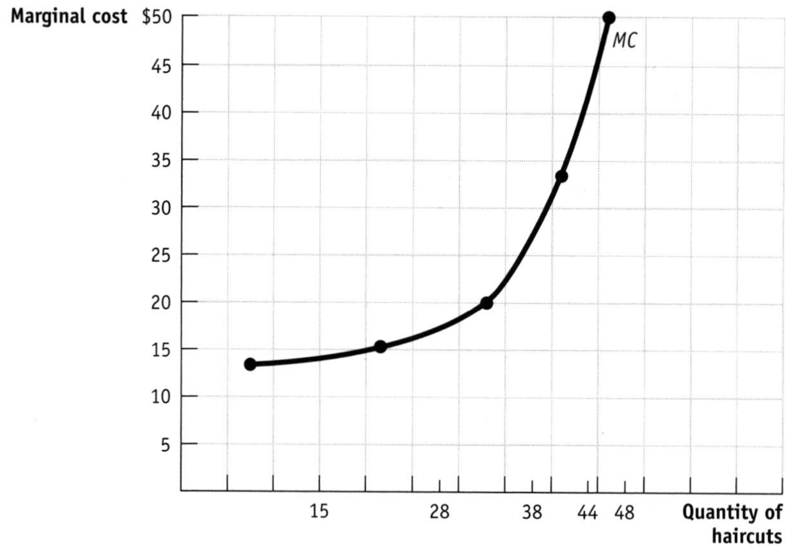

As output gets larger, the effect of diminishing marginal returns to the variable input causes *MC* to increase.

e.

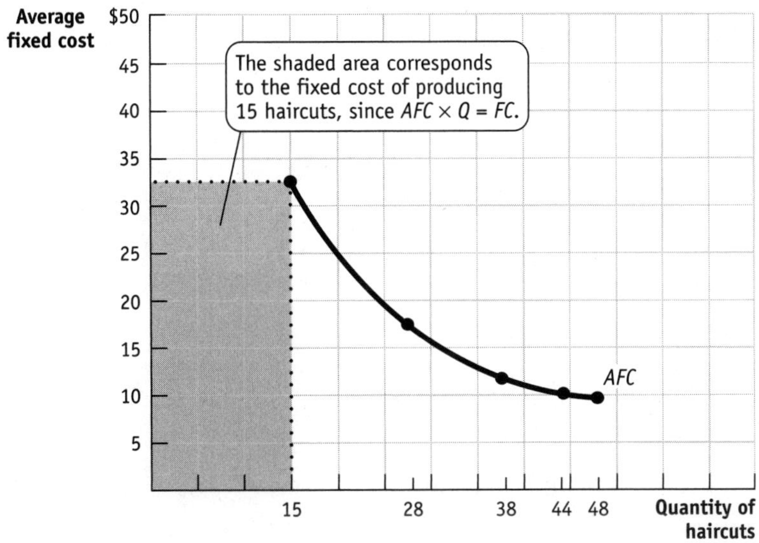

f.

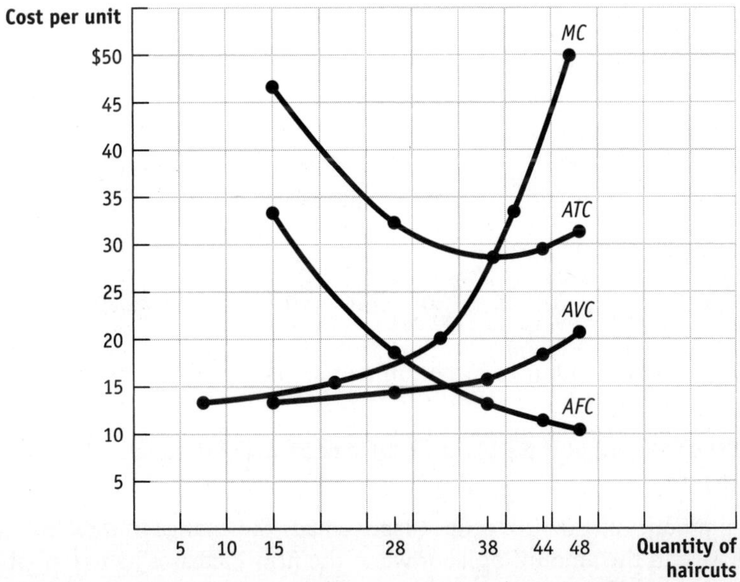

The *ATC* curve intersects the *MC* curve at the minimum point on the *ATC* curve.

2. **a.** The cost of the one-year lease does not change during the year no matter what level of output the firm produces. This is a fixed cost.

b. Annual property taxes are set yearly and are not based on the level of production of the firm. This is a fixed cost.

c. The cost of metal varies as the level of output the firm produces varies. This is a variable cost.

d. The machine still has a long, useful life and is capable of meeting the production demands of the firm. The cost of this machine does not vary with the level of production. This is a fixed cost.

e. This is a variable cost since, as the output of cookies increases, the firm finds that it uses more sugar.

3. Marginal cost provides the slope measure of the *TC* curve at a particular level of output: marginal cost at low levels of output may fall as output increases, but eventually as output increases, the marginal cost of producing this output rises. Marginal product is the slope measure of the total product curve at a particular level of variable input usage: marginal product eventually declines as the level of variable input increases because of diminishing marginal returns to the variable input.

4. **a.**

Quantity of labor (units)	Quantity of capital (units)	Quantity of output	*VC* ($)	*FC* ($)	*AVC* ($)	*AFC* ($)	*ATC* ($)	*TC* ($)	*MC* ($)
0	5	0	0	10		—	—	10	
									0.50
1	5	10	5	10	0.50	1.00	1.50	15	
									0.63
2	5	18	10	10	0.56	0.56	1.11	20	
									0.83
3	5	24	15	10	0.63	0.42	1.04	25	
									1.25
4	5	28	20	10	0.71	0.36	1.07	30	
									2.50
5	5	30	25	10	0.83	0.33	1.17	35	
									5.00
6	5	31	30	10	0.97	0.32	1.29	40	

b. The price of the variable input is $5 per unit since the variable cost equals $15 when 3 units of labor are hired.

c. The price of the fixed input is $2 per unit since the fixed cost equals $10 when 5 units of capital are hired.

d. The marginal product of the fifth unit of labor equals the change in total output divided by the change in the amount of labor when the firm increases its use of labor from 4 units to 5 units, or (2 units of output)/(1 unit of labor), for a marginal product of 2.

e. The marginal cost of producing the twenty-fourth unit of output is equal to the change in total cost divided by the change in output, or ($5)/(6 units of output), for a marginal cost of $0.83.

5. The spreading effect refers to the ability to spread the fixed cost over all the production of the firm. When the firm produces a few units, the fixed cost is not spread over very many units and therefore the average fixed cost is relatively high; when the firm produces a large number of units, the fixed cost is spread over these units and the average fixed cost is therefore much smaller. This means that the spreading effect is not of great importance when producing a lot of output, but it can have a significant effect at lower levels of production. The diminishing returns effect describes the effect on average variable cost of producing larger amounts of output. To produce larger amounts of output the firm must hire more variable input, but each additional unit of the variable input is less productive than the previous unit, and therefore as output increases, average variable cost also increases. The diminishing returns effect gets more pronounced the greater the level of production.

6. **a.** True. If average total cost is decreasing, this must be because the marginal cost of producing another unit of output is less than the average total cost of producing the current level of output. When an additional unit of output is produced in these circumstances, this causes the average total cost to fall.

b. False. Marginal cost can be increasing but still be less than average total cost.

c. False. Average fixed cost decreases as output increases since fixed cost is constant for the firm and does not change as the level of output changes.

d. False. Fixed cost does not change for the firm no matter what level of output they produce.

e. True. As the firm produces more output, it must hire additional units of its variable input, which causes its variable cost to increase.

Answers to Module Review Questions

1. **Answer c.** Fixed costs are those costs that do not vary as output varies. Terry's fixed costs include his capital costs of $600 a month and his rent of $200 a month: neither of these costs change for Terry no matter what level of output he produces. In contrast, Terry's use of labor varies as he changes his level of production, and when he hires additional labor his variable costs are altered.

2. **Answer b.** There are no fixed costs in the long run, only variable costs; there isn't some dollar amount that exists as a limit to variable costs; and capital or labor can be variable in the short run. What does distinguish variable costs from fixed costs is that variable costs vary as the level of output varies: a firm wishing to produce more of a good in the short run does so by hiring more units of the variable input.

3. **Answer b.** Larry's Auto Shop's fixed cost equals his total cost when output is zero, since the firm does not hire any of the variable input if it decides to not produce any output. When Q equals zero, Larry's total cost equals $50, and therefore Larry's fixed cost must equal $50. Fixed cost does not change as the level of output produced by the firm changes.

4. **Answer a.** When output is zero, fixed cost equals total cost and Larry's fixed cost is therefore $50. Larry's variable cost can therefore by expressed as $10Q^2$ since $TC = FC + VC$. When Q equals 1, VC is $10; when Q equals 2, VC is $40.

5. **Answer a.** As the firm produces greater levels of output, its costs increase because it must employ more and more units of the variable input to produce that output. Yet as it employs more of the variable input, it finds that each additional unit of the variable input is less productive than the last unit hired, which therefore leads total cost to increase at an increasing rate.

6. **Answer b.** Jimmy's fixed cost is equal to the number of units of the fixed input he hires times the price of the fixed input. Jimmy hires 10 units of capital, irrespective of his level of production, and so his fixed cost equals $100.

7. **Answer b.** By definition, variable cost for a firm varies as the level of production varies, which eliminates answer (a). Variable cost may or may not be greater than fixed cost. Variable cost increases as the level of output increases because of the diminishing marginal returns to the variable input.

8. **Answer d.** Total cost for producing any level of output can be found by summing variable cost and fixed cost for that level of output. Jimmy's fixed cost equals $100 and his variable cost is $400 when he produces 700 units of output, so Jimmy's total cost of producing 700 units of output is $500. The total cost of producing 600 units of output is $400. Jimmy's total cost of producing 600 units of output is less than his total cost of producing 700 units of output.

9. **Answer d.** The marginal cost of producing the last unit of output is equal to the change in total cost divided by the change in output. The total cost of producing 700 units is $500 and the total cost of producing 600 units is $400: the change in total cost is $100. The change in output is 100 units. Thus, the marginal cost of producing the seven-hundredth unit of output is $100/(100 units of output), or $1 per unit of output.

10. **Answer c.** As output increases, the marginal cost of producing that level of output also increases because the marginal product of the variable input is falling. This is due to the diminishing marginal returns to the variable input.

11. **Answer b.** *FC* does not vary as the level of production varies, but average fixed cost declines as output increases since $AFC = FC/Q$ and Q is increasing.

12. **Answer b.** The spreading effect refers to the idea that since fixed costs are constant at all short-run levels of output this implies that the *AFC* will decline as output increases, since those constant fixed costs will be spread over a larger number of units of output. The spreading effect does not influence the *AVC* or the *MC*.

13. **Answer c.** The diminishing returns effect refers to the idea that as the firm increases its production in the short run it must hire additional units of the variable input, but that as the firm's usage of the variable input increases it finds that additional units of the variable input are less productive than the preceding unit. This means that the firm's *AVC* eventually rises due to the variable cost of production increasing faster than the increase in the level of output.

14. **Answer b.** At high levels of output, the firm's *ATC* curve increases, indicating that the spreading effect, which causes *AFC* to fall as output increases, is not as strong as the diminishing returns effect, which causes *AVC* to rise as output increases.

15. **Answer c.** At the minimum-cost output, average total cost equals marginal cost since the minimum-cost output is the level of output at which average total cost is minimized. At outputs lower than the minimum-cost output, average total cost is falling as output increases, which implies that the marginal cost of producing an additional unit of output is less than the average total cost of producing that output. At outputs greater than the minimum-cost output, average total cost is rising as output increases, which implies that the marginal cost of producing an additional unit of output is greater than the average total cost of producing that output. The average variable cost is not at its minimum point at the minimum-cost output, and the average fixed cost does not have a minimum point since it declines as the level of output increases.

module **23**

Long-Run Costs and Economies of Scale

BEFORE YOU READ THE MODULE

Summary

This module discusses the distinction between short run and long run and explores how short-run costs differ from long-run costs for a firm. The module also develops the idea of returns to scale and then analyzes the relationships between inputs, outputs, and costs in the long run.

Module Objectives

Objective #1. The long-run costs for a firm are all variable costs, since in the long run all inputs can be adjusted. Thus, long-run total costs are equivalent to long-run variable costs.

Objective #2. The long-run average total cost (*LRATC*) curve illustrates the relationship between output and average total cost when fixed cost has been chosen to minimize the average total cost at every level of output. The *LRATC* curve is U-shaped: when *LRATC* is decreasing as output increases, the firm experiences increasing returns to scale; when *LRATC* is increasing as output increases, the firm experiences decreasing returns to scale; and when *LRATC* is constant as output increases, the firm experiences constant returns to scale. Figure 23.1 illustrates the *LRATC* curve and returns to scale: for outputs from 0 units to Q_1, this firm has increasing returns to scale and decreasing costs; for outputs from Q_1 units to Q_2, this firm has constant returns to scale and constant costs; and for outputs greater than Q_2, this firm has decreasing returns to scale and increasing costs.

Figure 23.1

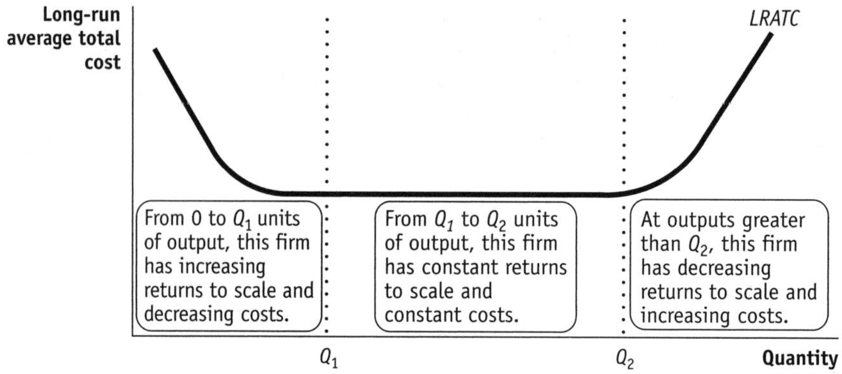

- A firm that has increasing returns to scale in its range of production finds that as its production level increases, its cost of production falls: this firm benefits from getting larger. A firm with increasing returns to scale finds that an equal proportionate increase in all its inputs will result in a greater-than-proportionate increase in its output: for example, a doubling of all of the firm's inputs causes the firm's output to more than double, and therefore the firm's *ATC* decreases.
- A firm that has decreasing returns to scale in its range of production finds that as its production level increases, its cost of production increases: this firm benefits from staying relatively small. A firm with decreasing returns to scale finds that an equal proportionate increase in all its inputs will result in a less-than-proportionate increase in its output: for example, a doubling of all of the firm's inputs causes the firm's output to less than double, and therefore the firm's *ATC* increases.
- A firm that has constant returns to scale in its range of production finds that a proportionate increase in all its inputs results in a proportionate increase in its output: for example, if all inputs are doubled, then the firm's output also doubles, and therefore the firm's *ATC* stays constant.

Objective #3. Returns to scale for a firm depend on the firm's production technology. Increasing returns to scale arise because of increasing specialization that is possible at large output levels or because of large initial set-up costs that must be incurred to produce any output or because of network externalities. Decreasing returns to scale arise due to problems of coordination and communication as the level of production increases.

Key Terms

long-run average total cost curve a graphical representation showing the relationship between output and *average total cost* when *fixed cost* has been chosen to minimize average total cost for each level of output.

economies of scale long-run average total cost declines as output increases.

increasing returns to scale long-run *average total cost* declines as output increases (also referred to as *economies of scale*).

Notes

Key Terms *(continued)*

Notes

decreasing returns to scale long-run *average total cost* increases as output increases (also known as *diseconomies of scale*).

constant returns to scale long-run *average total cost* is constant as output increases.

AFTER YOU READ THE MODULE

Tips

Tip #1. A firm's returns to scale identifies whether the firm can reduce its costs by increasing its level of production. Firms that have increasing returns to scale benefit from being relatively large, while firms with decreasing returns to scale find that getting larger is detrimental to them since as their output levels expand their average costs rise.

- Consider a firm with increasing returns to scale: when this firm doubles its inputs, it doubles its costs. But when inputs are doubled, this firm can produce more than double its original level of output. This implies that its *ATC*, which is equal to *TC*/*Q*, will decrease since *TC* has doubled while Q has more than doubled.
- Consider a firm with decreasing returns to scale: when this firm doubles its inputs, it doubles its costs. But when inputs are doubled, this firm can only produce less than double its original level of output. This implies that its *ATC*, which is equal to *TC*/*Q*, will increase since *TC* has doubled while Q has less than doubled.

Tip #2. Students often mix up the concepts of diminishing marginal returns to an input and returns to scale. Remember that diminishing returns to an input is based on changing the level of one input while holding constant the levels of all other inputs: diminishing returns to scale is a short-run concept since at least one input is being held constant. Returns to scale, in contrast, is a long-run concept based on an equal proportionate increase in all inputs and the effect of this change on the firm's level of output.

WORKED PROBLEMS

1. Nancy operates a bakery. She employs 10 workers and has two ovens and three mixers. Consider these the only relevant inputs she uses to make her bread. With these inputs she can make 1,000 loaves of bread each week. Each worker earns $200 per week; the rental price of an oven is $1,000 per week; and the rental price of a mixer is $500 per week. Nancy knows that if she increases her employees to 20 workers and brings in two additional ovens and three additional mixers, she will be able to produce 2,500 loaves of bread each week. She has asked you to analyze the decision she faces with regard to expanding her bakery by hiring more workers and renting additional capital equipment. She is interested in hearing about the returns to scale her bakery will produce with this proposed expansion; the effect on her average total costs and her total costs of this proposed expansion; and your recommendation about what she should do. She knows she can sell as many loaves of bread each week as she is able to produce, so do not worry about the demand for her product.

STEP 1: Calculate Nancy's current total costs and average total costs based upon the amount of labor and capital she currently employs.

Nancy has labor costs of $2,000 per week (10 employees each making $200 per week) and capital costs of $3,500 (two ovens that cost $1,000 each and three mixers that cost $500 each). Thus, her total cost for these inputs is $5,500. Her average total cost for the 1,000 loaves of bread she can produce each week from these inputs is ($5,500/1,000 loaves of bread), or $5.50 per loaf of bread.

STEP 2: Calculate Nancy's total costs and average total costs based upon the amount of labor and capital she will employ if she expands her bakery.

Before doing this calculation, an observant reader might notice that all of the inputs have doubled (twice as much labor, twice as many ovens, twice as many mixers), while output has more than doubled (1,000 loaves of bread to 2,500 loaves of bread). This implies that the firm's total costs should double and its average total cost of production should fall. Let's do the calculation to see whether this reasoning proves correct.

Twenty employees will cost $4,000 per week (20 employers each making $200 per week); four ovens will rent each week for $4,000 (each oven rents for $1,000 per week); and six mixers will each rent for $3,000 per week (each mixer rents for $500 per week). Total cost will therefore equal $11,000 (twice the original total cost of $5,500). Average total cost equals total cost divided by quantity of output produced, or $11,000/2,500 loaves of bread. Thus, average total cost equals $4.40 per loaf of bread if Nancy expands by hiring twice as much labor and investing twice as much capital. Our results verify our earlier reasoning.

STEP 3: Analyze Nancy's returns to scale by comparing her original average cost of production to the average cost of production if she expands her bakery.

When Nancy's bakery is expanded by a proportionate increase in the inputs she uses, she finds that her average total cost decreases. This implies that Nancy's bakery produces increasing returns to scale as she increases her level of production. That is, as Nancy produces at a larger scale of operation, her cost per loaf of bread produced decreases.

STEP 4: Make a recommendation as to whether Nancy should expand her bakery.

Nancy's firm is operating in the range of increasing returns to scale, which means that, expanding the operation will decrease the unit costs of production. Nancy should expand her bakery to take advantage of these increasing returns to scale, given the assumption that she can sell as much bread as the bakery produces.

2. Suppose the firm represented in the table below is operating in the long run. This firm produces widgets using only capital and labor. The table provides information about possible combinations of capital and labor the firm can use to produce widgets. For this problem assume that no matter how much capital or labor the firm uses, the price of these inputs does not change.

Units of capital	Units of labor	Quantity of widgets
10	20	1,000
15	30	2,500
30	60	4,000
50	100	5,000

Suppose this firm is initially using 10 units of capital and 20 units of labor but it is considering increasing its use of capital to 15 units and its use of labor to 30 units. How will this expansion affect this firm's average total cost of production? Can you conclude anything about this firm's returns to scale as it contemplates this expansion? Suppose the firm alternatively considered increasing its use of capital to 50 units and its use of labor to 100 units. Assuming that demand for widgets is not an issue for this firm, how will this proposed expansion affect the firm's average total cost of production compared with its initial situation?

STEP 1: Analyze how the proposed use of 15 units of capital and 30 units of labor will affect this firm's total costs of production. Then analyze the impact of this proposed change in scale on this firm's long-run average total cost of production.

When this firm considers expanding from using 10 units of capital and 20 units of labor to 15 units of capital and 30 units of labor, it is increasing its use of inputs by a factor of 1.5. This will increase the firm's total costs of production by the same factor, 1.5. The effect of this increase on the cost per widget (the average total cost of production) will depend not only on total cost but also on the level of production. The table tells us this new, higher level of input usage results in widget production increasing from 1,000 to 2,500, a factor of 2.5. Therefore, this proposed expansion in input usage will decrease the long-run average total cost: As total cost increased by a factor of 1.5, total production increased by a factor of 2.5, so that the long-run average total cost of production is decreasing as the scale of production increases.

STEP 2: Given your analysis in Step 1, decide whether this firm will have increasing returns to scale, decreasing returns to scale, or constant returns to scale if it expands from using 10 units of capital and 20 units of labor to using 15 units of capital and 30 units of labor.

Since this firm's long-run average total cost of production decreases as the firm uses additional inputs and increases its production from 1,000 pillows to 2,500 pillows, the firm has increasing returns to scale over this range of production. That is, as the firm expands production from 1,000 pillows to 2,500 pillows, its long-run average total cost decreases.

STEP 3: Analyze how the proposed expansion of using 50 units of capital and 100 units of labor will affect this firm's total costs of production. Then analyze the impact of this proposed change in scale on this firm's long-run average total cost of production.

When this firm considers expanding from using 10 units of capital and 20 units of labor to 50 units of capital and 100 units of labor, it is increasing its use of inputs by a factor of 5. This increased use of inputs will increase the firm's total costs of production by the same factor, 5. The effect of this increased cost on the cost per widget (the average total cost of production) will depend not only on total cost but also on the level of production. The table tells us that this new, higher level of input usage results in widget production increasing from 1,000 to 5,000, an increase by a factor of 5. Therefore, this proposed expansion does not alter the firm's long-run average total cost of production from the production level of 10 units of capital and 20 units of labor.

STEP 4: Given your analysis in the first three steps of this problem, explain how it is possible for this firm to decrease its long-run average total cost as it expands from producing 1,000 widgets to 2,500 widgets but to see no change in its long-run average total cost if it expands from producing 1,000 widgets to producing 5,000 widgets.

Initially these two outcomes may appear to be contradictory. But recall that the long-run average total cost curve is U-shaped: at low levels of output, average total cost decreases as output increases and the firm reaps increasing returns to scale; and at higher levels of output, it increases as output increases and the firm sees decreasing returns to scale. For this firm we are considering two possible expansions from the base production capacity of 10 units of capital and 20 units of labor. With the first expansion, to using 15 units of capital and 30 units of labor, the firm is expanding over a range of output for which it has increasing returns to scale; with the second expansion, to using 50 units of capital and 100 units of labor, the firm is expanding over a range of output for which it has decreasing returns to scale.

Problems and Exercises

1. Suppose the firm represented in the table below is operating in the long run. This firm produces chairs and uses wood and labor to produce these chairs. Some production information is provided in the table. Assume the price of wood and the price of labor do not change.

Quantity of wood	Quantity of labor	Quantity of chairs
4 units	5 units	20 chairs
8 units	10 units	45 chairs
12 units	15 units	90 chairs
24 units	30 units	150 chairs

   a. If this firm is currently using 4 units of wood and 5 units of labor, does it experience increasing, decreasing, or constant returns to scale if it increases its wood use to 8 units and its labor use to 10 units? Explain your answer.

b. Is this firm's *LRATC* curve downward sloping, upward sloping, or constant in the range of production described in part (a)?

c. If this firm is currently using 8 units of wood and 10 units of labor and it increases the use of both inputs by 50%, will the firm experience increasing, decreasing, or constant returns to scale?

d. Is this firm's *LRATC* curve downward sloping, upward sloping, or constant in the range of production described in part (c)?

e. Suppose this firm is currently using 12 units of wood and 15 units of labor to produce chairs, and then the firm increases its input usage by 100% for both inputs. Will the firm experience increasing, decreasing, or constant returns to scale?

f. Is this firm's *LRATC* curve downward sloping, upward sloping, or constant in the range of production described in part (e)?

2. Sarah has two possible technologies she can use to produce her output. One of the technologies relies heavily on equipment and machinery: this equipment and machinery, although expensive, is able to produce large quantities of output in a short amount of time. The alternative technology is more labor intensive: this technology does not utilize such expensive capital equipment and it is able to produce smaller quantities of output in the same amount of time. Sarah is trying to figure out which method will result in lower costs per unit for her business. What would your advice to Sarah be given this information?

3. Emilio's Fine Dining is an internationally recognized gourmet restaurant. The restaurant is well known for its exquisite food and fine service. On any given night Emilio's can serve a maximum of 60 patrons and for the past five years it has been impossible to dine at Emilio's without a reservation made at least two months ahead of time. Given how successful this restaurant is and how many people want to dine here, why doesn't Emilio's expand their dining room to accommodate more customers? Use your knowledge of economies of scale to explain your answer.

BEFORE YOU TAKE THE TEST

Module Review Questions

1. The firm's *LRATC* curve illustrates the relationship between output and
   a. average total cost when fixed cost has been chosen to minimize average total cost for each level of output.
   b. marginal cost when fixed cost has been chosen to minimize average total cost for each level of output.
   c. average total cost when variable cost has been chosen to minimize average total cost for each level of output.
   d. average total cost when marginal cost has been chosen to minimize average total cost for each level of output.

2. When the firm's *LRATC* curve is downward sloping over its range of production, this implies that
   a. when all of the firm's inputs are increased proportionately, the firm's level of production will increase, but by a smaller factor than the increase in the firm's inputs.
   b. when all of the firm's inputs are doubled, the firm's level of production will more than double.
   c. when all of the firm's inputs are tripled, the firm's level of production may or may not increase.
   d. the firm is experiencing decreasing returns to scale over this range of production.

3. A firm finds that past a certain level of production its *LRATC* curve is upward sloping. Which of the following is true?
   a. The firm in this range of production experiences decreasing returns to scale.
   b. Increased specialization allows the firm to operate a larger scale of operation.
   c. The set-up costs of entering this industry must be quite high.
   d. Answers (a), (b), and (c) are all true.

4. Which of the following statements is true?
   I. In the short run, a firm can experience increasing, decreasing, or constant returns to scale.
   II. If a firm doubles all of its inputs with the result that its output doubles, then this firm has constant returns to scale.
   III. Decreasing returns to scale are due to coordination and communication problems.
   a. Statements I and II are true.
   b. Statement II is true.
   c. Statements II and III are true.
   d. Statements I, II, and III are true.

5. Fixed cost
   a. varies with the level of output produced.
   b. is always equal to 20% of a firm's total cost.
   c. in the short run accounts for the majority of a firm's average total cost of production.
   d. plus variable cost is equal to the firm's short-run total cost of production.

6. A firm is currently producing 20 units of output. Its average fixed cost is equal to $4 per unit of output and its average total cost is equal to $16 per unit of output. The firm's variable cost is equal to

a. $12 per unit of output.
b. $20 per unit of output.
c. $240.
d. $400.

7. A firm has fixed costs of $20 in the short run. It finds that its average variable cost is equal to $12 when it produces 30 units of output and its average variable cost is equal to $15 when it produces 31 units of output. Given this information, what is this firm's marginal cost of producing the thirty-first unit of output?

a. There is not enough information given to calculate the marginal cost of production.
b. The marginal cost of production is $3 when the firm produces its thirty-first unit of output.
c. The marginal cost of production is $105 when the firm produces its thirty-first unit of output.
d. The marginal cost of production is $15 when the firm produces its thirty-first unit of output.

ANSWER KEY

Answers to Problems and Exercises

1. a. In this question, the firm is doubling both inputs (4 units of wood to 8 units of wood, 5 units of labor to 10 units of labor) and the firm finds that this leads to more than double the amount of output (20 chairs to 45 chairs). This firm is experiencing increasing returns to scale, since as the scale or size of operation gets larger, the firm's unit cost of production falls.

   b. This firm's *LRATC* curve is downward sloping over this range of output.

   c. A 50% increase in the use of inputs would result in the firm using 12 units of wood and 15 units of labor. With a 50% increase in inputs the firm finds that its output increases from 45 chairs to 90 chairs, which is a 100% increase in the level of output. The firm experiences increasing returns to scale over this range of output.

   d. This firm's *LRATC* curve is downward sloping over this range of output.

   e. The firm changes its wood usage from 12 units of wood to 24 units of wood and its labor usage from 15 units of labor to 30 units of labor. Output changes from 90 chairs to 150 chairs. The increase in output is less than 100%, so this firm experiences decreasing returns to scale over this range of production.

   f. This firm's *LRATC* curve is upward sloping over this range of output.

2. The two technologies reflect different fixed costs of production: the first technology has high fixed costs due to the technology being dependent on equipment and machinery; the second technology has low fixed costs due to the technology relying primarily on labor. If Sarah plans to produce a relatively small amount of output then the more labor-intensive technology will be the lower cost per unit option; if Sarah plans to produce a larger quantity of output then the more capital-intensive technology will lead to a lower cost per unit as the level of output produced increases. Sarah will need to decide what level of output she is going to produce in order to make a good decision about the appropriate technology.

3. Emilio's purposefully seems to be adhering to a small size scale of operation. Given that there is plenty of evidence that demand for the restaurant is high and steady there must be some overriding reason that prevents Emilio's from expanding its seating capacity. The most likely reason is that there is something about fine dining that leads to a small scale of operation: that is, decreasing returns to scale set in at low levels of output. Emilio's likely finds that there are limits to its ability to coordinate and operate a larger scale food operation. One can imagine that coordinating the timing of gourmet meals might prove more challenging the larger the number of meals served; similarly, communicating with wait staff, chefs, and house managers would also be more difficult the larger the number of seats in the restaurant. As these costs of coordination and communication increase this leads to higher costs per unit as output increases: Emilio's elects to stay relatively small since this is where their costs per unit of output are minimized.

Answers to Module Review Questions

1. **Answer a.** This is the definition of the *LRATC* curve, which identifies the lowest average total cost of production for every level of output, assuming that the firm has the freedom to set its fixed input at the optimal level for each level of output.

2. **Answer b.** As the firm increases its production the firm's cost rises, but if the *LRATC* curve is downward sloping this implies that the increase in output must be proportionately greater than the increase in total cost. In this range of output, the firm has increasing returns to scale.

3. **Answer a.** When a firm's *LRATC* curve is upward sloping this means that increasing the firm's level of production will raise the average total cost of producing the good, and the firm does not benefit from getting larger. In this case the firm has decreasing returns to scale. Decreasing returns to scale arise primarily because of problems of coordination and communication. When a firm has high set-up costs, this implies that the firm is likely to have increasing returns to scale and decreasing average total cost over a large range of outputs. The firm in this example has increasing average total cost.

4. **Answer c.** Statement II is the definition of constant returns to scale, and statement III identifies the primary reasons for the decreasing returns to scale. Returns to scale is a long-run phenomenon and thus statement I, with its focus on the short run, is incorrect.

5. **Answer d.** Fixed cost is a short-run cost that does not vary as the level of production changes. Examples of fixed cost include the rental payment a firm makes for a building, the cost of a piece of equipment, or a flat tax that the business pays irrespective of its level of production. Fixed costs may be a small part of a firm's total cost of production or it may be a large part of a firm's total cost of production.

6. **Answer c.** The firm's average total cost is equal to the sum of the firm's average fixed cost plus its average variable cost. Thus, the firm's average variable cost equals average total cost minus average fixed cost. In this example the firm's average variable cost is equal to \$12 per unit of output. To find the variable cost of production multiply the firm's average variable cost times its level of production: thus, \$12 per unit output times 20 units of output gives us variable cost of \$240.

7. **Answer c.** To calculate the marginal cost of producing the thirty-first unit of output you need to first calculate the total cost of producing the thirtieth unit of output and the total cost of producing the thirty-first unit of output. Then, you can calculate the change in total cost for the firm as it produces one more unit. From the information we are given we can calculate the variable cost of producing 30 units as (\$12/unit)(30 units) = \$360. The total cost of producing 30 units is therefore equal to *FC* + *VC*, or \$20 + \$360, or a total of \$380. The variable cost of producing 31 units is equal to (\$15/unit)(31 units) = \$465. The total cost of producing 31 units is therefore equal to *FC* + *VC*, or \$20 + \$465 = \$485. The marginal cost of producing the thirty-first unit is therefore equal to (\$485 – \$380)/(31 – 30) = \$105.

module 24

Introduction to Market Structure

BEFORE YOU READ THE MODULE

Summary

This module discusses a system of market structure based upon the number of firms in the market and the degree to which the good offered in the market by different producers is differentiated. Using this system of market structure the module then describes the four primary types of market structure based on these two characteristics: perfect competition where there are many firms all producing an identical product; monopoly where there is a single firm producing a product for which there are no close substitutes; oligopoly where there are a few firms that may or may not produce a differentiated product; and monopolistic competition where there are many firms producing differentiated products.

Module Objectives

Objective #1. There are four principal models of market structure: perfect competition, monopoly, oligopoly, and monopolistic competition. These four types of market structure are distinguished by the number of firms in the market and whether the goods offered in the market are identical or differentiated.

- In monopoly, a single producer produces a single, undifferentiated product. In oligopoly, a few producers sell products that may or may not be differentiated. In monopolistically competitive markets, many producers sell differentiated products. In perfect competition, many producers produce identical products.
- The number of firms in the market is determined by the long-run conditions that make it difficult for new firms to enter the market: these conditions include government regulations that limit entry, the presence of increasing returns to scale in production, technological superiority that limits potential competition, or the control of necessary resources or inputs. When these conditions are present, the market structure tends to be monopolistic or oligopolistic.

Objective #2. A perfectly competitive industry is an industry in which both the producers and consumers in that industry are price takers. A price-taking producer is one whose actions cannot affect the market price of the good sold. A price-taking firm can sell as many units of the good as it would like at the prevailing market price. A price-taking consumer is a consumer who cannot influence the market price of the good by their actions. The market price is therefore unaffected by the actions of either individual producers or individual consumers.

- For an industry to be perfectly competitive there must be many producers in that industry, and no one of these producers can have a large market share of the industry's output.
- For an industry to be perfectly competitive consumers must regard the products produced in that market as being equivalent. The product sold in a perfectly competitive industry is a standardized product or commodity, and consumers must view each producer's product as a perfect substitute for any other producer's product.
- Most perfectly competitive industries also have easy entry of new firms into the industry and exit of existing firms from the industry in the long run. This is referred to as free entry and exit.

Objective #3. A monopoly is a market characterized by having a single producer of the good, when the good has no close substitutes. Monopolists, unlike perfectly competitive firms, know that their actions affect the market price, and they take this fact into account when deciding how much to produce.

Objective #4. Positive economic profits earned by the monopolist continue in the long run because effective barriers to entry prevent new firms from entering the industry. There are four principal barriers to entry: (1) the monopoly controls a scarce resource or input that prevents new firms from being able to compete in the industry; (2) the monopolist enjoys increasing returns to scale and therefore can spread its fixed cost over a larger volume of output, resulting in the monopolist having lower average total costs than potential competitors; (3) the monopolist enjoys technological superiority over its potential competitors; and (4) the monopolist is protected from competition due to government-created barriers.

- Increasing returns to scale results in lower costs of production as the size of the firm increases. In the case of a monopoly with increasing returns to scale, the single firm finds that its cost of production falls throughout the relevant range of production. Any potential competitor would face higher costs per unit. Natural monopolies are an example of a monopoly that benefits from increasing returns to scale.
- With technological superiority some monopolists also experience network externalities, which is a condition that arises when the value to a consumer of a good increases as the number of people who use the good increases. This advantage may allow the producer to become a monopolist.
- The most important government-created barrier to entry takes the form of patent protection. A similar type of protection afforded producers is the copyright.

Objective #5. Oligopolies are characterized as an industry in which there are a few producers. Each of these individual producers has some market power (like a monopoly) that enables them to affect market prices, but each of these producers also competes against the other producers in the industry. This competition is different from perfect competition in that each producer is aware of the other firms in the industry and recognizes that each firm's behavior affects the other firms. The key aspect of oligopoly is the tension between cooperation and competition: each firm must decide whether and to what degree it wants to cooperate or compete with the other firms in their industry.

Objective #6. With an oligopolistic industry what matters is not the size of the firm, but rather the number of firms serving the industry. Oligopolies primarily exist because each firm benefits from increasing returns to scale and these returns to scale result in a few producers in the industry rather than many small-scale producers in the industry. Analysis of oligopoly presents several challenging puzzles not presented in our analysis of perfectly competitive markets or monopolies.

Objective #7. The Herfindahl–Hirschman Index (HHI) allows economists to measure the degree of concentration in an industry. This index is the square of the share of market sales summed over the firms in the industry. An HHI greater than 1,800 indicates an oligopoly; an HHI between 1,000 and 1,800 indicates a somewhat competitive market; and an HHI less than 1,000 indicates a strongly competitive market. When a proposed merger is likely to significantly increase the HHI over 1,000, the merger is closely analyzed and is likely to be disallowed by government antitrust enforcement.

Objective #8. A monopolistically competitive industry is composed of many competing firms selling differentiated products with free entry and exit of firms in the long run. The three essential characteristics of monopolistic competition are a large number of producers, differentiated products, and free entry and exit of firms in the long run. Analysis of this market structure reveals that in some ways it resembles perfect competition and in other ways it resembles monopoly.

Key Terms

Notes

price-taking firm a firm whose actions have no effect on the market price of the good or service it sells.

price-taking consumer a consumer whose actions have no effect on the market price of the good or service he or she buys.

perfectly competitive market a market in which all participants are price-takers.

perfectly competitive industry an industry in which all producers are price-takers.

market share the fraction of the total industry output accounted for by a given producer's output.

standardized product output of different producers regarded by consumers as the same good; also referred to as a *commodity.*

commodity output of different producers regarded by consumers as the same good; also referred to as a *standardized product.*

free entry and exit describes an industry that potential producers can easily enter or current producers can leave.

monopolist a firm that is the only producer of a good that has no close substitutes.

monopoly an industry controlled by a *monopolist.*

Key Terms *(continued)*

Notes

barrier to entry something that prevents other firms from entering an industry. Crucial in protecting the profits of a *monopolist.* There are four types of barriers to entry: control over scarce *resources* or *inputs,* increasing returns to scale, technological superiority, and government-created barriers such as *licenses.*

natural monopoly a *monopoly* that exists when *increasing returns to scale* provide a large cost advantage to having all output produced by a single firm.

patent a temporary monopoly given by the government to an inventor for the use or sale of an invention.

copyright the exclusive legal right of the creator of a literary or artistic work to profit from that work; like a *patent,* it is a temporary monopoly.

oligopoly an industry with only a small number of producers.

oligopolist a firm in an industry with only a small number of producers.

imperfect competition a market structure in which no firm is a *monopolist,* but producers nonetheless have *market power* they can use to affect market prices.

Herfindahl–Hirschman Index, or **HHI** is the square of each firm's share of market sales summed over the industry. It gives a picture of the industry market structure.

monopolistic competition a market structure in which there are many competing producers in an industry, each producer sells a differentiated product, and there is *free entry and exit* into and from the industry in the *long run.*

AFTER YOU READ THE MODULE

Tips

Tip #1. The market structure of an industry depends upon two dimensions: 1) the number of firms in the market, and 2) the degree of product differentiation in the market. Review the different types of market structure presented in this module and focus on these two dimensions for each type of market structure.

Tip #2. For a market structure to be perfectly competitive two conditions must be met: 1) there must be many firms with no firm having significant market share; and 2) the product produced in the industry must be standardized.

Tip #3. Monopolies exist because of barriers to entry. Barriers to entry are due to control of a scarce resource or input, economies of scale, technological superiority, or government-created barriers.

Tip #4. To characterize an industry as monopolistically competitive, that industry must have a large number of firms that sell differentiated products. The industry must also have free entry or exit of firms in the long run.

WORKED PROBLEMS

1. For each of the following situations, fill in the accompanying table. You are asked to determine what type of industry each situation represents and whether the product is differentiated. Choose perfect competition, monopoly, oligopoly, or monopolistic competition for the type of industry and differentiated, undifferentiated, or not applicable for the product differentiation column. If the product is differentiated, describe how the product is differentiated: differentiated by style or type; differentiated by location; or differentiated by quality.

Situation	Type of industry	Is product differentiated, and if so, how is it differentiated?
Dress shops for teenagers at malls		
Gasoline stations in a town of 200,000 people		
Meat market in a community of 20 people		
100,000 corn growers in a country		
Gasoline station located on a toll road		
Colleges and universities in a country		

STEP 1: Review the characteristics of each type of industry before filling out the column. Also, review what it means to have a differentiated product.

STEP 2: Now, fill in the table, recognizing that if there is only one producer in the market, the market structure is a monopoly; that if there are many producers none of whom has market power and the good is an identical product, then the market is a perfectly competitive market; that if there are a few producers, the market is an oligopoly; and that if there are many producers producing differentiated products, the market is monopolistically competitive.

The completed table follows.

Situation	Type of industry	Is product differentiated, and if so, how is it differentiated
Dress shops for teenagers at malls	Monopolistic competition	Differentiated by style or type; differentiated by quality
Gasoline stations in a town of 20,000 people	Oligopoly	Differentiated by location
Meat market in a community of 20 people	Monopoly	Not applicable
100,000 corn growers in a country	Perfect competition	Not differentiated
Gasoline station located on a toll road	Monopoly	Not applicable
Colleges and universities in a country	Monopolistic competition	Differentiated by style or type; differentiated by quality; and differentiated by location

2. Suppose the market for widgets in the United States has eight producers. The following table provides the market share of each of these producers. You have been asked to calculate the Herfindahl–Hirschman Index (HHI) for the widget industry. In addition, Firms 1, 2, and 4 have proposed to the U.S. Justice Department a merger of their three firms. You have been asked to calculate the HHI for this industry if this merger is allowed. Based on your two calculations, what do you think the U.S. Justice Department's position on this merger will be?

Firm	Firm's market share (percent)
1	10
2	8
3	14
4	15
5	16
6	20
7	15
8	2

STEP 1: Start by calculating the HHI for the widget industry, given the provided market shares. Then determine, according to its HHI, whether the widget industry is a strongly competitive market, a somewhat competitive market, or an oligopoly.

To find the HHI for the industry, recall that the HHI is the square of each firm's share of market sales summed over all of the firms in the industry. Thus, the HHI for the widget industry based on the current numbers would be HHI = $10^2 + 8^2 + 14^2 + 15^2 + 16^2 + 20^2 + 15^2 + 2^2 = 1{,}470$. The U.S. Justice Department's guidelines state that an industry with an HHI of less than 1,000 is a strongly competitive industry, an industry with an HHI between 1,000 and 1,800 is considered a somewhat competitive market, and an industry with an HHI greater than 1,800 is an oligopoly. Since the HHI for the widget industry is between 1,000 and 1,800, the industry would be considered somewhat competitive.

STEP 2: Create a new table providing the new market shares in the widget market if the proposed merger takes place.

For the new table, merge firms 1, 2, and 4 into a new firm 1, and then enter the other firms' market shares in the table as well.

Firm	Firm's market share after merger (percent)
1 (combines original firms 1, 2, and 4)	33
3	14
5	16
6	20
7	15
8	2

STEP 3: Calculate the new HHI for the widget industry based on the new market shares. Then determine, according to the new HHI, whether the widget industry would be a strongly competitive market, a somewhat competitive market, or an oligopoly.

The new HHI after the merger would be equal to HHI = $33^2 + 14^2 + 16^2 + 20^2 + 15^2 + 2^2 = 2{,}170$. Given the guidelines given in Step 1, this industry would move from being considered somewhat competitive to being considered an oligopoly, since its HHI is increasing from 1,470 to 2,170.

STEP 4: Provide a statement of what the U.S. Justice Department's position on this proposed merger is likely to be, given the two HHI numbers you have calculated.

The U.S. Department of Justice will likely turn down this proposed merger, since the merger transforms the widget industry from a somewhat competitive industry to an oligopolistic industry.

Problems and Exercises

1. What does it mean to be a price-taking firm? What does it mean to be a price-taking consumer? What is the relationship between market share and price taking?

2. The model of perfect competition is based on two necessary conditions and a third condition that is often present as well. Identify each of these conditions and then briefly discuss their importance in the model.

3. Suppose there is a single firm producing a good for which there are no close substitutes. This firm is currently earning positive economic profit in the short run. Why does this firm care about the existence of barriers to entry in its market? Explain your answer.

4. A firm wishes to increase the price it charges for its product, and it wishes to restrict the level of output available to consumers. What must be true if this firm is to be successful?

5. Briefly review the four general types of barriers to entry and how each of these types effectively restricts the level of competition the monopolist faces.

6. An industry has 10 producers producing differentiated products, but all the products in the industry are generally viewed by consumers as soft drinks. What kind of market structure does this industry have, and why would you define the market structure in this way?

7. Each of the 10 producers in question 6 has 10% of the market sales in the soft drink industry. What is the Herfindahl–Hirschman Index (HHI) for this industry? Does this HHI change your opinion about what kind of market structure this industry represents? Explain your answer.

8. Four of the 10 producers in question 6 each have 20% of the market sales in the soft drink industry while, of the remaining six firms, one firm has 5% of the market sales in the industry and the other five firms each have 3% of the market sales. What is the HHI for this industry? Does this HHI change your opinion about what kind of market structure this industry represents? Explain your answer.

9. Four of the 10 producers in question 6 each have 20% of the market sales in the soft drink industry while, of the remaining six firms, one firm has 5% of the market sales in the industry and the other five firms each have 3% of the market sales. Two of the firms that currently each have 20% of the market sales propose to merge. What would the change in the HHI be if this merger was approved? Would the merger have any effect on the industry?

10. Two of the 10 producers in question 6 each have 30% of the market sales in the soft drink industry while, of the remaining eight firms, one firm has 25% of the market share, another firm has 3% of the market share, and the remaining six firms each have 2% of the market share. What is the HHI for this industry? Does this HHI change your opinion about what kind of market structure this industry represents? Explain your answer.

11. Oligopoly is characterized by having a few firms in the industry. What is the best explanation for why these industries only have a few firms?

12. Why are fast-food restaurants considered an example of a monopolistically competitive industry? What key attributes need to be present to have a monopolistically competitive industry?

13. How are fast-food restaurants similar; that is, why are they all considered to be part of the fast-food industry? How are fast-food restaurants differentiated; that is, why are the meals they sell considered to be differentiated from each other?

14. What aspect of the fast-food restaurant business is competitive? What aspect of the fast-food restaurant business is monopolistic?

BEFORE YOU TAKE THE TEST

Module Review Questions

1. Perfect competition requires that
   a. producers be able to enter or exit an industry in the short run.
   b. producers be able to distinguish their product from a rival producer's product.
   c. producers have no ability to exert influence over the market price of the product.
   d. consumers compete for the producers' product.

2. Which of the following describes a perfectly competitive industry?
   a. Elementary school students are only allowed to attend the school in their attendance area.
   b. Water for household use is sold by the local water utility.
   c. The price of wine is determined by global supply and demand. A small share of the total world production of wine is produced in a local valley by ten companies.
   d. The price of oil is determined by global supply and demand. A total of five companies produce the world's supply of oil.

3. Which of the following statements is true?
   I. The model of supply and demand is a model of a perfectly competitive market.
   II. In the model of supply and demand, some producers may be able to affect the price of the good.
   III. In the model of supply and demand, some consumers may be able to affect the price of the good.
   a. Statement I is true.
   b. Statements II and III are true.
   c. Statements I, II, and III are true.
   d. None of these statements is true.

4. An industry is characterized by having a few firms, each producing a differentiated product. The market structure for this industry is most likely
   a. perfect competition.
   b. monopoly.
   c. oligopoly.
   d. monopolistic competition.

5. Monopoly and oligopoly are the typical market structures that occur when there are
   a. no significant entry barriers.
   b. significant entry barriers.

6. A barrier to entry is
   a. always a man-made obstacle to the entry of new firms into a competitive industry.
   b. a term referring to the firm's private property and the firm's right to exclude people from entering this private property.
   c. something that effectively keeps new firms from entering an industry.
   d. only relevant in perfectly competitive industries.

7. A network externality is a situation in which the value of the good ________ as more people use the good.
   a. increases
   b. decreases

8. Patents and copyrights
   a. protect the rights of inventors and writers.
   b. harm consumers of the patented or copyright-protected articles because these articles are more expensive to consumers.
   c. provide an incentive for research and development as well as creative work.
   d. All of the statements are true.

9. An industry characterized by having a few firms, each with some market power, is an example of (a)n
   a. monopoly, since the firms have some market power.
   b. perfectly competitive industry, since there is more than one firm in the industry.
   c. monopolistically competitive industry, since the firms compete with one another while at the same time they have some market power.
   d. oligopoly, since the firms have market power and can therefore affect the market price, but there are only a few firms, so each firm recognizes the interdependence between firms.

10. The formation of an oligopoly is primarily due to the
    a. control of an essential input or resource used in the production of the good.
    b. existence of increasing returns to scale in the industry.
    c. effective entry barrier posed by copyrights or patents.
    d. Answers (a), (b), and (c) are all correct.

11. There are 10 firms in an industry and five of these firms each have sales equal to 10% of the total market. Two of the other five firms each have sales equal to 20% of the total market, two of the other five firms each have sales equal to 3% of the total market, and the remaining firm has sales equal to 4% of the total market. What is the HHI for this industry?
    a. 100
    c. 4,152
    b. 1,334
    d. 1,000

12. There are 10 firms in an industry and five of these firms each have sales equal to 10% of the total market. Two of the other five firms each have sales equal to 20% of the total market, two of the other five firms each have sales equal to 3% of the total market, and the remaining firm has sales equal to 4% of the total market. If two of the firms with market share of 10% each were to merge, what would the new HHI equal?
    a. 1,534
    c. 1,000
    b. 1,334
    d. 1,743

13. A monopolistically competitive industry is characterized by having
    a. many firms, each producing a differentiated product and operating in an industry with free entry and exit in the short run.
    b. a few firms, each producing a differentiated product but with each firm having market power and the ability to set the price of the good it sells.
    c. a very large number of firms that produce very similar products and that always elect to produce the profit-maximizing amount of output in both the short run and the long run.
    d. None of the answers is true about a monopolistically competitive industry.

ANSWER KEY

Answers to Problems and Exercises

1. A price-taking firm is a firm that is so small relative to the entire market that it has no influence on the market price. This firm accepts the price of the good that is determined by the interaction of the market demand and the market supply. A price-taking consumer is a consumer whose purchases in a market are so small relative to the entire market that they can exert no influence on the market price. A price-taking consumer is one that accepts the market-determined price as the price they will pay for the good. Market share refers to the fraction of the total industry output represented by a producer's output: when no producer has significant market share, this implies that no producer is able to influence market prices.

2. The model of perfect competition requires that producers be price takers and that the good being produced in the market is a standardized product. These two conditions imply that no producer can exert influence on the market price and that any producer who raises their price above the market price will find that they lose all their sales to other producers. A third condition that is often present in a perfectly competitive industry is free entry and exit of firms in the long run. Free entry and exit in the long run ensures that economic profit will equal zero in the long run. Firms enter the industry in the long run if there are positive short-run profits, and they exit the industry in the long run if there are negative short-run profits.

3. This firm is a monopoly in that there is only one producer, and this producer is producing a good for which there are no close substitutes. However, if there are no barriers to entry, then this monopoly will not persist since new firms will be attracted to this industry in the long run due to the existence of positive economic profit. Substantial barriers to entry can prevent the firm from facing competition, and it therefore can continue to sustain its positive economic profit into the long run.

4. A firm can choose to restrict its output and raise its price, but if it competes in an industry where there are many firms and where there are close substitutes for its product, the firm will find that raising price and restricting output is not beneficial to them in terms of their profitability. What makes it possible for a firm to restrict output and raise price is the presence of market power that enables the firm to affect the market outcome.

5. Control of an essential resource or input is a very effective barrier to entry, since new firms would be unable to produce the product if they do not have access to this resource or input. The presence of increasing returns to scale also serves as an effective barrier to entry, since the firm that has a larger volume of sales will find that its average total cost of production is lower than a firm with a smaller volume of sales: increasing returns to scale implies that the firm benefits from its large scale of production, which makes it difficult for would-be competitors to enter the industry and compete. Technological superiority can also act an as effective barrier to entry: firms that maintain a consistent technological superiority over potential competitors can establish themselves as monopolists. Lastly, the government may create effective barriers to entry in the form of patents or copyright protections.

6. This industry is characterized as having just a few producers, and although the products are differentiated, they are closely related and can be viewed as substitutes for one another. Because of the small number of firms, this industry would be viewed as an oligopoly, although this classification is dependent on the share of market sales that each firm has. If the market is dominated by several of these firms, then the industry is definitely an oligopoly, but if the market is divided evenly among these ten firms, then the industry, despite its small number of firms, would act more like a perfectly competitive industry than an oligopolistic one.

7. The HHI for this industry is equal to the square of the share of market sales summed over the firms in the industry, or HHI = $(10)^2 + (10)^2 + (10)^2 + (10)^2 + (10)^2 + (10)^2 + (10)^2 + (10)^2 + (10)^2 + (10)^2 = 1{,}000$. An HHI of 1,000 indicates that the industry is on the boundary between a strongly competitive market (HHI of less than 1,000) and a somewhat competitive market (HHI greater than or equal to 1,000 but less than 1,800). The calculation of the HHI changes the appraisal of the market structure from oligopolistic, based on the number of firms in the industry, to more competitive, based on the division of market share.

8. The HHI for this industry is equal to $(20)^2 + (20)^2 + (20)^2 + (20)^2 + (5)^2 + (3)^2 + (3)^2 + (3)^2 + (3)^2 + (3)^2 = 1{,}670$. This HHI places this group of firms in the somewhat competitive market category. To be considered an oligopoly, the HHI must be over 1,800.

9. The HHI before the merger equals 1,670 (see problem 3). The HHI after the merger would equal $(40)^2 + (20)^2 + (20)^2 + (5)^2 + (3)^2 + (3)^2 + (3)^2 + (3)^2 + (3)^2 = 2{,}470$, or a change of 800 from the initial index. This would represent a significant increase in the market concentration in this industry, and the industry would move from a somewhat competitive market structure to an oligopolistic market structure.

10. The HHI for this industry equals $(30)^2 + (30)^2 + (25)^2 + (3)^2 + (2)^2 + (2)^2 + (2)^2 + (2)^2 + (2)^2 + (2)^2 = 2{,}458$. This HHI is over 1,800 and so the industry would be classified as an oligopoly. Notice that when a few firms account for a relatively large amount of the market share the HHI increases rapidly. Compare your calculations in problems 7, 8, and 9.

11. An industry typically has a few firms because the industry is one in which firms have increasing returns to scale: firms benefit from being relatively large, which implies that the total market is usually easily served by just a few firms rather than many small firms.

12. Fast-food restaurants are a good example of a monopolistically competitive industry because there are many firms in the industry, each producing a differentiated product, and there is free entry and exit in the industry in the long run. The key attributes of monopolistically competitive industries are a large number of firms, a differentiated product, and free entry or exit of firms in the long run.

13. Here the answers may vary quite a bit depending on what attributes you have focused on. Fast-food restaurants typically offer relatively cheap meals, in easily accessible locations, at fast speed with little waiting. The food is often easy to eat on the run or to have as carryout. Fast-food restaurants differ from one another in the type of food they serve (e.g., Mexican, hamburgers, Italian). There may also be small price variations that distinguish one restaurant from another.

14. Here again the answers may vary depending on what you focus on in your response. The fast-food restaurant industry is competitive in that there are many firms producing within this industry and each competes to satisfy more or less the same demand—the demand for quick, tasty food. The fast-food restaurant industry is also monopolistic since each firm sells a product that is differentiated from the products of other producers, and this differentiation results in each firm having some degree of market power.

Answers to Module Review Questions

1. **Answer c.** Perfect competition does not require free entry and exit, but it is often present in the long run in a perfectly competitive industry. The output produced in a perfectly competitive industry is a standardized commodity: consumers cannot distinguish one producer's output from another producer's output. Consumers are price taking, and the market price equates the quantity demanded at that price with the quantity supplied at that price. Perfectly competitive industries are characterized by producers being price takers.

2. **Answer c.** Only answer (c) provides a description of price-taking behavior on both the producer and the consumer side of the model.

3. **Answer a.** A basic underlying assumption of the model of supply and demand is that neither consumers nor producers can affect the price of the good. Producers and consumers are price takers, which eliminates statements II and III.

4. **Answer c.** Oligopolies are characterized by having just a few firms in the industry. These firms may produce differentiated products or they may produce identical products.

5. **Answer b.** Entry barriers effectively protect an industry from potential competition from new firms. Entry barriers may be due to government regulation, increasing returns to scale in production, technological superiority, or the control of some essential resource or input.

6. **Answer c.** Barriers to entry may be man-made: for example, legislation may grant patents or copyrights to a particular business or individual. But barriers to entry do not act as an obstacle to new firm entry in a competitive industry, since we assume this kind of industry has free entry and exit in the long run, which eliminates answers (a) and (d). Answer (b) is not true: barriers to entry are not about people's rights to trespass at a business site. Answer (c) is a general definition of barriers to entry.

7. **Answer a.** A network externality is a situation where one person's use of a good is enhanced when other people elect to also use the good. This is the result of interconnections or networks existing between the users of the good. The more users of the good, the more networks or connections are created.

8. **Answer d.** Patents and copyrights are intended to protect the work of inventors and artists. This work is costly in terms of time and resources and would not be undertaken if the inventors and artists did not receive compensation for their creations. However, patents and copyrights create a temporary monopoly and therefore restrict the level of output available while raising the price of the good: both of these effects are harmful to consumers.

9. **Answer d.** This is just a definitional question. The industry described is not a perfectly competitive industry because there are only a few firms and these firms all possess some market power: in a perfectly competitive industry there are many firms and none of these firms has market power. The industry is not a monopoly because a monopolistic industry has a single producer of the good. The industry is not monopolistically competitive because there are not enough firms in the market.

10. **Answer b.** Although oligopolies may arise because of an entry barrier based on scarce resources or government protection in the form of copyrights or patents, it is far more likely that the oligopoly arises due to the presence of returns to scale that results in the firms in the industry producing at a large scale relative to the overall market demand for the product.

11. **Answer b.** The HHI is equal to $(10)^2 + (10)^2 + (10)^2 + (10)^2 + (10)^2 + (20)^2 + (20)^2 + (3)^2 + (3)^2 + (4)^2 = 1{,}334$.

12. **Answer a.** The HHI would equal $(10)^2 + (10)^2 + (10)^2 + (20)^2 + (20)^2 + (20)^2 + (3)^2 + (3)^2 + (4)^2 = 1{,}534$.

13. **Answer d.** Each of the answers (a) through (c) contains some type of error. For example, answer (a) is correct except for the fact that entry and exit occur in the long run. Answer (b) is correct except for the fact that there are more than a few firms in a monopolistically competitive industry. Answer (c) is incorrect because the firms in a monopolistically competitive industry typically produce highly differentiated products.

module 25

Perfect Competition

BEFORE YOU READ THE MODULE

Summary

This module focuses on the model of perfect competition and in particular, on the determination of the profit-maximizing level of output. The module then discusses how to determine whether the perfectly competitive firm is making positive or negative profits.

Module Objectives

Objective #1. Marginal analysis can be used to compute the profit-maximizing level of output. To do this analysis, marginal revenue and marginal cost must be calculated. Recall that marginal cost (*MC*) is the change in total cost divided by the change in output.

- The profit-maximizing level of output corresponds to that level of output at which marginal revenue equals marginal cost. Marginal revenue measures the addition to total revenue from selling one more unit of the good while marginal cost measures the addition to total cost from producing one more unit of the good. When marginal revenue is greater than marginal cost the firm's benefit from producing this last unit of output is greater than the cost of producing this last unit: the firm should expand output to include this unit of production. When marginal revenue is less than marginal cost the firm's benefit from producing another unit of output is less than the cost of producing this last unit: the firm should not expand output to include this additional unit of production. It is only when marginal revenue equals marginal cost for the last unit of output produced that the firm earns its highest level of profit.
- The producer's optimal output rule states that profit is maximized by producing that level of output at which marginal revenue equals marginal cost for the last unit produced. That is, the firm should produce that level of output where $MR = MC$. This can be restated as: the firm's profit-maximizing level of output is where $P = MC$, since for the perfectly competitive firm P equals MR. Figure 25.1 illustrates the profit-maximizing level of output (q) for a perfectly competitive firm.

Figure 25.1

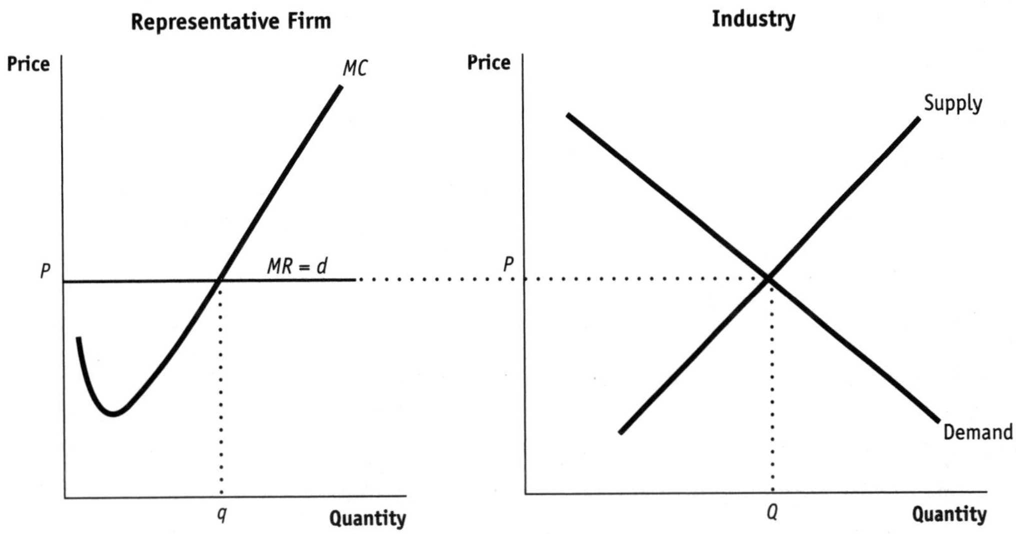

Objective #2. The profit-maximization rule identifies the level of output that results in maximizing the firm's profit, but it does not tell the producer whether they should produce at all. To answer this question, the firm needs to look at whether it is profitable or unprofitable to produce. The decision to produce or not is based on the firm's economic profit and not its accounting profit. The cost curves that the firm uses to make its production decisions are cost curves that include all costs, implicit and explicit. Given the firm's cost curves, whether it is profitable in the short run to produce depends on whether the market price of the good is more or less than the firm's average total cost.

- The firm makes a profit whenever its total revenue is greater than its total cost. The firm breaks even whenever its total revenue is equal to its total cost. The firm incurs a loss whenever its total revenue is less than its total cost.

Key Terms

marginal revenue the change in total revenue generated by an additional unit of output.

optimal output rule profit is maximized by producing the quantity of output at which the marginal revenue of the last unit produced is equal to its marginal cost.

price-taking firm's optimal output rule the profit of a price-taking firm is maximized by producing the quantity of output at which the market price is equal to the *marginal cost* of the last unit produced.

marginal revenue curve a graphical representation showing how marginal revenue varies as output varies.

Notes

AFTER YOU READ THE MODULE

Tips

Tip #1. It is critical that students understand the optimal output rule for a price-taking firm. The firm in order to profit-maximize must produce that quantity where marginal revenue equals marginal cost. If the firm produces less output than this it will not be maximizing its profits since at a lower level of output the addition to total revenue from selling one more unit of the good will be greater than the addition to total cost from producing one more unit of the good: the firm can increase its profits by producing a higher level of output. If the firm produces more output than this it will not be maximizing its profits since at a level of output where *MR* is less than *MC* it will find that the addition to total revenue from selling one more unit of the good will be less than the addition to total cost from producing one more unit of the good: the firm can increase its profits by producing a lower level of output.

Tip #2. When a firm produces at its minimum average total cost, this implies that the firm earns a normal economic profit. The firm's minimum average total cost occurs at that level of output where the firm's *ATC* curve intersects its *MC* curve.

WORKED PROBLEMS

1. A perfectly competitive market structure is characterized by having many producers, where none of these producers has a large market share. In addition, this type of market is characterized by its standardized product. Explain why these two characteristics are necessary for a market to be considered perfectly competitive.

STEP 1: Start by considering the impact on a market when that market has just a few firms or at least one firm that has significant market share. How would either of these events affect the market?

If there were just a few firms in a market, then it is likely that each firm would be very aware of what the other firms were doing in the market. With just a few firms in the market, it is likely that any action taken by one of the firms would influence market prices and therefore significantly alter the overall amount of the good supplied in the market. Similarly, if there was a single firm with significant market share in an industry with many firms, this single firm could still influence market price and thereby affect the market quantity of the good. In a market with many firms, none of which has significant market share, all firms will be price takers: each firm will sell its output at the market-determined price.

STEP 2: Why is a standardized product a necessary condition for a perfectly competitive industry?

With a standardized product, consumers view the good as the same no matter which producer provides the good. Thus, consumers will be willing to pay only the market price for the good since each producer's product is a perfect substitute for every other producer's product.

2. Perfectly competitive firms maximize their profit when they produce that output at which their marginal revenue is equal to their marginal cost. Explain verbally why firms realize their greatest profit when they produce this particular quantity.

STEP 1: **Start by reviewing what marginal revenue means for the firm.**

Marginal revenue is the addition to total revenue that a firm earns when it sells an additional unit of output. Marginal revenue can be calculated by looking at the change in total revenue that occurs when the firm sells one more unit of the good. Firms make their production decisions by looking at how producing and selling an additional unit of the good changes their cost and their revenues.

STEP 2: **Now, review what marginal cost means for the firm.**

Marginal cost is the addition to total cost that a firm incurs when it produces an additional unit of output. Marginal cost can be calculated by looking at the change in total cost that occurs when the firm produces one more unit of the good. Firms make their production decisions by looking at how producing and selling an additional unit of the good changes their cost and their revenues.

STEP 3: **Put the two concepts developed in Steps 1 and 2 together to create an explanation for why producing that quantity at which marginal cost equals marginal revenue results in maximum profit for the firm.**

By producing that level of output at which marginal cost equals marginal revenue, firms are selecting that level of output at which the addition to total cost from producing one more unit of the good equals the addition to total revenue from selling one more unit of the good. Any other level of output will not maximize profit. To see this, consider what happens if the firm produces that level of output at which marginal revenue is greater than marginal cost: if the firm were to produce an additional unit of the product and sell that unit, it would add more to its total revenue than it would add to its total cost. The firm realizes that, if marginal revenue is greater than marginal cost at its current level of output, then the firm should increase its level of production. If the firm produces that level of output at which marginal cost is greater than marginal revenue, then it is clearly producing too many units of the good. By reducing its level of production, it can enhance its profitability.

Problems and Exercises

1. Use the following graph of a perfectly competitive firm to answer this set of questions.

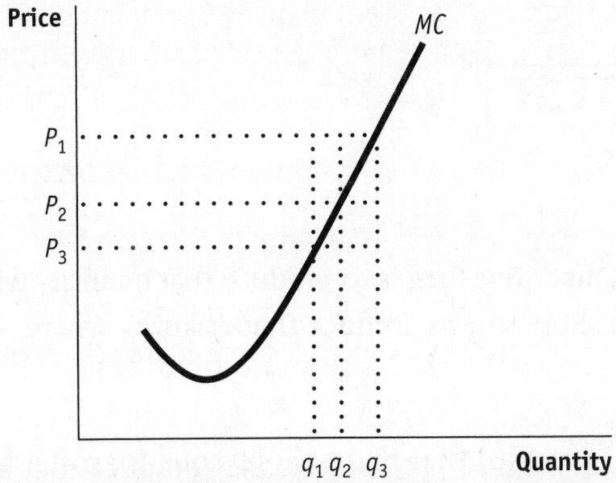

a. Suppose that the market price is equal to P_2. In the short run what level of output will this firm produce? Explain your answer.

b. Suppose that the market price increases to P_1. How will this firm respond to the change in the market price? Explain your answer.

c. Suppose that the market price decreases to P_3. How will this firm respond to the change in the market price? Explain your answer.

2. A perfectly competitive firm is described as a price taker and as a price taker it can sell as many units of output as it would like at the market price. Explain how this is possible. Why is there no limit to how many units the firm can sell in the market?

3. Why is the demand curve for a perfectly competitive firm drawn as a horizontal line at the market price?

BEFORE YOU TAKE THE TEST

Module Review Questions

1. The optimal output rule for a perfectly competitive firm is to produce that quantity where

a. $MR = MC$ in the long run, but in the short run to produce that quantity where $MC = ATC$.

b. $MC = ATC$ in the short run.

c. $MR = MC$ no matter what the period, provided that marginal revenue is greater than average variable cost.

d. $MR = MC$ no matter what the period, provided that marginal revenue is greater than average total cost.

2. Production is profitable in the short run whenever price is greater than
   a. average total cost.
   b. marginal cost.
   c. average variable cost.
   d. average fixed cost.

3. A perfectly competitive firm's minimum-cost output corresponds to the level of output at which
   a. fixed cost is minimized.
   b. variable cost is minimized.
   c. average total cost is minimized.
   d. total cost is minimized.

4. A perfectly competitive industry is characterized as
   a. having many sellers where no individual seller has a large market share.
   b. having many buyers where no individual buyer has market power.
   c. having firms that always produce that quantity where marginal revenue equals marginal cost.
   d. Answers (a) and (b) are both correct.
   e. Answers (a), (b), and (c) are all correct.

5. A perfectly competitive firm's marginal cost for a particular quantity of production is calculated as
   a. the change in fixed cost divided by the change in output.
   b. the change in total cost divided by the change in output.
   c. the change in average total cost divided by the change in output.
   d. the change in average fixed cost divided by the change in output.

6. Suppose that when a perfectly competitive firm produces 10 pens its cost of production is equal to $24 and when it produces 12 pens its cost of production is equal to $30. If the price of pens is equal to $3 then this firm should
   a. produce no more than 10 pens.
   b. produce at least 12 pens.

7. For a perfectly competitive firm, suppose that the price per unit the firm can sell its product for is greater than the cost per unit of producing that quantity of the product. Then, it must be the case that if this firm produces this quantity the firm will
   a. earn a negative economic profit.
   b. earn a positive economic profit.
   c. earn a normal economic profit.

ANSWER KEY

Answers to Problems and Exercises

1. a. The profit-maximizing perfectly competitive firm will use the optimal output rule to determine the level of output that it will produce given the market price. When the market price is P_2, the firm will interpret this market price as its marginal revenue, and it will maximize its profits by producing output so that MR equals MC. In the graph this occurs at q_2.

   b. If the market price increases to P_1, the firm will still use the optimal output rule to determine the level of output that it should produce in order to maximize its profits. When the market price is P_1, the representative firm will maximize its profits by producing output so that MR equals MC, or in the graph, at q_3.

   c. If the market price decreases to P_3, the firm will still use the optimal output rule to determine the level of output that will maximize its profits. When the market price is P_3, the representative firm will maximize its profits by producing so that MR equals MC, or in the graph, at q_1.

2. In a perfectly competitive industry each firm produces a level of output that is very small compared to the total level of output produced in the industry. This means that no one firm can affect the market price: each firm finds that it must sell its product at the market price. But, it also means that each firm can sell as much of the good as it would like at this market price since its level of production is quite small compared to the overall level of industry production.

3. The demand curve for a perfectly competitive firm is drawn as a horizontal line at the market price since from the firm's perspective it can sell as much of the good as it would like at the market price. The firm knows that it will be unable to sell the good at a price higher than the market price: since its product is identical to the product sold by the other firms in the industry no one will be willing to buy its product at a higher price since they can get the product at the market price. The firm also recognizes that there is no reason to sell its product at a price below the market price since customers in this market are willing to pay the market price for the good.

Answers to Module Review Questions

1. **Answer c.** The profit-maximizing firm, if it produces, always produces that quantity where $MR = MC$. The profit-maximizing firm produces in the short run, provided that the market price is equal to or greater than the firm's average variable cost. The firm makes a positive economic profit if the market price is greater than average total cost, and it earns a negative economic profit if the market price is less than average total cost.

2. **Answer a.** The firm makes positive economic profit whenever the market price is greater than the firm's average total cost, and it makes negative economic profit whenever the market price is less than the firm's average total cost.

3. **Answer c.** The firm's minimum-cost output occurs where the cost per unit (its average total cost) is minimized. The firm's average total cost is minimized at the output level that corresponds to the firm's break-even price.

4. **Answer e.** A perfectly competitive firm maximizes its profit by producing an output level where marginal cost equals marginal revenue for the last unit of the good produced. Perfectly competitive industries are characterized as having many buyers and many sellers where no one of these entities has market power. Both firms and consumers are price takers.

5. **Answer b.** Marginal cost is defined as the change in total cost divided by the change in output. Note that since fixed cost is constant, it does not affect marginal cost. Marginal cost is determined by the change in variable cost that occurs as the level of output changes. Thus, one can calculate marginal cost as the change in variable cost divided by the change in output and get exactly the same results as you would get from calculating marginal cost as the change in total cost divided by the change in output. Answer (a) is incorrect since fixed cost does not change as the level of output changes. Answers (c) and (d) are incorrect since marginal cost is not based on average costs.

6. **Answer b.** From the information you are given you can calculate the marginal cost of the firm producing 12 pens instead of 10 pens: *MC* = (change in total cost)/(change in total output) = $6/2 units of output = $3/unit of output. The firm's marginal revenue is equal to the market price of $3 since the firm is a price-taking perfectly competitive firm. To firm will profit-maximize by producing where *MR* = *MC*. This occurs at 12 pens and not 10 pens.

7. **Answer b.** When price per unit is greater than cost per unit this implies that the firm is earning more money selling the output then it is incurring in costs. The firm must therefore be earning a positive economic profit.

module 26

Graphing Perfect Competition

BEFORE YOU READ THE MODULE

Summary

This module fully develops the model of perfect competition. It shows how to determine a perfectly competitive firm's profit or loss from a graph. The module also discusses how a firm decides whether or not it should produce in the short run or shut down its production.

Module Objectives

Objective #1. The firm's profitability can be expressed in terms of averages. Profit = $TR - TC$, and if both sides of this equation are divided by output (Q), this results in profit/Q = $TR/Q - TC/Q$. TR/Q is average revenue, which for a perfectly competitive firm is the market price (P) since the average price for the price-taking firm exactly equals the market-determined price. TC/Q is equal to the average total cost (ATC) of producing the level of output. This equation provides a means for comparing the price of the good to the average total cost: when the price is greater than the average total cost, the firm earns a positive profit; when the price is equal to the average total cost, the firm breaks even; and when the price is less than the average total cost, the firm incurs a loss. Figure 26.1 illustrates three situations: a firm earning a positive economic profit ($P > ATC$), a firm earning zero economic profit ($P = ATC$), and a firm earning negative economic profit ($P < ATC$).

Figure 26.1

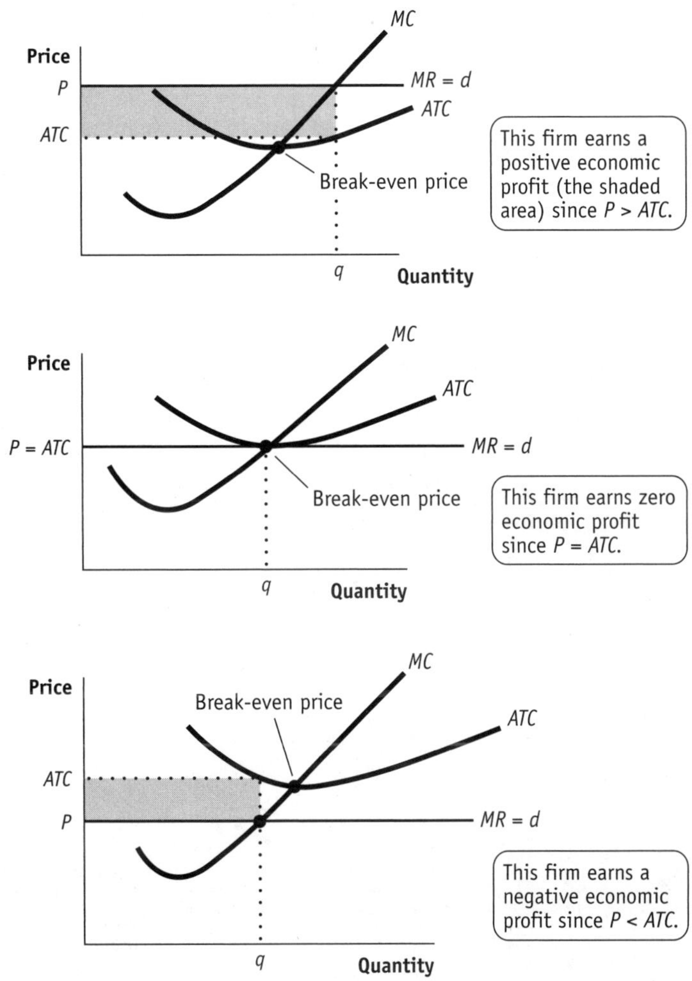

- The firm breaks even, or earns a zero economic profit, if the market price is equal to the minimum of the firm's average total cost; the firm earns a negative profit if the price is less than the minimum of the firm's average total cost; and the firm earns a positive profit if the price is greater than the minimum of the firm's average total cost. Figure 26.1 illustrates these three possibilities and the resultant profit situation for the firm. The minimum point of the average total cost is called the break-even price because it identifies the price at which the firm breaks even (earns a zero economic profit).

Objective #2. In the short run, a perfectly competitive firm incurs its fixed costs whether or not it produces, while it can reduce its variable costs by deciding not to produce. The firm would therefore want to base its production decision in the short run on whether it can cover its variable cost of production: when the firm's revenues do not cover all of its variable cost of production, then the firm will lose money on its fixed cost as well as some of its variable cost; when the firm's revenues cover all of its variable cost of production, then the firm will lose money only on that part of its fixed cost that the remaining revenue does not cover. In the short run, the firm will be willing to produce only if its revenue is sufficient to cover all of its variable cost of production. This concept can be summarized by the following guidelines:

- In the short run, when the market price is less than the minimum point of the firm's average variable cost (*AVC*) curve, then the firm should shut down and produce 0 units of output. Its short-run costs will therefore equal its fixed cost and the firm will minimize its losses.

- In the short run, when the market price is greater than or equal to the minimum point of the firm's *AVC* but is less than the minimum point of the *ATC*, then the firm should produce the level of output at which $P = MC$. This level of output will result in negative economic profits in the short run, but these negative profits will be equal to or less than the firm's fixed cost.
- Figure 26.2 illustrates the short-run production decisions for these two possibilities.

Figure 26.2

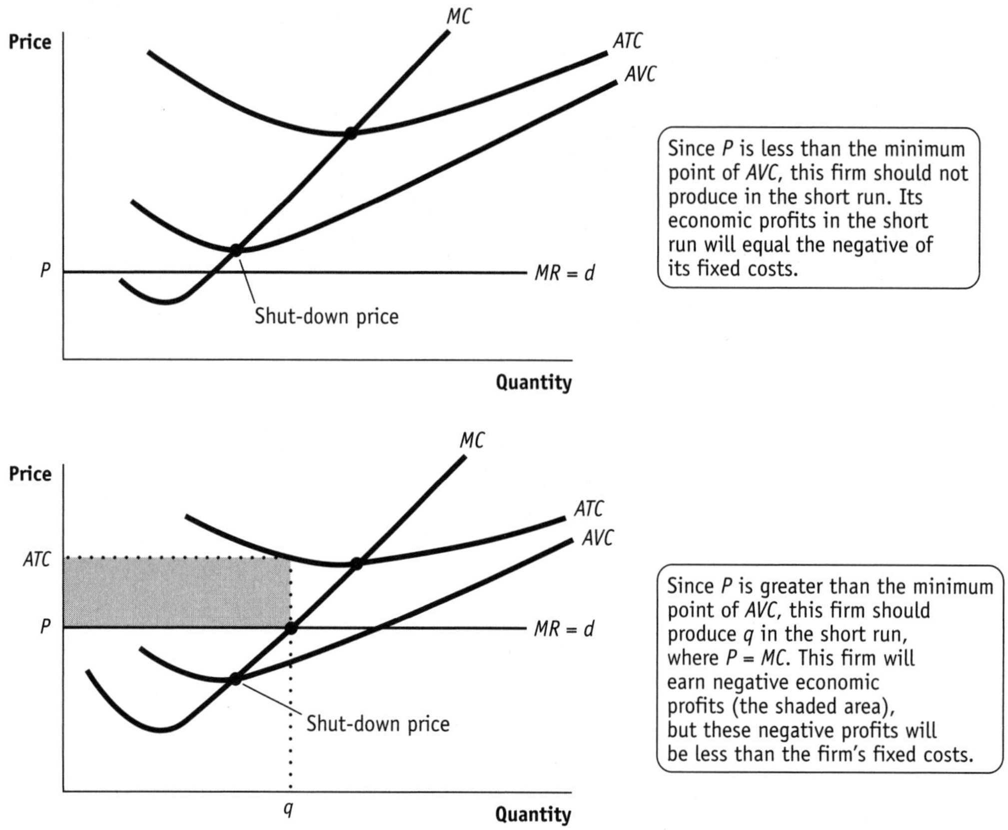

- To summarize, when price is between the minimum point of the *AVC* and the minimum point of the *ATC*, the firm will lose money (earn a negative economic profit) in the short run, but it will lose less money by producing in the short run than it would lose if it decided to shut down in the short run. This decision is similar to the decision to ignore sunk costs: the firm's fixed cost cannot be changed in the short run, so they should be ignored by the firm when the firm makes its short-run production decision.

Objective #3. The firm's short-run supply curve corresponds to the firm's *MC* curve when the market price is equal to or above the shut-down price (the minimum point of the *AVC* curve). The firm's short-run supply curve for market prices less than the shut-down price is the vertical axis: the firm will produce 0 units of output when the market price is less than the shut-down price.

Objective #4. The short-run industry supply curve shows the quantity that producers supply at each price, holding the number of producers constant at a given level.

Key Terms

break-even price the market price at which a firm earns zero profits.

shut-down price the price at which a firm ceases production in the short run because the market price has fallen below the minimum *average variable cost.*

Notes

AFTER YOU READ THE MODULE

Tips

Tip #1. This module advances the use of cost concepts in analyzing firm behavior. You may find it helpful to work with the graphs depicting the short-run economic behavior of the perfectly competitive market: these graphs can serve as a roadmap for directing your analyses of how a firm responds to economic events. Students often find that a quick sketch of a representative firm and the industry provides insight into solving a challenging problem.

- Figure 26.3 illustrates an example of this type of quick sketch for a perfectly competitive industry in the short run. In this example, the firm is earning a negative economic profit since the price the good is sold for is less than the average total cost of producing the good. Here's the analysis for this sketch: the industry demand and supply curves determine the equilibrium price (*P*) in the market and the equilibrium market quantity (*Q*). Firms are price takers, so they will sell their output at *P* and their *MR* curve is a horizontal line drawn at that price. Firms will select their profit-maximizing level of output (*q* for the representative firm in our sketch) by producing the quantity at which $MR = MC$, or where $P = MC$. The firm can then calculate its profit by comparing its *P* to its *ATC* at the level of production that was chosen. In this example $P < ATC$, so the firm must be making negative economic profit. The shaded area in the graph represents this negative economic profit.

Figure 26.3

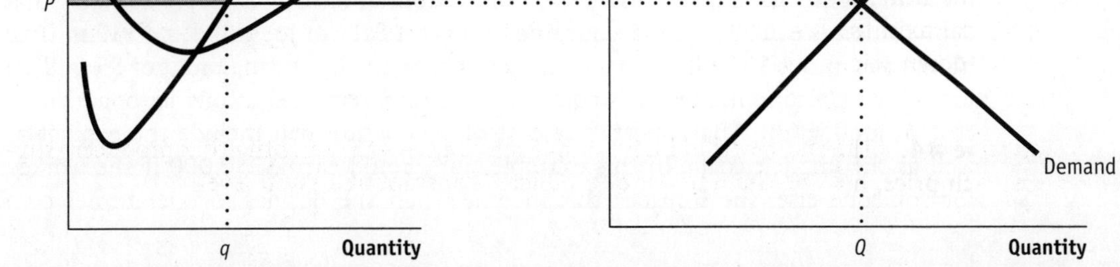

- Figure 26.3 could be redrawn to illustrate a short-run equilibrium where the representative firm earns positive economic profit, or it could be redrawn so that the representative firm earns zero economic profit. These three short-run scenarios are important for you to be able to construct and understand: being able to construct the graph and read the graph is vital for your ability to understand this material.

Tip #2. The short-run production conditions for a perfectly competitive firm can be summarized as follows:

- When $P >$ minimum *AVC* or the shut-down price, the firm produces in the short run. If $P >$ minimum *ATC*, the firm is covering all of its variable cost as well as its fixed cost of production. If $P <$ minimum *ATC* but is still above the minimum *AVC*, the firm is covering all of its variable cost and part of its fixed cost.
- When $P =$ minimum *AVC* or the shut-down price, the firm is indifferent between producing in the short run and shutting down in the short run. The firm's revenue is just enough to cover its variable cost of production. The firm's profit is thus equal to the negative of its fixed cost.
- When $P <$ minimum *AVC* or the shut-down price, the firm shuts down production in the short run since it cannot cover its variable cost of production. The firm's profit when it produces 0 units of output in the short run is equal to the negative of its fixed cost.

WORKED PROBLEMS

1. Sally and Joe are local business people who supply computer software design services to their community as well as to other customers located throughout the world. Sally and Joe are well aware that their firms are just two of many, many firms that offer similar services. Currently, Sally's and Joe's firms have revenues of $10 million a year and operating costs of $5 million. Sally and Joe both estimate that if they used their time to work for someone else, they could each earn an annual salary of $250,000. Furthermore, Sally and Joe both have $2 million apiece of their own money invested in their firms, and if they were to sell their firms, they could invest this money, with each earning 10% profit a year. Sally and Joe want to calculate their accounting profit and their economic profit. They then want to make a prediction about their firms' future prospects with regard to economic profitability. Can you help them out? Assume that Sally's and Joe's firms are identical and assume that depreciation is equal to zero.

STEP 1: Sally and Joe want information about their accounting profit and their economic profit. This requires that you distinguish between explicit costs and implicit costs.

Accounting profits include only explicit costs: recall that explicit costs are those costs that involve the actual laying out of money. Accounting profit is equal to the firm's revenues minus its explicit costs and depreciation. Since this example assumes that depreciation is equal to zero, accounting profits for Sally or Joe will equal $10 million in revenue minus $5 million in operating costs, or an accounting profit of $5 million for the year. Economic profit is equal to the firm's revenues minus its opportunity cost of production. The opportunity cost of production will include the explicit as well as the implicit costs. In this example, Sally could earn $250,000 if she worked for someone else: she foregoes this income when she decides to operate her own company. In addition, she could take her $2 million that is currently invested in the company and, instead of operating her company, invest it and earn $200,000 a year in interest. Thus, Sally's opportunity cost of having her own business is $450,000 a year. Joe has identical opportunity costs. Sally's economic profit from running her business is equal to $10 million – ($5 million + $450,000), or $4,550,000 a year.

STEP 2: Make a prediction about the profitability of Sally's and Joe's firms in the future. This requires you first to determine if their firms are perfectly competitive and then to make a prediction as to whether you expect entry or exit into the computer software industry in the future.

Perfect competition requires that no individual producer have a large market share. In the case of Sally and Joe, this is true. Perfect competition also requires that the product being produced in the industry is a standardized product: one could argue that the software produced by Sally and Joe is not a standardized product, but the actual product that their firms are providing is computer services to generate needed software. There are many firms in the world that can potentially offer this type of service to potential customers. The industry in which Sally and Joe operate seems to meet the criteria necessary to be characterized as a perfectly competitive industry.

Perfectly competitive industries have free entry and exit. This means that new firms can enter the industry easily and that existing firms can exit the industry. When there are positive economic profits in a perfectly competitive industry, new firms will enter the industry and price will fall. Price will continue to fall until economic profits for firms in the industry are equal to zero. Since Sally and Joe are currently earning positive economic profits, new firms will enter the industry and Sally's and Joe's economic profits will fall.

2. Sally's Doughnuts, a firm selling doughnuts in a perfectly competitive market, knows that its cost curves can be represented by the following graph. But Sally is not clear as to how to use this information to determine whether she should produce doughnuts in the short run. Examine the graph and then advise Sally as to whether she should produce. Be sure to reference relevant prices as well as how different prices will affect whether Sally's short-run profits will be positive, negative, or equal to zero in the short run. Include a discussion of the break-even price and the shut-down prices and what these points imply about Sally's profits.

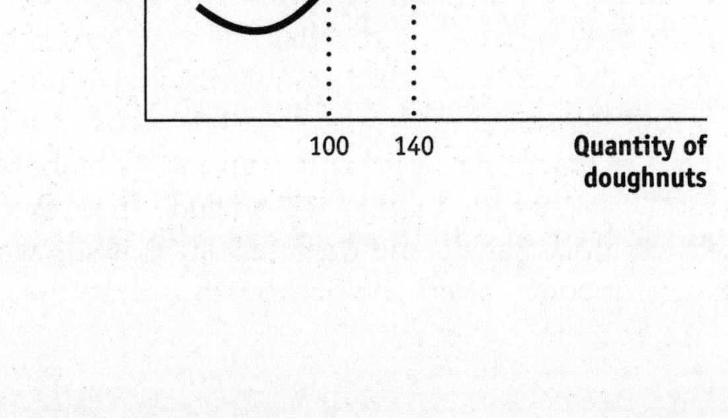

STEP 1: Refer to the relationship between the cost curves for a perfectly competitive firm and its *MR* curve. In your review pay close attention to the relationship between the market price, the cost curves, and how economic profits are determined.

The text discusses the optimal output rule for a perfectly competitive firm: The firm should produce where *MR* equals *MC*. The perfectly competitive firm's *MR* curve will be a horizontal line drawn at the market price, which is determined by the intersection of the market demand and supply curves. Where the market price intersects the minimum point of the firm's average total cost curve, total revenue is equal to total cost, since the price per unit equals the cost per unit. At that point the firm's revenue will cover all of its fixed and variable costs, and the firm will earn zero economic profits. This minimum point of the average total cost curve is the break-even price: the firm will break even, or earn zero economic profit, at this market price.

Where the market price intersects the minimum point of the firm's average variable cost curve, total revenue is equal to variable cost of production, since the price per unit equals the variable cost. Revenue will cover all variable cost, but it will not cover any fixed cost, and the firm will earn negative economic profits equal to the negative of its fixed costs. This minimum point of the average variable cost curve is the shut-down price, since the firm will earn negative economic profits equal to the negative of its fixed costs if the market price goes through this minimum point. Recall that in the short run, if the firm decides to produce nothing, it will still incur its fixed costs; thus, no matter whether the firm produces at the minimum point of its average variable cost curve or produces nothing, its economic profits will equal the negative of its fixed costs.

If the market price intersects the marginal cost curve below the shut-down price, the firm will choose to shut down in the short run and not produce any output. The firm makes this choice because its total revenue will not cover all of its variable costs. The firm will only be willing to produce in the short run if it can earn enough revenue to cover the variable cost of production.

If the market price intersects the marginal cost curve above the break-even price, the firm will choose to produce where *MR* equals *MC*, and the firm will earn positive economic profit in the short run, since the firm's price per unit will be greater than its cost per unit.

STEP 2: Examine the graph and determine where the break-even price is. Determine the price and the quantity associated with this break-even price and then explain the relationship between the firm's total revenue and its total cost if the firm produces and sells the level of output associated with the break-even price.

The break-even price in the graph occurs when the market price is $1 per unit (1 unit is equal to 1 doughnut). When the market price is $1, the firm's *MR* curve is a horizontal line. This horizontal line intersects the minimum point of the firm's average total cost curve. Sally will maximize her profit by producing where *MR* equals *MC*: she will produce 140 doughnuts and charge the market-determined price of $1 per doughnut. Her price per unit will be equal to her cost per unit: Sally will earn zero economic profit when she produces at her break-even price.

STEP 3: Examine the graph and determine where the shut-down price is. Determine the price and the quantity associated with this shut-down price and then explain the relationship between the firm's total revenue and its total cost if the firm produces and sells at the level of output associated with the shut-down price.

The shut-down price lies where the market price is $0.50 per unit. When the market price is $0.50, the firm's *MR* curve is a horizontal line. This horizontal line intersects the minimum point of the firm's average variable cost curve. Sally will maximize her profit by producing the quantity whose *MR* equals *MC*: She will produce 100 doughnuts and charge the market-determined price of $0.50 per doughnut. Her price per unit will be equal to her variable cost per unit: Sally will earn negative economic profits equal to the negative of her fixed costs when she produces at her shut-down price.

STEP 4: From the graph identify the market price that results in Sally shutting down her firm in the short run and producing zero units of output. Explain why Sally would make this choice rather than continuing to produce in the short run.

From Step 3 we know that the shut-down price occurs when the market price is at $0.50 per doughnut. If the price falls below this level, Sally should shut down her firm in the short run because production at a price lower than $0.50 results in Sally's revenues not covering her variable costs of production. Sally will be unwilling to produce in the short run unless she can earn enough revenue to cover her variable cost; Sally is willing not to cover her fixed costs in the short run, but she must cover her variable costs in order to be willing to produce.

STEP 5: Summarize your findings for Sally and give her explicit advice about when she should produce and when she should shut down. In addition, advise Sally about the relationship between her economic profits and her production decision.

When price is greater than $1 per unit, Sally should produce more than 140 doughnuts. She will earn positive economic profit in the short run. When price is equal to $1 per unit, Sally should produce 140 doughnuts (where her *MR* curve intersects her *MC* curve), and she will earn zero economic profit in the short run. When price is less than $1 and greater than or equal to $0.50, Sally should produce between 100 units and 140 units, depending upon where her *MR* curve intersects her *MC* curve. She will earn negative economic profit in the short run. When price is less than $0.50 per unit, Sally should shut down in the short run, and her economic profit will be equal to the negative of her fixed costs.

Problems and Exercises

1. The market for ice cream is a perfectly competitive market. Suppose the short-run industry supply curve is given by the equation $P = (1/7{,}500)Q$ while the short-run industry demand curve is given by the equation $P = 4 - (1/2{,}500)Q$ where P is the price of a unit of ice cream and Q is units of ice cream. Furthermore, you are told that a representative firm's total cost is given by the equation $TC = 9 + (.5)q^2$ and its marginal cost curve is given by the equation $MC = q$ where q is the quantity of ice cream produced by the firm.
   a. Given this information what is the equilibrium market price and equilibrium market quantity in this perfectly competitive market in the short run?

b. How many units of ice cream will a representative firm produce in the short run?

c. What are the fixed costs for a representative firm in this industry? Explain how you found your answer.

d. Given the market price you determined in part (a) and the rest of your work on this problem, will this firm earn positive, negative, or zero economic profit in the short run?

2. A perfectly competitive firm is trying to decide whether it should produce in the short run. It knows that its fixed cost of production is equal to $2,500. It also knows that its variable cost of production for the profit-maximizing level of output is equal to $3,500. At the market price of $40 it will profit-maximize by producing 100 units of output. What advice would you give this firm about whether it should produce in the short run or not? Make sure you also advise the firm about its level of profitability in the short run.

3. A perfectly competitive firm is trying to decide whether it should produce in the short run. It knows that its fixed cost of production is equal to $450. It also knows that its average variable cost of production for the profit-maximizing level of output is equal to $40. At the market price of $50 it will profit-maximize by producing 100 units of output. What advice would you give this firm about whether it should produce in the short run? Make sure you also advise the firm about its level of profitability in the short run.

4. Use the following graph of a perfectly competitive firm to answer this set of questions.

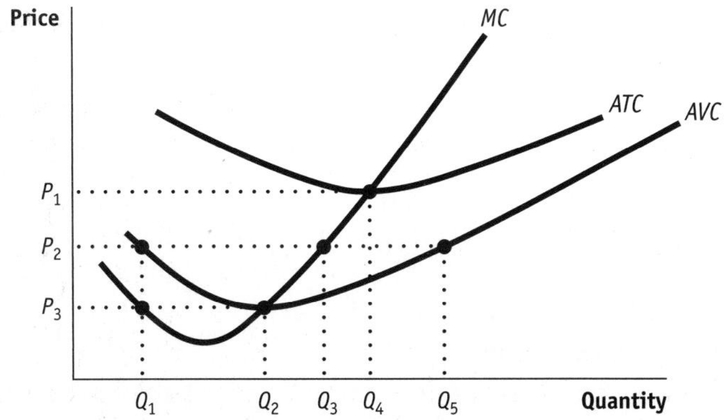

a. Suppose that the market price in this perfectly competitive industry is equal to P_2. In the short run what level of output will this representative firm produce? Describe this representative firm's profits in the short run.

b. Suppose that you are told that a representative firm in this perfectly competitive industry is making a normal profit in the short run. What is the market price and what quantity of output does the representative firm produce given this information?

c. Suppose that market price in this competitive industry is currently less than P_3. In the short run what will this representative firm choose to do? Explain your answer.

BEFORE YOU TAKE THE TEST

Module Review Questions

1. A firm in the short run must decide whether it should produce any level of output. This means that the firm must

a. equate marginal revenue to marginal cost to decide its level of output.

b. consider whether its revenue is sufficient to cover its total costs of production.

c. consider whether its revenue is sufficient to cover its average fixed costs of production.

d. consider whether its revenue is sufficient to cover its variable costs of production.

2. A firm making its short-run decision about whether to produce should ignore its
a. fixed costs.
b. variable costs.
c. average costs.
d. marginal costs.

3. A perfectly competitive firm finds that its break-even price occurs at \$22 while its shut-down price is at \$12. You are told that the market demand curve in this industry is $P = 30 - (1/30)Q$ and the market supply curve is $P = (1/15)Q$. In the short run this firm will
a. produce, since it is covering its variable costs of production.
b. produce, since it can earn positive economic profits.
c. produce, since it is covering its fixed costs of production.
d. shut down, since it is not covering its fixed costs of production.

4. For a firm to profit-maximize, it must also be true that
a. the firm is cost-minimizing.
b. the market price is greater than the shut-down price.
c. the market price is equal to the break-even price.
d. the firm is earning a positive accounting profit.

5. In the short run, the individual supply curve for a perfectly competitive firm is that firm's
a. *MC* curve at or above the shut-down price.
b. *ATC* curve above the *MC* curve.
c. *ATC* curve below the *MC* curve.
d. *MR* curve at or above the shut-down price.

6. The short-run industry supply curve for a perfectly competitive market is
a. perfectly elastic, since buyers can purchase as many units of the good as they desire at the prevailing market price.
b. equal to the horizontal sum of the supply curves of the individual producers.
c. equal to the horizontal sum of the individual firms' *MC* curves at and above the *AVC*.
d. Answers (b) and (c) are both true.

7. Suppose there are two firms in a perfectly competitive industry and that each of these two firms have a *MC* curve that can be expressed as $MC = 2q$, where q is the level of output produced by the firm. Furthermore, suppose that the minimum point of the *AVC* curve occurs at \$10. If these two firms comprise the industry (a simplification to make the calculation easier), which of the following equations describes the industry supply curve where Q refers to the market quantity and *P* refers to the market price?
a. $P = 2Q$ for $Q \geq 5$
b. $P = Q$ for $Q \geq 5$
c. $P = Q$ for $Q \geq 10$
d. $P = 2Q$ for $Q \geq 10$

8. Which of the following statements for a perfectly competitive industry is true?

I. In the short run, the number of firms in the industry is fixed.

II. For a constant-cost industry, the market supply curve in the short run is a horizontal line.

III. In a short-run market equilibrium, the quantity supplied equals the quantity demanded.

a. Statement I is true.

b. Statements I and II are true.

c. Statements I and III are true.

d. Statements I, II, and III are true.

9. Suppose a perfectly competitive industry with constant costs is initially in long-run equilibrium. Demand for the product produced in this industry increases due to a change in tastes and preferences. In the short run this will result in

a. the product selling for a higher price, each firm producing more of the good, and positive economic profits for the firms in the industry.

b. the product selling for a higher price; each firm in the industry producing the same level of the good as they did initially, since their capital is fixed; and each firm earning positive economic profit.

c. the product selling for a higher price initially, but the industry will attract new firms, which will cause the price to fall back to its original level.

d. the price staying constant, since the firms in this industry are price-takers, and the output of each firm increasing; therefore each firm will earn positive economic profit.

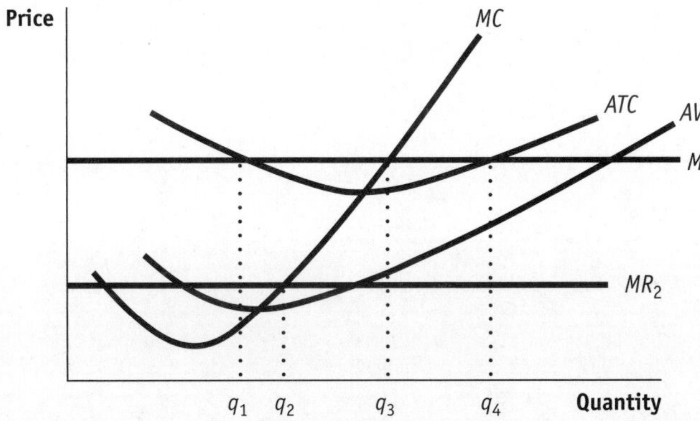

10. Use the above graph of a perfectly competitive firm in the short run to answer this question. If the firm's marginal revenue is MR_1, then this firm profit-maximizes by producing __________ units of output, and its economic profit will be __________.

a. q_1; zero

b. q_2; positive

c. q_3; positive

d. q_4; positive

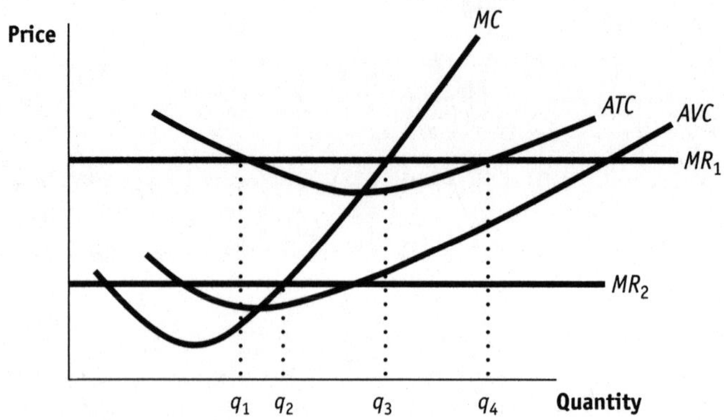

11. Use the above graph of a perfectly competitive firm in the short run to answer this question. If the firm's marginal revenue is MR_2, then this firm profit-maximizes by producing _________ units of output, and its economic profit will be _________.

a. q_1; negative

b. q_2; negative

c. q_3; zero

d. q_4; negative

ANSWER KEY

Answers to Problems and Exercises

1. **a.** To find the equilibrium market price and quantity set the market demand curve equal to the market supply curve. Thus, 4 – (1/2,500)Q = (1/7,500)Q, or Q = 7,500. Use this quantity in either the market demand curve or the market supply curve to find the equilibrium price: for example, $P = 4 - (1/2{,}500)(7{,}500) = \$1$.

   b. To find how many units of ice cream a representative firm will produce in the short run remember that the firm is a price-taker. That is, the firm will sell the good at the market price and the market price will be the firm's *MR* curve. Thus, *MR* = $1. The firm will profit-maximize by producing that quantity where *MR* = *MC*. Or, 1 = *q*.

   c. The firm's fixed costs are that part of its total cost that do not change as the level of output changes. The firm's *TC* is given as $TC = 9 + (.5)q^2$. Note that the term $(.5)q^2$ will have a different value as the value of q changes: this term expresses the firm's variable cost of production. The firm's fixed cost is equal to $9.

   d. To calculate the firm's profit in the short run we need to find the firm's total revenue (*TR*) and the firm's total cost (*TC*). The firm's *TR* is equal to the price times the quantity or, in this case, ($1 per unit of output)(1 unit of output) = $1. The firm's *TC* = $9 + (.5)(1)^2 = \$9.50$. The firm earns a negative economic profit: *TR* = *TC* = –$8.50.

2. In the short run, the firm should produce provided its total revenue is sufficient to cover its variable cost of production. For this scenario the firm's total revenue is equal to ($40/unit)(100 units) or $4,000. The firm's total revenue is great enough to cover its variable cost of production of $3,500. The firm should produce in the short run. In the short run the firm will earn a negative economic profit since its total costs will equal $6,000 while its total revenue will only equal $4,000. The firm will produce in the short run however since it can do nothing about its fixed costs in the short run: if the firm were to produce zero units of output the firm's profits would be equal to –$2,500 (its loss on its fixed costs). The firm when it produces 100 units in the short run incurs losses of only $2,000 which is better than it would achieve were it to shut down and produce nothing.

3. If the firm produces 100 units of output at a market price of $50, its total revenue will equal $5,000. The firm's variable costs of production at this level of output will equal ($40 per unit of output)(100 units of output) = $4,000. The firm's variable costs are less than its total revenue so the firm should produce in the short run. The firm's total cost of production will equal $4,450 which is less than its total revenue of $5,000. The firm will earn a positive economic profit in the short run of $550.

4. **a.** If the market price is P_2 then the firm will produce that quantity where *MR* equals *MC*. Since *MR* is equal to the market price for a perfectly competitive firm this means that the firm will produce Q_3 units of the good. At Q_3 the price per unit is less than the cost per unit and the representative firm will earn negative economic profits in the short run.

   b. If the firm is making normal economic profits this implies that the price per unit must be equal to cost per unit. This will occur at the break-even price: the break-even price is where the *ATC* curve crosses the *MC* curve. Thus, for the above firm the break-even price is at a price of P_1 and a quantity of Q_4.

   c. If the market price is less than P_3 this representative firm will choose to shut down in the short run since the revenue it earns at this price level is not sufficient to cover its variable costs of production.

Answers to Module Review Questions

1. **Answer d.** In the short run, the firm ignores its fixed cost since it cannot alter these costs. The firm decides whether it should produce in the short run by checking to see if its revenue is sufficient to cover its variable cost. If the revenue will not cover these variable costs, the firm can opt to shut down and incur only the fixed cost of production in the short run.

2. **Answer a.** In the short run, the firm will ignore its fixed cost since in the short run the fixed inputs cannot be altered. In the short run, the firm is able to alter its hiring of the variable input and, hence, its variable cost.

3. **Answer a.** Solving for the market equilibrium price using the market demand and supply curve yields a price of $20. This price is less than the break-even price and greater than the firm's shut-down price. The firm will produce in the short run since the market price is great enough to cover its variable cost of production (since the price exceeds the shut-down price). But the firm will earn negative profits because the market price is less than its break-even price, and therefore the price is not high enough for the firm to cover all of its variable cost and all of its fixed cost.

4. **Answer a.** Profit maximization implies that the firm must be minimizing its costs. In addition, profit maximization requires that the firm produce the level of output where $MR = MC$.

5. **Answer a.** The firm decides how much to supply by equating the market price to its *MC* curve, since the market price is the firm's *MR* curve. The firm produces in the short run provided that the market price is equal to or greater than its shut-down price, or its *AVC*. Thus, the firm's short-run supply curve is its *MC* curve at or above the point of intersection with its *AVC* curve.

6. **Answer d.** The supply curves of the individual producers are their *MC* curves at or above the shut-down price. To find the industry supply curve, simply horizontally sum together these individual supply curves.

7. **Answer c.** The market supply curve is found by horizontally summing the individual supply curves. The firm's supply curve is given by $MC = 2q$, provided that the price is greater than the minimum point of the *AVC*, or in this case provided that the price is equal to or greater than $10. So at a price of $10, each firm is willing to produce 5 units, for a total of 10 units. At a price of $20, each firm is willing to produce 10 units, for a total of 20 units. Thus, the industry supply curve is $P = Q$ for outputs greater than or equal to 10 units.

8. **Answer c.** In a perfectly competitive industry, the number of firms in the industry is fixed and constant in the short run. Entry of new firms or the exit of existing firms can only occur in the long run. Market equilibrium, whether in the short run or long run, occurs at that price and quantity combination where the quantity demanded equals the quantity supplied. However, in the short run, a constant-cost industry will have an upward-sloping market supply curve because the production of a greater level of output must entail increasing costs due to the diminishing returns to the variable input.

9. **Answer a.** The increased demand for the good will cause the market demand curve to shift to the right, leading to a higher equilibrium level of output in the market and a higher equilibrium price. The firms in this industry are price takers, and they will take the price they receive from the market and see where this price intersects their *MC* curve (recall that for a perfectly competitive firm the market price is equal to the marginal revenue) to select the profit-maximizing level of output. The firms will produce a higher level of output relative to their initial level, and they will earn positive economic profit.

10. **Answer c.** The perfectly competitive firm sets marginal revenue equal to marginal cost and produces that level of output (q_3). When the firm produces q_3 units, the market price is greater than the average total cost of production for this level of output, and the firm will earn positive economic profit.

11. **Answer b.** The perfectly competitive firm sets marginal revenue equal to marginal cost and produces that quantity of output (q_2). When the firm produces q_2 units of output, the market price is less than the average total cost of production for this level of output, and the firm will earn negative economic profit.

module 27

Long-Run Outcomes in Perfect Competition

BEFORE YOU READ THE MODULE

Summary

This module analyzes the perfectly competitive industry in the long run and then examines how industry behavior differs between the short run and the long run. The module also develops the industry supply curve in the short run as well as the long run.

Module Objectives

Objective #1. In the long run a firm can in a perfectly competitive industry exit the industry or a new firm can enter the industry. Firms will exit the industry if the market price is consistently less than the break-even price, or the minimum point of the firm's *ATC* curve. In other words, firms will exit the industry in the long run if they are consistently making negative economic profit in the short run. Firms will enter the industry if the market price is consistently greater than the break-even price. That is, firms will enter the industry in the long run if existing firms are consistently making positive economic profit in the short run.

Objective #2. The long-run market equilibrium in a perfectly competitive industry corresponds to the situation in which the quantity supplied equals the quantity demanded given that sufficient time has elapsed for producers to either enter or exit the industry. In the long-run market equilibrium, all existing producers and all potential producers have fully adjusted to their optimal long-run choices, and therefore there is no incentive for producers to either exit or enter the industry. Thus, the long-run industry supply curve shows the quantity supplied by the industry at each price, given that producers have had time to enter or exit the industry.

- In an industry that has constant costs across the industry, the long-run industry supply curve is perfectly elastic. The long-run industry supply curve can be drawn as a horizontal line at the break-even price.

- In an industry that has increasing costs across the industry, the long-run industry supply curve is upward sloping. This reflects the fact that some input is in limited supply, and as the industry expands, this results in higher prices for that input and therefore higher costs for the firms producing in that industry.
- Regardless of whether the industry is a constant-cost or increasing-cost industry, the long-run industry supply curve is flatter than the short-run industry supply curve. Entry of new firms in the long run results in greater levels of output and therefore lower prices than in the short run, and the exit of existing firms in the long run results in lower levels of output and therefore higher prices than in the short run.

Objective #3. Perfect competition leads to three conclusions about the cost of production and efficiency.

- When the perfectly competitive industry is in equilibrium, the value of marginal cost is the same for all firms. Since firms produce that output where marginal cost equals the market price, and since all firms are price takers, this implies that all firms must have the same marginal cost value in equilibrium.
- In the long run, all firms in a perfectly competitive industry earn zero economic profit due to free entry and exit. The existence of positive economic profits in the short run acts as an incentive for new firms to enter the industry. The existence of negative profits in the short run acts as an incentive for existing firms to exit the industry. This entry and exit continues until economic profits for all firms in the industry equal zero.
- The long-run market equilibrium in a perfectly competitive industry is efficient because there are no mutually beneficial transactions that are not exploited. In the long-run equilibrium in a perfectly competitive industry, costs are minimized and no resources are wasted.

Key Terms

Notes

industry supply curve a graphical representation that shows the relationship between the price of a good and the total output of the industry for that good.

short-run industry supply curve a graphical representation that shows how the *quantity supplied* by an industry depends on the market price, given a fixed number of producers.

short-run market equilibrium an economic balance that results when the *quantity supplied* equals the *quantity demanded,* taking the number of producers as given.

long-run market equilibrium an economic balance in which, given sufficient time for producers to enter or exit an industry, the *quantity supplied* equals the *quantity demanded.*

long-run industry supply curve a graphical representation that shows how *quantity supplied* responds to price once producers have had time to enter or exit the industry.

AFTER YOU READ THE MODULE

Tips

Tip #1. Figure 27.1 provides a sketch of the long-run equilibrium in a perfectly competitive industry. (This is also the same sketch for a short-run situation where the representative firm earns zero economic profit.) In this example, the firm is earning a zero economic profit because the price the good is sold for is equal to the average total cost of producing the good. Here's the analysis for this sketch: the industry demand and supply curves determine the equilibrium price (*P*) in the market and the equilibrium market quantity (*Q*). Firms are price takers, so they will sell their output at *P* and their *MR* curve is a horizontal line drawn at that price. Firms will select their profit-maximizing level of output (*q* for the representative firm in our sketch) by producing the quantity at which *MR* = *MC*, or where *P* = *MC*. The firm can then calculate its profit by comparing its *P* to its *ATC* at the level of production that was chosen. In this example, *P* = *ATC*, so the firm must be making zero economic profit.

Figure 27.1

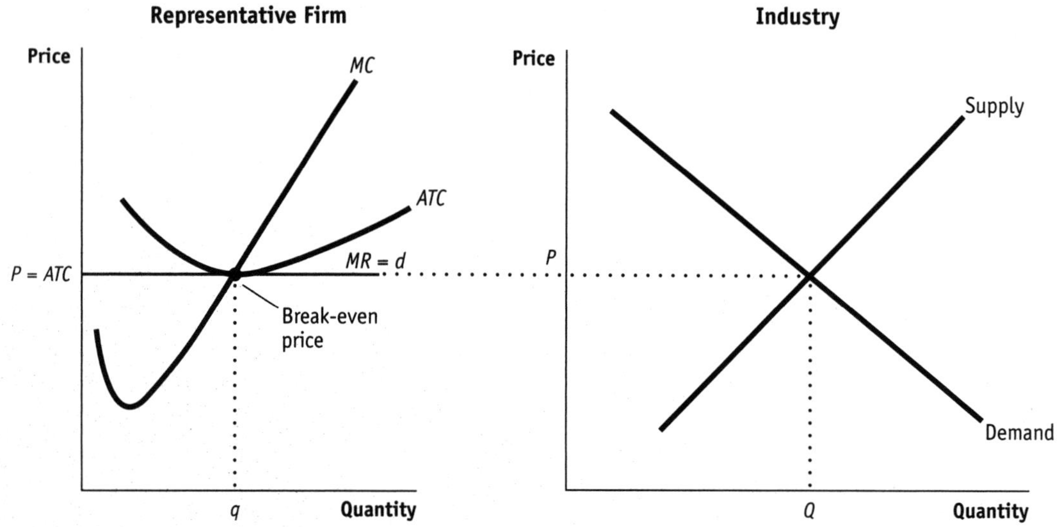

Tip #2. In the short run in a perfectly competitive industry, there is no entry or exit of firms. Thus, positive or negative economic profits can persist in the short run. However, in the long run there is entry and exit. It is important to understand how this affects the short-run situation for a perfectly competitive industry.

- Figure 27.2 analyzes the effect of the exit of firms in the long run. Here's the analysis: the representative firm is initially producing *q* and selling this output at *P*, resulting in the firm earning negative economic profit in the short run. In the long run, some of the existing firms exit the industry due to these negative economic profits, and this causes the market supply curve to shift to the left, which causes the market price to rise to P_2 and the market quantity to fall to Q_2. The representative firm that remains in the industry now faces a higher price for its output and therefore a new *MR* curve (MR_2). The firm will select its profit-maximizing output by equating MR_2 to *MC*: the firm will produce q_2 units of the good. The firm will earn zero economic profit, since in the long run the industry will have firms exit until all remaining firms produce at their break-even price. Notice that the firms that remain in the industry produce a higher level of output than they did initially (q_2 versus *q*), while the overall industry production of the good has fallen (Q_2 versus Q) due to firms exiting the industry. It is important to be able to construct these graphs and make the logical arguments implied by them. Make sure you study and work through these graphs until they are very familiar to you.

Figure 27.2

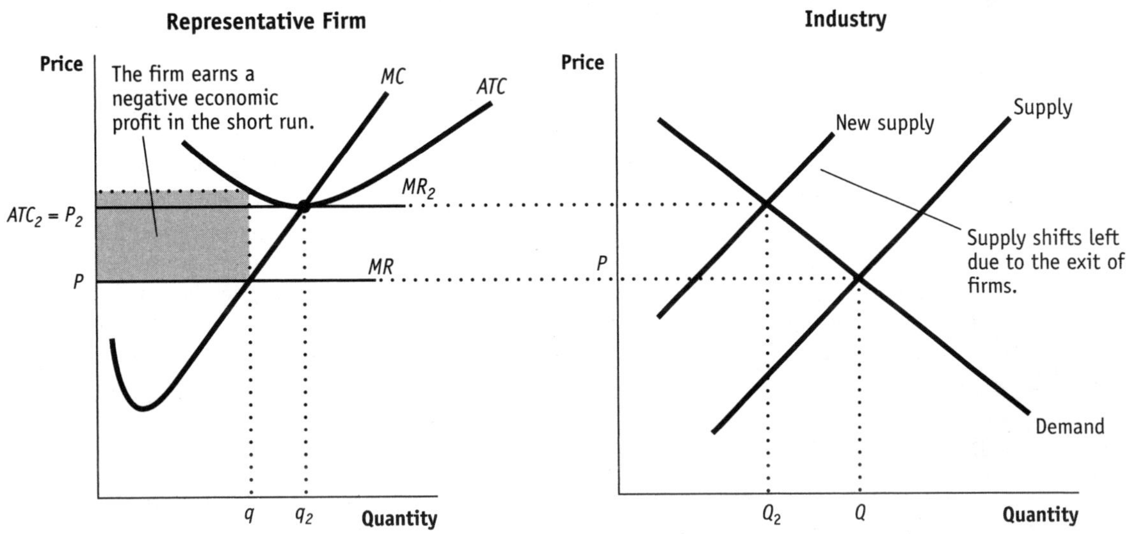

- Figure 27.3 is a graph that represents the long-run equilibrium adjustment when the representative firm earns a positive economic profit in the short run, thereby resulting in the entry of new firms in the long run. Here's the analysis: the representative firm is initially producing q and selling this output at P, resulting in the firm earning positive economic profit in the short run. In the long run, some new firms enter the industry because of these positive economic profits, causing the market supply curve to shift to the right, which causes the market price to fall to P_2 and the market quantity to rise to Q_2. The representative firm in the industry now faces a lower price for its output and therefore a new MR curve (MR_2). The firm will select its profit-maximizing output by equating MR_2 to MC: the firm will produce q_2 units of the good. The firm will earn zero economic profit, since in the long run the industry will have firms enter until all firms in the industry produce at their break-even price. Notice that the firms in the industry produce a lower level of output than they did initially (q_2 versus q), while the overall industry production of the good has risen (Q_2 versus Q) due to firms entering the industry. It is important to be able to construct these graphs and make the logical arguments implied by them. Make sure you study and work through these graphs until they are very familiar to you.

Figure 27.3

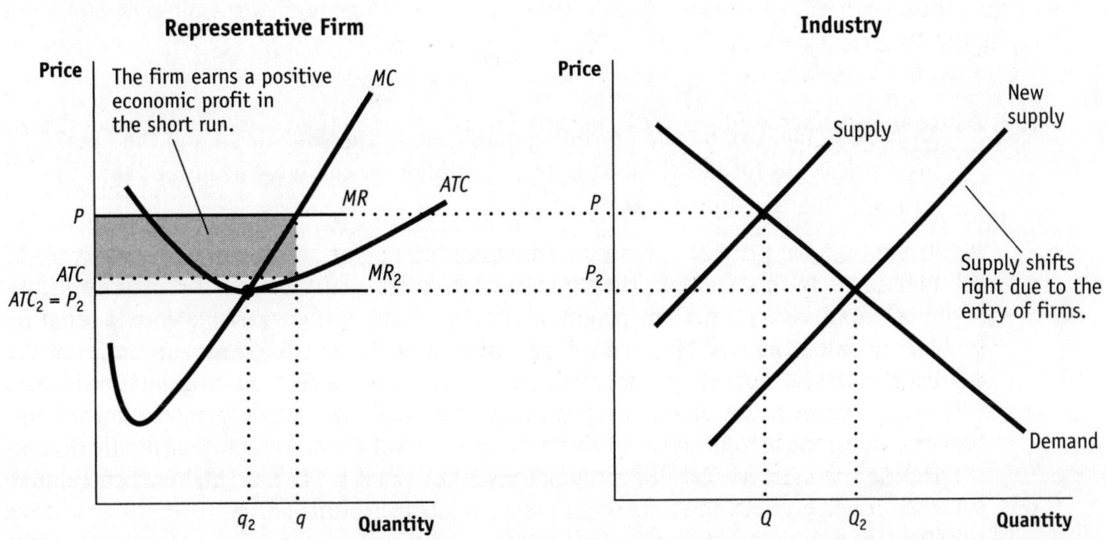

Tip #3. The profitability conditions for a perfectly competitive firm can be summarized as follows:

- When $P >$ minimum *ATC* or the break-even price, the firm earns a positive economic profit in the short run and firms enter the industry in the long run.
- When $P =$ minimum *ATC* or the break-even price, the firm earns zero economic profit in the short run and firms do not enter or exit the industry in the long run.
- When $P <$ minimum *ATC* or the break-even price, the firm earns a negative economic profit in the short run and firms exit the industry in the long run.

WORKED PROBLEMS

1. The following figure shows three curves, *MC, ATC,* and *AVC:* they are for the firm in a perfectly competitive market, where all firms in this industry have identical cost curves. Use the information given in the figure to answer the following questions. Identify what the shut-down price for this firm is in the short run and, if the firm operates at its shut-down price, how many units of output the firm will produce. Identify what the break-even price for this firm is in the short run, and identify the level of output the firm will produce if it operates at its break-even price. Identify the market price at which you know with certainty that this firm will exit the industry. If there are no changes in this firm's costs, what is the long-run equilibrium market price in this industry? What must be true for the firm in order for a particular market price to be the long-run equilibrium price?

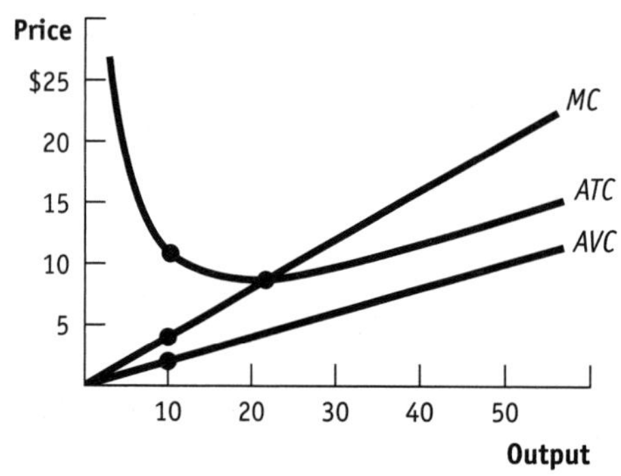

STEP 1: Identify on the preceding graph where the shut-down and the break-even prices are for the firm. At both prices identify the level of output that the firm will choose to produce.

The shut-down price corresponds to the minimum point on the firm's average variable cost curve. In this example, the firm's average variable cost is not a U-shaped curve. Its minimum point occurs when output is at zero and average variable cost is equal to \$0 per unit of output. The firm will continue to produce in the short run until price is equal to \$0 per unit of output since at any other price the firm will receive enough revenue to cover its variable costs of production. As long as price is greater than \$0, the firm will choose to produce in the short run: it will choose its level of production by setting the market price (or marginal revenue) equal to its marginal cost curve, and then it will produce the level of output associated with this point.

The break-even price corresponds to the minimum point on the firm's average total cost curve. In this example, the break-even price is when price is equal to \$8 per unit and the firm is producing 20 units of output. When the market price is equal to \$8, then the firm will equate its marginal revenue (which is equal to the market price, or in this case \$8) to its marginal cost: it will produce 20 units and make zero economic profit since its total revenue will exactly equal its total cost of production.

STEP 2: Identify the market price at which you know this firm will exit the industry in the short run.

The firm will exit the industry whenever the market price falls to a level at which the firm can no longer earn sufficient revenue to cover all of its variable costs of production. In this example, the firm will have enough revenue to cover its variable costs of production at any price that is greater than zero. So, the firm will not choose to exit the industry unless price falls to zero.

STEP 3: Identify the long-run equilibrium price for this firm and then discuss what must be true for this firm to be at its long-run equilibrium price.

For the firm to be at its long-run equilibrium price, it must be earning revenues that exactly equal its economic costs. This will occur only when it produces that level of output associated with the minimum point of its average total cost curve and then sells that output at the price associated with this point. At this point, its total revenue (price times quantity) will exactly equal its costs (average total cost times quantity) since the market price will be equal to the average total cost of producing that level of output.

2. Suppose that the following graphs illustrate both the market for gadgets and a representative firm's cost curves in this market. Furthermore, suppose this market is a perfectly competitive market with constant costs. From the graphs, identify whether this is a long-run or short-run equilibrium. Then, determine the firm's level of production in the short run and its level of short-run profits. What do you expect will happen to price, market quantity, the representative firm's level of production, and profits in the long run? Explain how this market will adjust in the long run. Finally, draw the short-run equilibrium situation and the long-run equilibrium situation on two different graphs. On these graphs, label the market price, market quantity, firm level of production, and area of profit if there is a profit.

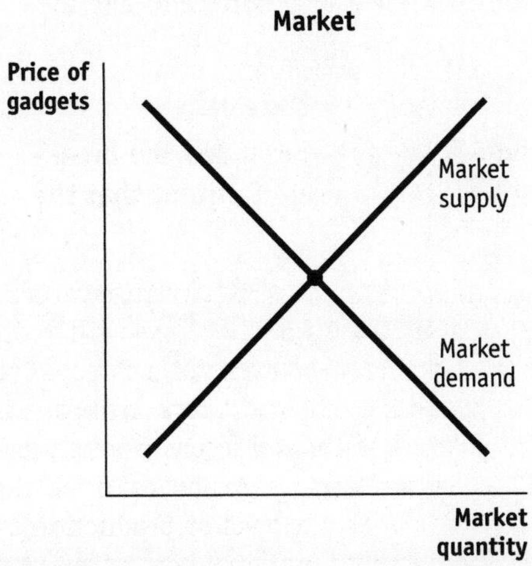

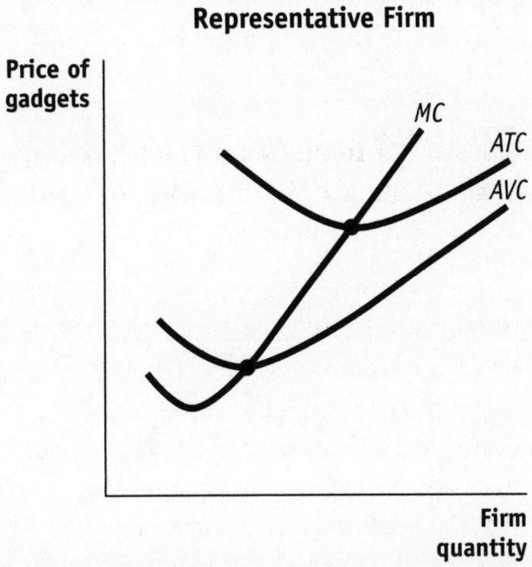

STEP 1: Determine whether the preceding graphs represent a long-run or short-run equilibrium.

These graphs represent a short-run equilibrium since the market price, P_1, is less than the minimum point of the average cost curve. This indicates that the price per unit is less than the cost per unit: the firm is earning negative economic profits. Since in the long run, perfectly competitive firms earn zero economic profits, we know that these graphs are not depicting a long-run equilibrium in this market.

STEP 2: Determine the firm's level of production and profit in the short run.

In the short run, the firm will produce that quantity at which its marginal revenue curve intersects its marginal cost curve. For the firm, the marginal revenue curve is equal to the market price. The firm will sell the good for the market price and earn total revenue equal to the market price times its level of output. The firm's total cost will be equal to its average total cost of production times its level of production. For this firm, its total cost is greater than its total revenue in the short run: the firm will earn negative economic profit in the short run.

STEP 3: Determine what will happen to price, market quantity, the firm's level of production, and the profits of the firm in the long run.

In the long run, a firm in a perfectly competitive industry will earn zero economic profit. In this case, this will be the result of the exiting of firms from the industry. As firms exit the industry, the market supply curve shifts to the left until the market equilibrium price is just equal to the firm's break-even price. The firm's break-even price is the price that intersects the minimum point on the firm's average total cost curve. Market price will rise, market quantity will decrease, the level of production for the firms remaining in the industry will increase, and profits will equal zero.

STEP 4: Provide an explanation of the long-run equilibrium process.

In the long run, firms will exit the industry due to the presence of short-run negative profits. This exit will shift the market supply curve to the left, resulting in an increase in the equilibrium market price and a decrease in the equilibrium market quantity. This entry will occur until a representative firm in the industry is earning zero profit.

STEP 5: Provide a graph of the short-run equilibrium in this market. In this graph, label the market price, market quantity, firm level of production, and area of profit if there is a profit.

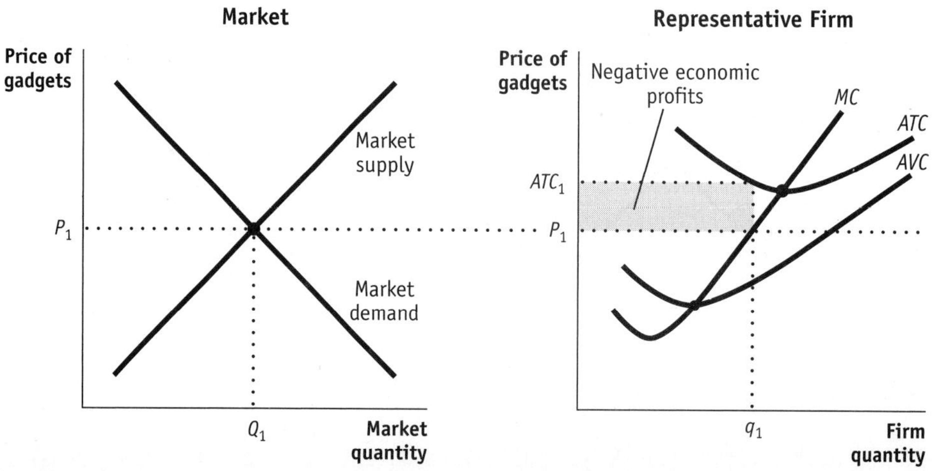

STEP 6: **Provide a graph of the long-run equilibrium in this market. In this graph, label the market price, market quantity, firm level of production, and area of profit if there is a profit.**

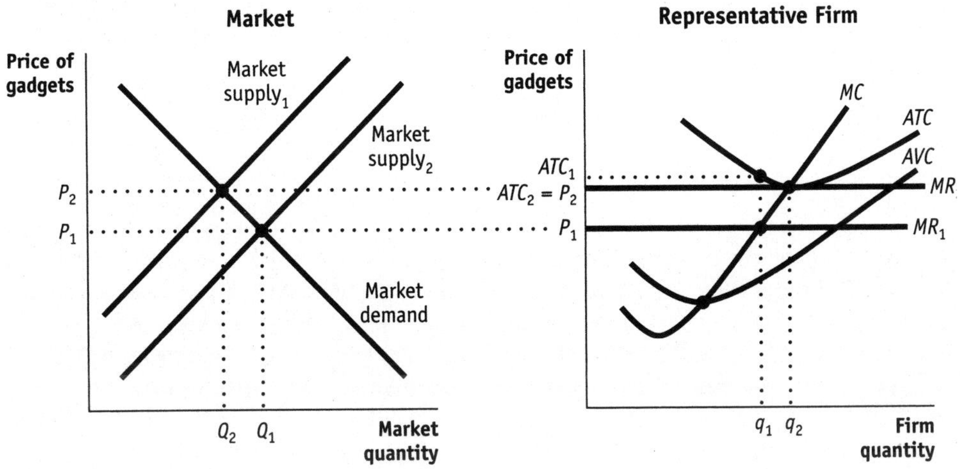

Problems and Exercises

1. Use the graphs below of a perfectly competitive market in a constant-cost industry to answer this set of questions.

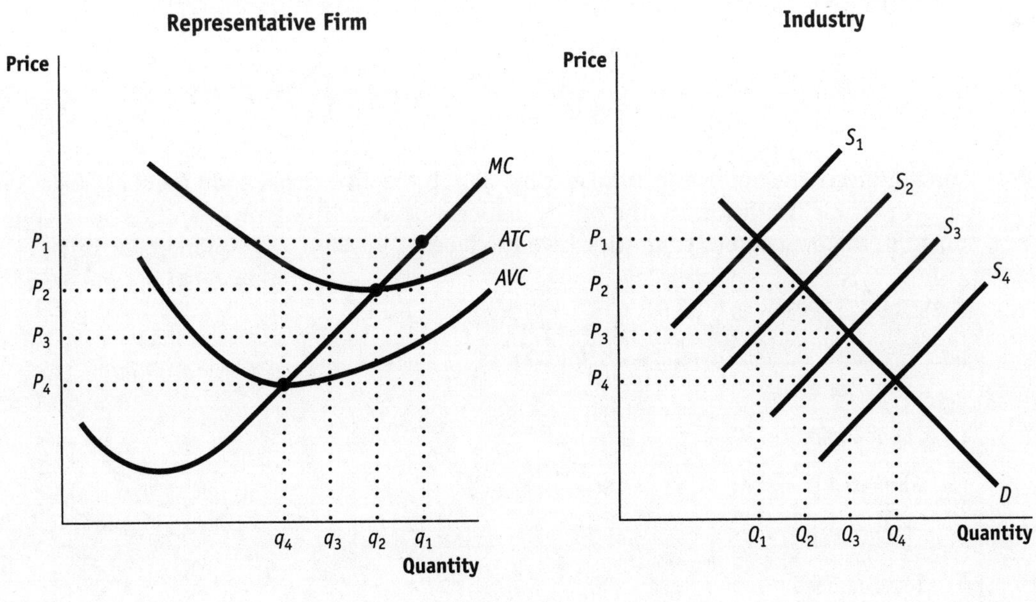

a. Suppose in the short run the industry supply curve is given by S_1. Identify the short-run equilibrium market price and quantity, the quantity produced by the representative firm, and whether the firm is making positive, negative, or zero economic profits. Holding everything else constant, what will happen in the long run in this industry? In your answer to this question, identify the long-run equilibrium price and quantity in the industry, the quantity produced by the firm in the long run, and the level of profits for the firm in the long run.

b. Suppose in the short run the industry supply curve is given by S_4. Identify the short-run equilibrium market price and quantity, the quantity produced by the representative firm, and whether the firm is making positive, negative, or zero economic profits. Do you know with certainty what this firm's profits equal in the short run? Holding everything else constant, what will happen in the long run in this industry? In your answer to this question, identify the long-run equilibrium price and quantity in the industry, the quantity produced by the firm in the long run, and the level of profits for the firm in the long run.

c. You are told that this representative firm is currently making negative economic profits in the short run, but that it is covering all of its variable costs of production and some of its fixed costs. Given the price choices in the preceding graph, what is the current price for this good? In the long run will there be entry of new firms into the industry or will existing firms exit the industry? Explain your answer.

2. You are given the following information about the five firms that produce soda in Bigtown. These five firms are the only producers of soda in Bigtown, and all soda consumed in Bigtown comes from these five producers.

Name of company	Quantity of soda sold (cans per month)
Fizzy Water	150
Cool Tonics	200
Carbonated Bliss	100
Mom's Pop	450
Taste of Eden	100

a. Given the information in the table would you characterize the market for soda in Bigtown as perfectly competitive? Explain your answer.

b. Suppose market share is defined as the percentage of total sales represented by a firm's sales of soda over the given period. Calculate the market share of each of the companies producing soda in Bigtown.

c. Is the soda produced in this market likely to be standardized? Explain your answer.

3. The market for books is perfectly competitive and a constant-cost industry. The short-run industry supply curve is given by the equation $P = 4 + Q$, while the industry demand curve is given by the equation $P = 100 - Q$, where P is the market price and Q is the market quantity. The representative firm's MC curve can be written as $MC = 4 + 2q$, and its TC is given by the equation $TC = 36 + 4q + q^2$, where q is the quantity produced by the firm.

a. What is the equilibrium price and the equilibrium market quantity for this good in the short run?

b. Given the market price you calculated in part (a), what is the profit-maximizing quantity, q, for a representative firm to produce in the short run? What rule did you use to calculate this profit-maximizing level of output?

c. Is this firm making positive, negative, or zero economic profit in the short run? Sketch a diagram of the market and the representative firm. In these diagrams identify the equilibrium price, the market quantity, the firm quantity, the firm's *ATC* curve (a sketch of this is fine), the firm's *MC* curve, and the firm's profits, if there are any.

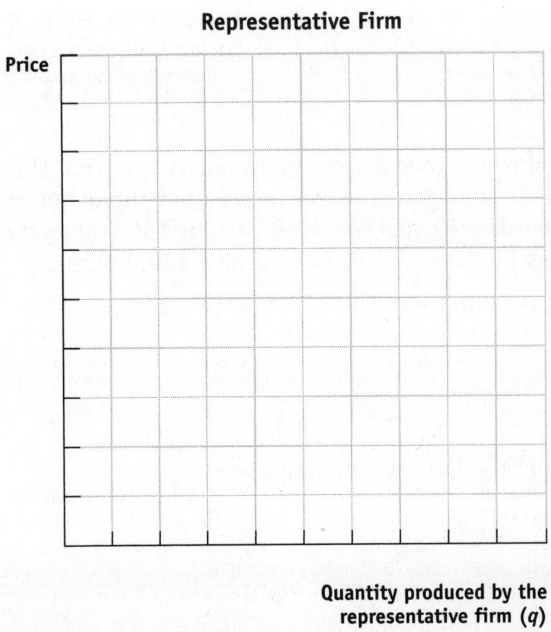

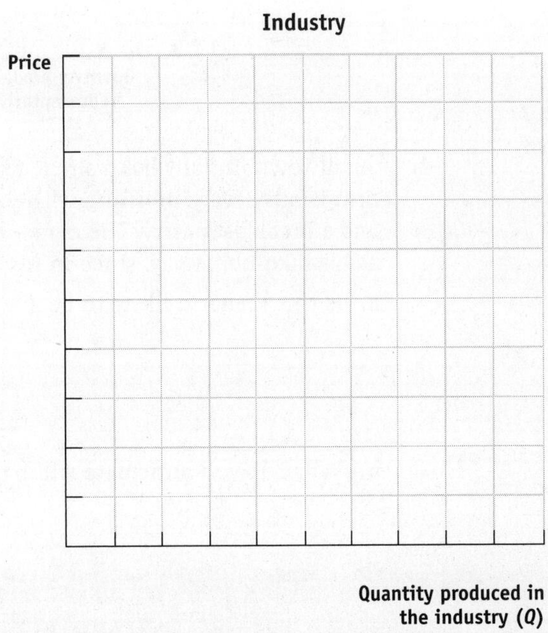

d. If all the firms are identical in this industry, how many firms are in the industry in the short run?

e. What is the long-run price, the long-run market quantity, the long-run quantity produced by a representative firm, and the long-run number of firms in the industry?

f. Draw a sketch illustrating the long-run equilibrium for this industry and for a representative firm.

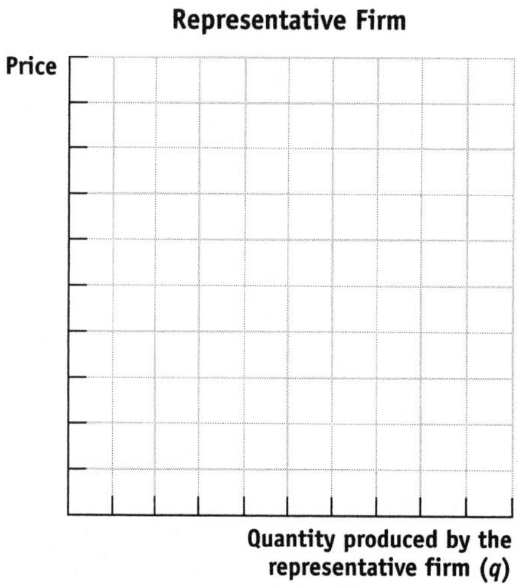

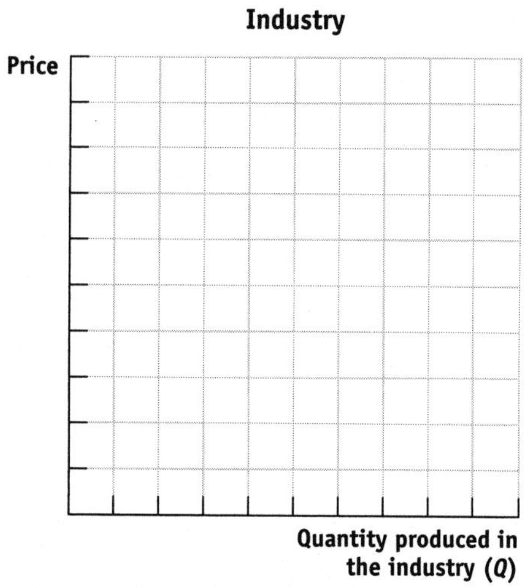

4. Small Town initially has a single firm that serves good coffee and wonderful pastries. This firm is busy every morning with long lines of customers eager to get a hot cup of coffee and a breakfast pastry. The owner of the café is excited that he is earning $50,000 a year as his take-home pay, since in his former job he managed to earn only $30,000.

a. Is this scenario likely to be a long-run equilibrium situation? Explain your answer.

b. What do you anticipate will happen in the long run in Small Town?

c. The owner of the café is interviewed 10 years after the initial story about his success. The reporter finds out that the café owner is no longer in business providing coffee and pastries. Can you think of a possible story to explain this owner's departure from the business? (Hint: the owner did not choose to retire—he simply exited the industry during this 10-year period.)

5. For the most part, our model of perfect competition focuses on constant-cost industries. Is the assumption of constant costs in the long run a plausible assumption for the types of industries that most closely resemble perfect competition? Explain your answer.

6. In the long run, the model of perfect competition predicts that all firms in an industry will earn zero economic profits. Why would firms be willing to continue to produce in the long run if their economic profits are equal to zero?

BEFORE YOU TAKE THE TEST

Module Review Questions

1. In recent years, there has been an increased demand for organic produce due to concerns about health issues related to food consumption. Holding everything else constant, in the short run this demand should lead to __________, while in the long run __________.

a. increases in the price of organic produce; entry of firms into the industry will reduce the price of organic produce

b. increases in the price of organic produce; exit of firms from the industry will further increase the price of organic produce

c. decreases in the price of organic produce; entry of firms into the industry will further reduce the price of organic produce

d. decreases in the price of organic produce; exit of firms from the industry will increase the price of organic produce

2. Suppose a perfectly competitive firm in the short run sells its product for a price that is less than the minimum point on its *ATC* curve. Which of the following statements is true?

a. The firm will shut down in the short run since it is not covering all of its costs.

b. Some firms in this industry will exit the industry in the long run, and the exiting will continue until the market price increases and is equal to the break-even price on the *ATC* curve.

c. The firm will shut down in the short run only if the price is greater than the shut-down price but less than the break-even price.

d. Some firms in this industry will exit the industry in the long run, and the exiting will continue until the market price increases and is equal to the shut-down price on the *ATC* curve.

3. Suppose a perfectly competitive industry with constant costs is initially in long-run equilibrium. Demand for the product produced in this industry increases due to a change in tastes and preferences. In the long run this will result in

a. the industry output of this good increasing, the price staying constant due to the entry of new firms into the industry, and each firm in the industry earning positive economic profits.

b. the industry output of this good increasing, the price staying constant due to the entry of new firms into the industry, and each firm in the industry earning negative economic profits.

c. the industry output of this good increasing, the price staying constant due to the entry of new firms into the industry, and each firm in the industry earning zero economic profit.

d. the industry output of this good increasing, the firm level of output increasing, the price increasing, and each firm in the industry earning zero economic profit.

4. Which of the following statements about a perfectly competitive firm is true?

I. A firm profit-maximizes by producing that output where $MR = MC$.

II. A firm will produce in the short run provided that the price of the good exceeds its average variable cost.

III. A firm in the long run can make positive economic profits.

a. Statement I is true.
b. Statements I and II are true.
c. Statements I and III are true.
d. Statements I, II, and III are true.

5. A perfectly competitive firm will exit the industry in the long run if the

a. firm's marginal revenue is consistently less than the firm's marginal cost.
b. market price is consistently less than the break-even price.
c. firm's fixed cost cannot be eliminated in the long run.
d. firm's marginal cost is consistently less than the firm's marginal revenue.

6. The long-run market equilibrium in a perfectly competitive industry with identical firms results in all firms

a. earning zero economic profit.
b. producing the quantity associated with their break-even price.
c. producing the profit-maximizing quantity at which $MR = MC$.
d. All of the statements are true.

7. A constant-cost industry in a perfectly competitive market can be identified by its

a. horizontal long-run market supply curve.
b. horizontal long-run market demand curve.
c. upward-sloping long-run market supply curve.
d. downward-sloping long-run market supply curve.

ANSWER KEY

Answers to Problems and Exercises

1. **a.** The equilibrium price is P_1 and the equilibrium quantity is Q_1 in the market. The representative firm produces the quantity at which $MR = MC$, or $P_1 = MC$, since for a perfectly competitive firm $MR = P$. The representative firm produces q_1. The firm earns positive economic profit since $P_1 > ATC$ for q_1 units of output. In the long run, new firms will enter the industry, since the existence of positive economic profits creates an incentive for more competition. As firms enter the industry, the industry supply curve will shift to the right from S_1 to S_2, which will result in a decrease in the market price from P_1 to P_2. The equilibrium output in the industry will increase to Q_2 while the representative firm will decrease its production to q_2. The level of economic profits will equal zero in the long run for the firms in the industry.

b. The equilibrium price is P_4 and the equilibrium quantity is Q_4 in the market. The representative firm finds that the market price goes through its shut-down price at P_4(the minimum point of the *AVC* curve), and therefore the firm needs to decide whether or not it wants to produce in the short run. With either choice, the firm will earn negative economic profits equal to the negative of their fixed costs. The firm will produce q_4 units since $MR = MC$ at this level of output. In the long run, firms will exit the industry, causing the industry supply curve to shift to the left to S_2. This will cause the market price to increase to P_2, the market quantity to decrease to Q_2, and the level of production for each firm remaining in the industry to increase to q_2. Economic profits will equal zero in the long run for each firm.

c. Looking at the graph we know that P_4 corresponds to the price that goes through the shut-down price, which implies that the firm covers all of its variable cost, but none of its fixed cost. At P_1, the firm earns a positive economic profit and thus its revenues are greater than the sum of its fixed cost and variable cost. P_2 corresponds to the price that goes through the break-even price: the firm's total revenue is exactly equal to its total cost and therefore the firm is covering all of its variable cost and all of its fixed cost. That leaves P_3, and from the graph we see that P_3 is a price that lies between the break-even price and the shut-down price: the firm will receive enough revenue to cover all of its variable cost and some of its fixed cost. In the long run, firms will exit this industry until the supply curve shifts left from S_3 to S_2. The remaining firms in the industry will earn zero economic profits in the long run.

2. **a.** No, this market is not perfectly competitive since there are not many producers and at least one of them has substantial market share (Mom's Pop accounts for 45% of total soda sales in Bigtown).

b.

Name of company	Market share
Fizzy Water	15%
Cool Tonics	20
Carbonated Bliss	10
Mom's Pop	45
Taste of Eden	10

c. No, the soda will likely be quite differentiated since customers distinguish between these companies' products (for example, Mom's Pop really outsells every other business in the industry).

3. a. To find the equilibrium price and quantity in the market, use the market demand and supply equations. Solving $100 - Q = 4 + Q$ for Q gives you the equilibrium quantity of 48 units. Substituting this quantity into either the demand or the supply equation gives you the equilibrium price of $52.

b. The profit-maximizing level of output for the firm is found by equating marginal revenue to marginal cost. For the price-taking firm, marginal revenue is equal to the market price. Thus, $52 = 4 + 2q$, or q (the quantity produced by the representative firm) is 24 units.

c. Profit is equal to $TR - TC$. Total revenue for this firm is ($52)(24) = $1,248, and total cost is equal to $ATC \times q$ or $TC = (36/q + 4 + q)(q) = (36/24 + 4 + 24)(24) = \$708$. This firm makes positive profits equal to $540.

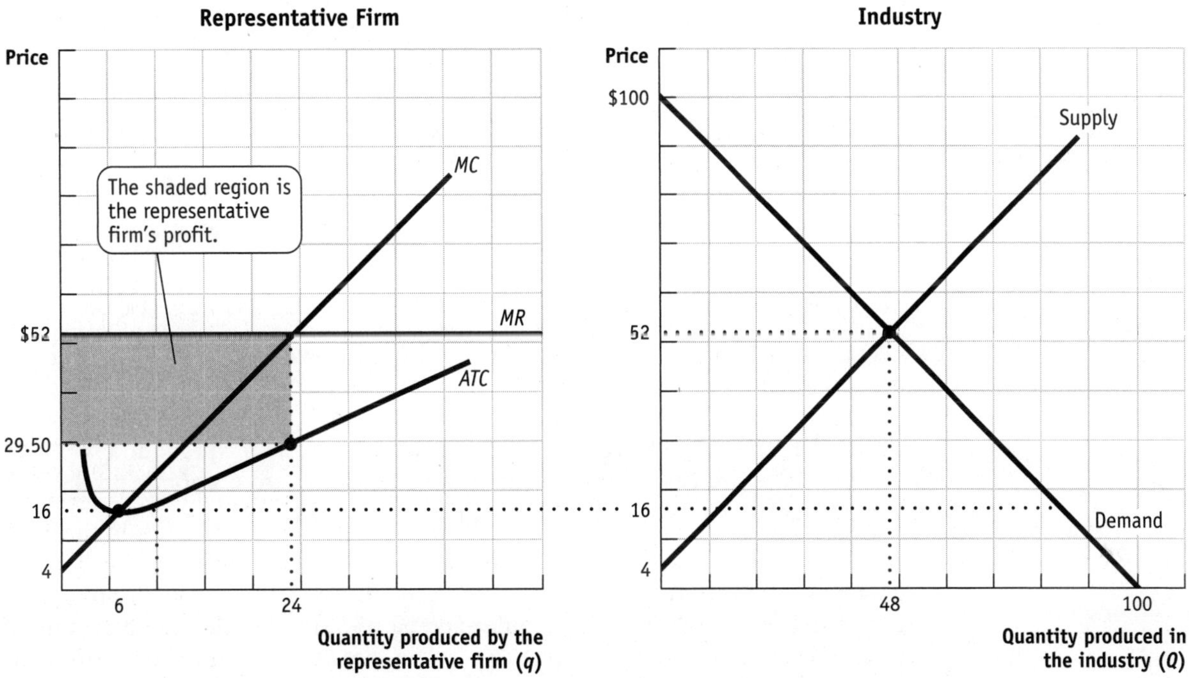

d. The representative firm produces 24 units in the short run when it profit-maximizes, while the total market quantity produced is 48 units. This implies that if all firms are identical and produce 24 units of output, then it will take two firms to produce the market quantity (this is a simplified example with just a few firms to make the math easier).

e. In the long run, the representative firm will earn zero economic profits due to the entry of new firms into the industry. For this to be true, the firm must produce at its break-even price where $MC = ATC$. You can find the average total cost by dividing total cost by the firm's quantity, q. Thus, $TC = 36 + 4q + q^2$ gives us $ATC = 36/q + 4 + q$. $MC = 4 + 2q$, so we can set $MC = ATC$ and have $4 + 2q = 36/q + 4 + q$. Solving this equation gives us $36/q = q$, or $q^2 = 36$. The positive quantity that solves this equation is $q = 6$. So, the long-run quantity produced by the representative firm is 6 units. The long-run equilibrium price is the price at which $MC = ATC$ for this firm, so if q equals 6 units, then the long-run price is $4 + 2(6) = \$16$. At a price of $16 the quantity demanded in the market is 84 units. If each firm produces 6 units and a total of 84 units are produced, then there are 14 firms in the industry.

f.

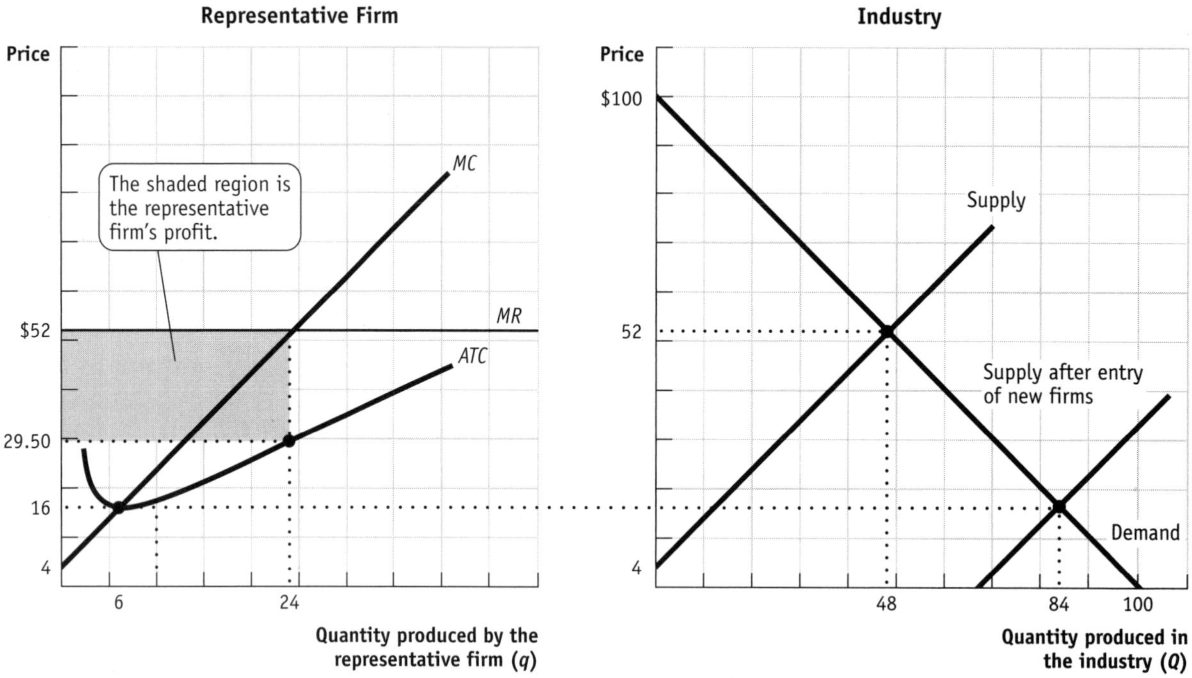

4. **a.** This is not likely to be a long-run equilibrium since the owner of the café is earning a return that is greater than his opportunity cost. He knows that when working for someone else the best he can do is to earn \$30,000, and so the \$50,000 he earns running his coffee shop suggests that he is earning positive economic profit and that over the long run this profit should be reduced until he earns zero economic profit, provided that there is free entry into the market for coffee shops.

b. In the long run, entry of new firms should occur, which should reduce the level of profit to zero for all the firms in the industry. This scenario is based on there being no barriers to entry, and in the case of providing coffee and pastries this is a plausible assumption. Entry should continue until all owners of the coffee shops that are in business earn their opportunity cost and until the level of economic profit for the firms equals zero.

c. The model of perfect competition suggests that all firms in the industry in the long run will earn zero economic profit. But some firms may be driven from the industry if they find their costs of production are greater than the cost of production for other firms. It is likely that this owner found that he simply could not compete with the new firms entering the industry and that he was forced to exit the industry in the long run because other firms could provide coffee and pastries at somewhat lower cost than he was able to achieve. This helps us understand the frequent exit of established businesses from an industry: it is not at all unusual for a city to have restaurants or other business enterprises in markets with competition go out of business.

5. The assumption of constant costs for an industry implies that new firms can enter the industry without causing the costs of production for both the existing firms and these new firms to increase. This is an important assumption to consider: implicitly it is saying that it is possible for all these firms to increase their hiring of labor and capital without affecting the price of that labor or that capital. Is this plausible? It is probably not a bad assumption for many productive enterprises in which the amount of labor and capital used is small relative to the total pool of labor and capital used in the economy. It is probably a poor assumption when the amount of labor and capital used in the industry accounts for a large percentage of the total pool of labor and capital used. Perfect competition, with its assumption of price-taking behavior on the part of producers and consumers, is likely to be a modeling situation in which each individual firm's hiring of labor and capital is unlikely to exert upward pressure on the prices of those inputs.

6. Earning zero economic profits in the long run is not a bad outcome for existing firms in an industry. Rather, this level of profit allows each factor of production (including the owner) to earn a return that is equal to their opportunity cost. Thus, when a firm earns zero economic profit this does not suggest that the firm is performing at a less than ideal level, but that all inputs used by the firm are being compensated at a level equal to their worth as measured by their opportunity costs. In contrast, a firm earning positive economic profit (a possibility in the short run) is receiving a level of compensation that exceeds their opportunity costs: this suggests that an inadequate amount of resources are being devoted to this production since the value placed on the goods being produced exceeds the costs of producing the good. As more resources are devoted to the production of this good through the entry of new firms, the level of economic profit falls until it is at a level where these inputs are valued at their opportunity cost.

Answers to Module Review Questions

1. **Answer a.** When the demand for organic produce increases, this causes a rightward shift in the demand curve, which results in the price of organic produce increasing in the short run. In the long run, however, new producers will enter this industry, which will cause the supply curve to shift to the right, thereby lowering the price of organic produce.

2. **Answer b.** In the short run, if the price is less than average total cost, then firms in this perfectly competitive industry earn negative economic profit. These negative economic profits will lead some firms to exit the industry in the long run until the firms remaining in the industry earn zero economic profits. This implies that price will equal the minimum point of the *ATC* curve or the break-even price. The shut-down price is not on the *ATC* curve, as given in answer (d), but is instead on the *AVC* curve.

3. **Answer c.** In the long run, this industry will experience the entry of new firms because the increase in tastes and preferences for this good will cause the short-run price of the good to increase, resulting in the existing firms earning positive economic profit. But these profits will act as a signal to potential firms to enter, and this entry will shift the market supply curve to the right, causing the price to fall back to its initial level. Firms in the long run will produce the same level of output as they did initially, but there will be more firms in the industry, which will lead to an increase in the industry level of output. Firms in the long run will earn zero economic profit.

4. **Answer b.** Perfectly competitive firms produce that level of output where, for the last unit produced, the addition to total revenue (the marginal revenue) just equals the addition to total cost (the marginal cost). Perfectly competitive firms do not produce in the short run if the market price is less than the shut-down price, or the minimum point of the *AVC* curve. In the long run, a perfectly competitive firm will earn zero economic profit due to the entry of firms in the event of positive short-run economic profit or the exit of firms in the event of negative short-run economic profit.

5. **Answer b.** In the long run, a firm can sell its plant and equipment and exit the industry, and it will choose to exit the industry, if the market price does not cover its average total cost of production, or in other words, its break-even price.

6. **Answer d.** In the long run, entry or exit will occur in the perfectly competitive industry until all firms in the industry earn zero economic profit. Since all firms earn zero economic profit this implies that all firms are producing at the point where price equals average total cost, which can only occur at the break-even price, since firms must also be producing the profit-maximizing quantity where $MR = MC$.

7. **Answer a.** A perfectly competitive industry with constant costs is an industry that can expand its output in the long run without incurring higher or lower costs per unit. This implies that the long-run market supply curve for this industry will be horizontal.

module 28

Monopoly in Practice

BEFORE YOU READ THE MODULE

Summary

This module develops the model of monopoly, a situation in which there is a single producer of the good. This module explores how the monopolist determines its profit-maximizing price and output. The module also considers how to determine whether the monopoly is operating at a profit or a loss.

Module Objectives

Objective #1. In contrast to perfect competition, a monopolist produces a smaller quantity and charges a higher price for its product. The monopolist is able to charge a price that is greater than the competitive price because it has market power: it is the only producer of the good and the good has no close substitutes. By charging a higher price and restricting output, the monopolist is able to increase its profit while maintaining positive profits in the long run.

Objective #2. The monopolist's demand curve for its product is the market demand curve, since it is the only provider of the good in the market. Since the monopolist's demand curve is downward sloping, this implies that the monopolist can only sell additional units of the good by lowering the price on all the units it sells: this results in the monopolist's marginal revenue (*MR*) curve being beneath the monopolist's demand curve. An increase in production by a monopolist has two opposing effects on revenue: a quantity effect and a price effect.

- When the monopolist sells one more unit of the good, this increases its revenue by the price at which the unit is sold: this is the quantity effect.
- When the monopolist sells one more unit of the good, it must reduce the price on all units sold, which decreases revenue: this is the price effect.
- A firm with market power will find that its *MR* curve always lies beneath its demand curve due to the price effect.
- At low levels of output the quantity effect is stronger than the price effect, and the monopolist will find that its total revenue increases as it increases its level of production.

- At high levels of output the price effect is stronger than the quantity effect, and the monopolist will find that its total revenue decreases as it increases its level of production.
- Figure 28.1 illustrates a linear demand curve for a monopolist as well as the monopolist's *MR* curve. Notice that the *MR* curve bisects the distance between the origin and the horizontal intercept of the demand curve. This implies that the slope of the *MR* curve is twice the slope of the demand curve. Notice also that the *y*-intercept for the demand curve and the *MR* curve are the same.

Figure 28.1

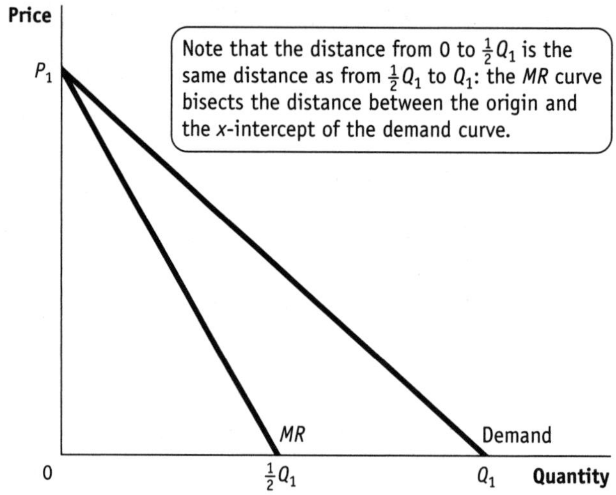

Objective #3. The monopolist maximizes profit by producing the output at which marginal revenue equals marginal cost ($MR = MC$) for the last unit produced while charging the price consumers are willing to pay for this output. The profit-maximizing price-quantity combination is always a point on the demand curve. Figure 28.2 illustrates this concept.

Figure 28.2

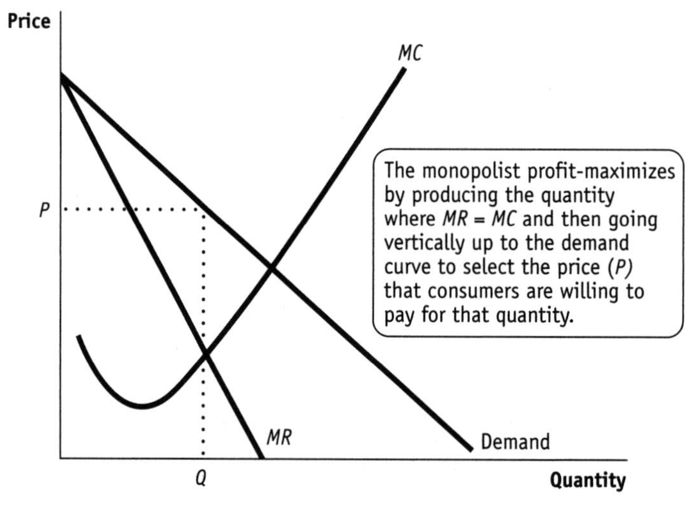

Objective #4. Just as with perfect competition, the monopolist's profits are equal to total revenue minus total cost ($TR - TC$). However, the monopolist can earn profits in the short run as well as the long run since there are effective barriers to entry that protect the monopolist from competition. Figure 28.3 illustrates a monopolist's profit: note that when the price the monopolist charges is greater than its average total cost, then the monopolist earns positive economic profit.

Figure 28.3

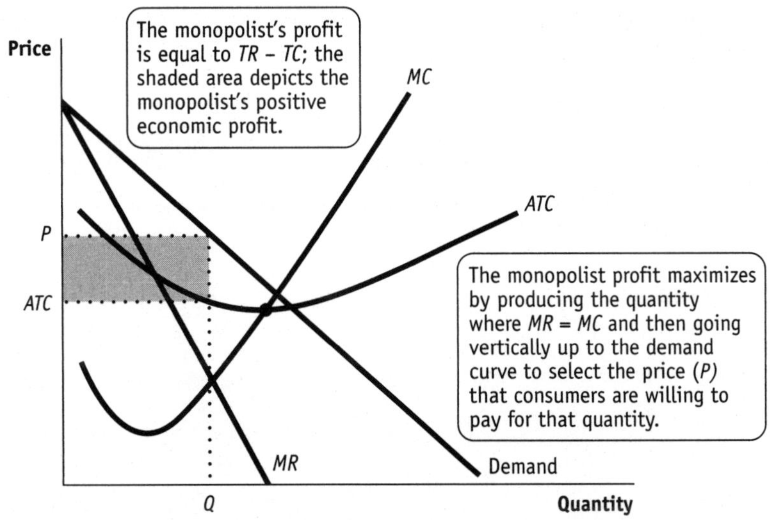

Objective #5. In a perfectly competitive industry, each firm equates the marginal cost to the price of the good; in contrast, in a monopoly the price of the good is always greater than the marginal cost at the profit-maximizing level of output. This tells us that the monopolist is not producing the efficient level of output, since the price consumers are willing to pay for the last unit produced is greater than the cost of producing the last unit. Too few resources are being devoted to the production of the monopolist's product. A monopoly, compared with a perfectly competitive industry, restricts output, charges a higher price for the product, and earns a profit that is not eliminated through the entry of new firms in the long run.

AFTER YOU READ THE MODULE

Tips

Tip #1. It is important that you understand why the monopolist has a downward-sloping *MR* curve that lies beneath the monopolist's demand curve and how to find this *MR* curve. When the monopolist thinks about increasing the amount of the good it supplies to the market, it knows that it will increase its revenue when it sells this additional unit of the good. But it also knows that to sell more units of the good it will need to lower the price on all the units of the good it sells, so the decision to sell a larger amount of the good has two effects—one effect adds to the monopolist's revenue, but the second effect decreases the monopolist's revenue. Review this analysis until you understand it and can express it clearly.

Tip #2. To find the monopolist's *MR* curve is a relatively simple matter if the demand curve for the monopolist is linear. For a linear demand curve, the *MR* curve has the same *y*-intercept as the demand curve and twice the slope of the demand curve. For example, if the demand curve is expressed as $P = 1{,}000 - 2Q$, then the *MR* curve is $MR = 1{,}000 - 4Q$. Another way of expressing this idea is to realize that the *MR* curve bisects the horizontal distance between the origin and the *x*-intercept of the demand curve. Figure 28.4 illustrates this concept.

Figure 28.4

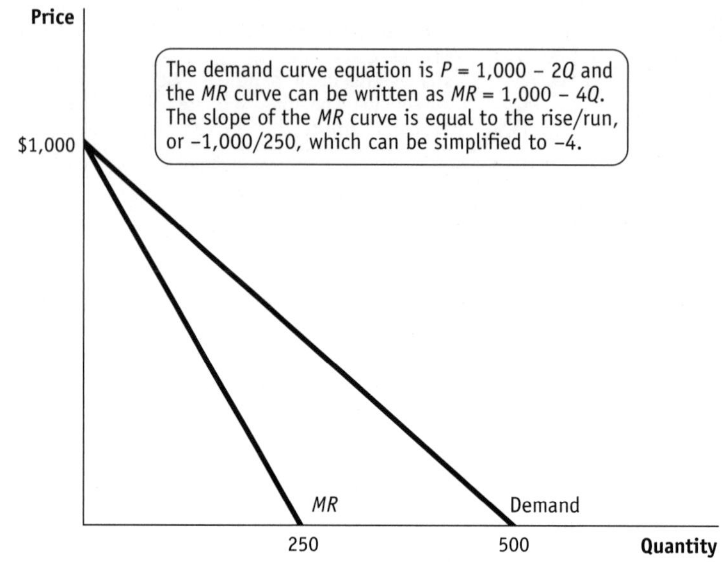

Tip #3. Notice the relationship between the elasticity of the linear demand curve and its *MR* curve. Marginal revenue is positive in the elastic portion of the demand curve, marginal revenue equals zero at the unit-elastic point (the midpoint) of the demand curve, and marginal revenue is negative in the inelastic portion of the demand curve.

Tip #4. This module continues the use of cost curves and marginal analysis. If you are still having trouble with the terminology related to cost curves, or with your understanding and use of these concepts, you should return to the earlier module covering production and cost and review this material. To work successfully with this material, you must have a very strong understanding (and not just memorization) of these underlying concepts.

WORKED PROBLEMS

1. The following graph represents the market demand for Claire's Keepsakes, a monopoly gift store in a resort community. (Claire's is the only gift store in the region.) The graph also includes Claire's cost curves. You are asked to provide guidance to Claire on the profit-maximizing output and price and to identify for her the profits she would earn at the price and output combination. Finally, she would like to know what happens to her profits if the market demand shifts to the right because of an increase in the number of vacation travelers to her region.

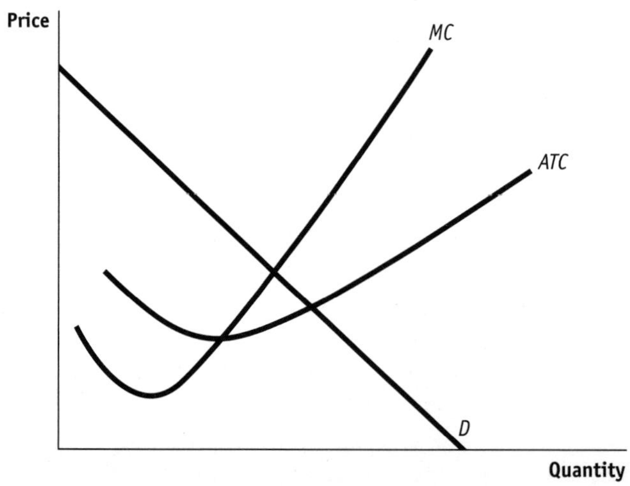

STEP 1: Use the graph to determine the profit-maximizing quantity, *Q*, and the profit-maximizing price, *P*. Explain how you found the profit-maximizing output and price.

To find the profit-maximizing output for the monopolist, first construct the marginal revenue curve. For a linear demand curve, the *MR* curve will share the *y*-intercept with the demand curve and bisect the distance from the origin to the *x*-intercept of the demand curve. The firm will maximize profit by producing the quantity at which *MR* equals *MC* and then pricing the good at the price on the demand curve associated with this quantity. The following figure illustrates the firm's *MR* curve and the profit-maximizing quantity, Q, and profit-maximizing price, *P*.

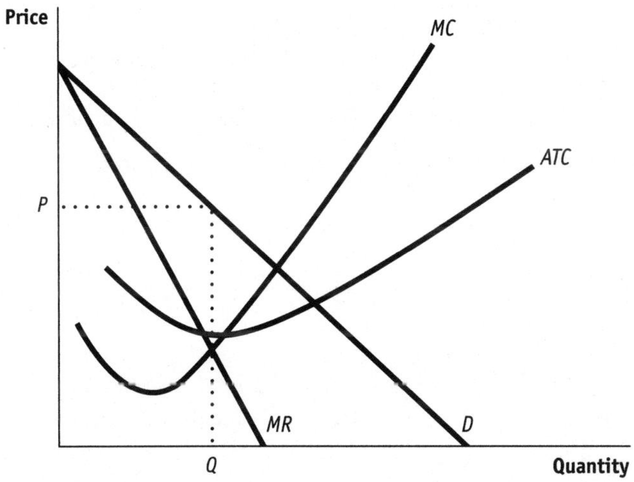

STEP 2: In the graph, determine Claire's profits and explain how you found these profits.

To find the firm's profits you need to find the firm's total revenue (*TR*) and the firm's total cost (*TC*). The firm's $TR = P \times Q$, and the firm's total cost can be calculated as $ATC \times Q$. The difference between *TR* and *TC* is the firm's profits. The firm's *ATC* of producing Q units is marked on the following graph. The shaded area represents the firm's profits. Claire's Keepsakes earns positive economic profits.

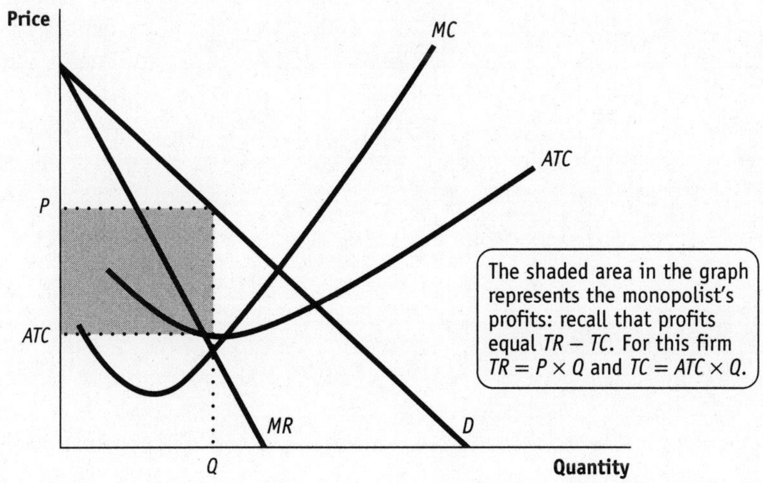

STEP 3: Redraw the graph with the same cost curves but with a demand curve, *D′*, that has shifted to the right of *D*. Determine the profit-maximizing output and price for this new demand curve and explain how you found this profit-maximizing output and price.

When the monopolist's demand curve shifts to the right, this shift will also cause the monopolist's *MR* curve to shift to the right. In the following graph, you can see the shift in the demand curve from D_1 to D_2 as well as the shift in the *MR* curve from MR_1 to MR_2. The monopolist will still profit maximize by producing that level of output where *MR* equals *MC*. In this case, the monopolist will equate MR_2 to *MC* and produce Q_2 units of output. The monopolist then charges the price, P_2, which is the price demanders are willing to pay when they demand Q_2 units of output. The monopolist calculates its profits by calculating its total revenue ($P_2 \times Q_2$) and then subtracting its total costs ($ATC_2 \times Q_2$). The profits are marked in the graph as the shaded area. Note that when the demand curve for the monopolist's product shifts to the right and everything else is held constant, that this results in higher profits for the monopolist.

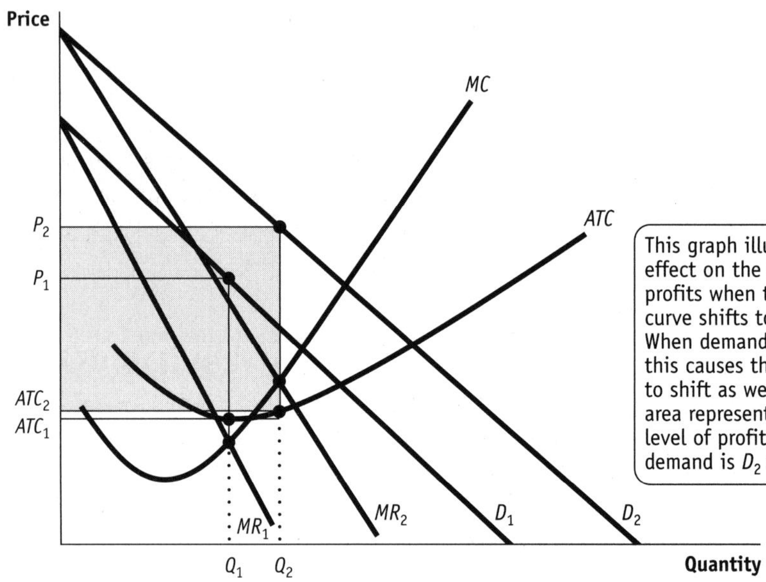

This graph illustrates the effect on the monopolist's profits when the demand curve shifts to the right. When demand shifts right, this causes the *MR* curve to shift as well. The shaded area represents the new level of profits when demand is D_2 and not D_1.

STEP 4: In the new graph, determine Claire's profits now that demand has shifted further to the right. Compare Claire's initial profit situation to what her profit situation will be if there is an increase in demand for her product.

If you compare the shaded profits shown in Step 2 to the shaded profits shown in Step 3, it is easy to verify that Claire's profits increase when the demand curve for her product shifts to the right. The monopolist is now selling more units of the good and selling each unit at a higher price: profits increase.

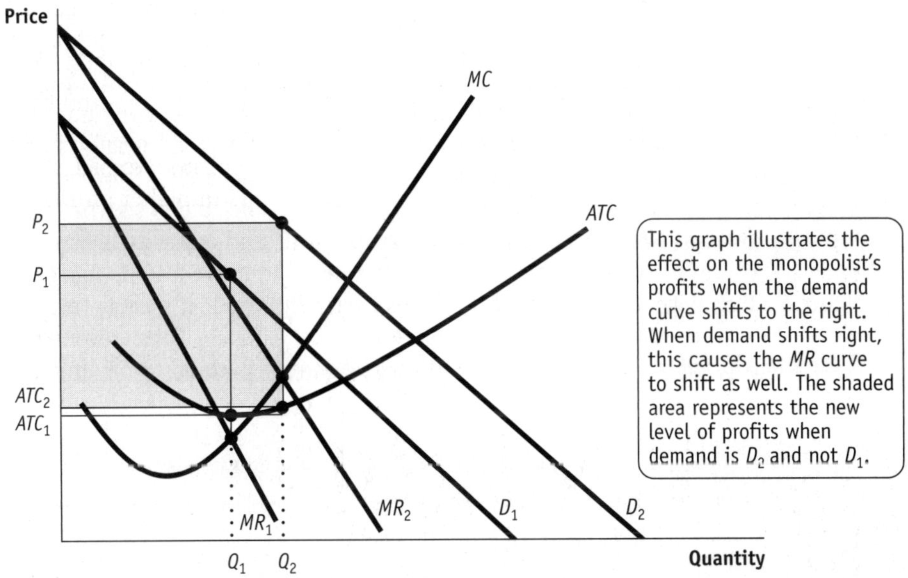

2. Consider Frankie's Toy Shop, the only toy shop in a community. Frankie's enjoys a monopoly in the provision of educational toys in this community. The market demand curve for Frankie's Toy Shop is given by the equation $Q = 100 - 2P$, where Q is the units of educational toys demanded per week and P is the price per educational toy. Frankie has asked you to provide a detailed report about the relationship between selling different quantities of output in this market each week and the effect on the total revenue Frankie's will earn at each output. Frankie would like you to help him understand the relationship between total revenue and the elasticity of demand his store faces as well as the relationship between the quantity of toys he sells and his marginal revenue. Frankie learns best from strong graphical images, so when it would be helpful, be sure to provide a graph to illustrate these concepts.

STEP 1: Start by constructing a demand schedule showing the relationship between different prices that Frankie's might charge and the number of educational toys demanded each week at these prices. Use this information to calculate total revenue at each price.

The following table illustrates the demand schedule for Frankie's Toy Shop as well as the total revenue that the Toy Shop will earn at each of the prices included in the table.

Price	Quantity (units)	Total revenue
$40	20	$ 800
30	40	1,200
20	60	1,200
10	80	800

STEP 2: From the information in Step 1 calculate the value of marginal revenue, or the change in total revenue from selling one additional unit of the good. Draw a graph illustrating the general relationship between the demand curve for the monopolist's product and its marginal revenue curve. Draw another graph illustrating what happens to total revenue as output increases.

The prices and quantities in the table in Step 1 give a sense of what is happening to marginal revenue at specific prices and quantities. As price decreases from \$40 to \$30, the total revenue is increasing. We could calculate the marginal revenue as [(\$1,200 – \$800)/(40 units – 20 units)] = \$20 per unit. If we repeated this calculation for the price decrease from \$20 to \$10, we would find that total revenue is decreasing and marginal revenue is equal to [(\$800 – \$1,200)/(80 units – 60 units)], or –\$20 per unit. From this exercise with discrete data points we could conclude that as price decreases, marginal revenue is not constant. Marginal revenue initially is positive, but as price continues to decrease, it eventually becomes negative. If you included more prices and quantities in the table in Step 1, you would be able to see that total revenue is at its greatest when price is equal to \$25 per unit and quantity is equal to 50 units. The next graphs illustrate this monopolist's demand curve and its marginal revenue curve along with the relationship between the monopolist's total revenue and its level of output. Marginal revenue is equal to 0 (hence, total revenue is maximized) when price is equal to \$25 per unit and quantity is equal to 50 units.

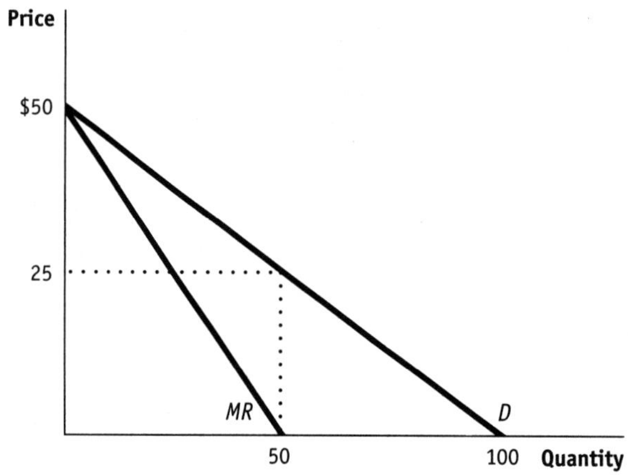

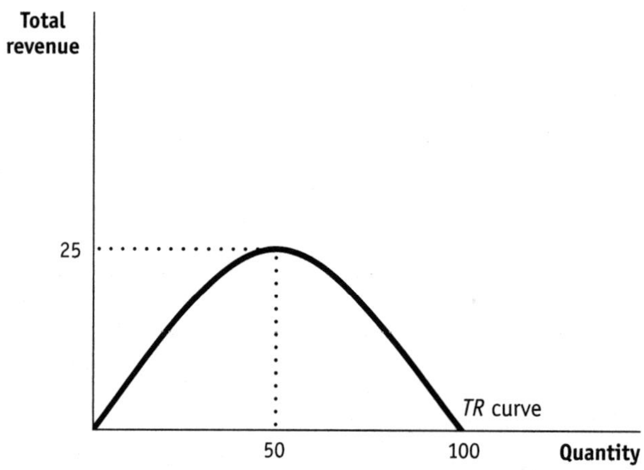

STEP 3: Then use these graphs to interpret the relationship between total revenue, marginal revenue, and elasticity of demand.

Recall that a downward-sloping demand curve is elastic above its midpoint, unit elastic at its midpoint, and inelastic below its midpoint. Also recall that total revenue increases when the price decreases in the elastic region of the demand curve. Since total revenue is increasing as price decreases, marginal revenue must have a positive value. Recall also that total revenue is maximized at the unit-elastic point (or the midpoint) of the demand curve. This implies that marginal revenue must have a value of zero. Finally, as price decreases in the inelastic region, total revenue decreases; hence, marginal revenue must have a negative value. Study the two graphs in Step 2 to verify these concepts. Frankie's Toy Shop will maximize its revenues by charging $25 per unit and selling 25 units since this price and output combination represents the midpoint, or unit-elastic point, on the demand curve for this monopolist.

3. A monopolist needs to know whether selling his product at two different prices, rather than a single price, will affect his profits. The monopolist recognizes that the demand curve for his product is given by the equation $P = 1{,}000 - 2Q$, and furthermore, he knows that there are no fixed costs of producing the good and that the marginal cost of producing the good is given by the equation $MC = 100$. First, the monopolist would like you to calculate the profit-maximizing price and quantity for the good sold at a single price. The monopolist would also like to know what his profits will equal if he pursues a single-price policy. He then would like you to contrast this outcome with what will happen if he is willing to sell a total of 225 units, with the first 100 units sold at a price of $800 per unit. Then, he'll sell the second 125 units at whatever single price he can get after he sells the first 100 units. You must decide what this second price is and then determine what the monopolist's profits will be if he pursues this two-price policy. The monopolist asks that you provide him with a graph of each of these scenarios so that he can analyze the effect of these two policies. Finally, which policy will you recommend to this monopolist if his goal is to maximize his profit?

STEP 1: Draw a graph representing the monopolist's demand curve and his marginal cost curve.

This graph will be your base graph from which you will analyze the rest of this problem. It is important to start with this graph so that you have a clear image to guide your analysis. The graph that follows provides an image of the monopolist's demand curve and the marginal cost curve.

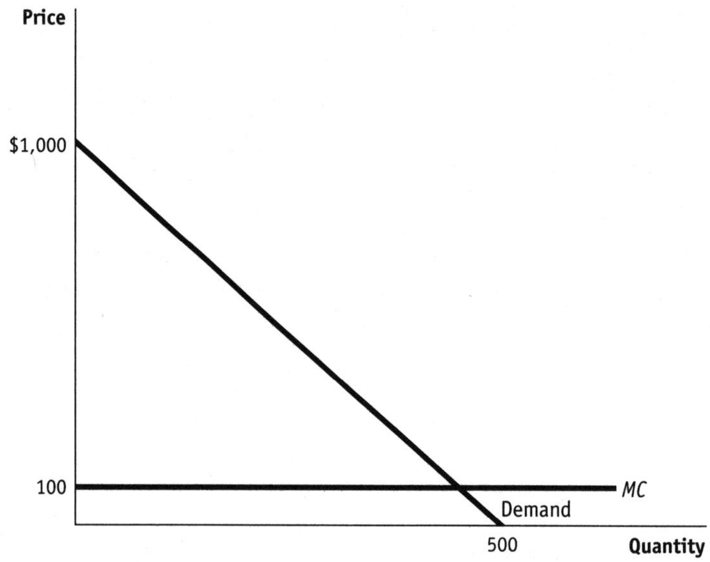

STEP 2: Find the single price monopolist's marginal revenue (*MR*) curve and draw it in your graph.

Recall that if the single-price monopolist's demand curve is linear, then its *MR* curve will share the same *y*-intercept as the demand curve and have twice the slope of the demand curve. Thus, the *MR* curve for this monopolist is given by the equation $MR = 1{,}000 - 4Q$. The graph that follows illustrates the single-price monopolist's demand curve, *MC* curve, and *MR* curve.

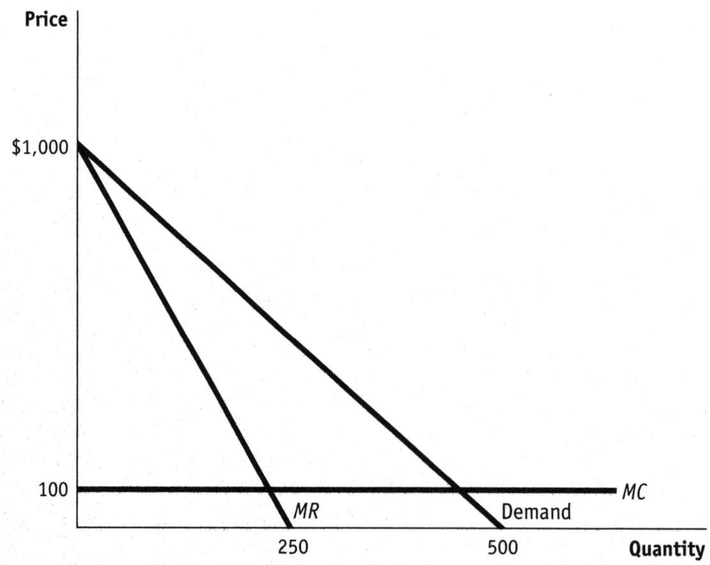

STEP 3: Identify the profit-maximizing quantity for the single-price monopolist. Then, determine the price that the monopolist will charge if he produces this quantity.

To find the profit-maximizing quantity for a single-price monopolist, you will want to equate MC to MR. Thus, $100 = 1{,}000 - 4Q$, or $Q = 225$. To find the price for this level of output, substitute this quantity into the demand curve: $P = 1{,}000 - 2Q = 1{,}000 - 2(225) = \$550$ per unit. The following graph illustrates these profit-maximizing levels if the monopolist is charging a single price.

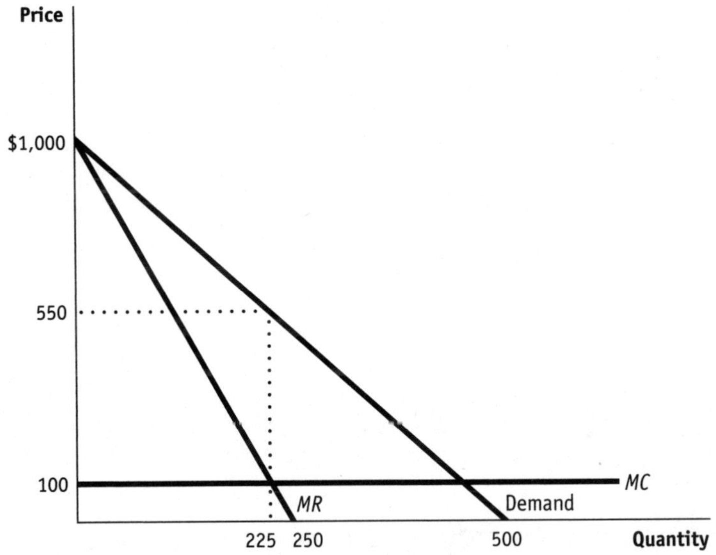

STEP 4: **Calculate the single-price monopolist's total costs, total revenue, and monopoly profits.**

We know that the cost of each additional unit produced by this monopolist is \$100. So, if the monopolist produces 225 units, the total cost of producing these units will be given by (\$100 per unit)(225 units) = \$22,500. Since *MC* is horizontal and there are no fixed costs, this implies that marginal cost is equal to average total cost. To calculate total revenue, we simply need to multiply the number of units produced by the price per unit: (225 units)(\$550 per unit) = \$123,750. The single-price monopolist's profit will be equal to *TR* minus *TC*, or \$123,750 – \$22,500, which is equal to \$101,250. The following graph illustrates the single-price monopolist's profits.

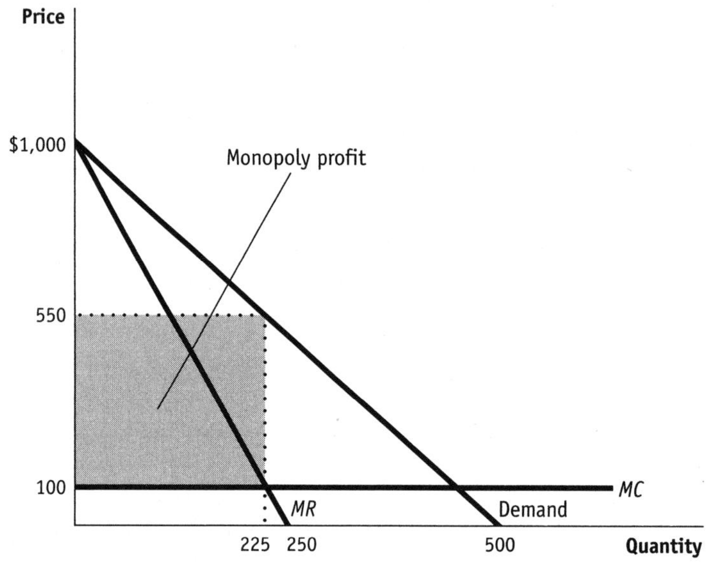

STEP 5: **Draw a picture of the monopolist's demand curve and the *MC* curve. On this graph label a price of \$800 and determine the quantity of the monopolist's product that is demanded at this price. Then, label a quantity of 225 units and mark what price corresponds to this quantity on the monopolist's demand curve. From your graph determine the two prices the monopolist will charge if he charges \$800 per unit for the first 100 units he sells and he is willing to sell another 125 units at a different price.**

In this step, you are providing yourself with a visual map of the various calculations you will need to do to answer this question. On the graph, you will want to determine the quantity that is demanded at a price of \$800 per unit, as well as the price that people in this market are willing to pay when a total of 225 units of the good are provided by the monopolist. In the graph that follows, you can see that when the price of the good is \$800 there are 100 units demanded. We could also see this by using the demand equation: when price is \$800 then we have $800 = 1{,}000 - 2Q$, and solving for Q, we get $Q = 100$ units. When the quantity demanded is 225 units we can use the demand equation to solve for the price: thus, $P = 1{,}000 - 2Q = 1{,}000 - 2(225) = \$550$ per unit. Carefully examine the following graph to see these price and quantity combinations. The monopolist will be able to sell the first 100 units at a price of \$800 per unit, and he can sell an additional 125 units (for a total of 225 units sold in all) for a price of \$550 per unit.

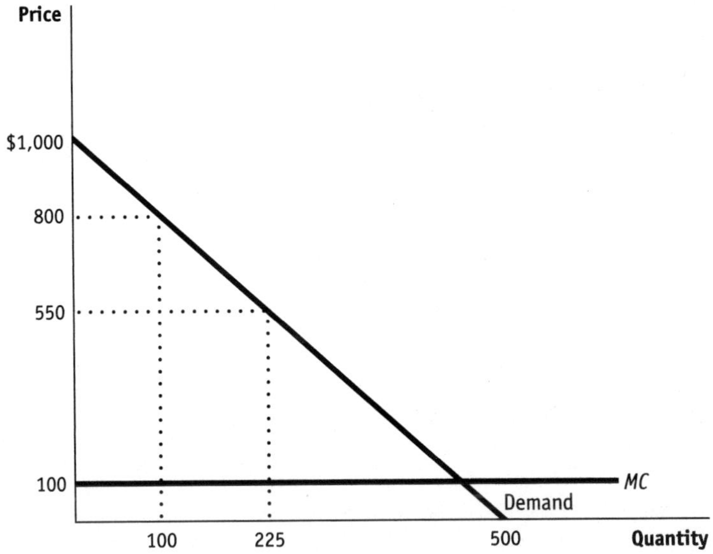

STEP 6: Calculate the total costs, total revenue, and monopoly profits for this monopolist when he sells the good at two different prices: $800 per unit for the first 100 units and $550 per unit for the next 125 units.

We know that the cost of each additional unit produced by this monopolist is $100. So, if the monopolist produces 225 units, the total cost of producing these units will be ($100 per unit)(225 units) = $22,500. Since *MC* is horizontal and there are no fixed costs, this implies that marginal cost is equal to average total cost. To calculate total revenue, we simply need to multiply the number of units produced by the price per unit and remember that this time we have two different prices and two different quantities: (100 units)($800 per unit) + (125 units)($550 per unit) = $148,750. The monopolist who charges two prices ($800 per unit for the first 100 units and $550 per unit for the next 125 units) will earn profits equal to *TR* minus *TC*, or $148,750 – $22,500, which is equal to $126,250. The following graph illustrates the monopolist's profits when he charges these two different prices.

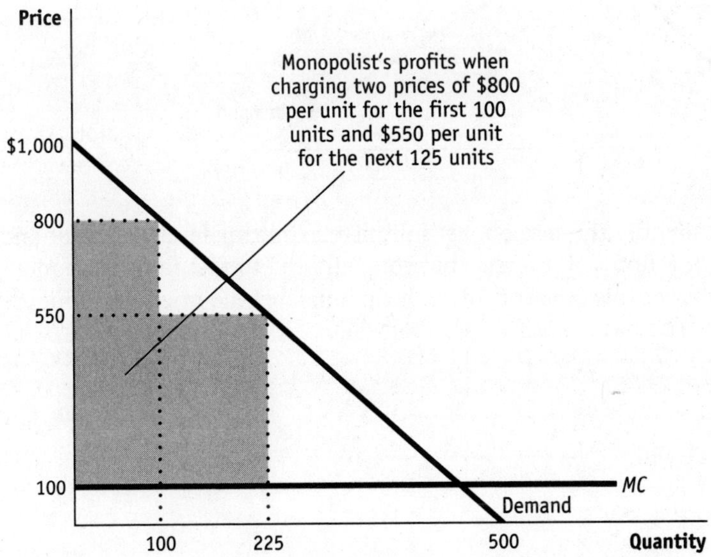

STEP 7: Based on your calculations, make a recommendation as to which pricing scheme will be best for the monopolist.

Clearly a two-price policy results in greater profits for the monopolist than a single-price policy. With the single-price policy the monopolist earns profits of $101,250, while with the two-price policy outlined in this problem the monopolist earns profits of $126,250.

Problems and Exercises

1. The graph below represents a monopolist's cost curves and the demand curve for the monopolist's product. Use this graph to answer this set of questions.

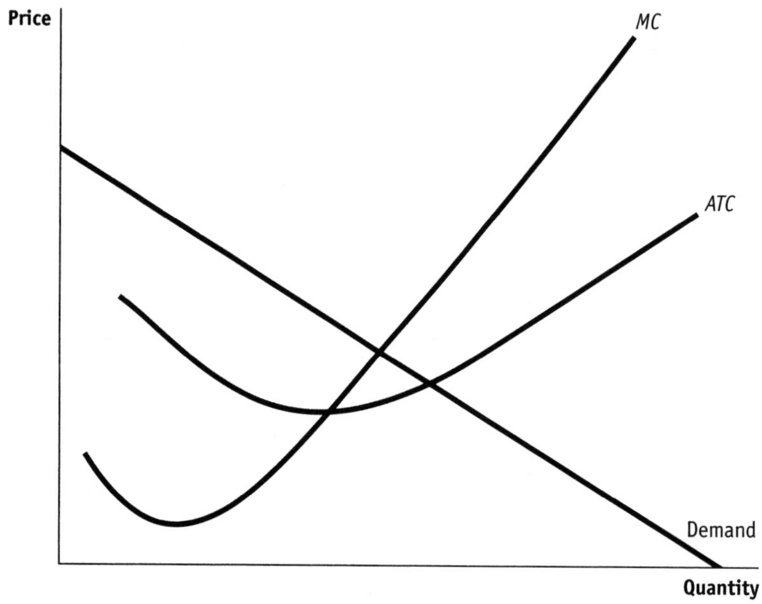

a. On the above graph, identify the monopolist's profit-maximizing level of output and label this amount Q_M. (Hint: don't forget that you will need to first find the monopolist's *MR* curve to answer this question.) On the graph, label the price the monopolist will charge for the good as P_M.

b. Does this monopolist make positive, negative, or zero economic profit in the short run? Identify the area that represents profits in the above graph if the firm earns positive or negative profit.

c. What do you expect will happen to the monopolist in the long run? In your answer, be sure to identify what happens to the firm's profits, level of production, and price.

d. A newspaper runs an article on the benefits of consuming the product this monopolist produces. The result of this article is that demand for this product shifts to the right at every price. Redraw your graph with the old and the new demand curves, and then analyze what happens to output, price, and profits for this firm. Label the new output Q_M', the new price P_M', and identify the area that represents the firm's profits.

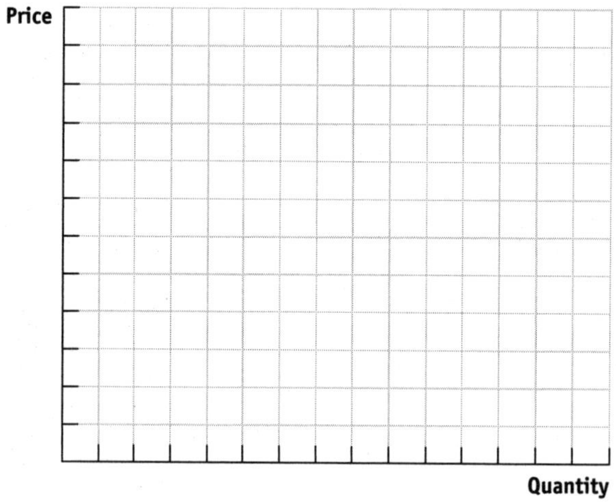

e. Given your answer in part (d), is there an incentive for a monopolist to try to increase the demand for its product?

2. Perfectly competitive firms and monopolies are both assumed to profit maximize. How does the perfectly competitive firm decide on the optimal price and quantity for profit maximization? How does the monopolist decide on the optimal price and quantity for profit maximization? What are the efficiency implications of these two decisions? In your answer to this last question, be sure to comment on the relationship between price and marginal cost for the last unit the firm produces.

3. Suppose a monopolist has a linear market demand curve. At the midpoint of this demand curve, the elasticity of demand is unit-elastic. What do you know about the marginal revenue of the monopolist when the elasticity of demand is equal to 1? If the demand for this monopolist is elastic, what do you know about the marginal revenue for this monopolist? If the demand for this monopolist is inelastic, what do you know about the marginal revenue for this monopolist?

4. A monopolist finds that the demand for its product at the current level of production is elastic. Will this monopolist increase or decrease its revenue if it lowers the price at which it sells its product? Explain your answer making reference to the quantity effect as well as the price effect. Which of these two effects is dominant in this situation?

BEFORE YOU TAKE THE TEST

Module Review Questions

1. The demand for the monopolist's product
   a. is downward sloping.
   b. equals the market demand curve.
   c. is equal to the firm's *MR* curve.
   d. All of the statements are true.
   e. Answers (a) and (b) are true.

2. In contrast to perfect competition, a monopolist charges a
   a. higher price and produces a larger quantity.
   b. higher price and produces a smaller quantity.
   c. lower price and produces a larger quantity.
   d. lower price and produces a smaller quantity.

3. A monopolist is debating whether to lower the price it charges for its product. Which of the following statements is true?
   I. When the monopolist lowers its price, the quantity effect always increases the monopolist's total revenue provided that the monopolist is producing in the elastic region of its demand curve.
   II. When the monopolist lowers its price, the price effect initially causes total revenue to increase, but eventually the price effect causes total revenue to fall.
   III. The monopolist does not need to worry about the quantity or price effect when debating what price to charge for its product, since it is the only producer of the good.

   a. Statement I is true.
   b. Statement II is true.
   c. Statements I and II are true.
   d. Statement III is true.

4. A monopolist estimates that the price elasticity of demand for its product is less than 1. This monopolist knows that an increase in the price of its good will __________ its total revenue.

   a. increase
   b. decrease

5. Which of the following statements is true about a monopolist with a linear demand curve?
   I. The more elastic the demand for a monopolist's product, the closer the market price will be to marginal revenue for this firm.
   II. Once the elasticity of demand for a monopolist falls below 1, the value of marginal revenue is negative.
   III. At the midpoint of the monopolist's demand curve, the firm's marginal revenue is equal to zero.

   a. Statement I is true.
   b. Statement II is true.
   c. Statements I and II are true.
   d. Statements I and III are true.
   e. Statements I, II, and III are true.

6. Which of the following statements is true?
   I. A monopolistically competitive market structure is composed of many firms producing differentiated products.
   II. A perfectly competitive firm profit maximizes by producing the level of output where $MR = MC$.
   III. A monopolist profit maximizes by charging the price where $MR = MC$.

   a. Statements I and II are true.
   b. Statements I and III are true.
   c. Statements II and III are true.
   d. Statements I, II, and III are true.

ANSWER KEY

Answers to Problems and Exercises

1.

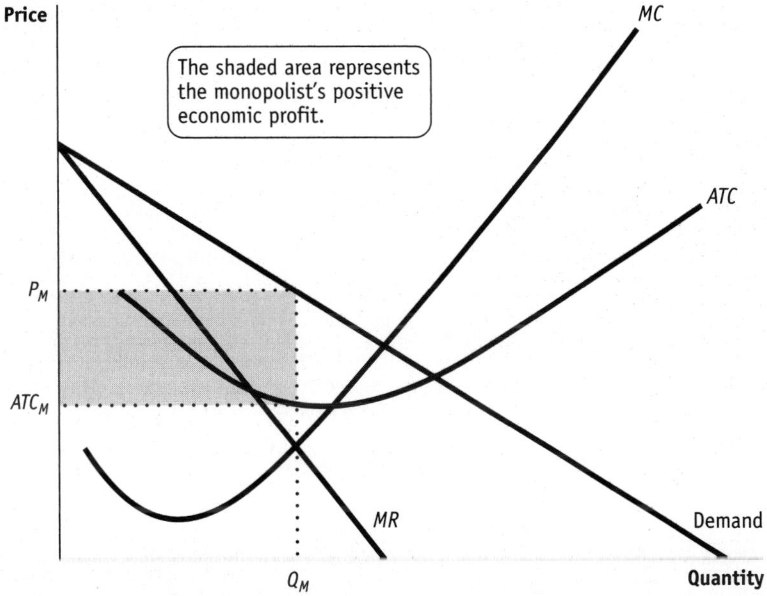

a. See the above graph.

b. This monopolist earns positive economic profit since the price it receives on each unit (P_M) is greater than its average total cost (*ATC*) of production (ATC_M on the graph).

c. This monopolist will continue to earn positive economic profits because there is an effective barrier to entry to this industry that prevents the firm from having to compete with other producers. The firm's profits will continue at the level given in the graph, and the firm's price and quantity decision will remain unchanged.

d.

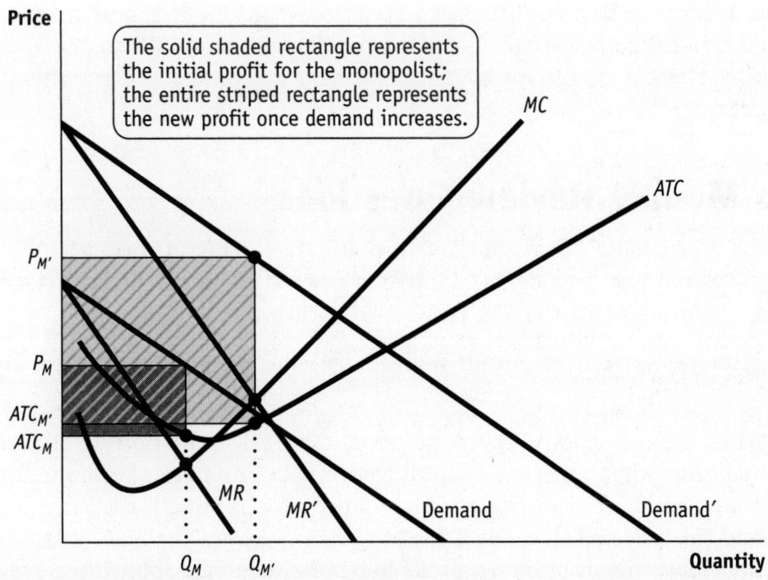

e. Holding everything else constant, if the monopolist can increase the demand for its product, it can charge a higher price, produce more units of the good, and increase the level of economic profits it earns.

2. The perfectly competitive firm is a price-taking firm and must charge the market-determined price for its output. It then chooses the profit-maximizing level of output given this price. The profit-maximizing level of output for the perfectly competitive firm is where $MR = MC$, or where $P = MC$, since $P = MR$ for a perfectly competitive firm.

A monopoly can set its own price, subject to market demand for its product. It determines its profit-maximizing level of output by equating marginal cost to marginal revenue, and then charges the price consumers are willing to pay for this level of output. The monopolist finds this price by going vertically up to the demand curve from its selected level of output and charging the price on its demand curve that is associated with this level of output.

A perfectly competitive firm produces an efficient level of output, since $P = MC$ for the last unit of output it produces. This implies that the price consumers are willing to pay for the last unit produced is equal to the cost of producing this last unit: consumers and producers value this last unit equivalently, which tells us that the right amount of resources is being allocated to the production of this good. A monopoly, in contrast, produces an inefficient level of output, since $P > MC$ for the last unit of output it produces. This implies that the price consumers are willing to pay for the last unit produced is greater than the cost of producing this last unit: the value the consumers place on this last unit exceeds the cost of producing this last unit. More resources should be devoted to the production of this good.

3. The *MR* curve for a monopolist with a linear demand curve shares the *y*-intercept with the demand curve and has twice the slope of the demand curve. If you plot this *MR* curve and the demand curve on the same graph, you will find that the *MR* curve intersects the horizontal axis at a quantity that is the quantity found at the midpoint of the demand curve. Thus, when demand is unit-elastic (at its midpoint), marginal revenue equals zero. When demand is elastic, marginal revenue is positive, and when demand is inelastic, marginal revenue is negative.

4. When the demand for the product is elastic, the monopolist can increase its revenue by selling the good for a lower price. When the monopolist lowers its price, it sells more units than it did at a higher price: this quantity effect positively increases the monopolist's revenue. When the monopolist lowers its price, it must cut the price on all units sold: this price effect negatively impacts the monopolist's revenue. When demand is elastic, the quantity effect is dominant over the price effect, resulting in the monopolist's revenues increasing.

Answers to Module Review Questions

1. **Answer e.** The monopolist's demand curve is the market demand curve and it is downward sloping. The monopolist's demand curve is not the monopolist's *MR* curve, however, since for the monopolist the *MR* curve lies beneath the demand curve.

2. **Answer b.** Monopolies restrict output and charge consumers higher prices for their product.

3. **Answer a.** When the monopolist lowers its price, it can sell more units of the good and these additional units will always make a positive contribution to total revenue. However, when the monopolist lowers its price, it finds that it now has to cut the price on all the units it sells and this price effect reduces the total revenue from the units that previously would have sold for a higher price. To profit maximize, the monopolist must select the price off the demand curve that corresponds to the quantity where $MR = MC$.

4. **Answer a.** When price elasticity of demand is less than 1, the demand curve is relatively inelastic. An increase in price in the inelastic region of the demand curve results in total revenue increasing.

5. **Answer e.** All three of these statements are true and rely on a thorough knowledge of the meaning of elasticity and its relationship to total revenue. The elastic region of the demand curve occurs at prices that are greater than the price at the midpoint of the demand curve: at higher prices, the demand is more elastic. In this region of the demand curve, the *MR* curve lies closer to the demand curve. When the elasticity of demand has a value of less than 1, this signifies that demand is inelastic and a fall in the price of the good will cause total revenue to decrease, which implies that marginal revenue is negative. The midpoint of the linear demand curve is the unit-elastic point: this is where total revenue is maximized, and therefore the change in total revenue, MR_1, is equal to zero.

6. **Answer a.** The first statement is the definition of monopolistic competition. The second statement correctly states the profit-maximizing rule used by perfectly competitive firms when selecting their optimal output level. The third statement is false: monopolies profit-maximize when they produce the level of output where $MR = MC$ and then charge the price on their demand curve that is associated with this level of output.

module 29

Monopoly and Public Policy

BEFORE YOU READ THE MODULE

Summary

This module continues the discussion of monopoly begun in the previous module. The module compares perfect competition and monopoly and examines how these two different market structures result in different outcomes with respect to social welfare. The module also discusses how policymakers address the problems posed by monopoly.

Module Objectives

Objective #1. Monopoly causes a net loss to the economy because the cost to the consumer is greater than the gain to the monopolist. The existence of a monopoly creates a deadweight loss due to the monopolist's restriction of output and its ability to charge a higher price for its product relative to the quantity and price decision made by a perfectly competitive firm. The deadweight loss created by the monopolist occurs because some mutually beneficial transactions do not occur: this is evident when we recall that for the last unit produced by the monopolist, the marginal cost of producing that unit is less than the price consumers are willing to pay for that unit. Because monopoly is inefficient, government policy often is used to offset some of the undesired effects of monopoly. Figure 29.1 indicates for a monopolist the areas that correspond to consumer surplus, producer surplus, and deadweight loss.

Figure 29.1

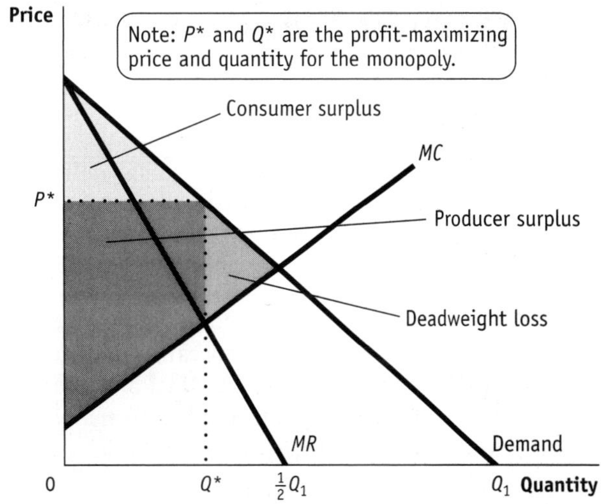

Objective #2. If an industry is not a natural monopoly, then the best method for avoiding monopoly outcomes is to prevent monopoly from arising or to break up the monopoly if it already exists. Government policies used to prevent or eliminate monopolies are known as antitrust policy.

Objective #3. If an industry is a natural monopoly, then breaking up the monopoly is not a clearly beneficial idea since large-scale producers have lower average total cost than smaller-scale producers. Two policy methods are used for regulating natural monopolies: public ownership and regulation.

- With public ownership, the government establishes a public agency to provide the good and to protect consumers' interests. With public ownership, it is possible to set the price at the efficient level so that $P = MC$ for the last unit being produced by the natural monopoly. Unfortunately, publicly owned natural monopolies are not always successful at minimizing their costs or at providing high-quality products. Publicly owned companies may also end up serving political interests.
- Regulation typically takes the form of price regulation, where the private company is regulated with regard to what prices it can charge for the product. Local utilities are frequently regulated in this way. With price regulation the monopolist produces a higher level of output and sells this output at a lower price, provided that the regulated price is set at a level greater than the firm's marginal cost and is high enough that the firm at least breaks even on total output. Price regulation increases the area of consumer surplus because the regulation reduces the monopolist's profit and results in more output at lower prices. The price set by regulators is ideally set so that price equals average total cost, but monopolies have an incentive to exaggerate their costs to regulators, making it difficult for regulators to ascertain this ideal price. Additionally, regulated monopolies often provide inferior quality to consumers.

Key Terms

public ownership when goods are supplied by the government or by a firm owned by the government to protect the interests of the consumer in response to *natural monopoly.*

price regulation a limitation on the price a *monopolist* is allowed to charge.

Notes

AFTER YOU READ THE MODULE

Tips

Tip #1. A monopoly reduces social welfare because it restricts output and charges a higher price than would occur if the product was produced in a perfectly competitive market. The area of deadweight loss measures the loss in social welfare.

Tip #2. A natural monopoly is a situation in which a single firm can produce the market output at a lower price than can two or more firms. This reduction in the costs of production is due to economies of scale: a single firm can reap the benefits of large-scale production better than multiple smaller firms. Natural monopolies tend to be either owned by the public or regulated with regard to what prices they can charge for their product.

WORKED PROBLEMS

1. Monty's Dry Cleaners is the only dry cleaning establishment in Tuxedoville. Monty knows that the market demand curve for dry cleaning in Tuxedoville is given by the equation $P = 100 - Q$. Furthermore, assume that Monty has no fixed costs and that his marginal costs of production are equal to $10. Monty seeks your advice on what his profit-maximizing price and quantity are. In addition, Monty would like to know what his economic profit is in this market. In addition to calculating these values, provide Monty with a calculation of the deadweight loss and the consumer surplus due to his operating as a monopoly.

STEP 1: Start by drawing a graph of Monty's demand curve for his product and his *MC* curve. Then find the marginal revenue curve for Monty's Dry Cleaners.

The following graph gives Monty's demand curve and *MC* curve. Since $MC = 10$, this implies that Monty's *MC* curve is a horizontal line that intersects the vertical axis at $10 per unit. His *MR* curve is also drawn in: to find his *MR* revenue, recall that for a straight-line demand curve, the *MR* curve shares the *y*-intercept with the demand curve and bisects the horizontal axis between the origin and the *x*-intercept of the demand curve. Thus, the *y*-intercept for the demand curve is at $100 per unit, which will also be the *y*-intercept for the *MR* curve. The *x*-intercept for the demand curve is at 100 units and the *x*-intercept for the *MR* curve will be half this number, or 50 units.

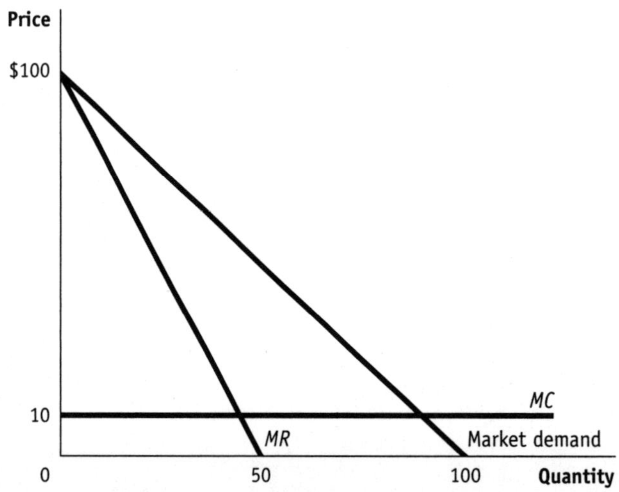

STEP 2: Identify the profit-maximizing quantity, the quantity at which marginal revenue equals marginal cost. Use the demand curve to find the price that Monty should charge for this quantity.

Monty will want to produce that quantity at which $MR = MC$, and then charge the price that demanders are willing to pay for this quantity. The following graph illustrates this profit-maximizing price and quantity. We can solve for the specific price and quantity by first writing an equation for the *MR* curve and then setting this *MR* curve equal to the *MC* curve. Thus, $MR = 100 - 2Q$, and if $MR = MC$, then $Q = 45$. Substituting a quantity of 45 into the demand curve, we get a price of \$55. The profit-maximizing quantity is 45 units and the profit-maximizing price is \$55. The following graph identifies these profit-maximizing levels.

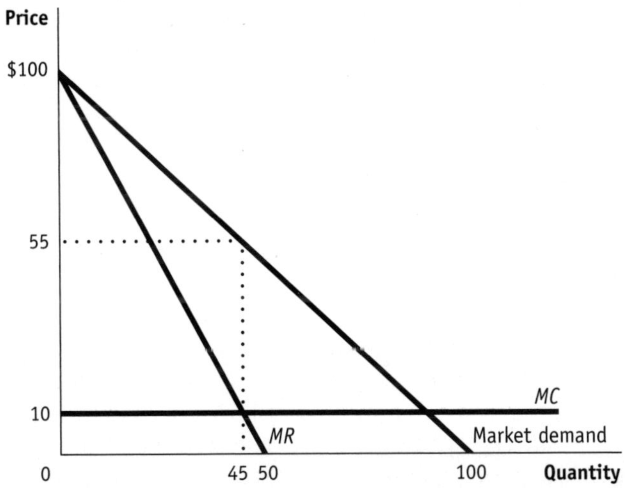

STEP 3: Calculate Monty's total costs and total revenues and then use these figures to calculate the profit he will make.

To calculate Monty's total costs, start by recognizing that the cost of each additional unit is \$10. Since there are no fixed costs, this implies that producing 45 units will cost Monty \$450. (Since *MC* is horizontal and there are no fixed costs, this implies that marginal cost is equal to average total cost.) To calculate Monty's total revenue, multiply the price per unit times the number of units: (\$55 per unit)(45 units) = \$2,475. Monty's profit is equal to total revenue minus total cost, or \$2,475 – \$450 = \$2,025. In the following figure, the shaded area represents Monty's profit.

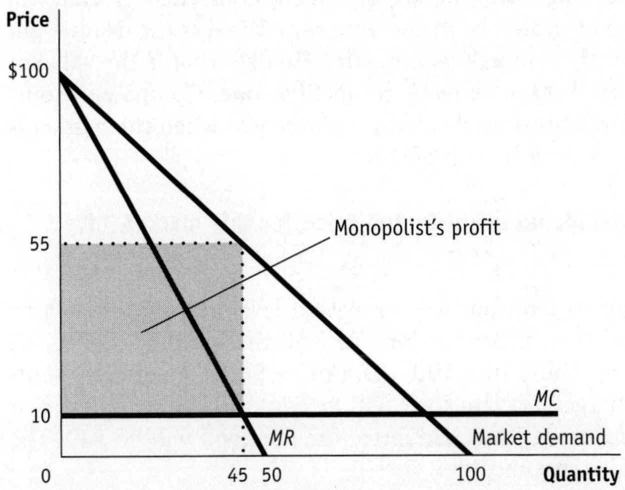

STEP 4: Using your graph identify the area that corresponds to deadweight loss and then calculate a value for this area. Also, identify the area that corresponds to consumer surplus and then calculate a value for this area.

Deadweight loss is the area that corresponds to the loss in consumer and producer surplus that results when not all mutually beneficial transactions take place. In this case, the deadweight loss is solely a loss in consumer surplus: if the dry-cleaning industry was a perfectly competitive industry, more units of output would be produced and these units would sell for a price equal to *MC*. The following figure represents the deadweight loss due to monopoly. The value of this deadweight loss is equal to (1/2)($55 per unit – $10 per unit)(90 units – 45 units) = $1,012.50.

The consumer surplus in the dry-cleaning market will be equal to that area that is beneath the demand curve but above the price consumers pay. In this market, consumers are paying $55 per unit of dry cleaning. The following graph indicates the area that corresponds to consumer surplus. The value of this area is equal to (1/2)($100 per unit – $55 per unit)(45 units) = $1,012.50.

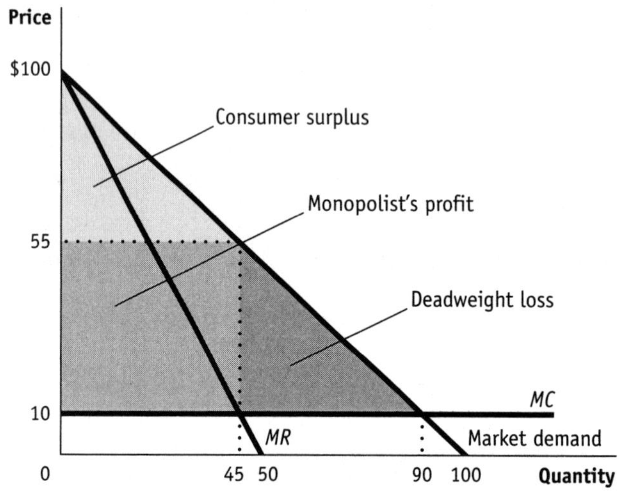

2. Suppose that the dry-cleaning market in Tuxedoville is a perfectly competitive industry and not the monopoly described in problem 1. Suppose that the market demand curve for the industry is $P = 100 - Q$ and the *MC* of a representative firm is given by the equation $MC = 10$. How much dry cleaning will be produced in this perfectly competitive industry given this information? What will be the price of dry cleaning if this market is perfectly competitive? What will the individual firm's level of profits be in the long run? What is the deadweight loss equal to in this perfectly competitive industry? Finally, what is the value of consumer surplus if the market is a perfectly competitive one? Compare the outcome in this perfectly competitive market with the outcome when the market is served by the monopolist Monty from problem 1.

STEP 1: Find the profit-maximizing quantity and price for this market, given the preceding information.

In a perfectly competitive industry, output will be at that level of output at which price is equal to the marginal cost of production. To find this output, equate the demand curve to the *MC* curve: thus, $10 = 100 - Q$, or $Q = 90$. In a perfectly competitive industry, the price charged for the good will be equal to the marginal cost of producing the last unit of output: thus, the price for the good will be $10. The following graph illustrates this outcome.

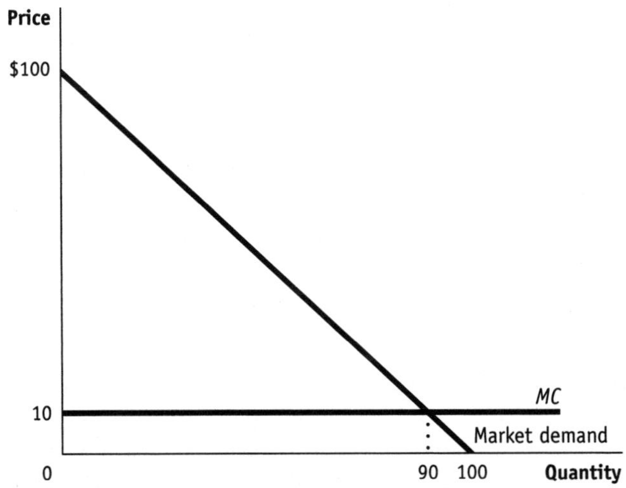

STEP 2: Find the individual firm's level of profit in the long run as well as the deadweight loss in the industry. Calculate the value of consumer surplus when this market is a perfectly competitive market.

In a perfectly competitive industry, firms earn zero economic profit in the long run due to entry and exit of firms. There is no deadweight loss in a perfectly competitive industry since all mutually beneficial transactions are taking place. The value of consumer surplus is equal to the area that is underneath the demand curve and above the price that consumers pay for the product. In this case, that area's value is equal to (1/2)($100 per unit – $10 per unit)(90 units) = $4,050. The following graph indicates the area that corresponds to consumer surplus.

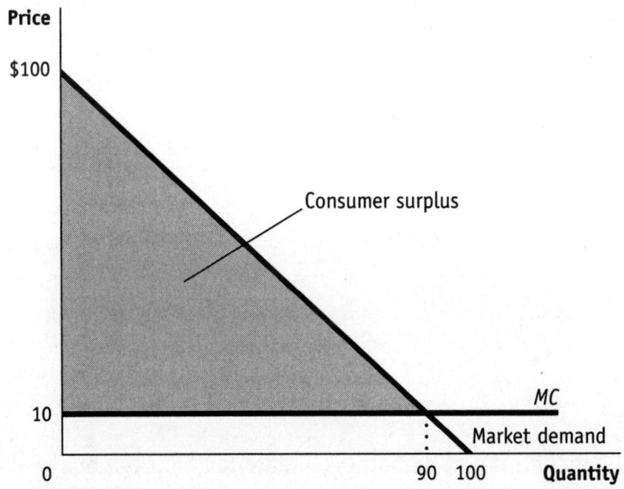

STEP 3: Compare the outcome of this market when it is perfectly competitive with when it is served by a monopolist.

Price is lower and output higher when this industry is perfectly competitive than when it is a monopoly. With perfect competition, the area of consumer surplus is larger and there is no deadweight loss. Thus, monopoly reduces consumer surplus, creates a deadweight loss, prevents mutually beneficial transactions from taking place, and results in higher prices and lower outputs than would be the case if the industry were a perfectly competitive industry. Monopoly also results in positive economic profit for producers.

Problems and Exercises

1. Assuming identical costs, what is the monopolist's effect on price and quantity compared to a perfectly competitive industry? Draw two sketches, with one sketch illustrating the perfectly competitive industry and its equilibrium market price and market quantity, and the other sketch illustrating the monopoly and its market price and market quantity. On both sketches, identify the area that corresponds to the consumer surplus, producer surplus, and deadweight loss.

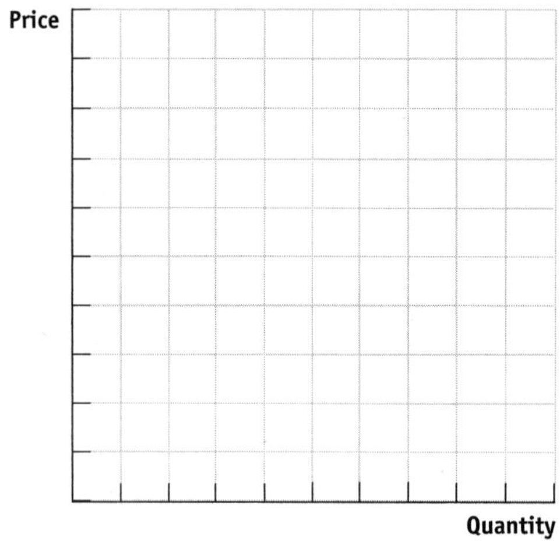

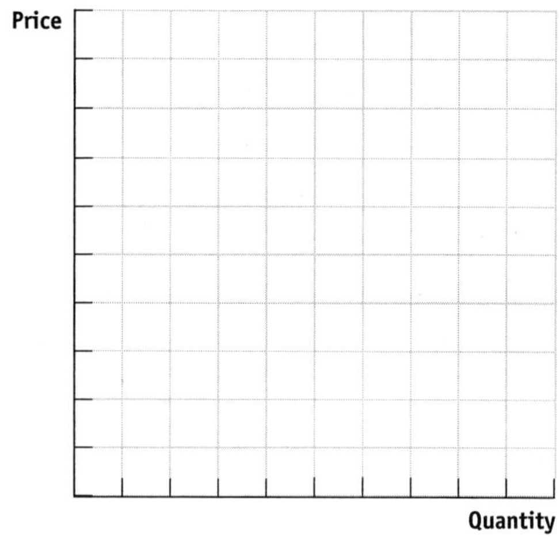

2. For the last unit produced by a monopolist, what is the relationship between the price consumers are willing to pay for this unit versus the cost of producing this last unit of the good? What is the implication of this relationship with regard to the allocation of resources to this monopoly?

3. Suppose the following table describes the market demand schedule for a monopoly.

Price ($)	Quantity demanded (units)
1,000	0
800	200
600	400
400	600
200	800
0	1,000

a. Draw a graph of this market demand schedule for the monopoly.

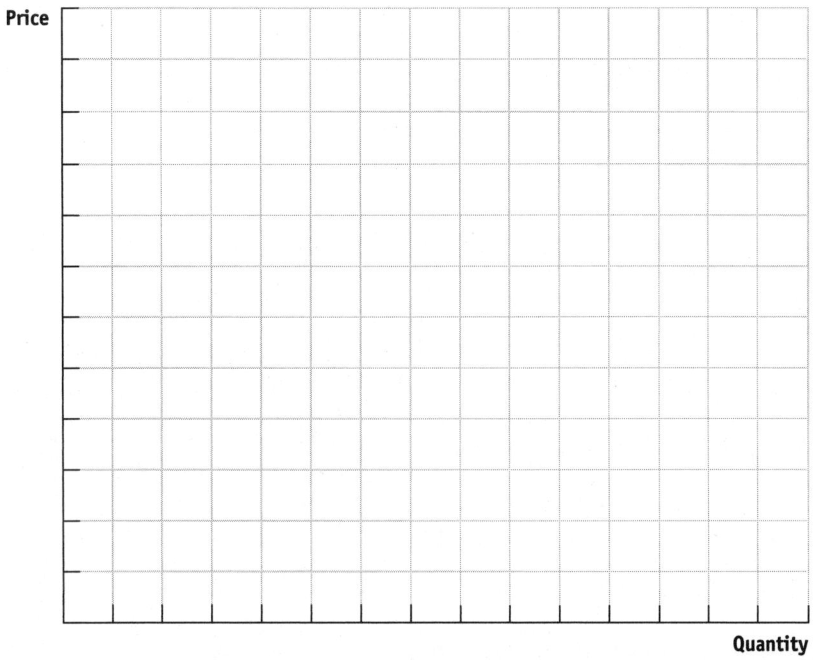

b. Compute the firm's total revenue and marginal revenue figures for the table below. For the marginal revenue figures, use the midpoint method.

Price ($)	Quantity demanded (units)	Total revenue ($)	Marginal revenue (dollars per unit)
1,000	0		
800	200		
600	400		
400	600		
200	800		
0	1,000		

c. Draw the monopolist's marginal revenue curve on the graph you drew in part (a) of this problem.

d. Write an equation for this monopolist's market demand curve and for its *MR* curve. Compare these two equations. What is true about the *y*-intercept of these two equations? What is the relationship between the slope of the demand curve and the slope of the *MR* curve?

e. If the firm's marginal cost is constant and equal to $200, what is this monopolist's profit-maximizing level of output and what price will this monopolist charge for this good? Label this quantity and this price on your graph.

f. On your graph you drew in part (a), shade in the area that corresponds to the consumer surplus and label it clearly. On this same graph, shade in the area that corresponds to producer surplus and label it clearly. Shade in the area that corresponds to deadweight loss and label it clearly.

g. Calculate the value of consumer surplus, producer surplus, and deadweight loss for this monopoly.

4. Suppose the following table describes the market demand schedule for a monopoly.

Price ($)	Quantity demanded (units)
1,000	0
800	400
600	800
400	1,200
200	1,600
0	2,000

a. Draw a graph of this market demand schedule for the monopoly.

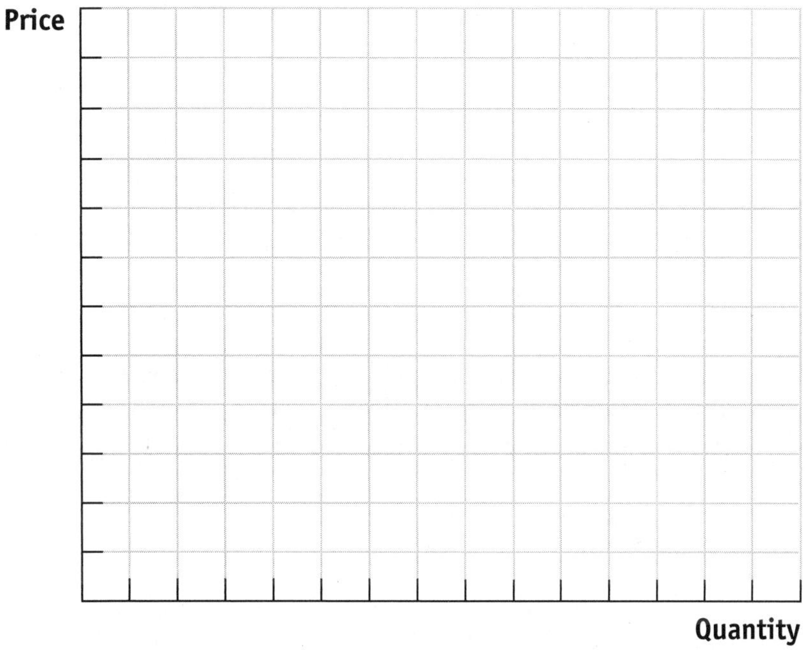

b. Compute the firm's total revenue and marginal revenue figures for the table below. For the marginal revenue figures, use the midpoint method.

Price ($)	Quantity demanded (units)	Total revenue ($)	Marginal revenue (dollars per unit)
1,000	0		
800	400		
600	800		
400	1,200		
200	1,600		
0	2,000		

c. Draw the monopolist's marginal revenue curve on the graph you drew in part (a) of this problem.

d. Write an equation for this monopolist's market demand curve and for its *MR* curve. Compare these two equations. What is true about the *y*-intercept of these two equations? What is the relationship between the slope of the demand curve and the slope of the *MR* curve?

e. If the firm's marginal cost is constant and equal to $200, what is this monopolist's profit-maximizing level of output and what price will this monopolist charge for this good? Label this quantity and this price on your graph.

f. On the graph you drew in part (a), shade in the area that corresponds to the consumer surplus and label it clearly. On this same graph, shade in the area that corresponds to producer surplus and label it clearly. Shade in the area that corresponds to deadweight loss and label it clearly.

g. Calculate the value of consumer surplus, producer surplus, and deadweight loss for this monopoly.

5. Use the diagrams below to answer this set of questions. The left-hand graph depicts a monopoly with its market demand curve and its *MC* curve. The right-hand graph depicts a perfectly competitive industry with the same market demand curve and the *MC* curve for a representative firm. These two graphs are intended to allow you to compare a monopoly to a perfectly competitive industry.

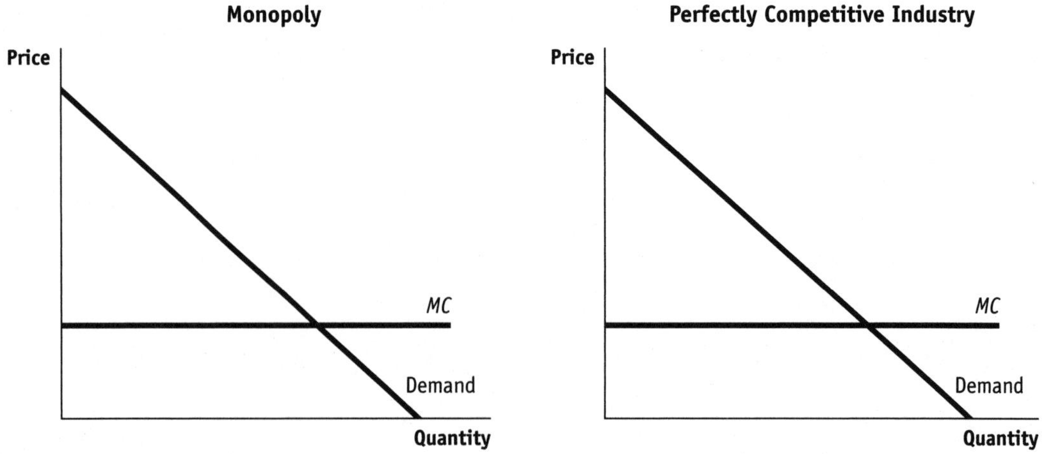

a. On each graph, identify the market level of output. On the first graph, label this output level Q_M, and on the second graph, label this output level Q_{PC}. (Hint: remember that you must first identify the *MR* curve before selecting the quantity that will be produced.)

b. On each graph, identify the market price for the good. On the first graph, label this price P_M, and on the second graph, label this price P_{PC}.

c. Compare the level of production and the price of the good in the two markets. Which market outcome is better for consumers? Explain your answer.

d. Is there a deadweight loss in either of the two graphs? If there is a deadweight loss, shade in the relevant area on the graph.

6. Discuss two different government policies for dealing with a natural monopoly. Describe each policy and then discuss any limitations or shortcomings that might arise from the implementation of the policy.

7. Use the graph below to answer this set of questions. Because of increasing returns to scale, the firm in the graph is a natural monopoly.

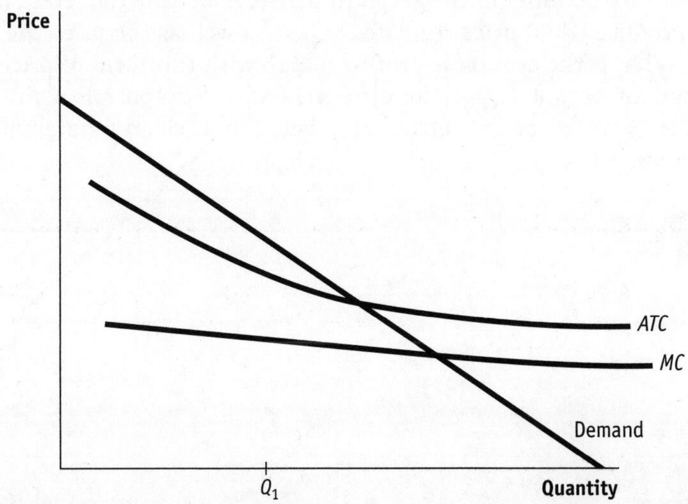

a. Why does this firm's increasing returns to scale result in its being a natural monopoly?

b. Suppose that Q_1 units are provided in this market. On the graph provided, indicate the area that represents the total cost of production if this amount is produced by a single firm. Indicate the area that represents the total cost of production if this amount is produced by five identical firms. Is there an advantage to having a single firm produce this level of output versus having five firms produce this level of output?

c. Suppose this firm acts like a profit-maximizing monopolist. On the graph, find the quantity the monopolist will produce, and label this quantity Q_M. Also identify the price the monopolist will charge (P_M) and identify the area that represents the monopolist's profits, if there are any profits.

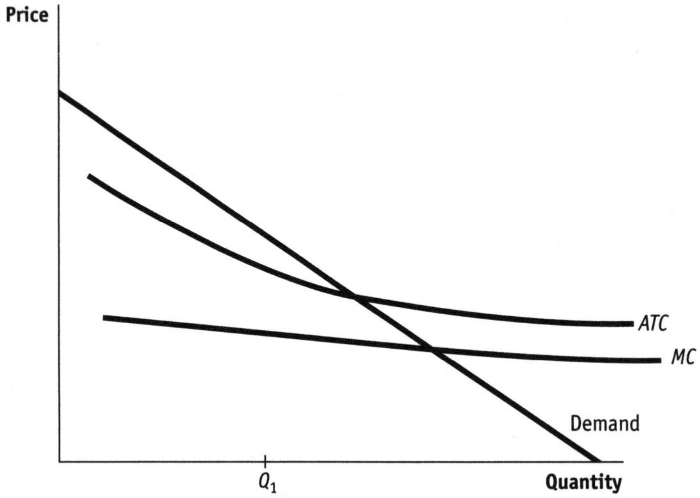

d. Suppose this firm is price regulated so that the price charged is exactly equal to the average total cost of production. On the graph in part (c), identify the level of output the firm will produce when price regulated (Q_{PR}) as well as the price the firm will charge (P_{PR}). What is the economic profit equal to with this form of price regulation? Is the level of output (Q_{PR}) the efficient level of output? Explain your answer making sure to reference the relationship between price and marginal cost for the last unit produced.

e. Suppose this firm is price regulated so that the price charged is exactly equal to the marginal cost of production. On the graph in part (c), identify the level of output that the firm will produce with this regulation (Q_{MC}) as well as the price the firm will charge (P_{MC}). Identify on the graph any area of profit that the firm earns with this form of price regulation. Is the level of output (Q_{MC}) the efficient level of output? Explain your answer making sure to reference the relationship between price and marginal cost for the last unit produced. Will the natural monopolist be willing to produce this level of output at this price? Can you think of a way to get the natural monopolist to produce this level of output?

BEFORE YOU TAKE THE TEST

Module Review Questions

1. A firm that experiences increasing returns to scale

a. finds that its average total cost of production decreases throughout the relevant region of production.

b. will find it advantageous to produce a relatively large amount of output rather than a relatively small amount of output.

c. will benefit from a larger volume of sales.

d. Answers (a), (b), and (c) are all true.

2. A natural monopoly

a. profit maximizes when it produces the quantity where $MR = MC$.

b. experiences decreasing costs throughout the relevant region of output.

c. is a monopoly whose *ATC* curve declines over the output levels at which price is greater than or equal to average total cost.

d. All of the statements are true.

3. An industry is characterized by having average total cost that decreases as output increases. In this industry, the output can be produced at the lowest cost if ________ produce(s) the total market output.

a. many identical firms

b. a single firm

c. a large number of firms

d. a few firms

4. An industry is characterized by having average total cost that decreases as output increases. This is due to large

a. variable costs that are more easily borne by a single producer of the good.
b. fixed costs that are more easily borne by a single producer of the good.
c. marginal costs that are more easily borne by a single producer of the good.
d. fluctuations in revenue that create market instability in the industry, which results in many firms exiting the industry and leaving a single firm to produce the good.

Use the graph of a monopolist below to answer the next four questions.

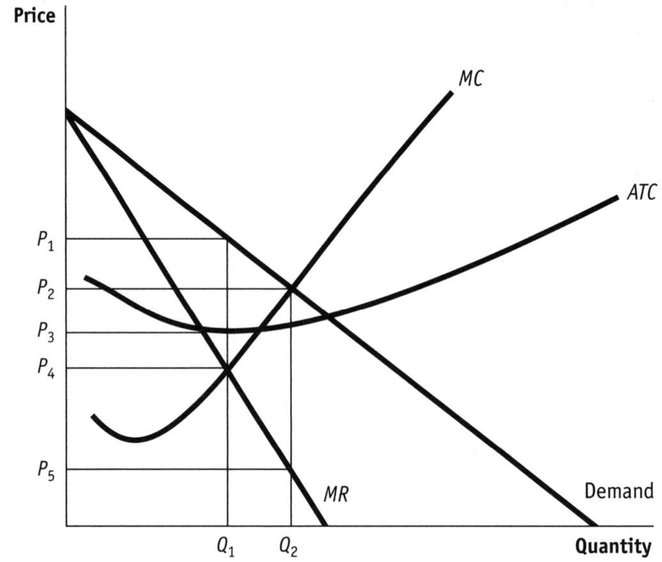

5. This monopolist will produce the profit-maximizing level of output _________ and sell each unit for _________.

a. Q_1; P_1.
b. Q_1; P_2.
c. Q_2; P_2.
d. Q_1; P_4.

6. If this monopolist were to act as if it was a perfectly competitive industry, then it would produce _________ units of the good and charge _________ for each unit.

a. Q_1; P_2
b. Q_1; P_1
c. Q_2; P_2
d. Q_2; P_5

7. The deadweight loss associated with this monopoly can be measured as the area

a. $(1/2)(P_2/\text{unit} - P_4/\text{unit})(Q_2 \text{ units} - Q_1 \text{ units})$.
b. $(1/2)(P_1/\text{unit} - P_4/\text{unit})(Q_1 \text{ units})$.
c. $(1/2)(P_2/\text{unit} - P_4/\text{unit})(Q_1 \text{ units})$.
d. $(1/2)(P_1/\text{unit} - P_4/\text{unit})(Q_2 \text{ units} - Q_1 \text{ units})$.

8. This monopolist earns

a. positive economic profit equal to area $(P_1/\text{unit} - P_3/\text{unit})(Q_1 \text{ units})$.
b. positive economic profit equal to area $(P_1/\text{unit} - P_4/\text{unit})(Q_1 \text{ units})$.
c. negative economic profit equal to area $(P_1/\text{unit} - P_3/\text{unit})(Q_1 \text{ units})$.
d. negative economic profit equal to area $(P_1/\text{unit} - P_4/\text{unit})(Q_1 \text{ units})$.

Use the following information to answer the next four questions. The demand curve for a monopolist is given by $P = 100 - Q$, while the monopolist's marginal cost is $MC = 3Q$. At the profit-maximizing level of output for the monopolist, the average total cost of production is equal to \$70.

9. This monopolist's *MR* curve can be written as

a. $MR = 100 - Q$.

b. $MR = 200 - Q$.

c. $MR = 100 - (1/2)Q$.

d. $MR = 100 - 2Q$.

10. For this monopolist the profit-maximizing level of output is equal to ________ units and the market price for this output is ________.

a. 20; \$80

b. 20; \$60

c. 25; \$75

d. 50; \$50

11. Profits for this monopolist equal

a. \$400.

b. \$200.

c. \$10.

d. \$20.

12. The deadweight loss associated with this monopoly

a. cannot be calculated from the information given.

b. is unimportant, since the monopoly is protected from competition by the existence of effective barriers to entry.

c. equals \$50.

d. equals \$25.

13. A natural monopoly is a monopoly that occurs because of increasing returns to scale. Which of the following statements are true for a natural monopoly?

a. Public ownership, although a policy often used for dealing with natural monopoly, may result in poor service and a failure to minimize the cost of providing the good.

b. Price regulation of a natural monopoly, which limits the price charged for the product, is capable of increasing the total amount of the good available while simultaneously reducing the price of each unit.

c. A natural monopolist that is price regulated will only be willing to supply the good if the regulated price is equal to or greater than the average total cost of producing its output.

d. Answers (a), (b), and (c) are all true.

ANSWER KEY

Answers to Problems and Exercises

1. A perfectly competitive industry produces a greater quantity of the good and sells this good at a lower price than a monopoly with the same cost curves. The figures below contrast the outcomes for these two types of market structures based on the same market demand curve. In the first figure, the perfectly competitive industry sets the market equilibrium price and quantity where the quantity demanded equals the quantity supplied. This figure also indicates this price and quantity combination and indicates the areas that correspond to consumer and producer surplus.

Market Outcome for a Perfectly Competitive Industry

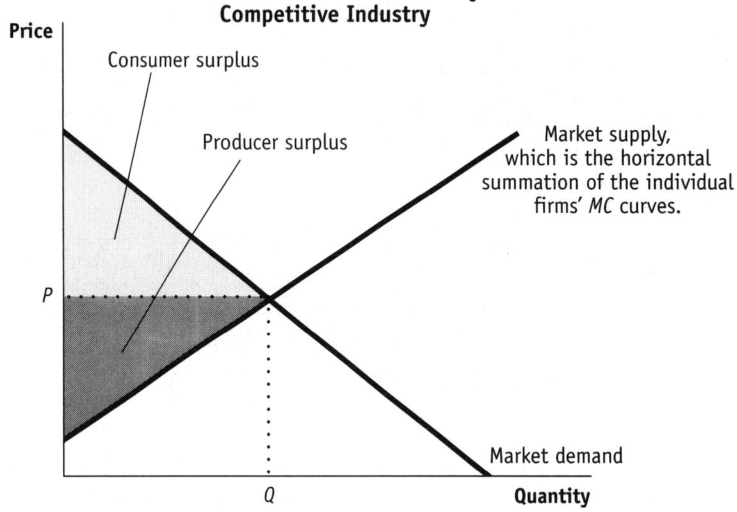

In contrast, the monopoly selects its output by equating *MR* to *MC* and then setting price by taking this quantity and looking at what price consumers are willing to pay for this quantity. The figure below illustrates the monopoly situation. Note that the monopoly results in a higher price, a lower quantity, and the creation of a deadweight loss relative to the market being served by a perfectly competitive industry.

Market Outcome for a Monopoly

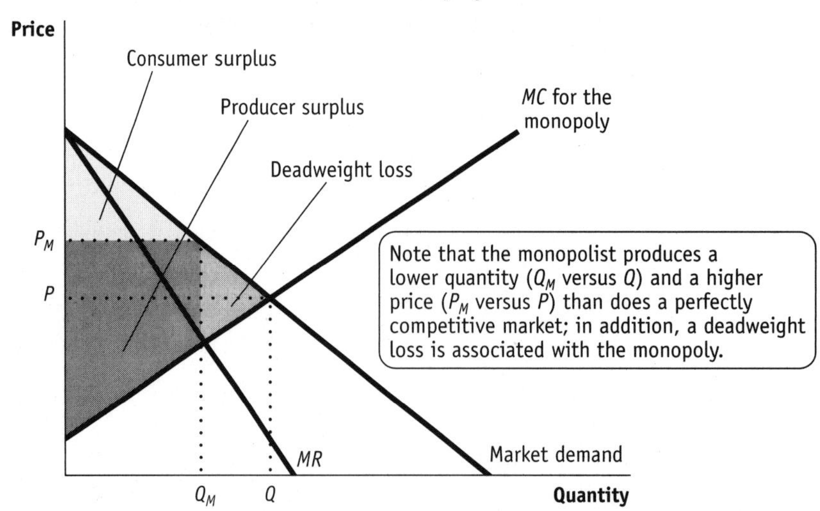

2. For the last unit produced by the monopolist, the price consumers are willing to pay for this unit is greater than the marginal cost of producing this last unit. Refer back to the graph of the monopoly given in the answer to problem 1 to see this. The implication is that the value consumers place on this last unit, as measured by the price they are willing to pay, is greater than the cost of producing this last unit, as measured by the marginal cost incurred by the firm when it produces this unit. Thus, too few resources are being allocated to the production of this good, since the value to the consumer exceeds the cost to the producer of producing this last unit. This is not surprising, since one of the effects of a monopoly is to restrict output to a lower level than would be produced with perfect competition.

3. **a.**

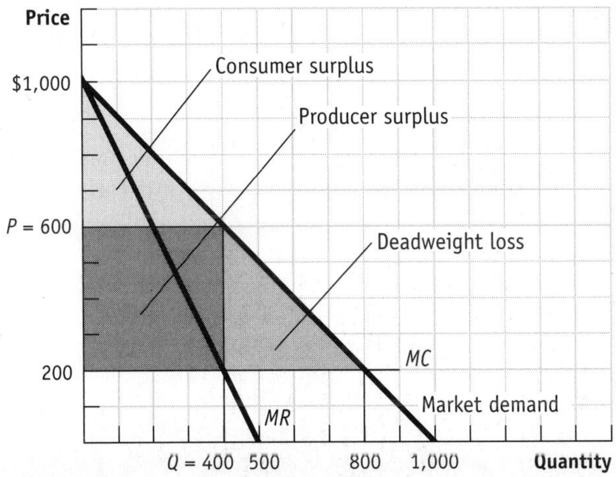

b.

Price ($)	Quantity demanded (units)	Total revenue ($)	Marginal revenue (dollars per unit)
1,000	0	0	
			800
800	200	160,000	
			400
600	400	240,000	
			0
400	600	240,000	
			–400
200	800	160,000	
			–800
0	1,000	0	

c. See the graph in part (a).

d. The monopolist's demand curve is $Q = 1{,}000 - P$, or written in slope-intercept form, it is $P = 1{,}000 - Q$. The monopolist's *MR* curve is $MR = 1{,}000 - 2Q$. The *y*-intercept for the monopolist's demand curve is the same as the *y*-intercept for the monopolist's *MR* curve if the demand curve is linear. The slope of the *MR* curve is twice the slope of the demand curve provided that the demand curve is linear.

e. The monopolist profit maximizes by producing the level of output where $MR = MC$ and then moving up to the demand curve to charge the price associated with this level of output. Thus, if $MC = 200$ and $MR = 1{,}000 - 2Q$, then the profit-maximizing quantity is 400 units. To find the monopolist's price, substitute 400 for Q in the demand equation: the monopolist's price is $600.

f. See the graph in part (a).

g. Consumer surplus = (1/2)($400 per unit)(400 units) = $80,000; producer surplus = ($400 per unit)(400 units) = $160,000; deadweight loss = (1/2)($400 per unit)(400 units) = $80,000

4. a.

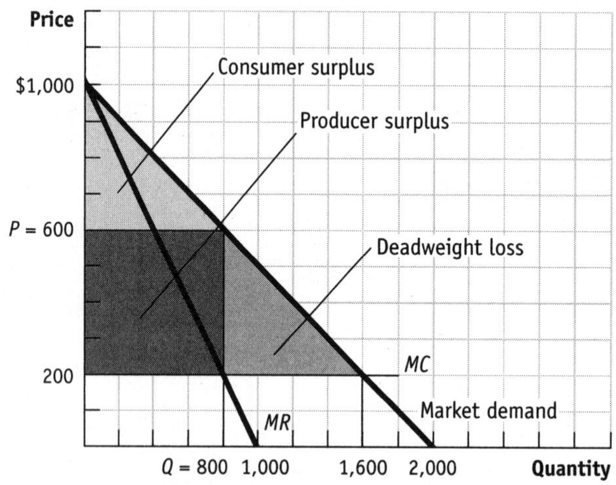

b.

Price ($)	Quantity demanded (units)	Total revenue ($)	Marginal revenue (dollars per unit)
1,000	0	0	
			800
800	400	320,000	
			400
600	800	480,000	
			0
400	1,200	480,000	
			−400
200	1,600	320,000	
			−800
0	2,000	0	

c. See the graph in part (a).

d. The monopolist's demand curve is $Q = 2{,}000 - 2P$, or written in slope-intercept form, it is $P = 1{,}000 - (1/2)Q$. The monopolist's *MR* curve is $MR = 1{,}000 - Q$. The *y*-intercept for the monopolist's demand curve is the same as the *y*-intercept for the monopolist's *MR* curve if the demand curve is linear. The slope of the *MR* curve is twice the slope of the demand curve provided that the demand curve is linear.

e. The monopolist profit maximizes by producing the level of output where $MR = MC$ and then moving up to the demand curve to charge the price associated with this level of output. Thus, if $MC = 200$ and $MR = 1{,}000 - Q$, then the profit-maximizing quantity is 800 units. To find the monopolist's price, substitute 800 for Q in the demand equation: the monopolist's price is $600.

f. See the graph in part (a).

g. Consumer surplus = (1/2)($400 per unit)(800 units) = $160,000; producer surplus = ($400 per unit)(800 units) = $320,000; deadweight loss = (1/2)($400 per unit)(800 units) = $160,000

5. a, b.

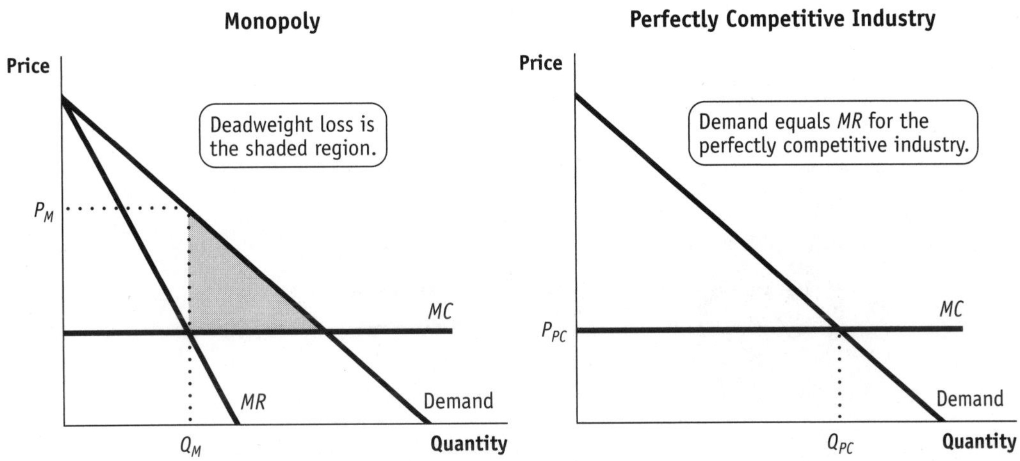

c. The perfectly competitive market produces a higher level of output and charges a lower price for this output than does the monopoly. Consumers prefer the outcome of the perfectly competitive industry since they have more output and pay lower prices.

d. The monopoly has a deadweight loss, which is the shaded area in the graph. Notice that the monopoly's level of production occurs where $P > MC$. This implies that consumers would like to have more of the good, since they are willing to pay more for another unit of the good than the marginal cost of producing that additional unit of output. Whenever price is not equal to marginal cost for the last unit produced, there is a deadweight loss, since the market is not producing the socially optimal level of output.

6. There are two primary government policies for dealing with natural monopolies: public ownership and price regulation.

With public ownership, the natural monopoly is operated by a public agency that has a mandate to provide the good while also protecting consumers' interests. A publicly owned natural monopoly can set prices based on efficiency and not profit maximization. However, a publicly owned natural monopoly may fail to keep costs down or to offer high-quality products.

Price regulation limits the price that natural monopolies can charge for their good. Price regulation takes the form of setting a price ceiling so that the natural monopoly provides more of the regulated good at a lower price than would occur with an unregulated natural monopoly. Price regulation is difficult because the regulators do not have the required information to be able to set price at exactly that point where $P = ATC$. In addition, price-regulated natural monopolies have a tendency to inflate their costs to regulators and to provide inferior-quality products.

7. a. This firm's increasing returns to scale means that the firm can reduce its average cost of production by producing larger levels of output. The firm's *ATC* curve is downward sloping over the relevant region of production. This suggests that we should expect to see large-sized firms serving this industry, or more likely, a single firm providing the product because of the cost advantages of being a large producer.

b.

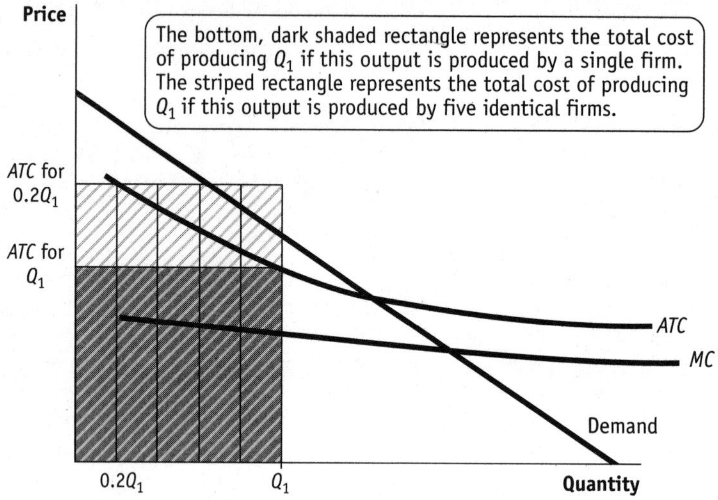

A single producer can produce the total amount of Q_1 at substantially lower cost than can five identical firms. Because of increasing returns to scale, it is far less costly to have a single producer than many producers in this market.

c. The natural monopolist acting as a profit-maximizing monopolist earns positive economic profit. See the graph below for Q_M, P_M, and the area that represents these profits. Also notice that you must draw in the firm's *MR* curve in order to identify the quantity and price for this monopolist.

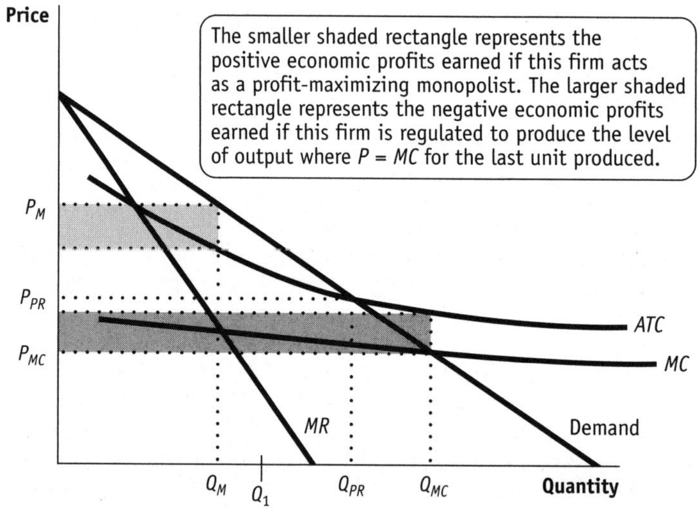

d. When this natural monopoly is price regulated to produce the quantity where price equals average total cost, the firm earns zero economic profit. This level of output (Q_{PR}) is not the efficient level of output, however, since for the last unit produced P_{PR} is greater than the marginal cost of producing this last unit. This indicates that this price-regulated monopolist is not producing enough of the good, since the value consumers place on this last unit is greater than the cost of producing this last unit.

e. When this natural monopoly is price regulated to produce that quantity where price equals *MC*, the firm earns negative economic profit, but it produces the efficient level of output, since $P = MC$ for the last unit produced. However, the natural monopolist will be unwilling to produce this level of output since it incurs negative economic profit. The natural monopolist would be willing to produce this level if it received a subsidy equal to its negative economic profit. This would allow the firm to break even and produce the efficient level of output.

Answers to Module Review Questions

1. **Answer d.** Increasing returns to scale implies that the average cost of producing the good decreases as the level of production increases: the *ATC* curve is downward sloping throughout the relevant region of production. Thus, firms benefit from producing larger amounts of output (or having larger volumes of sales), since each unit of this output is cheaper on average to produce than would be the case with a smaller level of output.

2. **Answer d.** A natural monopoly has increasing returns to scale over all the levels of output at which price is greater than or equal to average total cost. This implies that as its level of production increases its cost per unit declines. It is cheaper for a single firm to produce the total output for the market than it is for multiple firms to produce this level of total output.

3. **Answer b.** This industry is a decreasing-cost industry that is best served by having a single producer supply the good, since a single producer can produce the good at the lowest cost.

4. **Answer b.** When an industry is characterized as having average total cost that decreases as output increases, this is due to large fixed costs that result in larger levels of output being produced at lower cost per unit than smaller levels of output.

5. **Answer a.** The monopolist profit maximizes when it produces the level of output where $MR = MC$ and then prices this level of output by charging the price on the demand curve that is associated with this level of output. $MR = MC$ at Q_1, and P_1 is the price that is associated with Q_1 on the demand curve.

6. **Answer c.** If this monopolist were to act as if it was a perfectly competitive industry, then it would produce the level of output where marginal cost intersected the demand curve, because this would represent the efficient level of output where the marginal cost of the last unit produced equals the price from selling the last unit of the good. It would sell these Q_2 units of the good for the price on the demand curve (P_2) that is associated with this level of output.

7. **Answer d.** The deadweight loss associated with this monopoly is the area that represents the loss in total surplus due to the market being served by a monopoly instead of a perfectly competitive industry. This surplus loss is the area $(1/2)(P_1/\text{unit} - P_4/\text{unit})(Q_2 \text{ units} - Q_1 \text{ units})$.

8. **Answer a.** This monopolist earns positive economic profit since the price it charges for the good (P_1) is greater than the average total cost of producing Q_1 units of the good. To calculate profits you can use the formula $TR - TC = \text{profits}$, or you can calculate the product of the quantity produced times the difference between the price of each unit and the average total cost of producing these units. Using this latter method, the price of each unit is P_1, the average total cost of each unit is P_3, and the number of units produced is Q_1. Thus, profit is $(P_1/\text{unit} - P_3/\text{unit})(Q_1 \text{ units})$.

9. **Answer d.** For a monopolist with a linear demand curve, the *MR* curve has the same *y*-intercept as the demand curve, and its slope is twice the slope of the demand curve. The *y*-intercept of the demand curve is 100 and the slope of the demand curve is (–1). The *MR* curve has a *y*-intercept of 100 and its slope is (–2). The *MR* curve can be written as $MR = 100 - 2Q$.

10. **Answer a.** The profit-maximizing monopolist will produce the quantity where $MR = MC$ and then price this level of output by going to its demand curve: $MR = 100 - 2Q$, and

$MC = 3Q$; thus, $Q = 20$ units. Substituting 20 for Q in the demand equation and solving for P gives us the monopolist's market price for this good: $P = \$80$.

11. **Answer b.** Profit can be calculated by multiplying the level of output times the difference between the price of the good and the average total cost of producing the good. Thus, (20 units)($80 per unit – $70 per unit) gives a profit of $200.

12. **Answer c.** There is a deadweight loss due to the monopoly. It is the area that represents the efficiency loss due to the market not operating as a perfectly competitive market. The efficient level of output in this market is 25 units (where the *MC* curve intersects the demand curve). The deadweight loss is equal to (1/2)($80 per unit – $60 per unit)(25 units – 20 units) = $50.

13. **Answer d.** Public ownership of a natural monopoly does not often work as a solution to the problem because it offers little incentive for the natural monopolist to keep costs down and produce high-quality products. Price regulation of a natural monopolist is a policy that can result in lower prices and greater quantities, provided that the regulated price allows the natural monopolist to at least break even. Provided the regulated price is equal to or greater than the average total cost of production, the natural monopolist will be able to make zero or positive economic profits and will therefore be willing to produce the good.

module 30

Price Discrimination

BEFORE YOU READ THE MODULE

Summary

This module discusses the meaning of price discrimination and why price discrimination is so common when producers have market power. The module discusses the effects of price discrimination on a market.

Module Objectives

Objective #1. Price discrimination refers to a situation in which a firm with market power charges different prices to different customers. Instead of offering the good at a single price, the firm with market power offers the good at multiple prices depending on the characteristics of the consumer. The firm will find that its profit increases if it charges a higher price to the consumers of the good who have price-inelastic demand, and a lower price to the consumers of the good who have price-elastic demand. Common techniques for price discrimination include:

- Advance purchase restrictions—the earlier you purchase, the lower the price you pay.
- Volume discounts—the larger the quantity you buy, the lower the price per unit.
- Two-part tariffs—you pay an annual fee plus the cost of whatever items you purchase, thereby effectively creating a volume discount.

Objective #2. Perfect price discrimination occurs when the monopolist is able to capture the entire consumer surplus. The greater the number of prices the monopolist charges, the more money it extracts from consumers. In addition, the greater the number of prices the monopolist charges, the closer the lowest price will get to the marginal cost of producing the last unit of the good. A monopolist who practices perfect price discrimination does not cause any inefficiency, since the marginal cost of producing the last unit exactly equals the price of this last unit. But with perfect price discrimination, the consumer's surplus is equal to zero since this entire surplus is captured by the producer.

Key Terms

single-price monopolist a *monopolist* that offers its product to all consumers at the same price.

price discrimination charging different prices to different consumers for the same good.

perfect price discrimination a situation in which a monopolist charges each consumer his or her willingness to pay—the maximum that the consumer is willing to pay.

Notes

AFTER YOU READ THE MODULE

Tips

Tip #1. A monopoly that can practice price discrimination will find that this results in the profits of the monopoly increasing relative to their level as a single-price monopolist. A monopolist who practices price discrimination will charge a higher price to those consumers with more inelastic demand and a lower price to those consumers with more elastic demand.

Tip #2. A perfect price-discriminating monopolist produces the socially optimal amount of output since for the last unit produced the *MR* is equal to the *MC*. Although this is the socially optimal amount of the good, the perfect price discriminating monopolist captures all of the consumer surplus. The result is that monopoly profits are enhanced relative to the single-price monopolist result while simultaneously the socially optimal amount of the good is produced.

WORKED PROBLEMS

1. A monopolist needs to know whether selling his product at two different prices, rather than a single price, will affect his profits. The monopolist recognizes that the demand curve for his product is given by the equation $P = 1{,}000 - 2Q$, and furthermore, he knows that there are no fixed costs of producing the good and that the marginal cost of producing the good is given by the equation $MC = 100$. First, the monopolist would like you to calculate the profit-maximizing price and quantity for the good sold at a single price. The monopolist would also like to know what his profits will equal if he pursues a single-price policy. He then would like you to contrast this outcome with what will happen if he is willing to sell a total of 225 units, with the first 100 units sold at a price of \$800 per unit. Then, he'll sell the second 125 units at whatever single price he can get after he sells the first 100 units. You must decide what this second price is and then determine what the monopolist's profits will be if he pursues this two-price policy. The monopolist asks that you provide him with a graph of each of these scenarios so that he can analyze the effect of these two policies. Finally, which policy will you recommend to this monopolist if his goal is to maximize his profit?

STEP 1: Draw a graph representing the monopolist's demand curve and his marginal cost curve.

This graph will be your base graph from which you will analyze the rest of this problem. It is important to start with this graph so that you have a clear image to guide your analysis. The graph that follows provides an image of the monopolist's demand curve and the marginal cost curve.

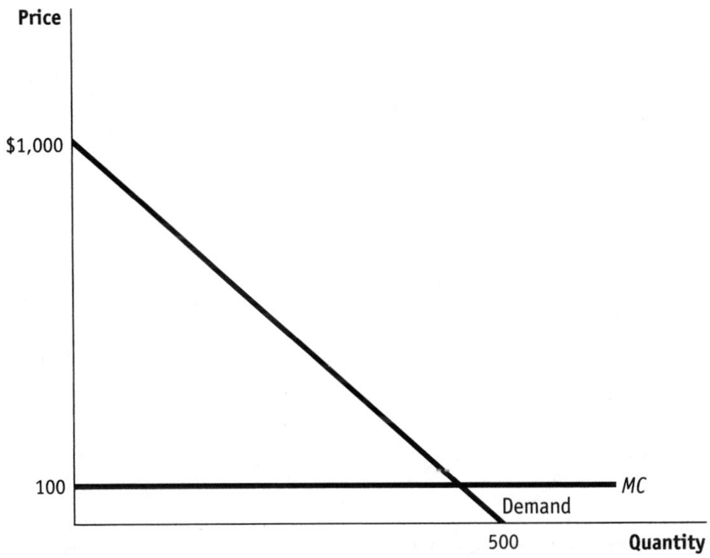

STEP 2: Find the single price monopolist's marginal revenue (*MR*) curve and draw it in your graph.

Recall that if the single-price monopolist's demand curve is linear, then its *MR* curve will share the same *y*-intercept as the demand curve and have twice the slope of the demand curve. Thus, the *MR* curve for this monopolist is given by the equation $MR = 1{,}000 - 4Q$. The graph that follows illustrates the single-price monopolist's demand curve, *MC* curve, and *MR* curve.

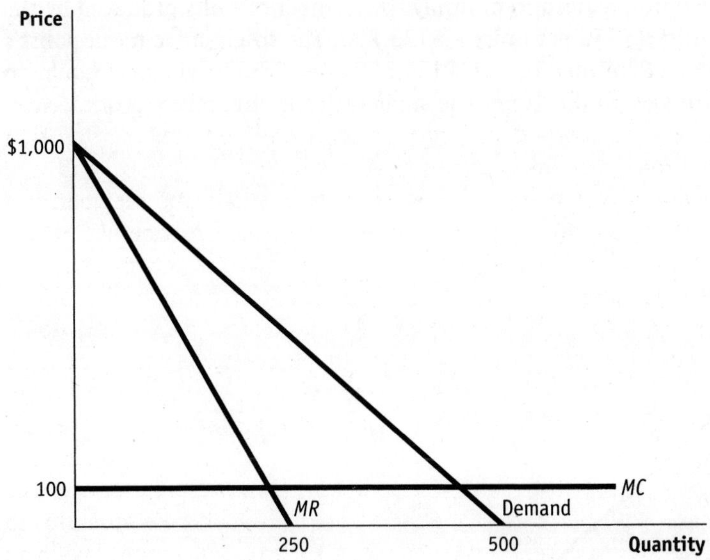

STEP 3: Identify the profit-maximizing quantity for the single-price monopolist. Then, determine the price that the monopolist will charge if he produces this quantity.

To find the profit-maximizing quantity for a single-price monopolist, you will want to equate *MC* to *MR*. Thus, $100 = 1{,}000 - 4Q$, or $Q = 225$. To find the price for this level of output, substitute this quantity into the demand curve: $P = 1{,}000 - 2Q = 1{,}000 - 2(225) = \$550$ per unit. The following graph illustrates these profit-maximizing levels if the monopolist is charging a single price.

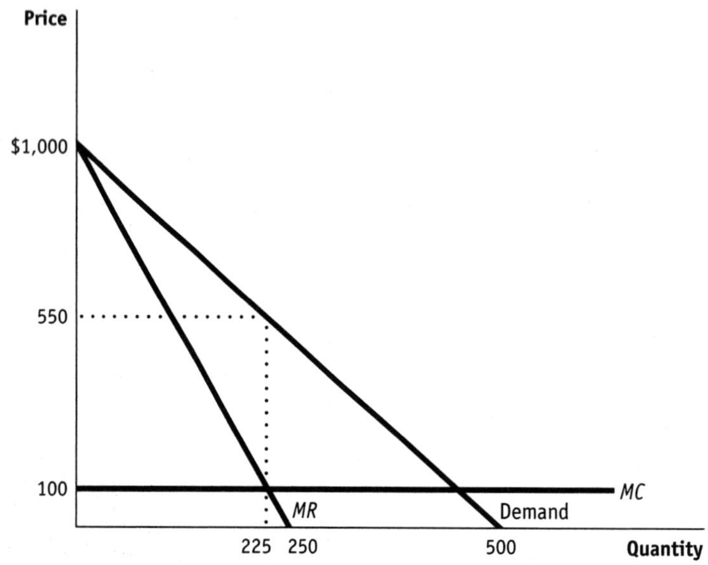

STEP 4: Calculate the single-price monopolist's total costs, total revenue, and monopoly profits.

We know that the cost of each additional unit produced by this monopolist is \$100. So, if the monopolist produces 225 units, the total cost of producing these units will be given by (\$100 per unit)(225 units) = \$22,500. Since *MC* is horizontal and there are no fixed costs, this implies that marginal cost is equal to average total cost. To calculate total revenue, we simply need to multiply the number of units produced by the price per unit: (225 units)(\$550 per unit) = \$123,750. The single-price monopolist's profit will be equal to *TR* minus *TC*, or \$123,750 – \$22,500, which is equal to \$101,250. The following graph illustrates the single-price monopolist's profits.

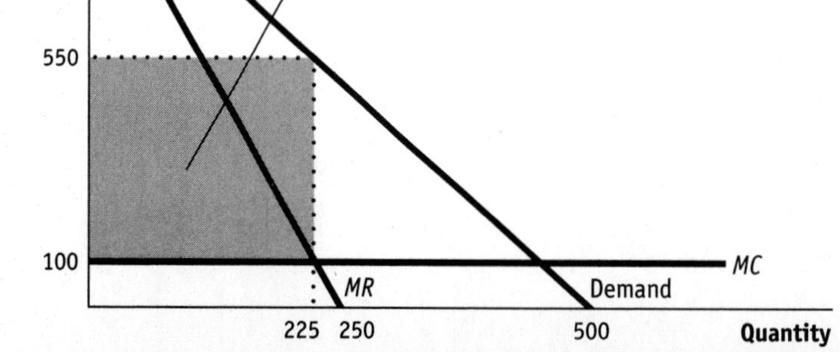

STEP 5: Draw a picture of the monopolist's demand curve and the *MC* curve. On this graph label a price of \$800 and determine the quantity of the monopolist's product that is demanded at this price. Then, label a quantity of 225 units and mark what price corresponds to this quantity on the monopolist's demand curve. From your graph determine the two prices the monopolist will charge if he charges \$800 per unit for the first 100 units he sells and he is willing to sell another 125 units at a different price.

In this step, you are providing yourself with a visual map of the various calculations you will need to do to answer this question. On the graph, you will want to determine the quantity that is demanded at a price of \$800 per unit, as well as the price that people in this market are willing to pay when a total of 225 units of the good are provided by the monopolist. In the graph that follows, you can see that when the price of the good is \$800 there are 100 units demanded. We could also see this by using the demand equation: when price is \$800 then we have $800 = 1{,}000 - 2Q$, and solving for Q, we get $Q = 100$ units. When the quantity demanded is 225 units we can use the demand equation to solve for the price: thus, $P = 1{,}000 - 2Q = 1{,}000 - 2(225) = \$550$ per unit. Carefully examine the following graph to see these price and quantity combinations. The monopolist will be able to sell the first 100 units at a price of \$800 per unit, and he can sell an additional 125 units (for a total of 225 units sold in all) for a price of \$550 per unit.

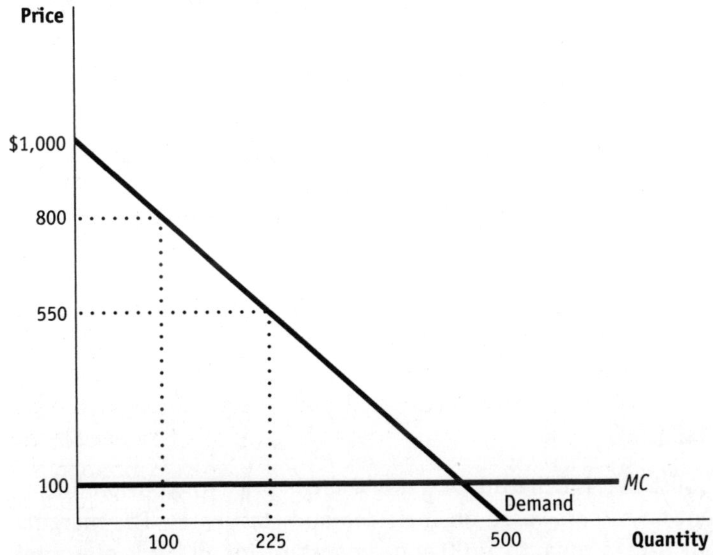

STEP 6: Calculate the total costs, total revenue, and monopoly profits for this monopolist when he sells the good at two different prices: \$800 per unit for the first 100 units and \$550 per unit for the next 125 units.

We know that the cost of each additional unit produced by this monopolist is \$100. So, if the monopolist produces 225 units, the total cost of producing these units will be (\$100 per unit)(225 units) = \$22,500. Since *MC* is horizontal and there are no fixed costs, this implies that marginal cost is equal to average total cost. To calculate total revenue, we simply need to multiply the number of units produced by the price per unit and remember that this time we have two different prices and two different quantities: (100 units)(\$800 per unit) + (125 units)(\$550 per unit) = \$148,750. The monopolist who charges two prices (\$800 per unit for the first 100 units and \$550 per unit for the next 125 units) will earn profits equal to *TR* minus *TC*, or $148,750 – $22,500, which is equal to $126,250. The following graph illustrates the monopolist's profits when he charges these two different prices.

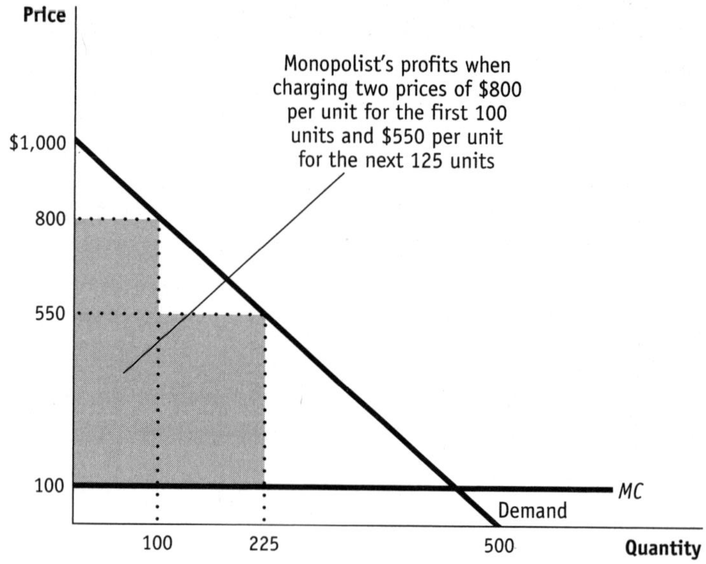

STEP 7: Based on your calculations, make a recommendation as to which pricing scheme will be best for the monopolist.

Review Steps 4 and 6 so that you can compare what happens to profit for the monopolist under the two alternatives.

Clearly a two-price policy results in greater profits for the monopolist than a single-price policy. With the single-price policy the monopolist earns profits of $101,250, while with the two-price policy outlined in this problem the monopolist earns profits of $126,250.

Problems and Exercises

1. Suppose you are a monopolist that is debating charging a single price for your product or different prices to different customers based on their demand elasticities. The marginal cost of production for your firm is equal to $200 and is constant for all levels of output. The market demand curve is $P = 1{,}000 - 2Q$.

a. If you charge a single price, what price and quantity would you select given the above information? What does the firm's total revenue equal? What do the firm's profits equal with this pricing policy?

b. Suppose you could charge one group of buyers in this market a price of $600 and a second group of buyers a price of $400. Using the information you have, calculate the number of units of the good the monopolist will sell to the group willing to pay $600 per unit and the number of units of the good the monopolist will sell to the group willing to pay $400 per unit. What does the firm's total revenue equal if it sells the good at two prices instead of a single price? What do the firm's profits equal with this pricing policy?

c. Given your findings in parts (a) and (b), is it advantageous for this firm to sell the good at two different prices? Explain your answer.

d. Does the price discrimination outlined in part (b) increase or decrease consumer surplus? What does your answer tell you about the efficiency of price discrimination relative to the efficiency of a single-price, profit-maximizing monopolist? You may find it helpful to draw sketches of the situation in part (a) and part (b) to compare the areas of consumer surplus. What is the value of consumer surplus in the two situations?

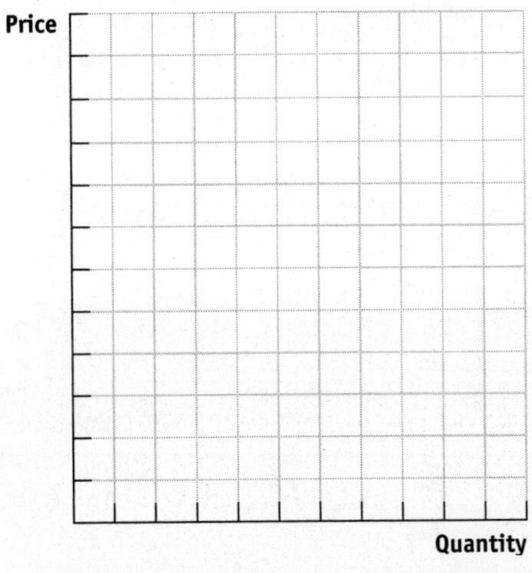

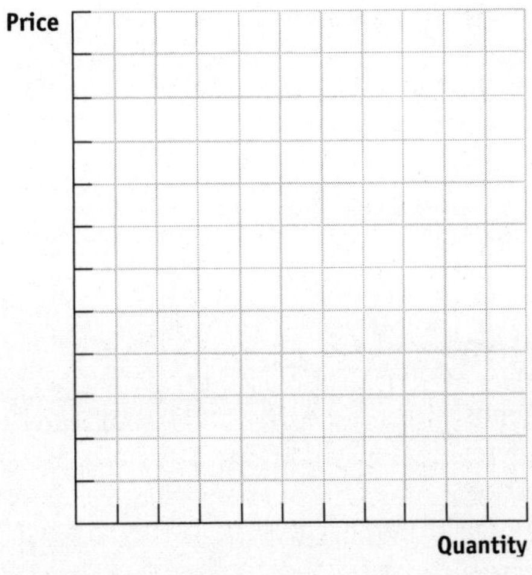

2. Why does a price-discriminating monopolist charge a higher price to consumers with less elastic demand and a lower price to consumers with more elastic demand?

3. Suppose the demand in a market is given by $P = 200 - 2Q$, while the supply in this market is given by $P = 2Q$.

   a. What is the value of consumer surplus and producer surplus in this market if price is determined through the interaction of supply and demand and the market is perfectly competitive?

   b. Suppose this market is served by a monopolist who is able to practice perfect price discrimination. What level of output will this perfectly price-discriminating monopolist produce? How does this level of output compare with the level of output produced in part (a)? Is the level of output produced efficient? Justify your answer.

   c. Calculate the value of consumer and producer surplus in this market if the producer is a perfectly price-discriminating monopolist. Sketch a graph of the two situations: the consumer and producer surplus under the conditions described in part (a) and the consumer and producer surplus under the conditions described in part (b).

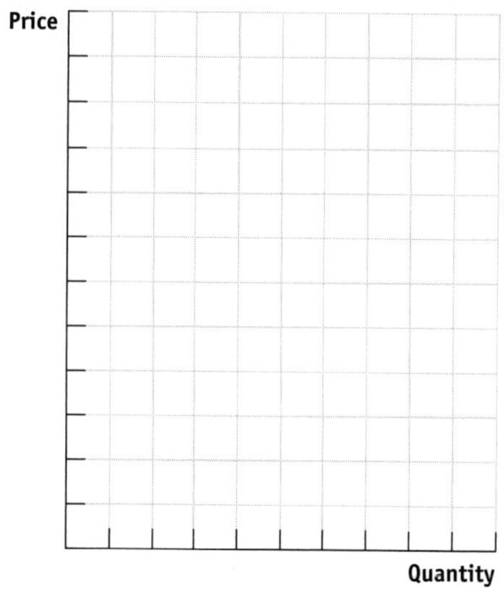

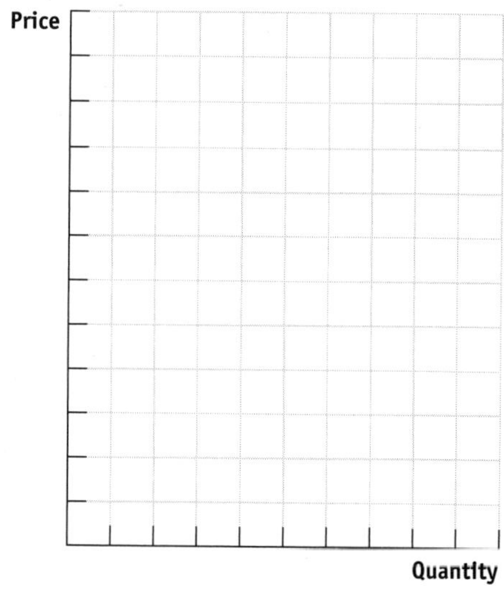

BEFORE YOU TAKE THE TEST

Module Review Questions

1. Which of the following statements is true?
   I. A perfectly competitive industry produces an efficient level of output, since $P = MC$ for the last unit produced in this industry.
   II. A monopoly produces an efficient level of output, since $MR = MC$ for the last unit produced by this monopoly.
   III. A perfectly price-discriminating monopolist produces an efficient level of output, since the value consumers are willing to pay for the last unit sold is equal to the cost of producing this last unit.
   a. Statement I is true.
   b. Statements I and II are true.
   c. Statements I and III are true.
   d. Statements I, II, and III are true.

Use the following information to answer the next three questions. An airline company is the only airline serving a market between several small cities. This monopolist finds that it can sell 500 tickets at a price of \$300. The company also knows that it could sell an additional 200 tickets at \$150. The marginal cost of providing a seat is \$100.

2. If this airline company is only allowed to offer tickets at a single price, the company should sell ________ tickets at a price of ________ and earn economic profits of ________.
   a. 700; \$300; \$140,000
   b. 500; \$150; \$25,000
   c. 700; \$150; \$35,000
   d. 500; \$300; \$100,000

3. If this airline company is allowed to offer tickets at different prices, what is the maximum amount of profit this airline company can earn?
   a. \$100,000
   b. \$110,000
   c. \$35,000
   d. \$180,000

4. When this company price discriminates,
   a. it increases its level of profit.
   b. it increases consumer surplus.
   c. it reduces the deadweight loss associated with being a monopoly.
   d. Answers (a), (b), and (c) are all true.

5. Joe's price elasticity of demand for airplane travel is equal to 2, and Beth's price elasticity of demand for airplane travel is equal to 1.3. If the airline companies are allowed to price-discriminate, we would anticipate that if Joe and Beth are both traveling to the same location and leaving from the same airport,
   a. they will both pay the same price for an airline ticket.
   b. Joe will pay a higher price for an airline ticket.
   c. Beth will pay a higher price for an airline ticket.
   d. it is unclear who will pay the higher price for an airplane ticket.

Use the following graph of a monopolist to answer the next two questions.

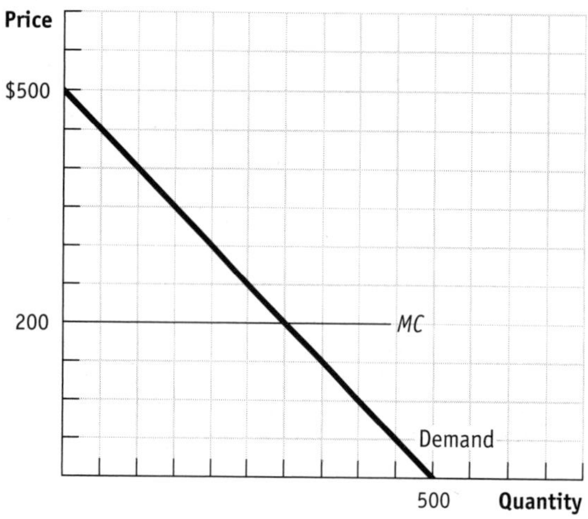

6. If this monopolist profit maximizes, it will produce __________ units of output, charge a price of __________, provide a producer surplus equal to __________, provide a consumer surplus equal to __________, and create a deadweight loss equal to __________.
   a. 250; $250; $31,250; $31,250; $0
   b. 150; $350; $22,500; $11,250; $11,250
   c. 150; $350; $11,250; $22,500; $11,250
   d. 300; $200, $0; $45,000; $0

7. If this monopolist practices perfect price discrimination, it will produce __________ units, charge a price of __________ for the last unit produced, provide a producer surplus equal to __________, provide a consumer surplus equal to __________, and create a deadweight loss equal to __________.
   a. 300; $200; $0; $45,000; $0
   b. 300; $200; $45,000; $0; $0
   c. 250; $200; $43,750; $0; $1,250
   d. 250; $200; $0; $43,750; $1,250

ANSWER KEY

Answers to Problems and Exercises

1. **a.** The monopolist would produce the profit-maximizing level of output where $MR = MC$. For this monopolist the MR curve is $MR = 1{,}000 - 4Q$ and $MC = 200$. Thus, the profit-maximizing level of output is $Q = 200$. The profit-maximizing price can be found by substituting this level of output into the demand equation and solving for price: $P = \$600$. The firm's total revenue is equal to \$120,000. Since the MC curve is a horizontal line, this implies that the firm's ATC is also a horizontal line at $ATC = \$200$. The firm's total cost of producing 200 units is therefore \$40,000, and the firm earns a profit of \$80,000.

b. You could still sell 200 units for a price of \$600. But now you can sell additional units for a price of \$400. To see how many additional units you can sell, first substitute \$400 into the demand equation for the price to solve for how many units will be demanded in this market at a price of \$400. A total of 300 units will be demanded, but 200 of these units can be sold for a price of \$600. Thus, 100 additional units can be sold at a price of \$400. The firm's total revenue is equal to (200 units)(\$600 per unit) + (100 units)(\$400 per unit), or \$160,000. The firm's total cost is equal to (300 units)(\$200 per unit), or \$60,000, and the firm earns a profit of \$100,000.

c. The single-price monopolist earns a lower level of profit (\$80,000) than does the monopolist that price discriminates and charges more than one price in this market. In the case of the price-discriminating monopolist that charges two different prices (\$600 and \$400), the level of profits is \$100,000. It definitely pays to price discriminate.

d. Price discrimination increases the area of consumer surplus and therefore results in a better outcome for the consumer. The price discriminator produces a more efficient level of output than does the single-price, profit-maximizing monopolist. Consumer surplus is equal to \$40,000 for the single-price monopolist and \$50,000 for the price-discriminating monopolist. The figure below illustrates the two situations.

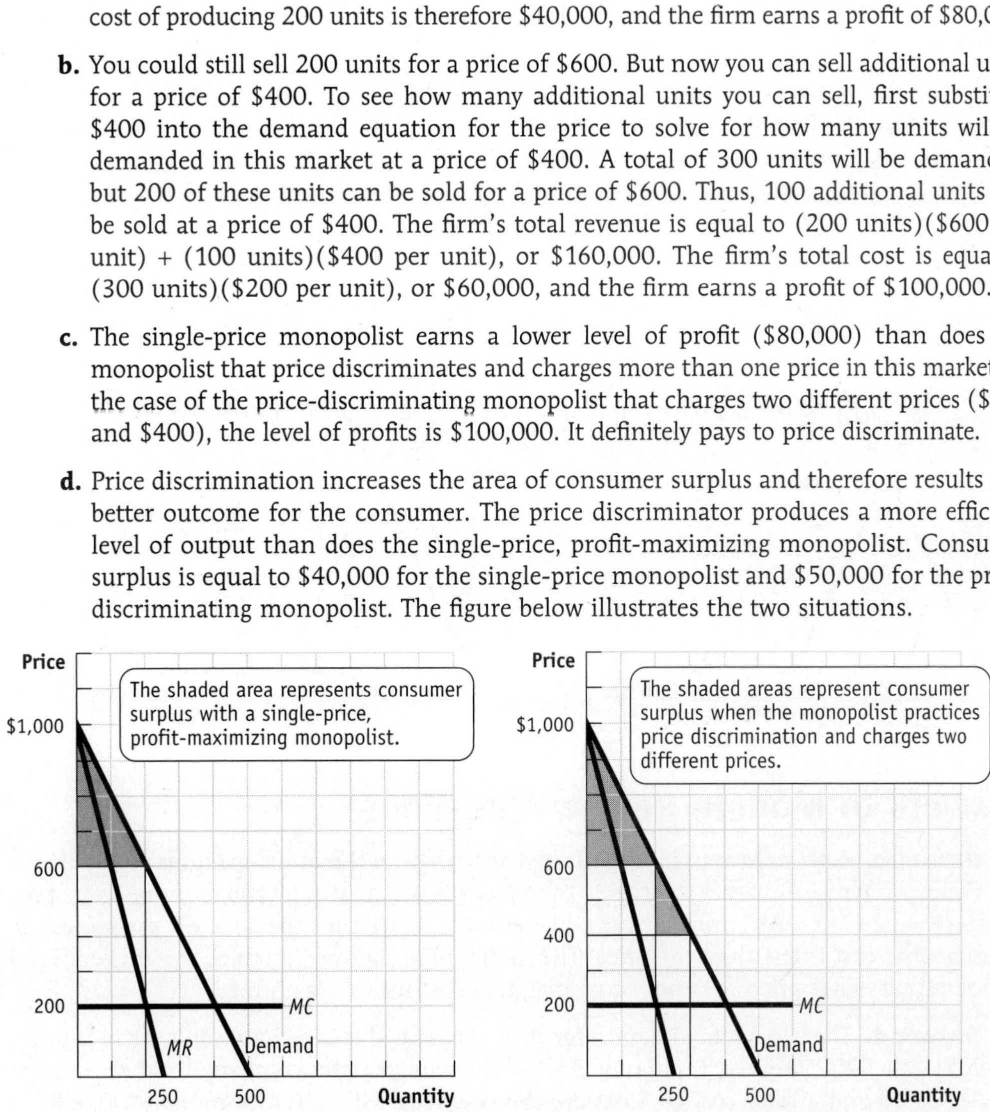

2. Consumers with relatively elastic demand are price sensitive: a little change in the price causes a relatively large change in the quantity demanded of the good. Consumers with relatively inelastic demand are not price sensitive: a change in the price of the good causes little change in the quantity demanded of the good. Thus, the price-discriminating monopolist finds that it is better to charge a high price to consumers with inelastic demand and a low price to consumers with elastic demand.

3. **a.** The value of consumer surplus is \$2,500 and the value of producer surplus is \$2,500.

   b. The monopolist will produce 50 units of output, since this is the level of output where the demand equals the marginal cost. In this case, the marginal revenue for the perfectly price-discriminating monopolist is the market demand curve, since it receives marginal revenue equal to the price of the good for each unit of the good sold. To select the profit-maximizing level of output, the perfectly price-discriminating firm will set marginal revenue equal to marginal cost and produce that level of output. This will result in the same level of output being produced by the market in part (a). Since the price the consumer pays for the last unit produced is exactly equal to the cost of producing this last unit, this is an efficient level of output. Both the perfectly competitive market and the perfectly price-discriminating monopolist produce the efficient level of output.

   c. The value of producer surplus for the perfectly price-discriminating monopolist is \$5,000, which is the sum of the consumer and producer surplus when the market is perfectly competitive. The value of consumer surplus is \$0. The figures below illustrate the two situations.

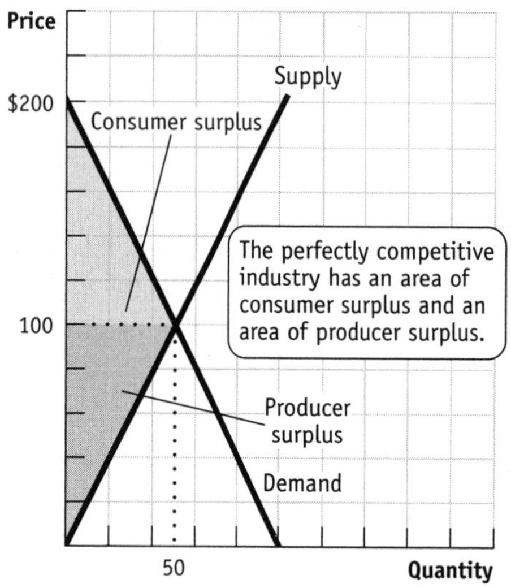

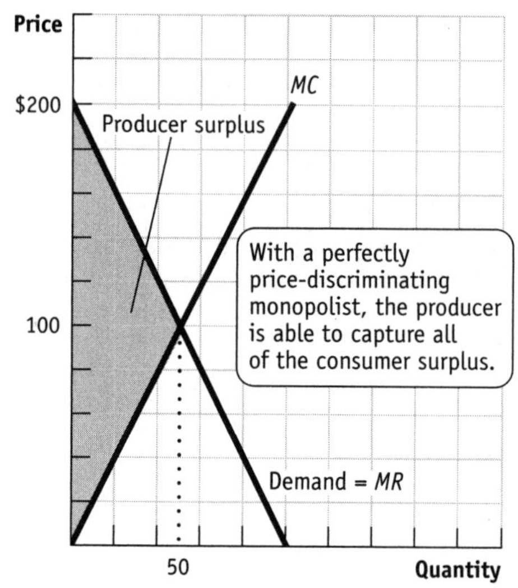

Answers to Module Review Questions

1. **Answer c.** Both statements I and III arc true based on the profit-maximization rule for these two types of market structures. Statement II is not true: although monopolies produce where $MR = MC$, they charge a higher price, so that for the last unit produced, the marginal cost is less than the price. The monopolist does not produce the efficient level of output, since price does not equal marginal cost for this last unit.

2. **Answer d.** The best profit situation for this company, if it can charge only a single price, is to sell 500 tickets at a price of \$300. This will give the company total revenue of \$150,000 and a total cost of \$50,000: the company will earn a profit of \$100,000. In contrast, if the company sells 700 tickets, they must drop the price to \$150 for all the tickets. Then the company would earn profits of \$35,000, since its total revenue would equal \$105,000 and its total cost would equal \$70,000.

3. **Answer b.** When the company sells tickets at \$300 and at \$150, it can sell 700 tickets in all. It can sell the first 500 tickets for \$300 and then an additional 200 tickets for \$150. The total revenue for the company from these sales equals \$180,000, and its total cost equals \$70,000. The firm's profit equals \$110,000.

4. **Answer d.** From question 3, you know that price discrimination increases the company's profitability. In addition, when the company expands the number of tickets it offers, this results in improving the market outcome for consumers. This is measured by an increase in consumer surplus as well as a reduction in the deadweight loss associated with the monopoly.

5. **Answer c.** Price elasticity of demand measures price sensitivity. Because Joe's price elasticity of demand is greater than Beth's price elasticity of demand, we know that Joe is more price sensitive. With regard to airline tickets, this indicates that Beth's travel is less negotiable than Joe's travel and therefore that Beth can anticipate she will pay more for an airline ticket than Joe.

6. **Answer b.** The monopolist profit-maximizes by producing the quantity where $MR = MC$. The MR curve for this monopolist is $MR = 500 - 2Q$. So the monopolist will produce 150 units, and it will sell these units for a price of \$350 (substitute 150 units into the demand curve to find the price the monopolist will charge). The graph below indicates the areas that correspond to consumer surplus, producer surplus, and deadweight loss.

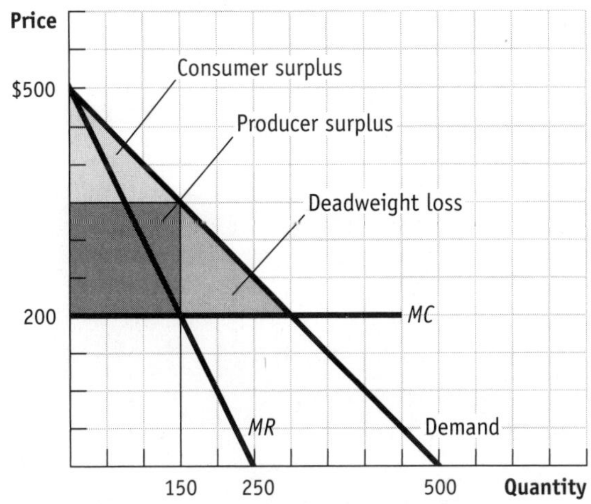

7. **Answer b.** The perfect price discriminator captures all of the consumer surplus by producing the level of output where MC = demand. In this case, the perfectly price-discriminating firm will produce 300 units and charge a price of \$200 for the last unit produced. The graph below indicates the area that corresponds to producer surplus. There is no consumer surplus or deadweight loss associated with perfect price discrimination.

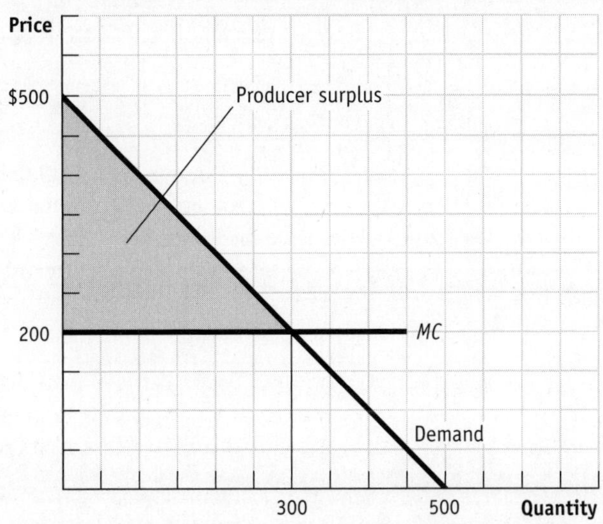

module 31

Oligopoly

BEFORE YOU READ THE MODULE

Summary

This module explores oligopoly, a market structure characterized by a few firms producing a product that may or may not be differentiated. The module discusses the incentives for oligopolists to act cooperatively or competitively and the results of these actions on the level of oligopoly profits. The module explores why oligopolists have an incentive to engage in behavior that reduces their combined profit.

Module Objectives

Objective #1. Oligopolies are characterized as an industry in which there are a few producers. Each of these individual producers has some market power (like a monopoly) that enables them to affect market prices, but each of these producers also competes against the other producers in the industry. This competition is different from perfect competition in that each producer is aware of the other firms in the industry and recognizes that each firm's behavior affects the other firms. The key aspect of oligopoly is the tension between cooperation and competition: each firm must decide whether and to what degree it wants to cooperate or compete with the other firms in their industry.

Objective #2. With an oligopolistic industry what matters is not the size of the firm, but rather the number of firms serving the industry. Oligopolies primarily exist because each firm benefits from increasing returns to scale and these returns to scale result in a few producers in the industry rather than many small-scale producers in the industry. Analysis of oligopoly presents several challenging puzzles not presented in our analysis of perfectly competitive markets or monopolies.

Objective #3. The simplest type of oligopoly to analyze is a duopoly, a situation in which there are only two firms in the industry. These two firms face two strategies: they can decide to cooperate with each other or they can decide to compete with each other by adopting noncooperative behavior. By cooperating and forming a cartel, these two firms can work together to select the level of output that will maximize their joint profits. Even with an agreement to cooperate, the firms will each find that they have an incentive to cheat on this arrangement. Cartels are inherently unstable because each firm recognizes that they have an incentive to produce more of the good than was agreed. Like a monopolist, each firm in an oligopoly recognizes that selling a greater amount of output creates both a quantity and a price effect; however, the price effect is smaller for the oligopolist than it is for the monopolist, which means that the marginal revenue from selling additional units of the good is higher for the oligopolist than it would be for the monopolist. Ultimately, collusion is more profitable than noncooperative behavior, but it is difficult to achieve since formal agreements to collude are illegal in many nations. Some oligopolies find ways to collude without a formal agreement.

Key Terms

interdependent the outcome (profit) of each firm depends on the actions of the other firms in the market.

duopoly an *oligopoly* consisting of only two firms.

duopolist one of the two firms in a *duopoly.*

collusion cooperation among producers to limit production and raise prices so as to raise one another's profits.

cartel an agreement among several producers to obey output restrictions in order to increase their joint profits.

noncooperative behavior actions by firms that ignore the effects of those actions on the profits of other firms.

Notes

AFTER YOU READ THE MODULE

Tip

Tip #1. This module entails less certainty about how the market structure works relative to the modules on perfect competition and monopoly. After you study the module, you should have an appreciation for the puzzles presented by the oligopolistic market structure. These puzzles typically reflect the trade-offs between cooperation and competition and the benefits firms receive from these two strategies.

WORKED PROBLEMS

1. Suppose there is an industry in which there are just a few producers and each of these producers is aware of the others. Why might it be worthwhile for these producers to cooperate in making decisions to produce the monopoly price and quantity of the good in this market? Why might it be difficult for these producers to be able to adhere to this monopoly-level pricing and production decision?

STEP 1: Review the benefits of forming a cartel and why it is beneficial in an industry characterized as having just a few firms for those firms to cooperate and produce the monopoly level of its output and price and then divide up this level of production among the different firms.

A successful cartel can restrict output and raise the price above the level that would exist without a cartel. That implies that the successful cartel can generate higher joint profits for the firms that are in the cartel.

STEP 2: List the reasons that undermine the ability of a cartel to collude.

It is highly difficult to maintain a cartel agreement among the different firms since each firm faces an incentive to cheat on the cartel arrangement. Cartels find it particularly hard to collude when there are large numbers of firms, complex products or pricing schemes, and differences in interests among the firms in the cartel, as well as when buyers have some degree of bargaining power.

2. Suppose there are two identical gas stations in Smallville and they both know that the demand curve for gasoline in their market is given by the equation $P = 10 - .02Q$. Furthermore, suppose that both firms have constant marginal cost equal to \$2 per gallon of gasoline provided in the market. The two firms are willing to share the market equally, and the two firms want your advice as to what the profit maximizing quantity and price would be if they successfully collude and share the market evenly. They would also like to know what their profits would be under this plan. In your calculation, assume fixed cost is equal to \$100 for each firm. After making these calculations, the two firms ask you what will happen to price, quantity, and profits for each firm if one of the firms decides to increase its production by 50 additional gallons, while the other firm continues to produce its initial agreed upon level.

STEP 1: Start this problem by calculating the profit-maximizing quantity and price for this market if the two firms collude, divide the market in half, and in effect, act like a monopoly through the implementation of this agreement.

To find the profit-maximizing overall quantity for this market, we will want to equate *MR* to *MC*. We know that $MC = \$2$, but we have to find the *MR* curve for the market. If the two firms collude and act as a single firm in determining this profit-maximizing level of output, they will effectively be looking for the profit-maximizing quantity that a monopolist would produce. Thus, if the demand curve is $P = 10 - .02Q$, then the *MR* curve would be $MR = 10 - .04Q$. Setting $MR = MC$, we get $10 = .04Q = 2$, or $Q = 200$ gallons of gasoline. When a total of 200 gallons of gasoline is produced, demanders are willing to pay a price of \$6 per gallon (to see this, plug 200 gallons into the demand curve: $P = 10 - .02(200) = \$6$ per gallon). Thus, under this collusive arrangement, each firm will produce 100 gallons (half of the total production) and charge a price of \$6 per gallon.

STEP 2: Given the price and quantity you calculated in Step 1, find the level of profits for each firm as well as the total level of profits in the industry if both firms adhere to their agreement.

To find the total profits for the industry, remember that profits are equal to total revenue (*TR*) minus total cost (*TC*). *TR* for the industry will equal the product of price and quantity, or ($6 per gallon)(200 gallons), or a *TR* of $1,200. *TC* for the industry will equal the sum of variable cost and fixed cost. The fixed cost is equal to 2($100), since there are two firms and each has fixed costs of $100. The variable cost for the industry will be equal to ($2 per gallon)(200 gallons), since when *MC* is constant this implies that *MC* is equal to average variable cost. Thus, variable costs equal $400. *TC* for the industry is therefore $600. Profits for the industry, when both firms adhere to the collusive agreement to split the market, are equal to $600.

Alternatively, we can calculate the profit for a single firm by recognizing that the single firm's *TR* is equal to ($6 per gallon)(100 gallons), or $600, and the single firm's *TC* is equal to $100 plus ($2 per gallon)(100 gallons), or $300. The single firm's profit is therefore equal to $300. Since there are two identical firms and they each make $300 in profits, this implies that total profit is $600.

STEP 3: Determine the price and the profits for each firm, and the total profits in the market if one of the firm's adheres to the collusive agreement, while the other firm increases its production by 50 gallons of gasoline.

Suppose firm 1 cheats on the arrangement and decides to produce 50 extra gallons of gasoline, while firm 2 upholds the agreement. Firm 1 will therefore produce 150 gallons of gasoline, while firm 2 produces 100 gallons. Total gasoline production in this market will therefore be 250 gallons of gasoline. From the demand curve, we can see that the price in the market for 250 gallons of gasoline will be $5 per gallon of gasoline ($P = 10 - .02(250) = \$5$ per gallon).

Firm 1 will produce 150 gallons of gasoline, sell each gallon for $5 per gallon, have total revenue of $750, total cost of $400 (to see this, recall that $TC = FC + VC = 100 +$ ($2 per gallon)(150 gallons) = $400), and firm profits of $350.

Firm 2 will produce 100 gallons of gasoline, sell each gallon for $5 per gallon, have total revenue of $500, total cost of $300 (to see this, recall that $TC = FC + VC = 100 +$ ($2 per gallon)(100 gallons) = $300), and firm profits of $200.

Joint profits if firm 1 cheats on the arrangement and increases its production by 50 gallons will be $550, which is less than the two firms earned in joint profits when they both adhered to the collusive agreement. But, notice that by cheating, firm 1 has now captured more profits than firm 1 would have received when firm 1 adhered to the agreement. Cheating is worthwhile if it can be done without the other firm retaliating by also cheating.

Problems and Exercise

1. Suppose there are only two firms in an industry that produces gasoline. To make the analysis simpler, assume that once the companies have incurred the fixed costs of production the marginal cost of producing another gallon of gasoline is equal to zero. Suppose the demand for gasoline in this market is equal to $Q = 10{,}000 - 1{,}000P$.

a. Draw a graph of the industry demand curve, and draw the *MC* curve for the industry as well.

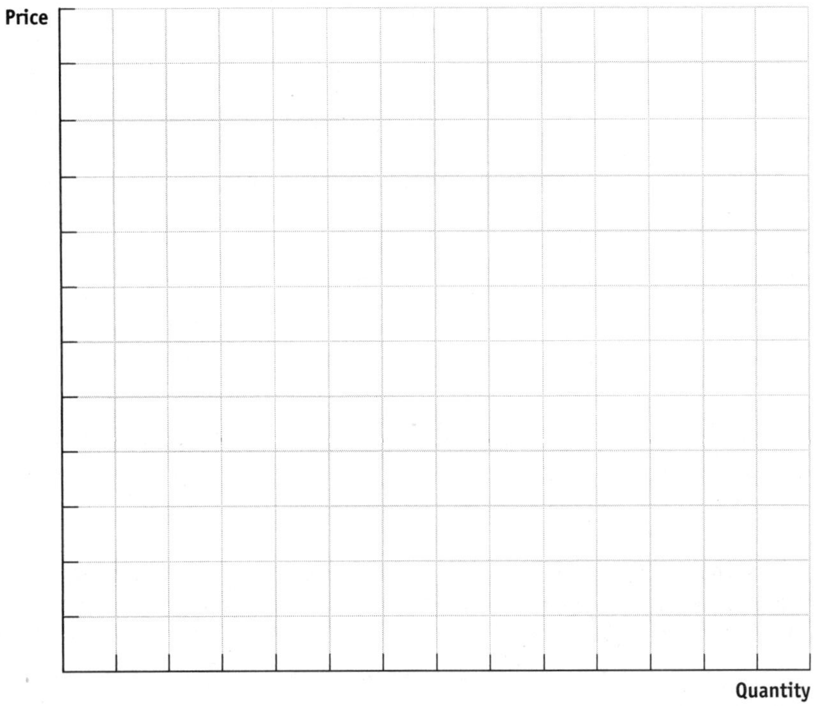

b. If these two firms acted like perfectly competitive firms, how many units would they produce altogether? What would the total revenue for the two firms equal?

c. Suppose these two firms are able to form a cartel in which they agree to produce the profit-maximizing level of output and then split the market evenly. What is the total amount of output these two firms will produce if they agree to split the market? What is the price of gasoline? What will be the total revenue received by each firm if they agree to split the market and neither firm cheats on this agreement? Are the two firms better off if they agree to this arrangement?

d. On a graph, indicate the market quantity Q^* that these two firms will produce under the arrangement described in part (c). On this same graph, indicate the market price P^* that will be charged for the gasoline.

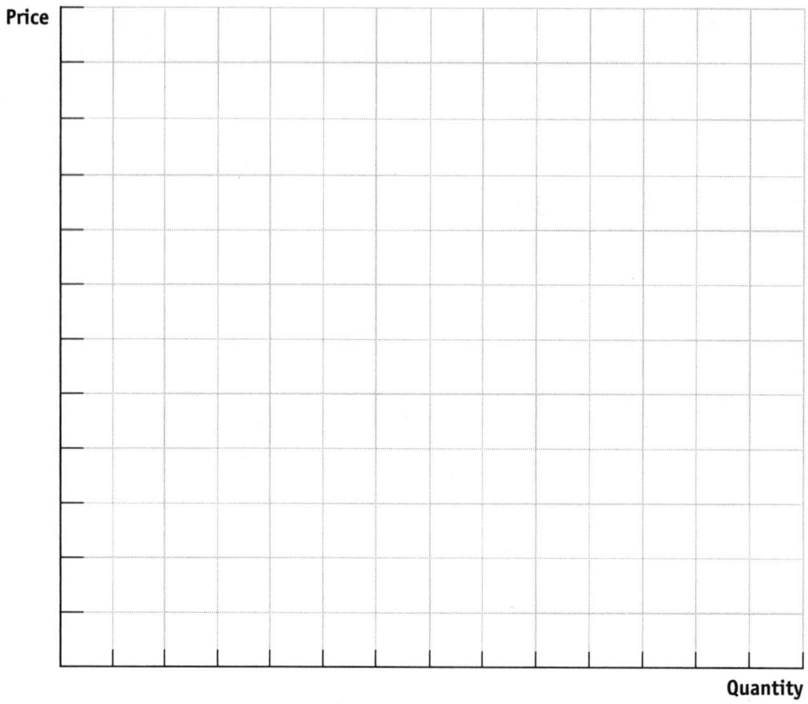

2. Suppose the two firms in problem 1 agree to form a cartel as described in part (c) of that problem, but that one of the firms decides to cheat on the arrangement by producing 3,500 gallons of gasoline instead of the agreed-upon 2,500 gallons of gasoline.

a. What will happen to the total amount of gasoline produced by the two firms?

b. What will happen to the price of gasoline when one firm increases its production to 3,500 gallons while the other firm continues to produce 2,500 gallons?

c. What is the total revenue received by the firm that produces 3,500 gallons of gasoline? What is the total revenue received by the firm that produces 2,500 gallons of gasoline? Is cheating on the cartel arrangement by one firm beneficial to both firms? Explain your answer. When one firm cheats on the cartel, what happens to the level of total profits?

d. Once the second firm realizes what the first firm has done, what do you imagine might be the second firm's response? Why are cartels unstable?

e. Are these two firms exhibiting quantity competition (Cournot behavior) or price competition (Bertrand behavior)?

3. Suppose there are two firms in an industry that produces nuclear generators. Furthermore, suppose that each of these firms is able to produce a maximum of 20 generators a year because of their productive facility. Would you predict that these two firms could successfully collude on price without a formal agreement? Why or why not?

BEFORE YOU TAKE THE TEST

Module Review Questions

1. Suppose there is a duopoly and that the two firms in this duopoly collude. The firms have agreed to collude most likely as a means to
   a. stabilize prices.
   b. stabilize quantities.
   c. maximize each firm's profits.
   d. maximize their joint profits.

2. Suppose there is a duopoly and that the two firms in this duopoly have formed a cartel. This cartel will likely be
   a. quite stable, since there are only two firms and they are each aware of each other's actions.
   b. unstable, since both firms have an incentive to cheat on the cartel arrangement.

3. When a monopolist lowers price, the monopolist experiences both a quantity and a price effect from this action. When a firm in a cartel lowers price, it also experiences a quantity and a price effect from this action. With respect to the monopoly's experience, the firm in a cartel finds that the
   a. quantity effect is a negative effect on total revenue.
   b. price effect is a larger positive effect on total revenue for the firm in the cartel than it is for the monopolist.
   c. price effect is a smaller negative effect on total revenue for the firm in the cartel than it is for the monopolist.

4. Firms in an oligopoly have a choice of competing with one another or cooperating with one another. Which strategy is typically more profitable to the individual firms in the industry?
   a. Compete
   b. Cooperate

Use the following information to answer the next three questions. Suppose there are two identical firms in an industry and that the market demand curve in the industry is $Q = 2{,}000 - 2P$. The marginal cost of producing the good in this industry is constant and equal to $200.

5. If each firm produces the same amount and the two firms collude with one another, what is the profit-maximizing quantity and price for this industry?

a. 1,600 units of output; $200
b. 800 units of output; $200
c. 800 units of output; $600
d. 1,000 units of output; $500

6. When these two firms collude with each other, what is the level of profit received by each firm?

a. $320,000
b. $480,000
c. $160,000
d. $240,000

7. Suppose one of the firms in this industry decides to cheat on the agreement to collude. Instead of selling its product for $600, this firm decides to increase its production and sell its output for a price of $400. If the other firm continues to produce 400 units, the new price for the product will equal __________, the cheating firm's profits will equal __________, and the noncheating firm's profits will equal __________.

a. $600; $160,000; $80,000
b. $600; $80,000; $160,000
c. $400; $160,000; $80,000
d. $400; $80,000; $160,000

ANSWER KEY

Answers to Problems and Exercises

1. a.

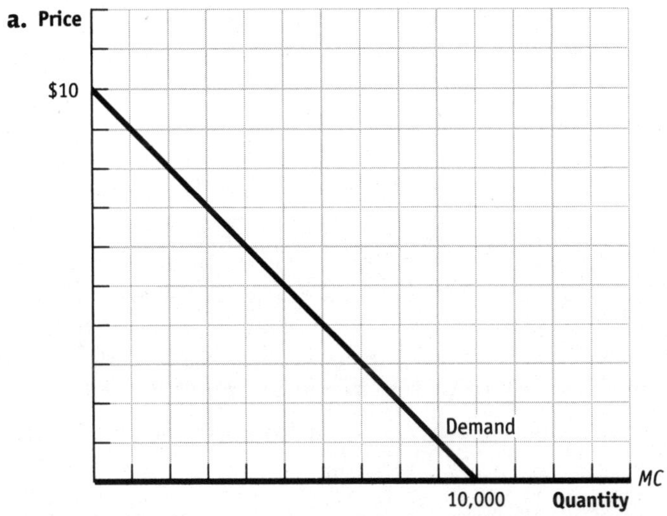

b. If the two firms acted like perfectly competitive firms, they would produce the quantity where the demand curve intersects the *MC* curve: they would produce a total of 10,000 gallons of gasoline. The price of this gasoline would be \$0 since in a perfectly competitive industry $P = MR = MC$ in the market equilibrium. The total revenue for both firms would equal \$0.

c. If the two firms collude and split the market, they will produce a total of 5,000 gallons of gasoline since this is the profit-maximizing amount of gasoline. To find this quantity remember that you need to equate the *MR* curve to the marginal cost. But this time, the two firms act together like a monopolist, so you need to first construct the monopolist's *MR* curve: $MR = 10 - 0.002Q$. $MR = MC$ at an output of 5,000 gallons. The firms then price this output by going up to the market demand curve and selecting the price on the demand curve that is associated with 5,000 gallons of gasoline. This price will be \$5 per gallon of gasoline. The total revenue received by each firm if they split the market evenly is (1/2)(\$5 per gallon)(5,000 gallons) = \$12,500. Each firm's *ATC* is equal to the sum of their fixed costs and their variable costs, and since the firm's *MC* is equal to 0, this implies that the firm's *AVC* is also equal to 0. The firm's profit will therefore equal total revenue minus fixed cost. Clearly, colluding leaves both firms better off than they would be under the scenario described in part (b).

d.

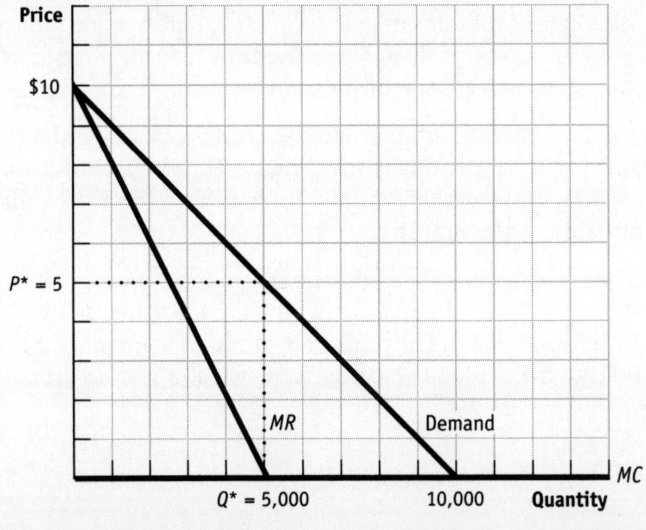

2. a. The total amount produced by the two firms will now be 6,000 gallons of gasoline.

   b. When 6,000 gallons of gasoline are produced, the market price decreases to \$4 per gallon of gasoline. To see this, remember that the demand curve can be written as $P = 10 - 0.001Q$, and when $Q = 6{,}000$ gallons this implies that $P = \$4$ per gallon.

   c. The total revenue of the firm that produces 3,500 gallons is now equal to \$14,000, while the total revenue of the firm that produces 2,500 gallons is equal to \$10,000. The firm that cheats on the cartel benefits since its total revenue increases from \$12,500 to \$14,000. The firm that maintains the cartel arrangement is hurt when the other firm cheats because its total revenue falls from \$12,500 to \$10,000. Notice that cheating causes the overall level of joint profits for the cartel to fall from \$25,000 to \$24,000: the two firms are no longer joint profit-maximizing.

   d. The second firm is likely to match the first firm's production decision, which will cause price and therefore total revenue to fall further. The two firms may persist in this price-cutting behavior until they reach the perfectly competitive result where 10,000 gallons of gasoline are produced and the market price is \$0. Cartels are inherently unstable due to the incentives both firms face to cheat on the cartel.

   e. The two firms are exhibiting price competition and Bertrand behavior since they are competing with regard to the price at which they offer the good.

3. Since both firms are constrained with regard to their ability to alter the level of output they produce, neither firm needs to worry about the other firm suddenly increasing its level of output and decreasing the price of its product. The two firms should be able to divide the market with relative ease while pricing their product above marginal cost. This will enable both firms to earn a positive economic profit.

Answers to Module Review Questions

1. **Answer d.** The two firms collude in order to set price and quantity so that the total amount of profits earned by the two firms is maximized. This does not imply that either firm is necessarily maximizing their own profits, since the market may not be divided evenly between the two firms.

2. **Answer b.** Cartels are inherently unstable because the firms in the cartel have decided to set price and quantity at a level where the marginal revenue from the last unit produced is greater than the marginal cost of producing the last unit. Each firm recognizes that it can expand production and earn more revenue than the costs it generates, so each firm is likely to deviate from the agreed-upon production level.

3. **Answer c.** The price effect is a negative effect on total revenue, since as the firm (whether a monopolist or a firm in a cartel) reduces price on all the units it sells in order to sell more units of the good, this causes total revenue to fall. The quantity effect on total revenue is a positive effect for either type of firm: when the firm reduces price to sell more units of the good, the extra sales increase the firm's total revenue.

4. **Answer b.** Cooperation is the superior strategy because with cooperation the firms can work to maximize the joint profits of the oligopoly. When each firm acts in its own self-interest and adopts a compete strategy, this typically leads to price decreases that erode the general level of profitability in the industry.

5. **Answer c.** The firms will profit-maximize by producing the quantity where $MR = MC$ and then selecting the price from the demand curve at that quantity. For the industry the MR curve is $MR = 1{,}000 - Q$ while $MC = 200$. The profit-maximizing quantity for the industry is 800 units. Plugging 800 into the demand equation for Q yields a market price of \$600.

6. **Answer c.** The total amount of profit for the industry is equal to total revenue minus total cost. When the firms produce 800 units and sell these units at a price of $600, their total revenue equals $480,000. Their total cost is equal to ($200 per unit)(800 units), or $160,000. The total profit then for the two firms is $320,000, and each firm, since they are identical, earns $160,000 in profits.

7. **Answer c.** When the cheating firm decreases the price for the good to $400, the quantity demanded in the market increases to 1,200 units. Since the noncheating firm is still producing 400 units, the cheating firm will increase its production to 800 units. The good will sell for $400 and the cheating firm's total revenue will equal $320,000, its total cost will equal $160,000, and its profit will equal $160,000. The noncheating firm will sell 400 units at a price of $400, its total revenue will equal $160,000, its total cost will equal $80,000, and its profit will equal $80,000.

module 32

Game Theory

BEFORE YOU READ THE MODULE

Summary

This module discusses game theory and its usefulness in exploring some of the issues confronting oligopolies. The module develops the concept of the prisoner's dilemma. Finally the module explores how repeated interactions between oligopolists can result in collusive behavior even though there is no formal agreement to collude.

Module Objectives

Objective #1. Oligopolistic firms are interdependent: one firm's profit depends on what its competitors do and vice versa. This interdependence can be modeled using game theory, in which a payoff matrix is constructed to represent the different outcomes that each firm achieves depending on the decisions made by the other firms. In this module, game theory is used to model this interdependence between two firms. The prisoner's dilemma is an example of game theory in which each player in the game has an incentive to cheat or take an action that benefits the player at the other player's expense, and the outcome of this behavior leaves both players worse off than they would have been if neither player had cheated. This example helps illustrate the peculiar, and often puzzling, behavior of oligopolistic firms. Figure 32.1 illustrates a payoff matrix between player 1 and player 2. Both players have a choice of two strategies—strategy 1 and strategy 2—and the payoff for each player is given in the individual cells, with player 1's payoff given first, followed by player 2's payoff.

Figure 32.1

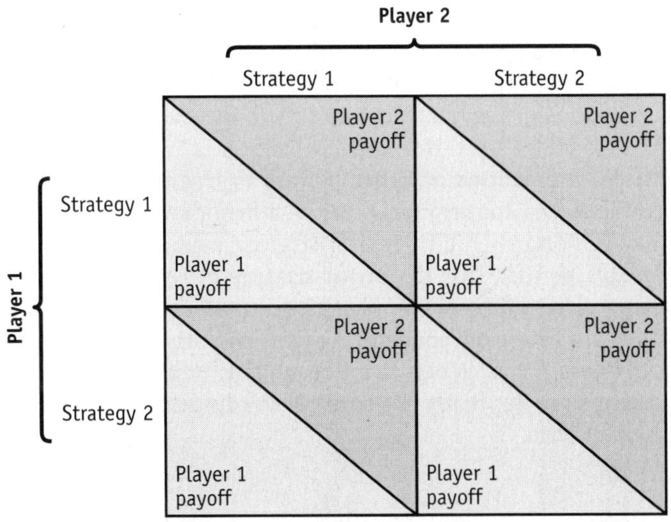

Objective #2. A dominant strategy is a strategy that the player will adhere to no matter what the other players do. When each player takes the strategy that is best for them given the actions of the other players, this generates a game equilibrium that is referred to as a Nash equilibrium. The Nash equilibrium is a noncooperative equilibrium, since none of the players take into account the effects of their actions on the other players. Figure 32.2 illustrates a payoff matrix for two firms, firm 1 and firm 2, where both firms are deciding whether they should cooperate or compete with one another. Each cell provides information about the level of profits the firms earn depending on their strategy. Both firm 1 and firm 2 have dominant strategies: they will both compete, since their profit is greater when electing this strategy no matter what strategy the other firm chooses. However, when both firms select this strategy, their total profits fall below the level they could achieve if both firms were willing to commit to the strategy to cooperate. The Nash equilibrium for this game leaves both firms worse off than they would be if it were possible for them to creditably maintain the other strategy.

Figure 32.2

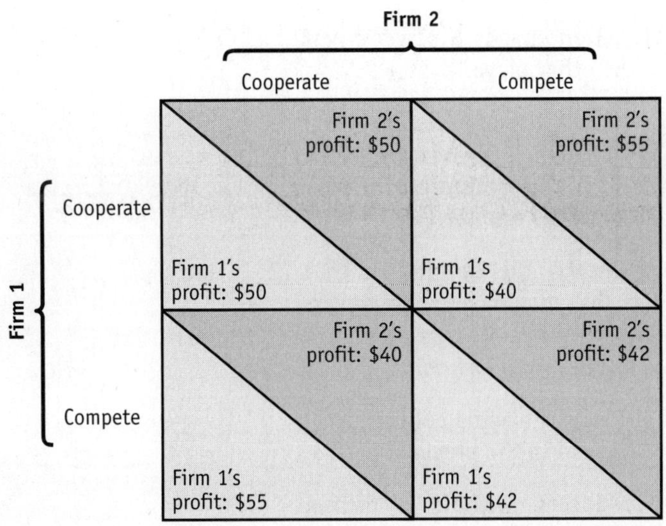

Objective #3. Some games are played only once (Figure 32.2 is an example of this kind of game). These one-shot games do not offer the complexities found in games that are played multiple times. For businesses that hope to stay in business for many years, game theory suggests the need to consider strategic behavior that takes into account the impact of the firm's decision on the future actions of other players in the game. These multishot games often start with firms behaving cooperatively. When a firm deviates from cooperative behavior, the other firms may respond with a tit-for-tat strategy wherein they repeat what the other firm did in the previous period. This tit-for-tat strategy offers a reward to firms for cooperative behavior while punishing firms who opt to cheat on the other firms. Over time each firm recognizes that they are better off cooperating with the other firms in the industry rather than competing with these firms. When firms reach this point, this is referred to as tacit collusion, since the firms are implicitly colluding with one another without the necessity of a formal, explicit agreement.

Key Terms

game theory the study of behavior in situations of *interdependence.* Used to explain the behavior of an *oligopoly.*

payoff in *game theory,* the reward received by a player (for example, the profit earned by an *oligopolist*).

payoff matrix in *game theory,* a diagram that shows how the *payoffs* to each of the participants in a two-player game depend on the actions of both; a tool in analyzing *interdependence.*

prisoner's dilemma a game based on two premises in which (1) each player has an incentive to choose an action that benefits itself at the other player's expense; and (2) both players are then worse off than if they had acted cooperatively.

dominant strategy in *game theory,* an action that is a player's best action regardless of the action taken by the other player.

Nash equilibrium in *game theory,* the *equilibrium* that results when all players choose the action that maximizes their *payoffs* given the actions of other players, ignoring the effect of that action on the *payoffs* of other players; also known as *noncooperative equilibrium.*

noncooperative equilibrium in *game theory,* the *equilibrium* that results when all players choose the action that maximizes their *payoffs* given the actions of other players, ignoring the effect of that action on the *payoffs* of other players; also known as *Nash equilibrium.*

tit for tat in *game theory,* a strategy that involves playing cooperatively at first, then doing whatever the other player did in the previous period.

tacit collusion cooperation among producers, without a formal agreement, to limit production and raise prices so as to raise one anothers' profits.

Notes

AFTER YOU READ THE MODULE

Tip

Tip #1. Students often find reading a payoff matrix challenging. Here's a suggestion for making this task easier. First, consider the payoff matrix from player 1's perspective as two separate columns: each column represents player 2 taking a particular strategy and sticking with it, while player 1's task is to decide which of the available strategies is the best strategy for player 1 to pursue. For example, Figure 32.3 represents the payoff matrix given in Figure 32.2 from firm 1's perspective.

Figure 32.3

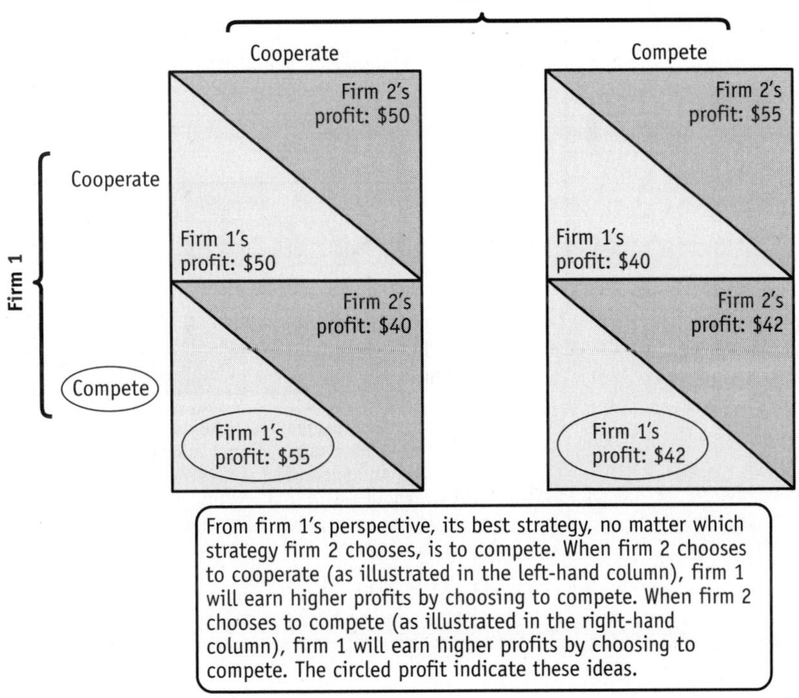

Now, consider the payoff matrix from player 2's perspective as two separate rows: each row represents player 1 taking a particular strategy and sticking with it, while player 2's task is to decide which of the available strategies is the best strategy for player 2 to pursue. Figure 32.4 represents the payoff matrix given in Figure 32.2 from firm 2's perspective.

Figure 32.4

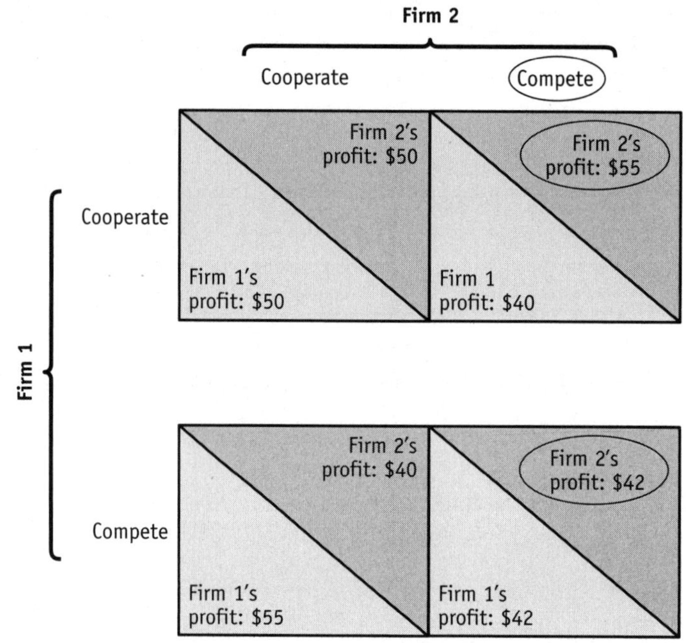

From firm 2's perspective, the best strategy is to compete no matter which strategy firm 1 adopts. If firm 1 adopts the strategy to cooperate (as illustrated in the top row of the diagram), firm 2 earns higher profits by adopting the strategy to compete. If firm 1 adopts the strategy to compete (as illustrated in the bottom row of the diagram), firm 2 earns higher profits by adopting the strategy to compete. The circled profits identify firm 2's best profit situations depending on firm 1's strategy.

WORKED PROBLEM

1. Suppose there are two firms in an industry and they are both trying to decide whether they will advertise. Firm A and firm B know that if both firms advertise, each firm will earn $1,000 in profits. However, if only one firm advertises, then the firm that advertises will earn $0 in profits (the advertising costs will overwhelm the additional revenue), while the other firm that is not advertising will earn $2,000 in profits (since it will sell more of the good but not have to pay for the expensive advertising). If both firms decide not to advertise, then each firm will earn $500 in profits since people will, in general, be less aware of their product. You have been asked to organize these data into a payoff matrix and then determine the dominant strategies for firm A and for firm B, Finally, you have been asked to determine whether these two firms are likely to end up maximizing their joint profits.

STEP 1: **Create a payoff matrix illustrating the given information.**

To create the payoff matrix, first determine what the strategy choices are for each of the firms. In this example, both firms can choose between Advertising or Not Advertising. Then, construct a matrix similar to the one illustrated in Figure 32.1 of your text. The payoff matrix is as follows.

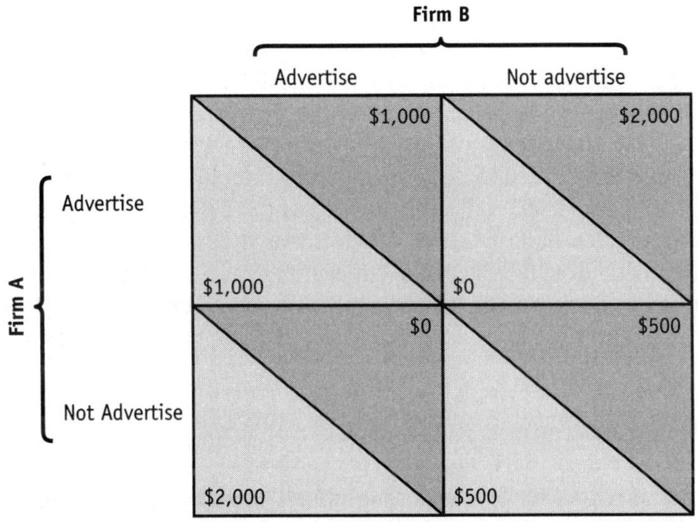

Remember that the first number in the cell represents the payoff for firm A, while the second number in the cell represents the payoff for firm B. Thus, in the top right corner, the cell contains the numbers "$0" and "$2,000." The $0 is the level of profits that firm A earns when firm A advertises and firm B does not advertise. The $2,000 is the level of profits that firm B earns when firm A advertises and firm B does not advertise.

STEP 2: **Analyze what Firm A's dominant strategy is, given the payoff matrix you created in Step 1.**

Recall from the Tip section of the Study Guide that the analysis of the payoff matrix from firm A's perspective is as if firm A is considering two separate columns.

In the first column, firm B is assumed to be adopting the strategy of "Advertise" and the question that firm A asks itself is, "Is it better for us to advertise or not advertise, given that firm B is going to advertise?" Firm A sees that if it advertises and firm B advertises, then firm A will earn $1,000 in profit; firm A sees that, if it does not advertise while firm B advertises, then firm A will earn $2,000 in profit. Firm A concludes that if firm B is going to advertise, then the best strategy for firm A is to not advertise.

In the second column, firm B is assumed to be adopting the strategy of "Not Advertise" and the question that firm A asks itself is, "Is it better for us to advertise or not advertise, given that firm B is going to not advertise?" Firm A sees that if it advertises and firm B does not advertise, then firm A will earn $0 in profit; firm A sees that if it does not advertise and firm B does not advertise, then firm A will earn $500 in profit. Firm A concludes that if firm B is not going to advertise, then the best strategy for firm A is to not advertise.

Firm A concludes that, irrespective of what firm B does, firm A should not advertise. Firm A has a dominant strategy of Not Advertise.

STEP 3: Analyze what firm B's dominant strategy is, given the payoff matrix you created in Step 1.

Recall from the Tip section of the Study Guide that the analysis of the payoff matrix from firm B's perspective is as if firm B is considering two separate rows.

In the first row, firm A is assumed to be adopting the strategy of "Advertise" and the question that firm B asks itself is, "Is it better for us to advertise or not advertise, given that firm A is going to advertise?" Firm B sees that if it advertises and firm A advertises, then firm B will earn $1,000 in profit; firm B sees that if it does not advertise while firm A advertises, then firm B will earn $2,000 in profit. Firm B concludes that if firm A is going to advertise, then the best strategy for firm B is to not advertise.

In the second row, firm A is assumed to be adopting the strategy of "Not Advertise" and the question that firm B asks itself is, "Is it better for us to advertise or not advertise, given that firm A is going to not advertise?" Firm B sees that if it advertises and firm A does not advertise, then firm B will earn $0 in profit; firm B sees that if it does not advertise and firm A does not advertise, then firm B will earn $500 in profit. Firm B concludes that if firm A is not going to advertise, then the best strategy for firm B is to not advertise.

Firm B concludes that, irrespective of what firm A does, firm B should not advertise. Firm B has a dominant strategy of Not Advertise.

STEP 4 Determine the outcome for this situation, given your analysis in Steps 1 and 2. Then, comment on whether this outcome results in the two firms maximizing their joint profits.

Both firm A and firm B will pursue their dominant strategy and they will both choose to not advertise. This means that each of these firms will earn a profit of $500 or a joint profit of $1,000. This is not the optimal outcome, however, if the goal of the firms is to maximize their profits: if the two firms advertise, then their individual profit would be $1,000 and their joint profit would be $2,000. This example illustrates the prisoner's dilemma, in which the outcome of the game is suboptimal because of each firm's incentive to take an action that benefits itself.

Problems and Exercises

1. The following payoff matrix provides information about the profits Apple Growers and Johnny Appleseed Company earn based on the advertising strategy the companies adopt. The first entry in the matrix cell gives the profits of Apple Growers, and the second entry provides the profits of Johnny Appleseed Company.

		Johnny Appleseed Company	
		Advertise	Not advertise
Apple Growers	Advertise	$700 / $500	$710 / $440
	Not Advertise	$600 / $550	$610 / $580

a. If these two firms could collude with one another and decide jointly on their advertising strategy with the goal of maximizing their joint profits, what combination of strategies results in the greatest joint profit for these two companies?

b. Which strategy is Apple Growers' dominant strategy?

c. Which strategy is Johnny Appleseed Company's dominant strategy?

d. What is the Nash equilibrium for this game?

2. Two firms, firm A and firm B, compete against each other in a duopoly. These two firms have been in competition with each other for many years, and they anticipate that they will continue to compete against each other for many more years. Both firms are faced with two strategies they can pursue: they can either always cheat or they can pursue a strategy of tit for tat in which one firm punishes the other firm whenever the other firm cheats. Both firms are faced with two strategies they can pursue: they can either "Always Cheat" or they can pursue a strategy of "Tit for Tat" in which one firm punishes the other firm whenever the other firm cheats. Suppose that the payoff for playing the strategy of "Always Cheats" results in each firm earning profits of $100 a year. If one firm plays the strategy of "Tit for Tat" while the other firm plays the strategy of "Always Cheats," the cheating firm will earn $150 the first year but only $90 for each subsequent year, while the "Tit for Tat" firm will earn $90 the first year but $100 for each subsequent year. If both firms play the "Tit for Tat" strategy, they will earn $130 a year.

   a. Create a payoff matrix for firm A and firm B showing the profits these two firms earn given the strategies that are open to each of them.

   b. Suppose that firm A anticipates that firm B is going to choose the strategy to always cheat. Given firm B's choice, what is firm A's best strategy if these two firms compete for a single year? Is this still the best choice if firm A and firm B are competing with each other for many other years?

   c. Suppose that firm B anticipates that firm A is going to choose the strategy to always cheat. Given firm A's choice, what is firm B's best strategy if these two firms compete for a single year? Is this still the best choice if firm A and firm B are competing with each other for many other years?

   d. If firm A chooses the tit-for-tat strategy, what is the best strategy for firm B to choose? If firm B chooses the tit-for-tat strategy, what is the best strategy for firm A to choose?

3. Cool Cola and Peppy Soda are the only two soft drink makers in a market. Both companies are trying to decide what price to charge for their 12-ounce drinks. If both companies charge $1.00 per drink they can each sell 5,000 units of the drink. If one of the companies charges $.90 per drink, that company can sell 10,500 units of the drink while the other company sells no units of the drink. If both companies charge $.90 per drink they each will sell 5,300 units of the drink.

   a. Create the payoff matrix for Cool Cola and Peppy Soda showing the total revenue that each firm receives when it sets its price at either $1.00 per unit or $.90 per unit. In the payoff matrix enter Cool Cola's revenues as the first entry in each cell.

   b. What choice of strategy will result in the joint revenue of the two companies being maximized?

c. What choice of strategy will be the dominant strategy for Cool Cola?

d. What choice of strategy will be the dominant strategy for Peppy Soda?

e. What will be the chosen strategy for both companies given the information you have been given?

BEFORE YOU TAKE THE TEST

Module Review Questions

Use the following information to answer the next three questions. The following payoff matrix indicates the level of profits earned by Printers Press and Typesetters, the only two firms in the printing industry in an economy. The level of profits for each firm depends on whether they cooperate or compete with each other.

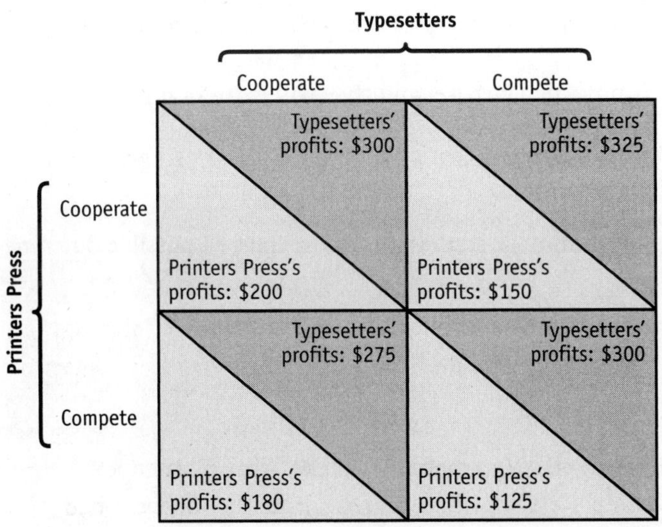

1. What is Printers Press's dominant strategy?

a. Compete

b. Cooperate

c. Printers Press does not have a dominant strategy.

2. What is Typesetters' dominant strategy?
   a. Compete
   b. Cooperate
   c. Typesetters does not have a dominant strategy.

3. When Printers Press and Typesetters pursue their dominant strategies, the sum of their joint profits is
   a. maximized.
   b. not maximized.

Answer the next three questions based on the following information. Two firms are the only producers in a market. Each firm is trying to decide whether to advertise. If firm B advertises, firm A earns $2,000 in profit if firm A does not advertise and $1,800 if firm A advertises (the advertising increases its costs more than its revenues). If firm B does not advertise, firm A earns $2,200 in profit if firm A does not advertise and $2,000 if firm A advertises. If firm A advertises, firm B earns $3,000 in profit if firm B does not advertise and $2,700 if firm B does advertise. If firm A does not advertise, firm B earns $2,600 if firm B does not advertise and $2,400 if firm B does advertise.

4. What is firm B's dominant strategy?
   a. Advertise
   b. Do not advertise
   c. Firm B does not have a dominant strategy.

5. What is the Nash equilibrium for this game?
   a. Firm A and firm B will not advertise, and they will earn joint profits of $4,800.
   b. Firm A will advertise, firm B will not advertise, and they will earn total profits of $5,000.
   c. Firm A will not advertise, firm B will advertise, and they will earn total profits of $4,400.
   d. Firm A and firm B will advertise, and they will earn total profits of $4,500.

6. For these two firms, choosing the dominant strategy results in the best possible outcome with respect to total profits.
   a. True
   b. False

7. In the prisoner's dilemma,
   a. both players have an incentive to cheat no matter what the other player does.
   b. when both players cheat, both players are worse off than if neither of them had cheated.
   c. The prisoner's dilemma is a helpful tool for understanding one-shot games.
   d. Answers (a), (b), and (c) are all true.

8. When firms in an oligopoly pursue a tit-for-tat strategy, this implies that each firm will

a. continue to pursue its strategy no matter what the other firms in the oligopoly choose to do.

b. punish other firms if they cheat on the tacit agreement that the firms have with one another.

c. behave cooperatively, but will then mimic what the other player did in the previous period.

d. Answers (b) and (c) are both true.

9. Firms in an oligopoly that expect to compete with one another for an extended period will

a. choose a noncooperative strategy, since they do not like competing with other firms and they hope this will drive some firms out of the industry.

b. choose a tit-for-tat strategy that evolves into all firms cooperating, since they realize this is their best strategy if they are to be in the same industry for an extended period.

c. engage in price wars in hopes that some firms will be driven from the industry, leaving a smaller number of firms to collude with one another.

d. often ignore one another, since they cannot do anything about the fact that they are competing in the same industry.

10. In recent years, many colleges have felt the need to build impressive student centers and athletic facilities on their campuses. Each college realizes that if they do not build these facilities while other colleges do build them, the nonbuilding college will be less competitive and less attractive to prospective students. This is an example of a(n)

a. arms race.

b. exclusive dealing.

c. tacit collusion.

d. antitrust activity.

ANSWER KEY

Answers to Problems and Exercises

1. a. When both companies pick the strategy to advertise, joint profits are maximized since the profits in this cell of the matrix equal $1,200 and the three other cells result in joint profits that are less than this amount.

   b. Apple Growers' dominant strategy is to not advertise. If Johnny Appleseed Company selects the strategy to advertise, Apple Growers will earn greater profit by choosing to not advertise. If Johnny Appleseed Company selects the strategy to not advertise, Apple Growers will earn greater profit by choosing to not advertise. No matter which strategy Johnny Appleseed Company selects, Apple Growers will be best off choosing to not advertise.

   c. Johnny Appleseed Company's dominant strategy is to not advertise. If Apple Growers selects the strategy to advertise, Johnny Appleseed Company will earn greater profit by choosing to not advertise. If Apple Growers selects the strategy to not advertise, Johnny Appleseed Company will earn greater profit by choosing to not advertise. No matter which strategy Apple Growers selects, Johnny Appleseed Company will be best off choosing to not advertise.

   d. Both companies will choose to not advertise, and they will earn joint profits of $1,190 instead of the $1,200 that they could earn if they could communicate and collude with each other, and both choose to advertise as their strategy.

2. a.

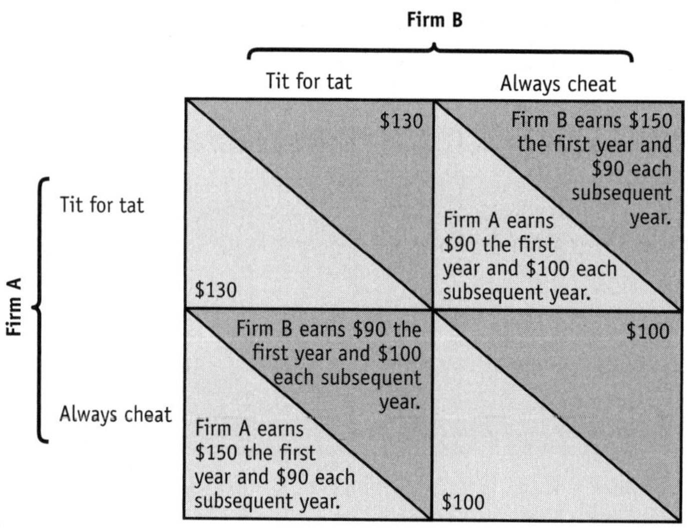

   b. Firm A's best strategy, if the two firms compete for a single year and if firm B chooses to always cheat, is to also choose the strategy to always cheat. But, firm A's best strategy if the two firms compete for many years and firm B chooses to always cheat, is still to pursue the strategy of always cheating. Notice though that this result does not result in the best outcome for both firms. Both firms, if they plan to compete for many years, would be better off choosing the strategy of tit for tat since that results in the greatest level of profits for each firm over time.

   c. Firm B's best strategy, if the two firms compete for a single year and if firm A chooses to always cheat is to also choose the strategy to always cheat. But, firm B's best strategy if the two firms compete for many years and firm A chooses to always cheat, is still to pursue the strategy of always cheating. Notice though that this result does not result in the best outcome for both firms. Both firms, if they plan to compete for many years, would be better off choosing the strategy of tit for tat since that results in the greatest level of profits for each firm over time.

d. If one firm chooses tit for tat, then the other firm is better off also choosing tit for tat.

3. a.

		Charge $1.00 per drink	Charge $.90 per drink
Peppy Soda	Charge $1.00 per drink	$5,000, $5,000	$0, $9,450
Cool Cola	Charge $.90 per drink	$9,450, $0	$4,770, $4,770

b. Joint revenues will be maximized when both companies charge $1.00 per drink since joint revenue will equal $10,000 at that price.

c. The dominant strategy for Cool Cola is to charge $.90 per drink no matter what Peppy Soda's strategy. When Peppy Soda charges $1.00 per drink, Cool Cola's revenue will be greater if it charges $.90 per drink. When Peppy Soda charges $.90 per drink, Cool Cola's revenue will be greater if it charges $.90 per drink.

d. The dominant strategy for Peppy Soda is to charge $.90 per drink no matter what Cool Cola's strategy. The reasoning is the same as was given in answer (c) for Cool Cola.

e. Both companies will charge $.90 per drink and earn joint revenue of $9,540 instead of the $10,000 in joint revenue they could earn by both charging $1.00 per drink.

Answers to Module Review Questions

1. **Answer b.** No matter which strategy Typesetters pursues, Printers Press is better off adhering to a strategy to cooperate since it will leave the company with the highest level of profits.

2. **Answer a.** No matter which strategy Printers Press pursues, Typesetters is better off adhering to a strategy to compete since it will leave the company with the highest level of profits.

3. **Answer b.** When both companies pursue their dominant strategies, they earn a total of $475 profit, which is less than they would earn if they both pursue the strategy to cooperate.

4. **Answer b.** No matter which strategy firm A pursues, firm B's dominant strategy is to not advertise, since firm B earns greater profits by pursuing this strategy.

5. **Answer a.** Both firms will pursue their dominant strategy to not advertise, and this will result in the sum of total profits of $4,800.

6. **Answer b.** The best possible outcome with respect to the sum of total profits occurs when the two firms earn $5,000 in profits. This happens when firm A chooses to advertise while firm B chooses to not advertise.

7. **Answer d.** Answers (a) and (b) are true because of the nature of the prisoner's dilemma, whereas answer (c) underscores the idea that modeling a game that is only played once is easier than modeling a game that is played multiple times.

8. **Answer d.** In the tit-for-tat strategy, the firms in general cooperate with one another, but they will retaliate if a firm elects to not cooperate. This retaliation takes the form of mimicking whatever the other firm has done in the previous period.

9. **Answer b.** When a small number of firms realize that they will be competing for an extended period, these firms have a tendency to elect to cooperate with one another. Often the firms realize this is their best strategy after they have been the recipient of the tit-for-tat strategy, which effectively punishes noncooperating firms.

10. **Answer a.** When the different college campuses compete with regard to facilities, they are engaging in an arms race, since campuses that refuse to build these facilities find that they lose their position in the college admissions game. Exclusive dealing refers to a firm's contracting with businesses to sell only its product, thereby creating a miniature monopoly situation for the firm. Tacit collusion refers to firms agreeing to market price and market quantity without a formal agreement: this is not really applicable here since colleges keep trying to outdo one another in creating the best facilities. Antitrust activity refers to government action to limit market power or monopoly in a market.

module **33**

Oligopoly in Practice

BEFORE YOU READ THE MODULE

Summary

This module discusses the relationship between oligopolies and antitrust policy. It also considers the factors that limit tacit collusion. The module also examines the cause and effect of price wars, product differentiation, price leadership, and nonprice competition. Finally, the module discusses the importance of oligopoly in the real world.

Module Objectives

Objective #1. An oligopolist would prefer to have no firms to compete against. An oligopolist can distinguish its product through differentiation: the more differentiated the firm's product, the closer the market structure is to monopoly.

Objective #2. The United States legally restricts the behavior of oligopolistic firms and prohibits the creation of monopolies. The Sherman Antitrust Act of 1890 marks the beginning of antitrust policy and the government's commitment to prevent oligopolistic industries from becoming monopolies or behaving like monopolies.

Objective #3. Although tacit collusion is common, it is hard for firms to push prices up to the monopoly level due to a number of different factors. Monopolistic prices are hard to achieve for at least four reasons: (1) when there are many firms in the industry, firms are less likely to behave cooperatively; (2) when firms produce a variety of products and offer these products at different prices it is hard to discern when a firm is cheating on the tacit agreement; (3) firms do not always agree on what is fair and in their interests, and this can lead to firms deviating from the tacit agreement; and (4) firms may find that the buyers of their products are large enough relative to the entire market to be able to bargain for lower prices. When tacit collusion breaks down, this is often due to price wars in which each firm reduces the price of its product below the cooperative level. In a worse-case scenario prices can fall below the noncooperative level as each seller tries to drive the other sellers out of the business.

Objective #4. Another form of oligopolistic behavior is that of price leadership. Here a firm acts to set the price tacitly for the whole industry. In industries that follow a price leadership model, the firms often compete with each other with regard to other product characteristics. This nonprice competition injects competition into an otherwise cooperative environment.

Key Terms

antitrust policy legislative and regulatory efforts undertaken by the government to prevent oligopolistic industries from becoming or behaving like *monopolies.*

price war a collapse of prices when *tacit collusion* breaks down.

product differentiation the attempt by firms to convince buyers that their products are different from those of other firms in the industry. If firms can so convince buyers, they can charge a higher price.

price leadership a pattern of behavior in which one firm sets its price and other firms in the industry follow.

nonprice competition competition in areas other than price to increase sales, such as new product features and advertising; especially engaged in by firms that have a tacit understanding not to compete on price.

Notes

AFTER YOU READ THE MODULE

Tips

Tip #1: The Sherman Antitrust Act of 1890 was intended to break up existing monopolies and prevent the formation of new ones. This act reflected recognition that monopolies led to higher prices and restricted outputs in markets. Although the United States established this antimonopoly position a long time ago, only relatively recently have other countries, particularly those in the European Union, recognized the benefits of restricting monopoly power.

Tip #2: It is normal to see tacit collusion among the firms in an oligopolistic industry. This tacit collusion leads to higher prices than would prevail if there were no collusion, but the prices do not typically rise to the monopolistic level. Tacit collusion is more difficult to achieve, however, in these circumstances: (1) As the number of firms in the industry increases, the incentive to cooperate decreases. (2) Complex products and pricing schemes make it hard to discern when a firm cheats on the pricing arrangement. (3) The interests of the firms in the oligopoly may diverge. (4) Buyers may have bargaining power.

Tip #3: Firms in an oligopolistic industry recognize that they can increase their market power through product differentiation. This product differentiation allows competition based on how the products differ rather than on price differences. When product differentiation is possible, many firms follow a price leadership model in which one firm establishes prices for the general type of product and the other firms follow its pricing lead.

WORKED PROBLEMS

1. Joey and Suey are the only producers of chocolate fudge in their small country. They have decided to charge $5 per pound of fudge, since this is the price that will maximize their joint profits. Joey and Suey have little trouble maintaining this pricing agreement. Can you detail the four factors that make tacit agreement easier to achieve and how these factors help make their tacit collusion relatively stable?

STEP 1: Review the meaning of *tacit collusion* and apply this definition to Joey and Suey's situation.

Tacit collusion is cooperation among producers, without a formal agreement, to limit production and raise prices so as to raise each other's profits. Because Joey and Suey are the only two producers of fudge in this market, by cooperating with each other with regard to how much fudge they produce and what price they charge, they can maximize their total level of profits.

STEP 2: Discuss four factors that determine how successful firms will be in achieving tacit collusion.

Tacit collusion is difficult to maintain among a large number of firms. In this example there are only two firms, so it is easy for Joey to know what Suey is doing and vice versa. Joey and Suey can easily recognize the advantages of cooperating with each other and tacitly colluding on price and quantity.

Tacit collusion is more difficult to maintain when there are complex products and pricing schemes. In this example there is only one general product, fudge, and the pricing scheme of $5 per pound is straightforward. This makes it easy for Joey and Suey to know if the other firm is cheating on the tacit agreement to collude.

Tacit collusion is more difficult to maintain if the firms in the industry have different interests. In this example both Joey and Suey are interested in maximizing their profits, and they both realize that this goal will be best met by tacitly colluding with each other on price and output decisions.

Finally, tacit collusion is more difficult to maintain if buyers of the product have substantial bargaining power. In this example, we do not know anything about buying power, but it is likely that the market is not dominated by a buyer or a group of buyers who exert substantial bargaining power in the industry.

Thus, Joey and Suey are likely to find it easy to tacitly collude with regard to their pricing and production decisions.

2. In 1890, Congress passed the Sherman Antitrust Act. What were the two primary goals of this act? Why was Congress interested in addressing these two goals?

STEP 1: Review the history of the Sherman Antitrust Act.

Prior to the passage of the Sherman Antitrust Act in 1890, several key industries in the United States formed cartels and eventually trusts designed to limit competition. Industry leaders in these companies recognized that by forming these arrangements they could effectively charge monopoly prices and earn monopoly profits. Congress recognized that these arrangements had the effect of limiting price competition in these markets.

STEP 2: Identify the two primary goals of the Sherman Antitrust Act.

The Sherman Antitrust Act was intended (1) to prevent the formation of more monopolies and (2) to break up existing monopolies.

STEP 3: Discuss why the government thought these two goals should be addressed.

The government considered that further monopolization within particular markets would result in prices being too high, production being too low, and monopoly profits not being eliminated through competition. The government wanted an environment that would eliminate this concentration of market power.

Problems and Exercises

1. What kinds of factors can make it hard for a group of firms in an oligopolistic industry to achieve tacit collusion? Discuss four different factors that make this difficult.

2. What is price leadership? How does price leadership resolve the oligopoly's problem of deciding how to set the optimal price? If the firms follow a price leadership model, how do the firms then compete with one another if they all offer the good at the same price?

3. Why is it unlikely that restaurants in a town of 300,000 people will form a cartel and fix prices? Why is it likely that OPEC, the Organization of Petroleum Exporting Countries, may be successful at times with raising the price of petroleum in world markets?

4. In a situation where there is tacit collusion among competing firms in an industry, do you expect the price for the industry product to be as high as the price would be if the industry was a monopoly? Why or why not?

BEFORE YOU TAKE THE TEST

Module Review Questions

1. The Sherman Antitrust Act of 1890 was
   a. aimed at preventing the creation of more monopolies.
   b. intended to provide legislation to help break up existing monopolies.
   c. the beginning of antitrust policy in the United States.
   d. Answers (a), (b), and (c) are all true statements.

2. Which of the following makes tacit agreements more difficult to achieve in an industry?
   a. The existence of just a few firms that each produce similar products.
   b. The existence of a buyer with significant buying power in the industry.
   c. The existence of just a few firms that have interacted over time and have developed strong ties of trust and respect.
   d. The existence of a few firms that produce one product with a relatively simple pricing policy for this product.

3. In an oligopolistic industry that practices price leadership, the competition between firms is apt to be
   a. price competition, as firms jockey for the right to be the price leader.
   b. quantity competition, as firms compete to gain market share at whatever price the price leader has established.
   c. nonprice competition, as firms strive to differentiate their product from the products produced by competing firms.
   d. All of the above forms of competition occur in the price leadership model.

4. By limiting price competition, firms can
   a. reduce the level of wasted output they would otherwise produce.
   b. increase their level of profitability.
   c. avoid creating a harmful cartel.

5. In a trust
   a. there is only one owner of the firm.
   b. shareholders of all the major companies in an industry place their shares in the hands of a board of trustees that control the companies.
   c. shareholders of all the major companies in an industry vote to have a single board of trustees to control the companies.
   d. Answers (a), (b), and (c) are all correct.
   e. Answers (a) and (b) are both correct.
   f. Answers (a) and (c) are both correct.

6. The first act passed by Congress to address the issue of industry concentration was the
   a. Government Competitive Business Act.
   b. Sherman Antitrust Act.
   c. Anti-Rockefeller Act.
   d. Monopoly Prohibition Act.

7. Industries in which there are just a few firms rarely manage to collude enough to push prices to the monopoly level. This failure may be due to
   a. too many firms in the industry making it hard to coordinate and maintain a monopoly level of prices in the industry.
   b. the presence of complex products and pricing schemes in the industry.
   c. firms in the industry having different interests and different perceptions as to what is a fair way to distribute profits in their industry.
   d. buyers having bargaining power in the industry.
   e. All of the answers are correct.

ANSWER KEY

Answers to Problems and Exercises

1. When there are a large number of firms in the oligopoly it is harder for the firms to reach an agreement about price and quantity decisions for the industry, and it is harder for firms to ascertain when other firms are cheating on the agreement. In addition, when there are more firms in the oligopoly, this indicates that the barriers to entry are low and that existing firms face the threat of new entry, which acts as a brake on raising price to monopolistic levels.

   When the oligopoly produces a number of different products and engages in more than one pricing scheme, this makes it harder for firms to have perfect collusion. It also makes it difficult to know with certainty when firms in the oligopoly are cheating on the tacit agreement.

   In addition, firms in an oligopoly may not share the same perspective and reach the same conclusion about what is fair. Some firms may feel that the quantity they are assigned to produce under the tacit agreement is too low, and they may feel they deserve to be able to produce more of the product. This type of disagreement causes the tacit agreement to quickly break down.

   Finally, in some oligopolistic markets there are buyers with significant market power that may be able to offset some of the market power held by the oligopoly. This makes it difficult for the oligopoly to maintain prices that are higher than the marginal cost of producing the good.

2. Price leadership is a situation in which one of the firms in the oligopoly takes a leadership role in setting the price of the product and then the other firms in the industry follow this price when setting the price of their products. This resolves the issue of how to determine the optimal price for the oligopoly, because once the price leader assumes that position, the other firms simply need to follow the lead of this firm. In the price leadership model, the price of the good is roughly the same across all firms, but each firm is free to differentiate and distinguish their product from their competitors' products. The firms under a price leadership model engage in nonprice competition.

3. In a town of 300,000 people it is difficult to imagine restaurants successfully forming a cartel because there will be too many restaurants to easily enforce the agreement. In contrast, OPEC has a relatively small number of members so it is relatively easy to ascertain whether members are adhering to the cartel price agreement.

4. In a situation where there is tacit collusion among competing firms in an industry you would expect the price for the industry product to be lower than the price would be if the industry was a monopoly because agreements to tacitly agree to set price tend to be unstable with firms cheating on the arrangement. When firms cheat on the arrangement the result is that the cheating firm offers the good at a lower price than the price that has tacitly been agreed to. This pushes the price downwards away from the monopoly level price.

Answers to Module Review Questions

1. **Answer d.** All three of these statements are true by definition.

2. **Answer b.** The presence of a buyer with significant buying power lessens the ability of the firms to set price above the competitive level. When there are just a few firms, it is relatively easy for these firms to cooperate with regard to price and quantity decisions. Similarly, if firms have a long relationship with one another, they are apt to have developed tacit agreements about how the market is to be divided and what pricing and

production decisions the firms will follow. Production of a single product with a simple pricing scheme makes a tacit agreement easier to create in a market than does the production of multiple products with more complicated pricing schemes.

3. **Answer c.** The price leadership model theorizes that the price is set by a firm in the industry and that this price is then used as the industry price. Firms do not compete with regard to price in this model, but instead compete with regard to the nonprice aspects of their product: the special features as well as the advertising campaigns that portray the quality of their product over their rivals' products.

4. **Answer b.** When firms limit price competition they are effectively trying to create a cartel situation where price of the good is determined by firms cooperating with one another rather than competing with one another. This cooperation potentially can enable firms to produce the profit-maximizing level of output and price that a monopolist would charge: by limiting price competition the firms can enlarge their joint profits.

5. **Answer b.** This is the definition of a trust as given in the text. Shareholders do not vote to give control to the board of trustees that instead place their shares in the hands of a board of trustees that then administers the companies as a single entity.

6. **Answer b.** The first act passed by Congress was the Sherman Antitrust Act of 1890. Shareholders do not vote to give control to the board of trustees. Shareholders place their shares in the hands of a board of trustees. The first trust was developed at John D. Rockefeller's Standard Oil Company.

7. **Answer e.** All of the factors listed in question 7 are factors that make it difficult for a group of firms in an industry to collude and set price in the industry at the monopoly level. The text describes each of these factors and how they limit a group of firms' ability to set price.

module 34

Monopolistic Competition

BEFORE YOU READ THE MODULE

Summary

This module introduces the model of monopolistic competition and discusses the determination of prices and profits in monopolistic competition in both the short run and the long run. The module compares perfectly competitive markets to monopolistically competitive markets in order to illustrate how monopolistically competitive markets can lead to inefficiency and excess capacity.

Module Objectives

Objective #1. Because monopolistically competitive firms sell differentiated products, each firm has some degree of market power and therefore faces a downward-sloping demand curve for its product. In fact, product differentiation is the only way monopolistically competitive firms acquire market power. This implies that these firms, like a monopoly, have some power to set the price they charge for their product. However, these firms also face competition, and due to free entry and exit in the long run will find that their long-run economic profit is equal to zero. There is no tendency toward collusion in a monopolistically competitive market since all firms recognize that new firms can enter the industry in the long run.

Objective #2. In the short run, a monopolistically competitive firm produces the level of output where marginal revenue equals marginal cost ($MR = MC$) and then prices this output by going up to its demand curve. The monopolistically competitive firm's *MR* curve lies beneath its demand curve (you find it exactly the same way you found the *MR* curve for the monopoly). This firm will earn positive economic profits if price is greater than average total cost, and negative economic profits if price is less than average total cost. The monopolistically competitive firm acts exactly like a monopoly in the short run. Figure 34.1 illustrates a monopolistically competitive firm in the short run earning positive economic profits, while Figure 34.2 illustrates a monopolistically competitive firm in the short run earning negative economic profits.

Figure 34.1

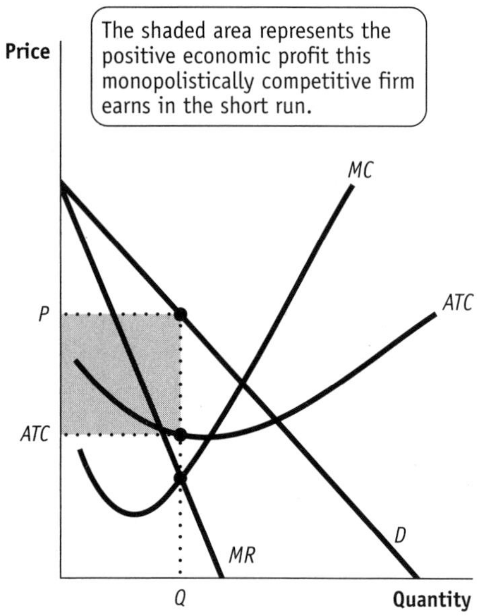

Figure 34.2

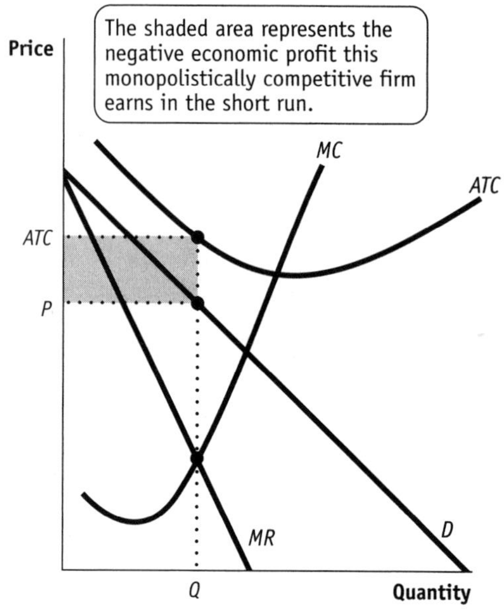

Objective #3. In the long run, the monopolistically competitive firm earns zero economic profit due to the entry or exit of firms.

- If the monopolistically competitive firm earns positive economic profit in the short run, this acts as a signal for other firms to enter the industry. The entry of firms into the industry causes the demand curve for each existing firm to shift to the left so that at every price fewer units of their product are demanded. This process continues until there has been enough entry so that each firm's price equals average total cost. Figure 34.3 illustrates both the short-run and the long-run equilibrium for a monopolistically competitive firm with positive economic profits in the short run. Notice that this firm produces a smaller level of output and sells its good at a lower price in the long run than it did in the short run.

Figure 34.3

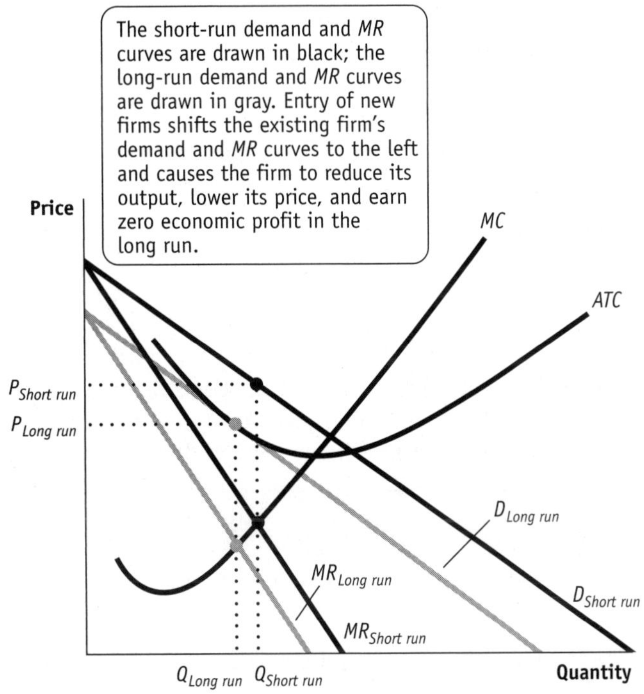

- If the monopolistically competitive firm earns negative economic profit in the short run, this acts as a signal for some of the firms in the industry to exit in the long run. This exit of firms from the industry causes the demand curve for each remaining firm to shift to the right so that at every price more units of their product are demanded. This process continues until there has been enough exiting so that each remaining firm's price equals its average total cost. Figure 34.4 illustrates both the short-run and the long-run equilibrium for a monopolistically competitive firm with negative economic profits in the short run. Notice that this firm produces a higher level of output and sells this output at a higher price in the long run than it did in the short run.

Figure 34.4

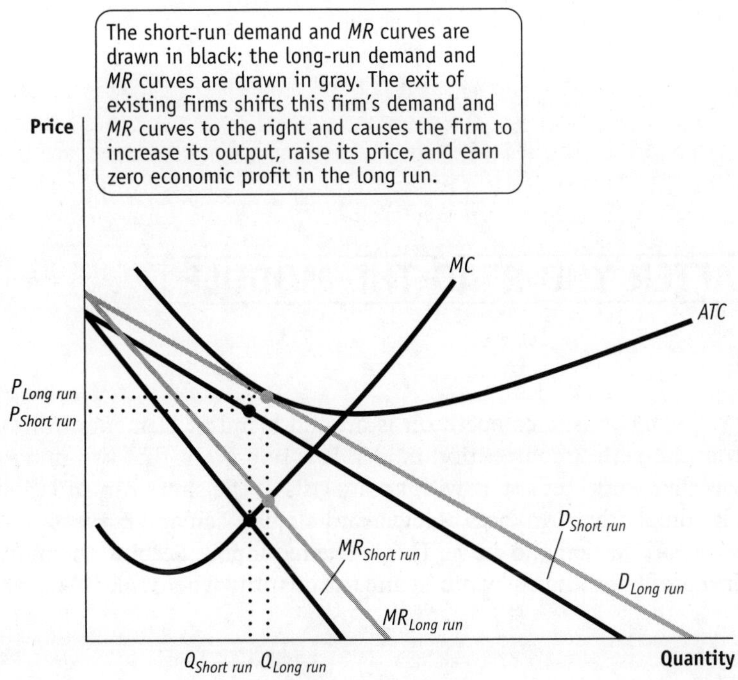

Objective #4. In the long run, each firm in a monopolistically competitive industry acts like a monopolist in setting marginal revenue equal to marginal cost and producing the quantity of output so as to maximize profits. However, in the long run the producers earn zero economic profits, unlike the long-run result for monopoly.

Objective #5. The long-run equilibrium in monopolistic competition also resembles the perfect competition result, since firms earn zero economic profit and their price equals average total cost. But there is a critical difference between long-run equilibrium in perfect competition and long-run equilibrium in a monopolistically competitive industry: in perfect competition, price is equal to the minimum of average total cost, while in monopolistic competition, price is equal to average total cost but not at the minimum-cost point of the average total cost (*ATC*) curve. The monopolistically competitive firm has excess capacity in the long run even though it earns zero economic profit; this excess capacity is another way of saying that the monopolistically competitive firm is not producing at minimum cost. This excess capacity of the monopolistically competitive firm arises from the cost of providing variety in the industry: the excess capacity is a sign of wasteful duplication that could be eliminated if there were fewer firms in the industry offering less-differentiated products. Yet consumers enjoy this diversity of products and it is valuable to them.

Objective #6. In the long run, the perfectly competitive firm produces at a level where price equals marginal cost, while the monopolistically competitive firm produces at a level where price is greater than marginal cost. The monopolistically competitive firm in the long run is interested in selling more units of the good, since price is greater than marginal cost for the last unit produced. This helps us understand why monopolistically competitive firms advertise their products.

Key Terms

zero-profit equilibrium an economic balance in which each firm makes zero profit at its profit-maximizing quantity.

excess capacity when firms produce less than the output at which *average total cost* is minimized; characteristic of *monopolistically competitive* firms.

Notes

AFTER YOU READ THE MODULE

Tips

Tip #1. Monopolistic competition is an odd blend of elements from the monopoly model and from the perfect competition model. It is important that you understand these elements and how they work. Let's start with an analysis of the short-run situation. First, the monopolistically competitive firm faces a downward-sloping demand curve and, therefore, a *MR* curve that is beneath its demand curve. This is like monopoly. Second, the monopolistically competitive firm profit-maximizes by producing the quantity where $MR = MC$. This is like both perfect competition and monopoly. Third, the price the monopolistically competitive firm charges for its good is found by taking the profit-maximizing quantity and looking at the demand curve for the price associated with that quantity. This is exactly what a monopoly does. In the short run, the monopolistically competitive firm exactly mimics the behavior of a monopoly. So, just remember your work with monopoly and apply those same rules. In the short run, the monopolistically competitive firm can earn positive, negative, or zero economic profit.

Tip #2. In the long run, the monopolistically competitive firm is subject to entry of new firms into the industry and the exit of existing firms from the industry. This is a characteristic that makes the monopolistically competitive industry resemble perfect competition. But there's an important distinction: even though economic profit equals zero in the long run for both market structures, the monopolistically competitive firm faces a downward-sloping demand curve, which means that price and marginal revenue are not the same for this firm. It implies that even when the monopolistically competitive firm earns zero economic profit in the long run, it charges a price that is greater than its marginal cost. This is different from the result found in perfect competition. Also, in perfect competition in the long run, price = MR = MC = minimum ATC. In monopolistic competition in the long run, MR = MC and price = ATC, but price is not equal to marginal cost and price is not equal to the minimum average total cost.

Review these two tips thoroughly until you have mastered them and understand the implications of the points made in each tip.

WORKED PROBLEMS

1. In the small town of Urbana, there are 10 fast-food restaurants: Jolly Bob's Jerk Chicken, Famous Dan's BBQ, Smokey Jack's Burgers, Tijuana Fats Tacos, Quik Stop Burgers, The True Dog, Noodles and More, Dumplings Galore, Veggie Burger Hut, and Snack Shack. These 10 restaurants are located throughout the community. Currently, all of the restaurants are earning sufficient revenues to cover their variable costs of operation, but they are not covering their fixed costs of operation. You have been asked to describe the market for fast food in Urbana and to describe the degree of differentiation in this market. You have also been asked to comment on what you think will happen in the long run in this market. In particular, what do you anticipate will happen in the long run to the number of firms in the market, and the level of profits for firms in the fast-food market in Urbana.

STEP 1: Describe the market for fast food in Urbana as well as the degree of product differentiation in this market.

Urbana has many fast-food restaurants for the size of its community, and these fast-food restaurants are differentiated by their location and by the type of food they serve. Although we do not have any information about the relative quality of these 10 restaurants, it is certainly possible that the fast-food industry in Urbana is also differentiated by quality.

STEP 2: Describe the short-run profit situation for firms in the fast-food industry in Urbana.

From the given information, we know that the 10 fast-food restaurants are currently earning sufficient revenue to cover their variable costs of production: this implies that all 10 restaurants are willing to produce in the short run, since their revenues are sufficient to cover the variable costs of production. However, we also know that each restaurant's revenues are not sufficient to cover the variable costs and the fixed costs: this tells us that each restaurant is earning negative economic profits in the short run.

STEP 3: Describe the long-run adjustment mechanism for this industry given its short-run profit situation.

As the industry moves from the short run to the long run, some of the restaurants will decide to exit the industry, since they are not earning sufficient revenues to cover all of their costs of production. As firms exit the industry, the remaining firms will experience this exiting of firms as a rightward shift in their own demand curves. As the remaining firms' demand curves shift to the right, this shift will cause each firm that remains in the industry to eventually produce at a price and quantity level that will result in the firm earning zero economic profit.

STEP 4: Describe what will happen to the profits of fast-food restaurants in Urbana in the long run.

As the remaining firms in the industry adjust to the rightward shift of their demand curve, they will find that they are earning just enough revenue to offset their total costs: in the long run, the firms remaining in the fast-food industry in Urbana should expect to see their economic profits equal to zero.

2. Beauty Concepts, a beauty salon in a large midwestern city, has come to you for advice. Beauty Concepts knows that the demand for its product is given by the equation $Q_D = 100 - P$ and that its total cost (TC) of production is described by the equation $TC = 10 + 4Q + 2Q^2$. Beauty Concepts also knows that its marginal cost of production is $MC = 4 + 4Q$. Beauty Concepts is one of many beauty salons in this city, and each of these salons is differentiated by location, style, and quality. Beauty Concepts would like you to advise it as to what price and quantity it should charge in the short run, what level of profits you anticipate it will make in the short run, and then, finally, what the long-run outcome for this firm is likely to be. The owners of Beauty Concept are visually oriented people and would find it helpful if you could provide a graph to illustrate their short-run situation.

STEP 1: Calculate the short-run profit maximizing price and quantity for Beauty Concepts. Remember that you will need to find the firm's marginal revenue to find the firm's profit-maximizing quantity.

To find the profit-maximizing quantity, you will want to first find the firm's marginal revenue curve. To do this, start by rewriting the demand curve in slope intercept form: $P = 100 - Q_D$. The marginal revenue curve for a firm with a downward-sloping linear demand curve will have the same y-intercept and twice the slope of this demand curve. Thus, $MR = 100 - 2Q$. To find the profit-maximizing level of output, equate the firm's MR curve to its MC curve: $100 - 2Q = 4 + 4Q$, or Q (the profit-maximizing quantity) equals 16 units. To find the price that the firm should charge for this level of output, put this quantity into the firm's demand curve: $P = 100 - 16$, or P is equal to \$84 per unit of output. Beauty Concepts should produce 16 units of output and sell each unit for a price of \$84.

STEP 2: Draw a graph that represents the short-run situation for Beauty Concepts. When you draw your graph remember that you will need to depict the marginal revenue curve for Beauty Concepts. This graph can just be a sketch and does not need to be drawn to scale.

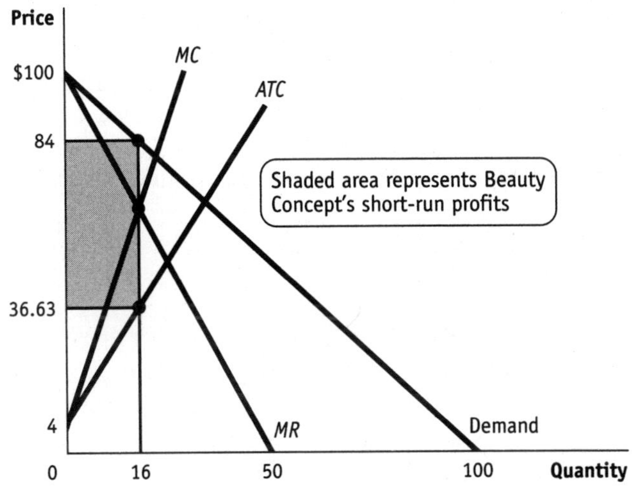

In sketching the graph for Beauty Concepts, it should be a relatively easy matter to draw in the demand curve and, if you remember that the marginal revenue curve for a downward-sloping demand curve has the same *y*-intercept as the demand curve and twice the slope of the demand curve, the marginal revenue curve should not be hard to draw. More challenging in this example is the marginal cost curve and the average total cost curve. The marginal cost curve is a linear relationship with *y*-intercept of 4 and slope of 4. The average total cost curve in the preceding graph has been sketched in: the average total cost curve is not linear, but for the sake of directing the work we need to do the preceding line will be sufficient. From both Step 1 and the graph, we see that $MR = MC$ when output is 16 units. When output is 16 units, people are willing to pay $84 per unit of the good. The only thing we need to calculate that we do not already know is the value of average total cost when the firm produces 16 units. But, we have the equation for *ATC* and can simply plug our value of Q = 16 into that equation. Thus, $ATC = (10/16) + 4 + 2(16) = \$36.63$. I have marked this *ATC* on the graph. From the graph and our calculations, we know that the price per unit is $84 while the cost per unit is $36.63; this implies that the firm is making positive profits in the short run.

STEP 3: Calculate the short-run profits for Beauty Concepts.

From Steps 1 and 2 we know that the price per unit is $84, the number of units produced is 16 units, and the *ATC* of producing 16 units is $36.63 per unit. We can use this information to calculate the short-run profits for the firm. Recall that profit equals total revenue (*TR*) minus total cost (*TC*). *TR* is equal to price times quantity or, in this case ($84 per unit)(16 units), or $1,344. *TC* is equal to average cost per unit times quantity or, in this case ($36.625 per unit)(16 units) = $586. Short-run profit for the firm is equal to $1,344 – $586, or $758.

STEP 4: Describe what the long-run situation is likely to be for Beauty Concepts.

In the long run, we can expect entry of firms into the industry until all firms in the industry earn zero economic profit. As new firms enter the industry, Beauty Concepts's demand curve will shift in toward the origin until eventually the profit-maximizing quantity will be that quantity at which the price per unit is equal to the average cost per unit, and economic profits are therefore equal to zero.

3. Suppose you are given the following graph of the demand curve and cost curves for Imperial China, a restaurant featuring Chinese food located in a large city. Imperial China is one of many restaurants in this city. You are asked to use this graph to help Imperial China decide on the optimal short-run course of action. Imperial China's owners are interested in what their short-run quantity of production should be, as well as what their short-run profits will be. They also want advice as to whether they should produce in the short run. Use the provided graph to illustrate the firm's short-run price, quantity, and profits. Finally, the owners want your predictions about the likely outcome for the restaurant in the long run.

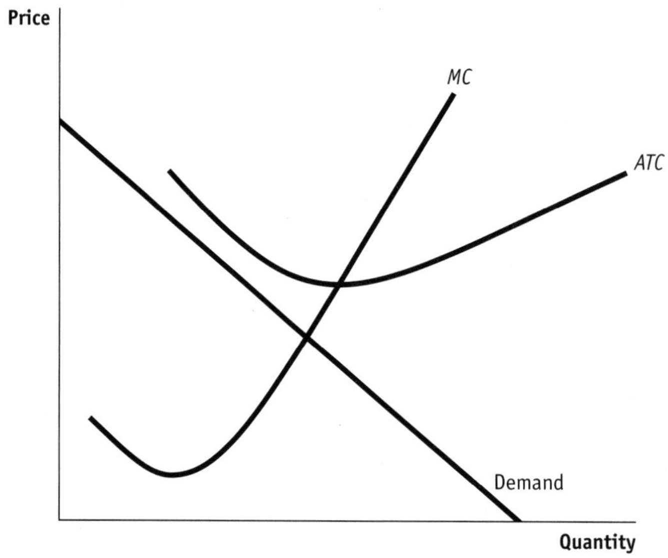

STEP 1: Calculate the profit-maximizing price and quantity for Imperial China in the short run. Indicate this price and quantity on the graph provided for you.

To identify the profit-maximizing level of output, you will first need to find the firm's marginal revenue (*MR*) curve. Remember that this curve will share the *y*-intercept of the demand curve and bisect the distance between the origin and the *x*-intercept of the demand curve if the demand curve is linear. Once you have drawn the *MR* curve, it is a simple matter to find where *MR* = *MC*: the firm should produce the quantity associated with this point. The firm will charge the price on the demand curve associated with this quantity. The following graph illustrates the firm's *MR*, and the profit-maximizing quantity and price.

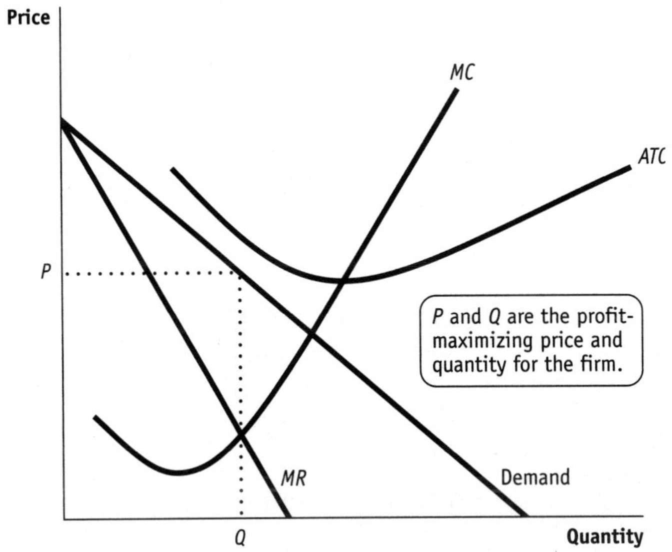

STEP 2: Calculate the firm's short-run profits and indicate these profits on the graph provided for you.

To find the firm's profit, we will need to calculate the firm's *TR* and the firm's *TC*. *TR* is equal to *P* × Q, while *TC* is equal to *ATC* × Q. Remember that *ATC* can be found by going up from the quantity being produced to the firm's average total cost curve, and then reading the *ATC* value off the *y*-axis. Short-run profit for this firm is negative, since the price per unit the good sells for is less than the cost per unit of producing the good. The negative economic profit is shaded in the graph that follows.

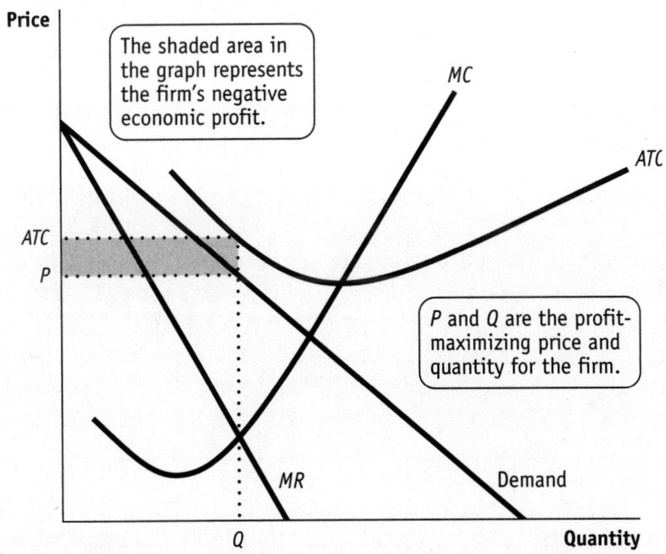

STEP 3: Advise Imperial China's owners as to their best short-run course of action.

In the short run, Imperial China will want to produce since its revenue is sufficient to cover all of its variable cost of production and some of its fixed cost of production. If Imperial China shuts down, in the short run it will have a profit equal to its negative fixed cost, and it will therefore be losing more money than if the restaurant produces Q units of output.

STEP 4: Advise Imperial China's owners as to the likely long-run outcome for their restaurant.

In the long run, restaurants will exit the industry and the remaining restaurants will see their demand curves shift to the right until economic profit is equal to zero for the restaurants remaining in the industry. Imperial China will want to exit the industry in the long run unless enough other restaurants have exited the industry by that time to have restored Imperial China's profit level to zero.

Problems and Exercises

1. Suppose the existing firms in the fast-food restaurant business are currently earning positive economic profit in the short run.

a. Draw a graph representing a monopolistically competitive firm in this situation. Identify the price of the good and the output the firm produces in the short run and the area that represents this firm's profit.

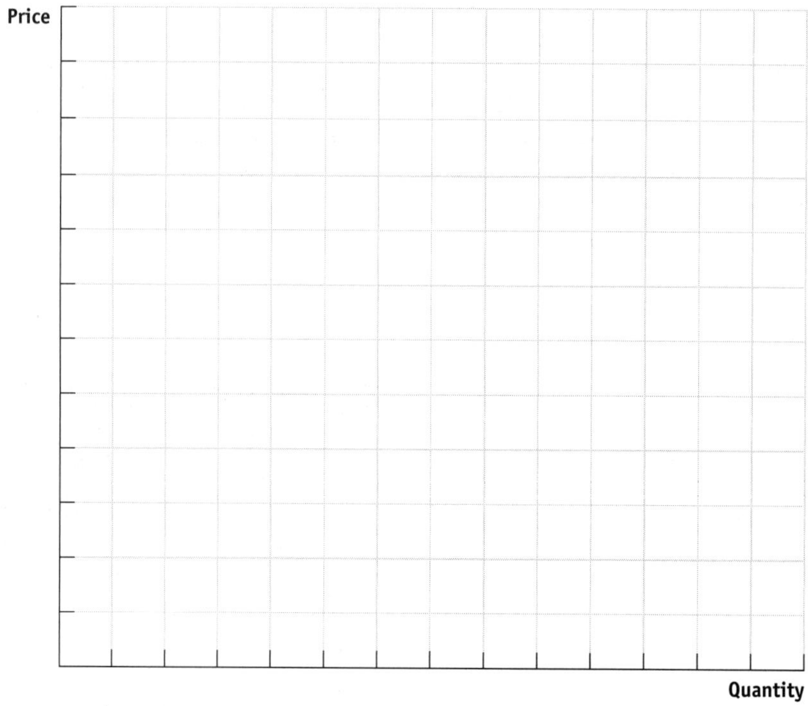

b. What do you anticipate will happen in the long run in this industry? How will the industry price and quantity change in the long run? How will each firm's profit change in the long run?

c. Draw a graph representing a monopolistically competitive firm in long-run equilibrium. Identify the price of the good and the quantity the firm sells in the long run. What is the relationship between price and marginal cost for this firm in the long run? What is the relationship between price and average total cost for this firm in the long run?

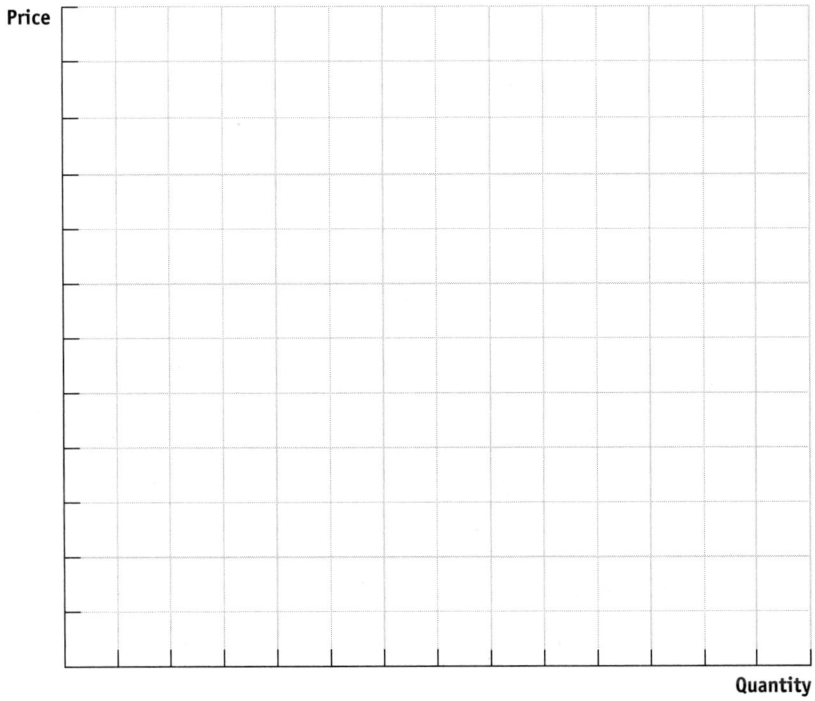

2. Suppose the existing firms in the fast-food restaurant business are currently earning negative economic profit in the short run.

   a. Draw a graph representing a monopolistically competitive firm in this situation. Identify the price of the good and the output the firm produces in the short run and the area that represents this firm's profit.

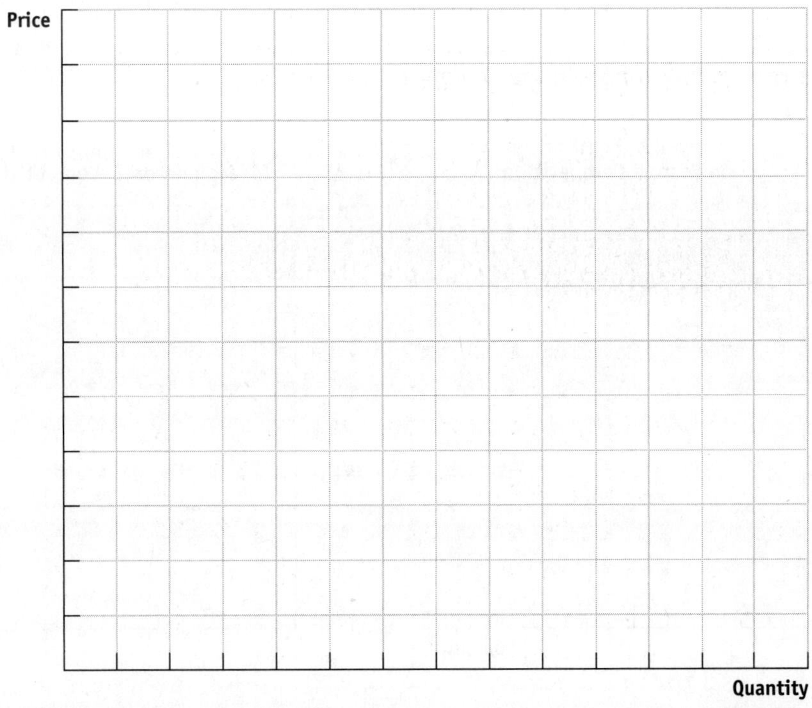

   b. What do you anticipate will happen in the long run in this industry? How will the industry price and quantity change in the long run? How will each firm's profit change in the long run?

c. Draw a graph representing a monopolistically competitive firm in long-run equilibrium. Identify the price of the good and the quantity the firm sells in the long run. What is the relationship between price and marginal cost for this firm in the long run? What is the relationship between price and average total cost for this firm in the long run?

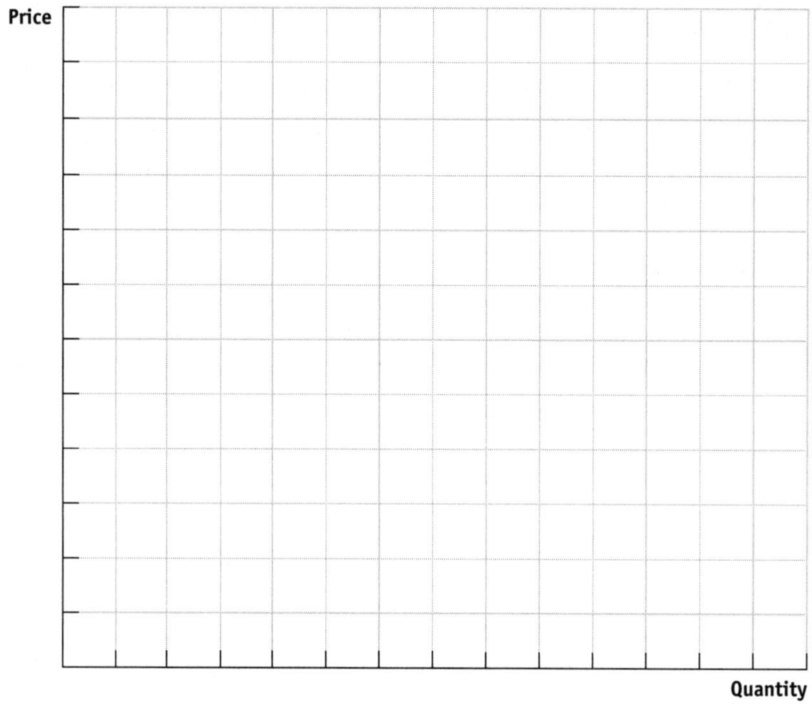

3. **a.** Compare the long-run equilibrium for a monopolistically competitive firm with the long-run equilibrium for a perfectly competitive firm. How are these two equilibriums similar? How are these two equilibriums different? Draw two sketches depicting the long-run equilibrium for these two market structures.

Long-Run Equilibrium in Perfect Competition

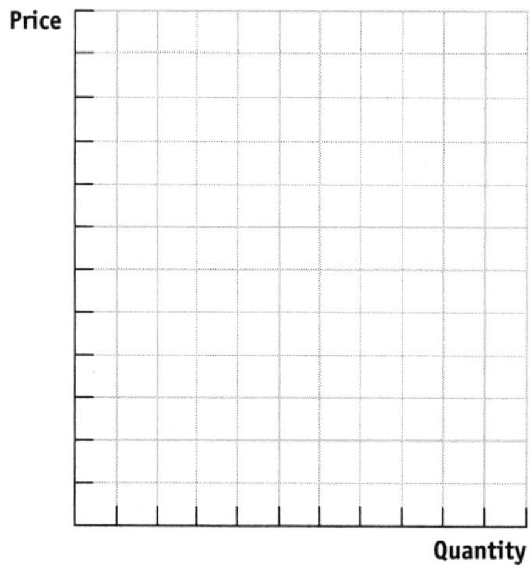

Long-Run Equilibrium in Monopolistic Competition

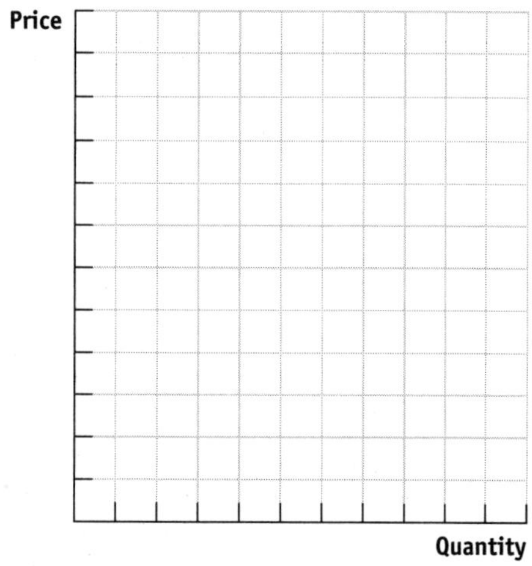

b. Compare the long-run equilibrium for a monopolistically competitive firm with the long-run equilibrium for a monopoly. How are these two equilibriums similar? How are these two equilibriums different? Draw two sketches depicting the long-run equilibrium for these two market structures.

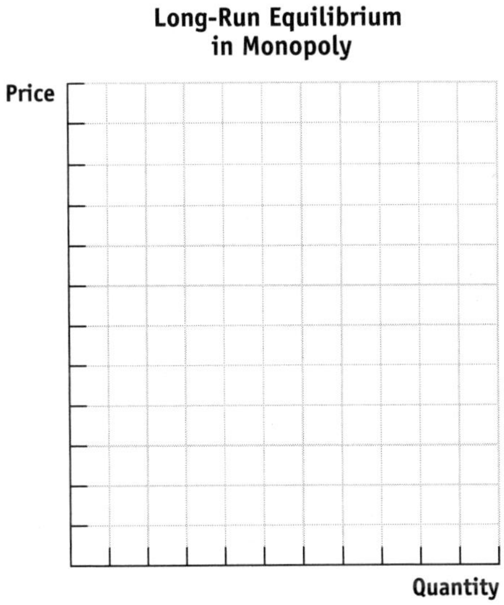

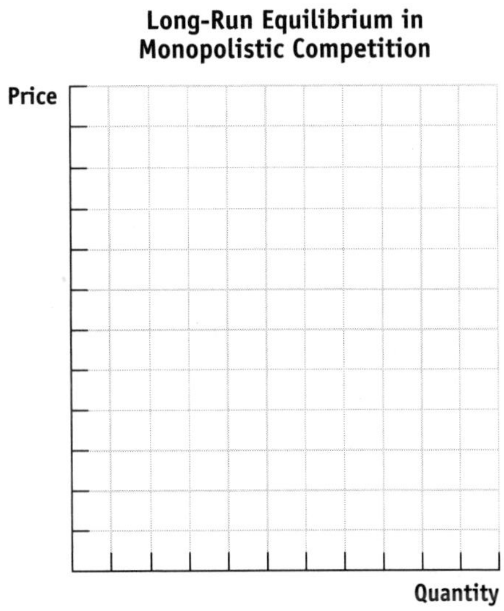

4. Suppose the demand curve for a monopolistically competitive firm is given by the equation $Q = 100 - 2P$. Furthermore, suppose this firm's marginal cost can be expressed by the equation $MC = 2Q + 2$, while the firm's total cost (TC) is $TC = 100 + Q^2 + 2Q$.

a. In the short run, what level of output will this firm produce? (Hint: remember, you must first find the firm's *MR* curve before you can identify the profit-maximizing level of output.)

b. In the short run, what price will the firm charge for its product?

c. In the short run, what will this firm's profit equal?

d. Describe what will happen in the long run to this monopolistically competitive firm.

5. Use the graph below of a monopolistically competitive firm to answer the next set of questions.

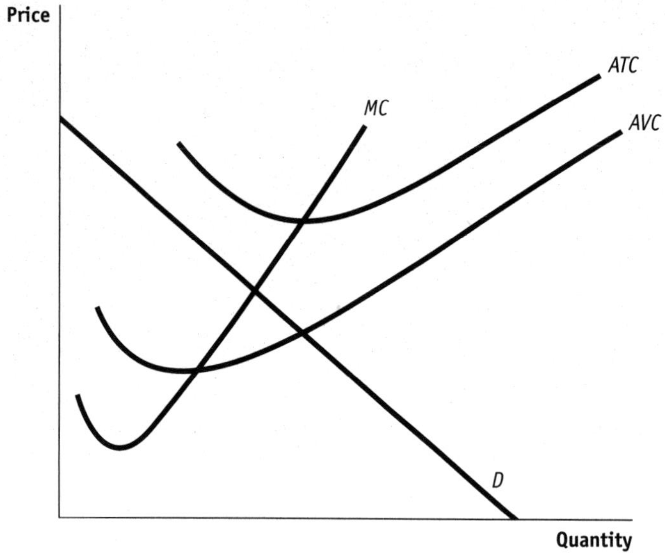

a. Label the profit-maximizing level of output and price for this firm in the short run.

b. Identify any profits the firm is making in the short run and decide whether these profits are positive or negative.

c. Draw the long-run equilibrium situation on this graph. Identify the long-run profit-maximizing quantity and the long-run price. What will this firm's profits equal in the long run?

d. Did entry or exiting of firms occur in the long run in this problem? Explain your answer.

6. What does it mean to say that a monopolistically competitive firm in the long run produces at a quantity where the firm has excess capacity? Is this a good or a bad outcome?

BEFORE YOU TAKE THE TEST

Module Review Questions

1. Monopolistic competition is a market structure

a. that makes a trade-off between lower prices and greater product diversity.

b. in which each firm produces the quantity where $MC = MR$.

c. in which firms earn zero economic profit in the long run.

d. Answers (a), (b), and (c) are all true.

2. Which of the following statements is true for a monopolistically competitive firm?

I. In the short run, the firm earns a positive economic profit whenever price is greater than average total cost.

II. In the short run, the firm produces at the minimum-cost level of production where $MR = MC$.

III. Monopolistically competitive firms engage in collusion so that they can set price at a level that is greater than marginal cost.

a. Statement I is true.

b. Statements I and II are true.

c. Statements I and III are true.

d. Statements I, II, and III are true.

3. Monopolistically competitive firms resemble perfectly competitive firms because

a. in the long run they earn zero economic profit.

b. in the long run they produce at the minimum-cost point of their *ATC* curves.

c. they compete with other firms that offer similar products.

d. Answers (a), (b), and (c) are all true.

4. Monopolistically competitive firms resemble monopolies because

a. their *MR* curves lie beneath their demand curves.

b. they charge a price that is greater than their marginal cost of production.

c. entry and exit of firms in the long run ensure that profits are equal to zero in the long run.

d. Answers (a), (b), and (c) are all true.

e. Answers (a) and (b) are true.

5. Monopolistically competitive firms

a. have no limit as to what price they can charge for the good they produce, since this good is highly differentiated from any other firm's product.

b. charge the highest price people are willing to pay for the good based on the demand curve for the good.

c. are price takers and must accept the market price that is determined in the industry.

d. do not worry about what price to charge and instead focus the bulk of their attention on deciding what the profit-maximizing level of output is for the firm.

Use the following information to answer the next five questions. A monopolistically competitive firm's demand for its product is equal to $Q = 100 - P$, and its marginal cost of production is equal to $MC = 20 + 2Q$. The firm's total cost is equal to $TC = Q^2 + 20Q + 10$.

6. What is this monopolistically competitive firm's fixed cost?

a. Fixed cost cannot be calculated from the above information.

b. $Q^2 + 20Q$

c. 10

d. The monopolistically competitive firm need not consider the distinction between fixed cost and variable cost.

7. What is the profit-maximizing level of output in the short run?

a. 100 units

b. 80 units

c. 50 units

d. 20 units

8. What is the profit-maximizing price for this firm in the short run?

a. \$100

b. \$80

c. \$60

d. \$20

9. In the short run, this firm earns

a. positive economic profits.

b. negative economic profits.

c. zero economic profits.

10. In the long run, this firm's demand curve will shift to the

a. right because of entry of new firms into the industry.

b. left because of the entry of new firms into the industry.

Use the following diagram of a monopolistically competitive firm to answer the next four questions.

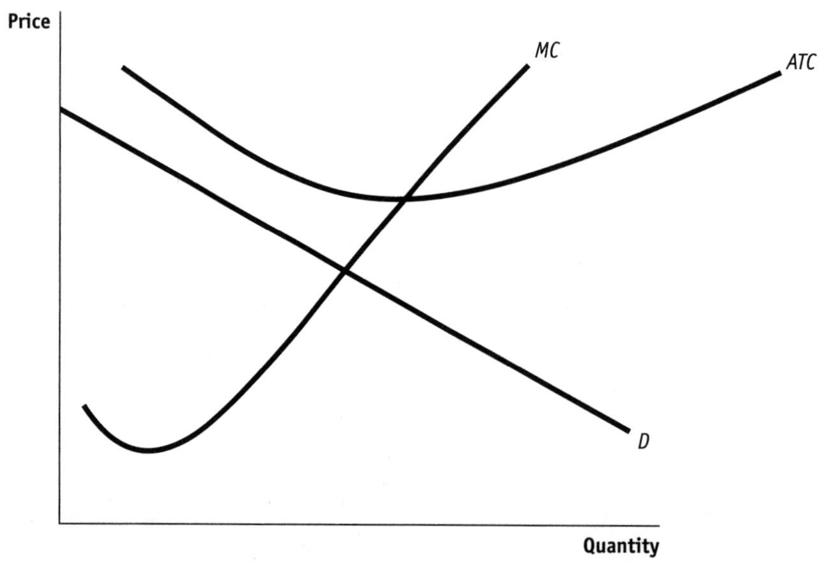

11. To identify the profit-maximizing output for this firm in the short run, this graph needs
a. the market price identified.
b. the *MR* curve identified.
c. the *AVC* curve identified.
d. All of the answers are true.
e. Answers (b) and (c) are true.

12. Assuming this firm produces in the short run, this firm will earn
a. negative economic profit, since its price is less than its average total cost.
b. positive economic profit, since its price is greater than its marginal cost.
c. zero economic profit, since entry of new firms will drive the profits of all firms down to that level where each firm earns zero economic profit.
d. zero economic profit, since the exit of firms will cause profits of all existing firms to increase until all the firms left in the industry earn zero economic profit.

13. Assuming this firm produces in the short run, this firm will
a. find that it is interested in selling more units of the good, since *MR* = *MC* at its selected level of production.
b. find advertising worthwhile if it increases sales, since it is producing at a quantity where price is less than marginal cost.
c. be enthusiastic about increasing its sales, since it currently is producing a quantity where marginal cost is less than price.
d. be reluctant to advertise, since this will only increase the costs that the firm has to pay.

14. Relative to a perfectly competitive firm, a monopolistically competitive firm produces
a. its product at a higher price.
b. where its average total cost is increasing as output increases.
c. at a point where the firm has excess capacity.
d. Answers (a), (b), and (c) are all true.
e. Answers (a) and (c) are true.

ANSWER KEY

Answers to Problems and Exercises

1. a.

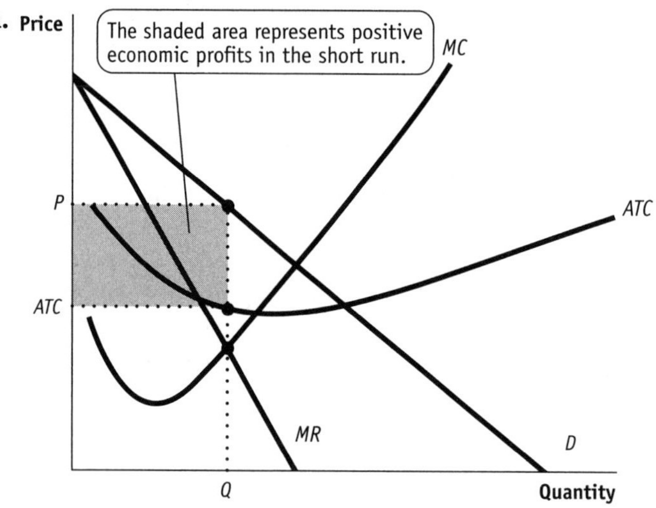

b. In the long run, new firms will enter this industry because the short-run positive economic profits act as a signal for firms to enter the industry. As firms enter the industry, each existing firm in the industry will see the demand for its product shift to the left as some of its customers stop demanding its product and start demanding the new firm's product. As the demand curve shifts to the left, this will also cause the *MR* curve to shift to the left. This process will continue until the firm earns zero economic profit in the long run. The firm will sell its product at a lower price and produce a smaller quantity of the good because of the entry of the new firms into the industry.

c. In the long run, the monopolistically competitive firm will continue to charge a price that is greater than its marginal cost. In the long run, the price of the product will equal the average total cost of producing the product, but the price will not equal the minimum point of the *ATC* curve. These two results indicate that the firm will continue to be interested in selling more units of the good, since price is greater than marginal cost for the last unit produced (hence, advertising will pay off if it increases the demand for the firm's product), and that the firm has excess capacity since it is not producing at the minimum point of its *ATC* curve. The figure below illustrates the long-run equilibrium for a monopolistically competitive firm.

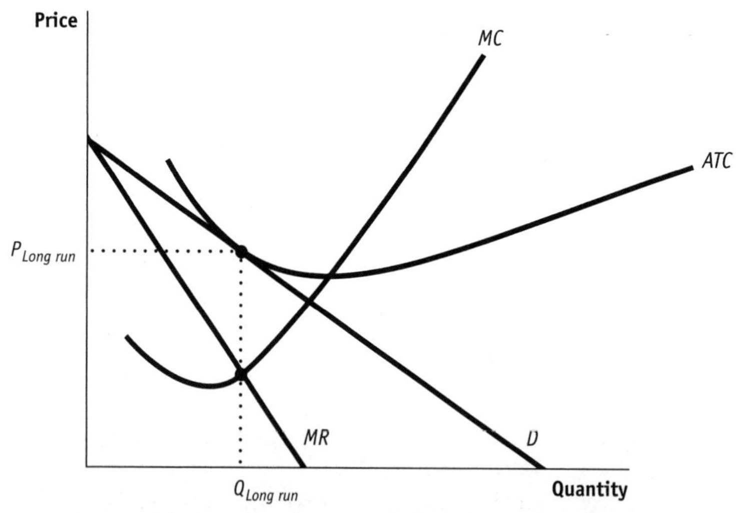

2. a.

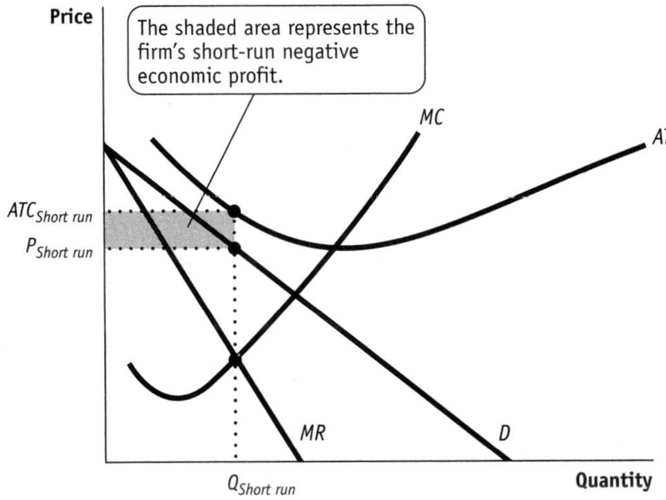

b. In the long run, some existing firms will exit this industry because the short-run negative economic profits act as a signal for firms to exit the industry. As firms exit the industry, each remaining firm in the industry will see the demand for its product shift to the right as some of the customers from exiting firms begin demanding its product and stop demanding the exiting firm's product. As the demand curve shifts to the right, this will also cause the *MR* curve to shift to the right. This process will continue until the firm earns zero economic profit in the long run. The firm will sell its product at a higher price and produce a larger quantity of the good because of the exit of existing firms from the industry.

c. In the long run, the monopolistically competitive firm will continue to charge a price that is greater than its marginal cost. In the long run, the price of the product will equal the average total cost of producing the product, but the price will not equal the minimum point of the *ATC* curve. These two results indicate that the firm will continue to be interested in selling more units of the good, since price is greater than marginal cost for the last unit produced (hence, advertising will pay off if it increases the demand for the firm's product), and that the firm has excess capacity since it is not producing at the minimum point of its *ATC* curve. The figure below illustrates the long-run equilibrium for a monopolistically competitive firm.

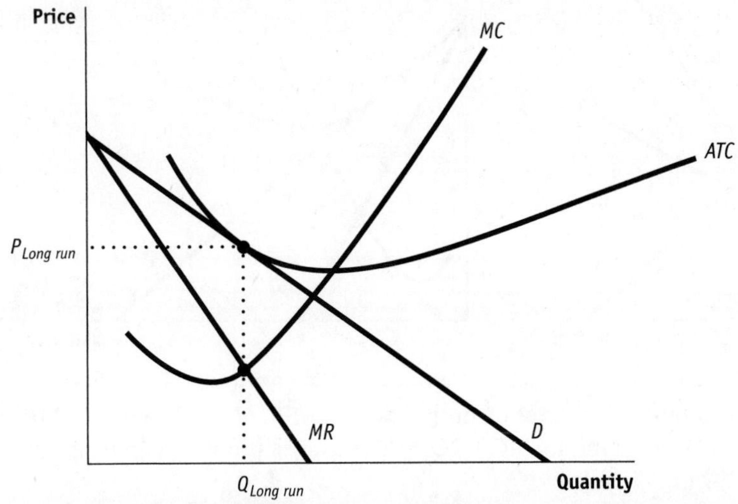

3. a. In the long run, both market structures produce the profit-maximizing level of output where $MR = MC$, and both market structures earn zero economic profit in the long run. However, the monopolistically competitive firm in the long run does not produce at the level where price is equal to marginal cost, while the perfectly competitive firm does. In addition, the perfectly competitive firm produces the long-run level of output at the minimum-cost point on its *ATC* curve, while the monopolistically competitive firm produces in the decreasing cost portion of its *ATC* curve. The monopolistically competitive firm has excess capacity in the long run since it does not produce at the minimum-cost point of its *ATC* curve. The two sketches below illustrate the long-run situation for the two types of market structures.

Long-Run Equilibrium in Perfect Competition **Long-Run Equilibrium in Monopolistic Competition**

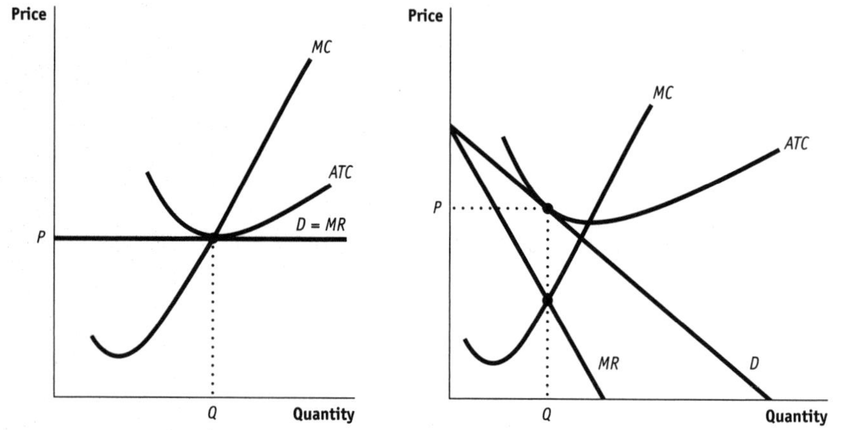

b. In the long run, the monopolistically competitive firm and the monopoly are remarkably similar except for one very important difference. In the long run, entry and exit of firms ensures that the monopolistically competitive firm earns zero economic profit, while the monopoly, protected from competition by barriers to entry, is able to continue to maintain its positive profits into the long run. The two graphs below illustrate the long-run situation in the two market structures.

Long-Run Equilibrium in Monopoly **Long-Run Equilibrium in Monopolistic Competition**

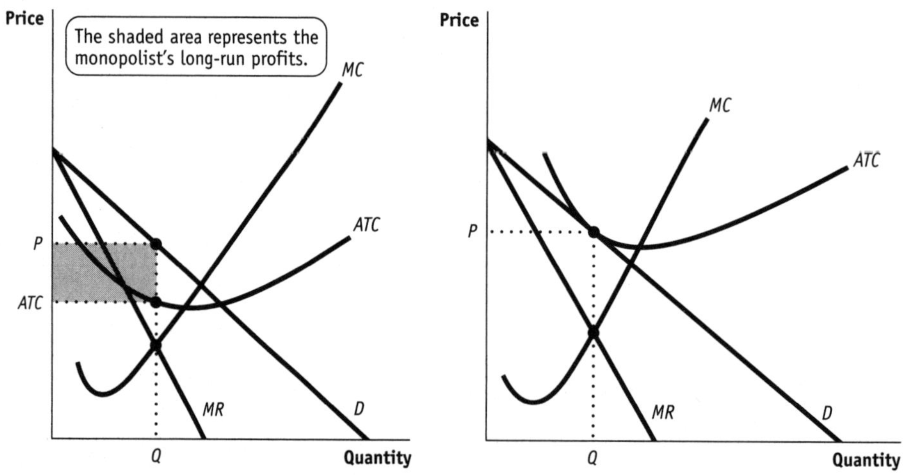

4. **a.** The firm will produce the level of output where $MR = MC$. The firm's MR curve is given by $MR = 50 - Q$, and its $MC = 2Q + 2$. Thus, the profit-maximizing level of output for this firm is 16 units.

b. The firm sets its price by taking its profit-maximizing level of output and plugging this value into its demand curve. When $Q = 16$, price is equal to \$42.

c. The firm earns total revenue of \$672 and its total cost equals \$388, so the firm's short-run economic profits are equal to \$284.

d. In the short run, this firm earns positive economic profit, which acts as a signal for other firms to enter this industry in the long run. Entry will continue until each existing firm's demand curve shifts to the left far enough to result in each firm earning zero economic profit at the profit-maximizing level of output.

5. a–c.

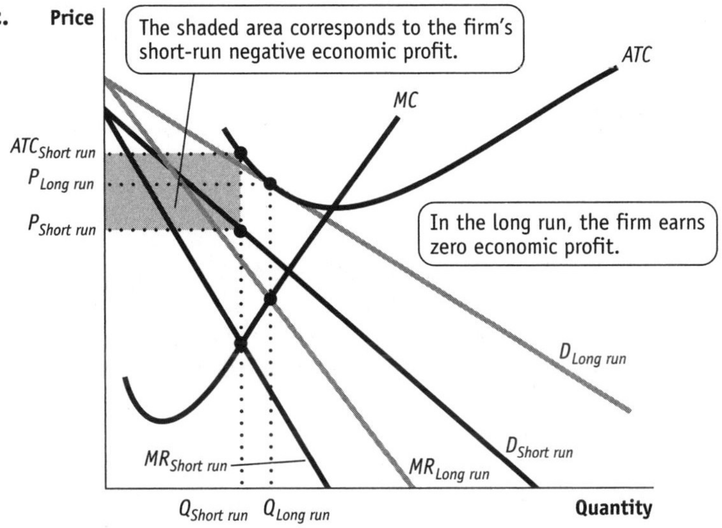

The firm earns negative economic profit in the short run since price is less than average total cost at the short-run profit-maximizing quantity.

In the long run, this firm earns zero economic profit since price is equal to *ATC* at the long-run profit-maximizing quantity.

d. Exiting of firms occurred in the long run because there were too many firms initially serving this monopolistically competitive industry. Firms exited because they were earning negative economic profits; exiting continued until the remaining firms were able to break even.

6. When a firm produces at a quantity at which the firm has excess capacity, this indicates that at the current level of production the *ATC* curve is decreasing as output increases. This implies that the firm could produce a higher level of output at lower unit cost. This indicates that the firm is not fully utilizing its productive capacity, and carries with it an implication of waste. But the monopolistically competitive firm produces at excess capacity because of the product differentiation that occurs in the industry and, even though this leaves each firm with excess capacity, it also leaves consumers with greater choice and greater variety, which are highly valued by the consumer. Consumers are willing to pay a higher price for the product in order to have this variety.

ANSWER KEY

Answers to Module Review Questions

1. **Answer d.** Monopolistic competition results in higher prices for the goods that are produced, but there is more variety in the produced goods than you would see in a perfectly competitive market. Thus, monopolistic competition is a market structure that trades off lower prices for greater product diversity. Monopolistically competitive firms profit-maximize by producing the quantity where $MC = MR$. In the long run, there is entry and exit of firms in a monopolistically competitive industry, which ensures that economic profits equal zero in the long run.

2. **Answer a.** Whenever a firm produces at an output level where price is greater than average total cost, the firm earns a positive profit (statement I). In a monopolistically competitive industry, the firm does not produce at the minimum-cost level of production in

the short run or the long run: firms produce the quantity where $MR = MC$ in order to maximize profit, and then determine their level of profit by comparing price to average total cost (statement II). Collusion does not occur in a monopolistically competitive market due to the number of firms and the fact that there is free entry into the industry (statement III).

3. **Answer a.** Monopolistically competitive firms do not produce at the minimum-cost point on the *ATC* curves in the short run or the long run. Instead these firms produce in the decreasing-cost portion of their *ATC* curve: this implies that each firm has excess capacity. Although monopolistically competitive firms compete with other firms, this is different from the competition that perfectly competitive firms engage in: the monopolistically competitive firms differentiate their product, and each firm has some market power. In perfect competition, firms sell identical products and no firm has market power.

4. **Answer e.** The monopolistically competitive firm faces a downward-sloping demand curve for its product because the product is differentiated from the products produced by competing firms. This implies that the *MR* curve for the monopolistically competitive firm lies beneath the demand curve. Like a monopolist, the monopolistically competitive firm produces the level of output where $MR = MC$ and then prices this output by going to the demand curve, which results in price being greater than marginal cost. There is no entry and exit of firms in a monopoly in the long run: this is the biggest difference between a monopolistically competitive firm and a monopoly in the long run.

5. **Answer b.** Monopolistically competitive firms first select their profit-maximizing level of output by equating marginal revenue with marginal cost, and then they go to the demand curve to see what price people are willing to pay given this level of output. The firms cannot charge more than the price on the demand curve associated with their level of production because people are not willing to pay more than the price on the demand curve. Monopolistically competitive firms are not price takers because they have some market power. Monopolistically competitive firms act to maximize profits by producing the right quantity and charging the right price.

6. **Answer c.** Fixed cost (*FC*) is the cost the firm incurs when output is equal to zero units. If $Q = 0$ in the above total cost equation, then $TC = FC = 10$. Answer (d) is incorrect since the monopolistically competitive firm, just like the perfectly competitive firm or the monopoly, is unwilling to produce when its total revenue does not cover its variable cost of production.

7. **Answer d.** To find the profit-maximizing level of output in the short run, you need to equate marginal revenue with marginal cost. Marginal revenue for this firm is $MR = 100 - 2Q$, so equating marginal revenue with marginal cost yields $Q = 20$ units.

8. **Answer b.** The profit-maximizing price is found by substituting the profit-maximizing quantity, 20 units, into the demand equation, $P = 100 - Q$. When $Q = 20$ units, then $P = \$80$.

9. **Answer a.** In the short run, this firm produces 20 units and then sells these units at a price of \$80. The firm's total revenue equals \$1,600 and its total cost equals \$810. The firm earns a positive profit of \$790.

10. **Answer b.** Since the firm is earning positive economic profits in the short run, this will lead to the entry of new firms in the long run. As new firms enter the industry, this firm's demand curve will shift to the left because some of this firm's customers will decide to buy a competitor's product: this firm will find that at every price, it sells less of its good than it did before the entry of the new firms.

11. **Answer e.** To find the profit-maximizing level of output for this firm in the short run requires that we equate marginal revenue with marginal cost. So the marginal revenue curve must be identified. But the firm will not produce in the short run if the price it can charge for its product is less than the average variable cost of producing that product (recall this from your previous work with monopolies), since the firm will be unwill-

ing to hire the variable input if its revenue is not sufficient to cover the cost of this variable input.

12. **Answer a.** This firm will earn negative economic profit in the short run because the price it charges for its product is less than the cost per unit (average total cost) of producing this product. Entry and exit of firms is a long-run characteristic of this market structure, not a short-run characteristic.

13. **Answer c.** A monopolistically competitive firm's profit-maximizing quantity occurs where $MR = MC$, but the price that the firm charges for its product is found by going up to the demand curve at this quantity. This implies that the firm produces a quantity for which price is greater than marginal cost, and therefore the firm will be enthusiastic about increasing its sales as long as price remains above marginal cost.

14. **Answer e.** The monopolistically competitive firm produces a quantity where price is greater than marginal cost, while a perfect competitive firm produces a quantity where price equals marginal cost. The monopolistically competitive firm produces a quantity where the average total cost is downward sloping: this indicates that the firm is producing in the decreasing-cost portion of its cost curve and not the increasing-cost portion of its cost curve. When the monopolistically competitive firm produces in the decreasing-cost portion of its cost curve, this indicates that the firm could expand its level of production and thereby reduce its cost per unit, which implies that the firm has excess productive capacity.

module 35

Product Differentiation and Advertising

BEFORE YOU READ THE MODULE

Summary

This module discusses why monopolistic competitors and oligopolists differentiate their products. The module also considers the costs and benefits from advertising and the creation of brand names.

Module Objectives

Objective #1. Product differentiation takes three general forms: differentiation by style or type, differentiation by location, and differentiation by quality. Differentiation by style or type creates products that are imperfect substitutes for one another. Differentiation by location offers essentially identical products that are differentiated by their proximity and convenience to the buyer. Differentiation by quality provides a range of products that are of different quality levels to buyers. No matter what type of product differentiation we consider, the monopolistically competitive market structure is characterized by competition among sellers and a more diverse array of products.

Objective #2. Advertising is worthwhile in industries where firms have some degree of market power. Advertising may help to establish the quality of a firm's product. Advertising may also convey important information. The establishment of a brand name may be a way of signaling quality to a consumer.

Key Term

brand name a name owned by a particular firm that distinguishes its products from those of other firms.

Notes

AFTER YOU READ THE MODULE

Tips

Tip #1: In a monopolistically competitive industry, product differentiation enables firms to reduce price competition. Firms that can successfully differentiate their product from other products enhance their market power. With greater market power the firm can charge higher prices and earn more economic profit. Essentially, product differentiation allows firms in a monopolistically competitive industry to insulate themselves from competition.

Tip #2: Products can be differentiated by their style or type, by their location, by their quality, or by a combination of these. For example, a fast-food restaurant clearly differentiates its products from those of other fast-food restaurants through the type of food it offers. This same restaurant may also differentiate itself from its competitors by location and by quality.

Tip #3: Advertising is worthwhile in industries with product differentiation. Advertising may be informative or persuasive. Even advertising that is primarily persuasive may provide to purchasers an indirect signal of the item's quality. Firms that can pay stars to advertise their product suggest that their firm is solvent and their product is likely of greater quality than that of a competitor that cannot afford an expensive advertising campaign. Brand names similarly convey an indirect message about the good's quality.

WORKED PROBLEMS

1. In Smalltown the Sunday newspaper runs advertising circulars about this week's sales at area grocery stores. These circulars list the sale prices, the days of the sale, and the items that are specially priced during the sale. How do these advertising circulars help the grocery stores differentiate their products? Why would the grocery stores be willing to increase their costs of production by buying advertising? What kind of indirect signal does this type of advertising send to readers?

STEP 1: Review the relationship between product differentiation and advertising and then relate how this kind of advertising campaign can contribute to product differentiation.

Product differentiation may be a matter of style or type, location, or quality. The advertising circular has the potential to help the firm differentiate its product from its rivals' in terms of the style or type of the product (what items are on sale this week), the location of its stores (the sale is occurring on Friday at our store on the east side of town), and quality (we have more and better items on sale this week than you will find in our competitor's advertising circular). By informing potential customers of the items on sale, the grocery store distinguishes its products from those of its competitors.

STEP 2: Discuss why firms are willing to advertise even though it raises their costs of production.

A successful advertisement will add to the firm's costs, but it will also differentiate the firm's product from that of its rivals. This product differentiation will reduce the intensity of price competition as people are drawn to the store by the advertised specials. Shoppers will buy the discounted items, but they are also likely to purchase other full-priced items while in the store. This product differentiation will enable the monopolistically competitive firm to acquire some market power.

STEP 3: Discuss how advertising in the Sunday newspaper is a form of indirect signal for the advertising firm. Then elaborate on what the indirect signal is in this example.

The advertising campaign is an indirect signal of the firm's capacity. Since advertising costs the firm money, the advertising campaign tells potential customers that the firm has resources that will likely contribute to the quality of the product offered by the firm. It also communicates to potential customers that the firm has a presence in the market, and customers who are dissatisfied with the product probably can return to the firm and have their complaint successfully addressed.

2. Jonette is considering purchasing a bicycle. She knows she can get a bike at a discount store for $100, or she can go to the Bike Shop and get a name brand bike for $600. Why would Jonette consider purchasing the more expensive bike?

STEP 1: Review the general concept of product differentiation and apply it to this situation.

A product may be differentiated by style or type, by location, or by quality. In this example Jonette may be comparing two very different bicycles. The bikes may differ by style and/or quality: The less expensive bicycle may be have lower-quality components, may not have as many gears, may be heavier, or may lack features that increase the value of the final product (for example, lights, fenders, reflectors, a carrier). The bicycles may also reflect location: the discount store may be a considerable drive from Jonette's house and the Bike Shop local.

STEP 2: Review the significance of a brand name and analyze the benefits of consuming a name brand product in this example.

A brand name distinguishes the product from the products of other firms. Jonette may decide that it is worth spending more money on a bicycle to get one made by a known entity. She may interpret the brand name as an indirect symbol of quality, the longevity of the firm's production in the industry, and an indicator that should a problem with the bicycle develop, she will be able to talk to someone at the firm who can make sure her complaint is addressed.

Problems and Exercises

1. In Smalltown there are three different gas stations owned by different people. One is located on the west side of town, one is on the east side of town, and one is on the south side of town. They all sell three types of identical gasoline, and their business hours are the same. Are these three firms differentiated?

2. The fast-food industry has many different restaurants selling many different types of food. These restaurants are also located in different places. What types of differentiation are represented by the fast-food industry?

3. Monopolistic competition is particularly noteworthy because of the degree of product differentiation one finds in this type of market structure. Why do firms find it profitable to differentiate their product? Why do consumers like this variety?

4. Some monopolistically competitive firms differentiate their product according to quality. Describe what this means and why a firm might find this a profitable type of differentiation.

5. How did General Motors overtake Ford as the dominant auto manufacturer of the twentieth century? Relate its strategy to the issue of differentiation.

6. How does advertising and the establishment of a brand name assure the potential customer of the quality of the good?

BEFORE YOU TAKE THE TEST

Module Review Questions

1. When monopolistically competitive firms differentiate their products, this is
   a. unprofitable, since differentiation costs money.
   b. unprofitable in the short run, since monopolistically competitive firms make zero economic profits in the short run.
   c. profitable in the short run, so long as consumers differ in their tastes.
   d. wasted effort, since consumers would be just as happy with identical products as they are with differentiated products.

2. Which of the following statements is true about monopolistically competitive industries that produce differentiated products?
   I. Monopolistically competitive industries with differentiated products are characterized as having competition among sellers.
   II. Monopolistically competitive industries with differentiated products are industries that find there is value in diversity.
   III. Monopolistically competitive industries with differentiated products are able to sustain short-run positive economic profits into the long run.
   a. Statement I is true.
   b. Statement II is true.
   c. Statement III is true.
   d. Statements I and II are true.
   e. Statements I and III are true.

3. When Henry Ford produced his cars, he maximized his economies of scale, while General Motors decided to produce with excess capacity. This resulted in
   a. Ford being able to produce cheaper cars than General Motors initially, since Ford did not diversify the product it provided.
   b. General Motors facing a trade-off between offering cars at a lower price with less differentiation or selling cars at a higher price with greater differentiation.
   c. consumers ultimately finding they preferred product differentiation as General Motors sold more cars than Ford.
   d. Answers (a), (b), and (c) are all true.

4. Advertising in a monopolistically competitive industry
   a. is worthwhile if it gets consumers to buy more of the product.
   b. may provide helpful information that consumers can use when making their purchasing decisions.
   c. is costly and of little use.
   d. is often an indirect signal as to the dependability of the individual firm that elects to advertise its products.
   e. Answers (a), (b), and (d) are all true.

5. Firms differentiate their products because
   a. differentiation leads to lower costs of production.
   b. people have different tastes and preferences.
   c. differentiation enhances competition between firms in an industry.
   d. Answers (a), (b), and (c) are all correct answers.

6. Monopolistically competitive firms
   a. offer greater variety of products than do perfectly competitive firms.
   b. produce their level of output at greater cost per unit in the long run than do perfectly competitive firms.
   c. in the long run produce at a level of output where there is excess capacity.
   d. Answers (a), (b), and (c) are all correct answers.

7. Which of the following statements is true?
   a. A perfectly competitive firm has an incentive to advertise.
   b. A monopolistically competitive firm by advertising can shift the demand curve for their product to the right.
   c. A perfectly competitive industry has an incentive to advertise.
   d. Answers (a), (b), and (c) are all correct.
   e. Answers (b) and (c) are both correct.
   f. Answers (a) and (c) are both correct.

8. A brand name
   a. helps to differentiate their product in a consumer's mind.
   b. often is the most important asset a company possesses.
   c. creates market power.
   d. conveys information.
   e. All of the answers are correct.

ANSWER KEY

Answers to Problems and Exercises

1. Yes, the type of differentiation these three firms illustrate is differentiation by location. Each of these three firms is located in a different part of the community, which differentiates them even though they sell very similar products.

2. This industry is characterized by having differentiation by style or type as well as differentiation by location.

3. As long as people have different tastes and preferences, firms will find it profitable to offer differentiated products. Variety is appealing to people primarily because people have different tastes and preferences.

4. Differentiation based on quality is the idea that firms can choose to produce a similar product with a range of quality. Some firms find it profitable to produce the product with very high standards of quality, while other firms produce a similar product that has a much lower standard of quality. Consumers can then select the level of quality they desire by selecting the product whose quality most closely resembles the desired level of quality. Consumers' tastes and preferences are thus served more closely when firms decide to produce a product with different quality levels.

5. Although Ford was the first car company in the United States to produce an affordable car, Ford only produced one basic model of car. General Motors innovated by producing a variety of styles and colors so that consumers could purchase a car that was reflective of their personal tastes and preferences. By differentiating its product, General Motors was able to become the dominant car producer in the twentieth century.

6. If a firm can afford to make an expensive advertisement about their product or expend the resources to create a brand name, this indicates to the potential buyer that the firm is able to stand behind its product. These actions serve to establish the quality of the firm's products from the consumers' perspective.

Answers to Module Review Questions

1. **Answer c.** As long as people's preferences are not identical, firms will find it profitable in the short run to produce a wide variety of goods so that people can select items that maximize their satisfaction given these preferences.

2. **Answer d.** Statements I and II are descriptive of monopolistically competitive industries with differentiated products. Statement III is not true because, in the long run, entry will drive economic profit to zero even if the firms in the industry produce differentiated products.

3. **Answer d.** This is a recap of the "Economics in Action" sidebar in the text that discusses the competition between Ford and General Motors.

4. **Answer e.** Advertising is costly, but if it is of little use, then firms would realize this and decide to forgo their advertising expenditures. Advertising may encourage consumers to purchase a product they otherwise would not purchase, it may provide consumers with information about the product or the firm, and it can indicate that the firm is large enough and successful enough to be able to afford an advertising campaign. The consumer may view this last aspect as a way for the firm to convey its reliability, and therefore the reliability of its product.

5. **Answer b.** Differentiation increases the costs of production for a firm while decreasing the amount of competition between different firms in an industry. Firms find it worthwhile to differentiate their products because individuals have different tastes and preferences and are willing to pay somewhat more in order to satisfy these preferences.

6. **Answer d.** Monopolistically competitive firms differentiate their products and therefore provide greater variety than is found in perfectly competitive market structures where the firms produce identical products. The cost of this variety is that these firms end up producing at higher cost per unit in the long run than would occur if they did not differentiate their product. This higher cost per unit indicates that the monopolistically competitive firm has excess capacity: their production process could produce at a lower cost per unit if the firm were to produce a greater amount of output.

7. **Answer e.** A perfectly competitive firm does not have an incentive to advertise since it can sell as much of its product as it wishes at the market price. A perfectly competitive industry does have an incentive to advertise since through advertising it can shift the market demand curve for the product to the right, and holding everything else constant, increase the quantity of the good being sold. A monopolistically competitive firm has an incentive to advertise since it has market power. This market power means that it faces a downward-sloping demand curve. Through advertising the monopolistically competitive firm can shift the demand curve for its product to the right.

8. **Answer e.** Brand names are a means for companies to help consumers identify their product: brand names convey information, create market power, and often end up being the greatest asset a firm possesses because of the important information the name conveys to the potential buyer. The brand name differentiates the product from its competitors.

module 36

Externalities

BEFORE YOU READ THE MODULE

Summary

This module describes positive and negative externalities and the effect of these externalities in the marketplace. The module also discusses why the presence of externalities often requires the intervention of government. The module also presents the Coase theorem which explains how private individuals can sometimes remedy externalities.

Module Objectives

Objective #1. Many activities produce pollution as a side effect of these activities. One of the problems with pollution is that it inflicts a cost on the entire society, and this cost is typically not borne by the companies or individuals who generate the pollution. The module explores how to determine the optimal amount of pollution by developing the concepts of the marginal social cost of pollution and the marginal social benefit of pollution. Pollution generates costs as well as benefits to society.

- The marginal social cost of pollution is the additional cost imposed on society of an additional unit of pollution. The marginal social cost of pollution is an upward-sloping line, since each additional unit of pollution represents a greater cost to society as the environment deteriorates.
- The marginal social benefit of pollution is the additional benefit to society from an additional unit of pollution. Cleaning up pollution requires the use of scarce resources that would otherwise be used to produce goods and services. From a producer's perspective, the benefit from emitting one more unit of pollution is measured by the costs the producer saves from not having to buy and install expensive pollution-control equipment. One can measure the marginal social benefit of an additional unit of pollution by finding out what is the highest willingness to pay for the right to emit this unit of pollution among all the polluters in the society. Polluters know that to avoid polluting requires using scarce resources and therefore reduction of pollution carries a cost. The marginal social benefit of pollution is a downward-sloping line: when pollution is negligible, then an additional unit of pollution has a high benefit to society; when there is a lot of pollution, then an additional unit of pollution brings little benefit to society.

- The optimal amount of pollution for a society is the level of pollution at which the marginal social cost of pollution is equal to the marginal social benefit of pollution. Figure 36.1 illustrates these concepts.

Figure 36.1

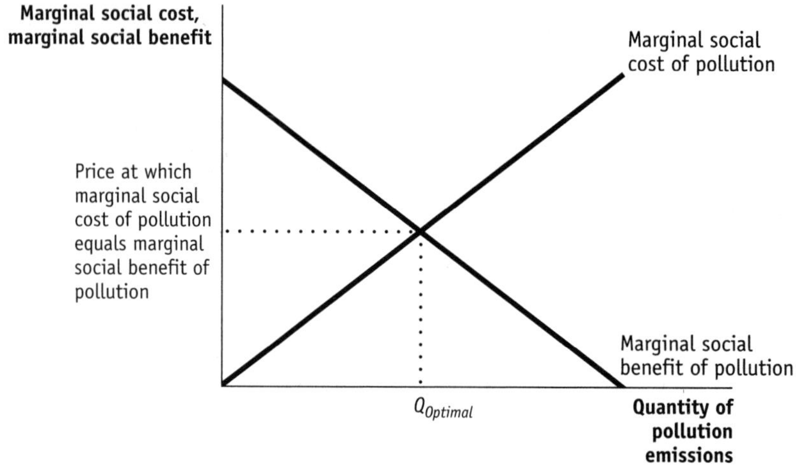

- It is unlikely that the market will generate the optimal amount of pollution, because those who produce the pollution do not have to compensate those who bear the costs of the pollution. The polluting producer can pass along the pollution costs to all members of society, and thus the market, left to its own devices, will result in too much pollution.
- In the absence of government intervention, polluters will pollute up to the point where the marginal social benefit of pollution is equal to zero. The market outcome is represented in Figure 36.2: note that the market level of pollution is greater than the optimal level of pollution, and that the market level of pollution is inefficient since, at this level of pollution, the marginal social cost of pollution is greater than the marginal social benefit of pollution.

Figure 36.2

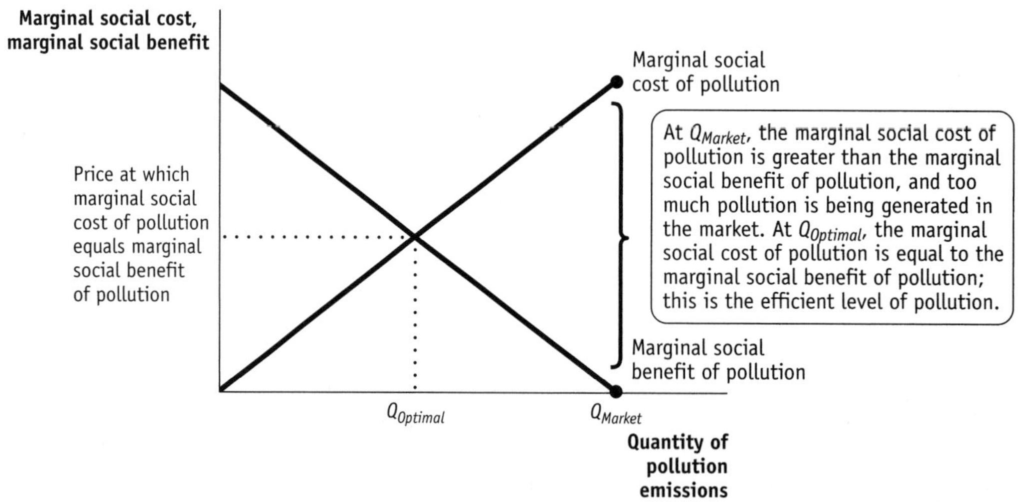

Objective #2. According to the Coase theorem, the private sector can correct externalities and produce the efficient level of the good, provided that transaction costs are sufficiently low. The Coase theorem states that externalities need not lead to inefficiencies since people have an incentive to make mutually beneficial transactions, which leads individuals to take externalities into account when making decisions, provided that the transaction costs are not too great. When individuals take into account externalities when making decisions, this is referred to as internalizing the externality. Internalization of the externality does not occur if the cost of communication between the affected parties is too high, if the cost of making a legally binding agreement is too great, or if there are costly delays in the bargaining. When transaction costs prevent people from internalizing the externality, then the government must intervene to correct the market and its failure to internalize the externality.

Key Terms

marginal social cost of pollution the additional cost imposed on society as a whole by an additional unit of pollution.

marginal social benefit of pollution the additional gain to society as a whole from an additional unit of pollution.

socially optimal quantity of pollution the quantity of pollution that society would choose if all the costs and benefits of pollution were fully accounted for.

external cost an uncompensated cost that an individual or firm imposes on others; also known as *negative externalities.*

external benefit an uncompensated benefit that an individual or firm confers on others; also known as *positive externalities.*

externalities *external benefits* and *external costs.*

negative externalities *external costs.*

positive externalities *external benefits.*

Coase theorem the proposition that even in the presence of *externalities* an *economy* can always reach an *efficient* solution as long as *transaction costs* are sufficiently low.

transaction costs the costs to individuals of making a deal.

internalize the externality when individuals take into account *external costs* and *external benefits.*

Notes

AFTER YOU READ THE MODULE

Tips

Tip #1. The key concept in this chapter is the idea that markets fail to produce the optimal amount of the good whenever there is a cost or a benefit that the market fails to include in its reckoning when deciding what the optimal quantity of the good will be in the market. A negative externality occurs when there is some kind of cost that is not internalized in the market, and a positive externality occurs when there is some kind of benefit that is not internalized in the market. When there is an externality in the market that is not internalized, the market does not produce the efficient level of output because it is not producing the level of output where the marginal social cost of production is equal to the marginal social benefit of consumption.

Tip #2. Another key concept of this chapter is that the optimal amount of a good for a market to produce is that amount, where the marginal social cost of producing that good (*MSC*) is equal to the marginal social benefit from consuming that good (*MSB*). If the market produces where the *MSC* is greater than the *MSB*, then the market is producing too much of the good and there is a negative externality that the market has failed to internalize. If the market produces where the *MSC* is less than the *MSB*, then the market is producing too little of the good and there is a positive externality that the market has failed to internalize.

Tip #3. Students often are surprised that the optimal amount of pollution is not zero units. Remember that it is important to analyze this issue by using our now-familiar marginal analysis. The optimal amount of pollution will be that amount where the marginal social benefit of the last unit of pollution is equal to the marginal social cost of that pollution. An alternative way of thinking about the optimal amount of pollution is to realize that if we were to eliminate all pollution, the last units of pollution that were eliminated would be very costly to eliminate while yielding very small amounts of benefits to society.

WORKED PROBLEMS

1. Josie just went to hear an eminent economist speak on pollution issues. She was surprised to hear that the optimal amount of pollution was not zero units. The speaker talked about the relationship between pollution's marginal social cost and marginal social benefit, and she suggested to the audience that the market was unlikely to provide the socially optimal amount of pollution. Josie has asked you to explain these concepts to her: In particular she wants you to explain the meaning of the marginal social cost of pollution, the marginal social benefit of pollution, and the socially optimal amount of pollution. She would prefer that you help her understand these ideas without using graphs.

STEP 1: Define the terms *marginal social cost of pollution, marginal social benefit of pollution,* and *socially optimal amount of pollution.*

The marginal social cost of pollution is the additional cost to society of producing one more unit of pollution. This is a measure in dollars of the cost of an additional unit of pollution to everyone in that society. The marginal social benefit of pollution is the additional benefit to society from producing one more unit of pollution. This is a measure in dollars of the benefits of an additional unit of pollution to everyone in that society. The socially optimal amount of any good is the amount at which the marginal social cost of producing the last unit equals the marginal social benefit of consuming the last unit produced. Therefore, at the socially optimal amount of pollution, its marginal social cost is equal to its marginal social benefit.

STEP 2: Discuss the relationship between the marginal social cost of pollution and its marginal social benefit and why the socially optimal amount of pollution is the amount at which its marginal social cost equals its marginal social benefit.

As discussed in Step 1, the socially optimal amount of any good is the amount of the good at which the marginal social cost of production equals the marginal social benefit of consumption. When the marginal social cost of producing the good is greater than the marginal social benefit of consuming it, the market is producing too much of the good because the cost to society of an additional unit is greater than its value to society. When the marginal social cost of producing the good is less than the marginal social benefit of consuming it, the market is producing too little of the good because the cost to society of an additional unit is less than its value to society.

STEP 3: Explain why the market is unlikely to produce the socially optimal amount of pollution.

The market is unlikely to produce the socially optimal amount of the good because the market fails to internalize the negative externality. That is, those who produce the pollution do not have to compensate those who bear its costs. The producer who pollutes passes along the costs of that pollution to all members of society rather than bearing its costs. Without any government intervention, the producer will continue to pollute until the marginal social benefit of pollution from the last unit of the good produced is zero. Thus, there will be too much pollution: Its marginal social cost will exceed its marginal social benefit.

2. Suppose you are given the following table about a community's marginal social benefit and marginal social cost of pollution from an industrial facility. From this you are asked to advise the community as to its socially optimal range of pollution. You are also asked to provide insight into the likely level of pollution if the government does not restrict the level of allowable pollution.

Quantity of emissions (tons)	Marginal social benefit	Marginal social cost
0	$250	$ 0
100	200	40
200	150	80
300	100	120
400	50	160
500	0	200

STEP 1: Review the relationships among the marginal social cost of pollution, the marginal benefit of pollution, and the socially optimal amount of pollution.

The socially optimal amount of pollution is the level at which the marginal social cost of an additional unit is equal to its marginal social benefit. The socially optimal amount of pollution will therefore occur at the intersection of its marginal social cost curve and its marginal social benefit curve.

STEP 2: In the table, determine the range of pollution emissions that contains the socially optimal amount of pollution. Explain how you determine this range and why you are unable to determine precisely the socially optimal amount of pollution.

When pollution emissions are equal to 200 tons, the marginal social benefit of pollution ($150) is greater than its marginal social cost ($80). This tells us that this community would be better off if there was more pollution, since the social cost to the community is less than the social benefit to the community. When pollution emissions are equal to 300 tons, the opposite is true: The marginal social benefit ($100) is less than the marginal social cost ($120). This tells us that this community would be better off if there was less pollution than 300 tons, since the social cost to the community of this amount of pollution is greater than its social benefit to the community. Thus, the socially optimal amount of pollution is somewhere between 200 tons and 300 tons of emissions. To find the precise socially optimal amount of pollution would require us to solve mathematically for the intersection of the marginal social cost curve and the marginal social benefit curve.

STEP 3: Describe the level of pollution this community will have if there is no government intervention to limit it. Explain why this will be the level of pollution produced in this community.

This producer will produce the level of output at which the marginal social benefit of pollution is zero if there is no government intervention to limit pollution. Given the table, that means that this producer will emit 500 tons of pollution, which exceeds the range given for the socially optimal amount of pollution in Step 2.

3. Kelly loves dogs and has recently looked into buying a new pup. Unfortunately, Smithie, Kelly's neighbor, loathes dogs and would really prefer that Kelly not have a puppy. Suppose that the value to Kelly of having a dog can be measured as $1,500, while the value to Smithie of not having a dog can be measured as $2,000. Using the concepts underlying the Coase theorem, determine whether Kelly will get the new pup. In addition, explain why it does not matter in the resolution of this matter whether Kelly has the right to own a dog or Smithie has the right to forbid ownership of a dog. Assume for the sake of this discussion that Kelly and Smithie can easily talk to each other and that each has a complete measure of the value of having or not having a dog.

STEP 1: Review the Coase theorem and its implications.

According to the Coase theorem, provided that transaction costs are sufficiently low, the private sector can correct externalities and produce the efficient level of the good. In this example the externality is that Kelly is unlikely to take into account Smithie's dislike of dogs. But we are told that Smithie and Kelly can easily to talk to each other and that each of them knows how they would value either having a dog (Kelly) or not having a dog (Smithie). We assume from this that the transactions costs are low and therefore it should be theoretically possible for Kelly and Smithie to have a private-sector solution that will correct for the externality represented by the dog.

STEP 2: Analyze the situation based upon Kelly's having the right to own a dog. Explain how this disagreement can be resolved so that both parties are satisfied.

We start with the assumption that Kelly has the right to own a dog. And given Kelly's feelings about dogs, we know that she is ready to go out and pick up that pup. But Smithie really does not care for dogs, and so we can imagine that Smithie comes to Kelly and tells her that he is willing to compensate Kelly if Kelly is willing to give up the dog. They discuss this and realize that Kelly is willing to give up the dog provided she gets at least $1,500 and Smithie is willing to pay as much as $2,000 not to have the dog. Kelly and Smithie will resolve this problem by having Smithie compensate Kelly at a level sufficient to stop Kelly from getting the puppy.

STEP 3: Analyze the situation based upon Smithie's having the right to forbid dog ownership. Explain how this disagreement can be resolved so that both parties are satisfied.

Here we start with the assumption that Smithie has the right to keep his neighbor from owning a dog. But Kelly really wants a dog, and so we can imagine Kelly coming to Smithie and telling him she is willing to compensate Smithie for the nuisance. They discuss this and realize that Kelly is willing to pay up to $1,500 to have a dog but that Smithie must be compensated at least $2,000 to be willing to have the dog next door. Kelly will not get the dog, since the amount she is willing to pay for the right to own the dog is less than the amount Smithie must have to be willing to have the dog.

STEP 4: Summarize your findings. Will there be a dog or not?

Whether the property rights reside with Kelly or with Smithie, we can see that this scenario ends with no dog for Kelly. If Kelly wants a dog, she will have to compensate Smithie with at least $2,000, and dog ownership is not worth so much to Kelly.

Problems and Exercises

1. Suppose the following table provides information about the marginal social benefit of pollution and the marginal social cost of pollution for a society. Assume that both the marginal social benefit of pollution and the marginal social cost of pollution are linear relationships.

Quantity of pollution emissions (tons)	Marginal social benefit of pollution	Marginal social cost of pollution
0	$1,000	$ 0.0
2,000	800	133.3
4,000	600	266.7
6,000	400	400.0
8,000	200	533.3
10,000	0	666.7

a. What is the marginal social benefit from emitting pollution?

b. What is the marginal social cost of emitting pollution?

c. When 3,000 tons of pollution emissions are emitted, what is the marginal social benefit of this pollution? What is the marginal social cost of this level of pollution emissions? Is this an efficient level of pollution emissions for this society? Explain your answer.

d. When 9,000 tons of pollution emissions are emitted, what is the marginal social benefit of this pollution? What is the marginal social cost of this level of pollution emissions? Is this an efficient level of pollution emissions for this society? Explain your answer.

e. What is the efficient level of pollution emissions for this society?

2. Use the information given in problem 1 to answer this set of questions.

a. Draw a graph of the marginal social benefit (*MSB*) of pollution and the marginal social cost (*MSC*) of pollution where *MSB* and *MSC* are measured on the vertical axis and the quantity of pollution emissions is measured on the horizontal axis.

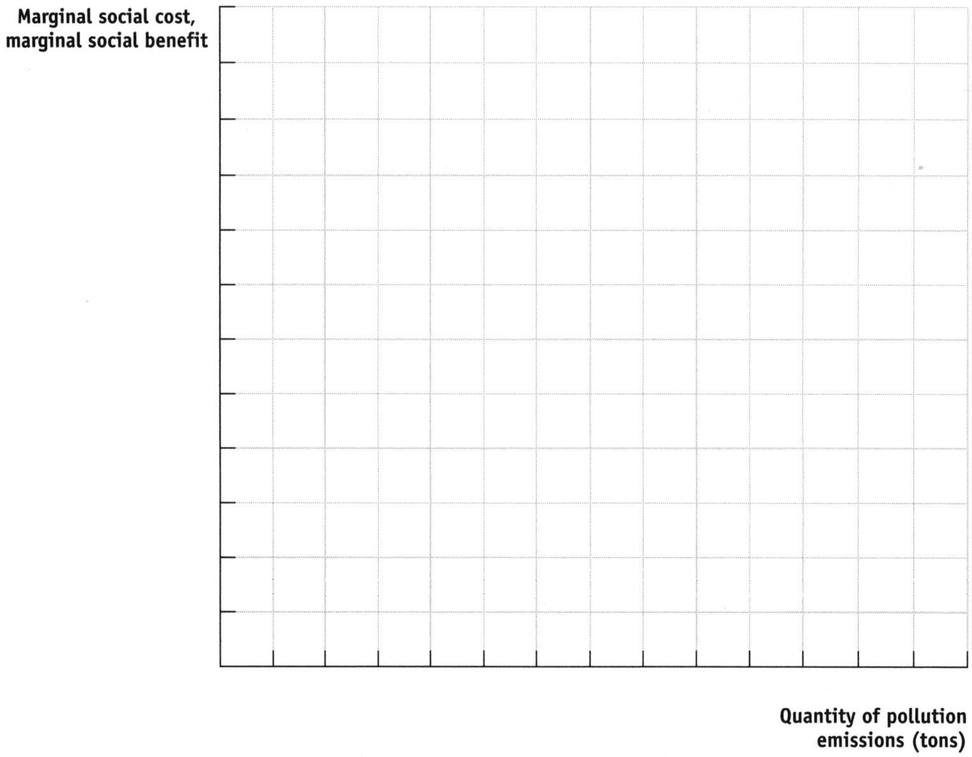

b. Label the socially optimal amount of pollution emissions in the graph you drew in part (a).

c. Will the socially optimal amount of pollution be produced in this market if there is no government intervention? Explain your answer.

3. In a market economy without government intervention, why will there be too much pollution?

4. Why does talking on a cell phone while driving create a negative externality?

5. Joan loves dogs and decides that she is going to buy a dog. She analyzes the benefit she will get from owning a dog and values the benefit of owning a dog at $500. Joan's next-door neighbor loathes dogs and is vehemently opposed to dogs being in the neighborhood. This neighbor, Mike, views the cost of an additional dog in the neighborhood as being $800. According to the Coase theorem, is it possible for Joan and Mike to amicably resolve this dilemma about the dog ownership? In your answer, identify how this conflict can be resolved provided that the rights to dog ownership are well defined. Also, in your answer consider how it does not matter who owns the rights to dog ownership provided that these rights are well defined.

BEFORE YOU TAKE THE TEST

Module Review Questions

1. The optimal amount of pollution is
   a. the amount of pollution where the marginal social benefit of the pollution exceeds the marginal social cost of the pollution.
   b. zero units of pollution, since pollution is harmful to people.
   c. the amount of pollution where the marginal social benefit of the pollution is less than the marginal social cost of the pollution.
   d. the amount of pollution where the marginal social benefit of the pollution equals the marginal social cost of the pollution.

Use the figure below to answer the next two questions.

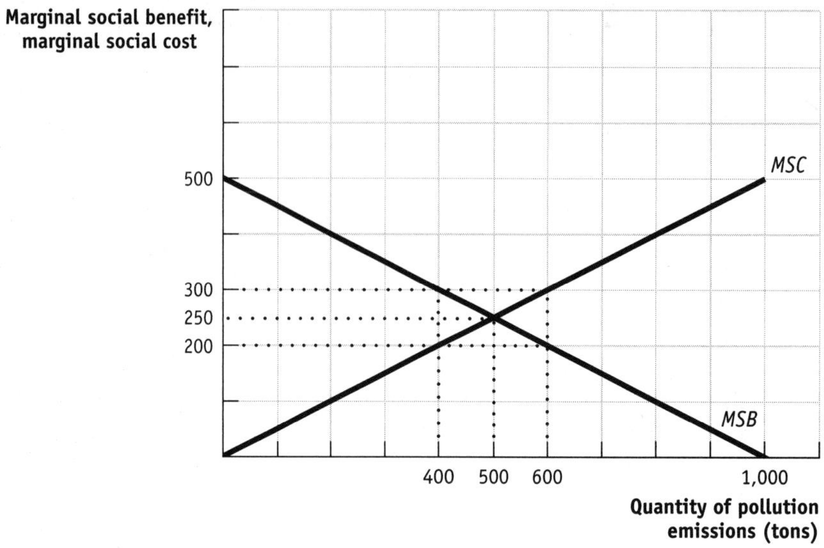

2. The socially optimal amount of pollution emissions in the above graph is
a. 400 tons.
b. 500 tons.
c. 600 tons.

3. When 400 tons of pollution are emitted,
a. the marginal social cost of pollution is less than the marginal social benefit of pollution.
b. this economy would be better off producing more pollution emissions.
c. this economy would be worse off producing more pollution emissions.
d. Answers (a) and (b) are true.
e. Answers (a) and (c) are true.

4. When there is an external cost, like pollution, the market if there is no government intervention will
a. produce too much of the good.
b. produce too little of the good.

5. Pollution avoidance refers to
a. the decision to live one's life so as to minimize the amount of pollution that is generated.
b. the monetary and input costs of reducing pollution.
c. the decision to forgo producing a good or service because of the pollution that would be generated by that production.
d. Answers (a), (b), and (c) are all true.
e. Answers (a) and (b) are true.
f. Answers (b) and (c) are true.

6. External costs are referred to as
   a. externalities.
   b. negative externalities.
   c. positive externalities.
   d. inefficiencies.

7. Which of the following statements is true?
   a. The Coase theorem shows that the outcome in a case with externalities does not depend on the legal rights; it only depends on the legal rights being clearly defined.
   b. The Coase theorem indicates that issues with regard to externalities can be resolved if the costs of communication between the involved parties is small, if the costs of making legally binding agreements is small, and if the costs of bargaining are small.
   c. The Coase theorem indicates that problems with externalities can be resolved provided that there are well-defined property rights and transactions costs are low.
   d. Answers (a), (b), and (c) are all true.
   e. Answers (b) and (c) are both true.
   f. Answers (a) and (c) are both true.

ANSWER KEY

Answers to Problems and Exercises

1. **a.** The marginal social benefit from emitting pollution is the measure of the additional benefit a society gets from one more ton of pollution. It can be measured in terms of the cost that must be incurred by a society in order to not produce this ton of pollution: to produce less pollution, a society must use some of its scarce resources that could have been used to produce other goods and services. The marginal benefit of emitting pollution is the amount of money a society would save if it were allowed to emit an additional ton of pollution.

   b. The marginal social cost of emitting pollution is equal to the sum of the highest willingness to pay among all members of this society to avoid that ton of pollution. The marginal social cost of emitting pollution measures the true marginal cost of the pollution. Another way of expressing the marginal social cost of pollution is that this measures the additional cost imposed on all of the society of an additional ton of pollution.

   c. Since this level of pollution emissions is not listed in the table, you have to extrapolate from the numbers in the table or write an equation for the marginal social benefit of pollution and the marginal social cost of pollution. Extrapolating from the table, you can see that the marginal social benefit of 2,000 tons of pollution is \$800 per ton, and the marginal social benefit of 4,000 tons of pollution is \$600 per ton: you could infer that the marginal social benefit of 3,000 tons of pollution is therefore \$700 per ton. Or you write the equation for the marginal social benefit of pollution as $MSB = 1{,}000 - 0.1Q$, where *MSB* is the marginal social benefit of pollution and Q is the quantity of pollution emissions. Then, substituting 3,000 into the equation for Q, *MSB* is equal to \$700 per ton of pollution emissions. Using a similar technique for the marginal social cost of pollution, $MSC = (1/15)Q$, where *MSC* is the marginal social cost of pollution emissions. When Q equals 3,000, *MSC* equals \$200 per ton of pollution emissions. This is not an efficient level of pollution emissions since the marginal social benefit is greater than the marginal social cost: too little pollution emissions are being produced at this level, since the marginal social benefit of more pollution emissions is greater than the marginal social cost of pollution emissions.

   d. Using the equations found in part (c), the marginal social benefit of 9,000 tons of pollution emissions is equal to \$100 per ton of pollution emissions, while the marginal social cost of 9,000 tons of pollution emissions is equal to \$600 per ton of pollution emissions. This is not an efficient level of pollution emissions since the marginal social benefit is less than the marginal social cost: too much pollution emissions are occurring in this society.

   e. The efficient level of pollution emissions for this society is the level where the marginal social benefit is equal to the marginal social cost. This occurs at 6,000 tons of pollution emissions where the marginal social benefit and the marginal social cost are both \$400 per ton of pollution emissions.

2. a, b.

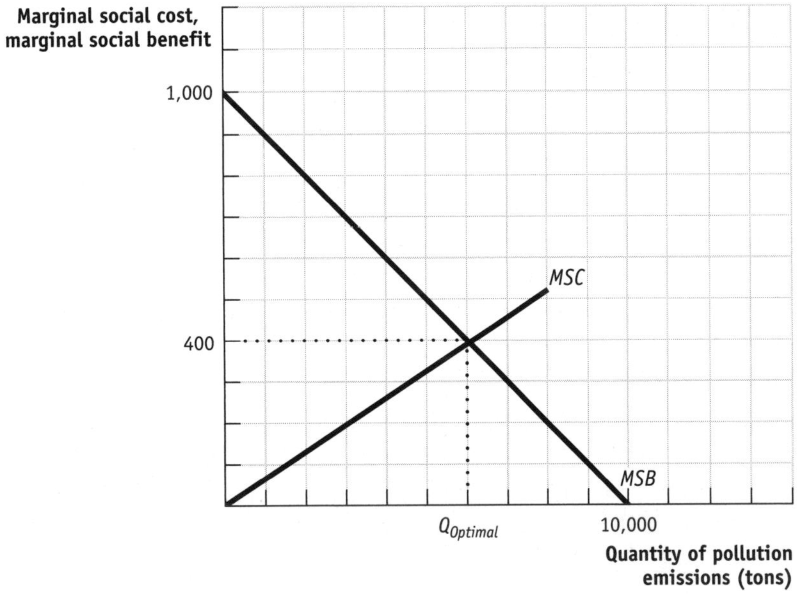

c. No, the optimal level of pollution emissions will not be produced in this economy without government intervention since producers do not have any incentive to take into account the costs of pollution that they impose on other people.

3. When there is no government intervention to limit pollution producers have no incentive to take into account the costs of pollution that their production imposes on others in the society. Because of this manufacturers will produce more pollution than is optimal for the society. In a market economy without government intervention to protect the environment, only the benefits of pollution are taken into account in choosing the quantity of pollution. This means that too much pollution will be produced.

4. Talking on a cell phone while driving creates a negative externality since the talking driver is taking an action that has potentially serious consequences not only for the driver but for other members of society. The externality arises because the driver does not consider this potentially harmful consequence to others when they decide to talk and drive.

5. To answer this question, we first have to look at the requirements for the Coase theorem: for an externality situation to be resolved by the two transacting parties, the transaction cost must not be too high and the property rights must be well defined. The two neighbors can easily talk to each other, and we can start by assigning the property rights to dog ownership to the potential dog owner. This would mean that Joan has the right to purchase a dog. But Mike could approach Joan and tell her that he is willing to compensate her an amount sufficient to persuade her not to purchase the dog. Mike can offer Joan any amount greater than \$500 but less than \$800, and both Joan and Mike will be better off. Given Joan's marginal benefit of owning the dog and Mike's marginal cost of another dog in the neighborhood, the two parties, if they are free to discuss this transaction at reasonable cost, will decide that Joan will not purchase the dog and instead will receive compensation for forgoing the consumption of a canine. If the property rights to dog ownership rest with Mike and he therefore gets to decide whether a neighbor gets to own a dog, we get the same result. Joan is only willing to pay Mike up to \$500 for the right to buy the dog, and since Mike must receive at least \$800 to be willing to have a dog in the neighborhood, Joan will not purchase the dog. The thrust of the Coase theorem is that externality issues can be resolved if the parties are well identified, the transaction costs are not high, and the property rights are well defined.

Answers to Module Review Questions

1. **Answer d.** When the marginal social benefit of pollution is greater than the marginal social cost of pollution, too little pollution is being produced. When the marginal social benefit of pollution is less than the marginal social cost of pollution, too much pollution is being produced. It is optimal to produce the amount of pollution where the marginal social benefit of the pollution equals the marginal social cost of the pollution. Zero units of pollution would only be optimal if the marginal social benefit of the pollution is equal to $0.

2. **Answer b.** The socially optimal amount of pollution emissions is the amount of pollution where the marginal social benefit from the pollution equals the marginal social cost of the pollution.

3. **Answer d.** The socially optimal amount of pollution emissions is 500 tons where the marginal social benefit of pollution equals the marginal social cost of pollution. At 400 tons, the marginal social benefit of pollution equals $300 per ton, while the marginal social cost of this pollution equals $200 per ton. This society would be better off producing more pollution emissions.

4. **Answer a.** When a productive enterprise generates pollution the market will produce too much of the good unless there is government intervention to limit the amount of allowed pollution.

5. **Answer b.** Pollution avoidance refers to the cost to society of reducing the amount of pollution that is generated. Reduction of pollution-creating activities implies the use of money as well as inputs to reduce pollution rather than using this money and these inputs to produce something else. That is, there is a societal cost to the choice to avoid pollution.

6. **Answer b.** An external cost is a situation where firms or consumers generate costs that are not borne by them but are instead borne by society. These external costs are referred to as negative externalities since they affect in a negative way people who are not directly involved in the transaction. They affect people who are therefore external to the transaction.

7. **Answer d.** These are all true answers. The Coase theorem states that the problem of externalities can be solved provided that property rights are well defined and provided that transactions costs are low. Transaction costs include the cost of bargaining, the cost of making legal agreements, and the cost of communication between the involved parties.

module 37

Externalities and Public Policy

BEFORE YOU READ THE MODULE

Summary

This module explores the economic inefficiency that arises from positive and negative externalities when these externalities are not corrected. The module also considers several alternative methods for correcting externalities. The module makes the case for government intervention in the form of emissions taxes, tradable permits, or Pigouvian subsidies as an efficient means of correcting externalities. The module also discusses environmental standards as an inefficient government policy. Finally, the module looks at network externalities as an important feature of high-tech industries.

Module Objectives

Objective #1. A principal source of market failure occurs when the market fails to take into account side effects or externalities of consumption or production decisions. A negative externality is a side effect that imposes costs on others, and a positive externality is a side effect that provides benefits to others. When externalities are present, the market fails to produce the optimal amount of the good: in the case of a negative externality, the market produces too much of the good if it does not take into account the externality; in the case of a positive externality, the market produces too little of the good if it does not take into account the externality. When the externality can be directly observed, then it can be regulated through direct controls, taxation, or subsidization. When the externality cannot be directly observed, then the government must implement policies that aim at generating the right amount of the activity that produces the externality. This module discusses these two approaches—targeting the side effect versus targeting the original activity—as it reviews different policies available to the government to correct the problem presented by externalities.

Objective #2. The government can reduce the amount of pollution by enforcing environmental standards, which are rules that protect the environment by specifying what actions need to be taken by producers and consumers. Although effective, these standards are not efficient since they do not incorporate the costs of reducing pollution. Economists believe that pollution can be reduced at lower cost through the use of taxes and tradable permits.

- Emissions taxes are taxes that depend on the amount of pollution a firm produces. An emissions tax is more efficient than an environmental standard, since the emissions tax ensures that the marginal benefit of pollution is equal for all sources of pollution while the environmental standard does not consider the marginal benefit of pollution when it is enforced. Figure 37.1 illustrates the differences between these two approaches using two different firms, firm A and firm B, that both produce pollution but have different marginal social benefit of pollution curves. The graph on the left illustrates the environmental standard approach: pollution for all firms in the society must, by law, be reduced to 450 units for each firm. With this standard, however, notice that the marginal social benefit of reducing pollution is different for the two firms: for firm A the marginal social benefit is $225 for the last unit of pollution emissions, while for firm B the marginal social benefit is $450 for the last unit of pollution emissions. The graph on the right illustrates the emissions tax approach using an emissions tax of $300 per unit of pollution: each unit of pollution emitted is taxed, and polluters reduce their pollution by considering the tax versus the benefit of the pollution. Both firm A and firm B select the level of pollution emissions where the emissions tax is equal to their marginal social benefit from pollution: for firm A this corresponds to a reduction in pollution emissions of 600 units, while for firm B this corresponds to a reduction in pollution emissions of 300 units. The total amount of pollution reduction is the same in both programs (900 units), but the emissions tax is efficient since all producers reduce pollution to the point where the marginal social benefit of pollution is exactly equal to the tax.

Figure 37.1

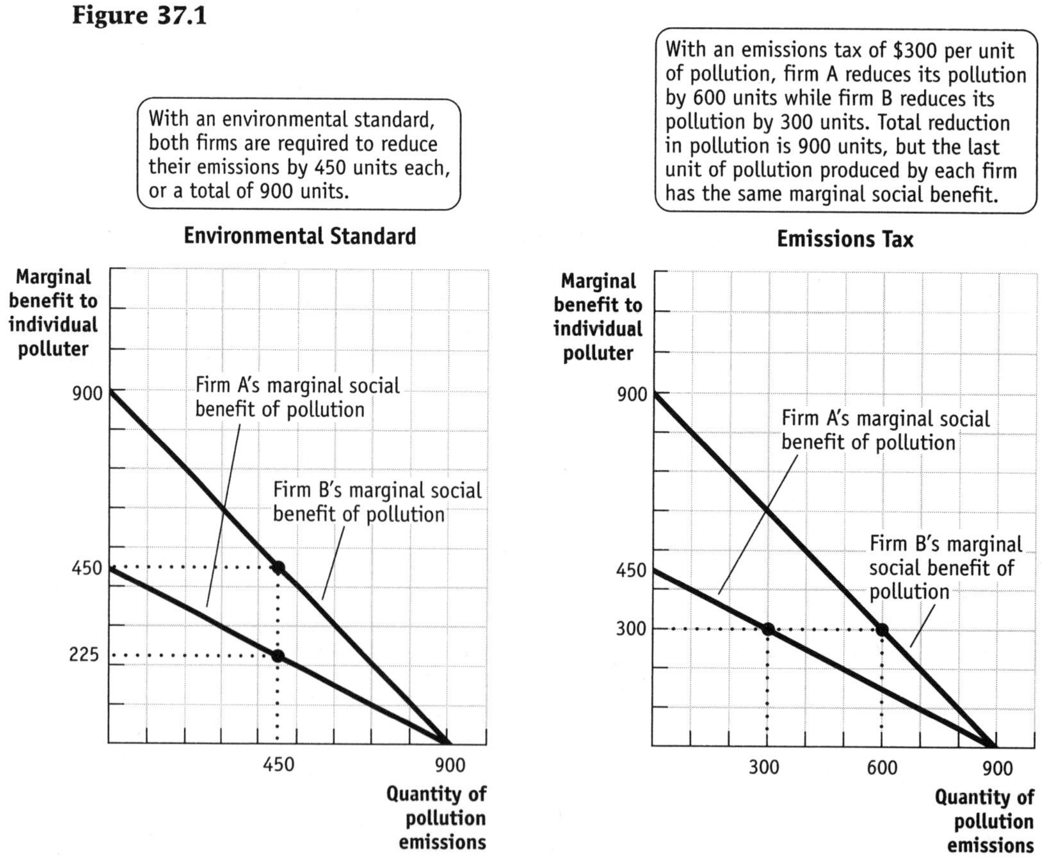

- Taxes can be used to reduce any kind of activity that generates a negative externality. This use of taxes to address the problem of negative externality is referred to as a Pigouvian tax. Although effective as a policy, Pigouvian taxes are difficult to implement since government officials do not always know with certainty what level of tax is the efficient level of tax.
- Tradable emissions permits are licenses granted by the government that give the holder of the license permission to emit limited quantities of the pollutant. These tradable emissions permits can be bought and sold by the polluters. In essence, the government determines the legal amount of pollution and then sells permits equal to this amount of pollution. Producers who pollute must own permits granting them the right to generate their level of pollution. Producers can either purchase the right to pollute or they can clean up their production and eliminate the polluting activity. Firms that find the cost of reducing pollution greater than the cost of buying the permits will buy the permits. Firms that find the cost of reducing pollution less than the cost of buying the permits will eliminate their pollution. Since the level of pollution is limited by the amount of permits in the market, this results in producers basing their decision about whether or not to pollute on the costs of reducing their pollution. In effect, the government creates a market in the right to pollute by using tradable emissions permits. The greatest challenge for government when implementing a tradable emissions permit program is determining the optimal number of permits for the economy: issue too many permits, and pollution is not reduced enough; issue too few permits, and pollution is reduced too much.
- Both emissions taxes and tradable emissions permits create an incentive for producers to create and use less-polluting technology.
- Cap-and-trade systems are another name for tradable emissions permits. In this case, the government issues a cap, or a total amount of pollutant that can be emitted; then the government issues tradable emissions permits and enforces a rule that polluters must hold a number of permits equal to the amount of the pollutant they emit. This policy is effective with pollution that is dispersed, but it is less effective with pollution that is geographically localized. As with any policy, policymakers also face political pressure to set the level of the cap at either too high or too low a level. Finally, these measures to reduce pollution require a high degree of monitoring and compliance if the policy is to be effective.

Objective #3. When an activity generates an external cost, or a cost incurred by someone other than the people directly involved in the transaction, the market produces too much of the good. This situation of an external cost is an example of a negative externality. Figure 37.2 illustrates a negative externality. From the producers' perspective, the market supply curve represents the private costs they incur when they produce the good. However, when this good is produced there are also social costs that the producers do not include in their costs of production. The result is a difference between the market supply curve and the true marginal social costs of production. The market, when it fails to correct for the externality, produces Q_{Market}, which is more than $Q_{Optimal}$. Notice that at Q_{Market} the marginal social benefit of consuming the last unit of the good produced (as measured by the demand curve) is less than the marginal social cost of producing this last unit. Too much of this good is being produced by the market, and therefore too many resources are being devoted to its production. This negative externality can be remedied by applying the appropriate Pigouvian tax, equal to the externality per unit of the good produced, on producers so that $Q_{Optimal}$ is produced by the market. The application of this tax on the market causes the market to internalize the negative externality.

Figure 37.2

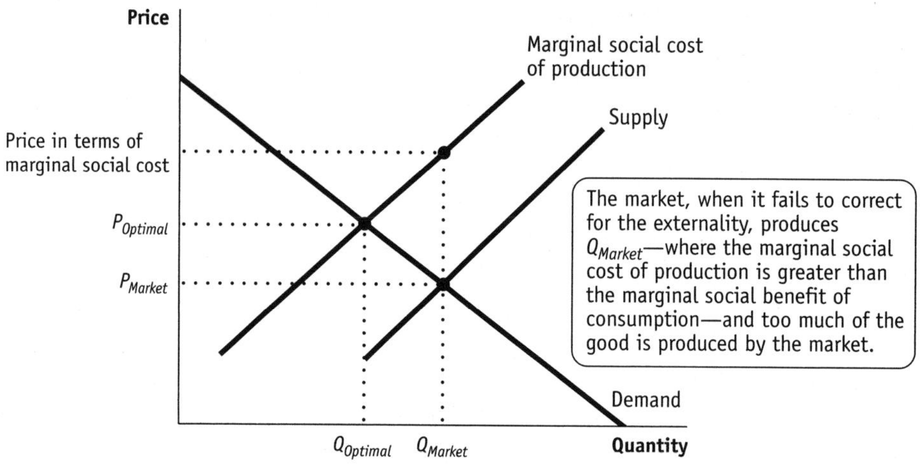

Objective #4. When an activity generates an external benefit, or a benefit received by someone other than the people directly involved in the transaction, the market does not produce enough of this good. This situation of an external benefit is an example of a positive externality. In the case of a positive externality, the government must target the original activity rather than the external benefit because the external benefit can be difficult or impossible to measure. For example, the external benefit from people getting vaccinated is a reduction in the spread of disease among the whole population, but it is impossible to measure how many people benefit from an individual getting vaccinated. When individuals consider getting vaccinated, they consider only the benefits they directly receive and do not include the external benefits the vaccination provides to other people. This implies that people will consume less than the ideal level of vaccinations because they do not include the external benefits.

- This scenario can be illustrated by thinking about the demand curve that represents the private benefits that individuals receive from the vaccination and the demand curve that includes the private benefits as well as the external benefits. Figure 37.3 illustrates the case of a positive externality: in the graph the quantity produced by the market is Q_{Market}, and the optimal quantity, where the marginal cost of producing the last unit is equal to the marginal social benefit from consuming the last unit, is given by $Q_{Optimal}$. This situation of a positive externality can be corrected by application of the optimal Pigouvian subsidy, a subsidy equal to the positive externality cost per unit of the good. The application of this subsidy in this market causes the market to internalize the externality.

Figure 37.3

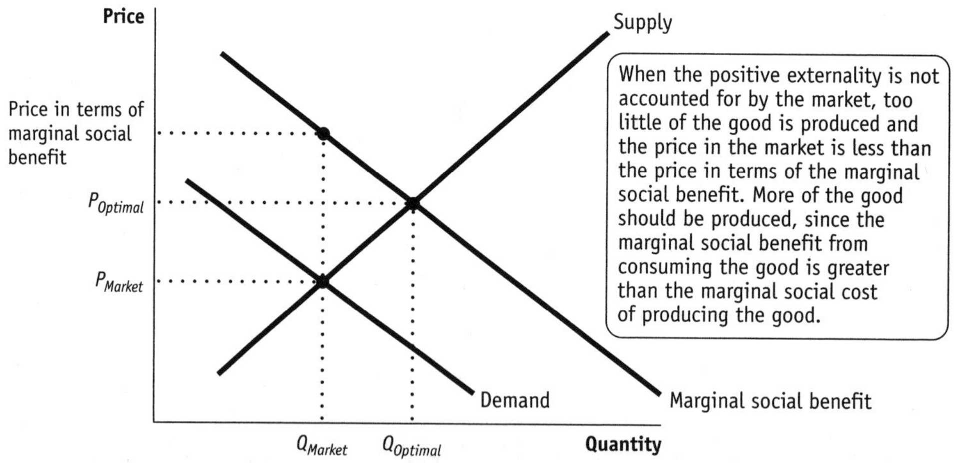

Objective #5. The creation of knowledge poses the greatest single source of external benefits in the modern economy. Technology spillover is a term that describes the spread of knowledge among individuals and firms: technology spillover measures the external benefit that occurs when new knowledge is discovered in one application and then this knowledge is used in other applications. Some people advocate for an industrial policy that would support specific industries due to the existence of these technology spillover effects. This industrial policy would amount to subsidization or reductions in competition from foreign producers through the imposition of trade restrictions for specific industries deemed to generate these technology spillovers. Economists are not strong advocates of industrial policy because it is hard to identify with certainty positive externalities, and because these policies may result in the promotion of industries with political power rather than industries that create technology spillovers.

Objective #6. A final type of externality is that of network externalities. A network externality occurs when the value of a good to a consumer increases as more people own or use the good. These types of externalities frequently occur in technology-driven sectors of the economy. With a network externality, the marginal benefit to the individual is dependent on the number of other individuals who use the good. A good with a network externality also exhibits positive feedback: as more people use the good, even more people are inclined to use the good, and if fewer people use the good, then even fewer people are inclined to use the good. The good's ultimate success or failure is self-reinforcing: a well-accepted good becomes ever more accepted, while a poorly received good is quickly abandoned because of this positive feedback effect. Companies recognize the importance of network externalities and the positive feedback effect, and they sometimes offer a new product at a very low price in hopes of generating a strong network effect.

Key Terms

environmental standards rules established by a government to protect the environment by specifying actions by producers and consumers.

emissions tax a tax that depends on the amount of pollution a firm produces.

Pigouvian taxes taxes designed to reduce *external costs.*

tradable emissions permits *licenses* to emit limited quantities of pollutants that can be bought and sold by polluters.

Pigouvian subsidy a payment designed to encourage activities that yield *external benefits.*

technology spillover an *external benefit* that results when knowledge spreads among individuals and firms.

network externality the increase in the value of a good to an individual is greater when a large number of others own or use the same good.

positive feedback the condition in which success breeds greater success and failure breeds greater failure.

Notes

AFTER YOU READ THE MODULE

Tips

Tip #1. The key concept in this module is the idea that markets fail to produce the optimal amount of the good whenever there is a cost or a benefit that the market fails to include in its reckoning when deciding what the optimal quantity of the good will be in the market. A negative externality occurs when there is some kind of cost that is not internalized in the market, and a positive externality occurs when there is some kind of benefit that is not internalized in the market. When there is an externality in the market that is not internalized, the market does not produce the efficient level of output because it is not producing the level of output where the marginal social cost of production is equal to the marginal social benefit of consumption.

Tip #2. Negative externalities can occur on the production or the consumption side of the model of supply and demand. For example, when a producer produces a good whose production generates substantial pollution and the producer does not take into account the cost of this pollution, then there is a negative externality on the production or cost side of the market. This implies that the producer's supply curve does not represent the true societal costs of producing the good. Alternatively, a consumer can engage in behaviors that inflict a negative benefit on others: for instance, the decision to drink alcoholic beverages and then operate a car has potential negative consequences for others in the community. In this case, the demand curve for the individual does not take into account the negative externality imposed by the individual's consumption decision. In either case (the negative externality on the production side of the model or the negative externality on the consumption side of the model), the market produces too much of the good when the externality is not accounted for in the market. Figure 37.4 illustrates these two examples. Imposition of the appropriate Pigouvian tax will correct the market outcome and result in the market producing the optimal amount of the good where the marginal social benefit from consuming the last unit of the good is equal to the marginal social cost of producing the last unit of the good.

Figure 37.4

In the graphs below, *MSC* is the marginal social cost of production, Supply is the marginal private cost of production, *MSB* is the marginal social benefit of consumption, Demand is the marginal private benefit of consumption, Q_{MKT} is the quantity produced by the market, Q_{OPT} is the optimal quantity to produce, P_{MKT} is the market-determined price, and $P_{Opt\text{-}tax}$ is the optimal price. $P_{Opt\text{-}tax}$ includes the Pigouvian tax.

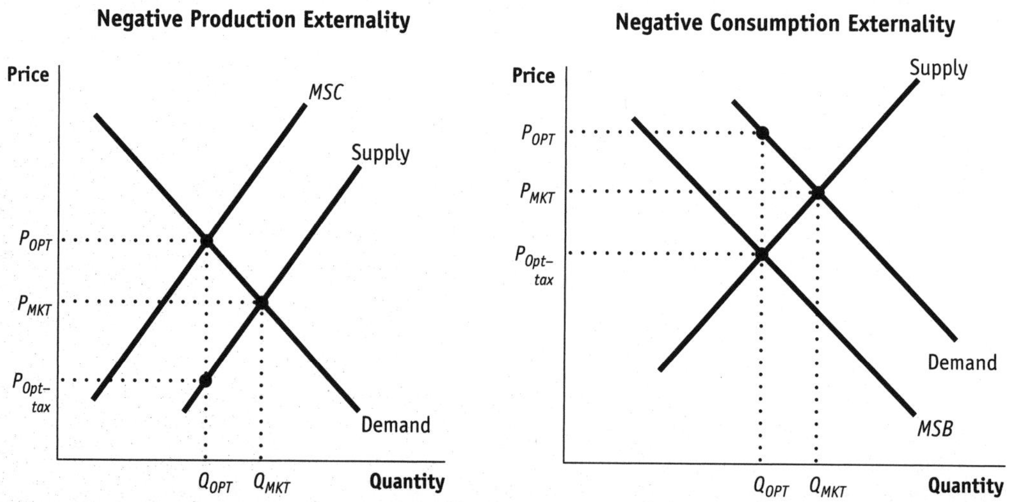

Tip #3. Positive externalities can occur on the production or the consumption side of the model of supply and demand. For example, when a producer produces a good whose production generates technology spillovers and the producer does not take into account the benefit of this technology spillover on the rest of the economy, then there is a positive externality on the production or cost side of the market. This implies that the producer's supply curve does not represent the true societal costs of producing the good. Alternatively, a consumer can engage in behaviors that inflict a positive benefit on others: for instance, the decision to maintain the exterior of one's house results in positive externalities with regard to the property values for neighboring properties. In this case, the demand curve for the individual does not take into account the positive externality created by the individual's consumption decision. In either case (the positive externality on the production side of the model or the positive externality on the consumption side of the model), the market produces too little of the good when the externality is not accounted for in the market. Figure 37.5 illustrates these two examples. Imposition of the appropriate Pigouvian subsidy will correct the market outcome and result in the market producing the optimal amount of the good where the marginal social benefit from consuming the last unit of the good is equal to the marginal social cost of producing the last unit of the good.

Figure 37.5

In the graphs below, *MSC* is the marginal social cost of production, Supply is the marginal private cost of production, *MSB* is the marginal social benefit of consumption, Demand is the marginal private benefit of comsumption, Q_{MKT} is the quantity produced by the market, Q_{OPT} is the optimal quantity to produce, P_{MKT} is the market-determined price, and $P_{Opt\text{-}subsidy}$ is the optimal price. $P_{Opt\text{-}subsidy}$ includes the Pigouvian subsidy.

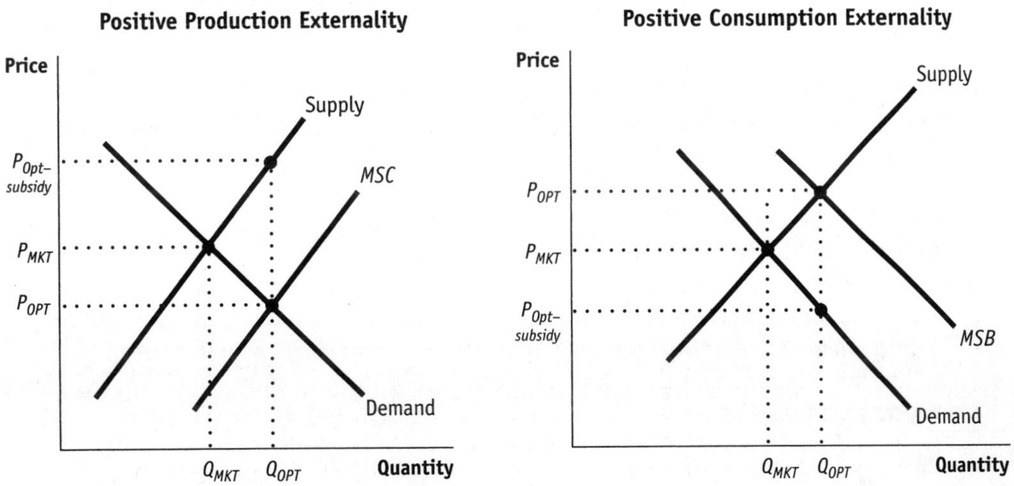

WORKED PROBLEMS

1. Utopia strives to be a perfect society. Recently citizens in Utopia have had a heated debate about pollution in their society. Members of a group called Fresh Air advocate for the elimination of all pollution, since this is critical to Utopia's actually being a perfect society. Rivals in an alternative group argue that this is a decision that is economically imperfect, since it would result in the elimination of units of pollution where the marginal benefit of the pollution reduction is less than the marginal cost of that pollution reduction. The two groups have called you in to give a general presentation on the nature of pollution and how

they should best determine the optimal amount of pollution for their society. They also want you to advise them on strategies for eliminating pollution to this level and as well as advise them about the optimal strategy for this pollution reduction.

STEP 1: To discuss the optimal amount of pollution reduction, you will need to compare the marginal benefit from an additional unit of pollution with the marginal cost of an additional unit of pollution. You will want to identify the market amount of pollution as well as the socially optimal amount of pollution.

The marginal social benefit curve of pollution slopes downward: at very low levels of pollution the benefits to society of that pollution are very high, while at high levels of pollution the benefits to society of that pollution are very low. Since it takes scarce resources to reduce pollution, the more pollution that is allowed in an economy, the fewer resources that are diverted to pollution reduction. The marginal social benefit of pollution thus measures how an additional unit of pollution emissions depends on the quantity of pollution emissions.

The marginal social cost of pollution is an upward-sloping line measuring the additional cost to society of an additional unit of pollution. At high levels of pollution, an additional unit of pollution results in a large change in cost to society; at low levels of pollution, an additional unit of pollution results in a small change in cost to society.

The optimal amount of pollution is at that level where the marginal benefit of pollution is just equal to the marginal cost of pollution. When the marginal benefit of pollution is greater than the marginal cost of pollution, this tells us that an additional unit of pollution yields additional benefits that exceed the additional costs of that unit of pollution: in this case, it is optimal for society to allow an additional unit of pollution. When the marginal benefit of pollution is smaller than the marginal cost of pollution, this tells us that an additional unit of pollution yields additional costs that exceed the additional benefits of that unit of pollution: in this case, it is optimal for society to reduce pollution by this additional unit. It is only when the marginal social benefit of pollution is equal to the marginal social cost of pollution that society has produced the optimal amount of pollution.

The market-determined amount of pollution is that amount where the marginal benefit of pollution is equal to zero. That is, the market will provide that amount of pollution where an additional unit of pollution yields zero social benefits: the market will fail to take into account the marginal social cost of this pollution. The following graph illustrates these ideas.

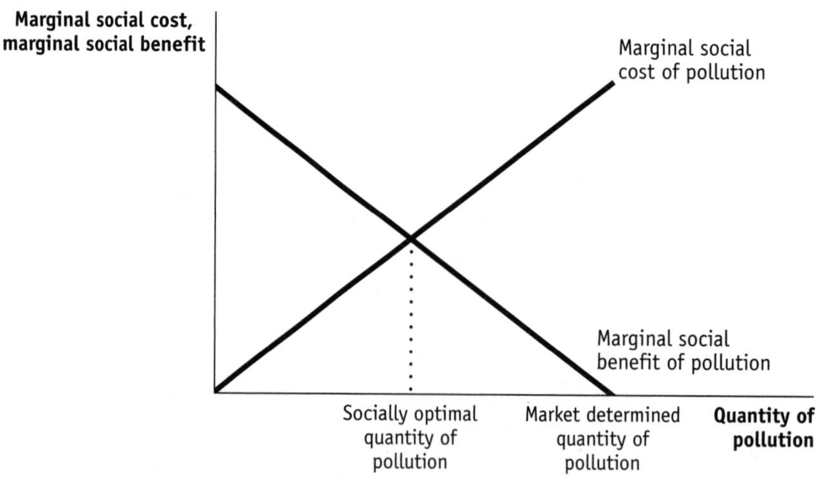

STEP 2: Now that you have identified the optimal amount of pollution, you can turn your attention to policies that can help Utopia reach this goal.

There are three basic policies that could be utilized to reach the optimal amount of pollution in Utopia: environmental standards, emissions taxes, and tradable emissions permits.

Environmental standards impose rules about what levels of pollution are admissible: although successful at reducing pollution, these standards are less efficient than other methods of pollution abatement since the other methods of pollution abatement allow society to reach the same reduced level of pollution at lower cost to society. This inefficiency occurs because most environmental standards are inflexible and do not allow reductions in pollution to be achieved at minimum cost.

Emissions taxes are taxes that depend on the amount of pollution that a firm produces. When the emissions taxes are set at the level that represents the marginal social cost of pollution, this provides firms with an incentive to internalize the externality imposed by the pollution and to take into account the true costs to society of this pollution. An emissions tax approach is efficient in contrast to an environmental standards approach, since it provides an incentive for firms to produce that level of pollution where the marginal benefit of that pollution is equal for all sources of pollution. Each firm will reduce the amount of pollution they emit until its marginal benefit from that pollution equals the marginal social cost of that pollution as measured by the emissions tax.

Tradable emissions permits are licenses that allow license holders to emit limited quantities of pollutants. These permits can be bought and sold by polluters. In effect, tradable emissions permits create a market for pollution: those who are willing to pay high prices for the right to pollute can enter this market and purchase the right to emit that pollution. This market will enable firms with different costs of reducing pollution to engage in mutually beneficial transactions: those that can reduce pollution cheaply will sell their rights to pollute to firms that find their costs of pollution reduction relatively high. Provided that the government does not issue too many permits or too few permits, a tradable emissions permit policy can efficiently result in pollution being reduced to the socially optimal amount, since it provides an incentive for those who can reduce their pollution most cheaply to do so.

From an efficiency standpoint, emissions taxes or tradable emissions permits are superior to environmental standards.

2. Childhood vaccination benefits the recipient of the vaccination since it reduces or eliminates the possibility that the child will contract a serious childhood disease. Childhood vaccination also generates external benefits since vaccinations reduce the probability that other people will develop the disease since there are fewer possible transmitters of the disease. Suppose that the market demand curve for childhood vaccination is given by the equation $Q = 1{,}000 - 2P$. But, this market demand curve fails to take into account the marginal social benefit (*MSB*) of childhood vaccinations that accrue to society: these marginal social benefits include an additional $100 per vaccination in benefits than what is represented by the market demand curve. Suppose also that the marginal social cost (*MSC*) for childhood vaccinations is given by the equation $P = (1/3)Q$. Identify the amount of vaccinations the market will supply as well as the price of these vaccinations. Then compute the socially optimal amount of vaccinations and the price associated with this optimal amount. Finally, suppose the government decides to subsidize consumers of childhood vaccinations. What would be the optimal Pigouvian subsidy per vaccination if the goal of the government was to get the market to provide the socially optimal amount of childhood vaccinations? Use a graph to illustrate your answers to this problem, but provide numerical answers to each of the questions as well.

STEP 1: **Use the market demand curve and *MSC* equations to solve for the market equilibrium quantity and market equilibrium price.**

Rewrite the *MSC* as $Q = 3P$ and then set the *MSC* equal to the market demand curve to get $P = 200$. Then use this price to find the market quantity of vaccinations: $Q_{Market} = 600$. Because there is an external benefit in this market, we know that the market provided quantity and the market determined price will be too low. Consumers in this market undervalue childhood vaccinations and therefore do not consume the socially optimal quantity of vaccinations since they do not take into account the external benefits that accrue to society at large from childhood vaccination.

STEP 2: **Sketch a graph of the market for childhood vaccinations using the numerical values you calculated in Step 1 to guide your sketch. In your graph indicate the market demand curve for vaccinations, the *MSC* for vaccinations, and the *MSB* from vaccinations.**

Start by drawing the market demand curve. Close inspection of this demand curve reveals that the *x*-intercept of the demand curve is 1,000 and the *y*-intercept of the demand curve is 500. Then, draw in the *MSC:* it has a *y*-intercept of zero. From Step 1, you know the equilibrium price and quantity in the market: mark these levels on your graph. Then, draw in the *MSB* for childhood vaccinations: since the marginal external benefit of a vaccination is \$100 per vaccination greater than the market demand curve, this will result in the *MSB* of vaccination curve being parallel to the demand curve, with a *y*-intercept that is \$100 greater than the original *y*-intercept of 500. The following graph illustrates these curves.

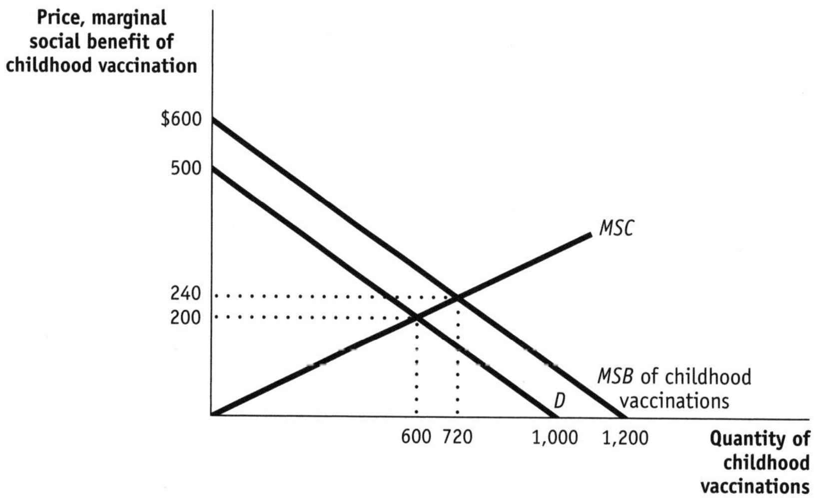

STEP 3: **Identify what the optimal Pigouvian subsidy would be if the government intervenes with the intention of providing a payment that is designed to encourage vaccinations to that level that would include the social benefits of vaccinations.**

From the preceding graph, we can see that the optimal amount of childhood vaccinations is 720 units when all the social benefits from vaccinations are included. Suppliers are willing to supply this amount of the good if they receive a price of \$240. Demanders are only willing to pay a price of \$140 for this level of vaccination (\$240 minus the social benefit or, alternatively, use the demand curve and the quantity equal to 720 to find the price that demanders are willing to pay). The government would need to provide a subsidy equal to this price difference ($100) for the optimal amount of vaccinations to be provided through a Pigouvian subsidy.

3. Joe's Garage provides a number of car services including oil changes. Some of the dirty oil often finds its way into a nearby stream, and this pollution is harmful to the wildlife that frequents the area. Joe does not make any effort to clean up this pollution, since this clean up would only add to his cost and the pollution does not directly affect him or his business. Thus, Joe, when he considers his supply curve, does not incorporate the social costs of his production. The demand for Joe's services at this shop is given by $P = 50 - Q$, where Q is a measure of the number of units of car services Joe provides. The demand curve reflects the marginal social benefit (*MSB*) of consuming Joe's services. The supply of services at Joe's shop is given by the equation $P = 4Q$. The pollution cost is estimated to be equal to $5 per unit of car services provided. Recently, a local community group has formed with the intention of identifying polluters and then designing and legislating Pigouvian taxes to correct these situations of negative externalities that are not accounted for by the market. You are asked to help this organization first identify the cost of Joe's pollution to the community as well as the deadweight loss from this pollution (you may need to review your notes from previous chapters on deadweight loss). Then, the organization would like you to identify the optimal amount of car services and the optimal Pigouvian tax to achieve this level of car services. You may find it helpful to draw a sketch indicating the demand (which in this example is also the *MSB* curve) and supply curves for Joe's Garage as well as the marginal social costs of providing these car services. How much revenue will the government receive if the government imposes this Pigouvian tax, and how does this amount of revenue compare to the social costs that arise from this production?

STEP 1: Identify the amount of car services and the price for these car services currently provided by Joe's Garage.

To find the amount of car services and the price of these car services that will be provided by the market, use the demand and supply curves. Using these two equations, we find that the price of car services is equal to $40 and the equilibrium quantity of car services in the market is 10 units.

STEP 2: Identify the cost of the pollution to the community that arises from the current production at Joe's Garage.

Since each unit of car services generates $5 in pollution costs (the social costs), the cost of the pollution to the community is equal to (10 units)($5/unit) or $50.

STEP 3: Identify the socially optimal amount of car services to provide if the social costs of providing these services are taken into account.

The socially optimal amount of car services to provide is equal to that amount of car services where the *MSB* of car services is just equal to the *MSC* of car services. To find this quantity, we must first find the *MSC* of the car services. Since each car service generates an additional social cost of $5 per unit, we can think of these additional social costs as simply shifting the initial supply curve upwards by this additional social cost per unit. Thus, if the initial supply curve is $P = 4Q$, the *MSC* of providing car services will be given by the equation $P = 5 + 4Q$. Notice that the *y*-intercept of the *MSC* curve is simply the original *y*-intercept of the supply curve plus the additional social cost per unit. This will be true provided that the additional social cost is a constant amount per unit of the good provided. The optimal amount of car services to provide can be found by using the *MSB* and *MSC* curves: the optimal amount of car services to provide is 9 units.

STEP 4: Identify the deadweight loss to society of this pollution.

To find the deadweight loss, you will want to think about the area that represents in this case the overproduction of the good by the market. In the following graph, the market quantity (Q_{MKT}) and the socially optimal quantity (Q_{OPT}) are identified along with the market price (P_{MKT}) and the price that would reflect the marginal cost to society of car services (P_{MSC}). The deadweight loss in this graph is shaded: notice that at Q_{MKT}, the true marginal cost to society of car services is greater than the market price: the price people are willing to pay for this last unit of the good is less than the cost to society of producing this last unit of the good. This indicates that too many car services are being provided by the market. This same argument will hold true until the quantity produced is reduced to Q_{OPT}, where the true marginal cost of producing the last unit of car services is exactly equal to the price consumers are willing to pay (P_{OPT}). Study this graph carefully.

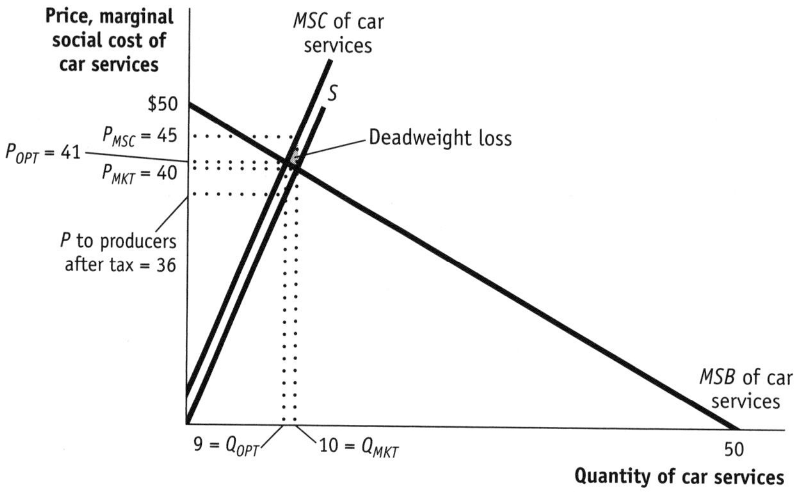

STEP 5: Identify the optimal Pigouvian tax to apply in this situation to have the optimal amount of car services provided by Joe's Garage.

The optimal Pigouvian tax will be equal to the additional social cost of providing the car services, or $5 per unit. Suppliers will charge consumers $41 per unit of car services, send $5 per unit of car services to the government, and then keep $36 per car services. With this tax and pricing arrangement, suppliers will be willing to supply 9 units of car services (the socially optimal amount), since they will receive the amount ($36 per unit) that they must receive to supply this amount. Demanders will demand this amount if they pay $41 (use the *MSB* curve to verify that the price demanders are willing to pay for 9 units is $41). The price difference, $5 per unit, is the optimal Pigouvian tax.

STEP 6: Identify how much tax revenue the government gets when it implements the optimal Pigouvian tax on this market, and then compare this tax revenue with the social costs that occur when these car services are produced.

The tax revenue will equal the Pigouvian tax per unit times the number of units provided. Since the Pigouvian tax is equal to $5 per unit and 9 units are provided, the tax revenue is equal to $45. This is equivalent to the amount of social costs generated by this amount of car services. The government has collected enough tax revenue to compensate or remediate the pollution that Joe's Garage generates when it provides car services.

4. In Valley City there are two firms, firm A and firm B, that emit pollution emissions. The two firms have done a study of the marginal benefits of these pollution emissions, and the following graph provides each firm's marginal benefit of pollution. Without government intervention, each firm would choose to produce 1,000 tons of pollution emissions where the marginal benefit of an additional unit of pollution is zero for both firms. Citizens in Valley City want to reduce the pollution emissions by 50%, and have asked the government to institute either an environmental standard that will achieve this goal or an emissions tax. The government of Valley City has asked you to analyze both proposals and advise it as to how each firm will react to the two proposals. The government also needs you to identify what the numeric value of the tax needs to be to reach the goal of a 50% reduction in pollution. In addition, the government seeks your guidance as to which proposal will provide the more efficient outcome.

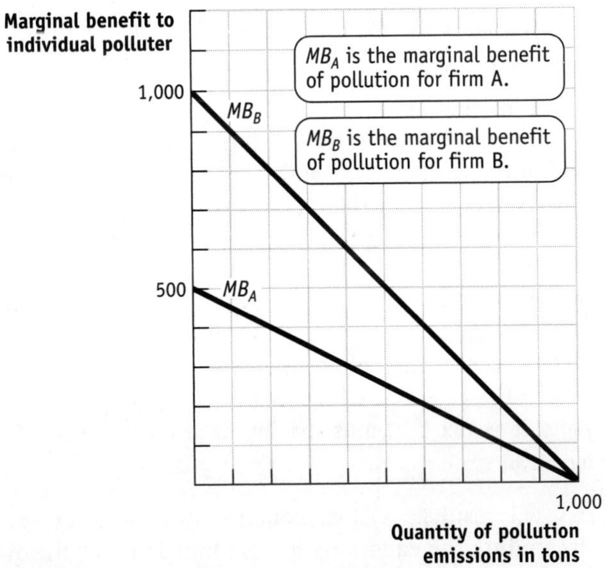

STEP 1: Determine the environmental standard that must be imposed on these two firms to reduce total emissions by 50%.

Without any intervention by the government to force these firms to reduce their pollution emissions, both firms will choose to each produce 1,000 tons of pollution emissions, since this is where each firm finds that the marginal benefit of additional pollution emissions is equal to $0. So, without any government intervention, we know that total pollution emissions will be 2,000 tons. If the goal of Valley City is to reduce pollution emissions by 50%, then the total reduction in pollution emissions must be 1,000 tons. In this example, the environmental standard results in a reduction in pollution emissions for each firm of 50%: that is, each firm needs to reduce its pollution emissions by 500 tons. The following graph illustrates the environmental standard.

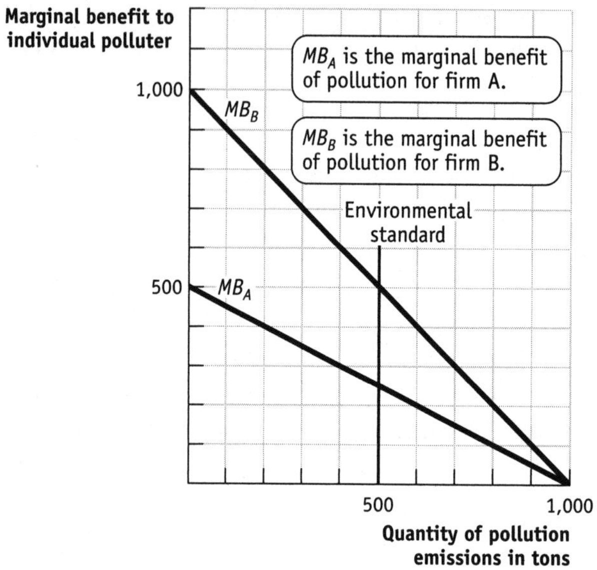

STEP 2: Analyze the efficiency of this environmental standard as a method for reducing pollution in Valley City.

When firm A reduces its pollution emissions to 500 tons, its marginal benefit from pollution is equal to \$250; when firm B reduces its pollution emissions to 500 tons, its marginal benefit from pollution is equal to \$500. This implies that there is a greater benefit from pollution to firm B than there is to firm A, or, in other words, the benefit of reducing pollution for firm A is not as costly as it is for firm B. This suggests that it is possible to achieve the same total reduction in pollution emissions at a cheaper cost than through the use of an environmental standard. The use of an environmental standard by Valley City to achieve its pollution emissions goal is not efficient, since it is not the lowest cost means of accomplishing this goal.

STEP 3: Determine the emissions tax that must be imposed on these two firms to reduce total emissions by 50%.

Finding the emissions tax that will result in a 50% reduction in pollution emissions is a bit of work. Let's start by finding the equations for the marginal benefit of pollution for each firm. Since each marginal benefit of pollution curve is linear in the given graph, this is a relatively simple matter.

$$MB_A = 500 - (1/2)Q_A$$
$$MB_B = 1{,}000 - Q_B$$

We also know that the total amount of pollution emissions Valley City wants is 1,000 tons and that this total must be achieved by firm A and firm B reducing their pollution emissions. We can write this relationship as

$$Q_A + Q_B = Q_{Total} = 1{,}000$$

Finally, the emissions tax results in each firm having the same marginal benefit from pollution for the last ton emitted: or,

$$MB_A = MB_B = \text{Emissions Tax}$$

Let's use these equations to find the emissions tax that Valley City must impose to reach its goal of a 50% reduction in pollution emissions.

Since $MB_A = MB_B$, we can write this as $500 - (1/2)Q_A = 1{,}000 - Q_B$. Rearranging this equation, we can rewrite this as $Q_A = 2Q_B - 1{,}000$. Then, we can make use of the relationship $Q_A + Q_B = 1{,}000$ and rearrange this equation to be $Q_A = 1{,}000 - Q_B$. Now, let's substitute $(1{,}000 - Q_B)$ for Q_A:

$$500 - (1/2)Q_A = 1{,}000 - Q_B$$
$$500 - (1/2)(1{,}000 - Q_B) = 1{,}000 - Q_B$$
$$3Q_B = 2{,}000$$
$Q_B = (2{,}000/3)$, or approximately 666.7 tons of pollution emissions

Once we have Q_B, we can find Q_A using the relationship $(1{,}000 - Q_B) = Q_A$:

$$Q_A = 1{,}000 - Q_B$$
$Q_A = 1{,}000 - (2{,}000/3) = (1{,}000/3)$, or approximately 333.3 tons of pollution emissions

Notice that $Q_A + Q_B$ equals 1,000 tons of pollution emissions: this is the amount of total pollution emissions that Valley City would like the policy to achieve.

Now, we need to find what the emissions tax must be to achieve this reduction in pollution emissions. Use the MB_A and MB_A equations for this. Thus,

$$MB_A = 500 - (1/2)Q_A = 500 - (1/2)(1{,}000/3) = \$333.33$$
$$MB_B = 1{,}000 - Q_B = 1{,}000 - (2{,}000/3) = \$333.33$$

An emissions tax of $333.33 will result in a 50% reduction in total pollution emissions in Valley City.

The following graph provides an illustration of this emissions tax and the work we have done.

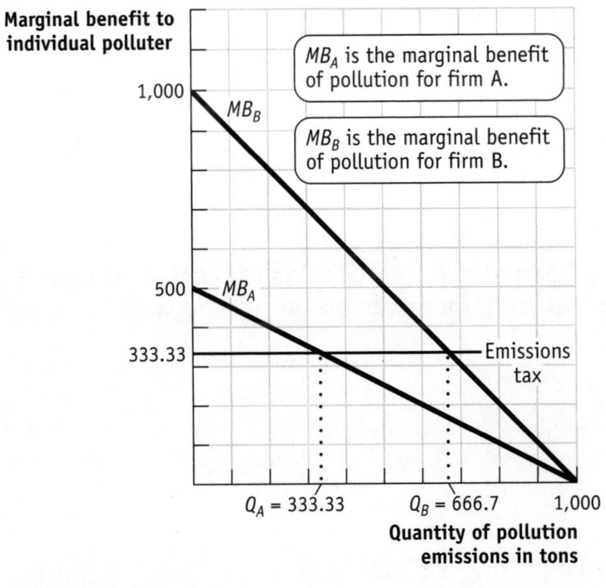

STEP 4: Analyze the efficiency of this emissions tax as a method for reducing pollution in Valley City.

With the emissions tax of $333.33 per unit of pollution emissions, we are able to reduce overall pollution emissions in Valley City by 50%, and, in addition, we are able to accomplish this goal and have both firms produce that level of pollution emissions, where their marginal benefit from pollution is equal. In our example, firm A reduces its pollution emissions more than firm B because the marginal benefit from pollution is less for firm A than it is for firm B. Firm B will generate 666.7 tons of pollution emissions, with a marginal benefit to pollution from the last unit being equal to $333.33, while firm A will generate 333.3 tons of pollution emissions, with a marginal benefit to pollution from the last unit being equal to $333.33. Firm A reduces its pollution by more than it would under an environmental standard and firm B reduces its pollution by less than it would under an environmental standard: in the end, the reduction in pollution emissions is equivalent with the two programs, but the total surplus in the market is greater with the emissions tax, since because the reduction in emissions has been achieved efficiently by having the firm that can reduce its pollution at lower cost reduce its pollution more.

STEP 5: Provide a statement as to the most efficient means for Valley City to achieve its pollution reduction goals.

Valley City can achieve its goal of a 50% reduction in pollution emissions using either an environmental standard or an emissions tax, but the emissions tax will accomplish this goal efficiently, while the environmental standard will not.

Problems and Exercises

1. Classify each of the following situations as positive or negative externalities; then identify whether the externality occurs on the demand or consumption side of the model or on the supply or production side of the model.
   a. A manufacturing plant spews toxic gas into the environment as a by-product of its production of furniture.
   b. A group of teenagers gather on Saturday to play loud music and congregate in a downtown park, making it difficult for other people in the town to enjoy thc park.
   c. A property owner fills his front yard with trash and old tires.

d. A company develops a new technology for producing its product, and the new technology can potentially help other companies produce more efficiently.

e. School-age children in a community do not get immunized prior to attending school.

f. A neighbor decorates the outside of her house with a tasteful holiday display.

g. A neighbor keeps his barking dog outside his house all day and all night.

h. Commercial fishermen catch too many fish and deplete the stock of fish.

2. What is a side effect? What does it mean when a market fails to take into account a side effect? What can you say about the level of production of the good in a market where there are side effects?

3. Suppose there are just two firms in Smalltown and both of these firms emit pollution as part of their productive process. Firm A's marginal social benefit from pollution is given by the equation $MSB = 100 - Q$, while firm B's marginal social benefit from pollution is given by the equation $MSB = 50 - 0.5Q$, where Q is the quantity of pollution emissions measured in tons.

   a. Draw a graph representing the marginal social benefit of pollution emissions for firm A and firm B.

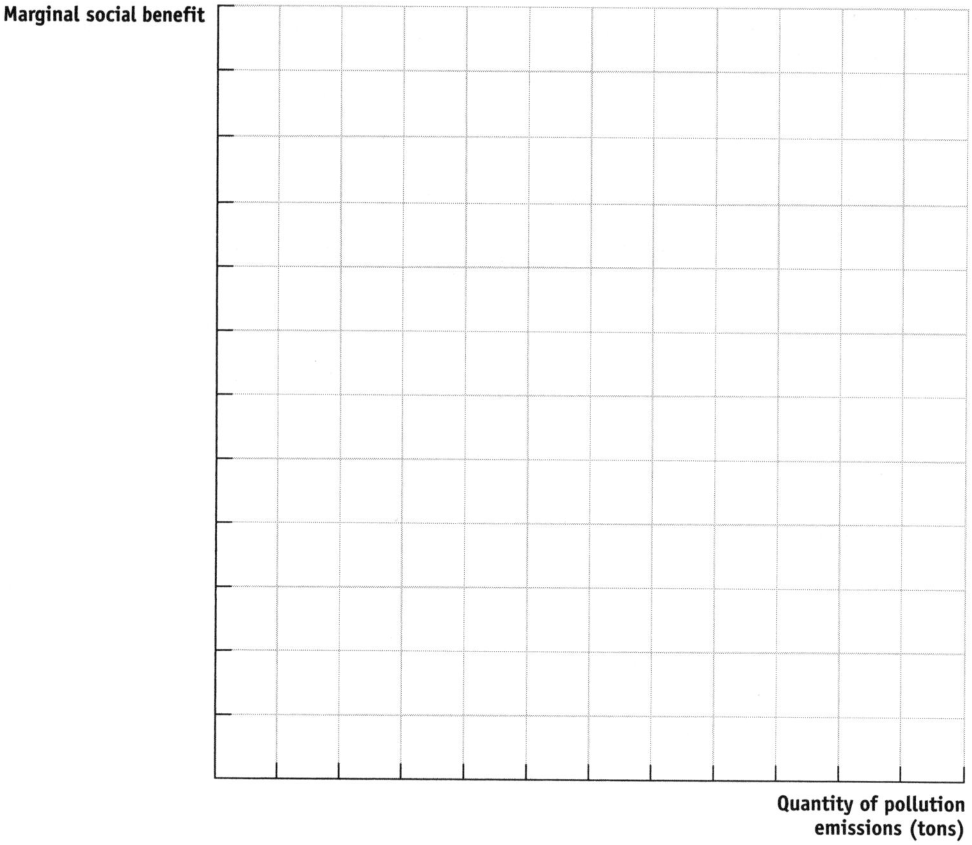

   b. Suppose the government in Smalltown decides to impose an emissions standard of 55 tons for every firm producing in Smalltown. How much of a reduction in pollution emissions will occur because of the imposition of this standard? Assume that prior to the emissions standard, firms produced the level of pollution emissions at which their marginal social benefit equaled $0.

   c. What is the marginal social benefit to firm A of the last ton of pollution it emits? What is the marginal social benefit to firm B of the last ton of pollution it emits?

   d. Is this an efficient method for reducing pollution emissions by this amount? Explain your answer.

4. Use the information given in problem 3 to answer this set of questions. Suppose that the government, instead of an emissions standard, imposes a tax on emissions of $30 per ton.

a. What will be the reduction in pollution emissions by firm A with the imposition of this tax?

b. What will be the reduction in pollution emissions by firm B with the imposition of this tax?

c. What will be the total reduction in pollution emissions with this tax?

d. Is this an efficient method for reducing pollution emissions by this amount? Explain your answer.

e. Draw a graph illustrating this tax. Identify firm A's and firm B's marginal social benefit from pollution emissions.

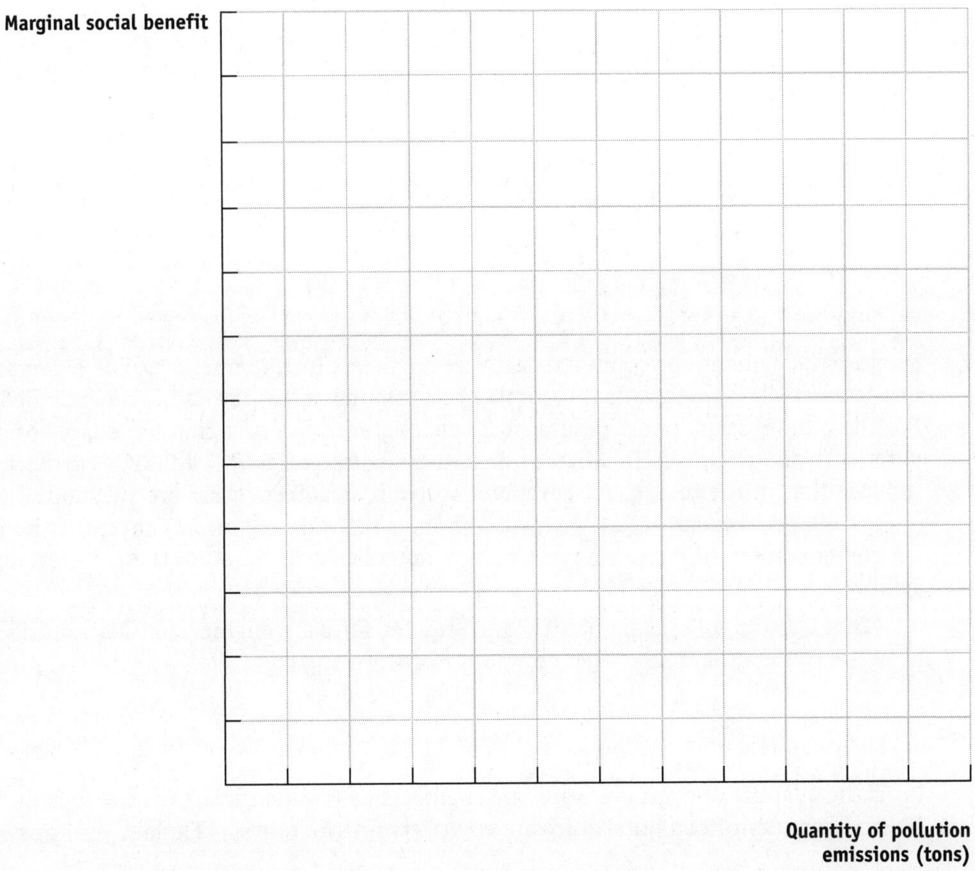

5. A recent article reports that drunken driving has risen in communities that have imposed smoking bans in their bars and taverns. The gist of the problem is that smokers who also drink are now driving longer distances to get to bars that allow them to smoke while they are drinking. Does the decision to impose a smoking ban on the bars and taverns in the community create an externality? What do you think motivated policymakers to impose this smoking ban?

6. Suppose the consumption of a good generates substantial external benefits due to the presence of side effects. Suppose the government wishes to help the market generate the socially optimal consumption of this good. Will the market by itself generate the socially optimal amount of this good? Explain your answer. What type of policy or policies might the government engage in to meet this goal?

7. Suppose the demand for computer software engineers in Micronesia can be expressed as $Q = 100 - 0.001P$, where Q is the number of computer software engineers demanded and P is the annual salary per computer software engineer. Suppose that the supply of computer software engineers in Micronesia can be expressed as $P = 4{,}000Q$. Furthermore, suppose that in the market for computer software engineers there are substantial technology spillovers equal to \$20,000 per computer software engineer. Currently, the market for computer software engineers does not take into account these technological spillovers.

   a. What is the equilibrium quantity of computer software engineers in Micronesia, and what is the annual salary per computer software engineer?

   b. Is the quantity of computer software engineers you found in part (a) the socially optimal quantity of computer software engineers for Micronesia? Explain your answer.

c. Draw a graph of the market for computer software engineers. In your graph draw a curve that represents the marginal private benefits (demand), a curve that represents the marginal social benefit (*MSB*), and a curve that represents supply. Identify the market quantity and market price as well as the socially optimal quantity and price.

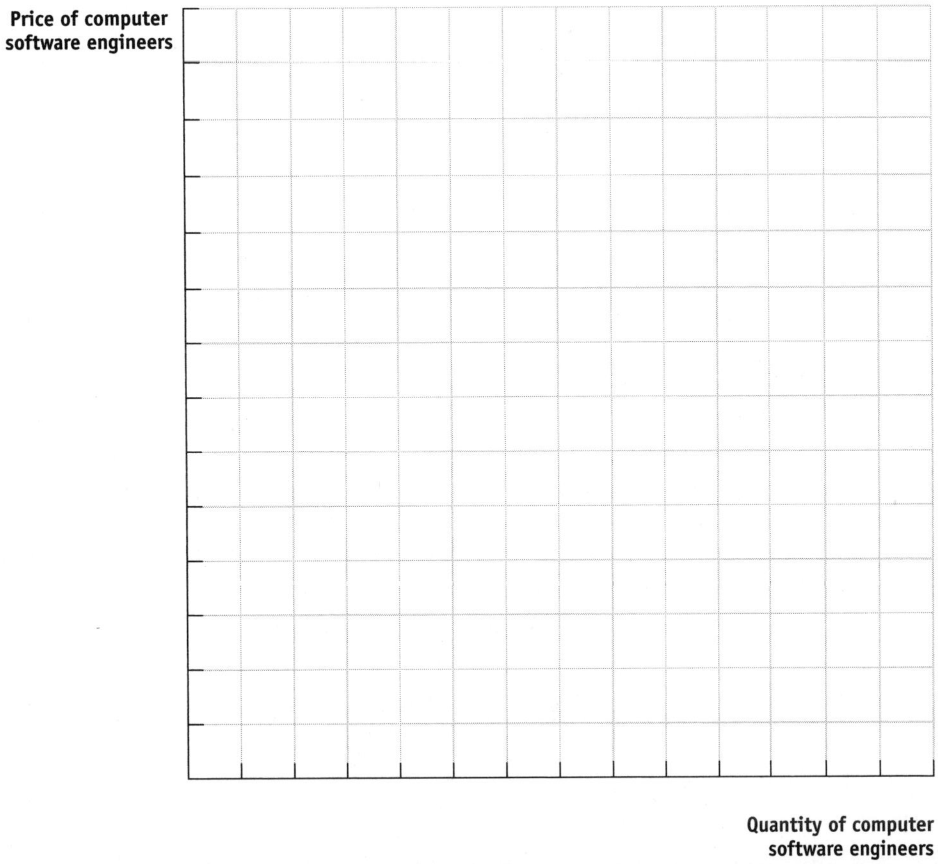

d. What is the optimal quantity of computer software engineers for Micronesia? Explain why you have chosen this quantity as the optimal quantity.

e. What policy could the government enact to enable Micronesia to produce this optimal quantity?

f. Graph the policy you described in part (e) on the graph below, and label this graph carefully and completely.

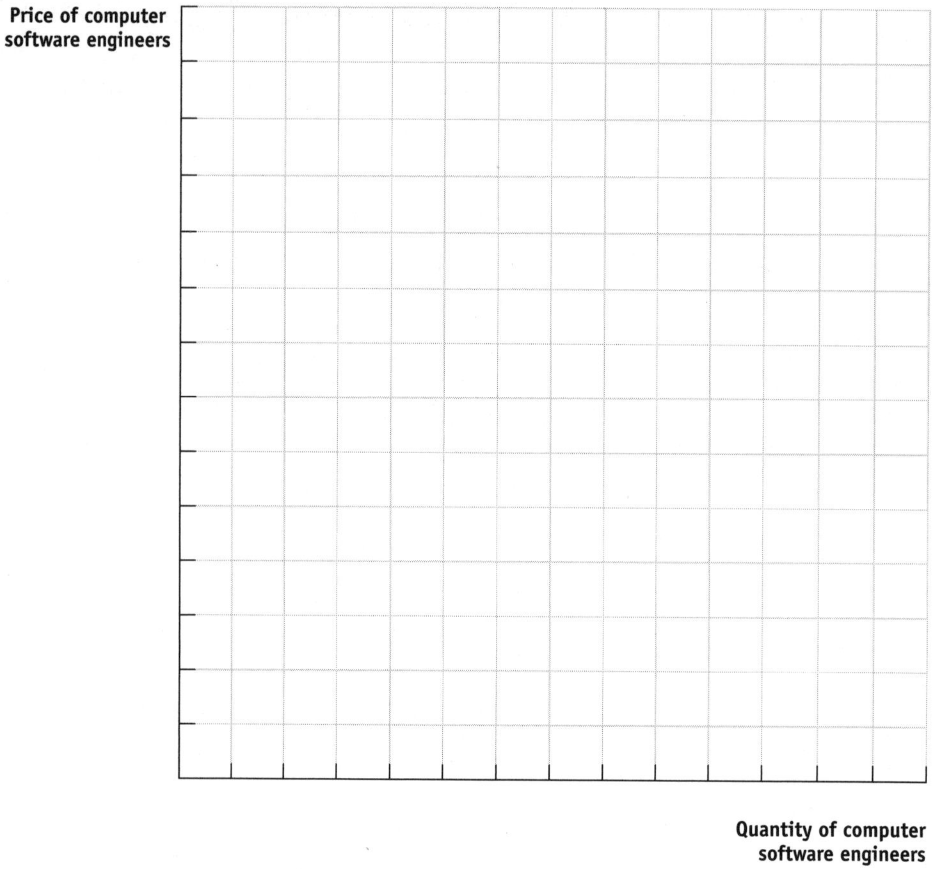

8. The following table is meant to summarize the market level of production for various situations that might occur due to the presence of externalities. In the table, *MSC* refers to the marginal social cost of production, Supply refers to the marginal private cost of production, *MSB* refers to the marginal social benefit from consuming the good, and Demand refers to the marginal private benefit from consuming the good. Read each scenario and then decide whether the market produces thc socially optimal amount of the good, too much of the good, or too little of the good. Fill in the second column with the relevant description of the market's production decision.

Situation	Market Produces
Demand = *MSB* and Supply = *MSC*	
Demand > *MSB* and Supply = *MSC*	
Demand < *MSB* and Supply = *MSC*	
Demand = *MSB* and Supply < *MSC*	
Demand = *MSB* and Supply > *MSC*	

9. In the 1980s, there were two competing technologies for watching movies at home. The Beta system and the VHS system competed with each other for this particular market. Eventually, the VHS system became the dominant system, and those individuals who had purchased the Beta system found it difficult to find movies using this technology to show at home.

a. Is there an externality issue lying behind this story? If so, what kind of externality issue is it?

b. How would the term *positive feedback* apply to this situation?

c. Describe how this competition for the market for movies shown at home ultimately illustrates a network externality.

BEFORE YOU TAKE THE TEST

Module Review Questions

1. The gain to society of an additional unit of pollution is best measured by

a. an emissions tax.

b. an emissions standard.

c. the marginal social benefit of pollution.

d. the socially optimal quantity of pollution.

Use the figure below to answer the next question.

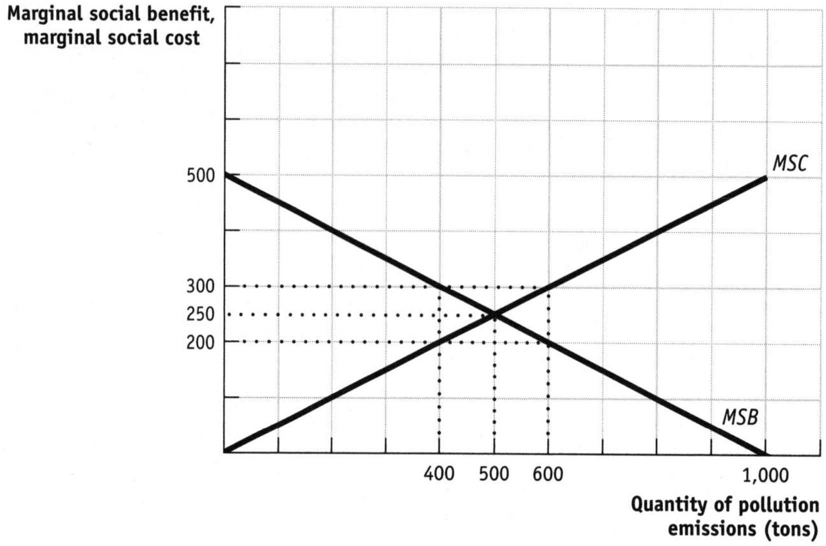

2. What is the appropriate emissions standard for this economy if there is only one producer in the economy and the goal is to produce the efficient level of pollution emissions?

a. 400 tons of emissions

b. 500 tons of emissions

c. 600 tons of emissions

d. 0 tons of emissions

3. A government wants to enact a policy that will lead to a reduction in pollution emissions. One policy entails establishing an emissions standard, and another policy entails implementation of an emissions tax. Which of the following statements is true?

I. An emissions standard and an emissions tax are equally efficient methods for reducing pollution emissions.

II. An emissions standard ensures that the marginal social benefit of pollution is equal for all sources of pollution.

III. An emissions tax does not ensure that the marginal social benefit of pollution is equal for all sources of pollution.

a. Statement I is true.

b. Statements I and II are true.

c. Statements I and III are true.

d. Statements I, II, and III are true.

e. None of the statements is true.

4. When two firms have different marginal social benefits from pollution, this implies that

a. an equal reduction in pollution by both firms is not efficient.

b. one firm can reduce its level of pollution by a larger amount and still find that its marginal social benefit of pollution is equal to the other firm's marginal social benefit of pollution.

c. an emissions tax is more efficient than an emissions standard.

d. All of the statements are true.

5. Taxes that are designed to reduce external costs are known as
   a. excise taxes.
   b. income taxes.
   c. Pigouvian taxes.
   d. emissions taxes.

6. Suppose a government decides to issue a limited number of tradable pollution permits. Which of the following statements is true?
   a. Firms that can easily and at low cost reduce their level of pollution will find it beneficial to purchase these tradable pollution permits.
   b. When the government issues these tradable pollution permits, it effectively creates a market for the right to pollute.
   c. Firms that sell their tradable pollution permits do not fully understand the costs they will incur when they try to reduce the level of pollution they create.
   d. None of the statements is true.

7. Which of the following tools is likely to encourage firms to find less-polluting technology?
   a. Emissions standards
   b. Emissions taxes
   c. Tradable pollution permits
   d. All of the above will create incentives for firms to find less-polluting technology.
   e. Emissions taxes and tradable pollution permits will create incentives for firms to find less-polluting technology.

8. Which of the following statements is true?
   a. In contrast to the cost of a negative externality like pollution, the benefit from a positive externality is easier to measure, since people like to reveal the amount of positive benefits they receive from different activities.
   b. The benefit from a positive externality is difficult to measure, since these benefits cannot be directly observed.

9. When the consumption of a good generates positive external benefits, the market tends to produce
   a. too much of the good, since there are positive external benefits from the consumption of the good.
   b. too little of the good, since the market does not take into account the positive external benefits from the consumption of the good.

10. Joe really does not enjoy school and is thinking about dropping out this spring. Joe's consumption of formal education is likely to
    a. be the efficient amount of education, since Joe knows best the level of benefit he receives from attending school.
    b. be at too high a level, since Joe has always been an indifferent student and a student who has rarely been engaged in getting an education.
    c. be at too low a level, since Joe only considers his private benefits from getting an education and not the social benefits that society receives when he gets an education.
    d. reflect his family's benefit from his getting an education, and his family thinks they will get a greater benefit if Joe drops out and gets a job. From his family's perspective, this would be an efficient outcome.

Use the following information to answer the next three questions.

Residents of Smalltown recognize that there are private benefits to exercise, and they estimate that the marginal private benefits from exercise can be represented by the demand curve $P = 100 - 0.05Q$, where P measures the marginal private benefit and Q is hours of exercise per year. Exercise also generates positive external benefits for the community because it reduces health care costs, lowers the obesity rate, and results in a more energetic and engaged community. The marginal external benefit from a unit of exercise is estimated to have a value of $10 per hour of exercise. The supply curve for exercise can be represented by the equation $P = 0.05Q$, where P measures the marginal private cost of exercise and Q is hours of exercise per year.

11. The market for exercise will not include the marginal social benefits from exercise without some type of intervention. How many hours of exercise per year will be provided by the market, and what is the price demanders are willing to pay for each unit of exercise consumed?

a. 0 hours of exercise; $100

b. 50 hours of exercise; $1,000

c. 1,000 hours of exercise; $50

d. 2,000 hours of exercise; $0

12. What is the socially optimal amount of exercise per year for Smalltown?

a. 0 hours of exercise

b. 1,000 hours of exercise

c. 1,100 hours of exercise

d. 2,000 hours of exercise

13. Smalltown decides it is important for the community to consume the socially optimal amount of exercise. Smalltown therefore decides to enact a policy of

a. subsidizing everyone who exercises with a payment of $10 per hour of exercise.

b. taxing everyone who exercises with a tax payment of $10 per hour of exercise.

c. mandating that everyone exercise an additional 10 hours per year.

d. reducing the price of each hour of exercise by $20.

14. Policymakers decide they wish to encourage the consumption of an activity that generates positive externalities. Which of the following statements is true?

I. An excise tax on each unit of the good consumed helps the policymaker achieve the socially optimal amount of consumption of this good.

II. A subsidy per unit of the good consumed helps the policymaker achieve the socially optimal amount of consumption of this good.

III. Intervention in this market by the policymaker results in a socially less-optimal outcome for this market, since government intervention in any market results in a deadweight loss.

a. Statement I is true.

b. Statement II is true.

c. Statement III is true.

d. None of the statements is true given this situation.

Answer the next three questions based on the following diagram of the market for bottled water that comes from aquifers deep underground. In the production of this product, the level of water in these aquifers is drawn down at a rate faster than the water can be replenished. This action results in a negative externality on the nearby communities that depend on these aquifers for their water, since the producers of the bottled water do not consider the effect of their production on the community's water source. In the graph below, Supply represents the marginal private cost of producing the good, *MSC* represents the marginal social cost (the external as well as private cost) of producing the good, and Demand represents the marginal social benefit from consuming the good. Assume that the externality per unit of the good produced is a constant amount per unit of bottled water.

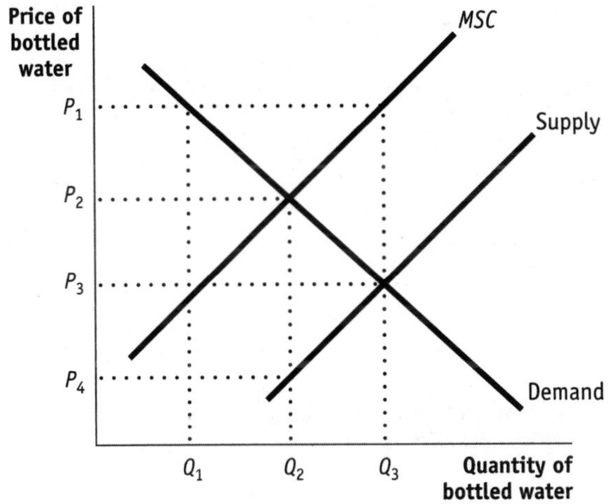

15. Without government intervention in this market, the market will provide _________ bottles of bottled water at a price of _________ per bottle.
    a. Q_1; P_1
    b. Q_2; P_2
    c. Q_2; P_4
    d. Q_3; P_3

16. What is the socially optimal level of output for this market?
    a. Q_1
    b. Q_2
    c. Q_3

17. At the market-determined level of production in the above market, the deadweight loss due to the negative externality can be expressed as the area
    a. $(1/2)(P_1 - P_3)Q_3$.
    b. $(1/2)(P_2 - P_4)(Q_3 - Q_2)$.
    c. $(1/2)(P_2 - P_4)Q_2$.
    d. $(1/2)P_2(Q_3 - Q_2)$.

18. A network externality is a situation

a. in which the value of a good to the consumer is dependent on how many other people also consume the same type of good.

b. that often arises in the markets for transportation and communication.

c. in which the marginal benefit from the consumption of the good depends on the number of other individuals who also use the good.

d. Answers (a), (b), and (c) are all true statements.

19. A community is debating the construction of several bike paths in the community. These bike paths would be separate from the roadway system in the community. As the community creates more bike paths linking different parts of the city, they expect this will lead to

a. negative externalities, as more and more people on bikes interfere with other forms of transportation.

b. positive feedback, due to the network externalities that will come from more and more people being able to move around the community efficiently on the bike paths.

c. more people deciding to bike to different locations, since the bike paths will make this form of transportation both safer and more convenient.

d. Answers (b) and (c) are both true.

20. A network externality is a situation in which the value of the good as more people use the good

a. increases.

b. decreases.

ANSWER KEY

Answers to Problems and Exercises

1. **a.** This is a negative production externality.

b. This is a negative consumption externality.

c. This is a negative consumption externality.

d. This is a positive production externality.

e. This is a negative consumption externality.

f. This is a positive consumption externality.

g. This is a negative consumption externality.

h. This is a negative production externality.

2. A side effect is a situation in which the market fails to take into account a cost or a benefit from some action. This results in the market failing to produce the right amount of the good, because the market either does not correctly measure the cost to society of producing the good or the benefit to society of consuming the good. When side effects are present in a market, this implies that the market produces either too much of the good (the situation when the side effect is a hidden cost) or too little of the good (the situation when the side effect is a hidden benefit).

3. **a.**

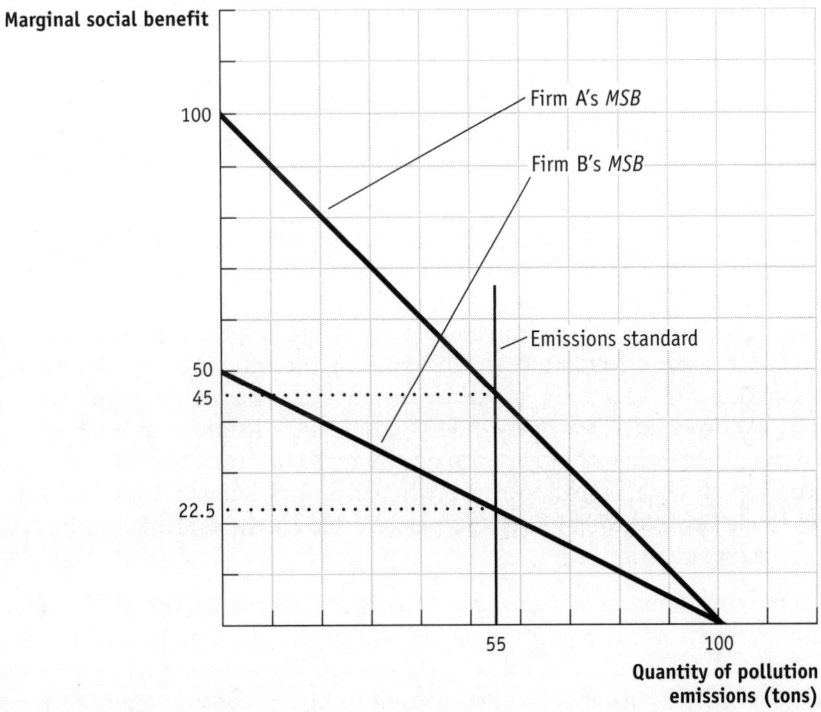

b. Each firm will reduce its emissions by 45 tons, for a total of 90 tons.

c. The marginal social benefit for firm A is $45, and the marginal social benefit for firm B is $22.50.

d. No, this is not efficient since the marginal social benefit of pollution emissions reduction is not equivalent across all the firms in the economy.

4. **a.** Firm A will reduce pollution emissions by 30 units.

   b. Firm B will reduce pollution emissions by 60 units.

   c. The total reduction in pollution emissions will be 90 units (note that this is the same level of pollution reduction achieved with the emissions standard in problem 3).

   d. This is an efficient method for reducing pollution emissions since each firm's marginal social benefit of pollution is the same for the last unit of pollution they emit.

   e.

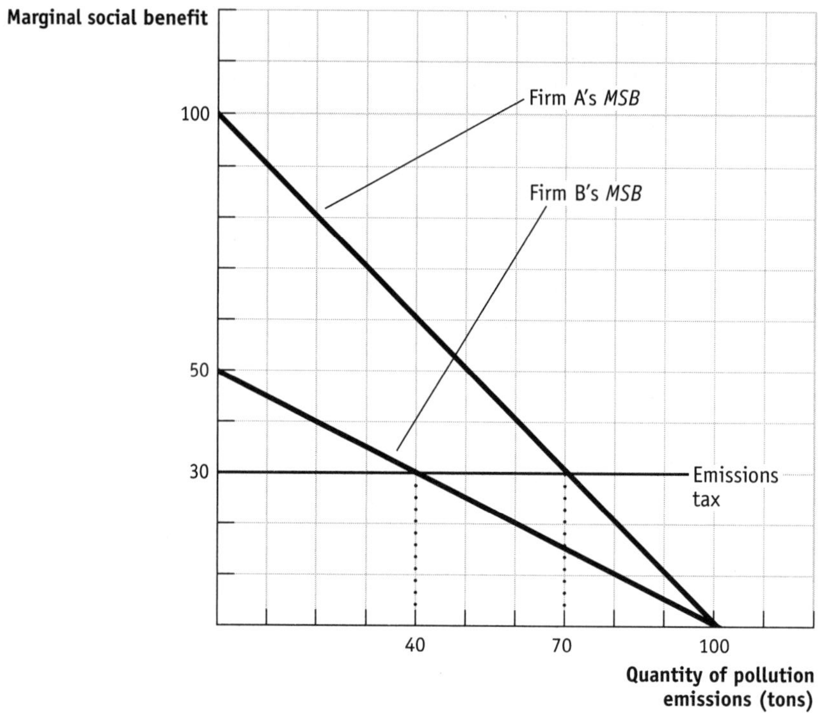

5. This is quite ironic in that the smoking ban was likely motivated by a desire to reduce the negative externality of secondhand smoke in bars and taverns. The policymakers considered the situation of smoking in the bar and identified that this behavior created a cost that was imposed on nonsmokers. By imposing this smoking ban, they would eliminate this side effect. However, in imposing the smoking ban they did not consider how smokers might react. If smokers view smoking as a highly important complement to their bar experience, they may indeed drive longer distances to be able to both smoke and drink. Then, when they get back on the road they impose a side effect, or negative externality, on others in the form of their drunk driving. Which side effect is more costly to society and to the third parties affected by these drinkers who also smoke is an interesting question!

6. When the consumption of a good generates external benefits, the good is underproduced in the market, since the positive side effects of the consumption of the good are not included in the market's determination of the equilibrium quantity of the good. The government needs to pursue policies that result in higher consumption of the good, which in turn affect the quantity of the side effect produced. The government can achieve this result by targeting the activity, or consumption of the good, by offering subsidies to consumers to encourage a higher level of consumption.

7. **a.** The equilibrium quantity in the market is where the quantity demanded equals the quantity supplied, or where 100,000 – 1,000Q = 4,000Q. Solving this equation, Q equals 20 computer software engineers. The annual salary for a computer software engineer can be found by using either the demand or the supply curve, and substituting in 20 for the quantity. Thus, the annual salary for a computer software engineer is $80,000.

b. The quantity found in part (a) is not the socially optimal amount of computer software engineers, since the market does not take into account the side effects of the positive externality that arises from the technology spillover. The market quantity equates demand and supply, instead of equating the marginal social benefit to the marginal social cost.

c.

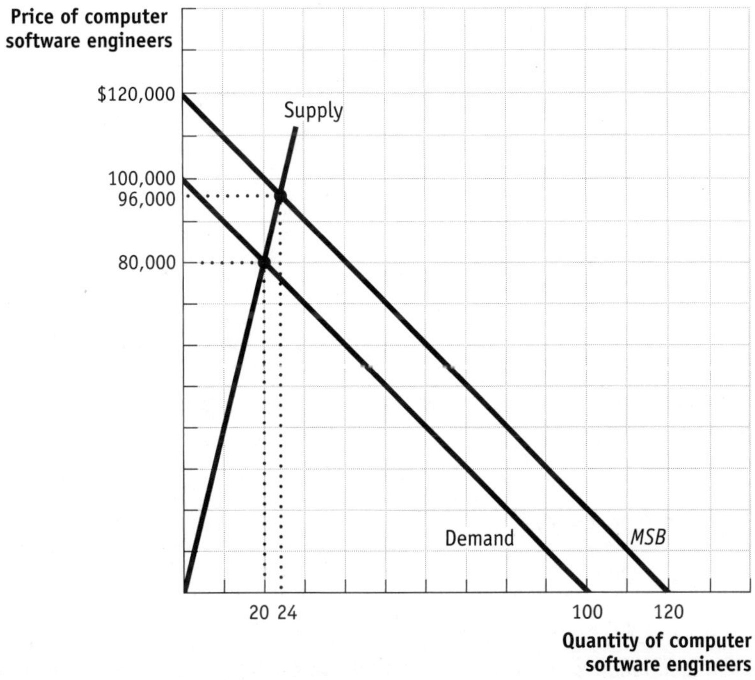

d. The optimal quantity of computer software engineers is where the marginal social benefit equals the marginal social cost. To find this quantity, first write an equation that expresses the marginal social benefit. This equation is $P = 120{,}000 - 1{,}000Q$ since the marginal social benefit curve has the same slope as the market demand curve but a *y*-intercept of 120,000 instead of 100,000. Setting the marginal social benefit curve equal to the supply curve yields the following: 120,000 – 1,000Q = 4,000Q, or Q = 24. When there is an external benefit from the consumption of the good, too few units of the good are consumed in the market: in this case, the optimal quantity of computer software engineers is 24 and not the market-determined quantity of 20 engineers.

e. The government could subsidize the demanders of computer software engineers so that they would effectively view the market demand curve for computer software engineers as being $P = 120{,}000 - 1{,}000Q$. This would entail paying a subsidy of $20,000 for every computer software engineer demanded. With this subsidy the government would effectively internalize the positive externality.

f.

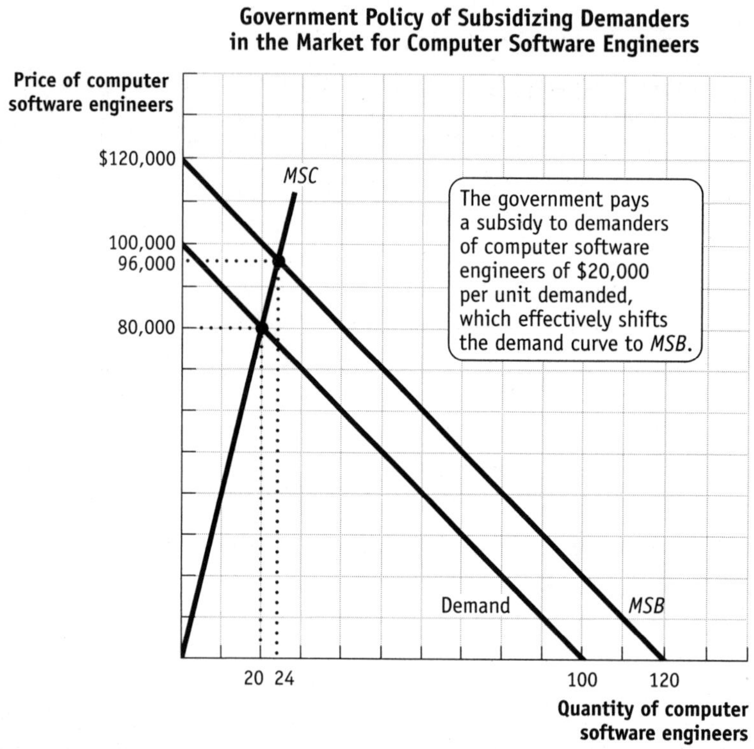

8.

Situation	Market Produces
Demand = *MSB* and Supply = *MSC*	The market produces the socially optimal amount of the good.
Demand > *MSB* and Supply = *MSC*	The market produces too much of the good.
Demand < *MSB* and Supply = *MSC*	The market produces too little of the good.
Demand = *MSB* and Supply < *MSC*	The market produces too much of the good.
Demand = *MSB* and Supply > *MSC*	The market produces too little of the good.

9. **a.** The externality issue is that the value of either of these systems for watching movies at home depends on how many other people have bought a particular system. For example, as more and more people purchase the VHS system, video stores are likely to stock more movies recorded with this system, and owners of the VHS system find that they have more movie choices. The system that gets more converts benefits from this wider usage.

b. *Positive feedback* refers to the idea that as more people purchase a product, other people are more likely to purchase the product. In this example, as more people purchased the VHS system, other people decided to adopt this technology for their own movie viewing: the value of the VHS system rose as more people purchased the system.

c. There is a network externality at play in this example, since as the network of users expands, the marginal benefit for each user of the good increases. This ultimately leads to one of the technologies becoming the dominant technology, which effectively drives the other technology out of the market.

Answers to Module Review Questions

1. **Answer c.** This is just the definition of the marginal social benefit of pollution.

2. **Answer b.** The socially optimal amount of pollution emissions is 500 tons of emissions.

3. **Answer e.** An emissions standard is not as efficient as an emissions tax because it does not ensure that the marginal social benefit of pollution is equal for all sources of pollution. In contrast, an emissions tax is a tax that results in the marginal benefit of pollution being equal across all sources of pollution.

4. **Answer d.** When two firms have different marginal social benefit from pollution curves, this tells us that the marginal social benefit from reducing pollution by a set amount is different between the two firms. It is therefore more efficient to have the firms reduce pollution by different amounts until the marginal social benefit of pollution is the same for both firms. An emissions standard requires that both firms reduce pollution by an equal amount without regard to the marginal social benefit of pollution.

5. **Answer c.** This is a definitional question. Pigou, an economist, emphasized that the appropriate tax could eliminate the hidden costs imposed by negative externalities.

6. **Answer b.** Firms will sell their permits if it is easy and inexpensive for them to reduce their pollution, since the permits are more valuable to firms that find the cost of reducing their level of pollution high. Firms that sell their pollution permits understand and have analyzed the costs associated with pollution reduction and have determined that they are better off selling the permits rather than using the permits. The government effectively decides what level of pollution it wants, and then creates a market for the right to pollute within this limit.

7. **Answer e.** Emissions standards are applied uniformly across all producers and therefore do not offer any incentive for producers to find new technology to reduce their pollution levels. In contrast, emissions taxes and tradable pollution permits provide a system of incentives that rewards those firms that find ways to reduce their levels of pollution or find cost-effective methods for pollution reduction.

8. **Answer b.** The positive benefit from the externality cannot be directly observed and measured, while it is possible to measure the external costs due to a negative externality such as pollution.

9. **Answer b.** When a good produces positive external benefits, the market does not include these benefits and therefore tends to undervalue the benefits from the consumption of the good. The market therefore results in too little of the good being produced.

10. **Answer c.** Joe's education reaps benefits not only for Joe and his family, but also for society. Joe will likely be able to better provide for himself with more education; he is likely to be a more productive member of society when he gets more education; and he will likely contribute more to society as a better-educated individual. Joe's education has both private and social benefits, but Joe is likely to consider only the private benefits and therefore select too low a level of education; from an efficiency standpoint the optimal amount of education is where the marginal social benefit of the education is equated to the marginal social cost of the education.

11. **Answer c.** To find the number of hours of exercise consumed in this market, set the demand curve equal to the supply curve: $100 - 0.05Q = 0.05Q$. This results in $Q =$ 1,000 hours of exercise with price equal to \$50.

12. **Answer c.** The socially optimal amount of exercise is the amount of exercise where *MSB* = Supply (since there are no marginal social costs to include in this problem). Thus, to solve this question you must find the marginal social benefit of exercise, which is equal to the demand curve plus the marginal external benefit. The marginal external benefit is \$10 per unit, so this means that the *MSB* curve can be expressed as $MSB = 110 - 0.05Q$. Setting this equation equal to the supply curve yields $110 - 0.05Q = 0.05Q$. Thus, the socially optimal amount of exercise is 1,100 hours of exercise.

13. **Answer a.** When Smalltown subsidizes the consumption of exercise by an amount equal to the social benefit of the additional hour of exercise, it effectively causes the demand curve for exercise to shift to the right, resulting in more hours of exercise being demanded at every price. With a subsidy of \$10 per hour of exercise, the subsidy exactly equals the marginal social benefit of an hour of exercise, and thus this subsidy results in the residents of Smalltown consuming the socially optimal amount of exercise.

14. **Answer b.** When there is a positive externality, the government can encourage the consumption of the good by legislating a subsidy for the consumption of the good. Without the subsidy too little of the good is consumed, and therefore the government intervention in this market can move the market closer to the socially optimal outcome.

15. **Answer d.** The market without intervention will provide the amount of bottled water where Supply = Demand, or Q_3 units at a price of P_3.

16. **Answer b.** The socially optimal level of output for this market is where *MSC* = Demand for the last unit produced, which occurs when the quantity is Q_2.

17. **Answer b.** The deadweight loss is the area that represents the efficiency loss due to the externality. When the market produces Q_3 units of the good, the marginal social cost of the last unit is greater than the marginal social benefit from the last unit. This difference can be represented by the distance $(P_1 - P_3)$ or by the distance $(P_2 - P_4)$ since the externality per unit of the good produced is assumed to be constant. The market produces Q_3 units instead of the socially optimal Q_2 units, so the deadweight loss can be calculated as $(1/2)(P_2 - P_4)(Q_3 - Q_2)$.

18. **Answer d.** These statements are all definitional: network externalities often arise in transportation and communication systems, since these systems become more effective when more people use the particular system. This implies that one person's benefit from consuming an additional unit of the good is affected by the consumption decisions of other people with regard to this good.

19. **Answer d.** Since the bike paths are separate from the roadway system, this will likely not create negative externalities related to the bikes interfering with other forms of transportation. But as more and more miles of bike paths are created, this will make transportation by bicycle more feasible and will lead to positive feedback from the network effects.

20. **Answer a.** A network externality is a situation where one person's use of a good is enhanced when other people elect to also use the good. This is the result of interconnections or networks existing between the users of the good. The more users of the good, the more networks or connections are created.

module 38

Public Goods and Common Resources

BEFORE YOU READ THE MODULE

Summary

This module explores two characteristics, the property of rivalness and the property of excludability, that are key to determining whether or not a market can provide the efficient level of the good. The module uses these characteristics to explore the problems presented by public goods, common resources, and artificially scarce goods.

Module Objectives

Objective #1. The characteristics of a good determine whether or not the market can provide the good efficiently. When a good is excludable and rival, the market can provide the good efficiently. A good is excludable when suppliers of the good can prevent people who do not pay for the good from consuming the good. Since the good is excludable, suppliers can charge consumers of the good a price, which gives the producers an incentive to supply the good. A good is rival when a person's consumption of the good means that no other consumer can consume that same unit of the good. Since the good is rival this implies that it is efficient for consumers to pay a positive price equal to the good's marginal cost of production. Private goods are both excludable and rival, and hence, the market provides the efficient quantity of a private good.

Objective #2. A public good is a good that benefits many people whether or not they have paid for it and whose benefits to an individual are not affected by how many other people are consuming the good. Thus, a public good is nonrival, because one consumer's consumption of the good does not change the level of benefits available to other consumers of the good, and it is nonexcludable, since an individual can consume the good once it is produced whether or not they have paid for the good. These two differences result in the market being unable to provide the efficient amount of the good. Because public goods are nonexcludable they suffer from the free-rider problem: this free-rider problem results in firms being unwilling to produce the good since they know it will be possible for consumers to consume the good without paying for it once the good is produced. Because public goods are nonrival in consumption it is inefficient to charge people for consuming these goods, since the marginal cost of another person consuming the good is zero.

Objective #3. A common resource is a good that many people consume whether or not they have paid for the good and whose consumption by each person reduces the amount of the good available to other people. The common resource is, thus, nonexcludable but rival in consumption since people can consume the good even though they have not paid for it, but their consumption of the good reduces the amount of the good available to others. Common resources are subject to overuse by individuals because individuals will continue to consume units of the good until their marginal benefit from consumption of the common resource is equal to zero. In choosing this level of consumption, individuals ignore the cost their actions inflict on society. Common resources thus present a problem of a negative externality in which individuals consume an inefficiently high amount of the good because they ignore, or fail to internalize, the external costs they impose on other members of society. In the case of a common resource, society must intervene in the market to find a way to get individual users of the resource to take into account the costs they impose on others. This intervention could be in the form of a Pigouvian tax, a system of tradable licenses for the use of the common resource, or through the assignment of property rights to the common resources. This last intervention, the assignment of property rights, gives the holder of the property rights the ability to limit the use of the common resource and, thus, prevent the overuse of this resource.

Objective #4. Artificially scarce goods are those goods that are excludable but nonrival in consumption. These are goods that must be paid for in order for the consumer to consume the good but whose consumption does not diminish the ability of other consumers to consume the same unit of the good. Since the artificially scarce good is nonrival in consumption, the marginal cost of an individual's consumption is zero. When the supplier charges a price for this good, the price is therefore greater than the individual's marginal cost, which results in too few units of the good being consumed. The case of the artificially scarce good is similar to that of the natural monopoly in which the average total cost is greater than the marginal cost within the relevant output range. For both the artificially scarce good and the natural monopoly, the producers in these situations are willing to produce only if they can charge a price that is greater than the marginal cost of producing the good, but this price implies that the producer is producing an inefficiently low amount of output.

Objective #5. When a good is either nonexcludable or nonrival, the market does not produce the efficient quantity of the good.

- When a good is nonexcludable, this creates a free-rider problem in which consumers are not willing to pay for the good but instead want to free ride on those who do pay for the good. When consumers free-ride, too little of the good is produced in the market.
- When a good is nonrival in consumption, the cost of providing an additional unit of the good is zero because the good is nonrival. When consumers are forced to pay a price that is greater than zero, they end up demanding too little of the good and the market therefore produces an inefficient quantity of the good.

Objective #6. A public good may be provided through voluntary contributions or by self-interested individuals or firms who produce them with the hope of earning money through some indirect means. For example, broadcast television is produced by firms who earn money through advertisement rather than payments from consumers who watch the televised programming. A public good may also be provided through social encouragement or social pressure. Many public goods are provided by the government and funded through taxation. This provision of public goods by the government is a crucial role for the government: without government provision these public goods would either not be provided or would be provided at levels that are inefficiently low.

Objective #7. Governments must decide whether to provide the public good and how much of the public good to provide. The optimal level of public good provision is the level where the marginal social benefit of the public good is equal to the marginal cost of producing the public good. In the case of a public good, the marginal social benefit from the public good is the sum of the individual marginal benefits that are enjoyed by all consumers of that unit. Since the public good is nonrival, the benefit an individual receives from the consumption of the public good does not diminish the benefit another individual receives from consuming the same unit of the public good. Therefore, the marginal social benefit from consumption of the public good is always greater than the marginal private benefit from the consumption of the public good: individual self-interest does not result in the provision of the efficient quantity of public goods because of this divergence between the marginal public and marginal private benefit from the consumption of the public good. This is similar to the problem presented by positive externalities: the market does not provide the efficient amount of the public good or the efficient amount of a good with a positive externality because the marginal social benefit received by all consumers of another unit of the good is greater than the price the producer would receive from providing that unit of the good. The market produces too little of either type of good.

Objective #8. Governments decide on the optimal amount of the public good to provide by estimating the social benefits and the social costs of providing the public good. This process is known as cost-benefit analysis. Although it is relatively easy to estimate the cost of providing the public good, it is much more difficult to estimate the benefits from the provision of the public good. Individuals have an incentive to not answer truthfully about the benefits they receive from a public good because of the nature of the public good.

Key Terms

excludable referring to a good, describes the case in which the supplier can prevent those who do not pay from consuming the good.

rival in consumption referring to a good, describes the case in which one unit cannot be consumed by more than one person at the same time.

private good a good that is both *excludable* and *rival in consumption.*

nonexcludable referring to a good, describes the case in which the supplier cannot prevent those who do not pay from consuming the good.

nonrival in consumption referring to a good, describes the case in which the same unit can be consumed by more than one person at the same time.

free-rider problem when individuals have no *incentive* to pay for their own consumption of a good, they will take a "free ride" on anyone who does pay; a problem with goods that are *nonexcludable.*

public good a good that is both *nonexcludable* and *nonrival in consumption.*

Notes

Key Terms *(continued)*

common resource a *resource* that is *nonexcludable* and *rival in consumption.*

overuse the depletion of a *common resource* that occurs when individuals ignore the fact that their use depletes the amount of the resource remaining for others.

artificially scarce good a good that is *excludable* but *nonrival in consumption.*

Notes

AFTER YOU READ THE MODULE

Tips

Tip #1. This module looks at four types of goods—private goods, public goods, common resources, and artificially scarce goods—from the perspective of whether or not the good is rival in consumption and excludable. To understand this module, it is essential that you have a firm grasp on what it means to be rival in consumption versus nonrival in consumption and excludable versus nonexcludable.

- When a good is rival, this means that one person's consumption of the good effectively prevents another consumer from consuming that same unit of the good. Hamburgers and ice cream cones are two examples of goods that are rival: when Sally eats her hamburger or her ice cream cone this means that Joe cannot eat the same hamburger or the same ice cream cone. Joe and Sally are rivals with regard to the consumption of the hamburger or the ice cream cone.
- When a good is nonrival, this means that one person's consumption of the good does not prevent another consumer from consuming the same unit of the good. Sally and Joe can both enjoy the light from the lighthouse in their community without diminishing the consumption benefits received by the other person from their consumption of the same light. Sally and Joe are not rivals with regard to the consumption of the light from the lighthouse.
- A good is excludable if a supplier can prevent someone from consuming the good if they do not pay for it. Sally can enjoy her fast-food hamburger only if she pays for it. The restaurant will exclude her from the consumption of the hamburger if she cannot first pay for the hamburger. Hamburgers are therefore excludable as well as rival.
- A good is nonexcludable if a supplier cannot prevent someone from consuming the good if they do not pay for it. Residents of a community can benefit from a tornado warning siren even if they do not pay for this siren. It is impossible to exclude the nonpayers from the benefits of consuming this good even though they have not paid for it.

Tip #2. To find the demand curve for a public good requires that you vertically sum the individual demand curves for this public good. In contrast to a private good for which the market demand curve is found by horizontally summing the individual consumer demand curves, the public good requires the vertical summation of the individual consumer demand curves. The private good is rival in consumption, so that when we find the market demand curve we essentially ask how many units do demanders want of this good at a particular price. We repeat this process for different prices until we have identified the market demand curve for the private good. The public good, in contrast, is nonrival in consumption. This means that the market demand for the public good at any quantity is equal to the sum of the prices individuals are willing to pay for this particular amount of the public good. This nonrival characteristic of public goods implies that the market demand for public goods is found by considering the sum of what people are willing to pay for each level of public good provision. Figure 38.1 illustrates this idea for a public good when there are two individuals in the market for this good: D_1 represents the first person's demand for the public good, while D_2 represents the second person's demand for the public good, and D_3 represents the total demand for the public good.

Figure 38.1

To find the market demand curve for a public good, sum the individual demand curves for the good. To sum the demand curves, hold quantity constant (for example, Q_1) and then see what price each individual is willing to pay for this quantity. Thus, individual 1's marginal benefit from consuming Q_1 units of the public good is P_2, while individual 2's marginal benefit from consuming Q_1 units of the good is P_4. Together the marginal social benefit from Q_1 units is equal to $P_2 + P_4$.

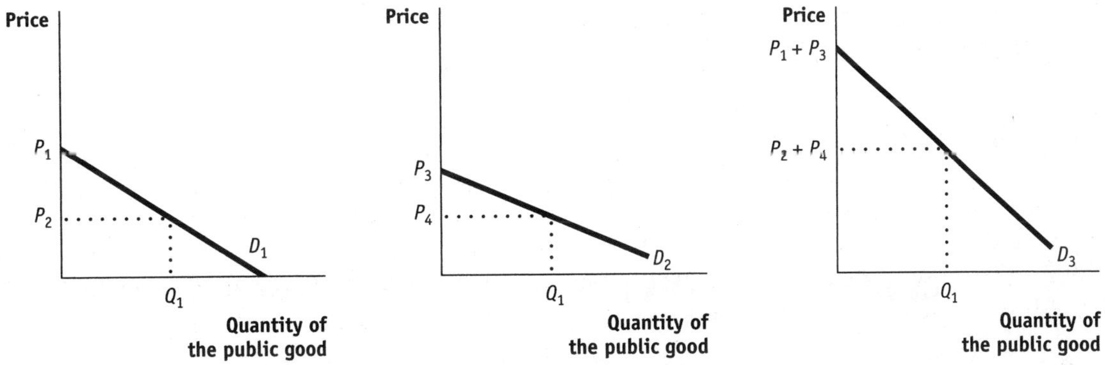

WORKED PROBLEMS

1. Suppose a community is composed of two individuals, Sam and Betty. Furthermore, suppose that in this community there is a recognized need for lighthouse services since the community is located on a rocky seashore. Both Betty and Sam fish daily and would benefit from the lighthouse service. Suppose that Betty's marginal benefit curve for these lighthouse services is given by the equation $P = 10 - Q$ while Sam's marginal benefit curve for these lighthouse services is given by the equation $P = 5 - (1/2)Q$. If the marginal social cost of providing lighthouse services is equal to \$6, what is the optimal amount of lighthouse services to provide in this market? In your answer provide the marginal social benefit of lighthouse services to the community. In addition, identify how much Betty and Sam should contribute per unit of lighthouse services if the optimal amount of lighthouse service is provided. You may find a graph depicting Sam's and Betty's marginal benefit curves, as well as the marginal social benefit curve for lighthouse services and the curve for the marginal social cost of lighthouse services, to be helpful.

STEP 1: Draw graphs of Betty's and Sam's marginal benefit curves from these lighthouse services.

When you draw these two graphs you will want to orient them so that one graph is above the other graph. You will want to do this to make it easier to think about vertically summing the two marginal benefit curves to create the marginal social benefit curve. The two marginal benefit curves will be summed vertically, since lighthouse services are a public good: lighthouse services are nonrival and nonexcludable. The following figures give the two marginal benefit curves.

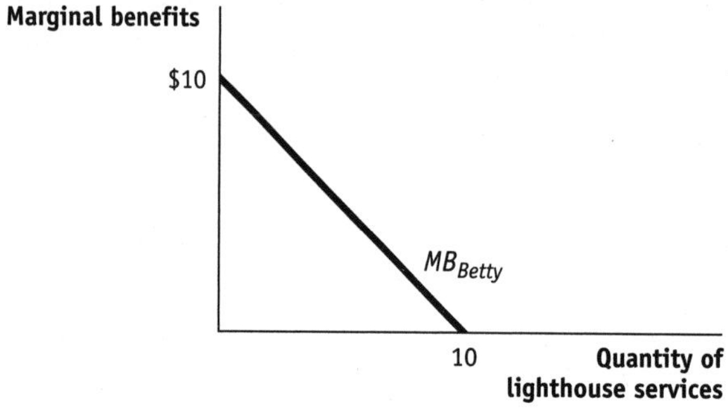

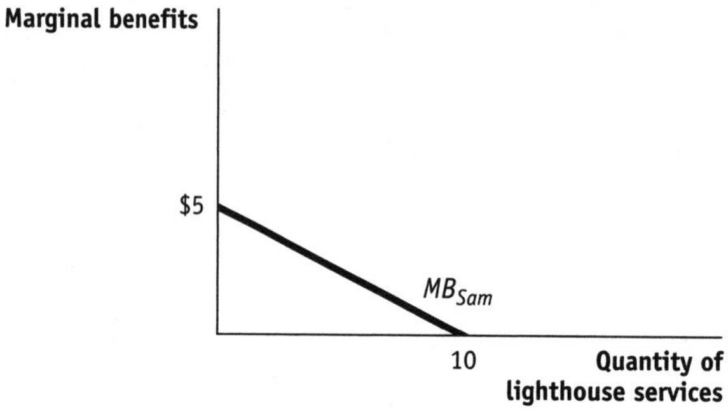

STEP 2: Based upon the graphs you drew in Step 1, draw a marginal social benefit curve for lighthouse services in this community.

To find the marginal social benefit curve, select a quantity and then ask how much Betty is willing to pay for this quantity and how much Sam is willing to pay for this quantity. Sum these two payments together to find the marginal social benefit of this quantity of lighthouse services. The two marginal benefit curves are summed vertically since the good is nonrival: both Betty and Sam can consume the lighthouse services without reducing the amount of these services available to the other. The following figure provides this marginal social benefit curve.

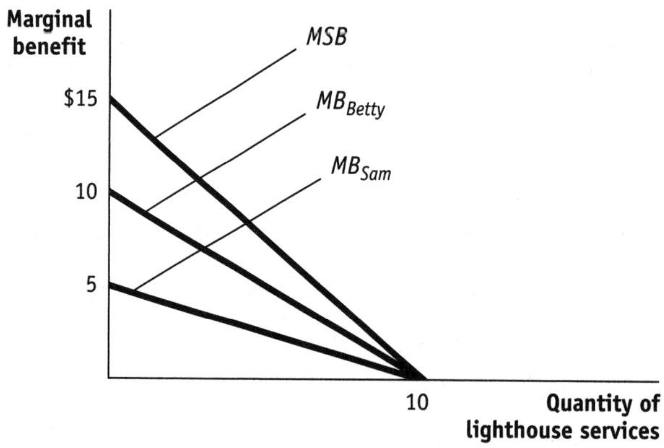

STEP 3: Draw the marginal social cost of lighthouse services in the graph you drew in Step 2 and find where the marginal social cost of lighthouse services intersects with the marginal social benefit of lighthouse services. Where these two curves intersect will be the optimal amount of lighthouse services to provide to this community.

Since the marginal social costs of lighthouse services are equal to $6, this is a horizontal line. To find where this horizontal line intersects the marginal social benefit from lighthouse services, you will find it helpful to write an equation for the marginal social benefit. This equation is $MSB = 15 - (3/2)Q$. Equate MSC to MSB, or $MSC = 6$ to $MSB = 15 - (3/2)Q$, to find the optimal amount of lighthouse services. Thus, the optimal amount of lighthouse services is equal to 6 units. The following graph illustrates these ideas.

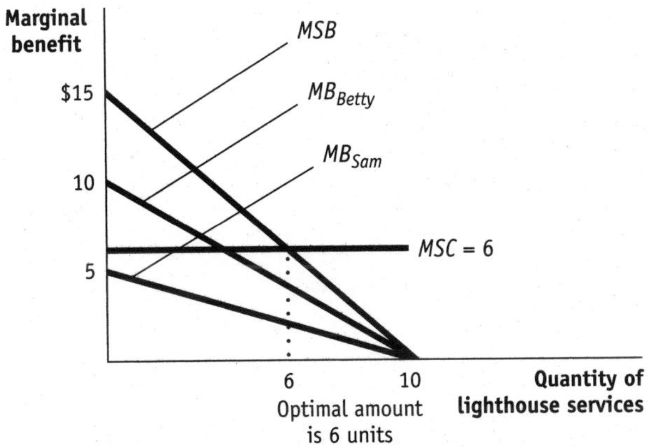

STEP 4: Identify how much Betty and Sam should contribute for each unit of lighthouse services that are provided when the optimal amount of lighthouse services is provided.

Now that we know the optimal amount of lighthouse services (6 units), we can ask Betty and Sam how much they are each willing to contribute for each unit of lighthouse services. Since Betty's marginal benefit from lighthouse services is given by $P = 10 - Q$, this indicates that when Q is equal to 6 units she is willing to contribute $4 per unit of services provided. Since Sam's marginal benefit from lighthouse services is given by $P = 5 - (1/2)Q$, this indicates that when Q is equal to 6 units he is willing to contribute $2 per unit of services provided. Notice that together they are willing to contribute a total of $6 per unit of lighthouse services, and this is exactly what the marginal social cost of providing each unit of lighthouse services is! The following graph identifies the contribution Betty and Sam are willing to make when the optimal amount of lighthouse services is provided.

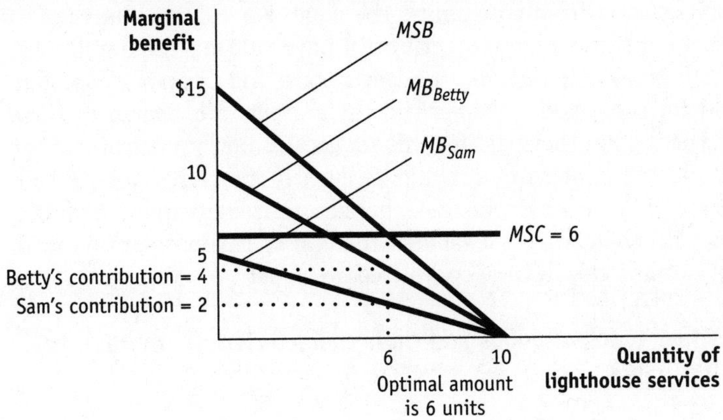

2. You have been asked to complete the following table for a presentation to your community about different types of goods. In the table, you are asked to identify whether the item is nonrival or rival in consumption, whether the item is nonexcludable or excludable, and finally, based on these characteristics,

whether the good is a private good, an artificially scarce good, a common resource, or a public good.

Item	Nonrival or rival in consumption	Nonexcludable or excludable	Type of good
Snowplowing of city streets			
Street lights in your town			
The Sports Channel (a cable television channel you must pay for to receive)			
Rain forests			
Wild elephants in Africa			
Wild salmon			
Clean air			

STEP 1: Review the meanings of rival and nonrival in consumption, and then decide for each item whether the item is rival or nonrival in consumption.

A good is rival in consumption when the same unit of the good cannot be consumed by more than one person at the same time. For example, an ice cream cone that is enjoyed by Mary cannot simultaneously be enjoyed by Tom. In the preceding table, when the city plows snow from the streets all the residents in the city can enjoy this service at the same time. This is true also for streetlights: your consumption of the light from the streetlight does not diminish my consumption of that same light from the streetlight. Fill in the first column of the table based on these examples, and then compare your answers with the completed table at the end of this problem. Wait to compare your answers until after you have completed all steps!

STEP 2: Review the meaning of nonexcludable and excludable, and then decide for each item whether the item is nonexcludable or excludable.

A good is excludable when the producers or suppliers of the good can prevent people who have not paid for the good from consuming the good. For example, at the fast food restaurant I cannot consume a hamburger until I have paid for the hamburger. In contrast, I can benefit from a community's sewer system and clean water system even if I have not paid for these goods. When the city's streets are cleared of snow everyone benefits, whether or not they paid for this service. Similarly, everyone in the community can consume the light from streetlights even if they have not paid for these lights. Fill in the second column of the table, based on these examples, and then compare your answers with the completed table at the end of this problem. Wait to compare your answers until after you have completed all steps!

STEP 3: Review the four types of goods and their characteristics, and then fill in the last column of the table.

A private good is both rival in consumption and excludable. A common resource is rival in consumption but nonexcludable. An artificially scarce good is nonrival in consumption but excludable. A public good is nonrival in consumption and nonexcludable. Since you have already characterized each of these goods with regard to whether they are rival or nonrival in consumption, as well as whether they are excludable or nonexcludable, it should be a relatively easy matter to apply the definitions of the various types of goods to determine the type of good each item represents. Fill in the final column of the table based on these definitions, and then compare your answers with the completed table at the end of this problem. Wait to compare your answers until after you have completed all steps!

Here is the completed table.

Item	Nonrival or rival in consumption	Nonexcludable or excludable	Type of good
Snowplowing of city streets	Nonrival	Nonexcludable	Public good
Street lights in your town	Nonrival	Nonexcludable	Public good
The Sports Channel (a cable television channel you must pay for in order to receive the signal)	Nonrival	Excludable	Artificially scarce good
Rain forests	Rival	Nonexcludable	Common resource
Wild elephants in Africa	Rival	Nonexcludable	Common resource
Wild salmon	Rival	Nonexcludable	Common resource
Clean air	Rival	Nonexcludable	Common resource

3. Your professor in economics has been asked to provide a review session for the upcoming examination. But your professor is reluctant to do this because she says it is liable to result in a free-rider problem. One of your friends is not sure what the professor means by this statement. Can you help your friend understand what the problem is, and can you think of anything the professor could do to reduce the free-rider problem?

STEP 1: Review the definition of the free-rider problem.

The free-rider problem refers to the situation that occurs when individuals have no incentive to pay for their own consumption of a good and instead decide to take a "free ride" on someone else who has paid for that good. The free-rider problem arises because of the nonexcludability of the good: once the good is provided, no one can be prevented from consuming the good even if he or she has not paid for it. For example, once a system of national defense is in place, it is impossible to exclude people living in the country from enjoying its benefits even if they have not paid to support the national defense. Some people will not want to pay taxes to support national defense, since they know that they can free ride on other people's provision of funds for it. Another example would be one roommate deciding not to clean the apartment because she knows that once her roommate cleans the apartment she will be able to reap the benefits of a clean apartment even though she has not done her part to get it clean: she has instead been a "free rider" by benefitting from her roommate's effort.

STEP 2: Discuss how a review session might result in a free-rider problem.

At the review session, it is likely that the professor will provide some sort of guidance about the topics to study as well as the topics that are less important. The professor may also help the student who hasn't started preparing for the exam reduce the amount of time he needs to prepare through the professor's explanations and examples. Other students may do the work of identifying the difficult or challenging topics on the exam, saving the free-riding student from the effort needed to identify these topics. Many students may decide to attend the review session in order to free ride on the work done by the professor and their fellow students.

STEP 3: Discuss ways the professor could reduce the free-rider problem while still providing a review session for the upcoming exam.

The professor could require students to submit a set of questions to her prior to the review session, and these questions could act as the student's ticket to the review session. The professor could offer review assistance: for example, the "review session" could consist of the professor being available during office hours to answer questions asked by individual students who come in to see her. The professor could also rule out any "fishing questions": these are questions like "Will the exam include questions on this topic?" or "Is this a concept that we need to study?" In brief, the professor would likely try to create an environment where the good is no longer nonexcludable: to get the information from the review session would require that students pay for that information through their efforts to prepare for the review session.

Problems and Exercises

1. For each of the following situations, determine whether the good in the situation is (1) excludable or nonexcludable, and (2) nonrival in consumption or rival in consumption.

a. A community erects a lighthouse to guide ships navigating near its rocky shoreline.

b. A country builds a national defense system of missiles.

c. A community builds a toll road that has low levels of use.

d. A community builds a toll road that has high levels of use.

e. A radio station broadcasts the baseball game.

f. A community builds a non-toll road that has high levels of use.

g. Police protection is hired for a community.

h. The environment of a community is improved.

2. What does it mean when a good is nonexcludable? Explain in your own words what this means.

3. What does it mean when a good is nonrival in consumption? Explain in your own words what this means.

4. Markets provide private goods efficiently since the market price is equal to the marginal cost of producing the good. Why do markets fail to produce the efficient level of public goods?

5. Jimmy and Beth are the only residents of Smalltown. They both think the community would benefit from more parks, but neither Jimmy nor Beth are willing to contribute money to buy land to turn into parks since they both realize that once a park is provided they can enjoy the park even though they have not paid for the park.

   a. Describe Jimmy and Beth's behavior and why it represents a problem when trying to provide parks in their community.

   b. Suppose Jimmy reveals that his marginal benefit from one park is equal to \$50 per park, his marginal benefit from two parks is equal to \$25 per park, and his marginal benefit from three parks is equal to \$0 per park. Beth reveals that her marginal benefit from one park is equal to \$60 per park, her marginal benefit from two parks is equal to \$40 per park, and her marginal benefit from three parks is equal to \$20 per park. What is the marginal social benefit of two parks equal to in their community? Explain how you found this answer.

   c. Suppose the information in part (b) is still true. Jimmy and Beth analyze the cost of providing parks in their community and they find that the marginal social cost of providing parks is constant and equal to \$55. What is the socially optimal amount of parks for this community? Explain how you got this answer.

   d. If Jimmy and Beth are both willing to reveal their preferences with regard to parks (that is, they will tell the truth about the marginal private benefit they receive from the parks), will they both contribute to getting the socially optimal amount of parks for their community?

6. What two characteristics do private goods have that make it possible for markets to efficiently provide the good, and why are these characteristics so important?

7. Big Sports is a television company that has won the rights to broadcast next season's football games in the Big Group college football conference. To watch these televised games, viewers need to subscribe to the Super Cable package that costs an additional $15 per month.

a. Does Big Sports and its televised games represent a public good, a common resource, or an artificially scarce good? Explain your answer and why you have classified Big Sports in this manner.

b. What price is the efficient price for consumers to pay for watching these football games? Explain your answer.

c. Does Big Sports produce the socially optimal, or efficient, level of televised football games for the Big Group college football conference? Explain your answer. If the level of production is not the socially optimal amount, is the amount produced in the market greater than or less than the socially optimal amount? Explain your answer.

8. In which of the following situations is the free-rider problem likely to arise? Explain for each situation that has a free-rider problem why this occurs and what the nature of the free-rider problem is.

a. The parent-teacher association at your child's elementary school is looking for parent volunteers to direct a fundraiser to raise money to replace the playground equipment.

b. Local community organizers are seeking people to serve on a committee to improve the beauty of the community through gardening and landscaping efforts.

c. The local hamburger joint is testing a new sandwich on its menu.

d. A local group is organizing a Saturday morning spring cleanup of the lakeshore in their community.

9. Several sub-Saharan African countries are worried about their elephant population decreasing over time due to the hunting and killing of these elephants for their ivory tusks. Elephants tend to roam over relatively large areas to seek food, which makes it difficult to manage the elephant population. One country proposes creating a large elephant refuge area where the elephants can roam and be protected by law from the hunting of elephants. Another country proposes assigning property rights to the elephants to specific individuals: these individuals would own specific elephants and would be allowed to provide these elephants for slaughter if they so desired. There is an active market for ivory, but at this time the market is strictly an underground, or illegal, market since the ivory that is supplied has been obtained by illegally killing the elephants.

a. What is the nature of the problem of dwindling elephant population in sub-Saharan Africa? Explain your answer.

b. Of the two policies, which one is more likely to result in the greatest reduction in illegal killing of elephants? Why?

c. Which proposal assigns property rights to the ownership of elephants? Why is the assignment of property rights important in resolving the problem of the declining elephant population?

BEFORE YOU TAKE THE TEST

Module Review Questions

1. A public good is a good

a. that benefits many people whether or not they have paid for it.

b. whose benefits to any particular individual do not depend on how many other individuals benefit from the good.

c. that is nonrival in consumption and nonexcludable.

d. Answers (a), (b), and (c) are all true statements.

2. In the case of a common resource,
   a. one person's consumption of the common resource reduces the amount of the common resource available to other consumers.
   b. one person cannot be excluded from consuming the common resource because it is nonrival in consumption.
   c. one person can exclude others from consuming the common resource if they have not paid for the consumption of the common resource.
   d. it represents the same type of problem found in a market when positive externalities are associated with the good.

3. When the price of a good is greater than its marginal cost of provision, the market for this good is producing
   a. the socially optimal amount of the good.
   b. too little of the good.
   c. too much of the good.
   d. as optimal an amount of output as is possible given the circumstances.

4. For a market to efficiently deliver a good, the good must be
   a. rival in consumption.
   b. excludable.
   c. nonrival in consumption.
   d. nonexcludable.
   e. (a) and (b)
   f. (c) and (d)

5. Madison has a number of city parks that are open to the public at no charge. Throughout the year these parks are often crowded, with long lines at the play structures. These public parks represent a good that is
   a. nonrival and nonexcludable.
   b. nonrival and excludable.
   c. rival and nonexcludable.
   d. rival and excludable.

6. Madison is in the middle of tornado country and, because of the imminent danger of tornadoes, has decided to invest in a tornado siren system. This tornado siren system is an example of a good that is
   a. nonrival in consumption and nonexcludable.
   b. nonrival in consumption and excludable.
   c. rival in consumption and nonexcludable.
   d. rival in consumption and excludable.

7. The Illinois Tollway that connects Rockford to Chicago is constantly congested with traffic jams. Motorists must pay a toll fee to use the Tollway. The Tollway is a good that is characterized as
   a. rival in consumption and nonexcludable.
   b. rival in consumption and excludable.
   c. nonrival in consumption and nonexcludable.
   d. rival in consumption and nonexcludable.

8. Mason Street is a quiet residential street that is only three blocks long. There is no toll for driving on Mason Street, and the street gets very little traffic except from the people who live on the street. Mason Street is

a. nonrival in consumption and nonexcludable.
b. rival in consumption and excludable.
c. nonrival in consumption and excludable.
d. rival in consumption and nonexcludable.

9. Sally and Sue live in an apartment and neither of them likes to clean the apartment nor do the dishes. After several weeks of living like this, the apartment does get really dirty. Sally often wishes the apartment was clean, but she does not do anything to clean up the apartment because she figures if she is only patient enough Sue will clean the apartment. Which of the following statements is true?

a. Sue free-rides on Sally when it comes to getting the apartment cleaned up.
b. Sally free-rides on Sue when it comes to getting the apartment cleaned up.
c. Since there are only two people in the apartment, the free-rider problem is not important because eventually Sally and Sue will clean the apartment.
d. Free ridership is a problem that only arises in a society that is trying to provide a public good.

10. Joey's elementary school is organizing a fundraiser to raise the funds needed to refurbish the library. Each parent has been asked to contribute two hours of their time toward the fundraiser, but very few parents have come forward to help out. Which of the following statements is true?

a. Their children will benefit from the refurbishment of the library irrespective of whether or not their parents volunteer their time.
b. If the parents do not volunteer, someone else will and then they and their children can free-ride on the other parents' work.
c. The school will suffer from the free-rider problem and will not raise the optimal amount of funds due to the parents' free riding.
d. Answers (a), (b), and (c) are all true statements.

11. When a good is nonexcludable, the market produces

a. too much of the good.
b. too little of the good.

12. New Glarus has just built and opened a toll road connecting New Glarus to Old Glarus. This toll road is never congested no matter what time of day or what day of the week it is. Since the toll road is both nonrival in consumption and excludable, it is an example of an artificially scarce good. The marginal cost of letting an additional driver use the toll road is equal to

a. the toll.
b. zero.
c. the toll divided by the number of drivers currently using the toll road.
d. the toll divided by the population of the two communities.

13. New Glarus has just built and opened a toll road connecting New Glarus to Old Glarus. This toll road is never congested no matter what time of day or what day of the week it is. Since the toll road is both nonrival in consumption and excludable, it is an example of an artificially scarce good. Drivers who might benefit from using this toll road will

a. not use the toll road as much as is socially optimal since the toll is greater than the marginal cost of allowing these drivers to use the road.

b. use the toll road at the socially optimal level since the toll is sufficient to cover the costs of providing the road.

c. free-ride on other drivers.

Use the following information to answer the next three questions.

Suppose Joe's marginal private benefit from national defense is given by the equation $P = 100 - Q$, where Q refers to the amount of military goods and P refers to the price Joe is willing to pay for each unit of military goods. Mary's marginal private benefit from national defense is given by the equation $P = 50 - 0.5Q$. Furthermore, suppose the marginal social cost of providing an additional unit of military goods is constant and equal to \$60.

14. Which equation represents the marginal social benefit (*MSB*) from military goods if Joe and Mary are the only two individuals in the economy? (Hint: draw two graphs of the individual demand curves for Joe and Mary; then draw a third graph that adds these two individual demand curves together.)

a. $MSB = 66.67 - 0.33Q$

b. $MSB = 150 - 1.5Q$

c. $MSB = 100 - Q$

d. $MSB = 50 - 0.5Q$

15. What is the socially optimal amount of national defense for this economy?

a. 90 units of military goods

b. 80 units of military goods

c. 170 units of military goods

d. 60 units of military goods

16. Suppose both Joe and Mary are truthful about their preferences with regard to national defense and they both fully reveal the marginal benefits they receive from national defense. Furthermore, suppose the socially optimal amount of national defense is produced in this economy. What price per unit of national defense will Joe be willing to pay?

a. \$100

b. \$60

c. \$40

d. \$20

17. Which of the following statements about public goods is true?

I. Public goods can be provided efficiently by the market or by the government.

II. Public goods can be provided through voluntary contributions or by self-interested individuals or firms.

III. Some public goods can be provided through social encouragement or pressure.

a. Statement I is true.

b. Statements II and III are true.

c. Statements I, II, and III are true.

d. Statements I and II are true.

e. Statements I and III are true.

Use the following graph of a public good to answer the next three questions. Assume that Joe and Sarah are the only two people who live in their community and that this graph represents Joe's marginal benefit from the public good, Sarah's marginal benefit from the public good, and the total marginal social benefit from the public good. In addition, the marginal cost of producing an additional unit of the public good is constant and equal to P_4.

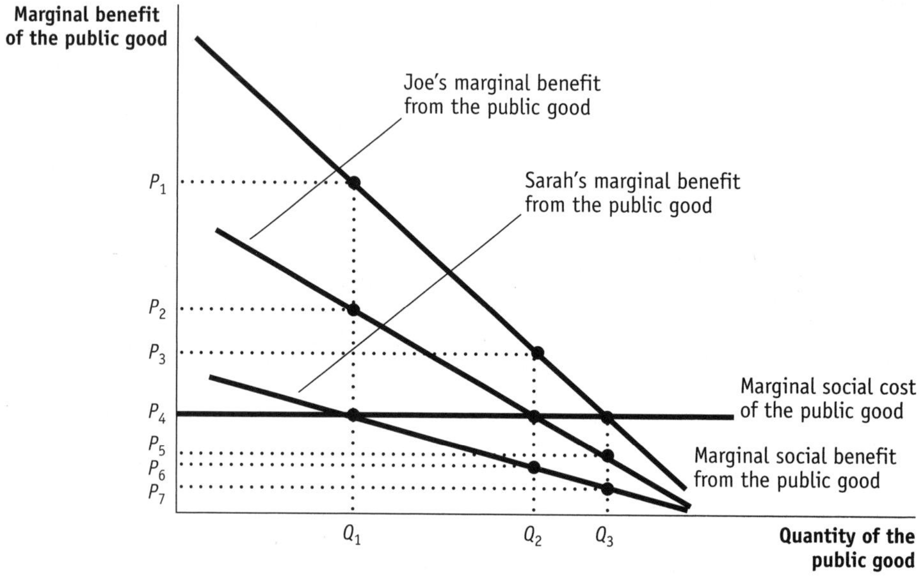

18. At Q_1, the marginal social benefit from this last unit of the public good

a. is equal to P_1 or the sum of $P_2 + P_4$.

b. is greater than the marginal social cost of producing this last unit of the public good.

c. exceeds the marginal social cost of producing another unit of the public good, which tells us that this community is not producing enough of the public good.

d. Answers (a), (b), and (c) are all true statements.

19. What is the socially optimal amount of the good; and, if both Sarah and Joe contribute to the provision of the public good an amount that equals the marginal benefit they get from the last unit of the good they consume, how much will Joe contribute per unit of the public good?

a. Q_1; P_2

b. Q_1; P_4

c. Q_2; P_4

d. Q_3; P_4

e. Q_3; P_5

20. Given the information in the above graph, who places a higher value on the public good represented in the graph?

a. Joe

b. Sarah

21. A community is trying to decide whether to install lighting at one of the local city parks. Government officials estimate that the marginal social benefit from installing the lighting will be $100, but that the marginal social cost of installing the lighting will be $105. This community

a. should conduct another study to see if the numbers come out better, since clearly it would be great to have a well-lit park.

b. should not install the lighting at this time since the marginal benefit from the lighting is less than the marginal cost of installing the lighting.

c. will not install the lighting since the market will provide the lighting.

d. should install the lighting because the cost-benefit analysis did not take into account the tendency of individuals to free-ride on the provision of the public good.

22. Fishermen in Oceania report dwindling supplies of their favorite fish. These fishermen fish in open water with no limits placed on who can fish in the water and how many fish can be taken from the sea. This is an example of a(n)

a. artificially scarce good, since good fisheries management could eliminate the fish scarcity.

b. public good, since no one is paying to fish in the water and no one can be excluded from fishing in the water.

c. common resource, since the fishing grounds are nonexcludable but rival in consumption.

d. private good, since each fisherman catches his own fish, and then markets them at the local fish market.

23. A good that is nonexcludable but rival in consumption is a(n)

a. public good.

b. positive externality.

c. artificially scarce good.

d. common resource.

24. In the case of a common resource, the market tends to

a. overconsume the good, since the good is nonexcludable but rival in consumption.

b. underconsume the good, since the good is nonexcludable but rival in consumption.

25. London recently started charging drivers a fee to drive in certain parts of the city during high-traffic times of day. This fee effectively seeks to address the problem of traffic congestion. This fee has successfully reduced traffic congestion in the areas of London where it has been applied. By imposing this fee, government officials have

a. encouraged consumers to drive less than they otherwise would.

b. encouraged consumers to drive at times when traffic congestion is less of a problem.

c. made a common resource excludable: those who pay for the right to drive can drive, and those unwilling to pay must forgo driving.

d. Answers (a), (b), and (c) are all true.

26. In the case of a common resource, the market does not recognize that

a. marginal social cost is greater than the private cost of providing the last unit of the good.

b. marginal social benefit is greater than the marginal benefit individuals receive from consuming the last unit of the good.

c. marginal social benefit and marginal social cost are both ignored by the market.

d. the marginal benefits and marginal costs from consumption of the good are ignored.

27. The market can correct the problem posed by common resources by
- a. imposing the appropriate Pigouvian tax on the good.
- b. creating a system of tradable licenses for the right to this common resource.
- c. assigning property rights to this common resource, thereby making the good an excludable good.
- d. Answers (a), (b), and (c) are all feasible corrections to the problem posed by common resources.

28. Economists are excited because they have just discovered a good that is nonrival in consumption but excludable. This good
- a. will be very expensive, since it is such a rare good.
- b. should be free, since the marginal cost of an individual's consumption of this good is equal to zero if this good is to be produced at the socially optimal level of production.
- c. will be overproduced in this market, since the price of the good is less than the marginal cost of providing the good.
- d. will be efficiently produced in this market, since the good is excludable and a price can therefore be assigned to the good by the market.

ANSWER KEY

Answers to Problems and Exercises

1. a. Nonexcludable and nonrival

   b. Nonexcludable and nonrival

   c. Excludable and nonrival

   d. Excludable and rival

   e. Nonexcludable and nonrival

   f. Nonexcludable and rival

   g. Nonexcludable and rival

   h. Nonexcludable and nonrival

2. A good is nonexcludable when once the good is produced individuals can enjoy the consumption of this good even if they do not pay for the good. Once people realize a good is nonexcludable, they will free-ride on other people who are willing to pay for the good, knowing that once the good is provided they will be able to consume it even if they have not paid for the good.

3. A good is nonrival in consumption if more than one person can consume the same unit of the good without diminishing the benefits of consuming the good for other people. Most of the goods we have discussed thus far in the text are private goods for which one person's consumption of the good means that no one else can consume that unit: this implies that consumers are rivals when they consume private goods. In the case of a good that is nonrival, consumers are not rivals and many people can enjoy the benefits from the same good.

4. A public good is both nonexcludable and nonrival in consumption. This means that consumers can consume the good without paying for the good and that consumers are not rivals with one another in the consumption of the good. This nonrival characteristic of public goods results in the marginal social benefit from the public good being greater than the demand for the public good at all levels of public good provision. This implies that the market does not produce the efficient amount of the public good because it does not equate the marginal cost of producing the good to the marginal social benefit from consuming it. Too few units of the public good are provided by the market.

5. a. Both Jimmy and Beth are free-riding on this issue of park provision. They both realize that once the parks are provided they can enjoy the park even if they have not contributed to the creation of the park. When people free-ride, too little or none of the good gets produced. In this case, if neither Jimmy nor Beth are willing to contribute, then the community will end up with no new parks.

   b. The marginal social benefit of two parks is equal to the sum of Jimmy's and Beth's marginal benefits from two parks: Jimmy's marginal social benefit from two parks is equal to $25 per park while Beth's marginal social benefit from two parks is equal to $40 per park, for a total marginal social benefit from two parks of $65 per park.

   c. Since the marginal cost of providing parks is constant and equal to $55 per park, parks should be provided as long as the marginal social benefit from the park is greater than or equal to the marginal cost of providing the park. In this case, two parks will be provided since the marginal social benefit of two parks is equal to $65 per park while the marginal cost of providing two parks is $55 per park. Three parks will not be provided because the marginal social benefit of three parks is only $20 per park while the marginal social cost of three parks is $55 per park.

d. Yes, if both Jimmy and Beth reveal their preferences they will each contribute, since they each assign a positive marginal benefit to two parks. Jimmy will likely contribute less than Beth because the marginal benefit he receives from two parks is less than the marginal benefit that Beth receives from two parks.

6. Private goods are both rival in consumption and excludable. A good that is rival in consumption is a good whose benefit from consumption can only be enjoyed by the individual consuming it. This quality of being rival in consumption implies that individuals must pay a positive price to consume the good. When a good is excludable, this means that no individual can enjoy the benefits from consuming the good without first paying for the good. These two characteristics allow private goods to be produced efficiently in the market because producers can set a price for these goods that is equal to the marginal cost of producing the good.

7. **a.** Since the televised games are available only if the consumer pays for the cable package, these games are an excludable good. But the televised games are nonrival in consumption since one individual's viewing of the game does not diminish the ability of another viewer to watch the game. Thus, Big Sports and its televised games represent an artificially scarce good, since these goods are excludable but nonrival in consumption.

b. The efficient price for consumers would be zero since the marginal cost of delivering the televised games to another consumer is zero. At a price of zero, however, Big Sports has no incentive to provide the games. Big Sports will only provide the games if they can charge consumers a positive price.

c. Big Sports does not produce the optimal amount of the good since the price they charge ($15 per month) is greater than the marginal cost of producing an additional televised game ($0). Since price is greater than marginal cost this indicates that too little of the good is being produced, because the value consumers place on the last unit produced is greater than the cost of producing the last unit.

8. **a.** There is a free-rider problem in this situation because the final good (the playground equipment) is nonexcludable. Too few parents will come forward to volunteer their time because the parents all realize that once the playground equipment is installed, all the children at the school will be able to use the equipment even if their parents did not help in the fundraising effort. If the free-rider problem is too severe, the school will not get the new playground equipment.

b. There is a free-rider problem in this situation because the final good (a more beautiful community) is nonexcludable. Too few people will come forward to help with this effort since everyone in the community realizes that if the community is made more beautiful, then everyone in the community can enjoy this beauty even if they did not help in the effort to create a more beautiful community. The community will likely continue to have its blemishes and eyesores and not achieve the socially optimal amount of community beauty.

c. There is no free-rider problem with this situation since the new sandwich is excludable.

d. There is a free-rider problem in this situation because the final good (a cleaner lake and a cleaner lakeshore) is nonexcludable. Too few people will come forward to help clean up the lakeshore because people in the community realize that once the lakeshore is cleaned up, everyone in the community can enjoy this cleaner lakeshore even if they have not contributed to this outcome. The lakeshore will not be cleaned to the socially optimal level.

9. **a.** The population of elephants in Africa is dwindling because of the illegal harvesting of their tusks (which can only be done by killing the elephants). This occurs because the elephants represent a common resource: anyone can kill an elephant and benefit from harvesting the tusks since no one owns the elephants. This common resource leads to overharvesting of the elephants and, hence, a decline in the elephant population.

b. Assigning property rights to elephant ownership will likely prove more effective than setting up an elephant refuge, since the owner of the elephant recognizes that the elephant has value and will therefore take care of the elephant to preserve that value. The owner would likely try to ensure that the elephant stays nearby, where it would be difficult for someone to come along and kill the elephant. In contrast, the refuge would consolidate the area in which elephants are found, making it easier for poachers to find the elephants.

c. The second proposal assigns property rights for elephant ownership. Assigning property rights helps to eliminate the problem of nonexcludability, since theoretically no one will have access to the elephant, or its tusks, unless they pay for the elephant.

Answers to Module Review Questions

1. **Answer d.** Public goods are nonrival in consumption and nonexcludable. These two characteristics imply that people can benefit from the good even if they did not pay for it (nonexcludable) and that the benefits any individual gets from the good do not depend on whether or not another individual is benefiting from the good (nonrival in consumption).

2. **Answer a.** The common resource is a situation in which the good is rival in consumption but nonexcludable. In the case of the common resource, individuals overuse the common resource, which creates a negative externality on everyone else who would benefit from the use of the common resource.

3. **Answer b.** When the price of the good is greater than its marginal cost this tells us that too little of the good is being produced since the value consumers place on the good (the price they are willing to pay) is greater than the cost of producing an additional unit of the good. This situation arises with monopoly, oligopoly, public goods, and artificially scarce goods.

4. **Answer e.** Goods that are both rival in consumption and excludable are private goods and can be produced efficiently by the market. Goods that lack one or both of these characteristics are not efficiently provided by the market.

5. **Answer c.** The parks are open to the public at no charge, so they are nonexcludable. But they are often congested with long lines, which implies that the parks are rival in consumption. One child's use of the play structure reduces the available benefits of the play structure for another child.

6. **Answer a.** Once the tornado siren system is in place, everyone living in Madison will be able to benefit from the system even if they did not contribute to its production, so it is nonexcludable. The good is also nonrival in consumption since one person's consumption of the signal from the siren system does not reduce the available benefit to other people from consuming the same signal from the siren system.

7. **Answer b.** The Tollway is rival in consumption, since one person's use of the Tollway reduces the benefit of using the Tollway for other people due to the high level of congestion. The Tollway is also excludable since no one can drive on the Tollway without paying the toll.

8. **Answer a.** Since there is no charge to drive on Mason Street, it is an example of a nonexcludable good: anyone can enjoy driving on the street even though they have not paid for the street. Mason Street is also nonrival in consumption since it is never congested: this means that one person's use of the street does not diminish the level of benefits available to someone else who wishes to use the street.

9. **Answer b.** Sally free-rides: she does not want to contribute to cleaning the apartment, but she enjoys the benefits of a clean apartment once Sue gets everything cleaned. Free ridership can occur in all sorts of transactions and is not limited to the situation posed by a public good.

10. **Answer d.** These statements are all true. When a good is nonexcludable, people tend to free-ride. Once the library is refurbished, there is no way that the school can prevent those children from using the library whose parents did not help out with the fundraiser. When the good is nonexcludable, too little of the good is provided without intervention in the market because of the free-rider problem.

11. **Answer b.** When a good is nonexcludable, people tend to free-ride and rely on others to provide the good. Because people free-ride, the market undervalues the benefit from the good, and therefore produces too little of the good.

12. **Answer b.** Since the toll road is nonrival in consumption, the marginal cost of letting another driver use the road is equal to zero. When an additional driver on this toll road is forced to pay the toll, this payment is higher than the marginal cost of allowing them to consume the good.

13. **Answer a.** Drivers will not consume as many drives on the toll road as is socially optimal since the price they must pay to use the road (the toll) is greater than the marginal cost of allowing them to use the road (zero). They will not be free-riding since the toll road is excludable and people can only free-ride when the good is nonexcludable.

14. **Answer b.** To find the *MSB* curve, you need to vertically sum the two individual demand curves for the public good (national defense is a public good since it is nonrival in consumption and nonexcludable). An easy point to find on the *MSB* curve is the *y*-intercept, since it equals the sum of the *y*-intercepts from the two individual demand curves: in this case, the *y*-intercept is equal to 150. Then, given the two individual demand curves, when 100 units of military goods are demanded, both Joe and Mary are not willing to pay anything for this quantity of military goods. Thus, the *MSB* curve intersects the *x*-axis at 100 units of military goods. The *MSB* curve is therefore $MSB = 150 - 1.5Q$.

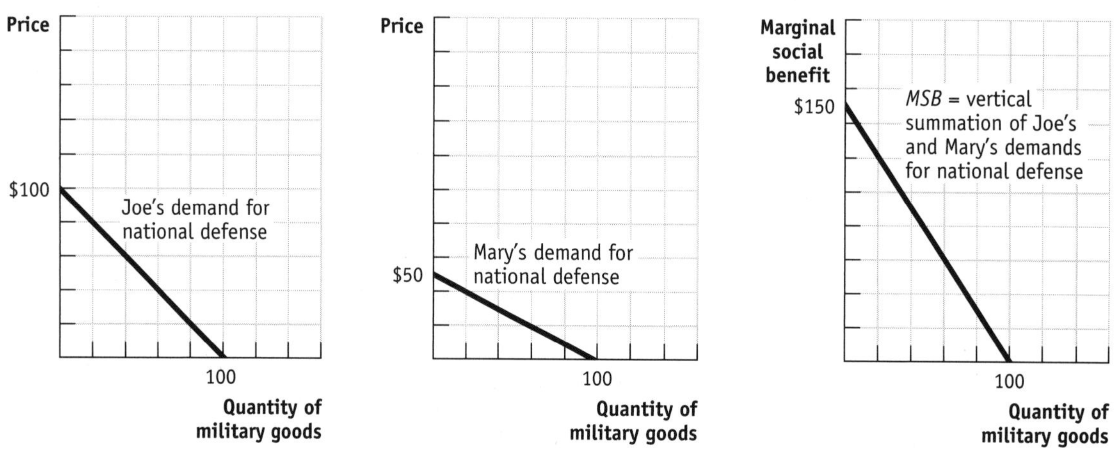

15. **Answer d.** To find the socially optimal amount of national defense for this economy, you must find where the marginal social benefit equals the marginal social cost. Or, $150 - 1.5Q = 60$, and therefore Q equals 60 units of military goods.

16. **Answer c.** Since the socially optimal amount of national defense in this problem is 60 units (see question 15), we can find Joe's willingness to pay by substituting this quantity into his demand curve. Thus, Joe's demand for national defense is given by $P = 100 - Q$, and when Q equals 60 units of military goods, Joe is willing to pay a price of $40 per unit of military goods.

17. **Answer b.** Public goods are not provided for by the market because they are nonrival in consumption and nonexcludable. But public goods may be provided through voluntary contributions, through the self-interested behavior of individuals or firms, or through social encouragement or pressure. For example, some conservation efforts occur through voluntary contributions or through firm activity in which the firm hopes to be able to

make money in some indirect way through their efforts to increase conservation. Many people do not litter and actually pick up litter because of social encouragement or pressure. Having less litter is a public good—nonrival in consumption and nonexcludable—and this "good" to some degree is produced by moral suasion.

18. Answer d. It is a relatively easy task to measure the marginal social benefit of producing Q_1 units of the good: you simply need to go vertically up from Q_1 units to the marginal social benefit curve and then read the *y*-intercept value for this level of public good production. The marginal social benefit from the public good curve is constructed by adding the marginal benefit that Joe receives from the public good to the marginal benefit that Sarah receives from the public good: this is equal to $P_2 + P_4$. The marginal social cost of producing an additional unit of the public good is equal to P_4, so the marginal social cost is less than the marginal social benefit. This implies that too little of the public good is being produced.

19. Answer e. The socially optimal amount of the public good is that amount of the public good where the marginal social benefit is equal to the marginal social cost. This is true at Q_3. Joe's marginal benefit from the public good can be found by going vertically up from Q_3 units to Joe's marginal benefit from the public good curve and then reading off the *y*-intercept value for this point.

20. Answer a. Joe's marginal benefit from the public good is greater than Sarah's marginal benefit from the public good: he places a higher value on the public good since the public good yields greater benefits to him.

21. Answer b. When the marginal social benefit is less than the marginal social cost, the good should not be produced. One hopes that the cost-benefit study was well conducted and took into account the tendency for individuals to free-ride on the provision of the public good, since the cost-benefit study would have little value if it was based on poor analysis.

22. Answer c. The fishermen face a problem of a common resource, since all of them use the sea where the fish are located. Since no one owns the fishing rights to the sea and there is no way to limit the amount of fishing in the sea, there is too much fishing. This leads to the quantity of fish available decreasing due to overfishing: a natural outcome of a situation in which the good is nonexcludable but rival. When one fisherman catches a fish, that fish is no longer available for some other fisherman to catch.

23. Answer d. This is the simple definition of a common resource.

24. Answer a. A common resource is overconsumed because individuals cannot be charged for using the good, while at the same time individuals recognize that they are rivals with other individuals for the good. Individuals ignore the cost of their use of the good on the rest of society, which leads them to overuse the good.

25. Answer d. By charging a price for the right to drive in the city during high-traffic hours, London officials have effectively raised the price of driving. This causes individuals to drive less, and it also encourages them to shift their driving to times when the fee is lower (i.e., times when there is less traffic). London officials recognize that traffic congestion is a sign of a common resource problem, and this policy attempts to make a nonexcludable good excludable.

26. Answer a. With a common resource, the marginal cost of consuming an additional unit of the good does not take into account the social cost of this consumption on other individuals. This implies that there is a divergence between the marginal social cost of consuming an additional unit of the good and the marginal cost to the individuals of consuming an additional unit of the good. The market equates the marginal social benefit of consuming the good with the consumer's marginal cost of consuming the good, rather than equating the marginal social benefit to the marginal social cost.

27. Answer d. Common resources essentially present the same type of problem as those presented by a negative externality. As with a negative externality, the problem of common resources can be eliminated through assigning property rights, or by creating a system of licenses granting the holder the right to use the common resource, or by taxing the users of the common resource.

28. Answer b. When a good is excludable but nonrival in consumption, the market fails to produce the efficient level of the good. The marginal cost of an individual's consumption of this good equals zero since the good is nonrival in consumption: one individual's consumption of the good does not diminish the benefits available to another consumer from consuming the same good. But producers are only willing to produce the good if they can charge for the good: this implies that the price in the market is greater than the marginal cost of the good, and therefore the market-determined quantity of the good is smaller than is socially optimal. To get the socially optimal amount of the good requires that the price of the good be equal to zero.

module **39**

The Economics of the Welfare State

BEFORE YOU READ THE MODULE

Summary

This module is highly descriptive in its focus on what the welfare state is and the rationale for the welfare state. The module defines poverty and then examines the causes and the consequences of poverty. The module also looks at income inequality in America from a historical perspective. The module discusses the impact of programs such as Social Security, Medicare, and Medicaid on poverty and income inequality. Lastly, the module examines the political and philosophical debate over the size of the welfare state.

Module Objectives

Objective #1. The welfare state is a term used to describe the collection of government programs aimed at reducing or alleviating economic hardship. A large portion of government spending in wealthy countries consists of government transfers that provide financial aid to individuals designated by the government as in need of government assistance. These individuals may be poor, unemployed, elderly, or may be experiencing large health care expenses. There are two major rationales for the welfare state: (1) to help alleviate income inequality and (2) to help alleviate economic insecurity. Programs designed to alleviate income inequality by aiding the poor are known as poverty programs; programs designed to alleviate economic insecurity by providing protection against unpredictable distress are known as social insurance programs. Both types of programs are closely related to the ability-to-pay principle, which is used to justify progressive taxation that requires those with higher incomes to pay a greater fraction of their income in taxes than those with low incomes. The programs of the welfare state redistribute income from some people to other people.

Objective #2. Debate over the size and extent of the welfare state typically focuses on two points of contention. The first point of disagreement is over how large a role the government should play in alleviating economic inequality and economic insecurity. Even conservatives who believe in the limited role of government typically support some welfare state programs.

The second point of disagreement is over the effects of welfare state programs on the incentives to work and save. Just as in the case of taxes, the provision of welfare state programs can create substantial deadweight losses, and thus the economic cost of welfare state programs can be considerably greater than the direct monetary cost of providing these programs.

Objective #3. Poverty is defined in the United States as the minimum amount of annual income that is considered adequate to purchase the necessities of life. When a family's income falls below the poverty line, that family is considered poor. By several different measures the United States has an unusually high poverty rate. The data on poverty in the United States shows a strong association between poverty and the lack of adequate employment. Part-time work typically lacks benfits such as health plans, paid vacation days, and retirement benefits, and in addition, these workers often are paid an hourly wage that is lower than comparable full-time work. These part-time workers are the working poor—those workers whose income falls at or below the poverty line. The causes of poverty in the United States include

- Low levels of education;
- Lack of proficiency in speaking English;
- The existence of gender and racial discrimination; and
- Bad luck, which causes the wage-earner to lose a job or a family member to develop a serious medical problem.

Impoverished people experience

- A lack of health care that can disrupt schooling and affect the ability to work; and
- A lack of access to affordable housing, which leads to disrupted schooling and work schedules for family members.

Poverty is often self-perpetuating: the children of the poor start at such a disadvantage relative to other Americans that it's very hard for them to achieve a better life.

Objective #4. Income in the United States is unequally distributed. Mean household income, or average household income, is equal to the total income of all U.S. households divided by the number of U.S. households. This measure is skewed upward by the inclusion of highly wealthy households. A better measure of income inequality is median household income. Median household income in the United States is the level of income earned by the household in the exact middle of the income distribution. Median household income is not skewed by the inclusion of very high or very low household incomes. Another measure of income inequality is the Gini coefficient: a country with a perfectly equal distribution of income would have a Gini coefficient of zero, whereas a country where all income went to a single person would have a Gini coefficient of one. Countries with relatively low Gini coefficients have less income inequality than countries with relatively high Gini coefficients.

Objective #5. High income inequality implies that some people in the economy do not benefit from the overall level of prosperity in a country. High income inequality is also associated with political instability. Income inequality is best measured over a long period rather than a short period, since the income of individual families fluctuates over time. In addition, a family's income varies over its life cycle: family income is relatively low at the beginning of the family's working years and rises over time; eventually, family income drops during the retirement years. Year-to-year fluctuations in income do highlight a significant issue even for affluent families, which is economic insecurity.

Objective #6. Economic insecurity refers to year-to-year fluctuations in income. These fluctuations impact both poor families and more affluent families. Two common causes of economic insecurity are job loss and medical problems that require expensive treatment.

Objective #7. Economic inequality over the past hundred years evidences three trends: during the 1930s and 1940s, economic inequality fell; during the 35 years after World War II economic inequality did not change; and during the last 30 years or so, economic inequality has risen. Economic inequality declined sharply in the late 1930s and early 1940s because of the imposition of special controls on wages and prices during World War II. This Great Compression was a period characterized by growing economic equality. During the past thirty years, economic inequality has grown: one argument for this change focuses on technological change, which has increased the demand for highly skilled workers while reducing the demand for low-skilled workers. In addition, the growth of international trade may have further compressed the wages of low-skilled labor while increasing the wages of highly skilled workers. Finally, rising immigration may also contribute to growing economic inequality. However, technological change, international trade, and increased immigration do not account for the growing economic gap among highly educated workers.

Objective #8. The three largest programs in the U.S. welfare state are Social Security, Medicare, and Medicaid.

Welfare state programs can be divided into two groups based on whether the program is means tested. Means-tested programs are poverty programs designed to help those with low incomes, whereas non-means-tested programs are programs whose benefits are available to everyone without regard to their income. Examples of means-tested poverty programs include:

- Monetary aid to poor families with children, which is given by the Temporary Assistance for Needy Families (TANF) program. This program is available only to those poor families with children, and this assistance is available only for a limited period.
- Negative income tax, which is a program that supplements the earnings of low-income working families. This Earned Income Tax Credit (EITC) provides additional income to millions of workers.

Both TANF and EITC address concerns about the provision of welfare and the impact poverty programs have on work incentives: work incentives are less impacted by limiting the amount of time a family can receive TANF or by supplementing the income low-wage workers receive (the EITC). Examples of non-means-tested programs include Social Security, which is a program that guarantees retirement income to qualifying older Americans. Social Security also provides benefits to disabled workers and the survivors of workers who have died. Social Security benefits are determined by a formula that gives high earners more than low earners, but with a sliding scale so that the program is relatively more generous for low earners than for high earners.

Welfare programs can also be divided into two groups based on whether the benefits of the program are in-kind benefits (such as the provision of health care to Medicare and Medicaid clients) or in-cash benefits.

Objective #9. There is political debate about how large the welfare state should be. Those arguing for a small welfare state believe that government's role is to maintain the rule of law, provide public goods, and control externalities. Other arguments for a relatively small welfare state focus on the trade-off between efficiency and equity: the ability-to-pay principle reduces the incentive to increase a family's income by working hard or by making risky investments, whereas provision of generous welfare programs creates adverse work incentives for low-income individuals. In addition, the creation of a large welfare state requires more tax revenue and therefore higher tax rates than does the creation of a small welfare state. One way to hold down the cost of the welfare state is to use means-tested benefits so that these benefits are made available only to those who need them. This method is not fail-safe since it may create a notch, which is a situation in which earning more actually leaves a family worse off.

Key Terms

poverty threshold the annual income below which a family is officially considered poor.

poverty rate the percentage of the population with incomes below the *poverty threshold.*

welfare state the set of government programs designed to alleviate economic hardship.

government transfer a payment from a government to an individual or a family.

poverty program a government program designed to aid the poor.

social insurance program a government program designed to provide protection against unpredictable financial distress.

mean household income the average income across all households.

median household income the income of the household lying at the exact middle of the *income distribution.*

Gini coefficient a number that summarizes a country's level of income inequality based on how unequally income is distributed across quintiles.

means-tested a program in which benefits are available only to individuals or families whose incomes fall below a certain level.

in-kind benefit a benefit given in the form of goods or services.

negative income tax a government program that supplements the income of low-income working families.

private health insurance a contract under which individuals pay a fixed amount annually to a private company that agrees to compensate the individuals for certain medical expenses.

Notes

AFTER YOU READ THE MODULE

Tips

Tip #1. This module discusses two measures of central tendency: the mean and the median. To find the mean, add up all the observed values for a variable and then divide this value by the number of observations. The mean, or simple average, is highly impacted by extremely low or high values. To find the median, first list all the observed values from lowest value to highest value and then find the middle observation in this ranking so that half of the observed values are below the median value and half are above the median value. The median value is not impacted adversely by extremely low or extremely high values. For purposes of measuring average income, the median average income is a far more accurate measure than is the mean average income.

Tip #2. There are two general kinds of benefit programs provided by the government: in kind and in cash. In-kind benefit programs provide benefits in the form of goods or services, whereas in-cash benefit programs provide benefits in the form of monetary payments.

Tip #3. A government program is means tested when there is a list of criteria the recipient must satisfy in order to participate in the program and receive the program's services.

Tip #4. In implementing welfare state programs, government officials are concerned about some potential negative consequences of these programs. Consider the potential effect of welfare state programs on the incentive to work and the incentive to save, as well as the potential deadweight loss that may arise from the implementation of welfare state programs.

WORKED PROBLEMS

1. Suppose you have been asked to do a study about the income distribution in the small town of Whynot. Whynot has a population of 15 people and each of these people work. The town authorities have collected information on the yearly income earned by each of the individuals who live in Whynot, and they have asked you to compile a report providing the mean and median income for the town. The information on yearly income is given in the following table.

Individuals in Whynot	Yearly income for each individual (in U.S. dollars)
Josie Jones	10,000
Amanda Adobe	20,000
Larry Lasso	14,000
Stuart Stevens	80,000
Karla Kitchener	30,000
Bart Bellows	40,000
Miranda Miracle	44,000
Sam Smith	30,000
Talia Telefono	50,000
Carolyn Cantrell	60,000
Nobel Nasmith	8,000
Debby Delores	8,000
Urban Vincent	10,000
Ella Fitzhugh	12,000
George Hazard	25,000

In the midst of compiling your data, you are told that Sam Smith just had one of his inventions patented and, because of the technological innovation represented by this patent, Sam's yearly income has risen to $5,000,000. You are asked to recalculate the mean and median income of Whynot after this event. Finally, the authorities in Whynot have asked you to evaluate the meaning of the new results you have found relative to the old results: in your report, provide an explanation of what these numbers actually tell you about the income distribution in Whynot.

STEP 1: Review the definition of median and mean before calculating the initial mean income and median income for Whynot.

To calculate the median value, you first rank the data you have from smallest value to largest value (or from largest value to smallest value) and then find the value that is in the middle of this ranking. The median income in Whynot would be the income earned by the person whose income places him or her in the ranked list at the eighth position: this person has seven people earning more than he or she does and seven people earning less than he or she does.

To calculate the mean value from a set of data, you sum all of the values for that variable and then divide by the number of values that you have. In this example, to find the mean income in Whynot, you would sum the yearly income of all 15 people and then divide that number by 15.

STEP 2: **Reorder the initial set of data from lowest income to highest income so that you can easily find the median income for the community.**

Individuals in Whynot	Yearly income for each individual (in U.S. dollars)
Nobel Nasmith	8,000
Debby Delores	8,000
Josie Jones	10,000
Urban Vincent	10,000
Ella Fitzhugh	12,000
Larry Lasso	14,000
Amanda Adobe	20,000
George Hazard	25,000
Karla Kitchener	30,000
Sam Smith	30,000
Bart Bellows	40,000
Miranda Miracle	44,000
Talia Telefono	50,000
Carolyn Cantrell	60,000
Stuart Stevens	80,000

STEP 3: **Identify the median income for Whynot, based on the preliminary data.**

From Step 1, we know that the median income is that income earned by the eighth person in the table, since this person is at the exact middle of the income distribution, with seven people earning more than he or she does and seven people earning less than he or she does. George Hazard is the eighth person in the income distribution and he earns $25,000. The median income for Whynot is $25,000.

STEP 4: **Calculate the mean income for Whynot, based on the preliminary data.**

To find the mean, we need to first sum the income earned by all 15 people in Whynot. Adding the values given in either table, we get $441,000. We then divide $441,000 by 15 to find the mean income: the mean income is $29,400.

STEP 5: Alter the set of data from Step 2 so that it now includes Sam Smith's higher income.

Individuals in Whynot	Yearly income for each individual (in U.S. dollars)
Nobel Nasmith	8,000
Debby Delores	8,000
Josie Jones	10,000
Urban Vincent	10,000
Ella Fitzhugh	12,000
Larry Lasso	14,000
Amanda Adobe	20,000
George Hazard	25,000
Karla Kitchener	30,000
Bart Bellows	40,000
Miranda Miracle	44,000
Talia Telefono	50,000
Carolyn Cantrell	60,000
Stuart Stevens	80,000
Sam Smith	5,000,000

STEP 6: Identify the median income for Whynot based on this new data.

Despite the enormous increase in Sam Smith's income, there is no effect on the median income in Whynot. George Hazard is still the individual whose income places him in the exact middle of the income distribution for this community.

STEP 7: Calculate the new mean income for Whynot based on this new data.

First, we will need to recalculate the sum of the income in Whynot. Initially, we calculated $441,000, but we need to now subtract out Sam Smith's income of $30,000 and replace it with his new income of $5,000,000. The new total income for Whynot is $5,411,000. Dividing this number by 15, we get the new mean income as $360,733.

STEP 8: Compare and contrast the new mean and median income in Whynot to the initial mean and median income in Whynot.

Sam Smith's substantial increase in income has not affected the median income in Whynot, but it has affected the mean income. This example illustrates how these two measures of central tendency can be quite different from a given set of data. Is the measure of mean income or median income more helpful in this situation? The mean income, particularly once Sam's income increases, gives a distorted view of income in this community. Clearly, most people's income does not approach the mean income of $360,733. In this example, the median income of $25,000 is a more accurate reflection of the income distribution. Imagine what would happen to average mean income in Whynot if Sam Smith decided to relocate to New York City: instead of a mean income of $360,733, we would have a mean income of $29,357 (found by dividing $411,000 by 14 people).

2. This problem is intended to illustrate the adverse selection death spiral. Suppose that Sarah owns a business that employs 100 people. Sarah would like to provide health insurance for her workers. To do this, she knows that she will need to collect payments from each of these workers so that the sum of the payments she collects is equal to the amount that will be needed to cover the medical costs of this group of people. To make this problem easier, let's assume that we are only looking at the expenses that will be incurred in one year. Sarah anticipates that 2% of the people who work for her company will face substantial medical expenses this year and that the cost of these medical expenses will be $500,000 per person. She also anticipates that 8% of the people who work for her company will face moderate medical expenses this year of $10,000 per person. The remaining 90% of the people who work for her will experience normal preventative care expenses of $2,000 per person. Sarah has asked you to provide her with answers to a number of questions. First, how much money will she need to collect from each worker if all the workers decide to get health insurance from her and all workers pay an equal amount for their health insurance? Second, if half the healthy people she employs decide not to get health insurance, how much money will she need to collect from the workers who get health insurance and what will each worker pay if he or she each contributes an equal amount for his or her health insurance? And, finally, given these calculations, help provide Sarah with an argument for why everyone must be in the pool if she is going to provide health insurance for her workers.

STEP 1: First, calculate the total cost of health care this year for Sarah's workers given the information she provided.

Sarah estimates that 2% of her workers will face substantial medical expenses for the year: 2% of her workers is equal to two workers, so the total cost of health care for these workers will be $1,000,000 ($500,000 per worker). Sarah estimates that 8%, or eight workers, will face moderate health care expenses of $10,000 per worker this year: thus, the total cost of health care for this set of workers will be $80,000 this year. Sarah estimates that 90%, or 90 workers, will face normal health care expenses of $2,000 per worker this year: thus, the total cost of health care for this set of workers will be $180,000 this year. Total cost of health care for all 100 workers will therefore be equal to $1,000,000 + $80,000 + $180,000, or $1,210,000.

STEP 2: Given the cost you calculated in Step 1, now calculate the payment each worker must make if all workers contribute the same amount for their health insurance.

If all 100 people who work for Sarah pay an equal amount for their health care insurance this year, they will each pay $12,100. If you are thinking about this example, you may already see that this is a great deal for those individuals who face significant health issues this year ($500,000 versus $12,100) and not a very good deal for those individuals who face moderate or normal health issues this year. Of course, you may also realize that people may not know with certainty which type of individual they are: no one can be certain that he or she will be lucky enough to be in the normal group—an accident can quickly catapult any one of us into the category with significant health problems.

STEP 3: Calculate the total cost of health care this year for Sarah's insured workers if half the healthy workers decide not to buy insurance through Sarah's business.

We still have two people with significant health care expenses for the year, for a total of $1,000,000, and eight people with moderate health care expenses for the year, for a total $80,000. That leaves half the 90 people with normal health care expenses staying in the program for health insurance at a cost to the program of $90,000 (45 people, each incurring medical expenses of $2,000 per year). Total cost of health care will therefore be equal to the sum of $1,000,000 + $80,000 + $ 90,000, or $1,170,000.

STEP 4: Given the cost you calculated in Step 3, now calculate the payment each insured worker must make if all insured workers contribute the same amount for their health insurance.

To find the payment each insured worker must make if all insured workers contribute the same amount for their health insurance, we must take the cost calculated in Step 3 and divide it by the number of insured workers, which is 55 in the given scenario: $1,170,000 divided by 55 is equal to $21,273. Take a moment and think about this figure: clearly, this is a bargain if you know you are only of the people facing significant health issues this year, but if you think you might be a person facing moderate or normal health issues this year, you are apt to decide you do not want this health insurance because of its cost. As others make the same decision, an adverse selection death spiral occurs: only the most expensive individuals to insure remain in the pool of insured workers, and the cost of providing insurance to this group grows prohibitively expensive.

STEP 5: Provide Sarah with an argument for why all of her workers must contribute to the health insurance plan if it is going to be feasible.

Reread the answer to Step 4: when individuals who are relatively low cost to insure drop out of the insurance pool, the remaining individuals in the pool become increasingly more expensive to insure. Remember that none of us can know for sure whether we will be an individual with significant health issues or a person with normal health care issues: when many people decide to opt out of the insured pool of individuals, then the cost of providing insurance to the pool of people who want insurance gets too expensive. The pool of people desiring insurance is apt to be adversely selected, with the pool containing a greater percentage of people with significant health issues than would be the case if everyone were included in the pool.

Problems and Exercises

1. For each of the following programs, decide whether the program is a poverty program or a social insurance program.

a. The Unemployment Compensation Program, which provides a payment equal to a fraction of the individual's income when the individual loses his job.

b. Medicaid, which pays medical expenses for low-income individuals who meet the means-tested criteria.

c. Medicare, which pays the medical expenses for all eligible elderly individuals regardless of their income.

d. Food stamps, which provides subsidies to low-income families who meet the means-tested criteria in order to help them purchase food items.

2. The following table provides information about the distribution of income in a small economy for three years.

Name	First year	Second year	Third year
Mary	$ 10,000	$12,000	$12,000
Ellen	12,000	12,000	12,000
Bob	8,000	10,000	12,000
Xiao	100,000	60,000	12,000
Sarah	4,000	8,000	12,000
Maria	20,000	12,000	12,000
Carlos	15,000	12,000	12,000
Juan	12,000	10,000	12,000
Hon Ho	9,000	45,000	12,000

a. Calculate the mean and median income for each of the three years.

b. Does the same individual earn the median income in each of the years?

c. In which year(s) is the mean as good a measure of income distribution as the median? Explain your answer.

d. In which year(s) is the mean not as good a measure of income distribution as the median? Explain your answer.

e. Since the median is the same for all three years, does this imply that the underlying income distribution is the same in all three years?

f. Calculate the mean income over the entire three years. Is this a better measure than the mean income for each specific year? Explain your answer.

3. Identify two rationales for the existence of welfare state programs. After identifying these two rationales, discuss the type of program—poverty or social insurance—that is designed to address the underlying economic issue of the rationale.

4. Describe the relationship between welfare state programs and the incentives to work and save. Is there a potential for the creation of deadweight loss from the implementation of welfare state programs?

5. Identify four sources of poverty.

6. For each of the following programs, identify whether the program is an example of a program offering in-kind benefits or in-cash benefits.

   a. The Unemployment Compensation Program, which provides a payment equal to a fraction of the individual's income when the individual loses his job.

   b. Medicaid, which pays medical expenses for low-income individuals who meet the means-tested criteria.

   c. Medicare, which pays the medical expenses for all eligible elderly individuals regardless of their income.

   d. Food stamps, which provides subsidies to low-income families who meet the means-tested criteria in order to help them purchase food items.

7. Suppose the government of Utopia is concerned about income distribution issues in Utopia's economy. Government officials propose implementing a negative income tax that will consist of all individuals receiving a $10,000 payment from the government while simultaneously requiring that all individuals pay a flat tax of 25% of their total income including the government payment. For instance, an individual who earns $0 in income would receive a $10,000 payment from the government and would then pay 25% of their income after the government subsidy to the government. Thus, this individual would pay $2,500 to the government and would have $7,500 in after-tax income. The table below summarizes this transaction for this individual.

Initial income	Government subsidy	Total before tax income	Tax	After-tax income
$0	$10,000	$10,000	$2,500	$7,500

a. Following the same reasoning as outlined in the above information, fill in the following table based on the implementation of this program.

Initial income	Government subsidy	Total before tax income	Tax	After-tax income
$ 0	$10,000	$10,000	$2,500	$7,500
10,000				
20,000				
30,000				
40,000				
50,000				
60,000				

b. At what initial level of income does the individual find that their tax payment to the government exactly equals the $10,000 subsidy?

c. This negative income tax is designed to provide an incentive for low-income people to work. Do you think this program meets this goal? Explain your answer.

8. Suppose the government of Utopia is concerned about income distribution issues in Utopia's economy. Government officials propose implementing a negative income tax that will consist of all individuals receiving a $10,000 payment from the government while simultaneously requiring that all individuals pay a flat tax of 20% of their total income including the government payment. For instance, an individual who earns $0 in income would receive a $10,000 payment from the government and would then pay 20% of their income after the government subsidy to the government. Thus, this individual would pay $2,000 to the government and would have $8,000 in after-tax income. The table below summarizes this transaction for this individual.

Initial income	Government subsidy	Total before tax income	Tax	After-tax income
$0	$10,000	$10,000	$2,000	$8,000

a. Following the same reasoning as outlined in the above information, fill in the following table based on the implementation of this program.

Initial income	Government subsidy	Total before tax income	Tax	After-tax income
$ 0	$10,000	$10,000	$2,000	$8,000
10,000				
20,000				
30,000				
40,000				
50,000				
60,000				

b. At what initial level of income does the individual find that their tax payment to the government exactly equals the $10,000 subsidy? Compare your result in problem 7(b) with your result in problem 8(b): what is the effect of reducing the flat tax rate on the break-even income?

9. Edenville, a small country of 100 people, decides that it will provide health care insurance to all 100 people who live in Edenville. Each person living in Edenville will be charged a health care premium that is the same for all individuals. Initially, everyone in Edenville endorses this plan and willingly makes the required payment. In Edenville, 20% of the population never gets sick and never incurs any medical expenses; 40% of the population gets sick occasionally, and the yearly medical expense for this group is $500 per person; and the last 40% of the population gets sick often, and the yearly medical expense for this group is $5,000 per person. Initially, no one in Edenville knows which category of health they represent.

a. If Edenville is to collect a sufficient amount of money to cover all of the medical expenses of their population during the year, how much money will they need to collect?

b. If Edenville charges each resident the same amount for health care insurance, what will the premium be per person?

Suppose people in Edenville become aware of whether they are in the healthy group, the relatively healthy group, or the sick group. Base your answers to the following questions on these individuals having this knowledge.

c. Suppose the healthy individuals petition the government to be exempt from the health care program. They argue that 100% of their premium pays medical expenses that are incurred by other people in the population. If the healthy individuals leave the insurance pool, what level of insurance premium will the government need to collect to be able to pay all of the medical costs that will be incurred in Edenville in a year's time?

d. Consider the premium you calculated in part (c). Is the level of this premium an amount that the remaining less-healthy and sick individuals will still be willing to pay? Explain your answer and provide a logical argument to support your answer.

e. If both the healthy and the relatively healthy individuals opt out of the health care program, what level of premium per person will the sick group need to pay to cover all of the medical expenses that are incurred in Edenville during the year? Will this group be willing to pay this amount? Assume that individuals opting out of the program will still incur medical expenses as stated and that these medical treatments will be given.

BEFORE YOU TAKE THE TEST

Module Review Questions

1. The welfare state refers to

a. Temporary Assistance to Needy Families.

b. Social Security.

c. the Earned Income Tax Credit.

d. the collection of government programs that are aimed at alleviating economic hardship.

2. Government transfers are

a. payments to the government that provide support to the poor, to the unemployed, to the elderly, and to those needing assistance in paying medical bills in a society.

b. payments by the government to the poor, to the unemployed, to the elderly, and to those needing assistance in paying medical bills in a society.

c. the collection of programs that are aimed at alleviating economic hardship.

d. Answers (a), (b), and (c) are all correct.

3. Suppose the government taxes a family that earns $500,000 and collects a tax equal to $2,000. The government then provides a family that earns $23,000 an extra $2,000. Which of the following statements is true?

a. The $2,000 is equally valuable to both families since it represents the same amount of purchasing power to both families.
b. The $2,000 is more highly valued by the high-income family since they know and appreciate more fully the merits of a higher income.
c. The $2,000 is more highly valued by the low-income family because they received these dollars without having to perform extra work or any tangible service. It was "free" to them.
d. The $2,000 is likely to make a greater difference in the quality of life for the low-income family than for the high-income family.

4. The government recently announced a program aimed at reducing the percentage of families earning incomes below the poverty line. The announced program is an example of a

a. poverty program.
b. social insurance program.

5. The government recently announced a program aimed at providing financial resources to workers who have been temporarily laid off from their jobs. The announced program is an example of a

a. poverty program.
b. social insurance program.

6. Which of the following statements is true?

I. A major rationale for the welfare state is the desire to achieve economic equality for all members of a society.
II. A major rationale for the welfare state is the desire to achieve a just distribution of income for all members of a society.
III. A major rationale for the welfare state is the desire to alleviate income inequality.
IV. A major rationale for the welfare state is the desire to alleviate economic insecurity.

a. Statement I is true.
b. Statement II is true.
c. Statement III is true.
d. Statement IV is true.
e. Statements I and III are true.
f. Statements III and IV are true.
g. Statements I, III, and IV are true.
h. Statements I, II, III, and IV are true.

7. Which of the following statements is true?

I. Only political conservatives support the creation of welfare state programs.
II. Only political liberals support the creation of welfare state programs.
III. Both political conservatives and liberals support the creation of welfare state programs, although the two groups differ as to the appropriate extent of these programs.

a. Statement I is true.
b. Statement II is true.
c. Statement III is true.

8. To be considered poor in the United States, your household income
  a. must be below $30,000.
  b. must be below the minimum amount deemed adequate to purchase the necessities of life.
  c. must fall below the poverty threshold.
  d. Answers (a), (b), and (c) are all true.
  e. Answers (b) and (c) are true.

9. The poverty threshold is the same for individuals and for families.
  a. True
  b. False

10. Which of the following statements is true?
  I. Since 1980, income inequality in the United States has diminished substantially.
  II. Since 1980, income inequality in the United States has remained relatively constant.
  III. Since 1980, income inequality in the United States has increased substantially.
  a. Statement I is true.
  b. Statement II is true.
  c. Statement III is true.
  d. None of the statements is true.

11. Which of the following is a relative measure of poverty?
  a. A person is considered poor when his or her income is below a designated level of income, or poverty threshold.
  b. A person is considered poor when his or her household income is less than half of his or her country's median household income.

12. Compared with other wealthy countries, the United States has a(n)
  a. unusually low poverty rate.
  b. unusually high poverty rate.
  c. similar poverty rate.

13. Which of the following is not a cause of poverty?
  a. Lack of education
  b. Lack of proficiency in speaking English
  c. Racial and gender discrimination
  d. Bad luck
  e. Answers (a), (b), (c), and (d) are all causes of poverty.

14. In the United States, the average household income in 2011 was more than $68,000. This means that

a. half of all households in the United States earned less than $68,000, and half of all households in the United States earned more than $68,000.

b. no household in the United States was poor, since all households on average earned $68,000, which is clearly not an impoverished level of income.

c. if there are households below the poverty threshold in the United States, then the distribution of income in the United States must be highly unequal.

d. households earning less than the poverty threshold are not making enough effort to earn an income to support themselves.

15. Median household income is equal to

a. the total income of all households in a country divided by the total number of households.

b. the income of the household in the exact middle of the income distribution.

16. Income inequality

a. is often associated with political instability.

b. means that not everyone benefits from the country's prosperity.

c. is impossible to measure, and therefore public policy should not be based on reducing income inequality.

d. Answers (a) and (b) are both true.

17. Income inequality among households in the United States

a. is greater if it is measured over a shorter period than over a longer period.

b. is the same if it is measured over a shorter period than over a longer period.

c. is smaller if it is measured over a shorter period than over a longer period.

d. has an unpredictable pattern when measurements from a short period are compared with measurements gathered over a longer period.

18. Economic insecurity

a. may be the result of a sudden loss of income.

b. may be the result of a sudden surge in expenses.

c. is often caused by significant, and costly, medical problems.

d. Answers (a), (b), and (c) are all true.

19. Income inequality in the United States

a. has not varied significantly over the past eighty years.

b. fell during the 1930s and 1940s, was stable for about thirty-five years after World War II, and then fell again during the last thirty years.

c. fell during the 1930s and 1940s, was stable for about thirty-five years after World War II, and then rose during the last thirty years.

d. rose during the 1930s and 1940s, was stable for about thirty-five years after World War II, and then fell again during the last thirty years.

20. A means-tested welfare state program is one that

a. is available to all individuals in the country.

b. is available to those individuals in the country with income or wealth below a certain threshold.

c. is available to those individuals in the country with income or wealth above a certain threshold.

d. does not reduce the level of income inequality in a country.

21. The main welfare state program that provides assistance to low-income families with children is

a. the Aid to Families with Dependent Children program (AFDC).

b. the Temporary Assistance for Needy Families program (TANF).

c. Social Security.

d. Medicare.

22. Which of the following programs in not means tested?

a. Social Security

b. Temporary Assistance for Needy Families

c. Supplemental Security Income

d. Earned Income Tax Credit

23. Which of the following statements is true?

a. In the United States, the combination of tax and transfer programs essentially leaves the income distribution unchanged.

b. In the United States, the individuals who pay taxes tend to be different from the individuals receiving transfer payments, and the income distribution in the United States is affected by these tax and transfer programs.

c. In the United States, the welfare state has little, if any, impact on income distribution.

d. In the United States, the welfare state is administered in such a way that there is no efficiency cost to the programs supported by the welfare state.

24. The program that provides health insurance coverage to all Americans aged 65 and older, regardless of their income, is

a. Medicaid.

b. Medicare.

25. Welfare state programs that aid the poor often face the problem in which earning more actually leaves the family worse off. This "notch" problem acts like a

a. low marginal tax rate on the income received by the poor family.

b. high marginal tax rate on the income received by the poor family.

ANSWER KEY

Answers to Problems and Exercises

1. **a.** This is a social insurance program, since it is aimed at stabilizing income for all working individuals rather than targeting poor individuals.

   b. This is a poverty program, since it is aimed at providing medical care for the poor, who are identified by meeting a set of standards that assesses the means of these individuals.

   c. This is a social insurance program, since it is aimed at stabilizing income for all eligible elderly individuals rather than targeting poor elderly individuals.

   d. This is a poverty program, since it is aimed at providing subsidized food to the poor, who are identified by meeting a set of standards that assesses the means of these individuals.

2. **a.**

	First year	Second year	Third year
Mean	$21,111	$20,111	$12,000
Median	12,000	12,000	12,000

   b. No, only Ellen earns the median income in each of the years. Since everyone receives the median income. In the first year, Juan and Ellen both earn the median income. In the second year, Mary, Ellen, Maria, and Carlos all earn the median income.

   c. In the third year the mean and the median provide the same measure of $12,000; more important, income is evenly distributed in the third year, with all individuals receiving the same amount of income, so the mean does not distort the income of the average person since everyone has the same income.

   d. In the first and second years, the mean is not as good a measure of the income distribution as the median since in both of these years some individuals earn substantially more than the median income, which results in the mean income being much higher than the median income. In the first year, Xiao earns an income that is substantially greater than the median income, and in the second year Xiao and Hon Ho both earn incomes that are greater than the median income.

   e. No, the underlying distribution of income is different in the three years even though the median income is the same.

   f. The mean income for the entire three-year period is $17,741. This is a better measure of average income than the average from any one year since it smooths out the fluctuations in average income that occur from year to year.

3. The two rationales for welfare state programs are the alleviation of income inequality and the alleviation of economic insecurity. Poverty programs are designed to reduce income inequality, whereas social insurance programs are designed to provide protection against unpredictable economic distress.

4. Welfare state programs, designed to reduce income inequality and/or economic insecurity, may affect people's desire to work and save. When individuals know that the government will provide support when the individual lacks economic means, this lessens the incentive for the individual to be prudent with regard to their saving while also potentially affecting the individual's desire to work. These negative aspects of welfare state programs result in the creation of deadweight losses similar to the losses that are created when the government imposes taxes.

5. Poverty may be caused by lack of education, lack of English language proficiency, the presence of gender or racial discrimination, or due to bad luck.

6. **a.** The Unemployment Compensation Program provides dollars to the recipient, and the recipient is free to choose how he or she wishes to spend these dollars. This is an in-cash benefit program.

   b. Medicaid provides health care services to the poor. This is an in-kind benefit program.

   c. Medicare provides health care services to eligible elderly individuals. This is an in-kind program.

   d. Food stamps help recipients purchase food at reduced cost. Since this aid can only be used on food purchases, it is an example of an in-kind benefit program.

7. **a.**

Initial income	Government subsidy	Total before tax income	Tax	After-tax income
$ 0	$10,000	$10,000	$ 2,500	$ 7,500
10,000	10,000	20,000	5,000	15,000
20,000	10,000	30,000	7,500	22,500
30,000	10,000	40,000	10,000	30,000
40,000	10,000	50,000	12,500	37,500
50,000	10,000	60,000	15,000	45,000
60,000	10,000	70,000	17,500	52,500

   b. When individuals earn $30,000, they receive the $10,000 payment from the government but must also pay $10,000 to the government in taxes. Their initial income and their after-tax income is $30,000.

   c. For low-income individuals this program provides an incentive to work, since it enhances the individual's income for any income level less than $30,000.

8. **a.**

Initial income	Government subsidy	Total before tax income	Tax	After-tax income
$ 0	$10,000	$10,000	$ 2,000	$ 8,000
10,000	10,000	20,000	4,000	16,000
20,000	10,000	30,000	6,000	24,000
30,000	10,000	40,000	8,000	32,000
40,000	10,000	50,000	10,000	40,000
50,000	10,000	60,000	12,000	48,000
60,000	10,000	70,000	14,000	56,000

   b. When individuals earn $40,000, they receive a payment from the government of $10,000 but must also pay 20% of their total income of $50,000 to the government. When the flat tax rate is lowered, it raises the level of the break-even income.

9. **a.** The total medical expenses in Edenville for the year are equal to $220,000 ($20,000 are the medical expenses associated with the relatively healthy group, and $200,000 are the medical expenses associated with the sick group).

   b. If each person contributes the same amount, the premium will equal $2,200 per person. This premium is $2,200 more than the healthy person wants to pay for health care insurance, $1,700 more than the relatively healthy person wants to pay for health care insurance, and $2,800 less than the total cost of care that the sick person will incur during the year.

c. If the 20 healthy people leave the pool, the $220,000 in medical costs must be paid by the remaining eighty people. The premium per person would therefore equal $2,750. This is $2,250 more than the value of the health care insurance that the relatively healthy person receives and $2,250 less than the cost of providing health care to the relatively sick individual.

d. Referring back to answer (c), the health care premium is higher than the cost of providing health care for the relatively healthy individual and lower than the cost of providing health care for the sick individual. The relatively healthy individual will not be willing to pay the premium, whereas the sick individual will find this insurance program a bargain.

e. If only the 40 sick people are left in the program, the health care insurance premium will be equal to $5,500. This amount is $500 more than the cost of providing health care to the sick individual (the sick individual is now paying for his or her own health care as well as the health care of the relatively healthy individual). This group will not be willing to pay this amount, since it is greater than their individual medical costs.

Answers to Module Review Questions

1. **Answer d.** *Welfare state* is a general term that encompasses all the various programs the government operates that are designed to lessen economic hardship.

2. **Answer b.** *Government transfers* refers to the payments made by the government to different individuals who qualify for government support, which provides economic support to the poor, to the elderly, to those who are unemployed, and to those needing assistance in paying their medical bills. The collection of programs that are aimed at alleviating economic hardship is the welfare state.

3. **Answer d.** The high-income family may have to forgo a few things when they pay this tax, but they will not be giving up necessities. On the other hand, the low-income family will find this additional income represents a significant difference in their quality of life: it will enable this family to purchase goods and services they otherwise could not afford. The low-income family finds that a marginal dollar is worth more to them than it is to the high-income family.

4. **Answer a.** Programs directed at reducing economic inequality are poverty programs, whereas programs designed to provide protection against unpredictable distress are known as social insurance programs.

5. **Answer b.** Programs directed at reducing economic inequality are poverty programs, whereas programs designed to provide protection against unpredictable distress are known as social insurance programs.

6. **Answer f.** The two major rationales for the welfare state are the alleviation of income inequality and the alleviation of economic insecurity. These two goals do not necessarily imply the achievement of an equal distribution of income or a just distribution of income.

7. **Answer c.** Liberals and conservatives both believe that some level of welfare state programs need to exist: conservatives typically favor less extensive programming, and liberals typically favor more extensive programming.

8. **Answer e.** The poverty threshold is defined as the minimum annual income that is considered adequate to purchase the necessities of life. The dollar amount of this poverty threshold is not static, but changes as the price of goods and services change. If your household income falls below the poverty threshold, then your household is considered poor.

9. **Answer b.** The poverty threshold depends on the size and the composition of a family. For example, the poverty threshold for an individual is a lower dollar amount than it is for a family of four.

10. **Answer c.** Since 1980, income inequality in the United States has increased substantially.

11. **Answer b.** A relative measure of poverty is a poverty definition that compares the individual's level of income with the level of income received by other individuals in the country. An absolute measure of poverty is one based on a dollar amount.

12. **Answer b.** By either relative or absolute measures, the United States has an unusually high poverty rate.

13. **Answer e.** The major causes of poverty are lack of education and English language proficiency, racial and gender discrimination, and bad luck.

14. **Answer c.** Answer (a) is the definition of the median household income. Answers (b) and (d) are nonsense answers: the average household income figure for a country tells you nothing about whether there are poor households in the country, nor does it tell you anything about the effort poor people expend on earning an income.

15. **Answer b.** Half of all households in the income distribution earn less income than the median income, and half of all households in the income distribution earn more income than the median income.

16. **Answer d.** Income inequality means that income is unequally distributed among residents of a country and therefore not everyone benefits from the country's general prosperity. Income inequality is also associated with political instability, since income inequality often creates tension between the wealthy members of the society and the less-wealthy members of the society.

17. **Answer a.** Incomes of many families vary over time, so measurements of income inequality that averages income over a longer period smooths out these income fluctuations and results in a lower measure of income inequality.

18. **Answer d.** All four answers are associated with economic insecurity that arises because of a sudden decrease in income (job loss) or a sudden surge in expenses (particularly associated with expensive medical problems).

19. **Answer c.** This is just a factual question, and you should refer back to the text to see that income inequality fell during the 1930s and 1940s, was stable during the 35 years after World War II, and then rose during the last 30 years.

20. **Answer b.** A means-tested welfare state program is one that requires recipients to meet an income or wealth requirement: if the individual's income or wealth is lower than the program's established threshold, then the individual is eligible for the program; if the individual's income or wealth is greater than the program's established threshold, then the individual is not eligible for the program. Therefore, a means-tested welfare state program is not available to all individuals in the country. A well-designed means-tested welfare state program should reduce income inequality in a country.

21. **Answer b.** The welfare state program that provides assistance to low-income families with children is called TANF. This program replaced AFDC during the 1990s and is an attempt to rectify the negative incentives in the AFDC program.

22. **Answer a.** Social Security guarantees retirement income and is available to all qualifying older Americans. The other three programs are means tested.

23. **Answer b.** The U.S. welfare state programs do impact the income distribution, primarily because the individuals who pay the bulk of taxes are different from the individuals who receive transfer payments from the government. The tax systems to support the welfare state programs and the actual programs both create economic inefficiency, since they alter the incentives that individuals face with regard to their work and leisure choices.

24. Answer b. Medicaid provides health insurance coverage to those Americans who are poor and who meet the means-tested criteria for receiving this insurance. Medicare is the health insurance program for the elderly, and it is not a means-tested program.

25. Answer b. The "notch" problem occurs when a poor family that has been receiving aid from a program increases its earnings and finds that this increase in earnings leads to a reduction in the level of aid they receive from the government. This situation makes the family worse off, and the resultant effect on the family is much like the result you would see if the family was subjected to a high marginal tax rate on their additional earnings.

module 40

Factor Markets

BEFORE YOU READ THE MODULE

Summary

This module introduces factor markets and then discusses how resources like land, labor, and capital are traded in these factor markets. The module discusses the determination of the factor distribution of income and how the demand for a factor of production is determined.

Module Objectives

Objective #1. There are four principle categories of resources.

- Land, a resource that is provided by nature.
- Labor, the resource that is the work done by human beings.
- Capital, the value of assets used by a firm in producing its output; physical capital refers to manufactured resources such as equipment, buildings, tools, and machines, while human capital refers to the improvement in labor created by education and knowledge.
- Entrepreneurship, a risk-taking activity that brings together resources for innovative production.

Objective #2. Factor markets and factor prices are critical in determining the allocation of resources among competing uses. There are two features that make factor markets special. First, the demand for a factor is a derived demand: this demand depends on or is derived from firms' decisions about how much output to produce. Second, factor markets are, for most of us, the source of the largest share of our income. Factor prices play a key role in determining the income distribution in our economy, since it is these factor prices that determine how the total income in an economy is divided among labor, land, and capital.

- In the United States, payments to labor account for most of the economy's total income. Seventy percent of total income in the United States takes the form of "compensation of employees": this figure has been relatively stable for the past 35 years. Much of the return to labor is a return on human capital: the data on labor compensation does not distinguish between the return to labor and the return to human capital, but most economists believe that human capital has become the most important factor of production in modern economies.

Objective #3. Firms should hire additional factors of production provided that the marginal cost of the additional factor is less than or equal to the marginal benefit from hiring the additional factor. In a competitive factor market, the marginal cost of an additional unit of a factor is the factor's price: in the case of a competitive labor market, the marginal cost of an additional worker is that worker's wage rate. This equilibrium wage rate is determined by the intersection of the labor supply curve with the labor demand curve: at the equilibrium wage, the quantity of labor supplied is equal to the quantity of labor demanded. In the market for capital and the market for land, the equilibrium factor price also reflects an equilibrium between the quantity supplied of the factor and the quantity demanded of the factor.

- In a competitive labor and product market, the marginal benefit of hiring an additional worker is equal to the value of the marginal product (*VMPL*) of that worker: the value of the marginal product of a worker is that worker's marginal product of labor times the price of the firm's output. This calculation is expressed by the formula below:

  $$VMPL = P \times MPL$$

  A firm should continue to hire additional units of labor until the *VMPL* is equal to the wage rate or until

  $$VMPL = W$$

- The firm will apply this general concept when making a decision about hiring any factors of production: the firm should hire additional units of the factor until the point at which the value of the marginal product of the last unit of the factor hired is exactly equal to the factor's price. If the level of output produced by the firm is chosen so that price equals marginal cost, then it is also true that at this output the value of the marginal product of each factor will be equal to the factor's price.

Objective #4. The *VMPL* curve is downward sloping: for example, as additional units of labor are hired, the *VMPL* of labor decreases due to diminishing marginal returns to labor. Although hiring additional units of labor allows the firm to expand its production of output, output eventually increases at a diminishing rate, which implies that the marginal product of labor will decrease. Since in a perfectly competitive output market the firm is a price taker, this implies that as the firm increases its hiring of labor, the *VMPL* of labor must eventually decline since the constant price is being multiplied by smaller values for the marginal product of labor. The *VMPL* of labor curve is the firm's demand curve for labor. Figure 40.1 illustrates a representative firm in the market for labor: this labor market is assumed to be perfectly competitive, and therefore the firm accepts the equilibrium wage (W_E) as the wage it will pay when it hires a unit of labor. The *VMPL* of labor curve is the firm's individual demand for labor curve. The firm selects the amount of labor it wishes to hire (n) by equating the *VMPL* of labor with the equilibrium wage, since the equilibrium wage represents the marginal cost of hiring an additional unit of labor. The firm's factor demand curve will shift with changes in the price of the goods being produced, with changes in the supply of other factors, and with changes in the level of technology.

Figure 40.1

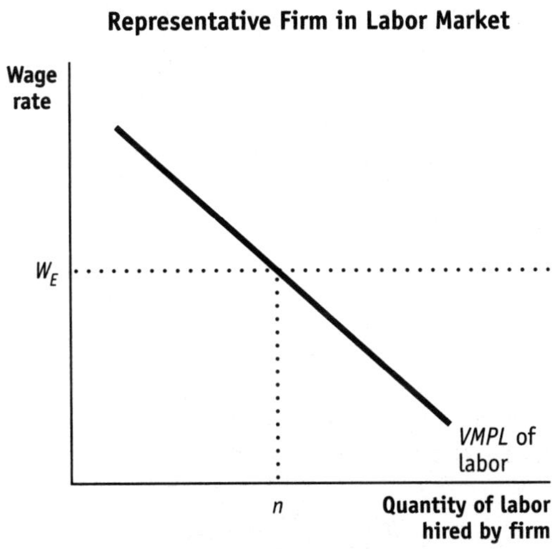

- An increase in the price of the firm's product will cause the *VMPL* curve for the factor to shift to the right, since each marginal product value for the factor will be multiplied by a higher price, and the profit-maximizing firm will hire more of the factor at a given factor price than it did initially. Figure 40.2 illustrates the effect of an increase in the price of the firm's product on the firm's hiring decision with regard to labor: n is the initial level of labor hired by the firm and n_2 is the amount of labor hired by the firm after the change in the price of the firm's product.

Figure 40.2

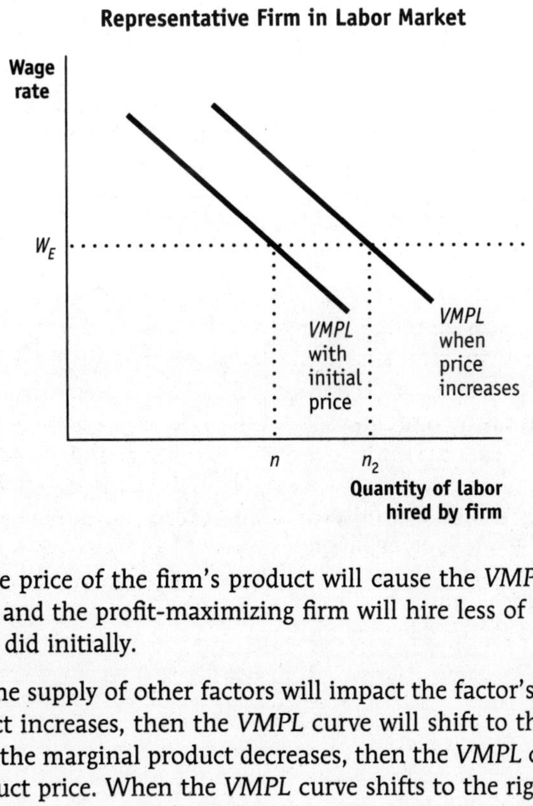

A decrease in the price of the firm's product will cause the *VMPL* curve for the factor to shift to the left, and the profit-maximizing firm will hire less of the factor at a given factor price than it did initially.

- An increase in the supply of other factors will impact the factor's marginal product: if the marginal product increases, then the *VMPL* curve will shift to the right for a given product price, and if the marginal product decreases, then the *VMPL* curve will shift to the left for a given product price. When the *VMPL* curve shifts to the right, then the profit-maximizing firm will hire more of that factor at a given factor price. If the *VMPL* curve shifts to the left, then the profit-maximizing firm will hire less of that factor at a given factor price. Figure 40.3 illustrates the change in the firm's hiring of labor when the marginal product of labor increases: the firm initially hires n units of labor but then increases its hiring of labor to n_2 when the marginal product of labor increases.

Figure 40.3 Representative Firm in Labor Market

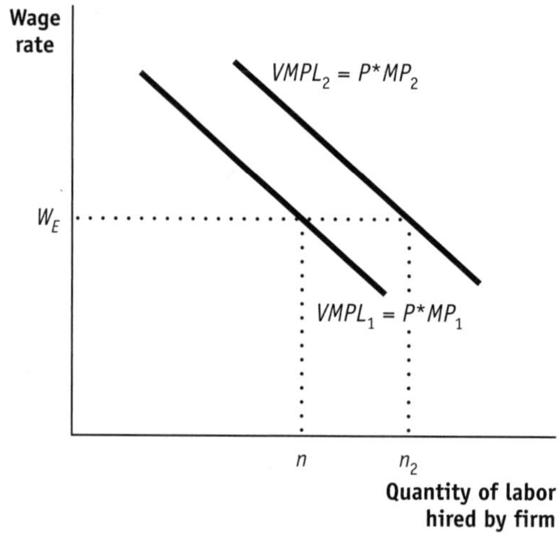

- A change in technology may shift the *VMPL* curve to the left or to the right, depending on the effect of the technological change on the factor's *VMPL*. Thus, technological change may increase or decrease the demand for a given factor of production.

Key Terms

physical capital manufactured productive resources, such as buildings and machines; often referred to simply as "capital."

human capital the improvement in labor created by education and knowledge that is embodied in the workforce.

derived demand for a factor results from (or is derived from) the demand for the output being produced.

factor distribution of income the division of total income among labor, land, and capital.

value of the marginal product the value of the additional output generated by employing one more unit of a given factor, such as labor.

value of the marginal product curve a graphical representation showing how the *value of the marginal product* of a factor depends on the quantity of the factor employed.

Notes

AFTER YOU READ THE MODULE

Tips

Tip #1. One of the key tips for working with factor markets is to recognize that the demanders in these markets are firms while the suppliers in these markets are individuals. Firms demand the services of land, labor, and capital, and households (or individuals) supply these services. This is in contrast to output markets where the demanders of the outputs are households and the suppliers of outputs are firms.

Tip #2. Section 13 introduces new vocabulary that many students find difficult to understand and remember. Review this vocabulary and the definitions until you feel confident about the meaning and use of the new terms that are introduced.

Tip #3. Review the factors that shift the factor demand curve. It is critical to your understanding of this material that you know these factors that result in the demand curve shifting.

WORKED PROBLEMS

1. Harriet works for Acme Publishing, and she has been asked to provide the company with a description of the relationship between the value of the marginal product of labor and the quantity of labor the firm hires. Harriet is also asked to analyze the optimal amount of labor for the firm to hire given that the market wage rate is $80. Harriet has been provided with the following data, and she must calculate first the marginal product of labor and then the value of the marginal product of labor. She must provide a table relating these values to the quantity of labor hired along with a graph of the relationship. Harriet also knows that Acme Publishing is a firm in a perfectly competitive industry and that the price of its product in this industry is $10 per unit.

Quantity of labor	Quantity of output
0	0
1	10
2	18
3	24
4	28
5	30

STEP 1: Review the definition of the marginal product of labor and the value of the marginal product of labor.

The marginal product of labor is defined as the change in total output divided by the change in labor. In the table the change in labor from one row to the next is a single unit, and thus the marginal product of labor will be measured as the change in output as the level of labor increases by one unit. The value of the marginal product of labor is defined as the product of the price of the firm's product times its marginal product of labor. In this example the price of the firm's product is given as $10 per unit, and this will be the price used in calculating the value of the marginal product of labor for this firm.

STEP 2: Calculate the marginal product of labor and the value of the marginal product of labor for Acme Publishing, and then put your findings in a table.

The following table provides the marginal product of labor and the value of the marginal product of labor for Acme Publishing.

Quantity of labor	Quantity of output	Marginal product of labor	Value of the marginal product of labor
0	0		
		10	$100
1	10		
		8	80
2	18		
		6	60
3	24		
		4	40
4	28		
		2	20
5	30		

STEP 3: Graph the relationship between the value of the marginal product of labor and the quantity of labor. Base your graph on the data you calculated in Step 2.

In graphing this relationship, measure the value of the marginal product of labor on the vertical axis and the quantity of labor on the horizontal axis. The following graph depicts the value of the marginal product curve for Acme Publishing.

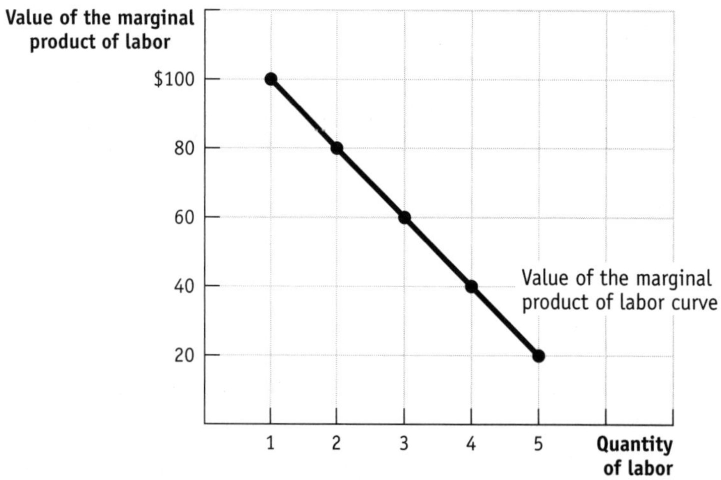

STEP 4: Given that the market wage rate is $80, determine the optimal amount of labor Acme Publishing should hire.

Acme Publishing should hire the amount of labor that will set the value of the marginal product of labor equal to the market wage rate. Given that the market wage rate is $80, Acme Publishing should hire two units of labor.

2. Harriet has just finished her analysis of Acme Publishing's value of the marginal product of labor curve when her supervisor tells her that the price of their final product has increased to $20. Harriet has been asked to explain to her supervisor the impact of this price change on the firm's value of the marginal product of labor curve. Harriet will need to provide a table contrasting the impact of the two different prices on the firm's value of marginal product of labor along with a graph depicting the two value of marginal product of labor curves. Finally, Harriet has been asked to determine the optimal amount of labor to hire if the market wage rate is $80 and the product price is $20.

STEP 1: Start by revising the table from problem 1 by adding a column showing the value of the marginal product of labor when the price of the product is $20.

Here is the revised table:

Quantity of labor	Quantity of output	Marginal product of labor	Value of the marginal product of labor when product price is $10	Value of the marginal product of labor when product price is $20
0	0			
		10	$100	$200
1	10			
		8	80	160
2	18			
		6	60	120
3	24			
		4	40	80
4	28			
		2	20	40
5	30			

STEP 2: **Revise the graph in problem 1 so that it shows both curves for value of marginal product of labor. Indicate which curve reflects a product price of $10 and which curve reflects a product price of $20.**

Here is the revised graph. The value of the marginal product of labor curve shifts to the right when the price of the product increases.

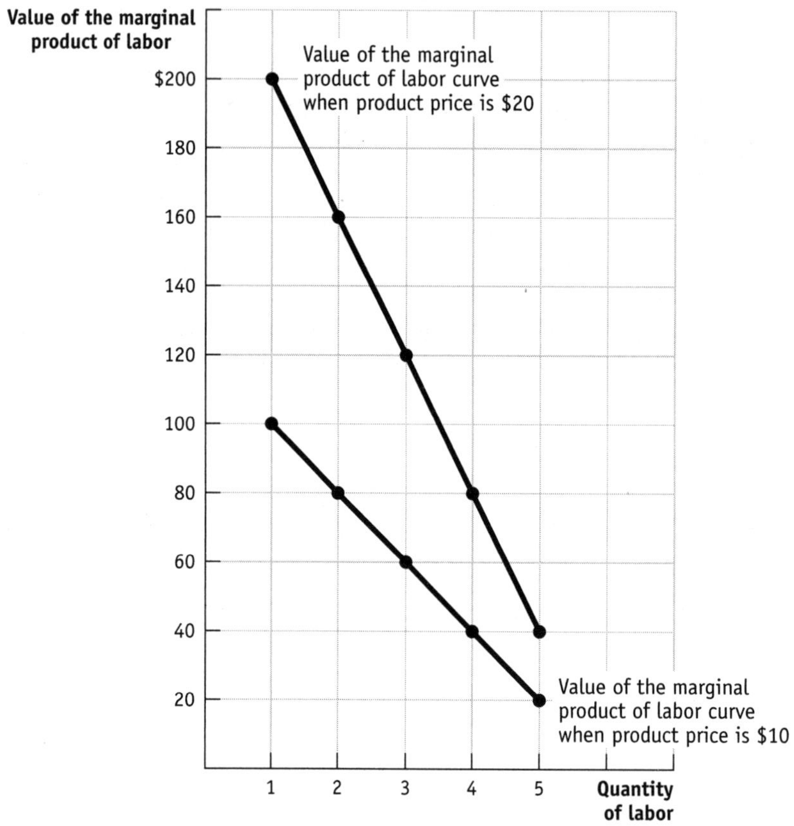

STEP 3: **Provide a statement that explains the impact of a change in the price of the product on a firm's value of marginal product of labor curve, holding everything else constant.**

When the price of the firm's product increases, the value of marginal product of labor curve shifts to the right; when the price of the firm's product decreases, the value of marginal product curve shifts to the left.

STEP 4: **Determine the optimal amount of labor for Acme Publishing to hire if the market wage rate is $80 and the price of its product is $20.**

Acme Publishing will want to hire the amount of labor that sets the value of the marginal product of labor equal to the wage rate it must pay. This will occur when Acme Publishing hires 4 units of labor; it is more profitable for Acme Publishing to hire more labor now that its product is selling for a higher price.

Problems and Exercises

1. What is a derived demand? How is this term used to describe the demand for the services of land, labor, and capital?

2. Sarah operates a coffeehouse and her production function per week is given in the table below. The current equilibrium weekly wage in the labor market is $400 per week, and Sarah sells each cup of coffee for $3 at her coffeehouse.

Quantity of labor (workers)	Quantity of coffee (number of cups)
0	0
1	300
2	450
3	550
4	600

a. Find the marginal product of labor for each worker and the value of the marginal product of each worker. Put your findings in the table below.

Quantity of labor (workers)	Marginal product of labor (cups of coffee per worker)	Value of the marginal product of labor (dollars per worker)
0	—	—
1		
2		
3		
4		

b. How many workers should Sarah hire?

c. Suppose the equilibrium wage rate fell to $300 per week. How would this change in the equilibrium wage rate affect Sarah's hiring decision? Describe in words how Sarah would determine how much labor she should hire.

3. Mike operates a sandwich shop and his production function is given in the table below. Suppose that the equilibrium weekly wage in the labor market is $300 a week and that Mike sells his sandwiches for $5 each.

Quantity of labor (workers)	Quantity of sandwiches (number of sandwiches)
0	0
1	100
2	180
3	240
4	290

a. Using the above information, fill in the following table.

Quantity of labor (workers)	Marginal product of labor (sandwiches per worker)	Value of the marginal product of labor (dollars per worker)
0	—	—
1		
2		
3		
4		

b. Draw the value of the marginal product of labor curve for Mike's sandwich shop. Use this graph to determine how many workers Mike should hire at his sandwich shop.

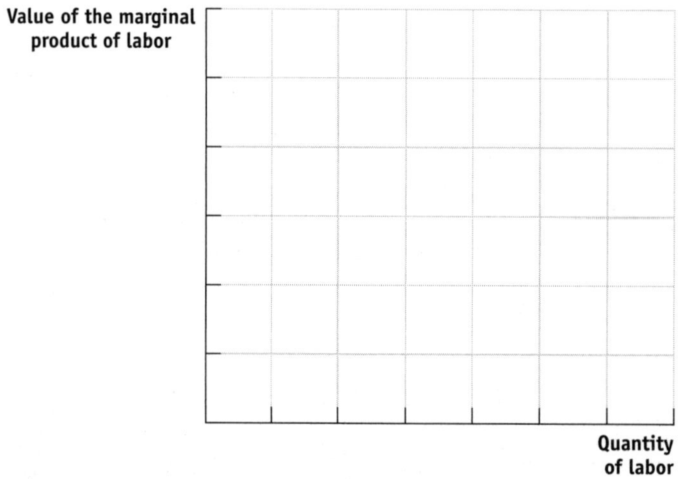

c. Suppose that the price of sandwiches falls to $4 a sandwich. Draw a new graph illustrating Mike's value of the marginal product of labor. How will this price change affect the amount of labor Mike chooses to hire?

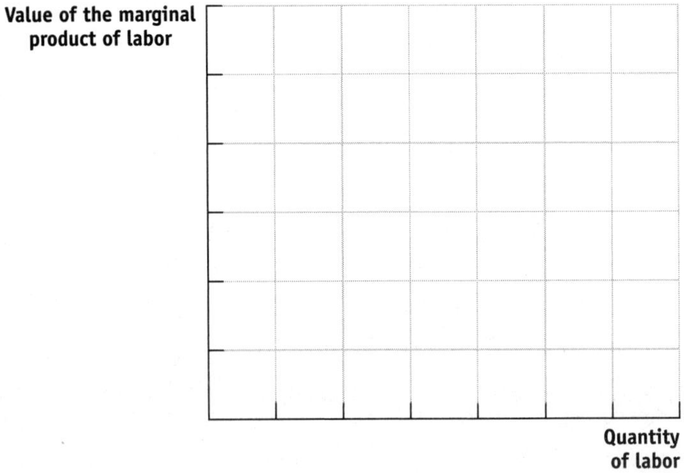

4. For each of the following situations, decide what the effect of the situation is on the firm's value of the marginal product of labor curve and on the amount of labor the firm will hire. Assume that the labor and product markets are both perfectly competitive for each of these situations.

a. The labor hired by the firm has an increase in its level of human capital.

b. The price of the firm's product decreases.

c. The technology used to produce the product changes and less labor is needed to produce each level of output than was necessary initially.

d. The firm decides to increase its use of capital.

BEFORE YOU TAKE THE TEST

Module Review Questions

1. Human capital is
   a. the machines, tools, equipment, and buildings that humans own and that they use to produce goods and services.
   b. the improvement in labor that reflects education and knowledge.
   c. relatively unimportant in determining labor's share of total income.
   d. a resource that is provided by nature since human capability is an innate endowment.

2. Capital, from an economist's perspective, refers to
   a. the dollars a household has invested in the stock market.
   b. the value of assets that are used by a firm to produce its output.
   c. both human and physical capital.
   d. Answers (a), (b), and (c) are all true.
   e. Answers (b) and (c) are both true.

3. The improvement in labor that is due to greater education and knowledge is referred to as
   a. physical capital, since the labor has physically made the effort to get more education and knowledge.
   b. human capital, since more educated and knowledgeable labor is more productive.

4. The demand for a factor of production is
   a. dependent on the demand for the output the labor produces.
   b. a derived demand.
   c. dependent on the available supply of that factor.
   d. Answers (a), (b), and (c) are all true.
   e. Answers (a) and (b) are true.

5. The factor distribution of income
   a. describes the share to total income received by land, labor, and capital.
   b. indicates that total income in the economy is evenly divided between land, labor, and capital.
   c. indicates that most household income reflects the selling of labor.
   d. Answers (a), (b), and (c) are all true.
   e. Answers (a) and (c) are true.
   f. Answers (b) and (c) are true.

6. Labor's share of income in the United States over the past 35 years has
   a. remained relatively stable at about 70% of total income.
   b. increased rapidly until finally leveling off at 70% of total income.
   c. declined significantly until finally leveling off at 70% of total income.
   d. fluctuated from year to year and shows no discernible constancy.

7. An input is different from a factor of production since
   a. an input can be used over and over again by a business or an individual to earn income.
   b. a factor of production can be used over and over again by a business or an individual to earn income.

Answer the next five questions based on the following information.

In this question, assume the product market is perfectly competitive and that the labor market is also perfectly competitive. Furthermore, assume that the price of the firm's product is \$10. The schedule for the firm's total product with respect to labor is given in the table below.

Quantity of labor (number of workers)	Quantity of output
0	0
1	50
2	80
3	100
4	110
5	105

You are also told that the labor demand curve and labor supply curve for the labor market are given by the following equations, where W is the wage rate and N is the number of workers hired:

$$\text{Market labor demand curve: } W = 400 - N$$

$$\text{Market labor supply curve: } W = N$$

8. What is the value of the marginal product of labor for the fourth worker?
   a. \$500
   b. \$300
   c. \$200
   d. \$100

9. What is the marginal product of labor for the third worker?
   a. 50 units of output per unit of labor
   b. 30 units of output per unit of labor
   c. 20 units of output per unit of labor
   d. 10 units of output per unit of labor

10. What is the equilibrium wage rate in this labor market?
    a. \$500 per worker
    b. \$300 per worker
    c. \$200 per worker
    d. \$100 per worker

11. How many units of labor will this perfectly competitive, profit-maximizing firm choose to hire given the previous information?

a. one worker

b. two workers

c. three workers

d. four workers

12. Suppose that the demand for this firm's product increases. Holding everything else constant, this firm

a. will continue to hire the same number of workers.

b. will hire more workers, since the increased demand for its product causes the value of the marginal product of labor curve to shift to the right.

c. will hire fewer workers, since the increased demand for its product causes the value of the marginal product of labor curve to shift to the left.

d. may increase, decrease, or continue to hire the same number of workers.

13. A firm realizes that it has diminishing returns to labor. This means that

a. its total output decreases as it hires additional units of labor.

b. the marginal product of labor curve for this firm is downward sloping.

c. its total output increases as it hires additional units of labor, but it increases at a decreasing rate.

d. Answers (a) and (b) are both true.

e. Answers (b) and (c) are both true.

14. Suppose the marginal cost of hiring an additional unit of labor is $10 while the value of the marginal product from hiring this additional unit of labor is $12. To profit-maximize, this firm should hire

a. more labor.

b. less labor.

15. The equilibrium wage rate in the labor market is $18. A perfectly competitive firm sells its product for $8. Furthermore, suppose that the marginal product of the sixth unit of labor is 3 units of output while the marginal product of the ninth unit of labor is 2 units of output. This firm should hire

a. fewer than 6 units of labor.

b. more than 9 units of labor.

c. more than 6 units of labor but fewer than 9 units of labor.

d. 6 units of labor.

e. 9 units of labor.

16. Suppose the marginal cost of an additional unit of a factor is greater than the value of the marginal product of that additional unit of the factor. This means that hiring this additional unit of the factor will add more to the firm's

a. costs than to the firm's revenue.

b. revenue than to the firm's costs.

17. The firm's demand curve for labor is equal to the

a. firm's marginal product of labor curve.

b. firm's value of the marginal product of labor curve.

c. firm's marginal cost of hiring labor curve.

d. market-determined equilibrium wage rate.

18. A firm experiences a change in technology. This

a. may cause the firm's demand for an input to increase or decrease depending on the nature of the technological change.

b. causes the firm's demand for an input to increase due to this technological change.

c. causes the firm's demand for an input to decrease due to this technological change.

d. does not affect the firm's demand for other inputs since the firm chooses how much of an input to demand based on its production function without regard to the technology that is available to the firm.

ANSWER KEY

Answers to Problems and Exercises

1. A derived demand is a demand that is dependent on the demand for some other good or service. The demand for factors of production such as land, labor, and capital is a derived demand, since the demand firms for these different factors of production are dependent on the output choice that firms make. Firms only demand the level of labor, capital, or land that they need depending on the level of output they choose to produce.

2. a.

Quantity of labor (workers)	Marginal product of labor (cups of coffee per worker)	Value of the marginal product of labor (dollars per worker)
0	—	—
1	300	900
2	150	450
3	100	300
4	50	150

b. Sarah should continue to hire workers provided that the value of the marginal product of the additional worker is greater than or equal to the cost of hiring an additional worker. When Sarah hires the first worker, the cost of hiring that worker is $400 per week, but the value of the marginal product of the first worker is $900 per week: Sarah will want to hire the first worker. When Sarah considers hiring the second worker, the cost of hiring that worker is $400 per week, but the value of the marginal product of the second worker is $450 per week: Sarah will want to hire the second worker. But when Sarah considers the third worker, she finds that the marginal cost of hiring the third worker ($400 per week) is greater than the value of the marginal product from this third worker ($300): Sarah will not want to hire this third worker.

c. Sarah would decide how much labor to hire by comparing the additional cost of hiring the labor with the additional revenue from hiring the labor: Sarah would continue to hire labor provided that the value of the marginal product of the last unit of labor hired is greater than or equal to the marginal cost of hiring the last unit of labor. When the equilibrium wage rate falls to $300 per week, Sarah will find that the profit-maximizing amount of labor to hire is three workers.

3. a.

Quantity of labor (workers)	Marginal product of labor (sandwiches per worker)	Value of the marginal product of labor (dollars per worker)
0	—	—
1	100	$500
2	80	400
3	60	300
4	50	250

b.

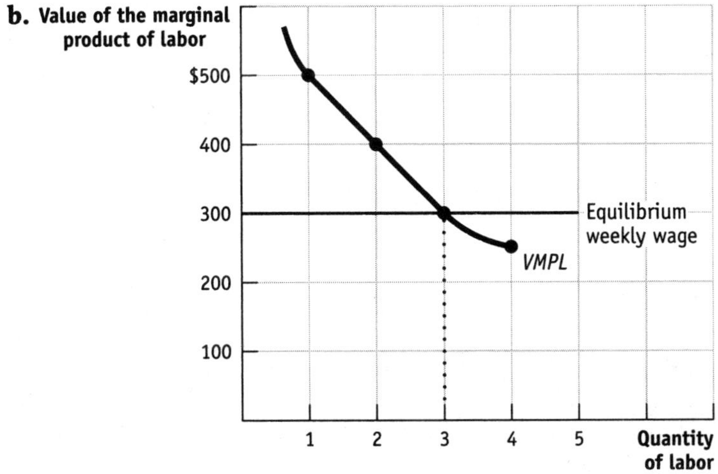

Mike should hire three workers given his production function and the above information.

c. When the price of sandwiches decreases from $5 per sandwich to $4 per sandwich, this changes Mike's value of the marginal product of labor curve. The new values are given in the table below.

Quantity of labor (workers)	Marginal product of labor (sandwiches per worker)	Value of the marginal product of labor (dollars per worker)
0	—	—
1	100	$400
2	80	320
3	60	240
4	50	200

This price change causes the *VMPL* curve to shift to the left: at every wage rate Mike will demand fewer units of labor. The figure below gives the new *VMPL* curve.

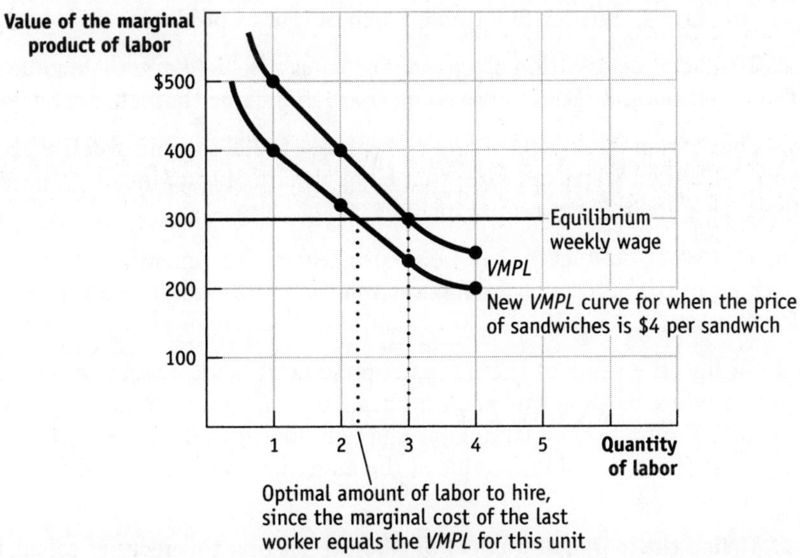

Mike will choose to hire less labor when the price of sandwiches falls to $4: if he has to hire whole units of labor, he will choose to hire two workers when the price of his product decreases to $4 per unit.

4. a. When the firm's labor experiences an increase in its human capital, this means that the labor becomes more productive and the marginal product of labor increases at each level of labor used. This increase in the marginal product of labor causes the value of the marginal product of labor curve to shift to the right and at any given wage rate the firm will now hire more labor than it did initially.

   b. When the price of the firm's product decreases, this causes the firm's value of the marginal product of labor curve to shift to the left. At any given wage rate the firm will now hire less labor than it did initially.

   c. The firm now needs less labor than it did before the technology change: this implies that the firm's demand for labor, its value of the marginal product of labor curve, will shift to the left, with the firm hiring less labor than it did initially at the prevailing wage rate.

   d. When the firm increases its use of capital, this causes the marginal product of labor to increase at every level of labor usage since each unit of labor will now have more capital to work with. This increase in the marginal product of labor causes the value of the marginal product of labor curve to shift to the right, with the firm hiring more labor at any given wage rate.

Answers to Module Review Questions

1. **Answer b.** Human capital refers to the improvement in labor that is the result of education and knowledge, while physical capital refers to manufactured resources such as machines, tools, equipment, and buildings. An individual's human capital determines the level of compensation the individual receives and is therefore highly important in determining the share of total income that labor receives. The resource that is provided by nature is referred to as land.

2. **Answer e.** Capital refers to human and physical capital. From an economist's perspective, capital does not refer to dollars that have been invested in the stock market, but instead refers to the equipment that companies purchase from the dollars they raise in the stock market.

3. **Answer b.** Human capital refers to the improvement in labor due to increased education and knowledge.

4. **Answer e.** Demand for a factor is a derived demand, since the demand for this factor comes from the firm's decision about how much output to produce.

5. **Answer e.** The factor distribution of income indicates the share of total income received by each factor. The largest factor share is the share of income that labor receives.

6. **Answer a.** The data on labor income as a percentage of total income over the past thirty-five years in the United States indicates that labor's share of total income has been relatively stable and is about 70% of total income.

7. **Answer b.** Factors of production can be used repeatedly to generate income, while an input is used up in the process of production and therefore cannot be a source of future income for its owner.

8. **Answer d.** To find the value of the marginal product of labor, you must first calculate the marginal product of labor and then multiply the marginal product of labor by the price of the firm's output. The marginal product of labor for hiring the fourth worker is equal to 10 units of output and the value of the marginal product of labor for the fourth worker is equal to $100.

9. **Answer c.** To find the marginal product of labor, recall that this requires calculating the ratio of the change in total product divided by the change in labor. When the firm hires the third worker, the change in total product is equal to 100 units of output minus 80

units of output, or a change of 20 units of output. The change in labor is equal to one unit since the firm changes the amount of labor it uses from two units of labor to three units of labor. Thus, the marginal product of labor for the third worker is equal to 20 units of output from this additional unit of labor.

10. Answer c. To find the equilibrium wage rate in this market, set the market labor demand curve equal to the market labor supply curve and solve for the equilibrium wage rate. Thus, $400 - N = N$, or $N = 200$. Plugging this value of N into either equation and solving for W, the equilibrium wage rate is \$200 per worker.

11. Answer c. The firm will choose to hire labor up until that point where the value of the marginal product of the last unit of labor hired is equal to the equilibrium wage rate. The equilibrium wage rate is \$200 per worker and the value of the marginal product of labor is equal to \$200 per worker when the firm hires three workers.

12. Answer b. When the firm's price increases due to the increase in demand for the firm's product, this causes the value of the marginal product of labor curve to shift to the right. At every wage rate, the firm will now want to hire more units of labor than it did prior to the change in the demand for its product.

13. Answer e. A firm has diminishing returns to labor when its output increases as more labor is hired, but with the output increasing at a diminishing rate. Since the increase in output is smaller and smaller with each additional unit of labor hired, this results in a downward-sloping marginal product of labor curve.

14. Answer a. Since the value of the marginal product of labor is greater than the marginal cost of this additional unit of labor, the firm will enhance its profit by hiring additional units of labor. The firm should continue to hire more units of labor until the marginal cost of the last unit of labor hired is equal to the value of the marginal product of this last unit of labor.

15. Answer c. The firm should hire labor until the marginal cost of the additional unit of labor is equal to the value of the marginal product of the last unit of labor hired. The firm's marginal cost of hiring an additional unit of labor is equal to the wage rate of \$18. The value of the marginal product of labor when the firm hires six units of labor is equal to \$24: the firm should hire more than six units of labor. The value of the marginal product of labor when the firm hires nine units of labor is equal to \$16: the firm should hire fewer than nine units of labor.

16. Answer a. When the marginal cost of the factor is greater than the value of the marginal product of the factor, this means that the firm's costs increase more than the firm's revenue if the firm hires this additional unit of the factor. The firm will not want to hire this unit since the addition to the firm's costs from hiring this unit exceeds the addition to its revenue from hiring the unit.

17. Answer b. The firm's demand curve for labor is found by multiplying the firm's marginal product of labor by the market price of the firm's output: this is the value of the marginal product of labor curve.

18. Answer a. Technological change can cause the firm's demand for an input to shift out or to shift in: for example, when the gas engine was invented the demand for horses decreased, but when the personal computer was invented the demand for information technology workers increased.

module **41**

Marginal Productivity Theory

BEFORE YOU READ THE MODULE

Summary

This module discusses labor market applications of the marginal productivity theory of income distribution before exploring the sources of wage disparity and the role and effect of discrimination in the labor market.

Module Objectives

Objective #1. The marginal productivity theory of income distribution says that each factor is paid the value of the output generated by the last unit of that factor employed in the factor market as a whole. This is equivalent to saying that each factor is paid the value of its marginal product. This theory implies that the division of income among the economy's factors is not arbitrary, but is instead determined by each factor's marginal productivity at the economy's equilibrium.

Objective #2. There are two main objections to the marginal productivity theory of income distribution.

- In the real world, there are wide disparities in income among people, and some people believe that some of this income disparity is not due solely to differences in marginal productivity.
- Some people believe that the marginal productivity theory of income distribution is based on a moral justification for the distribution of income and they reject the theory because they believe that the resultant distribution of income is not fair or appropriate.

Objective #3. In the United States, there are wide disparities in income between genders and across ethnic groups. Some of this wage disparity can be explained by the following three sources of wage disparity:

- The existence of compensating differentials, where wages are higher or lower depending on how attractive or unattractive the job is;

- The existence of differences in talent, with very talented individuals commanding higher salaries and less-talented individuals commanding lower salaries; and
- The existence of differences in human capital, where individuals with high levels of human capital receive relatively higher wages than those individuals with low levels of human capital.

Objective #4. Earnings differences arising from differences in human capital may not be fair or just: individuals who receive poor education because of their socioeconomic status or their race may have labor markets that are well described by marginal productivity theory but whose resultant distribution of income is viewed by many people as unfair.

Objective #5. Some people believe that wage differences cannot be fully explained by compensating differentials, differences in talent, and differences in human capital. They argue that wage differences may also reflect market power, efficiency wages, and discrimination.

- Some workers earn higher wages than otherwise similar workers because of the role of unions that successfully negotiate higher wages and better working conditions for their members. The union is able to exert some market power, which raises wages for this group.
- Some employers pay efficiency wages as a means to motivate their workers. An efficiency wage is a wage that exceeds the equilibrium wage: the worker who receives an efficiency wage is motivated to work harder in order to retain their job. In markets that pay an efficiency wage there is unemployment of labor since there are more people who are willing to supply labor at the efficiency wage than there is demand for labor.
- Discrimination in labor markets is possible when there is market power or when the labor market fails to work efficiently. In both the case of a market with union power and a market that pays efficiency wages there is an excess supply of labor, making it possible for employers to discriminate among job applicants since there are more job applicants than there are jobs.

Key Terms

marginal productivity theory of income distribution theory that every factor of production is paid the equilibrium value of its marginal product.

equilibrium value of the marginal product the additional value produced by the last unit of a factor employed in the *factor market* as a whole.

compensating differentials wage differences across jobs that reflect the fact that some jobs are less pleasant or more dangerous than others.

unions organizations of workers that try to raise wages and improve working conditions for their members by bargaining collectively.

efficiency-wage model a model in which some employers pay an above-equilibrium wage as an *incentive* for better performance.

Notes

AFTER YOU READ THE MODULE

Tip

Tip #1. There are many potential explanations for wage disparity. Wages may differ because of compensating differentials, differences in talent, or differences in human capital. Wage differences may also exist because of the existence of market power where either the suppliers of labor have market power (for example, unions) or where the demanders of labor have market power (for example, health maintenance organizations). Wage differences may also reflect firms' decisions to pay efficiency wages where the wage rate is greater than the market wage rate: an efficiency wage is paid in order to motivate a worker to work hard in a situation where it might be difficult to evaluate the worker's performance. Finally wage differences may be the result of discrimination.

WORKED PROBLEMS

1. Josie's Specialty Products must hire labor in a perfectly competitive labor market in which the labor demand and labor supply curves are described by the following equations, where L is the quantity of labor in hours and W is the hourly wage rate:

Labor Demand: $L = 2000 - 100W$
Labor Supply: $L = 100W$

Furthermore, Josie's knows that it can sell its product for $2.50 per unit in a perfectly competitive product market. Josie's has approached you for your advice as to how many hours of labor Josie's should hire. Josie's has provided you with the following information about the relationship between the number of hours of labor hired and the marginal product of labor.

Hours of labor	Marginal product of labor
0	
	10
1	
	8
2	
	6
3	
	4
4	
	2
5	

Given that information, help Josie's determine the optimal amount of labor to hire, as well as the wage rate it should pay per unit of labor. In addition, provide an explanation of why your answer represents the optimal amount of labor for Josie's to hire.

STEP 1: Think about the overall steps you will need to perform to determine the optimal amount of labor for Josie's to hire.

To determine the optimal amount of labor for Josie's to hire, you will need to calculate both the equilibrium wage rate (*W*) in the labor market as well as the value of the marginal product of labor (*VMPL*) for the firm, since the optimal amount of labor to hire is that amount of labor, where the $VMPL = W$. To find the equilibrium wage rate, you will need to use the information on the labor market. To find the value of the marginal product of labor, you will need the information about the marginal product of labor as well as the price of the product. You will then use both the wage rate and the value of the marginal product of labor to determine the optimal amount of labor for Josie's to hire.

STEP 2: Find the equilibrium wage rate (*W*) in the labor market.

To find the equilibrium wage rate in the labor market, you will equate the labor supply curve to the labor demand curve. Thus, $2000 - 100W = 100W$, or $W = \$10$ per hour of labor.

STEP 3: Find the value of the marginal product of labor (*VMPL*) for Josie's.

To find the *VMPL*, you need both the price of the product ($2.50 per unit) and the marginal product of labor. The *VMPL* is equal to the price of the product times the marginal product of labor. The following table provides the *VMPL* for Josie's.

Hours of labor	Marginal product of labor	Value of the marginal product of labor
0		
	10	25
1		
	8	20
2		
	6	15
3		
	4	10
4		
	2	5
5		

STEP 4: To find the optimal amount of labor for Josie's to hire, equate the firm's *VMPL* to the equilibrium wage rate in the labor market. Then, identify the amount of labor associated with this *VMPL*.

Thus, $VMPL = W$ and, since $W = \$10$ per unit of labor, we need the *VMPL* to also equate \$10 per unit of labor. The *VMPL* equals this amount when Josie's hires 4 units of labor.

STEP 5: Explain why your answer represents the optimal amount of labor for Josie's to hire.

Josie's will want to continue to hire additional units of labor as long as the value of the additional output this additional labor produces is greater than or equal to the wage that must be paid that unit of labor. Thus, if the *VMPL* is greater than the equilibrium wage rate, this indicates that the value of the output produced by the additional unit of labor is greater than the wage rate: it is therefore cost effective for the firm to hire this additional unit of labor. Josie's will find that its optimal amount of labor to hire is that amount of labor, where the *VMPL* is equal to the equilibrium wage rate.

2. After helping identify the optimal amount of labor for Josie's Specialty Products in problem 1 to hire, you have been asked to continue your consulting work with the firm. Josie's tells you that it anticipates that the market price for its product will rise to \$5 per unit next year and the firm would like you to advise it on the effect this price increase will have on its labor hiring decisions. Josie's does not anticipate any other changes in either the labor market or the product market. Josie's asks that you provide it with an explanation about the effect of the change in product price on its labor employment.

STEP 1: Review the underlying relationship that determines the optimal amount of labor for Josie's to hire.

The optimal amount of labor for a firm to hire is that amount of labor that corresponds to the firm's *VMPL* equaling the equilibrium wage rate. This is optimal because it equates the value of the additional output the firm gets from hiring an additional unit of labor to the additional cost the firm incurs when it hires an additional unit of labor. When the *VMPL* is greater than the wage rate this indicates that the increase in production made possible by the hiring of an additional unit of labor has a greater value than the cost of hiring this additional unit of labor: the firm should hire more labor. And when the *VMPL* is less than the wage rate this indicates that the increase in production made possible by the hiring of an additional unit of labor has a smaller value than the cost of hiring this additional unit of labor: the firm should hire less labor. It is only when the firm hires the amount of labor, where the *VMPL* equals the wage rate that the firm has hired the optimal amount of labor.

STEP 2: Recalculate the firm's *VMPL* now that the product price is $5 per unit of output.

The following table provides the new *VMPL*. Recall that the *VMPL* is equal to (the price of the product)(the marginal product of labor).

Hours of labor	Marginal product of labor	Value of the marginal product of labor
0		
	10	50
1		
	8	40
2		
	6	30
3		
	4	20
4		
	2	10
5		

STEP 3: Determine the optimal amount of labor for Josie's to hire.

The optimal amount of labor for Josie's to hire is five units of labor, since the firm's *VMPL* when it hires five units of labor is equal to $10 per unit of labor and is therefore equal to the equilibrium wage rate in the market.

3. For each of the following scenarios, determine whether the wage inequality is due to compensating differentials, differences in talent, differences in human capital, the presence of unions, the payment of efficiency wages, or the presence of discrimination. Provide a brief explanation for each of your answers. Assume that there is no other relevant information than what is given for each scenario.

Scenario	Explanation of wage differential
Mary pays her babysitter twice the hourly babysitting rate in her community	
Harvey earns a wage 50% higher than other firefighters in his job as a firefighter fighting dangerous wildfires	
Susie earns $2.00 more per hour than the women she works with who are doing the same job but happen to be members of a minority race	
Steve and Joe have identical job responsibilities, but Steve's hourly wage rate is higher because of his membership in a union	
Both Mary and Terry work as physical therapists, but Mary has completed all the years of training while Terry is still in training; Mary earns a higher wage	

STEP 1: Review the explanations for wage disparity provided in your text prior to selecting an explanation for the wage disparities noted in the preceding table.

Wages may differ for a variety of reasons. Here is a quick synopsis of these reasons.

Wages differ because of compensating differentials when these wage differences are due to differences in the attractiveness of the job. Jobs that are more dangerous or more unpleasant will pay more than jobs requiring the same skills but in circumstances that are less dangerous or less unpleasant.

Wages differ because of talent when individuals earn different amounts based on their abilities or talents. Individuals possessing great talent will receive higher payment than individuals doing the same job but with less skill or talent.

Wages differ because of differences in human capital when the wage differentials reflect the workers' different levels of education and training. Workers with more education or more training possess greater amounts of human capital and will typically earn higher wages than a person with less human capital.

Wages differ because of the influence of unions when union members receive higher wages than do nonunion workers for the same kind of work.

Wages sometimes differ because the employer is paying an efficiency wage: in this case, the employer compensates the worker with a higher wage than the market wage to provide an incentive for the worker to perform the job at a very high standard. Often efficiency wages are paid to employees who are performing important work in a setting in which it is difficult for the employer to frequently assess how well the employee is doing.

Wages may differ because of discrimination: some workers may receive lower pay than others for the same work solely because of discrimination, based on their race, gender, ethnicity, or some other characteristic.

STEP 2: Having reviewed the different causes of wage differentials, fill in the second column in the given table.

Here is the completed table.

Scenario	Explanation of wage differential
Mary pays her babysitter twice the hourly babysitting rate in her community	Efficiency wage: Mary cannot frequently assess how well the babysitter performs this very important job, so Mary offers the babysitter an efficiency wage to encourage the sitter to be very conscientious in carrying out the job duties
Harvey earns a wage 50% higher than other firefighters in his job as a firefighter fighting dangerous wildfires	Compensating wage: fighting dangerous wildfires is typically more dangerous than fighting fires in more controlled situations, and so the wage differential reflects the fact that the job is more dangerous and more unattractive than jobs requiring the same skills
Susie earns $2.00 more per hour than the women she works with who are doing the same job but happen to be members of a minority race	Discrimination: based on the information given, Susie's higher wage is due to her racial identity and not to any particular talent or skill
Steve and Joe have identical job responsibilities, but Steve's hourly wage rate is higher because of his membership in a union	Union membership: union membership can result in union members earning higher wages for the same job than nonunion members
Both Mary and Terry work as physical therapists, but Mary has completed all the years of training while Terry is still in training; Mary earns a higher wage	Human capital differences: Mary has more years of education and training and her wage, based on the given information, is due to this difference in her human capital compared with Terry's human capital

Problems and Exercises

1. What are three sources of wage disparity?

2. A friend of yours argues that there is great wage disparity in your economy and that therefore the marginal productivity theory of income distribution is not true since it results in a highly unfair and inequitable income distribution. What do you think about this argument?

3. How are unions and efficiency wages similar with regard to their effects on a labor market?

4. Joe hires labor in a perfectly competitive labor market. Joe and all the other employers in his economy would prefer to hire only men that are the same race as they are (assume that all the employers are of the same race). Why would Joe likely decide not to continue this policy of discrimination in this market?

5. Historically, how is discrimination institutionalized in most economies?

BEFORE YOU TAKE THE TEST

Module Review Questions

1. In a perfectly competitive labor market, the equilibrium wage is the wage at which
   a. the quantity of labor demanded is equal to the quantity of labor supplied.
   b. all people who work in the labor market earn a living wage.
   c. the wage is equal to the value of the marginal product of labor.
   d. Answers (a), (b), and (c) are all true.
   e. Answers (a) and (c) are true.

2. The marginal productivity theory of income distribution states that
   a. each factor is paid a payment equal to that factor's marginal productivity.
   b. each factor is paid a payment equal to the value of the output generated by the last unit of that factor employed in the factor market as a whole.
   c. factor income is distributed evenly and equally across all factors.
   d. all factors are paid less than the value of their marginal product.

3. Which of the following provide an explanation for wage disparities?
   a. Compensating differentials
   b. Differences in talent
   c. Differences in human capital
   d. Answers (a), (b), and (c) are all true.
   e. Answers (a) and (c) are both true.

4. The marginal productivity theory of income distribution provides a moral justification for the prevailing income distribution.
   a. True
   b. False

5. When a union effectively bargains for a wage rate greater than the equilibrium wage rate, this implies that the
   a. union has market power in the labor market.
   b. labor market has an excess supply of labor at the prevailing wage rate.
   c. union may have created a situation that makes employer discrimination more feasible.
   d. Answers (a), (b), and (c) are all true.
   e. Answers (a) and (b) are both true.

6. There are three sources of wage disparities across occupations and individuals. They are

a. compensating differentials, talent differences, and human capital differences.

b. compensating differentials, differences in income tax treatment, and human capital differences.

c. compensating differentials, differences in the riskiness of the job, and human capital differences.

d. differences in the riskiness of the job, differences in income tax treatment, and human capital differences.

7. *Human capital* refers to

a. formal education.

b. on-the-job training.

c. work experience.

d. Answers (a), (b), and (c) are all true.

8. Differences in wages due to human capital are wage differences that are "fair."

a. True

b. False

ANSWER KEY

Answers to Problems and Exercises

1. Wage disparity may be due to compensating differentials, where jobs requiring similar education and experience may pay quite different wages because some of the jobs are less pleasant and attractive than the other jobs. Jobs that are unattractive or dangerous typically pay more than jobs that are more attractive and less dangerous.

   Wage disparity may also be due to differences in talent. Someone who is particularly talented with regard to their occupation will likely command a higher wage than someone who has less talent in the same occupation.

   Wage disparity may also be due to differences in human capital. Workers with more human capital will receive a higher wage than workers with less human capital.

2. Although there may be large disparities in income in a society, that does not negate the marginal productivity theory of income distribution. Wage disparities may arise from compensating differentials, differences in talent, and differences in human capital. The marginal productivity theory provides a theory about the determination of the income distribution, but it does not provide a moral or normative judgment about that income distribution. The income distribution might be quite uneven and still support the marginal productivity theory.

3. Both unions and efficiency wages result in a situation in which the wage rate paid is greater than the equilibrium wage rate. This creates a situation where there is an excess supply of labor at the wage rate. The union is able to raise wages above the equilibrium level because the union has market power, while the efficiency wage increases wages above the equilibrium level in order for the wage to serve as a motivator to employees to work harder than they might otherwise choose to do.

4. When Joe limits his hiring decisions to a subgroup of the total population, he effectively reduces the total supply of labor available to him. Since all the other employers are doing the same thing, they effectively have shifted the supply of labor curve to the left and have to pay a higher wage rate than would be the case if they were willing to hire anyone regardless of race and gender (provided they are qualified). Joe will find that by stopping his policy of discrimination he can reduce his cost of labor and therefore enhance the profitability of his enterprise.

5. Discrimination typically results from the acceptance and institutionalization of discriminatory practices by the government. The government passes laws that allow or create discrimination, and it is the government's support of these laws that allows this discrimination to continue.

Answers to Module Review Questions

1. **Answer e.** In a perfectly competitive labor market, the equilibrium wage occurs at the point where the demand for labor intersects the supply of labor: at this wage the quantity of labor demanded is equal to the quantity of labor supplied. This wage is also equal to the value of the marginal product of labor, or the value produced by the last unit of labor employed in the labor market as a whole. The equilibrium wage may or may not be a living wage.

2. **Answer b.** The marginal productivity theory says that each factor is paid the value of the output generated by the last unit of that factor employed in the factor market as a whole: some factors are therefore paid an amount that is less than their marginal product. The marginal productivity theory is useful in explaining the economy's underlying distribution of income and why that income is not evenly distributed among the different factors of production: instead, the economy's distribution of income is determined by each factor's marginal productivity at the economy's equilibrium.

3. **Answer d.** Wage disparities may arise because of compensating differentials, differences in talent, or differences in human capital.

4. **Answer b.** The marginal productivity theory of income distribution does not provide any analysis of whether the underlying income distribution is fair or equitable: the theory simply posits that factors of production receive a payment equal to the value of the marginal productivity of the last unit of the factor hired in the factor market as a whole.

5. **Answer d.** When the union is successful at raising the wage rate above the equilibrium wage rate, this implies that the union has market power in the labor market. It also implies that at the prevailing wage rate there will be more job applicants than there are jobs: there will be an excess supply of labor. When there is an excess supply of labor, this creates a situation in which it is easier for firms or employers to discriminate, since there are more job applicants than there are jobs.

6. **Answer a.** Compensating differentials refer to wage differences due to the attractiveness of the job and/or the riskiness or danger of the job. Talent differences refer to wage differences due to individuals having differences in talent: high-talented individuals receive higher wages than low-talented individuals doing the same job. Differences in human capital in the form of education and talent also explain wage differences. Although different individuals face different income tax treatment depending upon their wages this tax treatment does not explain why these individuals receive different wages. Differences in the riskiness of jobs will cause wages to differ but this difference in wages is explained as part of compensating differentials.

7. **Answer d.** Human capital refers to the acquisition of knowledge and skill through formal education, on-the-job training, and work experience.

8. **Answer b.** Earning differences that are due to human capital differences are not necessarily "fair." A society in which certain groups of individuals receive substandard educations will find that earnings between groups do differ due to differences in human capital. Many people would argue that the resultant distribution of income is not fair since it reflects discrimination in the educational system.

module 42

The Market for Labor

BEFORE YOU READ THE MODULE

Summary

This module focuses on the labor market and the determination of the equilibrium wage rate. The module considers how a worker's time allocation decision determines the individual supply of labor curve. The module also discusses the relationship between the individual supply of labor curve and the market supply of labor curve.

Module Objectives

Objective #1. An individual's decision about how much labor to supply is a decision about time allocation and how the individual chooses to divide their time among different activities. When an individual chooses to work, the individual earns income; when an individual chooses not to work, they increase their consumption of leisure time. For an individual, the optimal amount of labor to supply occurs when the marginal utility of one hour of leisure is equal to the marginal utility the individual gets from the goods their hourly wage can purchase.

Objective #2. An increase in the individual's wage rate may result in the individual supplying more labor or less labor. The higher wage increases the opportunity cost of an hour of leisure—the amount of money the individual gives up if he chooses to work one less hour. The higher wage also generates an income effect: the individual can purchase the same amount of goods and services while working fewer hours. The individual increases the quantity of labor they supply when the wage rate increases if the substitution effect is stronger than the income effect. The individual decreases the quantity of labor they supply when the wage rate increases if the income effect is stronger than the substitution effect. Thus, as the wage rate increases, the individual's supply of labor curve may be upward sloping or downward sloping depending on which of these effects is dominant.

Objective #3. The labor supply curve in a labor market is the horizontal summation of the individual labor supply curves in that market. The labor supply curve in a labor market shifts with changes in preferences and social norms with regard to people's willingness to work, changes in population, changes in opportunities, or changes in wealth.

- The labor supply curve shifts to the right if people's preferences for work increase or if the social norms change so that more people decide it is socially appropriate to work.
- The labor supply curve shifts to the right with an increase in population since the increase in population increases the pool of workers available at any given wage rate.
- The labor supply curve shifts to the right if this labor market represents a superior alternative compared to other labor markets, and the labor supply curve shifts to the left if this labor market represents a less favorable alternative compared to other labor markets.
- The labor supply curve shifts to the left with an increase in wealth, since the increase in wealth enables individuals to purchase more normal goods, including leisure.

Objective #4. When the product market is perfectly competitive then the wage rate is equal to the value of the marginal product of labor at equilibrium. But, when the labor market is not perfectly competitive, then the equilibrium amount of labor occurs where the marginal revenue product of labor is equal to the marginal factor cost of labor.

Objective #5. A monopsony occurs when a firm operates in an imperfectly competitive labor market where the firm is large enough to affect the market wage rate. A monopsonist will hire that amount of labor where the marginal revenue product of labor is equal to the marginal factor cost of labor and then it will pay a wage equal to the market wage rate at that quantity of labor. The result is that the wage in this imperfectly competitive labor market is less than the marginal factor cost of labor.

Key Terms

time allocation the decision about how many hours to spend on different activities, which leads to a decision about how much labor to supply.

leisure the time available for purposes other than earning money to buy marketed goods.

individual labor supply curve a graphical representation showing how the quantity of labor supplied by an individual depends on that individual's wage rate.

marginal revenue product of labor (*MRPL*) equals the marginal product of labor times the marginal revenue received from selling the additional output. The marginal revenue product of land and the marginal revenue product of capital are equivalent concepts.

monopsonist a single buyer in a market.

monopsony a market in which there is only one buyer.

Notes

AFTER YOU READ THE MODULE

Tips

Tip #1. When the wage rate increases in the labor market, this causes both an income and a substitution effect for the individual. The wage increase causes the price of an hour of leisure to increase since the individual will now give up a greater amount of income if they elect to increase their consumption of leisure. Thus, the wage increase causes the individual to substitute away from leisure, the relatively more expensive good, toward income, the relatively cheaper good. However, the wage increase also creates an income effect: when the wage increases, the individual's income rises at every level of work effort and this increase in income causes the individual to demand more units of leisure, which is a normal good. Depending on the relative strength of the income and substitution effects, the individual may elect to work more or work less when the wage rate increases.

Tip #2. Profit-maximizing firms face two basic profit-maximizing rules. The first rule states that the firm will profit-maximize when it produces the level of output at which marginal revenue equals marginal cost. The second rule says that a firm will profit-maximize when it hires the level of factors at which the marginal cost of an additional unit of that factor is equal to the value of the marginal product of that factor. Although one of these rules focuses on the optimal output level while the other focuses on the optimal factor use, the two rules amount to the same principle: undertake production or hiring of a factor only up to the point where the marginal cost of that production or that factor usage is less than or equal to the marginal benefit from that production or that factor usage. By this point in the semester this should be a familiar concept.

Tip #3. This module contains challenging new vocabulary. You will want to thoroughly review this vocabulary and also make sure you understand how to mathematically calculate the value of some of the terms like the marginal revenue product of labor.

WORKED PROBLEM

1. Kerry currently earns $3 an hour, and you have been asked to help Kerry construct a graph depicting her time allocation budget line. She is only interested in looking at this time allocation budget line for a single day: assume that Kerry can choose to work the entire 24 hours, take the entire 24 hours as leisure, or any combination thereof. In a graph, show Kerry's time allocation budget line, BL_1, with income measured on the vertical axis and leisure measured on the horizontal axis. Suppose that when Kerry earns $3 an hour she is willing to work eight hours. In your graph, label the point that represents this work/leisure decision as point *A*. At point *A*, what is Kerry's income and how many hours of leisure does she have? Now, suppose that the government decides to put a tax of 33% on Kerry's wage rate. What is Kerry's new wage rate after tax? In your graph, draw Kerry's new time allocation budget line, BL_2. Suppose that, with the new government policy, Kerry is willing to work 10 hours. What will Kerry's after tax income be, and how many hours of leisure will she have? Label this new work/leisure decision point in your graph as point *B*. Given this information, is the substitution effect or the income effect stronger for Kerry? Finally, is Kerry's labor supply curve downward sloping or upward sloping? Explain your answer and provide a graph of this labor supply curve.

STEP 1: In a graph, draw Kerry's time allocation budget line BL_1 measuring income on the vertical axis and leisure hours on the horizontal axis.

To construct Kerry's time allocation budget line, you need to know the number of hours that are available to Kerry for work or leisure, as well as the hourly wage rate. From the given information, we know that Kerry has 24 hours available to divide between work and leisure and that she earns a wage rate of \$3 per hour. If Kerry works all 24 hours, and therefore, has zero hours of leisure, she can earn a total of \$72. If Kerry works zero hours, then she can have 24 hours of leisure but no income. These are not the only choices available to Kerry: for example, she could choose to work 16 hours and have eight hours of leisure: on her time allocation budget line, we would want to graph this as the point with eight hours of leisure and \$48 of income. The graph shown after Step 6 illustrates BL_1, which is the line that represents all the possible trade-offs between consumption of leisure and income for Kerry when she earns \$3 an hour and has 24 hours.

STEP 2: In your graph, label point *A* where Kerry works eight hours that day. Identify how many hours of leisure Kerry has that day and also what her income is.

When Kerry works eight hours she earns (\$3/hour)(8 hours/day), or \$24. If Kerry is working eight hours, she has 16 hours a day to devote to leisure. Point *A* has been marked on the graph shown after Step 6.

STEP 3: Analyze the effect of a tax of 33% on Kerry's wage rate. Once you have analyzed how this tax affects Kerry's wage rate, construct BL_2, Kerry's new time allocation budget line.

When the government imposes a tax of 33% on Kerry's wage rate, this results in her after-tax rate falling to \$2 per hour. She earns \$3 per hour but must send the government 33% of this hourly wage rate. The government gets \$1 for every hour that Kerry works and Kerry keeps the remaining \$2 per hour for herself. If Kerry is now earning \$2 per hour, then her budget line will pivot down toward the origin. If Kerry works all 24 hours, then she can earn a maximum of \$48. If she chooses to work zero hours, then she will still be able to have 24 hours of leisure. The new time allocation budget line, BL_2, has been drawn on the graph at the end of Step 6.

STEP 4: In your graph, label point *B* where Kerry works 10 hours at the new after-tax wage rate. Identify how many hours of leisure Kerry has and also what her income is.

If Kerry decides to work for 10 hours, this implies that she will earn \$20 in after-tax income since her after-tax wage rate is \$2 per hour. If Kerry is working 10 hours, she will have 14 hours available for leisure. Point *B*, corresponding to this work/leisure choice, has been marked on the graph following Step 6.

STEP 5: Examine your graph to determine whether the income effect or the substitution effect is stronger for Kerry.

The income effect is stronger than the substitution effect: as Kerry's wage rate decreases, she opts to work more hours and take fewer leisure hours. As the wage rate falls, the substitution effect causes Kerry to substitute toward more leisure since leisure has now become relatively cheaper; as the wage rate falls, Kerry's income decreases, and this causes Kerry to consume less leisure and more work. From the graph, we can see that overall Kerry ends up consuming less leisure and working longer hours, and this tells us that the income effect is therefore stronger for Kerry than the substitution effect.

STEP 6: Determine whether Kerry's labor supply curve is upward sloping or downward sloping, and then draw a graph of this labor supply curve.

Kerry's labor supply curve is downward sloping. When the wage rate is \$3 per hour Kerry works eight hours, and when the wage rate is \$2 per hour Kerry works 10 hours. If you graph these two points with the wage rate on the vertical axis and the hours of labor on the horizontal axis, you will find that Kerry's supply of labor curve is downward sloping. Examine the two figures that follow: the first provides Kerry's time allocation budget lines and the optimal points, *A* and *B*, while the second figure provides a graph of Kerry's supply of labor curve.

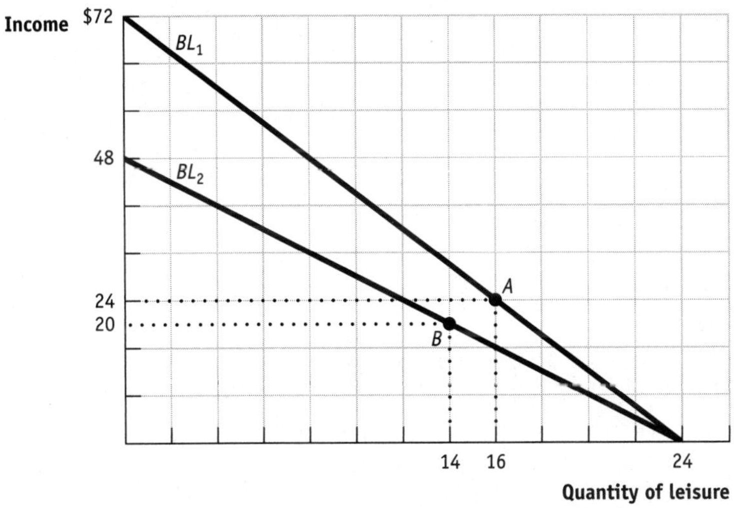

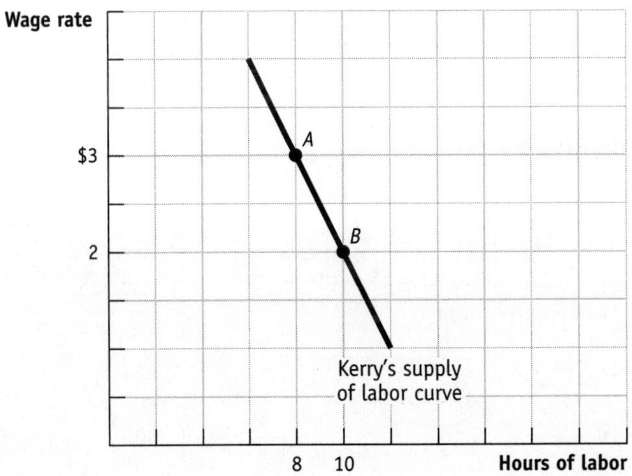

Problems and Exercises

1. Suppose that Mark finds that he is willing to work 40 hours a week when his wage rate is $10 an hour, but when the wage rate increases to $15 an hour Mark finds that he is only willing to work 36 hours a week.

   a. If you were to draw Mark's labor supply curve given this information, what would it look like? In the graph below, measure wage rate per hour on the vertical axis and quantity of labor hours per week on the horizontal axis.

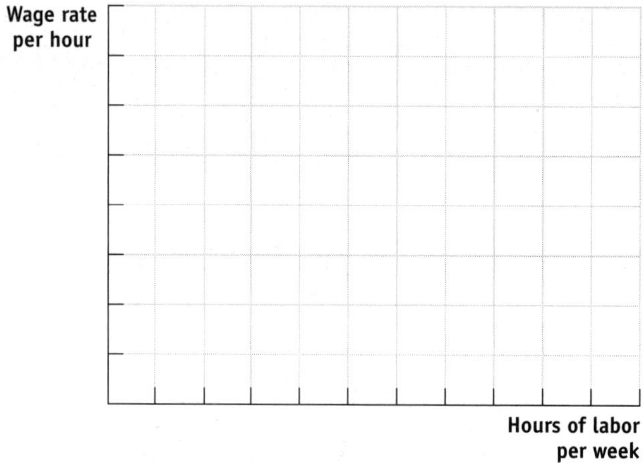

   b. Given this information, what do you know about the income effect relative to the substitution effect of this change in wage rates for Mark?

   c. What happens to the opportunity cost of an hour of leisure when Mark's wage rate increases from $10 an hour to $15 an hour?

   d. Describe the income effect of this wage increase.

2. Suppose that Susan finds that she is willing to work 40 hours a week when her wage rate is $10 an hour, but when the wage rate increases to $15 an hour Susan finds that she is willing to work 44 hours a week.

a. What is Susan's weekly income when the wage rate is $10 an hour? What is Susan's weekly income when the wage rate is $15 an hour?

b. If you were to draw Susan's labor supply curve given this information, what would it look like? In the graph below, measure wage rate per hour on the vertical axis and quantity of labor hours per week on the horizontal axis.

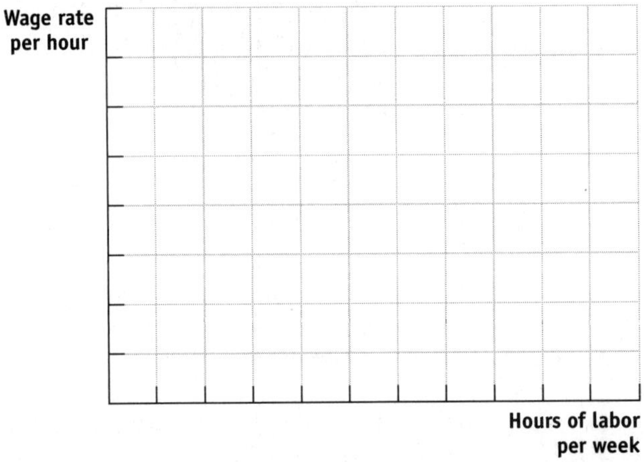

c. Given this information, what do you know about the income effect relative to the substitution effect of this change in wage rates for Susan?

d. Why would Susan choose to work longer hours when the wage rate is $15 an hour rather than $10 an hour?

3. Suppose that a labor market is composed of two individuals: Sam and Anne. Sam's and Anne's individual supply of labor curves can be described by the following two equations:

Sam's supply of labor: $W = 5 + (1/4)N$

Anne's supply of labor: $W = 5 + (1/6)N$

where W is the wage rate and N is the number of hours worked per week. Furthermore, you are told that the equilibrium wage rate in this labor market is \$15 an hour.

a. Find the market supply of labor curve assuming that Sam and Anne are the only two individuals supplying labor in this market.

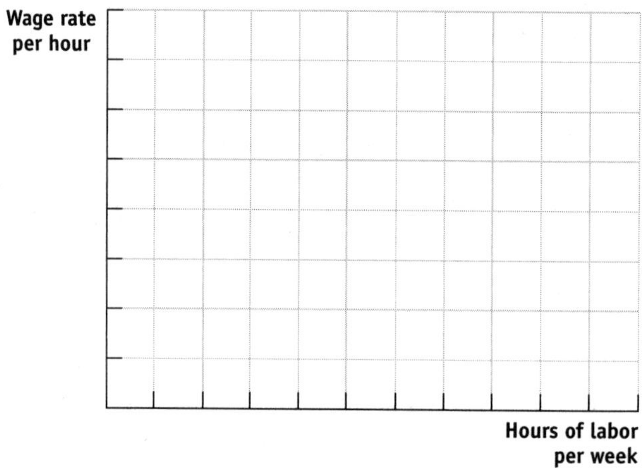

b. What is the total amount of labor supplied in this market at the equilibrium wage rate?

c. What is Sam's weekly income given this equilibrium wage rate?

d. What is Anne's weekly income given this equilibrium wage rate?

BEFORE YOU TAKE THE TEST

Module Review Questions

1. An individual's decision about how much labor to supply is a decision

a. about time allocation.

b. made by firms when they hire labor.

c. that is independent of the individual's preferences with regard to leisure.

d. Answers (a), (b), and (c) are all true.

e. Answers (b) and (c) are both true.

2. Leisure is

a. a normal good, since as an individual's income rises the individual consumes more leisure.

b. an inferior good, since as an individual's income rises the individual consumes less leisure.

3. For an individual, the optimal amount of labor to supply is the amount of labor at which, for the last hour of labor supplied, the marginal utility of an additional hour of leisure is

a. equal to the marginal utility the individual gets from consuming the goods that their hourly wage allows them to purchase.

b. greater than the marginal utility the individual gets from consuming the goods that their hourly wage allows them to purchase.

c. less than the marginal utility the individual gets from consuming the goods that their hourly wage allows them to purchase.

4. Carolyn's marginal utility from an additional hour of leisure is 20 utils, while her marginal utility from the income earned from working an additional hour is 25 utils. Carolyn should

a. work an additional hour, since her additional utility is greater if she devotes this hour to work instead of leisure.

b. choose to consume an additional hour of leisure, since an hour of leisure must always be preferred to an hour of work.

5. When an individual's labor supply curve is backward bending (that is, downward sloping) this implies that the individual's income effect is

a. stronger than the individual's substitution effect.

b. weaker than the individual's substitution effect.

6. With regard to an individual's labor supply curve, the substitution effect of a wage increase refers to the

a. decrease in the price of leisure relative to the price of other goods.

b. change in the opportunity cost of an hour of leisure relative to an hour of other goods.

c. incentive for the individual to consume less leisure and instead work longer hours.

d. Answers (b) and (c) are both true.

7. Which of the following statements is true?
   a. A worker will always choose to work as many hours as possible.
   b. A worker may not work as many hours as possible because the worker has other uses for their time besides work.
   c. The decision about whether to work or not is a decision about time allocation.
   d. Answers (a) and (c) are both true.
   e. Answers (b) and (c) are both true.

8. At the individual's optimal level of labor supply
   a. the marginal utility from an additional hour of leisure is equal to the marginal utility he receives from the goods that his hourly wage can purchase.
   b. the marginal utility from an additional hour of leisure is greater than the marginal utility he receives from the goods that his hourly wage can purchase.
   c. the marginal utility from an additional hour of leisure is less than the marginal utility he receives from the goods that his hourly wage can purchase.
   d. Answers (a), (b), and (c) are all possible.

9. In an imperfectly competitive labor market firms should hire workers until
   a. firms will pay workers more than the marginal factor cost of labor.
   b. firms will pay workers the marginal factor cost of labor.
   c firms will pay workers less than the marginal factor cost of labor.

ANSWER KEY

Answers to Problems and Exercises

1. **a.** As Mark's wage rate is bid up, the number of hours of labor he supplies decreases. This implies that Mark's labor supply curve is downward sloping, since the wage rate and the number of hours worked are inversely related to each other over this range of wages. The figure below illustrates Mark's supply of labor curve.

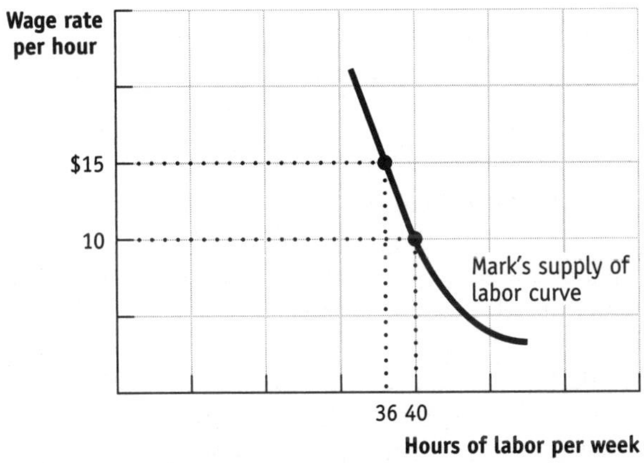

b. The income effect is stronger than the substitution effect over this range of wages. As Mark's wage is bid up, Mark chooses to consume more leisure and less work: the substitution effect of a higher wage makes an hour of leisure relatively more expensive and would tend to encourage Mark to work more and take fewer hours of leisure, but the income effect of a higher wage is that Mark can earn more income working the same number of hours. Since Mark chooses to work fewer hours, it must be the case that the income effect is dominant over the substitution effect in this case.

c. The opportunity cost of an hour of leisure increases when the wage rate increases: for each additional hour of leisure Mark consumes, he is now giving up $15 in lost wages instead of $10. Leisure has gotten relatively more expensive.

d. The income effect of this wage increase is that Mark can earn the same amount of income as he had initially while working fewer hours. For instance, if he works 40 hours a week for $10 an hour he will earn $400, but if his wage increases to $15 an hour he can earn $400 a week by working only 26.67 hours a week. In Mark's case, he chooses to consume a bit more income (36 hours at $15 an hour gives him $540 a week in income) plus 4 more hours of leisure.

2. **a.** When the wage rate is $10 an hour, Susan's weekly income is $400. When the wage rate is $15 an hour, Susan's weekly income is $660.

b. Susan's labor supply curve is upward sloping: as the wage rate increases, the quantity of labor supplied increases. The figure below illustrates Susan's supply of labor curve.

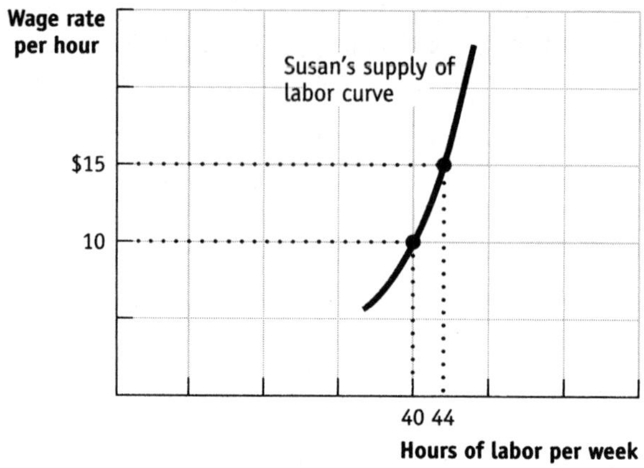

c. The income effect is dominated by the substitution effect in this example. As the opportunity cost of consuming an additional hour of leisure increases with the increase in the wage rate, Susan opts to work longer hours: the relative price of leisure has risen and Susan moves toward consuming the extra goods made possible by her higher income rather than consuming more leisure. When the substitution effect dominates the income effect for a wage increase, this leads to the supply of labor curve being upward sloping.

d. Susan chooses to work longer hours because the marginal utility she receives from the additional goods she can purchase with her higher income is greater than the marginal utility she receives from consuming additional hours of leisure.

3. **a.** The market supply of labor curve is equal to the horizontal summation of the individual supply of labor curves. To find this labor supply curve, you might find it helpful to sketch a graph of Sam's labor supply curve and a graph of Anne's labor supply curve. When the wage rate is \$5 an hour, neither Sam nor Anne will supply any labor: the wage rate is too low to convince either of them to work. When the wage rate rises to \$10 an hour, Sam is willing to supply 20 hours of work a week while Anne is willing to supply 30 hours of work a week. Thus, at a wage rate of \$10 an hour, the total amount of labor supplied in the market is 50 hours a week. From this information you now know two points on the market supply of labor curve: (50 hours a week, \$10 an hour) and (0 hours a week, \$5 an hour). Use this information to find the market supply of labor curve: $W = 5 + (1/10)N$. The figure below illustrates Sam's supply of labor curve, Anne's supply of labor curve, and the market supply of labor curve.

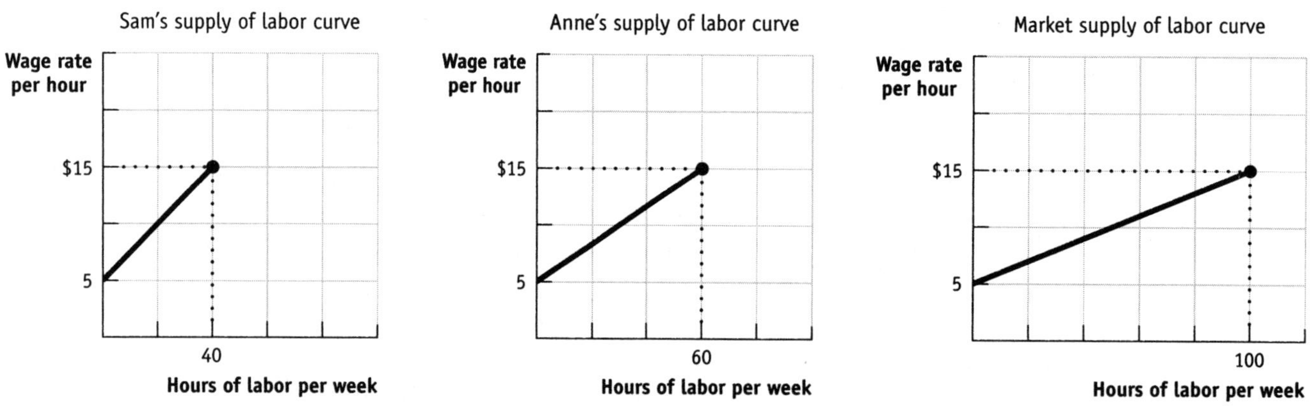

b. When the wage rate is $15 an hour, the total amount of labor supplied in the market is equal to 100 hours a week.

c. To find Sam's weekly income, we first need to know how many hours Sam will work at the equilibrium wage rate of $15 an hour. From Sam's supply of labor curve, we find that Sam is willing to supply 40 hours of work a week at this wage rate, which implies that Sam will earn $600 a week.

d. To find Anne's weekly income, we first need to know how many hours Anne will work at the equilibrium wage rate of $15 an hour. From Anne's supply of labor curve, we find that Anne is willing to supply 60 hours of work a week at this wage rate, which implies that Anne will earn $900 a week.

Answers to Module Review Questions

1. **Answer a.** The individual's decision about how much labor to supply is based on the individual's decision about time allocation and how the individual wishes to divide their time between different activities. The individual chooses to work and earn dollars that they can then use to purchase goods or to not work and instead consume leisure. The individual therefore faces a trade-off between additional income or additional leisure.

2. **Answer a.** Leisure is considered a normal good: as income rises, most people would choose to consume more leisure.

3. **Answer a.** The individual should supply an additional hour of labor if the marginal utility of an hour of leisure is less than the marginal utility received from the goods that their hourly wage allows them to purchase. The individual should not supply an additional hour of labor if the marginal utility of an hour of leisure is greater than the marginal utility received from the goods that their hourly wage allows them to purchase. The individual provides the optimal amount of labor when the marginal utility of an hour of leisure is equal to the marginal utility from the goods that their hourly wage allows them to purchase.

4. **Answer a.** In making her optimal labor supply decision, Carolyn should compare her marginal utility from an additional hour of work to her marginal utility from the income earned from an additional hour of leisure: since the income earned from work provides a greater increase in utility than leisure in this example, Carolyn should choose to work an additional hour.

5. **Answer a.** When the income effect is stronger than the substitution effect, an increase in the wage rate causes an individual to supply fewer hours of labor, and thus, the individual's labor supply curve is downward sloping.

6. **Answer d.** The substitution effect with respect to an individual's labor supply decision refers to the opportunity cost of one good (leisure) in terms of the other goods the individual can purchase by working an additional hour. When the individual's wage rate increases, this implies that an additional hour of leisure is now relatively more expensive and the individual will substitute away from leisure and toward working longer hours due to the change in the relative price of leisure.

7. **Answer e.** The decision to work is one that entails the worker making a choice about how best to allocate their time among competing uses. When an individual chooses to work that means that the individual cannot use that time for other uses: the individual must weigh the benefits of working an additional hour against the costs of working that additional hour. That is, the individual will want to consider what they are giving up when they decide to work an additional hour.

8. **Answer a.** The individual when making his decision about how many hours to work and how many hours to devote to leisure will consider what the addition to his total utility is from an additional hour of leisure versus the addition to his total utility from working

an additional hour and taking those earnings and buying goods. He will utility maximize by allocating his time so that these two marginal utilities are equal. If the marginal utility of an additional hour of leisure is greater than the marginal utility he gets from the goods that his hourly wage from an additional hour of work provides he will be happier if he chooses to devote more of this time to leisure and less of his time to work. The same logic applies if his marginal utility from the goods that his hourly wage from an additional hour of work is greater than his marginal utility from an additional hour of leisure: in this case, he should work more and take fewer hours of leisure.

9. **Answer c.** In an imperfectly competitive labor market a firm will hire labor until the marginal revenue product of labor equals the marginal factor cost of labor. In an imperfectly competitive labor market, the firm must offer a higher wage to hire more workers, so the marginal factor cost curve is above the labor supply curve. The optimal amount of labor to hire in this kind of labor market is that quantity where the marginal revenue product equals the marginal factor cost. Firms will then pay the wage required to have this amount of labor: this wage will be less than the marginal factor cost of labor.

module 43

The Cost-Minimizing Input Combination

BEFORE YOU READ THE MODULE

Summary

This module discusses how firms determine their optimal input mix. The module develops the cost-minimizing rule for hiring inputs. To cost-minimize firms adjust their hiring of inputs until the marginal product per dollar is equal for all inputs.

Module Objectives

Objective #1. Earlier in the text you learned about substitutes and complements. Recall that if there are two goods these goods are considered substitutes for each other if an increase in the price of one good leads to the quantity demanded of the other good increasing. Two goods are considered complements for each other if an increase in the price of one good leads to the quantity demanded of the other good decreasing. This module introduces the concept of substitutes and complements in production. Here we consider two inputs and how a change in the price of one input alters the firm's decision about how much of the other input to use. For example:

- Two inputs are substitutes for each other when the price of one input rises and this leads to a increase in the demand for the other input.
- Two inputs are complements to each other when the price of one input rises and this leads to a decrease in the demand for the other input.

Objective #2. A firm decides on the optimal amount of inputs to use and the combination of inputs to use by analyzing what combination of inputs leads to the minimization of the firm's cost for the level of output they wish to produce. The cost-minimization rule to hire inputs until the marginal product of one input per dollar spent on that input is equal to the marginal product of any other input per dollar spent on that input. Thus, if the two inputs are capital and labor then the firm will cost-minimize by hiring that amount of labor and capital such that the marginal product of labor per dollar spent on labor is equal to the marginal product of capital per dollar spent on capital.

Objective #3. A firm cannot be profit maximizing unless it is also cost minimizing.

Key Terms

cost-minimization rule hire factors so that the marginal product per dollar spent on each factor is the same; a firm uses this rule to determine the cost-minimizing combination of inputs.

Notes

AFTER YOU READ THE MODULE

Tip

Tip #1. This module continues the use of marginal analysis: this time the module uses this type of analysis to determine the optimal combination of inputs to hire in order to produce a given level of output. The analysis tells us that firms should hire each input until the marginal product of that input per dollar spent on that input is equivalent for all inputs. By this time in the course you should be comfortable with this use of marginal analysis: refer this concept paying close attention to why these marginal products per dollar spent must be equivalent. This is the same logic that we used when analyzing why consumers will maximize their utility by choosing the combination of goods so that the marginal utility per dollar is equal for all goods.

WORKED PROBLEMS

1. Suppose that First National, a local bank, is trying to decide between two options for delivering banking services to its customers. Option A utilizes more capital in the form of ATMs, while option B utilizes more labor in the form of bank tellers. First National knows that the rental price for an ATM is $500 per month and that the wage rate for a teller is $2,000 per month. Option A depends upon using 10 ATMs and three tellers, while option B uses two ATMs and eight tellers. First National has asked you to do an analysis of the cost of these two options that will guide them in making their decision as to which option they should adopt for their business.

STEP 1: Organize the given data into a table showing the input usage for each option.

The two options for First National can be delineated in a table that indicates the capital and labor usage for each option. The table below illustrates these two options.

Bank Tellers and ATMs		
	Capital (ATMs)	Labor (Bank Tellers)
	Rental rate = $500/month	Wage rate = $2,000/month
Option A	10 ATMs	3 tellers
Option B	2 ATMs	8 tellers

STEP 2: Calculate the cost of providing bank services using each option. Provide an organized summary of these costs.

The table below provides the cost calculation for each option.

Cost Calculation for Each Option Available to First National			
Option A	Cost of capital	10 × \$500	\$5,000
	Cost of labor	3 × \$2,000	\$6,000
	TOTAL COST		\$11,000
Option B	Cost of capital	2 × \$500	\$1000
	Cost of labor	8 × \$2,000	\$16,000
	TOTAL COST		\$17,000

STEP 3: Based upon the cost of each option, advise the management of First National as to which option results in lower costs.

Option A would cost First National \$11,000 per month, while option B would cost First National \$17,000 per month. First National should opt to use the more capital-intensive option A, since it results in lower costs for the firm.

2. Cindy's Candy Shop calculates that the marginal product of hiring one more unit of labor is 30 units of output, while the marginal product of hiring one more unit of capital equipment is 60 units of output. Cindy's Candy Shop hires labor for \$5 per unit and rents capital equipment for \$12 per unit. Given this information, should Cindy's Candy Shop increase its use of labor or its use of capital equipment? Explain the reasoning behind your answer.

STEP 1: Review the cost-minimization rule prior to answering this question.

The cost-minimization rule directs business owners to hire factors of production so that the marginal product per dollar spent on each factor is the same. In other words, business owners should hire factors so that the amount of output produced per dollar spent on the factor is the same for all factors: any other hiring choice results in higher costs for the business and therefore cannot minimize cost.

STEP 2: Compare the ratio of the marginal product of labor to its wage rate with the ratio of the marginal product of capital equipment to its rental rate.

The ratio of marginal product of labor to wage rate is (30 units of output)/(\$5 per unit), or six units of output per dollar spent on labor. The ratio of marginal product of capital equipment to rental rate of capital equipment is (60 units of output)/(\$12 per unit) or five units of output per dollar spent on capital equipment. The ratio of marginal product of labor to wage rate is larger than the ratio of marginal product of capital equipment to rental rate in this example.

STEP 3: Determine whether Cindy's Candy Shop should hire more labor or more capital equipment, and then explain the reasoning behind your answer.

Cindy should hire more labor, since for each dollar spent on labor her output increases by more than it does for each dollar spent on capital equipment.

Problems and Exercises

1. Widget Enterprises is trying to determine which of three production processes it should adopt in order to produce 1,000 widgets this month. The three production processes are given in the table below. They have asked for your help in evaluating which process is the least-cost process for their business.

Production Process	Units of capital	Units of labor
I	25	22
II	40	10
III	20	35

a. Suppose that you know that the cost of capital is $100 per unit and the cost of labor is $150 per unit. Use this information to complete the following table.

Production Process	Total cost of capital	Total cost of labor	Total cost of production
I			
II			
III			

b. Given your calculations in (a), which production process should Widget Enterprises adopt?

c. Suppose that the price of capital increases to $200 per unit of capital. Intuitively how do you think Widget Enterprises will respond to this increase in capital? Assume that capital and labor are substitutes in production.

d. Given the change in the price of capital described in (c), recalculate the cost of production for Widget Enterprises using the three different production processes that were provided in (a). Fill in the following table with your calculations.

Production Process	Total cost of capital	Total cost of labor	Total cost of production
I			
II			
III			

e. Was the prediction you made in (c) supported by the calculations you made in (d)? Explain your answer.

2. Suppose Wheel Enterprises produces bicycles. They calculate that the marginal product of labor at their level of current production is equal to 40 bicycles per unit of labor. Furthermore, they know that the price of labor is $10 per unit of labor. In addition, Wheel Enterprises knows that the marginal product of capital at their current level of production is equal to 20 bicycles per unit of capital. The price of capital is equal to $15 per unit of capital. Wheel Enterprises is trying to decide if they are cost minimizing and, if they are not, what they should do.

a. Are they cost minimizing for their current level of production? Explain your answer.

b. What do you suggest that they should do given the above information if their goal is to cost minimize?

BEFORE YOU TAKE THE TEST

Module Review Questions

1. The optimal combination of inputs for a firm to use when producing its output is

a. an equal amount of labor and capital.

b. more labor than capital since capital is often very expensive.

c. more capital than labor since capital is more productive than labor.

d. that combination of labor and capital where the marginal product of each input per dollar spent on the input is equal at the current level of production.

2. A capital-intensive operation

a. relies more heavily on the use of capital than on the use of labor.

b. relies more heavily on the use of labor than on the use of capital: since there is less capital the capital is used more intensively.

3. A firm uses both labor and capital to produce its output. Suppose that the firm is currently hiring 10 units of labor where the price per unit of labor is equal to $20. Furthermore, the firm is currently hiring 5 units of capital where the rental price of capital is $50 per unit of capital. When the price of labor rises to $25 the firm decides to increase its hiring of capital even though it plans to continue to produce exactly the same amount of output. This tells us that

a. labor and capital are substitutes for each other.

b. labor and capital are complements for each other.

c. the firm initially was not cost minimizing.

d. the firm initially was not profit maximizing.

4. When Joe hires an additional unit of labor he finds that the marginal product of the capital he uses in his business increases. Joe can conclude that labor and capital in his business are

a. complements.

b. substitutes.

5. The cost-minimization rule states that a firm should hire factors so that the

a. average product per dollar spent on each factor is the same.

b. marginal product per dollar spent on each factor is the same.

c. total product per dollar spent on each factor is the same.

d. total cost of each factor is the same.

6. Suppose that for an additional dollar spent on capital the firm can increase its production by 10 units while for every additional dollar spent on labor the firm can increase its production by eight units. If this firm wants to increase its production it should

a. hire more labor.

b. hire more capital.

ANSWER KEY

Answers to Problems and Exercises

1. a.

Production Process	Total cost of capital	Total cost of labor	Total cost of production
I	$2,500	$3,300	$5,800
II	4,000	1,500	5,500
III	2,000	5,250	7,250

b. From part (a) we can see that Widget Enterprises should adopt production process II since it results in the lowest cost of production for this level of output.

c. If the price of capital increases, holding everything else constant, this should result in Widget Enterprises hiring more labor and less capital in order to produce its output at least cost.

d.

Production Process	Total cost of capital	Total cost of labor	Total cost of production
I	$5,000	$3,300	$8,300
II	8,000	1,500	9,500
III	4,000	5,250	9,250

e. Given the data found in (d), Widget Enterprises should change its production process from II to I since production process I is now cheaper than production process II. Production process I uses more labor than production process II, while production process II uses more capital than production process I. As capital gets more expensive we can anticipate that the firm will move toward a less capital-intensive production process and away from a more capital-intensive production process.

2. **a.** To answer this question we should start by first calculating the marginal product of labor divided by the wage rate: thus, 40 bicycles per unit of labor divided by $10 per unit of labor gives us 4 bicycles per dollar. This tells us for every dollar that Wheel Enterprises spends on labor they can produce 4 bicycles. Next, calculate the marginal product of capital divided by the price of capital: thus, 20 bicycles per unit of capital divided by $15 per unit of capital gives us 1.3 bicycles per dollar. This tells us for every dollar that Wheel Enterprises spends on capital they can produce 1.3 bicycles. Wheel Enterprises gets more production per dollar spent on labor and this implies that Wheel Enterprises would be able to reduce their costs by using a more labor-intensive, less capital-intensive production process.

   b. Wheel Enterprises should choose a production process that uses more labor and less capital than they are currently using. They should hire more labor and less capital.

Answers to Module Review Questions

1. **Answer d.** The optimal amount of labor and capital to use when producing its output is dependent upon the marginal product of each input relative to each input's price. The firm will want to select that amount of each input where the marginal product of that input per dollar spent on that input is equal for all inputs.

2. **Answer a.** Capital-intensive production implies that the firm uses more capital and less labor to produce its output.

3. **Answer a.** Labor and capital are substitutes for each other in production since as the price of labor rises the firm substitutes away from the relatively more expensive labor and towards the relatively cheaper capital. From the information given we cannot conclude that the firm is not cost minimizing or not profit maximizing: to know this with certainty we would need to know what the marginal product of each input per dollar spent on the input is equal to in the initial situation.

4. **Answer a.** When the hiring of an additional unit of an input increases the marginal product of a different input, that tells us that the two inputs are complements to each other. When the marginal product of the input increases this means that this input has become more productive: in this case the increase in productivity is due to that input having more of the other input to work with—the other input complements this input.

5. **Answer b.** The firm will cost-minimize by hiring each factor to that the marginal product per dollar spent on each factor is the same. To see this imagine that the marginal product per dollar spent on labor is equal to 10 units of output per dollar while the marginal product per dollar spent on capital is equal to five units of output per dollar. The firm could expand its production by hiring more labor and less capital since the marginal product per dollar spent on labor is greater than the marginal product per dollar spent on capital.

6. **Answer b.** Since the marginal product of capital per dollar spent on capital is greater than the marginal product of labor per dollar spent on labor the firm can increase its production more cheaply by hiring capital rather than labor. That is, the addition to total output from hiring an additional dollar of capital is greater than the addition to total output from hiring an additional dollar of labor.

module 44

The Time Value of Money

BEFORE YOU READ THE MODULE

Summary

This module discusses the concept of present value and then it discusses a method measuring costs and benefits when these costs and benefits arrive in the future.

Module Objectives

Objective #1. The present value calculation is a method for evaluating the value today of a payment to be received or made at some point in the future. This calculation is useful when comparing the benefits and costs from an activity when these benefits and costs arrive at different points in time. By using present values in evaluating a project, you can evaluate the project as if all the costs and benefits from the project were occurring today rather than at different times.

- The present value calculation recognizes that a dollar held today is worth more than a dollar held a year from now. You can use the interest rate to compare the value of a dollar today to a dollar received at some point in the future: the interest rate measures the cost to you of delaying the receipt of a dollar of benefit, or the benefit to you of delaying the payment of a dollar of cost.
- Suppose you lend out $\$x$ today with the expectation that you will be repaid a dollar a year from now. The dollar you receive a year from now should be equal to $\$x$ plus the interest you receive from the borrower. If interest rate is represented as r, then we can express this idea as follows: the payment you receive a year from now (\$1) equals $x(1 + r)$. Thus $\$x$ is the present value of the \$1 you receive a year from now, and the present value of a payment of \$1 made a year from now is $\$x = 1/(1 + r)$. This method converts future dollars into their present values so that the time factor issue can be eliminated when making decisions. The present value concept can be expanded to a number of years. For example, the present value of a payment made N years from now is (future value)$/(1 + r)^N$.
- The net present value is the present value of current and future benefits minus the present value of current and future costs. When comparing potential projects, the project with the highest net present value is financially the most attractive project to undertake.

Key Terms

present value the amount of money needed at the present time to produce, at the prevailing *interest rate*, a given amount of money at a specified future time.

net present value the *present value* of current and future benefits minus the present value of current and future costs.

Notes

AFTER YOU READ THE MODULE

Tip

Tip #1. The calculation of present value is a calculation that allows you to compare a stream of payments occurring over time to another stream of payments occurring over some other period of time. This calculation is highly useful, and you should practice using it until you are comfortable with the concept as well as the technique.

WORKED PROBLEMS

1. Jason purchased a CD (certificate of deposit) for \$100 at his local bank this morning. Jason was told that the CD would be redeemable a year from now and would earn 5% interest over this period. How much will Jason receive a year from now, when he redeems this CD? Suppose that instead of the interest rate being 5% for the year, it was 8%. How would this change in interest rate affect Jason?

STEP 1: Review the concept of present value prior to analyzing this question.

\$X today is worth (\$X)(1 + interest rate) a year from now. \$X today is worth (\$X)(1 + interest)(1 + interest) two years from now if the annual interest rate is constant. In general, then, given a constant annual interest rate, \$X today is worth (\$X)$(1 + \text{interest})^n$, where n is the number of years.

STEP 2: Calculate the amount Jason will receive a year from now, when he redeems his \$100 CD. Base your calculation on a 5% interest for the year.

Jason will receive \$100(1 + 0.05), or \$105, a year from now.

STEP 3: Calculate the amount Jason would receive a year from now, when he redeemed his CD, if the CD earned 8% interest for the year.

Jason would receive \$100(1 + 0.08), or \$108, a year from now if he bought a \$100 CD today and received an annual interest rate of 8%.

STEP 4: Generalize the impact of an increase in interest rates on the future value of a payment.

The value of the future payment Jason receives increases as the annual interest rate increases, holding everything else constant. Jason receives a higher return on his deposited money when the interest rate is higher, holding everything else constant.

2. Suppose you know that the annual interest rate is 5% and suppose you have a friend who is willing to promise to pay you $1,000 a year from now. Given this information, how much would you be willing to lend to this friend today?

STEP 1: Review the concept of present value prior to analyzing this question.

An amount of \$X today is worth (\$X)(1 + interest rate) a year from now, and \$X today is worth (\$X)(1 + interest)(1 + interest) two years from now if the annual interest rate is constant. In general, then, provided the annual interest rate is constant, \$X today is worth (\$X)(1 + interest)^n, where n is the number of years.

STEP 2: Calculate the present value of $1,000 received a year from now given an interest rate of 5%.

The present value of \$1,000 received a year from now given the interest rate of 5% can be calculated as \$X = (\$1,000)/(1 + 0.05), or \$952.38.

STEP 3: Provide a verbal interpretation of your finding in Step 2.

Given an interest rate of 5% and a promise to repay $1,000 a year from now, you are willing to lend your friend $952.38 today. A year from now this $952.38, if it were put into an account earning 5% for the year, would be worth $1,000, exactly the amount your friend has promised to repay you if you make the loan.

Problems and Exercises

1. Mary offers to pay Joe $1,000 a year from now if he will loan her money today. Suppose Joe wants to earn 10% interest and there is no inflation over this period. What is the maximum amount Joe will lend Mary, given her offer?

2. Sarah borrows $1,000 from Joe at the beginning of the year and promises to repay him at the end of five years. She also agrees to pay him an annual interest rate of 12%. What is the total amount Joe will receive at the end of the fifth year?

3. Joe can't decide between two financial options: he can loan Sarah $1,000 as outlined in problem 2, or he can invest the $1,000 in a new venture. He estimates that during the first year the venture will earn 5% interest, during the second and third years it will earn 10% interest, and during the fourth and fifth years it will earn 18% interest. Evaluate these two options for Joe and then make a recommendation based on this evaluation.

4. You have won the lottery and you can receive your winnings as a single payment of $2 million in cash now or you can receive a payment of $500,000 a year for five years starting now. The interest rate is constant and equal to 10% per year. Which payment plan do you prefer?

5. Does your decision in problem 4 change if the interest rate is constant and equal to 8% instead of 10%? Explain your answer.

6. Does your decision in problem 4 change if the interest rate is constant and equal to 15% instead of 10%? Explain your answer.

BEFORE YOU TAKE THE TEST

Module Review Questions

Use the following information to answer the next two questions.

Marty borrows \$1,000 from Harry on January 1, 2010, and promises to repay Harry on December 31, 2014, a payment that will result in Harry earning an annual rate of interest of 10%.

1. Which of the following expressions correctly states the value of Marty's payment on December 31, 2014?

a. $(\$1,000)(1 + 10)$

b. $(\$1,000)/(1 + 0.10)^5$

c. $(\$1,000)(1 + 0.10) + (\$1,000)(1 + 0.10)^2 + (\$1,000)(1 + 0.10)^3 + (\$1,000)$
$(1 + 0.10)^4 + (\$1,000)(1 + 0.10)^5$

d. $(\$1,000)(1 + 0.10)^5$

2. Suppose Harry tells Marty he will lend him the money if he earns an annual rate of interest of 12%. This will result in Marty paying Harry a

a. smaller amount than if the interest rate were 10%.

b. larger amount than if the interest rate were 10%.

3. Holding everything else constant, the present value of a future payment increases when the interest rate rises.

a. True

b. False

Use the following information to answer the next three questions.

Courtney's Computers is thinking about whether they should invest in a new software program. Development of this program will require an initial expenditure of \$4 million now but will result in annual profits of \$2 million for three years.

4. No matter what the interest rate, Courtney's Computers should invest in this new software since the profits from this new software far outweigh the costs of developing this software.

a. True

b. False

5. Given the above information and an interest rate of 20%, Courtney's Computers should

a. invest in the development of this new software.

b. not invest in the development of this new software.

6. Given the above information and an interest rate of 20%, the net present value of this new software for Courtney's Computers is equal to

   a. –\$2 million.
   b. \$2 million.
   c. \$0.21 million.
   d. –\$0.21 million.

7. When considering a new investment project, companies

   a. do not care if the net present value is positive or negative provided the interest rate is at least 10%.
   b. are willing to undertake investment projects only when the interest rate is 5% or lower.
   c. ignore the interest rate.
   d. None of the statements is correct.

ANSWER KEY

Answers to Problems and Exercises

1. To calculate this value, use the present value formula: PV = (future value)/(1 + r). Thus, PV = ($1,000)/(1 + 0.10) = $909.09. Joe will be willing to lend Mary $909.09 today, given her offer.

2. The future value Joe will receive equals ($1,000)(1 + 0.12)^5, or $1,762.34.

3. From problem 2, we know Joe will earn a total of $762.34 if he loans Sarah $1,000 for five years. To evaluate what Joe should do requires a calculation of the value of the second option. This second option is a bit more complicated to calculate than the loan to Sarah. At the end of the first year, this option is worth ($1,000)(1 + 0.05), or $1,050. This amount remains with the venture, and at the end of the second year the value of this option will equal ($1,050)(1 + 0.10). At the end of the third year the value of this option will equal ($1,050)(1 + 0.10)(1 + 0.10), or $1,270.50. At the end of the fourth year the value of this option is ($1,270.50)(1 + 0.18), and at the end of the fifth year the value of this option is ($1,270.50)(1 + 0.18)(1 + 0.18) or $1,769.04. Subtracting out Joe's initial investment of $1,000 yields Joe a net income of $769.04. Since this amount is greater than what he receives from Sarah, Joe should invest in the new venture.

4. To compare these payments requires calculating the present value of the future payments you would receive if you opted for five payments over time instead of a single payment now. The present value of these payments is $500,000 + ($500,000)/(1.1) + ($500,000)/(1.1)^2 + ($500,000)/(1.1)^3 + ($500,000)/(1.1)^4, or $2,084,933. You will receive a larger total payment if you choose to receive the lottery winnings over a five-year period.

5. No, the decision does not change, although this change in the interest rate does change the present value of the stream of payments received over five years. The present value of this stream of payments is now equal to $500,000 + ($500,000)/(1.08) + ($500,000)/(1.08)^2 + ($500,000)/(1.08)^3 + ($500,000)/(1.08)^4, or $2,122,077. A decrease in the interest rate makes the stream of payments over five years even more attractive to you.

6. Yes, when the interest rate increases to 15%, this makes the single payment option more valuable than the stream of five payments. To see this, compare the single payment of $2 million to the present value of the stream of payments. The present value of the payments over five years is equal to $500,000 + ($500,000)/(1.15) + ($500,000)/(1.15)^2 + ($500,000)/(1.15)^3 + ($500,000)/(1.15)^4, or $1,927,489, which is less than $2 million.

Answers to Module Review Questions

1. **Answer d.** This is a simple illustration of the present value formula.

2. **Answer b.** When the interest rate increases, this means the cost of borrowing money has risen and therefore the amount of money to be paid back will rise.

3. **Answer b.** The present value of a future payment decreases when the interest rate rises, since the higher interest rate means that a smaller amount today will accumulate to a larger amount in the future.

4. **Answer b.** Whether an investment project should be undertaken depends on the benefits as well as the costs associated with the investment project. It is possible that even though this project has positive projected profits, the cost of borrowing funds to undertake the project will exceed these projected profits.

5. **Answer a.** If you compute the net present value for the project, the value is a positive number and therefore the project should be undertaken. This computation is done in the answer to question 6.

6. **Answer c.** To compute the net present value entails calculating the present value of the benefits and the present value of the costs and then subtracting the present value of the costs from the present value of the benefits. The present value of the benefits is equal to $(2)/(1+0.2)+(2)/(1+0.2)^2+(2)/(1+0.2)^3$, and the present value of the costs is equal to 4. The difference between these two present values is approximately $0.21 million.

7. **Answer d.** None of the answers is true. Companies decide to undertake investment projects when the net present value is a positive number for the given interest rate.

module 45

The Economics of Information

BEFORE YOU READ THE MODULE

Summary

This module considers the special problems created by private or asymmetric information, a situation in which some people possess information that is unknown or unavailable to other people. The module discusses the problem of adverse selection (the "lemons problem") as well as the problem of moral hazard. The module explores how the problems associated with asymmetric information can be addressed through screening and monitoring.

Module Objectives

Objective #1. Markets fail when there is private information, a situation in which some people know things that other people do not know. Private information, or asymmetric information, distorts economic decisions and may prevent mutually beneficial transactions from taking place. Two types of problems arise because of private information.

- Adverse selection arises from possessing private information about the way things are.
- Moral hazard arises from possessing private information about what people do.

Objective #2. Adverse selection problems occur because the potential sellers know more about the quality of what they are selling than do the potential buyers. The potential sellers have an incentive to offer low-quality items for sale. Health insurance companies in particular face significant adverse selection problems since individuals seeking health insurance possess private information about their health that is hard for the insurance company to obtain. This asymmetric information results in healthy people opting not to purchase health insurance and leaving the insurance company with exactly the customers it wishes to avoid—those individuals with higher-than-average risk of needing significant health care. When the insurance company increases the premium on health insurance policies, this drives out more of the relatively healthy customers: this process can eventually lead to the collapse of the health insurance market. Strategies for reducing the problem of adverse selection include:

- screening, which entails the use of observable information to make inferences about private information;
- signaling, when people who represent a good prospect for the business do some action they would not do if they were not a good prospect; and
- the use of reputation to indicate that the business is one whose product is not adversely selected.

Objective #3. Moral hazard arises when an individual has private information about their own actions when someone else bears the cost of the individual's actions. The individual acts in a morally hazardous manner with respect to the other party since the individual's actions create a cost for this other party. To correct for the problem of moral hazard, the individuals with private information must be given a personal stake in what happens so that they have an incentive to exert effort even when others cannot verify they have done so. For instance, a car insurance company can require a deductible: an individual who is a careless driver will incur the deductible expense even though they are insured. This potential deductible expense encourages the individual to drive with greater care and therefore, reduce the moral hazard the car insurance company faces.

Key Terms

private information information that some people have that others do not.

adverse selection occurs when an individual knows more about the way things are than other people do. Adverse selection problems can lead to market problems: private information leads buyers to expect hidden problems in items offered for sale, leading to low prices and the best items being kept off the market.

screening using observable information about people to make inferences about their *private information;* a way to reduce *adverse selection.*

signaling taking some action to establish credibility despite possessing *private information;* a way to reduce *adverse selection.*

reputation a long-term standing in the public regard that serves to reassure others that *private information* is not being concealed; a valuable asset in the face of *adverse selection.*

moral hazard the situation that can exist when an individual knows more about his or her own actions than other people do. This leads to a distortion of incentives to take care or to expend effort when someone else bears the costs of the lack of care or effort.

deductible a sum specified in an insurance policy that the insured individual must pay before being compensated for a claim; deductibles reduce *moral hazard.*

Notes

AFTER YOU READ THE MODULE

Tip

Tip #1. Students often find the concepts of adverse selection and moral hazard challenging to identify. Think about these two concepts using a time frame that focuses on whether the situation is occurring before the transaction or after the transaction.

- Adverse selection occurs before the transaction between the two parties: because of asymmetric information, one party to the transaction possesses information that the other party does not have and can not easily access. Because of this imbalance in information, the party possessing the private information faces an incentive to offer low-quality products in the market due to the fact that the other party cannot readily identify whether the product is of low or high quality. This leads to a breakdown in the market, since buyers will grow increasingly reluctant to purchase the product as the product becomes adversely selected from the buyers' perspective.
- Moral hazard occurs after the transaction, when one party to the transaction acts in a manner that is detrimental, or morally hazardous, to the desired outcome for the other party. For example, a person contracts for automobile insurance and once the insurance is in place, drives less carefully. This is a morally hazardous behavior from the perspective of the insurance company, since it is likely to lead to higher expenses for the insurance company due to the individual having a higher probability of a car accident.
- The key to distinguishing between these two concepts is to recognize that the timing of the information issue is essential. Adverse selection occurs before the transaction and moral hazard after the transaction.

WORKED PROBLEMS

1. Suppose Peter owns a company that employs 50 people. Peter would like to provide health insurance to his employees, and he is busy trying to calculate what premium his employees will need to pay for everyone to be insured. He estimates that 2% of his employees will have major health issues this year, resulting in expenditures of $500,000 per person in health care costs. Another 10% of his employees are likely to have some health care expenses for the year, and he estimates the cost per person in this group will be $20,000. He predicts the final 88% of his employees will be quite healthy and only have well-care visits resulting in a health care cost per person in this group of $1,000. Peter asks you to figure out what each employee must pay as a premium if all employees join the plan and if all employees contribute an equivalent amount. He also asks you to advise him about what he should do with regard to the health insurance premiums if 20% of the population decides to drop out of the system. He also seeks your analysis on any issues this health insurance plan is likely to face when he begins to implement the plan. Finally, make sure you relate this analysis to issues of adverse selection.

STEP 1: Calculate the total cost of health care for Peter's employees for the coming year, based on the given information.

To find the total cost of health care for Peter's employees, we need to add up the costs of care for each of the individual employees. First, 2% of Peter's employees face major health care expenses of $500,000: that is, one of his employees can be expected to generate $500,000 in expenses for the coming year. Another 10% of his employees, or five employees, will generate expenses of $20,000 per person. The remaining 88% of his employees, or 44 employees, will generate expenses of $1,000 per person. The following table summarizes these findings.

	Number of employees	Annual health care expense
2% of Peter's employees	1	$500,000
10% of Peter's employees	5	100,000
88% of Peter's employees	44	44,000
Total annual health care expense		644,000

STEP 2: Given the health care costs you calculated in Step 1, calculate the cost of the health insurance premium if all employees participate in the plan and the cost will be evenly divided across all workers.

The total annual health care expense is $644,000, and if this cost is divided evenly across all of Peter's employees, then each employee will need to contribute $12,880 this year.

STEP 3: Given the cost of the premium you calculated in Step 2, analyze how Peter's employees will respond to the plan.

For any employees anticipating major or significant health care expenses for the coming year, the health care plan is a good opportunity: Peter's single employee with major health care expenses will have these expenses of $500,000 completely covered if he or she makes a health care insurance contribution of $12,880. For the 5% of employees with significant health care issues, this is still a good deal: without the health care insurance, these individuals would expect to pay $20,000 a year and now they will only need to pay $12,880. But, for individuals without health care issues, this plan is much more expensive than if they self-insure. They will not like having to participate in the plan.

Of course, none of these employees necessarily know to which group they belong. Each might be just a step away from a serious medical issue and, if Peter's employees recognize this, they may be less resistant to his plan. It is likely that those individuals who believe themselves to be in the healthy category will want to opt out of the health insurance plan. As these healthy employees exit the plan, the employees who continue to participate are adversely selected: the percentage of employees with significant health issues will rise.

STEP 4: Calculate the total cost of health care for Peter's employees for the coming year if 20% of his employees decide not to participate in the health insurance program.

We will assume that the 20% who decide to not participate in the plan are in the group of healthy employees. Thus, there will now be 40 employees in the plan and the annual cost of health care provision for them is given in the following table.

	Number of employees	Annual health care expense
Employees with major health care issues	1	$500,000
Employees with significant health care issues	5	100,000
Healthy employees	34	34,000
Total annual health care expense		634,000

The total annual health care expense when 20% of Peter's employees choose to not participate in the health insurance program is now $634,000.

STEP 5: Given the health care costs you calculated in Step 3, calculate the cost of the health insurance premium if 20% of Peter's employees decide to not participate in the health insurance plan.

The total annual health care expense is $634,000, and if this cost is divided evenly across 40 of Peter's employees, then each employee in the plan will need to contribute $15,850 this year. This is a substantial increase in the cost of this plan for participating employees: the cost of the health insurance plan has risen by 23%.

STEP 6: Explain the impact of adverse selection in this example.

The design of this program results in healthier individuals opting out of the program. When employees leave the program, the cost of providing health care insurance to the remaining employees increases. This exiting of employees from the program results in an even greater incentive for more exiting: the pool of insured workers becomes increasingly expensive to insure, since the less costly healthy employees are no longer participating in the program. The participants in the health care insurance program are adversely selected. This helps explain why many health care insurance reforms mandate full participation by everyone in the program.

2. Jeremy just got his driver's license, and he really wants to go see his friends. His parents reluctantly agree to let him go. Their reluctance stems from their fear that Jeremy is still a very inexperienced driver and that he sometimes acts a bit impulsively. If Jeremy gets in the family car and drives 40 miles over the speed limit, how does this pose a moral hazard problem for his parents?

STEP 1: Review the meaning of moral hazard prior to analyzing this situation.

Moral hazard refers to occasions when an individual fails to act carefully or to make an appropriate effort, and that failure results in others bearing a cost for that behavior.

STEP 2: Identify where the moral hazard is in this example.

If Jeremy drives over the speed limit, he puts himself and other people at risk of injury. In addition, his speeding may endanger the safety of the family car. The moral hazard arises because Jeremy's parents do not know what Jeremy will do once he is away from their supervision.

Problems and Exercises

1. Why do companies often offer warranties covering their products during the first year or two that a person owns the product?

2. For each of the following situations, determine if this is a problem of adverse selection or moral hazard.

a. Recently, colleges in many parts of the United States have decided to forgo standardized tests and instead make their admission decisions based on the information that prospective students send to them.

b. Mary has a midnight curfew and at 11:55 P.M. she realizes that if she does not get home by midnight, she will be grounded. She drives home at 80 miles per hour to make the curfew.

c. Josie knows she needs major medical surgery, but when she investigates different health insurance policies, she does not reveal that she needs this surgery.

d. Jeremy wrecked his car three summers ago and is now selling the car. In his advertisement, he does not mention that the car was in a wreck and needed substantial repair.

3. For each of the following situations, identify whether the situation is an illustration of moral hazard or adverse selection. Explain your answer.

a. It is final exam week at Everyman's University. Professor Smith is surprised to receive 10 emails the day before his final exam is scheduled. In the emails, there are five students who report being too sick to take the exam and three students who report family members that have died and whose funerals will require their missing the final exams. All eight of these students have requested extensions on the deadline to complete the final exam. The other two emails have questions about the material covered on the exam.

b. Susy received early admission to the college of her choice. During the rest of her senior year in high school, Susy did not attend class regularly and her grades fell significantly.

c. Molly makes one-of-a-kind handbags. She sells her handbags at temporary stands she sets up around the country as she travels. She is rarely in the same community more often than every two to three years.

BEFORE YOU TAKE THE TEST

Module Review Questions

1. Many products are sold with warranties. These warranties are

a. a way for the producer to signal that the product is of high quality.

b. a form of consumer insurance.

c. a way of minimizing the consumer's expected utility from consuming the product.

d. Answers (a), (b), and (c) are all true answers.

e. Answers (a) and (b) are true answers.

2. Adverse selection can be reduced by
   a. the use of screening, where potential demanders of a product collect information about the product prior to purchasing the product.
   b. the use of signaling by suppliers of the product, where the signal acts to provide the potential demander with information about the quality of the product.
   c. the seller developing a reputation for a high-quality product and high-quality service for that product.
   d. Answers (a), (b), and (c) are all methods that can reduce adverse selection.

3. Susy just got her driver's license and has begged her parents to let her take the family car out for a drive. Susy's parents are likely to be worried that this situation represents a potential
   a. adverse selection problem, since Susy has only recently learned to drive.
   b. moral hazard problem, since once Susy is out with the car, the parents have no certainty that Susy will drive in a manner that is safe and careful.

4. Harold is starting a car insurance company and is offering to provide 100% coverage to his customers. Harold is likely to encounter a
   a. moral hazard problem given this offer.
   b. adverse selection problem given this offer.

5. The use of a deductible in an insurance policy helps to reduce the problem of
   a. adverse selection.
   b. moral hazard.

6. A car insurance company offers a variety of policies that each have different insurance premiums and different deductibles. These policies allow the company to
   a. effectively screen their customers and gather private information that would otherwise not be available to the insurance company.
   b. effectively discriminate between low-risk individuals and high-risk individuals.
   c. provide a set of incentives to buyers to engage in less risky behavior from the insurance company's perspective.
   d. Answers (a), (b), and (c) are all true.

Use the following information to answer the next three questions.

Suppose that there is a used car market and in this market half of the cars for sale are lemons (that is, a car of poor quality) and half of the cars for sale are cherries (that is, a car of high quality).

7. In this market suppose buyers are not able to distinguish between a lemon car and a cherry car. Which of the following statements is true?
   a. The price offered for a used car by a buyer will be lower than the value of the cherry car to its owner.
   b. The price offered for a used car by a buyer will be greater than the value of the lemon car to its owner.
   c. Over time in this market there will be more lemon cars than cherry cars.
   d. Answers (a), (b), and (c) are all true statements.

8. Over time, if buyers are not able to distinguish lemon cars from cherry cars in this market, then

a. the market will eventually be composed only of cherry cars.

b. the market will eventually be composed only of lemon cars.

c. buyers will have an equal likelihood of purchasing a lemon or a cherry car.

d. buyers will exit the market and not purchase any cars.

9. This set of questions focuses on asymmetric information and, in particular, the problem associated with

a. adverse selection.

b. moral hazard.

ANSWER KEY

Answers to Problems and Exercises

1. The warranty is a way for the company to signal their reliability: the warranty lets consumers know that the company stands behind its product. This helps alleviate consumers' fears that the product is of low quality or adversely selected from their consumers' perspective.

2. **a.** There is an information problem here in that colleges will be making their decisions based on the information they receive from prospective students: these students have an incentive to embellish these details, particularly if there is no way for the college to verify the validity of their claims. This is an adverse selection problem.

   b. This is a moral hazard problem since Mary acts in a morally hazardous manner when she drives 80 miles per hour. This is morally hazardous since Mary may injure other people or may kill herself: neither of these outcomes is what Mary's parents intended when they established the curfew.

   c. This is an adverse selection problem since Josie possesses private information that the prospective insurer does not have. Josie represents an adversely selected potential customer for the insurance company since she is likely to be expensive to insure.

   d. This is an adverse selection problem since Jeremy possesses information about the status of the car that potential buyers do not have access to.

3. **a.** Professor Smith is apt to think this is an adversely selected pool of students given the timing of the issues that have been raised. Students who are poorly prepared for the final exam may think that waiting to take the final exam will improve their score. It is more likely that poorly prepared students will seek this option than well-prepared students.

   b. This is a moral hazard problem. Susy is acting in a morally hazardous manner from the perspective of the college. The college admitted her based on her record: her new behavior is generating a very different kind of record, one that is not the image or record that the college felt they were choosing when making their admission decision.

   c. This is an adverse selection issue for would-be consumers of Molly's handbags. Since she is rarely in the same place, buyers of her product will find it difficult to contact her and get needed repairs or adjustments if the bags prove faulty. Under these types of circumstances, it would not be surprising to find that the quality of the wares offered for sale is lower than what one would find in a traditional storefront.

Answers to Module Review Questions

1. **Answer e.** Warranties serve as a signal of the quality of the good as well as providing consumer insurance for those who purchase the good. When warranties cover the cost of repair or replacement, this effectively increases the consumer's expected utility from consuming the good.

2. **Answer d.** Screening, signaling, and the establishment of a good reputation are all effective methods for reducing the problem of adverse selection, since all three of these methods provide information to the potential buyer about the quality of the product.

3. **Answer b.** The moral hazard problem occurs after the transaction: if Susy gets permission to take the family car out for a drive, the parents do not know with certainty what Susy will do with the car once she is out of sight. Susy may drive carefully and act in a

manner that is not morally hazardous to her parents, but she may also take this opportunity to drive too fast and end up wrecking the car, or even worse, wrecking the car and killing herself or others. The moral hazard problem arises because the parents do not know what Susy will do once she is away from their supervision.

4. **Answer a.** When Harold offers 100% coverage to his customers, he effectively creates an environment where the customers have little incentive to drive carefully since any damage that they experience due to their driving will be covered by the insurance they purchased. The customers are apt to behave in a manner that is morally hazardous to Harold, since the customers may not operate their vehicles as carefully as Harold would desire given that Harold is insuring the vehicles.

5. **Answer b.** The deductible serves to give individuals a stake in the outcome of their decision making: the deductible gives the individual a reason to exert effort to avoid behaviors that would hurt the insurance company.

6. **Answer d.** When the insurance company offers a choice of policies with different premiums and deductibles, the insurance company can screen its customers by having its customers sort themselves based on the private information that the customers possess. In addition, this allows those customers who represent a high risk to identify themselves when they seek an insurance policy with a low deductible. Lastly, the deductibles act as an incentive for insured drivers to drive with care to avoid incurring the deductible expense.

7. **Answer d.** If buyers cannot discern whether the car is a lemon or a cherry, they will offer a price that is lower than the value of the car if it is a cherry and higher than the value of the car if it is a lemon. Over time sellers of high-valued cars will decide that it is not worthwhile to offer their cars: this implies that over time there will be more lemon cars in the used car market.

8. **Answer b.** If buyers are not able to distinguish a lemon car from a cherry car they will not be willing to pay the full value of a cherry car to a seller since there is a strong chance that the car they are purchasing is a lemon. Suppliers of cherry cars will be less willing to supply cherry cars while suppliers of lemon cars will continue to be willing to supply the lemon cars. Over time this market will suffer from a problem of adverse selection in which the market becomes characterized as being composed of the adversely selected product (in this case, the lemon cars).

9. **Answer a.** This is an example of adverse selection where the asymmetric or imperfect information creates a situation in which mutually beneficial transactions do not take place because of the asymmetry of information in the market. Over time, the used car market becomes characterized as a market composed of adversely selected products from the demander's perspective: the market will fail unless demanders can secure good information about the quality of the used cars being offered for sale in this market.